Making world history come alive by tell[ing] stories of global travelers

Voyages in World History uses the themes of movement and contact to illustrate the most important topics in world history. Authors Valerie Hansen and Kenneth R. Curtis use the compelling stories of individual men and women throughout history to help students understand the movement of people, ideas, and goods. By focusing on one traveler in each chapter, the authors provide an engaging framework to help students understand the variety of people, places, and events that have shaped world history.

The Second Edition of **Voyages in World History** blends the text's proven approach with new content:

- A new *Context and Connections* feature in each chapter shows students how various people and events are relevant to each other and to the larger themes throughout the book

- The mobile *Voyages Map App* complements the text and allows interactive exploration of historic people and sites using Google Earth™

- Popular features such as *Visual Evidence in Primary Sources, World History in Today's World,* and *Movement of Ideas Through Primary Sources* are updated with new content

Available in three versions:

Complete Edition
978-1-133-60781-6

Volume 1: To 1600
978-1-133-60782-3

Volume 2: Since 1500
978-1-133-60783-0

"I like that Hansen and Curtis teach from the primary sources. This makes the historical narrative concrete and appealing to students. This corresponds well to the way I teach history."

Frans van Liere, Calvin College

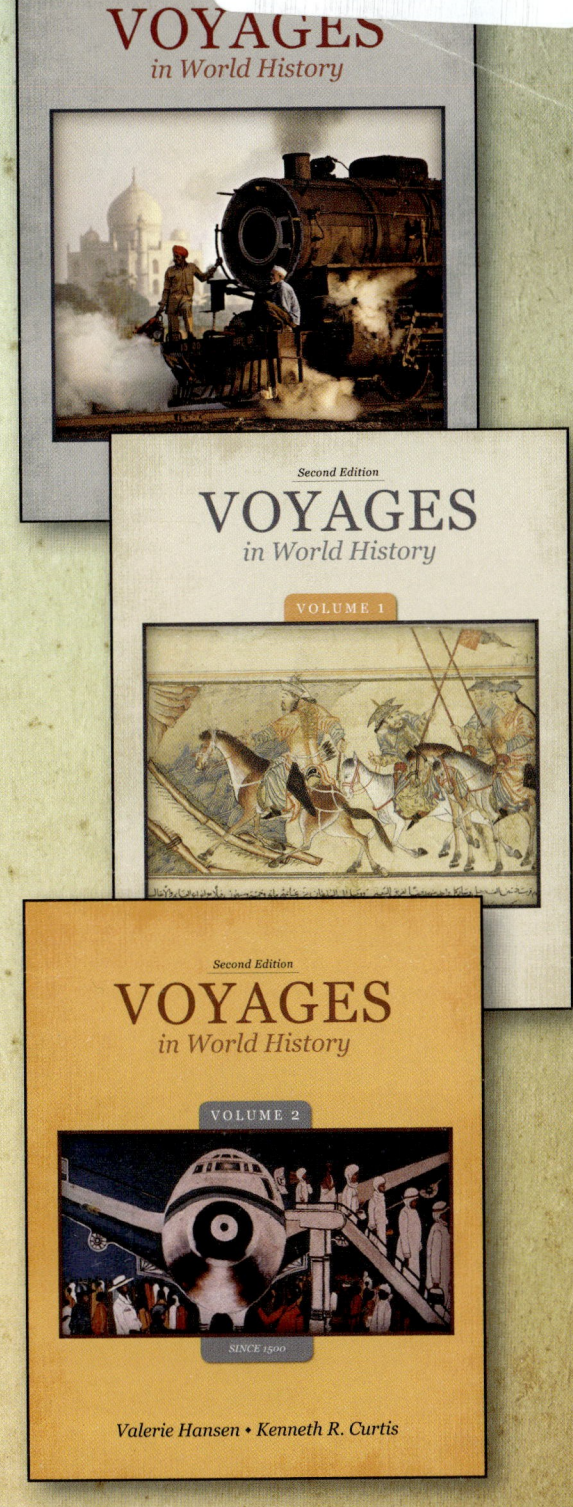

The *Voyages Map App* lets students be a part of the exploration

The *Voyages Map App* allows students to explore the past as they follow the voyages taken by the travelers highlighted in the text. Using Google Earth™, students are transported to historic sites and locations visited by the travelers and learn about each location's monuments, architecture, and historic significance.

"[The Map App is] a useful tool that goes beyond the traditional map and allows the student to engage with historically significant geographical locations."

Salvador Diaz,
Santa Rosa Junior College

The *Voyages Map App* includes:

- Review questions
- Flash cards
- Timelines
- Quizzes

- **91% of students report that the map app increases their understanding of material in the textbook**

- **86% of instructors say the app is valuable to students' educational experience**

"I really like how interactive the app is. I like it when technology brings history to life. I really appreciate how the app has comprehensive quizzes— these always help me make sure I've retained the material, so I would definitely use the app."

Allyx Nicolici,
student at California State University Sacramento

Vivid accounts of travelers provide compelling context about historical events that shaped our world

Travelers—merchants, poets, rulers, adventurers, missionaries, and scholars and their voyages—provide a framework for each chapter that draws students into the stories of world history.

8 Hindu and Buddhist States and Societies in Asia, 100–1000

In 838, at the age of forty-five, the Japanese monk **Ennin** (EN-nin) (793–864) joined a Japanese delegation that was the last of nearly twenty official delegations sent to China by the Japanese government. The Japanese emperors wanted to learn the reasons for the success of the Tang dynasty (618–907), the most powerful empire in East Asia and a model for all rulers hoping to strengthen their own governments. The Tang dynasty blueprint for rule drew on the earlier Qin/Han blueprint (see Chapter 4) but added other elements, most importantly state support for Buddhism. The Japanese delegation of over thirty people included both officials and monks like Ennin, who hoped to study with knowledgeable teachers and to obtain copies of books not available in Japan. Eleven days after the four ships departed from the modern Japanese port of Fukuoka, it began to rain:

The east wind was blowing fiercely, and the waves were raging high. The ship was suddenly dashed up onto a shoal. In trepidation we immediately lowered sail, but the corners of the rudder snapped in two places, while the waves from both east and west battered the ship a[nd]... the blade of the rudder was stuck... was about to break up, we cut dow[n]... rudder. The ship straightway floa[ted]... waves came from the east, the sh[ip]... when they came from the west, it...

Portrait of Ennin

[From Edwin O. Reischauer, trans., *Ennin's Diary: The Record of a Pilgrimage to China in Search of the Law* (New York: Ronald Press Company, 1955).]

Travelers provide crucial comparisons between their own societies and those they visited. One traveler is featured in every chapter, and six travelers have been changed for the second edition. For example, in Chapter 8, "Hindu and Buddhist States and Societies in Asia," readers are introduced to Ennin, a Japanese Buddhist monk who goes to China to study.

Each chapter begins with a detailed map that illustrates the traveler's route.

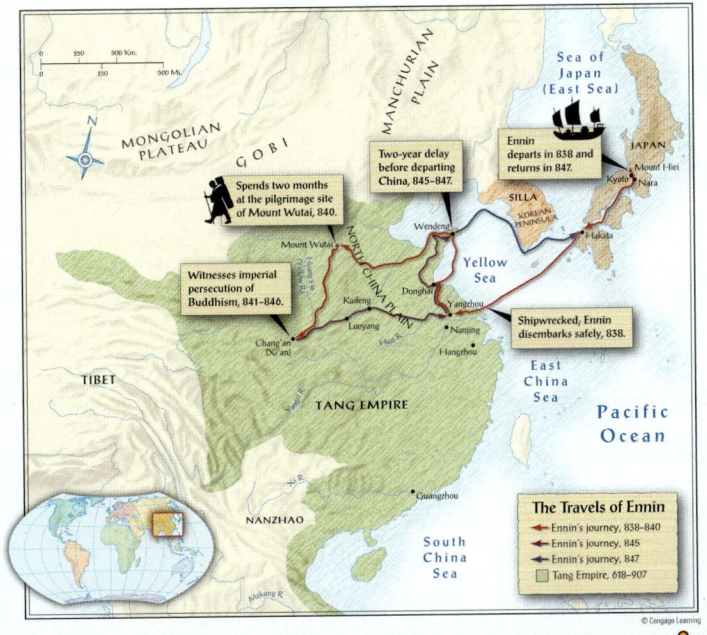

*"I love the approach. My department has recently taken a more global history approach to world civ and [*Voyages in World History*] seems well suited to this approach."*

LaQuita Saunders,
Arkansas State University

Join this chapter's traveler on "Voyages," an interactive tour of historic sites and events:
www.cengagebrain.com

Preview 3

Teaching students how to think critically about the past

Using detailed images and discussion questions, *Visual Evidence in Primary Sources* features help students identify and examine historical evidence within artifacts, works of art, and architecture.

Borobudur: A Buddhist Monument in Java, Indonesia

The largest Buddhist monument in the world lies not in the homeland of the Buddha in India but over 1,000 miles (1,600 km) to the southeast at Borobudur on the island of Java in Indonesia. The Shailendra (SHAI-len-drah) kings (ca. 775–860) built the monument out of volcanic rock sometime in the eighth or ninth century, just as they were consolidating their rule. When they moved their capital to a different location in east Java, they abandoned the magnificent complex, and it lay unknown until the early nineteenth century, when Sir Thomas Raffles, founder of Singapore, saw it covered with mold and lichen plants in the middle of a dense forest.

Since no surviving documents explain the meaning of the elements of the monument, analysts must study the different sections of the enormous structure to reconstruct its possible meaning. Rising over 100 feet (31.5 m) above the ground, the monument rests on a large squarish base measuring 400 feet (122 m) on each side. The overall effect resembles the ziggurat temples of Mesopotamia. Staircases at the center of each level lead up to the next, and visitors walk around each level for a total of 3 miles (5 km) until they reach the top.

The lowest level of the monument, originally below ground, depicts an underground hell for those who do not obey Buddhist teachings. The four square terraces above contain over 2,500 panels, most showing scenes from the earlier lives of the Buddha. Monks and guides probably explained the meaning of these scenes to pilgrims. Near the top, the visitor reaches the three terraces holding seventy-two bodhisattvas, each sitting under a bell-shaped stone with holes to look through. At the top of the monument stands an empty stupa, which may have originally held a relic.

Borobudur was a pilgrimage site for people all over Southeast Asia. Pilgrims brought simple clay objects in the shape of stupas and buried them underground at the site. Archaeologists have unearthed 2,397 clay stupas and 252 clay tablets with writing on them. Pilgrims also buried clay pots and sheets of silver covered with written Buddhist charms, either to keep away evil spirits or to bring good health. The many languages on the tablets indicate that people came from great distances to see Borobudur and to make offerings to the Buddha who came to be worshiped so far from his original home.

Most analysts concur that the monument was designed to lead pilgrims from the underworld, shown in the base, up through the five platforms showing human existence, through the world of the seventy-two bodhisattvas, to the single Buddha on top who had attained enlightenment. While the content of the different panels is clearly inspired by Buddhism, the design of the monument, with its multiple ascending levels, is distinctly local. No other Buddhist monument is like it.

Borobudur is made of 2 million separate blocks of yellow-brown andesite, volcanic rock found throughout Java. Each year over 70 inches (2 m) of rain falls on the rocks, creating the perfect environment for moss and lichen to thrive. Between 1973 and 1983, with UNESCO support, workers dismantled the monument, removed and cleaned each of the blocks, and restored the monument for the third time since its rediscovery in the early 1800s.

QUESTION FOR ANALYSIS

» *How had Buddhist worship at stupas changed from the first century B.C.E. at Sanchi (see "Visual Evidence in Primary Sources," Chapter 3) to the eighth and ninth centuries at Borobudur?*

206

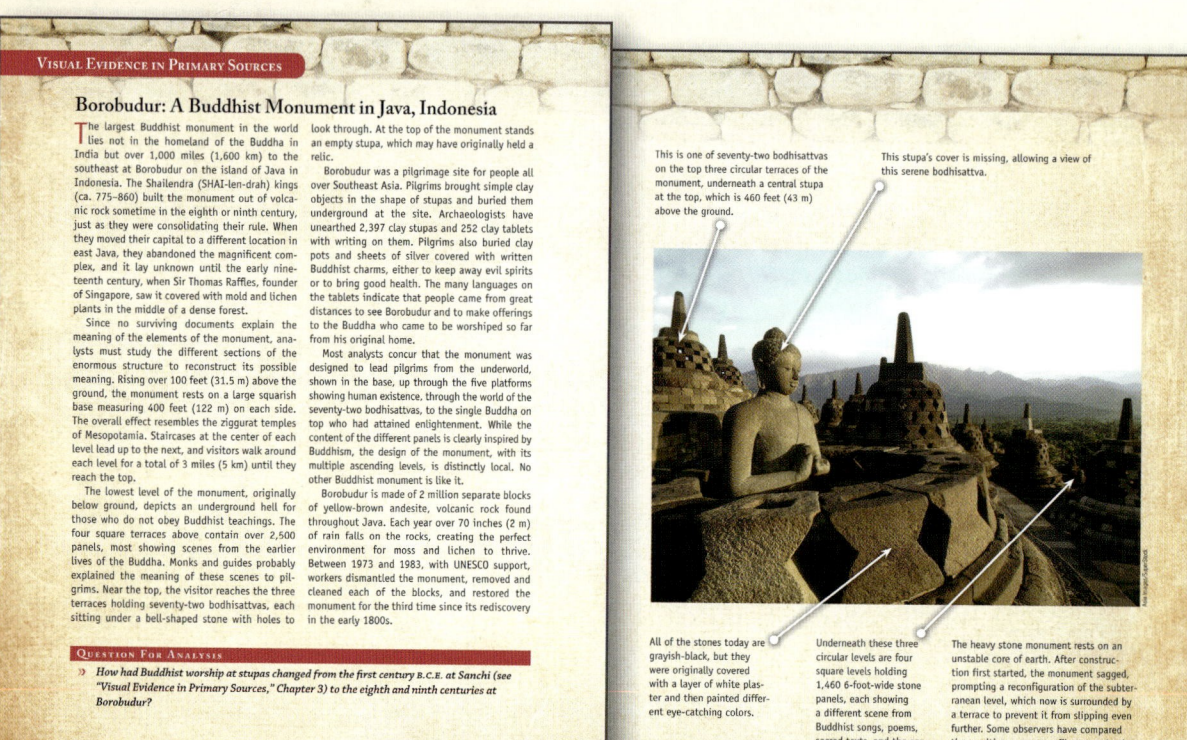

This is one of seventy-two bodhisattvas on the top three circular terraces of the monument, underneath a central stupa at the top, which is 460 feet (43 m) above the ground.

This stupa's cover is missing, allowing a view of this serene bodhisattva.

All of the stones today are grayish-black, but they were originally covered with a layer of white plaster and then painted different eye-catching colors.

Underneath these three circular levels are four square levels holding 1,460 6-foot-wide stone panels, each showing a different scene from Buddhist songs, poems, sacred texts, and the earlier lives of the Buddha.

The heavy stone monument rests on an unstable core of earth. After construction first started, the monument sagged, prompting a reconfiguration of the subterranean level, which now is surrounded by a terrace to prevent it from slipping even further. Some observers have compared the resulting uneven profile to a cake that did not rise properly.

207

Teaching Buddhism in a Confucian Society

Monks frequently told stories to teach ordinary people the tenets of Buddhism. The story of the Indian monk Maudgalyayana (mowd-GAH-lee-yah-yah-nah) survives in a Sanskrit version, composed between 300 B.C.E. and 300 C.E., and a much longer Chinese version from a manuscript dated 921. This story has enormous appeal in China (it is frequently performed as Chinese opera or on television) because it portrays the dilemma of those who wanted to be good Confucian sons as well as good Buddhists. Maudgalyayana may have been filial, but he was unable to fulfill his Confucian obligations as a son because he did not bear a male heir. The Buddhist narrator takes great pains to argue that he can still be a good son because Confucian offerings have no power in a Buddhist underworld.

In the Sanskrit version, Maudgalyayana, one of the Buddha's disciples, realizes that his mother has been reborn in the real world and asks the Buddha to help her to attain nirvana. Maudgalyayana and the Buddha travel to find the mother, who attains nirvana after hearing the Buddha preach.

In the Chinese version, the protagonist retains his Indian name but acts like a typical Chinese son

in every respect. The tale contrasts the behavior of the virtuous, if slightly dim, Maudgalyayana with his mother, who never gave any support to her local monastery and even kept for herself money that her son had asked her to give the monks. As a filial son, he cannot believe her capable of any crime, and he searches through all the different compartments of the Chinese hell to find her. Unrepentant to the very end of the tale, she explains that traditional Confucian offerings to the ancestors have no power in the underworld. Only offerings to the Buddhist order, such as paying monks to copy Buddhist texts, can help to ease her suffering. At the end of the story, the Buddha himself frees her from the underworld, a grim series of hells that do not exist in the Sanskrit original.

Sources: John Strong, "Filial Piety and Buddhism: The Indian Antecedents to a 'Chinese' Problem," in *Traditions in Contact and Change: Selected Proceedings of the XIVth Congress of the International Association for the History of Religions*, ed. Peter Slater and Donald Wiebe (Winnipeg, Man.: Wilfrid Laurier University Press, 1980), p. 180; from *Tun-huang Popular Narratives*, by Victor H. Mair. Copyright © 1983 Cambridge University Press. Reprinted with permission of Cambridge University Press.

Sanskrit Version

From afar, [Maudgalyayana's mother] Bhadrakanya [bud-DRAH-kahn-ee-ya] saw her son, and, as soon as she saw him, she rushed up to him exclaiming, "Ah! At long last I see my little boy!" Thereupon the crowd of people who had assembled said: "He is an aged wandering monk, and she is a young girl—how can she be his mother?" But the Venerable Maha Maudgalyayana replied, "Sirs, these skandhas* of mine were fostered by her; therefore she is my mother."

Then the Blessed One, knowing the disposition, propensity, nature and circumstances of Bhadrakanya, preached a sermon fully penetrating the meaning of the Four Noble Truths. And when Bhadrakanya had heard it, she was brought to the realization of the fruit of entering the stream.

*skandhas The five aggregates—form, feelings, perceptions, karmic constituents, and consciousness—which in Buddhism are the basis of the personality.

QUESTIONS FOR ANALYSIS

» *What are the main differences between the Indian and Chinese versions?*
» *How do they portray the fate of the mother after her death?*
» *What is the Chinese underworld like?*

214

Movement of Ideas Through Primary Sources features include an excerpt from one or more primary sources with discussion questions. This feature encourages students to develop the core historical skill of primary source analysis.

Preview 4

Connections between the world today and historical events are illustrated in *World History in Today's World*. Instructors can use this feature to spark discussion about why world history matters today.

WORLD HISTORY IN TODAY'S WORLD

A World with Two Dalai Lamas?

The Dalai Lama, perhaps the most famous Buddhist teacher in the world, is the spiritual leader of Tibet's 6 million Buddhists. Tibetan Buddhists believe that he is the manifestation of Avalokiteshvara (whose Tibetan name is Chenrezig), the bodhisattva of compassion and patron saint of Tibet. Born in Tibet in 1935, the current Dalai Lama, His Holiness Tenzin Gyatso, was identified as the new Dalai Lama when he was three years old.

Following the traditional process, senior monks searched for children born near the time the previous Dalai Lama had died. These monks showed many children the possessions of the deceased Dalai Lama alongside other items that had not belonged to him. Tenzin Gyatso successfully identified the previous Dalai Lama's possessions, crying out loud "It's mine, it's mine." This and other indications persuaded the search team that the child was indeed the reincarnation of the deceased Dalai Lama, and Tenzin Gyatso left his parents to live in a local monastery and study Buddhism. In 1940 he traveled to Lhasa, the Tibetan capital, where he was formally named the spiritual leader of Tibet at a ritual in the Potala Palace. In 1959, when the People's Republic of China established direct administration of the region, the Dalai Lama left Tibet and has since lived in exile in Dharamsala, India, along with several thousand other Tibetans.

How will the next Dalai Lama be chosen? The Dalai Lama has advocated changing the traditional process so that someone who does not live in Tibet—perhaps even a non-Tibetan—could succeed him. Adamantly opposed to this proposal, the Chinese officials who govern Tibet argue that the next Dalai Lama should be chosen following the traditional process. Many observers believe that the Tibetan exile community and the Chinese government will each choose their own candidate, with the result that two men will claim to be the legitimate successor of the Dalai Lama.

As is true of the Dalai Lama, certain men head individual schools of Buddhists, but no single person claims to lead all the world's Buddhists. Scholars of religion are not certain how to calculate the total number of Buddhists but estimate it at 350 million, with 100 million in China and 90 million in Japan. While many modern Chinese or Japanese, if asked, may identify themselves as Buddhists, they visit Buddhist temples only rarely and devote less time to religious devotion than do Tibetan Buddhists.

Sources: The New York Times; www.dalailama.com; www.adherents.com.

CONTEXT AND CONNECTIONS

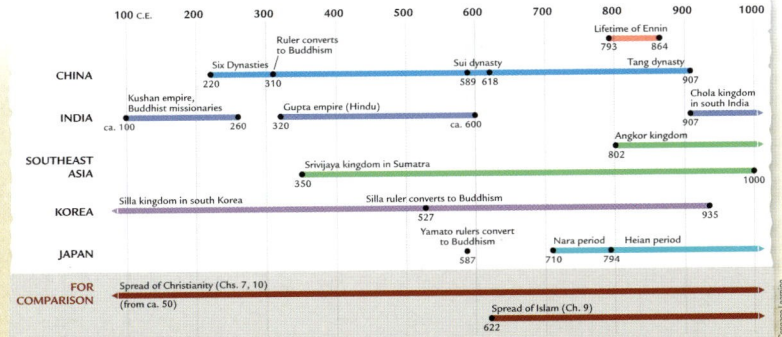

Students will better understand historical events and global patterns with the new *Context and Connections* feature. Found at the end of each chapter, the timeline and analysis guides students as they make connections among regions.

The Place of Buddhism and Hinduism in World History

In the year 100, the only Buddhists in the world lived in India and Sri Lanka; by the year 1000, Buddhist teachings had spread throughout the entire region encompassing India, coastal and inland Southeast Asia, China, Tibet, Korea, and Japan. When the Japanese monk Ennin traveled in China between 838 and 847, he encountered Buddhist monks from north and south India, Sri Lanka, Central Asia, Japan, Korea, and, of course, China. Between 380 and 400, the Roman woman Egeria had traveled as a pilgrim to Jerusalem to see where Jesus had lived and to visit monasteries in Turkey (see Chapter 7). Ennin's reasons for going on pilgrimage differed. His purpose was not to see where the Buddha had lived, but to study and obtain books so that he could understand complex Buddhist teachings more completely.

Chinese monasteries hosted Indian monks who taught Sanskrit, the language of many texts from India, but, as the centuries passed, more and more Buddhist texts were translated into Chinese. A beginning student of Sanskrit, Ennin read these texts in Chinese. Like Greek and Latin in the Christian world, Sanskrit and Chinese were spoken and written throughout the Buddhist world. Ennin found that he could brush-talk by writing Chinese characters with almost every Buddhist he met.

Buddhism became a major world religion during the same centuries as Christianity did. No single event in Buddhist history marked a turning point like the Edict of Milan in 313 or the 380 decree making Christianity the official religion of the Roman empire (see Chapter 7). Instead, drawn by the chakravartin ideal,

*"I have recommended the book to many colleagues. I think that **Voyages** presents us with a compelling and refreshing approach to world civilizations. Here is a text that my students might actually read."*

Derek Maxfield, Genesee Community College

Voyages in World History is supported by a carefully developed package of student learning resources.

Aplia

Aplia prompts history students to contextualize and analyze information. The exercises, written by trained historians who have taught undergraduates, ensure that students think critically and draw conclusions rather than merely memorize historical facts.

- Auto-assigned and graded activities hold students accountable for the material before class, increasing their effort and preparation.

- Primary source-based activities encourage critical thinking.

- Interactive maps provide practice interpreting this key historical medium.

- Grades are automatically recorded and instructors can monitor class performance and individual student performance on a topic-by-topic basis.

- Map and writing tutorials guide students through the process of interpreting information and effectively communicating their ideas within the framework of the history discipline.

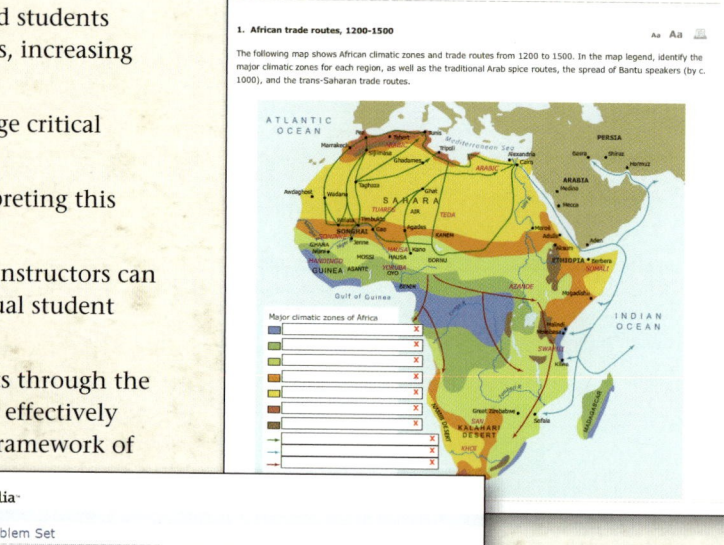

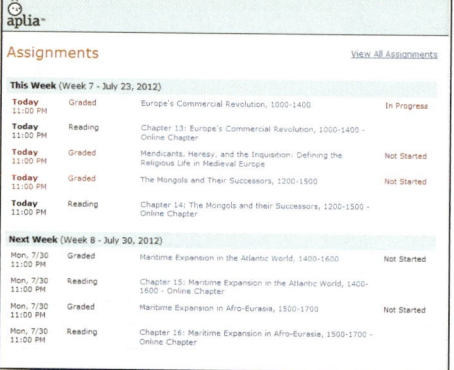

- **88% say it is easy to integrate into their class plans**
- **85% say that it saves them time**
- **79% say that it is user-friendly and requires little to no training**

*"I think that **Aplia**, when used in conjunction with the text, is probably one of the best web-based platforms. The students who came to class prepared were already thinking about the material and were prepared to tackle 'bigger questions'."*

Mari Nicholson-Preuss,
University of Houston–Downtown

World History

Engaging. Trackable. Affordable.

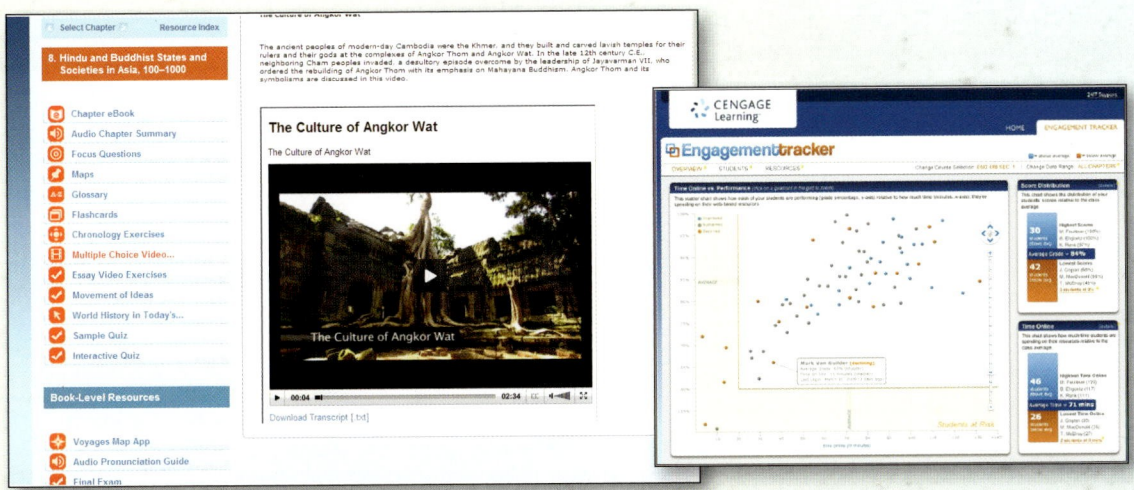

Complement your text and course content with study and practice materials. Cengage Learning's History **CourseMate** brings course concepts to life with interactive learning, study, and exam preparation tools that support the printed textbook. Watch student comprehension soar as your class works with the printed textbook and the textbook-specific website. **CourseMate** goes beyond the book to deliver what you need!

CourseMate has unique features!

- Use Engagement Tracker to monitor student engagement in the course and watch student comprehension soar as your class works with the printed textbook and the textbook-specific website.

- An interactive eBook allows students to take notes, highlight, search, and interact with embedded media (such as quizzes, flash cards, primary sources, and videos).

Learn more at www.cengage.com/coursemate.

CengageBrain.com

Save students time and money—direct them to **CengageBrain.com**, a single destination for more than 10,000 new textbooks, eTextbooks, eChapters, study tools, and audio supplements. Students have the freedom to purchase a la carte exactly what they need, when they need it.

World History

Create an affordable and customized online reader in minutes!

CourseReader lets you choose from thousands of primary and secondary sources—including permissions-cleared readings, audio, and video selections.

CourseReader is Cengage Learning's easy, affordable way to build your own online customizable reader. Select exactly and only the material you want your students to work with. Each selection can be listened to (using the "Listen" button) to accommodate varied learning styles. Instructors can even add their own notes to readings to direct students' attention or ask them questions about a particular passage. Each primary source is accompanied by an introduction and questions to help students understand the reading.

With **CourseReader**, you can:

- Easily search and preview source material for your course

- Publish your notes to students, assign due dates, assemble and re-order selections, archive readers from previous terms, and adapt them for future classes

- Provide students with pedagogical support, including descriptive introductions that add context to many of the primary source documents, and critical-thinking and multiple-choice questions that reinforce key points

- Utilize Editor's Choice selections as time-saving starting points

Learn more and view a demo!
www.cengage.com/coursereader

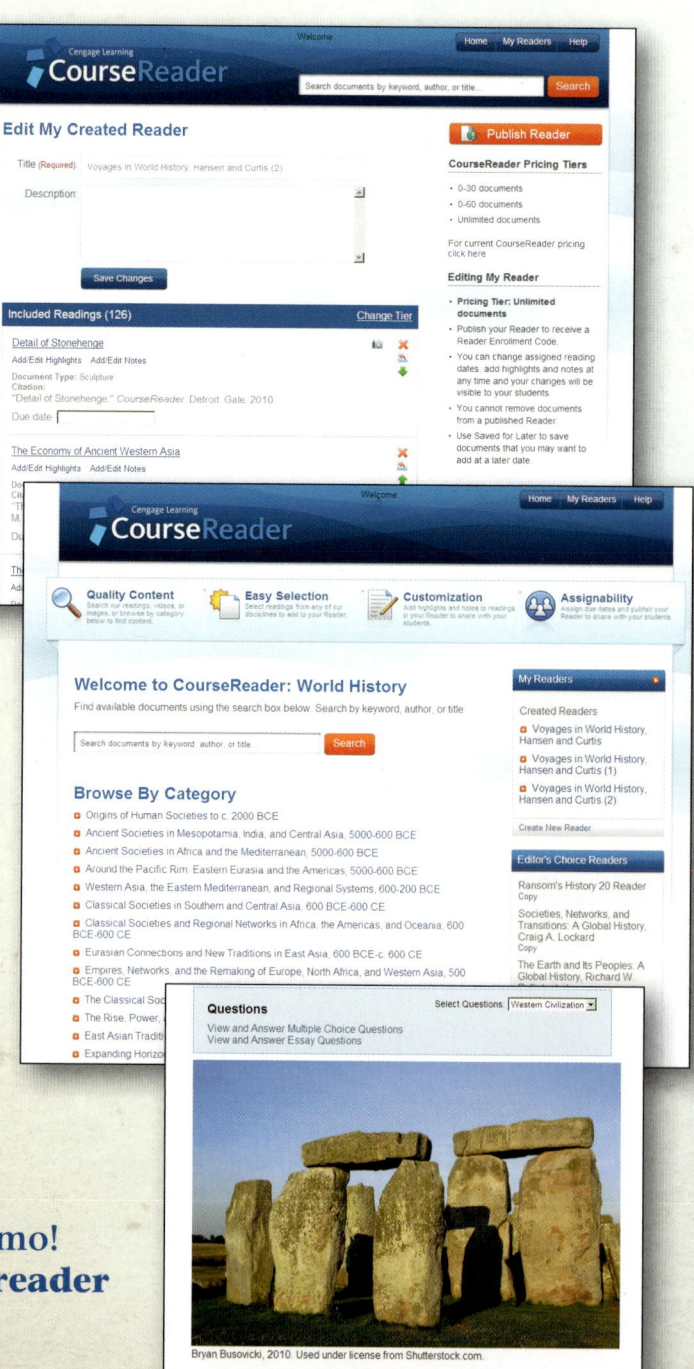

VOYAGES
in World History

Second Edition

Valerie Hansen
YALE UNIVERSITY

Kenneth R. Curtis
CALIFORNIA STATE UNIVERSITY LONG BEACH

WADSWORTH
CENGAGE Learning·

Australia • Brazil • Japan • Korea • Mexico • Singapore • Spain • United Kingdom • United States

WADSWORTH
CENGAGE Learning·

Voyages in World History, **Second Edition**
Valerie Hansen, Kenneth R. Curtis

Editor-in-Chief: Lynn Uhl

Senior Publisher: Suzanne Jeans

Acquiring Sponsoring Editor: Brooke Barbier

Development Editor: Jan Fitter

Associate Development Editor: Clint Attebery

Assistant Editor: Jamie Bushell

Editorial Assistant: Katie Coaster

Managing Media Editor: Lisa Ciccolo

Marketing Manager: Melissa Larmon

Marketing Coordinator: Lorreen R. Towle

Marketing and Communication Director: Talia Wise

Senior Content Project Manager: Carol Newman

Senior Art Director: Cate Rickard Barr

Manufacturing Planner: Sandee Milewski

Senior Rights Acquisition Specialist: Jennifer Meyer Dare

Production Service/Compositor: Lachina Publishing Services

Text and Cover Designer: RHDG | Riezebos Holzbaur

Cover Image: Train in India with soldier riding up front/Steve McCurry/Magnum Photos NYC107630.

For product information and technology assistance, contact us at
Cengage Learning Customer & Sales Support, 1-800-354-9706
For permission to use material from this text or product,
submit all requests online at **cengage.com/permissions**
Further permissions questions can be emailed to
permissionrequest@cengage.com

Library of Congress Control Number: 2012943412

Student Edition:

ISBN-13: 978-1-133-60781-6

ISBN-10: 1-133-60781-0

Wadsworth
20 Channel Center Street
Boston, MA 02210
USA

Cengage Learning is a leading provider of customized learning solutions with office locations around the globe, including Singapore, the United Kingdom, Australia, Mexico, Brazil, and Japan. Locate your local office at: **www.cengage.com/global.**

Cengage Learning products are represented in Canada by Nelson Education, Ltd.

For your course and learning solutions, visit **www.cengage.com**.

Purchase any of our products at your local college store or at our preferred online store **www.cengagebrain.com**.

Instructors: Please visit **login.cengage.com** and log in to access instructor-specific resources.

Printed in Canada
1 2 3 4 5 6 7 16 15 14 13 12

BRIEF CONTENTS

CONTENTS

CHAPTER **1**

The Peopling of the World, to 4000 B.C.E.   2

Traveler: *Mungo Man*

CHAPTER **2**

The First Complex Societies in the Eastern Mediterranean, ca. 4000–550 B.C.E.   26

Traveler: *Gilgamesh*

Photo credits: Courtesy Jim Bowler / The Schøyen Collection, MS 1989 www.schoyencollection.com

CHAPTER **3**

Ancient India and the Rise of Buddhism, 2600 B.C.E.–100 C.E.   56

Traveler: *Ashoka*

CHAPTER **4**

Blueprint for Empire: China, 1200 B.C.E.–220 C.E.   82

Traveler: *First Emperor of the Qin Dynasty*

CHAPTER **5**

The Americas and the Islands of the Pacific, to 1200 C.E.   108

Traveler: *Mau Piailug*

CHAPTER **6**

New Empires in Iran and Greece, 2000 B.C.E.–651 C.E.   136

Traveler: *Herodotus*

CHAPTER **7**

The Roman Empire and the Rise of Christianity, 509 B.C.E.–476 C.E.

166

Traveler: *Polybius*

CHAPTER **10**

The Multiple Centers of Europe, 500–1000   256

Travelers: *Gudrid and Thorfinn Karlsefni*

CHAPTER **11**

Expanding Trade Networks in Africa and India, 1000–1500   286

Traveler: *Ibn Battuta*

CHAPTER **12**

China's Commercial Revolution, ca. 900–1276   *316*

Traveler: *Li Qingzhao*

CHAPTER **13**

Europe's Commercial Revolution, 1000–1400   *342*

Travelers: *Peter Abelard and Heloise*

CHAPTER **14**

The Mongols and Their Successors, 1200–1500

370

Traveler: *William of Rubruck*

CHAPTER **15**

Maritime Expansion in the Atlantic World, 1400–1600 *402*

Traveler: *Christopher Columbus*

CHAPTER **16**

Maritime Expansion in Afro-Eurasia, 1500–1700 *434*

Traveler: *Matteo Ricci*

Photo credits: Hulton-Deutsch Collection/Corbis / From *Memoirs of Halide Edib* by Halide Adivar Edib (N.J.: Gorgias Press). Reprinted by permission of Gorgias Press

Photo credits: Australian War Memorial, Negative Number P00885.001 / © Stefano Rellandini/Reuters/Corbis

Maps

WORLD HISTORY IN TODAY'S WORLD

PREFACE

What makes this book different from other world history textbooks?

- Each chapter opens with a narrative about a Traveler, whose real-life story is woven throughout the chapter. The *Voyages Map App* then continues the journey online by using Google Earth™ to transport students to historic sites and locations visited by the Travelers, allowing students to explore the past and make connections to the world today.

- Shorter than most world history textbooks, this survey still covers all of the major topics required in a world history course, as well as others we have found to be of interest to our students.

- The book's theme of movement highlights cultural contact and is reinforced in both the *Voyages Map App* and the chapter features, Movement of Ideas Through Primary Sources and Visual Evidence in Primary Sources, which teach analytical skills by inviting students to compare viewpoints.

- The chapter-ending Context and Connections feature, new in the second edition, will help students better understand the connections among different regions and periods, as well as global effects and trends.

- The print text reinforces the online experience, which includes the *Voyages Map App, Aplia™,* and *CourseMate.* See the Ancillaries section below for full details on each.

- *CourseReader: World History* and *Hansen's Editor's Choice CourseReader* are available with the text and allow instructors to build their own customized online reader. See the Ancillaries section for details.

- Innovative maps in the text show each Traveler's route while inviting students to think analytically about geography and its role in world history, and the *Voyages Map App* brings the maps to life online.

- A beautiful, engaging design features an on-page glossary, a pronunciation guide, and chapter-opening focus questions (with answers supplied online for review). These tools help students grasp and retain the main ideas of the chapters.

This world history textbook will, we hope, be enjoyable for students to read and for instructors to teach. We have focused on thirty-two different people and the journeys they took, starting forty thousand years ago with Mungo Man in Australia (Chapter 1) and concluding in the twenty-first century with Chinese artist Ai Weiwei. Each of the thirty-two chapters introduces multiple focus points. First, the Traveler's narrative introduces the home society and the new civilizations visited, demonstrating our theme of the movement of people, ideas, trade goods, and artistic motifs and the results of these contacts. We introduce other evidence, often drawn from primary sources (marked in the running text with italics in this edition), to help students reason like historians. Each chapter also covers changes in political structure, the spread of world religions, and prevailing social structure and gender relations. Other important topics include cultural components and the effects of technology and environment.

The chapter-opening narratives enhance the scope and depth of the topics covered. The Travelers take us to Tang China with the Japanese Buddhist monk Ennin, to Africa and South Asia with the hajj pilgrim Ibn Battuta, to Peru with the cross-dressing soldier and adventurer Catalina de Erauso, across the Atlantic with the African Olaudah Equiano, and to Britain during the Industrial Revolution with the Russian anarchist Mikhail Bakunin. Their vivid accounts are important sources about these long-ago events that shaped our world. Almost all of these travel accounts are available in English translation, listed in the suggested readings at the end of each chapter.

Students new to world history, or to history in general, will find it easier, we hope, to focus on the experience of thirty-two individuals before focusing on the broader trends in their societies and their place in world history. The interactive *Voyages Map App* further engages the new student.

Instead of a canned list of dates, each chapter covers the important topics at a sensible and careful pace, without compromising coverage or historical rigor. Students compare the Traveler's perceptions with alternative sources, and so awaken their interest in the larger developments. Our goal was to select the most compelling topics and engaging illustrations from the entire record of human civilization, and present them in a clear spatial and temporal framework, to counter the view of history as an interminable compendium of geographical place names and facts.

We have chosen a range of Travelers, both male and female, from all over the world. These individuals help cast our world history in a truly global format, avoiding the Eurocentrism that prompted the introduction of world history courses in the first place. Many Travelers were well born and well educated, and many were not.

Our goal in focusing on the experience of individual Travelers is to help make students enthusiastic about world history, while achieving the right balance between the Traveler's experience and the course material. We measure our success by all the encouragement we have received both from instructors who teach the course and from students.

We aspire to answer many of the unmet needs of professors and students in world history. Because our book is not encyclopedic, and because each chapter begins with a narrative of a trip, our book is more readable than its competitors, which strain for all-inclusive coverage. They pack so many names and facts into their text that they leave little time to introduce beginning students to historical method. Because our book gives students a chance to read primary sources in depth, particularly in the Movement of Ideas Through Primary Sources feature, instructors can spend class time teaching students how to reason historically—not just imparting the details of a given national history. Each chapter includes focus questions that make it easier for instructors new to world history to facilitate interactive learning. Students can review answers to those questions online.

Our approach particularly suits the needs of young professors who have been trained in only one geographic area of history. Our book does not presuppose that instructors already have broad familiarity with the history of each important world civilization.

Theme and Approach

Our theme of movement and contact is key to world history because world historians focus on connections among the different societies of the past. The movement of people, whether in voluntary migrations or forced slavery, has been one of the most fruitful topics for world historians, as are the experiences of individual Travelers. Their reactions to the people they met on their journeys reveal much about their home societies as well as about the societies they visited.

Our focus on individual Travelers illustrates the increasing ease of contact among different civilizations with the passage of time. This theme highlights the developments that resulted from improved communications, travel among different places, the movement of trade goods, and the mixing of peoples. Such developments include the movement of world religions, mass migrations, and the spread of diseases like the plague. *Voyages* shows how travel has changed over time—how the distance covered by travelers has increased at the same time that the duration of trips has decreased. As a result, more and more people have been able to go to societies distant from their own.

Voyages and its integrated online components examine the different reasons for travel over the centuries. While some people were captured in battle and forced to go to new places, others visited different societies to teach or to learn the beliefs of a new religion like Buddhism, Christianity, or Islam. This theme, of necessity, treats questions about the environment: How far and over what terrain did early man travel? How did sailors learn to use monsoon winds to their advantage? What were the effects of technological breakthroughs like steamships, trains, and airplanes—and the use of fossil fuels to power them? Because students can link the experiences of individual Travelers to this theme, movement provides the memorable organizing principle for the book, a principle reinforced in the interactive online journeys offered by the *Voyages Map App*.

Having a single theme allows us to provide broad coverage of the most important topics in world history. Students who use this book will learn how empires and nations grew in power or influence, and how their governmental organization differed. Students need not commit long lists of rulers' names to memory: instead they focus on those leaders who created innovative political structures. This focus fits well with travel, since the different Travelers were able to make certain journeys because of the political situation at the time. For example, William of Rubruck was able to travel across all of Eurasia because of the unification brought by the Mongol empire, while the size and strength of the Ottoman empire facilitated Evliya Çelebi's travels to Vienna and Egypt and across southwest Asia.

Many rulers patronized religions to increase their control over the people they ruled, allowing a smooth introduction to the teachings of the major world religions. Volume 1 introduces the major religions and explains how originally regional religions moved across political borders to become world religions. Volume 2 provides context for today's complex interplay of religion and politics and the complex cultural outcomes that occurred when religions expanded into new world regions. The final two chapters analyze the renewed contemporary focus on religion, as seen in the rise of fundamentalist movements in various parts of the world. Our focus on Travelers offers an opportunity to explore their involvement with religion, and *Voyages'* close attention to the religious traditions of diverse societies, often related through the Travelers' tales, will give students a familiarity with the primary religious traditions of the world.

The topic of gender is an important one in world history, and throughout, *Voyages* devotes extensive space to the experience of women. Although in many societies literacy among women was severely limited, especially in the premodern era, we have included as many women Travelers as possible. In addition, extensive coverage of gender allows students to grasp the experience of ordinary women.

Features

We see the features of this book as an opportunity to help students better understand the main text, and to expand that understanding as they explore the integrated online features. Here, we describe the features in the printed book. Details about online features are found in the Ancillaries section below.

Chapter Opening Map

At the beginning of each chapter a map illustrates the route of the Traveler using imaginative graphics. The opening section of each chapter also provides a biographical sketch for the chapter's Traveler, a portrait, and a passage from his or her writings (or, if not available, a passage about the individual). This feature should capture the student's attention at the outset of each chapter.

Movement of Ideas Through Primary Sources

This feature offers an introduction, an extensive excerpt from one or more primary sources, and discussion questions. The chosen passages emphasize the movement of ideas, usually by contrasting two different explanations of the same idea. The feature aims to develop the core historical skill of analyzing original sources. Topics include "The Five Pillars of Islam," as described in the Hadith of Gabriel

and by a contemporary Chinese encyclopedia, and "Gandhi and Nehru on Progress and Civilization."

Visual Evidence in Primary Sources

The goal of this feature is to train students to examine an artifact, a work of art, or a photograph and to glean historical information from the find or artwork. A close-up photograph of the Chinese terracotta warriors, for example, shows students how the figurines were mass produced, yet have individual features. Portraits of George Washington and Napoleon Bonaparte lead students to analyze the symbolism they contain and how the portraits serve as *representations* of political power. Discussion questions help students analyze the information presented.

World History in Today's World

This brief feature picks an element of modern life with roots in the period under study. We chose topics interesting to students (for example, "Avatar: Then and Now" and "The Jasmine Revolution and the Arab Spring"), and we highlight their relationship to the past. This feature should provide material to trigger discussion and help instructors explain why world history matters, since students often have little sense that the past has anything to do with their own lives.

Changes in the Second Edition

Every chapter of this new edition has been carefully checked and revised for readability and clarity of language. In every chapter, topics and subtopics have been added or elaborated on, and recent scholarship has been incorporated throughout the text. Some highlights of specific changes in the second edition follow.

- A chapter-closing Context and Connections feature consists of a narrative conclusion supported by the chapter's timeline. The concluding essay makes broad connections and offers global and temporal context for the topics and regions discussed in the chapter and in other chapters, so that students will appreciate the global implications of each chapter. The timeline includes a new section showing events from other regions or periods to help students place that chapter's material in a larger historical framework.

- A total of eight Visual Evidence in Primary Sources features and eleven Movement of Ideas Through Primary Sources features have been replaced. Nearly all of the World History in Today's World features have been replaced.
- Approximately 25 percent of the illustrations have been replaced with new images, with an eye toward visual interest and engagement.
- Chapter 1 has a new Traveler, Mungo Man (and Mungo Woman), allowing a focus on the earliest migration to Australia and the use of boats.
- Chapter 5's new Traveler, Mau Piailug (1932–2010), was a contemporary Polynesian navigator who, like Polynesian voyagers before 1350, used only traditional methods—the stars, ocean currents, and so on—and no navigational instruments. The chapter also incorporates expanded coverage of the preclassic Maya, in particular of the El Mirador site.
- Chapter 8 has a new Traveler, Ennin, a Japanese monk who traveled in China to study Buddhism, and the chapter has been revised to further strengthen the core theme of Buddhism across regions.
- In Chapter 11, the coverage of the Delhi sultanate has been significantly expanded, including the addition of a new map.
- Chapter 14 includes a new map of Zheng He's voyages and Ming dynasty China and new coverage of the Pax Mongolica.
- Chapter 17 has a new Traveler, Evliya Çelebi, a widely traveled Ottoman diplomat.
- Chapter 23 has a new Traveler, Mikhail Bakunin, the Russian anarchist, and anarchism has been added to the coverage of nineteenth-century ideologies. A new table clearly demonstrates the massive shift of production from east to west.
- In Chapter 26, the opening section introducing the New Imperialism has been overhauled to more fully and clearly depict the "big picture." New material covers the Pacific Islands, Australia, and New Zealand.
- Chapters 27–29 include additions to emphasize the repression and violence of communist regimes in the Soviet Union and Cuba.
- Chapter 32 has been overhauled and updated, and shortened by roughly 10 percent. The new Traveler is Ai Weiwei, the world-renowned Chinese artist persecuted by the Chinese government for his support of individual freedom. Protest and democracy are now a major theme of the chapter.

Ancillaries

A wide array of supplements accompany this text to help students better master the material and to help instructors teach from the book:

Instructor's Resources

Power Lecture DVD with ExamView® and JoinIn®
ISBN-10: 1285057066 | ISBN-13: 9781285057064
This dual platform, all-in-one multimedia resource includes the Instructor's Resource Manual; the Test Bank, prepared by Dolores Grapsas of New River Community College, which includes key term identification, multiple-choice, true/false, essay, and map questions; Microsoft® PowerPoint® slides of both lecture outlines and images and maps from the text that can be used as offered or customized by importing personal lecture slides or other material; and *JoinIn* PowerPoint slides with clicker content. Also included is ExamView, an easy-to-use assessment and tutorial system that allows instructors to create, deliver, and customize tests in minutes. Instructors can build tests with as many as 250 questions using up to 12 question types, and using ExamView's complete word-processing capabilities, they can enter an unlimited number of new questions or edit existing ones.

eInstructor's Resource Manual

Prepared by Jim Simon of Genesee Community College. This manual has many features, including instructional objectives, chapter outlines, lecture topics and suggestions, classroom activities and writing assignments, exercises analyzing primary sources , activities for the Traveler, activities for the map app, map activities, geography questions, audiovisual biographies, suggested readings, and Internet resources. Available on the instructor's companion website.

CourseMate

ISBN-10: 1285060822 | ISBN-13: 9781285060828 PAC
ISBN-10: 1285060806 | ISBN-13: 9781285060804 IAC
ISBN-10: 1285060741 | ISBN-13: 9781285060743 SSO
Cengage Learning's History CourseMate brings course concepts to life with interactive learning, study, and exam preparation tools that support the printed textbook. History CourseMate includes an integrated eBook, interactive teaching and learning tools (including quizzes, flashcards, videos, and more), and EngagementTracker, a first-of-its-kind

tool that monitors student engagement in the course. Learn more at www.cengagebrain.com.

Aplia™
ISBN-10: 1285068726 | ISBN-13: 9781285068725
1-term PAC
ISBN-10: 128506867X | ISBN-13: 9781285068671
1-term IAC
ISBN-10: 1285068599 | ISBN-13: 9781285068596
2-semester PAC
ISBN-10: 1285068505 | ISBN-13: 9781285068503
2-semester IAC

Aplia is an online interactive learning solution that improves comprehension and outcomes by increasing student effort and engagement. Founded by a professor to enhance his own courses, Aplia provides automatically graded assignments with detailed, immediate explanations on every question. The interactive assignments have been developed to address the major concepts covered in *Voyages in World History, Second Edition* and are designed to promote critical thinking and engage students more fully in their learning. Question types include questions built around animated maps, primary sources such as newspaper extracts, or imagined scenarios (like engaging in a conversation with Benjamin Franklin or finding a diary and being asked to fill in some blank words); more in-depth primary source question sets that address a major topic with a number of related primary sources; and questions that promote deeper analysis of historical evidence. Images, video clips, and audio clips are incorporated in many of the questions. Students get immediate feedback on their work (not only what they got right or wrong, but why), and they can choose to see another set of related questions if they want to practice further. A searchable ebook is available inside the course as well, so that students can easily reference it as they are working. Map-reading and writing tutorials are available as well to get students off to a good start.

Aplia's simple-to-use course management interface allows instructors to post announcements, upload course materials, host student discussions, email students, and manage the gradebook; personalized support from a knowledgeable and friendly support team also offers assistance in customizing assignments to the instructor's course schedule. To learn more and view a demo for this book, visit www.aplia.com.

CourseReader
CourseReader is an online collection of primary and secondary sources that lets you create a customized electronic reader in minutes. With an easy-to-use interface and assessment tool, you can choose exactly what your students will be assigned—simply search or browse Cengage Learning's extensive document database to preview and select your customized collection of readings. In addition to print sources of all types (letters, diary entries, speeches, newspaper accounts, etc.), the collection includes a growing number of images and video and audio clips.

Each primary source document includes a descriptive headnote that puts the reading into context and is further supported by both critical thinking and multiple-choice questions designed to reinforce key points. For more information visit www.cengage.com/coursereader.

CengageBrain.com
Save your students time and money. Direct them to www.cengagebrain.com for choice in formats, savings, and a better chance to succeed in your class. *CengageBrain.com*, Cengage Learning's online store, is a single destination for more than ten thousand new textbooks, eTextbooks, eChapters, study tools, and audio supplements. Students have the freedom to purchase á la carte exactly what they need when they need it. Students can save 50 percent on the electronic textbook, and can pay as little as $1.99 for an individual eChapter.

Student Resources

Voyages Map App
ISBN-10: 1285055934 | ISBN-13: 9781285055930 PAC
ISBN-10: 1285055977 | ISBN-13: 9781285055978 IAC
ISBN-10: 128505590X | ISBN-13: 9781285055909 SSO
This interactive app guides students through the voyages taken by historical Travelers, allowing them to explore and examine the past. Using Google Earth™, students are transported to historic sites and locations visited by the Travelers and learn about each location's monuments, architecture, and historic significance. The app includes review questions, flashcards, and timelines to help students further understand the Travelers and their importance. After students visit the historic sites and analyze the map from each chapter, a Journey Quiz helps them evaluate their understanding of the location and events.

The *Voyages Map App* is available with CourseMate and is available for purchase at the iTunes® store.

Book Companion Site
ISBN-10: 113393899X | ISBN-13: 9781133938996
This is a website for students that features a wide assortment of resources to help students master the subject matter. The website, prepared by Jim Simon of Genesee Community College, includes a glossary, flashcards, sample quizzes, focus questions, critical thinking questions, maps, and primary sources.

Cengage Learning eBook
This interactive, multimedia eBook links out to rich media assets such as video and MP3 chapter summaries. Through this eBook, students can also access chapter objectives, chapter overviews, focus questions, a glossary, primary source documents, audio chapter summaries, zoomable and animated maps, web field trips, and more than twenty-five videos. Available at www.cengagebrain.com.

Doing History: Research and Writing in the Digital Age, Second Edition
ISBN-10: 1133587887 | ISBN-13: 9781133587880
Prepared by Michael J. Galgano, J. Chris Arndt, and Raymond M. Hyser of James Madison University. Whether you're starting down the path as a history major, or simply looking for a straightforward and systematic guide to writing a successful paper, you'll find this text to be an indispensible handbook to historical research. This text's "soup-to-nuts" approach to researching and writing about history addresses every step of the process, from locating your sources and gathering information to writing clearly and making proper use of various citation styles to avoid plagiarism. You'll also learn how to make the most of every tool available to you—especially the technology that helps you conduct the process efficiently and effectively. The second edition includes a special appendix linked to CourseReader (see above), where you can examine and interpret primary sources online.

The History Handbook, Second Edition
ISBN-10: 049590676X | ISBN-13: 9780495906766
Prepared by Carol Berkin of Baruch College, City University of New York, and Betty Anderson of Boston University. This book teaches students both basic and history-specific study skills, such as how to read primary sources, research historical topics, and correctly cite sources. Substantially less expensive than comparable skill-building texts, *The History Handbook* also offers tips for Internet research and evaluating online sources.

eAudio History Handbook
ISBN-10: 084006344X | ISBN-13: 9780840063441
Printed Access Card for eAudio History Handbook
ISBN-10: 1111471266 | ISBN-13: 9781111471262

Writing for College History
ISBN-10: 061830603X | ISBN-13: 9780618306039
Prepared by Robert M. Frakes of Clarion University. This brief handbook for survey courses in American history, Western civilization/European history, and world civilization guides students through the various types of writing assignments they encounter in a history class. Providing examples of student writing and candid assessments of student work, this text focuses on the rules and conventions of writing for the college history course.

The Modern Researcher, Sixth Edition
ISBN-10: 0495318701 | ISBN-13: 9780495318705
Prepared by Jacques Barzun and Henry F. Graff of Columbia University. This classic introduction to the techniques of research and the art of expression is used widely in history courses, but is also appropriate for writing and research methods courses in other departments. Barzun and Graff thoroughly cover every aspect of research, from the selection of a topic through the gathering, analysis, writing, revision, and publication of findings, presenting the process through actual cases that put the subtleties of research in a useful context, not as a set of rules. Part One covers the principles and methods of research; Part Two covers writing, speaking, and getting one's work published.

Reader Program
Cengage Learning publishes a number of readers, some containing exclusively primary sources, others devoted to essays and secondary sources, and still others providing a combination of primary and secondary sources. All of these readers are designed to guide students through the process of historical inquiry. Visit www.cengage.com/history for a complete list of readers.

Rand McNally Historical Atlas of the World
ISBN-10: 0618841911 | ISBN-13: 9780618841912
This valuable resource features more than seventy maps that portray the rich panoply of the world's history, from preliterate times to the present. They show how cultures and civilizations were linked and how they interacted. The maps make it clear that history is not static. Rather, it is about change and movement across time. The maps show change by presenting the dynamics of expansion, cooperation, and conflict. This atlas includes maps that display the world from the beginning of civilization; the political development of all major areas of the world; expanded coverage of Africa, Latin America, and the Middle East; the current Islamic world; and world population changes in 1900 and 2000.

Acknowledgments

It is a pleasure to thank the many instructors who read and critiqued the manuscript through its development, as well as those who reviewed and class tested Aplia, CourseReader, and the *Voyages Map App*:

Mark Baker, California State University Bakersfield
Jessica Weaver Baron, Saint Mary's College
Albert Bauman, Hawai'i Pacific University
Christopher Bellito, Kean University
Robert Bond, Cuyamaca College
Marjan Boogert, Manchester College
Maryann Brink, University of Massachusetts-Boston
Paul Buckingham, Morrisville State College
Jochen Burgtorf, California State University Fullerton
Celeste Chamberland, Roosevelt University
Annette Chamberlin, Virginia Western Community College
Patty Colman, Moorpark College
Marcie Cowley, Grand Valley State University
Matthew Crawford, Kent State University
Brian Daugherity, Virginia Commonwealth University
Katie Desmond, Feather River College
Salvador Diaz, Santa Rosa Junior College
Kimberly Dowdle, Jackson State University
Jeffrey Dym, Sacramento State University
Don Eberle, Bowling Green State University
Angela Feres, Grossmont College
Christopher Ferguson, Auburn State University
Christina Firpo, California Polytechnic State University
Nancy Fitch, California State University Fullerton
Candace Gregory-Abbott, California State University Sacramento
Eric Gruver, Texas A&M University
Kenneth Hall, Ball State University
Ellen J. Jenkins, Arkansas Tech University
Phyllis Jestice, University of Southern Mississippi
Gustavo Jimenez, Los Angeles Mission College
Michael Kinney, Calhoun Community College

Mark Lentz, University of Louisiana-Lafayette
Jodie Mader, Thomas More College
Susan Maneck, Jackson State University
Christopher Mauriello, Salem State University
Derek Maxfield, Genesee Community College
Alexander Mirkovic, Arkansas Tech University
Houston Mount, East Central University
Stephen Neufeld, California State University Fullerton
Mari Nicholson-Preuss, University of Houston
Bill Palmer, Marshall University
Sean Perrone, Saint Anselm College
Dave Price, Santa Fe College
Elizabeth Propes, Tennessee Technological University
Carey Roberts, Arkansas Tech University
Anne Rose, Grand Valley State University
LaQuita Saunders, Arkansas State University
Charles Scruggs, Genessee Community College
Scott Seagle, Chattanooga State Community College
Tatiana Seijas, Miami University
Al Smith, Modesto Junior College
Jeffrey Smith, Lindenwood University
David Stefancic, Saint Mary's College
Pamela Stewart, Arizona State University
Julie Tatlock, Mount Mary College
Lisa Tran, California State University Fullerton
Sarah Trembanis, Immaculata University
Sarah Tucker, Washburn University
Timothy Wesley, Pennsylvania State University
Robert Wilcox, Northern Kentucky University
James Williams, University of Indianapolis
Kent Wright, Arizona State University

Valerie Hansen would also like to thank the following for their guidance on specific chapters: Haydon Cherry, Yale University; Stephen Colvin, London University; Fabian Drixler, Yale University; Benjamin Foster, Yale University; Karen Foster, Yale University; Paul Freedman, Yale University; Phyllis Granoff, Yale University; Thomas R. H. Havens, Northeastern University; Stanley Insler, Yale University; Mary Miller, Yale University; Frederick S. Paxton, Connecticut College; Stuart Schwartz, Yale University; Koichi Shinohara, Yale University; Francesca Trivellato, Yale University; and Anders Winroth, Yale University.

The study of world history is indeed a voyage, and Kenneth Curtis would like to thank the following for helping identify guideposts along the way. First, thanks to colleagues in the World History Association and the Advanced Placement World History program, especially Omar Ali, University of North Carolina Greensboro; Ross Dunn, San Diego State University; Alan Karras, University of California, Berkeley; Patrick Manning, University of Pittsburgh; Laura Mitchell, University of California, Irvine; Heather Salter-Streets, Washington State

University; Peter Stearns, George Mason University; Merry Wiesner-Hanks, University of Wisconsin-Milwaukee; and Anand Yang, University of Washington. Ken would especially like to commemorate the scholarly stimulation, friendship, and generous spirit of the late Jerry Bentley of the University of Hawai'i. He would also like to acknowledge the support of his colleagues in the history department at California State University Long Beach, especially those who aided with sources, translations, or interpretive guidance: Houri Berberian, Craig Hendricks, Ali Igmen, Andrew Jenks, Timothy Keirn, Margaret Kuo, Sharlene Sayegh, and Donald Schwartz.

The authors would also like to thank the many publishing professionals at Wadsworth/Cengage Learning who facilitated the publication of this book, in particular: Jan Fitter, whose desire to get it right shaped this second edition; our original editor, Nancy Blaine, for guiding us through the entire process from proposal to finished textbook, and her able successor Brooke C. Barbier, who supervised the revisions; Jean Woy, for the extraordinary historical judgment she brought to bear on the first edition; Carol Newman, for shepherding the book through the final, chaotic pre-publication process; Charlotte Miller, who oversaw creation of the book's distinctive maps; and Jamie Bushell, who coordinated preparation of the many online ancillaries.

In closing, Valerie Hansen would like to thank Brian Vivier for doing so much work on Volume 1; the title of "research assistant" does not convey even a fraction of what he did, always punctually and cheerfully. She dedicates this book to her children, Lydia, Claire, and Bret Hansen Stepanek, and their future educations.

Kenneth Curtis would like to thank Francine Curtis for her frontline editing skills and belief in the project, and his mother, Elizabeth J. Curtis, and siblings Jane, Sara, Margaret, Jim, Steve, and Ron for their love and support. In recognition of his father's precious gift of curiosity, Ken dedicates this book to the memory of James Gavin Curtis.

About the Authors

Valerie Hansen

Valerie Hansen teaches Chinese and world history at Yale University, where she is professor of history. Her main research goal is to draw on nontraditional sources to capture the experience of ordinary people. In particular she is interested in how sources buried in the ground, whether intentionally or unintentionally, supplement the detailed official record of China's past. Her books include *The Open Empire: A History of China to 1600* (2000) and *The Silk Road: A New History* (2012). In the past decade, she has spent three years in China: 2005–2006 in Shanghai on a Fulbright grant, and 2008–2009 and 2011–2012 teaching at Yale's joint undergraduate program with Peking University. Life in China offers many pleasures. It's wonderful to be able to show students to actual places on field trips and not simply look at PowerPoint slides during class.

Kenneth R. Curtis

Kenneth R. Curtis received his Ph.D. from the University of Wisconsin-Madison in African and Comparative World History. His research focuses on colonial to postcolonial transitions in East Africa, with a particular focus on the coffee economy of Tanzania. He is professor of history and Liberal Studies at California State University Long Beach, where he has taught world history at the introductory level, in special courses designed for future middle and high school teachers, and in graduate seminars. He has worked to advance the teaching of world history at the collegiate and secondary levels in collaboration with the World History Association, the California History/Social Science Project, and the College Board's Advanced Placement World History program.

Note on Spelling

Students taking world history will encounter new names of people, terms, and places from languages that use either different alphabets or no alphabet at all (like Chinese) and that have multiple variant spellings in English. As a rule, we have opted to give names in the native language of whom we are writing about, not in other languages.

Our goal has been to avoid confusing the reader, even if specific decisions may not make sense to expert readers. To help readers, we provide a pronunciation guide on the first appearance of any term or name whose pronunciation is not obvious from the spelling. There is also an audio pronunciation guide on the text's companion website. A few explanations for specific regions follow.

The Americas

Only after 1492 with the arrival of Columbus and his men did outsiders label the original residents of the Americas as a single group. For this reason, any word for the inhabitants of North and South America is inaccurate. We try to refer to individual peoples whenever possible. When speaking in general terms, we use the word *Amerindian* because it has no pejorative overtones and is not confusing.

Many place names in Spanish-speaking regions have a form in both Spanish and in the language of the indigenous peoples; whenever possible we have opted for the indigenous word. For example, we write about the *Tiwanaku* culture in the Andes, not *Tiahuanaco*. In some cases, we choose the more familiar term, such as *Inca* and *Cuzco*, rather than the less-familiar spellings *Inka* and *Cusco*. We retain the accents for modern place names.

East Asia

For Chinese, we have used the pinyin system of romanization. However, on the first appearance of a name, we alert readers to nonstandard spellings, such as Chiang Kai-shek and Sun Yat-sen, that have already entered English.

For other Asian languages, we have used the most common romanization systems (McCune-Reischauer for Korean, Hepburn for Japanese). Because we prefer to use the names that people called themselves, we use *Chinggis Khan* for the ruler of the Mongols (not *Genghis Khan*, which is Persian) and the Turkish *Timur the Lame* (rather than *Tamerlane*, his English name).

West Asia and North Africa

Many romanization systems for Arabic and related languages like Ottoman Turkish or Persian use an apostrophe to indicate specific consonants (*ain* and *hamza*). Because it is difficult for a native speaker of English to hear these differences, we have omitted these apostrophes. For this reason, we use *Quran* (not *Qur'an*).

VOYAGES in World History

Second Edition

1

The Peopling of the World, to 4000 B.C.E.

From the earliest moments of human history our ancestors were on the move. Archaeologists continue to debate when the earliest anatomically modern humans moved out of Africa and how they populated the rest of the world. One of the most distant places our ancient forebears reached—probably around fifty thousand years ago—was Australia. In 1974 a team of archaeologists from Australia National University discovered the remains of a male near Mungo (muhn-GO) Lake in the southeastern Australian state of New South Wales. He is known as **Mungo Man**; Mungo Woman is the cremated remains of a female that the team's lead archaeologist, J. M. Bowler, found at the site several years earlier. Here, Bowler describes the moment he spotted Mungo Man's skull sticking out of the ground:

Mungo Man

(Courtesy Jim Bowler)

*P*rolonged and heavy rains during 1973 had swept across the eroded dune surface, uncovering a new crop of archaeologic and other prehistoric finds. At a point some 500 m [1,600 ft] east of the Lake Mungo I cremation/burial site [of Mungo Woman] the late afternoon sun was highlighting a small white object protruding through the sandy surface. . . . Closer examination revealed the object to be the exposed left side of a carbonate-encrusted human cranium. The central area of

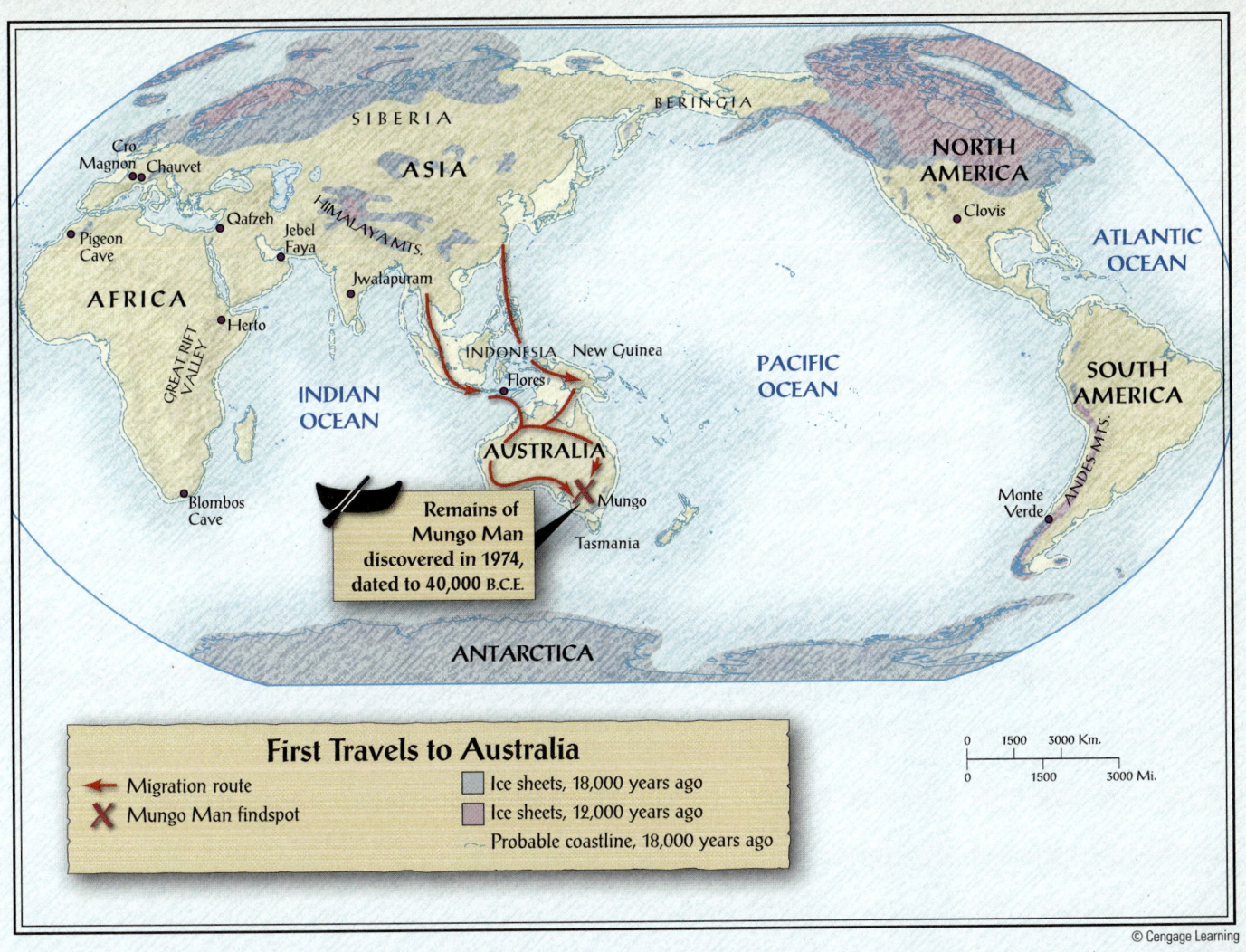

First Travels to Australia

← Migration route

✖ Mungo Man findspot

☐ Ice sheets, 18,000 years ago

☐ Ice sheets, 12,000 years ago

〜 Probable coastline, 18,000 years ago

Remains of Mungo Man discovered in 1974, dated to 40,000 B.C.E.

© Cengage Learning

Join this chapter's traveler on "Voyages," an interactive tour of historic sites and events:
www.cengagebrain.com

exposed bone protruded some 2–3 cm above the eroded surface. Much of the bone was coated with a thin layer of calcrete which was pinkish in color, a feature not known from carbonate of similar age elsewhere. . . .[*]

[*]J. M. Bowler and A. G. Thorne, "Human Remains from Lake Mungo: Discovery and Excavation of Lake Mungo III," in *The Origin of the Australians*, ed. R. L. Kirk and A. G. Thorne (Atlantic Highlands, N.J.: Humanities Press Inc., 1976), p. 128.

Mungo Man
Remains of a male found near Mungo Lake in the southeastern Australian state of New South Wales, dated to about 40,000 B.C.E.

ocher
A reddish-brown iron-based pigment that ancient peoples used to color the soil and to decorate cave walls.

Even on that first day, Professor Bowler noticed that the soil around the burial had a pinkish tinge, which turned out to be the remains of **ocher** (OH-kerh), a reddish-brown mineral element ancient peoples used to color the soil. The site dates to 40,000 B.C.E., some 10,000 years after Australia was first settled. (As is common among world historians, this book uses B.C.E. [Before Common Era] for dates prior to the year 1 of the first century, and C.E. [Common Era] for dates from the year 1 forward. Older books use B.C. [Before Christ] and A.D. [Anno Domini, In the Year of Our Lord].) The peopling of Australia marked an important phase in the history of humankind: people had advanced to the point where they could plan into the future. They could construct boats or rafts to take them across the 60 miles (100 km) of water separating Australia from the Eurasian landmass at the time.

By 150,000 B.C.E., anatomically modern people had fully developed in Africa. Starting between 80,000 and 60,000 B.C.E., our ancestors arrived in Asia. They later reached Australia and Europe at the same time. The Western Hemisphere was settled much later.

Since none of these early peoples could read and write, no documents survive. But archaeological evidence, including cave paintings and ancient tools, makes it possible to reconstruct the early history of humanity. In addition, new information derived from genetic material called deoxyribonucleic acid (DNA) has allowed scientists to reconstruct the peopling of the world with unprecedented accuracy.

Focus Questions

» *When did anatomically modern humans arise in Africa, and when did they first behave in recognizably human ways?*

» *How and when did the first humans settle Asia, Australia, Europe, and the Americas?*

» *How and where did humans begin to cultivate plants? How did agriculture's impact vary around the world?*

The First Anatomically Modern Humans in Africa, ca. 150,000 B.C.E.

Homo sapiens sapiens
Biological term for modern human beings belonging to the genus *Homo*, species *sapiens*, and subspecies *sapiens*.

hominins
Term referring to all humans and their ancestors but not to chimpanzees, gorillas, or orangutans.

When the species **Homo sapiens sapiens** (HO-mo SAY-pee-uhnz SAY-pee-uhnz), anatomically modern humans, first appeared in central and southern Africa some 150,000 years ago, they lived side by side with other animals and other **hominins**, a general term referring to humans and their ancestors. But in important respects they were totally different from their neighbors, for they learned to change their environment with radically new tools and skills. Their departure from Africa, their first art works, their hunting prowess, and their trade networks are all signs of recognizably human behavior.

Predecessors to the First Anatomically Modern Humans

Because ancient human remains are rare, in 1997 paleontologists (pay-lee-on-TAHL-oh-gists), scientists who study life in the distant past, were extremely pleased to excavate three skulls dating to 160,000

B.C.E. at the Herto site of Ethiopia. Slightly different in shape and dimensions from the skulls of modern humans, the Herto skulls (from two adults and one child) represent the immediate predecessors to modern humans and thus show that the *Homo sapiens sapiens* species arose first in Africa. Concluding that all modern people are descended from this group, one of the excavating archaeologists commented: *"In this sense, we are all African."*[1]

Scientists use the concept of **evolution** to explain how all life forms, including modern humans, have come into being. In the nineteenth century, Charles Darwin proposed that natural selection is the mechanism underlying evolutionary change. He realized that variations exist within a species and that certain variations increase an individual's chances of survival. We know that genetic mutations, or permanent, transmissible changes to genetic material, cause DNA to change, and so all variations, beneficial or not, are passed along to offspring. Because those individuals within a population who possess beneficial traits—perhaps a bigger brain or more upright posture—are more likely to survive, they will have more offspring. And because traits are inherited, these offspring will also possess the beneficial traits. Those individuals lacking those traits will have few or no offspring. As new mutations occur within a population, its characteristics will change and a new species can develop from an earlier one, typically over many thousands or even millions of years. The species closest to modern human beings today is the chimpanzee, whose cells contain nuclei with DNA that overlaps with 98.4 percent of human DNA. But humans and chimpanzees have developed separately for some seven million years.

Biologists use four different subcategories when classifying animals: family, genus (JEAN-uhs, the Latin word for "group" or "class"), species, and then subspecies. Members of the primate family, modern humans belong to the genus *Homo* ("person" in Latin), the species *sapiens* ("wise" or "intelligent" in Latin), and the subspecies *sapiens*, so the correct term for modern people is *Homo sapiens sapiens*. Members of the same species can reproduce, while members of two different species cannot. Since modern humans are now the only living subspecies in the *Homo sapiens* species, scholars often abbreviate the name to *Homo sapiens*. Here, we will continue to say *Homo sapiens sapiens* because we are discussing periods when other subspecies were alive.

Compared to those of modern humans, the skulls found at the Herto site are slightly larger, the faces are longer, and the brow is more pronounced. Because of these differences, paleontologists have tentatively identified a new subspecies, *Homo sapiens idaltu*. (*Idaltu* means "elder" in the Awash language spoken in Herto today.)

The Herto site was on the edge of a shallow, freshwater lake that was home to crocodiles, fish, and hippopotamuses, and buffalo lived on the land. The site's residents used stone tools to remove flesh from the hippopotamus, and the only child's skull had tool marks as well, an indication that flesh had been removed from it. Some scientists have speculated that the Herto residents practiced cannibalism, but it is more likely that they left marks on the skull as part of the ritual preparation of the dead.

> **evolution**
> Model proposed by Charles Darwin to explain the development of new species through genetic mutation and natural selection.

Anatomically Modern Humans

Sometime around 150,000 years ago, anatomically modern humans appeared in Africa. These people were physically the same as modern humans: their build, the size of their brains, and their physical appearance were identical to ours.

Analysis of genetic material has provided crucial information that supplements what we can learn by analyzing archaeologically excavated remains. When a man and a woman have a child, most of their DNA recombines to form a new sequence unique to their baby, but some DNA passes directly from the mother to the child in mitochondrial DNA, or mtDNA. By analyzing mtDNA, geneticists have identified a single female ancestor, known as **mitochondrial Eve**, whom all living humans have in common. Mitochondrial Eve lived in West Africa near modern Tanzania. Eve was not the first anatomically modern female; she was the first anatomically modern female whose daughters gave birth to daughters, and so on through the generations, allowing her mtDNA to pass to every person alive today. The total number of anatomically modern humans alive during Eve's lifetime was surprisingly small: about 10,000 or 20,000 people. And the total number of humans seems to have stayed at that level for more than one hundred thousand years, until the development of agriculture (discussed later in this chapter) made it possible to support a larger population.

mitochondrial Eve The first female ancestor shared by all living humans, who was identified by analysis of mitochondrial DNA.

The Beginnings of Modern Human Behavior

Scientists debate when these members of our species first began to act like modern humans. The ability to plan ahead is the most important indicator of human behavior, and additional clues lie in the ability to modify tools to improve them, the existence of trade networks, the practice of making art, the ritual of burying the dead, and the ability to speak. Early *Homo sapiens sapiens* had larynxes, but they did not begin to speak until sometime between 100,000 and 50,000 B.C.E. We cannot know precisely when because the act of speaking produces no lasting evidence in the archaeological record. Instead, paleontologists have identified certain human activities, such as organizing hunting parties to trap large game, as sufficiently complex to require speech. Speech may have begun because of a single genetic mutation; scientists have identified a single gene on the Y-chromosome (FOXP$_2$) that only men carry. This finding suggests that women would have had to learn language by interacting with men.

Our forebears began to leave Africa around 100,000 B.C.E., perhaps even earlier. In 2011, archaeologists found tools at the Jebel Faya site in modern United Arab Emirates that date to about 125,000 B.C.E. and resemble those made in Africa by anatomically modern humans. Because water levels differed at this time, only 3 miles (5 km) of water separated the Arabian peninsula from Africa. However, archaeologists have yet to unearth any human fossils, so they are not certain who made these tools.

Remains of anatomically modern humans have surfaced at Qafzeh (KAHF-seh) cave, a site near Nazareth in Israel. It is most likely that multiple generations traveled short distances and kept on moving into new environments. Their ability to do so testifies to the growing sophistication of *Homo sapiens sapiens* at this time. However, DNA analysis of the Qafzeh remains has demonstrated that the site's residents are not the ancestors of modern humans. Most likely, their community died out sometime after they left Africa.

Several sites in South Africa have produced evidence of distinctly human behavior dating to around 75,000 B.C.E. Animal remains at the site indicate that anatomically modern humans had developed spears and arrows sufficiently powerful to kill local antelope and seals. Distinctive stones have been found 18 miles (30 km) from where they were mined, an indication of early trade networks. Most revealingly, the humans living on the site of Blombos Cave in South Africa showed a capacity for symbolic thinking, as evidenced in the production of art objects. (See the feature "Visual Evidence in Primary Sources: The First Art Objects in the World.")

How Modern Humans Populated Asia, Australia, and Europe

To be able to migrate out of Africa and displace existing populations in Asia and Europe, modern humans had to behave differently from their forebears. Long-distance migration required forward planning and most likely speech. As the modern humans left Africa, they modified existing tools to suit new environments, and they devised boats or rafts to cross bodies of water. After crossing into Asia between 80,000 and 60,000 years ago, they proceeded to modern Indonesia, Papua New Guinea, and Australia, which they reached 50,000 years ago, the same time that they reached Europe. Europe was colder than Asia, and it was inhabited by Neanderthals, whom the modern humans displaced by 25,000 years ago. They traveled to the Americas last, reaching there by at least 14,000 B.C.E., if not earlier.

The Settling of Asia, 80,000–60,000 B.C.E.

Although some early humans left Africa around 100,000 B.C.E., the first humans who established lasting settlements left between 80,000 and 60,000 B.C.E. Why did they leave? Was there a dramatic event that prompted their journey?

The earliest concrete archaeological evidence of the migration to Asia comes from Jwalapuram, India, where tools—but no human remains—dating to 74,000 B.C.E. have been found. The 215 stone tools and a piece of ocher are nearly identical to those found in Africa, an important clue to the origins of the travelers.

Archaeologists found these tools under a layer of volcanic ash about 1 yard (1 m) deep. Thermoluminescent dating, which measures the radiation emitted by an object, determined that the ash deposit was left by a volcanic eruption occurring some 73,000 years ago in Toba, Indonesia, which caused the world's temperatures to lower significantly. Some archaeologists believe that the effects of this eruption were so profound that they forced people to leave Africa.

Others propose a less dramatic explanation: the peoples living near the coast of Africa, near Djibouti and Somalia, crossed a land bridge to the Arabian peninsula (water levels were lower then) and continued to hug the coast of the Indian Ocean, eating shellfish and tropical fruit as they made their way south. These analysts point out that the tools from Jwalapuram found immediately below and above the ash level are very similar, suggesting that local humans survived the eruption and no cataclysm occurred. The first humans to leave Africa probably did so without realizing they were leaving one landmass and going to another: they simply followed the coastline in search of food.

The Settling of Australia, ca. 50,000 B.C.E.

Homo sapiens sapiens were sufficiently versatile that they could adjust to new, even cold, habitats, and their improved hunting skills allowed them to move to new places. The farthest they traveled from Africa was to Australia. One of the most isolated places on earth, this continent provides a rich environment for animals, such as kangaroos, that are found nowhere else in the world. No animals from Eurasia, except for rodents and modern humans, managed to reach Australia.

How *Homo sapiens sapiens* journeyed to Australia is still a mystery. Oceans then lay about 250 feet (76 m) below modern levels, and the body of water dividing

The First Art Objects in the World

One site in Africa—Blombos Cave in South Africa—has produced some of the earliest art objects in the world. The Blombos Cave site, on the coast about 186 miles (300 km) east of Cape Town, dates to 100,000 B.C.E. and was occupied for long periods after that. The surface of this chunk of ocher (opposite, top) bears a geometric design of triangles between three parallel lines. This pure design, with no functional purpose, points to the capacity for abstract thinking.

The occupants of Blombos Cave fished and hunted and made sets of fine bone tools, all of the same size. First they cut bone with stone tools and then polished it with leather and abrasive powder. They also mixed ocher with animal fat and some charcoal in abalone shells to make the earliest known paint in the world.* What did they use the ocher for? To color the earth? As a type of makeup? Whatever its use, it was entirely decorative, evidence of an early human desire to make something beautiful.

At Blombos archaeologists found nineteen snail shells, about the size of a kernel of corn, each with a hole through it (opposite, bottom). Traces of wear at the ends of the shells indicate that they were originally strung together to make a strand of beads, worn perhaps on the wrist or at the neck. The beads also show traces of ocher. The beads, archaeologists speculate, may have functioned at Blombos as they do among the Ju/'hoansi people who live in the Kalahari Desert in Botswana and who are sometimes called Bushmen. Speakers of a language with many click sounds, the Ju/'hoansi present ostrich shell beads to other groups with whom they hope to form alliances.

The scientist who discovered these shells argued convincingly that these are very early signs of human creativity. A recent discovery suggests that they may be more than that. In 2007, archaeologists excavating the Pigeon Cave site in Morocco have found similar shells dated between 91,000 and 74,000 years ago. These beads also have holes, abrasion marks at the ends where they were strung together, and traces of ocher. They are not from exactly the same species of snail as those from Blombos Cave, but the two species of snail look identical to the naked eye (one can see the differences between them only with a microscope). Other undated finds of similar shells in Israel and Algeria suggest that a trading network that spanned Africa and Israel may have existed as early as 82,000 years ago.

The chunk of ocher, the bone tools, and the beads from Blombos reveal that their makers were able to produce beautiful objects because they had the time and energy left over after meeting basic subsistence needs. These early objects clearly display the artistic impulses of their makers and suggest that *Homo sapiens sapiens* engaged in the recognizably human activity of making art objects as early as 75,000 B.C.E. and possibly even before.

*John Noble Wilford, "In African Cave, Signs of an Ancient Paint Factory," *New York Times*, October 13, 2011.

QUESTION FOR ANALYSIS

» *Which evidence from the archaeological record (including, but not limited to, the objects discussed here) do you find most convincing as the earliest indication of people becoming recognizably human? Why?*

This is a block of red ocher, a pigment made from iron oxide. Now the color of rust, the surface would have originally been a vivid blood red. This block, 2.5 inches (6 cm) long, formed a small crayon that was used, perhaps, to decorate the body.

Anna Zieminski/AFP/Getty Images

The abstract triangle markings may be purely decorative or may represent a way to count something, perhaps the passage of days.

This object was found in Blombos Cave, some 186 miles (300 km) from Cape Town, where the cave's occupants hunted and fished around 75,000 B.C.E.

(Courtesy, UiB Global, University of Bergen, Norway)

Australia from the Greater Southeast Asian landmass was at least 60 miles (100 km) across, indicating that these humans could cover short distances by raft or boat. Making even a simple boat required complex skills such as cutting timber and lashing pieces of wood together. These ancient travelers probably first made boats for fishing, which they did with nets, and then used the boats to travel longer distances. Both fishing and boat journeys required forward planning. Yet no watercraft from this time have been found, possibly because any remains have disintegrated.

Once they reached Australia, the early settlers did not stay on the coast but moved inland rapidly, reaching the site of Mungo, in southeast Australia, by 50,000 years ago. There, J. M. Bowler found the grave of Mungo Man near an ancient campsite marked by hearths. The living arranged the body of Mungo Man carefully, positioning his hands over his crotch.

Mungo Man was buried in a grave colored by reddish ocher, the same mineral element used to make the ocher implement at Blombos Cave. Bowler explained, *"We believe the pink staining to be due to the scattering of a quantity of red ochre over the cadaver in the prepared grave. Small lumps of ochre were recovered but it is likely the bulk of the ochre was scattered over the cadaver as a powder."*[*]

religion
Belief system that holds that divine powers control the environment and people's futures.

The living, then, deliberately colored the soil around the grave. Burials, which began as early as 100,000 B.C.E., are another important indicator of human behavior because they suggest the presence of religious beliefs. The defining characteristic of **religion** is the belief in a divine power or powers that control or influence the environment and people's lives. The most reliable evidence is a written text demonstrating religious beliefs, but early humans did not write. They did, however, bury their dead, most likely because they believed in an afterlife, a major component of many religious belief systems.

Nearby was a woman (Mungo Woman), whose burnt remains constitute the earliest known example of human cremation. The bones of Mungo Woman underwent a multistep process: the living burned her bones, crushed them, burned them a second time, and then buried them—possibly because they wanted to ensure that her spirit never returned to bother the living. Or perhaps they cremated the dead in the hope that their souls could proceed safely to the next world. Whatever their reasons, the complexity of the process points to the ability to plan and carry out multistep operations, a defining characteristic of modern human behavior.

The residents of the Mungo site used grinding stones to sharpen their cutting tools, a breakthrough in tool manufacture; they employed ground-edge axes to cut down trees and clear small plots of land. Like the residents of Blombos, they wore and traded shell beads, and they established long-distance trade networks linking Australia with Tasmania and New Guinea.

The Settling of Europe, 50,000–25,000 B.C.E.

Early humans followed two routes into Europe: one went around the Mediterranean Sea, and the other followed the Danube River into eastern Europe. Starting around 50,000 B.C.E., the humans living in Europe began to organize hunts of migrating animals in the fall to provide meat during the winter. They continued to refine the advanced hunting technologies of their African forebears, who had formed large, organized hunting parties that killed big game with sharp-pointed spears. In addition to hunting, the migrants also gathered wild plants.

The earliest *Homo sapiens sapiens* found so far in Europe are called Cro Magnon (CROW MAG-nahn), after the site, dating to around 38,000 B.C.E., where their

---

*J. M. Bowler and A. G. Thorne, "Human Remains from Lake Mungo: Discovery and Excavation of Lake Mungo III," in *The Origin of the Australians,* ed. R. L. Kirk and A. G. Thorne (Atlantic Highlands, N.J.: Humanities Press Inc., 1976), p. 129.

remains were first found in southwest France. Their methods of obtaining food show that they were better able to think about the future than earlier hunting groups. Cro Magnon bands traveled to rivers and coasts to catch fish. As they moved in search of more game and fish, they built new types of houses and developed better clothes. One of their most important innovations was the bone needle, which they used to sew snug-fitting fur clothing to protect them from the cold winters of Europe.

The Cro Magnon also produced the extraordinary cave paintings of Chauvet (SHOW-vay) in southern France (dated to 30,000 B.C.E.), which show the different animals they hunted: mammoths (various types of extinct elephants), lions, and rhinoceroses. Some paintings are decorated with patterns of dots or human handprints. Other cave sites, such as the well-known Lascaux (las-KOH) (15,000 B.C.E.) site in southwestern France, show horses, bison, and wild goats, suggesting that ancient hunters targeted different animals during different seasons. (See also the feature "Movement of Ideas Through Primary Sources: The Worship of Goddesses?")

An Ancient Artist at the Chauvet Caves of France Traces of charcoal from the battling woolly rhinoceros (*lower right*) have been dated to about 30,000 B.C.E., making this one of the earliest cave paintings found anywhere in the world. The panel also portrays the same horse in four different poses, rare sketches done by an individual artist. Many of the paintings in the Chauvet caves display this artist's distinctive style.

Jean Clottes/AP Images

Yet some scientists have loudly voiced their skepticism, largely because the stone tools found at the site are much more sophisticated than any associated with earlier hominins. They suggest, instead, that the skeleton may be that of a small *Homo sapiens sapiens* afflicted with a disorder called microcephaly (my-cro-SEPH-uh-lee) that results in a shrunken brain and other deformities. This controversial find shows how a single discovery can prompt radical revision of the scientific consensus on human evolution. Even if *Homo floresiensis* gains recognition as a new hominin species, it died out by 12,000 B.C.E., leaving *Homo sapiens sapiens* as the sole surviving human species on the planet.

The Settling of the Americas, ca. 14,000–12,000 B.C.E.

*H*omo sapiens sapiens* reached the Americas much later than they did any other landmass. The earliest confirmed human occupation in the Western Hemisphere dates to about 12,000 B.C.E., some forty thousand years after the settling of the Eurasian landmass and Australia.[3] Accordingly, all human remains found so far in the Americas belong to the *Homo sapiens sapiens* species. Scholars are not certain which routes the early settlers took, when they came, or if they traveled over land or by water.

One theory is that humans reached America on a land bridge from Siberia to Alaska: **Beringia** (bear-in-JEE-uh), now below water, which connected the tip of Siberia in Russia with the northeastern corner of Alaska. Today Beringia is covered by a 50-mile-wide (80-km-wide) stretch of the Bering Sea. The water in this part of the Bering Sea is shallow, consistently less than 600 feet (182 m) deep. As the earth experienced different periods of extended coldness, called Ice Ages, ocean water froze and covered such northern landmasses with ice. During these periods the ocean level declined and the ancient Beringia landmass emerged to form a large land bridge between Siberia and North America, measuring over 600 miles (1,000 km) from north to south. What are now islands of the Bering Sea then stood as giant peaks on the Beringia landmass.

The first migrations to the New World may have occurred in 14,000 B.C.E. or even earlier, and they certainly took place by about 12,000 B.C.E., when ice still covered much of Beringia. Much of North America was covered by sheets of ice over 10,000 feet (3,000 m) thick. Some scientists believe that an ice-free corridor between ice masses allowed movement through today's Canada. Others hypothesize that the ancient settlers hugged the coast, traveling in boats covered by animal skins stretched tight over a wooden pole frame. Boats would have allowed the settlers to proceed down the coast from Beringia to South America, disembarking and pitching temporary camps where no ice had formed.

Monte Verde, Chile: How the First Americans Lived, 12,000 B.C.E. The best evidence for this first wave of migration comes from far down the west coast of the Americas, from a settlement called **Monte Verde, Chile**, which lies only 9 miles (14 km) away from the Pacific coast, south of the 40th parallel. Forming a bony spine running along the western edge of the Americas, the Rocky Mountains and the Andes Mountains formed a barrier that kept the first settlers in the coastal zones west of the mountain chain. Early humans probably traveled down the west coast of North and South America in small boats.

Beringia
Landmass now submerged below water that connected the tip of Siberia with the northeastern corner of Alaska.

Monte Verde, Chile
Earliest site in the Americas, where evidence of human occupation has been found dating to 12,000 B.C.E.

Monte Verde is the most important ancient site in the Americas for several reasons. First, without a doubt it contains very early remains. Lying under a layer of peat, it also preserves organic materials like wood, skin, and plants that almost never survive. Finally, and most important, professional archaeologists have scrupulously recorded which items were found at each level, following the key principle of **stratigraphy**. This principle means that, at an undisturbed site, any remains found under one layer are earlier than anything from above that layer.

Monte Verde's undisturbed state made it an excellent place from which to collect samples for carbon-14 testing. **Carbon-14** is an isotope of carbon present at a fixed percentage in a living organism. Because this percentage declines after death, one can determine the approximate age of an archaeological sample by analyzing the percentage of carbon-14 in it. Carbon-14 dates always include a plus/minus range because they are not completely accurate: the farther back in time one goes, the less accurate the dating is. (This book gives only one date for ease of presentation.) Carbon-14 analysis of evidence from Monte Verde gave an approximate date of 12,000 B.C.E. for the lowest level definitely occupied by humans.[4]

Although no human remains have been found at Monte Verde so far, the footprints of a child or a young teenager were preserved on the top of a level dated to 12,000 B.C.E. This finding provides indisputable evidence of human occupation. The twenty to thirty residents of Monte Verde lived in a structure about 22 yards (20 m) long that was covered with animal skins; the floor was also covered with skins. The residents used poles to divide the structure into smaller sections, probably for family groups, and heated these sections with fires in clay hearths. There they prepared food that they had gathered: wild berries, fruits, and wild potato tubers. An even lower layer with stone tools has been dated to approximately 31,000 B.C.E., but the evidence for human occupation is less convincing than the human footprints from the higher level. If people lived at the site at this time, then the Americas may have been settled much earlier than the 14,000 B.C.E. date that is widely accepted today.

A separate building, shaped like a wishbone, stood about 100 feet (30 m) away from the large structure. The residents hardened the floor of this building by mixing sand, gravel, and animal fat to make a place where they could clean bones, produce tools, and finish animal hides. Healers may have treated the ill in this building, too, since the floor contained traces of eighteen different plants, some chewed and then spit out, as though they had been used as medicine.

The unusual preservation of wood at Monte Verde means that we know exactly which tools the first Americans used. The site's residents mounted stone flakes onto wooden sticks, called hafts. They also had a small number of more finely worked spear points. Interestingly, Monte Verde's residents used many round stones, which they could have easily gathered on the beach, for slings or bolos. A bolo consists of a long string made of hide with stones tied at both ends. Holding one end, early humans swung the other end around their heads at high speed and then released the string. If on target, the spinning bolo wrapped itself around the neck of a bird or other animal and killed it.

The residents of Monte Verde hunted mastodon, a relative of the modern elephant that became extinct about 9000 B.C.E. They also foraged along the coast for shellfish, which could be eaten raw. In the initial stages of migration, the settlers found a coastal environment much more hospitable than an inland one because they could forage for many different types of food at the beach. Hunting parties could leave for long periods to pursue mastodon and other large game, confident that those left behind had ample food supplies.

stratigraphy
Archaeological principle that, at an undisturbed site, material from upper layers must be more recent than that from lower layers.

carbon-14
Isotope of carbon whose presence in organic material can be used to determine the approximate age of archaeological samples.

A Powerful Ancient Weapon: The Atlatl The residents of the Monte Verde site used the atlatl spear-thrower to kill game. The atlatl had two parts, a long handle with a cup or hook at the end, and a spear tipped with a sharp stone point. The handle served as an extension of the human arm, so that the spear could be thrown farther with much greater force.

(Illustration by Eric Parrish from James E. Dixon, *Bones, Boats and Bisons: Archaeology and the First Colonization of Western North America*, Albuquerque: University of New Mexico Press, 1999, p. 153, figure 6-1)

The main weapon used to kill large game at Monte Verde and other early sites was the atlatl (AHT-latt-uhl), a word from the Nahuatl (NAH-waht) language spoken in central Mexico. The atlatl was a powerful weapon, capable of piercing thick animal hide, and was used for thousands of years.

The Rise of Clovis and Other Regional Traditions, 11,000 B.C.E.

By 11,000 B.C.E., small bands of people had settled all of the Americas. They used a new weapon in addition to the atlatl: wooden sticks with sharp slivers of rock, called microblades, attached to the shaft. Studies of different sites have determined that while the people in these regions shared many traits in common, different technological traditions also existed in different North American regions. Each left behind distinct artifacts (usually a spear point of a certain type).

Like the residents of Monte Verde, these later peoples combined hunting with the gathering of wild fruits and seeds. They lived in an area stretching from Oregon to Texas, with heavy concentration in the Great Plains, and hunted a wide variety of game using atlatl tipped with stone spear points. Archaeologists call these characteristic spear points the **Clovis technological complex**, named for Clovis, New Mexico, where the first such spear points were found. It is difficult to estimate the number of residents at a given location, but some of the Clovis sites are larger than earlier sites, suggesting that as many as sixty people may have lived together in a single band.

Clovis technological complex
The characteristic stone spear points that were in use around 11,000 B.C.E. across much of modern-day America.

The Clovis spear points impress all viewers with their beauty: their makers chose glassy rocks of striking colors to craft finely worked stone points. Foraging bands covered large stretches of territory, collecting different types of stone and carrying them far from their areas of origin. The Clovis peoples buried some of these collections in earth colored by ocher, the same mineral element used by the ancient peoples of South Africa and Australia. Archaeologists working at later Clovis sites throughout the Great Plains have also found a different type of stone blade lodged in bison bones. It seems that, as mammoth and mastodon became extinct, the residents shifted to hunting bison.

The migrations to the Americas ended when the world's climate warmed quickly at the end of the Wisconsin Ice Age. After 8300 B.C.E., the sea level rose, so that by 7000 B.C.E. most of Beringia lay under water once again. The only regions of the world that had not yet been settled were the islands of the Pacific (see Chapter 5). After 7000 B.C.E., the ancestors of modern Amerindians dispersed over North and South America, where they lived in almost total isolation from the rest of the world until 1492.

The Emergence of Agriculture, 9400–3000 B.C.E.

The development of **agriculture**, when people planted the first seeds and harvested the resulting crops using domesticated animals, marked a crucial breakthrough in the history of humankind. Before it, all ancient peoples were hunters and gatherers, constantly in motion, whether following herds of wild animals or gathering wild berries and plants. Over thousands of years, early peoples in different parts of the globe experimented first by gathering certain plants and planting their seeds, which anthropologists refer to as cultivation, and raising and hunting selected animals, a process called domestication.

Eventually some of these peoples began to plant seeds in specific locations and to raise tame animals that could help them harvest their crops. Only when a society committed to both processes did it become an agricultural society. Many others continued to forage for all their food. For example, in the spring, hunter-gatherers in New Guinea planted the seeds of a particularly desirable crop, such as bananas, and then moved on, returning in the fall to harvest the ripened fruit. This is cultivation but not agriculture, because they did not raise crops or animals full-time. For those who adopted agriculture, the cultivation of crops caused a dramatic increase in human populations, who first lived in small farming villages and then in towns.

Archaeologists have found evidence of cultivation that arose independently in at least eight places: in western Asia around 9400 B.C.E., as we will see in this chapter (see Map 1.1); in Mesoamerica, the Peruvian Andes, and the Yellow River Valley of China around 8000 B.C.E.; in the Indus River Valley in today's Pakistan between 6500 and 5000 B.C.E.; in New Guinea around 5000 B.C.E.; in the eastern Sahara around 8000 B.C.E.; and in sub-Saharan Africa, in the Middle Niger Valley, around 2000 B.C.E. In the Middle Niger, people formed larger communities even as they continued to forage for food; they planted millet but never engaged in intensive, full-time cultivation.

The Domestication of Plants and Animals, ca. 9400–7000 B.C.E.

The first people in the world who learned how to plant seeds, domesticate animals, and cultivate crops were the Natufians (NAH-too-fee-uhnz), who lived in Palestine and southern Syria by 12,500 B.C.E. (see Map 1.2). Hunters and gatherers, they harvested fields of grain, particularly wild barley and emmer wheat. They also picked fruits and nuts and hunted wild cattle, goats, pigs, and deer.

The Natufians used small flint blades mounted on wooden handles to cut down the stands of wild barley and emmer wheat, and they ground the harvested grain in stone mortars with pestles. Because they knew how to make advanced stone tools, archaeologists class them as **Neolithic**, literally "New Stone Age," people who, unlike earlier peoples, practiced agriculture. Gradually the Natufians began to modify their way of life so that they could support a growing population.

Around 9400 B.C.E., the Natufians began to cultivate their first crop: figs. In 2006, archaeologists found nine dried figs that had been preserved after being burnt in a

agriculture
The planting of seeds and harvesting of crops using domesticated animals.

Neolithic
"New Stone Age," the archaeological term for societies that used stone tools and practiced agriculture.

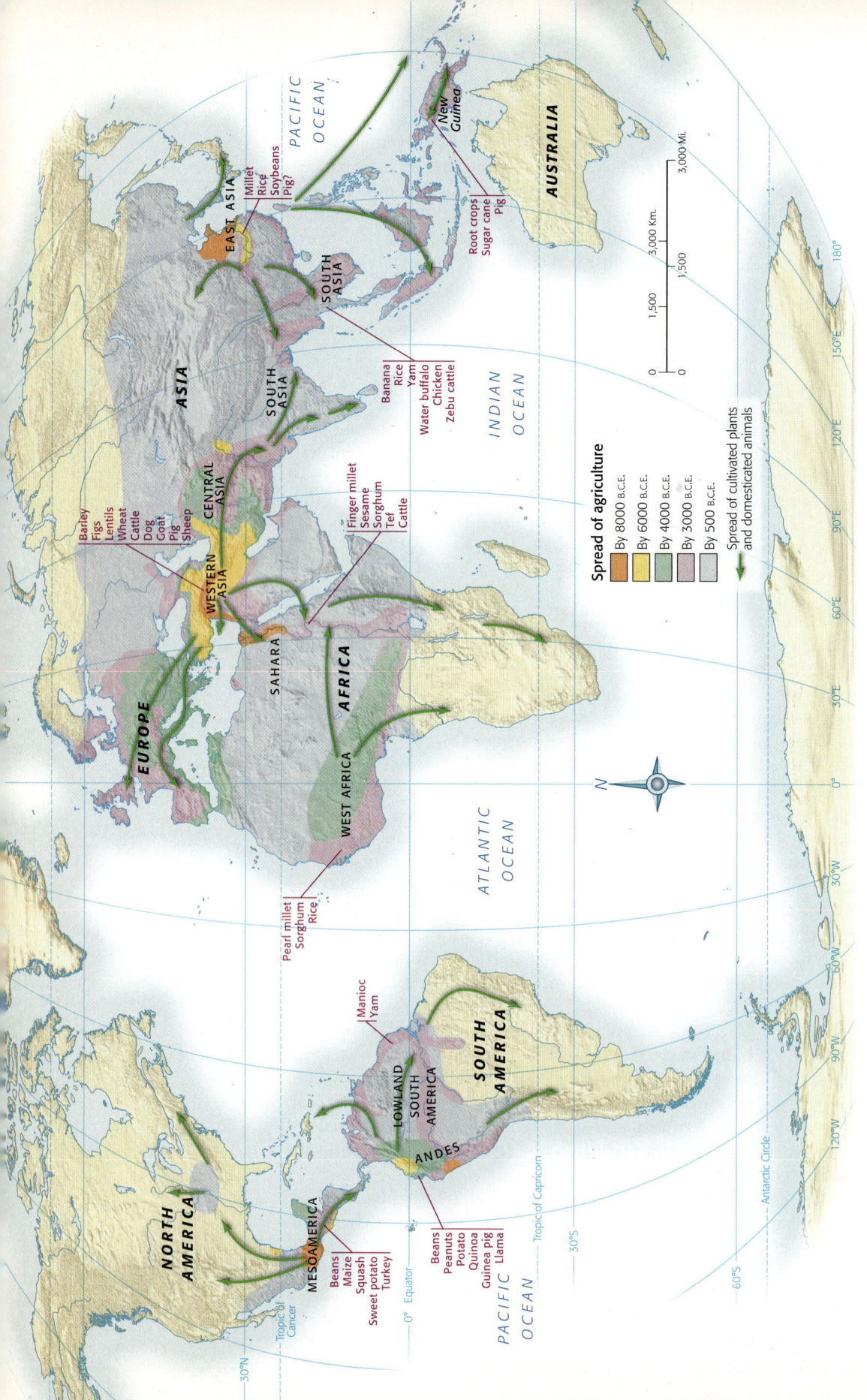

MAP 1.1 Early Agriculture Agriculture developed independently at different times in the different regions of the world. In some places, like western Asia, residents gradually shifted to full-time cultivation of crops and raising domesticated animals, while in others, like New Guinea, they continued to hunt and gather. (© Cengage Learning)

Spread of agriculture

- By 8000 B.C.E.
- By 6000 B.C.E.
- By 4000 B.C.E.
- By 3000 B.C.E.
- By 500 B.C.E.

Spread of cultivated plants and domesticated animals

3,000 Km.
3,000 Mi.
1,500
1,500
0
0

EAST ASIA
Millet
Rice
Soybeans
Pig?

WESTERN ASIA
Barley
Figs
Lentils
Wheat
Cattle
Dog
Goat
Pig
Sheep

SOUTH ASIA
Banana
Rice
Yam
Water buffalo
Chicken
Zebu cattle

SAHARA
Finger millet
Sesame
Sorghum
Tef
Cattle

WEST AFRICA
Pearl millet
Sorghum
Rice

New Guinea
Root crops
Sugar cane
Pig

LOWLAND SOUTH AMERICA
Manioc
Yam

ANDES
Beans
Peanuts
Potato
Quinoa
Guinea pig
Llama

MESOAMERICA
Beans
Maize
Squash
Sweet potato
Turkey

ASIA
CENTRAL ASIA
SOUTH ASIA
EUROPE
AFRICA
NORTH AMERICA
SOUTH AMERICA
AUSTRALIA

PACIFIC OCEAN
INDIAN OCEAN
ATLANTIC OCEAN
PACIFIC OCEAN

Tropic of Cancer
Equator
Tropic of Capricorn
Antarctic Circle

30°N
0°
30°S
60°S

0° 30°E 60°E 90°E 120°E 150°E 180°
30°W 60°W 90°W 120°W

N

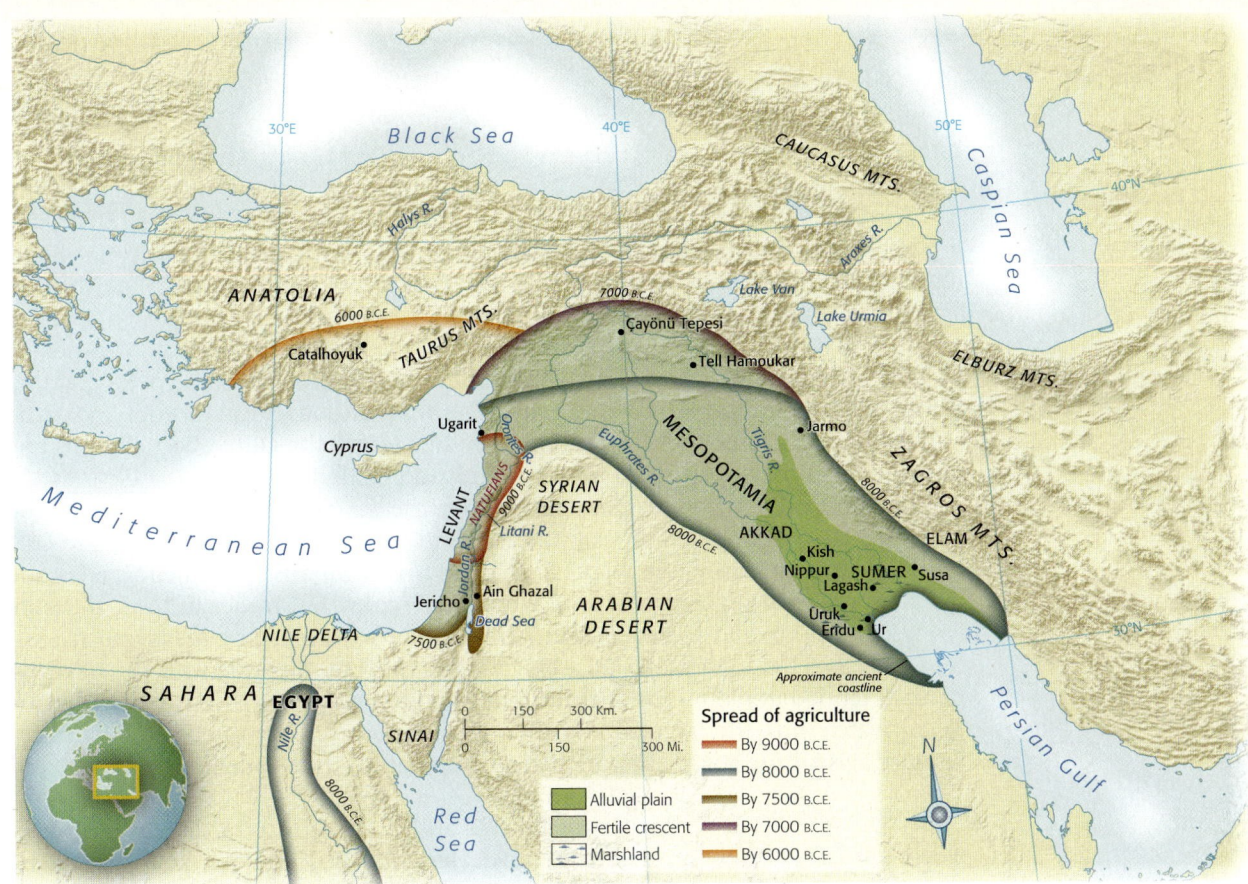

MAP 1.2 **Ancient Southwestern Asia** The Natufians, who lived in Palestine and southern Syria, began to harvest wild crops around 12,500 B.C.E. and gradually learned how to raise animals and plant crops over the next several thousand years. Agriculture eventually spread beyond the Levant and Mesopotamia to southern Anatolia, where agriculturalists built the world's earliest city at Catalhoyuk. (© Cengage Learning)

fire. These figs, because of a mutation, had no fertile seeds but tasted sweet; unless someone planted a branch from a fig tree in the ground, this type of fig would have died out the following season. Since the figs did not die out, we know that someone deliberately planted them. The Natufians did not have to stay near the fig trees they planted; they could continue to hunt and gather as before and simply had to visit the fig trees from time to time to collect the fruit and plant new branches.

The next crop they cultivated—grain—had a far greater impact because it replaced basic elements in their diet. At first, the Natufians gathered wild grain where it grew naturally. But wild grain had two flaws: the stems were so weak that their seeds easily fell to the ground, and thick husks made it difficult to remove the kernels of grain from inside the seeds. The Natufians gradually started to weed these naturally occurring stands of grain and to plant extra seeds in them. The Natufians picked seeds from tall plants, a practice that eventually fostered the growth of wheat with stronger stems. Similarly, they favored plants whose kernels had thinner husks, which eventually fostered the growth of grain that was easier to harvest and winnow. The wheat and barley they planted began to diverge from their wild prototypes.

People took thousands of years to master the two major components of farming: domesticating animals and planting crops. The first step to domesticating wild animals was simply to stop killing young female animals. Then people began to watch over wild herds and kill only those animals that could no longer breed. Eventually, the Natufians began to feed the herds in their care. The dog was the first animal to be tamed, around 10,000 B.C.E., and its function was to help hunters locate their prey.

After several thousand years, villagers had domesticated goats, sheep, and cattle. All these animals produced meat, and sheep produced wool that was woven into cloth.

The size of excavated Natufian sites suggests that groups as large as 150 or 250 people—far larger than the typical hunting and gathering band of 30 or 40—lived together in settlements as large as 10,800 square feet (1,000 sq m). The shift to agriculture almost always caused a dramatic increase in population.

After 8300 B.C.E., possibly because of a sustained period of dryer weather, it became increasingly difficult for the Natufians to continue gathering wild grain as before. Some Natufians returned to a life of hunting undomesticated crops and gathering wild plants, a possible indication that they found the cultivation of crops too difficult. Still others intensified their planting and gathering of wheat and barley.

By 8000 B.C.E. many peoples throughout the eastern Mediterranean, particularly near the Zagros (ZAH-groes) Mountains in modern Turkey, had begun to cultivate wheat and barley (see Map 1.2). Unlike the Natufians, these peoples did not live near pre-existing stands of wild wheat and barley but rather in more difficult living conditions that forced them to experiment with planting seeds and raising crops. Peoples living in marginal areas, not the most fertile areas with the heaviest rainfall, tended to plant crops because they had to innovate. Once they had begun to cultivate crops, the larger size of their villages forced them to continue farming because agriculture could support a larger population than foraging.

The First Larger Settlements, 7000–3000 B.C.E. Between 8300 and 7500 B.C.E., the largest Natufian settlement was Jericho (JEHR-ih-koh), near the Jordan River in the present-day West Bank, where as many as one thousand people may have lived in an area of 8–10 acres (.03–.04 sq km).[5] Residing in mud-brick dwellings with stone foundation bases, the residents of Jericho planted barley and wheat, possibly along with figs and lentils, at the same time they continued to hunt wild animals. The more grains they ate, the more their bodies needed salt, which they collected by evaporating water from the Dead Sea.

The residents of Jericho dug a wide ditch and built a wall at least 8 feet (2.5 m) high around their settlement to protect their accumulated resources from wild animals, human enemies, or possibly both. They also built a 28-foot (8.5-m) tower inside the wall that may have served as a lookout post. The ditches, the wall, and the tower all show the ruler's ability to mobilize laborers and supplies for large-scale construction.

Around 7250 B.C.E., more than one thousand people lived at the site of Ain Ghazal (AYN GUH-zahl) near Amman, Jordan, which also covered 10 acres (.04 sq km). In 6500 B.C.E., the site had become twice as large, and by 6000 B.C.E. it was three times as large. Like the residents of Jericho, the people of Ain Ghazal planted wheat, barley, and lentils, even as they continued to hunt for wild animals and gather wild plants. They also raised their own domesticated goats.

The residents of Ain Ghazal detached the heads of some of the dead and buried them in pits under their houses—perhaps these were ancestors they especially revered—but they threw away other intact corpses without removing their heads. Two ritual pits held groups of unusual human figurines, made from plaster around a tree-branch core; some were as tall as 3 feet (.9 m), with distinctive shell eyes. These practices all suggest that the living believed that they could maintain communication with the dead.

By 7000 B.C.E. early farmers were living in villages in western Turkey and the region of the Levant (the eastern shore of the Mediterranean in today's Lebanon and Israel). Their residents could depend on rainfall to support their crops, and

Photo by John Tsantesi, courtesy Dr. Gary O. Rollefson, Whitman College, Walla Walla, Washington

The Earliest Depictions of People? The Plaster Statues of Ain Ghazal, Jordan Dating to 6500 B.C.E., these figures were probably used in rituals and commemorated the dead. Their makers fashioned a core of reeds and grass, covered it with plaster, and then painted clothes and facial features on it. The eyes, made from inlaid shells with painted dots, are particularly haunting.

they continued to forage as they raised their own herds. By far the largest settlement in the region was at **Catalhoyuk** (CHAH-tal-her-yerk) in south-central Anatolia, where some five thousand people were living in 6000 B.C.E.

Catalhoyuk did not resemble earlier settlements. Unlike Jericho, it had no external wall or surrounding moats. The residents lived in mud-brick dwellings touching each other, and the exteriors of the houses on the perimeter of the town formed a continuous protective wall.

Frequently whitewashed, the walls of the Catalhoyuk dwellings depicted animals, hunters, gods, and even the earliest known landscape painting of a volcano exploding. Of the more than one hundred rooms that have been excavated, forty had plaster models of bull or ram heads mounted on the walls or paintings showing women giving birth to rams or bulls. These rooms may have served as shrines where residents worshiped bulls and rams.

The different types of houses at Catalhoyuk indicate that some residents had more wealth than others. The wealthy buried their dead with jewelry and tools, while the poor interred only their dead bodies. At the same time that they worked in the fields, some families worked bone tools, wove cloth, or made clay pots, which they could trade for other goods, especially obsidian, a naturally occurring volcanic glass. Ancient peoples treasured obsidian because they could use it to make sharp knives and beautiful jewelry.

Catalhoyuk
The world's largest early settlement, with a population of 5,000 in 6000 B.C.E., located in modern Turkey.

The World's First Town: Catalhoyuk, Turkey This artist's reconstruction shows what Catalhoyuk looked like in 6000 B.C.E., when it had a population of around five thousand people. The settlement had no streets, and the houses had no doors at ground level. Instead, residents walked on top of the roofs to get from one place to another. Entering houses through a hole in the roof, they climbed down a ladder to get inside. (Courtesy Catalhoyuk Research Project, Institute of Archaeology, University College, London)

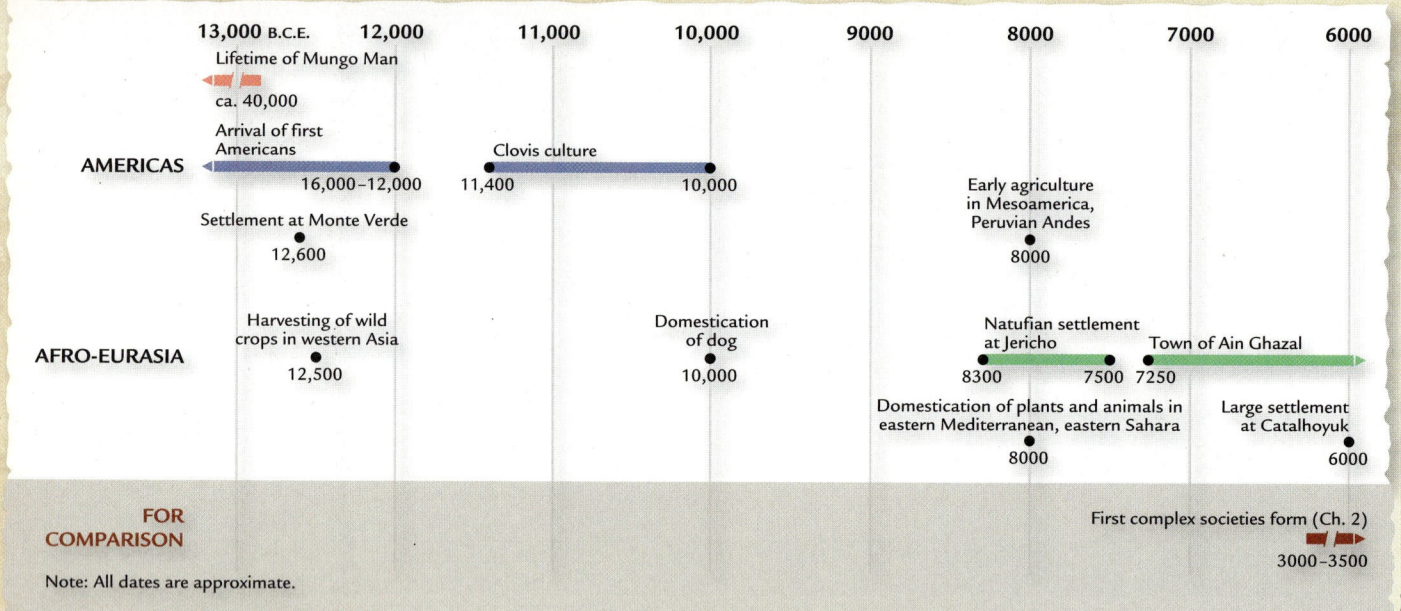

Timeline (13,000 B.C.E.–6000 B.C.E.)

AMERICAS
- Lifetime of Mungo Man — ca. 40,000
- Arrival of first Americans — 16,000–12,000
- Settlement at Monte Verde — 12,600
- Clovis culture — 11,400–10,000
- Early agriculture in Mesoamerica, Peruvian Andes — 8000

AFRO-EURASIA
- Harvesting of wild crops in western Asia — 12,500
- Domestication of dog — 10,000
- Natufian settlement at Jericho — 8300–7500
- Town of Ain Ghazal — 7250
- Domestication of plants and animals in eastern Mediterranean, eastern Sahara — 8000
- Large settlement at Catalhoyuk — 6000

FOR COMPARISON
- First complex societies form (Ch. 2) — 3000–3500

Note: All dates are approximate.

© Cengage Learning

The Significance of Early Human Migrations for World History

Mungo Man and Mungo Woman are among the earliest exemplars of human behavior. Their discovery shows that, by 50,000 B.C.E., when they arrived in Australia, *Homo sapiens sapiens* were certainly behaving like modern humans—planning for the future, engaging in multistep activities, and imagining an afterlife. Anatomically modern humans had arisen in western Africa sometime around 150,000 B.C.E., and they began to behave in recognizably human ways tens of thousands of years later, when they hunted large game, crafted the world's first art objects, built large trade networks, and started to speak.

Our forebears had to build small boats or rafts to cross some 60 miles (100 km) of ocean to reach Australia, but they did not have to adapt to a different climate. However, when *Homo sapiens sapiens* entered Europe in 50,000 B.C.E., they had to adjust to colder temperatures, and they encountered the Neanderthals already living there. The trip into the Americas, which also required some migrants to travel by boat, occurred in 14,000 B.C.E. at the latest.

The total worldwide population of humans remained low—an estimated 10,000–20,000—as they settled all of the world's regions except for the islands of the Pacific. The population only began to increase after the introduction of agriculture. Many peoples of the world continued to hunt and gather as the major way of securing food. The Natufians were the first to shift to agriculture, around 8000 B.C.E., and their settlements at Jericho and Ain Ghazal were larger than any earlier human settlements. Catalhoyuk, the largest early settlement, was the result of the spread of agriculture to Turkey. In a few places in the world, the development of agriculture would lead to the rise of a complex society, as we will see in Chapters 2 through 5.

The remains of Mungo Man testify to the settlement of Australia, one of the most distant journeys ancient humans took. The movement of humans from Africa to almost every corner of the globe was a long one, requiring over one hundred thousand years. One theme is constant: our ancestors were always on the move. They followed herds, crossed rivers, traveled by boat, and ultimately covered enormous distances at a time when their most powerful weapon was a stone hand ax and the fastest means of locomotion was running. From their beginnings, humans have always been voyagers who traveled the world.

Voyages on the Web: Mungo Man

The Voyages Map App follows the traveler's journeys using interactive study tools, including 360-degree panoramic views of historic sites, zoomable maps, audio summaries, flash cards, and quizzes.

Key Terms

Mungo Man (2)
ocher (4)
Homo sapiens sapiens (4)
hominins (4)
evolution (5)
mitochondrial Eve (6)

religion (10)
Neanderthals (14)
Beringia (16)
Monte Verde, Chile (16)
stratigraphy (17)
carbon-14 (17)

Clovis technological complex (18)
agriculture (19)
Neolithic (19)
Catalhoyuk (23)

For Further Reference

Bowler, J. M., and A. G. Thorne. "Human Remains from Lake Mungo: Discovery and Excavation of Lake Mungo III." In *The Origin of the Australians*, ed. R. L. Kirk and A. G. Thorne. Atlantic Highlands, N.J.: Humanities Press, 1976.

Davidson, Iain, and William Noble. "Why the First Colonisation of the Australian Region Is the Earliest Evidence of Modern Human Behaviour." *Archaeology in Oceania* 27, no. 3 (October 1992): 135–142.

Dillehay, Tom D., et al. "Monte Verde: Seaweed, Food, Medicine, and the Peopling of South America." *Science* 320, no. 5877 (May 2008): 784–789.

Dixon, E. James. *Bones, Boats, and Bison*. Albuquerque: University of New Mexico Press, 1999.

Fagan, Brian M. *The Great Journey: The Peopling of Ancient America*. Gainesville: University Press of Florida, 2004.

Haynes, G. *Early Settlement of North America: The Clovis Era*. New York: Cambridge University Press, 2002.

Klein, Richard, with Blake Edgar. *The Dawn of Human Culture*. New York: John Wiley, 2002.

Scarre, Chris. *The Human Past: World Prehistory and the Development of Human Societies*. 2d ed. London: Thames and Hudson, 2009.

Stiebing, William H. *Ancient Near Eastern History and Culture*. New York: Pearson/Longman, 2009.

Stringer, Chris, and Peter Andrews. *The Complete World of Human Evolution*. London: Thames and Hudson, 2006.

Tattersall, Ian. *The World from Beginnings to 4000 B.C.E.* New York: Oxford University Press, 2008.

Wells, Spencer. *Deep Ancestry: Inside the Genographic Project*. Washington, D.C.: National Geographic, 2006.

White, Randall. *Prehistoric Art: The Symbolic Journey of Humankind*. New York: Harry N. Abrams, 2003.

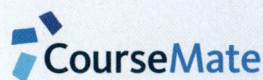 Go to the CourseMate website at **www.cengagebrain.com** for additional study tools and review materials—including audio and video clips—for this chapter.

2

The First Complex Societies in the Eastern Mediterranean, ca. 4000–550 B.C.E.

The epic *Gilgamesh* (GIL-ga-mesh), one of the earliest recorded works of literature, captures the experience of the people of Mesopotamia (mess-oh-poh-TAME-ee-ah), who established one of the first complex societies in the world. **Mesopotamia** (Greek for "between the rivers") is the region between the Tigris (TIE-gris) and Euphrates (you-FRAY-teez) Rivers in today's Iraq and eastern Syria. The epic *Gilgamesh* indicates that the people in this region remembered what life was like before the rise of cities. It describes the unlikely friendship between two men: Enkidu (EN-kee-doo), who lives in the wild like an animal, and **Gilgamesh**, the king of the ancient city Uruk (OO-rook), located in modern-day Warka in southern Iraq. Ruler of the walled city during a time between 2700 and 2500 B.C.E., Gilgamesh enjoys the benefits of a complex society: wearing clothing, drinking beer, and eating bread. Early in the epic, when a hunter complains to Gilgamesh that Enkidu is freeing the animals caught in his traps, Gilgamesh sends the woman Shamhat, a priestess at the main temple of Uruk, to introduce Enkidu to the pleasures of life:

Gilgamesh Killing a Bull
(The Schøyen Collection, MS 1989 www.schoyencollection.com)

*E*nkidu, born in the uplands,
	Who feeds on grass with gazelles,
Who drinks at the water hole with beasts, . . .
Shamhat looked upon him, a human-man,
A barbarous fellow from the midst of the steppe:
Shamhat loosened her garments,
She exposed her loins, he took her charms, . . .
After he had his fill of her delights,
He set off towards his beasts.
When they saw him, Enkidu, the gazelles shied off,

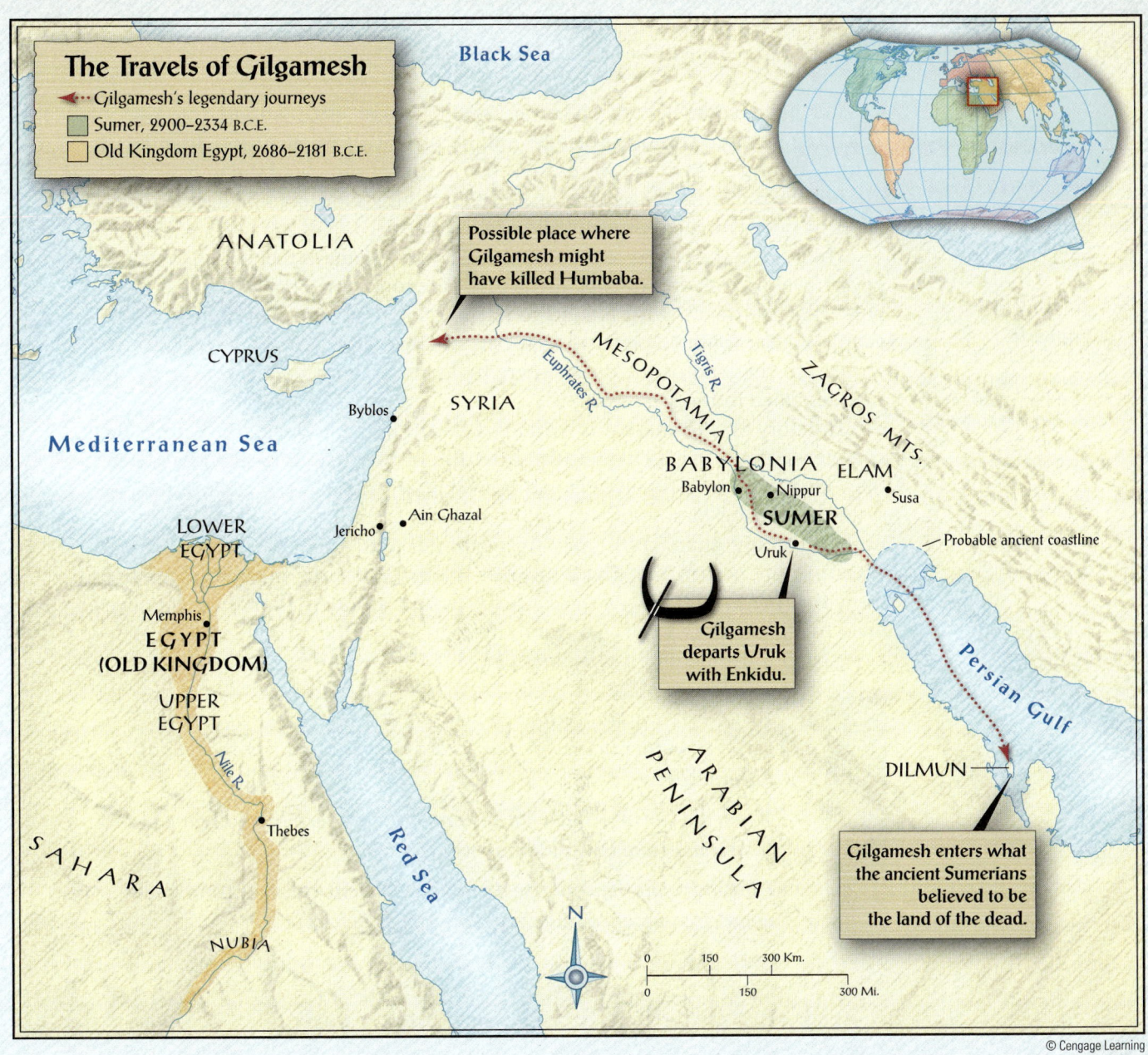

The Travels of Gilgamesh

- ◄····· Gilgamesh's legendary journeys
- Sumer, 2900–2334 B.C.E.
- Old Kingdom Egypt, 2686–2181 B.C.E.

Black Sea

ANATOLIA

CYPRUS

Mediterranean Sea

Byblos

SYRIA

Possible place where Gilgamesh might have killed Humbaba.

MESOPOTAMIA

Euphrates R.

Tigris R.

ZAGROS MTS.

BABYLONIA   ELAM
Babylon   Nippur   Susa
SUMER
Uruk   Probable ancient coastline

Jericho   Ain Ghazal

LOWER
EGYPT

Memphis

EGYPT
(OLD KINGDOM)

UPPER
EGYPT

Nile R.

Thebes

SAHARA

Red Sea

NUBIA

ARABIAN
PENINSULA

Gilgamesh departs Uruk with Enkidu.

Persian Gulf

DILMUN

Gilgamesh enters what the ancient Sumerians believed to be the land of the dead.

N

0   150   300 Km.
0   150   300 Mi.

© Cengage Learning

Join this chapter's traveler on "Voyages," an interactive tour of historic sites and events:
www.cengagebrain.com

The wild beasts of the steppe shunned his person. . . .
Enkidu was too slow, he could not run as before,
But he had gained reason and expanded his understanding.[*]

[*]Excerpt from *The Epic of Gilgamesh*, translated by Benjamin R. Foster. Copyright © 2001 by W.W. Norton & Company. Used by permission of W.W. Norton & Company, Inc.

Mesopotamia
Greek for "between the rivers": the region between the Tigris and Euphrates Rivers in today's Iraq and eastern Syria.

Gilgamesh
Name of a historic king of Uruk (modern-day Warka, Iraq) who ruled between 2700 and 2500 B.C.E. Also the name of an epic about him.

After his encounter with Shamhat, Enkidu immediately adopts the ways of those living in complex societies and becomes Gilgamesh's close friend. First written around 2100 B.C.E., *Gilgamesh* is not a strict chronicle of the historic king's life, but the romanticized version of a legendary king's life, complete with appearances by different gods who control human fate.

The hero of the epic is constantly in motion. Gilgamesh makes two long journeys, traveling overland by foot and across water on a small boat he guides with a pole. First, he travels with Enkidu to kill the ferocious monster Humbaba, who guards a cedar forest somewhere to the west. Then, after Enkidu dies, Gilgamesh voyages to the land of the dead, where he learns about a flood surprisingly like that described in the Hebrew Bible.

The story of Gilgamesh was written by people living in one of the world's first complex societies. This chapter traces the rise of the first cities, then city-states, then kingdoms, and finally regional powers that interacted in an international system spanning Mesopotamia, Egypt, and the eastern coast of the Mediterranean, including Anatolia (the western section of present-day Turkey), Crete, and Greece in the Aegean Sea. These societies were significantly more complex than those that preceded them. As the centuries passed, an international system developed in which envoys traveled from one ruler to another and merchants transported goods throughout the region.

Focus Questions

» *What were the similarities in political structures, religion, and social structure in Mesopotamia and Egypt? What were the main differences?*

» *When did the international system of the eastern Mediterranean take shape, and how did it function?*

» *How did monotheism arise among the ancient Hebrews, and under what circumstances did they record their beliefs?*

The Emergence of Complex Society in Mesopotamia, ca. 3100–1590 B.C.E.

As we have seen in the previous chapter, the settlements of the eastern Mediterranean increased in size gradually, reaching some five thousand people living in Catalhoyuk by 6000 B.C.E. Eventually some villages became larger than the surrounding villages and thus became centers. In time these centers grew to house twenty thousand inhabitants or more. By 3100 B.C.E. even larger urban centers had formed in southern Mesopotamia, where the first city of forty or fifty thousand people was located at Uruk. Here complex society took shape.

complex society
Society characterized by a large urban center with specialized labor and social stratification, as well as the belief that rulers and deities were entitled to the surpluses the society produced.

Scholars define a **complex society** as a large urban center with a population in the tens of thousands whose residents pursue different occupations, the mark of specialized labor. Some have higher social positions than others, an indication of social stratification. Some earlier definitions of complex society required the presence of a writing system, but today the term also covers urban societies without writing systems. In recent years, analysts have stressed that, unlike Neolithic societies, early complex societies had much larger surpluses—of both material goods and labor—and believed that their rulers, their gods, and their human representatives, the priests, were entitled to a large share of these surpluses.

The shift from a simpler society to a complex one took thousands of years. Complex societies interest historians because they had larger populations than simple societies and their residents often left behind written records that allow historians to study how they changed over time, the major topic of historical writing. The world's first complex societies appeared in Mesopotamia and Egypt at about the same time, before 3000 B.C.E.; this chapter first considers Mesopotamia.

City Life in Ancient Mesopotamia

The first settlers came to southern Mesopotamia from the eastern Mediterranean and western Turkey. They found the environment harsh. Each year not enough rain fell to support intensive farming, and no wild grain grew naturally in the marshlands. In addition, the Tigris and Euphrates Rivers tended to flood in the late summer, when crops were ripening, and the floodwaters often washed away the settlers' homes.

The settlers responded by developing channels to control the water. They settled along the shore of the Euphrates, which flowed less rapidly than the Tigris, and dug channels for the river's floodwater, through which they could move the water to fields far from the river. Using irrigation, these early farmers permanently settled the lower Mesopotamian plain between 6000 and 5000 B.C.E.

Their first villages were small, but by 4000 B.C.E. some villages had grown into walled urban centers of over ten thousand people. The farmland within the walls could not produce enough food for the growing population, so the urban centers came to depend on surplus food grown by the residents of the surrounding villages. The food was stored in temples. Excavations reveal that temples had a main chamber surrounded by multiple rooms for the storage of grain. In exchange for this food, the cities provided the villages with military protection from raids by neighboring cities.

Historians use the term **city-state** for a city whose ruler governs both the city center and the surrounding countryside. Kings descended from prominent families, like Gilgamesh, ruled these city-states, often with the support of temple priests and in consultation with other prominent families (see page 33). The first kings were probably successful military leaders who continued to rule in peacetime.

city-state
A city whose ruler governs both the city center and the surrounding countryside.

Ancient texts simply call Gilgamesh's city of Uruk "the city," because no other city rivaled Uruk in size or importance between 3400 and 3000 B.C.E., the dates of the Uruk period. One of the most ancient cities to be excavated by archaeologists, Uruk meets the definition of a complex society: its population numbered between forty and fifty thousand, and its inhabitants had specialized occupations and were divided by social level. The surrounding countryside provided a large surplus of grain that the ruler and temple leadership distributed to the residents of the city.

The opening section of *Gilgamesh* provides a vivid description of the region's greatest city:

Go up, pace out the walls of Uruk,
Study the foundation terrace and examine the brickwork.
Is not its masonry of kiln-fired brick?
And did not seven masters lay its foundations?
One square mile of city, one square mile of gardens,
One square mile of clay pits, a half square mile of Ishtar's dwelling,
*Three and a half square miles is the measure of Uruk!**

Uruk, then, contained 1 square mile each of land occupied by residences, farmland, and clay pits, with the remaining half square mile taken by the temple of Ishtar, the city's guardian deity. (The Sumerian mile does not correspond exactly to the modern mile.)

Dating to 700 B.C.E., the most complete version of the *Gilgamesh* epic is a retelling of the original story, and historians must use archaeological data to supplement the information it provides about early Uruk. Although the epic claims that the walls were made from fired bricks, the actual walls were made from sun-dried mud brick. In roughly 3000 B.C.E., the city had a wall 5 miles (9.5 km) long. Enclosing approximately 1,000 acres (400 ha), it was by far the largest city in the world at the time. Much of it consisted of open farmland.

Farming required year-round labor and constant vigilance. Unlike Neolithic farmers, whose tools were made from bone, wood, or stone, Mesopotamian farmers had much more durable tools made of **bronze**, an alloy of copper and tin. In addition to axes used to cut down trees and clear fields, they used bronze plow blades to dig the furrows and bronze sickles to harvest the grain.

Archaeologists are not certain where the **wheel** was first invented. One of the most important tools used by the Mesopotamians, it first appeared sometime around 3500 B.C.E. in a wide area extending from Mesopotamia to the modern European countries of Switzerland, Slovenia, Poland, and Russia. The earliest wheeled vehicles were flat wooden platforms that moved on two logs pulled by laborers. By 3000 B.C.E. the Mesopotamians were using narrow carts, usually with four solid wooden wheels, to move loads, both within city-states and over greater distances. By 2500 B.C.E. they had begun to add spokes to wheels, which allowed for much greater speed.

Built in the floodplain of the Euphrates, Uruk had no tall trees suitable for lumber, little stone, and almost no mineral deposits. The epic tells of Gilgamesh and Enkidu's overland journey to the wooded home of the monster Humbaba to obtain lumber, and the real-life inhabitants of Uruk shipped wood in carts or by boat first from the highlands of northern Mesopotamia, near the Zagros (ZAH-groes) Mountains, and later from the forests of Lebanon.

At Uruk, archaeologists have found extensive evidence of occupational diversity and social stratification, both important markers of a complex society. Large quantities of broken pottery found in the same area suggest that potters lived and worked together, as did other craftworkers like weavers and metalsmiths. Because people received more or less compensation for different tasks, some became rich while others stayed poor. Poorer people lived in small houses made of unfired mud bricks and mud plaster, while richer people lived in fired-brick houses with kitchens and many rooms. They hosted guests in large reception rooms in which they served lavish meals with bread, washed down with generous quantities of beer.

bronze
An alloy of copper and tin used to make the earliest metal tools.

wheel
An important innovation in transport dating to 3500 B.C.E.

---

*Excerpt from *The Epic of Gilgamesh*, translated by Benjamin R. Foster. Copyright © 2001 by W.W. Norton & Company. Used by permission of W.W. Norton & Company, Inc.

"Enkidu did not know how to eat bread, / Nor had he ever learned to drink beer!" the author of *Gilgamesh* exclaims in amazement. Having grown up in the wild, Enkidu had never tasted these two basic foodstuffs of the Sumerians, both made from barley and wheat. The Sumerians were the first people in the world to make beer.

Gilgamesh vividly describes Enkidu's first taste of beer:

Enkidu drank seven juglets of the beer.
His mood became relaxed, he was singing joyously,
He felt light-hearted and his features glowed.[*]

The Sumerians drank beer constantly. The rations provided by the king to royal messengers included beer, bread, and onions. Temple-goers offered clay jars full of beer to their gods, and Sumerians regularly gave wedding presents ranging from 5 to 10 gallons (20–40 liters) of beer, or one-third to two-thirds of a modern keg.

The Beginnings of Writing, 3300 B.C.E.

People living in southern Mesopotamia developed their writing system sometime around 3300 B.C.E., making it the earliest in the world. Scholars call the language of the first documents Sumerian, after **Sumer**, a geographical term referring broadly to the ancient region of southern Mesopotamia. It is not always easy to determine whether a given sign constitutes writing in ancient script. Markings on pottery, for example, look like writing but may be only the sign of the person who made the pot. A sign becomes writing only when someone other than the writer associates a specific word or sound with it.

Sumer
A geographical term from Akkadian meaning the ancient region of southern Mesopotamia.

We can track the invention of writing in Mesopotamia because the residents used clay, a material that, once baked, was virtually indestructible. At first, sometime between 4000 and 3000 B.C.E., the ancient Sumerians used small clay objects of different shapes to keep track of merchandise, probably animals being traded or donated to a temple. Eventually they began to incise lines in these objects to stand for a certain number of items. Later, they placed these small objects in a bag made from a clay sheet and incised these bags, while still soft, on the outside to indicate their contents. These markings did not yet constitute written language because they could be understood in different ways; one had to cut open the clay bag, after it had hardened, to find out what was inside.

The transition to written language came when people drew a picture on a flat writing tablet that represented a specific animal and could not be mistaken for anything else. The first documents in human history, from a level dating to 3300 B.C.E., depict the item being counted with a tally next to it to show the number of items. Temple accountants needed writing to record increasingly sophisticated transactions, like the number and type of animal or the amount of grain donated on successive days.

By 3300 B.C.E., a full-blown writing system of more than seven hundred different signs had emerged. Some symbols, like an ox-head representing an ox, are clearly pictorial, but many others are not. The word *sheep*, for example, was a circle with an *X* inside it (see Figure 2.1).

Over time, the marks lost their original shapes, and by 700 B.C.E. each symbol represented a certain sound; that is, it had become phonetic. We call this later

---

[*]Excerpts from *The Epic of Gilgamesh*, translated by Benjamin R. Foster. Copyright © 2001 by W.W. Norton & Company. Used by permission of W.W. Norton & Company, Inc.

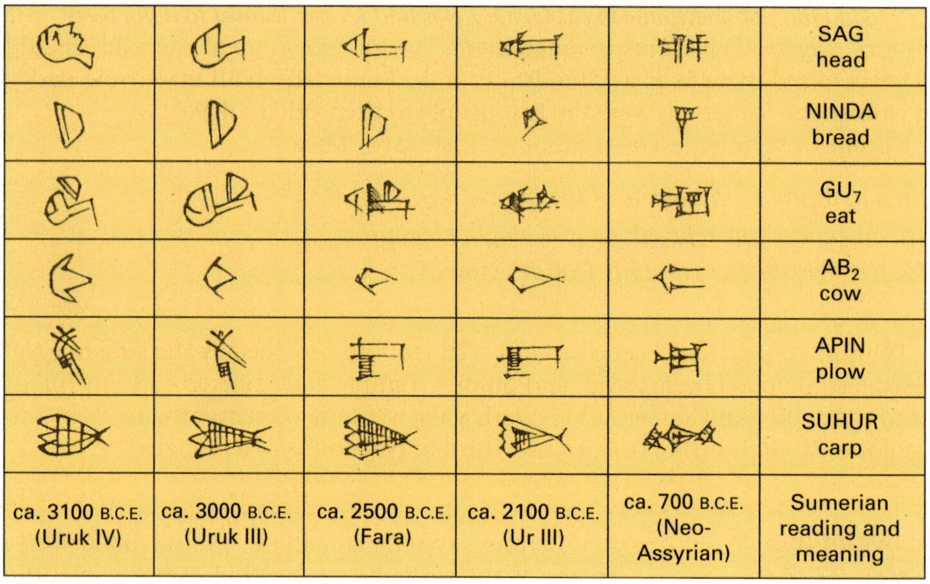

					SAG head
					NINDA bread
					GU$_7$ eat
					AB$_2$ cow
					APIN plow
					SUHUR carp
ca. 3100 B.C.E. (Uruk IV)	ca. 3000 B.C.E. (Uruk III)	ca. 2500 B.C.E. (Fara)	ca. 2100 B.C.E. (Ur III)	ca. 700 B.C.E. (Neo-Assyrian)	Sumerian reading and meaning

FIGURE 2.1 Cuneiform The Mesopotamians first made small pictures, or pictographs, to write, but these symbols gradually evolved into combinations of lines that scribes made by pressing a wedge-shaped implement into wet clay. The cuneiform forms from 700 B.C.E. hardly resemble their original pictographic shapes from 3100 B.C.E. (From J. N. Postgate, *Early Mesopotamia: Society and Economy at the Dawn of History*, Routledge, 1992, p. 63. Reprinted with permission of Taylor and Francis Books Ltd.)

cuneiform
The term, meaning "wedge-shaped," for the writing system of Sumer in its late stages, when the script became completely phonetic.

writing **cuneiform** (cue-NAY-i-form), meaning "wedge-shaped," because it was made by a writing implement pressed into clay. These early records, most of them temple accounts, allow us to understand early Sumerian religion and how the ancient Sumerians distributed their surplus wealth.

Sumerian Religion

The people of ancient Sumer believed that various gods managed different aspects of their hostile environment. The most powerful god, the storm-god, could control storms and flooding. Like human beings, the Sumerian gods had families who sometimes lived together in harmony and sometimes did not.

The largest building in Uruk was the temple to Ishtar, the protective deity of Uruk and the storm-god's daughter. Sumerian temple complexes sometimes housed a thousand priests, priestesses, and supporting laborers. The largest structure inside each temple was a ziggurat, a stepped platform made from bricks. Throughout the year both rich and poor participated in different festivals and ceremonies presided over by priests and priestesses.

The human king played an important role in Sumerian religion because he was believed to be the intermediary between the gods and human beings. The epic describes Gilgamesh as two-thirds divine, one-third human, an indication that the Sumerians did not believe that parents contributed equal shares to their offspring. He was sufficiently attractive that Ishtar proposed marriage to him. He brusquely turned her down, pointing out that each of her previous lovers had come to a bad end.

Ishtar persuaded her father to retaliate by sending the Bull of Heaven to punish Gilgamesh and destroy Uruk. Gilgamesh's friend Enkidu killed the bull, to the delight of Uruk's residents but to the dismay of the gods, who then convened in council. The storm-god decided that Enkidu had to die.

Before he died, Enkidu dreamed of the world of the dead:

To the house whence none who enters comes forth,
On the road from which there is no way back,
To the house whose dwellers are deprived of light,
Where dust is their fare and their food is clay.
They are dressed like birds in feather garments,
Yea, they shall see no daylight for they abide in darkness.*

This description provides certain evidence—not available for earlier, preliterate societies—that the Sumerians believed in an afterworld.

When Enkidu dies, the heartbroken Gilgamesh renounces life in complex society: *"Now that you are dead, I will let my hair grow matted / I will put on a lion skin and roam the steppe!"* Resolving to escape death, he travels a great distance over mountains and desert to reach the entrance to the underworld, believed to be near modern-day Bahrain. At the end of his journey, Gilgamesh meets Utanapishtim (OO-tah-nah-pish-teem), who tells him of a great flood that occurred because the storm-god became angry with humankind. Utanapishtim managed to escape because another divinity secretly informed him in time to build a boat. Hearing this story from Utanapishtim, a human being to whom the gods granted immortality, Gilgamesh realizes that he, like all human beings, must die, and returns to Uruk to rule the city-state.

Sumerian Government

The ruler of each city-state claimed to rule with the support of the local guardian deity, but an early version of *Gilgamesh* makes clear that he actually ruled in consultation with one or more assemblies. Faced with a demand from a neighboring kingdom to surrender, Gilgamesh consults with two separate assemblies, one of elders, one of younger men. While the elders oppose Gilgamesh's decision to go to war, the younger men support him.

During the Early Dynastic period, between 2900 and 2334 B.C.E., settlers moved out of Uruk to build new city-states closer to supplies of lumber and precious metals. Because transportation was slow and communication difficult, these satellite cities had their own rulers but maintained trade ties with the mother cities. Thirty-five different city-states, each with a temple and its own guardian deity, traded and increasingly warred with one another. Higher city walls, increasing numbers of bronze weapons, and more artistic depictions of battle victories indicate regular warfare among these city-states.

The first ruler to conquer all the city-states and unify the region was **Sargon of Akkad** (r. 2334–2279 B.C.E.). Sargon (SAHR-gone) and the Akkadians ruled the world's first **empire**, defined as a large territory with subject peoples of different languages and different religious traditions. He and his descendants ruled over southern Mesopotamia for slightly over one hundred years until their empire broke apart. As surviving inscriptions show, Sargon changed the language of administration from Sumerian to Akkadian (uh-KAY-dee-uhn), named for his home city of Akkad (AHK-cad), and Akkadian replaced Sumerian as the language of daily life.

Sargon of Akkad
(r. 2334–2279 B.C.E.)
The first ruler to unify Mesopotamia. Changed the language of administration to Akkadian.

empire
A large territory in which one people rule over other subject peoples with different languages and different religious traditions.

---

*Excerpts from *The Epic of Gilgamesh*, translated by Benjamin R. Foster. Copyright © 2001 by W.W. Norton & Company. Used by permission of W.W. Norton & Company, Inc.

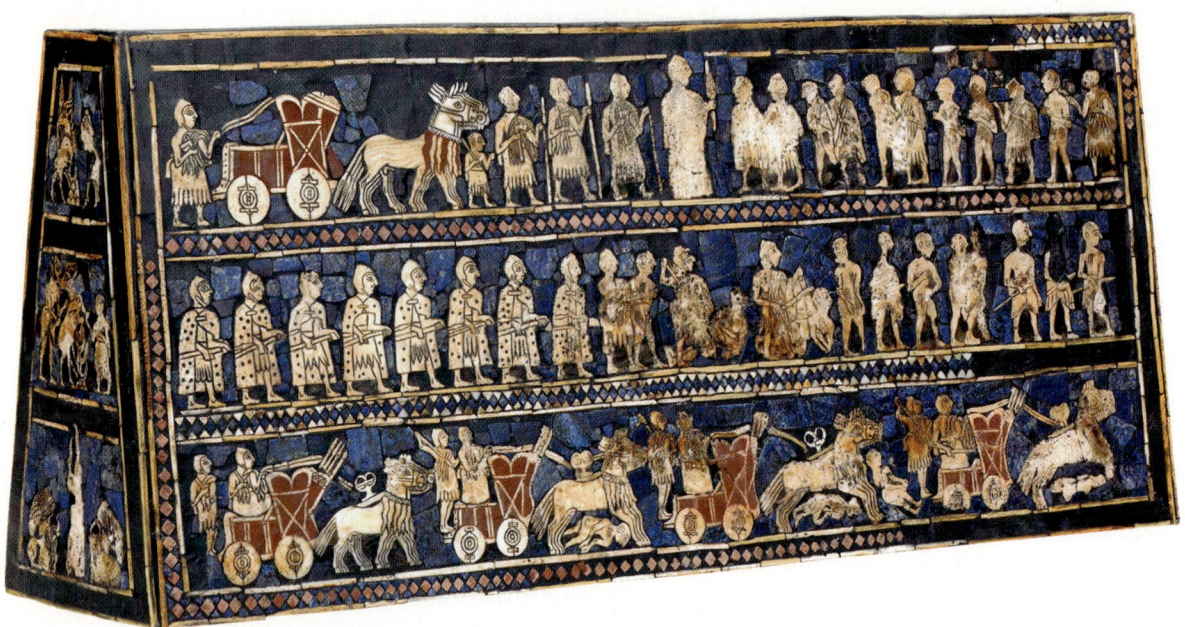

Documenting the Violence of War: The Standard of Ur This object tells a story of war in different panels read from bottom to top. Notice the trampled bodies of the enemy under the feet of the donkeys on the bottom frame. The battle continues in the middle, and, on the top, officials present prisoners to a larger-than-lifesize king. (© British Museum, London/Art Resource, NY)

The Babylonian Empire, 1894–1595 B.C.E.

After the fall of the Akkadian empire, Mesopotamia again broke into several different kingdoms. Sometime around 2200 B.C.E., a new city, Babylon, located north of Uruk on the Euphrates, gained prominence. Babylon was a small city-state ruled by a succession of kings until the great military and legal leader Hammurabi (ham-u-ROB-ee) (r. 1792–1750 B.C.E.) unified much of Mesopotamia.

Hammurabi is famous, even today, for the laws that he issued. Many people have heard of a single provision in Hammurabi's law—"an eye for an eye"—but few realize that the original document contained nearly three hundred articles on a host of topics, including the treatment of slaves, divorce, criminal punishments, and interest rates on loans.

Although Hammurabi's laws are often called a "code," the texts of many surviving decisions indicate that judges did not actually consult them. The king carved different legal cases onto stone tablets as proof of his divine rule and as model cases for future kings to study.

The laws recognized three different social groups, who received different punishments for the same crime. The most privileged group included the royal family, priests, merchants, and other free men and women who owned land. In the middle were commoners and peasants, and at the bottom were slaves.

The original wording of the famous eye-for-an-eye clause says, *"If an awālu [freeman] should blind the eye of another awālu [freeman], they shall blind his eye."*[1] This is the law of exact retaliation: if you bring harm to someone else, the identical wound shall be your punishment. It operated only among social equals. If a freeman destroyed the eye of a commoner, he paid only a moderate fine. If he destroyed the eye of a slave or broke one of his bones, then he had to pay the owner half of the slave's value, an even lesser amount. The laws stipulated the payment of fines in fixed amounts of silver or grain because coins did not yet exist.

As trade increased in the years after 2000 B.C.E., the Babylonian law codes on regulations governing commerce became more detailed. The main trading partners of the Babylonians lay to the southeast and included communities in the Persian Gulf and modern-day Afghanistan, who exported copper, the blue semiprecious mineral lapis lazuli, and other metals and precious stones in exchange for Mesopotamian textiles.

Hammurabi's laws also provide insight into marriage and the roles and status of women. Marriage had to be recorded in a written contract to be legally valid. Women were entitled to a share of their father's and/or mother's property, either as a gift when they married or as a share of the father's wealth upon his death. Punishment for adultery was severe: if a wife was found "lying with" someone other than her husband, she and her lover were tied together and thrown into water to drown; she was permitted to live if her husband allowed it.

At the same time, the law afforded women certain legal rights: if a woman was accused of adultery and denied it (and was not found with a lover), she could take an oath of innocence before a god and return to her husband's house unpunished. A wife could initiate divorce on the grounds that her husband failed to support her or had committed adultery. If the judge found that her husband had taken a lover but she had not, the divorce would be granted.

The tablets reveal only how Hammurabi hoped his laws would operate, not how they actually did. Historians call this a prescriptive source because it reports what should happen, and they value descriptive sources that tell what actually did happen. One case, recorded shortly before Hammurabi's reign on a clay tablet found at Nippur, is valuable precisely because it shows how the legal system actually functioned. Three men—a barber, a gardener, and a third person whose occupation is not mentioned—killed a temple official named Lu-Inanna. They confessed to the victim's wife, but she, for unstated reasons, failed to report the crime.

Eventually the murderers were apprehended and the case came before the assembly of Nippur. A group of about ten men, including a bird-hunter, a porter, and a gardener, argued against the murderers: *They who have killed a man are not worthy of life. Those three males and that woman [the widow] should be killed in front of the chair of Lu-Inanna.* An official and a gardener, whose different social ranks show the mixed composition of the assembly, spoke on the wife's behalf: *Granted that the husband . . . had been killed, but what had the woman done that she should be killed?*[2] The assembly decided that the murderers should be punished but that the wife was innocent.

Southern Mesopotamia came to be known as Babylonia. Yet Hammurabi's dynasty was short-lived. It officially ended in 1595 B.C.E., when the Hittites (see page 45) sacked the city. Although the pace and extent of trade continued to increase, between 3300 and 1500 B.C.E. Mesopotamia remained politically apart from the other kingdoms of the eastern Mediterranean, as well as from Egypt, its neighbor to the west.

Egypt During the Old and Middle Kingdoms, ca. 3100–1500 B.C.E.

Complex society arose in Egypt at about the same time as in Mesopotamia—3100 B.C.E.—but under much different circumstances. The people of Egypt never lived in city-states but rather in a unified kingdom made possible by the natural geography of the Nile River Valley. Their god-king was called the **pharaoh**. Although Egypt did not have the large cities so characteristic of early complex societies, its society was highly stratified, with great differences between the poor and the rich. Large construction projects, like the building of the pyramids, required the same kind of occupational specialization so visible in Mesopotamian cities. The less tangible aspects of complex societies—the belief that the ruler governed with the support of the gods and that his subjects owed him their surplus—were also present in ancient Egypt.

In certain periods Egypt was unified under strong rulers. Historians call these periods "kingdoms." In other times, called "intermediate periods," the presiding pharaoh did not actually govern the entire region. The pharaohs of the Old Kingdom, between 2686 and 2181 B.C.E., ruled the Nile Valley from the Delta to the first impassable rapids; those who ruled during the Middle Kingdom, between 2040 and 1782 B.C.E., controlled an even larger area. Even today historians do not agree about the dates of individual dynasties. Thus the dates given in this book, although accepted by many, are only approximate.[3]

pharaoh
The god-king who ruled the unified kingdom of Egypt from at least 3100 B.C.E.

The Central Role of the Nile

The Egyptian climate is mild, and the country is protected by natural barriers: deserts on three sides and the Mediterranean Sea on the fourth. Fed by headwaters coming from Lake Victoria and the Ethiopian highlands, the Nile flows north, and its large delta opens onto the Mediterranean. Along the river are six steep, perilous, unnavigable rapids called cataracts (see Map 2.1). Lying 620 miles (1,000 km) upstream, the First Cataract formed a natural barrier between Egypt and **Nubia**, an ancient kingdom, sometimes called Kush, that straddled modern Egypt and Sudan (see page 42). Egypt was divided into three parts: Lower Egypt (the Delta region north of present-day Cairo), Upper Egypt (which ran from the First Cataract to the Delta), and Nubia.

Because almost no rain falls anywhere along the Nile, farmers had to tap the river to irrigate their wheat and barley fields, which were near the river. Two types of soil filled the banks of the Nile: "the black land," averaging one-quarter mile (.65 sq km) on both sides, consisted of very fertile soil, each year renewed by the river's deposits of silt; beyond the black land lay the red land, which was less fertile. Beyond the red land lay uncultivable desert.

The Nile, with its annual summer floods, was a much more reliable source of water than the Tigris and Euphrates in Mesopotamia; thus the Egyptians had no equivalent of the vengeful Mesopotamian storm-god who ordered the flood in *Gilgamesh*. The Egyptians began to cultivate the floodplain of the Nile between 4400 and 4000 B.C.E. Their calendar had three seasons, each 120 days long: "Inundation," "Emergence of the Fields from Waters," and "Drought." During "Emergence," farmers used irrigation to move the Nile waters to their fields and planted seeds, which they harvested during the "Drought" season.

Nubia
Region south of the First Cataract on the Nile, in modern-day Egypt and Sudan; was an important trading partner of Egypt.

hieroglyphs
The writing system of ancient Egypt, which consisted of different symbols, some pictorial and some phonetic, used on official inscriptions.

papyrus
A convenient but perishable writing material made from a reed that grew naturally along the Nile.

Egyptian Government and Society: Unity Without City-States

By 3100 B.C.E. the Egyptians were writing using **hiero-glyphs** (pictorial and phonetic symbols). Egyptian hieroglyphs are so different from Sumerian writing that the two societies probably developed writing independently. The surviving record does not explain how writing developed in Egypt because the Egyptians used the perishable writing material of **papyrus** (pah-PIE-rus), made by pressing together the inner stems of the papyrus reed that grew along the banks of the Nile. The dried fibers bonded to form a lightweight, convenient writing material that was far more fragile than the clay tablets of Mesopotamia. Most of the surviving sources for Egyptian history were carved into stone.

Ancient historians credited the legendary founder of the First Dynasty (3200–3000 B.C.E.), Narmer (NAR-mer), with consolidating the entire Nile Valley into a single kingdom. One of the earliest records is a piece of slate dating to around 3100 B.C.E. that uses hieroglyphs to indicate the king's name. Later, by 2500 B.C.E., Egyptians were using two writing systems: pictorial hieroglyphs, and a cursive form, called hieratic ("priestly"). Hieroglyphs were reserved for public writing on monuments and plaques.

Considerable uncertainty persists in our knowledge of Egypt. Many scholars today think that Egypt may have been unified as early as 3500–3200 B.C.E. It seems likely that Upper Egypt and Lower Egypt originally formed two separate regions. Over time various rulers of Upper Egypt gradually conquered more of the Delta until they unified Egypt.

Egypt was united under the rule of one man, the pharaoh. As a god-king, the pharaoh presided over rituals to the Egyptian gods. In theory, the pharaoh removed the gods' statues from their shrines in each temple, dressed them, fed them, and prayed to them. In the evening he fed them again before returning them to their shrines. In practice, the pharaoh performed these rites in the capital and delegated his duties to priests throughout Egypt.

Since the pharaoh's family members shared his semidivine status, pharaohs often married their closest kin, including their sisters and mothers. They also took multiple wives. The frequency of intermarriage meant that a single woman could simultaneously be the wife of the serving pharaoh,

MAP 2.1 Ancient Egypt and Nubia The Nile River lay at the heart of ancient Egypt, but one could not sail all the way from its headwaters in Lake Victoria and the Ethiopian highlands to the Delta at the Mediterranean. Because no boat could cross the sheer vertical rapids called cataracts, the First Cataract formed a natural barrier between Egypt and Nubia, the region to the south where many gold fields were located. (© Cengage Learning)

the mother of the future pharaoh, and the daughter of the previous one. For example, the wife of King Tutankhamen (too-tunk-AH-muhn), Ankhesenamen (ON-kays-ah-muhn), was also his half-sister.

The pharaoh's chief adviser, the vizier, was the only person permitted to meet with the pharaoh alone. Since the pharaoh was often occupied with ritual duties, the vizier handled all matters of state. He was assisted by a variety of higher- and lower-ranking officials, many of whom came from the same small group of families.

Egypt was divided into some forty districts, each ruled by a governor with his own smaller establishment of subordinate officials and scribes. Scribes were among the few Egyptians who could read and write. Legendary for its record keeping, the Egyptian government employed a large number of scribes to keep detailed papyrus records of every conceivable item. The demand for scribes was so great that the government often hired people from nonofficial families, and some of these managed to be promoted to higher office, a rare chance for social mobility in Egyptian society.

Craftspeople and farmers formed the illiterate majority of Egyptian society. Slavery was not widespread. Those who worked the land gave a share of their crop to the pharaoh, the owner of all the land in Egypt, and also owed him labor, which they performed at fixed intervals on roads and royal buildings.

The Rosetta Stone   This stone, dating to 196 B.C.E., provided the key to deciphering Egyptian hieroglyphs because it gives the same government regulations in ancient Greek, a phonetic version of Egyptian called demotic, and hieroglyphs. In fact, the stone contains a fourth, often-overlooked inscription: "Captured in Egypt by the British Army in 1801." The British took the stone from the French, who had found it, which is why the stone is in the British Museum today.

(British Museum, London/Eric Lessing/Art Resource, NY)

The Old Kingdom and Egyptian Belief in the Afterlife, 2686–2181 B.C.E.

The five hundred years of the Old Kingdom, between 2686 and 2181 B.C.E., marked a period of prosperity and political stability for Egypt. No invasions occurred during this time. The Old Kingdom is also called the Pyramid Age because government officials organized the construction of Egypt's most impressive monuments at this time.

Egyptians believed that each person had a life-force (*ka*) that survived on energy from the body. When the body died, Egyptians preserved it and surrounded it with food so that the life-force could continue. The Great Pyramid was built between 2589 and 2566 B.C.E. to house the life-force of the pharaoh Khufu (KOO-fu), also called Cheops (KEY-ops).

Covering an area of 571,211 square feet (53,067 sq m), the Great Pyramid stands 480 feet (147 m) tall. It contains an estimated four million stone blocks ranging from 9.3 tons (8,445 kg) to 48.9 pounds (22.2 kg) in weight.[4] Approximately fifteen to twenty thousand laborers, both male and female, worked on the pyramids each year during the Inundation season. None of these laborers were slaves. About five thousand skilled workers and craftsmen worked full-time, while the rest rotated in and out.[5]

The size of his funerary monument provides a tangible measure of each ruler's power. The government had to organize the labor of all the workers and coordinate the shipment of large stones to the site of the pharaoh's tomb. Projects like the

Great Pyramid of Khufu (Cheops): How Did the Egyptians Do It? The Great Pyramid contains some 4 million stone blocks, which the builders moved by means of a system of ramps and poles. They managed to construct a perfectly level base by pouring water into a grid of channels, some still visible here.

building of the Great Pyramid required a level of social organization and occupational specialization characteristic of early complex societies.

The earliest surviving Egyptian mummy dates to 2400 B.C.E., just after the time of the Great Pyramid, and happens to be one of the best preserved, with his facial features and even a callus on his foot still visible. During the Old Kingdom, only the pharaoh and his family could afford to preserve their corpses for eternity, but in later centuries, everyone in Egypt, whether rich or poor, hoped to travel to the next world with his or her body intact. Detailed descriptions of mummification date from much later, around 450 B.C.E., when the Greek traveler Herodotus (he-ROD-uh-tuhs) visited Egypt (see Chapter 6). Both mummies and, in some cases, their coffins reveal information about Egyptian society over thousands of years (see page 46).

Egyptians believed that the dead had to appear before Osiris (oh-SIGH-ruhs), the god of the underworld, who determined who could enter the realm of eternal happiness. Compiled in the sixteenth century B.C.E. yet drawing on materials dating back to 2400 B.C.E., the *Book of the Dead* contained detailed instructions for what the deceased should say on meeting Osiris. At the moment of judgment, the deceased should deny having committed any crime:

I have not committed evil against men.

I have not mistreated cattle.

I have not committed sin in the place of truth [that is, a temple or burial ground].

I have not blasphemed a god. . . .

I have not made (anyone) sick.

I have not made (anyone) weep.

I have not killed. . . .

I have not held up water in its season [that is, denied floodwaters to others].

I have not built a dam against running water. . . .*

The list reveals the offenses thought most outrageous by the Egyptians: diverting water from the irrigation channels belonging to one's neighbor constituted a major infraction.

During the First Intermediate Period (2180–2040 B.C.E.), Old Kingdom Egypt broke apart into semi-independent regions ruled by rival dynasties. The pharaoh was unable to appoint regional governors because certain families refused to give up government posts they had retained for multiple generations. Nor could the pharaoh collect as much revenue as his predecessors, possibly because sustained drought reduced agricultural yields.

Egyptian Expansion During the Middle Kingdom, 2040–1782 B.C.E.

In 2040 B.C.E. the ruler based in Thebes (modern-day Luxor) reunited Egypt and established what became known as the Middle Kingdom (2040–1782 B.C.E.), the second long period of centralized rule. Egypt's trade with other regions increased dramatically. Like Mesopotamia, Egypt had few natural resources and was forced to trade with distant lands to obtain wood, copper, gold, silver, and semiprecious stones. Its main trading partners were modern-day Syria and Lebanon to the north and Nubia to the south (see Map 2.1). At the height of the Middle Kingdom, the pharaoh sent his armies beyond Egypt for the first time, conquering territory in Palestine and Nubia. Various Middle Kingdom rulers conquered and governed the regions south of the First and Second Cataracts.

Sometime around 2000 B.C.E., Egyptian sources begin to mention the kingdom of Kush, another name for Nubia, whose capital lay south of the Third Cataract. During the Middle Kingdom, trade goods coming from sub-Saharan Africa, including panther and other rare animal skins, gold, ivory from elephant tusks, and slaves, traveled through Nubia, overland around the cataracts, and down the Nile to Egypt.

By 1720 B.C.E., the Middle Kingdom had weakened, most likely because a group of immigrants from Syria and Palestine, whom the Egyptians called Hyksos (HICK-sos) (literally "chieftains of foreign lands"), settled in the Delta. Historians call the years between 1782 and 1570 B.C.E. the Second Intermediate Period. The Hyksos had horse-drawn chariots with spoked wheels as well as strong bows made of wood and bone, while the Egyptians had no carts and only wooden bows. The Hyksos formed an alliance with the Nubians and ruled Egypt from 1650 to 1570 B.C.E.

---

*Excerpt from the *Book of the Dead* from James B. Pritchard (ed.), *Ancient Near Eastern Texts Relating to the Old Testament*, Third Edition With Supplement. Copyright © 1950, 1955, 1969, renewed 1978 by Princeton University Press. Reprinted by permission of Princeton University Press.

The International System, 1500–1150 B.C.E.

Around 1500 B.C.E., western Asia entered a new stage of increasingly sophisticated material cultures and extensive trade. During the third period of centralized rule in Egypt, the New Kingdom (1570–1069 B.C.E.), Egypt had more dealings with the other kingdoms of the eastern Mediterranean than in previous periods. Pharaohs of the Eighteenth Dynasty (1570–1293 B.C.E.) exchanged diplomatic envoys with rulers in Crete, Cyprus, and Anatolia and brought captured foreigners from the Mediterranean and Nubia to serve in the Egyptian army and to work as slaves.

Egypt's main rivals in the region were the Hittites (see page 45), who were based in Anatolia, Turkey, and Syria (see Map 2.2). Egypt reached its greatest extent at this time, governing a swath of territory that included small kingdoms in Palestine, Lebanon, and Syria, as well as Nubia. For five hundred years, the states of the eastern Mediterranean enjoyed a period of relative tranquility as they intensified their trade and diplomatic contacts to form what has been called the first international system.

MAP 2.2 **The International System, ca. 1500–1250 B.C.E.** Wen-Amun's journey from Egypt to Lebanon and Cyprus in around 1130 B.C.E. (see page 45) shows the ease with which individuals moved in the region of the eastern Mediterranean. International credit networks made it possible for Egyptian merchants to send gold, silver, linen, and papyrus to Lebanon, meaning that Wen-Amun did not have to return to Egypt to collect them. (© Cengage Learning)

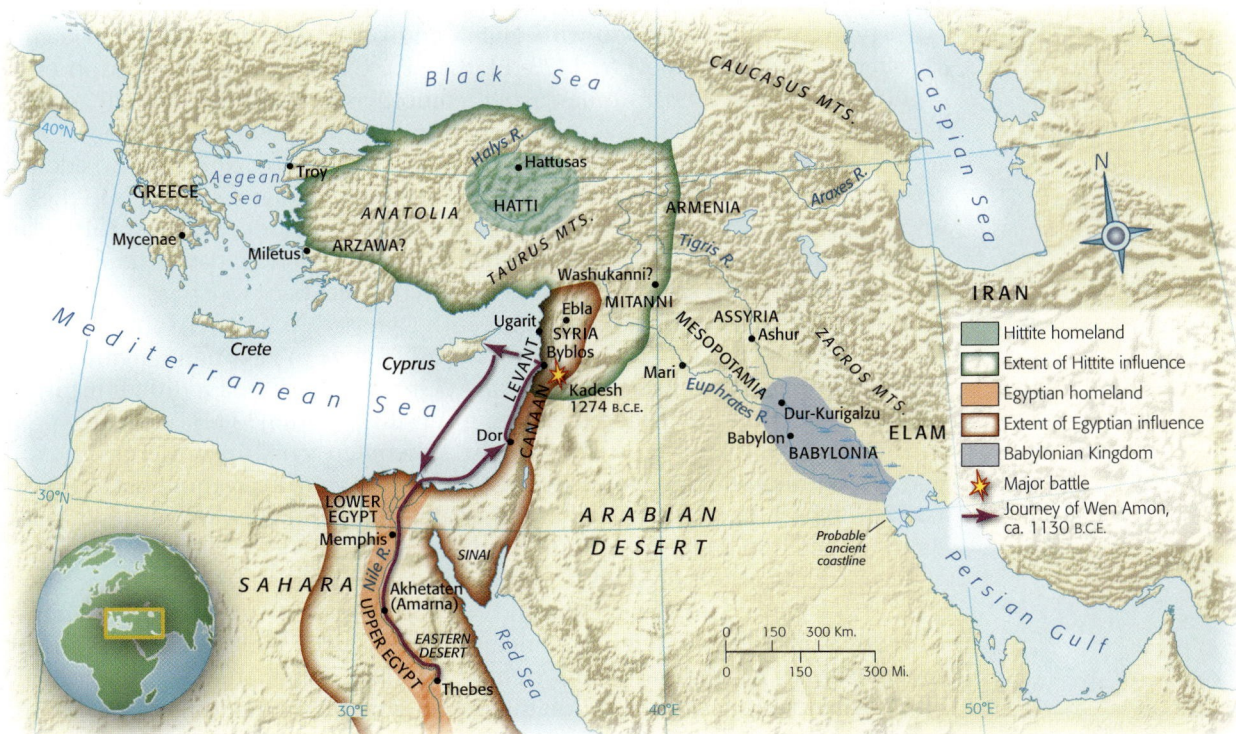

New Kingdom Egypt and Nubia, 1570–1069 B.C.E.

During the New Kingdom period, Egypt continued to expand into Nubia. After eliminating the kingdom of Kush as a rival, Egypt destroyed its capital and extended control all the way to the Fourth Cataract. Nubia's most valuable natural resource was gold, which the pharaohs required in large amounts.

The pharaohs of the Eighteenth Dynasty venerated the sun-god Amun-Ra (AH-muhn–RAH) above all other deities because they believed that he had enabled them to expel the Hyksos from Egypt and establish their dynasty. They built an enormous temple at Karnak to house the image of Amun-Ra. Every day the temple's priests carried the bathed image around the temple, and once a year they sent the main image of Amun-Ra in an elaborate barge along the Nile to the capital at Thebes.

The Egyptians believed that the most appropriate offerings to Amun-Ra were made from gold because gold was the color of the sun. Being indestructible, gold also represented immortality. Living people who wore gold became like gods, and the Egyptians buried the dead with multiple gold ornaments in the hope that they would live forever. While Egypt had some gold mines (see Map 2.1), Nubia had many more, and New Kingdom pharaohs were able to exploit these mines to the fullest extent.

After conquering Nubia, the pharaohs of the Eighteenth Dynasty worked to transform Nubia into an Egyptian society: they brought the sons of Nubian chiefs to Egypt, where they studied the Egyptian language, received Egyptian names, worshiped Egyptian deities like Amun-Ra, and wore Egyptian linen clothing, made from the flax plant, and other adornments. When they returned home, they served the Egyptians as administrators. (See the feature "World History in Today's World: The Benefits of Lead-Based Eye Makeup.")

Egypt continued to trade with Nubia and other regions during the reign of Hatshepsut (hat-SHEP-soot) (r. 1473–1458 B.C.E.), the only woman pharaoh of the Eighteenth Dynasty. Older women, whether mothers or aunts, occasionally served as regents when the pharaoh was too young to rule on his own, but Hatshepsut ruled for a full fifteen years as pharaoh. She imported gold, ebony, and cedar to add new rooms at Amun-Ra's temple at Karnak and build a spectacular new temple in the Valley of the Kings, where the New Kingdom pharaohs were buried. She was particularly proud of an expedition that she dispatched to Punt (in modern-day Ethiopia), which brought exotic goods such as monkeys and myrrh trees back to Egypt.

One ruler near the end of the Eighteenth Dynasty, Akhenaten (ah-ken-AHT-n) (r. 1352–1336 B.C.E.), introduced an important change to Egyptian religion. Rather than accepting Amun-Ra as the supreme deity, he worshiped a different form of the sun-god, whom he called the "living sun-disk," "Aten" (AHT-n) in Egyptian. In the past analysts erroneously thought Akhenaten worshiped Aten as the only god. In fact, he continued to worship other gods as well, even though Aten clearly ranked highest among them. After Akhenaten's death, Egyptians restored Amun-Ra to his position as the most important deity.

During the New Kingdom period, Egypt established a series of alliances with the various powers in the region and occasionally went to war with them. An extraordinary find of 350 letters concerning diplomatic matters makes it possible to reconstruct the international system of the time. Akhenaten addressed the rulers of Babylonia, Assyria, and Anatolia, who governed kingdoms as powerful as Egypt, as "brother," an indication that he saw them as his equals, while he reserved the term *servant* for smaller, weaker kingdoms in Syria and Palestine.

The Benefits of Lead-Based Eye Makeup

Could lead-based eye makeup actually help the user? For generations, scientists have assumed that lead-based makeup had to be dangerous. They scoffed at the ancient Egyptian use of lead eye makeup, which dates back at least to the time of Nefertiti, wife of Akhenaten, and probably earlier.

Analysis of fifty-two samples held in the Louvre museum in Paris, done in 2010, identified four different lead-based chemicals in ancient Egyptian eye makeup. Galena produced dark shades and added shine, while cerussite, laurionite, and phosgenite made lighter shades. One chemist explained: "Lead and arsenic, among other metals, make beautiful color pigments. . . . Because they make an attractive color and because you can create a powder with them, it makes sense to use it as a skin colorant."

Lead in small doses was not enough to poison the user, these researchers explain. The average life expectancy of the Egyptians was under forty, long before mild exposure to lead would cause cancer. In fact, the lead in eye makeup helped to protect the eyes—at least in the short term. The Nile's floodwaters harbored dangerous bacteria that could enter the eye and cause conjunctivitis and related illnesses. But because the lead makeup killed bacteria, it helped to prevent eye infections.

Aware of the protective function of eye makeup, Egyptians credited the makeup with healing powers granted, they believed, by the gods Horus and Ra. The makers of eye makeup recited prayers to these gods as they mixed the makeup, hoping to enhance its protective functions.

Two of these lead-based elements, laurionite and phosgenite, do not occur naturally: the Egyptians synthesized them specifically for use in eye makeup. The authors of the report concluded, saying: "It is no wonder that 'kemej,' the Egyptian word that referred to the Egyptian land and to the black earth of the Nile valley, was handed to us via the Greeks and then the Arabs to eventually coin our present 'chemistry.'"

Sources: Sindya N. Bhanoo, "Ancient Egypt's Toxic Makeup Fought Infection, Researchers Say," *New York Times*, January 19, 2010; Christian Amatore, Philippe Walter, "Finding Out Egyptian Gods' Secret Using Analytical Chemistry: Biomedical Properties of Egyptian Black Makeup Revealed by Amperometry at Single Cells," *Analytic Chemistry* 82, no. 2 (2010): 457–460. Reprinted by permission of the American Chemical Society.

Many of the letters concern marriage among royal families. Akhenaten tried to persuade other rulers to send their daughters to marry Egyptian men, but he did not ask for their sons because Egyptians would not allow Egyptian women to marry non-Egyptians. Even though the arrangement was unequal, the rulers usually sent their daughters because they wanted gold, and only Egypt had gold (obtained from Nubia).

The Kingdom of Nubia, 800 B.C.E.–350 C.E.

Much weaker after 1293 B.C.E., when the Eighteenth Dynasty ended, Egypt eventually lost control of Nubia. For several centuries no centralized power emerged in Nubia, but around 800 B.C.E. a political center formed at Napata, the administrative center from which the Egyptians had governed Nubia during the New Kingdom.

Seeing themselves as the rightful successors to the pharaohs of the Eighteenth Dynasty, the rulers of Nubia conquered Egypt under King Piye (r. 747–716 B.C.E.). King Taharqo (690–664 B.C.E.) ruled over Nubia at its peak. The builder of an elaborate cult center to Amun-Ra, King Taharqo also revived the building of pyramids,

Nubia, Land of Pyramids Modern Sudan has more pyramids—a total of 223—than Egypt. Modeled on those of Old Kingdom Egypt, the Nubian tombs are steeper and originally had a layer of white plaster on their exterior. Starting in the mid-700s B.C.E. and continuing to 370 C.E., the Nubian rulers of Kush built pyramids over their tombs, which were in the ground—unlike the Egyptian tombs, which were constructed above ground and inside the pyramids (contrast with Cheops's tomb shown on page 39). (Martin Gray/NGS Image Collection)

a practice that had long since died out in Egypt. His pyramid was the largest ever built by the Nubians, standing 160 feet (49 m) tall.

The Nubians continued to erect pyramids even after 300 B.C.E., when they shifted their capital from Napata to Meroë. By 300 B.C.E. the Nubians had developed their own writing system, called Meroitic (mer-oh-IT-ick), which combined hieroglyphs with hieratic script. Scholars know how to pronounce the Meroitic script because it is phonetic, but they cannot understand it because its structure differs from all living languages.

The royal cemetery at Meroë contains the pyramids of thirty kings and eight queens. As was common throughout sub-Saharan Africa, the Nubian dynasties practiced matrilineal succession in which the king was succeeded by his sister's son. (In a patrilineal system, the son succeeds the father.) If the designated successor was too young to rule, the king's sister often ruled in his place. Nubian queens did everything the male kings did, including patronizing temples, engaging in diplomacy, and fighting in battle.

The kingdom of Meroë thrived because it was able to tax the profitable trade between sub-Saharan Africa and the Mediterranean, but it broke apart in the fourth century C.E., possibly because the trade was diverted to sea routes it did not control. Located south of Egypt, Nubia had little contact with the different states of the eastern Mediterranean to the north of Egypt. Accordingly, it did not actively participate in the system of international alliances that had begun to take shape as early as 1500 B.C.E.

The Hittites, 2000–1200 B.C.E.

During the New Kingdom period, Egypt's rulers frequently wrote to the rulers of a powerful new kingdom based in Anatolia and Syria, the **Hittites**. The language of the Hittites belonged to the Indo-European language family, meaning that its structure resembled that of Latin, Greek, and Sanskrit (see Chapter 3). The Hittites were the first speakers of an Indo-European language to establish a complex society in western Asia.

The Hittites were able to do so because, sometime around 2000 B.C.E., they learned how to work **iron**. With a much higher melting point (2,786 degrees Fahrenheit, 1,530 degrees Celsius) than other metals, iron could not be melted and then poured into molds like bronze. Metalsmiths heated iron and hammered it into the shape of the tool or weapon needed, a process that removed impurities in the metal. Much stronger than bronze weapons, the iron weapons of the Hittites were highly prized.

The Hittite empire reached its greatest extent between 1322 and 1220 B.C.E., when the Hittites controlled all of Anatolia and Syria. In the thirteenth century B.C.E. the Hittite ruler wrote to the ruler of the Assyrians to apologize for not sending any unworked iron. Instead he sent a single blade, an indication of iron's value at the time.

The Hittites had another advantage over their enemies: they had mastered the art of chariot warfare. Two horses pulled a chariot that carried three men (a driver and two warriors). While consolidating their rule in Anatolia, the Hittites sent only a small number of chariots into battle. By the Battle of Kadesh in 1285 B.C.E., when the Hittites faced the Egyptians, the ruler commanded 2,500 chariots.[6] Egyptian documents claim that the pharaoh Ramesses II (r. 1290–1224 B.C.E.) had triumphed, but Egypt gained no territory, an indication that the Hittite and Egyptian forces were probably evenly matched. After the Battle of Kadesh, Egypt signed a treaty with the Hittites, who sent a Hittite princess to marry Ramesses II.

The Hittite kingdom came to an end in 1200 B.C.E. when their capital fell to outsiders. Historians are not certain who the invaders were, but they note a period around 1200–1150 B.C.E. of prolonged instability throughout western Asia. Egyptian sources mention attacks by "sea peoples," and Egypt lost control of both Syria-Palestine to the north and Nubia to the south.

Wen-Amun's Voyage to Lebanon and Cyprus, 1130 B.C.E.

Even in the centuries after 1200, Egypt continued to enjoy extensive trade relations with the Mediterranean, as we can see in the earliest detailed account of an actual voyage, recorded on a torn papyrus dating to 1130 B.C.E.[7] In that year, an Egyptian priest named Wen-Amun (one-AH-muhn) traveled down the Nile and caught a ship across the Mediterranean to Lebanon to buy cedar for the Amun-Ra temple at Karnak, which had so much money and land that it was independent of the pharaoh's authority. (See the feature "Visual Evidence in Primary Sources: Reading the Mummy of Hornedjitef: High Priest at Karnak.")

On arriving at a port in modern-day Lebanon, Wen-Amun realized that a shipmate had stolen almost 9 pounds (4 kg) of gold and silver—all the money Wen-Amun had with him to buy the lumber for the temple. Desperate, he sailed to the next port, where he stole some silver. When the victims reported the theft to their king, he detained Wen-Amun.

Hittites
A people based in Anatolia, Turkey, and Syria who spoke the Indo-European language of Hittite and learned to work iron around 2000 B.C.E. The Hittite empire reached its greatest extent between 1322 and 1220 B.C.E. and ended around 1200 B.C.E.

iron
A metal used to make farm tools and weapons; iron smelting was an important technology because iron implements were much more durable than those made of bronze.

Reading the Mummy of Hornedjitef: High Priest at Karnak

Mummies possess an undying fascination because we always want to know about the person wrapped up inside the linen straps. Often, though, crucial information is missing because the mummy has been separated from its coffin or accompanying burial goods. One extraordinary example, held in the British Museum, survives with its exterior and interior cases intact, as well as a papyrus text, 18 inches (.45 m) tall and 16 feet (4.9 m) long, from the *Book of the Dead*, instructing the deceased how to travel to the next world.

The biography on the interior coffin gives the name of the deceased, Hornedjitef (ca. 240 B.C.E.), and all his official titles. As a high priest at the temple of Amun at Karnak, Hornedjitef was one of the few people who could handle the statue of Amun, which was carried outside the temple during processions. Hornedjitef's tomb text does not mention his family, but most of the Amun temple priests married and had children.

Because the museum staff did not want to damage Hornedjitef's mummy, they did not unwrap it. Instead, they performed a nondestructive CAT scan. Hornedjitef's body was intact; a few missing teeth and wear on the rest provide a key indicator that he was between fifty and sixty at the time of death. (The cause of death is unknown.) His spinal column was misshapen by chronic arthritis, which must have been extremely painful.

The scan revealed the precise location of several items: rings on Hornedjitef's left hand and left big toe, protective amulets on his neck, and a scarab, which had slipped away from its proper placement over his heart. Before he was buried, his organs were removed through an incision in the abdomen so that they could be dried and treated with preservatives; the embalmers then wrapped the organs in their own linen cases and replaced them in their original locations. His wrapped stomach, lungs, and heart were all visible on the CAT scan. (In earlier periods, embalmers buried the wrapped body parts in a separate container called the canopic chest; Hornedjitef had one, but it contained broken pottery and no body parts—perhaps the embalmers included the chest simply to observe tradition.) Using a hook, the embalmers removed his brain through the nasal cavity and filled the skull about halfway with resin.

As was fitting for a man of his high station, Hornedjitef received the most expensive treatment offered to the dead by embalmers. After removing his organs, they rinsed the body and covered it with natron (NAY-tron), a crystallized form of potassium carbonate that kept the corpse dry. After forty days, bandagers spent two weeks wrapping the body in linen before placing it in a coffin. In the less expensive option, the embalmers simply injected the body with cedar oil, which caused the internal organs to decay and to be expelled through the anus. Bandaging and burial followed. The poorest Egyptians could only afford to have the internal organs expelled and the corpse buried unbandaged.

QUESTIONS FOR ANALYSIS

» *What kind of information about the world of the living and their ideas about the dead can historians learn from the primary source of Hornedjitef's mummified body and interior coffin?*

» *Historians always consider the issue of typicality. With his lavish mummification, which social level does Hornedjitef represent? Why is it not appropriate to use the information from Hornedjitef's mummy to analyze the burial customs of the Egyptian poor?*

This funerary mask does not show Hornedjitef at death, but the younger man he hoped to be reborn as.

This wooden case is made of sycamore.

This shows the sky goddess Nut with her hands stretched above her head.

This artificial beard is attached to his funerary mask with straps. Priests shaved off all their body hair, including beards, because body hair was believed to be unclean.

This is a list of the planets and the stars.

This section lists the constellations and protective gods and shows scenes of the zodiac.

This winged scarab beetle represents the sun god, who grants life. The eight baboons standing on the beetle's wings worship the sun god.

This text gives Hornedjitef's biography in hieroglyphs. As "overseer of the abattoir" at the Karnak temple to Amun, he ensured that the meat from animals killed at the temple was used correctly in ceremonies.

This spell to unite the soul and the body in the underworld comes from Chapter 89 of the *Book of the Dead*.

This space is for the feet of the mummy.

Then something unusual happened. A young boy at court was suddenly afflicted by seizures, and the king's advisers concluded that Amun-Ra was responsible. Their explanation reveals that the Egyptian deity's reputation had spread far beyond Egypt. The local ruler made a proposal: if Wen-Amun sent to his home temple for funds, he would be allowed to depart. The credit network of the local merchants was sufficiently sophisticated that Wen-Amun was able to write home to request that another ship bring him gold, silver, ten linen garments, and five hundred rolls of papyrus to cover the cost of the lumber.

When Wen-Amun set off for home, his ship was blown off course to the island of Cyprus. There he met an Egyptian interpreter, who explained his predicament to the ruler, and Wen-Amun managed somehow to make his way back home. Thus even during this time of instability, the international system of the period functioned smoothly enough that people could obtain credit and travel in the eastern Mediterranean.

Syria-Palestine and New Empires in Western Asia, 1200–500 B.C.E.

Several kingdoms occupied the land along the eastern shore of the Mediterranean where modern-day Palestine, Israel, Lebanon, and Syria are located. They participated in the international system, but always as minor players in a world dominated by kings of larger powers such as Egypt, Assyria, Babylonia, and Anatolia. Around 1000 B.C.E. a smaller complex society arose in the eastern Mediterranean that was notable for its innovation in religion.

monotheism
Belief in only one god.

This lightly populated and politically weak region was important because it was the homeland of the ancient Hebrews or Israelites. The Hebrews were the first people in the eastern Mediterranean to practice **monotheism**, or belief in only one god, whom they called Yahweh (YAH-way) in Hebrew (God in English). Belief in a single god underlay the religious teachings recorded in the Hebrew Bible (called the Old Testament by Christians). Hebrew monotheism would profoundly shape both Christian and Islamic teachings (see Chapters 7 and 10).

The History of the Ancient Hebrews According to the Hebrew Bible

Geographers call the region bordering the eastern Mediterranean the Levant (see Map 2.3). The most populated section of the Levant was the strip of land 30–70 miles (50–110 km) wide along the Mediterranean coast. The northern section, between the Orontes River and the Mediterranean, formed Lebanon, while the land west of the Jordan River formed Israel and Palestine. Israel and Palestine stretched only 250 miles (400 km) from north to south, with the southern half consisting almost entirely of desert. Its population around 1000 B.C.E. has been estimated at 150,000, and its largest city, Jerusalem, reached its maximum population of 5,000 in 700 B.C.E.[8]

The Hebrew Bible was written sometime around 700 B.C.E., and its current text dates to around 500 B.C.E.[9] Historians and archaeologists of Israel and Palestine disagree sharply about the value of the Bible as a historical source. Some view everything in the Bible as true, while others do not credit the accounts of the Bible unless they are confirmed by other documentary or archaeological evidence. World historians rarely have as much material for a given society as they have for ancient

Israel and Palestine, and they often rely on orally transmitted sources far more recent than the Hebrew Bible.

The first book of the Hebrew Bible, Genesis, traces the history of the ancient Hebrews from the earth's creation. The Hebrew Bible contains a later version of the flood story that closely resembles that in *Gilgamesh*. Archaeologists have not found evidence of a single flood as described in either *Gilgamesh* or the Hebrew Bible; most think the flood narrative collapses repeated floods in the Tigris and Euphrates into a one-time calamity. (See the feature "Movement of Ideas Through Primary Sources: The Flood Narrative in the *Epic of Gilgamesh* and the Hebrew Bible.")

The most important event in their history, the ancient Hebrews believed, was God's choice of Abraham to be the leader of his people. Abraham, like his direct ancestor Noah, spoke directly to God and agreed to be the leader. God, in turn, made Abraham promise that all his descendants would be circumcised.

The Hebrew Bible teaches that Abraham and his wife Sarah had no children. God promised that Sarah would give birth to a son, even though Abraham was one hundred years old and Sarah ninety. When their son Isaac was born, she was overjoyed. Abraham had one son, Ishmael, with Sarah's maid Hagar, but Sarah sent Hagar away after the birth of Isaac.

God then subjected Abraham to the most severe test of all: he asked him to sacrifice his son Isaac as an offering. Abraham led his young son up into the mountains and prepared the sacrificial altar. At the moment when he was about to kill Isaac, the Bible records, God, speaking through an angel, commanded: *"Do not lay your hand on the boy or do anything to him; for now I know that you fear God, since you have not withheld your son, your only son, from me'"* (Genesis 22:12). Abraham untied Isaac.

The Bible's dramatic account of Isaac's rescue reflects a crucial change in Israelite religious observance. In an earlier time, the ancient Hebrews sacrificed animals and perhaps even children to their gods. An inscription dating to the eighth century B.C.E. from modern-day Lebanon records that during a plague the priests advised the local ruler to sacrifice a son or a grandson, in addition to an animal offering, to end the disease.[10] In later times, when the Isaac story was recorded, the Hebrews abandoned child sacrifice. The Bible gives no dates for the events it describes.

After the ancient Hebrews came to Israel, the book of Exodus claims that they went to Egypt and then returned to Israel under the leadership of the patriarch

MAP 2.3 The Assyrian and Neo-Babylonian Empires at Their Greatest Extent The rulers of the Assyrian empire were the first in the eastern Mediterranean to resettle subject populations. Their successors, the Neo-Babylonians, continued the practice and resettled many subject peoples, including the Hebrews, in their capital at Babylon. (© Cengage Learning)

---

*All quotations from the Bible are from the New Revised Standard Version. Revised Standard Version of the Bible, Copyright © 1952 [2nd edition, 1971] by the Division of Christian Education of the National Council of the Churches of Christ in the United States of America. Used by permission. All rights reserved.

The Flood Narrative in the *Epic of Gilgamesh* and the Hebrew Bible

The striking similarities in the two versions of the flood story demonstrate that the Hebrew Bible drew on oral traditions circulating throughout Mesopotamia. The most complete version of the *Epic of Gilgamesh* was written in 700 B.C.E., but it drew on written versions dating to at least 2100 B.C.E. and even earlier oral traditions. Like the *Epic of Gilgamesh*, the Bible had a long history of oral transmission before being recorded in its current version around 500 B.C.E. Some of its oldest content may have circulated orally as early as 1200 B.C.E., when the ancient Hebrews first settled what is now modern Israel.

The two accounts of the flood differ most notably in their depiction of the divine. In the *Epic of Gilgamesh*, multiple gods squabble and the god Enki warns Utanapishtim that the storm-god Enlil is sending the flood to destroy his home city of Shuruppak. In the Bible, one god decides to punish all of humanity except for Noah and his family.

Sources: The Epic of Gilgamesh, translated by Benjamin R. Foster. Copyright © 2001 by W.W. Norton & Company. Used by permission of W.W. Norton & Company, Inc., pp. 85–89; Genesis 6:11–19; Genesis 7:17–18; Genesis 8:1–3; Genesis 8:6–12. All quotations from the Bible are from the New Revised Standard Version. Revised Standard Version of the Bible, Copyright © 1952 [2nd edition, 1971] by the Division of Christian Education of the National Council of the Churches of Christ in the United States of America. Used by permission. All rights reserved.

The Flood Story in *Gilgamesh*

Instructions to Utanapishtim for Building the Ark

O Man of Shuruppak, son of Ubar-Tutu,
Wreck house, build boat,
Forsake possessions and seek life,
Belongings reject and life save!
Take aboard the boat seed of all living things.
The boat you shall build,
Let her dimensions be measured out:
Let her width and length be equal,
Roof her over like the watery depths.

The Length of the Flood

Six days and seven nights
The wind continued, the deluge and windstorm leveled the land . . .
The sea grew calm, the tempest stilled, the deluge ceased.

The End of the Flood

When the seventh day arrived,
I [Utanapishtim] brought out a dove and set it free.

The dove went off and returned,
No landing place came to its view so it turned back.
I bought out a swallow and set it free,
The swallow went off and returned,
No landing place came to its view, so it turned back.
I brought out a raven and set it free,
The raven went off and saw the ebbing of the waters.
It ate, preened, left droppings, did not turn back.
I released all to the four directions,
I brought out an offering and offered it to the four directions.
I set up an incense offering on the summit of the mountain,
I arranged seven and seven cult vessels,
I heaped reeds, cedar, and myrtle in their bowls.

The Flood Story in the Bible

Instructions to Noah for Building the Ark

Now the earth was corrupt in God's sight, and the earth was filled with violence. And God saw that the earth was corrupt; for all flesh had corrupted its ways upon the earth. And God said to Noah, "I have determined to make an end of all flesh, for the earth is filled with violence because of them; now I am going to destroy them along with the earth. Make yourself an ark of cypress wood; make rooms in the ark, and cover it inside and out with pitch. This is how you are to make it: the length of the ark three hundred cubits, its width fifty cubits, and its height thirty cubits•. Make a roof for the ark, and finish it to a cubit above; and put the door of the ark in its side; make it with lower, second, and third decks. For my part, I am going to bring a flood of waters upon the earth, to destroy from under heaven all flesh in which is the breath of life; everything that is on the earth shall die. But I will establish my covenant with you; and you shall come into the ark, you, your sons, your wife, and your sons' wives with you. And of every living thing, of all flesh, you shall bring two of every kind into the ark, to keep them alive with you; they shall be male and female."

The Length of the Flood

The flood continued forty days on the earth; and the waters increased, and bore up the

• **cubit**   A measure about 3 feet (1 m) long. The ark was approximately 450 feet (137 m) long, 75 feet (23 m) wide, and 45 feet (14 m) tall.

ark, and it rose high above the earth. The waters swelled and increased greatly on the earth; and the ark floated on the face of the waters. . . .

But God remembered Noah and all the wild animals and all the domestic animals that were with him in the ark. And God made a wind blow over the earth, and the waters subsided; the fountains of the deep and the windows of the heavens were closed, the rain from the heavens was restrained, and the waters gradually receded from the earth. At the end of a hundred fifty days the waters had abated.

The End of the Flood

At the end of forty days Noah opened the window of the ark that he had made and sent out the raven; and it went to and fro until the waters were dried up from the earth. Then he sent out the dove from him, to see if the waters had subsided from the face of the ground; but the dove found no place to set its foot, and it returned to him to the ark, for the waters were still on the face of the whole earth. So he put out his hand and took it and brought it into the ark with him. He waited another seven days, and again he sent out the dove from the ark; and the dove came back to him in the evening, and there in its beak was a freshly plucked olive leaf; so Noah knew that the waters had subsided from the earth. Then he waited another seven days, and sent out the dove; and it did not return to him any more.

QUESTION FOR ANALYSIS

» *What are the similarities between the two versions of the flood story? What are the differences? Explain why the later version diverges from the original.*

Moses. Since no archaeological evidence confirms that a single migration out of Egypt occurred, many scholars suggest that the Exodus may have been a series of migrations.

The History of the Ancient Hebrews According to Archaeological Evidence

The earliest archaeological evidence of the ancient Hebrews dates to between 1300 and 1100 B.C.E. In 1300 B.C.E. approximately twelve to fifteen thousand people lived in three hundred small villages on previously unoccupied hillsides in the southern Levant; by 1100 B.C.E. the population had mushroomed to seventy-five to eighty thousand.[11] No urban centers existed. Most of the residents had tools made of bronze, flint, and occasionally iron. Archaeologists have analyzed the bones they deposited in refuse pits and have found that no more than 1 percent are pig, an indication that the taboo on eating pork that is recorded in the Hebrew Bible may already have been in effect.

The few inscriptions found so far reveal that the residents wrote ancient Hebrew, a Semitic language. An Egyptian inscription dated 1210 B.C.E. lists several different defeated peoples living in modern-day Lebanon, one of whom it calls "Israel peoples,"[12] most likely the residents of the hill country.

Although the Bible portrays the ancient Hebrews as practitioners of monotheism from ancient times on, archaeological evidence indicates that they, like all the other peoples of the eastern Mediterranean, worshiped several different deities. The most important were the storm-god, called El or Ba'al (BAHL), and his wife, a fertility goddess. In this early period, some of the Israelites also worshiped a storm-god named Yahweh.

The Bible describes the ancient Hebrews as living under a united monarchy that linked both the north and the south. King David built a shrine to Yahweh in Jerusalem, which his successor Solomon (r. 960–920 B.C.E.) rebuilt and expanded. After Solomon's death the kingdom broke into two parts: Judah in the south with its capital at Jerusalem, and Israel in the north.

Archaeologists have not found evidence of a united kingdom under the rule of either David or Solomon. But a significant change did occur sometime between 1000 and 900 B.C.E., when complex society first took shape in the region. The main evidence, as in Mesopotamia, is the formation of large urban centers with massive walls and impressive gates. At this time what had been a loose tribal confederacy became a small kingdom, complete with a bureaucracy and intermediate-level cities.

The residents of both Judah and Israel worshiped Yahweh, but in the ninth century two distinct groups formed. One, consisting of the rulers and probably most of their subjects, continued to worship Yahweh as one of many gods. The other, called the prophetic school, strongly believed that Yahweh was the most important god.

The Assyrian Empire, 911–612 B.C.E.

The two kingdoms of Israel and Judah remained separate and independent until 721 B.C.E., when the Assyrians, whose homeland was in northern Mesopotamia, conquered southern Mesopotamia, Egypt, and the kingdoms of Israel and Judah. Like the Hittites, the Assyrians had iron weapons. In addition, their cavalry was particularly powerful because it was the first true army on horseback. The cavalry soldiers rode bareback since neither saddles nor stirrups had been invented.

Unlike the various conquerors of the eastern Mediterranean before them, the Assyrians did not simply send in armies and subjugate enemy territory. Because the

Assyrian ruler saw himself as the representative of the gods, he asked the rulers of foreign territories to submit voluntarily to him and his deities. Those who surrendered he treated gently, but his troops were infamous for their cruel treatment of those who resisted. Soldiers skinned captives alive, removed their eyes or cut off their hands and feet, and impaled others on stakes. These atrocities served as a warning to those who had not yet been conquered: if they surrendered quickly, they could avoid such barbarities. Such treatment was justified, the Assyrians believed, because the subject populations were resisting the gods, not just a human king.

Once the Assyrians had conquered a given region, they forcibly resettled the conquered rulers and skilled craftsmen to another part of the empire. The original intent in the ninth century was to fill up the lightly populated sections of the empire; later, resettlement was simply a demonstration of the ruler's power. Several hundred thousand people were resettled in this way, including many people from Israel and Judah who were sent to Assyria.

The last Assyrian king, Asshurbanipal (as-shur-BAH-nee-pahl) (r. 668–627 B.C.E.), built one of the world's earliest libraries, which consisted of over 1,500 texts for his own private use. In the 1850s, British excavators found the most complete set of clay tablets of the *Gilgamesh* epic, and the basis of all modern translations, in the ruins of Asshurbanipal's palace.

The Babylonian Captivity and the Recording of the Bible, 612–539 B.C.E.

The Neo-Babylonians conquered the Assyrians and established their capital at Babylon. Their most powerful ruler was Nebuchadnezzar II (r. 605–562 B.C.E.), who rebuilt the city of Babylon, repaired its temples, and constructed magnificent hanging gardens. Nebuchadnezzar II (nab-oo-kuhd-NEZ-uhr) extended his empire all the way to Syria, Palestine, and Lebanon. He sacked Jerusalem twice, in 597 and 586 B.C.E., and destroyed much of the city. He leveled Solomon's Temple and, like the Assyrians, deported thousands of Hebrews to Babylon, in what is known today as the Babylonian Exile or Babylonian Captivity.

The exiled Hebrews living in Babylon were not allowed to return to Israel, but otherwise they had some freedom of movement, and some seem to have prospered as merchants or farmers. The exiled community reached a new understanding of their past. Many of the tales they told, including those about Noah and Abraham, had episodes in which God punished the ancient Hebrews for failing to follow his instructions, and they interpreted the Assyrian and Neo-Babylonian conquests in the same light. The Israelite community, the prophets explained, had strayed from righteousness, which they defined as ethical behavior.

The Hebrew Bible took shape during these years. Some parts, such as the book of Deuteronomy, already existed in written form, but the exiles recorded the core of the modern Hebrew Bible, from Genesis to 2 Kings. The first five books of the Bible, known either as the Torah in Hebrew or the Pentateuch in Greek, stress that God is the only god and that he will not tolerate the worship of any other gods. This pure monotheism was the product of specific historical circumstances culminating in the Babylonian Exile and the recording of the Bible.

The Neo-Babylonians were the last dynasty to rule from Babylon. In 539 B.C.E. Cyrus the Great, the leader of the Persians, conquered Mesopotamia, and the entire Neo-Babylonian empire came under Persian rule (see Chapter 6). In 538 B.C.E. Cyrus allowed the Hebrews to return to Judah, bringing the Babylonian Captivity to an end, and he ordered the rebuilding of the Temple in Jerusalem. The word **Jew**, derived from the Hebrew *Yehudhi*, literally means a member of the nation of Judah. After 538 B.C.E., it came to refer to all Hebrews.

Jew
A term (derived from Hebrew) that originally meant a member of the nation of Judah and later came to refer to all Hebrews.

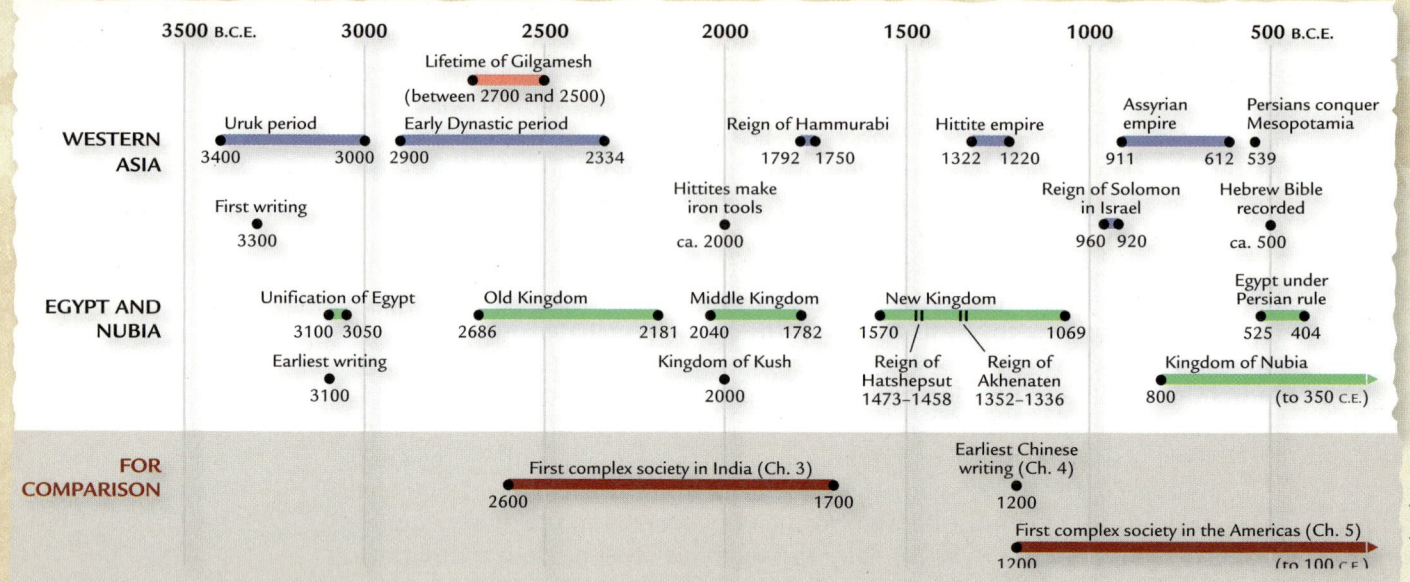

The Place of Mesopotamia and Egypt in World History

The epic *Gilgamesh* contrasts the experience of the king Gilgamesh, who governs a complex society, with that of his friend Enkidu, who grew up in the wild. Composed at a time in which people in complex societies lived adjacent to those in the wild, the epic vividly portrays the sharp differences between life inside and outside the world's first city-states. As the chapter opening shows, once Enkidu sleeps with the priestess named Shamat, he immediately becomes a member of a complex society; the next morning, the gazelles that had been his original companions avoid him. Both men go on a long journey to kill the monster Humbaba. When Enkidu dies, Gilgamesh dons fur clothing and enters the wild, leaving the life of complex society behind—until he realizes that he, too, ultimately will die. Chastened, he returns to rule his city-state.

Those living in the cities ate bread and drank beer made from cultivated grain, the fruits of the world's first agricultural societies, which arose in West Asia starting in 12,500 B.C.E., the time of the Natufians (see Chapter 1). In city-states like Gilgamesh's Uruk, people with similar occupations resided together in different neighborhoods, as did members of similar social strata. Complex society had a more abstract side: the people living in Mesopotamian city-states believed that they owed payments of grain to the gods and to their intermediary, the king, and the king, in turn, had an obligation to govern them. They also knew the qualities of a good king, qualities that Gilgamesh lacks at the beginning of the epic and slowly acquires as he matures.

Cuneiform, used in Mesopotamia, and hieroglyphs, used in Egypt, were the world's two earliest writing systems. But the complex society of the Egyptians differed from that of the Mesopotamians. Sometime around 3500 B.C.E., the earliest pharaohs unified the Nile Valley, and city-states never existed in Egypt. As the different types of burial show, Egyptians had different occupations and occupied different social levels, both marks of complex society. The corpses of high-ranking priests such as Hornedjitef received the most extensive mummification and survive intact even today. At the pinnacle of Egyptian society, the pharaoh collected both taxes and labor from his subjects; over ten thousand laborers worked on the final resting place of pharaoh Khufu (Cheops), one of the world's largest and longest-lasting monuments.

Both the Mesopotamians and the Egyptians believed in multiple deities. Yet the *Gilgamesh* story of a flood sent by the storm-god Enlil was also told in a different form by the ancient Hebrews living in West Asia, who invoked only one god, Yahweh, whose deeds are recounted in the Bible.

Complex societies are historically significant because they attained much higher population densities than those of peoples who did not pursue agriculture full-time. These societies also produced some of the largest and most important monuments in human history, whether the ziggurats of Mesopotamia or the pyramids of Egypt and Nubia. The coming chapters will analyze the varying experiences of peoples living in other regions of the world: in India (Chapter 3), in China (Chapter 4), and in Mexico, the Andes, the modern-day United States, and the islands of the Pacific (Chapter 5). As different as these places were and are, there are underlying commonalities. Before the rise of agriculture, the region's residents lived by foraging. Their populations were low, and they lived in bands of under one hundred people. In most cases they left few lasting traces. In each place, the transition to complex society produced radically different results, each with far-reaching implications for the world we live in today.

Voyages on the Web: Gilgamesh

The Voyages Map App follows the traveler's journeys using interactive study tools, including 360-degree panoramic views of historic sites, zoomable maps, audio summaries, flash cards, and quizzes.

Key Terms

Mesopotamia (26)
Gilgamesh (26)
complex society (28)
city-state (29)
bronze (30)
wheel (30)

Sumer (31)
cuneiform (32)
Sargon of Akkad (33)
empire (33)
pharaoh (36)
Nubia (36)

hieroglyphs (37)
papyrus (37)
Hittites (45)
iron (45)
monotheism (48)
Jew (53)

For Further Reference

Andrews, Carol. *Egyptian Mummies*. Cambridge, Mass.: Harvard University Press, 2004.

Brewer, Douglas J. *Ancient Egypt: Foundations of a Civilization*. 1st ed. Harlow, England; New York: Pearson/Longman, 2005.

Brewer, Douglas J., and Emily Teeter. *Egypt and the Egyptians*. New York: Cambridge University Press, 1999.

Casson, Lionel. *Travel in the Ancient World*. Baltimore: Johns Hopkins University Press, 1994.

Dever, William G. *What Did the Biblical Writers Know and When Did They Know It? What Archaeology Can Tell Us About the Reality of Ancient Israel*. Grand Rapids, Mich.: William B. Eerdmans, 2001.

Foster, Benjamin R. *The Epic of Gilgamesh: A Norton Critical Edition*. New York: W. W. Norton, 2001.

Kramer, Samuel Noah. *History Begins at Sumer: Thirty-nine Firsts in Recorded History*. Philadelphia: University of Pennsylvania Press, 1988.

Manzanilla, Linda, ed. *Emergence and Change in Early Urban Societies*. New York: Plenum Press, 1997.

Postgate, J. N. *Early Mesopotamia: Society and Economy at the Dawn of History*. New York: Routledge, 1992.

Richards, Janet, and Mary Van Buren, eds. *Order, Legitimacy, and Wealth in Ancient States*. New York: Cambridge University Press, 2000.

Shaw, Ian. *The Oxford History of Ancient Egypt*. New York: Oxford University Press, 2004.

van de Mieroop, Marc. *A History of the Ancient Near East, ca. 3000–323 B.C.* Malden, Mass.: Blackwell Publishing, 2007.

van de Mieroop, Marc. *A History of Ancient Egypt*. Chichester, West Sussex, England; Malden, Mass.: Wiley-Blackwell, 2011.

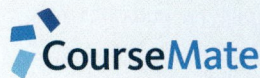 Go to the CourseMate website at **www.cengagebrain.com** for additional study tools and review materials—including audio and video clips—for this chapter.

3

Ancient India and the Rise of Buddhism, 2600 B.C.E.–100 C.E.

For the first eight years he was king, **Ashoka** (r. 268–232 B.C.E.) led his armies on a series of campaigns in north and central India that culminated in a ferocious struggle in Kalinga (kuh-LING-uh) in modern-day Orissa on India's eastern coast. Victorious at last but appalled by the losses on both sides, Ashoka (uh-SHO-kuh) made a decision that would affect world history long after his Mauryan (MORE-ee-ahn) dynasty (ca. 320–185 B.C.E.) came to an end: he chose to embrace the teachings of Buddhism.

Because the ancient Indians used perishable materials like palm leaves for writing, we have no written documents before the third century B.C.E. from South Asia (including the modern countries of India, Pakistan, Bangladesh, Nepal, Sri Lanka, Bhutan, and the Maldives). However, throughout his reign, Ashoka had his ideas carved on both large and small stones, called rock edicts, and later on stone pillars. Thus Ashoka's inscriptions provide the fullest record of a single individual's thoughts and movements in South Asia before the modern era. Shortly after conquering Kalinga, in an inscription carved in 260 B.C.E., Ashoka explained his decision to follow Buddhism:

Ashoka and His Wife Dismounting from Elephant

(Dinodia Photo Library)

*W*hen he had been consecrated eight years the Beloved of the Gods, the king Ashoka, conquered Kalinga. A hundred and fifty thousand people were deported, a hundred thousand were killed and many times that number perished. Afterwards, now that Kalinga was annexed, the Beloved of the Gods very earnestly practiced dharma, desired dharma, and taught dharma. On conquering Kalinga the Beloved of the Gods felt remorse, for, when an independent country is conquered the slaughter, death, and deportation of the people is extremely grievous to the Beloved of the Gods, and weighs heavily on his mind.

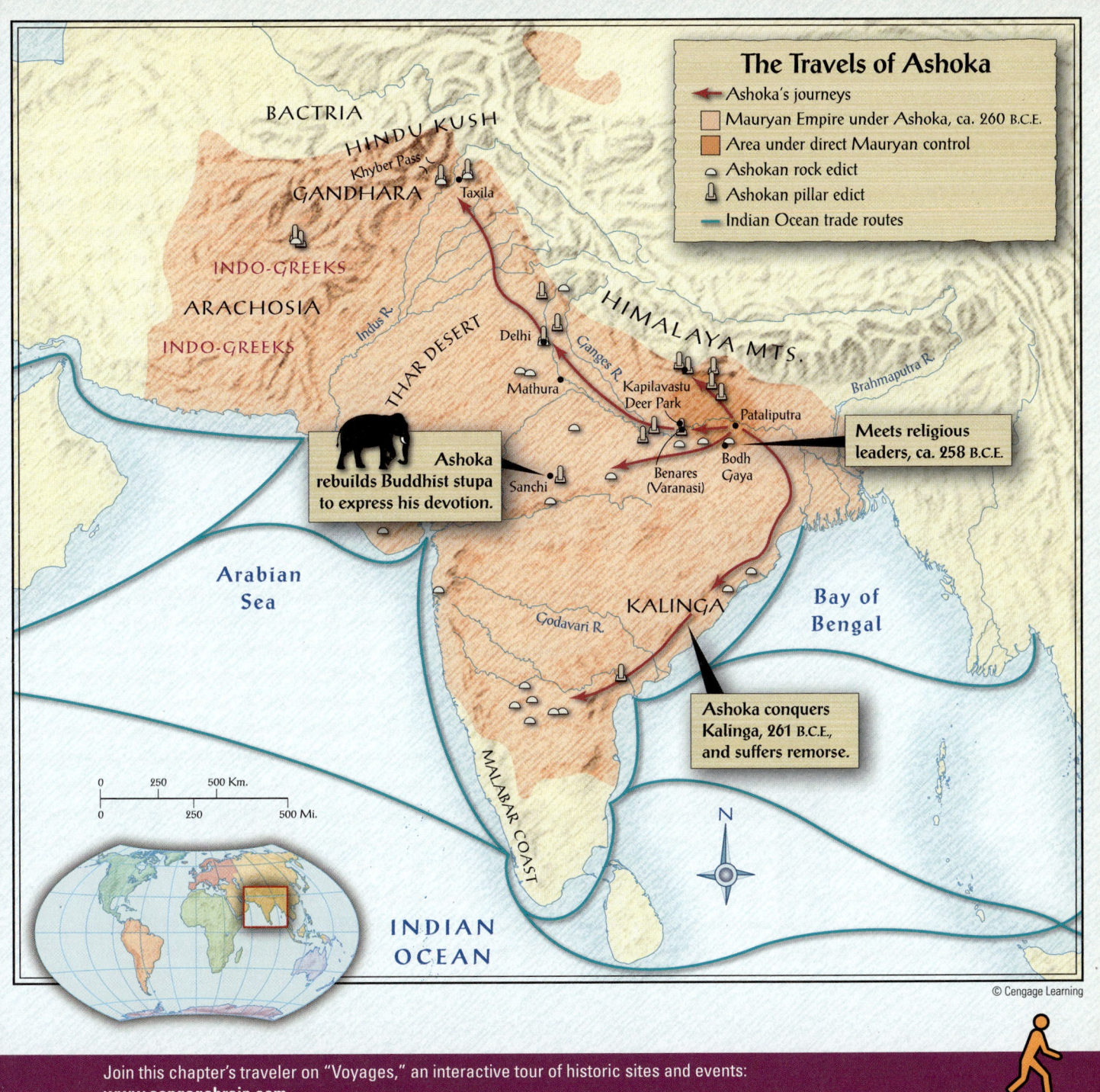

The Travels of Ashoka

← Ashoka's journeys
■ Mauryan Empire under Ashoka, ca. 260 B.C.E.
■ Area under direct Mauryan control
⚱ Ashokan rock edict
⚱ Ashokan pillar edict
— Indian Ocean trade routes

BACTRIA
HINDU KUSH
Khyber Pass
GANDHARA
Taxila
INDO-GREEKS
ARACHOSIA
INDO-GREEKS
Indus R.
THAR DESERT
Delhi
Mathura
HIMALAYA MTS.
Brahmaputra R.
Ganges R.
Kapilavastu
Deer Park
Pataliputra

Meets religious leaders, ca. 258 B.C.E.

Ashoka rebuilds Buddhist stupa to express his devotion.

Sanchi
Benares (Varanasi)
Bodh Gaya

Arabian Sea

Godavari R.
KALINGA
Bay of Bengal

Ashoka conquers Kalinga, 261 B.C.E., and suffers remorse.

0   250   500 Km.
0   250   500 Mi.

MALABAR COAST

N

INDIAN OCEAN

© Cengage Learning

Today if a hundredth or a thousandth part of those people who were killed or died or were deported when Kalinga was annexed were to suffer similarly, it would weigh heavily on the mind of the Beloved of the Gods.*

*Excerpt from *Aśoka and the Decline of the Mauryas*, ed. Romila Thapar, 1973, pp. 255–256. Reprinted with permission of Oxford University Press India, New Delhi.

Ashoka
(r. 268–232 B.C.E.) The third king of the Mauryan dynasty (ca. 320–185 B.C.E.), the first Indian ruler to support Buddhism.

dharma
A Sanskrit term meaning correct conduct according to law or custom; Buddhists, including Ashoka, used this concept to refer to the teachings of the Buddha.

The concept of **dharma** occurs repeatedly in Ashoka's inscriptions. He uses the word to mean the teachings of the Buddha, but more broadly it means correct conduct according to law or custom, which is how many people in South Asia would have understood it. Dharma was also an important concept in Hinduism, the major religion that arose in India after Buddhism declined (see Chapter 8).

Ashoka governed an unusually large area. Riding on an elephant, he traveled along the trunk roads that radiated out like spokes on a bicycle wheel from his capital at Pataliputra (puh-TAH-lee-poo-truh). For much of its history South Asia was divided into separate regions governed by various rulers; only a few dynasties, like the Mauryan, succeeded in uniting the region for brief periods. Although not politically unified, Indians shared a common cultural heritage: living in highly developed cities, many spoke Sanskrit or related languages, recited religious texts in those languages, and conceived of society in terms of distinct social ranks.

In contrast to rulers of the city-states of ancient Mesopotamia (see Chapter 2), the kingdom of ancient Egypt, and the Neo-Assyrian and Neo-Babylonian empires, South Asian rulers exercised much less direct control over their subjects. Instead, leaders like Ashoka ruled by example, often patronizing religion to show what good monarchs they were. Indeed, religion provided one of the major unifying forces in the often-disunited South Asia. This chapter first discusses the ancient Vedic religion of India and then the exciting alternatives that appeared around the fifth century: Buddhism and Jainism (JANE-is-uhm). It concludes by discussing the Indian Ocean trade network.

Focus Questions

» *What evidence survives of social stratification at the Indus Valley sites? How did the Indo-Aryans describe the social stratification in their society?*

» *What were the main teachings of the Buddha?*

» *Why did Ashoka believe that supporting Buddhism would strengthen the Mauryan state?*

» *Who were the main actors in the Indian Ocean trade? What types of ships did they use? Along which routes? To trade which commodities?*

The Origins of Complex Society in South Asia, 2600–500 B.C.E.

We can glimpse the origins of South Asian social structures and religious traditions from archaeological evidence in the Indus River Valley dating to between 2600 and 1700 B.C.E. One of the most important urban sites lies near the modern Pakistan village of Harappa (ha-RAHP-pa). The Harappan culture extended over a wide area that included parts of present-day Pakistan, India, and Afghanistan (see Map 3.1). The people of the Indus Valley society used the same script, but, because archaeologists have not deciphered their writing system, we do not know what cultural forces bound them together. We learn more about ancient Indian society from evidence dating to 1500 B.C.E., when people in India, though never politically unified, came to share certain religious beliefs and conceptions of society. The pattern they established at that time held for much of Indian history.

Complex Society in the Indus River Valley, 2600–1700 B.C.E.

Long before the continents assumed their current configuration, India was a separate, diamond-shaped island located south of what would become the Eurasian landmass. Over time, the tectonic plate carrying India shifted north until it collided with the Eurasian landmass, forming a massive chain of mountains, the Himalayas. Mount Everest, at 29,028 feet (8,848 m), is the highest mountain in this chain. The South Asian landmass, often called a subcontinent, can be divided into three geographical regions: the high and largely uninhabited mountains to the north, the heavily populated plains of the Indus and Ganges (GUN-geez) (Ganga) Rivers, and the southern peninsula, which is not as densely settled.

The Indian subcontinent has two great rivers: the Indus to the west and the Ganges to the east. The headwaters of both rivers start in the high Himalayas and drain into the sea, with the Indus flowing into the Arabian Sea and the Ganges into the Bay of Bengal. The earliest farmers planted wheat and barley on the hillsides of what is now western Pakistan. The domestication of plants and animals, sometime between 6500 and 5000 B.C.E., made it possible for the people to create larger settlements in the valley of the Indus River.

India's pattern of rainfall differed from that in Mesopotamia and Egypt. Much of the annual rainfall came in several months in late summer or fall, called the **monsoon** season, and a second period came in the winter months. Indus Valley farmers had to build water storage tanks and measure out the water carefully until the next monsoon came. Like the Mesopotamians and the Egyptians, the Indus Valley residents learned to make pottery and to work metal, usually copper and bronze.

In the 1920s British and Indian archaeologists began to excavate huge mounds of brick and debris near the town of Harappa in the **Indus River Valley**. They uncovered the remains of a large urban settlement built from mud brick, complete with walls, drainage systems, open plazas, and avenues several yards (meters) across. Subsequent excavations have revealed that at its height Harappa had an area of over 380 acres (150 ha) and a population between forty and eighty thousand.[1] Archaeologists have found over fifteen hundred settlements belonging to the Indus River Valley society, the largest complex society of its time on the Indian subcontinent. Mohenjo-daro (mo-HEN-juh DAH-ro), the second-largest site of the Harappan settlements, was perhaps the most impressive. Unlike other cities of the ancient world, the cities of the Indus River Valley provided drinking water, bathing facilities, and sewer drains to all their residents, not just a privileged few.

We know frustratingly little about the people who occupied the Harappan sites because their script has yet to be deciphered. Seals with the same signs have been found at different sites throughout the Indus River Valley, suggesting that the region shared a common writing system. Archaeologists have identified 400 to 450 signs. But this number is puzzling; 400 signs is more than an alphabet (most alphabets contain fewer than 50 letters) yet fewer than a pictorial writing system (the earliest, simplest phase of Sumerian writing had 700 signs). Scholars wonder

monsoon
A term referring both to seasonal winds in South Asia blowing northeast in spring and early summer and southwest in fall and winter, and to the heavy seasonal rains they bring.

Indus River Valley
Site of the earliest complex society on the Indian subcontinent (2600–1700 B.C.E.), characterized by brick cities, drainage systems, open plazas, and broad avenues.

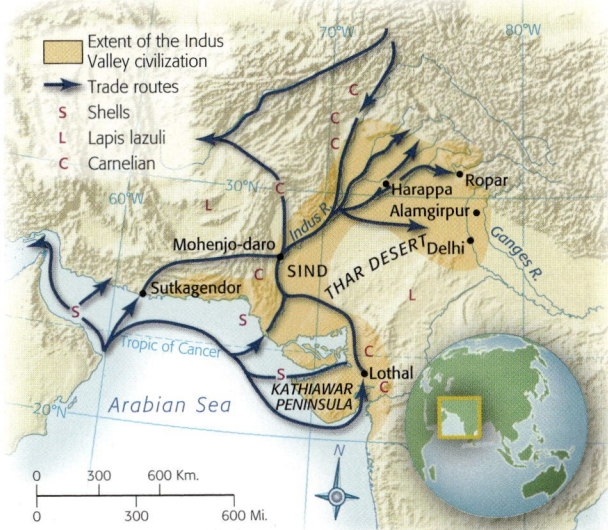

MAP 3.1 Indus River Valley Society Between 2600 and 1700 B.C.E., the Indus River Valley society covered a large area in modern-day India and Pakistan. The most important sites were at Mohenjo-daro and Harappa. The region exported carnelian and lapis lazuli to Mesopotamia and to the northeast and imported shells in return. (© Cengage Learning)

whether these mysterious signs stood for an individual word, syllable, or sound. Since no key giving their meaning in another language has yet been found, they are almost impossible to decipher.

A seal made in the Indus River Valley was found at the Mesopotamian city-state of Ur from a level occupied in 2600 B.C.E. The ancient peoples of the Indus River Valley were heavily involved in trade, and the people of Mesopotamia were among their most important trading partners. The residents of ancient Mesopotamia imported carnelian and lapis lazuli from the Indus Valley, and shells traveled in the opposite direction (see Map 3.1).

The absence of written documents makes it difficult to reconstruct either the social structure or the religious practices of the residents of the Indus River Valley. As in Mesopotamia, craftsmen who made similar goods seem to have lived in the same residential quarter. There is clear archaeological evidence of social stratification, one of the hallmarks of cities and complex societies. The people who had more possessions than others lived in bigger houses and were buried in graves with more goods.

Beginning in 1900 B.C.E., the large urban sites of the Harappan society become smaller. The characteristic Indus River pottery vessel types give way to new shapes and decorative patterns. Some of the pots have graffiti markings in Indus Valley script, indicating that the script remained in use.

With incontrovertible evidence of social stratification, occupational specialization, and large urban centers, the Indus River Valley sites certainly meet our definition of a complex society. Although the people were probably not united under a single ruler, they shared a common system of weights and measures, standardized brick size, and urban planning. Shared cultural practices in the absence of political unification characterized later South Asian societies as well.

The "Great Bath" at Mohenjo-daro, Pakistan   One of the most impressive ruins from the Harappan period (2600–1700 B.C.E.), the Great Bath is misnamed. Measuring 40 feet (12 m) high and 23 feet (7 m) wide, it was a water tank—not a pool or a bathing area. It held water for the ritual use of the city's residents, who bathed in a nearby building.

Copyright J. M. Kenoyer. Courtesy Department of Museum and Archaeology, Government of Pakistan

Can You Decipher the Harappan Seals of Mohenjo-daro, Pakistan?
These five seals have Indus Valley writing above several figures (*from top left to right, clockwise*): a unicorn, a rhinoceros, an elephant, a water buffalo, and a short-horned bull. A water fountain, possibly with a square sieve on top, stands below the unicorn's mouth; other animals eat from feeding troughs on the ground. No one has yet deciphered the symbols of the Indus Valley writing system.

The Spread of Indo-European Languages

Our understanding of the South Asian past becomes much clearer with the first textual materials in the Indo-European language of **Sanskrit**. Linguists place languages whose vocabulary and grammatical structures are most closely related into the same language family. If you have studied French or Spanish, you know that many words are related to their English counterparts. English, French, and Spanish all belong to the Indo-European language family, as do ancient Greek, Latin, Hittite, and Sanskrit. The Indo-European languages contain many core vocabulary words related to English, such as the words for mother, father, and brother (see Table 3.1). If you study a non-Indo-European language, like Chinese or Arabic, few words will resemble any word in English, and word order may be different.

Sometime in the distant past, thousands of years ago, a group of herding peoples who spoke Indo-European languages began to leave their homeland, possibly the Pontic steppe north of the Black Sea. Horse-drawn carts gave these peoples a technological edge because they could cover far more ground than most of their contemporaries, who did not know how to breed horses or drive wheeled carts.

The distribution of Indo-European languages over Eurasia shows how far these peoples went: Russia, most of Europe, Iran, and north India, but not southern India or East Asia (see Map 3.2). By at least 2000 B.C.E., those going west reached Anatolia, where they spoke Hittite. Those going east passed through Iran and arrived in north India sometime between 1500 and 1000 B.C.E., where they spoke Sanskrit. The modern inhabitants of the region speak a range of Indo-European languages descended from Sanskrit, including Hindi (HIN-dee), while those in south India speak Dravidian (druh-VID-ee-uhn) languages, which belong to a different language family. When linguists first discovered the similarities among Latin, Greek, and Sanskrit in the early nineteenth century, they assumed that the speakers of

Sanskrit
A language, such as Latin, Greek, and English, belonging to the Indo-European language family and spoken by Indo-Aryan migrants to north India around 1500–1000 B.C.E.

TABLE 3.1 Related Words in Various Indo-European Languages

English	Latin	Greek	Sanskrit
mother	mater	meter	matar
father	pater	pater	pitar
brother	frater	phrater	bhratar
sister	soror	(unrelated)	svasar
me	me	me	ma
two	duo	duo	duva
six	sex	hex	shat
seven	septem	hepta	sapta

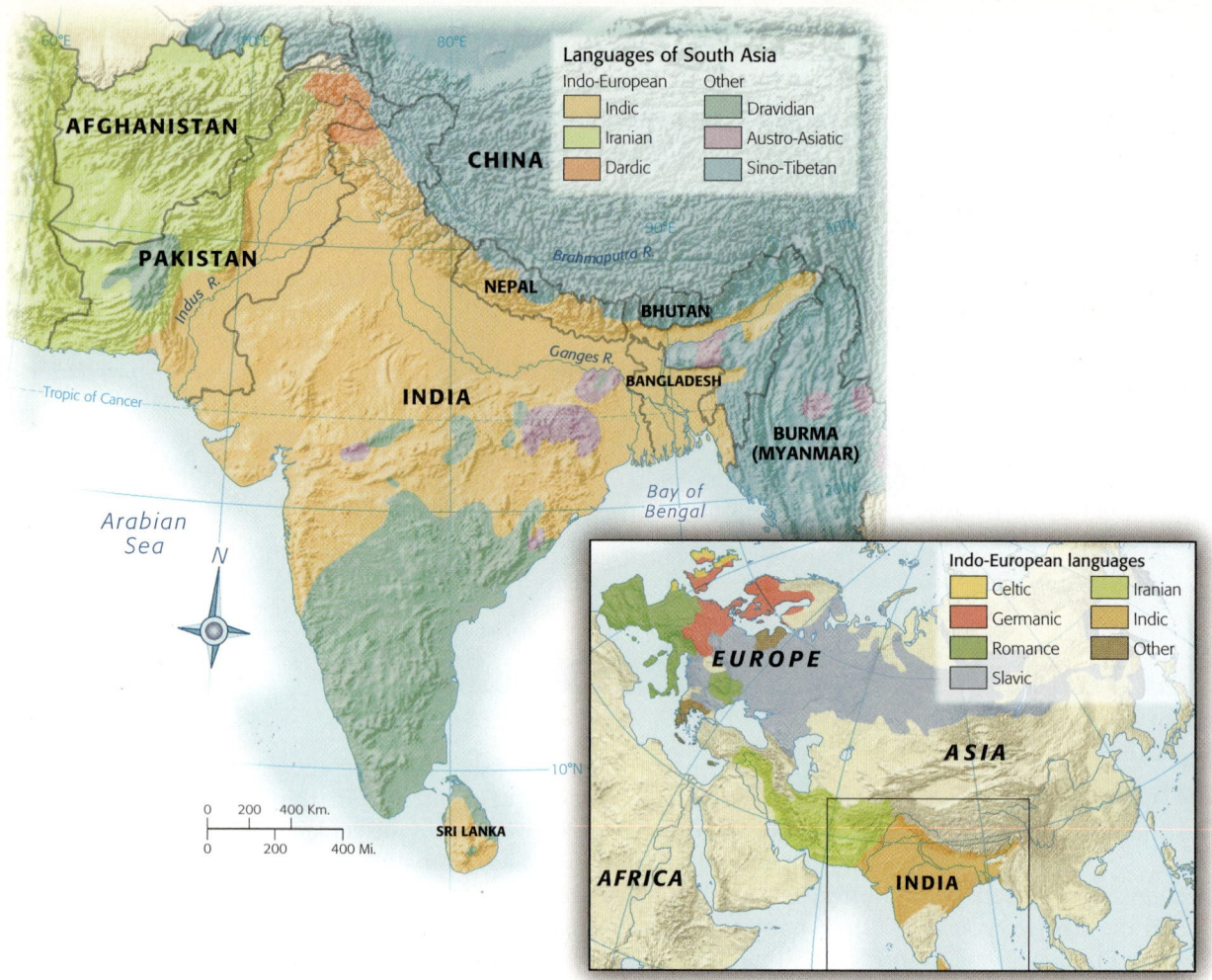

MAP 3.2 Distribution of Languages in Modern South Asia Most people living in the northern regions of modern South Asia speak Indo-European languages, including Hindi and Urdu, while those living in the south speak Dravidian languages like Tamil and Telegu. The dominance of Indo-European languages in much of today's Eurasia is the result of migrations occurring over three thousand years ago. (© Cengage Learning)

Indo-European languages invaded and wiped out the indigenous peoples. Modern scholars have since proposed variations on the original conquer-and-destroy model. Perhaps, when the Indo-European speakers migrated into a new region, their superior technology convinced the local peoples to adopt the newcomers' language.

The Indo-European Migrations and Vedic Culture, 1500–1000 B.C.E.

Rig Veda
A collection of 1,028 Sanskrit hymns, composed around 1500–1000 B.C.E. but written down around 1000 C.E. One of the most revealing sources about Indo-Europeans who settled in north India.

The Indo-European migrants left us the ***Rig Veda*** (RIG VAY-duh), a collection of 1,028 hymns that were preserved because the priests who sang them passed them down orally from one generation to the next. They date to around 1500 to 1000 B.C.E., the probable time of the Indo-European migrations to South Asia, yet they were not written down until more than two thousand years later, perhaps in 1000 C.E.[2] The word *hymn* is slightly misleading, since Vedic hymns touch on many everyday activities, including sex and gambling. Accordingly, they reveal much about ancient society.

Linguists have concluded that the Sanskrit of the older hymns varies slightly from the later hymns, making it possible to determine the order of their composition.

The earlier hymns mention many place names to the west of those included in the later hymns, an indication that the migrants came first to northwest India and later to all of north India.

These migrants sometimes called themselves "Aryan," a Sanskrit word whose meaning is "noble" or "host." While modern researchers think that many and varied peoples spoke Indo-European languages, the propagandists of Nazi Germany wrongly imputed a racial unity to what was a linguistic group. Always mindful that we know nothing of their appearance, it is best to refer to these migrants as Indo-Aryans because their language belonged to the Indo-Aryan branch of the Indo-European language family.

Scholars have named the religion of the Indo-Aryans Vedic (VAY-dick), from the *Rig Veda*. The roots of Hinduism, a major religion in modern South Asia, lie in **Vedic religion**, but the religious practices of the early Indo-Aryans differed from later Hinduism, discussed in Chapter 8. Many scholars of South Asian religion date the rise of Hinduism to the seventh century C.E., after the decline of Buddhism.[3]

Many Vedic rituals focused on the transition between day and night or between seasons. A priest had to make the correct offering to the appropriate deity to ensure that the sun would rise each day or that at the winter solstice the days would begin to grow longer. The deities mentioned in the *Rig Veda* include the war-god, Indra (IN-druh), the god of fire, the sun-god, and the god of death, as well as many minor deities. Rituals honoring these gods could last several days and involve intricate sequences of steps, including animal sacrifice. The Brahmin (BRAH-min) priests who performed them were paid handsomely by local rulers. There was no single ruler in Vedic society. Instead a number of kings ruled small territories by collecting taxes from farmers to finance these lavish ceremonies.

The *Rig Veda* provides a few valuable hints about social organization. The original Indo-European migrants were **nomads** who migrated seasonally from place to place to find grass for their animals. Carrying their tents with them, they usually did not farm but tended their herds full-time. The most important animal in their society was the horse, which pulled the carts that transported their families and possessions across Eurasia. According to some hymns, some people began to cultivate grain after settling in India.

One early hymn, addressed to Indra, gives a clear sense of the diverse occupations of the Indo-European speakers:

> *Our thoughts bring us to diverse callings, setting people apart: the carpenter seeks what is broken, the physician a fracture, and the Brahmin priest seeks one who presses Soma.*[*]

Soma was an intoxicating beverage, possibly made from ephedra (AY-fay-druh) leaves, that was drunk at ceremonies. This poem shows that Vedic society included carpenters, doctors, Brahmin priests, and people who prepared the ritual drink.

The position of women in Vedic society was probably not much lower than that of men. Girls could go out unsupervised in public. Both girls and boys received an education in which they memorized hymns and studied their meaning, yet only male specialists recited hymns in public ceremonies. One hymn instructs educated girls to marry educated husbands. Girls could sometimes even choose

Vedic religion
Religious belief system of Indo-European migrants to north India; involved animal sacrifice and elaborate ceremonies to ensure that all transitions in the natural world—day to night, or one season to the next—proceeded smoothly.

nomads
A term for people who migrate seasonally from place to place to find grass for their animals. They do not usually farm but tend their herds full-time.

---

[*]From *The Rig Veda: An Anthology of One Hundred and Eight Hymns*, selected, translated, and annotated by Wendy Doniger O'Flaherty (Penguin Classics, 1981). Copyright © Wendy Doniger O'Flaherty, 1981. Reprinted with permission of Penguin Group/UK.

their own husbands, provided they had obtained permission from their mother and father. Women could inherit property, and widows could remarry.

Changes After 1000 B.C.E.

The later hymns, composed perhaps around 1000 B.C.E. as the former nomads settled down to a life of agriculture, indicate that social roles in Vedic society became more fixed, and women's freedom declined. Eventually people came to be classed into four different social groups, called **varna** (VAR-nuh), that were determined by birth. The literal meaning of *varna* is "color," reflected in the modern English word *varnish*. One hymn, "The Hymn of the Primeval Man," explains that when the gods dismembered a cosmic giant, they created each varna from a different part of his body:

> *When they divided the man, into how many parts did they apportion him?*
> *What do they call his mouth, his two arms and thighs and feet?*

> *His mouth became the Brahmin; his arms were made into the Warrior, his thighs the People, and from his feet the Servants were born.**

varna
From the Sanskrit word for "color": the four major social groups of ancient Indian society, ranked in order of purity (not wealth or power): Brahmin priests at the top, then warriors, then farmers and merchants, and finally dependent laborers.

This passage sets out the major social groups of late Vedic society, ranked in order of purity (not wealth or power): Brahmins were the purest because they conducted Vedic rituals; the warrior category included the kings who sponsored the rituals. The farmers and merchants ("the People") were supposed to farm the land and tend the herds. The fourth varna of dependent laborers, many of whom were the region's original residents, served all the varna above them. Like all documents, however, this hymn has a distinct point of view: a Brahmin priest composed it, and it is not surprising that he placed Brahmins at the top of the social hierarchy.

India's caste system has changed greatly over the last three thousand years. There is no exact equivalent in Indian languages of the English word *caste*, which comes from the sixteenth- to seventeenth-century Portuguese word *castas*, meaning breed or type of animal or plant. Most Indians would say that the word **jati** (JAH-ti), sometimes translated as "subcaste," comes closest.

jati
A term, sometimes translated as "sub-caste," for groups of five thousand to fifteen thousand people in modern India. Many, but not all, Indians marry someone from the same jati and share meals on equal footing only with people of the same jati.

People in a jati sometimes specialize in a certain occupation, but many jati have members with several different occupations, and some jati have completely given up their traditional occupations in favor of something new. Jati usually range in size from five thousand to fifteen thousand people. Many, but not all, people in modern South Asia find their spouse through an arranged marriage with someone from the same jati. People often socialize within their own jati and share meals together.

If asked to identify their own caste, most South Asians would name their jati first and then perhaps add the varna. Most outside observers tend to exaggerate the rigidity of caste in modern India. Castelike groups exist within other modern societies, too, although we often fail to recognize how many people in non-Indian societies, including the United States, also tend to marry spouses from similar social and economic backgrounds.

---

*From *The Rig Veda: An Anthology of One Hundred and Eight Hymns*, selected, translated, and annotated by Wendy Doniger O'Flaherty (Penguin Classics, 1981). Copyright © Wendy Doniger O'Flaherty, 1981. Reprinted with permission of Penguin Group/UK.

Different changes took place in the centuries after about 1000 B.C.E., when the later poems in the *Rig Veda* were composed. Iron came into widespread use and, as in Mesopotamia, iron tools proved much more effective at clearing land than bronze or copper ones, making the settlement of the lower Ganges Valley possible. Between 1000 and 500 B.C.E. the residents of the lower valley cleared much of the forest cover so that they could intensively pursue agriculture there. The sedentary peoples, armed with horses and iron weapons, continuously extended the area of cultivated land. Higher agricultural yields prompted an increase in population and a boom in trade, as shown by the appearance of the first coins around 500 B.C.E., at the same time as in China (see Chapter 4) and the Persian empire (see Chapter 6).

This period also saw other challenges to the old order. Composed between 900 and 600 B.C.E., the *Upanishad* (oo-PAHN-ih-shahd) texts claim to be linked to the Vedic tradition but introduce entirely new ideas. These texts turn inward, away from costly sacrificial rituals. One new and exciting idea was that souls transmigrated: according to the doctrine of **karma**, people's acts in this life determined how they would be reborn in the next. New gods appeared and are still worshiped by Hindus today. Unlike the gods of the *Rig Veda*, these gods intervene actively in human affairs and sometimes assume human form.

karma
The sum of one's deeds in this and all earlier existences that determines one's rebirth in the next life.

The *Mahabharata* (muh-HAH-bah-ruh-tuh) and the *Ramayana* (ruh-MAH-yuh-nuh), the two great Sanskrit epics, began to be composed at this time, although they were recorded only in the fourth century C.E. The *Mahabharata*, over 100,000 verses in length, describes a long-running feud between two clans. Its major theme is dharma, or right conduct. The epic vividly enacts some of the most basic conflicts in the human psyche as the characters struggle to understand what it means to be good and what the consequences of evil actions might be. We see men and women struggling with the question of whether it even matters if a person is actively trying to change the world, or whether perhaps everything is simply fated to be the way it is.

One part of the *Mahabharata*, the *Bhagavad Gita* (bug-GAH-vud GEEH-tuh), was often read as an independent work. Composed around 200 C.E., it tells the story of a battle between two armies. One leader hesitates before the battle: his dharma is to fight, but he will not be able to escape from the cycle of death and rebirth if he kills any of his relatives fighting on the other side. The deity Krishna, in human form as a chariot driver, argues that each person should fulfill his dharma, or his given role, in life. Then Krishna appears as a deity and urges the warrior to devote himself fully to worshiping him. Krishna's teaching later became a key tenet in Hinduism. (See the feature "World History in Today's World: Avatar: Then and Now.")

The much-shorter *Ramayana* tells of a great king, Rama (RAH-muh), whose wife is abducted by a demon king. Rama fights to get Sita (SEE-tuh) back, but when he defeats the demon king he greets her coldly and explains that he cannot take her back because, although a married woman, she has lived alone with her captors. After ordering a pyre of wood to be built, she jumps into the flames, but the fire-god lifts her from the flames and presents her to Rama. Only then does he accept that she has remained loyal to him. In the centuries after their initial composition, both the *Mahabharata* and the *Ramayana* spawned many versions throughout South Asia and even Southeast Asia, and today's television versions captivate millions of viewers.

Avatar: Then and Now

Why does your electronic persona in a video game have the Sanskrit name of *avatar*? In the *Bhagavad Gita*, deities assume human form so that they can intervene in the world of the living. The god Vishnu, who later became one of the most important deities in Hinduism, explains that he takes human form whenever he needs to reestablish cosmic order:

Whenever righteousness wanes and unrighteousness increases I send myself forth.
In order to protect the good and punish the wicked,
In order to make a firm foundation for righteousness,
I come into being age after age. (4.7–8)

The god's avatar is human, and so it lacks the full power of the deity.

In 1985, the designers of the game *Habitat* coined the word *avatar* for the player's online persona. At the time, almost all video games were text only. *Habitat* pioneered the use of simple cartoon avatars who could perform basic commands and represent the player in the virtual world of the game. Video games have become much more sophisticated since then—avatars are now three-dimensional and can speak—but the basic concept is unchanged. As the ancient Indian gods controlled their avatars who lacked all the gods' powers, so too do human operators command their virtual avatars.

Set in the year 2154, the 2009 film *Avatar* introduced yet another meaning for the word. The writer and director James Cameron used *avatar* to refer to distant, hybrid bodies linked genetically to humans who control them simply by thinking. In Cameron's conception, the humans exist in the same world as their avatars—something not true of either the ancient Indian avatars or their video-game successors.

Sources: From the *Bhagavad Gita*: David Kinsley. "Avatāra." From Jones, Lindsay (Editor). *Encyclopedia of Religion*. 15 Volume Set, 2E. © 2005 Cengage Learning. Reprinted by permission; Lori Kendall, "Avatar," in *Encyclopedia of New Media: An Essential Reference to Communication and Technology*, ed. Steve Jones (Thousand Oaks, Calif.: Sage Publications, 2003), p. 21.

Jainism
An Indian religion founded around the same time as Buddhism that emphasizes right faith, right knowledge, and right conduct: a key tenet is not to harm any living beings.

Different teachers continued to debate new religious concepts in succeeding centuries. Between the sixth and fourth centuries B.C.E., **Jainism**, an Indian religion with some two million followers today, took shape. Mahavira, the founder of the Jains (JANES), went from place to place for twelve years, testing himself and debating ideas with other ascetics. After thirteen months he stopped wearing even a single garment and wandered naked for eleven years before reaching liberation from the bondage of human life. He died, it is thought, in his seventies after voluntarily renouncing food and water. Jains believe in right faith, right knowledge, and right conduct, and they emphasize the obligation to harm no living beings. They abstain from eating and drinking at night, when it is dark, so that they will not kill any insects by mistake.

The Rise of Buddhism

Buddha
The founder of the Buddhist religion, Siddhartha Gautama (ca. 600–400 B.C.E.); also called the Buddha, or the enlightened one.

Also living in this time of religious ferment was the founder of the Buddhist religion, Siddhartha Gautama (sid-DAR-tuh gow-TA-muh), or the Buddha. The word **Buddha** literally means "the enlightened or awakened one." The religion that he founded became one of the most influential in the world, and Ashoka's decision to support Buddhism marked a crucial turning point in the religion's history. Buddhism spread to Sri Lanka, Central Asia, Southeast Asia, and eventually to China and Japan, where it continued to thrive after it declined in its Indian homeland. Today Japan, Tibet, and Thailand have significant Buddhist populations, and growing Buddhist communities live in Europe and North America.

We know many details about the Buddha's life but cannot be sure which are facts and which myths because all our sources date to several centuries after his death and were recorded by Buddhist monks and nuns. Born at a time when India was not politically unified, the Buddha did not intend to found a religion that would bind Indian society together. His stated goal was to teach people how to break out of the endless cycle of birth, death, and rebirth.

The Life of the Buddha

Born along the southern edge of the Himalaya Mountains in today's Nepal, the Buddha lived to almost eighty. Scholarly consensus puts the death of the Buddha at around 400 B.C.E.

The legend of his life, known to all practicing Buddhists, recounts that his mother dreamed of a white elephant with a lotus flower in his trunk. The wise men she consulted explained that she would give birth to either a great monarch or a great teacher. One seer predicted that, if he learned about human problems, he would become a teacher; this prediction prompted his parents to raise him inside a walled palace precinct so that he would never see any signs of suffering or illness. He grew up, married, and fathered a child.

One day when he was driving inside the palace park with his charioteer, he saw an extremely elderly man, then a man who was very ill, and then a corpse being taken away to be cremated. A fourth encounter, with a wandering ascetic who wore a simple robe but who looked happy, gave Siddhartha hope, and he resolved to follow the ascetic's example. For six years he subjected himself to all kinds of self-mortification. Then he decided to stop starving himself and meditated under a tree, later known as the Tree of Wisdom (also called a bodhi tree), for forty-nine days. He gained enlightenment and explained how he had done so.

The Teachings of the Buddha

According to much later Buddhist tradition, the Buddha preached his first sermon in the Deer Park near Benares (buh-NAR-us) in the Ganges Valley to five followers, who, like him, were seeking enlightenment. First he identified two incorrect routes to knowledge: extreme self-denial and complete self-gratification. The Buddha preached that his listeners should leave family life behind and follow him, and they should live simple lives, avoiding the strenuous fasts and self-mortification advocated by other ascetic groups.

He explained that one could escape from the endless cycle of birth, death, and rebirth by following a clear series of steps, called the Noble Eightfold Path. Like a doctor, the Buddha diagnosed suffering in the First Noble Truth, analyzed its origins in the Second Noble Truth, stated that a cure exists in the Third Truth, and explained that cure in the Fourth Noble Truth: to follow the Noble Eightfold Path. This path consists of right understanding, right resolve, right speech, right action, right livelihood, right effort, right mindfulness, and right meditation. When people follow the Noble Eightfold Path and understand the Four Noble Truths, their suffering will end because they will have escaped from the cycle of life and rebirth by attaining **nirvana**, literally "extinction."

Buddhism shared with Jainism much that was new. Both challenged Brahminic authority, denied the authority of the Vedic hymns, and banned animal sacrifices. Vedic religious practice did not address the question of individual liberation; the goal of Vedic ritual was to make sure that the cosmos continued to function in an orderly way. In contrast, the Buddha preached that salvation was entirely the product of an individual's actions. He focused on the individual, outside of his or her family unit and any social group and without regard to his or her varna ranking.

nirvana
A Sanskrit word that literally means "extinction," as when the flame on a candle goes out. In Buddhism the term took on broader meaning: those who followed the Eightfold Path and understood the Four Noble Truths would gain true understanding.

A Mix of Sculptural Traditions from Gandhara, Afghanistan This Gandharan statue's posture is classically Buddhist: his legs are crossed so that both feet face up, the left hand grasps his robe, and the right makes a gesture meaning to dispel fear. But the facial expression, hair, and overall posture are drawn from Greco-Roman models already familiar to Gandharan sculptors for several centuries. Neither Buddhist nor Greco-Roman, the spokes in the halo behind the Buddha's head probably represent the sun's rays. (Image © The Metropolitan Museum of Art/Art Resource, NY)

The people who heard the Buddha preach naturally wanted to know how they could attain nirvana. He urged them to leave their families behind so that they could join him as monks in the Buddhist order. Those who followed him went from place to place, begging for their daily food from those who did not join the order. They lived nowhere permanently except during the monsoon months, when it was not practical to live by begging.

Only those monks who joined the Buddhist order could attain nirvana, the Buddha taught. His first followers were all men, but Buddhist sources record that the Buddha's aunt asked to join the Buddhist order. The Buddha refused her until his star disciple Ananda (uh-NAN-duh) intervened and persuaded him to change his mind. Later women did become Buddhist nuns, but they were always subordinate to men.

Those outside the order could not attain nirvana, but they could gain merit by donating food and money, the Buddha taught. Many kings and merchants gave large gifts in the hope of improving their lives, either in this world or in future rebirths.

This teaching marked a major departure from the pre-existing Vedic religion. According to the *Rig Veda*, Brahmins stood at the top of the ritual hierarchy, and those who ranked below them could do nothing to change their position. The Buddhists took a radically different view: a merchant, a farmer, or even a laborer who made a donation to the Buddhist order could enhance his or her standing. From its very earliest years, Buddhism attracted merchant support, and communities of Buddhists often lived near cities, where merchants had gathered.

The Buddha forbade his followers to worship statues or portraits of him. Instead, they worshiped at the four sites that had been most important during the Buddha's life: where he was born, where he gained enlightenment, where he preached the first sermon, and where he died. Before his death the Buddha had instructed his followers to cremate him and bury his ashes under a bell-shaped monument built over a burial mound, called a stupa (STEW-pah). The first generation of Buddhists divided the Buddha's remains under many different stupas, where they honored him by circling the stupa in a clockwise direction, a practice called circumambulation (pradaksina) (pra-DUCKSH-ee-nah). To gain merit, they walked a fixed number of circuits with their right arm, thought to be more pure than the left, facing the stupa. They also left flowers, incense, and clothing on the stupas, where they lit lamps and played music as an expression of their devotion. (See the feature "Visual Evidence in Primary Sources: The Buddhist Stupa at Sanchi.")

Beginning in the first and second centuries C.E., sculptors began to make images of the Buddha himself. One group in north India portrayed the Buddha as a young man, while another, active in the Gandhara (gahn-DAHR-ah) region of modern Pakistan and Afghanistan, was influenced by later copies of Greek statues brought by Alexander the Great and his armies in the fourth century B.C.E.

The Mauryan Empire, ca. 320–185 B.C.E.

Mauryan dynasty (ca. 320–185 B.C.E.) A dynasty that unified much of the Indian subcontinent. Relying on trunk roads, it exercised more control in the cities than in the countryside.

During the Buddha's lifetime, Buddhism was but one of many different teachings circulating in India. The support of Ashoka, the third ruler of the **Mauryan**

dynasty, founded by Ashoka's grandfather, transformed Buddhism into the most influential religion of its day. Ashoka's adoption of Buddhism as the state religion promoted cultural unity and strengthened his political control. The Mauryans came to power at a time when trade was increasing throughout the region, and Buddhism was able to succeed because it appealed to merchants. The Mauryans created the first large state in India, extending over all of north India (see the map on page 57).

Surprisingly few materials about the Mauryans survive. As a result, historians continue to debate the amount of control the Mauryan empire exercised over the regions it conquered. Local rulers may have retained considerable power. In addition to archaeological excavations, our major sources are the partial report of a Greek ambassador named Megasthenes (ME-gas-thuh-nees), written after 288 B.C.E., and Ashoka's rock edicts.

Life and Society in the Mauryan Dynasty, ca. 300 B.C.E.

In 320 B.C.E. the grandfather of Ashoka, a general named Chandragupta (chuhn-druh-GOOP-tuh) Maurya (r. ca. 320–297 B.C.E.), defeated another general and gained control of his territory and his capital Pataliputra (modern-day Patna [PUTT-nuh]), located on the Ganges. After Chandragupta Maurya took power, his forces fought those of Seleucus I (seh-LOO-kuhs) (321–281 B.C.E.), a general who succeeded Alexander the Great (see Chapter 6) in Mesopotamia. After making peace, Seleucus in 302 B.C.E. sent an ambassador named Megasthenes to the Mauryan court at Pataliputra, where he stayed for fourteen years.

Megasthenes wrote a work entitled *Indika* (IN-dick-uh), which provides a detailed description of Pataliputra in approximately 300 B.C.E., some thirty years before Ashoka ascended to the throne. Archaeological excavations early in the twentieth century around Patna revealed clear evidence of large fortification walls, including large reinforcing wooden trusses, and the city occupied some 20 square miles (50 sq km). Pataliputra's size impressed Megasthenes deeply. Unfortunately, Megasthenes's original work does not survive; we know it only from passages quoted by later Greek and Roman writers.

Within the capital the Mauryans exercised considerable control. Most of their officials supervised trade and commerce, the major source of Mauryan revenue. Market officials, concentrated at marketplaces in the capital, collected taxes and regulated weights and measures to ensure that no one was cheated. They encouraged merchants to sell only one type of good by charging them twice as much tax as if they sold more, and they levied fines on those merchants who passed off old goods as newly made.

The passages from Megasthenes that have come down to us take a detached tone: he includes no personal anecdotes. His account of the officials who watched over the foreigners comes closest to describing his own life in Pataliputra:

> *Those of the second branch attend to the entertainment of foreigners. To these they assign lodgings, and they keep watch over their modes of life by means of those persons whom they give to them for assistants. They escort them on the way when they leave the country, or, in the event of their dying, forward their property to their relatives. They take care of them when they are sick, and if they die bury them.* *

We may surmise that city officials gave Megasthenes a servant.

---

*J. W. McCrindle, *Ancient India as Described by Megasthenes and Arrian* (London: Trübner, 1877), p. 87.

The Buddhist Stupa at Sanchi

The oldest and best-preserved stupa in India is at Sanchi, near Bhopal, India. The Buddha never visited Sanchi during his lifetime, but Ashoka chose it as the site of a new stupa for the relics of the Buddha, because Sanchi lay on the main route between Pataliputra and the western coastal ports and had frequent visitors. Ashoka ordered the remains of the Buddha removed from their original resting place and placed in a new burial mound, which was covered with a layer of sandstone and had a wooden railing around it. He also placed a pillar edict on the site.

The site today looks the way it did after extensive renovations done during the first century B.C.E. A square stone wall with a central gate on each side surrounds the main burial mound; beautifully carved stone pillars decorate each of the gates (see opposite). In addition to the main stupa, Sanchi contains two other large stupas and hundreds of smaller ones, where monks seeking to share the Buddha's merit were buried. Buddhists believe that visiting a stupa holding someone's remains brings them closer to the deceased.

Built in the first century B.C.E., the Southern Gate at Sanchi contains three horizontal sections held up by the two main vertical posts. The carvings, which illustrate people and animals worshiping the Buddha, are wonderfully lifelike. The artists working at Sanchi exercised great ingenuity. They showed scenes from the Buddha's life, but never directly the Buddha himself. In his dying instructions, the Buddha forbade his followers to worship representations of him.

After looking at the friezes, worshipers climbed a flight of steps to reach a railed walkway. The pillars and gates at Sanchi contain hundreds of inscriptions from Ashoka's time and later, recording the names of those making a donation to pay for part of a railing or a frieze in the hope of gaining Buddhist merit. All those who circumambulated the stupa shared this same goal.

QUESTION FOR ANALYSIS

» *How did people of different social ranks (Ashoka, monks, nuns, and ordinary people) express their devotion to Buddhism at different places—the friezes of the gates, the pillars, the walkways, and the stupa itself—at the site of Sanchi?*

The Southern Gate at Sanchi marked one of the entrances to the main stupa at the site. After looking at the detailed reliefs on the front and back, worshipers followed the path around the burial mound to reach stairs that led up to the walkway that led all the way around the stupa.

The stupa mound was first built over the remains of the Buddha in the third century B.C.E. and attained its current size—120 feet (36.5 m) in diameter and 54 feet (16.5 m) high—one hundred years later.

Robert Harding World Imagery/Alamy

The Southern Gate was built in the first century B.C.E. The high quality of the vivid carvings makes this one of the great, and one of the earliest, surviving monuments of Buddhist art in India.

This railing surrounds the interior walkway on which worshipers circumambulated the stupa. Individual stones bear the names of contributors—including monks, nuns, and merchants—who made donations to finance the building of the walkway.

According to Megasthenes, the military section of the government was the same size as the urban section: thirty men, divided into six branches, each with its own area of responsibility—navy, supplies, infantry, cavalry, war chariots, and elephants. If true, and we have no independent source to verify this information, this is a tiny number of officials: still, historians value Megasthenes's reports for their plausibility and detail. Elephants fascinated Megasthenes, who devoted many lines to their capture, training, loyalty to their masters, and general care; when on active duty, he reports, they consumed rice wine and large quantities of flowers.

Megasthenes's descriptions of Indian society have long puzzled analysts. He identifies seven ranks within Indian society: (1) philosophers, (2) farmers, (3) herdsmen, (4) artisans, (5) soldiers, (6) spies, and (7) councillors. This overlaps only slightly with the varna scheme described in the *Rig Veda* some seven hundred years earlier, with its four ranks of Brahmin, warriors, merchants and farmers, and dependent servants. Three of Megasthenes's groups (herdsmen, artisans, and spies) do not even appear in the varna ranking.

The top-ranking group, according to Megasthenes, was the smallest: the king's advisers, military generals, and treasury officials, who were *"the most respected on account of the high character and wisdom of [their] members."** The placement at the top of the ranking suggests that this was the group Megasthenes spoke to directly.

Ranking second were the "philosophers," or religious practitioners. They performed sacrifices and funerals, and Megasthenes explains that the Brahmins among them married and had children but lived simply. Another group of religious practitioners underwent various privations, such as abstaining from sexual intercourse or sitting in one position all day. The Jains would have belonged to this group. Finally, a third group followed the Buddha, *"whom they honor as a god on account of his extraordinary sanctity."** Megasthenes devotes only a few sentences to the Buddhists, an indication that they had only a small following in 300 B.C.E.

Conceptions of caste, Megasthenes suggests, were much more fluid than many of our surviving sources, which almost always place Brahmins at the top, would indicate. Megasthenes lists five other groups (farmers, herdsmen, artisans, soldiers, and spies) without ranking them in any way. The farmers, the largest group, were exempt from military service but paid a land tax to the king as well as one-quarter of all their crops. Megasthenes concludes his list by saying, *"No one is allowed to marry out of his own caste, or to exercise any calling or art except his own,"** an indication of the strength of caste identities in this early period.

Mauryan Control Outside the Capital

The Mauryans exercised close supervision over the rural areas in the immediate vicinity of the capital, but not over all of north India. Megasthenes reports that the kingdom contained three different types of territory: those ruled directly by the Mauryan king, those territories where the local king was allowed to remain in place with reduced powers, and local republics, in which an assembly made the decisions for everyone. This description of the Mauryans suggests an empire quite different from that of the Assyrians (see Chapter 2). Whereas the Mauryans exercised direct rule in only a limited area, the Assyrians were so powerful that they could forcibly resettle large groups of people throughout their empire.

The Ashokan inscriptions were written after Megasthenes left India (most likely between 260 and 232 B.C.E.). They were placed in the capital, in northwest

*J. W. McCrindle, *Ancient India as Described by Megasthenes and Arrian* (London: Trübner, 1877), pp. 43, 105, 44.

An Ashokan Column from Vaishali, Bihar, India   This pillar, made of polished red sandstone, stands 60 feet (18.3 m) high. Capped with a lion, it was visible in all four directions. This and the other stone columns Ashoka commissioned are the first monuments worked in stone anywhere in ancient India. Some scholars have wondered if Ashoka knew of other stone monuments in neighboring regions like Iran.

India in the Punjab (PUHN-juhb) region, on the east and west coasts, and in central India (see the map on page 57).

Earlier analysts often assumed that the monuments outlined the territory under Mauryan control. Recently, however, historians have realized that Mauryan control was greatest in the region about Pataliputra. Control also extended to the trade routes linking the capital with outlying trade centers, along which the Mauryans could have dispatched officials to markets to collect sales taxes. But the regions lying in between the trade routes were controlled lightly, if at all.

The Mauryan empire remained a decentralized one in which local people continued to speak their own languages. Ashoka drafted the texts of his inscriptions in his native language of Magadhi (muh-GUH-dee), a language related to Sanskrit. They were then translated into the different Prakrit (PRAH-krit) vernaculars used in north India, which are all descended from Sanskrit. Some in the northwest were translated into Greek, a European language, and Aramaic, a western Asian language, because the local population spoke both languages.

Ashoka drafted short, medium, and lengthy versions of each edict so that his local officials could decide which one to use. Officials sometimes left out passages from the original to save space, Ashoka realized, and the officials at Kalinga did not even put up the text cited at the beginning of this chapter about Ashoka's bloody conquest of the region, possibly because they did not want to antagonize the local population. The text survives in the long version in the capital, an important reminder that central governments may issue prescriptive orders but local officials do not necessarily implement them.

The inscriptions report that Ashoka sent officials to inspect outlying regions every three to five years. He claims to have built new roads, along which his men planted trees and dug wells, and he encouraged his officials to discover new medicinal herbs and plant them where they had not previously been cultivated. Ashoka and the other Mauryan rulers did not mint their own coins; rulers in each locality did.

Ruling by Example: The Ceremonial State

chakravartin
Literally "turner of the wheel," a Buddhist term for the ideal ruler who patronized Buddhism but never became a monk.

Ashoka was the first major Indian ruler to support Buddhism. The ideal ruler followed Buddhist teachings and made donations to the Buddhist order, which he did not join. Nor did he renounce his family. The Buddhists called such a ruler a **chakravartin** (chah-kruh-VAR-tin), literally "turner of the wheel," a broad term indicating that the sovereign ruled over a wide territory. Ashoka's inscriptions fully express his ideal of ruling by example. Every measure he took had the same goal: to encourage his subjects to follow dharma, which he described in this way:

> *There is no gift comparable to the gift of dharma, the praise of dharma, the sharing of dharma, fellowship in dharma. And this is—good behavior towards slaves and servants, obedience to mother and father, generosity towards friends, acquaintances, and relatives and towards shramanas [shrah-MUH-nuhz; Buddhists and other renunciants] and Brahmins, and abstention from killing living beings.*[*]

Many subsequent rulers, particularly in South and Southeast Asia, followed Ashoka's example.

ceremonial state
State whose ruler sponsored religious observances and construction of religious edifices in the hope that his subjects would willingly acknowledge him as ruler. Usually contrasted with rulers who depended on sheer force to govern.

Historians call this type of rule a "**ceremonial state**" to contrast it with empires in which rulers exercised more direct control. The ruler of a ceremonial state sponsored religious observances and contributed money for the construction of religious edifices in the hope that his subjects would recognize his generosity and willingly acknowledge him as their leader.

Ashoka's inscriptions permit us to see how his devotion to Buddhism increased over time. As we have seen, the huge number of deaths in the battle of Kalinga (260 B.C.E.) filled him with remorse and he made a decision to follow the teachings of the Buddha. In the following year he promised to uphold the five most important precepts—not to kill, steal, commit adultery, lie, or drink alcohol—and became a **lay Buddhist** (upasaka). Anyone could become a lay Buddhist; one simply had to vow to uphold the five precepts and then continue in one's normal profession while living with one's family. Four distinct groups formed the early Buddhist order: monks and nuns were ordained, while male and female lay Buddhists were not.

lay Buddhist
A Buddhist devotee who observes the five precepts not to kill, steal, commit adultery, lie, or drink alcohol, but continues to live at home and does not join the Buddhist order.

In the tenth year of his reign, around 258 B.C.E., Ashoka decided to increase his devotion to Buddhism even further. Presumably along with learned Buddhists, he conducted a series of meetings with non-Buddhist "ascetics" engaged in different austerities, as well as with Brahmin priests, who continued to sacrifice animals. Ashoka discussed the teachings of the Buddha and gave them gifts to encourage

---

[*]Excerpt from *Aśoka and the Decline of the Mauryas*, ed. Romila Thapar, 1973, pp. 254–255. Reprinted with permission of Oxford University Press India, New Delhi.

them to convert to Buddhism. He used the same combination of persuasion and gift giving with elderly people and with ordinary people in the countryside. (See the feature "Movement of Ideas Through Primary Sources: The First Sermon of the Buddha and Ashoka's Fourth Major Rock Edict.")

Ashoka visited the Deer Park in Benares as well as the site of the Buddha's birth in present-day Nepal, where he built a stone fence and erected a stone pillar in memory of the Buddha. Another legend records that, as a sign of his devotion to Buddhism, Ashoka paid for the construction of 84,000 stupas, none of which survive, and later Buddhist rulers often emulated his chakravartin example by building monuments to express their devotion to Buddhism.

Ashoka's style of governing was very personal. One inscription describes how seriously he took the business of ruling and explains that his officials were free to interrupt him with public business no matter what he was doing. *"And whatever I may order by word of mouth, whether it concerns a donation or a proclamation, or whatever urgent matter is entrusted to my officers, if there is any dispute or deliberation about it in the Council, it is to be reported to me immediately, at all places and all times."* This inscription tells us that some officers could speak directly to the king and that there was a council, but not how it functioned. Another inscription proclaims the breadth of Ashoka's influence:

> *The Beloved of the Gods considers victory by dharma to be the foremost victory. And moreover the Beloved of the Gods has gained this victory on all his frontiers to a distance of six hundred yojanas [about 1,500 miles, or 2400 km], where reigns the Greek king Antiochus [in Syria], and beyond the realm of that Antiochus in the lands of four kings named Ptolemy [in Egypt], Antigonus [in Macedonia], Magas [of Cyrene], and Alexander [of Epirus]; and in the south over the Colas and the Pandyas as far as Ceylon.**

This inscription, composed between 256 and 254 B.C.E., claims that Ashoka had brought about "victory by dharma" far beyond his frontiers, as far west as the realms of Greek rulers in Egypt and Greece, and as far south as the island of Ceylon, modern Sri Lanka. Modern scholars concur that he may have sent missionaries, particularly to Sri Lanka, where oral accounts record their names.

We must keep in mind that Ashoka wrote his inscriptions and had them carved into huge, dramatic monuments to remind his subjects that he had the right to rule over them. The only external confirmation of their veracity comes from later Buddhist sources, which mention Ashoka's devotion to Buddhism. If Ashoka had violated his Buddhist vows, or if a certain region had risen up in rebellion during his reign, we can be sure that the inscriptions would not mention it. One recent analysis suggests that the inscriptions not be seen *"as solid blocks of historical fact, but as flightier pieces of political propaganda, as the campaign speeches of an incumbent politician who seeks not so much to record events as to present an image of himself and his administration to the world."*[4]

After Ashoka's death in 232 B.C.E., the Mauryan empire began to break apart; the Mauryans lost control of the last remaining section, the Ganges Valley, around 185 B.C.E. A series of regional kingdoms gained control, as was the usual pattern for much of South Asian history.

---

*Excerpt from *Aśoka and the Decline of the Mauryas*, ed. Romila Thapar, 1973, pp. 253, 256. Reprinted with permission of Oxford University Press India, New Delhi.

The First Sermon of the Buddha and Ashoka's Fourth Major Rock Edict

After gaining enlightenment under the Tree of Wisdom at Bodh Gaya, the Buddha preached his first sermon at the Deer Park at Benares. The Buddha's sermon presented the main teachings of Buddhism in a capsule form that could be translated into other languages when Buddhism spread beyond India to East and Southeast Asia. Because the language is easy to understand, this would have worked well as a spoken sermon, with repetition of important concepts to ensure the comprehension of his five followers, or bhikkhus (BEAK-kooz), whom he addressed. This text was transmitted orally by Buddhists in north India. Hundreds of monks met, first following the Buddha's death and then one hundred years later, to make sure that they were reciting the standard version of the sermon. The text was committed to writing only in the first century B.C.E. by monks in modern-day Sri Lanka, evidence that Buddhism had spread to south India and beyond by that time.

The Fourth Major Rock Edict provides a summary of Ashoka's beliefs. Some overlap with the Buddha's teachings in the First Sermon, while others differ. Although Ashoka himself embraced Buddhism, he reached out to both Buddhist and non-Buddhist subjects by erecting pillar and rock inscriptions throughout India. The location of his edicts provides a rough indication of how far Buddhist teachings reached during his reign.

Sources: From "The First Sermon of Buddha," from Walpola Rahula, *What the Buddha Taught*, Grove Atlantic, 1974, pp. 92–94. Copyright © 1959, 1974 by Wapola Rahula. Used by permission of Grove/Atlantic, Inc.; *Aśoka and the Decline of the Mauryas*, ed. Romila Thapar, 1973, pp. 251–252. Reprinted with permission of Oxford University Press India, New Delhi. (Some changes in spelling and capitalization made for the sake of consistency.)

The First Sermon of the Buddha

Thus I have heard. The Blessed One was once living in the Deer Park at Isipatana (the Resort of Seers) near Varanasi (Benares). There he addressed the group of five bhikkhus:

Bhikkhus, these two extremes ought not to be practiced by one who has gone forth from the household life. What are the two? There is devotion to the indulgence of sense-pleasures, which is low, common, the way of ordinary people, unworthy and unprofitable; and there is devotion to self-mortification, which is painful, unworthy and unprofitable.

Avoiding both these extremes, the Tathagatha [the Buddha] has realized the Middle Path: it gives vision, it gives knowledge, and it leads to calm, to insight, to enlightenment, to nirvana. And what is that Middle Path . . . ? It is simply the Noble Eightfold Path, namely, right view, right thought, right speech, right action, right livelihood, right effort, right mindfulness, right concentration. . . .

The Noble Truth of suffering (*dukkha*) is this: Birth is suffering; aging is suffering; sickness is suffering; death is suffering; sorrow and lamentation, pain, grief and despair are suffering; association with the unpleasant is suffering; dissociation from the pleasant is suffering; not to get what one wants is suffering—in brief, the five aggregates of attachment are suffering.

The Noble Truth of the origin of suffering is this: It is this thirst (craving) which produces re-existence and re-becoming, bound up with passionate greed. It finds fresh delight now here and now there, namely, thirst for sense-pleasures; thirst for existence and becoming; and thirst for non-existence (self-annihilation).

The Noble Truth of the cessation of suffering is this: It is the complete cessation of that very thirst, giving it up, renouncing it, emancipating oneself from it, detaching oneself from it.

The Noble Truth of the path leading to the cessation of suffering is this: It is simply the Noble Eightfold Path, namely right view; right thought; right speech; right action; right livelihood; right effort; right mindfulness; right concentration.

"This is the Noble Truth of Suffering (*dukkha*)"; such was the vision, the knowledge, the wisdom, the science, the light, that arose in me with regard to things not heard before. "This suffering, as a noble truth, should be fully understood"; such was the vision, the knowledge, the wisdom, the science, the light, that arose in me with regard to things not heard before. "This suffering, as a noble truth, has been fully understood"; such was the vision, the knowledge, the wisdom, the science, the light, that arose in me with regard to things not heard before. . . .

As long as my vision of true knowledge was not fully clear . . . regarding the Four Noble Truths, I did not claim to have realized the perfect Enlightenment that is supreme in the world. . . . But when my vision of true knowledge was fully clear . . . regarding the Four Noble Truths, then I claimed to have the perfect Enlightenment that is supreme in the world. . . . And a vision of true knowledge arose in me thus: My heart's deliverance is unassailable. This is the last birth. Now there is no more re-becoming (rebirth).

This the Blessed One said. The group of five bhikkhus was glad, and they rejoiced at his words.

The Fourth Major Rock Edict

In the past, the killing and injuring of living beings, lack of respect towards relatives, Brahmins and shramanas had increased. But today, thanks to the practice of dharma on the part of the Beloved of the Gods, the king Ashoka, the sound of the drum has become the sound of dharma, showing the people displays of heavenly chariots, elephants, balls of fire, and other divine forms. Through his instruction in dharma abstention from killing and non-injury to living beings, deference to relatives, Brahmins and shramanas, obedience to mother and father, and obedience to elders have all increased as never before for many centuries. These and many other forms of the practice of dharma have increased and will increase.

The Beloved of the Gods, the king Ashoka, his sons, his grandsons and his great grandsons will advance the practice of dharma, until the end of the world and will instruct in the law, standing firm in dharma. For this, the instruction in the law, is the most valuable activity. But there is no practice of dharma without goodness, and in these matters it is good to progress and not to fall back. For this purpose, the inscription has been engraved—that men should make progress in this matter, and not be satisfied with their shortcomings. This was engraved here when the Beloved of the Gods, the king Ashoka, had been consecrated twelve years.

QUESTIONS FOR ANALYSIS

» *What are the Four Noble Truths taught by the Buddha, and what is the relationship among them?*

» *What are the signs that the First Sermon was transmitted orally?*

» *Which Buddhist teachings did Ashoka think most important? What did he mean by dharma?*

In the second century B.C.E. a local chieftain unified the island of Sri Lanka for the first time. After being named king, he followed Ashoka's example and built a giant stupa like that at Sanchi as a monument to the Buddha. Also in the second century B.C.E., another patron of Buddhism, a ruler of Greek descent, unified a large territory in Afghanistan and Pakistan whose eastern edge included the former Mauryan capital at Pataliputra. These two rulers' patronage of Buddhism marked the first time Buddhism spread beyond the immediate territory of India.

South Asia's External Trade

India's geographic proximity to western Asia meant that outsiders came to South Asia in very early times, and conversely, Indian culture, particularly Buddhist teachings, traveled out from India on the same paths. In ancient times travelers seeking to enter South Asia had a choice of routes. Although the Himalaya Mountains in the north and extensive mountains in the northeast prevented large-scale overland trade, regular cultural contacts and the movement of valuable goods always continued. Land routes through the Hindu Kush (HIHN-doo KOOSH) in the northwest, including the Khyber (KAI-ber) Pass, allowed contacts between South Asia and Central Asia through what is today Afghanistan. These are the routes that allowed the expansion of Indo-European languages and that Megasthenes used when he came to India.

However, the most important mode of communication between South Asia and the rest of the world was by sea. By 100 C.E., if not earlier, mariners from South and Southeast Asia had learned to capture the monsoon winds blowing northeast in the spring and early summer, and southwest in the fall and winter, to carry on regular commerce and cultural interaction with Southwest Asia and Africa. If one caught the winds going west on a summer departure, one could return in the following winter as they blew east.

Finds of Harappan artifacts in the archaeological assemblages of early Sumer testify to the importance and age of these ancient sea routes across the Indian Ocean, connecting India with Mesopotamia, the Arabian Peninsula, and East Africa (see Map 3.1 on page 59). Merchants traveling the Indian Ocean usually sailed in small boats called **dhows** (DOWZ). With their teak planks held together by coconut fiber twine and tightly caulked, dhows had greater flexibility during storms than boats made from nailed wooden planks.

dhows
Small sailboats used in the Indian Ocean made from teak planks laid edge to edge, fastened together with coconut fiber twine, and caulked to prevent leaking.

Because no written descriptions of the ancient trade exist, archaeologists must reconstruct the trade on the basis of excavated commodities. Natural reserves of the semiprecious blue stone lapis lazuli exist only in the Badakhshan (BAH-duck-shan) region of northern Afghanistan, so we know that by 2600 B.C.E., if not earlier, trade routes linked Badakhshan with ancient Sumer, where much lapis lazuli has been found. Similarly, the red-orange semiprecious stone carnelian traveled from mines in Gujarat (GOO-juh-ruht), India, to Mesopotamian sites. The presence of Harappan seals and clay pots at Sumer reveals that the trade included manufactured goods as well as minerals. These goods traveled overland or by boat down the Indus River to the Arabian Sea, where they hugged the coast as they traveled west to the Persian Gulf. Ancient sea routes across the Indian Ocean connected India with Mesopotamia, the Arabian peninsula, and East Africa.

We learn much about the Indian Ocean trade during the first century C.E. from an unusual work called the *Periplus* (PAY-rih-plus) (literally "around the globe"), written in colloquial Greek not by a scholar but by an anonymous merchant living in Egypt around 50 C.E. The *Periplus* describes the routes sailors took from Egypt and the goods they traded at Indian ports.

Written explicitly for merchants, the *Periplus* is organized as a guidebook: port by port, down the East African coast, around the Arabian peninsula, and then to India. One-quarter of the book describes the trade with East Africa, one-quarter with Arabia, and one-half with India, the most important trading destination. In African and Arabian ports sailors could purchase ivory or gum resins like frankincense and myrrh, which were prized for their fragrance, but India offered far more goods than either Arabia or Africa. The author says almost nothing about social structure and little about government, other than the names of local rulers; he is much more interested in which commodities were for sale.

Analyzed carefully, however, the descriptions in the *Periplus* have much to tell us. For example, it summarizes the import trade on India's southwestern Malabar (MAH-lah-bar) coast. At the markets one could buy a yellow gem called peridot (PAY-ree-doh), clothing and textiles, coral, raw glass, copper, tin, lead, and wine. The author instructs his readers to bring money, and lots of it, to the southwestern coast because there were few opportunities for barter. Thousands of Roman silver and gold coins have been found on the south coast but not farther north, suggesting that the traders could barter in the north but had to pay Roman coins in the south (see Chapter 7). The author continues his discussion of the southwest coast by explaining the goods the region exported. Most of the items on the list, like pepper, pearls, ivory, and precious stones, are valuable even today.

Aimed at non-Indian readers, the *Periplus* gives the misleading impression that the Indian Ocean trade was controlled by foreigners, possibly because its author was a Greek living in Egypt who used Roman coins to purchase Indian goods. In fact, though, Indian merchants played an active role in the Indian Ocean trade.

At the end of the *Periplus*, the author describes one final destination:

Beyond this region, by now at the northernmost point, where the sea ends somewhere on the outer fringe, there is a very great inland city called Thina from which silk floss, yarn, and cloth are shipped by land . . . and via the Ganga River. . . . It is not easy to get to this Thina; for rarely do people come from it, and only a few.[5]

Thina? The spelling makes sense when one realizes that ancient Greek had no letter for the sound "ch," so the author had to choose either a "th" or an "s" for the first letter of the place whose name he heard from Indian traders. He opted for Thina. *China* was pronounced "CHEE-na" in Sanskrit (and is the source of our English word *China*).

The author thought Thina was a city, not a country, but he knew that silk was made there and exported. The *Periplus* closes with the admission that China lay at the extreme edge of the world known to the Greeks: *"What lies beyond this area, because of extremes of storm, bitter cold, and difficult terrain and also because of some divine power of the gods, has not been explored."* The India described in the *Periplus*, then, was a major trade center linking the familiar Roman empire with the dimly understood China.

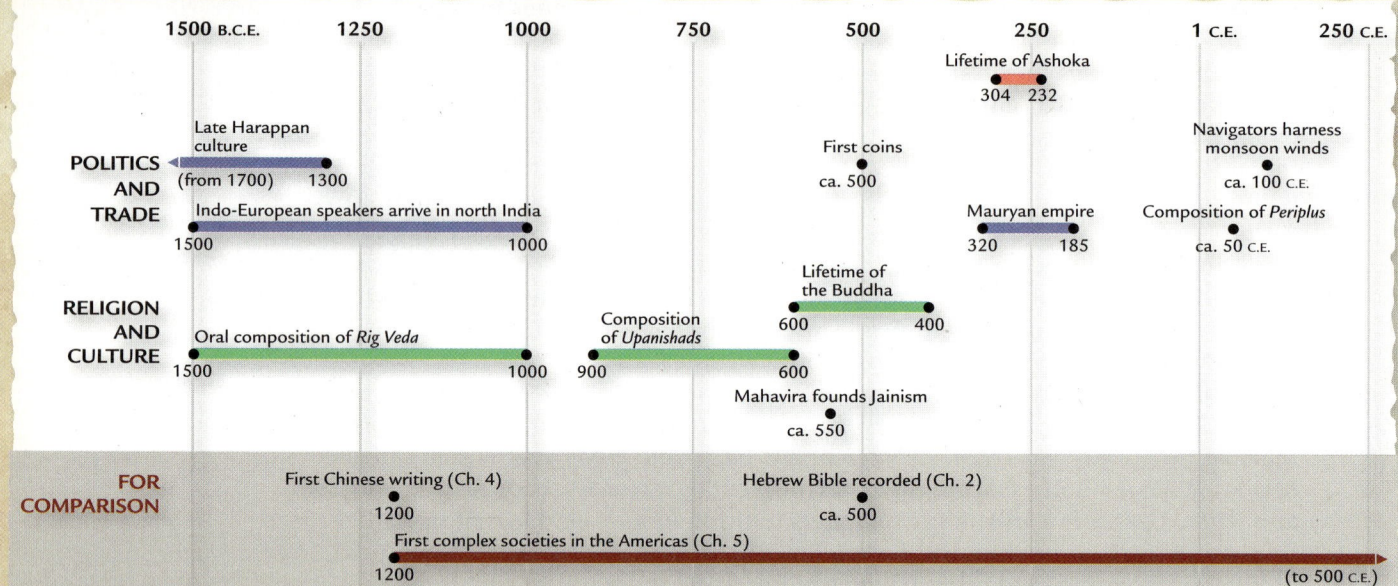

The Significance of Ancient India in World History

Ashoka's decision to patronize Buddhism in 260 B.C.E. marked a key juncture in world history: after Buddhism became the state religion of the Mauryan dynasty, it spread throughout the Ganges, northern Indus, and Godavari River Valleys. A century later, as kings in Sri Lanka and Afghanistan emulated Ashoka's example as a chakravartin ruler, Buddhism extended even farther. Eventually it would become a major world religion with adherents in South, Southeast, and East Asia (see Chapter 8).

The residents of the Indian subcontinent adopted agriculture between 6500 and 5000 B.C.E. Like the inhabitants of Mesopotamia (see Chapter 2), the people of the Indus River Valley's complex society did not have a single ruler but multiple rulers in different cities. The ruins of these ancient cities had distinct neighborhoods for people of varying occupations and social levels, but because the Indus River Valley script has not been deciphered, we do not know how the residents conceived of these different social groupings. Most distinctive, the sophisticated water system of their largest settlement at Mohenjo-daro provided clean water for drinking and bathing as well as sewage facilities for all residents, regardless of social level.

The introduction of Sanskrit by Indo-Aryan migrants between 1500 and 1000 B.C.E. brings Indian ideas about social rank into clearer focus. The hymns of the *Rig Veda* explain the system of four ranked varna for different occupations. Local kings ruled by patronizing Brahmin priests who performed complex rituals on their behalf, a hallmark of complex societies whose members believed that their rulers were entitled to the surplus they produced.

In a ceremonial state, the king patronized priests in the hope that his subjects would support his rule because of his ties to religious specialists. Ashoka's exercise of chakravartin rule made the Mauryans a full-fledged ceremonial state. Both Egypt and ancient Mesopotamia also had elements of ceremonial states: the pharaoh was thought to be a god-king whose rituals ensured the well-being of his kingdom, and the rulers of ancient Sumer made regular offerings to the temples in their city-states.

The Greek ambassador Megasthenes reported that the kingdom had three types of territory: that ruled directly by the Mauryan king, that governed by local rulers with reduced powers who acknowledged the sovereignty of the Mauryan king, and local republics. Even under Ashoka, one of ancient India's most

80

powerful rulers, India was not politically united, but its different regions maintained shared cultural traditions. This pattern held for many periods in South Asian history.

Although surrounded by water on two sides and bounded by mountains to the north, ancient India had extensive contacts with its neighbors. Trade of carnelian, lapis lazuli, and shells with Mesopotamia dated back to at least 2500 B.C.E. Sometime before the year 100 C.E., the understanding of the monsoon winds made it possible for ships to sail to India from Egypt and to sail west of India to China. In China, as the next chapter will show, only a few decades after Ashoka put up his stone pillars, a different ruler erected stones carved with texts asserting his virtue, but he exercised far greater control over his subjects than did Ashoka.

VOYAGES ON THE WEB: Ashoka

The Voyages Map App follows the traveler's journeys using interactive study tools, including 360-degree panoramic views of historic sites, zoomable maps, audio summaries, flash cards, and quizzes.

KEY TERMS

Ashoka (56)
dharma (58)
monsoon (59)
Indus River Valley (59)
Sanskrit (61)
Rig Veda (62)
Vedic religion (63)

nomads (63)
varna (64)
jati (64)
karma (65)
Jainism (66)
Buddha (66)
nirvana (67)

Mauryan dynasty (68)
chakravartin (74)
ceremonial state (74)
lay Buddhist (74)
dhows (78)

FOR FURTHER REFERENCE

Basham, A. L. *The Wonder That Was India: Survey of the Culture of the Indian Sub-continent Before the Coming of the Muslims.* New York: Grove Press, 1959.

Casson, Lionel. *The Periplus Maris Erythraei Text with Introduction, Translation, and Commentary.* Princeton: Princeton University Press, 1989.

Davis, Richard. *Global India Circa 100 CE: South Asia in Early World History.* Ann Arbor: Association for Asian Studies, Inc., 2009.

Elder, Joe. "India's Caste System." *Education About Asia* 1, no. 2 (1996): 20–22.

Fussman, Gerard. "Central and Provincial Administration in Ancient India: The Problem of the Mauryan Empire." *Indian Historical Review* 14 (1987–1988): 43–72.

Kenoyer, Mark. *Ancient Cities of the Indus Valley Civilization.* Karachi, Pakistan: Oxford University Press, 1998.

Liu, Xinru. *Ancient India and Ancient China: Trade and Religious Exchanges, A.D. 1–600.* Delhi: Oxford University Press, 1988.

O'Flaherty, Wendy Doniger. *The Rig Veda: An Anthology.* New York: Penguin Books, 1981.

Pearson, Michael. *Eyes Across the Water: Navigating the Indian Ocean.* Pretoria, South Africa: Unisa Press, 2010.

Thapar, Romila. *Aśoka and the Decline of the Mauryas.* Delhi: Oxford University Press, 1973.

Thapar, Romila. *Early India: From the Origins to AD 1300.* Berkeley: University of California Press, 2003.

FILMS

The Little Buddha.

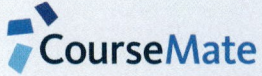 CourseMate Go to the CourseMate website at **www.cengagebrain.com** for additional study tools and review materials—including audio and video clips—for this chapter.

4

Blueprint for Empire: China, 1200 B.C.E.–220 C.E.

In 221 B.C.E., the **First Emperor of the Qin dynasty** (259–210 B.C.E.) united China for the first time and implemented a blueprint for empire that helped to keep China together for much of the following two thousand years. The future emperor, named Zheng (JUHNG), was born in the Qin (CHIN) territory in the town of Xianyang (SHYEN-yahng) in Shaanxi (SHAHN-shee) province, western China. Prince Zheng's father, one of more than twenty sons of a regional ruler in west China, lived as a hostage in a city 360 miles (580 km) to the east because it was customary for younger sons to be sent to the courts of allied rulers. Two years after Zheng's birth, during an attack on this city, his father escaped home, and his mother and the young prince went into hiding. Six years later they returned to Xianyang, and in 246 B.C.E., on the death of his father, Prince Zheng ascended to the Qin throne at the age of thirteen. For the first nine years he governed with the help of adult advisers until he became ruler in his own right at the age of twenty-two.

During his reign he went on five different expeditions. At the top of each mountain he climbed, he erected a stone tablet describing his many accomplishments and asserting widespread support for his dynasty. Unlike Ashoka's pillar and stone inscriptions, the Qin tablets were placed on remote mountaintops where the intended audience of ancestors could view them. One of these tablets read as follows:

First Emperor of the Qin Dynasty
(British Library, London/HIP/Art Resource, NY)

*I*n His twenty-sixth year [221 B.C.E.]
He first unified All under Heaven—
There was none who was not respectful and submissive.
He personally tours the distant multitudes,
Ascends this Grand Mountain

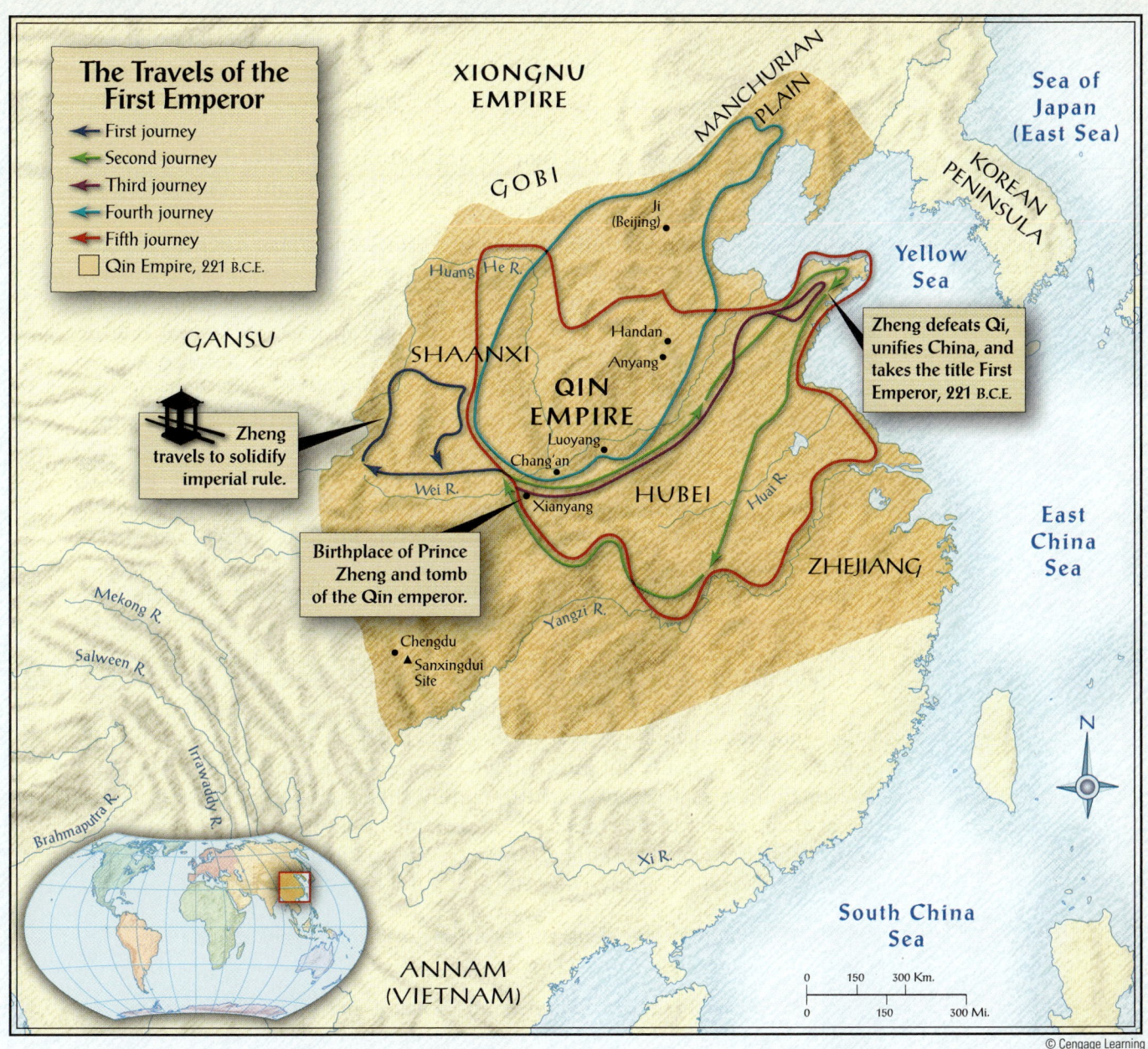

The Travels of the First Emperor

- ← First journey
- ← Second journey
- ← Third journey
- ← Fourth journey
- ← Fifth journey
- ☐ Qin Empire, 221 B.C.E.

XIONGNU EMPIRE

GOBI

MANCHURIAN PLAIN

Sea of Japan (East Sea)

KOREAN PENINSULA

Ji (Beijing)

Huang He R.

GANSU

SHAANXI

Handan

Anyang

QIN EMPIRE

Luoyang

Chang'an

Xianyang

Wei R.

HUBEI

Huai R.

Yellow Sea

Zheng defeats Qi, unifies China, and takes the title First Emperor, 221 B.C.E.

East China Sea

Zheng travels to solidify imperial rule.

Birthplace of Prince Zheng and tomb of the Qin emperor.

ZHEJIANG

Yangzi R.

Mekong R.

Salween R.

Irrawaddy R.

Brahmaputra R.

Chengdu

▲ Sanxingdui Site

Xi R.

South China Sea

ANNAM (VIETNAM)

N

| 0 | 150 | 300 Km. |
| 0 | 150 | 300 Mi. |

© Cengage Learning

Join this chapter's traveler on "Voyages," an interactive tour of historic sites and events:
www.cengagebrain.com

And all round surveys the world at the eastern extremity. . . .
May later ages respect and follow the decrees He bequeaths
And forever accept His solemn warnings.

*Excerpt from Martin Kern, *The Stele Inscriptions of Ch'in Shih-huang: Texts and Ritual in Early Chinese Imperial Representation*
(New Haven: American Oriental Society, 2000), pp. 18–23. Reprinted with permission of the American Oriental Society,
http://www.umich.edu/~aos/.

First Emperor of the Qin dynasty Founder of the Qin dynasty (221–207 B.C.E.) and the first ruler to unify ancient China. Eliminated regional differences by creating a single body of law and standardizing weights and measures.

The new emperor traveled overland in a sedan-chair carried by his servants and along rivers by boat. By the time he finished his last journey, he had crisscrossed much of the territory north of the Yangzi (YAHNG-zuh) River in modern-day China.

His unusual childhood must have affected Prince Zheng, but surviving sources convey little about his personality except to document his single-minded ambition. After taking the throne, he led the Qin armies on a series of brilliant military campaigns. They fought with the same weapons as their enemies—crossbows, bronze armor, shields, and daggers—but the Qin army was a meritocracy. A skilled soldier, no matter how low-ranking his parents, could rise to become a general, while the son of a noble family, if not a good fighter, would remain a common foot soldier for life.

The Qin was the first dynasty to vanquish all of its rivals, including six independent kingdoms, and unite China under a single person's rule. The First Emperor eliminated regional differences by creating a single body of law for all his subjects, standardizing all weights and measures, and even mandating a single axle width for the ox- and horse-drawn carts. He coined a new title, *First Emperor* (*Shi Huangdi*), because he felt that the word *king* did not accurately convey his august position. The First Emperor intentionally stayed remote from his subjects so that they would respect and obey him.

On his deathbed, the First Emperor urged that his descendants rule forever, or "ten thousand years" in Chinese phrasing. Instead, peasant uprisings brought his dynasty to an end in three years. The succeeding dynasty, the Han dynasty, denounced Qin brutality but used Qin governance to rule for four centuries. Subsequent Chinese rulers who aspired to reunify the empire always looked to the Han as their model. Unlike India, which remained politically disunited for most of its history (see Chapter 3), the Chinese empire endured for over two thousand years. Whenever it fell apart, a new emperor put it back together.

Focus Questions

» *What different elements of Chinese civilization took shape between 1200 and 221 B.C.E.?*

» *What were the most important measures in the Qin blueprint for empire?*

» *How did the Han rulers modify the Qin blueprint, particularly regarding administrative structure and the recruitment and promotion of officials?*

» *Which neighboring peoples in Central, East, and Southeast Asia did the Han dynasty conquer? Why was the impact of Chinese rule limited?*

The Origins of Chinese Civilization, 1200–221 B.C.E.

Agriculture developed independently in several different regions in China circa 7000 B.C.E. In each region, as elsewhere in the world, people began to harvest seeds occasionally before progressing to full-time agriculture. By 1200 B.C.E., several independent cultural centers had emerged. One, the Shang (SHAHNG) kingdom based in the Yellow River (Huang He) Valley, developed the Chinese writing system. Many elements of Chinese civilization—the writing system, the worship of ancestors, and the Confucian and Daoist systems of belief—developed in the years before China was united in 221 B.C.E.

Early Agriculture, Technology, and Cuisine to 1200 B.C.E.

North China was particularly suited for early agriculture because a layer of fine yellow dirt, called loess (LESS), covers the entire Yellow River Valley, and few trees grow there. The river carries large quantities of loess from the west and deposits new layers each year in the last 500 miles (900 km) before the Pacific Ocean. As a result, the riverbed is constantly rising, often to a level higher than the surrounding fields. Sometimes called "China's River of Sorrow," the Yellow River has been dangerously flood-prone throughout recorded history.

Three major climatic zones extend east and west across China (see the map on page 83). Less than 20 inches (50 cm) of rain falls each year on the region north of the Huai (HWHY) River; about 40 inches (1 m) per year drops on the middle band along the Yangzi River; and over 80 inches (2 m) a year pours on the southernmost band of China and Hong Kong. This differential pattern of rainfall is due to the monsoon winds off the ocean: the water-laden winds first cross south China, where they drop much of their water; by the time they reach the north, they are carrying much less water. The climate of the Yellow River was probably hotter and wetter than it is today. Elephants and rhinoceros both lived there as late as 1000 B.C.E.

Sometime around 8000 B.C.E., the residents of north China began to deliberately cultivate millet, a domesticated grass with seeds that can be made into gruel, baked as bread, or cooked as noodles. Wheat and millet cultivation extended as far north as Manchuria and as far south as Zhejiang (JEH-jeeahng), near the mouth of China's other great river, the Yangzi, where in 7000 B.C.E. the first rice was planted. As in Mesopotamia, Egypt, and India, some communities turned to full-time agriculture while others continued to forage for food (see Chapters 2 and 3).

The different implements found in various regions suggest great cultural diversity within China between 7000 and 2000 B.C.E. Around 4500 B.C.E., those living in the Yangzi River delta raised silkworms and spun silk. Around 3000 B.C.E., craftsmen in the same region sanded chunks of jade to make exquisite jade tubes. On the Shandong peninsula, far to the west, two early urban centers emerged around 2500 B.C.E., with three layers of smaller settlements around them, suggesting an interlocking city system.

These different peoples started out as small, egalitarian tribal groups who farmed intermittently. They evolved to larger settled groups with clearly demarcated social levels living in large urban settlements, demonstrating all the elements of complex society described in Chapter 2.

Like the Mesopotamians, the early Chinese lived inside walled cities. Starting around 2000 B.C.E., they made machetes, shovels, and plow-blades from bronze. Ancient Chinese bronze casters mastered the exacting technology of mixing copper, tin, and lead in differing ratios to cast harder and softer bronze objects: daggers had to be hard, while mirrors could only be polished sufficiently to see one's reflection if they were soft.

The early Chinese conducted frequent rituals in which they made offerings of food and drink. Whether for ritual offerings or daily use, they used two types of vessels for foodstuffs: flat bronze vessels for grain (usually wheat or millet) and baskets and wooden and pottery vessels for meat and vegetables. This division of foods between starch and dishes made from cut-up meat and vegetables continues among Chinese chefs to the present day, an example of a characteristic cultural practice that originated in this early time. Combining component parts in various ways to produce a slightly different product each time, the chef tosses precut meat and vegetables into a wok, stir-fries them, and uses an array of sauces to make a large number of dishes, each with a different name and recognizable taste.

Shang dynasty cooks used many of the same tools as today's cooks—knives, stirring utensils, and bronze cooking pots. However, rather than stir-frying, they steamed and braised food. Those who presided over Shang rituals used chopsticks, one of the hallmarks of East Asian culture, to move food from large serving vessels to smaller plates. People then ate the food with their hands. Ordinary diners began to use chopsticks as eating utensils sometime around 200 B.C.E., the time of the first stir-fried food.

Shang dynasty
China's first historic dynasty. The earliest surviving records date to 1200 B.C.E., during the Shang. The Shang king ruled a small area in the vicinity of modern Anyang, in Henan province, and granted lands to allies in noble families.

oracle bones
The earliest surviving written records in China, scratched onto cattle shoulder blades and turtle shell bottoms, or plastrons, to record the diviners' interpretations of the future.

Early Chinese Writing in the Shang Dynasty, ca. 1200 B.C.E.

As modern Chinese cuisine has an ancient history, so too do Chinese characters, which constitute the world's writing system with the longest history of continuous use. When did the Chinese first speak Chinese? Archaeologists cannot be certain, because the only certain evidence about ancient language is the presence of writing. The first recognizable Chinese characters appeared on bones dating to around 1200 B.C.E. (Some pots dating to circa 2000 B.C.E. are illustrated with different pictures, but these were probably potters' marks and not written characters.) The bones came from near the modern city of Anyang (AHN-yahng) in the central Chinese province of Henan (HUH-nahn), the core region of China's first historic dynasty, the **Shang dynasty** (1766–1045 B.C.E.). The discovery and deciphering of these bones, first found in 1899, mark one of the great intellectual breakthroughs in twentieth-century China.

Many ancient peoples around the world used oracles to consult higher powers, and scholars call the excavated bones "**oracle bones**" because the Shang ruler used them to forecast the future. To do so the Shang placed a heated poker on cattle shoulder blades and turtle shell bottoms, or plastrons, and interpreted the resulting cracks. They then recorded on the bone the name of the ancestor they had consulted, the topic of inquiry, and the outcome. It was an extremely difficult feat, and we still do not know how the ancient Chinese incised characters on these bones with the bronze tools available to them.

Since 1900 more than 200,000 oracle bones, both whole and fragmented, have been excavated in China. The quantities are immense—1,300 oracle bones concern

The Earliest Records of Chinese Writing Starting around 1200 B.C.E., ancient Chinese kings used the clavicle bones of cattle (as shown here) and the bottom of turtle shells to ask their ancestors to advise them on the outcomes of future events, including battles, sacrifices, their wives' pregnancies, and even their own toothaches. After applying heat, the fortune-tellers interpreted the resulting cracks and wrote their predictions—in the most ancient form of Chinese characters—directly on the bones and turtle shells. (Lowell Georgia/Corbis)

Inputting Chinese Characters

Before the advent of computers, many reformers called for the abolition of Chinese characters and their replacement with an alphabet. A major problem was typesetting: a Chinese newspaper font had over seven thousand different characters, and typing them was slow and costly. In many cases the typist had to spend valuable time searching through drawers of type for a rare character.

Computers have made it much easier to type Chinese. Most people input Chinese characters by pronunciation. Since a single pronunciation can refer to a number of different words (characters), typing the pronunciation of one character can generate as many as a hundred choices: you then choose the character you need from an on-screen selection that offers the most frequently used characters first with unusual characters later. Since the computer remembers the characters you frequently use, the longer you work on a given computer, the faster you can type. The latest computers and smartphones also recognize handwriting so that you can copy an unknown character on a keypad and the computer will identify the character.

But the fastest way to input, used by professional typists, is to use the shape of the character, not the sound. One popular system organizes characters by stroke: all characters that start with a given stroke form a group, and the typist chooses the correct character. Today, the most skilled Chinese typists can input at a rate of over one hundred characters per minute, about the same as for English.

Most helpful to scholars of ancient Chinese characters are online dictionaries of ancient Chinese characters that allow you to look up a single character and see all the different ways it was written in the past. Take the character wang 王, for example, which means "king" and appears in the photograph of the oracle bone. In this case the oracle bone character looks just like the modern character, which has three parallel horizontal lines bisected by a vertical stroke, but the "Chinese Etymology" website developed by Richard Sears, a nonlinguist based in Tennessee, documents over four hundred variants of the character used in the past three thousand years.

Source: http://www.chineseetymology.org.

---

rainfall in a single king's reign. Their language is grammatically complex, suggesting that the Shang scribes had been writing for some time, possibly on perishable materials like wood. Shang dynasty characters, like their modern equivalents, have two elements: a radical, which suggests the broad field of meaning, and a phonetic symbol, which indicates sound. Like Arabic numerals, Chinese characters retain the same meaning even if pronounced differently: 3 means the number "three" even if some readers say "trois" or "drei." (See the feature "World History in Today's World: Inputting Chinese Characters.")

During the Shang dynasty only the king and his scribes could read and write characters. Presenting the world from the king's vantage point, some oracle bones treat affairs of state, like the outcomes of battles, but many more touch on individual matters, such as his wife's pregnancy or his own aching teeth. The major religion of the time was **ancestor worship**. The Shang kings believed that their recently dead ancestors could intercede with the more powerful long-dead on behalf of the living.

ancestor worship
The belief in China that dead ancestors could intercede in human affairs on behalf of the living. Marked by frequent rituals in which the living offered food and drink to the ancestors in the hope of receiving help.

Shang Dynasty Relations with Other Peoples

Historians of China have ingeniously combined the information in oracle bones with careful analysis of Shang archaeological sites to piece together how Shang government and society functioned between 1200 and 1000 B.C.E. Before the bones were studied, the main source for early Chinese history was a book entitled *Records of the Grand Historian*, written in the first century B.C.E. by **Sima Qian** (SUH-mah CHEE-EN)

Sima Qian
The author of *Records of the Grand Historian*, a history of China from ancient legendary times to the first century B.C.E.

(145–ca. 90 B.C.E.). Combining information drawn from several extant chronicles, Sima Qian wrote a history of China from its legendary founding sage emperors through to his lifetime. He gave the founding date of the Shang dynasty as 1766 B.C.E. and listed the names of the Shang kings but provided little detail about them. Setting a pattern for all future historians, Sima Qian believed that there could be only one legitimate ruler of China at any time and omitted any discussion of regional rulers who coexisted with the Shang and other dynasties.

In fact, though, the Shang exercised direct control over a relatively small area, some 125 miles (200 km) from east to west, and the Shang king sometimes traveled as far as 400 miles (650 km) away to fight enemy peoples. Beyond the small area under direct Shang control lived many different non-Shang peoples whose names appear on the oracle bones but about whom little is known. Shang kings did not have a fixed capital but simply moved camp from one place to another to conduct military campaigns against these other peoples.

Early Chinese Bronzeworking The ancient Chinese combined copper, tin, and lead to make intricate bronze vessels like this wine container, which dates to circa 1050 B.C.E. and was found buried in the hills of Hunan (HOO-nan), in southern China. Analysts are not sure of the relationship between the tiger-like beast and the man it embraces. The man's serene face suggests that the beast is communicating some kind of teaching—not devouring him. (Musée Cernuschi, Paris/Scala/Art Resource, NY)

Many oracle bones describe battles between the Shang and their enemies. When the Shang defeated an enemy, they took thousands of captives. The fortunate worked as laborers, and the less fortunate were killed as an offering. One oracle bone asks the ancestors' opinion about the number of human sacrifices necessary—ten? twenty? thirty?—and gives the name of the conquered people.

Shang subjects interred their kings in large tombs with hundreds of sacrificed corpses. Even in death they observed a hierarchy. Placed near the Shang king were those who accompanied him in death, with their own entourages of corpses and lavish grave goods. Royal guards were also buried intact, but the lowest-ranking corpses, most likely prisoners of war, had their heads and limbs severed.

The Shang were but one of many peoples living in China around 1200 B.C.E. Yet since only the Shang left written records, we know much less about the other peoples. Fortunately an extraordinary archaeological find at the Sanxingdui (SAHN-shing-dway) site near Chengdu (CHUHNG-dew), in Sichuan (SUH-chwan) province, offers a glimpse of one of the peoples contemporary with the Shang. Inside the ancient city walls, archaeologists found two grave pits filled with bronze statues, bronze masks, and elephant tusks that had been burnt and cut into sections. Like the Shang, the people at the Sanxingdui site lived in small walled settlements.

The people of Sanxingdui also made bronze masks more than a yard across with huge protruding eyes, whose significance no one can explain satisfactorily. Whereas the Shang made no human statues, the bronze metallurgists at Sanxingdui did. Unlike the Shang, the people at Sanxingdui do not seem to have practiced human sacrifice, nor do they appear to have had a writing system, although some archaeologists hope in the future to find samples of their writing.

The Zhou Dynasty, 1045–256 B.C.E.

The oracle bones are most plentiful during the period from 1200 to 1000 B.C.E. and diminish in quantity soon after 1000 B.C.E. In 1045 B.C.E. a new dynasty, the **Zhou dynasty**, overthrew the Shang. The Grand Historian Sima Qian wrote the earliest detailed account of the Zhou (JOE) conquest, long after the fact, in the first century B.C.E. Claiming that 48,000 Zhou troops were able to defeat 700,000 Shang troops because the Shang ruler was corrupt and decadent, Sima Qian alleged that the last Shang ruler killed his enemies and roasted them on a rack or cut them into mincemeat before eating them. Historians question his account because of his clear bias against the Shang.

Sima Qian's description set a pattern followed by all subsequent historians: vilifying the last emperor of a fallen dynasty and glorifying the founder of the next. According to Sima Qian, the Zhou king was able to overthrow the Shang because he had obtained the **Mandate of Heaven**. A new god, worshiped by the Zhou ruling house but not previously worshiped by the Shang, Heaven represented the generalized forces of the cosmos, rather than the abode of the dead. China's rulers believed that Heaven would send signs—terrible storms, unusual astronomical events, famines, even peasant rebellions—before withdrawing its mandate. But because the recipient of the Mandate of Heaven could only be known after the fact, it often served as a retrospective justification for overthrowing a dynasty by force.

Many other states coexisted with the Zhou dynasty (1045–256 B.C.E.), the most important being the Qin, who would first unify China. The long period of the Zhou dynasty is usually divided into the Western Zhou, 1045–771 B.C.E., when the capital was located in the Wei (WAY) River Valley, and the Eastern Zhou, from 771 to 256 B.C.E., because the second Zhou capital was east of the first.

During Zhou rule, the people writing Chinese characters gradually settled more and more territory at the expense of other peoples. Because the final centuries of the Zhou were particularly violent, the period from 481 to 221 B.C.E. is commonly called the Warring States Period. Yet constant warfare brought benefits, such as the diffusion of new technology. As in India, the spread of iron tools throughout China enabled people to plow the land more deeply and to settle in new areas. Agricultural productivity increased, and the first money—in the shape of knives and spades but not round coins—circulated around 500 B.C.E., also at roughly the same time as in India.

Changes in warfare brought massive social change. Since the time of the Shang, battles had been fought with chariots, and only boys who grew up in wealthy households had the time and the resources to learn how to guide a galloping horse pulling a chariot with three men into battle. But in the sixth and fifth centuries B.C.E., as they went farther south, armies began to fight battles in muddy terrain where chariots could not go. The most successful generals were those, regardless of family background, who could effectively lead armies of ten thousand foot soldiers into battle. At this time ambitious young men studied strategy and general comportment with tutors, one of whom became China's most famous teacher, **Confucius** (551–479 B.C.E.).

Confucianism

Confucius was born in 551 B.C.E. in Shandong (SHAHN-dohng) province. His family name was Kong (KOHNG); his given name, Qiu (CHEE-OH). (*Confucius* is the English translation of *Kong Fuzi* [FOO-zuh], or Master Kong, but most Chinese refer to him as Kongzi [KOHNG-zuh], which also means Master Kong.) Confucius's students have left us the only record of his thinking, a series of conversations he had

Zhou dynasty The successor dynasty to the Shang that gained the Mandate of Heaven and the right to rule, according to later Chinese historians. Although depicted by later generations as an ideal age, the Zhou witnessed considerable conflict.

Mandate of Heaven The Chinese belief that Heaven, the generalized forces of the cosmos (not the abode of the dead), chose the rightful ruler. China's rulers believed that Heaven would send signs before withdrawing its mandate.

Confucius (551–479 B.C.E.) A teacher who made his living by tutoring students. Known only through *The Analects*, the record of conversations with his students that they wrote down after his death.

with them, which are called *The Analects*, meaning "discussions and conversations." Recently scholars have begun to question the authenticity of the later *Analects* (especially chapters 10–20), but they agree that the first nine chapters probably date to an earlier time, perhaps just after Confucius's death in 479 B.C.E.

Some recent archaeological discoveries of philosophical writings on bamboo slips contain exact phrases from *The Analects*. These finds show that Confucius was only one of many teachers active at the time, and archaeologists are hopeful that they will unearth more texts showing exactly how *The Analects* took shape.

Confucianism is the term used for the main tenets of Confucius's thought. The optimistic tone of *The Analects* will strike any reader. Acutely aware of living in a politically unstable era, Confucius did not advocate violence. Instead, he emphasized the need to perform ritual correctly. Ritual is crucial because it allows the gentleman, the frequent recipient of Confucius's teachings, to express his inner humanity (a quality sometimes translated as "benevolence," "goodness," or "man at his best"). Since Confucius is speaking to his disciples, he rarely explains what kind of rituals he means, but he mentions sacrificing animals, playing music, and performing dances.

Confucius's teachings do not resemble a religion so much as an ethical system. Filial piety, or respect for one's parents, is its cornerstone. If children obey their parents and the ruler follows Confucian teachings, the country will right itself because an inspiring example will lead people toward the good. (See the feature "Movement of Ideas Through Primary Sources: *The Analects* and Sima Qian's Letter to Ren An.")

Confucius was also famous for his refusal to comment on either the supernatural or the afterlife:

> *Zilu [ZUH-lu; a disciple] asked how to serve the spirits and gods. The Master [Confucius] said: "You are not yet able to serve men, how could you serve the spirits?"*
> *Zilu said: "May I ask you about death?"*
> *The Master said: "You do not yet know life, how could you know death?"*[*]

If we define religion as the belief in the supernatural, then Confucianism does not seem to qualify. But if we consider religion as the offering of rituals at different turning points in one's life—birth, marriage, and death—then Confucianism qualifies as a religion.

Daoism

Many of Confucius's followers were also familiar with the teachings of **Daoism** (DOW-is-uhm) (alternate spelling Taoism), the other major belief system of China before unification in 221 B.C.E. The earliest Daoist texts excavated so far, dated to 300 B.C.E., were found in tombs alongside Confucian texts, an indication that the deceased did not necessarily think of Daoism and Confucianism as separate religions. Both Confucius and the leading Daoist teachers spoke about the "Way," a concept for which they used the same word, *dao* (DOW).

For Confucius, the Way denoted using ritual to bring out one's inner humanity. In contrast, the Way of the early Daoist teachers included meditation, breathing techniques, and special eating regimes. They believed that if one learned to

---

Confucianism
The term for the main tenets of the thought of Confucius, which emphasized the role of ritual in bringing out people's inner humanity (a quality translated variously as "benevolence," "goodness," or "man at his best").

Daoism
A Chinese belief system dating back to at least 300 B.C.E. that emphasized the "Way," a concept expressed in Chinese as "dao." The Way of the early Daoist teachers included meditation, breathing techniques, and special eating regimes.

---

[*]Excerpt from *The Analects of Confucius*, translated by Simon Leys. Copyright © 1997 by Pierre Ryckmans. Used by permission of W.W. Norton & Company, Inc.

control one's breath or the life-force present in each person, one could attain superhuman powers and possibly immortality. Some said that immortals shed their human bodies much as butterflies cast off pupas. Such people were called Perfect Men. One early Daoist text, *Zhuangzi* (JUAHNG-zuh), named for the author of its teachings, Master Zhuang (JUAHNG), describes such people: *"The Perfect Man is godlike. Though the great swamps blaze, they cannot burn him; though the great rivers freeze, they cannot chill him."*[1]

Funny and ironic, *Zhuangzi* describes many paradoxes, and the question of knowledge—of how we know what we think we know—permeates the text. One anecdote describes how Zhuang dreamt he was a happy butterfly. When he awoke he was himself, *"But he didn't know if he was Zhuang Zhou [Zhuangzi] who had dreamt he was a butterfly, or a butterfly dreaming he was Zhuang Zhou."*

Zhuangzi often mocks those who fear death because they cannot know what death is actually like; he dreams that a talking skull asks him, *"Why would I throw away more happiness than that of a king on a throne and take on the troubles of a human being again?"* *Zhuangzi*'s amusing tales underline how profoundly gloomy was the Daoist view of death, which pictured it as a series of underground prisons from which no one could escape.

The other well-known Daoist classic, *The Way and Integrity Classic*, or *Dao-dejing* (DOW-deh-jing), combines the teachings of several different masters into one volume. It urges rulers to allow things to follow their natural course, or *wuwei* (WOO-way), often misleadingly translated as "nonaction": *"Nothing under heaven is softer or weaker than water, and yet nothing is better for attacking what is hard and strong, because of its immutability."*[2] In the centuries leading up to 221 B.C.E., no Daoist church had a recognized leader, but many Daoist masters had disciples, and *Zhuangzi* and *The Way and Integrity Classic* offer a glimpse of the wide variety of teachings circulating alongside Confucian teachings in China at that time.

Qin Rulers Unify China, 359–207 B.C.E.

While Confucian and Daoist thinkers were proposing abstract solutions to end the endemic warfare, a third school, the Legalists, took an entirely different approach based on their experience governing the Qin homeland in western China. In 359 B.C.E., the statesman Shang Yang (SHAHNG yahng), the major adviser to the Qin ruler, implemented a series of reforms reorganizing the army and redefining the tax obligations of all citizens. Those reforms made the Qin more powerful than any of the other regional states in China, and it gradually began to conquer its neighbors. The First Emperor implemented Shang Yang's blueprint for rule both as the regional ruler of the Qin and as emperor after the unification of China in 221 B.C.E.

Prime Minister Shang Yang's Reforms, 359–221 B.C.E.

In 359 B.C.E., Prime Minister Shang Yang focused on the territory under direct Qin rule. The government sent officials to register every household in the Qin realm, creating a direct link between each subject and the ruler. Once a boy resident in the Qin region reached the age of sixteen or seventeen and a height of 5 feet (1.5 m), he had to serve in the military, pay land taxes (a fixed share of the crop), and perform labor service, usually building roads, each year. To encourage people to inform on each other, Shang Yang divided the population into mutual responsibility groups of five and ten: if someone committed a crime but was not apprehended, everyone in the group was punished.

The Analects and Sima Qian's Letter to Ren An

Unlike Buddhism, which has the first sermon of the Buddha (see Chapter 3), Confucianism has no short text that summarizes its main teachings. Throughout history students read and memorized *The Analects* because it was thought to be the only text that quoted Confucius directly. Each chapter contains ten to twenty short passages, often dialogues between Confucius and a student, and each passage is numbered. The first chapter introduces the most important Confucian teachings, including respect for one's parents, or filial piety.

Living more than three hundred years after Confucius's death, the Grand Historian Sima Qian wrestled with the issue of how to best observe the tenets of filial piety. Convicted of treason because he defended a general who had surrendered to the Xiongnu, he was offered a choice: he could commit suicide or he could undergo castration. In the excerpts from this letter to his friend Ren An, whom he called Shaoqing (shaow-ching), he explains why he chose castration even though it brought shame to his ancestors. According to Confucian teachings, one's body was a gift from one's parents, and each person was obliged to protect his body from any mutilation. But Sima Qian's father had begun *The Records of the Grand Historian*, and he chose physical punishment so that he could complete his father's project.

Sources: Excerpts from *The Analects of Confucius*, translated by Simon Leys. Copyright © 1997 by Pierre Ryckmans. Used by permission of W.W. Norton & Company, Inc.; Published in *Sima Qian, Records of the Grand Historian, Han Dynasty I* (tr. Burton Watson) Copyright © 1993 Columbia University Press. Reprinted with permission of Columbia University Press and the Research Centre for Translation, The Chinese University of Hong Kong.

Chapter One of *The Analects*

1.1. The Master said: "To learn something and then to put it into practice at the right time: is this not a joy? To have friends coming from afar: is this not a delight? Not to be upset when one's merits are ignored: is this not the mark of a gentleman?"

1.2. Master You said: "A man who respects his parents and his elders would hardly be inclined to defy his superiors. A man who is not inclined to defy his superiors will never foment a rebellion. A gentleman works at the root. Once the root is secured, the Way unfolds. To respect parents and elders is the root of humanity."

1.3. The Master said: "Clever talk and affected manners are seldom signs of goodness."

1.4. Master Zeng said: "I examine myself three times a day. When dealing on behalf of others, have I been trustworthy? In intercourse with my friends, have I been faithful? Have I practiced what I was taught?"

1.5. The Master said: "To govern a state of middle size, one must dispatch business with dignity and good faith; be thrifty and love all men; mobilize the people only at the right times."

1.6. The Master said: "At home, a young man must respect his parents; abroad, he must respect his elders. He should talk little, but with good faith; love all people, but associate with the virtuous. Having done this, if he still has energy to spare, let him study literature."

1.7. Zixia said: "A man who values virtue more than good looks, who devotes all his energy to serving his father and mother, who is willing to give his life for his sovereign, who in intercourse with friends is true to his word—even though some may call him uneducated, I still maintain he is an educated man."

1.8. The Master said: "A gentleman who lacks gravity has no authority and his learning will remain shallow. A gentleman puts loyalty and faithfulness foremost; he does not befriend his moral inferiors. When he commits a fault, he is not afraid to amend his ways."

1.9. Master Zeng said: "When the dead are honored and the memory of remote ancestors is kept alive, a people's virtue is at its fullest."

1.10. Ziqing asked Zigong: "When the Master arrives in another country, he always becomes informed about its politics. Does he ask for such information, or is it given him?"

Zigong replied: "The Master obtains it by being cordial, kind, courteous, temperate, and deferential. The Master has a way of enquiring which is quite different from other people's, is it not?"

1.11. The Master said: "When the father is alive, watch the son's aspirations. When the father is dead, watch the son's actions. If three years later, the son has not veered from the father's way, he may be called a dutiful son indeed."

1.12. Master You said: "When practicing the ritual, what matters most is harmony. This is what made the beauty of the way of the ancient kings; it inspired their every move, great or small. Yet they knew where to stop: harmony cannot be sought for its own sake, it must always be subordinated to the ritual; otherwise it would not do."

1.13. Master You said: "If your promises conform to what is right, you will be able to keep your word. If your manners conform to the ritual, you will be able to keep shame and disgrace at bay. The best support is provided by one's own kinsmen."

1.14. The Master said: "A gentleman eats without stuffing his belly; chooses a dwelling without demanding comfort; is diligent in his office and prudent in his speech; seeks the company of the virtuous in order to straighten his own ways. Of such a man, one may truly say that he is fond of learning."

1.15. Zigong said: "'Poor without servility; rich without arrogance.' How is that?"

The Master said: "Not bad, but better still: 'Poor, yet cheerful; rich, yet considerate.'"

Zigong said: "In the *Poems*, it is said: 'Like carving horn, like sculpting ivory, like cutting jade, like polishing stone.' Is this not the same idea?"

The Master said: "Ah, one can really begin to discuss the *Poems* with you! I tell you one thing, and you can figure out the rest."

1.16. The Master said: "Don't worry if people don't recognize your merits; worry that you may not recognize theirs."

Sima Qian's Letter to Ren An

A man has only one death. That death may be as weighty as Mount Tai, or it may be as light as a goose feather. It all depends on the way he uses it. Above all, a man must bring no shame to his forebears. Next he must not shame his person, or be shameful in his countenance, or in his words. Below such a one is he who suffers the shame of being bound, and next he who bears the shame of prison clothing. . . . Lowest of all is the dire penalty of castration, the "punishment of rottenness"! . . .

It is the nature of every man to love life and hate death, to think of his parents and look after his wife and children. Only when he is moved by higher principles is this not so. Then there are things that he must do. Now I have been most unfortunate, for I lost my parents very early. With no brothers or sisters, I have been left alone and orphaned. And you yourself, Shaoqing, have seen me with my wife and child and know I would not let thoughts of them deter me. Yet the brave man does not necessarily die for honor, while even the coward may fulfill his duty. Each takes a different way to exert himself. Though I might be weak and cowardly and seek shamelessly to prolong my life, I know full well the difference between what ought to be followed and what rejected. . . . But the reason I have not refused to bear these ills and have continued to live, dwelling in vileness and disgrace without taking leave, is that I grieve that I have things in my heart that I have not been able to express fully, and I am ashamed to think that after I am gone my writings will not be known to posterity.

QUESTIONS FOR ANALYSIS

» *According to* The Analects, *how should a gentleman conduct himself? How should a son treat his parents?*

» *According to Sima Qian, how should a virtuous person live? Why does he choose castration over suicide?*

Most people in ancient China took it for granted that the son of a noble was destined to rule and the son of a peasant was not, but the Legalists disagreed. Renouncing a special status for "gentlemen," they believed that the ruler should recruit the best men to staff his army and his government. In keeping with **Legalism**, Qin officials recognized no hereditary titles, not even for members of the ruler's family.

Instead the Qin officials introduced a strict meritocracy, which made their army the strongest in China. A newly recruited soldier might start at the lowest rank, but if he succeeded in battle, he could rise in rank and thereby raise the stature of his household. Because Qin rules tolerated no value judgments, which could be biased, a soldier had to present the heads of all those enemy soldiers he had killed before he could advance. The more heads he presented, the higher he rose in the army. This reorganization succeeded brilliantly because each soldier had a strong incentive to fight. Starting in 316 B.C.E., the Qin polity began to conquer neighboring lands and implement Shang Yang's measures in each new region.

Legalist philosophers valued the contributions of the farmer-soldiers most highly because they paid taxes and were the backbone of the army. Accordingly, Legalist thinkers ranked peasants just under government officials, or scholars, who could read and write. Because artisans made objects peasants needed, like baskets and tools, they ranked third, and merchants, who neither worked the land nor manufactured the goods they traded, ranked at the bottom of society.

This ranking is prescriptive, reflecting how Legalist thinkers thought society should be, not descriptive, how it actually was. Any Chinese peasant would gladly have changed places with a merchant because merchants did not perform arduous physical labor and could afford better clothes and food. Although the Legalist ranking, like the explanation of varna in the Indian "Hymn of the Primeval Man" (see Chapter 3), did not reflect reality, it persisted throughout Chinese history.

Legalism
A school of thought, originating in the fourth century B.C.E. and associated with Qin dynasty rulers, that emphasized promotion for officials and soldiers alike on the basis of merit and job performance, not heredity.

The Policies of the First Emperor, 221–210 B.C.E.

In 246 B.C.E., Prince Zheng, the future First Emperor, ascended to the Qin throne and launched a series of military conquests that culminated with the defeat of his final rival, the ruler of Qi (modern-day Shandong), in 221 B.C.E. Prince Zheng then named himself First Emperor. Determining what happened during the Qin founder's eleven-year reign (221–210 B.C.E.) poses great challenges because immediately after his death Sima Qian portrayed him as one of the worst tyrants in Chinese history who murdered his opponents, suppressed all learning, and adamantly opposed Confucian virtues. This view of the First Emperor prevails today, but the evidence *from* his reign (as opposed to that composed *after* it) suggests that the First Emperor conceived of himself as a virtuous ruler along Confucian lines.

After 221 B.C.E., the stone tablets the emperor placed on high mountaintops recorded his view of his reign:

> *The way of good rule is advanced and enacted;*
> *The various professions achieve their proper place,*
> *And all find rule and model.*
> *His great principle is superb and shining.**

---

*Excerpt from Martin Kern, *The Stele Inscriptions of Ch'in Shih-huang: Texts and Ritual in Early Chinese Imperial Representation* (New Haven: American Oriental Society, 2000), pp. 19–20. Reprinted with permission of the American Oriental Society, http://www.umich.edu/~aos/.

Each line invoked Confucian learning. "Superb and shining" is a title used by the first ruler of the Zhou, and the First Emperor adopted it because he, too, hoped to be perceived as the virtuous founder of a new dynasty.

To compose the stone inscriptions, the Qin emperor commissioned a team of scholars who drew on all the classical learning of China's different regions that had taken shape in the previous millennium, including Confucius's teachings. One of the inscriptions claims, *"The way of filial piety is brilliantly manifest and shining!"** According to Confucian teachings, the ruler's main role was to lead his subjects in ritual, and the Qin emperor assumed this role each time he put up a stone tablet.

The Qin emperor placed these monuments in the far corners of his realm to demonstrate that he directed all of his subjects, both those in the Qin homeland and those recently conquered, in correct ritual observance. Unlike the Ashokan inscriptions in different languages, all the Qin inscriptions were written in Chinese because the Qin enforced linguistic standardization throughout their empire. And whereas Ashoka's inscriptions were phrased colloquially, the Qin inscriptions were rigidly formal, consisting of thirty-six or seventy-two lines, each with exactly four characters. The inscriptions use the characteristic Chinese technique of manufacture: their authors placed component parts, or characters, in various combinations to produce a slightly different text for each inscription. Although Ashoka's inscriptions were completed within the Qin emperor's lifetime, northern India lay some 1,000 miles (1,600 km) from the western edge of the Qin emperor's realm, and there is no evidence that the Mauryans inspired the First Emperor.

Qin dynasty sources demonstrate clearly that the First Emperor exercised far more control over his subjects than had his predecessors. Using government registers listing all able-bodied men, the First Emperor initiated several enormous public works projects, including 4,000 miles (6,400 km) of roads, roughly as many as the Romans built,[3] and long walls of pounded earth, the most readily available building material. The Qin emperor also used conscript labor to build his tomb, where he was buried in 210 B.C.E. (See the feature "Visual Evidence in Primary Sources: The Terracotta Warriors of the Qin Founder's Tomb.")

Many Qin subjects left their homes either to perform labor service on these different projects or to serve in the army, which had several hundred thousand conscripts and traveled as far north as modern-day Mongolia and as far south as Vietnam (as discussed later in this chapter). The central government sent supplies overland to its armies on the roads it built, but when the armies traveled too far, it became difficult to sustain their supply lines, and many died far from home in unsuccessful military campaigns.

Legalism and the Laws of the Qin Dynasty

The Qin ruler viewed the establishment of laws as one of his most important accomplishments. According to one inscription, he *"created the regulations and illuminated the laws"** as soon as he became emperor. Viewing law as a tool for strengthening the realm, the Legalists advocated treating all men identically, regardless of birth, because they believed that only the systematic application of one set of laws could control man's inherently evil nature. Subjects could not use law to challenge their ruler's authority because the only law for Legalists was the law of the ruler. They did not acknowledge the existence of a higher, divine law.

*Excerpt from Martin Kern, *The Stele Inscriptions of Ch'in Shih-huang: Texts and Ritual in Early Chinese Imperial Representation* (New Haven: American Oriental Society, 2000), pp. 13, 17. Reprinted with permission of the American Oriental Society, http://www.umich.edu/~aos/.

The Great Wall Then and Now Few people realize that the Great Wall that we see today (*right*) was built during the Ming dynasty (1368–1644), not during the Qin dynasty (221–207 B.C.E.). The Qin emperor ordered the construction of the Great Wall by linking together many pre-existing dirt walls. In the fifteenth through seventeenth centuries C.E., the Ming built with stone along the foundations of the Qin dirt walls. The remains of the Qin wall, which was made largely from pounded earth, survive in only a few places in China (*left*).

Qin dynasty
(221–207 B.C.E.) The first dynasty to rule over a unified China; heavily influenced by Legalist teachings that promoted soldiers and officials strictly on the basis of accomplishment, not birth.

In place for only fourteen years, the **Qin dynasty** (221–207 B.C.E.) did not have time to develop a governmental system for all of China, but it did create a basic framework. The First Emperor appointed a prime minister as the top official in his government. Different departments in the capital administered the emperor's staff, the military, and revenue. The Qin divided the empire into over forty military districts called commanderies, each headed by a governor and a military commander. They in turn were divided into districts, the smallest unit of the Qin government, which were governed by magistrates with the help of clerks. All these officials were charged with carrying out the new laws of the Qin.

Later historians described Qin laws as arbitrary and overly harsh; they were also surprisingly detailed, clearly the product of a government deeply concerned with following legal procedures carefully. Archaeologists working in Shuihudi (SHWAY-who-dee) town, in Hubei (WHO-bay) province, found a partial set of Qin dynasty laws dating to 217 B.C.E. in the tomb of a low-ranking clerk. This set of model cases illustrating legal procedures was written on bamboo slips preserved in stagnant water, with holes punched into them. They were then sewn together to form sheets that could be rolled up, similar to a modern placemat made from cord and reeds.

Each model case described in the Shuihudi materials is equally complex, pointing to the existence of established procedures for officials to follow before reaching a judgment. One text begins as follows:

Report. A, the wife of a commoner of X village, made a denunciation, saying, "I, A, had been pregnant for six months. Yesterday, in the daytime, I fought with the adult woman C of the same village. I, A, and C grabbed each other by the hair. C threw me, A, over and drove me back. A fellow-villager, D, came to the rescue and separated C and me, A. As soon as I, A, had reached my house, I felt ill and my belly hurt; yesterday evening the child miscarried."[4]

The text provides detailed instructions for investigating such a case. The legal clerk had to examine the fetus and consult with the local midwife; he also had to interrogate A and the members of her household to determine her condition.

The Shuihudi tomb also contained sections of the Qin legal code that make fine distinctions: the penalties for manslaughter (inadvertently killing someone) were lighter than those for deliberate murder. The determination of manslaughter hinged on whether the assailant had used an object lying at hand or had concealed his weapon, which indicated intent to murder. The fine legal distinctions among different types of murder resemble those in Hammurabi's laws (see Chapter 2). However, whereas in Babylon an assembly decided whether the accused was guilty of murder, in China the presiding official or clerk determined an individual's guilt.

Qin punishments were grisly. One could have one's foot cut off or one's nose severed for various offenses, and many of those sentenced to hard labor were not "complete," meaning that they were missing a limb. But if we consider the punishments in use elsewhere in the world at the time, such as Roman crucifixion, the Qin punishments were not unusual.

The Han Empire, 206 B.C.E.–220 C.E.

The Qin dynasty came to a sudden end in 207 B.C.E. with the suicide of the First Emperor's son. The following year, in 206 B.C.E., the new emperor founded the **Han dynasty**. Although the Han founder always depicted the Qin as a brutal dynasty, he drew on many Legalist precedents to create a blueprint that allowed him and his descendants to rule for four hundred years. The Han modified the Qin structure of central and local government and developed a mechanism for recruiting officials that linked education with bureaucratic advancement for the first time in Chinese history. Starting in 140 B.C.E. and continuing throughout the dynasty, Han emperors encouraged students and future officials to study the Confucian classics. The dynasty's support of learning encouraged the spread of Confucianism throughout the empire. The Confucian emphasis on education was so strong that the Chinese of that era schooled not only their sons but also, when they could, their daughters. Yet because the Han continued many policies of the Qin, it was a Legalist dynasty with a Confucian veneer.

Han dynasty
(206 B.C.E.–220 C.E.) The immediate successor to the Qin dynasty. Han rulers denounced Legalist governance but adopted much of the Qin blueprint for empire. Because of its long rule, the Han dynasty was a model for all subsequent dynasties.

Han Government and the Imperial Bureaucracy

After the death of the First Emperor, some regions, sensing weakness at the center, rebelled against the unpopular second Qin emperor. Eventually one man, formerly a low-ranking official under the Qin named Liu Bang (LEO bahng) (r. 206–195 B.C.E.), emerged as

The Terracotta Warriors of the Qin Founder's Tomb

The Qin emperor's tomb, sometimes called the eighth wonder of the world, was discovered in 1973 by a farmer digging a well. The enormous tomb is so big that archaeologists have to dig test pits to probe its dimensions. Test pit #1, shown to the right, contains over seven thousand soldiers of four types—foot soldiers, archers, charioteers, and soldiers riding on horseback—who staffed the emperor's terracotta army. Because the Qin emperor expected the afterlife to be exactly the same as his life, his tomb formed a miniaturized world in which he could pursue his usual activities, including commanding his troops in battle.

The terracotta warriors do not resemble the figurines placed in any Chinese tomb before or since, prompting much speculation about the identity of their creators. One intriguing possibility, recently proposed, is that the emperor used his plumbers, because the soldiers' legs greatly resemble clay water pipes found in the ruins of the Qin palace.

Over one thousand soldiers bear labels stamped into the clay by eighty-five foremen, who were presumably responsible for supervising their construction. One estimate suggests that it took eleven years for these foremen, each supervising some ten men, to make the entire army of over seven thousand figures.[*]

How did the Qin craftsmen make so many different soldiers in such a short time? As chefs in today's Chinese restaurants work with ingredients, they arranged thousands of prefabricated parts in various combinations to make a slightly different product each time. Archaeologists have identified two types of feet, three types of shoes and four types of boots, two types of legs, eight types of torso, and two types of armor used to make the mass-produced soldiers, whose bodies range from 5 feet 11 inches to 6 feet 5 inches (180 to 195 cm) tall.

Once a soldier's body was completed, a craftsman used clay to make his facial features. All the soldiers have individual faces, as if the craftsmen worked from living models. Yet the faces are idealized: no soldier has any wounds or scars. When the soldiers were completed, craftsmen painted them with bright colors, most of which have flaked off on the surrounding dirt.

The core of the tomb, where the Qin emperor himself was buried, has yet to be excavated, but writing one hundred years later, Sima Qian described it: "Artisans were ordered to install mechanically triggered crossbows set to shoot any intruder. With mercury the various waterways of the empire, the Yangzi and Yellow Rivers, and even the great ocean itself were created and made to flow and circulate mechanically."[†] Sima Qian also claimed that the son of the Qin founder ordered that the craftsmen who worked on the tomb be buried alive so that the tomb's exact location would remain secret. Archaeologists have not found human remains, but they continue to announce new discoveries, most recently of clay wrestlers and tumblers who performed for the emperor's pleasure in the next world.

[*] Lothar Ledderose, *Ten Thousand Things: Module and Mass Production in Chinese Art* (Princeton: Princeton University Press, 2000), pp. 69–70.

[†] Maxwell K. Hearn, "The Terracotta Army of the First Emperor of Qin," in *The Great Bronze Age of China: An Exhibition from the People's Republic of China,* ed. Wen Fong (New York: Metropolitan Museum of Art, 1980), p. 357.

QUESTION FOR ANALYSIS

» *How do the terracotta warriors illustrate the Chinese technique of using prefabricated component parts to mass-produce multiple objects that differ from each other?*

This ordinary soldier's head was made by combining molded forms of the front and the back and smoothing them together. Like all Chinese, he did not cut his hair, considered to be a gift from his parents, but bound it in intricate patterns on the back and top of his head.

His headdress indicates that this figure is an officer. This group of nine statues includes at least three officers who stand at the front of their unit so that they can lead their subordinates into battle.

A roof of wooden beams was originally built over the entire army and then covered with mats, a layer of sand and chalk, and finally a layer of dirt.

This missing head reveals how the hollow statues were made. The armor, lower skirt, and legs were made from sheets of clay in a construction technique originally used by palace plumbers for water pipes.

© Alfo Garozzo/Cuboimages srl/Alamy

Each Qin soldier wore a uniform consisting of a gown to the knees, leather armor on the upper torso, short pants, leg guards, and a headdress (never a helmet).

This officer's hands originally held weapons, most likely wooden spears or staffs, which have since disintegrated.

leader of the rebels and founded the Han dynasty in 206 B.C.E. Liu Bang was one of only two emperors (the other founded the Ming dynasty in 1368) to be born as a commoner. When he and his forces entered the Qin capital, he assured the capital's residents:

> *You elders have long suffered under the harsh laws of Qin. . . . I make an agreement with you that the law shall consist of only three sections: He who kills others shall die; he who harms others or steals from them shall incur appropriate punishment. For the rest, all other Qin laws shall be abolished.*[5]

Like a modern politician's campaign promise, this statement does not provide an accurate description of Han law, which actually retained many provisions of Qin law.

When the Han forces took power, they faced the immediate problem of staffing a government large enough to govern the empire. They adopted the Legalist structure of a central government with the emperor at the head and a prime minister (sometimes called a chancellor) as the top official. Underneath the prime minister were three main divisions: collection of taxes, supervision of the military, and recruitment of personnel.

The Han dynasty ruled for four hundred years, with only one interruption by a relative of the empress, named Wang Mang (WAHNG mahng), who founded his own short-lived Xin (SHIN) ("new") dynasty (9–23 C.E.). During the first two hundred years of the Han, called the Former Han or the Western Han (206 B.C.E.–9 C.E.), the capital was in Chang'an (CHAHNG-ahn). After Wang Mang was deposed, the original ruling family of the Han dynasty governed from the new capital of Luoyang (LWAW-yahng). The Later Han (25–220 C.E.) is also called the Eastern Han because Luoyang was some 300 miles (500 km) east of Chang'an.

The Han empire exercised varying amounts of control over the 60 million people under its rule. Immediately after taking over, the Han founder ceded about half of Qin territory to independent kings. He divided the remaining territory into one hundred commanderies and subdivided them into fifteen hundred prefectures, where a magistrate registered the population, collected revenues, judged legal disputes, and maintained irrigation works.

To get a government position during the Han dynasty, the first step was to get a referral. Men already serving in the government suggested younger men of good reputation, usually from wealthy families with large landholdings, to staff lower positions in prefectural offices. There they could learn how government functioned. The Han was the first Chinese dynasty to require that officials study classical writings on ritual, history, and poetry, as well as *The Analects*. Although these texts did not teach the nuts-and-bolts workings of local government, which remained Legalist in all but name, officials embraced the Confucian view that knowledge of these classic texts would produce more virtuous, and thus better, officials.

In 124 B.C.E., one of the most powerful Han emperors, Emperor Wu (also known as Han Wudi) (r. 140–87 B.C.E.), established the **Imperial Academy** to encourage the study of Confucian texts. At first the Academy consisted of five scholars, called Academicians, who specialized in the study of a given text, and the fifty students who studied with them. Within one hundred years the number of students at the Academy ballooned to several thousand. Ambitious young men already in the government realized that knowledge of Confucian texts, demonstrated by success in examinations conducted by the Imperial Academy, could advance their careers.

Imperial Academy
Established in 124 B.C.E. by the Han emperor, Emperor Wu (r. 140–87 B.C.E.), to encourage the study of Confucian texts.

The study of Confucian texts was aided by the invention of paper. The earliest examples of Chinese paper found by archaeologists date to the second century B.C.E. Ragpickers who washed and recycled old fabric left fibers on a screen to dry and accidentally discovered how to make paper. Initially, the Chinese used paper for wrapping fragile items, not as a writing material. But by 200 C.E. paper production had increased so much that people used paper, not bamboo slips, for letter writing and books.

With the adoption of paper as the primary writing material, the culture of learning in China shifted from an oral to a written one. In the early years, Han dynasty teachers taught students to memorize texts and recite them orally, but by the end of the dynasty they were reading books. When one poet in the first century B.C.E. submitted a written poem to the court as a gift, the emperor could not imagine that someone would commit a poem to writing without first reciting it in person. By the end of the dynasty, though, writing literary works on paper without reciting them had become commonplace. Paper was one of China's most important inventions; it spread from China to the Islamic world in the eighth century C.E. and finally to Europe only in the eleventh century.

Ban Zhao's *Lessons for Women*

During the first century C.E., the Later Han capital of Luoyang became an important literary center where young men came to study. One of the most famous literary families was that of the poet and historian Ban Biao (BAHN-beeow) (d. 54 C.E.), who had three children: twin boys and a daughter. One of the boys followed in his father's footsteps, while his twin became a successful general. Their sister, **Ban Zhao** (BAHN jow) (ca. 45–120 C.E.), was the most famous woman writer of her day. She is best known for her work *Lessons for Women*, which Chinese girls continued to read for centuries after her death.

Ban Zhao wrote *Lessons for Women* when in her mid-fifties. It contained everything she would like to have known when she married at age fourteen. Ban Zhao's main theme is clear: women exist to serve their husbands and their in-laws, whom they should always obey and with whom they should never quarrel. Yet Ban Zhao's ideal woman was also literate. She began her book by advising her readers to copy down her instructions, sure evidence that they could read and write. She criticized men who taught only their sons to read:

> Yet only to teach men and not to teach women—is that not ignoring the essential relation between them? . . . It is the rule to begin to teach children to read at the age of eight years. . . . Only why should it not be that girls' education as well as boys' be according to this principle?[6]

This is an eloquent call to teach girls to read at the same age as boys (age seven; eight in Chinese reckoning includes the time in the womb).

We must remember that Ban Zhao differed from her contemporaries in several ways. For one, she had studied with her father the historian and was sufficiently skilled that she completed his manuscript after he died. When married, she bore children, but she was widowed at a young age and became a tutor to the women at the imperial court. When a woman took power as regent, Ban Zhao advised her on matters of state.

Ban Zhao
(45–120 C.E.) A historian and the author of *Lessons for Women*, a book that counseled women to serve men and advocated education for girls starting at the age of seven.

Ban Zhao and the female regent did not have typical careers. Still, their unusual lives show that it was possible for women to take on male roles under certain circumstances. The literacy rate during the first century could not have exceeded 10 percent among men, but *Lessons for Women* was read, and Ban Zhao's ideal of literate women stayed alive in subsequent centuries. Well-off families made every effort to educate their daughters, if only to allow them to study a few years with their brothers' tutors; of course, few laboring people could afford to do so.

Extending Han Rule to Mongolia, Vietnam, and Korea

As the Qin and Han dynasties left their successors with a blueprint of how to govern the empire, the territories they conquered established boundaries that would define Chinese territory for centuries to come. After conquering six independent kingdoms to form their empire, the Qin controlled most of the land watered by the Yellow and Yangzi Rivers. Compare Qin dynasty China with Han dynasty China (see Map 4.1). The most visible difference is that the Han rulers controlled a narrow stretch of territory in the northwest, now Gansu (GAHN-sue) province and the Xinjiang (SHIN-jyahng) Autonomous Region. Han armies also extended the empire's borders northeast to control much of the Korean peninsula and south to modern-day Vietnam.

Conflict and Contact: The Han Dynasty and the Xiongnu Nomads, 201–60 B.C.E.

Xiongnu
Nomadic people north of China whose military strength derived from brilliant horsemanship. Defeated the Han dynasty in battle until 60 B.C.E., when their federation broke apart.

The Han dynasty gained much of this territory during its wars between 201 and 60 B.C.E. with the **Xiongnu** (SHEE-AWNG-new), a northern nomadic people who moved across modern-day Mongolia in search of grass to feed their sheep and horses. Only the Xiongnu had an army sufficiently powerful to threaten the Han, and they tried to conquer Chinese territory for the first century and a half of Han rule. Their military strength derived from their quick-footed horses and brilliant horsemanship, which enabled them to defeat the Chinese in battle after battle.

Having formed a confederation of the different tribal peoples living in Mongolia in Qin times, the Xiongnu fought their first battle with the Han soon after the founding of the dynasty. The Xiongnu won and after a temporary peace continued to launch military campaigns into China.

In 139 B.C.E. Emperor Wu dispatched an envoy named Zhang Qian (JAHNG chee-en) to Central Asia to persuade the Yuezhi (YOU-EH-juh) people to enter into an alliance against the Xiongnu. Zhang Qian reached the Yuezhi only after being held hostage by the Xiongnu for ten years. Although he failed to secure an alliance against the Xiongnu, he visited local markets and, to his surprise, saw Chinese goods for sale, certain evidence that merchants carrying Chinese goods had preceded him. Today most Chinese regard Zhang Qian as the person who discovered the Silk Road (see Chapter 8).

The Xiongnu supplied the Chinese with animals, hides, and semiprecious gems, particularly jade; in return the Chinese traded silk. The Chinese never succeeded, at least within the Chinese heartland, in breeding horses as strong as those the Xiongnu bred in the Mongolian steppe, probably because they did not have comparable grasslands. The Xiongnu threat came to a sudden end in 60 B.C.E.

because the huge Xiongnu confederation broke apart into five warring groups. Other nomadic peoples living in the grasslands to the north, like the Mongols, would intermittently threaten later dynasties.

Han Expansion to the North, Northwest, and South

The Han dynasty ruled China for over four hundred years. In certain periods, it was too weak to conquer new territories, but in other periods, particularly during the long reign of Emperor Wu, the army was so

MAP 4.1 **The Han Empire at Its Greatest Extent, ca. 50** B.C.E. The Han dynasty inherited all the territory of its predecessor, the Qin dynasty, and its powerful armies conquered new territory to the north in the Korean peninsula, to the west in the Taklamakan Desert, and to the south in modern-day Vietnam. *(© Cengage Learning)*

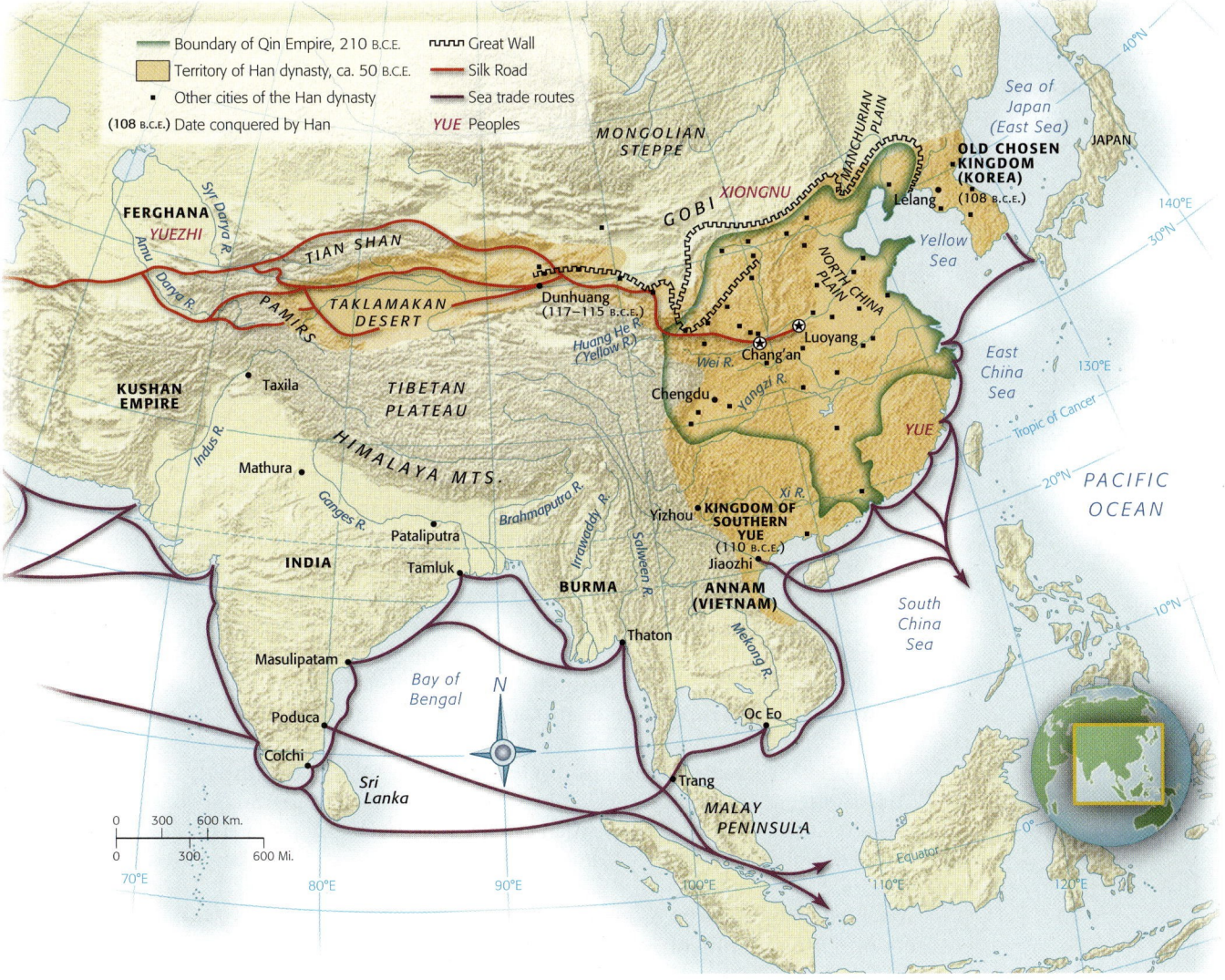

A Korean National Treasure This basket was found in the Chinese garrison town of Lelang, near Pyongyang in modern North Korea. Measuring 16 inches (39 cm) long and 9 inches (22 cm) high, the central band uses lacquer paint to depict ninety-four different paragons of filial piety and labels each in Chinese characters (a detail is shown here). These figures performed various good deeds for the benefit of their parents. The basket documents the spread of Confucianism to the Korean peninsula in the first and second centuries C.E. (Central Historical Museum, P'yongyang, North Korea/Werner Forman/Art Resource, NY)

strong that the emperor conquered new lands. Once the Han army had conquered a certain region, it established garrisons in the major towns. Chinese officials and merchants in these towns led Chinese-style lives, eating Chinese food and speaking Chinese, while the indigenous peoples largely continued to live as they had before. The officials living in the garrison towns exercised only tenuous control over the indigenous peoples, and if a local army retook a city, Chinese control could end suddenly. Han armies managed to take parts of the Taklamakan Desert, Korea, and Vietnam, but they ruled these borderlands only briefly. After 127 C.E., only a Han garrison at the city of Dunhuang (DUHN-hwahng), the outermost point of Chinese control, remained as the staging point for going farther west.

The region south of China, extending from modern-day Fujian (FOO-jee-en) province to Vietnam, differed from the northwest because one could reach it overland or, more easily, by sea. Much like camel caravans visited oases in their voyage west across the Taklamakan Desert, small boats, many propelled by oars, visited ports on the South China Sea, which offered a chance to rest, trade, and buy provisions for the next leg of the journey. Like all the rivers in Vietnam, the most important river, the Red River, drained from the mountains in the west to the South China Sea. High mountain chains separated the different river valleys, making overland transport much more difficult than sea travel.

The modern Chinese provinces of Guangdong (GWAHNG-dohng), Guangxi (GWAHNG-shee), and Yunnan (YUHN-nahn) were home to a regional people that the Chinese called Yue (YOU-EH), the ancestors of the Vietnamese. The Yue people had early (about 8000 B.C.E.) developed the cultivation of rice and were also avid sailors.

When the Qin armies conquered Vietnam before 207 B.C.E., they established centers of Chinese control in garrison towns. After 207 B.C.E., an independent kingdom also ruled by a Chinese leader, called the Southern Kingdom of Yue (Nam Viet), took over from the Qin. The kingdom was home to fishermen and traders who specialized in unusual goods like ivory tusks, pearls, tortoise shells, and slaves. After several attempts, the Han armies defeated this ruler and established garrison towns in 110 B.C.E.

While Vietnam marked the southern extent of Han territory, Korea marked the northern extent. Korea did not receive as much rainfall as Vietnam, and its climate was much cooler. Large, dense forests covered the region, and most early settlements were along rivers or on the coast, where residents could easily fish. Before 300 B.C.E., the region was home to several tribal confederations; then, during the third century B.C.E., the Old Choson (JOE-sohn) kingdom united much of the Korean peninsula north of the Han River, in what is today's North Korea. Qin armies defeated the Old Choson kingdom, and Han armies again conquered the region in 108 B.C.E., soon after gaining control of China.

Officials and merchants lived in a garrison city located in modern-day Pyongyang (BYOHNG-yahng), but the people outside the garrison were much less affected by the Chinese presence. Large, wealthy graves suggest that the people living on the Korean peninsula believed that the dead would travel to another realm. In one region they were buried with large bird wings so that they could fly to the next world.

In later periods (see Chapter 8), these three regions—northwest China, Vietnam, and Korea—would all join the Chinese cultural sphere and adopt the Chinese writing system. But during the Qin and Han dynasties Chinese influence was limited because the Chinese presence consisted only of military garrisons.

CONTEXT AND CONNECTIONS

The Significance of Ancient China in World History

The clearest indication of the First Emperor's legacy is the words we use even now for "China" and "Chinese." *China* entered English via the Sanskrit word *Chee-na*, the Indian pronunciation of *Qin*. Following the lead of the First Emperor, the Qin and Han dynasties created a blueprint for imperial rule that lasted for two thousand years. In the centuries after the fall of the Han, China was not always unified. But subsequent Chinese rulers always aspired to reunify the empire and conceived of China's physical borders as largely those of the Han dynasty at its greatest extent.

The Qin dynasty begun by the First Emperor introduced a centralized administration headed by the emperor, recorded the population in household registers, systematized weights and measures, and promoted officials strictly on the basis of merit. The

Qin also had a ceremonial state, as the emperor's sacrifices showed, but these measures affected everyone living in Qin territory and had far greater impact than any actions of the Mauryan dynasty in India (see Chapter 3).

The Han dynasty made one important change: officials had to pass examinations testing their knowledge of Confucianism before they could attain higher office. The Han extended its military control far to the west, establishing more sustained contacts with the peoples living along the Silk Road. Use of this route continued in later periods, peaking in the sixth through eighth centuries (see Chapter 8).

The Qin/Han blueprint for rule kept China unified for most of its long history. Even before the Qin unified China, the Chinese shared a cuisine, belief in the tenets of Confucianism, and a common

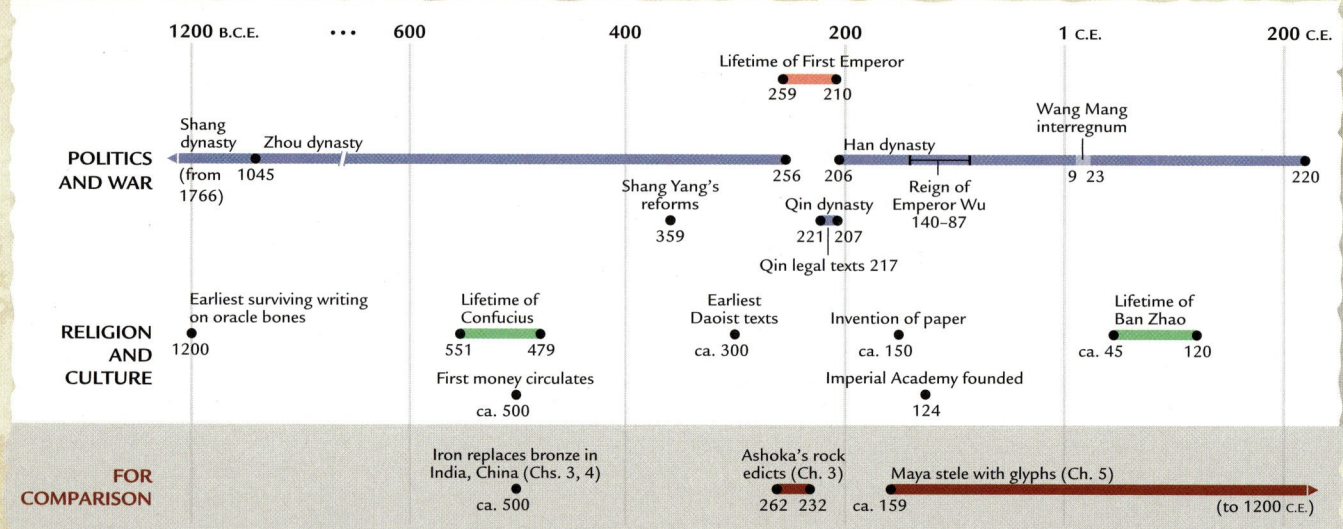

| | 1200 B.C.E. | ··· | 600 | 400 | 200 | 1 C.E. | 200 C.E. |

POLITICS AND WAR

Lifetime of First Emperor
259 — 210

Shang dynasty · Zhou dynasty
(from 1045
1766)

Han dynasty
256 206 · 9 23 · 220

Wang Mang interregnum

Shang Yang's reforms
359

Qin dynasty
221 207

Reign of Emperor Wu
140–87

Qin legal texts 217

RELIGION AND CULTURE

Earliest surviving writing on oracle bones
1200

Lifetime of Confucius
551 479

Earliest Daoist texts
ca. 300

Invention of paper
ca. 150

Lifetime of Ban Zhao
ca. 45 120

First money circulates
ca. 500

Imperial Academy founded
124

FOR COMPARISON

Iron replaces bronze in India, China (Chs. 3, 4)
ca. 500

Ashoka's rock edicts (Ch. 3)
262 232

Maya stele with glyphs (Ch. 5)
ca. 159 (to 1200 C.E.)

© Cengage Learning

writing system, which has remained in use, with some modifications, for over three thousand years. These all made China easier to unify than neighboring India. Just as a Chinese chef combines different precut ingredients to make distinctive dishes, other ancient innovations often made use of component parts to make final products that all varied slightly.

China's path to complex society followed the same pattern as in Mesopotamia, Egypt, and India, all societies on the Eurasian landmass (see Chapters 2 and 3). In about 8000 B.C.E. the Chinese began to cultivate millet and wheat in the north, and in 7000 B.C.E. they first grew rice in the south. Chinese farmers domesticated cattle, oxen, and horses to work

the land, and they made agricultural implements—plows, shovels, machetes—first of stone and then, around 2000 B.C.E., of bronze. Agriculture arose first in river valleys, and farmers used plows to prepare the land for seed, wheeled carts to carry things, and domesticated animals to work the land. Similarly, metallurgists learned how to work bronze before they mastered the higher temperatures necessary to smelt iron. In both China and India, iron replaced bronze around 500 B.C.E., the time when the first coins circulated. The next chapter will examine the experience of people living in the Americas and the Pacific islands, whose history took an entirely different course.

VOYAGES ON THE WEB: First Emperor of the Qin Dynasty

The Voyages Map App follows the traveler's journeys using interactive study tools, including 360-degree panoramic views of historic sites, zoomable maps, audio summaries, flash cards, and quizzes.

Key Terms

First Emperor of the Qin dynasty (82)
Shang dynasty (86)
oracle bones (86)
ancestor worship (87)
Sima Qian (87)

Zhou dynasty (89)
Mandate of Heaven (89)
Confucius (89)
Confucianism (90)
Daoism (90)
Legalism (94)

Qin dynasty (96)
Han dynasty (97)
Imperial Academy (100)
Ban Zhao (101)
Xiongnu (102)

For Further Reference

The Analects of Confucius. Simon Leys, trans. New York: W. W. Norton, 1997.

Eckert, Carter, et al. *Korea Old and New: A History.* Cambridge, Mass.: Harvard University Press, 1990.

Hansen, Valerie. *The Open Empire: A History of China to 1600.* New York: W. W. Norton, 2000.

Keightley, David N. *Sources of Shang History: The Oracle Bone Inscriptions of Bronze Age China.* Berkeley: University of California Press, 1978.

Kern, Martin. *The Stele Inscriptions of Ch'in Shih-huang: Text and Ritual in Early Chinese Imperial Representation.* New Haven: American Oriental Society, 2000.

Ledderose, Lothar. *Ten Thousand Things: Module and Mass Production in Chinese Art.* Princeton: Princeton University Press, 2000.

Schwartz, Benjamin. *The World of Thought in Ancient China.* Cambridge, Mass.: Harvard University Press, 1985.

Stark, Miriam. *Archaeology of Asia.* Hoboken, N.J.: Wiley-Blackwell, 2005.

Swann, Nancy Lee. *Pan Chao: Foremost Woman Scholar of China.* New York: American Historical Association, 1932.

Tao Te Ching: The Classic Book of Integrity and the Way. Victor Mair, trans. New York: Bantam Books, 1990.

Tarling, Nicholas, ed. *The Cambridge History of Southeast Asia.* Cambridge, England: Cambridge University Press, 1999.

Twitchett, Denis, and Michael Loewe, eds. *The Cambridge History of China.* Vol. 1, *The Ch'in and Han Empires 221 B.C.–A.D. 220.* New York: Cambridge University Press, 1986.

Films

The First Emperor of China from the Canadian Film Board. USA orders: 800–542–2164.

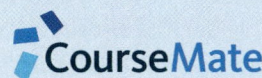

Go to the CourseMate website at **www.cengagebrain.com** for additional study tools and review materials—including audio and video clips—for this chapter.

5

The Americas and the Islands of the Pacific, to 1200 C.E.

In 1976 a group of Hawai'ians decided to celebrate the bicentennial of U.S. independence by crossing the Pacific from Hawai'i to Tahiti using the twin-hulled sailing canoes and navigation techniques of their ancestors. The greatest challenge was finding someone sufficiently skilled who could navigate without the assistance of a single instrument or map. Eventually, a former Peace Corps volunteer suggested that they contact his wife's cousin on the Micronesian island of Satawal (SAH-tah-wohl) in the Caroline island chain. The cousin, a man named **Mau Piailug** (MOW pee-EYE-lug) (1932–2010), had learned from his grandfather the art of navigating by using the stars, ocean currents, cloud patterns, and flight paths of birds. He frequently led short trips from one island in the Carolines to another.

The 3,337-mile (5,370-km) trip from Hawai'i to Tahiti was far longer than any trip Piailug had previously navigated, but after sailing for thirty-two days the voyagers' vessel, the *Hokule'a*, arrived safely in Tahiti, where 15,000 people, one-fifth of the island's population, turned out to celebrate the successful voyage. In a documentary film made that year, Piailug explained (through a translator) his feelings about the voyage:

Mau Piailug with Star Chart

(From Navigators: Pathfinders of the Pacific, a documentary film by Sanford Low. Courtesy, Documentary Educational Resources)

Our navigation is different from yours. I don't need a map or a sextant. I just use my head. I observe the ocean and the sky and I remember the words of my teachers.

The trip to Tahiti was very important for me. I know that people of Tahiti and Hawai'i once navigated as we do. They didn't use instruments. They navigated by the stars and the waves. I made the trip to show those people what their ancestors used to know and what we still know.

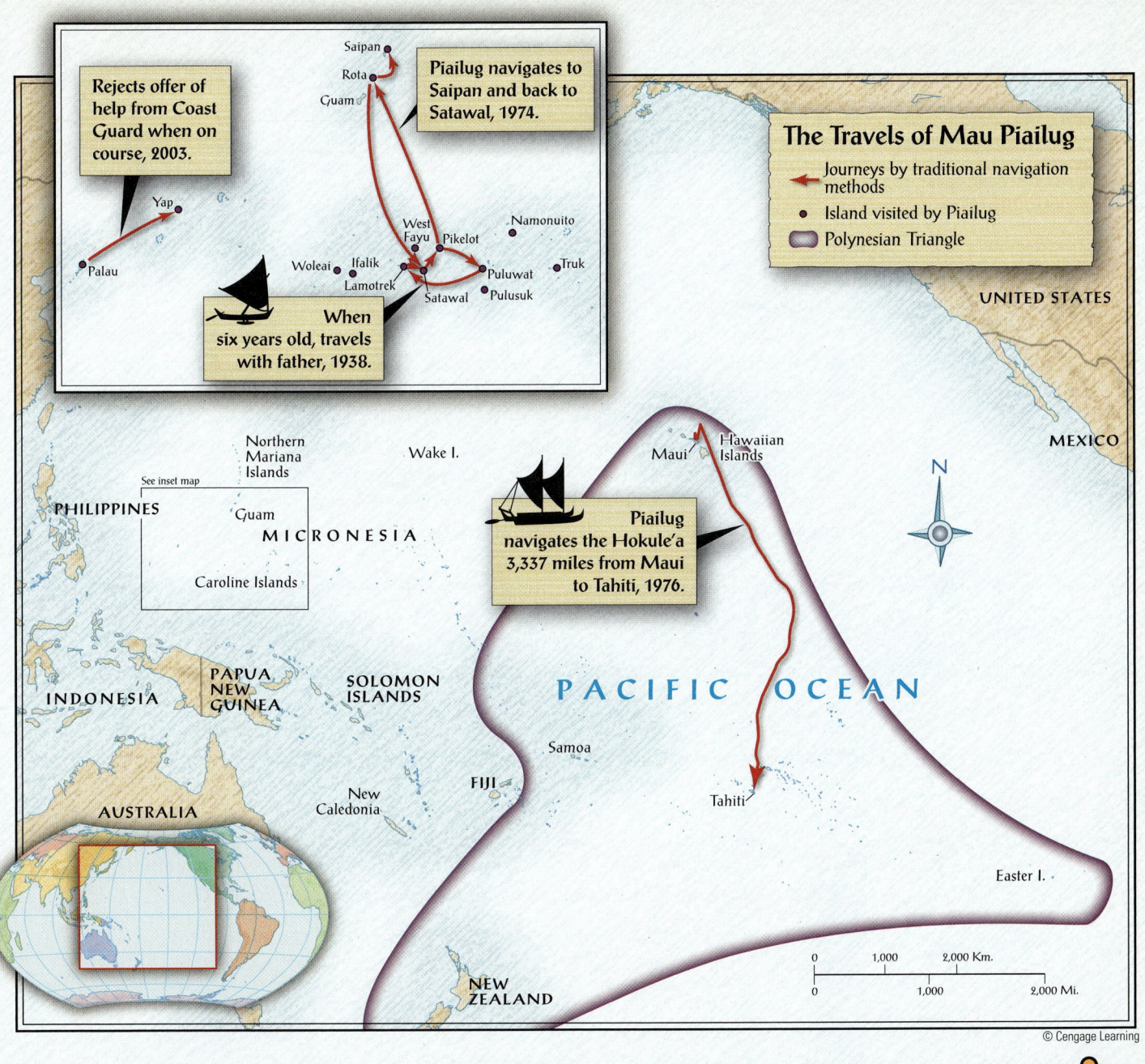

Rejects offer of help from Coast Guard when on course, 2003.

Piailug navigates to Saipan and back to Satawal, 1974.

When six years old, travels with father, 1938.

Saipan
Rota
Guam
Yap
Palau
West Fayu
Pikelot
Namonuito
Woleai
Ifalik
Lamotrek
Satawal
Puluwat
Pulusuk
Truk

The Travels of Mau Piailug

→ Journeys by traditional navigation methods

• Island visited by Piailug

▨ Polynesian Triangle

UNITED STATES

MEXICO

Piailug navigates the Hokule'a 3,337 miles from Maui to Tahiti, 1976.

Northern Mariana Islands
See inset map
Wake I.
Maui
Hawaiian Islands
N

PHILIPPINES
Guam
MICRONESIA
Caroline Islands

PAPUA NEW GUINEA
INDONESIA
SOLOMON ISLANDS

PACIFIC OCEAN

Samoa

FIJI

AUSTRALIA
New Caledonia

Tahiti

Easter I.

0   1,000   2,000 Km.
0   1,000   2,000 Mi.

NEW ZEALAND

© Cengage Learning

*The trip to Tahiti was very good because it will remind those people of what their ancestors did and make them want to learn about it.**

*Mau Piailug speaking through a translator in the film *The Navigators: Pathfinders of the Pacific,* directed by Sanford Low and Boyd Estus (Documentary Educational Resources [DER], 1976), 59 mins. Excerpt available online at http://www.der.org/films/navigators-preview.html. Reprinted by permission of Documentary Educational Resources.

Mau Piailug's homeland of Micronesia belonged to the vast area of the globe—North and South America and the islands of the Pacific—that developed in almost total isolation from Eurasia because, after approximately 7000 B.C.E., much of the ice covering the world's surface melted and submerged the Beringia ice bridge linking Alaska to Siberia (see Chapter 1). Drawing on oral testimony like Piailug's, on archaeological finds, and on surviving documents, archaeologists and historians have exercised great ingenuity in reconstructing the history of the American and Pacific peoples.

Complex societies arose in Mexico, the Andes, and the modern-day United States at different times and in different ways than in Eurasia. Hundreds, sometimes thousands, of years elapsed between the first cultivation of plants and the rise of cities. Archaeologists pay close attention to the American peoples who built large earthworks or stone monuments because their rulers had the ability to command their subjects to work on large projects. Similarly, although the peoples of the Pacific never built large cities, they conducted some of the world's longest ocean voyages across the Pacific and by 1350 had reached New Zealand, the final place on the globe to be settled by humans.

Differing from almost every other people of the Americas and the islands of the Pacific, the Maya developed one of the few writing systems used in the Americas before 1500. Some earlier peoples living in modern-day Mexico developed notational systems; much later, the Mexica (MAY-shee-kah) people of Mexico, often called the Aztecs, used a combination of pictures and visual puns to record events, but their writing system was not fully developed (see Chapter 15). Since historians know more about the Maya than any other society in the Americas or the Pacific islands, this chapter begins with their precursors and then proceeds to the Maya themselves.

Focus Questions

> » *How did the development of agriculture and the building of early cities in Mesoamerica differ from that in Mesopotamia, India, and China?*

> » *What has the decipherment of the Maya script revealed about Maya governance, society, religion, and warfare?*

> » *What were the similarities and differences among the complex societies of Mesoamerica, the northern peoples, and the Andes? What do they suggest about contact?*

> » *Where did the early settlers of the Pacific islands come from, and where did they go? What vessels did they use, and how did they navigate?*

The First Complex Societies of Mesoamerica, 8000 B.C.E.–500 C.E.

Unlike in Mesopotamia, Egypt, India, and China, agriculture in the Americas arose not in river valleys but in a plateau region, the highlands of Mexico, around 8000 B.C.E. The residents of Mexico continued to hunt and gather for thousands of years as they slowly began to cultivate corn, potatoes, cocoa beans, and other crops that grew nowhere else in the world. Large urban centers, one of the markers of complex society, first appeared in Mexico around 1200 B.C.E.

The Development of Agriculture, 8000–1500 B.C.E.

The people of Tehuacán (tay-wah-KAHN) in the modern state of Puebla (PWAY-bla), Mexico, initially harvested wild grasses with tiny ears of seeds. Their grinding stones, the first evidence of cultivation in the Americas, date to 8000 B.C.E. Just as the Natufians of western Asia had gradually domesticated wheat by harvesting certain wild plants with desirable characteristics (see Chapter 1), the residents of Tehuacán selected different grasses with more rows of seeds until they eventually developed a domesticated variety of maize sometime around 7000 B.C.E. (Specialists prefer the term *maize* to *corn* because it is more specific.) Unlike the early farmers of western Asia, the people of Tehuacán used no draft animals.

Maize spread from the Tehuacán Valley throughout the region of **Mesoamerica**. Located between the Atlantic and Pacific Oceans, Mesoamerica is bounded by barren desert north of modern Mexico. More rain falls in the east than in the west; because of the uneven rainfall, residents used irrigation channels to move water. Maize later reached north to Canada and south to the tip of South America.

Once planted, maize required little tending until the harvest. The hard dried kernels were ground or boiled and mixed with ground limestone into a paste, called nixtamal (NISH-ta-mal), that was used to make unleavened cakes. As the proportion of cultivated crops in the diet increased, the Mesoamericans gradually abandoned hunting and gathering. Eating little meat because they raised no domesticated animals, they cultivated squash and beans along with maize, three foods that together offered the same nutritional benefits (amino acids and vitamin B_{12}) as meat. The systematized cultivation of maize made it possible to support larger populations. By 2500 B.C.E., the population of Mesoamerica had increased by perhaps twenty-five times; the largest settlements had several hundred residents. By 1500 B.C.E., the Mesoamericans had adopted full-time agriculture.

If an ancient farmer from anywhere in Mesopotamia, China, or India had visited at this time, he or she would have been amazed to see that no one in Mesoamerica employed the familiar tools of farming—the plow, the wheel, or draft animals. Instead of the plow, the Mesoamericans used different types of digging sticks, and they dragged or carried things themselves. (The only wheels in the Americas appeared on children's toys around 500 C.E.)

Mesoamerica
The region that includes the southern two-thirds of modern Mexico, Guatemala, Belize, El Salvador, Honduras, Nicaragua, and Costa Rica.

Photograph K3670 © Justin Kerr

Maya Toy with Wheels The Maya certainly knew how wheels functioned, but they only used them on toys. This example is 5 inches (12.5 cm) tall. The tail was the mouthpiece for a whistle. Not certain why the Maya did not use the wheel for farming or transport, scholars have speculated that the wheel was not suited to the heavily forested terrain where the Maya lived.

Olmec
A complex society (1200–400 B.C.E.) that arose on the Gulf of Mexico coast from modern-day Veracruz to Tabasco. Known particularly for the massive colossal heads hewn from basalt.

The Olmec and Their Successors, 1200–400 B.C.E.

The **Olmec** peoples (1200–400 B.C.E.) built the first larger settlements along a 100-mile (160-km) stretch on the coast of the Gulf of Mexico (see Map 5.1). Raising two maize crops a year, the Olmec produced a large agricultural surplus, and the population also increased because of the nutritional benefits of the nixtamal diet.

Surviving colossal heads testify to the Olmec rulers' ability to mobilize their subjects for large labor projects. The Olmec used stone hammers to hew these heads from basalt. They are 5–10 feet (1.5–3.0 m) tall, and the largest weighs over 40 tons (36 metric tons). The nearest source of basalt lay more than 50 miles (80 km) to the northwest, and archaeologists surmise that Olmec laborers, lacking the wheel, carried the rock overland and built rafts to transport it along local rivers.

MAP 5.1 Complex Societies in the Americas, ca. 1200 B.C.E. Starting around 1200 B.C.E., complex societies arose in two widely separated regions in the Americas. In modern-day Mexico the Olmec hewed giant heads from basalt; in modern-day Peru, the Chavín built large temples decorated with statues combining human and animal body parts. (© Cengage Learning)

The Maya Calendar and the End of the World

According to the Maya calendar, the current Great Cycle began on August 11, 3114 B.C.E. and will end 5,125 years later on the winter solstice, December 21, 2012. The end of the current Great Cycle has triggered multiple doomsday scenarios. Search "2012" on amazon.com and you'll find over two hundred books predicting the demise of the world as we know it. Some foretell that a mysterious planet called Nibiru will collide with earth and destroy it. A disaster film called *2012*, made in 2009, presented an alternate terrifying scenario: particles pouring from the sun's surface caused the earth's crust to melt, and as Los Angeles collapsed and Yellowstone exploded, people desperately competed for one of four hundred thousand available places on escaping space arks.

Apprehensive? Go to YouTube and watch a film clip from NASA's Ames Research Center listing the different apocalyptic scenarios one by one. Listen as the professional astronomer David Morrison patiently explains why you have nothing to fear.

These pessimistic scenarios stem from popular reaction to the work of professional Maya scholars. The oral epic *Popul Vuh* begins by describing three separate efforts by the gods to make humans; they succeed only on their fourth attempt, when the current Great Cycle begins (see the feature "Movement of Ideas Through Primary Sources: The Ballgame in *Popul Vuh*," page 120). One of the most prominent American scholars in the field, Michael D. Coe, in the first 1966 edition of his classic book *The Maya*, wrote that "there is a suggestion . . . that Armageddon would overtake the degenerate peoples of the world and all creation on the final day of the thirteenth" and final baktun (a 394-year-long unit) of the current Great Cycle, and all would be destroyed.

New inscriptions have surfaced since 1966, though, that do give Long Count dates into the next Great Cycle, evidence that the Maya did not envision the world coming to an end. Most scholars and Mayans today concur that, when one Great Cycle ends, a new one will begin. NASA astronomer David Morrison's advice? "Don't worry about 2012 and enjoy 2013 when it comes."

Sources: Dennis Overby, "Is Doomsday Coming? Perhaps but Not in 2012," *New York Times*, November 17, 2009; "Niburu and Doomsday 2012: Questions and Answers with David Morrison," YouTube; Michael Coe, *The Maya* (New York: Praeger, 1966), p. 149.

Starting around 400 B.C.E., the peoples of Mesoamerica used two methods to count days: one cycle ran 365 days for the solar year, while the ritual cycle lasted 260 days. The solar year had 18 months of 20 days each with 5 extra days at the end of the year; the 260-day ritual cycle had 13 weeks of 20 days each.

If one combined the two ways of counting time so that both cycles started on the same day and ran their full course, 18,980 days, or 52 years, would pass before the two cycles converged again. The 52-year cycle had one major drawback: one could not record events occurring more than 52 years earlier without confusion.

Accordingly, the peoples of Mesoamerica developed the **Long Count**, a calendar that ran cumulatively, starting from a day far in the mythical past (whose equivalent is August 11, 3114 B.C.E.) and continuing to the present. (See the feature "World History in Today's World: The Maya Calendar and the End of the World.") The Long Count came into use in the fifth and fourth centuries B.C.E., when the successors to the Olmec built several monuments bearing Long Count dates. The inscriptions of Long Count dates use a mix of bars and dots to show the different units of the calendar: 400 years, 200 years, 1 year, 20 days, and 1 day.

Long Count
A calendar that ran cumulatively, starting from a day equivalent to August 11, 3114 B.C.E., and continuing to the present. Came into use in the fifth and fourth centuries B.C.E., when inscriptions of bars and dots showed different calendar units.

Teotihuacan, ca. 200 B.C.E.–600 C.E.

At the same time that the peoples along the coast were developing the Long Count and using glyphs, a huge metropolis arose at **Teotihuacan** (tay-oh-tee-WAH-kahn). Founded around 200 B.C.E., the city continued to grow until the year 650 C.E. Estimates of its population range between 40,000 and 200,000, certainly enough to qualify as a complex society. Teotihuacan's population made it the largest city in the Americas before 1500 but smaller than contemporary Rome's 1 million (see Chapter 7) or Luoyang's 500,000 during the Han dynasty (see Chapter 4). (See the feature "Visual Evidence in Primary Sources: The Imposing Capital of Teotihuacan.")

On Teotihuacan's neatly gridded streets, ordinary people lived in one-story apartment compounds whose painted white exteriors had no windows and whose interiors were covered with colorful frescoes. Divided among several families, the largest compounds housed over a hundred people; the smallest, about twenty. A plumbing system drained wastewater into underground channels along the street, eventually converging in aboveground canals. As is characteristic of complex societies, the compounds show evidence of craft specializations: for example, one was a pottery workshop.

One residential district in the city has atypical rounded houses instead of the more common apartment compounds and contains pottery similar to that in the Veracruz region. Since this type of dwelling has been found in many sites along the Gulf of Mexico, archaeologists surmise that this was a community of migrant workers from the Veracruz region that continued to make the characteristic pottery of their homeland.

We do not know whether Teotihuacan served as the capital of an empire, but it was certainly a large city-state. Sometime around 600 C.E. a fire, apparently caused by an internal revolt, leveled sections of the city, causing the residents to gradually move away.

Teotihuacan
The largest city in the Americas before 1500, covering 8 square miles (20 sq km), located some 30 miles (50 km) northeast of modern-day Mexico City. Was occupied from around 200 B.C.E. to 650 C.E. and had an estimated population at its height of 40,000–200,000.

The Maya, 300 B.C.E.–1200 C.E.

The **Maya**, like the other peoples of the Americas, differed from the Eurasian empires in that they created a remarkable complex society unaided by the wheel, plow, draft animals, or metal tools. Some scholars see the Olmec as a mother culture that gave both the Teotihuacan and Maya peoples their calendar, their writing system, and even their enormous flat-topped stepped pyramids—perhaps temples, perhaps palaces—of limestone and plaster packed with earth fill. Others disagree sharply, arguing that the Olmec, Teotihuacan, and Maya were neighboring cultures that did not directly influence each other. These ongoing debates combine with new discoveries to make Maya studies a lively field.

Some scholars also thought the Maya were a peace-loving people governed by a religious elite, until inscriptions dating between 250 and 910 C.E. were deciphered in the 1970s. Scholars today recognize the Maya's unrelenting violence but see it as no different from that of the Assyrian empire and Shang dynasty China.

Maya
Indigenous people living in modern-day Yucatán, Belize, Honduras, and Guatemala. Their complex society reached its height during the classic period, when they used a fully developed written language.

The Major Periods of Maya History and Maya Writing

Scholars specializing in Maya studies refer to the period from 250 to 910 as the classic age, because there are written inscriptions on monuments, and the period before 250 as the preclassic age. Recent discoveries are forcing scholars to reconsider these labels.

The urban complex of El Mirador and fifty surrounding satellite cities occupies 2,500 square miles (6,500 sq km) of jungle spanning northern Guatemala and the Campeche state in southwestern Mexico. The settlement, which covers 6 square miles (15.5 sq km), dates to 300 B.C.E.–200 C.E. and thus existed before the classic period. With an estimated population of at least one hundred thousand, El Mirador challenges the earlier view that all preclassic sites were small. The city had the enormous La Danta pyramid, compelling evidence of the ruler's ability to command labor (see the table "The World's Largest Pyramids," included in the feature "Visual Evidence in Primary Sources: The Imposing Capital of Teotihuacan"). The city's sophisticated system of water collection allowed the residents to attain much higher agricultural yields than their neighbors and fueled great prosperity. Because archaeologists are not certain whether the residents of El Mirador had a writing system (they have found some isolated glyphs), El Mirador is still considered a preclassic site. The city was abandoned sometime around 200 C.E.

In some Maya cities, such as Tikal (TEE-kal), but not in others, such as Copán (co-PAHN), construction of monuments and inscriptions stopped between 550 and 600, possibly because of a political or ecological crisis. This half-century marks the division between the early classic period (250–550) and late classic period (600–800), when the building of monuments resumed. The latest Maya monument with an inscription is dated 910, marking the end of the terminal classic period (800–910).

One of the great intellectual breakthroughs of the twentieth century was the decipherment of the Mayan script. (Scholars today use the word *Maya* to refer to the people and *Mayan* for the language they spoke.) Mayan glyphs did not look like any of the world's other writing systems. They were so pictorial that many doubted they could represent sounds. After twenty years of research and study, however, scholars realized in the 1970s that one could write a single Mayan word several different ways: entirely phonetically, entirely pictorially, or using a combination of both phonetic sounds and pictures. It is as if one could write *hat* in English by drawing a picture of a hat ⌂ or writing h + a + t, h + @ + t, or simply h + @.

***Popul Vuh* Frieze** In 2009, archaeologists from Idaho State University found a carved stucco panel 26 feet (8 m) long, depicting a scene from the Mayan oral epic *Popul Vuh*, in which one of the Hero Twins, wearing a jaguar headdress, swims with the severed head of his father. Dating to circa 200 B.C.E., the panel, part of the city's water collection system, shows that the tales of *Popul Vuh* circulated even in this early period. "It was like finding the Mona Lisa in the sewage system," reported the lead archaeologist.

Photo: D. McKay, © FARES 2009, used by permission

The Imposing Capital of Teotihuacan

The three magnificent pyramids of Teotihuacan, 30 miles (50 km) northeast of Mexico City, impress visitors even today. Lined with smaller pyramids, the broad Avenue of the Dead runs from the Pyramid of the Moon past the Pyramid of the Sun to the Feathered Serpent Pyramid. All of these names, including *Teotihuacan*, which means "the abode of the gods," were given by Nahuatl-speaking settlers from the north after their arrival sometime in the twelfth century (see Chapter 15).

Since we do not know what the original residents of the city called these structures and since no one has deciphered the few glyphs that appear on scattered stones, archaeologists have exercised great ingenuity in trying to understand the city's layout. Teotihuacan is unusual in that none of the city's rulers built monuments to themselves. Because deities of later peoples, like the Maya, were often associated with stars and planets, most concur that the city's orientation must have been astronomical, based on the different phases of Venus, the Morning Star honored by so many peoples in the Americas.

The discovery of more than two hundred skeletons under the Feathered Serpent Pyramid has shed new light on the building's purpose. The group with the most valuable jewelry appears to have the highest social status; another group that wears less valuable shell beads seems to rank lower. A third group of women had even less jewelry, while a fourth group consisted of uniformed men buried with large quantities of projectile points, most likely an army. The people in these groups assume different postures, some with their hands tied behind their backs, as if they had been killed before burial, possibly with the accompanying obsidian knives, blades, and piercing implements. Because looters dug two large trenches in the center of the Feathered Serpent Pyramid, archaeologists cannot be certain who was originally buried there, but the mass burials and valuable grave goods make it likely that this was the ruler's tomb. The dead buried at Teotihuacan, like the terracotta warriors of the Qin founder (see Chapter 4), appear to have served as a sacrificial army for the deceased ruler, who was buried circa 200 C.E. at the time of the pyramid's completion.

The World's Largest Pyramids

Name	Site	Date	Material	Height
Great Pyramid	Giza, Egypt	2580 B.C.E.	stone	480 ft (146 m)
La Danta	El Mirador, Guatemala	200 B.C.E.	cut stone and rock fill	230 ft (70 m)
Pyramid of the Sun	Teotihuacan	200 C.E.	volcanic rubble and earth	216 feet (66 m)
Tarharqa's Pyramid	Nuri, Nubia	664 B.C.E.	stone	160 feet (49 m)
Pyramid of the Moon	Teotihuacan	200 C.E.	volcanic rubble and earth	140 feet (43 m)
Pirámide Mayor	Caral	2600 B.C.E.	brick and earth	60 ft (18 m)

QUESTION FOR ANALYSIS

» *Compare and contrast the site of Teotihuacan with descriptions of the urban centers of other early complex societies in the Americas (Caral, Olmec, Maya in this chapter) and in Eurasia (Sumer, Chapter 2; Indus River Valley, Chapter 3; Shang dynasty, Chapter 4).*

With sides over 700 feet (213 m) long at the base, and over twenty stories high, the Pyramid of the Sun is one of the two largest structures in the Americas made before 1500 (the other is La Danta).

The Feathered Serpent Pyramid, also called the Quetzalcoatl Temple, has staircases up the side of the monument with stone facades and elaborate serpent heads dividing the different terraces.

The Citadel, opposite the Feathered Serpent Pyramid, was the political center of the city.

Georg Gerster/Photo Researchers, Inc.

The Avenue of the Dead, 50 yards (50 m) wide, extends for more than 3 miles (5.2 km) and connects the different pyramids of Teotihuacan.

Laborers made the Pyramid of the Moon in the same way that they made the Pyramid of the Sun: they piled up earth and rubble to form a pyramid shape, leveled off horizontal terraces, and then faced the surface with adobe and stone.

This modern ring road, the Periférico, was built in the 1960s to steer traffic away from the monuments.

Since 1973 Mayanists have learned to read about 85 percent of all surviving glyphs. Because inscriptions follow a set format, beginning with the rise of a particular ruler, it is possible to understand inscriptions at ruins throughout the Maya region. So far the focus on the history of royal dynasties unfortunately reveals little about ordinary people. Analysts are trying to bridge that immense information gap by ingeniously combining inscriptions and paintings from the classic period with information from European observers in the sixteenth century (see Chapter 15) and even ethnographic data on Maya peoples alive today.

Copán
A typical Maya city-state. At its peak in the eighth century, Copán had a population of 18,000–20,000 divided into sharply demarcated groups: the ruling family, the nobility, ordinary people, and slaves.

Maya Government and Society

Copán provides a good example of a typical Maya city-state, including a population divided into sharply demarcated groups: the ruling family, the nobility, ordinary people, and slaves. Copán reached its peak in the eighth century.

The ruler of Copán, who was also the commander of the army, ranked higher than everyone else. He decided when to ally with other city-states and when to fight them, as well as how to allocate the different crops and taxes received from the populace. When a ruler died, a council of nobles met to verify that his son or his younger brother was fit to rule. If a ruler died without an heir, the council appointed someone from one of the highest-ranking noble families to succeed him.

One ruler's tomb contained a deer-shaped vessel with traces of theobromine, a caffeine-like molecule found only in chocolate. Mesoamericans started preparing drinks made from pounded seeds from the cacao (*ka-ka-wa* in Mayan) tree as early as 600 B.C.E. and certainly by the early fifth century, the time of this ruler's tomb. The Maya did not sweeten the cacao drink but added spices and crushed chile peppers to make a variety of drinks they prized for their foam. The Maya believed that cacao could cure a variety of ills, including hemorrhoids and nervous tension.

Ranking just below the members of the ruling family, the nobles of Maya society lived in large, spacious houses such as those found in the section of Copán known as the House of the Officials. One typical compound there contains between forty and fifty buildings surrounding eleven courtyards. In judging a man's prominence, the Maya considered all of his relatives on both his father's and mother's side. The Mayan word for "nobles" means "he whose descent is known on both sides."[1]

Literate in a society where few could read or write, scribes came from the highest ranks of the nobility. When the king's armies did well in battle, the scribes enjoyed the best treatment that the king could give them. When the king's armies lost, they were often taken prisoner.

Only those scribes with mathematical skills could maintain the elaborate calendar. Having developed the concept of zero, Maya ritual specialists devised an extraordinarily sophisticated numerical system. Astronomers observed the stars and planets so closely that they could predict eclipses. They were particularly skilled in tracking the movements of Venus, which during some seasons appeared first in the evening before any stars, and in others was the last to disappear in the morning. The Maya used their knowledge of celestial bodies to determine auspicious days for inaugurating rulers, conducting elaborate religious ceremonies, or starting wars.

The most prosperous ordinary people became merchants specializing in long-distance trade. Salt was the one necessity the Maya had to import because their diet did not provide enough sodium to prevent a deficiency. They collected salt from the Yucatán beaches and shipped it in canoes along the ocean's shore and on interior rivers until it had to be carried by hand. Some of the items traded were luxury goods like jade, shells, and quetzal bird feathers, which flickered blue, gold, or green in the light.

The craft specialists who transformed these raw materials into finely worked goods lived in the small houses of ordinary people. The Maya first encountered gold around the year 800 and learned to work it, yet they made few items out of metal. They preferred green jade, which they carved and smoothed with saws made of coated string and different types of sandpaper.

The most important trade good in the Maya world was **obsidian**, a naturally occurring volcanic glass. The best material available to the Maya for making tools, obsidian could also be worked into fine art objects. Obsidian shattered easily, though, so the Maya also made tools from chert, a flintlike rock that was more durable.

Since Copán's urban inhabitants could not raise enough food to feed themselves, farmers who lived outside the city provided residents with maize and smaller amounts of beans, squash, and chili peppers. City dwellers had fruit gardens and were able occasionally to hunt wild game.

Because the Maya had no draft animals, most cultivators worked land within a day or two's walk from the urban center. Their fields marked the limit of each city-state's direct political control. Aerial photographs of the Yucatán, Mexico, and Belize have revealed raised fields dating back to the time of the Maya, which were farmed season after season. Much of this agricultural work was done by slaves. The lowest-ranking people in Maya society, slaves were prisoners of war who had been allowed to live and forced to work in the fields.

obsidian
A naturally occurring volcanic glass used by different peoples in the Americas to make fine art objects, dart tips, and knife blades sharper than modern scalpels. The most important good traded by the Maya.

The Religious Beliefs of the Maya

Many Maya rituals featured the spilling of royal blood, which the Maya considered sacred. Surviving paintings from throughout the Maya region depict women pulling thorny vines through their tongues and kings sticking either a stingray spine or a pointed bone tool through the tips of their penises. No surviving text explains exactly why the Maya thought blood sacred, but blood offerings clearly played a key role in their belief system.

One of the few Mayan sources that survives, an oral epic named ***Popul Vuh*** (POPE-uhl voo), or "The Council Book," features a series of games in which players on two teams moved the ball by hitting it with their hips and tried to get it past their opponents' end line. The Maya believed that the earth was recreated each time the hip ballgame was played, and the side seen as being tested by the gods, usually prisoners of war, always lost, after which their blood was spilled in an elaborate ceremony. (See the feature "Movement of Ideas Through Primary Sources: The Ballgame in *Popul Vuh*.")

Recorded nearly one thousand years after the decline of the Maya, the *Popul Vuh* preserves only a part of their rich legends, but scholars have used it in conjunction with surviving texts to piece together the key elements of the Maya belief system. All Maya gods, the *Popul Vuh* explains, are descended from a divine pair. The Lizard House, the father, invented the Mayan script and supported all learning, while his wife, Lady Rainbow, was a deity of weaving and medicine who also helped women endure the pain of childbirth. Their descendants, the Maya believed, each presided over a different realm: separate gods existed for merchants, hunters, fishermen, soldiers, and the ruling families. Maya rulers sacrificed their prisoners of war as offerings to these deities.

The Maya communicated with the dead using various techniques. Caves served as portals between the world of the living and the Xibalba Underworld described in *Popul Vuh*. One cave is 2,790 feet (850 m) long; its walls are decorated with drawings of the Hero Twins, the ballgame, and sexual acts. The Maya who visited this and other caves employed enemas to intoxicate themselves so they could see the dead. They performed these enemas by attaching bone tubes, found

Popul Vuh
One of the few surviving sources in the Mayan language, this oral epic features a series of hip ballgames between the gods and humans. Originally written in Mayan glyphs, it was recorded in the Roman alphabet in the 1500s.

The Ballgame in *Popul Vuh*

The complicated plot of the Maya oral epic *Popul Vuh* involves two sets of ball-playing twins: after disturbing the gods with their play, one pair go to the Xibalba (SHE-bal-ba) Underworld (derived from the Mayan word for "fear," "trembling"), where they die at the hands of One and Seven Death, the head lords of Xibalba. The severed head of one of these twins hangs on a tree from which its spittle magically impregnates Lady Blood, who gives birth to the second set of twins, Hunahpu (HOO-nah-pooh) and Xbalanque (sh-bal-on-kay). These Hero Twins, far more skillful than their father and uncle, at first trick the gods of the Underworld repeatedly and then defeat them in the ballgame described in the episode below. Eventually they also die, but because the gods grant them another life, they rise at the end of the narrative to become the sun and the moon, creating the upper world or cosmos.

The earliest archaeological evidence of the game comes from the Olmec site of El Manatí, located 6 miles (10 km) east of San Lorenzo, where a dozen rubber balls dating to around 500 B.C.E. were found. Almost every Maya city-state had a ball court, usually in the shape of an L, with walls around it, located near a major temple. The Maya played this soccer-like game with heavy rubber balls measuring 12 or 18 inches (33 or 50 cm) across. The Maya combined the liquid rubber from latex trees with sap from morning glory flowers to make rubber for different purposes: sandal soles had to be durable, rubber bands to attach blades

to shafts had to be resilient, and balls had to be bouncy. Sometimes the ball-makers used a human skull to make a hollow, less lethal, ball. The game spread throughout the Maya core region and as far north as Snaketown near Phoenix, Arizona, the home of an early Anasazi people who had two ball courts and rubber balls.

Since ball courts and balls do not provide enough information to understand how the game was played, anthropologists are closely studying the modern hip ballgames in the few villages near Mazatlán (ma-zat-LAN), Sinaloa (sin-A-loh-a) State in northwestern Mexico, where the game is still played. Two opposing teams of three to five players try to get the ball past the other team's end line. After serving with their hands, they propel the heavy rubber balls with their hips. Although players cover their hips with padding, the hips of modern players develop calluses and often become permanently bruised a deep-black color. We cannot be sure that everyone who played the game knew the story of the Hero Twins, but many players probably understood the game as a contest between two teams, one representing good, life, or the Hero Twins, and the other evil, death, or Xibalba, which was ultimately victorious.

This passage from the *Popul Vuh* describes the first test the twins must endure.

Source: Reprinted with the permission of Simon & Schuster, Inc., from POPUL VUH: The Definitive Edition of the Mayan Book of the Dawn of Life and the Glories of Gods and Kings, by Dennis Tedlock. Copyright © 1985, 1996 Dennis Tedlock. pp. 119–122.

First they entered Dark House.

And after that, the messenger of One Death brought their torch, burning when it arrived, along with one cigar apiece.

"'Here is their torch,' says the lord. 'They must return the torch in the morning, along with the cigars. They must return them intact,' say the lords," the messenger said when he arrived.

"Very well," they said, but they didn't burn the torch—instead, something that looked like fire was substituted. This was the tail of the macaw, which looked like a torch to the sentries. And as for the cigars, they just put fireflies at the tips of those cigars, which they kept lit all night.

"We've defeated them," said the sentries, but the torch was not consumed—it just looked that way. And as for the cigars, there wasn't anything burning there—it just looked that way. When these things were taken back to the lords:

"What's happening? Where did they come from? Who begot them and bore them? Our hearts are really hurting, because what they're doing to us is no good. They're different in looks and different in their very being," they said among themselves. And when they had summoned all the lords:

"Let's play ball, boys," the boys were told. And then they were asked by One and Seven Death:

"Where might you have come from? Please name it," Xibalba said to them.

"Well, wherever did we come from? We don't know," was all they said. They didn't name it.

"Very well then, we'll just go play ball, boys," Xibalba told them.

"Good," they said.

"Well, this is the one we should put in play, here's our rubber ball," said the Xibalbans.

"No thanks. This is the one to put in, here's ours," said the boys.

"No it's not. This is the one we should put in," the Xibalbans said again.

"Very well," said the boys.

"After all, it's just a decorated one," said the Xibalbans.

"Oh no it's not. It's just a skull, we say in return," said the boys.

"No it's not," said the Xibalbans.

"Very well," said Hunahpu. When it was sent off by Xibalba, the ball was stopped by Hunahpu's yoke [hip-pad].

And then, while Xibalba watched, the White Dagger came out from inside the ball. It went clattering, twisting all over the floor of the court.

"What's that!" said Hunahpu and Xbalanque. "Death is the only thing you want for us! Wasn't it *you* who sent a summons to us, and wasn't it *your* messenger who went? Truly, take pity on us, or else we'll just leave," the boys told them.

And this is what had been ordained for the boys: that they should have died right away, right there, defeated by that knife. But it wasn't like that. Instead, Xibalba was again defeated by the boys.

"Well, don't go, boys. We can still play ball, but we'll put yours into play," the boys were told.

"Very well," they said, and this was time for their rubber ball, so the ball was dropped in.

And after that, they specified the prize:

"What should our prize be?" asked the Xibalbans.

"It's yours for the asking," was all the boys said.

"We'll just win four bowls of flowers," said the Xibalbans.

"Very well. What kinds of flowers?" the boys asked Xibalba.

"One bowl of red petals, one bowl of white petals, one bowl of yellow petals, and one bowl of whole ones," said the Xibalbans.

"Very well," said the boys, and then their ball was dropped in. The boys were their equals in strength and made many plays, since they only had very good thoughts. Then the boys gave themselves up in defeat, and the Xibalbans were glad when they were defeated:

"We've done well. We've beaten them on the first try," said the Xibalbans. "Where will they go to get the flowers?" they said in their hearts.

"Truly, before the night is over, you must hand over our flowers and our prize," the boys, Hunahpu and Xbalanque, were told by Xibalba.

"Very well. So we're also playing ball at night," they said when they accepted their charge.

And after that, the boys entered Razor House, the second test of Xibalba.

QUESTIONS FOR ANALYSIS

» *What tricks do the Hero Twins play on the lords of the Xibalba Underworld? How do the Xibalba lords retaliate?*

» *What happens that is unexpected? Why do the twins lose?*

in large quantities at Maya sites, to leather or rubber bags filled with different liquids. Surviving drawings make it impossible to identify the liquids, but anthropologists speculate that the enema bags were filled with wine, chocolate, or hallucinogens made from the peyote cactus.

War, Politics, and the Decline of the Maya

In the past few decades, scholars have devoted considerable energy and ingenuity to sorting out the relationships among the sixty or so Maya city-states. A few key phrases appear in inscriptions: some rulers are said to be someone else's king, an indication that they accepted another king as their overlord or ruler. It is not clear what ties bound a subordinate ruler to his superior: marriage ties, loyalty oaths, military alliances, or perhaps a mixture of all three.

Because various rulers vied continuously to increase their territory and become each other's lord, the different Maya city-states devoted considerable resources to

Celebrating a Maya Victory in Battle   This colorful fresco in a Maya tomb in Bonampak, Mexico, commemorates the victory of the ruler, who wears an elaborate headdress and a jacket made from jaguar skin. He relentlessly thrusts his spear downward and grasps the hair of a prisoner whose outstretched hand implores his captor. These murals, which reveal so much about the lives of the Maya, were suddenly abandoned around 800, a time when work on many other monuments stopped abruptly, marking the end of the classic era. (© Charles and Josette Lenars/Corbis)

war. Armies consisted of foot soldiers whose weapons included spears with obsidian points, slingshots, and darts propelled by a spear-thrower. The Maya did not have the bow and arrow. On the most informal level of conflict, a group of soldiers might steal into enemy territory to take captives, while in formal battles, two opposing armies of infantry faced off and showered each other with darts or stones from slingshots. Traps and ambushes were common, and the fighters used both daggers and spears in hand-to-hand combat.

The goal of all Maya warfare was to obtain captives. In inscriptions rulers brag about how many captives they held, because they wanted to appear powerful. Low-born captives, if spared ritual sacrifice, were assigned to work in the maize fields of nobles, while prisoners of higher status, particularly those from noble families, might be held in captivity for long periods of time, sometimes as much as twenty years. However, many ordinary soldiers captured in warfare, and especially higher-ranking prisoners, could expect to suffer ritual bloodletting. Maya victors removed the fingernails of war captives, cut their chests open to tear out their hearts, and publicly beheaded them as sacrifices to their deities.

At the peak of Maya power in 750, the population reached 8 to 10 million. Sometime around the year 800, the Maya city-states entered an era of decline, evident because site after site has produced unfinished monuments abruptly abandoned by stoneworkers. So sudden was the decline that workers at some sites stopped carving after completing a single face of a square monument.

Archaeologists have different explanations for the Maya decline. In the seventh and eighth centuries, blocs of allied city-states engaged in unending warfare. The drain on resources may have depopulated the Maya cities. The fragile agricultural base depleted the nutrients in the fields close to the political centers. In some places, a sustained drought between 800 and 1050 may have dealt the final blow to the ecosystem.

Maya culture revived during the postclassic period (910–1200), and the city of Chichen Itza (CHEE-chen IT-za) in the northern Yucatán, which flourished between 1000 and 1200, combined classic elements of Maya and central Mexican architecture and city planning. The ball court at Chichen Itza measures 545 feet (166 m) by 223 feet (68 m), making it the largest ball court in the Americas. Although Maya culture did not die out after 1200, the Maya never again matched the social stratification, specialized occupations, and large urban centers of the classic period.

The Northern Peoples, 500 B.C.E.–1200 C.E.

Complex society arose north of the Rio Grande, in the area occupied by the modern United States and Canada, relatively late—after the decline of the Maya—and possibly as a result of contact with Mesoamerica. The North Americans planted maize as the Mesoamericans did, and their cities resembled their Maya counterparts. The first complex societies in North America, both dating to after 700 C.E., were the Mississippian culture in the central United States and the Anasazi (AH-nah-sah-zee) culture in the southwest United States.

Until about 500 B.C.E., the peoples living to the north continued to hunt and gather in small bands of around sixty people, much like the residents of Monte Verde, Chile (see Chapter 1), and as a result, their communities remained small. Then, from 500 B.C.E to 100 C.E., the Adena (uh-DEE-nuh) created earthworks along the Ohio River Valley in Ohio and Illinois. Some Adena mounds are perfect circles; others are shaped like animals.

The Adena did not farm, but their successors, the Hopewell peoples (200 B.C.E.–500 C.E.), cultivated maize, beans, and squash and built larger earthworks in the valleys of the Ohio, Illinois, and Mississippi Rivers. The taller and more elaborate Hopewell earthworks formed clusters of circles, rectangles, and polygons.

The Adena and Hopewell settlements were not large urban centers, but these earthworks demonstrate that their leaders could organize large-scale labor projects. Archaeologists have reconstructed the Hopewell trade routes by locating the sources of unusual items, such as alligator teeth and skulls from Florida, mapping the sites where those items appear, and then inferring the trade routes by linking the source with its various destinations. The Hopewell trading networks, more extensive than those of the Adena, extended from the Rocky Mountains to the Atlantic Ocean; with their neighbors to the south in modern-day Mexico, they traded conch shells, shark teeth, and obsidian.

Mississippian peoples

The first northern people (800–1450) to build large urban centers in the Mississippi River Valley.

Occupying over a hundred different sites concentrated in the Mississippi River Valley, the **Mississippian peoples** (800–1450) built the first large urban centers that characterize complex society in the north. Mississippian towns followed a Maya plan, with temples or palaces on earthen mounds around a central plaza. The Mississippian peoples were the first in the Americas to develop the bow and arrow, sometime around 900.

The largest surviving mound, in the Cahokia (kuh-HOKE-ee-uh) Mounds of Collinsville, Illinois (just east of St. Louis), is 100 feet (30 m) high and 1,000 feet (300 m) long. Its sheer magnitude testifies to the power the leaders had over their subjects. Cahokia, with a population of thirty thousand, held eighty-four other mounds, some for temples, some for mass burials. One mound contained the corpses of 110 young women, evidence of a sacrificial cult to either a leader or a deity.

The other major complex society of the north appeared in modern-day Colorado, Arizona, Utah, and New Mexico: the Anasazi. Their centers also show signs of contact with the Maya, most notably in the presence of ball courts. During the Pueblo period (700–1300), the Anasazi built two kinds of houses: pit houses carved out of the ground and pueblos made from bricks, mortar, and log roofs. One pueblo structure in Chaco, New Mexico, had eight hundred rooms in five stories and was home to one thousand residents. After 1150 the Anasazi began to build their pueblos next to cliff faces, as at Mesa Verde, Colorado. They used irrigation to farm, and their craftspeople made distinctive pottery, cotton and feather clothing, and turquoise jewelry.

Like so many other urban centers in the Americas, Cahokia Mounds and Mesa Verde declined suddenly after 1200, when their populations dispersed, and archaeologists do not know why.

The Peoples of the Andes, 3100 B.C.E.–1000 C.E.

Several complex societies arose, flourished, and collapsed between 3100 B.C.E. and 1000 C.E. in the Andean region, which includes modern-day Peru, Bolivia, Ecuador, Argentina, and Chile in South America. These complex societies predated the first Mesoamerican complex society of the Olmec by nearly two thousand years, indicating that the two regions developed independently of each other. All the Andean complex societies built city-states with large urban centers, though never on the scale of Teotihuacan.

The Andean mountain chain runs up the center of the Andean region, which extends east to the edge of the dense Amazon rainforest and west to the Pacific coast (see Map 5.1, page 112). Although at a higher altitude than Mesoamerica, this region has a similarly uneven distribution of rainfall. In the east, where rain falls heavily, the residents collected rainwater and brought it to their fields by a system of channels; to the west, almost none falls.

The main staple of the diet was potatoes, supplemented by squash, chili peppers, beans, and sometimes maize, which could grow only at lower altitudes. The earliest strains of domesticated squash date to about 8000 B.C.E. Sometime around 5000 B.C.E., the Andeans domesticated the llama and the alpaca. Both animals could carry loads of approximately 100 pounds (50 kg) over distances of 10–12 miles (16–20 km) a day. The Andeans never rode these animals, used them for farming, or raised them to eat. Their main source of animal protein was the domesticated guinea pig.

The earliest large urban settlement in the Americas, at the site of **Caral** (KA-ral) in the Andes, lies some 100 miles (160 km) north of Lima, the capital of modern Peru, and only 14 miles (22 km) from the Pacific coast. People have known about the site since the early twentieth century because its structures are prominent and so clearly visible from the air, but only in 2001 did archaeologists realize that it dated to 3100 B.C.E.

The Caral site contains five small pyramid-shaped structures and one large one: the Pirámide Mayor (pi-RAH-me-day my-your), which stands 60 feet (18 m) tall and covers 5 acres (.02 km) (see the table "The World's Largest Pyramids," included in the

Caral
The earliest complex society (3100–1800 B.C.E.) in the Americas, whose main urban center was located at Caral in modern-day Peru, in the Andes.

Latin America's First Civilization at Caral, Peru Since 1900 people have known about the Caral site, but only recently were archaeologists able to date the site to 3100 B.C.E. The circular amphitheater (on the right) was the major ceremonial center of the city; members of the audience sat in rows, and possibly even in box seats. Caral was a large city-state, with some twenty smaller communities in the immediate neighborhood. Archaeologists have found clear signs of social stratification: the wealthiest residents lived on the tops of the pyramids while the poorer residents lived on lower levels or on the outskirts of the town. (© George Steinmetz)

feature "Visual Evidence in Primary Sources: The Imposing Capital of Teotihuacan"). Inside the pyramid, archaeologists found a set of thirty-two carved flutes made from condor and pelican bone with decorations showing birds and monkeys, possibly deities. The three thousand or so people at the site included wealthy residents living in large dwellings on top of the pyramids, craftsmen in smaller houses at their base, and unskilled laborers in much simpler dwellings located around the perimeters of the town. Caral, like Uruk in Mesopotamia or Harappa in India, showed clear signs of social stratification. With some twenty smaller communities in the immediate vicinity, Caral was probably a city-state, not an early empire.

The history of the site reflects the rise-and-fall pattern so common to the early cities of the Americas and also to the Indus Valley (see Chapter 3). Agricultural improvements led to dramatic urban growth, followed by sudden decline. Usually no direct evidence reveals why a given city was abandoned, but drought and over-farming may have contributed. Caral was abandoned in 1800 B.C.E.

In 1200 B.C.E., nearly two thousand years after Caral was first occupied, a major urban center arose at **Chavín** (cha-VEEN), about 60 miles (100 km) north of Caral (see Map 5.1 on page 112). Chavín has large temples, some in the shape of a U, and impressive stone sculptures, which combine elements of different animals such as jaguars, snakes, and eagles with human body parts to create composite human-animal sculptures, possibly of deities.

In 350 B.C.E., during the last years of the Chavín culture, several distinct regional cultures arose on the south coast of Peru that are most famous for the Nazca (NAZ-ka) lines, a series of earthworks near the modern town of Nazca. The Nazca people scraped away the dark surface layer of the desert in straight-edged trenches to reveal a lighter-colored soil beneath, creating precise straight lines as long as 6 miles (10 km), as well as elaborate designs of spiders, whales, and monkeys, possibly offerings to or depictions of their gods. No one knows how people working on the ground created these designs, which are still visible from the air today. No large cities of the Nazca people have been found, but the Nazca lines, like the earthworks of the Adena and Hopewell peoples, show that their rulers were able to mobilize large numbers of laborers.

Occupied between 600 and 1000, the biggest Andean political center was at Tiwanaku (tee-wan-a-koo), 12 miles (20 km) south of Lake Titicaca (tit-tee-ka-ka), southern Bolivia, at the high altitude of 11,800 feet (3,600 m) above sea level. The rulers of the Tiwanaku city-state, archaeologists surmise, exercised some kind of political control over a large area extending through modern-day Bolivia, Argentina, northern Chile, and southern Peru. At its peak, Tiwanaku was home to some forty thousand people. Its farmers could support such a large population because they used a raised-field system: the irrigation channels they dug around their fields helped to keep the crops from freezing on chilly nights.

Sometime around 700 to 800, the Andean peoples, alone among the peoples living in the Americas, learned how to work metal intensively. Unlike the Maya, who worked with only gold, the Andeans discovered how to extract metallic ore from rocks and heat different metals to form alloys. They made bronze both by combining copper with tin, as was common in Eurasia, and also by combining copper with arsenic. One site in Peru, in continuous use after 700, had draft furnaces in which families melted fuel and metal ore together, producing slag with copper in it, which they extracted and worked into ingots, small sheets, or "ax money"—ax-shaped pieces of metal tied together in bundles and placed in tombs as an offering for the dead.

Andean graves have produced the only ancient metal tools found so far in the Americas. All were clearly designed for display. Most Andean metal was used to

Chavín
Andean complex society (1200–200 B.C.E.) in modern-day Peru. Best known for its temples and large stone sculptures of animals.

make decorations worn by people or placed on buildings, not for tools or weapons, which challenges yet another preconception prompted by the complex societies of Eurasia. In Mesopotamia, Egypt, India, and China, people switched to metal tools—first bronze, then iron—as soon as they learned to mine metal ore and make alloys. But the Andean peoples continued to use their traditional tools of wood and stone and used their newly discovered metal quite differently: for ceremonial and decorative purposes.

The Polynesian Voyages of Exploration, 1000 B.C.E.–1350 C.E.

The societies of the Americas discussed above, including the Maya, were land-based. Their residents used canoes for trips on inland waterways and for occasional voyages hugging the ocean shore, but they focused their energies on farming and building cities. In contrast, the peoples of the Pacific, who lived on the islands inside the Polynesian Triangle, spent much of their lives on the sea. Like the residents of the Americas, they developed in isolation from and quite differently from the Eurasians. Although their urban centers never became the large cities of complex societies, their societies were stratified and their leaders relied on their subjects for labor.

Humans had reached Australia in about 50,000 B.C.E. (see Chapter 1), and they ventured into the Pacific sometime after that. Starting around 1000 B.C.E., when the Fiji islands of Tonga and Samoa were first settled, early voyagers crossed the Pacific Ocean using only the stars to navigate and populated most of the Pacific islands. Their voyages resulted in one of the longest yet least-documented seaborne migrations in human history. How and why did these ancient voyagers travel so far? These questions have excited a century of lively debate and are far from settled.

The Settlement of the Polynesian Triangle

The islands of the Pacific fall into two groups: those lying off Australia and Indonesia—Micronesia (mike-ro-NEE-zhuh), Melanesia (mel-uh-NEE-zhuh), and New Guinea—and those within the **Polynesian Triangle**, an imaginary triangle linking Hawai'i, Easter Island, and New Zealand (see Map 5.2). With seventy times more water than islands, the Polynesian Triangle contains several thousand islands ranging in size from tiny uninhabited atolls to the largest, New Zealand, with an area of 103,695 square miles (268,570 sq km). The triangle's vast area can hold the continental United States twice over with room to spare.

The islands lying close to Indonesia and Australia were settled first. As the discovery of Mungo Man in Australia, which dates to circa 40,000 B.C.E., showed (see Chapter 1), ancient peoples could go from one island to the next in small craft. Since the islands of Micronesia and Melanesia were located close together, the next island was always within sight. But as these ancient settlers ventured farther east, the islands became farther apart: between Easter Island and Peru lie 2,250 miles (3,600 km) of open ocean. Sometime before 300 the first settlers reached Hawai'i, and after the year 400 they had reached Easter Island, or Rapa Nui (RA-pah nwee). Their final destination, in 1350, was New Zealand.

All the spoken languages within the Polynesian Triangle belong to the Oceanic language family. Languages within the Oceanic family differ only slightly among themselves; while the Hawai'ians say "kabu," meaning "forbidden" or

Polynesian Triangle An imaginary triangle with sides 4,000 miles (6,500 km) long linking Hawai'i, Easter Island, and New Zealand and containing several thousand islands.

MAP 5.2 Pacific Migration Routes Before 1500 Starting around 1000 B.C.E., the peoples living in Micronesia and Melanesia began to go to islands lying to the east in the Pacific Ocean. At first, they took canoes to the islands they could see with the naked eye. But later they traveled thousands of miles without navigational instruments, reaching Hawai'i before 300, Easter Island by 400, and New Zealand in 1350. (© Cengage Learning)

Lapita pottery
Named for a site in Melanesia, a low-fired brown pottery with lines and geometric decorations made with a pointed instrument. In use between 1500 and 1000 B.C.E., it reveals the direction of migration into the Pacific.

"prohibited," the Tahitian pronunciation is "tabu." (This word has entered English as *taboo*.)

Archaeologists have reconstructed the route of ancient migration, which started from Asia's Pacific coast and traveled east, by tracing the movement of a distinctive pottery with lines and geometric decorations made with a pointed instrument. This **Lapita** (la-PEE-tuh) **pottery** appears first in Melanesia in 1500 B.C.E. and then 500 years later on Tonga and Samoa.

Polynesian Seafaring Societies

Most observers agree that the original settlers must have traveled by canoe but do not know when canoes were first developed. Once their shape was perfected, it continued to be used for hundreds of years with no major modifications. Different peoples have used various coverings stretched over a light wooden frame: bark in heavily wooded areas like the temperate United States, and skins farther north, where trees were scarce. Today's fiberglass canoes have the same basic design.

double canoe
A sailing vessel made by connecting two canoes with rope to a wooden frame. Used by the ancestors of modern Polynesians for ocean voyages. Capable of speeds of 100–150 miles (160–240 km) per day.

Sometime in the first century C.E., the peoples of the Pacific developed a **double canoe**, which consisted of two canoes connected by a wooden frame lashed together with rope. More stable than single canoes, double canoes could also carry cargo on the platform between the two boats. A modern double canoe 50 feet (15 m) long can carry a load weighing 18,000 pounds (8,165 kg). Double canoes were propelled by a sail, an essential requirement for long ocean voyages, and could reach speeds of 100–150 miles (160–240 km) per day. Double canoes, however, had

National Library of Australia

drawbacks. Since they had no roofs, mariners would get wet during rainstorms. If one canoe sprang a leak and began to fill with water, it would sink, pushing the other canoe higher and the sinking canoe even lower. In storms the two canoes could easily break apart, resulting in the loss of all the baggage on the platform.

Europeans first described the villages of Tahiti and Hawai'i in the eighteenth century. Many historians assume that Polynesian life in earlier centuries resembled that in the eighteenth-century descriptions. The predominantly male chiefs and their kin lived lives of leisure, supported by gifts of food from the lower-ranking populace. Ordinary people tended crops in fields, which were often irrigated, and also hunted wildlife, mostly small birds.

The settlement of the Pacific resulted from both deliberate voyages and accidental exploration. Early settlers of both sexes must have traveled in boats, because otherwise the settlers could not have reproduced and populated the different islands. The settlers carried dogs and small rats because these animals became their main sources of protein. They found some islands when they were blown off course, most likely in storms.

The voyagers also carried plants, most likely in pots, to all the islands they reached. The staple crops of the Polynesian diet, breadfruit and taro, dispersed throughout the Pacific. Breadfruit, a seedless fruit with the texture of bread when baked, can be quite filling; taro is an edible starchy root plant that is pounded before being eaten. The distribution of two other plants points to early contacts between the Polynesian islands and South America: the sweet potato and the coconut. The sweet potato originated in South America and later spread throughout the Pacific; the coconut, in contrast, appeared first in Asia and later in Latin America.

Excavated chicken bones show that chickens lived in Chile between approximately 1304 and 1424. Prior to this find, many scholars believed that European settlers introduced chickens to the Americas in the 1500s (see Chapter 15), but the similarities between the Chilean and Polynesian chickens suggest that the first American chickens came from Polynesia.

The Polynesians may have followed large sea mammals, possibly orca or bottlenose dolphins, as they migrated for long periods over great distances. The first

European observers were struck by the Polynesians' ability to travel sometimes up to several hundreds of miles or kilometers to go deep-sea fishing.

etak
Traditional Polynesian system of navigation that uses the stars, clouds, waves, and bird flight patterns to steer on sea voyages.

Traditional Polynesian Navigation Techniques

In 1983, seven years after he guided the *Hokule'a* to Tahiti, Mau Piailug taught the traditional system of navigation, called **etak**, to an American named Steve Thomas. Piailug began by making a circular diagram from stones and palm fronds to teach Thomas the most important fifteen stars. Each star rose at one point and set on another on the circle; Piailug knew the trajectories through the night sky of over 150 stars. The start and end point for each star functioned exactly like the points on a compass: north, north by northeast, and so forth (see the photo on page 108).

Studying the skies and allowing for seasonal change, Polynesian navigators used the stars each night to determine their location; Piailug told Thomas which stars would be overhead for different journeys within the Caroline islands, to the Philippines in the west, and to Guam in the north. *"Then,"* Thomas reports, *"to my astonishment, he recorded the courses from Satawal [Piailug's home island] to Pikelot [a nearby island], then north to Hawai'i; from Hawai'i he delineated courses to North America, South America, Tahiti, the Marquesas, Samoa, and Japan. He told me he learned this wofanu [star course] from his grandfather."*

At the age of fifteen or sixteen, Piailug was formally initiated as a navigator: because no one after him received this recognition, Thomas called Piailug the last navigator. Although Piailug had not himself followed these different routes, the knowledge of these star courses enabled him to sail all the way from Hawai'i to Tahiti on his first attempt.

In its use of the stars, etak resembled navigation systems in use elsewhere, but the conceptual framework of etak was totally different. In Piailug's mind, his boat never moved through the water. Instead, the islands and water came to the boat and then went past it.

As every sailor knows, the stars are not always visible. Piailug summed up etak's main points: *"In good weather look to the stars. In bad weather look to the waves."*[2] Piailug kept a close eye on the ocean currents to determine his speed and the direction of travel. Very subtle changes in the waves contained valuable information: *"He tried to get me to see a kind of 'tightness' in the water—tiny ripples flowing on the surface, almost like the wrinkles on a weatherbeaten face."* Although Thomas could not detect it, he later checked navigational instruments and it turned out that Piailug was absolutely correct: the current was from the west. Using the etak system, Piailug used eight different patterns of ocean swells to determine his direction, particularly when he could not see the stars, whether in the daytime or on an overcast night.

Clouds also contained valuable information. One morning Thomas and Piailug woke up early before the sun was up.

On the walk up the beach, Piailug stopped to squat in the darkness. A large dark cloud was about to engulf the island, and he casually asked if I thought it would rain. I scrutinized the cloud carefully, wanting to give the right answer. I could feel a wave of cool air against my chest as the cloud approached, but if it was going to rain, I reasoned, this wave would be even cooler and would be followed by a distinctive smell. I said it wouldn't rain. He grunted approvingly.

*Steve Thomas, *The Last Navigator: A Young Man, an Ancient Mariner, and the Secrets of the Sea* (New York: H. Holt, 1987). Copyright © 1987, 2009 by Steve Thomas. All rights reserved. Reprinted by permission.

Piailug read the clouds just as he read the waves, and he was pleased when Thomas learned to do the same.

Once navigation by the stars brought boats close to land, etak navigators used other means to pinpoint the exact location of the islands. Certain birds nest on land and then fly far out to sea each day to look for fish before returning to their nests in the evening. Boobies fly 30–50 miles (50–80 km) each day; terns and noddies, 18–25 miles (30–40 km). Thomas learned that once sailing vessels sighted these birds, they would wait *"for dawn or dusk, and carefully observe the flight paths of the birds,"* which they could then follow to their destination.

The Polynesian system occasionally broke down. Typhoons caused the most problems; on one occasion, when a typhoon destroyed his vessel, Piailug and his crew waited five days in the water before they were rescued; a shark attacked and killed one of the crew. When Piailug was seventy-one, he led a short 250-mile (400-km) voyage between two nearby islands. When he failed to show up two weeks after the date of his expected return, his family asked the Coast Guard for help. Once located, the voyagers explained that they had encountered a typhoon whose strong winds delayed them. But Piailug knew their exact location: they were some 30 miles (50 km) from home and, exhausted as they were, they made their way back on their own. *"I wasn't worried. I knew right away that it was the weather,"* said Junior Coleman, a Hawai'ian who had earlier sailed with Piailug. *"I told people to remember who is involved here. He's the Yoda of the Pacific."*[3]

Piailug may have died, but the etak system of navigation did not die with him. Today members of the Polynesian Voyaging Society teach etak in Hawai'i's public schools as they continue to use it on long-distance voyages all over the Pacific.

The Mystery of Easter Island

Etak navigation techniques may have brought the ancestors of the Polynesians to the island chains of Hawai'i and Tahiti, but no one knows how they reached Easter Island, the easternmost inhabited island in the Pacific, which lies 1,300 miles (2,100 km) southeast of its nearest neighbor, Pitcairn Island, and 2,250 miles (3,600 km) off the coast of Chile. These distances are less than the 2,400 miles (3,800 km) between Hawai'i and Tahiti, but since Easter Island is a single island only 14 miles (23 km) across at its widest point and not part of an island chain, it would have been extremely difficult for ancient navigators to locate. It was probably settled in 300 by a small party of Polynesians blown far off their original course. Since linguists believe that the Easter Island language retains many more archaic features than that of its neighbors, the early settlers probably had little contact with the other peoples of Oceania after they arrived on Easter Island.

Easter Island has two names, neither of which is original. Most English speakers refer to it as Easter Island because a Dutch navigator first glimpsed the island on Easter Day, 1722. In the nineteenth century Polynesian sailors named the island Rapa Nui after the Polynesian Island Rapa, 2,400 miles (3,850 km) to the west, and this is the name currently in use by Polynesian speakers.

The people of Easter Island, like those elsewhere in the Pacific, subsisted on a diet of sweet potatoes, taro, and sugarcane supplemented by chicken, their only domesticated animal. Their garbage pits contain bones of dolphin, porpoise, and tuna, an indication that they also engaged in deep-sea fishing.

All early European visitors to Easter Island noticed the huge statues of volcanic tufa stone, called **moai** (MOH-ai), that dot the island, some taller than 70 feet (21 m).

moai
The name for the 887 statues, probably of ancestral leaders, made from tufa volcanic rock and erected on Easter Island around 1000. The largest are more than 70 feet (21 m) high and the heaviest weighs 270 tons.

The islanders—who had no metal, only tools of stone, wood, and bone—began to construct the statues during the island's most prosperous period, starting in 1000, when the population reached some fifteen thousand. The most recent count of the moai statues is 887.[4] Some stand on platforms that hold up to fifteen statues. The average weight is around 10 tons (9 metric tons), but the heaviest weighs a massive 270 tons (245 metric tons; it was never moved from its quarry). No two statues are identical. Some have designs showing tattoos and loincloths.

Local oral traditions hold that the statues portray ancestral leaders. The island was divided into small bands, whose leaders built the monuments as an expression of their power. Competition would account for the variation in height of the monuments; as leaders sought to outbuild one another, they erected ever-higher statues.

Moai Figures, Easter Island The giant stone figures, or moai, of Easter Island portray ancestral leaders. When alive, the leaders commissioned a statue of themselves that remained horizontal. After they died, the statues were placed in an upright position, and eye inlays of coral and other rock were inserted into the eye sockets. The chunk of red stone on the top of this moai represents a headdress.

Andreas M. Gross/Westend 61/Alamy

How could a Stone Age people with no metal tools make statues of such size and transport them? Earlier analysts proposed that the statues must have been brought by outsiders from South America or even outer space, but modern scholars concur that these statues were built and erected by indigenous peoples with no outside assistance. Sculptors used stone choppers and water to hew each statue's basic shape from the soft volcanic rock.

In 1998, Jo Anne Van Tilburg designed an experiment as innovative as the Polynesian Voyaging Society's sailing from Hawai'i to Tahiti. She found that between fifty and seventy people working five hours a day for a week could move a 12-ton (11-metric-ton) statue 9 miles (14.4 km). Some think that once the stone was at its destination, the Easter Islanders made a series of ramps from dirt, each steeper than the next, to move the statues into a standing position; others think they must have used ropes to hoist the statues into place. Tilburg's findings suggest that the islanders used a wooden frame, giant logs that functioned as rollers, or both to pull the statues from the quarry to their destinations. Although the island has no trees now, it did in the past. One of the largest was a type of palm tree that grew over 65 feet (20 m) tall.

Sometime around 1600 the Easter Islanders stopped making moai. In the end, the different chiefs made war against each other so intensively and for so long, pausing only to create these monuments, that they used up their resources. The activities of the Easter Islanders resulted in the total degradation of their environment: no trees or large animals remained in the eighteenth century. The only large bones available on the island were those of humans, which the islanders worked into fishhooks, and they used human hair to make ropes, textiles, and fishnets, a chilling demonstration of survival with few natural resources.

The Impact of Humans on New Zealand

New Zealand was the final island in the Pacific to be settled by humans. The first artifacts made by humans appear in a layer of volcanic ash dating to circa 1350. Studies of mitochondrial DNA (see Chapter 1) show that the indigenous Maori people of New Zealand were descended from some seventy different female ancestors in a founding population of more than one hundred settlers.

These settlers had a profound effect on the New Zealand environment. Like the Easter Islanders, they demonstrated that environmental damage is not simply a modern development. Within a century after their arrival, twenty different species of birds had died out, and hunters had killed more than 160,000 giant moa birds. Surviving skeletal remains indicate that some twenty different species of moa once flourished on the island; the tallest stood over 10 feet (3 m) tall. After the residents had eliminated the large birds, they preyed on large mammals like seals and sea lions until those populations were also depleted. The hunters then targeted smaller animals. As the supply of wild animals dwindled, the residents became more dependent on cultivation, destroying an estimated 40 percent of the island's forest cover.[5]

When the first Europeans arrived in the seventeenth and eighteenth centuries, they found many small warring bands leading an arduous existence that was the unintended result of their ancestors' overhunting and overfishing.

CONTEXT AND CONNECTIONS

The Different Path to Complex Societies in the Americas and the Pacific

When Mau Piailug steered the *Hokule'a* all the way from Hawai'i to Tahiti without using a single navigational instrument, his journey illustrated an important historical reality: the peoples of the Americas and the Pacific islands took paths to complex society different from those taken by peoples of Eurasia. The peoples who migrated to the Americas and the Pacific islands lived in almost total isolation from Eurasia until around 1500. During the long period of separation, they developed very different ways of adapting to their environments: they farmed differently than Eurasians, they used metal differently, and they navigated differently. Still, some of their societies had occupational diversity, social stratification, and large urban centers, the hallmarks of complex society.

Chapters 2–4 of this book analyze the rise of agriculture and of complex societies first in West Asia, then India, and then China. In each of these regions, agriculture arose in river valleys, and early farmers used tools and domesticated draft animals to raise their crops. Not so in the Americas. The peoples of Mesoamerica cultivated the earliest maize in the highlands and then moved down into river valleys; they never used the wheel, plow, or draft animals. The Andean peoples to the south domesticated both the alpaca and the llama, but they did not employ them as farm animals; the only animals they raised to eat were guinea pigs.

Another important difference lay in the use of metal. Western Asian, Indian, and Chinese metallurgists learned to work bronze, which has a lower

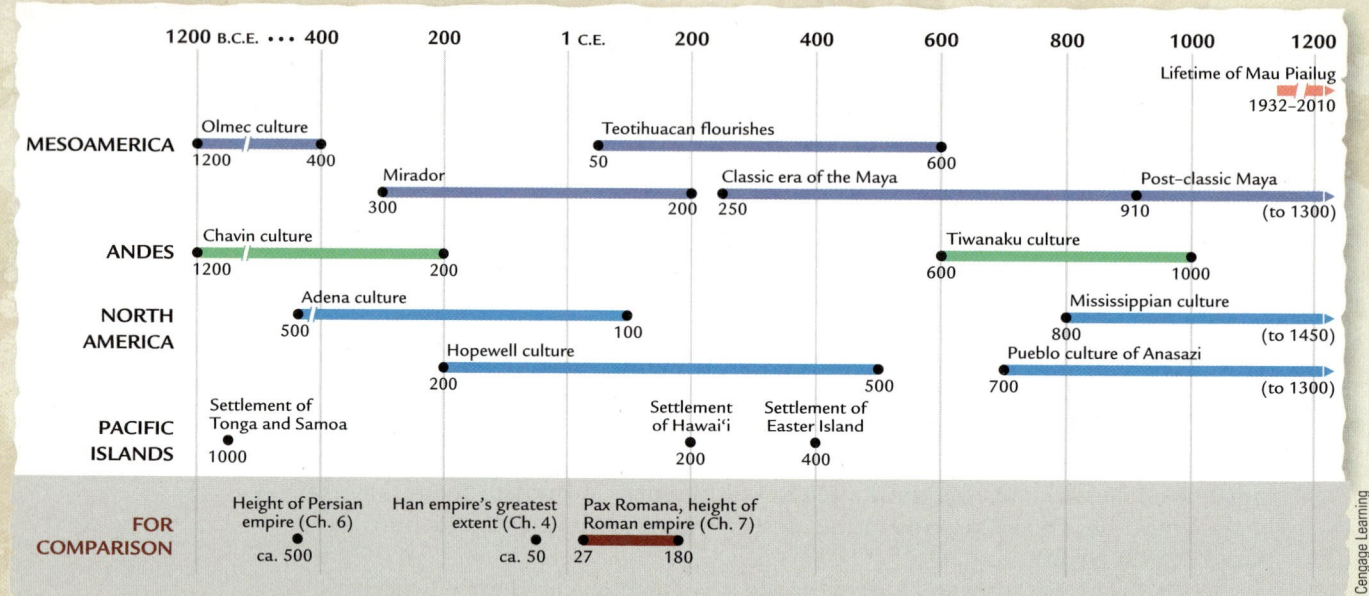

	1200 B.C.E. ••• 400	200	1 C.E.	200	400	600	800	1000	1200

Lifetime of Mau Piailug
1932–2010

MESOAMERICA
Olmec culture
1200 — 400
Teotihuacan flourishes
50 — 600
Mirador
300 — 200
Classic era of the Maya
250 — 910
Post-classic Maya
(to 1300)

ANDES
Chavin culture
1200 — 200
Tiwanaku culture
600 — 1000

NORTH AMERICA
Adena culture
500 — 100
Mississippian culture
800 — (to 1450)
Hopewell culture
200 — 500
Pueblo culture of Anasazi
700 — (to 1300)

PACIFIC ISLANDS
Settlement of Tonga and Samoa
1000
Settlement of Hawai'i
200
Settlement of Easter Island
400

FOR COMPARISON
Height of Persian empire (Ch. 6)
ca. 500
Han empire's greatest extent (Ch. 4)
ca. 50
Pax Romana, height of Roman empire (Ch. 7)
27 — 180

© Cengage Learning

melting point, before iron. Once they knew how to smelt iron, they made farm tools, particularly plow blades, from iron, which markedly increased agricultural productivity. In the Americas, by comparison, the Maya first worked gold around 800, but they made few implements from it, preferring knives of obsidian and ornaments of green jade and bird feathers. The Andean peoples had greater experience with metalworking: they made bronze from copper and tin, as the Eurasian peoples did, but also by mixing copper and arsenic, a combination not used in Eurasia. However, the Andean peoples reserved metal for ceremonial and decorative purposes. Like the peoples of Mesoamerica and the north, the Andean peoples preferred tools of wood, bone, and stone. The peoples of the Pacific also used wood, bone, and stone tools for farming and for large-scale projects like carving the moai statues of Easter Island from volcanic tufa stone and placing them upright.

As we have seen in this chapter, the peoples living on various continents developed radically different systems of navigation: as Mau Piailug

demonstrated, skilled navigators could cross the Pacific by making use of the information in the stars, waves, clouds, and bird flight patterns. As Chapters 10 and 15 will show, Viking navigators around the year 1000 and European navigators around the year 1500 also used some of these same clues. And while Piailug thought his boat stayed still and the water moved, the Europeans believed that their boats moved and the water stayed still. Whatever their thinking, they crossed the oceans in boats.

The settlement of New Zealand in 1350 by the Polynesian peoples marked the close of the first long chapter in world history: the settlement of all the globe's habitable regions, which began with the departure of the first anatomically modern humans from Africa over a hundred thousand years ago (see Chapter 1). After 1350, no unoccupied land was left other than Antarctica, where humans can survive only with the help of modern technology. After that date, whenever people migrating from their homeland to anywhere else in the world encountered indigenous peoples, conflict almost always resulted.

KEY TERMS

Mau Piailug (108)
Mesoamerica (111)
Olmec (112)
Long Count (113)
Teotihuacan (114)
Maya (114)

Copán (118)
obsidian (119)
Popul Vuh (119)
Mississippian peoples (124)
Caral (125)
Chavín (126)

Polynesian Triangle (127)
Lapita pottery (128)
double canoe (128)
etak (130)
moai (131)

FOR FURTHER REFERENCE

Brown, Chip. "El Mirador, the Lost City of the Maya." *Smithsonian*, May 2011, pp. 36–49.

Coe, Michael D. *The Maya*. 8th ed. New York: Thames and Hudson, 2011.

Coe, Michael D. *Mexico: From the Olmecs to the Aztecs*. New York: Thames and Hudson, 1984.

Fash, William L. *Scribes, Warriors and Kings: The City of Copán and the Ancient Maya*. Rev. ed. New York: Thames and Hudson, 2001.

Finney, Ben. *Hokule'a: The Way to Tahiti*. New York: Dodd, Mead, and Company, 1979.

Finney, Ben. *Voyage of Rediscovery: A Cultural Odyssey Through Polynesia*. Berkeley: University of California Press, 1994.

Flenley, John, and Paul Bahn. *The Enigmas of Easter Island: Island on the Edge*. New York: Oxford University Press, 2002.

Howe, K. R. *The Quest for Origins: Who First Discovered and Settled the Pacific Islands?* Honolulu: University of Hawai'i Press, 2003.

Jennings, Jesse D., ed. *The Prehistory of Polynesia*. Cambridge, Mass.: Harvard University Press, 1979.

Lewis, David. "Mau Piailug's Navigation of Hokule'a from Hawaii to Tahiti." *Topics in Culture Learning* 5 (1977): 1–23.

Martin, Simon, and Nikolai Grube. *Chronicle of the Maya Kings and Queens: Deciphering the Dynasties of the Ancient Maya*. 2d ed. New York: Thames and Hudson, 2008.

Oliphant, Margaret. *The Atlas of the Ancient World: Charting the Civilizations of the Past*. New York: Barnes and Noble Books, 1998.

Popol Vuh: The Definitive Edition of the Mayan Book of the Dawn of Life and the Glories of Gods and Kings. Denis Tedlock, trans. New York: Simon and Schuster, 1996.

Schele, Linda, and Mary Ellen Miller. *The Blood of Kings: Dynasty and Ritual in Maya Art*. Fort Worth: Kimball Art Museum, 1986.

Stuart, George E. "The Timeless Vision of Teotihuacan." *National Geographic* 188, no. 6 (December 1995): 3–38.

Sugiyama, Saburo. *Human Sacrifice, Militarism, and Rulership: Materialization of State Ideology at the Feathered Serpent Pyramid, Teotihuacan*. New York: Cambridge University Press, 2005.

Thomas, Steve. *The Last Navigator: A Young Man, an Ancient Mariner, and the Secrets of the Sea*. New York: H. Holt, 1987.

FILMS

The Navigators: Pathfinders of the Pacific
Nova: "Lost King of the Maya"
Nova: "Secrets of Lost Empires: Easter Island"

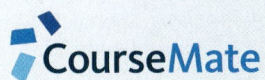

6

New Empires in Iran and Greece, 2000 B.C.E.–651 C.E.

Herodotus (heh-ROD-uh-tuhs) (ca. 485–425 B.C.E.) was born to a well-to-do literate family in Halicarnassus (HAH-lee-kar-nuh-suhs) (modern Bodrum), a city on the southwest coast of modern-day Turkey, which was home to a large Greek-speaking community. His hometown was part of the Persian empire ruled by the **Achaemenids** (ah-KEHM-uh-nid), which was far more diverse than any previous empire. It governed multiple peoples spread across Afro-Eurasia who spoke different languages and worshiped disparate religions, and so fully deserves to be called a world empire. Herodotus wrote his life's great work, *The Histories*, in Greek about his Persian rulers and their many subject peoples. The book opens with a statement of his goals:

Herodotus

(Antikensammlung Staatische Museen zu Berlin, Berlin, Germany/Bildarchiv Preussischer Kulturbesitz/Art Resource, NY)

*H*erodotus of Halicarnassus here displays his inquiry, so that human achievements may not become forgotten in time, and great and marvelous deeds—some displayed by Greeks, some by barbarians—may not be without their glory; and especially to show why the two peoples fought with each other.*

---

*From *The Histories* by Herodotus, translated by Aubrey de Sélincourt, revised with introductory matter and notes by John Marincola (Penguin Classics 1954, second revised edition 1996). Translation copyright 1954 by Aubrey de Sélincourt. Used by permission of Viking Penguin, a division of Penguin Group (USA) Inc., and David Higham Associates.

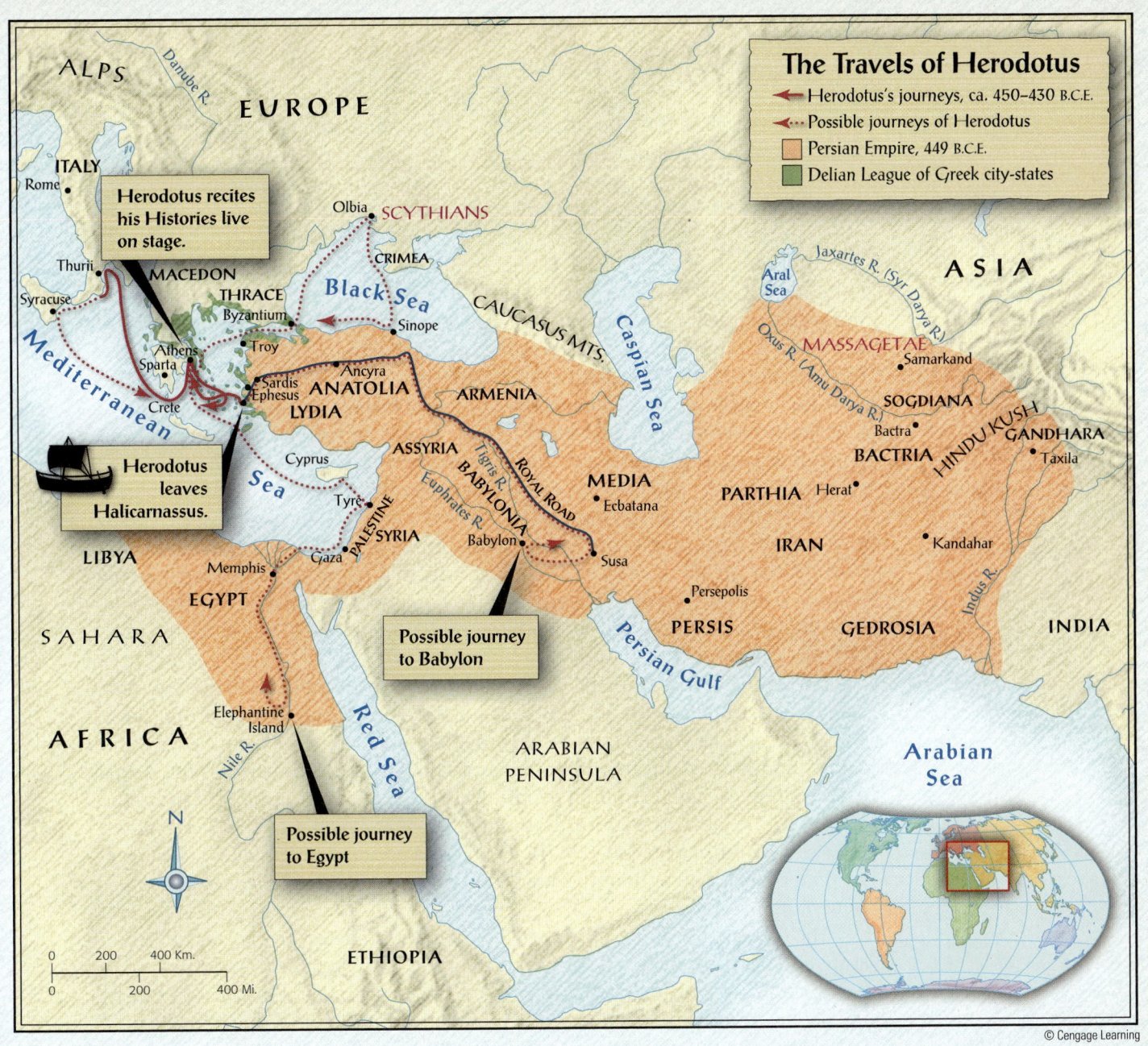

The Travels of Herodotus

→ Herodotus's journeys, ca. 450–430 B.C.E.
‹‹‹ Possible journeys of Herodotus
Persian Empire, 449 B.C.E.
Delian League of Greek city-states

Herodotus recites his Histories live on stage.

Herodotus leaves Halicarnassus.

Possible journey to Babylon

Possible journey to Egypt

ALPS
EUROPE
Danube R.
ITALY
Rome
Thurii
Syracuse
MACEDON
THRACE
Byzantium
Troy
Athens
Sparta
Crete
Mediterranean Sea
SCYTHIANS
Olbia
CRIMEA
Black Sea
Sinope
Sardis
Ephesus
ANATOLIA
LYDIA
Ancyra
ARMENIA
CAUCASUS MTS.
Caspian Sea
ASIA
Aral Sea
Jaxartes R. (Syr Darya R.)
MASSAGETAE
Oxus R. (Amu Darya R.)
Samarkand
SOGDIANA
Bactra
BACTRIA
HINDU KUSH
GANDHARA
Taxila
Cyprus
Tyre
PALESTINE
SYRIA
Gaza
Euphrates R.
Tigris R.
ASSYRIA
BABYLONIA
Babylon
ROYAL ROAD
MEDIA
Ecbatana
Susa
PARTHIA
Herat
IRAN
Kandahar
Indus R.
Persepolis
PERSIS
Persian Gulf
GEDROSIA
INDIA
LIBYA
Memphis
EGYPT
SAHARA
AFRICA
Elephantine Island
Nile R.
Red Sea
ARABIAN PENINSULA
Arabian Sea
ETHIOPIA

N

0   200   400 Km.
0   200   400 Mi.

© Cengage Learning

Herodotus chose the title *Historia* (hiss-TOR-ee-uh), which means "inquiry" or "investigation," not necessarily about the past, and this is the root of our word *history*. He calls the Persians "barbarians," but he is scrupulously even-handed: as the Greeks have performed "great and marvelous deeds," so too have the Persians.

Before recording his work, Herodotus performed sections before live audiences in the Greek city of Athens. The world's first stand-up historian, he narrated the events of the past to keep his audience entertained. Unlike other historians of his time, Herodotus makes it clear when he is including a hearsay account rather than his own observations and openly expresses doubt about some of the taller tales he presents. For this reason, the Roman orator Cicero (SIS-erh-oh) (106–43 B.C.E.) called Herodotus the father of history, a label he retains to this day.

Not a first-person travel account, *The Histories* presents the history, folklore, geography, plants, and customs of the known world in Herodotus's day. In addition to visiting Greece, he must have traveled along the Aegean coast of Turkey and to Italy. Egypt, the Crimean peninsula on the Black Sea, Sicily, Babylon, and North Africa are all places *The Histories* claims that he visited in person (see the map on page 137). Herodotus recorded his book on long rolls of papyrus sometime after 431 B.C.E. and died soon after, most likely around 425 B.C.E., in the town of Thurii, in the boot of Italy.

Herodotus devoted his life to explaining the success of the Persian empire, easily the largest and certainly the most powerful empire of its time. From 550 to 330 B.C.E. the Achaemenid dynasty governed a region extending from North Africa to the Indus Valley and from the Arabian Sea as far east as Samarkand in Central Asia. Between 30 and 35 million people lived in the Persian empire.[1] Up to around 500 B.C.E., the greatest western Asian empires—the Akkadians, the Babylonians, the Assyrians—had been based in the Tigris and Euphrates River Valleys (see Chapter 2); for more than a thousand years after 500 B.C.E., some of the largest empires were in Iran.

The Greeks were among the few who managed to defeat the powerful Persian army and resist conquest. In Athens, during the sixth and fifth centuries B.C.E., a new political system emerged, a system the Athenians called *democracy*, or rule by the people. Some thirty thousand men, but no slaves and no women, made decisions affecting the estimated three hundred thousand people living in Athens, 1 percent or less of the total population of the Persian empire.

The Achaemenid rulers developed a flexible type of empire that allowed them to conquer and rule the many different peoples of western Asia for more than two centuries, until the Macedonian king Alexander the Great defeated the Persians in 331 B.C.E. When Alexander came to power, democracy in Athens had already failed, and he took over Persian conceptions and structures of kingship intact. Unable to match the Achaemenid dynasty's feat of governing for two centuries, his empire broke apart after only thirteen years. Many different governments rose and fell in western Asia, but those that ruled the most territory for the longest periods of time—the successor states to Alexander, the Parthians, and the Sasanians—were all monarchies that drew much from the Persian empire.

Note that many of the answers this chapter proposes must be based on the work of Greek writers, including Herodotus, because so few sources in Persian survive.

» *What military and administrative innovations enabled the Achaemenid dynasty to conquer and rule such a vast empire?*

» *What were the important accomplishments of the Greek city-states? Consider innovations in politics, intellectual life, fine arts, and science.*

» *Who was Alexander, and what was his legacy?*

» *How did the Parthians and the Sasanians modify the Persian model of empire?*

The Rise of the Achaemenids in Iran, 1000–330 B.C.E.

After departing from their homeland somewhere in southern Russia (see Chapter 3), the Indo-European migrants broke into different branches, one of which arrived in the region of modern-day Iran in approximately 1000 B.C.E. These tribal people were largely nomads who did not plant crops but moved their sheep and camel flocks from pasture to pasture seeking fresh grass. Their language, Indo-Iranian, belonged to the same language family as Sanskrit, and their caste system resembled that of Vedic India (see Chapter 3) but had only three ranks: priests, rulers or warriors, and ordinary herders or farmers. Their herding way of life took maximum advantage of the high plateau environment of Iran, which had no major river valley comparable to the Nile, the Indus, or the Yellow Rivers. The tall mountains of Iran contain streams that drain into the high plateaus; many end in either salt lakes or trickle out into the desert.

Farming was only possible if farmers dug irrigation channels to collect water, and the first people who did so lived in the region of Persis in southwestern Iran. (*Iran* is the name of the larger geographic unit, while the English word *Persia* refers to the smaller region, the heartland, of Persis.)

Starting in 550 B.C.E. the Achaemenids created an empire far larger than any the world had seen before. Because the dynasty's founding ruler was from Persis, we refer to the Achaemenid realm as the Persian empire. It contained some of the world's most advanced cities, such as Babylon and Susa, and some of its most barren stretches, like the deserts of Central Asia. The key innovation in Achaemenid Persian rule was the use of **satraps**: after conquering a region, the Persians appointed a local governor, or satrap (SAH-trap), who was responsible for collecting taxes from the defeated and forwarding them to the capital at Susa. This flexible system suited the many different peoples of western Asia far better than the system used by the Qin and Han empires, which had identical districts all over China (see Chapter 4).

Zoroastrianism

Our best source for understanding the early migrants to Iran is *The Avesta* (uh-VEST-uh), a book that contains the core teachings of their religion, **Zoroastrianism** (zo-roe-ASS-tree-uhn-iz-uhm). Zoroastrianism, like Vedic religion, featured hymn singing and the performance of elaborate rituals but also held that the world was governed by two opposing forces: good and evil. Describing pastoral nomads active in eastern Iran, *The Avesta* portrays ancient Iran as having no cities or any political unit larger than a tribe.

satrap
The third Achaemenid ruler, Darius, divided his empire into provinces called *satrapies*, each administered by a governor, or satrap. The officials under the satrap were recruited locally, a hallmark of the Persian system.

The Avesta
A book, probably dating to circa 1000 B.C.E. and first recorded in writing around 600 C.E., whose title means "The Injunction of Zarathushtra," the founding prophet of Zoroastrianism. Contains hymns attributed to Zarathushtra himself, which provide our best guide to his original thought.

Zoroastrianism
Iranian religion named for Zarathushtra (in Persian; Zoroaster in Greek), who may have lived between 1500 and 700 B.C.E. He taught that a host of good deities and evil demons, all in perpetual conflict, populate the spiritual world.

Zoroastrianism is named for its founding prophet Zarathushtra (za-ra-THOOSH-tra) (in Persian; Zoroaster in Greek), who lived in the region of Herat, a city in the Iranian highland plateau now located in modern Afghanistan. Scholars have no way to determine when Zarathushtra lived, and informed estimates diverge widely. Sometime around 1000 B.C.E. seems a reasonable compromise. Three thousand years old, Zoroastrianism is one of the world's most ancient religions still practiced today.

Written in an extremely ancient form of Indo-Iranian, *The Avesta*, which means "The Injunction of Zarathushtra," contains a group of hymns attributed to the prophet Zarathushtra himself. First recorded sometime around 600, these hymns provide our best guide to Zarathushtra's original thought.

Zarathushtra believed in a supreme deity, **Ahura Mazda** (ah-HURR-uh MAZZ-duh), the Lord of Truth. Ahura Mazda gave birth to twin entities, the good spirit and the evil spirit. Zoroastrianism is dualistic because it posits two equal, opposing entities: a host of good deities and evil demons, all in perpetual conflict.

Each person, whether male or female, Zarathushtra taught, had to prepare for the day of judgment when everyone would appear before Ahura Mazda. Zarathushtra firmly believed in the ability of human beings to shape their world by choosing between the good and the bad. People who chose the good had to think good thoughts, do good deeds, and tell the truth. Herodotus remarked that young boys were taught to "speak the truth,"* the fundamental Zoroastrian virtue. Whenever anyone lied or did a bad deed, the evil spirit gained ground.

Much of Zoroastrian ritual involved fire altars. The Zoroastrians built three permanent fire altars, each dedicated to a different caste group. Male hereditary priests called Magi (MAHJ-eye) tended the fire to make sure that it never went out. If it did, an elaborate ritual was performed to relight the fire. Towns had fire altars, as did individual households, and worshipers fed fires five times a day, when they recited prayers. Because the Achaemenids supported these Zoroastrian priests, their state was also ceremonial (see Chapter 3).

The practice of reciting prayers ensured the transmission of the original wording of the sacred hymns for a full two thousand years before they were written down. The ancient core texts of Zoroastrianism are still recited by one of the most active communities of Zoroastrian believers today, the Parsis of modern Bombay (Mumbai), India. The Parsis (also spelled Parsees, which means Persian) left Iran after the Islamic conquest and moved to India sometime between the eighth and tenth centuries C.E. Ever since then they have recited two core prayers.

The first prayer stresses that people should choose the Lord of Truth, Ahura Mazda: *"Just as the lord in accord with truth must be chosen, so also the judgment in accord with truth. Establish a rule of actions stemming from an existence of good thinking for the sake of the Wise One [Ahura Mazda] and for the lord whom they established as pastor (Zarathushtra) for the needy dependents."* The second prayer continues this theme: *"Truth exists as the very best good thing. It exists under your will. Desire the truth for what is the very best truth."*[2] In short, truth is the highest good, and everyone has the ability to follow and promote the truth.

The funerary practices of the Zoroastrians differed from those of almost all other ancient peoples. Whereas most peoples buried their dead, Zoroastrians, believing that dead flesh polluted the ground, left corpses outside so that scavenging birds and dogs could eat the flesh; then they collected the cleaned bones and buried them.

Ahura Mazda
The name of the supreme deity of Zoroastrianism, the Lord of Truth, who created heaven and earth, day and night, and darkness and light. On the day of judgment, Zoroastrians believe, Ahura Mazda will judge each person's good and bad deeds.

*From *The Histories* by Herodotus, translated by Aubrey de Sélincourt, revised with introductory matter and notes by John Marincola (Penguin Classics 1954, second revised edition 1996). Translation copyright 1954 by Aubrey de Sélincourt. Used by permission of Viking Penguin, a division of Penguin Group (USA) Inc., and David Higham Associates.

The Military Success of the Persian Empire, 550–486 B.C.E.

In the centuries after Zarathushtra formulated his teachings, Iran remained a tribal society that had little contact with the neighboring empires of western Asia. In 612 B.C.E., an Iranian tribe called the Medes captured the Assyrian capital and brought Assyrian rule to an end. The Medes began to expand beyond Iran's borders into western Asia. In 550 B.C.E. the tribal leader **Cyrus** (r. 558–530 B.C.E.), from Persis, defeated the Medes and founded the Achaemenid dynasty, named for his ancestor Achaemenes.

When Cyrus founded his dynasty, his soldiers from Persis were obliged to serve in the king's army and to provide their own equipment. They served as foot soldiers, cavalrymen, archers, or engineers. They were not paid but were entitled to a share of the spoils from the cities they conquered.

As Cyrus's army conquered new territory, the army of citizen-soldiers became a paid full-time army staffed by Persians and other Iranians, the conquered peoples, and large contingents of Greek mercenaries. The most prestigious unit, the king's bodyguard, was called the *"Immortals, because it was invariably kept up to strength,"* Herodotus explains. *"If a man was killed or fell sick, the vacancy he left was at once filled, so that its strength was never more nor less than 10,000."* No records of the size of the army survive in Persian; Greek observers, prone to exaggerate, give figures as high as 2.5 million men, but the army certainly numbered in the hundreds of thousands, if not millions.

To bind their empire together physically, the Persians maintained an extensive network of roads that allowed them to supply the army no matter how far it traveled. Some were simple caravan tracks through the desert, while others, usually in or just outside the main cities like Babylon, were paved with bricks or rock. The main road, the Royal Road, linked the cities near the Aegean coast with the capital at Susa.

A system of government couriers made excellent use of these roads, as Herodotus remarks:

> There is nothing on earth faster than these couriers. The service is a Persian invention, and it goes like this, according to what I was told. Men and horses are stationed a day's travel apart, a man and a horse for each of the days needed to cover the journey. These men neither snow nor rain nor heat nor gloom of night stay from the swiftest possible completion of their appointed stage.*

Traveling at a breathtaking 90 miles (145 km) each day, government couriers could cover the 1,600 miles (2,575 km) of the Royal Road in less than twenty days, far more rapidly than the three months taken by ordinary travelers.[3] The couriers were crucial to the army's success because generals could communicate easily with one another across large expanses of territory.

The Persian army was responsible for a long string of military conquests. Cyrus began from his base in Persis, and by 547–546 B.C.E., his troops moved north and west into Anatolia (modern-day Turkey), an enormously wealthy region called Lydia. There, around 600 B.C.E., people minted **Lydian coins**, the first metal coins used anywhere in the world.

Cyrus
(r. 558–530 B.C.E.)
Founder of the Achaemenid dynasty in Iran. A native of Persis, Cyrus staffed his administration with many Persians as well as Medes, the tribe he defeated when he took power.

Lydian coins
The first metal coins in the world, dating to around 600 B.C.E. Made from electrum, a naturally occurring alloy of gold and silver collected from the riverbeds in Lydia, a region on the Aegean coast of modern-day Turkey.

---

*From *The Histories* by Herodotus, translated by Aubrey de Sélincourt, revised with introductory matter and notes by John Marincola (Penguin Classics 1954, second revised edition 1996). Translation copyright 1954 by Aubrey de Sélincourt. Used by permission of Viking Penguin, a division of Penguin Group (USA) Inc., and David Higham Associates.

Cyrus conquered the various Ionian ports on the eastern Aegean: Syria, Palestine, and Babylon. He did not attempt to change their cultures but made offerings to local gods and allowed his subjects to continue to worship as they had before, a key reason for the success of the Persian empire. He allowed the Jews to return home, ending the sixty-year-long Babylonian Captivity (see Chapter 2). Modern scholarship indicates that the Hebrew concepts of the afterlife and of the Devil arose after the Babylonian Captivity, and some attribute these new ideas to the influence of Zoroastrianism.

The Persian army was not invincible. In 530 B.C.E. it entered the unfamiliar terrain of Central Asia and attacked the Massagetae (mass-uh-GET-aye) peoples east of the Amu Darya River. Herodotus reports that the Persians were able initially to gain the advantage against the Massagetae tribes by offering them wine so that they fell drunk, but the fierce Massagetae recovered and defeated the Persians in hand-to-hand combat. Cyrus died while campaigning in Massagetae territory.

Darius's Coup, 522 B.C.E.

Darius I
(r. 522–486 B.C.E.) The third Achaemenid Persian ruler, who succeeded to the throne by coup. He conquered much territory in Eurasia but was unable to defeat the Scythians south of the Black Sea or the Greeks. He also reformed the empire's administrative structure.

When Cyrus's son Cambyses (kam-BEE-zuhs) died in 522 B.C.E., a group of Zoroastrian priests placed a Magi priest named Gaumata (GOW-mah-tah) on the throne. In the same year **Darius I** (r. 522–486 B.C.E.) led a group of six co-conspirators who killed the pretender. At the time of the murder the conspirators had not agreed on the political system they would implement. Herodotus (ca. 485–425 B.C.E.) recounted their lively discussion about the best form of government. While one suggested the democracy of the Greek city-state of Athens, another spoke up for rule by a few, or oligarchy (OLL-ih-gahr-key), the governing system of the city-state of Sparta. Darius (dah-RYE-uhs), the future king, vigorously defended rule by one man, or monarchy:

Take the three forms of government we are considering—democracy, oligarchy, and monarchy—and suppose each of them to be the best of its kind; I maintain that the third is greatly preferable to the other two. One ruler: it is impossible to improve upon that—provided he is the best. His judgment will be in keeping with his character; his control of the people will be beyond reproach; his measures against enemies and traitors will be kept secret more easily than under other forms of government. . . .

To sum up: where did we get our freedom from, and who gave it us? Is it the result of democracy, or oligarchy, or of monarchy? We were set free by one man, and therefore I propose that we should preserve that form of government, and, further, that we should refrain from changing ancient ways, which have served us well in the past.[*]

Herodotus could not possibly have known what was said in a secret conversation that occurred long before his birth in Persian, a language that he did not speak. He must have created this dialogue to enliven his narrative. Persuaded by Darius that monarchy was the best system, the conspirators agreed to choose the future king by seeing whose horse neighed first after the sun came up. Darius's wily groom made sure that his master's horse did so, and Darius became *king of kings*, the Persian term for the ruler of the empire.

---

[*]From *The Histories* by Herodotus, translated by Aubrey de Sélincourt, revised with introductory matter and notes by John Marincola (Penguin Classics 1954, second revised edition 1996). Translation copyright 1954 by Aubrey de Sélincourt. Used by permission of Viking Penguin, a division of Penguin Group (USA) Inc., and David Higham Associates.

Darius commemorated his accession to power in an extraordinary inscription at Behistun, the site of a steep cliff. Blocks of text in different languages around the large rock relief brag of the murder of the imposter-king. At the simplest level, Darius's message was obvious: if you oppose me, this is what will happen to you. Darius justified Gaumata's murder by appealing to a higher authority:

> *There was not a man, neither a Persian nor a Mede nor anyone of our family, who could have taken the kingdom from Gaumata the Magian. The people feared him greatly. . . . Then I prayed to Ahura Mazda. Ahura Mazda bore me aid. . . . Then I with a few men slew that Gaumata the Magian. . . . Ahura Mazda bestowed the kingdom upon me.*[4]

Darius's inscription differs from those of Ashoka (see Chapter 3) and the Qin founder (Chapter 4), both of whom had inherited the throne from their fathers. Darius, however, had killed the reigning king, and his distant family ties to Cyrus did not entitle him to the throne.

Justifying his rule by invoking Ahura Mazda, he also married Artystone (AR-tih-stoe-nay), daughter of Cyrus and half-sister of Cambyses, to bolster his claim to the Persian throne. Darius had several wives, but his favorite was Artystone, who possessed her own palace and wielded genuine authority within her own

Darius's Victory: The Stone Relief at Behistun, Iran In 522 B.C.E., Darius ordered this stone relief commemorating his victory over his rivals to be carved over 300 feet (100 m) above the road below. In it, Darius triumphantly places his left foot on the deposed Magi priest Gaumata, who lies dead on his back with his arms pointing vertically upward. The eight tribal leaders that Darius defeated are shown on the right; the larger figure with the pointed hat was added later. Above the human figures floats the winged Ahura Mazda, who looks on approvingly. (Robert Harding World Imagery)

estate. She organized banquets and trips, and sometimes the king would even take her with him on military campaigns.

Darius's use of languages also differed from that of Ashoka and the Qin founder. The text framing the Behistun relief appears in three languages: Elamite (EE-luhm-ite), the original language of administration of the Persians; Babylonian, the language they adopted as their administrative language; and Old Persian, which the royal family spoke at home. All three were written in cuneiform script. The Qin founder used a single language, confident that he could communicate with his subjects in Chinese; Ashoka had the same text translated into the different languages spoken in the various parts of the Mauryan empire.

But Darius ruled a multilingual empire in which people living in the same place spoke different languages. For this reason, Darius had rubbings of the inscription made and distributed translations of it throughout the empire. Most of Darius's subjects were illiterate; even the king had to have the Old Persian text read aloud to him. Darius's account in the Behistun inscription largely matches Herodotus's except for a few details.

Darius's Administration

During Darius's reign, the empire expanded to include Thrace in northern Greece and the Indus Valley in present-day Pakistan, but not the Scythian peoples living north of the Black Sea or the Greeks in Athens (see page 151). Fully aware of the challenges of governing his large empire, Darius instituted a series of far-reaching administrative reforms that held the Persian empire together for the better part of two centuries. He established a flexible administrative and taxation system and implemented a uniform law code for all his subjects.

Seeing himself as transmitting Ahura Mazda's laws to all his subjects, Darius appointed judges for life to administer those laws in his name. Just as on the day of judgment Ahura Mazda would judge each person's good and bad deeds, Persian judges were supposed to examine lawsuits carefully. They were to inquire deeply into the facts of a dispute and to reach a judgment that took into account a person's previous conduct. Accordingly, a man who had adhered to Zoroastrian teachings and told the truth his entire life was treated more leniently than one who had not.

As they reformed the courts, the Persians also changed the system of taxation. Herodotus explains:

> *During the reign of Cyrus and Cambyses there was no fixed tribute at all, the revenue coming from gifts only; and because of his imposition of regular taxes, and other similar measures, the Persians called Darius a huckster, Cambyses a master, and Cyrus a father; the first being out for profit wherever he could get it, the second harsh and arrogant, and the third, merciful and ever working for their well-being.**

We must remember that Cyrus had died nearly a century before Herodotus was writing and that Cambyses was reputed to be insane, a judgment with which Herodotus enthusiastically concurred. The view of Darius as a huckster contains an important element of truth: in seeking to put his empire on sound financial footing, Darius revolutionized the way the Persians collected taxes.

---

*Josef Wiesehöfer, *Ancient Persia from 550 BC to 650 AD*, trans. Azizeh Azodi (New York: I. B. Tauris, 2001), p. 63, citing Herodotus, *The Histories*, trans. Aubrey de Sélincourt, further rev. ed. (New York: Penguin Books, 1954, 1996), p. 89, Book III.

It was Darius who introduced satrapies, and the officials under the satrap were recruited locally, a hallmark of the Persian system. Darius required each satrap to submit a fixed amount of revenue each year. The taxes due from many of the different regions were assessed in silver, but Darius allowed several regions to pay some of their taxes in other items: Egypt, the empire's breadbasket, was required to forward 120,000 bushels of grain each year. The Indians, Herodotus explains, paid in gold dust, which they collected from riverbeds, while the Ethiopians submitted an annual quota of *"two quarts of unrefined gold, two hundred logs of ebony, and twenty elephant tusks."* Carved stone friezes at Persepolis (per-SEH-poe-lis), the site of the royal ritual center some 200 miles (360 km) west of Susa, illustrate beautifully the diversity of Darius's empire. (See the feature "Visual Evidence in Primary Sources: The Parade of Nations at Darius's Palace at Persepolis.")

After Darius died in 486 B.C.E., his son Xerxes (ZERK-sees) succeeded him. But in 465 B.C.E., Xerxes's younger son killed both his father and his elder brother. Royal assassinations occurred frequently over the next one hundred years, but the administrative structure the Persians originated allowed them to hold on to their empire until 331 B.C.E., when Alexander defeated them (see page 156).

Ancient Greece and the Mediterranean World, 2000–334 B.C.E.

A branch of the Indo-European speakers reached the Greek peninsula around 2000 B.C.E. The Greek speakers, as well as the Phoenicians (FOE-knee-shuns) (see page 148), were active traders in the Mediterranean. Although historians sometimes speak of the Phoenician and Greek "empires," neither people had a centralized administration governing many different peoples. Instead, both lived in scattered city-states, whose residents had sailed across the seas to establish new outposts that retained their ties to the mother city-state.

Although we tend to think of Greece as a single Greek-speaking entity, whether in earlier times or today, there was no unified nation called "Greece" in the ancient world. Greek speakers saw themselves as citizens of the city-state where they lived, such as Athens or Sparta. By the year 500 B.C.E. Athens emerged as the largest of over one hundred different Greek city-states, and only Athens had a democracy in which all male citizens, some 10 percent of the city's population, could participate equally. In addition to being a military power, Athens was also a cultural center renowned for its drama, art, and philosophy.

Greek Expansion in the Mediterranean, 2000–1200 B.C.E.

When the Indo-European speakers arrived in Greece, they found that the rocky land of the Greek peninsula, the Aegean coast of Turkey, and the islands of the Mediterranean offered little grass for their herds. No major rivers flowed in these areas. As the Indo-European migrants shifted from herding to farming, they used irrigation channels to distribute water over their fields. They usually planted barley, which was sturdier than wheat, in the lowlands, olive trees in the foothills, and grapes on the hillsides.

---

*From *The Histories* by Herodotus, translated by Aubrey de Sélincourt, revised with introductory matter and notes by John Marincola (Penguin Classics 1954, second revised edition 1996). Translation copyright 1954 by Aubrey de Sélincourt. Used by permission of Viking Penguin, a division of Penguin Group (USA) Inc., and David Higham Associates.

The Parade of Nations at Darius's Palace at Persepolis

To document his accomplishments, Darius built an enormous audience hall in Persepolis in modern-day Iran. The hall held 10,000 people and was 62,500 square feet (5,800 sq m), with a roof supported by columns more than 60 feet (20 m) high. Although the original wooden buildings, which were lavishly decorated with curtains, tiles, and paintings, no longer stand, the surviving stone reliefs show the many different peoples of the Persian empire coming to pay homage to their ruler.

The stairways leading to the audience hall have been called "perhaps the most perfect flight of stairs ever built."* Alongside the staircases, stone masons carved reliefs of twenty-three distinct peoples bringing gifts to the king to celebrate the coming of spring, one of the most important ritual occasions in the Zoroastrian calendar. On one side of the staircase the masons depicted the peoples of the empire as seen from the left, and on the facing side, as seen from the right. Each view of the procession occupies three tiers stretching 300 feet (92 m) long, making the frieze the largest mirror image in the world.

The top register, now partially destroyed, shows different regiments in the Persian army: the Persians and the Medes have different headdresses. The soldiers lead the king's horse, two empty chariots, a tent, and the throne for the king. The king himself is not shown.

*R. Ghirshman and E. Herzfeld, *Persepolis: The Achaemenian Capital* (Tehran: Mirdashti Farhangsara, 1999), p. 33.

On the lower tiers, trees divide the friezes into frames that show a small group of men from each place, wearing their native dress and led by a Persian or Median envoy. They carry local products as gifts for the king and guide a native animal. The animals reflect the great reach of the empire: horses from Syria, a humped bull and a wild donkey from Pakistan, a two-humped camel from Central Asia, and an antelope and a giraffe from Ethiopia. The animals are more detailed than the people, whose faces are the same and can be distinguished only by their clothing and different hairstyles.

The portraits capture the essence of the Persian empire. Each subject people occupies the same amount of space in the tableau; tall animals like giraffes are scaled down so that they take as much space as smaller animals like sheep and horses. Each group wears its national dress and offers its own distinctive gifts, while participating in a single procession designed to honor the Persian ruler.

The timing of the monument reveals something important about the Persian concept of empire. Darius began construction in 515 B.C.E., soon after he came to power, and the complex provided vivid testimony of his conquests of many different peoples. Xerxes completed the monument after the Greeks defeated the Persians in 480 B.C.E., but the Persian vision of empire remained unchanged. The omission of certain Greek peoples is the only indication that the expansion of the Persian empire had come to an end.

The facing page shows a small section of the frieze taken from the left side of the staircase.

QUESTION FOR ANALYSIS

» *How did the Persians and the Greeks illustrate their differing concepts of empire at Persepolis and the Acropolis? (For the Acropolis, see photo on page 154 and the feature "World History in Today's World: Returning the Elgin Marbles to Athens: The Case For and Against," page 155.)*

These Scythians, from the region north of the Black Sea, wear their characteristic pointed hoods and offer a fine horse.

This magnificent two-humped Bactrian camel follows Central Asians bearing cups and other gifts from the region east of the Caspian Sea.

These seven men from the impoverished Assyrian empire, defeated in 612 B.C.E., offer low-cost objects: a pair of rams, animal skins, and bowls.

© Corbis

The Ionians, from the Aegean coast of modern-day Turkey, offer folded bolts of cloth and bowls, most likely of gold.

These trees, like vertical lines in a comic strip, divide the different delegations in the Parade of Nations from one another. Each delegation is led by either a fully robed Mede, as in the bottom panel, or a bare-chested Persian guide, as directly above.

This Armenian groom keeps a close watch on this fine steed, while the countrymen behind him carry bolts of cloth.

The earliest trading centers of the Mediterranean have left ample archaeological evidence. Between 2000 and 1500 B.C.E., the Mediterranean island of Crete was home to a civilization with lavish palaces, well-built roads, bronze metallurgy, and a writing system called Linear A, which has not been deciphered. The archaeologist who discovered the site in the early twentieth century named the residents the Minoans (mih-NO-uhns) after the king Minos (mih-NOHS) who, Greek legends recounted, ruled a large empire with many ships. Archaeologists have found pottery made in the Minoan style all over the Mediterranean and western Asia, evidence of a wide-reaching Minoan trade network.

The Minoan civilization came to an abrupt end in 1500 B.C.E., probably because the Minoans were conquered by the Mycenaeans (1600–1200 B.C.E.), the earliest ancient civilization based on mainland Greece, in the city of Mycenae. The Mycenaeans (my-see-NEE-uhns) used Linear B script, which remained undeciphered until 1952. In that year, an architect and amateur cryptographer, Michael Ventris, realized what no one else had: Linear B was a dialect of Greek. He used his high school ancient Greek to decipher four thousand surviving clay tablets, which reveal much about the palace accounting system but little about Mycenaean society.

In his epic poems *The Odyssey* and *The Iliad*, the poet Homer (ca. 800 B.C.E.) described the Trojan Wars that took place centuries earlier between the Greeks and the Trojans living across the Aegean Sea in modern-day Turkey. Archaeologists are not certain whether the Trojan Wars occurred. If they did, it was during the time of the Mycenaean civilization. When the international system broke down in 1200 B.C.E. (see Chapter 2), Linear B fell into disuse, and the final archaeological evidence of Mycenaean culture dates to no later than 1200 B.C.E.

Phoenicians
A seagoing people who, around 900 B.C.E., expanded outward from their base on the Mediterranean coast of modern-day Lebanon. Their alphabet, which used only letters with no pictorial symbols, is the ancestor of the Roman alphabet.

The Phoenicians and the World's First Alphabet

Around this time, another seafaring people, the **Phoenicians**, appeared in the western Mediterranean. The Greeks called this people "red men," *Phoinikes*, or Phoenicians in English, most likely because they produced an extremely rare reddish-purple dye made from the glands of snails. The Phoenicians began to expand outward from their homeland in modern-day Lebanon around 900 B.C.E. They used a new type of writing system: an alphabet of twenty-two consonants. Unlike cuneiform, this alphabet had no pictorial symbols and depicted only sounds. Like many other scripts, Phoenician did not record vowels, which most native speakers can readily supply. (Consider the many abbreviations we use when texting.) The phonetic alphabet was surely one of the most influential innovations in the ancient world because it was much faster to learn an alphabet than to memorize a symbolic script like cuneiform.

By 814 B.C.E., the Phoenicians had established one outpost at Carthage (KAR-thudge) (modern-day Tunis in Tunisia) and subsequently built others at different ports along the North African coast as well as the southern coast of modern-day Spain (see Map 6.1). Herodotus credited the Phoenicians with the discovery that Africa was surrounded by water except where it joins Asia. He described a Phoenician voyage circumnavigating Africa sometime around 600 B.C.E.: *"Every autumn they [the voyagers] put in where they were on the African coast, sowed a patch of ground, and waited for next year's harvest. Then, having got in their grain, they put to sea again, and after two full years rounded Gibraltar in the course of the third, and returned to Egypt."*

˙From *The Histories* by Herodotus, translated by Aubrey de Sélincourt, revised with introductory matter and notes by John Marincola (Penguin Classics 1954, second revised edition 1996). Translation copyright 1954 by Aubrey de Sélincourt. Used by permission of Viking Penguin, a division of Penguin Group (USA) Inc., and David Higham Associates.

MAP 6.1 **Greek and Phoenician Settlement in the Mediterranean** Starting in 900 B.C.E., the Phoenicians expanded westward into the Mediterranean from their base along the eastern shore; they settled on the island of Sardinia and the North African shore. In 800 B.C.E., settlers from different Greek-speaking city-states left their homelands and formed more than 250 city-states in the eastern Mediterranean and Black Seas. (© Cengage Learning)

The Phoenicians founded new colonies by sending groups of men and women to coastal towns around the Mediterranean and even beyond.[5] We learn this from a Greek account about the Phoenician explorer Hanno, who set off from Carthage in 500 B.C.E. with sixty vessels and thirty thousand men and women. Hanno passed a river and two large gulfs and then captured three "gorillas," probably chimpanzees or baboons. Then he turned back. The vagueness of the description makes it difficult to know how far the Phoenicians traveled, but they may have reached Sierra Leone.

The veracity of both of these accounts—the Phoenician circumnavigation of Africa and the Phoenician colonization of West Africa—is much debated because of the lack of independent confirmation, but it is certain that the oceangoing Phoenicians transmitted their knowledge of geography along with their alphabet to the Greeks. The Phoenicians retained control of the western and southern Mediterranean until their defeat by ancient Rome in 202 B.C.E. (see Chapter 7).

The Rise of the Greek City-State, 800–500 B.C.E.

Since no materials in ancient Greek survive from between 1200 and 900 B.C.E., there is a gap in our knowledge. A new era in Greek history starts around 800 B.C.E., when various regions—including mainland Greece, the islands of the Aegean and the eastern Mediterranean, and the Aegean coast of Turkey—coalesced into city-states (*polis*; plural, *poleis*). The residents of these different places began to farm more intensively, and the resulting increase in agricultural production permitted a diversification of labor among the growing population: while the vast majority of people farmed the agricultural land around the cities, a tiny minority were able to settle inside walled cities. These cities had both markets for agricultural goods and temples to different gods. Each of these city-states, including the surrounding agricultural area, was small, with a population of between five and ten thousand people, but each was self-sufficient, having its own courts, law code, and army (see Map 6.1).

These city-states each had a guardian deity whose temple was located within the city walls. The Greeks believed in a pantheon of many gods headed by Zeus and his wife Hera. Each god possessed specific traits: Athena, the guardian god of Athens, was a goddess of war and of weaving. The Greeks told many myths about the gods and goddesses, often focusing on their attempts to intervene in the human world.

The citizens of the city-state gathered during festivals to offer animal sacrifices to the gods, with whom they communicated through prayers and oracles. The most celebrated oracle was at Delphi, on the Gulf of Corinth, where individuals and city-states consulted Apollo's priests to learn what would happen in the future before making any important decisions. People traveled all over the Aegean to pray for medical cures and to participate in temple festivals such as the Olympic games, which were held every four years starting in 776 B.C.E. at the temple to Zeus at Olympia in the Peloponnese.

An important breakthrough in shipbuilding that occurred around 800 B.C.E. facilitated such travel. Greek shipbuilders added a partial deck to boats that covered the center but left an open aisle along the sides. (Earlier boats, whether powered by oars or sails, had no decks.) Easily capable of traversing the Mediterranean, these improved boats made it possible for the citizens of the city-states of Greece to establish more than 250 different city-states along the coasts of the Mediterranean and Black Seas (see Map 6.1). Like Mesopotamian city-states, the Greek city-states remained linked to the mother city through trade. Ships carried olive oil, wine, and pottery produced by the Greeks to other regions, where they obtained lumber to make more ships.

During this period of vibrant growth and expansion, the Greeks adopted the Phoenician alphabet and added vowels. The first inscriptions in the new Greek alphabet date to 730 B.C.E. This new alphabet underlies many modern alphabets, including that of English, because the vowels and consonants could be used to represent the sounds of any language.

During the eighth and seventh centuries B.C.E., most Greek city-states were governed by powerful landowning families, but around 600 B.C.E. several city-states enacted reforms. Sparta became one of the first to grant extensive rights to its citizens. Only the descendants of original Spartans could be citizen-soldiers, who fought full-time and were not permitted to farm the land or engage in business. A second group, called "dwellers around," were descended from the first peoples to be conquered by the Spartans; entitled to own land, they also worked as craftsmen and traders but could not vote. The lowest-ranking group, full-time state slaves (Helots), cultivated the land of the citizens. Because their husbands were often away at war, Spartan women ran their estates and had more freedom than women in other city-states, yet they did not vote.

Future Spartan citizens joined the army as young children and received an austere military upbringing; only when they had successfully completed military training could they become citizens. Citizens (but not the state slaves) exercised a limited veto over the policies enacted by a council of elders who ruled in conjunction with two kings. When Darius and his co-conspirators debated the virtues of oligarchy, they were thinking of the Spartan government.

It took more than one hundred years for Athens to establish democracy. The most famous reformer, Solon (SOH-luhn), became the civilian head of state of Athens in 594 B.C.E. and launched a reform that abolished the obligation to pay one-sixth of one's crop as tax to the state. He also cancelled debts, which made it possible for former debtors to acquire and farm their own land. Athenian citizens formed four assemblies, defined by how much property they owned.

In 508 B.C.E., a group of aristocrats extended Solon's reforms further and established direct democracy. All citizens above the age of twenty—roughly thirty thousand men, or 10 percent of the population—could join the assembly, the lawmaking body. Many, however, were too busy to attend the frequent meetings, which occurred as often as forty times a year.

Women, who could not serve as soldiers or become citizens, never participated in the assembly. The women who enjoyed the greatest security were married; only children born to such couples were legitimate. Athenian men had many other sexual partners, both male and female: prostitutes whom they visited occasionally, concubines whom they supported financially, and slaves who could not say no to their owners.

Roughly two-fifths of Athens's population, some 120,000 people, were slaves, who also did not participate in the assembly. Many different types of slaves existed. Those who had skills and lived with their masters had less arduous lives than those who worked in the fields or in the silver mines, where working conditions were dangerous.

The Greco-Persian Wars, 490–479 B.C.E.

The Athenian army was particularly effective because it consisted of citizen-soldiers with a powerful commitment to defend their home city-state. Greek soldiers, called hoplites (HAHP-lites), could defeat the Persians in hand-to-hand combat because they had better shields, stronger armor, and more effective formations. The soldiers were divided into units, called phalanxes, eight men deep. If the first row of soldiers was broken, the row behind them pressed forward to meet the attack.

The first important Athenian victory came at the battle of Marathon in 490 B.C.E. The Persian ruler Darius sent a force to punish the Athenians for supporting an uprising against the Persians by the Greeks living on the east coast of the Aegean. The Athenian forces of eleven thousand men attacked the Persian army of twenty-five thousand when they were foraging for food and, in a stunning reversal of what every informed person expected, won a decisive victory on the plain of Marathon. (The English word *marathon* comes from a later legend about a messenger running over 20 miles [32 km] from Marathon to Athens to announce the victory.) Herodotus's tally of the casualties underlines the immensity of the Athenian victory: the Athenians lost 192 men; the Persians, 6,400.

After Darius died in 486 B.C.E., his son Xerxes (r. 486–465 B.C.E.) decided to avenge his father's defeat and gathered a huge army that he hoped would frighten the Greeks into surrendering. But Sparta and Athens for the first time organized a coalition of the Greek city-states that fought the Persians for control of a mountain pass north of Athens at Thermopylae (thuhr-MOP-uh-lie). The Greeks were eventually routed, but three hundred Spartans stood firm and fought to their deaths. The victorious Persians then sacked the deserted city of Athens.

The Greeks regrouped, and the Athenian naval commanders took advantage of their superior knowledge of the local terrain to secure a surprising Greek victory at Salamis. In recounting this battle, an important turning point in the war, Herodotus highlighted the role of **Artemisia** (ar-TEM-ee-zee-uh) (flourished 480 B.C.E.), the woman ruler of Halicarnassus (Herodotus's hometown), who had become queen upon the death of her husband and who, like all conquered peoples in the Persian empire, fought alongside the Persians. Artemisia commanded five of the Persians' 1,207 triremes (TRY-reems), three-story boats powered by rowers on each level. *"She sailed with the fleet,"* Herodotus explains, *"in spite of the fact that she had a grown-up son and that there was consequently no necessity for her to do so,"** implying that he would not have found her participation worthy of comment if her son had still been a child. Artemisia fascinated Herodotus because she differed so much from well-off Athenian women, who stayed indoors and devoted themselves to managing their households.

Hand-to-Hand Combat in Ancient Greece A naked Greek soldier, armed with only a shield and a spear, bests his Persian opponent, who wears a long-sleeved tunic and trousers. The Persian has just shot an arrow that missed its target. In fact, Greek soldiers did not fight naked; they wore armor. Vases depicting Greeks defeating Persians were extremely popular in the fifth century B.C.E., when the Greeks and Persians fought so many wars. (The Chicago Painter Pitcher (oinochoe) with Greek warrior attacking Persian archer, Greek, Classical Period, about 450 B.C. Ceramic, Red Figure Height: 19.3 cm; height with handle: 24 cm Museum of Fine Arts, Boston Francis Bartlett Donation of 1912, 13.196 Photograph © 2012 Museum of Fine Arts, Boston)

Herodotus employed contrasts to heighten his comparisons between Greeks and non-Greeks. The Athenians enjoyed the benefits of democracy while the Persians suffered under the tyranny of Xerxes. Greek men were strong while Persian men were weak, which is why Xerxes had to depend on Artemisia. In the inverted world of the war, the only Persian commander worthy of mention in Herodotus's eyes is the Greek woman Artemisia.

Contrary to all expectations, the Greeks defeated the Persians. Defeat, however, had little impact on the Persian empire except to define its western edge. Xerxes returned home to an empire just as large as his father's, and no Persian ruler after Xerxes ever succeeded in adding Greece to his empire.

Artemisia (flourished 480 B.C.E.) The woman ruler of Halicarnassus, on the Aegean coast of modern-day Turkey, who fought with the Persians against the Greeks at the Battle of Salamis.

Culture and Politics in Athens, 480–404 B.C.E.

During the century after the defeat of the Persians, Athens experienced unprecedented cultural growth. The new literary genre of Greek tragedy took shape, and the Athenians constructed the great temple to Athena on the Acropolis (uh-KRAW-poe-lis), the great bluff overlooking the city, as a lasting monument to Greek victory against the Persians.

In 472 B.C.E., the playwright Aeschylus (525–456 B.C.E.) wrote *The Persians*, the earliest Greek tragedy surviving today. Set in the Persian capital at Susa, the play

---

*From *The Histories* by Herodotus, translated by Aubrey de Sélincourt, revised with introductory matter and notes by John Marincola (Penguin Classics 1954, second revised edition 1996). Translation copyright 1954 by Aubrey de Sélincourt. Used by permission of Viking Penguin, a division of Penguin Group (USA) Inc., and David Higham Associates.

opens with a chorus of elderly men speculating about Xerxes's attempted invasion of Greece because they have had no news for so long. One-quarter of the way through the play, a lone messenger arrives and mournfully announces:

A single stroke has brought about the ruin of great
Prosperity, the flower of Persia fallen and gone.
Oh oh! To be the first to bring bad news is bad;
But necessity demands the roll of suffering
Be opened, Persians.

Writing only eight years after the war, Aeschylus (ESS-kih-luhs), himself a veteran, exaggerates the losses to make the audience sympathize with the Persians and emphasizes the shared humanity of the Persians and the Greeks. Xerxes's mother, the queen, struggles to understand why the Persians have lost: they have violated natural law, she eventually realizes, by trying to conquer what did not belong to them. *The Persians* is the first of over one hundred tragedies written during the fifth century B.C.E. by three great playwrights—Aeschylus, Sophocles (sof-uh-KLEEZ) (496–406 B.C.E.), and Euripides (you-RIP-uh-deez) (ca. 485–406 B.C.E.)—that show individuals, both male and female, coming to terms with their fates.

In 478 B.C.E., the Athenians formed the Delian (DEE-lih-yuhn) League, a group of city-states whose stated purpose was to drive the Persians from the Greek world. After several victories in the 470s against the Persians, the Persian threat was eliminated, prompting some of the league's members to withdraw. Athens invaded these cities and forced them to become its subjects. In the 460s a general named Pericles (PER-eh-kleez) (ca. 495–429 B.C.E.) emerged as the most popular leader in the city, and in 454 B.C.E. the Athenians moved the league's treasury to Athens, ending all pretense of an alliance among equals. This was the closest that Athens came to having an empire, but its possessions were all Greek-speaking, and its control was short-lived.

In 449 B.C.E., Pericles used the league's funds to finance a building campaign to make Athens as physically impressive as it was politically powerful. The centerpiece of the city's reconstruction, the Parthenon, was both a temple to Athena, the city's guardian deity, and a memorial to those who had died in the wars with Persia. Once completed, the Parthenon expressed the Athenians' desire to be the most advanced people of the ancient world. (See the feature "World History in Today's World: Returning the Elgin Marbles to Athens: The Case For and Against.")

The Spartans, however, felt that they, not Athens, should be the leader of the Greeks. Since the 460s, tensions had been growing between the two city-states, and from 431 to 404 B.C.E. Athens and Sparta, and their allied city-states, engaged in the protracted Peloponnesian War. Sparta, with the help of the Persians, finally defeated Athens in 404 B.C.E. The long and drawn-out Peloponnesian War wore both Sparta and Athens down, creating an opportunity for the rulers of the northern region of Macedon to conquer Greece (see page 156). In writing about the war, the historian **Thucydides** (460–395 B.C.E.) pioneered a more scientific approach to history by focusing exclusively on human, not divine, actors.

Thucydides
(460–395 B.C.E.) Author of *History of the Peloponnesian War*, a pioneering work.

---

*Reprinted with the permission of Simon & Schuster, Inc., from *The Persians* by Aeschylus, translated by Anthony J. Pedlecki. Copyright © 1970 by Prentice-Hall, Inc. All rights reserved.

Socrates
(469–399 B.C.E.) A great philosopher who believed that virtue was the highest good. He developed a method of instruction still in use today, in which teachers ask students questions without revealing the answers.

Plato
(429–347 B.C.E.) A student of Socrates and a teacher of Aristotle who used the Socratic method in his teaching, which emphasized ethics. He believed that students should use reason to choose the correct course of action.

Athens as a Center for the Study of Philosophy

Even during these years of conflict, Athens was home to several of the best-known philosophers in history: Socrates (469–399 B.C.E.) taught Plato (429–347 B.C.E.), and Plato in turn taught Aristotle (384–322 B.C.E.). Their predecessors, the earliest Greek philosophers, were active around 600 B.C.E. in the city-state of Miletus, just north of Halicarnassus on the eastern coast of the Aegean Sea. Members of this school argued that everything in the universe originated in a single element: some proposed water; others, air. Their findings may seem naive, but they were the first to believe in rational explanations rather than crediting everything to divine intervention, and the Athenian philosophers developed this insight further.

The Athenian philosopher **Socrates** (sock-ruh-TEEZ) wrote nothing down, so we must depend on the accounts of his student Plato (PLAY-toe). Socrates perfected a style of teaching, now known as the Socratic (suh-KRAT-ick) method, in which the instructor asks the student questions without revealing his own views. Many of the dialogues reported by Plato stress the Greek concept of *aretê* (virtue or excellence), which people can attain by doing right. Virtue was the highest good for Socrates, who believed that wisdom allows one to determine the right course of action.

Immediately after Sparta defeated Athens in the Peloponnesian War, a small group of men formed an oligarchy in Athens in 404–403 B.C.E., but they were overthrown by a democratic government. Late in Socrates's life, some of those in the new democratic government suspected the philosopher of opposing democracy because he had associated with those in the oligarchy they had overthrown. In 399 B.C.E. they brought him to trial on vague charges of impiety (not believing in the gods) and corrupting the city's youth. Found guilty by a jury numbering in the hundreds, Socrates did not apologize but insisted that he had been right all along. His death in 399 B.C.E. from drinking poisonous hemlock, the traditional means of execution, became one of the most infamous executions in history. Democratic rule in Athens ended in 322 B.C.E.

Plato continued Socrates's method of teaching by asking questions. He founded the Academy, a gymnasium where he could teach students a broad curriculum emphasizing ethics. Gymnasiums had begun simply as an open ground for soldiers to train, but they had evolved into schools for young boys where they engaged in exercise and studied texts. Plato taught that people could choose the just course of action by using reason to reconcile the conflicting

The Acropolis: A Massive Construction Project Completed in Only Fifteen Years Built between 447 and 432 B.C.E., the Parthenon was a two-roomed building surrounded by columns over 34 feet (10 m) tall; one of the interior rooms held a magnificent statue of Athena, now lost. Beautiful friezes inside the roofs and above the columns portrayed the legendary battles of the Trojan War, in which the Greek forces (symbolizing the Athenians and their allies) defeated the Trojans (the ancient counterpart of the Persian enemy).

Georg Gerster/Photo Researchers, Inc.

Returning the Elgin Marbles to Athens: The Case For and Against

Modern museums, particularly those with large collections acquired outside the home country, debate whether they should return archaeological treasures to the countries where they were originally found. The most controversial case is the Elgin Marbles, now held in the British Museum in London.

These statues and friezes, which were taken from Athens by Thomas Bruce, Seventh Earl of Elgin (the g is hard as in *girl*), between 1799 and 1810, came from the temple Pericles built to the goddess Athena on top of the Acropolis. The horizontal band above the columns holding up the roof holds multiple scenes of people and gods fighting in different mythical battles. This band of statuary originally stretched 524 feet (160 m) long; 247 feet (75 m) of it are on display in the British Museum, along with other statues and sections of buildings.

The museum acquired them in 1816, when the British Parliament authorized a payment to Lord Elgin, who had served from 1799 to 1803 as the British ambassador to the Ottoman empire, which governed Greece at the time. Elgin obtained permission from the Ottoman authorities to remove these objects. Even in 1816, critics charged that Elgin had bribed officials to obtain the marble statues, and in the 1980s the Greek minister of culture made a particularly impassioned plea for the return of the Elgin Marbles.

The year 2009 marked the opening of the New Acropolis Museum, which displays all the statues in Greece's possession as well as plaster casts of those that are now abroad. Everyone agrees that it is impossible to restore the much-damaged Parthenon to its original state; they concur as well that the marble sculptures belong indoors, away from the elements and air pollution, which can cause real damage.

If the Greek Ministry of Culture gets its way, the British Museum will return the Elgin Marbles to the new museum in Athens. Opposing the return, the trustees of the British Museum maintain that "the sculptures are part of everyone's shared heritage and transcend cultural boundaries." Being able to compare them with the art of other societies, the trustees believe, is a crucial element of understanding the world's past.

Sources: The British Museum website (www.britishmuseum.org); Greek Ministry of Culture website (www.culture.gr).

---

demands of spirit and desire. Reason alone determined the individual's best interests. Plato admitted boys to the Academy as well as some girls. Some scholars contend that all well-off Greek women could read and write, while others think that only a small minority could.

Plato's student **Aristotle** (AH-riss-tot-uhl) was not a native of Athens but was born in Macedon. He entered Plato's Academy at the age of seventeen in 367 B.C.E. and studied with him for twenty years, returning to Macedon after Plato's death in 347 B.C.E. There he later served as a tutor to Alexander, the son of the Macedonian ruler Philip (382–336 B.C.E.). Aristotle did not share Socrates's and Plato's optimism that knowledge alone would result in ethical behavior because he did not accept their view that human nature was good. He emphasized, instead, that people had to study hard so that they could gain control over their desires.

Aristotle
(384–322 B.C.E.) A Greek philosopher who encouraged his students to observe the natural world and explain logically how they proceeded from their starting assumptions. This system of reasoning shapes how we present written arguments today.

Aristotle had a broad view of what constituted a proper education. Observing the round shadow the earth cast on the moon during eclipses, he concluded that the earth was a sphere and lay at the center of the universe. He urged his students to observe live animals in nature and was one of the first to realize that whales and dolphins were mammals, a discovery ignored for nearly two thousand years. Aristotle required that his students identify their starting assumptions and explain logically how they proceeded from one point to the next. This system of reasoning remained influential in the Islamic world and Europe long after his death and continues to shape how we present written arguments today.

Alexander the Great and His Successors, 334–30 B.C.E.

In the course of his lifetime Aristotle witnessed the decline of Athens, which never recovered from the costs of the Peloponnesian War, and the rise of his native region of Macedon. Philip and his son **Alexander of Macedon** (also called Alexander the Great) were autocrats untouched by the Athenian tradition of democracy: as generals they ordered their professional armies to obey them and governed conquered territory as if the inhabitants were part of their army. Many scholars use the term *Hellenization* to describe the process by which societies, peoples, and places during Alexander's rule became more Greek (the Greek word for Greece is *Hellas*). As Alexander's army conquered territory, his Greek-speaking soldiers encountered many different peoples living in West, Central, and South Asia. Some settled in these regions and built communities that resembled those they had left behind in Greece. (See the feature "Movement of Ideas Through Primary Sources: Alexander's Hellenistic Policies in Central Asia.")

Recent historians have questioned this depiction of Alexander as a carrier of Greek culture, noting how much he emulated the Persians. Alexander portrayed himself as a defender of the Persian rulers' tradition and adopted many of their practices, sometimes to the dismay of his Greek followers. Newly discovered leather scrolls show that four years after defeating the Persians, Alexander's government issued orders under his name in the same format and language as their former rulers used.[6] The borders of his empire overlapped almost entirely with those of the Achaemenid empire, and his army, administration, and tax system were all modeled on those of the Persians. After his death, Alexander's empire broke into three major sections, each ruled by a successor dynasty that followed Persian practice.

Alexander of Macedon (r. 336–323 B.C.E.) Also known as Alexander the Great; son of Philip of Macedon. He defeated the last Achaemenid ruler in 331 B.C.E. and ruled the former Persian empire until his death.

Philip and Alexander: From Macedon to Empire, 359–323 B.C.E.

Lying to the north of Greece, Macedon was a peripheral region with no cities and little farming where Greek was spoken. Originally a barren region, it became a powerful kingdom under Philip II (r. 359–336 B.C.E.), who reorganized the army into a professional fighting force of paid soldiers. Philip and Alexander built empires by amassing wealth from the peoples they conquered.

Philip created, and Alexander inherited, an army more powerful than any of its rivals. Philip reorganized his army by training them to use close-packed infantry formations and by arming some of the infantry with pikes 17 feet (5 m) long. Alexander's infantry carried the same long pikes, and the infantry phalanx had fifteen thousand men who fought in rows and were almost invincible; 1,800 cavalry aided them by attacking the enemy on either side.

MAP 6.2 The Empires of Persia and Alexander the Great The Achaemenids (550–330 B.C.E.), the Parthians (247 B.C.E.–224 C.E.), and the Sasanians (224–651) all formed powerful dynasties in Iran. The largest (shown with a green border) was that of the Achaemenids. After conquering it in 330 B.C.E., Alexander of Macedon enlarged its territory only slightly. Under the Achaemenids, this large region remained united for over two hundred years; under Alexander, for only thirteen. After Alexander's death, the empire split into three separate empires. (© Cengage Learning)

Following his father's assassination in 336 B.C.E., Alexander defeated the Persian forces in 331 B.C.E., and in 330 B.C.E. one of the Persian satraps killed the last Achaemenid emperor, Darius III (r. 336–330 B.C.E.). This turn of events allowed Alexander to take over the Persian empire intact; he did not alter the administrative structure of satrapies. A brilliant military strategist, Alexander led his troops over 11,000 miles (18,000 km) in eight years, going as far as Egypt and north India, but did not significantly expand the territory of the Persian empire (see Map 6.2).

Alexander constantly wrestled with the issue of how to govern. Should he rule as a Macedonian or adopt the Persian model? To the horror of his Macedonian troops, he donned Persian clothing and expected them to prostrate themselves before him as the Persian subjects had honored their king. When his senior advisers protested, Alexander made one of many compromises during his thirteen-year reign: he required the Persians, but not the Macedonians, to prostrate themselves. Like the Persian kings, Alexander married women to cement his political alliances; his wife Roxane was a native of Samarkand, one of the cities that most vigorously resisted his rule.

The farther they traveled from Greece, the more unhappy Alexander's men grew. In 326 B.C.E., when they reached the banks of the Hyphasis River in India, they refused to go on, forcing Alexander to turn back. After a long and difficult march along the northern edge of the Indian Ocean, Alexander and the remnants of his army returned to Babylon, where Alexander died in 323 B.C.E.

Alexander's Hellenistic Policies in Central Asia

About four hundred years after the death of Alexander, the historian Plutarch (ca. 46–ca. 120) wrote two essays about him. The first appeared in Plutarch's *Lives*, an innovative collection of biographies that each paired one Greek with one Roman (in this case, Alexander the Great with the Roman leader Julius Caesar). The second, "On the Fortune of Alexander," appears in a collection of essays on moral topics. Writing as a Greek speaker under Roman rule, Plutarch is often remembered for his account of Hellenism, or Alexander's efforts to spread Greek culture to the non-Greek peoples of Central Asia. In fact, Plutarch devotes considerable attention to Alexander's efforts to win the support of the locals and not simply to force his policies on them, as Plutarch felt that Xerxes had.

Sources: Plutarch, *Greek Lives*, trans. Robin Waterfield (New York: Oxford University Press, 1998), pp. 355–356; Plutarch, *Moralia*, trans. Frank Cole Babbitt, vol. 4 (Cambridge, Mass.: Harvard University Press, 1957), pp. 397–401 (with some modifications to enhance readability).

"Alexander," from Plutarch's *Lives*

Alexander was worried about his troops refusing to continue with the campaign, so leaving the main body where it was, and taking only the best of them—20,000 foot-soldiers and 3,000 cavalrymen—with him into Hyrcania [the region south of the Caspian Sea], he won them over by telling them that at the moment the easterners could see them face to face, but that if all they did was cause havoc in Asia and then leave, the enemy would regard them as no better than women and not hesitate to attack them. Nevertheless, he left it up to them to leave if they wanted to, and asked that if they did so they should testify that in his attempt to make the whole world subject to the Macedonians, he had been left behind with his friends and those who were prepared to continue with the campaign. This is almost a verbatim quote from a letter of his to Antipater, and he goes on to say that after he had finished speaking they all shouted out loud, calling on him to take them wherever he wanted in the world. Once these elite troops had met this test of their loyalty, it proved easy to win over the main body of the army, which readily followed his lead.

After this, then, he began to assimilate his way of life even more closely with that of the locals, and also tried to get them to adopt Macedonian customs. He was of the opinion that while he was away on a lengthy expedition political stability would follow from fusion and co-operation, achieved through goodwill, rather than from the use of force. This is also why he issued instructions that 30,000 selected children were to learn Greek and to be trained in the use of Macedonian weaponry, and appointed a large number of people to oversee this project. Moreover, although what happened with Rhoxane occurred because he fell in love with her beauty and grace when he saw her dancing at a banquet, the marriage was also held to fit in quite well with the policy he was pursuing. For the easterners were reassured by the bond the marriage formed, and they particularly appreciated the self-restraint he demonstrated in refusing to lay a finger even on the only woman he ever fell for until it had been sanctioned by law.

"On the Fortune of Alexander"

Alexander did not follow the advice to treat the Greeks as if he were their leader, and other peoples as if he were their master; to have regard for the Greeks as for friends and kindred, but to conduct himself toward other peoples as though they were plants or animals; for to do so would have been to cumber his leadership with numerous battles and banishments and festering seditions. But, as he believed that he came as a heaven-sent governor to all, and as a mediator for the whole world, those whom he could not persuade to unite with him, he conquered by force of arms, and he brought together into one body all men everywhere, uniting and mixing in one great loving-cup, as it were, men's lives, their characters, their marriages, their very habits of life. He bade them all consider as their fatherland the whole inhabited earth, as their stronghold and protection his camp, as akin to them all good men, and as foreigners only the wicked; they should not distinguish between Greek and foreigner by Greek cloak and shield, or sword and jacket; but the distinguishing mark of the Greek should be seen in virtue, and that of the foreigner in iniquity; clothing and food, marriage and manner of life they should regard as common to all, being blended into one by ties of blood and children. . . .

But methinks I [Plutarch] would gladly have been a witness of that fair and holy marriage-rite, when Alexander brought together in one golden-canopied tent an hundred Persian brides and an hundred Macedonian and Greek bridegrooms, united at a common hearth and board. He himself, crowned with garlands, was the first to raise the marriage hymn as though he were singing a song of truest friendship over the union of the two greatest and most mighty peoples; for he, of one maid the bridegroom, and at the same time of all the brides the escort, as a father and sponsor united them in the bonds of wedlock.

Indeed at this sight I should have cried out for joy, "O dullard Xerxes, stupid fool that spent so much fruitless toil to bridge the Hellespont!˙ This is the way that wise kings join Asia with Europe; it is not by beams nor rafts, nor by lifeless and unfeeling bonds, but by the ties of lawful love and chaste nuptials and mutual joy in children that they join the nations together."

˙**Hellespont**   The strait at Byzantium.

QUESTIONS FOR ANALYSIS

» *What measures did Alexander use to expand Greek cultural influence?*

» *What did the Greeks learn from local peoples?*

159

The Legacy of Alexander the Great

The aftereffects of Alexander's conquests lasted far longer than his brief thirteen-year reign. Initially the greatest impact came from his soldiers. Thousands traveled with him, but thousands more chose to stay behind in different parts of Asia, often taking local wives. These men introduced Greek culture over a large geographic region.

Archaeologists have unearthed an entire Greek city in the Afghan town of Ai Khanum (aye-EE KAH-nuhm), which had all the characteristic buildings of a Greek town. The city's planners mounded dirt into an acropolis, or citadel, some 200 feet (60 m) high. Two guardian deities, statues of gods made by local artists following Greek prototypes, protected the city's Greek-style gymnasium, and a semicircular structure provided a place for the city's residents to watch theater, another defining feature of Greek life. A high-quality funerary text and text fragments preserved in the palace library testify to the locals' command of and interest in written Greek.

Other elements of the city, though, drew on different cultural traditions. Like other similar settlements, Ai Khanum included the local Iranian peoples along with descendants of Alexander's soldiers. The palace had long rows of Greek columns, but the layout, with its huge open spaces, was clearly Persian, modeled on Darius I's palace at Susa. Made from sun-baked bricks, stepped temples to Greek and various local deities were shaped like Babylonian ziggurats, not the stone temples of Greece. Founded in 300 B.C.E. by Alexander's successor Seleucus, Ai Khanum continued until 145 B.C.E., when a nomadic people attacked the city and burned the treasury.

After Alexander's death, his empire broke into three sections, each ruled by one of his generals (see Map 6.2): Egypt went to Ptolemy (TOHL-uh-mee), Greece and Macedon to Antigonas (an-TIG-uh-nass), and all other territories to Seleucus (seh-LOO-kuhs), who sent Megasthenes as his ambassador to the Mauryans in 302 B.C.E. (see Chapter 3). Each general founded a regional dynasty named for himself: the Ptolemies (TOHL-uh-meze), the Antigonids (an-TIG-uh-nidz), and the Seleucids (seh-LOO-sidz). These successor regimes continued to administer their territories using the Persian system of administration.

The city of Alexandria in Egypt, founded by Alexander in 332 B.C.E., became a major center of learning within the territory of the Ptolemies. At Alexandria, the Ptolemies built the Museum, a temple to the Muses (the goddesses of the arts), and they welcomed scholars in many different fields, including mathematics, medicine, astronomy, history, and geography. Their interactions produced many important scientific breakthroughs. Because of a long-standing Greek belief that dead bodies should not be touched, Greek scientists did not dissect human cadavers; Aristotle dissected only animal remains. In Alexandria, though, Greek scholars performed dissections on deceased prisoners, possibly inspired by Egyptian experts skilled in mummification (see Chapter 2).

Alexandria's library was particularly impressive because customs officials confiscated all papyrus rolls that travelers brought to Alexandria; the library retained the originals and returned copies to the owners. One librarian, the Greek astronomer Eratosthenes (eh-ruh-TOSS-thih-nees), took office in 240 B.C.E. Since Aristotle, the Greeks had believed that the earth was spherical, but they had no idea how big it was. Eratosthenes devised an ingenious experiment by which he concluded that the earth's circumference must be 250,000 stadia (24,427 miles, or 39,311 km), an error of less than 2 percent from the actual circumference of 24,857 miles (40,000 km) (see Figure 6.1). Eratosthenes' brilliant experiment taught the Greeks that the known world occupied only a small section of the earth's northern hemisphere.

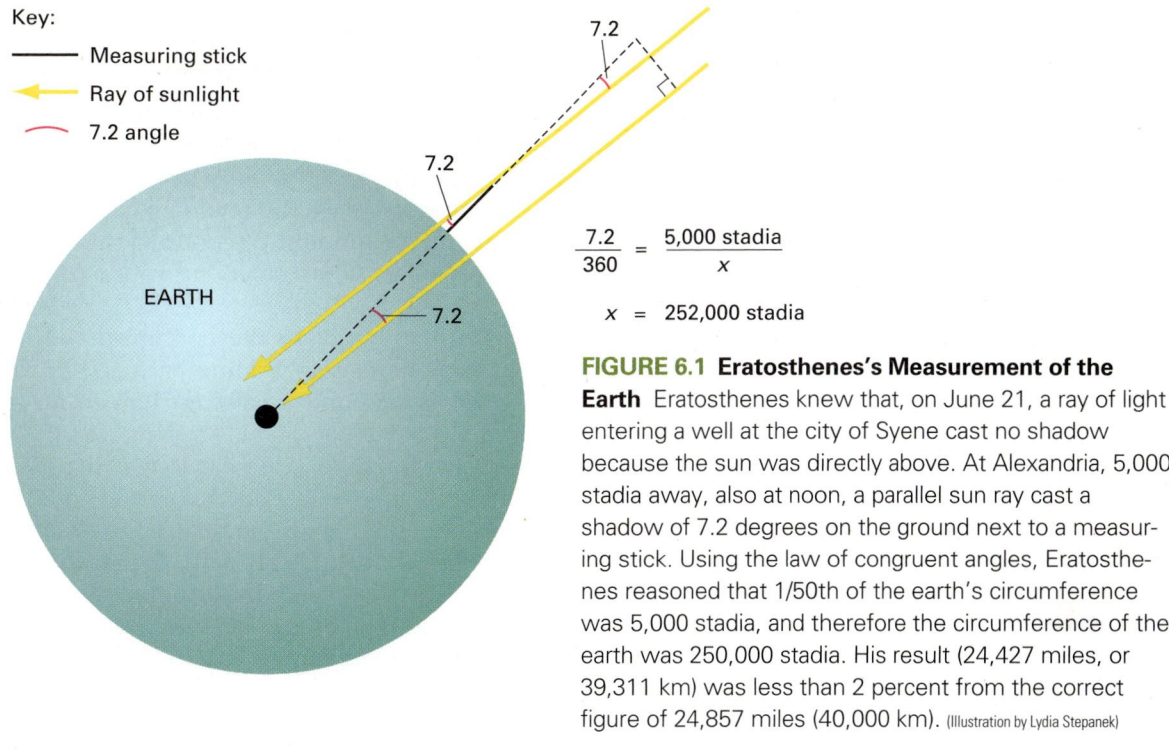

Key:
— Measuring stick
← Ray of sunlight
⌒ 7.2 angle

$$\frac{7.2}{360} = \frac{5,000 \text{ stadia}}{x}$$

$$x = 252,000 \text{ stadia}$$

FIGURE 6.1 Eratosthenes's Measurement of the Earth Eratosthenes knew that, on June 21, a ray of light entering a well at the city of Syene cast no shadow because the sun was directly above. At Alexandria, 5,000 stadia away, also at noon, a parallel sun ray cast a shadow of 7.2 degrees on the ground next to a measuring stick. Using the law of congruent angles, Eratosthenes reasoned that 1/50th of the earth's circumference was 5,000 stadia, and therefore the circumference of the earth was 250,000 stadia. His result (24,427 miles, or 39,311 km) was less than 2 percent from the correct figure of 24,857 miles (40,000 km). (Illustration by Lydia Stepanek)

The Parthians and the Sasanians, Heirs to the Persians, 247 B.C.E.–651 C.E.

A people based in northern Iran, the Parthians, took Iran from the Seleucids by 140 B.C.E. The **Parthians** (247 B.C.E.–224 C.E.) and then the **Sasanians** (224–651 C.E.) governed Iran for nearly nine hundred years. The two dynasties frequently emulated the Persians; they built monuments like theirs, retained their military and tax structures, and governed the different peoples under them flexibly. The Parthians followed the Persian precedent closely, while the Sasanians experimented more.

The homeland of a seminomadic people who lived in northern Iran, Parthia had been a satrapy within both the Persian and Seleucid empires. In 247 B.C.E., according to a legend, Arsaces I formed a conspiracy to found his own dynasty with six other men. It was no coincidence that he had exactly the number of conspirators that his role model Darius had. The dynastic founder and his successors eventually conquered the Tigris and Euphrates River Valleys and the Iranian plateau extending up to the Indus River Valley in Pakistan (see Map 6.2). Like the Persians, the Parthians were Zoroastrians who tended fire altars, but they allowed their subjects to practice their own religions.

The Parthians were celebrated for their fine and fast horses, which were heavily protected by armor. Parthian archers tricked the enemy by pretending to retreat and then turning backward on their mounts to shoot, in a display of archery prowess still known as the Parthian shot. Starting in the first century B.C.E. and

Parthians
(247 B.C.E.–224 C.E.) The ruling dynasty of Iran, who defeated the Seleucids and took over their territory in 140 B.C.E. Famous for their heavily armored cavalry, they posed a continuous problem for the Roman empire.

Sasanians
The ruling dynasty (224–651 C.E.) of Iran who defeated the Parthians and ruled for more than four centuries until the Islamic conquest of Iran. Introduced innovations such as nonsatrap royal lands and government support of Zoroastrianism.

continuing through the first and second centuries C.E., the Romans (see Chapter 7) attacked the Parthians at periodic intervals, but the powerful Parthian military always kept them at bay.

Parthian soldiers were retainers to the nobles, for whom they performed military service. The king, who called himself "king of kings" in the Persian tradition, stood at the top of Parthian society, and the upper nobility ranked just below him but above the lower nobility. Though not slaves, the retainers had to perform a certain amount of labor and to pay a fixed amount of goods to the nobles they served. Doctors, artists, singing storytellers, and traders formed a middle level between the nobles and the retainers.

Trade was important to the Parthians because they occupied the territory between the Greco-Roman world and their Asian trading partners. In times of peace with Rome the Parthians traded spices and textiles for Roman metals and manufactured goods.

The Parthians ruled for nearly five hundred years, far longer than the two-hundred-year reign of the Persians, and their rule came to an end in 224 when Ardashir, one of their satraps, overthrew them and founded the Sasanian empire (named for his ancestor, Sasan). After defeating the Parthians, the Sasanians incorporated the Parthian forces into their army, of which the armored cavalry continued to be the strongest section. The Sasanian rulers led their powerful army to conquer all the territory of the former Parthian empire, in addition to lands to the east and the northeastern Arabian peninsula.

Sasanian society remained as hierarchical as in earlier times under the Persians. The upper nobility was divided into four ranks, with the king's direct relatives ranking highest and those unrelated to the king lowest. Royal women continued to exercise considerable power, like their earlier Persian counterparts; some of the most powerful rulers' mothers were called "queen of queens." Under the upper nobility were a lower group of nobles, some of whom received their lands and positions directly from the king. The middle ranks included craftsmen, traders, doctors, and singers. At the bottom of society were the cultivators, who had to give a share of their crop to the nobles in addition to the taxes they paid.

Once the Sasanians conquered a region, they divided the territory into two types of land: some was reserved for the king, while that portion entrusted to a satrap was divided into smaller districts. Only on the royal lands could the king establish cities, which he populated with deported peoples, most often skilled craftsmen, drawn from prisoners of war. The practice of forcible resettlement had a long history in western Asia going back to the Assyrians and the Babylonians (see Chapter 2). The resettled peoples could not leave their assigned cities, but they were well paid and were free to marry local women, practice their own religions, and speak their native languages. These skilled craftsmen received high pay for their work as weavers and as builders and engineers who constructed roads and bridges.

Cognizant that many different peoples lived within their empire, the Sasanians encouraged the translation of certain books from Sanskrit, Greek, and Syriac (the language spoken in Mesopotamia). They appointed officials to supervise Zoroastrian observances in each province at the local level, and the state constructed fire altars all over the empire. These government policies made Sasanian Iran actively Zoroastrian, and the Sasanians had difficulty managing the great religious diversity of their subjects.

By the third century C.E. two new religions, each with sizable followings, appeared in Iran: Christianity (see Chapter 7) and Manichaeism (mah-nih-KEE-iz-uhm). Mani (mah-NEE) (216–ca. 274) was an Iranian preacher born in Mesopotamia who believed that his Manichaean teachings incorporated all the teachings of earlier prophets, including Zarathushtra, the Buddha, and Jesus Christ. Like Zoroastrianism, his was a dualistic system in which the forces of light and dark were engaged in a perpetual struggle. Ordinary people could strengthen the forces of light by supporting the Manichaean clergy, who ate only vegetarian food provided by the laity, lived celibate lives, and conducted Manichaean rituals.

The Sasanians saw both the Christians and the Manichaeans as threats because they had their own religious hierarchy and refused to perform Zoroastrian rituals. Some kings tried to strengthen Zoroastrianism by commissioning a written version of *The Avesta* to rival Manichaean scriptures and the Bible. Other rulers directly persecuted members of the two churches. The third major religious community, the Jews, fared better under the Sasanians and were allowed to govern their own communities as long as they paid their taxes. However, the Sasanians put down any challenge to the legitimacy of their rule.

Adherence to the Persian model of a flexible satrap-based empire allowed the Sasanians to rule for over four centuries. Suffering several military defeats and forfeiting large chunks of their empire, they survived until 651, when their capital at Ctesiphon fell to the Islamic armies of the caliphate (see Chapter 9).

The Sasanian Palace, Ctesiphon, Iran The ruins of the Sasanian palace at Ctesiphon demonstrate the ingenuity and great skill of the brickmasons, who came from all over the empire and were resettled there by the emperors. The vaulted arch stands 118 feet (36 m) high, making it one of the world's largest brick arches. Its open doorways and fine brickwork inspired Islamic architects, who incorporated these same features into early mosques. (Gerard Degeorge/akg-images)

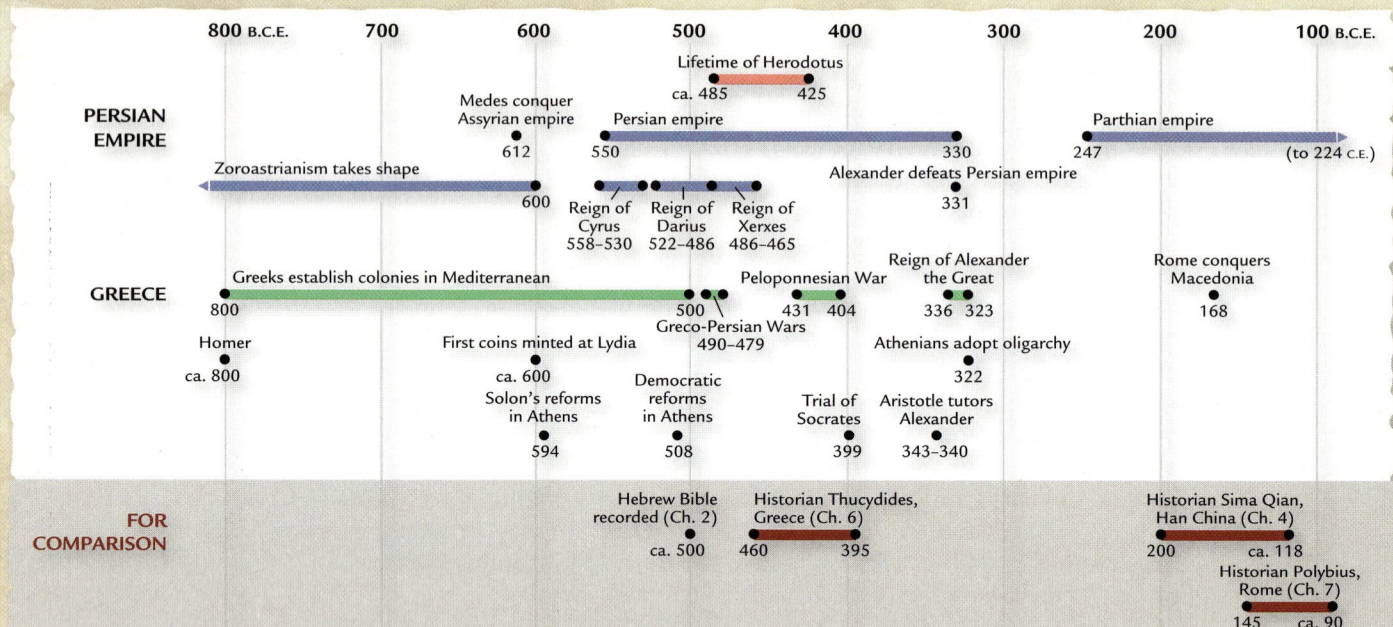

Persians and Greeks in the History of Empires

Born in the decade of the most intense fighting between Athens and the Persian empire, Herodotus devoted his life to understanding the conflict between the two. Although, as a Greek, Herodotus sympathized with the Athenians, he attributed the Persians' success in other conquests and in expanding their empire to their monarchical form of government and to the innovative policies of their early rulers: Cyrus, Darius I, and Xerxes. Herodotus did not travel for religious reasons; he went all over the Mediterranean to learn about the various peoples who resisted conquest by the Persians and those who succumbed to them. He earned his way as a stand-up historian: in front of live audiences, he recounted the stories that he later edited to form *The Histories*.

The division of the empire into satrapies allowed the Persians to govern 30–35 million subjects in an expanse centered on modern-day Iran that took in modern Egypt, Turkey, and Uzbekistan. The Persian empire was larger than any earlier or contemporary empire, and the rulers tolerated their subjects' diverse languages and religions. This flexible empire differed strongly from Chinese models, which assumed that all subjects spoke Chinese and shared the same religious orientation (see Chapters 4 and 8).

Although the Persian rulers were Zoroastrian and built fire altars throughout their realm, they granted religious freedom as long as their subjects paid their taxes to the center. Unlike in the Roman, Chinese, and Islamic empires to be discussed in Chapters 7, 8, and 9, the Persian rulers did not force or even encourage their subjects to convert to their religion. So Zoroastrianism never became a major world religion. Nor did the Persian kings require their subjects to use Persian, with the result that different languages continued to be spoken in various regions.

The Persians' tax system embodied this flexibility: while much of the empire paid taxes in silver, some regions substituted grain, gold dust, ebony logs, and even elephant tusks. The empire's subjects all served in the Persian army, which was formed of separate divisions for each of the regions in the empire. It was the most powerful military force of its day.

The peoples who avoided conquest by the Persians intrigued Herodotus: he wrote about both the fierce Massagetae who bested Cyrus and the Athenians who prevented successive Persian attempts to invade. The Athenians are notable for their many breakthroughs: the teaching methods of Socrates, the educational ideals of Plato, the scientific inquiries of Aristotle, the plays of Aeschylus, and the histories of both Thucydides and Herodotus. The participatory democracy of the Athenians was an important forerunner to modern democratic governments, although the vote was limited to only 10 percent of the population, all men. At most, only three hundred thousand people in the ancient world experienced Athenian democracy, at a time when a hundred times as many people lived under Persian rule.

For over a thousand years, the model of a flexible empire based on satrapies was so successful that the Persians, Alexander, the successor states, the Parthians, and the Sasanians all used it to govern their empires. During this time, a very different empire and a powerful military rival to both the Parthians and the Sasanians arose in Rome, as the next chapter will explain. The Romans defeated the last of the Antigonids in 168 B.C.E. and won Egypt from the Ptolemies in 30 B.C.E., but they never conquered the Iranian plateau, testimony to the lasting power of the Persian model for empire.

Voyages on the Web: Herodotus

The Voyages Map App follows the traveler's journeys using interactive study tools, including 360-degree panoramic views of historic sites, zoomable maps, audio summaries, flash cards, and quizzes.

Key Terms

Herodotus (136)
Achaemenids (136)
satrap (139)
The Avesta (139)
Zoroastrianism (139)
Ahura Mazda (140)

Cyrus (141)
Lydian coins (141)
Darius I (142)
Phoenicians (148)
Artemisia (152)
Thucydides (153)

Socrates (154)
Plato (154)
Aristotle (155)
Alexander of Macedon (156)
Parthians (161)
Sasanians (161)

For Further Reference

Allen, Lindsay. *The Persian Empire: A History*. London: The British Museum Press, 2005.

Bernard, Paul. "The Greek Colony at Aï Khanum and Hellenism in Central Asia." In *Afghanistan: Hidden Treasures from the National Museum, Kabul*, ed. Fredrik Hiebert and Pierre Cambon. Washington, D.C.: National Geographic, 2008, pp. 81–105.

Casson, Lionel. *Travel in the Ancient World*. Baltimore: Johns Hopkins University Press, 1994.

Davies, W. D., et al. *The Cambridge History of Judaism*. Vol. 1: *Introduction: The Persian Period*. New York: Cambridge University Press, 1984.

Gruen, Erich S. *Rethinking the Other in Antiquity*. Princeton: Princeton University Press, 2011.

Harley, J. B., and David Woodward. *The History of Cartography*. Vol. 1: *Cartography in Prehistoric, Ancient, and Medieval Europe*. Chicago: University of Chicago Press, 1987.

Herodotus. *The Histories*. Aubrey de Sélincourt, trans. Further rev. ed. New York: Penguin Books, 1954, 2003.

Hornblower, Simon, and Antony Spawforth. *The Oxford Companion to Classical Civilization*. New York: Oxford University Press, 1998.

Insler, Stanley. *The Gāthās of Zarathustra*. Leiden: E. J. Brill, 1975.

Kuhrt, Amélie. "The Achaemenid Persian Empire (c. 550–c. 330 B.C.E.): Continuities, Adaptations, Transformations." In *Empires: Perspectives from Archaeology and History*, ed. Susan Alcock. New York: Cambridge University Press, 2001, pp. 93–124.

Markoe, Glenn E. *Peoples of the Past: Phoenicians*. Berkeley: University of California Press, 2000.

Martin, Thomas R. *Ancient Greece from Prehistoric to Hellenistic Times*. New Haven: Yale University Press, 2000.

Nylan, Michael. "Golden Spindles and Axes: Elite Women in the Achaemenid and Han Empires." In *Early China/Ancient Greece: Thinking Through Comparisons*, ed. Steven Shankman and Stephen W. Durrant. Albany: State University of New York Press, 2002.

Pollitt, J. J. *Art and Experience in Classical Greece*. Cambridge: Cambridge University Press, 1972.

Wiesehöfer, Josef. *Ancient Persia from 550 BC to 650 AD*. Azizeh Azodi, trans. New York: I. B. Tauris, 2001.

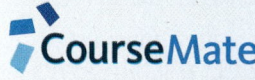

Go to the CourseMate website at **www.cengagebrain.com** for additional study tools and review materials—including audio and video clips—for this chapter.

7

The Roman Empire and the Rise of Christianity, 509 B.C.E.–476 C.E.

The events of 168 B.C.E. cut short the promising career of a young Greek statesman named **Polybius** (ca. 200–ca. 118 B.C.E.). In that year, after defeating the ruler of Macedon, the Romans demanded that the Greeks send over one thousand hostages to Italy for indefinite detention. Polybius (poh-LIH-bee-us) was deported to Rome, which remained his home even after his sixteen years of detention ended. His one surviving book, *The Rise of the Roman Empire*, explains why he felt that Rome, and not his native Greece, had become the major power of the Mediterranean:

Polybius

(Alinari/Art Resource, NY)

There can surely be nobody so petty or so apathetic in his outlook that he has no desire to discover by what means and under what system of government the Romans succeeded . . . in bringing under their rule almost the whole of the inhabited world, an achievement which is without parallel in human history. . . .

The arresting character of my subject and the grand spectacle which it presents can best be illustrated if we consider the most celebrated empires of the past which have provided historians with their principal themes, and set them beside the domination of Rome. Those which qualify for such a comparison are the following. The Persians for a certain period exercised their rule and supremacy over a vast territory, but every time that they ventured to pass beyond the limits of Asia they endangered the security not only of their empire but of their existence. . . . The rule of the Macedonians in Europe extended only from the lands bordering the Adriatic to the Danube, which would appear to be no more than a small fraction of the continent. Later, by overthrowing the Persian Empire, they also became the rulers of Asia; but although they were then regarded

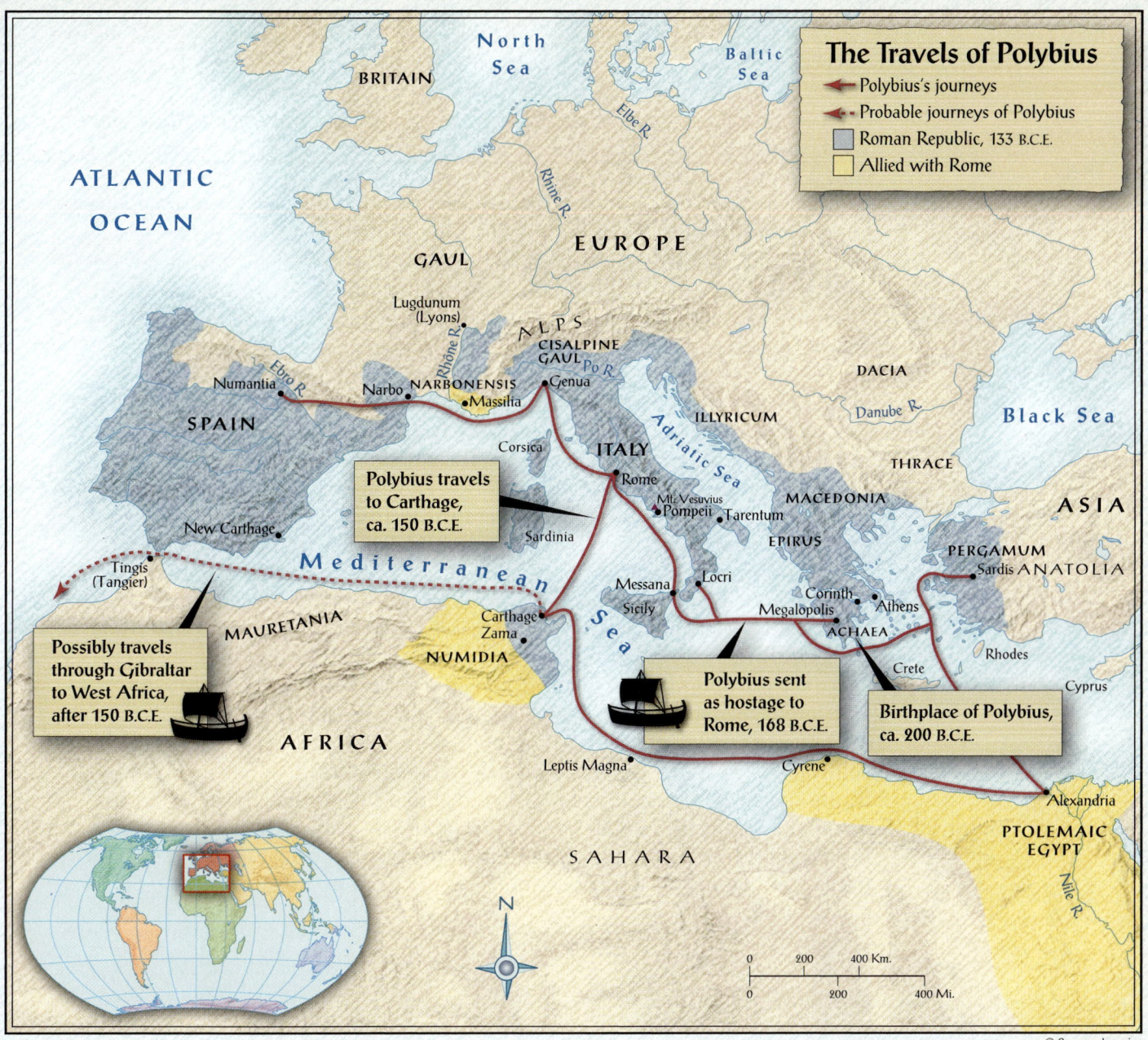

The Travels of Polybius

- → Polybius's journeys
- ‹·· Probable journeys of Polybius
- Roman Republic, 133 B.C.E.
- Allied with Rome

Polybius travels to Carthage, ca. 150 B.C.E.

Possibly travels through Gibraltar to West Africa, after 150 B.C.E.

Polybius sent as hostage to Rome, 168 B.C.E.

Birthplace of Polybius, ca. 200 B.C.E.

NORTH Sea
Baltic Sea
BRITAIN
ATLANTIC OCEAN
GAUL
EUROPE
Elbe R.
Rhine R.
Lugdunum (Lyons)
ALPS
CISALPINE GAUL
DACIA
Danube R.
Black Sea
Numantia
Ebro R.
Narbo
NARBONENSIS
Massilia
Genua
Po R.
ILLYRICUM
THRACE
ASIA
SPAIN
Corsica
ITALY
Rome
Adriatic Sea
MACEDONIA
PERGAMUM
New Carthage
Sardinia
Mt. Vesuvius
Pompeii
Tarentum
EPIRUS
Sardis ANATOLIA
Mediterranean Sea
Messana
Locri
Corinth
Megalopolis
Athens
Tingis (Tangier)
MAURETANIA
Carthage
Zama
Sicily
ACHAEA
Crete
Rhodes
NUMIDIA
Cyprus
AFRICA
Leptis Magna
Cyrene
Alexandria
SAHARA
PTOLEMAIC EGYPT
Nile R.
N

0   200   400 Km.
0   200   400 Mi.

© Cengage Learning

Join this chapter's traveler on "Voyages," an interactive tour of historic sites and events:
www.cengagebrain.com

as having become the masters of a larger number of states and territories than any other people before them, they still left the greater part of the inhabited world in the hands of others. . . . The Romans, on the other hand, have brought not just mere portions but almost the whole of the world under their rule, and have left an empire which far surpasses any that exists today or is likely to succeed it.[*]

[*]From *The Rise of the Roman Empire* by Polybius, translated by Ian Scott-Kilvert, selected with an introduction by F.W. Walbank (Penguin Classics, 1979), pp. 41–43. Copyright © Ian Scott-Kilvert, 1979. Reprinted with permission of Penguin Group/UK.

Polybius
(ca. 200–ca. 118 B.C.E.)
A Greek historian who was deported to Rome, where he wrote *The Rise of the Roman Empire*. Believed the task of the historian was to distinguish underlying causes of events.

Most historians today would challenge Polybius's decision to rank Alexander of Macedon above the Persians, whose empire he inherited (see Chapter 6). Polybius was also unaware of the Han dynasty in China (see Chapter 4), which had as many subjects as the Romans (around 55 million people). Yet Rome did bring under its rule "almost the whole of the world" if we grant that Polybius meant the entire Mediterranean region, including western Asia, North Africa, and much of Europe. Even after the empire broke apart, the Mediterranean remained a coherent geographical region with shared cultural and linguistic ties forged during the nearly one thousand years of Roman rule.

During his detention, Polybius stayed in the city of Rome, where he lived with the descendants of a prominent general. After 152 B.C.E., when he was freed, Polybius accompanied his host's grandson to modern-day Spain and Carthage in North Africa and probably sailed down the Atlantic coast of West Africa. (The chapter opening map shows Polybius's travels and the extent of the Roman empire after the conquests of Greece, Macedonia, and Carthage.) Travel around and across the Mediterranean was much more common in Polybius's lifetime than before, and it became even easier in the centuries after his death. Officials, soldiers, and couriers of the Roman empire proceeded along a network of straight paved roads that ringed the Mediterranean Sea, the heart of the Roman empire. Large boats crisscrossed the sea, while smaller vessels hugged its shore. Roman armies protected travelers from attacks, and the Roman navy lessened the threat of piracy.

During Polybius's lifetime Rome was a republic, but after his death, a century of political chaos culminated in the adoption of monarchy as the empire's new political system. In the beginning of the Common Era, the new religion of Christianity spread on roads and waterways throughout the Mediterranean region and eventually became the empire's official religion. The empire, increasingly unable to defend itself from powerful tribes in western Europe, moved to a new capital in the east and ultimately lost control of Rome and its western half.

Focus Questions

» *How did Rome, a small settlement in central Italy, expand to conquer and control the entire Mediterranean world of Europe, western Asia, and North Africa?*

» *How did the political structure of the Roman empire change as it grew?*

» *What were the basic teachings of Jesus, and how did Christianity become the major religion of the empire?*

» *What allowed Rome to retain such a large empire for so long, and what caused the loss of the western half of the empire?*

The Roman Republic, 509–27 B.C.E.

In its early years Rome was but one of many city-states on the Italian peninsula, but one with an unusual policy toward defeated enemies: once a neighboring city-state surrendered to Rome, Rome's leaders offered its citizens a chance to join forces with them. As a result of this policy, more and more men joined Rome's army, and it became almost unstoppable. By 272 B.C.E. Rome had conquered the Italian peninsula. In 202 B.C.E., after defeating Carthage, it dominated the western

Mediterranean, and in 146 B.C.E., after defeating a Greek coalition, it controlled the eastern Mediterranean as well. Those conquests were the crucial first step in the formation of the Mediterranean as a geographical region. After 146 B.C.E., Rome's armies continued to win territory, but the violence and civil wars of the first century B.C.E. brought an end to the republic in 27 B.C.E.

Early Rome to 509 B.C.E.

The city of Rome lies in the middle of the boot-shaped peninsula of Italy, which extends into the Mediterranean. One chain of mountains, the Apennines (AP-puh-nines), runs down the spine of Italy, while the Alps form a natural barrier to the north. Italy's volcanic soil is more fertile than Greece's, and many different crops flourished in the temperate climate of the Mediterranean. Several large islands, including Sardinia and Corsica, lie to the west of Italy; immediately to the south, the island of Sicily forms a natural stepping stone across the Mediterranean to modern-day Tunisia, Africa, only 100 miles (160 km) away.

Written sources reveal little about Rome's origins. The earliest surviving history of Rome, by Livy, dates to the first century B.C.E., nearly one thousand years after the site of Rome was first settled in 1000 B.C.E. The city's original site lay 16 miles (26 km) from the Tyrrhenian Sea at a point where the shallow Tiber River could be crossed easily. The seven hills surrounding the settlement formed a natural defense, and from the beginning people gathered there to trade.

Romans grew up hearing a myth, also recorded by Livy, about the founding of their city by two twin brothers, Romulus and Remus, grandsons of the rightful king. An evil king who had seized power ordered a servant to kill them, but the servant abandoned them instead. Raised by a wolf, the twins survived, and Romulus went on to found Rome in 753 B.C.E. This legend is not unique to Rome; it is a Romanized version of a western Asian myth. At this time, Rome consisted of small communities surrounded by walls.

During the sixth and fifth centuries B.C.E., when the Persian and the Greek empires were vying for power, Rome was an obscure backwater. Greek colonists had settled in southern Italy, and their cities were larger and far better planned than Rome. The Romans learned city planning, sewage management, and wall construction from their Etruscan neighbors to the north. The Etruscans modified the Greek alphabet to write their own language, which the Romans in turn adopted around 600 B.C.E. to record their first inscriptions in their native Latin, a language in the Indo-European family.

The Early Republic and the Conquest of Italy, 509–272 B.C.E.

The earliest form of government in the Roman city-state was a monarchy. The first kings governed in consultation with an assembly composed of men from Rome's most prominent and wealthiest families, the patricians (puh-TRISH-uhns), who owned large landholdings and formed a privileged social group distinct from the plebians (pluh-BEE-uhns), or commoners. Each time the king died, the patrician assembly chose his successor, not necessarily his son; the early kings included both Etruscans and Latins.

After overthrowing an Etruscan king, the Romans founded the **Roman republic** in 509 B.C.E. In a republic, unlike in a direct democracy like the assembly of Athens, the people choose the officials who govern. The power to rule was entrusted to two elected executives, called consuls, who served a one-year term. The consuls consulted regularly with an advisory body, the **Roman senate**, which was

Roman republic
Roman government between 509 and 27 B.C.E. Ruled by two elected executives who consulted regularly with the senate.

Roman senate
Roman governing body during the Roman republic, composed of some three hundred patricians. Later became an advisory body.

composed entirely of patricians, and less often with the plebian assembly, in which all free men, or citizens, could vote. The Romans never allowed a simple majority to prevail; instead they divided each assembly into smaller groups and reached a decision by counting the votes of the rich more heavily than the poor.

After 400 B.C.E., the republic continuously fought off different mountain peoples from the north who hoped to conquer Rome's fertile agricultural plain. The Celts or Gauls were residents of the Alps region who spoke Celtic, also an Indo-European language. In 387 B.C.E., Rome suffered a crushing military defeat at the hands of the Gauls, who took the city and left after plundering it for seven months.

Rome recovered and began to conquer other city-states. To speakers of Latin among their defeated enemies, the Romans offered all the privileges of citizenship and the accompanying obligations; those who did not speak Latin had to pay taxes and serve as soldiers but could not participate in the political system. This policy of actively incorporating conquered peoples differed from the Persian empire to the east, which never granted the conquered peoples the same privileged status as Persians and Medes.

The Romans learned much from the different peoples they conquered; they worshiped Greek gods, to whom they gave Roman names, and they adopted elements of Greek law. They also constructed roads linking Rome with their new possessions. Their policies led to military success, and by 321 B.C.E. Roman troops had gained control of the entire Italian peninsula except for the south (the toe and heel of the Italian boot), a region of heavy Greek settlement. It took almost fifty years before Rome conquered the final Greek city-state in Italy.

The Conquest of the Mediterranean World, 272–146 B.C.E.

In 272 B.C.E., the year that Rome gained control of the Italian peninsula, six different powers held territory around the coastline of the Mediterranean, and the residents of these different regions had no shared cultural identity. To the east, the three successors to Alexander still occupied territory: the Antigonids in Macedon, the Seleucids in Syria, and the Ptolemies in Egypt. In addition, two separate leagues of city-states controlled the Greek peninsula. Finally, Carthage controlled the north coast of Africa between today's Tunis and Morocco, the southern half of modern-day Spain, Corsica, Sardinia, and half of Sicily. An oligarchy (see page 142), **Carthage** prospered by taxing trade. Rome and Carthage, the only two actively expansionist states among these different powers, collided in 264 B.C.E.

In that year Rome sent troops to support one city-state in Sicily against a different city-state allied with Carthage, triggering the first of the **Punic Wars**. (The Latin word for Phoenicians was *Poeni*, the origin of the English word *Punic* [PYOO-nik].) Whereas Rome had an army of citizens who fought when they were not farming, Carthage's army consisted almost entirely of mercenary troops paid to fight. Previously a land power, Rome built its first navy of sailing ships powered by multiple levels of oarsmen. After more than twenty years of fighting—some on land, some on sea—Rome won control of Sicily in 241 B.C.E., but Carthage continued to dominate the Mediterranean west of Sicily.

Rome and Carthage faced each other again in the Second Punic War (sometimes called the Hannibalic War) from 218 to 202 B.C.E. This war matched two brilliant generals: Carthage's **Hannibal** (ca. 247–ca. 182 B.C.E.) with Rome's Scipio Africanus (SIP-ee-o ah-frih-KAHN-us) (236–183 B.C.E.). Writing about events that occurred before he was born, Polybius believed that, while an army might use a pretext to attack an enemy and a battle could begin a war, the historian should distinguish the underlying causes of war from both their pretexts and their

Carthage
A city in modern-day Tunisia originally founded by the Phoenicians. Rome's main rival for control of the Mediterranean.

Punic Wars
Three wars that Rome and Carthage fought between 264 and 146 B.C.E., all won by Rome.

Hannibal
(ca. 247–ca. 182 B.C.E.) A brilliant military strategist who led Carthage's armies over the Alps into Italy during the Second Punic War but lost to Rome in 202 B.C.E.

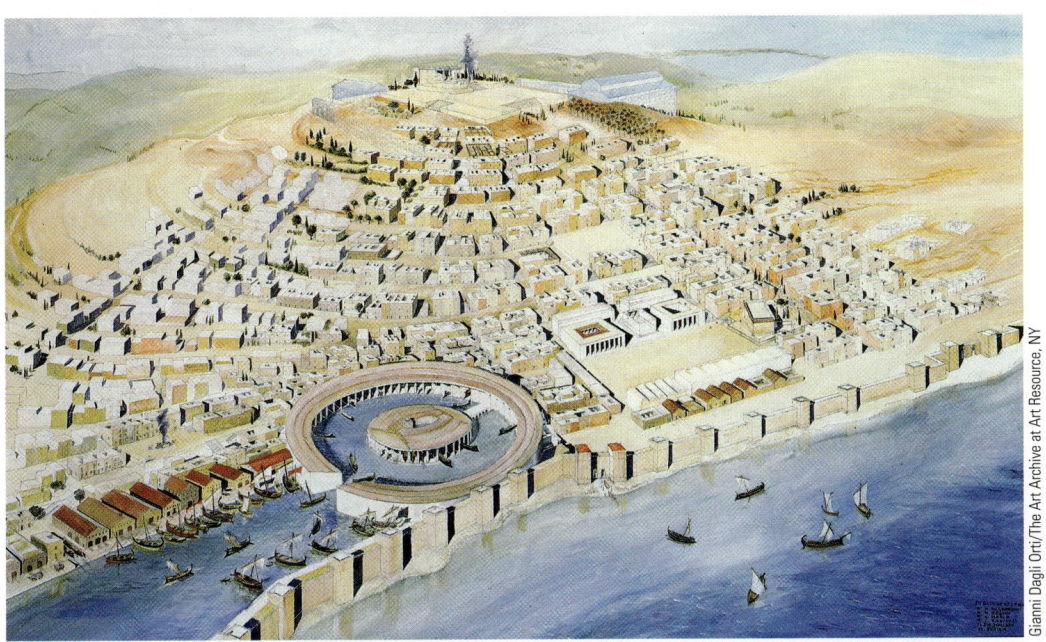

Gianni Dagli Orti/The Art Archive at Art Resource, NY

A Modern Reconstruction of the Port of Carthage The city's most prominent feature was its protected port. During peace, ships used the port behind the seawall, but during war, all the ships could retreat behind the city walls into the interior circular harbor, where they were well protected.

beginnings. The underlying cause of the Second Punic War, Polybius argued, dated back to Hannibal's childhood and his father's anger at losing the First Punic War.

From New Carthage (modern-day Cartagena) in Spain, Hannibal led a force of 50,000 infantry, 9,000 cavalry, and 37 elephants on a five-month march across southern France and then through the Alps. Polybius believed that the historian had to do on-site research; as he said, *"I . . . have personally explored the country, and have crossed the Alps myself to obtain first-hand information and evidence."** Polybius found Hannibal's decision to cross the Alps audacious: *"These conditions were so unusual as to be almost freakish,"* Polybius learned from interviews with the locals. *"The new snow lying on top of the old, which had remained there from the previous winter, . . . gave way easily, both because it was soft, having just fallen, and because it was not yet deep."** Many of Hannibal's men froze or starved to death, and Polybius estimated that less than half the original army, and a single elephant, survived the fifteen-day march through the Alps.

Carthage's army included Africans, Spaniards, Celts, Phoenicians, Italians, and Greeks. Although all of Hannibal's soldiers came from the Mediterranean region, Polybius noted that they *"had nothing naturally in common, neither in their laws, their customs, their language, nor in any other respect,"** because the region had not yet become a coherent unit. The varied composition of Hannibal's force intimidated the Romans. Polybius reported: *"The troops were drawn up in alternate companies, the Celts naked, the Spaniards with their short linen tunics bordered with purple—their national dress—so that the line presented a strange and terrifying appearance."**

---

*From *The Rise of the Roman Empire* by Polybius, translated by Ian Scott-Kilvert, selected with an introduction by F.W. Walbank (Penguin Classics, 1979), pp. 221–222, 227–228, 427–428, 271. Copyright © Ian Scott-Kilvert, 1979. Reprinted with permission of Penguin Group/UK.

Polybius attributed much of the Romans' success to the rules governing their army. Like the Qin army in China (see Chapter 4), the Roman commanders enforced a complex policy of rewards and punishments. Men who fought bravely in battle could win a spear, cup, or lance. The punishments for failure to fight were severe. If a group of men deserted, their commander randomly selected one-tenth of the deserters to be beaten to death. *"This is carried out as follows,"* explains Polybius. *"The tribune takes a cudgel and lightly touches the condemned man with it, whereupon all the soldiers fall upon him with clubs and stones, and usually kill him in the camp itself."* Fear of this punishment kept Roman soldiers at their posts even when defeat was certain.

Diminished as their numbers were by the trip across the Alps, Hannibal's army entered Italy and won several major battles in succession, yet Hannibal never attacked Rome directly. Finally, when the two armies met in 202 B.C.E. at Zama, on the North African coast, Rome defeated Carthage. In 201 B.C.E., Rome and Carthage signed a peace treaty that imposed heavy fines on Carthage, granted Carthage's holdings in Spain to Rome, and limited the size of its navy to only ten vessels. With the elimination of Carthage as a rival power, the Roman empire gained control of the entire western Mediterranean.

After the Second Punic War, Roman forces fought a series of battles with the three successor states to Alexander. Fighting in Greece and Anatolia, the Romans defeated the Seleucids in 188 B.C.E., yet allowed them to continue to rule in Syria. Rome defeated the Antigonids in 168 B.C.E., the year Polybius came to Rome as a hostage, and brought the Antigonid dynasty to an end. In the same year, Ptolemaic Egypt became a client state of Rome, nominally ruled by a Ptolemy king. Rome secured control of the eastern Mediterranean only in 133 B.C.E.

In 146 B.C.E. Rome defeated Carthage a third time. After he had taken the city, Scipio Aemilianus (SIP-ee-o ay-mill-YAN-us), the commander of Roman forces, ordered the city leveled and the survivors sent to Rome to be sold as slaves. The Roman senate passed a bill forbidding anyone to rebuild Carthage and in place of Carthage's empire established the province of Africa (the origin of the continent's name), an area of about 5,000 square miles (13,000 sq km) along the North African coast. As we have seen in previous chapters, conquering rulers frequently exacted a high price from the people of a newly subjugated territory, but the order to destroy a city and enslave all its inhabitants marked a new level of brutality.

Each conquest brought new territory to be administered by the Roman empire. Before the First Punic War, the newly conquered lands usually acquired the same governing structure as the city-state of Rome; in later periods the conquered territories, including Sicily, Sardinia, and Spain, were ruled as military districts by a governor, usually a former consul, appointed by the senate. The residents of these military districts did not receive citizenship.

Like the Persian satraps, each Roman governor was in charge of an extremely large area; the district of North Africa's 5,000 square miles stretched along the Mediterranean coastline of the three modern nations of Libya, Tunisia, and Algeria. The governor had a tiny staff: one official to watch over the province's finances, an advisory panel of the governor's friends and high-ranking clients, and a small entourage composed of lower-ranking freedmen or slaves. The low number of officials meant that the governor almost always left the conquered peoples' previous governmental structures in place.

---

*From *The Rise of the Roman Empire* by Polybius, translated by Ian Scott-Kilvert, selected with an introduction by F.W. Walbank (Penguin Classics, 1979), pp. 332–333. Copyright © Ian Scott-Kilvert, 1979. Reprinted with permission of Penguin Group/UK.

The greatest challenge for the provincial governors was the collection of taxes to be forwarded to Rome. Unlike the Persian satraps, who retained control over tax collection, the Roman governors delegated tax collection to others. The governors divided their provinces into regions and auctioned off the right to collect taxes in each region to the highest bidder. These tax farmers agreed to provide the governor with a certain amount of revenue; anything above that was theirs to keep. The residents of provinces suffered because the tax farmers took much more than they were entitled to. Most of the men who applied for the position of tax farmer belonged to a new commercial class of entrepreneurs and businessmen, called equites (EH-kwee-tays) because they were descended from soldiers who rode on horseback.

Roman Society Under the Republic

In 168 B.C.E., the family of the general Scipio Africanus persuaded the authorities to allow Polybius to stay with them. In *The Rise of the Roman Empire*, Polybius explains how he became acquainted with Scipio Aemilianus, the grandson of Scipio Africanus who later fought in the Third Punic War (ca. 185–ca. 129 B.C.E.). One day Scipio Aemilianus asked Polybius, *"Why is it, Polybius, that although my brother and I eat at the same table, you always speak to him, address all your questions and remarks in his direction and leave me out of them?"* Polybius responded that it was only natural for him to address the older brother, but he offered to help the eighteen-year-old Scipio Aemilianus launch his public career: *"I do not think you could find anybody more suitable than myself to help you and encourage your efforts."*

This conversation illustrates how influential Romans gained clients, or dependents not in their families. Clients were often newcomers to a city, traders, or people who wanted to break from their own families. Patrons had the same obligation to help their clients as the head of the family had to help his own family members. They gave their clients food and money or assistance with legal matters, and clients in turn demonstrated loyalty by accompanying their patrons to the Forum, the marketplace where the residents of every Roman town gathered daily to transact business.

Scipio Aemilianus, like most important patrons in Rome, belonged to an eminent patrician family. Both his father and mother were the children of consuls. When he met Polybius, he was living with his adoptive father, who was the head of his family, or the **paterfamilias** (pah-tehr-fah-MIL-lee-us). In Roman society only the paterfamilias could own property. He made all decisions affecting his wife, children, and son's wives, including, for example, the decision of whether the family could afford to raise a newborn baby or should deny it food and expose it to the elements. When the head of the family died, the sons might decide to split up the immediate family or to stay together under a new paterfamilias.

The Romans had two forms of marriage. Marriage among more prominent families, like the Scipios, required a formal contract stipulating that the father would recognize as heirs any children resulting from the match. More often a man and a woman simply moved in together and were recognized as married. Women were allowed to inherit, own, and pass on property in their own right, but under the stewardship of a male guardian, usually the paterfamilias. Roman men took only one wife, but the shorter life spans of the ancient world meant that remarriage among the widowed was common. Either the husband or wife could initiate

paterfamilias
The legal head of the extended family in Rome who made all decisions and was the only person who could own property.

---

*From *The Rise of the Roman Empire* by Polybius, translated by Ian Scott-Kilvert, selected with an introduction by F.W. Walbank (Penguin Classics, 1979), pp. 528–529. Copyright © Ian Scott-Kilvert, 1979. Reprinted with permission of Penguin Group/UK.

divorce, which was accomplished by simple notification; the main legal issue was the settlement of property. Scipio Aemilianus's parents divorced two or three years after his birth, but he remained close to both.

Roman women devoted considerable energy to educating their children, whose marriages they often helped to arrange. The biographer of **Cornelia**, the widowed aunt of Scipio Aemilianus, praised her for being *"proper in her behavior"* and *"a good and principled mother.'"* She refused to marry the ruler of Ptolemaic Egypt so that she could devote herself to her twelve children, of whom only three survived to adulthood. Late in her life, *"she had a wide circle of friends and her hospitality meant that she was never short of dinner guests. She surrounded herself with Greek and Roman scholars, and used to exchange gifts with kings from all over the world. Her guests and visitors used particularly to enjoy the stories she told of the life and habits of her father, Africanus.'"* Cornelia's example shows how Roman women were able to exert considerable influence even though they were formally barred from holding public office.

Well-off Roman households like the Scipios also owned slaves, who were usually captured in military campaigns abroad, brought to Rome, and sold to the highest bidder. Those who worked the fields or inside the homes of their masters were more fortunate than those who toiled in gold and silver mines, where mortality rates were high because the underground tunnels often collapsed. Some estimate that a ratio of three free citizens to one slave prevailed in the republic, one of the highest rates in world history.[1] Roman slaves rarely obtained their freedom, but those who did gained the full rights of citizens. However, many more slaves remained slaves for their entire lives, as did their children, because a child born to a slave mother, regardless of the father's status, remained a slave unless freed by the owner.

> **Cornelia**
> (ca. 190–100 B.C.E.)
> The mother of the Gracchus brothers, two reformers who sought to help Rome's poor; Cornelia exercised considerable political influence even though she, like all Roman women, did not hold public office.

The Late Republic, 146–27 B.C.E.

Polybius and his contemporaries were well aware of the strains on Roman society that came with the rapid acquisition of so much new territory. During the years of Rome's conquests, the political system of the republic had functioned well. But soon after the victories of 146 B.C.E., the republic proved unable to resolve the tensions that the expanding empire brought.

In the early years of the republic, most Roman soldiers lived on farms, which they left periodically to fight in battles. As the Roman army fought in more distant places, like Carthage, soldiers went abroad for long stretches at a time and often sold off their fields to rich landowners, who invested in large-scale agricultural enterprises that grew fruit or vegetables, pressed olive oil, or produced wine. With few freedmen for hire, the rich landowners turned increasingly to slaves, and privately held estates, called *latifundia* (lat-uh-FUN-dee-uh), grew larger and larger. The gulf widened between the well-off owners of *latifundia* estates and the ordinary people who had lost their land. Many of the landless moved to Rome, where they joined the ranks of the city's poor because they had no steady employment.

Cornelia's son Tiberius Gracchus (ty-BEER-ee-us GRAK-us) (ca. 169–133 B.C.E.) was one of the first to propose economic reforms to help the poor. Each time Rome conquered a new region, the government set aside large amounts of public land, much of it controlled by the wealthy landed families of the city. Tiberius wanted to give portions of this land to the poor.

Elected tribune in 133 B.C.E., Tiberius Gracchus brought his proposals before the plebian assembly, not the senate. The bill passed because Tiberius removed the

---

*Plutarch, *Roman Lives: A Selection of Eight Roman Lives,* trans. Robin Waterfield (New York: Oxford University Press, 1999), pp. 83, 115.

other tribune, who opposed the measure. Furious that he did not follow the usual procedures, a gang of senators and their supporters killed him. This was the first time since the founding of the republic that participants in a political dispute used murder as a weapon. Even after his death, calls for agrarian reform persisted. In 123 B.C.E. Tiberius's younger brother Gaius Gracchus (GUY-us GRAK-us) launched an even broader program of reform by which the state would provide low-cost grain to the poor living in Rome. He, too, was killed during violence that broke out between his supporters and their political opponents.

Polybius and his contemporaries were shocked by the sudden violent turn in Roman politics, but the trend grew only more pronounced in the first century B.C.E. To raise an army, one general, Marius (157–86 B.C.E.), did the previously unthinkable: he enlisted volunteers from among the working poor in Rome, waiving the traditional requirement that soldiers had to own land. Unlike the traditional farmer-soldiers, these troops had to be paid, and the leader who recruited them was obliged to support them for their entire lives. The troops eagerly looked forward to military campaigns because they received a share of the plunder each time they won a battle. Their loyalties were to the commander who paid them, not the republic.

After Marius died, Sulla, another general with his own private army, came to power. In 81 B.C.E. Sulla, not content to serve only a single year as consul, arranged for the senate to declare him **dictator**. In earlier periods, the senate had the power to name a dictator for a six-month term during a crisis, but Sulla used the position to secure his hold on the government. After Sulla's death in 78 B.C.E., different generals vied to lead Rome. The senate continued to meet and to elect two consuls, but the generals, with their private armies, controlled the government, often with the senate's tacit consent.

Large privatized armies staffed by the clients and slaves of generals conquered much new territory for Rome in the first century B.C.E. They defeated the much-weakened Seleucids in 64 B.C.E. in Syria, bringing the dynasty to an end, but they never defeated the powerful Parthian cavalry. The most successful Roman commander was **Julius Caesar** (100–44 B.C.E.), who conquered Gaul, a region that included northern Italy and present-day France. Although the Romans looked down on the peoples of Gaul as barbarians, or less civilized people who could not read and write, the Gauls participated actively in trade and had a strong economy. After his term as governor ended in Gaul, Caesar led his armies to Rome, and in 49 B.C.E. the senate appointed Caesar dictator. Between 48 and 44 B.C.E. Caesar continued as dictator and served as consul every other year.

Caesar named himself dictator for life in 44 B.C.E. This move antagonized even his allies, and a group of senators killed him in March that year. Caesar's death, however, did not end Rome's long civil war. In his will, Caesar had adopted as his heir his great-nephew Octavian (63 B.C.E.–14 C.E.), the future Augustus. In 30 B.C.E. Octavian conquered Egypt, ending the rule of the Ptolemies and making Egypt a province of the Roman empire.

dictator
A position given by the Roman senate before the first century B.C.E. to a temporary commander that granted him full authority for a limited amount of time, usually six months.

Julius Caesar
(100–44 B.C.E.) Rome's most successful military commander in the first century B.C.E. who was named dictator by the senate in 49 B.C.E.

The Roman Principate, 27 B.C.E.–284 C.E.

In 27 B.C.E. Octavian became the sole ruler of Rome. He had eliminated all his rivals and brought nearly a century of political chaos and civil war to a close. When the republic came to an end, he had to devise a new political system capable of governing the entire Mediterranean region. He never named himself emperor. Instead he called himself *"princeps"* (PRIN-keps), or first citizen. The new political structure he devised, in which he held almost all power over the empire, is called the **Roman principate** (PRIN-sih-pate) (government of the princeps). The principate remained in place until 284 C.E. Historians call the period between 27 B.C.E., when Octavian took power, and 180 C.E. the *Pax Romana* (PAHKS ro-MAHN-uh), or Roman Peace, because the entire Mediterranean region benefited from these centuries of stability. People moved easily across the empire, which became even more integrated as a result.

Roman principate
The system of government in Rome from 27 B.C.E. to 284 C.E., in which the *princeps*, a term meaning "first citizen," ruled the empire as a monarch in all but name.

The Political Structure of the Principate

Octavian wanted to establish a regime that would last beyond his own life. He hoped, too, to prevent a future general from seizing the government, yet he did not want to name himself perpetual dictator or king for fear that he would antagonize the Roman political elite. In 27 B.C.E. the senate awarded him a new title, **Augustus**, meaning "revered," the name by which he is usually known.

Augustus transferred the power to tax and control the armies from the senate to the princeps. Fully aware that the armies were dangerously big, Augustus ordered many soldiers demobilized and used his own private funds to buy land for them—some in Italy, some in the provinces. Augustus asserted the right to appoint all military leaders and the governors of the important provinces, thus ensuring that no one could form an army in the provinces and challenge him in Rome.

Augustus
The name, meaning "revered," that Octavian (63 B.C.E.–14 C.E.) received from the senate when he became princeps, or first citizen, of Rome in 27 B.C.E.

The one issue that Augustus did not resolve was who would succeed him: with no son of his own, he named his wife's son from a previous marriage as his heir, establishing a precedent that a princeps without a son of his own could name his successor. By chance, the three princeps who ruled from 98 to 161 did not have sons and so were able to choose their successors while still in office. The last century of the principate was not as smooth; between 211 and 284, the empire had thirty-six emperors, of whom nineteen were murdered, were executed, or died in battle with their successors.

The Social Changes of the Principate

Ever since the second century B.C.E., when the government classified Sicily and other new conquests as provinces, men in the provinces had not received the privileges of citizens. They did not have access to Roman courts, and they could not participate in the political system of Rome. In the first century C.E. Augustus deliberately increased the number of citizens by awarding Roman citizenship to discharged soldiers, many of whom lived outside Rome. On Augustus's death in 14 C.E. about 4 million people had become citizens,[2] and the number continued to increase until, in 212, the emperor granted citizenship status to all free men anywhere in the empire.

Roman law also changed during the course of the principate. Originally the magistrates and provincial governors who decided judicial cases applied Roman law to citizens and local law to noncitizens. They considered both unwritten laws, or customary practices, and written laws, which included laws passed by the senate or the plebian assembly, edicts from the emperor, and sometimes the writings of learned jurists. Many of the principles they developed still inform the modern practice of law. A person charged with a crime had the right to appear before a judge, who was to consider all the evidence fairly before deciding on the person's guilt. Everyone was innocent until proven guilty.

The Roman justice system did not, however, treat everyone equally. Over the course of the principate, the sharp differences of the republic among patricians, equites, and plebians gradually faded. As more people gained the rights of citizens, two new social groups subsumed the earlier divisions: the elite *honestiores* (hoh-NEST-ee-or-eez) and the *humiliores* (HUGH-meal-ee-or-eez), or the humble. Membership in these groups did not overlap with citizenship: noncitizen honestiores existed, as did citizen humiliores. Courts tended to treat the two groups very differently, allowing the wealthy to appeal their cases to Rome while sentencing the humble to heavier punishments for the same crime.

The years of the principate also saw some gradual changes in the legal position of women. Most people lived in small families consisting of a couple, their children, and whatever slaves or servants they had. On marriage, women moved in with their husbands but technically remained in their father's families and so retained the right to reclaim their dowries when their husbands died. Dowries were small, often about a year of the father's income, because daughters were entitled to a share of their father's property on his death, which granted them financial independence during the marriage.

Although they had greater control over their property than women in most other societies, Roman women continued to assume a subordinate role in marriage, possibly because many were much younger than their husbands. Men tended to marry in their late twenties and early thirties, women in their teens or early twenties. Most families arranged their children's marriages to form alliances with families of equal or better social standing.

Some marriages turned out to be quite affectionate, as made clear by one well-known writer in the first century who was also a lawyer, **Pliny the Younger** (ca. 61–113). Pliny (PLIE-nee) wrote to his wife's aunt about his wife Calpurnia:

> *She is highly intelligent and a careful housewife, and her devotion to me is a sure indication of her virtue. In addition, this love has given her interest in literature: she keeps copies of my works to read again and again and even learn by heart. She is so anxious when she knows that I am going to plead in court, and so happy when all is over! . . .*
>
> *Please accept our thanks for having given her to me and me to her as if chosen for each other.**

Pliny married in his forties, at the peak of his legal career, while Calpurnia, his third wife, was still a teenager. Teenage girls also engaged in various other cultural and recreational pursuits. (See the feature "Visual Evidence in Primary Sources: Girls' Sports in the Roman Empire.") Pliny's letter shows that Calpurnia was literate, as were many prominent Roman women.

Pliny the Younger (ca. 61–113) Roman lawyer and official famous for his letters describing life during the principate, especially the eruption of Mount Vesuvius in 79 C.E.

---

*Excerpt from *The Letters of the Younger Pliny*, translated with an introduction by Betty Radice (Penguin Classics 1963, reprinted 1969), pp. 126–127. Copyright © Betty Radice, 1963, 1969. Reprinted with permission of Penguin Books Ltd.

Girls' Sports in the Roman Empire

The wealthiest Romans lived in luxurious villas with beautiful floors paved with thousands of tiny mosaic tiles and individual cubes of colored glass, arrayed to form pictures. The world's largest set of late Roman mosaics survives intact at the Villa Romana del Casale in southern Sicily, which was built between 300 and 325 and is now a UNESCO World Heritage Site. A landslide in the 1100s buried the estate, preserving the floors of the villa in near-perfect condition. The luxurious estate is so large that many believe it was the private hunting lodge of an emperor, but it is also possible that the estate belonged to a provincial official.

The estate had four wings built around an open rectangular garden in the center. Six rooms, each with water at a different temperature from cool to boiling hot, formed the bathing complex. Not everyone in the Roman empire had indoor plumbing; poor people lived crowded together in small apartments without plumbing. But at a time when few people elsewhere in the world had even cold running water, the homes of the wealthy of the empire all had bathing rooms with both cold and hot water.

The floors of the Villa Romana del Casale depict daily-life scenes, such as a hunting scene that stretches some 210 feet (64 m) long, and also mythical scenes showing Roman gods. One unusual floor shows ten girls wearing bikini-like outfits engaged in different athletic events.

Did Roman girl athletes really wear such scant clothing? The only other Roman depiction of a woman in a two-piece suit is a statue of Venus, the goddess of love. In the absence of comparable images, one has to carefully consider the original context. The scenes of human activity at the Villa Romana del Casale are unusually lifelike: they show chariot races, the hunting of exotic animals like elephants and wild boar, and the mistress of the villa with her servants. Given the accuracy of these other mosaics, it seems likely that girls, at least in Sicily, wore the two-piece suits shown in this mosaic—suitable attire for vigorous physical activity.

QUESTION FOR ANALYSIS

» *Do you agree that the pictures of the girls in bikinis are realistic? Can you suggest any reasons why other images of girls in scanty clothing haven't been found?*

This geometric pattern is from a mosaic floor built on top of the floor showing the girls in bikinis.

This girl carries weights as she runs; her partner is about to throw her discus.

These two girls race each other.

The woman in the toga prepares to place a crown of flowers on the head of a girl who won a race in which competitors ran and at the same time used a stick to twirl a wheel on the ground.

This victorious girl has already received her crown and holds a palm.

These girls toss a ball back and forth.

Next to this room was a space for pipes that brought water to the large fountain in the garden and to the toilets.

Peter Barritt/Alamy

179

The Ruins at Pompeii: Lens into Life in a Provincial Roman Town

Pliny also wrote about the famous eruption from Mount Vesuvius, which he witnessed from his home in the Bay of Naples in the early afternoon on August 24, 79 C.E. He described the cloud of smoke as *"white, sometimes blotched and dirty, according to the amount of soil and ashes carried with it."* Many of the residents of nearby Pompeii (POMP-ay) did not recognize the danger and stayed in the town, and Pliny's uncle, Pliny the Elder, actually traveled to the site of the erupting volcano to see if he could rescue anyone.

When Pliny the Elder arrived, *"ashes were already falling, hotter and thicker as the ships drew near, followed by bits of pumice* [PUH-miss] *and blackened stones, charred and cracked by the flames."* That evening Pliny the Elder went to bed inside his house; he awoke to find his door blocked. His servants dug him out, and the entire household went outside; even though the sun had come up, the ash-filled sky was *"blacker and denser than any ordinary night."* The uncle tried to escape by boat, but the waves were too high, and he collapsed. Two days later, when the cloud lifted, Pliny the Elder had died, killed by the poisonous fumes from the volcano.

Pompeii and nearby Herculaneum are Italy's most popular archaeological sites, attracting 2.5 million visitors each year and offering a vivid glimpse of life in a provincial town during the first century C.E. Pompeii possessed all the important features of a typical Roman city: a theater, temples to Roman and non-Roman gods, baths, a gymnasium, an amphitheater, shops, paved streets, and a forum where the residents met each day and carried out their business transactions. The city's twenty thousand residents participated in a highly commercialized economy in which they bought and sold baked bread, wine, and local agricultural products. The site of Pompeii provides a valuable reminder of the high living standards of the Romans, even those living in a provincial town.

House of the Faun, Pompeii, Italy One of the loveliest surviving villas at Pompeii is the House of the Faun, named for the figure in the fountain. The well-off residents of Pompeii, a provincial Roman town, lived in luxurious villas like this one with hot and cold running water, lush gardens, and exquisite tiled fountains. (Casa del Faune, Pompeii, Italy/Scala/Art Resource, NY)

Travel and Knowledge of the Outside World

Romans had been traveling for business and pleasure ever since the conquests of the second century B.C.E., and travel continued to increase throughout the principate and contributed to the further integration of the Mediterranean world. The empire reached its largest extent in the second century C.E. (see Map 7.1), with an estimated population of 55 million people living in an area of 2 million square miles (5 million sq km).[3] Rome controlled not only the entire Mediterranean coast of North Africa, western Asia, and Europe, but also large amounts of territory inland from the Mediterranean—modern-day Spain, France, England, Germany west of the Rhine River, the Balkans, and Turkey.

*Excerpt from *The Letters of the Younger Pliny*, translated with an introduction by Betty Radice (Penguin Classics 1963, reprinted 1969), pp. 166–168. Copyright © Betty Radice, 1963, 1969. Reprinted with permission of Penguin Books Ltd.

Roman roads connected the different parts of the empire, and sea transport, although more dangerous, remained even cheaper. Travelers needed to carry only one type of currency, Roman coins. Just two languages could take them anywhere within the empire: Latin was used throughout the western Mediterranean and in Rome itself, while Greek prevailed in the eastern Mediterranean.

The appearance of new maps and guides testifies to the frequency of travel. Some simply listed each place on a given road and the distance to the next city; others portrayed the information visually. When papyrus was not available, the Romans used **parchment**, which was made by scraping the hair from the stretched skins of sheep, goats, or calves and then cleaning it. One of the longest surviving texts on parchment, the Peutinger Map, occupies a piece of parchment 13 inches (34 cm) wide and over 22 feet (6.75 m) long. It depicts the full 64,600 miles (104,000 km) of the empire's road system.

parchment
Writing material made by stretching, scraping, and cleaning animal skin.

The Peutinger Map: The Roman Equivalent of the Michelin Guide? This detail from the Peutinger Map shows Jerusalem, where many Christians traveled in the late 300s and 400s. (This is a twelfth- or thirteenth-century copy of a map dating to the 300s.) The cartographer devised symbols for the different types of lodging at each stopping place: a square building with a courtyard, for example, indicated the best kind of hotel. Modern guidebooks use exactly the same type of system.

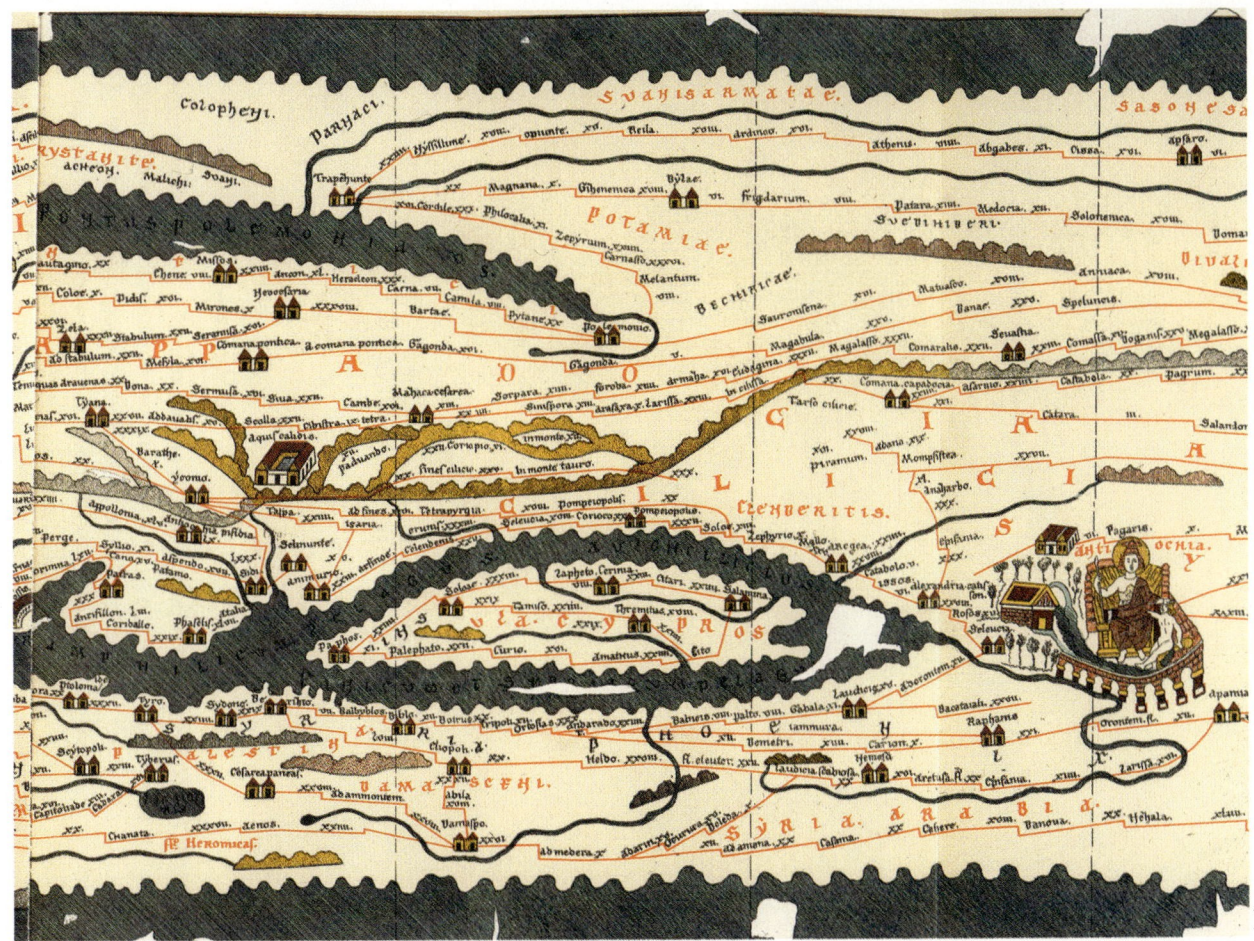

akg-images

MAP 7.1 The Roman Empire at Its Greatest Extent Some 55 million people lived in the 2 million square miles (5 million sq km) of the Roman empire in the second century c.e. A network of roads and shipping lanes bound the different regions together, as did a unified currency. Two common languages—Latin in the western Mediterranean and Greek in the eastern Mediterranean—helped to integrate the Mediterranean world even more closely. (© Cengage Learning)

Legend:
- Roman Empire by death of Augustus, 14 c.e.
- Territory added by death of Hadrian, 138 c.e.
- Territory gained and lost, with dates held
- Parthian Empire, ca. 200 c.e.
- ★ Major battle

The study of geography flourished throughout the empire and particularly in the city of Alexandria, Egypt, which continued to be a center of learning after the Roman conquest of Egypt in 30 B.C.E. The geographer Ptolemy (ca. 100–170) (not related to the Ptolemy royal family) devoted his life to collecting the longitudinal and latitudinal coordinates for eight thousand places. We do not know whether he made an actual map, but his work marked the high point of geographic knowledge in the Roman empire. China and Southeast Asia stood at the eastern edge of the world known to the Romans; the Canary Islands in the Atlantic Ocean at the western end. To the north lay the British Isles and the Scythian region (north of the Black Sea in Russia); to the south, below Ethiopia, Africa. Although he made some errors, Ptolemy knew where more places were located on the globe than did any geographer elsewhere in the world. His comprehensive knowledge of geography remained influential in the Islamic world (see Chapter 9) and Europe until 1500 (see Chapters 10 and 13).

The Rise of Christianity, ca. 30–284

During these years, the people who moved easily and widely throughout the Mediterranean world spread religious teachings. The Romans had their own gods, to whom officials offered regular sacrifices, and they worshiped many deities originating in other parts of the empire. Christianity began as a faith professed by a small group of Jews in the province of Judaea (joo-DAY-uh) and began to spread throughout the Mediterranean. The emperor Constantine's decision to support Christianity in 313 proved to be the crucial step in its extension throughout the Mediterranean world.

Roman Religion and Judaism

Throughout the republic and the principate, the state encouraged the worship of many different gods in the Roman polytheistic religion. Most Romans worshiped major deities, like Jupiter, the most powerful of all the gods, or Mars, the god of war, both of which have given their names to planets. Many of these gods were originally Greek; for example, Jupiter was the same as the Greek Zeus. Officials frequently spent tax monies to support public cults, sometimes honoring a deity and sometimes deifying current or former princeps.

In addition to their public obligations to state-supported gods, many people throughout the Mediterranean privately worshiped in mystery cults that drew on the symbolism of fertility deities. A female deity, sometimes with a male partner, disappeared in the fall and had to be coaxed to return in the spring. Mystery cults promised adherents immortality and a closer personal relationship with the divine. Cult deities not originally from Rome included Isis (EYE-sis), the Egyptian goddess of the dead, thought to have power to cure the sick, and Mithra (MIH-thruh), the Iranian sun-god sent by Ahura Mazda to struggle against evil. Gathering in small groups to sacrifice bulls, the worshipers of Mithra believed that the souls of the dead descended into earth before ascending into heaven.

Unlike almost everyone else in the Roman empire, Jews were monotheistic (see Chapter 2). Worshiping a single god, never depicted in images or paintings, Jews refused to worship any of the Roman gods or former princeps, a stance the Roman government tolerated. Their center of worship was the Jerusalem Temple, which housed their scriptures and survived the Roman conquest of Judaea in 63 B.C.E., when Judaea came under indirect Roman rule.

The discovery of the Dead Sea Scrolls, a group of texts on leather, papyrus, and copper, has revealed the diversity of beliefs among Jewish groups. The scrolls mention a Teacher of Righteousness, a figure who the authors believed would bring salvation, called a Messiah (muh-SIGH-uh) in Hebrew. Many Jewish groups at the time believed that a Messiah would come, yet they disagreed about how to identify him.

The Life and Teachings of Jesus, ca. 4 B.C.E.–30 C.E.

Jesus
(ca. 4 B.C.E.–30 C.E.)
Jewish preacher believed by Christians to be the Messiah, the figure who would bring salvation and, through atonement, eternal life to those who believed in him.

Almost every surviving record about early Christianity written before 100 C.E., whether about the life of **Jesus** or the early ministry, is written by a Christian believer.[4] The earliest sources about Jesus' life, and so the most reliable, are the four gospels of Mark, Matthew, Luke, and John, written between 70 and 110. Accordingly, historians use the gospels to piece together the chronology of Jesus' life, all the while remembering that, like sources about Zarathushtra or the Buddha, they were written by devotees, not outsiders.

The gospels relate that Jesus was born in Bethlehem around 4 B.C.E. to a well-off Jewish family who lived near the Sea of Galilee, where residents made a good living fishing. They say little about his life before about 26 C.E., when his cousin John the Baptist immersed him in the waters of the River Jordan. Although baptism later took on a specific meaning within Christianity, the Greek word *baptein* simply means "to wash in water" or "to immerse," and many ancient religions viewed bathing in water as a way to prepare believers for various rituals. Jewish tradition held that washing with water could cleanse someone of impurities—for example, when someone had touched a corpse—and the Jew could repeat the washing as often as needed. Modifying this tradition, at around the time Jesus lived, several Jewish groups required converts to undergo a single ritual bathing before they could enter the temple as Jews. Similarly, John, who claimed to be a prophet, urged Jews to undergo a one-time baptism in preparation for the kingdom of God.

In 28 and 29 C.E. Jesus began preaching publicly in Galilee and, like John, urged Jews to repent and undergo baptism. This marked the beginning of his life as a religious teacher. Illness was a sign of Satan's presence, Jesus taught, and many of the miracles recorded in the gospels are anecdotes about his curing the sick. Historians, particularly those who do not subscribe to the teachings of a given belief system, are often skeptical about whether the events described in miracle tales actually occurred. But they realize that many religious figures were able to win converts because of them.

As he explained in the Sermon on the Mount, Jesus welcomed the poor and downtrodden: *"Blessed are the poor in spirit, for theirs is the kingdom of heaven"* (Matthew 5:3). According to the gospels, Jesus' preaching in Galilee culminated in the feeding of five thousand supporters, possibly in the summer of 29 C.E. Jesus summed up his teachings succinctly in response to a Pharisee (FAIR-uh-see), a Jewish religious authority, who asked him what the most important commandment was:

*"You shall love the Lord your God with all your heart, and with all your soul, and with all your mind." This is the great and first commandment. And a second is like it: "You shall love your neighbor as yourself." (Matthew 22:36–39)**

---

*All quotations from the Bible are from the New Revised Standard Version. Revised Standard Version of the Bible, Copyright © 1952 [2nd edition, 1971] by the Division of Christian Education of the National Council of the Churches of Christ in the United States of America. Used by permission. All rights reserved.

Jesus also taught his followers that a time of great difficulty was coming and that God would send a Messiah to usher in a new age. *Christos* was the Greek word for Messiah, and Jesus came to be known as Jesus Christ because his followers believed that he was the Messiah. Jesus' teachings attracted converts because his egalitarian message promised salvation to all, including the poor, and welcomed all to join the new church, regardless of their background.

Jesus also wanted to reform and challenge the abuses he saw. His criticisms provoked the Jewish community leaders, who may also have feared that he would lead the residents of Palestine, where there was already a great deal of unrest, in an uprising against Roman rule. They asked the Roman governor, Pontius Pilate, to convict Jesus on the grounds that he claimed to be king of the Jews and thus posed a political threat to Rome. In 30 C.E., fearful of possible disorder, Pilate agreed to crucify Jesus. At the time of his death Jesus had been actively preaching for only three years.

On the third day after he died, Christians believe, and the gospels concur, that Jesus was resurrected, or raised from the dead. As the gospel of John explains: *"God so loved the world that he gave his only Son, so that everyone who believes in him may not perish but may have eternal life"* (John 3:16). This teaching, that Jesus died so that all believers will be able to overcome death, is called atonement, and it became one of the most important teachings of the Christian church.

The Early Church and the Travels of Paul

Jesus preached that a new age of salvation would come soon after his death, yet his disciples realized that they had to devise a governing structure for the church no matter how temporary they expected the wait to be. They established churches in Christian communities. Bishops headed these churches; below them were deacons and deaconesses, a position of genuine authority for the many women who joined the church.

The teachings of an early Christian leader, Paul, were highly influential. **Paul** (ca. 5–ca. 64) was born to a wealthy family of Roman citizens living in Tarsus in modern-day Turkey. Like many Jews living outside Judaea, Paul had grown up in a bilingual household in which both Greek and Hebrew were spoken, but he received a traditional education in Jerusalem.

As described in the book of Acts, the turning point in Paul's life came when Jesus appeared to him in a vision, probably in the year 38 C.E., as he traveled to Damascus. After deciding to become a Christian, Paul was baptized in Damascus. The Christian leadership in Jerusalem, however, never granted that Paul's vision was equal to their own experience of knowing Jesus personally and hearing him teach. Understandably suspicious of him, they sent Paul to preach in his native Tarsus in 48 C.E.

Paul initially focused on converting the Jewish communities scattered throughout the eastern half of the Mediterranean. His letters, written in Greek with the sophistication of an educated Roman, carried the teachings of Christianity to many fledgling Christian communities. When he arrived in a new place, he went first to the local synagogue and preached. (See the feature "Movement of Ideas Through Primary Sources: Early Christianity in the Eastern Provinces.") Whereas Jesus had preached to the poor and to slaves, Paul's potential audience consisted of more prosperous people. He did not call for the abolition of slavery or propose any genuine social reform. Accepting the right of the Roman empire to exist, he, like Jesus before him, urged his audiences to pay their taxes.

Paul
(ca. 5–ca. 64) An influential early Christian leader who traveled widely in modern-day Turkey, Cyprus, and Greece to teach about early Christianity.

---

*All quotations from the Bible are from the New Revised Standard Version. Revised Standard Version of the Bible, Copyright © 1952 [2nd edition, 1971] by the Division of Christian Education of the National Council of the Churches of Christ in the United States of America. Used by permission. All rights reserved.

MAP 7.2 The Spread of Christianity During his lifetime, Jesus preached in the Roman province of Judaea. After his death, Paul and other missionaries introduced Christian teachings to the eastern Mediterranean. By the late 300s, Christianity had spread throughout the Mediterranean, making it possible for pilgrims like Egeria (see page 192) to travel all the way from Rome to Jerusalem and Egypt, where she visited the earliest Christian monasteries. (© Cengage Learning)

Paul took advantage of the ease of travel within the Roman empire to propagate his views. A list of the cities he visited vividly conveys how much he traveled: Antioch, Iconium, Lystra, Derbe, and Ephesus in modern-day Turkey; Paphos on the island of Cyprus; and Thessalonica, Philippi, and Corinth in Greece. By the time Paul died, circa 64, a Christian community had arisen in many of the cities he visited. In Rome, according to Christian tradition, Jesus' apostle Peter, who died about the same time as Paul, headed the Christian community (see Map 7.2). A Jewish uprising in Judaea in 66 prompted the Roman authorities to intervene with great brutality: they destroyed the Jerusalem Temple in 70, and many Jews fled the city. After this year, Rome, Antioch, and Alexandria all became centers of the Christian church, which continued to be banned.

In subsequent centuries the Christian church expanded more than the spotty historical record indicates. Early Christian centers proliferated around the Mediterranean like the tips of icebergs, but surviving sources do not indicate how deep or wide the icebergs were at the base. The church grew steadily during the first, second, and third centuries C.E.

The Decline of the Empire and the Loss of the Western Provinces, 284–476

Although the principate was still nominally the structure of the government, the Pax Romana ended in the third century. In 226 Rome faced new enemies on its northern borders, as a Germanic tribal people called the Goths launched a series of successful attacks in the region of the Danube River. (In later centuries, the word *Goth* came to mean any social movement, whether Gothic architecture or today's Goth styles, that challenged existing practices.) The attacks by Germanic peoples continued in the following centuries. As a result, different Roman rulers repeatedly restructured the Roman empire and shifted the capital east. During these same centuries, they lifted the ban on Christianity and increasingly offered government support to the religion, which led to its further spread. Although the Romans lost chunks of their empire and even the city of Rome to barbarian invaders, the region of the Mediterranean remained a cultural unit bound by a common religion—Christianity—and the same two languages—Latin and Greek—that had been in use since the time of the republic.

Political Changes of the Late Empire

The principate came to a formal end early in the reign of Diocletian (r. 284–305). Diocletian (dy-oh-KLEE-shun) increased the size of Rome's armies by a third so that they could fight off their various enemies, including the Goths and the Sasanians, the dynasty established in Iran in 224. In 260, the Sasanians had captured the Roman emperor Valerian and forced him to crouch down so that the Sasanian emperor could step on his back as he mounted his horse. Realizing that the new threats made the empire too large to govern effectively, Diocletian divided the empire into an eastern and western half and named a senior emperor and a junior emperor to govern each half. This new structure of government, which replaced the principate, is called the tetrarchy (TEH-trar-kee) because there were four different emperors.

The structure of the tetrarchy did not make it easier to defend the empire. **Constantine** (272–337, r. 312–337), the son of one of the junior emperors named by Diocletian, defeated each of the other emperors in battle until he was the sole ruler of the reunited empire. In 330, to place himself near threatened frontiers, Constantine established a new capital 800 miles (1,300 km) to the east of Rome at Byzantium (bizz-AN-tee-um) on the Bosphorus, which he named for himself, Constantinople (modern-day Istanbul, Turkey).

At the time the population of Byzantium was around fifty thousand, while that of Rome was over 1 million. The move was strategic: it was difficult to maintain control of the empire from a base in Rome, and the emperors of the tetrarchy had already established individual capitals outside of Rome. Constantinople, located near the Danube and the Euphrates frontiers, could be defended more easily than Rome.

When Constantine died in 337, he left the empire to his three sons, who immediately began fighting for control. After the last son died in 364, no ruler succeeded in reuniting the empire for more than a few years at a time. In 395 the emperor formally divided the empire into western and eastern halves.

Constantine
(272–337, r. 312–337) Roman emperor who issued the Edict of Milan, the first imperial ruling to allow the practice of Christianity, and who shifted the capital from Rome to the new city of Constantinople (modern-day Istanbul, Turkey).

The fourth century was a time, particularly in the west, of economic decline. Repeated epidemics killed many in the overcrowded city of Rome. In addition, armies had difficulty recruiting soldiers. The central government, chronically short of revenues, minted devalued coins that contained far less metal than indicated by their face value. People living in regions where the use of coins had been common began to barter simply because fewer coins were in use. As the economy contracted, many urban dwellers moved to the countryside to grow their own crops.

During the fourth century, the armies of Germanic-speaking peoples repeatedly defeated the overstretched Roman army. These peoples, including the Vandals, the Visigoths and Ostrogoths (both branches of the Goths), and other tribes (see Map 7.3), lived north and west of the empire and spoke a variety of languages in the Germanic language family, but had no writing system (see Chapter 10).

Although Roman authors referred to the conquering armies by their tribal names, implying that they were quite different from the Romans, archaeologists in recent decades have found little material evidence of distinct invasions, prompting a revision of earlier views of tribal hordes of barbarian peoples invading civilized Rome. Scholars, led by Walter Goffart, now realize that the Goths and Vandals had lived alongside the Romans for centuries and adopted many of their customs. They now think that the migrations did occur, but they were not large-scale invasions by a single people, and only the leaders belonged to whatever groups the written sources name. The bulk of their followers belonged to multiple peoples with different customs, which is why they leave no distinctive footprint behind in the archaeological record.

Highly mobile and ferocious fighters, these peoples had little to defend and could devote their energies to attacking the long Roman frontier. In 410 the group Romans called Visigoths sacked Rome for three days and then retreated; this was the first time since the fourth-century B.C.E. attack of the Gauls (see page 170) that foreign armies had entered the city.

Religious Changes of the Late Empire

Diocletian launched the last persecution of Christianity in 303. In addition to ordering that Christian scriptures be destroyed and churches torn down, he called for the punishment of all practicing Christians.

In 311 Constantine defeated one of the other claimants to the throne. Initially he claimed to have had a vision of the Roman sun-god Apollo and the Roman numeral for 30, which is written XXX; he interpreted the vision to mean that Apollo chose him to rule for the next thirty years. However, Constantine later began to worship the Christian God along with Roman deities, and according to his biographer, a Christian bishop, what Constantine actually saw in his vision in 311 was a Christian cross.

Whatever the precise nature of Constantine's own beliefs, we know for certain that he ended Diocletian's persecution of Christianity in 313. With his co-emperor, Constantine issued the Edict of Milan, which compensated Christians for any property confiscated during Diocletian's persecution and officially allowed the practice of Christianity. Like Ashoka's decision to support Buddhism, this decision proved crucial to the spread of Christianity.

In 325 Constantine summoned different church leaders to Nicaea (ny-SEE-uh) (modern-day Iznik, Turkey) and encouraged them to reach an agreement about the nature of the Trinity, which consisted of God, Jesus Christ, and the Holy Spirit,

MAP 7.3 **The Migrations of Germanic-Speaking Peoples** Although the Romans looked down on the pre-literate Germanic-speaking peoples living on their borders, their armies proved surprisingly powerful and launched wave after wave of attacks on the empire and Rome itself. In 410, invaders the Romans called Visigoths came from the east and sacked Rome. In 430 migrants called Vandals attacked the city of Hippo on the North African coast. They went on to cross the Mediterranean and loot Rome for two weeks in 455. Historians have recently begun to debate whether terms like *Vandals* and *Visigoths* fully reflect the makeup of the invading groups. (© Cengage Learning)

often mentioned in the book of Acts in conjunction with healing and exorcism. The council drew up a basic statement of faith, the Nicene (ny-SEEN) Creed, which was worded specifically to assert that God and Jesus were made of the same substance and to counter the teachings of Arius (AHR-ee-us), a churchman from Alexandria, who maintained that God the Father was superior to Jesus and the Holy Ghost.[5] When Arius refused to sign the Nicene Creed, the Council of Nicaea excommunicated, or expelled, him from the church. In subsequent centuries the church convened many similar meetings to ensure doctrinal agreement among the different Christian branches.

Chi-rho symbol

An Easy-to-Miss Christian Message in a Medallion This medallion, dating to around 315, shows the Emperor Constantine with his horse and sword. The circle at the top of his helmet above the left eye is the chi-rho symbol, which combines the Greek letters chi (**X**) and rho (**P**), the first two letters in the Greek word for Christ. Chi-rho (☧) was used throughout the Christian world. This is one of the earliest coins with a Christian motif issued in the Roman empire, just after the Edict of Milan permitted Romans to be Christian. (Staatliche Muenzsammlung/akg-images)

During the third and fourth centuries, church leaders met to decide which books of the Bible, both in the Hebrew Bible (which Christians call the Old Testament) and the New Testament, should be included in the canon and which should be viewed as less reliable, or apocryphal. In 367 the bishop of Alexandria listed the twenty-seven books of the New Testament. This event marked the final step in the formation of the Bible.

In 380 Theodosius I, the last emperor to rule over both the eastern and western halves of the empire, issued the Edict of Thessalonica declaring Christianity, as defined by the Council at Nicaea, the official religion of the empire. In the following year Theodosius banned the worship of pagan deities and authorized the tearing down of temples.

In the fourth and fifth centuries Christian pilgrimages, often to Jerusalem, became increasingly popular even though travel was more difficult than in earlier, more peaceful centuries. In the early 300s, the emperor Constantine's mother traveled to Jerusalem, where she ordered the dismantling of pagan temples and the building of Christian churches. She also sponsored one of the world's earliest archaeological excavations to find the spot where Jesus had been crucified.

Travel was safe enough that ordinary women could also make the trip, as we learn from a travel account written by a woman named **Egeria**, who, sometime between 380 and 400, traveled all the way from her homeland in Spain to the Holy Land, the Christian name for Judaea (see Map 7.2). She went to Egypt, the Sinai, Jordan, and modern-day Turkey to visit the important sites of Judaism and early Christianity. After a three-year stay in Jerusalem, Egeria decided to continue her journey before returning home: *"by the will of God, I wished to go to Mesopotamia of Syria [modern-day Edessa, Turkey], to visit the holy monks who were said to be numerous there and to be of such exemplary life that it can scarcely be described."** The devout Egeria wanted to see monasteries because they were a new institution.

Egeria
(ca. 380–400) A Christian woman from Spain whose pilgrimage to the Holy Land and Egypt demonstrates the continued ease of travel in the late empire.

Christianity in North Africa

As Egeria's itinerary shows, North Africa had already become an important center of Christianity by the fourth century. (For more on how Christianity has moved, see the feature "World History in Today's World: The Changing Face of Christianity.") Early in the 300s, an Egyptian Christian founded the first monastic community whose members worked in the fields and prayed each day. Before this time, Christians who wanted to devote themselves full-time to a religious life had lived alone as hermits. In later centuries, monasteries became so popular that they spread from Egypt to all over the Mediterranean.

Egeria: Diary of a Pilgrimage, trans. George E. Gingras (New York: Newman Press, 1970), pp. 75–76.

The Changing Face of Christianity

Of the 7 billion people in the world today, 2.26 billion people identify themselves as Christian, making Christianity the world's largest religion. The degree of observance among Christians varies enormously: some Christians attend services at least once a week and possibly more often, while others have not been inside a church since being baptized.

Most early Christians lived in the Mediterranean region governed by the Roman empire. After the seventh century, Christianity's heartland shifted, as many people in North Africa and western Asia converted to Islam, while the number of Christians in Europe continued to grow.

Today the heartland of Christianity is shifting a second time, in what some scholars see as the rise of Southern Christianity in Africa, Latin America, and Asia, regions having higher birthrates than the Western Christian countries.

The area of greatest growth for Christians is unquestionably in Africa, where 46 percent of the population identifies itself as Christian (versus 9 percent in 1900). The fastest-growing sector of African Christianity is the Pentecostals.

If current trends continue, by the year 2025, Latin America will have the highest number of Christians, 623 million. Africa, with 595 million, will be second. Western Europe will have 513 million, and Asia 498 million. By that time, two-thirds of Christians will live in the Southern Christian regions.

Sources: chartsbin.com; Philip Jenkins, *The Next Christendom: The Coming of Global Christianity* (Oxford: Oxford University Press, 2002), pp. 2–3.

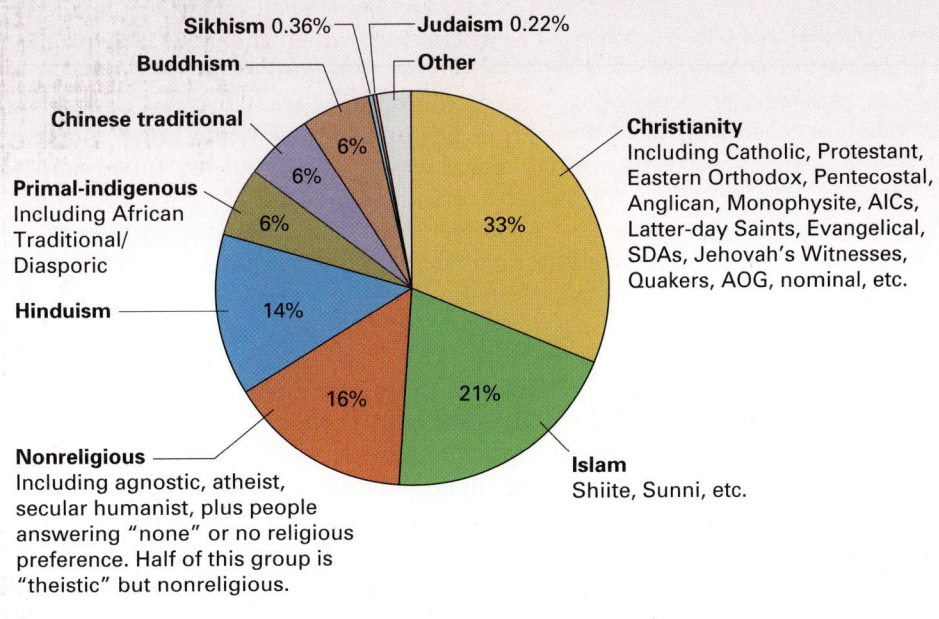

Sikhism 0.36%   **Judaism** 0.22%

Buddhism   **Other**

Chinese traditional

Primal-indigenous
Including African Traditional/Diasporic

Hinduism

Nonreligious
Including agnostic, atheist, secular humanist, plus people answering "none" or no religious preference. Half of this group is "theistic" but nonreligious.

Christianity
Including Catholic, Protestant, Eastern Orthodox, Pentecostal, Anglican, Monophysite, AICs, Latter-day Saints, Evangelical, SDAs, Jehovah's Witnesses, Quakers, AOG, nominal, etc.

33%

6%

6%

6%

14%

16%

21%

Islam
Shiite, Sunni, etc.

Chart from www.adherents.com. Used by permission.

Stone Stele at Aksum, Ethiopia Supported by a counterweight placed underground, this stone tower stands 67 feet (21 m) tall. It represents a building ten stories high, with closed windows and a door bolted shut. Notice the lock on the ground floor level. Some two hundred stone towers like this were built in the 300s and 400s, when the rulers of Aksum converted to Christianity, but unlike coins from the same period that show the cross, these towering monuments give no hint that the rulers who built them had converted to Christianity. (Werner Forman/Art Resource, NY)

Aksum
A center of Christianity in Ethiopia, one of the first places in the world outside the Roman empire to convert to Christianity in the early 300s.

Augustine
(354–430) Author of *The Confessions* and a prominent early Christian thinker who encouraged Christians to confess their sins.

One important Christian center lay to the east of Egypt in **Aksum**, in modern-day Ethiopia, whose rulers converted soon after Constantine issued the Edict of Milan. Their kingdom profited by taxing the trade from Egypt that went via the Red Sea to India. Merchants, who exported ivory from Africa and imported frankincense and myrrh from Arabia, encountered Christians while on trading voyages to the Mediterranean and introduced the religion to their countrymen.

The pre-Christian inscriptions commissioned by the rulers of Aksum mention local deities, including the southern Arabian goddess of the evening star, while the later ones mention the Lord of Heaven. One inscription, in Greek, names the Father, the Son, and the Holy Ghost, a definite indication of the ruler's support for Christianity. The Aksum Christians looked to the Egyptian church for leadership; the first bishop of Aksum and all his successors received their appointments from Egyptian bishops.

To the west of Egypt was another Christian center at Hippo, now Annaba, Algeria, home to one of the most important thinkers in early Christianity, **Augustine** (354–430). Educated in North Africa, Augustine wrote over 5 million words in his lifetime. His book *The Confessions* detailed his varied experiences, which included fathering a child and belonging to the Manichaean order (see page 163), before he joined the Christian church and became the bishop of Hippo. According to Augustine, God's grace was so great that all, no matter how much they had violated the church's teachings, would be forgiven if they joined the church. Augustine encouraged the practice of confessing one's sins to a member of the clergy, and confession became an important rite in early Christianity.

The Eastward Shift of the Empire's Center

In 430, the last year of Augustine's life, **Vandals** led a force of eighty thousand men from different Germanic-speaking tribes across the Mediterranean and laid siege to Hippo. Augustine described what he witnessed:

*whole cities sacked, country villas razed, their owners killed or scattered as refugees, the churches deprived of their bishops and clergy, and the holy virgins and ascetics dispersed; some tortured to death, some killed outright, others, as prisoners, reduced to losing their integrity, in soul and body, to serve an evil and brutal enemy.**

---

*Peter Brown, *Augustine of Hippo: A Biography* (London: Faber and Faber Limited, 2000), p. 430.

For Augustine, the invasions indicated the breakdown of the Roman empire and the end of the civilized world.

After taking Hippo, the invaders went on to conquer all of North Africa and the Mediterranean islands of Sardinia, Corsica, and Sicily. Whether or not it is accurate to call them all Vandals, their fighting techniques and looting were so brutal that the word *vandal* came to mean any deliberate act of destruction. In 455, the marauders moved north to Italy and sacked Rome for two weeks, exposing again the city's vulnerability.

For the next twenty years different Germanic-speaking groups gained control of the city and placed puppet emperors on the throne. In 476, the final emperor of the Western empire was deposed and not replaced. This date marks the end of the Western empire, and many earlier historians declared that the Roman empire fell in 476. Most recent historians, however, prefer not to speak in these terms. They note that the Eastern Roman empire, the Byzantine empire, continued to be governed from Constantinople for another thousand years (see Chapter 10).

The cultural center of the Mediterranean world, thoroughly Christianized by this time, had simply shifted once again—away from the Latin-speaking world centered on Rome to the Greek-speaking world, where it had been before Polybius was deported to Rome in 168 B.C.E.

> **Vandals**
> Leaders of a Germanic-speaking force that attacked North Africa in 430 and sacked Rome for two weeks in 455.

CONTEXT AND CONNECTIONS

The Roman Empire's Lasting Imprint on the Mediterranean

When Polybius compared the Roman empire with the empires of the Persians and Alexander the Great (see Chapter 6), he focused on the size of these three empires, noting correctly that the Roman empire was larger than the other two. Because of its different policies about citizenship and religion, the Roman empire also had greater lasting impact.

Three different governments—a republic, a principate, and a tetrarchy—ruled Rome for nearly one thousand years, and their approach to citizenship broadened over time. During the republic, the Roman government granted citizenship only to the Latin-speaking peoples of Italy. All conquered regions outside of Italy became military districts ruled by a governor. He, like the satrap of the Persian empire, was responsible for collecting taxes and forwarding them to the center.

In the early years of the principate, Augustus granted citizenship to discharged soldiers living outside of Rome, and subsequent emperors continued to increase the number of citizens until, in 212, all free men were granted citizenship. As citizens they were obliged to pay taxes; in return they gained access to the Roman legal system. The equal treatment of all citizens was unique to the Romans: the Persian rulers and Alexander of Macedon always treated the subject peoples of their empires differently.

During the republic and the principate, the Roman government supported the worship of different Roman deities and current or deceased princeps. Jesus lived in the early years of the principate, and even though after his death the government banned Christianity, the roads around the Mediterranean and the waterways across it provided wonderfully effective channels for the spread of Christian teachings. Two languages prevailed in the Roman empire: Latin in the west, Greek in the east. Constantine's decision to worship the Christian God and to rescind Diocletian's ban on Christianity was a crucial measure bringing the further spread of Christianity throughout the empire.

In the years after 313, Constantine encouraged church leaders to reach agreement about doctrinal

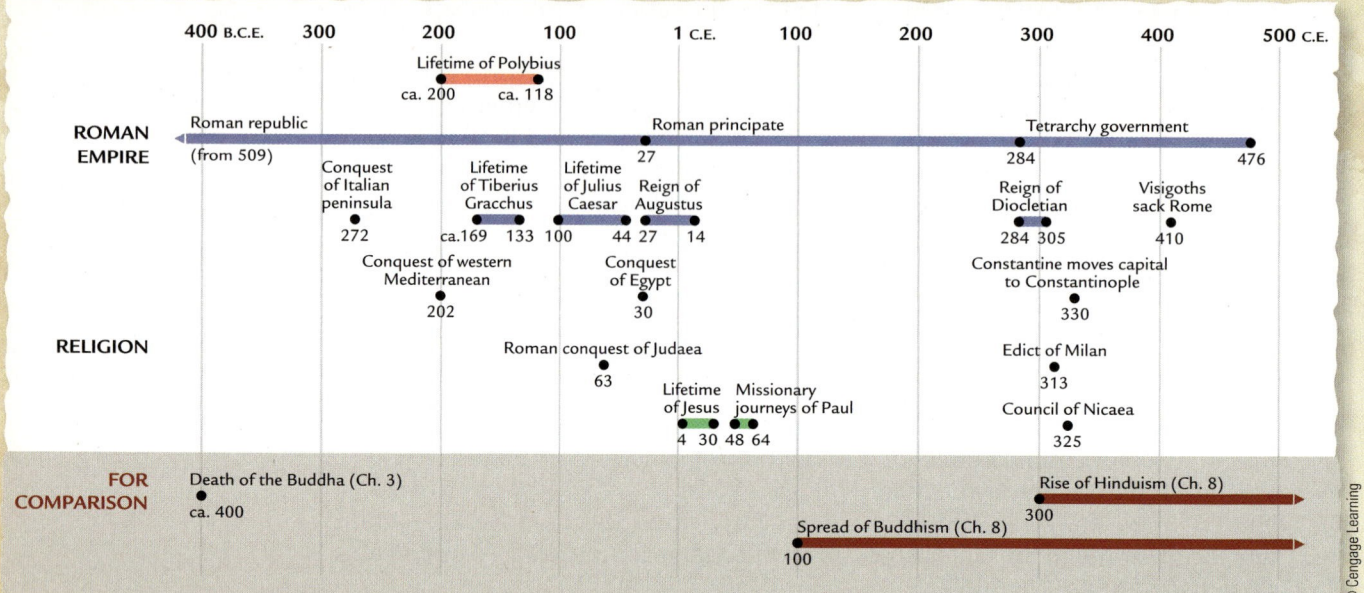

Lifetime of Polybius
ca. 200   ca. 118

ROMAN EMPIRE

Roman republic
(from 509)

Roman principate

Tetrarchy government
284   476

Conquest of Italian peninsula
272

Lifetime of Tiberius Gracchus
ca.169   133

Lifetime of Julius Caesar
100   44

Reign of Augustus
27   14

27

Reign of Diocletian
284 305

Visigoths sack Rome
410

Conquest of western Mediterranean
202

Conquest of Egypt
30

Constantine moves capital to Constantinople
330

RELIGION

Roman conquest of Judaea
63

Lifetime of Jesus   Missionary journeys of Paul
4   30   48 64

Edict of Milan
313

Council of Nicaea
325

FOR COMPARISON

Death of the Buddha (Ch. 3)
ca. 400

Rise of Hinduism (Ch. 8)
300

Spread of Buddhism (Ch. 8)
100

© Cengage Learning

matters, and the Council of Nicaea drew up the Nicene Creed and excommunicated those who disagreed with it. The Nicene interpretation of Christianity received imperial authorization in 380 when Emperor Theodosius issued the Edict of Thessalonica, which made Christianity the official religion of the Roman empire and banned all other religions. The ease of travel in the empire, even in the late 400s, facilitated pilgrimages for people like Egeria and contributed further to the spread of Christianity, which was well established in North Africa in the 400s, as shown by the inscriptions of Aksum and Augustine's *Confessions*.

The religious policies of the Romans differed from those of the Persians, who had built Zoroastrian altars throughout their large empire but allowed their subjects to worship their own religions. Similarly, Alexander of Macedon tolerated the worship of Greek and local deities. The granting of citizenship to subject peoples, the widespread use of Greek and Latin, and the imperial orders supporting Christianity were critical policies of the Roman empire that left a lasting legacy on the Mediterranean region long after the empire ended. Chapter 8 will analyze how decisions made by many different rulers led to the spread of two different religions, Buddhism and Hinduism, throughout Asia. Chapter 9 will explore the rise of Islam, which replaced Christianity in large sections of the former Roman empire in western Asia and North Africa only a few centuries after the eastward shift of the capital to Constantinople.

VOYAGES ON THE WEB: Polybius

The Voyages Map App follows the traveler's journeys using interactive study tools, including 360-degree panoramic views of historic sites, zoomable maps, audio summaries, flash cards, and quizzes.

Key Terms

Polybius (166)
Roman republic (169)
Roman senate (169)
Carthage (170)
Punic Wars (170)
Hannibal (170)
paterfamilias (173)

Cornelia (174)
dictator (175)
Julius Caesar (175)
Roman principate (176)
Augustus (176)
Pliny the Younger (177)
parchment (181)

Jesus (184)
Paul (185)
Constantine (189)
Egeria (192)
Aksum (194)
Augustine (194)
Vandals (194)

For Further Reference

Boardman, John, Jasper Griffin, and Oswyn Murray. *The Oxford History of the Roman World*. New York: Oxford University Press, 1986.

Casson, Lionel. *Travel in the Ancient World*. Baltimore: Johns Hopkins University Press, 1974.

Etherington, Norman. "Barbarians Ancient and Modern." *American Historical Review* 16, no. 1 (2011): 31–57.

Etienne, Robert. *Pompeii: The Day a City Died*. New York: Harry N. Abrams, 1992.

Frend, W. H. C. *The Rise of Christianity*. Philadelphia: Fortress Press, 1984.

Garipzanov, Ildar H., Patrick J. Geary, et al. *Franks, Northmen, and Slavs: Identities and State Formation in Early Medieval Europe*. Turnhout, Belgium: Brepols Publishers, 2008.

Goffart, Walter. *Barbarian Tides: The Migration Age and the Later Roman Empire*. Philadelphia: University of Pennsylvania Press, 2006.

Green, Bernard. *Christianity in Ancient Rome: The First Three Centuries*. New York: T & T Clark International, 2010.

Heather, Peter. *Empires and Barbarians*. London: Macmillan, 2009.

Kebric, Robert B. *Roman People*. 4th ed. New York: McGraw-Hill, 2005.

Lynch, Joseph H. *Early Christianity: A Brief History*. New York: Oxford University Press, 2010.

Polybius. *The Rise of the Roman Empire*. Ian Scott-Kilvert, trans. New York: Penguin Books, 1979.

Roberts, John. *The Oxford Dictonary of the Classical World*. New York: Oxford University Press, 2007.

Tingay, G. I. F., and J. Badcock. *These Were the Romans*. Chester Springs, Pa.: Dufour Editions, 1995.

Wilken, Robert L. *The Christians as the Romans Saw Them*. New Haven: Yale University Press, 2003.

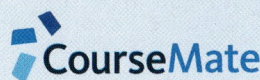 Go to the CourseMate website at **www.cengagebrain.com** for additional study tools and review materials—including audio and video clips—for this chapter.

8

Hindu and Buddhist States and Societies in Asia, 100–1000

In 838, at the age of forty-five, the Japanese monk **Ennin** (EN-nin) (793–864) joined a Japanese delegation that was the last of nearly twenty official delegations sent to China by the Japanese government. The Japanese emperors wanted to learn the reasons for the success of the Tang dynasty (618–907), the most powerful empire in East Asia and a model for all rulers hoping to strengthen their own governments. The Tang dynasty blueprint for rule drew on the earlier Qin/Han blueprint (see Chapter 4) but added other elements, most importantly state support for Buddhism. The Japanese delegation of over thirty people included both officials and monks like Ennin, who hoped to study with knowledgeable teachers and to obtain copies of books not available in Japan. Eleven days after the four ships departed from the modern Japanese port of Fukuoka, it began to rain:

Portrait of Ennin
(From Edwin O. Reischauer, trans., *Ennin's Diary: The Record of a Pilgrimage to China in Search of the Law* [New York: Ronald Press Company, 1955].)

The east wind was blowing fiercely, and the waves were raging high. The ship was suddenly dashed up onto a shoal. In trepidation we immediately lowered sail, but the corners of the rudder snapped in two places, while the waves from both east and west battered the ship and rolled it back and forth. Since the blade of the rudder was stuck in the ocean floor, and the ship was about to break up, we cut down the mast and cast away the rudder. The ship straightway floated with the waves. When the waves came from the east, the ship leaned over to the west, and when they came from the west, it inclined to the east. They washed

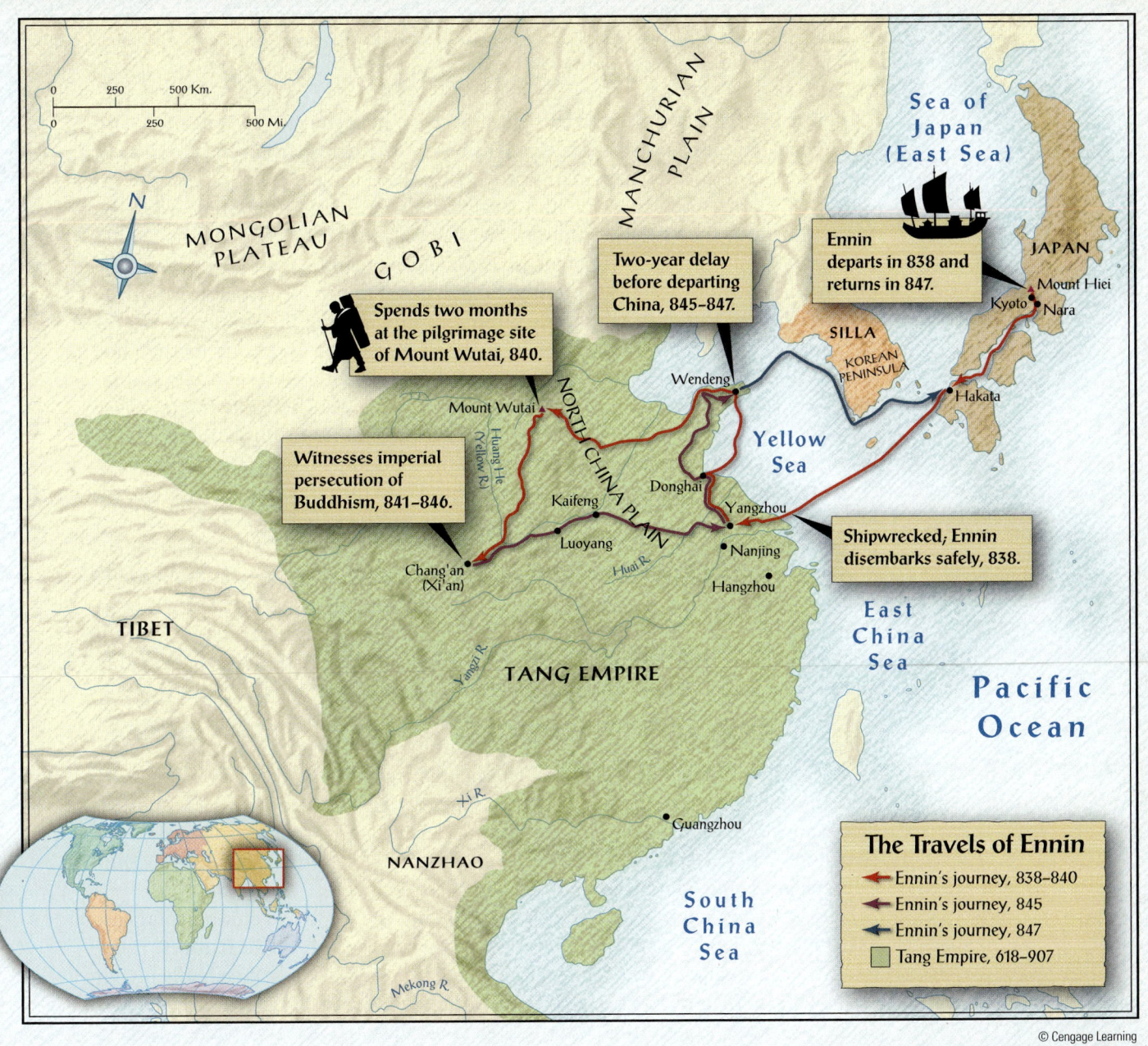

The Travels of Ennin

Spends two months at the pilgrimage site of Mount Wutai, 840.

Two-year delay before departing China, 845–847.

Ennin departs in 838 and returns in 847.

Witnesses imperial persecution of Buddhism, 841–846.

Shipwrecked; Ennin disembarks safely, 838.

- ← Ennin's journey, 838–840
- ← Ennin's journey, 845
- ← Ennin's journey, 847
- ☐ Tang Empire, 618–907

MONGOLIAN PLATEAU

GOBI

MANCHURIAN PLAIN

Sea of Japan (East Sea)

JAPAN

Mount Hiei

Kyoto • Nara

SILLA

KOREAN PENINSULA

Wendeng

Yellow Sea

Hakata

Mount Wutai

NORTH CHINA PLAIN

Huang He (Yellow R.)

Kaifeng

Donghai

Luoyang

Yangzhou

Huai R.

Nanjing

Chang'an (Xi'an)

Hangzhou

TIBET

Yangzi R.

TANG EMPIRE

East China Sea

Pacific Ocean

Xi R.

Guangzhou

NANZHAO

South China Sea

Mekong R.

© Cengage Learning

Join this chapter's traveler on "Voyages," an interactive tour of historic sites and events: www.cengagebrain.com

over the ship to a number beyond count. All on board put their faith in the Buddha and in the deities, and there was none but did pray.[*]

[*]Edwin O. Reischauer, trans., *Ennin's Diary: The Record of a Pilgrimage to China in Search of the Law* (New York: The Ronald Press, 1955), p. 6.

Ennin
(793–864) A Japanese monk who traveled to China between 838 and 847 to obtain original Buddhist texts.

Eventually the ship drifted to the Chinese coast, near the city of Yangzhou, and the Japanese reached shore safely. This was only the first of several shipwrecks Ennin survived, and he had many other setbacks during his seven-year stay in China: officials refused to grant him permission to visit the monastery where he wanted to study, he waited for months while officials debated whether he should proceed, and most frightening of all, he experienced an anti-Buddhist persecution.

As this chapter explains, Buddhism represented an important element of the revised Chinese blueprint for empire. After reuniting China, the Sui (SWAY) (589–617) and Tang (TAHNG) emperors introduced important additions to the Qin/Han synthesis of Legalist and Confucian policies, including civil service examinations, a new system of taxation, and a complex law code. They, like the Japanese emperor who sent Ennin in the delegation, also aspired to fulfill Ashoka's model of the ideal **chakravartin** king who patronized Buddhism (see Chapter 3).

chakravartin
Literally "turner of the wheel," a Buddhist term for the ideal ruler who patronized Buddhism but never became a monk.

When Ennin went home in 847, he had traveled over 3,000 miles (4,800 km). Ennin's detailed account of his trip supplements the official Chinese histories because it reveals so much about Buddhism in China and Japan. After he returned, Ennin became the third abbot of an enormous Buddhist monastery at Mount Hiei outside Kyoto, where he introduced new rituals that he had learned while in China. He was one of the most famous teachers in the Pure Land school of Buddhism, active in both China and Japan, which taught that all beings are capable of attaining Buddhahood, or enlightenment.

On his travels through China, Ennin encountered monks from many other Buddhist countries, including north and south India, Sri Lanka, Central Asia, Korea, and his homeland of Japan. The people traveling in this larger Buddhist world—which stretched from India and Nepal, where the Buddha had taught, to Japan and Korea and included China and Central Asia—had two languages in common: Sanskrit and Chinese. Ennin did not speak Chinese, but like all educated Japanese, he could read and write Chinese characters.

Silk Routes
Overland routes through Central Asia connecting China and India, as well as the sea routes around Southeast Asia, along which were transmitted teachings, technologies, and languages.

The overland routes through Central Asia—and the sea routes around Southeast Asia and extending to Japan and Korea—are known today as the **Silk Routes**. These routes were conduits not just for pilgrims like Ennin but also for merchants plying their goods, soldiers dispatched to fight in distant lands, and refugees fleeing dangerous areas. Most importantly, information about distant, powerful states traveled along these same routes. These travelers told of powerful rulers in India and China, whose accomplishments inspired chieftains in border areas to imitate them. These Asian leaders introduced new writing systems, law codes, ways of recruiting government officials, and taxation systems, often modifying them to suit their own societies. Some, like the rulers of Korea, Japan, and Tibet, patronized Buddhism and adopted Tang policies. Others, particularly in South and Southeast Asia, emulated South Asian monarchs and built temples to deities such as Shiva (SHIH-vah) and Vishnu (VISH-new), the most important deities in the emerging belief system of **Hinduism**.

Hinduism
Temple-based religious system that arose between 300 and 700 in India. Hinduism has two dimensions: public worship in temples to deities such as Shiva and Vishnu, and daily private worship in the home.

As rulers in Japan, Korea, and Tibet adopted the Tang blueprint, they gave money and land to Buddhist monks and monasteries, providing the crucial impetus for the belief system to spread throughout East and Southeast Asia between 200 and 1000. The individual decisions of these rulers resulted in the religious reorientation of the region. In 100, a disunited India was predominantly Buddhist, while the unified China of the Han dynasty embraced Legalist, Confucian, and Daoist beliefs. By 1000, the various kingdoms of India and Southeast Asia had become largely Hindu, while China, Japan, Korea, and Tibet had become Buddhist. This religious shift did not occur because one ruler of an intact empire, such as Constantine in the West, recognized a single religion. It was the result of many decisions taken in different places by multiple rulers, all of whom sought to strengthen their governments and so increase their power.

Focus Questions

» *How did Buddhism change after the year 100? How did Hinduism displace it within India?*

» *How did geography, trade, and religion shape the development of states and societies in Southeast Asia?*

» *How did the Sui and Tang dynasties modify the Qin/Han blueprint for empire?*

» *Which elements of the revised Chinese blueprint for empire did Korea and Japan borrow intact? Which did they modify?*

Buddhism, Hinduism, and Indian Rulers, 100–1000

By the year 100, India had broken up into different regional kingdoms, all much smaller than the Mauryan empire ruled by Ashoka (see Chapter 3) but bound by common cultural ties of Buddhism, social hierarchy, and respect for classical Sanskrit learning. Despite the claims of Ashokan inscriptions, the first evidence of the spread of Buddhism beyond South Asia dates to the Kushan empire (ca. 50–260), located in Pakistan, Afghanistan, and northwest India. The most important Kushan ruler, Kanishka (r. ca. 120–140), launched a missionary movement that propelled the new Greater Vehicle teachings of Buddhism into Central Asia and China.

Between 100 and 1000, Buddhism gained many adherents outside India but increasingly lost ground to new deities inside India. A Chinese monk who in the early 600s traveled to north India noticed Buddhism in decline everywhere, and he recorded, often regretfully, the rise of a new religion taught by Brahmins. We know this religion as Hinduism, a name not used until the nineteenth century, when British scholars of Indian religion coined the term for the religious practices of Indians who were not Zoroastrian, Christian, or Muslim.[1] By the year 1000, in many regions in India, particularly south India, the largest religious institutions were temples to Hindu deities such as Vishnu and Shiva.

The Rise of Greater Vehicle Teachings in Buddhism

Buddhism changed a great deal between Ashoka's time in the third century B.C.E. and Kanishka's reign in the second century C.E. Most importantly, Buddhist teachings no longer required an individual to join the Buddhist order to gain enlightenment. New interpreters of Buddhism referred to their own teachings as the Greater Vehicle (Mahayana) and denigrated those of earlier schools as the Lesser Vehicle (Hinayana, also called Theravada, meaning "the Tradition of the Elders").

The Buddha had taught that he was not a deity and that his followers should not make statues of him. Yet Indians began to worship statues of the Buddha in the first and second centuries C.E. (see Chapter 3). They also began to pray to **bodhisattvas** (BODE-ee-saht-vahz) for easier childbirth or the curing of illness. A bodhisattva—literally, a being headed for Buddhahood—refers to someone on the

bodhisattva
Buddhist term denoting a being headed for Buddhahood but postpones it to help others.

verge of enlightenment who chooses, because of his or her compassion for others, to stay in this world for this and future lives and help other sentient beings (the Buddhist term for all living creatures, including humans) to attain nirvana.

The proponents of the Greater Vehicle schools emphasized that Buddhists could transfer merit from one person to another: if someone paid for a Buddhist text to be recited, he or she acquired a certain amount of merit that could be transferred to someone else, perhaps an ill relative. Buddhist inscriptions frequently state that someone gave a gift to the Buddhist order in someone else's name.

During the early centuries of the Common Era, Buddhist monasteries appeared throughout India. Since monastic rules forbade the monks from working in the fields, most monasteries hired laborers to do their farming for them. One monastery erected a giant stone begging bowl by its front gate, where the monastery's supporters placed large gifts for the monks and nuns.

King Kanishka certainly supported the Buddhist order, and rich merchants probably did as well. Many Buddhist texts encouraged donors to make gifts of gold, silver, lapis lazuli, crystal, coral, pearls, and agate. These valuable items, often referred to as the Seven Treasures, were traded overland between India and China. The blue mineral lapis lazuli could be mined only in present-day Afghanistan, and one of the world's best sources of pearls was the island of Sri Lanka, just south of India.

The Buddhists, like the Christians at the Council of Nicaea, met periodically to discuss their teachings, and Buddhist sources credit Kanishka with organizing the Fourth Buddhist Council, whose primary task was to determine which versions of orally transmitted texts were authoritative. Because the few writing materials available in ancient India, such as leaves and wooden tablets, decayed in the tropical climate, monks who specialized in specific texts taught their disciples to memorize them.

The earliest Buddhists to arrive in China, in the first and second centuries C.E. (discussed later in this chapter), were missionaries from the Kushan empire. The Kushan dynasty was only one of many regional dynasties in India during the first to third centuries C.E. After 140, Kanishka's successors fought in various military campaigns, and Chinese sources report the arrival of refugees fleeing the political upheavals of their homeland in north India. In 260 the Sasanians (see Chapter 6) defeated the final Kushan ruler, bringing the dynasty to an end.

The Rise of Hinduism, 300–900

In the centuries after the fall of the Kushan dynasty, various dynasties arose in the different regions of South Asia, which continued to be culturally united even as it was politically divided. One of the most important was the **Gupta dynasty**, which controlled much of north India between 320 and 600. An admirer of the Mauryan dynasty (ca. 320–185 B.C.E.), Chandragupta (r. 319/320–ca. 330), the founder of the Gupta (GOOP-tah) dynasty, took the same name as the Mauryan founder and governed from the former capital at Pataliputra (modern-day Patna).

The Gupta rulers sponsored writers who used Sanskrit, which they saw as the language of higher learning. The Gupta period was the great age of Sanskrit, and India's most famous epics, the *Ramayana* and *Mahabharata* (see Chapter 3), both composed in Sanskrit, were written down in the fourth century.

In subsequent centuries, Sanskrit spread to Southeast Asia and China. During his travels in China, Ennin experienced several Buddhist rituals with Sanskrit chanting, and he encountered several different teachers of Sanskrit, all from India.

Gupta dynasty (ca. 320–600) Indian dynasty based in north India; emulated the earlier Mauryan dynasty and revived the use of the Sanskrit language. The Gupta kings pioneered a new type of religious gift: land grants to Brahmin priests and Hindu temples.

He believed they had a deeper knowledge of Buddhist teachings since they could read them in the original Sanskrit, and he himself started to study the language, with limited success.

In an important innovation, the Gupta rulers issued land grants to powerful families, Brahmins, monasteries, and even villages. These grants gave the holder the right to collect a share of the harvest from the cultivators who worked his land. Scribes developed a decimal system that allowed them to record the dimensions of each plot of land. Certainly by 876, and quite possibly during the Gupta reign, they also started to use a small circle to hold empty places; that symbol is the ancestor of the modern zero.[2] On the other side of the globe, the Maya started to use zero at roughly the same time (see page 118).

The Gupta rulers made many grants of land to Brahmins, members of the highest-ranking varna (see Chapter 3) who conducted rituals honoring Hindu deities like Vishnu and Shiva. The two deities, who appear only briefly in the *Rig Veda* of ancient India, became increasingly important in later times. Both deities took many forms with various names. Some Hindus claimed that the Buddha was actually an earlier incarnation of Vishnu.

Brahmin priests played an important role in Hindu worship, but unlike the Brahmins of Vedic times, who had conducted large public ceremonies with animal sacrifices, the Brahmins of the Gupta era performed offerings to Vishnu and Shiva at temples. These public ceremonies allowed local rulers to proclaim their power for all visiting the temple to see. The second dimension of Hindu worship was private worship in the home, in which devotees daily sang songs of love or praise to their deities. This strong personal tie between the devotee and the deity is known as **bhakti**. The main evidence for the rise of bhakti devotionalism is a large corpus of poems written in regional languages such as Tamil, a language of great antiquity spoken in the southernmost tip of India.

bhakti
Literally "personal devotion or love," a term for Hindu poetry or cults that emphasize a strong personal tie between the deity and a devotee, and did not use priests as intermediaries.

The Beginnings of the Chola Kingdom, ca. 900

In 907, the Tamil-speaking Chola (CHOH-lah) kings established their dynasty in south India. They were among the most powerful leaders who patronized Hindu temples. In their capital at Tanjore, the Chola rulers bestowed huge land grants on the Shiva temple because they hoped that their subjects would associate the generosity of the royal donors with the power of the deity.

The Tanjore temple to Shiva, like many other Hindu temples, had an innermost chamber, called the womb room, that housed a stone lingam, to which Hindu priests made ritual offerings. *Lingam* means "sign" or "phallus" in Sanskrit. On a concrete level, the lingam in the womb room symbolized the creative force of human reproduction; on a more abstract level, it stood for all the creative forces in the cosmos.

The Shiva temple lands lay in the agricultural heartland of south India and, when irrigated properly, produced a rich rice harvest whose income supported the thousands of Brahmins who lived in the temple. These Brahmins performed rituals in the temple, memorized and transmitted different texts, and taught local boys in temple schools.

The Chola kings controlled the immediate vicinity of the capital and possibly the other large cities in their district, but not the many villages surrounding the cities. Many of these villages were self-governing. But since their temples were subordinate to the larger temple in the Chola capital, they also acknowledged the Chola kings as their spiritual overlords.

Brihadeshwara Temple at Tanjore, with Womb Room
Rajaraja I (r. 985–1014) built this imposing temple (*below*) to Shiva at Tanjore. The temple's ornate exterior contrasts sharply with the austere interior. The innermost sanctuary of the Hindu temple, the womb room (*right*), held the lingam, on which devotees placed offerings, like the flowers shown here. A Hindu goddess sits on the peacock on the wall. Many temples allowed only Hindus, sometimes only Hindu priests, to enter the womb room.

Robert Harding World Imagery/Jupiter Images

Dinodia Photo Library

One of the most successful Chola rulers was Rajaraja (RAH-jah-rah-jah) I (r. 985–1014), who conquered much of south India and sent armies as far as Srivijaya (sree-VEE-jeye-ah) (modern Indonesia, on the southern Malay Peninsula and Sumatra). Although he did not conquer any territory there, the people of Southeast Asia learned of the Chola king's accomplishments from these contacts. As a direct result, local rulers encouraged priests literate in Sanskrit to move to Southeast Asia to build Hindu temples and teach them about Chola governance.

Buddhism, Hinduism, and Southeast Asian Rulers, 300–1000

The term *Southeast Asia* encompasses a broad swath of land in subtropical Asia and over twenty thousand islands in the Pacific. In most periods, travel among islands and along the shore was easier than overland travel, which was possible only on some of the region's major rivers. Most of the region's sparse population (an estimated fifteen people per square mile [six people per sq km] in the seventeenth century,[3] and even lower in earlier centuries) lived in isolated groups separated by forests and mountains, but the coastal peoples went on sea voyages as early as 1000 B.C.E.

Like India, Southeast Asia received heavy monsoon rains in the summer; successful agriculture often depended on storing rainwater in tanks for use throughout the year. While people in the lowlands raised rice in paddies, the different highland societies largely practiced slash-and-burn agriculture. Once farmers had exhausted the soil of a given place, they moved on, with the result that few states with fixed borders existed in Southeast Asia.

With no equivalent of caste, the shifting social structure of the region was basically egalitarian. From time to time, a leader unified some of the groups, dedicated a temple to either the Buddha or a Hindu deity, and adopted other policies in hopes of strengthening his new state.

Buddhist Kingdoms Along the Trade Routes

Merchants and religious travelers going from India to China (and back) by boat traveled along well-established routes (see Map 8.1 on page 208). Before 350, ships usually landed at a port on the Isthmus of Kra, and travelers crossed the 35-mile (56-km) stretch of land dividing the Andaman Sea from the Gulf of Thailand by foot before resuming their sea voyages.

Prevailing winds determined the schedule for merchants and pilgrims. During the spring and summer, while the Eurasian landmass heated up, travelers could follow the monsoon winds that blew toward India; during the fall and winter, as the landmass cooled, they followed the winds that blew away from the landmass and India. In Southeast Asia, ships waiting for the winds to change—sometimes with several hundred crew and passengers—needed food and shelter for three to five months, and port towns grew up to accommodate their needs. Local rulers discovered that they could tax the travelers, and merchants realized that there was a market for Southeast Asian aromatic woods and spices in both China and India.

Sometime after 350, the mariners of Southeast Asia discovered a new route between China and India, passing through either the Strait of Malacca or the Sunda Strait. Merchants and monks disembarked in the kingdom of Srivijaya in modern-day Indonesia, waited for the winds to shift, and then continued through the South China Sea to China. Srivijaya's ruler welcomed Buddhist travelers and made extensive contributions to local Buddhist monasteries as well as non-Buddhist deities. The Srivijayan kings called themselves "Lord of the Mountains" and "Spirit of the Waters of the Sea," titles from the local religious traditions. The kingdom of Srivijaya flourished between 700 and 1000. The Srivijaya kingdom traded with many regional kingdoms in central Java, where the world's largest Buddhist monument, at Borobudur (boh-roh-BUH-duhr), provides a powerful example of religious architecture connected with early state formation. (See the feature "Visual Evidence in Primary Sources: Borobudur: A Buddhist Monument in Java, Indonesia.")

The huge scale of Borobudur testifies to the wealth of the kingdom, which clearly benefited from its position on the main sea route between Tang dynasty China and the Islamic world. Archaeologists' discovery of a dhow wrecked in 826 near the island of Beilitung, Indonesia, offered an unusual snapshot of the sea trade. Like all dhows, the vessel had a square sail but no nails or wooden dowels: its wooden planks were sewn together with coconut fiber. It held over sixty thousand vessels, mostly ceramic, but also some of silver and gold, all made in China.

Borobudur: A Buddhist Monument in Java, Indonesia

The largest Buddhist monument in the world lies not in the homeland of the Buddha in India but over 1,000 miles (1,600 km) to the southeast at Borobudur on the island of Java in Indonesia. The Shailendra (SHAI-len-drah) kings (ca. 775–860) built the monument out of volcanic rock sometime in the eighth or ninth century, just as they were consolidating their rule. When they moved their capital to a different location in east Java, they abandoned the magnificent complex, and it lay unknown until the early nineteenth century, when Sir Thomas Raffles, founder of Singapore, saw it covered with mold and lichen plants in the middle of a dense forest.

Since no surviving documents explain the meaning of the elements of the monument, analysts must study the different sections of the enormous structure to reconstruct its possible meaning. Rising over 100 feet (31.5 m) above the ground, the monument rests on a large squarish base measuring 400 feet (122 m) on each side. The overall effect resembles the ziggurat temples of Mesopotamia. Staircases at the center of each level lead up to the next, and visitors walk around each level for a total of 3 miles (5 km) until they reach the top.

The lowest level of the monument, originally below ground, depicts an underground hell for those who do not obey Buddhist teachings. The four square terraces above contain over 2,500 panels, most showing scenes from the earlier lives of the Buddha. Monks and guides probably explained the meaning of these scenes to pilgrims. Near the top, the visitor reaches the three terraces holding seventy-two bodhisattvas, each sitting under a bell-shaped stone with holes to look through. At the top of the monument stands an empty stupa, which may have originally held a relic.

Borobudur was a pilgrimage site for people all over Southeast Asia. Pilgrims brought simple clay objects in the shape of stupas and buried them underground at the site. Archaeologists have unearthed 2,397 clay stupas and 252 clay tablets with writing on them. Pilgrims also buried clay pots and sheets of silver covered with written Buddhist charms, either to keep away evil spirits or to bring good health. The many languages on the tablets indicate that people came from great distances to see Borobudur and to make offerings to the Buddha who came to be worshiped so far from his original home.

Most analysts concur that the monument was designed to lead pilgrims from the underworld, shown in the base, up through the five platforms showing human existence, through the world of the seventy-two bodhisattvas, to the single Buddha on top who had attained enlightenment. While the content of the different panels is clearly inspired by Buddhism, the design of the monument, with its multiple ascending levels, is distinctly local. No other Buddhist monument is like it.

Borobudur is made of 2 million separate blocks of yellow-brown andesite, volcanic rock found throughout Java. Each year over 70 inches (2 m) of rain falls on the rocks, creating the perfect environment for moss and lichen to thrive. Between 1973 and 1983, with UNESCO support, workers dismantled the monument, removed and cleaned each of the blocks, and restored the monument for the third time since its rediscovery in the early 1800s.

QUESTION FOR ANALYSIS

» *How had Buddhist worship at stupas changed from the first century B.C.E. at Sanchi (see "Visual Evidence in Primary Sources," Chapter 3) to the eighth and ninth centuries at Borobudur?*

This is one of seventy-two bodhisattvas on the top three circular terraces of the monument, underneath a central stupa at the top, which is 460 feet (43 m) above the ground.

This stupa's cover is missing, allowing a view of this serene bodhisattva.

All of the stones today are grayish-black, but they were originally covered with a layer of white plaster and then painted different eye-catching colors.

Underneath these three circular levels are four square levels holding 1,460 6-foot-wide stone panels, each showing a different scene from Buddhist songs, poems, sacred texts, and the earlier lives of the Buddha.

The heavy stone monument rests on an unstable core of earth. After construction first started, the monument sagged, prompting a reconfiguration of the subterranean level, which now is surrounded by a terrace to prevent it from slipping even further. Some observers have compared the resulting uneven profile to a cake that did not rise properly.

MAP 8.1 **The Spread of Buddhism and Hinduism to Southeast Asia** Sea routes connected Southeast Asia with both India and China, facilitating travel by missionaries to the region and by devotees from the region. The regions closest to China, particularly Vietnam, became predominantly Buddhist, like China, while the rulers of other regions, including Cambodia, patronized both Buddhism and Hinduism, as did most rulers in India. (© Cengage Learning)

The pottery vessels were mass produced in five different Chinese kilns. The dhow contained large quantities of identical or similar items, such as 763 identical pots for ink, suggesting that they were to be sold in foreign markets, perhaps in the port of Basra on the Arabian Sea. Some of the motifs, like lotus leaves, were Buddhist; others, like inscriptions from the Quran in Arabic, were Islamic. The sea route from Guangzhou, where this ship most likely departed, to the Persian Gulf was the *"longest in regular use by mankind before the European expansion in the sixteenth century,"* according to a historian of early maritime trade.* While the coastal kingdoms of Southeast Asia had frequent contact with outsiders traveling the ocean routes, the interior kingdoms had much less.

Buddhist and Hindu Kingdoms of Inland Southeast Asia, 300–1000

Buddhist images made in stone appeared throughout interior Southeast Asia between 300 and 600. In the pre-Buddhist period, all the different societies of the region recognized certain individuals as "men of prowess" who used military skill and intelligence to rise to the leadership of their tribes. Sometimes a leader was so successful that various tribal leaders acknowledged him as a regional overlord.

Most societies in Southeast Asia recognized descent through both the mother and the father. In practice this meant that a nephew of a man of prowess had the same claim as a son to succeed him as the new leader. As a result, no group held together for very long. People were loyal to a given individual, not to a dynasty, and when he died, they tended to seek a new man of prowess to support.

Arab Seafaring in the Indian Ocean in Ancient and Early Medieval Times by George Fadlo Hourani, John Carswel.

Burial practices varied widely throughout Southeast Asia. In modern Cambodia alone, archaeologists have found evidence of cremation, burial in the ground, burial by disposal in the ocean, and exposure of the dead above ground. Many people conceived of a natural world populated by different spirits usually thought to inhabit trees, rocks, and other physical features. Specialists conducted rituals that allowed them to communicate with these spirits.

This was the world into which literate outsiders came in the fourth, fifth, and sixth centuries C.E. Most of the visitors, some identified as Brahmins, came from India and knew how to read and write Sanskrit. Southeast Asians also traveled to India, where they studied Sanskrit and returned after they memorized both sacred texts and laws. Inscriptions often refer to men literate in Sanskrit as *purohita*, a Sanskrit word meaning a chief priest, who conducted rituals for leaders and served as advisers or administrators. The teachings of bhakti encouraged devotees to study with a teacher, or purohita, so that they could get closer to the divinity they worshiped.

Men literate in Sanskrit brought different teachings—some we now identify as Buddhist, some as Hindu—to the rulers of Southeast Asia. We can see how they came together in the person of Jayavarman II (JAI-ah-var-mahn) (ca. 770–850), who ruled the lower Mekong basin in Cambodia between 802 and 850. Before the Mekong River empties into the South China Sea, much of its waters flow into

Bayon Gate, Angkor Thom, Cambodia In the 1180s and 1190s, the ruler Jayavarman VII built a series of monuments and temples, including this one at Angkor Thom, a fortified city just north of Angkor Wat. The figures on the road leading up to the Bayon Gate are Buddhist guardians: on the left stands a line of warrior deities; on the right, a row of gods. The faces on the four sides of the tower are those of a bodhisattva, but the multiple faces also seem Hindu, in an artful blending of Hindu and Buddhist imagery. (Robert Harding World Imagery/Alamy)

Tonle Sap (the Great Lake). The lake served as a holding tank for the monsoon rains, which were channeled into nearby rice fields.

Historians view Jayavarman II's reign as the beginning of the Angkor period (802–1431), named for the **Angkor dynasty**, whose rulers spoke the Khmer (KMEHR) language. Because Jayavarman II was a devotee of the Hindu deity Shiva, this dynasty is often called a Hindu dynasty. Shiva was believed to preside over the entire universe, with other less powerful deities having smaller realms. Similarly, Jayavarman II presided over the human universe as the overlord, while the chieftains in the surrounding region had their own smaller, but inferior, realms. Jayavarman II did not have to conquer them militarily to win their allegiance, because they acknowledged him as a bhakti teacher who could provide them with closer access to Shiva.

Devotees of Shiva built temples on sites where local spirits were thought to live. If the spirit inhabited a rock, that rock could be worshiped as the lingam of a new Shiva temple. In a Hindu ceremony to request children, devotees poured a sacred liquid over the lingam, a practice that echoed earlier fertility cults. The largest temple in the kingdom came to be known as Angkor Wat (ang-core WAHT). Built in the early twelfth century, it used motifs borrowed from Hinduism to teach its viewers that they were living during a golden age, when peace reigned and the Angkor dynasty controlled much of modern-day Cambodia. Jayavarman II also invoked Buddhist terminology by calling himself a chakravartin ruler. All subsequent Angkor kings, and many other Southeast Asian rulers, adopted this combination of Hindu and Buddhist imagery.

With the exception of Vietnam, which remained within the Chinese cultural sphere, Southeast Asia faced toward India, where Buddhism and Hinduism often coexisted. Buddhism and Hinduism came to Southeast Asia not because of conquest but because local rulers aspired to create new states as powerful as those they heard existed in India.

Angkor dynasty
Khmer-speaking dynasty in modern-day Cambodia founded by Jayavarman II. His combination of Hindu and Buddhist imagery proved so potent that it was used by all later Angkor kings.

Buddhism and the Revival of Empire in China, 100–1000

With the fall of the Han dynasty in 220, China broke up into different regions, each governed by local military leaders. When the first Buddhist missionaries from the Kushan empire arrived in China during the first and second centuries C.E., they faced great difficulties in spreading their religion. Buddhist teachings urged potential converts to abandon family obligations and adopt a celibate lifestyle, yet Confucian China was one of the most family-oriented societies in the world. The chakravartin ideal of the universal Buddhist ruler, though, appealed to leaders of regions no longer united under the Han dynasty. During the Sui dynasty, which reunited China, and its long-lived successor, the Tang dynasty, Chinese emperors introduced important additions to the Qin/Han blueprint for empire, additions that remained integral to Chinese governance until the end of dynastic rule in the early 1900s.

Buddhism in China, 100–589

The first Chinese who worshiped the Buddha did so because they thought him capable of miracles; some sources report that his image shone brightly and could fly through the air. The earliest Chinese document to mention Buddhism, from 65 C.E., tells of a prince worshiping the Buddha alongside the Daoist deity Laozi (see Chapter 4), indicating that the Chinese initially thought the Buddha was a Daoist deity.

The Han dynasty ended in 220, and no other regional dynasty succeeded in uniting the empire until 589. Historians call this long period of disunity the Six Dynasties (220–589). During the Six Dynasties, Buddhist miracle workers began to win the first converts. Historians of Buddhism treat these miracle accounts in the same way as historians of Christianity do biblical accounts (see Chapter 7). Nonbelievers may be skeptical that the events occurred as described, but people at the time found (and modern devotees continue to find) these tales compelling, and they are crucial to our understanding of how these religions gained their first adherents.

One of the most effective early missionaries was a Central Asian man named **Fotudeng** (d. 349), who claimed that the Buddha had given him the ability to bring rain, cure the sick, and foresee the future. In 310, Fotudeng managed to convert a local ruler named Shi Le (274–333). Shi Le asked Fotudeng to perform a miracle to demonstrate the power of Buddhism. A later biography explains what happened: *"Thereupon he took his begging bowl, filled it with water, burned incense, and said a spell over it. In a moment there sprang up blue lotus flowers whose brightness and color dazzled the eyes."** A Buddhist symbol, the lotus is a beautiful flower that grows from a root coming out of a dirty lake bottom; similarly, Fotudeng explained, human beings could free their minds from the impediments of worldly living and attain enlightenment. As usual with miracle tales, we have no way of knowing what actually happened, but Fotudeng's miracle so impressed Shi Le that he granted the Buddhists tax-free land so they could build monasteries in north China.

The son of a Xiongnu (SHEE-awng-new) chieftain (see Chapter 4), Shi Le could never become a good Confucian-style ruler because he spoke but could not read or write Chinese. Buddhism appealed to him precisely because it offered an alternative to Confucianism. He could aspire to be a chakravartin ruler.

Fotudeng tried to persuade ordinary Chinese to join the new monasteries and nunneries, but most people were extremely reluctant to take vows of celibacy. If they did not have children, future generations would not be able to perform ancestor worship for them. A Buddhist book written in the early sixth century, *The Lives of the Nuns*, portrays the dilemma of would-be converts. When one young woman told her father that she did not want to marry, he replied, *"You ought to marry. How can you be like this?"* She explained, *"I want to free all living beings from suffering. How much more, then, do I want to free my two parents!"*† But her father was not persuaded by her promise that she could free him from the endless cycle of birth, death, and rebirth. Many families made a compromise; they allowed one child to join the Buddhist order and transfer merit to the other children, who married and had children.

Buddhist missionaries found that they could use miracles to convert uneducated people like Shi Le, but they needed accurate Chinese translations of Buddhist texts in Sanskrit to impress China's scholars. No dictionaries or other translation aids existed. The first understandable translations in Chinese appeared only in the year 400, long after Buddhists had been active in China, when a monk who knew both Chinese and Sanskrit founded a translation bureau with teams of bilingual translators.

Buddhists continued to win converts during the fifth and sixth centuries. They gained support because Buddhist teachings offered more hope about the afterlife than did Confucian and Daoist teachings (see Chapter 4).

Fotudeng (d. 349) Central Asian Buddhist missionary who persuaded the ruler Shi Le to convert to Buddhism; Shi Le's decision to grant tax-free land to Buddhist monasteries was a crucial first step in the establishment of Buddhism in China.

---

*Valerie Hansen, *The Open Empire: A History of China to 1600* (New York: W. W. Norton, 2000), p. 159.

†*Lives of the Nuns: Biographies of Chinese Buddhist Nuns from the Fourth to Sixth Centuries: A Translation of the Pi-ch'iu-ni chuan,* compiled by Shih Pao-ch'ang, trans. Kathryn Ann Tsai (Honolulu: University of Hawai'i Press, 1994), pp. 20–21.

The original Indian belief in the transmigration of souls as expressed in the *Upanishads* (oo-PAHN-ih-shahdz; see Chapter 3) presumed that someone's soul in this life stayed intact and could be reborn in a different body. But the Buddhists propounded the no-self doctrine, which taught that there is no such thing as a fixed self. Each person is a constantly shifting group of five aggregates—form, feelings, perceptions, karmic constituents, and consciousness—that change from one second to the next. Accordingly, there is no self that can be reborn in the next life. This idea proved extremely difficult for people to grasp and was much debated as a result. Gradually, Chinese Buddhists abandoned the strict no-self doctrine and began to describe a series of hells, much like the indigenous Chinese concept of the underground prison, where people went when they died. (See the feature "Movement of Ideas Through Primary Sources: Teaching Buddhism in a Confucian Society.")

By the year 600, Buddhism was firmly implanted in the Chinese countryside. A history of Buddhism written in that year explained that three types of monasteries existed. In the largest 47 monasteries, completely financed by the central government, educated monks conducted regular Buddhist rituals on behalf of the emperor and his immediate family. In the second tier were 839 monasteries that depended on powerful families for support. The final category included over thirty thousand smaller shrines that dotted the Chinese countryside. Dependent on local people for contributions, the monks who worked in these shrines were often uneducated. The number of monks never exceeded more than 1 percent of China's total population, which was about 50 million in 600.[4]

China Reunified, 589–907

After more than three hundred years of disunity, the founder of the Sui dynasty reunified China in 589. Then, in less than thirty years, the **Tang dynasty** succeeded the Sui. The Sui and Tang emperors embraced the chakravartin ideal, for they hoped Buddhism would help to bind their many subjects together. The Tang emperors ruled more territory than any dynasty until the mid-eighteenth century, and Chinese openness to the influences of Central Asia made Tang art and music particularly beautiful.

Consciously modeling himself on the great chakravartin ruler Ashoka, whose support for the Buddhist order was well known in China, the Sui founder gave money for the construction of monasteries all over his empire. When the emperor turned sixty in 601, he ordered stupas for Buddhist relics to be built in thirty different places throughout the empire. At noon on the fifteenth day of the tenth month, each of the monasteries simultaneously conducted a ritual to honor the relics. Burning incense, the emperor welcomed 367 monks who attended the ceremony at the Daxing monastery in Chang'an (CHAHNG-ahn). He conducted identical rituals at fifty-three new monasteries in 602, and at another thirty in 604, the year he died.

When the emperor's son came to power, he led his armies on a disastrous campaign in Korea. He was soon overthrown by one of his generals, who went on to found the Tang dynasty. After only eight years of rule, in 626, the Tang founder's son, Emperor Taizong, overthrew his father in a bloody coup in which he killed one of his brothers and ordered an officer to kill another.

A talented general, Emperor Taizong led his armies on successive campaigns and extended Tang China's borders deep into Central Asia. Taizong was also able to fulfill the chakravartin ideal by making generous donations of money and land to Buddhist monasteries.

One of Taizong's greatest accomplishments was a comprehensive law code, the *Tang Code*, that was designed to help local magistrates govern and adjudicate disputes, a major part of their job. It taught them, for example, how to distinguish

Tang dynasty
Dynasty (618–907) that represented a political and cultural high point in Chinese history. The Tang emperors combined elements of the Qin/Han blueprint for empire with new measures to create a model of governance that spread to Tibet, Korea, and Japan.

between manslaughter and murder and specified the punishments for each. Tang dynasty governance continued many Han dynasty innovations, particularly respect for Confucian ideals coupled with Legalist punishments and regulations.

The *Tang Code* also laid out the **equal-field system**, which was the basis of the Tang dynasty tax system. Under the equal-field system, the government conducted a census of all inhabitants and drew up registers listing each household and its members every three years. Dividing households into nine ranks on the basis of wealth, it allocated to each householder a certain amount of land, some for temporary use until the next registers were compiled three years later, some for permanent use. It also fixed the tax obligations of each individual. Historians disagree about whether the equal-field system took effect throughout all of the empire, but they concur that Tang dynasty officials had an unprecedented degree of control over their 50 million subjects.

Emperor Taizong made Confucianism the basis of the educational system. By reserving the highest 5 percent of posts in the government for those who had passed written examinations on the Confucian classics, the Tang set an important precedent (see Chapter 12). Taizong combined the chakravartin ideal with Confucian policies to create a new model of rulership for East Asia.

One Tang emperor extended the chakravartin ideal to specific government measures: **Emperor Wu** (r. 685–705), the only woman to rule China as emperor in her own right. Many English-language books incorrectly refer to her as Empress Wu, even though she called herself emperor. Originally the wife of the emperor, she engineered the imperial succession so that she could serve first as regent to a boy emperor and then as emperor herself.

The chakravartin ideal appealed to Emperor Wu because an obscure Buddhist text, *The Great Cloud Sutra*, prophesied that a kingdom ruled by a woman would be transformed into a Buddhist paradise. (The word *sutra* means the words of the Buddha recorded in written form.) Emperor Wu ordered the construction of Buddhist monasteries in each part of China so that *The Great Cloud Sutra* could be read aloud. She issued edicts forbidding the slaughter of animals or the eating of fish, both violations of Greater Vehicle teachings. In 690, after five years as a Tang emperor, she proclaimed a new dynasty named the Zhou, and in 693 she officially proclaimed herself a chakravartin ruler. In 705 she was overthrown in a palace coup, and the Tang dynasty was restored. Documents and portrayals of the time do not indicate that Emperor Wu was particularly aware of being female. Like the female pharaoh Hatshepsut (see Chapter 2), Emperor Wu portrayed herself as a legitimate dynastic ruler.

> **equal-field system**
> The basis of the Tang dynasty tax system as prescribed in the *Tang Code*. Dividing households into nine ranks on the basis of wealth, officials allocated each householder a certain amount of land.

> **Emperor Wu**
> (r. 685–705) The sole woman to rule China as emperor in her own right; she called herself emperor and founded a new dynasty, the Zhou (690–705), that replaced the Tang dynasty until her death in 705, when the Tang dynasty was restored.

The Long Decline of the Tang Dynasty, 755–907

Historians today divide the Tang dynasty into two halves: 618–755 and 755–907. In the first half, the Tang emperors ruled with great success. They enjoyed extensive military victories in Central Asia, unprecedented control over their subjects through the equal-field system, and great internal stability. The first signs of decline came in the early 700s, when tax officials reported insufficient revenues from the equal-field system. In 751, the Tang sent an army deep into Central Asia, to Talas (modern-day Dzhambul, Kazakstan), to fight an army sent by the Abbasid caliph, ruler of much of the Islamic world (see Chapter 9). The Tang army lost the battle, which marked the end of Tang expansion into Central Asia.

The defeat drew little notice in the capital, where all officials were transfixed by the conflict between the emperor and his leading general, who was rumored to be having an affair with the emperor's favorite consort, a court beauty named Precious Consort Yang. In 755 General An Lushan led a mutiny of the army against the emperor. The Tang dynasty suppressed the rebellion in 763 but never regained

Teaching Buddhism in a Confucian Society

Monks frequently told stories to teach ordinary people the tenets of Buddhism. The story of the Indian monk Maudgalyayana (mowd-GAH-lee-yah-yah-nah) survives in a Sanskrit version, composed between 300 B.C.E. and 300 C.E., and a much longer Chinese version from a manuscript dated 921. This story has enormous appeal in China (it is frequently performed as Chinese opera or on television) because it portrays the dilemma of those who wanted to be good Confucian sons as well as good Buddhists. Maudgalyayana may have been filial, but he was unable to fulfill his Confucian obligations as a son because he did not bear a male heir. The Buddhist narrator takes great pains to argue that he can still be a good son because Confucian offerings have no power in a Buddhist underworld.

In the Sanskrit version, Maudgalyayana, one of the Buddha's disciples, realizes that his mother has been reborn in the real world and asks the Buddha to help her to attain nirvana. Maudgalyayana and the Buddha travel to find the mother, who attains nirvana after hearing the Buddha preach.

In the Chinese version, the protagonist retains his Indian name but acts like a typical Chinese son

in every respect. The tale contrasts the behavior of the virtuous, if slightly dim, Maudgalyayana with his mother, who never gave any support to her local monastery and even kept for herself money that her son had asked her to give the monks. As a filial son, he cannot believe her capable of any crime, and he searches through all the different compartments of the Chinese hell to find her. Unrepentant to the very end of the tale, she explains that traditional Confucian offerings to the ancestors have no power in the underworld. Only offerings to the Buddhist order, such as paying monks to copy Buddhist texts, can help to ease her suffering. At the end of the story, the Buddha himself frees her from the underworld, a grim series of hells that do not exist in the Sanskrit original.

Sources: John Strong, "Filial Piety and Buddhism: The Indian Antecedents to a 'Chinese' Problem," in *Traditions in Contact and Change: Selected Proceedings of the XIVth Congress of the International Association for the History of Religions*, ed. Peter Slater and Donald Wiebe (Winnipeg, Man.: Wilfrid Laurier University Press, 1980), p. 180; from *Tun-huang Popular Narratives*, by Victor H. Mair. Copyright © 1983 Cambridge University Press. Reprinted with permission of Cambridge University Press.

Sanskrit Version

From afar, [Maudgalyayana's mother] Bhadrakanya [bud-DRAH-kahn-ee-ya] saw her son, and, as soon as she saw him, she rushed up to him exclaiming, "Ah! At long last I see my little boy!" Thereupon the crowd of people who had assembled said: "He is an aged wandering monk, and she is a young girl—how can she be his mother?" But the Venerable Maha Maudgalyayana replied, "Sirs, these skandhas• of mine were fostered by her; therefore she is my mother."

Then the Blessed One, knowing the disposition, propensity, nature and circumstances of Bhadrakanya, preached a sermon fully penetrating the meaning of the Four Noble Truths. And when Bhadrakanya had heard it, she was brought to the realization of the fruit of entering the stream.

•**skandhas** The five aggregates—form, feelings, perceptions, karmic constituents, and consciousness—which in Buddhism are the basis of the personality.

QUESTIONS FOR ANALYSIS

» *What are the main differences between the Indian and Chinese versions?*

» *How do they portray the fate of the mother after her death?*

» *What is the Chinese underworld like?*

Chinese Version

This is the place where mother and son see
    each other: . . .
Trickles of blood flowed from the seven
    openings of her head.
Fierce flames issued from the inside of his
    mother's mouth,
At every step, metal thorns out of space
    entered her body;
She clanked and clattered like the sound of
    five hundred broken-down chariots,
How could her waist and backbone bear up
    under the strain?
Jailers carrying pitchforks guarded her to the
    left and the right,
Ox-headed guards holding chains stood on
    the east and the west;
Stumbling at every other step, she came
    forward,
Wailing and weeping, Maudgalyayana
    embraced his mother.
Crying, he said: "It was because I am unfilial,
You, dear mother, were innocently caused to
    drop into the triple mire of hell;
Families which accumulate goodness have a
    surplus of blessings,
High Heaven does not destroy in this man-
    ner those who are blameless.
In the old days, mother, you were hand-
    somer than Pan An•,
But now you have suddenly become haggard
    and worn;
I have heard that in hell there is much suffering,
Now, today, I finally realize, 'Ain't it hard,
    ain't it hard.'
Ever since I met with the misfortune of
    father's and your deaths,
I have not been remiss in sacrificing daily at
    your graves;
Mother, I wonder whether or not you have
    been getting any food to eat,
In such a short time, your appearance has
    become completely haggard."
Now that Maudgalyayana's mother had
    heard his words,
"Alas!" she cried, her tears intertwining as
    she struck and grabbed at herself:

• **Pan An**   A well-known attractive man.

"Only yesterday, my son, I was separated
    from you by death.
Who could have known that today we would
    be reunited?
While your mother was alive, she did not
    cultivate blessings,
But she did commit plenty of all the ten evil
    crimes•;
Because I didn't take your advice at that
    time, my son,
My reward is the vastness of this Avici Hell•.
In the old days, I used to live quite
    extravagantly,
Surrounded by fine silk draperies and
    embroidered screens;
How shall I be able to endure these hellish
    torments,
And then to become a hungry ghost for a
    thousand years?
A thousand times, they pluck the tongue
    from out of my mouth,
Hundreds of passes are made over my chest
    with a steel plough;
My bones, joints, tendons, and skin are
    everywhere broken,
They need not trouble with knives and
    swords since I fall to pieces by myself.
In the twinkling of an eye, I die a thousand
    deaths,
But, each time, they shout at me and I come
    back to life;
Those who enter this hell all suffer the same
    hardships.
It doesn't matter whether you are rich or
    poor, lord or servant.
Though you diligently sacrificed to me while
    you were at home,
It only got you a reputation in the village for
    being filial;
Granted that you did sprinkle libations of
    wine upon my grave,
But it would have been better for you to
    copy a single line of sutra."

• **ten evil crimes**   The ten worst offenses according
to Buddhist teachings.
• **Avici Hell**   The lowest Buddhist hell, for those
who had committed the worst offenses.

full control of the provinces. The equal-field system collapsed, and the dynasty was forced to institute new taxes that produced much less revenue.

Although the Tang dynasty was weaker after 755 than before, it remained quite powerful, especially in comparison to its neighbors in Korea, Japan, and Tibet. When, after 838, Ennin traveled around China, he encountered officials who zealously enforced the complex rules governing travelers. He initially tried to follow all the regulations, but when he realized that his hosts might not permit him to stay, he lied to them and said that he had missed a boat home. When ordained, all Buddhist monks took a vow promising to uphold the five precepts, which included not lying (see page 74), but Ennin invoked the Buddhist teaching of expedient means to justify his decision: it was more important for him to study Buddhism than to obey the emperor's regulations. His unusual candor makes his account particularly reliable: historians value a primary source whose author admits to being flawed.

China's wealth struck Ennin early in his travels. Just after his arrival, as he and his companions made their way to Yangzhou, they saw *"boats of the salt bureau laden with salt,"* tied three or four across, and stretching for over 10 miles (16 km). *"This unexpected sight is not easy to record. It was most extraordinary."*[*] The Japanese monk had simply never seen so much salt, a costly commodity, in the same place, and he could not conceive of a government that could control so many boats.

Ennin also visited the Tang capital of Chang'an. With a population of at least 500,000, the city was possibly the largest in the world (its only possible rival was Baghdad, in modern-day Iraq). Chang'an was laid out on a formal grid (see Figure 8.1). The major boulevards stretched 500 feet, or 150 meters, across—the width of

---

[*]Edwin O. Reischauer, trans., *Ennin's Diary: The Record of a Pilgrimage to China in Search of the Law* (New York: The Ronald Press, 1955), p. 20.

FIGURE 8.1 Layout of Chang'an and Heian (Kyoto)   Many rulers in East Asia followed Tang models very closely. Compare the city plans of Chang'an, the Tang capital, and Kyoto, the Heian capital. Both cities had square walls enclosing a gridded street plan, and the imperial palace was located in the north. Unlike Chang'an, Kyoto did not have a city wall or two central markets. (Figure 8.1 from Patricia Ebrey, Anne Walthall, and James Palais, *East Asia*, 2d ed. Copyright © 2009 by Wadsworth, a part of Cengage Learning, Inc. Reproduced by permission, www.cengage.com/permissions.)

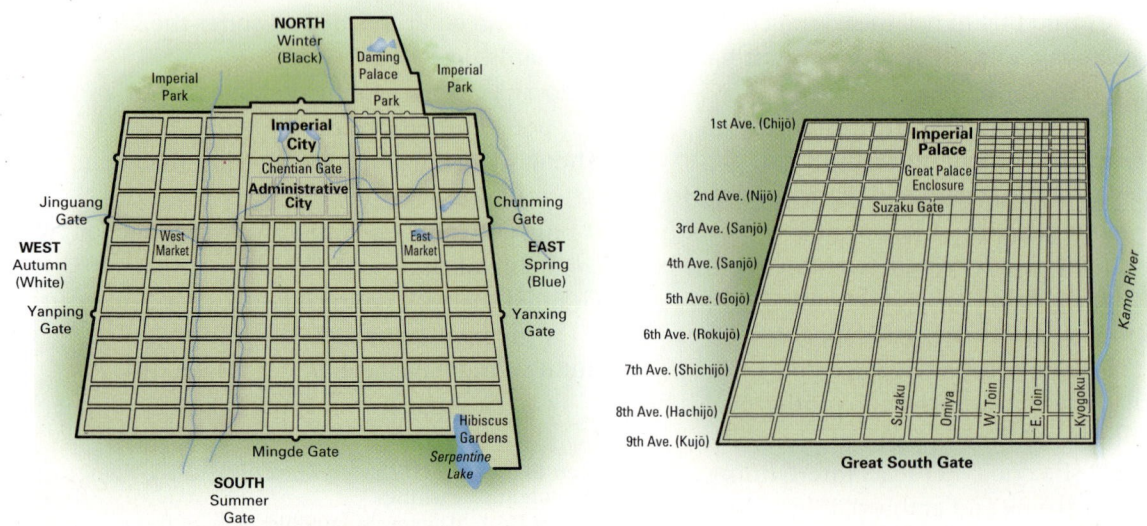

TANG CHANG'AN   HEIAN (KYOTO)

a modern forty-lane highway. The city had two markets, one to the west for mostly foreign goods, one to the east for domestic goods. In 843 Ennin heard about a fire in the Eastern Market that *"burned over four thousand houses in twelve alleyways westward from the gate of the Eastern Market Supervisor. Public and private money and gold, silver, silks, and drugs were all destroyed"*—an indication of both the market's population density and the goods for sale.

Among the goods for sale were printed books and calendars, the product of a new technology that originated in China and altered the course of world history. Ever since the founding of the religion, Buddhists had encouraged their followers to memorize and recite Buddhist teachings. In China devout Buddhists, seeking merit for themselves and their families, paid monks to copy texts. Sometime in the eighth century believers realized that they could make multiple copies of a prayer or picture of a deity if they used **woodblock printing**.

At first Buddhists printed multiple copies of single sheets; later they used glue to connect the pages to form a long book. The world's earliest surviving printed book, from 868, is a Buddhist text, *The Diamond Sutra*. During the Tang dynasty, almost all printing was religious, and Ennin bought both printed books and hand-copied manuscripts throughout his stay in China so that he could bring them to Japan, where books were scarce.

In 841, a new emperor, Emperor Wuzong, came to the throne and tried immediately to increase tax revenues by collecting taxes from the 300,000 tax-exempt monks and nuns. Observing these different anti-Buddhist measures, Ennin commented that the emperor *"hates Buddhism. He does not like to see monks."* The emperor ordered monks and nuns under fifty to leave the monasteries and return to lay life so that they could raise their own tax-paying families. Ennin agreed to return to lay life so that he could return to Japan. He put on non-Buddhist clothes and started to let his shaved head grow hair.

As happy as he was to return home, his main concern was the *"four hampers of writings"* that he had collected in his travels: *"I merely regret that I shall not be able to take with me the holy teachings I have copied."* If Chinese officials caught him with Buddhist books, they would surely confiscate them and possibly prevent him from going home.

Luckily for Ennin, in 846, just before his departure, the emperor Wuzong died. The new emperor permitted monasteries to reopen and monks to return to them.

Woodblock Printing This single sheet of paper is slightly larger than a standard 8½ by 11 sheet of computer paper today. With a drawing of a bodhisattva above and the words of prayers below, it demonstrates how believers used woodblock printing to spread Buddhist teachings. The new medium reproduced line drawings and Chinese characters equally well, and printers could make as many copies as they liked simply by inking the woodblock and pressing individual sheets of paper on it. The more copies they made, they believed, the more merit they earned.

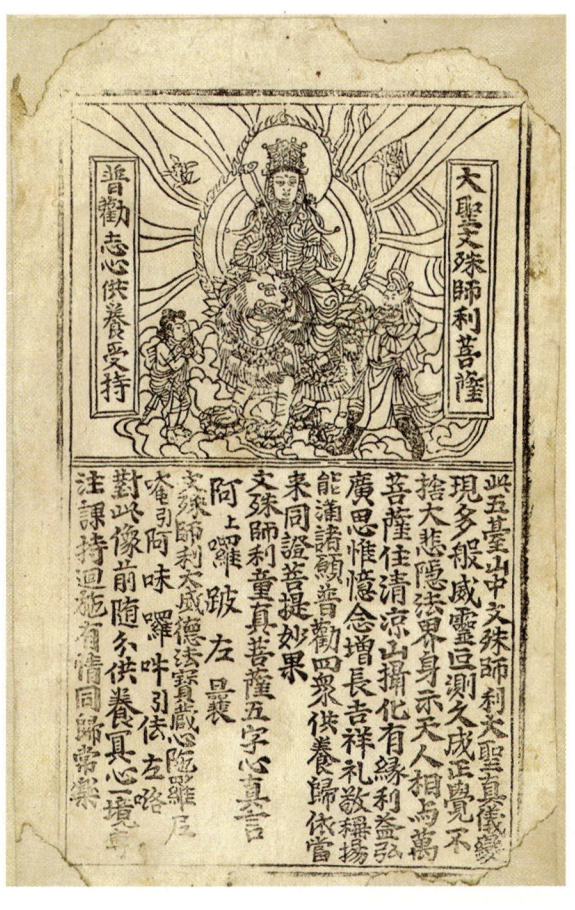

woodblock printing Printing technique developed by the Chinese in which printers made an image in reverse on a block of wood and then pressed the block onto sheets of paper. An efficient way to print texts in Chinese characters.

---

*Edwin O. Reischauer, trans., *Ennin's Diary: The Record of a Pilgrimage to China in Search of the Law* (New York: The Ronald Press, 1955), pp. 333, 343, 363.

Although severe, Wuzong's ban had few lasting effects. Ennin departed with most of his library intact.

After Ennin returned home in 847, no Tang emperor managed to solve the problem of dwindling revenues. In 907, when a rebel deposed the last Tang emperor, who had been held prisoner since 885, China broke apart into different regional dynasties and was not reunited until 960 (see Chapter 12). Even so, the Tang dynasty remained a powerful symbol for its neighbors and subsequent dynasties. It had stayed in power for nearly three centuries and governed more territory than any previous Chinese empire by combining support for Buddhist clergy and monasteries with strong armies, clear laws, and civil service examinations.

The Tibetan Empire, ca. 617–ca. 842

The rulers of the Tibetan plateau were among the first to adopt the Tang model of governance. Most of the Tibetan plateau lies within today's People's Republic of China, but historically it was a borderland not always under Chinese control. Located between the Kunlun Mountains to the north and the Himalayan Mountains to the south, the Tibetan plateau is high, ranging between 13,000 and 15,000 feet (4,000 and 5,000 m). Its extensive grasslands are suitable for raising horses, and barley can be grown in some river valleys. The inhabitants used knotted cords and tallies to keep records because they had no writing system.

Sometime between 620 and 650, during the early years of the Tang, a ruler named **Songtsen Gampo** (srong-btsan sgam-po) (ca. 617–649/650) unified Tibet for the first time and founded the Yarlung dynasty (ca. 617–ca. 842). Hoping to build a strong state, he looked to both India and China for models of governance. In 632, he sent an official to India to study Buddhism, who returned and introduced a new alphabet, based on Sanskrit, that enabled Tibetans to write their language for the first time.

Songtsen Gampo (ca. 617–649/650) Founder of the Yarlung dynasty in Tibet who introduced Buddhism and an alphabet to his subjects.

Songtsen Gampo learned that the Tang emperor had provided Chinese brides for the leaders of several peoples living in western China and demanded that he be given a Chinese bride, too. At first Emperor Taizong refused, but when a Tibetan army nearly defeated the Tang forces in Sichuan, he sent a bride in 641. Later sources credit this woman, the princess of Wencheng (ONE-chuhng) (d. 684), with introducing Buddhism to Tibet and call her a bodhisattva because of her compassion for Tibetans.

Her husband, Songtsen Gampo, realized that he could learn much more from China than Buddhist teachings. He requested that the Tang court send to his court men who could read and write, and he dispatched members of his family to Chang'an to study Chinese. The Chinese sent craftsmen to teach Tibetans how to make silk and paper and how to brew wine. For the first time Songsten Gampo recorded traditional laws on Chinese paper with ink. (See the feature "World History in Today's World: A World with Two Dalai Lamas?")

The Tibetan army took advantage of Tang weakness during the An Lushan rebellion and in 763 briefly invaded the capital of Chang'an before retreating. They conquered territory in western China, which they ruled for nearly a century until 842, when the confederation of peoples who had supported the Yarlung dynasty suddenly broke apart. The Tibetan experience demonstrates the utility of the Sui/Tang model of governance for a people in the early stages of state formation, and subsequent Tibetan dynasties periodically returned to it.

A World with Two Dalai Lamas?

The Dalai Lama, perhaps the most famous Buddhist teacher in the world, is the spiritual leader of Tibet's 6 million Buddhists. Tibetan Buddhists believe that he is the manifestation of Avalokiteshvara (whose Tibetan name is Chenrezig), the bodhisattva of compassion and patron saint of Tibet. Born in Tibet in 1935, the current Dalai Lama, His Holiness Tenzin Gyatso, was identified as the new Dalai Lama when he was three years old.

Following the traditional process, senior monks searched for children born near the time the previous Dalai Lama had died. These monks showed many children the possessions of the deceased Dalai Lama alongside other items that had not belonged to him. Tenzin Gyatso successfully identified the previous Dalai Lama's possessions, crying out loud "It's mine, it's mine." This and other indications persuaded the search team that the child was indeed the reincarnation of the deceased Dalai Lama, and Tenzin Gyatso left his parents to live in a local monastery and study Buddhism. In 1940 he traveled to Lhasa, the Tibetan capital, where he was formally named the spiritual leader of Tibet at a ritual in the Potala Palace. In 1959, when the People's Republic of China established direct administration of the region, the Dalai Lama left Tibet and has since lived in exile in Dharamsala, India, along with several thousand other Tibetans.

How will the next Dalai Lama be chosen? The Dalai Lama has advocated changing the traditional process so that someone who does not live in Tibet—perhaps even a non-Tibetan—could succeed him. Adamantly opposed to this proposal, the Chinese officials who govern Tibet argue that the next Dalai Lama should be chosen following the traditional process. Many observers believe that the Tibetan exile community and the Chinese government will each choose their own candidate, with the result that two men will claim to be the legitimate successor of the Dalai Lama.

As is true of the Dalai Lama, certain men head individual schools of Buddhists, but no single person claims to lead all the world's Buddhists. Scholars of religion are not certain how to calculate the total number of Buddhists but estimate it at 350 million, with 100 million in China and 90 million in Japan. While many modern Chinese or Japanese, if asked, may identify themselves as Buddhists, they visit Buddhist temples only rarely and devote less time to religious devotion than do Tibetan Buddhists.

Sources: *The New York Times*; www.dalailama.com; www.adherents.com.

Buddhism and the Tang Blueprint for Rule in Korea and Japan, to 1000

Because of the Han dynasty military garrisons in Korea, Koreans had some contact with China as early as the Qin and Han dynasties (see Chapter 4), while their neighbors to the east in Japan, who were surrounded by water, did not. The Japanese learned about many Chinese innovations from the Koreans.

In Korea and Japan, as in Tibet, rulers adopted the Tang blueprint for rule, including Buddhism, because they hoped to match the accomplishments (particularly the military success) of the Tang dynasty. Certain elements of the blueprint, like the patronage of Buddhism, were easy for them to adopt, but others, like the equal-field system, did not suit either Korean or Japanese society.

Buddhism and Regional Kingdoms in Korea

Three Kingdoms period
The period of Korean history from 313 to 668 when the Koguryo, Paekche, and Silla kingdoms all fought for control of the Korean peninsula and exercised profound cultural influence on Japan.

The northern part of the Korean peninsula remained under Chinese dominance until 313, when the king of the northern Koguryo (KOH-guh-ree-oh) region overthrew the last Chinese ruler. Because the Chinese presence had been limited to military garrisons, there was little lasting influence.

During this time, Korea was divided into different small chiefdoms on the verge of becoming states (see Map 8.2). The three most important ones were Koguryo (traditionally 37 B.C.E.–668 C.E.), Paekche (PECK-jeh; traditionally 18 B.C.E.–660 C.E.), and Silla (SHE-luh; traditionally 57 B.C.E.–935 C.E.). These "traditional" dates are based on much later legends, not contemporary evidence, which indicates that the three states largely coalesced after 300. The **Three Kingdoms period** started in 313, when the Koguryo kingdom expelled the last Chinese armies, and lasted until 668, when the Korean peninsula was unified for the first time.

After 300, these three kingdoms constantly vied with each other for territory and influence. Their campaigns extended all the way to the Japanese archipelago, where the Korean armies introduced new iron weapons like swords and spear points. In the centuries before gunpowder, heavy armor was a powerful military technology that protected soldiers from flying arrows and spears.

The Korean rulers adopted crucial elements of the Tang blueprint for rule during the Three Kingdoms period. They learned to read and write using Chinese characters and read them aloud using Korean pronunciation. Adopting Chinese-style written laws, they established Confucian academies where students could study Chinese characters, Confucian classics, the histories, and different philosophical works in Chinese. They also introduced Buddhism.

Before the adoption of Buddhism, the residents of the Korean peninsula prayed to local deities or nature spirits for good health and good harvests. The vast majority lived in small agricultural villages and grew rice. The ruling families of the Koguryo and Paekche kingdoms adopted Buddhism in the 370s and 380s for the same reasons: their rulers hoped to strengthen their dynasties and welcomed Buddhist missionaries from China. Like Chinese rulers, the Koguryo and Paekche kings combined patronage for Buddhism with support for Confucian education.

The circumstances accompanying the adoption of Buddhism by the **Silla** royal house illustrate how divided many Koreans were about the new religion. King Pophung (r. 514–540), whose name means "King who promoted the Dharma," wanted to patronize Buddhism but feared the opposition of powerful families who had passed laws against it.

MAP 8.2 Korea and Japan, ca. 550 The Japanese island of Kyushu lies some 150 miles (240 km) from the Korean peninsula, and the island of Tsushima provided a convenient stepping stone to the Japanese archipelago for those fleeing the warfare on the Korean peninsula. The Korean migrants introduced their social structure (with its bone-rank system) and Buddhism to Japan. (© Cengage Learning)

Sometime around 527, he persuaded one of his courtiers to build a shrine to the Buddha. However, since such activity was banned, the king had no choice but to order the courtier's beheading. The king and his subject prayed for a miracle. An early history of Korea describes the moment of execution: *"Down came the sword on the monk's neck, and up flew his head spouting blood as white as milk."* The miracle, we are told, silenced the opposition, and Silla became Buddhist in that year.[*]

By the middle of the sixth century, all three Korean kingdoms had adopted pro-Buddhist policies, and all sent government officials and monks to China, then divided into regional kingdoms, to learn how to govern. The three ruling dynasties built Buddhist monasteries in major cities and in the countryside, but ordinary people continued to worship the same local deities they had in pre-Buddhist times.

From 598 into the 640s, the Sui and Tang dynasties led several attacks on the Korean peninsula, all unsuccessful. In 660 the Silla kingdom allied with the Tang dynasty in hopes of defeating the Koguryo and Paekche kingdoms. Paekche was allied with the Japanese, and the Silla-Tang armies defeated the Paekche forces first in 660 and then in a major naval battle at Paekchon River in 663. The combined Silla-Tang forces did not reach Japan, but the defeat of Japan's navy—the greatest before 1600—caused the loss of four hundred Japanese ships and several thousand Japanese sailors.

A Formidable Korean Warrior This mounted cavalry soldier, a ceramic figurine from the Korean peninsula made in the fifth or sixth century C.E., displays the most up-to-date weaponry and armor of his time. Observe his saddle, the armor covering his legs (which consists of small plates of iron sewn together in parallel rows), and, in particular, the stirrups, a brand-new innovation that gave riders much greater control over their mounts. (Courtesy, National Museum of Korea)

After defeating the Paekche, the Silla-Tang armies conquered the Koguryo dynasty. By 675 the Silla forces had pushed Tang armies back to the northern edges of the Korean peninsula. This victory unified the Korean peninsula for the first time under Korean rule and ushered in a period of stability that lasted for two and a half centuries. Silla kings offered different types of support to Buddhism, with several following the example of Ashoka and the Sui founder in building pagodas throughout their kingdom.

Some elements of the Tang blueprint were not appropriate for the highly stratified Korean society of the seventh and eighth centuries. The **bone-rank system** classed all Korean families into one of seven categories. The true-bone classification was reserved for the highest-born aristocratic

---

[*]Ilyon, *Samguk Yusa: Legends and History of the Three Kingdoms of Ancient Korea,* trans. Tae-Hung Ha and Grafton K. Mintz (Seoul: Yonsei University Press, 1972), p. 188.

Silla
Korean kingdom that adopted Buddhism and united with the Tang dynasty in 660 to defeat the Koguryo and Paekche kingdoms, unifying Korea for the first time in 668.

bone-rank system
Korean social ranking system used by the Silla dynasty that divided Korean families into seven different categories, with kings coming from only the top group.

families, which included those eligible to be king. Below them were six other ranks in descending order.

The Silla rulers found that the redistribution of land every three years according to the equal-field system was not workable and that they could govern better if they granted entire villages forever to members of the true-bone families. In turn, the true-bone families paid the salaries of government officials, who then appointed other officials from the true-bone families. Civil service examinations became an important element of Korean society, but, unlike in Tang China, the authorities limited the exams to candidates from the highest-ranking families.

The Silla kingdom entered a period of decline after 780. From that time on, different branches of the royal family fought each other for control of the throne, and no one managed to rule for long.

The Emergence of Japan

Japan is an island chain, or archipelago, of four large islands and many smaller ones. Like Korea, which is only 150 miles (240 km) away, Japan had no indigenous writing system, so archaeologists must piece together the island's early history from archaeological materials and later sources like the *Chronicle of Japan* (*Nihon shoki*) (knee-HOHN SHOW-kee), a year-by-year account written in 720. The royal Yamato (YAH-mah-toe) house, the *Chronicle* claims, was directly descended from the sun-goddess Amaterasu (AH-mah-TAY-rah-suh). The indigenous religion of Japan, called Shinto (SHIN-toe), included the worship of different spirits of trees, streams, and mountains, as well as deceased rulers.

In the 300s and 400s, multiple chieftains, including the Yamato clan, ruled the different regions of Japan. Cultural influence from Korea to Japan accelerated in the fifth and sixth centuries, when many Koreans fled the political instability of the disunited peninsula to settle in the relative peace of Japan. In addition to military practices, the Korean refugees introduced techniques of governance relying on Chinese characters, law codes, and Buddhist teachings. Affecting all social groups, these changes had far-reaching effects.

The Yamato kings gave titles modeled on the Korean bone-rank system to powerful Japanese clans who were their military allies. They also allied with the Korean kingdom of Paekche against the Silla kingdom, which was geographically closest and so posed the greatest threat to Japan. Once the Paekche royal house adopted Buddhism, it began to pressure its clients, the Yamato clan, to follow suit. In 538, the Paekche ambassador brought a gift of Buddhist texts and images for the ruler of Japan, but the most powerful Japanese families hesitated to support the new religion. The conflict among supporters and opponents of Buddhism lasted for nearly fifty years, during which the Paekche rulers continued to send gifts of Buddhist writings, monks, and nuns.

The main supporters of Buddhism in Japan were the **Soga clan**, who were most likely of Korean ancestry and who supplied the Yamato rulers with wives. In 587, armed conflict broke out between the clans opposed to Buddhism and the Soga family, led by the thirteen-year-old prince Shotoku (SHOW-toh-ku) (574–622), too young to govern in his own right, and his mother, the regent. Prince Shotoku vowed that if the Soga clan was victorious, the government would support Buddhism. The pro-Buddhist forces won, and the Japanese court converted to Buddhism in 587.

Soga clan
Powerful Japanese family of Korean descent that ruled in conjunction with the Yamato clan from 587 to 645; introduced Buddhism to Japan.

Aware of the founding of the Sui dynasty and the subsequent reunification of China, Prince Shotoku sent the first Japanese delegation to China in 600. A large mission could have as many as five hundred participants, including officials, Buddhist monks, students, and translators. Some Japanese stayed in China for as long as thirty years before they returned home to teach their countrymen what they had learned. Three other missions went before the collapse of the Sui and the founding of the Tang dynasty in 618.

Acutely aware of China's military campaigns in Korea, successive Japanese rulers made several attempts to implement the Tang blueprint for rule. They sought to strengthen their country and also to enhance their own rule, because a Chinese-style emperor had much more power than a chieftain. In 645 the emperor announced that he would adopt the equal-field system and redistribute land every six years (rather than every three years as in the *Tang Code*), but he did not actually carry out these policies.

The 663 defeat of their Paekche allies galvanized the Japanese rulers, who realized that, if they did not adopt Chinese-style reforms, they could easily suffer the same fate. In 701, another Japanese ruler made an attempt to enforce the Tang blueprint for rule: this time he successfully issued a written law code, assigned rice-paddy land to individual households, and redistributed land every six years.

The changing design of Japanese capitals clearly illustrates the extent of Chinese influence. Before 710 the Japanese had occupied thirty-six capitals in 250 years. Houses were made with thatched roofs and wooden pillars buried directly in the dirt, where they rotted after only a few years. Every time a ruler died,

Horyuji Pagoda, Nara, Japan Built before 794, this five-story pagoda is possibly one of the oldest wooden buildings in the world. Like the stupa at the Indian site of Sanchi, it was built to hold relics of the Buddha. Not certain how the building survived multiple earthquakes without sustaining any damage, architects speculate that the central pillar is not directly connected to the ground below, allowing it to float slightly above the ground. (Robert Harding World Imagery/Alamy)

the new ruler shifted the capital, partially to escape the ghost of the deceased emperor. After 710 the Japanese adopted Chinese building practices, using tiled roofs and stone bases for timber columns so that they did not rot. They built a new capital at Nara, their first Chinese-style city with gridded streets, walls, and gates, which gives its name to the Nara period (710–784). Then in 784, they shifted the capital to modern Kyoto, where it remained for over one thousand years. Kyoto was called Heian (HEY-on), and the Heian period lasted from 784 to 1185 (see Figure 8.1, page 216).

Contact with China brought genuine risks, too. Starting in the 720s and then accelerating rapidly in the 730s, multiple smallpox epidemics broke out. Commentators knew that the disease originated in China and Korea. In earlier centuries Japan's population was dispersed over a wide area, so epidemic diseases could not spread. But the building of Chinese-style cities and growing population density resulting from the introduction of rice agriculture created the optimal conditions for epidemics. Japan's population reached around 5 million in the year 700, and some 25 percent of its people died in the epidemics.

In 749 a woman named Koken ascended to the throne when her father died of smallpox, and she herself died in 770 of the same disease. A devout Buddhist who became a nun, Empress Koken decided to generate Buddhist merit by printing 1 million copies of a Buddhist prayer (pronounced in Sanskrit but written in Chinese characters) and placing each of the prayers in a small wooden pagoda. She buried 100,000 pagodas each in ten different monasteries. Her act illustrates both the lasting power of the chakravartin ideal and the appeal of the brand-new technology of woodblock printing. She was the eighth woman to rule Japan as emperor, but when she died, the imperial family decided not to allow any more woman emperors because of persistent rumors of her sexual involvement with a Buddhist monk.

In the years after 800, the Japanese gradually departed from the Tang blueprint for rule. Although the *Tang Code* prescribed a militia staffed by farmer-soldiers who left their fields to fight part-time in battle, the emperor and his courtiers preferred to hire full-time bodyguards, who were the precursors of the samurai warriors. The government no longer redistributed land every six years; instead powerful families amassed large, permanent estates. The vast majority of the Japanese population continued to farm, while only a tiny minority, numbering in the thousands, lived in the capital and served the emperor as courtiers.

We know much more about the courtiers than any other group in early Japan because they produced almost all surviving records. Like them, Ennin wrote entirely in Chinese characters, which he pronounced in Japanese. During his travels in China, because he could not speak Chinese, he wrote everything down in Chinese characters. He called this "brush-talking."

Yet because Japanese, like Korean, was in a different language family, Chinese characters did not capture the full meaning of Japanese. In the ninth century, at the same time that Ennin was brush-talking in China, the Japanese developed an alphabet, called **kana** (KAH-nah), that allowed them to write Japanese words as they were pronounced.

kana
An alphabet developed in the ninth century that allowed the Japanese to write the pronunciation of words in Japanese.

In 1000, a Japanese woman named Murasaki Shikibu (MOO-rah-sock-ee SHE-key-boo) used kana to write one of the world's most important works of literature, *The Tale of Genji*, which some view as the world's first novel. The book relates the experiences of a young prince as he grows up. Lady Murasaki spent her entire life at court, and her novel reflects the complex system of etiquette that had developed among the Japanese aristocracy. For example, lovers in Genji choose sheets of paper from multiple shades, each with its own significance, before writing notes to each other. While the highest members of Japan's aristocracy could read and write—men using both Chinese characters and kana and women more often only kana—the vast majority of their countrymen remained illiterate.

By 1000, Japan, like Korea, had joined a larger East Asian cultural realm, in which people read and wrote Chinese characters and ate with chopsticks as the Chinese did. Although its rulers were predominantly Buddhist, they supported Confucian education, and their capital looked like Chang'an even if it was much smaller. After a brief period of using the *Tang Code* as a model of governance, the Japanese emperors abandoned the equal-field system and civil service exams in favor of a more Japanese system in which the emperor and his courtiers lived in the capital while they farmed out all military tasks to full-time warriors.

CONTEXT AND CONNECTIONS

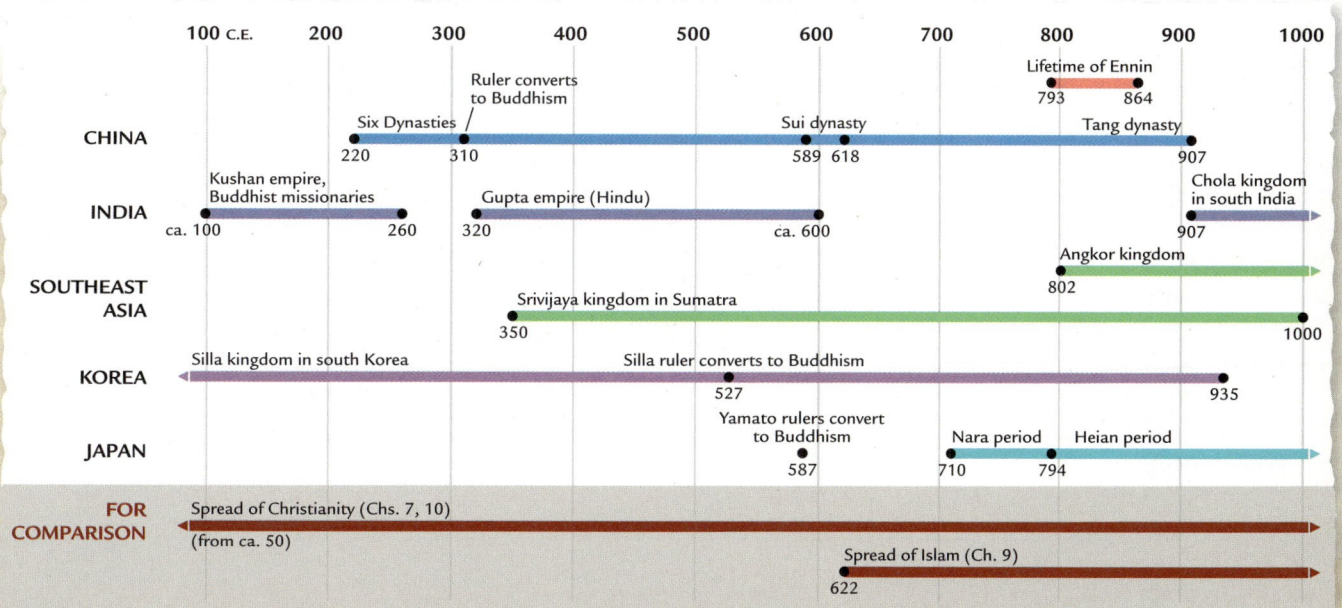

© Cengage Learning

The Place of Buddhism and Hinduism in World History

In the year 100, the only Buddhists in the world lived in India and Sri Lanka; by the year 1000, Buddhist teachings had spread throughout the entire region encompassing India, coastal and inland Southeast Asia, China, Tibet, Korea, and Japan. When the Japanese monk Ennin traveled in China between 838 and 847, he encountered Buddhist monks from north and south India, Sri Lanka, Central Asia, Japan, Korea, and, of course, China. Between 380 and 400, the Roman woman Egeria had traveled as a pilgrim to Jerusalem to see where Jesus had lived and to visit monasteries in Turkey (see Chapter 7). Ennin's reasons for going on pilgrimage differed. His purpose was not to see where the Buddha had lived, but to study and obtain books so that he could understand complex Buddhist teachings more completely.

Chinese monasteries hosted Indian monks who taught Sanskrit, the language of many texts from India, but, as the centuries passed, more and more Buddhist texts were translated into Chinese. A beginning student of Sanskrit, Ennin read these texts in Chinese. Like Greek and Latin in the Christian world, Sanskrit and Chinese were spoken and written throughout the Buddhist world. Ennin found that he could brush-talk by writing Chinese characters with almost every Buddhist he met.

Buddhism became a major world religion during the same centuries as Christianity did. No single event in Buddhist history marked a turning point like the Edict of Milan in 313 or the 380 decree making Christianity the official religion of the Roman empire (see Chapter 7). Instead, drawn by the chakravartin ideal, different Asian rulers made a series of individual decisions to support Buddhism.

First, sometime around 120, Kanishka, the Kushan ruler of north India, launched a missionary movement to introduce the teachings of Greater Vehicle Buddhism to Central Asia and China. Then, during the fourth and sixth centuries, rulers in different places converted to Buddhism: the Xiongnu leader Shi Le in north China, the rulers of the three Korean kingdoms of Koguryo, Silla, and Paekche, and the Yamato rulers of Japan. After the Sui emperor reunified the Chinese empire in 589, he conducted simultaneous rituals in monasteries to show the depth of his support for Buddhism.

Many of these events involved an element of belief, as individual rulers embraced Buddhist teachings, and some—like the Empress Koken of Japan—even became Buddhist nuns or monks. But these decisions also turned on nonreligious elements. The Tang blueprint for rule, as written in the *Tang Code*, offered a guide for the heads of smaller, weaker states who wished to become rulers as powerful as the Tang emperor. Rulers in Korea, Tibet, and Japan all issued local versions of the *Tang Code*.

In India, as more rulers endowed Hindu temples and patronized Brahmin priests, Hinduism gained in importance as Buddhism declined. Southeast Asian rulers combined both Hindu and Buddhist elements to sponsor magnificent religious monuments like Angkor Wat in Cambodia.

At the time of Ennin's visit, Buddhism had become so influential that the Chinese Emperor Wuzong ordered thousands of monks and nuns, who did not pay taxes, to return to lay life and generate income for his revenue-starved dynasty. On his death in 846, his successor immediately overturned all of his hostile measures, and Ennin was able to retrieve the books he cared about so deeply and take them to Japan.

By the year 1000, Buddhism, Hinduism, and Christianity had all spread far beyond the lands of their origin. Each is one of the largest religions in the world today (see "World History in Today's World," Chapter 7), and many Hindus and Buddhists live in Asia. In the next chapter we will consider yet another world religion that had spread by 1000 and that would have an equally profound impact on world history: Islam.

Voyages on the Web: Ennin

The Voyages Map App follows the traveler's journeys using interactive study tools, including 360-degree panoramic views of historic sites, zoomable maps, audio summaries, flash cards, and quizzes.

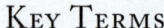

Key Terms

Ennin (198)
chakravartin (200)
Silk Routes (200)
Hinduism (200)
bodhisattva (201)
Gupta dynasty (202)
bhakti (203)

Angkor dynasty (210)
Fotudeng (211)
Tang dynasty (212)
equal-field system (213)
Emperor Wu (213)
woodblock printing (217)
Songtsen Gampo (218)

Three Kingdoms period (220)
Silla (220)
bone-rank system (221)
Soga clan (222)
kana (224)

For Further Reference

Ebrey, Patricia Buckley, Anne Walthall, and James B. Palais. *East Asia: A Cultural, Social, and Political History*. 2d ed. Boston: Wadsworth/Cengage Learning, 2009.

Farris, William Wayne. "Ancient Japan's Korean Connection." In *Sacred Texts and Buried Treasures: Issues in the Historical Archaeology of Ancient Japan*. Honolulu: University of Hawai'i Press, 1998, pp. 55–122.

Farris, William Wayne. *Japan to 1600: A Social and Economic History*. Honolulu: University of Hawai'i Press, 2009.

Hall, Kenneth R. *A History of Early Southeast Asia: Maritime Trade and Societal Development, 100–1500*. Lanham, Md.: Rowman and Littlefield, 2011.

Hansen, Valerie. *The Open Empire: A History of China to 1600*. New York: Norton, 2000.

Heng Chye Kiang. *Cities of Aristocrats and Bureaucrats*. Honolulu: University of Hawai'i Press, 1999.

Holcombe, Charles. *A History of East Asia*. New York: Cambridge University Press, 2011.

Kapstein, Matthew. *The Tibetan Assimilation of Buddhism: Conversion, Contestation, and Memory*. New York: Oxford University Press, 2000.

Keown, Damien. *Buddhism: A Very Short Introduction*. New York: Oxford University Press, 1996.

Krahl, Regina. *Shipwrecked: Tang Treasures and Monsoon Winds*. Washington, D.C.: Smithsonian Books, 2011.

Ray, Himanshu Prabha. "The Axial Age in Asia: The Archaeology of Buddhism (500 BC to AD 500)." In *Archaeology of Asia*, Miriam T. Stark, ed. Malden, Mass.: Blackwell, 2006, pp. 303–323.

Reischauer, Edwin O., trans. *Ennin's Diary: The Record of a Pilgrimage to China in Search of the Law*. New York: The Ronald Press, 1955.

Thapar, Romila. *Early India from the Origins to AD 1300*. Berkeley: University of California Press, 2003.

Washizuka, Hiromitsu, et al. *Transmitting the Forms of Divinity: Early Buddhist Art from Korea and Japan*. New York: Japan Society, 2003.

Worrall, Simon. "Made in China." *National Geographic Magazine* (June 2009): 112–123.

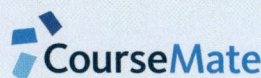 **CourseMate**

Go to the CourseMate website at **www.cengagebrain.com** for additional study tools and review materials—including audio and video clips—for this chapter.

9

Islamic Empires of Western Asia and Africa, 600–1258

Khaizuran (ca. 739–789) grew up as a slave girl but became the favored wife of the supreme religious and political leader of the Islamic world, the caliph Mahdi (MAH-dee), who reigned from 775 to 785 as the third ruler of the Abbasid (ah-BAHS-sid) caliphate (750–1258). As the wife of Mahdi and the mother of the caliph who succeeded him, Khaizuran (HAY-zuh-rahn) played an active role in court politics. A slave dealer brought her, while still a teenager, to Mecca, where she met Mahdi's father. He had come to perform the hajj pilgrimage, the religious obligation of all Muslims. When he inquired where she was from, she said:

Abbasid Singing Girl
(Digital Image © 2012 Museum Associates/ LACMA. Licensed by Art Resource, NY)

orn at Mecca and brought up at Jurash (in the Yaman).[*]

---

*Nabia Abbott, *Two Queens of Baghdad: Mother and Wife of Harun al-Rashid* (London: Al Saqi Books, 1986, reprint of 1946 original), p. 26, citing Jahiz (pseud.), *Kitab al-Mahasin wa Al-Addad,* ed. van Vloten (Leiden: E. J. Brill, 1898), pp. 232–233.

This is one of the few statements by Khaizuran that is preserved in the written record. Of course we would like to know more, but she left no writings of her own. The written record almost always says more about men than about women, and more about the prominent and the literate than about the ordinary and the illiterate. To understand the experience of everyone in a society, historians must exercise great ingenuity in using the evidence at hand. Khaizuran provides a rare opportunity to study the life of an ordinary Muslim woman who rose to become a leader in her own right.

The Travels of Khaizuran

- ← Khaizuran's journeys
- — Zubaydah's Road
- Islamic expansion under Muhammad, 622–632
- Islamic expansion, 632–661
- Expansion under Umayyad Caliphate, 661–750
- Abbasid Caliphate under Harun al-Rashid, 786–809

Khaizuran is sold as a slave and taken to Baghdad, 758 or 762.

Khaizuran leaves Baghdad on hajj pilgrimage, 776 and 778.

Khaizuran travels to Mecca, 750s.

© Cengage Learning

Join this chapter's traveler on "Voyages," an interactive tour of historic sites and events:
www.cengagebrain.com

In its support for Islam, the Abbasid dynasty played a role in world history similar to that of the Roman empire, which patronized Christianity (see Chapter 7), and the Tang dynasty in China, which supported Buddhism (see Chapter 8). Under the Abbasids, Islam became a world religion with millions of adherents in Africa, Europe, and Asia. At the peak of their power, around the year 800, the Abbasids governed some 35 or 40 million people living in North Africa and Southwest Asia.[1]

Khaizuran
Slave girl (ca. 739–789) who became the wife of the caliph Mahdi (r. 775–785), the third ruler of the Abbasid caliphate. Khaizuran played an active role in court politics.

Muhammad
(ca. 570–632) Believed by Muslims to be the last prophet who received God's revelations directly from the angel Gabriel. The first leader of the Muslim community.

But the Abbasid empire differed in a crucial way from either the Roman or the Tang empire. When the Roman emperor Constantine issued the Edict of Milan in 313, he recognized a religion already popular among his subjects. And when the early Tang emperors supported Buddhism, they did so because many Chinese had come to embrace Buddhism since its entry into China in the first century C.E. Yet the Roman and Tang emperors could withdraw their support for these religions, and they sometimes did.

In contrast, the Abbasid rulers were religious leaders who claimed a familial relationship with the prophet **Muhammad** (ca. 570–632) through his uncle Abbas (ah-BAHS). They could not withdraw their support from the Islamic religious community because they headed that very religious community. At the same time, they were also political leaders; the founder of the Abbasid dynasty seized power from the Umayyad (oo-MY-uhd) dynasty in 750. Even when the Abbasid caliphs no longer served as political leaders, they retained their religious role. Others could be king, but the Abbasids had a unique claim to being caliph.

This chapter will examine the history of Islam, from the first revelations received by Muhammad to the final collapse of the Abbasid empire in 1258.

Focus Questions

» *Who was the prophet Muhammad, and what were his main teachings?*

» *Between Muhammad's death in 632 and the founding of the Abba-sid caliphate in 750, what were the different ways that the Islamic community chose the new caliph?*

» *Which economic, political, and social forces held the many peoples and territories of the Abbasid caliphate together?*

» *After the fragmentation of the Abbasid empire in 945, which cul-tural practices, technologies, and customs held Islamic believers in different regions together?*

The Origins of Islam and the First Caliphs, 610–750

caliph
Literally "successor." Before 945, the caliph was the successor to Muhammad and the supreme political and religious leader of the Islamic world. After 945, the caliph had no political power but served as the religious leader of all Muslims.

Muhammad began to preach sometime around 613 and won a large following among the residents of the Arabian peninsula before his death in 632. The man who succeeded to the leadership of the Islamic religious community was called the **caliph** (KAY-lif), literally "successor." The caliph exercised political authority because the Muslim religious community was also a state, complete with its own government and a powerful army that conquered many neighboring regions. The first four caliphs were chosen from different clans on the basis of their ties to Muhammad, but after 661 all the caliphs came from a single clan, or dynasty, the Umayyads, who governed until 750.

The Life and Teachings of Muhammad, ca. 570–632

Muhammad was born into a family of merchants sometime around 570 in Mecca, a trading community in the Arabian peninsula far from any major urban center. At the time of his birth, the two major powers of the Mediterranean world were the Byzantine empire (see Chapter 10) and the Sasanian empire of the Persians (see Chapter 6).

On the southern edge of the two empires lay the Arabian peninsula, which consisted largely of desert punctuated by small oases. Traders traveling from Syria to Yemen frequently stopped at the few urban settlements, including Mecca and Medina, near the coast of the Red Sea. The local peoples spoke Arabic.

The population was divided between urban residents and the nomadic residents of the desert, called Bedouins (BED-dwins). The Bedouins moved from place to place, tending their flocks of sheep, horses, and camels, and were divided into different clans. Even though they no longer followed a nomadic way of life, many city people maintained a strong clan identity. Extensive trade networks connected the Arabian peninsula with Palestine and Syria, and both Jews and Christians lived in its urban centers.

All Arabs, whether nomadic or urban, worshiped protective deities that resided in an individual tree, a group of trees, or sometimes a rock with an unusual shape. One of the most revered objects was a large black rock in a cube-shaped shrine, called the Kaaba (KAH-buh), at Mecca, which was associated with Abraham, the patriarch described in the Hebrew Bible. In the 400s, one Egyptian observer, himself possibly an Arab, wrote that the Arabs believed they were descended from Abraham's son Ishmael (not Isaac, the man the Jews believed to be their ancestor) and that they refrained from eating pork. These monotheists were neither Jews nor Christians.[2]

While in his forties and already a wealthy merchant, Muhammad had a series of visions in which he saw a figure. Muslims believe that God spoke to Muhammad through the angel Gabriel, after which Muhammad called on everyone to submit to God. The religion founded on belief in this event is called Islam, meaning "submission" or "surrender." The Arabic word *allah* means "the god" and, by extension, "God." Early Muslims had contact with Jews, and their understanding of God shared much with Jewish and Christian conceptions.

Muslims do not call Muhammad the founder of Islam because God's teachings, they believe, are timeless. Muhammad taught that his predecessors included all the Hebrew prophets from the Hebrew Bible as well as Jesus and his disciples. Muslims consider Muhammad the last messenger of God, however, and historians place the beginning date for Islam in the 610s because no one thought of himself or herself as Muslim before Muhammad received his revelations. Muhammad's earliest followers came from his immediate family: his wife Khadijah (kah-DEE-juh) and his cousin Ali, whom he had raised since early childhood.

Unlike the existing religion of Arabia, but like Christianity and Judaism, Islam was monotheistic; Muhammad preached that his followers should worship only one God. He also stressed the role of individual choice: each person had the power to decide to worship God or to turn away from God. Those who submitted to God became the first Muslims. Men who converted to Islam had to undergo circumcision, a practice already widespread throughout the Arabian peninsula.

Islam developed within the context of Bedouin society, in which men were charged with protecting the honor of their wives and daughters. Accordingly, women often assumed a subordinate role in Islam. In Bedouin society, a man could repudiate his wife by saying "I divorce you" three times. Although women could not repudiate their husbands in the same way, they could divorce an impotent man.

Although Muhammad recognized the traditional right of men to repudiate their wives, he introduced several measures aimed at improving the status of women. For example, he limited the number of wives a man could take to four. His supporters explained that Islamic marriage offered this limited number of secondary wives far more legal protection than before Muhammad's reforms. He also banned the Bedouin practice of female infanticide. Finally, he instructed his

Certificate of Pilgrimage to Mecca
Islamic artists often ornamented manuscripts, tiles, and paintings with passages from the Quran. This document, written on paper, testifies that the bearer completed the pilgrimage to Mecca in 1207 and thus fulfilled the Fifth Pillar of Islam. Arabic reads from right to left; the red lines and dots guide the reader's pronunciation. (The Art Archive at Art Resource, NY)

female relatives to veil themselves when receiving visitors. Although many in the modern world think the veiling of women an exclusively Islamic practice, women in various societies in the ancient world, including Greeks, Mesopotamians, and Arabs, wore veils as a sign of high station.

Feuding among different clans was a constant problem in Bedouin society. In 620, a group of non-kinsmen from Medina, a city 215 miles (346 km) to the north, pledged to follow Muhammad's teachings in hopes of ending the feuding. Because certain clan leaders of Mecca had become increasingly hostile to Islam, even threatening to kill Muhammad, in 622 Muhammad and his followers moved to Medina. Everyone who submitted to God and accepted Muhammad as his messenger became a member of the umma (UM-muh), the community of Islamic believers.

This migration, called the *hijrah* (HIJ-ruh), marked a major turning point in Islam. All dates in the Islamic calendar are calculated in the year of the hijrah (Anno Hegirae, a Latin term usually abbreviated A.H.). (Because of the differences in the calendars, Islamic years often straddle two Common Era years. For example, 165 A.H. = 781–782 C.E.) The Islamic calendar calculated each year as twelve lunar months of 29.5 days each, with no adjustment for the remaining days (each solar year has 365.25 days). As a result, each day falls at a slightly different time each calendar year. For example, the first day of the month of Ramadan, when Muslims fast during daytime, falls ten or eleven days earlier than it did the previous year.

Muhammad began life as a merchant, became a religious prophet in middle age, and assumed the duties of a general at the end of his life. In 624, Muhammad and his followers fought their first battle against the residents of Mecca. Muhammad said that he had received revelations that holy war, whose object was the expansion of Islam—or its defense—was justified. He used the word **jihad** (GEE-hahd) to mean struggle or fight in military campaigns against non-Muslims. (In addition to its basic meaning of holy war, modern Muslims also use the term in a more spiritual or moral sense to indicate an individual's striving to fulfill all the teachings of Islam.)

In 630, Muhammad's troops conquered Mecca and removed all tribal images from the pilgrimage center at the Kaaba. Muhammad became ruler of the region and exercised his authority by adjudicating among feuding clans. The clans, Muhammad explained, had forgotten that the Kaaba had originally been a shrine to God dedicated by the prophet Abraham (Ibrahim in Arabic) and his son Ishmael. Muslims do not accept the version of Abraham's sacrifice given in the Old Testament, in which the elderly couple, Abraham and Sarah, have a son, Isaac, whom Abraham spares at God's command (see Chapter 2). In contrast, Muslims believe that Abraham offered God another of his sons: Ishmael, whose mother was the slave woman Hajar (Hagar in Hebrew). The pilgrimage to Mecca, or **hajj** (HAHJ), commemorates that moment when Abraham freed Ishmael and sacrificed a sheep in his place. Later, Muslims believe, Ishmael fathered his own children, the ancestors of the clans of Arabia.

The First Caliphs and the Sunni-Shi'ite Split, 632–661

Muhammad preached his last sermon from Mount Arafat outside Mecca and then died in 632. He left no male heirs, only four daughters, and did not designate a successor, or caliph. Clan leaders consulted with each other and chose Abu Bakr (ah-boo BAHK-uhr) (ca. 573–634), an early convert and the father of Muhammad's second wife, to lead their community. Because Abu Bakr could not receive divine revelations, he had to govern on the basis of what he and his advisers remembered of Muhammad's teachings. Although not a prophet, he held political and religious authority and also led the Islamic armies. Under Abu Bakr's skilled leadership, Islamic troops conquered all of the Arabian peninsula and pushed into present-day Syria and Iraq.

When Abu Bakr died only two years after becoming caliph, the Islamic community again had to determine a successor. This time the umma chose Umar ibn al-Khattab (oo-MAHR ib-in al-HAT-tuhb) (ca. 586–644), the father of Muhammad's third wife. Muslims brought their disputes to Umar, as they had to Muhammad. As the number of cases increased, the caliph appointed **qadi**, or jurists, who listened to the aggrieved parties, often after the close of Friday prayers in the Islamic house of worship, or mosque.

During Muhammad's lifetime, a group of Muslims had committed all of his teachings to memory, and soon after his death they began to compile them as the **Quran** (also spelled Koran), which Muslims believe is the direct word of God as revealed to Muhammad. In addition, early Muslims recorded testimony from Muhammad's friends and associates about his speech and actions. In the Islamic

jihad
(Arabic root for "striving" or "effort") A struggle or fight against non-Muslims. In addition to its basic meaning of "holy war," modern Muslims use the term in a spiritual or moral sense to indicate an individual's striving to fulfill all the teachings of Islam.

hajj
The pilgrimage to Mecca, required of all Muslims who can afford the trip. The pilgrimage commemorates that moment when, just as he was about to sacrifice him, Abraham freed Ishmael and sacrificed a sheep in his place.

qadi
A Muslim jurist.

Quran
The book that Muslims believe is the direct word of God as revealed to Muhammad. Written sometime around 650.

hadith
Testimony recorded from Muhammad's friends and associates about his speech and actions. Formed an integral part of the Islamic textual tradition, second in importance only to the Quran.

Five Pillars of Islam
The primary obligations of each Muslim as listed by Muhammad (specified on this page).

Sunnis
The larger of the two main Islamic groups that formed after Ali's death. Sunnis, meaning the "people of custom and the community," hold that the leader of Islam should be chosen by consensus and that legitimate claims to descent are only through the male line. Sunnis do not believe that Ali and Fatima's descendants can become caliph.

Shi'ites
The "shia" or "party of Ali," one of the two main groups of Islam, who support Ali's claim to succeed Muhammad and believe that the grandchildren born to Ali and Fatima should lead the community. Shi'ites deny the legitimacy of the first three caliphs.

textual tradition, these reports, called **hadith** (HAH-deet) in Arabic, are second in importance only to the Quran (kuh-RAHN).

Umar reported witnessing an encounter between Muhammad and the angel Gabriel in which Muhammad listed the primary obligations of each Muslim, which have since come to be known as the **Five Pillars of Islam**: (1) to bear witness to Allah as the sole god and to accept Muhammad as his messenger, (2) to pray five times a day in the direction of Mecca, (3) to pay a fixed share of one's income to the state in support of the poor and needy, (4) to refrain from eating, drinking, and sexual activity during the daytime hours of the month of Ramadan, and, (5) provided one has the necessary resources, to do the hajj pilgrimage to Mecca. (See the feature "Movement of Ideas Through Primary Sources: The Five Pillars of Islam.")

When Umar died in 644, the umma chose Uthman to succeed him. Unlike earlier caliphs, Uthman was not perceived as impartial. He gave all the top positions to members of his own Umayyad clan, which angered many. In 656, a group of soldiers mutinied and killed Uthman. With their support, Muhammad's cousin Ali, who was also the husband of his daughter Fatima, became the fourth caliph. Ali was unable to reconcile the different feuding groups, and in 661 he was assassinated. Ali's martyrdom became a powerful symbol for all who objected to the reigning caliph's government.

The political division that occurred with Ali's death led to a permanent religious split in the Muslim community. The **Sunnis**, the "people of custom and the community," held that the leader of the Islamic community could be chosen by consensus and that the only legitimate claim to descent was through the male line. In Muhammad's case, his uncles could succeed him, since he left no sons. Although Sunnis accept Ali as one of the four rightly guided caliphs that succeeded Muhammad, they do not believe that Ali and Fatima's children, or their descendants, can become caliph because their claim to descent was through the female line of Fatima.

Opposed to the Sunnis were the "shia" or "party of Ali," usually referred to as **Shi'ites** in English, who not only supported Ali's claim to succeed Muhammad but also believed that the grandchildren born to Ali and Fatima should lead the community. They denied the legitimacy of the three caliphs before Ali, who were related to Muhammad only by marriage, not by blood. The breach between Sunnis and Shi'ites became the major fault line within Islam that has existed down to the present.

Early Conquests and the Spread of Islam, 632–661

The early Muslims forged a powerful army that attacked non-Muslim lands, including the now-weak Byzantine and Sasanian empires, with great success. When the army attacked a new region, the front ranks of infantry advanced using bows and arrows and crossbows. Their task was to break into the enemy's frontlines so that the mounted cavalry, the backbone of the army, could attack.

In the first stage of conquest, the troops seized all the movable property of the conquered people and reserved a fixed share, called *zakat* (literally "purification," officially set at one-fifth), for the commander. The remaining four-fifths were distributed among the troops and provided a powerful incentive to keep on fighting. The caliph headed the army, which was divided into units of one hundred men and subunits of ten.

Once the Islamic armies pacified a new region, a process that sometimes took generations, the regional governor had to implement a more regular system of taxation. The Muslims levied the same tax rates on conquering and conquered peoples alike, provided that the conquered peoples converted to Islam.

Islam stressed the equality of all believers before God, and all Muslims, whether born to Muslim parents or converts, paid two types of taxes: one on the land, usually fixed at one-tenth of the annual harvest, and the zakat tax. From the one-fifth share of plunder originally set by Muhammad, the zakat tax evolved into a property tax with different rates for different possessions. Because the revenue from the zakat was to be used to help the needy or to serve God, it is often called an "alms-tax" or "poor tax." Exempt from the zakat alms tax, each individual non-Muslim paid a head tax, called a *jizya*, usually set at a higher rate than the taxes paid by Muslims.

Islamic forces conquered city after city and ruled the entire Arabian peninsula by 634. Then they crossed overland to Egypt from the Sinai Peninsula. By 642 the Islamic armies controlled Egypt, and by 650 they controlled an enormous swath of territory from Libya to Central Asia. In 650, they vanquished the once-powerful Sasanian empire.

The new Islamic state in Iran aspired to build an empire as large and long-lasting as the Sasanian empire, which had governed modern-day Iran and Iraq for more than four centuries. The caliphate's armies divided conquered peoples into three groups. Those who converted became Muslims. Those who continued to adhere to Judaism or Christianity were given the status of "protected subjects" (*dhimmi* in Arabic), because they too were "peoples of the book" who honored the same prophets from the Hebrew Bible and the New Testament that Muhammad had. Non-Muslims and nonprotected subjects formed the lowest group. Dhimmi status was later extended to Zoroastrians as well.

The Umayyad Caliphate, 661–750

Although the Islamic community had not resolved the issue of succession, by 661 Muslims had created their own expanding empire whose religious and political leader was the caliph. After Ali was assassinated in 661, Muawiya (mu-ah-WEE-ya), a member of the Umayyad clan like the caliph Uthman, unified the Muslim community. In 680, when he died, Ali's son Husain tried to become caliph, but Muawiya's son defeated him and became caliph instead. Since only members of this family became caliphs until 750, this period is called the Umayyad dynasty.

The Umayyads built their capital at Damascus, the home of their many Syrian supporters, not in the Arabian peninsula, the original homeland of Islam. Initially they used local languages for administration, but after 685 they chose Arabic as the language of the empire.

In Damascus, the Umayyads erected the Great Mosque on the site of a church housing the relics of John the Baptist (see Chapter 7). Architects modified the building's Christian layout to create a large space where devotees could pray toward Mecca. This was the first Islamic building to have a place to wash one's hands and feet, a large courtyard, and a tall tower, or minaret, from which Muslims issued the call to prayer. Since Muslims honored the Ten Commandments, including the Second Commandment, *"You shall not make for yourself a graven image,"* the Byzantine workmen depicted no human figures or living animals. Instead their mosaics showed landscapes in an imaginary paradise (see the photo on page 238).

---

*All quotations from the Bible are from the New Revised Standard Version. Revised Standard Version of the Bible, Copyright © 1952 [2nd edition, 1971] by the Division of Christian Education of the National Council of the Churches of Christ in the United States of America. Used by permission. All rights reserved.

Portraying Paradise on Earth: The Umayyad Mosque of Damascus The most beautiful building in the Umayyad capital of Damascus was the mosque, where some twelve thousand Byzantine craftsmen incorporated mosaics, made from thousands of glass tiles, into the building's structure. Notice how the trees grow naturally from the columns at the bottom of the photograph and how the twin windows allow viewers to glimpse the beautiful flowers on the ceiling above. These compositions portray the paradise that Muhammad promised his followers would enter after their deaths. (© Bernard O'Kane/Alamy)

The Conquest of North Africa, 661–750

Maghrib
The African coastal region facing the Mediterranean whose residents largely converted to Islam by the 1100s.

Under the leadership of the Umayyads, Islamic armies conquered the part of North Africa known as the **Maghrib**—modern-day Morocco, Algeria, and Tunisia—between 670 and 711, and then crossed the Strait of Gibraltar to enter Spain. Strong economic and cultural ties dating back to the Roman empire bound the Maghrib to western Asia. Its fertile fields provided the entire Mediterranean with grain, olive oil, and fruits like figs and bananas. In addition, the region exported handicrafts such as textiles, ceramics, and glass. Slaves and gold moved from the interior of Africa to the coastal ports, where they, too, were loaded into ships crossing the Mediterranean.

Arab culture and the religion of Islam eventually took root in North Africa, expanding from urban centers into the countryside. By the tenth century, Christians had become a minority in Egypt, outnumbered by Muslims, and by the twelfth century, Arabic had replaced both Egyptian and the Berber languages of the Maghrib as the dominant language. Annual performance of the hajj pilgrimage strengthened the ties between the people of North Africa and the Arabian peninsula. Pilgrim caravans converged in Cairo, from which large groups then proceeded to Mecca.

Islamic rule reoriented North Africa. Before it, the Mediterranean coast of Africa formed the southern edge of the Roman empire, where Christianity was the dominant religion and Latin the language of learning. Under Muslim rule,

North Africa lay at the western edge of the Islamic realm, and Arabic was spoken everywhere.

The Unified Abbasid Caliphate, 750–945

In 744, a group of Syrian soldiers assassinated the Umayyad caliph, prompting an all-out civil war among all those hoping to control the caliphate. In 750, a section of the army based in western Iran, in the Khurasan (HWER-us-sahn) region, triumphed and then shifted the capital some 500 miles (800 km) east from Damascus to Baghdad, closer to their base of support. Because the new caliph claimed descent from Muhammad's uncle Abbas, the new dynasty was called the Abbasid dynasty and their empire the **Abbasid caliphate**. Under Abbasid rule, the Islamic empire continued to expand east into Central Asia. At its greatest extent, it included present-day Morocco, Tunisia, Egypt, Saudi Arabia, Iraq, Iran, southern Pakistan, and Uzbekistan. In Spain, however, the leaders of the vanquished Umayyad clan established a separate Islamic state.

Abbasid caliphate
Dynasty of rulers (750–1258) who ruled a united empire from their capital at Baghdad until the empire fragmented in 945. They continued as religious leaders until 1258, when the last Abbasid caliph was killed by the Mongols.

Baghdad, City of Learning

The new Abbasid capital was built by the second Abbasid caliph Mansur (r. 754–775). Baghdad was on the Tigris River in the heart of Mesopotamia, near the point where the Tigris and Euphrates Rivers come closest together (see Chapter 2). Several canals linked the two rivers. Mansur explained his choice:

Indeed, this island between the Tigris in the East and the Euphrates in the West is the harbor of the world. All the ships that sail up the Tigris . . . and the adjacent areas will anchor here. . . . It will indeed be the most flourishing city in the world.[*]

Baghdad more than fulfilled his hopes. Located at the crossroads of Africa, Europe, and Asia, it was home to half a million residents including the majority Muslim community and smaller communities of Christians, Jews, and Zoroastrians. The city's residents lived side by side, celebrated each other's festivals, and spoke Arabic, Persian, Greek, and Hebrew.

Mansur, we learn from the historian Masudi,[3] *"was the first caliph to have foreign works of literature translated into Arabic,"* including Aristotle's works, the geography of Ptolemy, the geometry and physics of Euclid, various mathematical treatises, *"and all the other ancient works. . . . Once in possession of these books, the public read and studied them avidly."*[†] Caliphs, officials, and private individuals collected large numbers of books, sometimes holding several hundred thousand volumes in a single collection. Local scholars benefited from the support of both the caliph and the city's residents, who paid for the manuscripts to be copied and studied them in their schools. The city's cosmopolitan environment encouraged scholars to study the scientific and mathematical discoveries of Greece, India, and Mesopotamia. Historians call their collective efforts, which lasted several centuries, the **translation movement**. In translating astronomy, medical, mathematical, and geography books

translation movement
Between 750 and 1000, the effort by Islamic scholars, many living in Baghdad, to translate books on astronomy, medicine, mathematics, and geography from ancient Greek, Sanskrit, and Persian into Arabic.

*Jacob Lassner, *The Topography of Baghdad in the Early Middle Ages* (Detroit: Wayne State University Press, 1970), p. 127, citing the Islamic writer Ya'qubi.

†Paul Lunde and Caroline Stone, trans., *The Meadows of Gold: The Abbasids by Mas'udi* (New York: Kegan Paul International, 1989), p. 388.

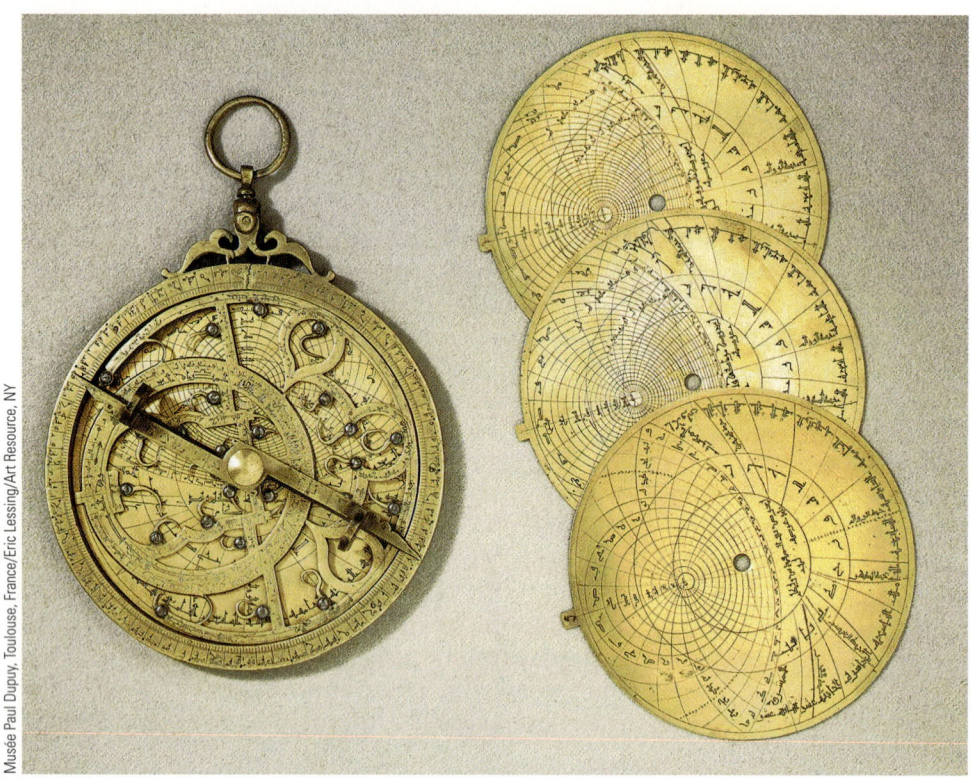

Musée Paul Dupuy, Toulouse, France/Eric Lessing/Art Resource, NY

Determining the Direction of Mecca: The Astrolabe This astrolabe, made in 1216, is a sophisticated mathematical device. After holding the astrolabe up to the sun to determine the angle of the sun's rays and thus fix the viewer's latitude on earth, one inserted the appropriate metal plate (this example has three) into the mechanism, which allowed one to chart the movement of the stars.

from ancient Greek, Sanskrit, and Persian into Arabic, they created a body of scientific knowledge unsurpassed in the world. Certain works by ancient Greek scholars, such as the medical scholar Galen, survive only in their Arabic translations. When, beginning in the eleventh and twelfth centuries, Europeans once again became interested in the learning of the Greeks, they gladly used the Arabic translations, which preserved the legacy of the past while adding many distinguished advances (see the feature "Movement of Ideas Through Primary Sources" in Chapter 13).

Islamic scholars also made many scientific and mathematical discoveries of their own. The great mathematician al-Khwarizmi (al-HWAR-iz-mee) (d. 830) combined the Indian and Babylonian number systems to create the world's first workable decimal system. Al-Khwarizmi invented algebra (from the Arabic word *al-jabr*, meaning "transposition"). He also developed a system of computation that divided complex problems into shorter steps, or algorithms (the word *algorithm* is derived from al-Khwarizmi's name).

One of the Five Pillars of Islam is to pray five times a day facing toward Mecca. Islamic scholars developed increasingly sophisticated instruments to determine this position for prayer. The **astrolabe** allowed observers to calculate their location on earth once they had set the appropriate dials for the date, the time of day, and the angle of the sun's course through the sky. The astrolabe also functioned as a slide rule, one of the world's first hand-held mathematical calculators. It became the most significant computational tool of its time.

astrolabe
Computational instrument that allowed observers to calculate their location on earth to determine the direction of Mecca for their prayers. Also functioned as a slide rule.

In a significant technological advance, a paper-making factory was opened in Baghdad in 794–795 that produced the first paper in the Islamic world, using Chinese techniques (see Chapter 4). Muslim scholars had previously written on either papyrus, a dried plant grown in Egypt, or the scraped and cleaned animal skin called parchment. Both were much more costly than paper, and the new writing material spread quickly throughout the empire. By 850, Baghdad housed one hundred paper-making workshops.

The low cost of paper greatly increased the availability of books. Manuals on agriculture, botany, and pharmacology contributed to the ongoing spread of agricultural techniques and crops from one end of the empire to the other. Cookbooks show the extent to which the empire's residents embraced Asian foodstuffs like rice, eggplant, and processed sugar. Cotton for clothing, grown by Persians at the time of the founding of the Abbasid dynasty, gradually spread to Egypt and, by the twelfth century, to West Africa.

Abbasid Governance

Baghdad, the city of learning, was the capital of an enormous empire headed by the caliph, who presided over the military, the bureaucracy, and the judiciary. His chief minister, or vizier, stood at the head of a bureaucracy based in the capital. In the provinces, the caliph delegated power to regional governors, who were charged with maintaining local armies and transmitting revenues to the center; however, they often tried to keep revenues for themselves.

In the early centuries of Islamic rule, local populations often continued their pre-Islamic religious practices. For example, in 750 fewer than 8 percent of the people living in the Abbasid heartland of Iran were Muslims. By the ninth century, the Muslim proportion of the population had increased to 40 percent, and in the tenth century to a majority 70 or 80 percent of the population.[4]

The caliphate offered all of its subjects access to a developed judicial system that implemented Islamic law. The caliph appointed a qadi for the city of Baghdad and a qadi for each of the empire's provinces. These judges were drawn from the learned men of Islam, or **ulama** (also spelled *ulema*), who gained their positions after years of study. The ulama took no special vows and could marry and have families. Some ulama specialized in the Quran, others scrutinized records of Muhammad's sayings in the hadith to establish their veracity, and still others concentrated on legal texts. Scholars taught at schools, and on Fridays, at the weekly services, the ulama preached to the congregation (women and men sat separately, with the men in front), and afterward they heard legal disputes in the mosques.

> **ulama**
> Learned Islamic scholars who studied the Quran, the hadith, and legal texts. They taught classes, preached, and heard legal disputes.

The judiciary enjoyed an unusually high position, for even members of the caliph's immediate family were subject to their decisions. In one example, an employee who bought goods for Zubaydah, the wife of the caliph Harun al-Rashid, refused to pay a merchant. When the merchant consulted a judge, the judge advised the merchant to file suit and then ordered the queen's agent to pay the debt. The angry queen ordered the judge transferred and Harun complied with his wife's request, but only after he himself paid the money owed to the merchant. A comparison with other contemporary empires demonstrates the power of the judiciary in the Abbasid empire: no Chinese subject of the Tang dynasty, for example, would have dared to sue the emperor.

Abbasid Society

When compared with its Asian and European contemporaries (see Chapters 8 and 10), Islamic society appears surprisingly egalitarian. It had divisions, of course: rural/urban, Muslim/non-Muslim, free person/slave. Apart from gender differences, however, none of these divisions were insurmountable. Rural people could move to the city, non-Muslims could convert to Islam, and slaves could be freed.

In the royal ranks, however, much had changed since the time of Muhammad, whose supporters treated him as an equal. The Abbasid rulers rejected the egalitarianism of early Islam to embrace the lavish court ceremonies of the Sasanians. To the horror of the ulama, the caliph received visitors from behind a curtained throne, and visitors had to kiss the ground in front of his throne even though only God, the learned Muslims felt, should receive such a form of submission. Equally reprehensible in the eyes of the ulama, his subjects addressed the caliph as "the shadow of God on earth," a title modeled on the Sasanian "king of kings." At the right of the caliph's throne stood an executioner, ready to kill any visitor who might offend the caliph.

The one group in Islamic society to inherit privileges on the basis of birth were those who could claim descent from Muhammad's family. All the Abbasid caliphs belonged to this group, and their many relatives occupied a privileged position at the top of Baghdad society. Descent from Muhammad did not bring any financial advantage; it simply commanded more respect.

Under the royal family, two large groups enjoyed considerable prestige and respect: the ulama, on the one hand, and the cultured elite on the other, including courtiers surrounding the caliph, bureaucrats staffing his government, and educated landowners throughout the empire. These groups often patronized poets, painters, and musicians, themselves also members of the cultured elite.

Like the caliph's more educated subjects, ordinary people varied in the extent of their compliance with the religious teachings of Islam. In the cities they worked carrying goods, and in the countryside they farmed. Most farmers prayed five times a day and attended Friday prayers at their local mosques, but they could not always afford to go on the hajj.

Farmers aspired to send their sons to study at the local mosque for a few years. Here, before starting work full-time as cultivators, they acquired the rudiments of Arabic so that they could recite the Quran. Families who educated their daughters did so at home. Boys who demonstrated scholarly ability hoped to become members of the ulama, while those gifted in mathematics might become merchants.

Muhammad and two of his immediate successors had been merchants, and trade continued to enjoy a privileged position in the Abbasid caliphate. Merchants were supposed to adhere to a high standard of conduct: to be true to their word and to sell merchandise free from defects. Many merchants contributed money for the upkeep of mosques or to help the less fortunate. Because Islamic law forbade usury (charging interest on loans), Muslim merchants used credit mechanisms like checks, letters of credit, and bills of exchange. While the most successful merchants became bankers and traders who specialized in large-scale transactions that spanned the empire, other merchants ran single shops or peddled their goods, some of which they made themselves, from town to town.

The shift of the capital to Baghdad in the eighth century brought a dramatic increase in trade within the empire and beyond. Long-distance merchants sent ships to India and China that were loaded with locally produced goods—such as Arabian horses, textiles, and carpets—and nonlocal goods, such as African ivory and Southeast Asian pearls. The ships returned with spices, medicines, and textiles. Islamic merchants were at home in a world stretching from China to Africa; Aladdin, the famous fictional hero of a tale from *The Thousand and One Nights*, was born in China and adopted by an African merchant. As also discussed in Chapter 8, as early as the ninth century, ships traveled routinely between the Arabian Sea and southern Chinese ports, and the China-Basra route was the longest regularly traveled sea route in the world before 1500.

Slavery

Much long-distance trade involved the import of slaves from three major areas: Central Africa, Central Asia, and central and eastern Europe, by far the largest source (see Map 9.1, page 245). The Arabs referred to the region of modern Poland and Bohemia as the "slave country." (The English word *slave* is derived from the Latin word for *slav*, because so many slaves were originally Slavic.)

Under the Abbasids, the coastal cities of East Africa, particularly those north of Madagascar, became Muslim, not because they were conquered by invading armies but because traveling merchants introduced Islam to them. The merchants came to the coast to buy slaves and other products, including gold and ivory. In many cases, the rulers converted first, and the population later followed.

Like Khaizuran, some Islamic slaves worked as servants or concubines. The caliph's household purchased thousands of slaves each year. The women entered the secluded women's quarters, or harem, in the palace. Other slaves labored in the fields, as soldiers, or—most dangerous of all—in mines.

Although Islamic teaching stressed the equality of all believers, slavery predated Muhammad and continued to exist throughout the years of the caliphate. Even when slaves converted to Islam, they continued, unless expressly freed by their masters, to serve as slaves.

All levels of society, from the caliph with his hundreds of female slaves down to the petty trader who could afford only one, respected the teaching that children born to a slave woman and a free Muslim father should be raised as free Muslims, provided that the father acknowledged the child as his. As a result, these children were granted identical rights as their siblings born to free Muslim mothers.

Harun al-Rashid was himself the child of a slave mother, Khaizuran. As a child, she learned to read and write because educated slaves could command a higher price on the slave market. When the caliph Mansur gave her to his son Mahdi sometime in the late 750s, Mahdi took an immediate liking to the young girl, who was *"slender and graceful as a reed,"*[*] the root meaning of her name *khaizuran*.

Politics of the Harem

Like most ordinary people living within the Abbasid empire, Khaizuran had grown up in a nuclear family headed by her father and his one wife, her mother. Islamic law permitted Muslim men to marry as many as four wives, but most men could afford to support only one. The caliphs took the four wives Islamic law entitled them to, and their enormous revenues permitted them to support unlimited numbers of concubines as well.

When Khaizuran joined the royal household, she left behind her life in the streets of Mecca, where women had some freedom of movement, and entered a world whose customs were completely unfamiliar. The higher a woman's class, the greater the degree of seclusion, and the caliph's wives were the most secluded of all. An army of eunuchs, or castrated men, guarded the secluded women's quarters and prevented illicit contact with any men. Khaizuran was free to leave the palace only on rare occasions, and then only under escort.

Only after giving birth to two sons, and only after she was certain of her status as one of the future caliph's favorites, did Khaizuran reveal that her mother, two

*Nabia Abbott, *Two Queens of Baghdad: Mother and Wife of Harun al-Rashid* (London: Al Saqi Books, 1986, reprint of 1946 original), p. 26, citing Jahiz (pseud.), *Kitab al-Mahasin wa Al-Addad*, ed. van Vloten (Leiden: E. J. Brill, 1898), pp. 232–233.

sisters, and a brother were still alive in Yemen. The caliph Mansur immediately summoned them to live in the palace and arranged for Khaizuran's sister to marry another of his sons. The sister subsequently gave birth to a daughter, whose nickname was "little butter ball," or Zubaydah.

Khaizuran's relations with her son Hadi soured soon after he, and not his brother Harun, became caliph in 785. Hadi was particularly upset to discover that his mother was meeting with his generals and courtiers on her own. He chastised her, saying:[5] *"Do not overstep the essential limits of womanly modesty. . . . It is not dignified for women to enter upon affairs of state. Take to your prayer and worship and devote yourself to the service of Allah. Hereafter, submit to the womanly role that is required of your sex."**

But Khaizuran did not back down. Hadi then asked his generals how they would feel if their mothers interfered in politics, and they all agreed,[6] *"Not any one of us would like that."** This description by the historian al-Tabari (al–TAH-bah-ree) (d. 923) suggests that all the commanders felt the same: that no woman, and certainly not Khaizuran, should intervene in matters of state. Contrary to the expectation of these men, Khaizuran did, however, intervene in court politics. Hadi died suddenly, in mysterious circumstances, and Khaizuran made sure that Harun succeeded him as caliph. (No one knows exactly how.)

Unlike her mother and her famous aunt Khaizuran, Zubaydah grew up entirely within the women's quarter of the palace. After her marriage to the caliph, she devoted herself to public works. While in Mecca, she contributed 1,700,000 dinars, or nearly eight tons of gold, from her own funds to construct a giant reservoir. She also ordered wells dug to provide hajj pilgrims with fresh water. The resulting stone water tunnels, running above and below ground for 12 miles (20 km), constituted a genuine feat of engineering. Finally, she made extensive repairs to the road linking Kufa, a city outside Baghdad, with Mecca and Medina, which is called **Zubaydah's Road** even today. (See the feature "Visual Evidence in Primary Sources: Zubaydah's Road.")

Zubaydah's Road
The pilgrimage road linking Kufa with Mecca and Medina that was rebuilt and improved by Queen Zubaydah.

The Breakup of the Abbasid Empire, 809–936

Like her mother-in-law Khaizuran, Zubaydah tried to manipulate the succession after Harun's death in 809, but she sided with the losing son, who was defeated by his brother Mamun in 813. The empire Mamun won, however, was not as prosperous as it appeared. The costs of governing the Abbasid empire often exceeded its revenues. Even during Harun's reign the caliphs were often forced to seek emergency loans. The central government frequently ran short of money because regional governors did not forward the taxes they collected to the caliph. The frequent civil wars between rivals for the caliphate destroyed the irrigation works that underpinned the agrarian economy, and, because no one rebuilt them, tax revenues continuously declined (see Map 9.1).

As a temporary expedient, the caliph occasionally appointed a tax farmer (see Chapter 7) to collect a fixed amount in a region where the caliph's bureaucrats had trouble raising revenue. In these cases the caliph still retained direct political control. If tax farmers failed to raise the necessary revenues, the caliph might go a step further and make an **iqta grant**, ceding all political control to the man who promised to collect taxes and pay a certain amount. The iqta (ICK-tah) grant

iqta grant
A grant given by the caliph to someone who promised to collect taxes from a certain region and pay the caliph a certain amount of money. Grant holders became military governors and rulers of their regions, over which the caliph had only nominal control.

---

*Nabia Abbott, *Two Queens of Baghdad: Mother and Wife of Harun al-Rashid* (London: Al Saqi Books, 1986, reprint of 1946 original), pp. 89–90, 92.

MAP 9.1 **The Breakup of the Abbasid Empire** Between 750 and 945, the Abbasid caliphate lost huge chunks of territory in North Africa, the Arabian peninsula, Iran, and Central Asia, yet a shared Islamic identity held the former empire together, as Ibn Jubayr learned in his 1183–1185 journey (see page 250). The people living in the empire's core around Baghdad imported slaves, many of whom converted to Islam, from Africa, northern Europe, and Central Asia.
(© Cengage Learning)

holder became the military governor and ruler of the area, and the caliph retained only nominal control. In 789 and 800, Harun granted independence to two Islamic states in North Africa in exchange for annual tax payments; his successors made similar arrangements with other regions. This was a dangerous innovation, far riskier than any grants the Persians had made to satraps or the Romans had made to tax farmers, because the iqta holders had no reason to support the empire.

Until the middle of the tenth century, none of the iqta holders directly challenged the authority of the caliph. Then, in 936, the caliph took the final step and ceded all his power to an Iraqi grant holder, giving him the title *commander of commanders*. The grant holder disbanded the entire Abbasid army and replaced it with an army loyal to himself. He eliminated the Abbasid bureaucracy as well, sentencing the last vizier to life imprisonment in a dungeon.

This new arrangement did not last long. In 945, the Buyids, a group of Shi'ite Iranian mercenaries based in the mountains south of the Caspian Sea, conquered Baghdad and took over the government. Rather than depose the caliphs and risk alienating their Muslim subjects, the Buyids retained them as figureheads who led the Islamic caliphate but had no political power. The caliph received a small allowance so that he could reside in his crumbling palace in Baghdad, and Islamic preachers continued to cite his name in their Friday prayers. The extensive territory of the Abbasid empire proved ungovernable as a single political unit, and it broke up into different regions, all still part of the Islamic cultural and religious world.

Zubaydah's Road

Zubaydah devoted considerable resources to the project that brought her lasting fame: the road linking Kufa, a city outside Baghdad, with Mecca and Medina. Although the road existed before her reign, she made so many improvements to it that it came to be called Darb Zubaydah, or Zubaydah's Road.

When Saudi archaeologists surveyed the desert in the 1970s, they found identifiable traces of a roadway 18 yards (17 m) wide. The road's builders had faced the challenge of designing a road for pedestrians even though it ran through long stretches of sand, some muddy ground, and rough lava fields. They cleared the road of stones, paved the sections of the road that went through the mud, and smoothed rough lava fields before covering them with soft sand on which pilgrims could easily walk. One archaeologist has called the project "the finest and most remarkable and extensive road system in the earlier period of Islamic history."[*]

[*]Saad A. al-Rashid, *Darb Zubaydah: The Pilgrim Road from Kufa to Mecca* (Riyad: Riyad University, 1980), p. 330.

The stones of the lava field were so sharp that they hurt the feet of the pilgrims and their camels.

After clearing the road, engineers covered it with a smooth layer of sand for the convenience of the pilgrims and their camels, who traveled over 700 miles (1,100 km).

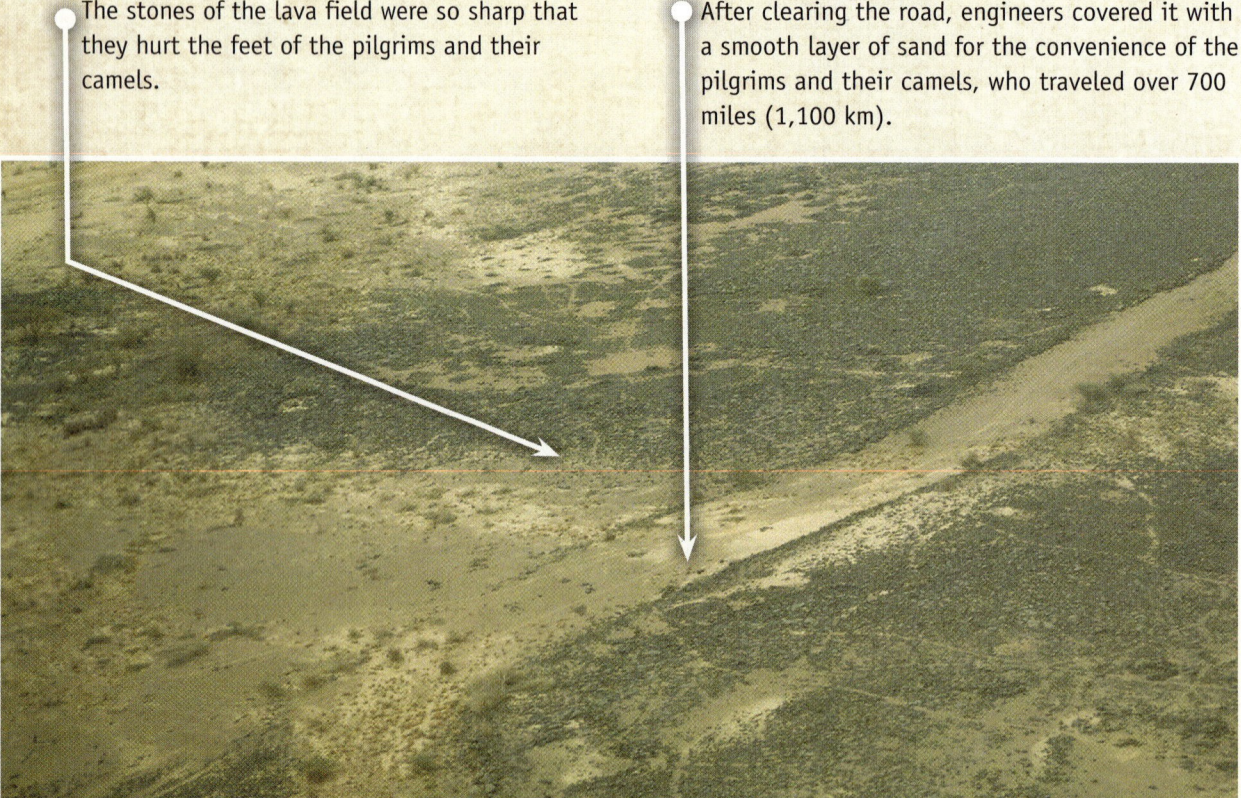

John Herbert

QUESTION FOR ANALYSIS

» *What preparations did hajj travelers going overland have to make, and how would these differ for those traveling by boat?*

Because Zubaydah was particularly concerned about poorer pilgrims who traveled the difficult route on foot, she added nine new rest stations at convenient intervals between existing stations, for a total of fifty-four rest stops. All the new stations had a pool, and they often included some kind of shelter and sometimes even a small mosque. This painting, from an illustrated thirteenth-century manuscript of collected anecdotes, shows what a resting place on the Darb Zubaydah might have looked like.

The nimbus, or cloud, behind the head was originally an Iranian artistic convention used to show royalty. In this picture, however, the nimbus seems purely decorative, since all the human figures have one.

Institute of Oriental Studies, St. Petersburg, Russia/The Bridgeman Art Library

This figure uses a bellows to light a fire below a cooking pot.

This is a shrine, most likely to a prominent Islamic teacher whose grave lies inside it, where Muslims came to pray.

Two camels bray with their mouths open. Although often ill-tempered, camels were the one draft animal that could withstand the hot, dry climate of the desert.

Inside a tent made from beautiful textiles, these two men lean on portable wooden furniture as they converse with each other.

Three camels feed from saddlebags placed on the ground. Able to survive for up to nine days without water, camels can carry loads over 300 pounds (140 kg).

247

The Rise of Regional Centers, 945–1258

Muslims found it surprisingly easy to accept the new division of political and religious authority. The caliphs continued as the titular heads of the Islamic religious community, but they were entirely dependent on temporal rulers for financial support. No longer politically united, the Islamic world was still bound by cultural and religious ties, including the obligation to perform the hajj. Under the leadership of committed Muslim rulers, Islam continued to spread throughout South Asia and the interior of Africa. Rulers all over the Islamic world continued to patronize Islamic scholars, and Islamic scholarship and learning, particularly in the field of geography, continued to thrive.

Regional Islamic States

In 1055, Baghdad fell to yet a different group of soldiers from Central Asia, the Turkish-speaking Seljuqs (also spelled Seljuks, and pronounced sell-JOOKs). Other sections of the empire broke off and, like Baghdad, experienced rule by different dynasties. In most periods, the former Abbasid empire was divided into four regions: the former heartland of the Euphrates and Tigris River basins; Egypt and Syria; North Africa and Spain; and the Amu Darya and Syr Daria River Valleys in Central Asia.

Two centuries of Abbasid rule had transformed these four regions into Islamic realms whose residents, whether Sunni or Shi'ite, observed the tenets of Islam. Their societies retained the basic patterns of Abbasid society. When Muslims traveled anywhere in the former Abbasid territories, they could be confident of finding mosques, being received as honored guests, and having access to the same basic legal system (even if some legal schools differed in their interpretations). As in the Roman empire, where Greek and Latin prevailed, just two languages could take a traveler through the entire realm: Arabic, the language of the Quran and high Islamic learning, and Persian, the Iranian language of much poetry, literature, and history.

Sometime around 1000, the city of Córdoba in Islamic Spain replaced Baghdad as the leading center of Islamic learning. The Umayyad capital from around 750 to 1031, Córdoba attracted many visitors because of its gardens, fountains, paved streets, and most of all, its running water (the first in Europe since the fall of Rome). Córdoba played a crucial role in the transmission of learning from the Islamic world to Christian Europe. Craftsmen learned how to make paper in the eleventh century and transmitted the technique to the rest of Europe. Córdoba's residents, both male and female, specialized in copying manuscripts and translated treatises from Arabic into Latin for European audiences.

The study of geography also flourished in the eleventh and twelfth centuries as Muslims learned about the most distant places within the Islamic community. The geographer **al-Bakri** (see Chapter 11), based in Córdoba, provided a rare, detailed description of Central Africa. His geographic work, entitled *The Book of Routes and Realms*, reported that the Central African kingdom of Ghana had a capital city with separate districts for Muslims and for local religious practitioners who prayed to images. He explained that although rulers often converted to Islam after contact with Muslim traders, their subjects, as in the case of the country of Mali, did not always follow suit.

This religious division between rulers who converted to Islam and subjects who did not held true in another major area that was brought into the Islamic world in the eleventh and twelfth centuries: Afghanistan, Pakistan, and north India. For example, when Muslim conquerors moved into north India from their base in Afghanistan, they tore down Hindu temples during the actual conquest,

al-Bakri
A Muslim geographer based in Córdoba whose *Book of Routes and Realms* is one of the earliest written sources about Africa.

National Library (Dar-al-Katub), Cairo, Egypt/Erich Lessing/Art Resource, NY

Map of Eurasia, 1182 This map, like all Islamic maps, is oriented with the south on top and the north below. It is a copy of a silver map made by the geographer al-Idrisi, which no longer survives. With greater precision than any other contemporary map, it shows the blue Mediterranean Sea in the middle with Africa above (notice the three sources of the Nile on the right) and Eurasia below.

but once they gained power they allowed Hindu temples to remain, even as they endowed mosques. Ordinary Indians continued to worship Hindu deities, while the ruling family, which was based in Delhi and were thus known as the Delhi sultanate, observed the tenets of Islam (see Chapter 11).

During this long period of division, Muslim cartographers made some of the most advanced maps of their day. Working in Sicily, the geographer al-Idrisi (1100–1166) engraved a map of the world on a silver tablet 3 yards by 1.5 yards (3 m by 1.5 m in size). Although the map was destroyed during his lifetime, the book al-Idrisi wrote to accompany his map is so detailed that scholars have been able to reconstruct much that appeared on his original map. Like all Islamic maps, his looks upside down to modern viewers, because he oriented the map to the south. His map showed the outlines of the Mediterranean, Africa, and Central Asia with far greater accuracy than contemporary maps made elsewhere in the world.

Ibn Jubayr's Hajj in 1183

By the twelfth century, different Islamic governments ruled the different sections of the former Abbasid empire. Since the realm of Islam was no longer unified, devout Muslims had to cross from one Islamic polity to the next as they performed

Ibn Jubayr
(1145–1217) Spanish courtier from Granada, Spain, who went on the hajj pilgrimage in 1183–1185. Wrote *The Travels* describing his trip to Mecca—the most famous example of a travel book, called a *rihla* in Arabic.

the hajj. Local Islamic rulers might take advantage of the pilgrims by charging them extra taxes, but sometimes they also facilitated the pilgrims' journey. Pilgrims were often unsure of the correct rituals to perform in Mecca, and as the number of pilgrims increased over the centuries, a new genre of book, called "travels" (*rihla* in Arabic), appeared that described the trip to Mecca and the most important rituals performed there, which bound Muslims from distant places together. (See the feature "World History in Today's World: Mecca's New Skyline.")

The most famous account of the hajj is *The Travels of Ibn Jubayr* (1145–1217), a courtier from Granada, Spain, who went on the hajj in 1183–1185. **Ibn Jubayr** (IH-buhn joo-BAH-eer) decided to go to Mecca to repent for drinking seven cups of wine, a drink forbidden to Muslims. He financed his trip with a gift of seven cups of gold coins received from the governor of Granada, his superior, who felt contrite about having forced Ibn Jubayr to drink so much. Ibn Jubayr's book serves as a guide to the

Mecca's New Look The illuminated clock face of the Royal Mecca Clock Tower, completed in 2011, looms high above the enclosure housing the cube-shaped shrine of the Kaaba, which means "cube" in Arabic. The Arabic writing on the clock face says "God is the Greatest." Muhammad instructed all Muslims who could afford the trip to make the pilgrimage to Mecca. (Salah Malkawi/The New York Times/Redux Pictures)

Mecca's New Skyline

Like many booming cities, Mecca has a new skyline. The most prominent building, just south of the Grand Mosque, is a replica of London's "Big Ben" bell tower called the Royal Mecca Clock Tower, which lies at the center of a new mall with a hotel and a prayer hall (see accompanying photo). All over the city, luxury high-rise apartments are going up that offer a view of the Grand Mosque: the better the view, the higher the price.

This wave of development has prompted criticism. One architect complained:

"The hajj was always supposed to be a time when everyone is the same. There are no classes, no nationalities. It is the one place where we find balance. You are supposed to leave worldly things behind you." Many fear that the new facilities will create a divided hajj experience, with the rich staying in air-conditioned luxury while the poor suffer in the heat.

The total number of hajj pilgrims is nearly 3 million. In 2010, 1.8 million Muslims traveled to Saudi Arabia, where over 1 million Saudis joined them. Because a non-Muslim once desecrated the mosque, the Saudis allow only Muslims to visit Mecca and Medina. The number of pilgrims would be even greater except that the government of Saudi Arabia limits the number of visas issued annually to one thousand pilgrims for each 1 million citizens in each country.

Twenty-three percent of the world's population, or 1.57 billion people, are Muslim, making Islam the world's second-largest and fastest-growing religion. The four countries with the greatest number of Muslims lie far from the heartland of Islam in Saudi Arabia: Indonesia (203 million), Pakistan (174 million), India (161 million), and Bangladesh (145 million). Egypt, with 79 million, and Nigeria, with 78 million, come next on the list, an indication that the world region with the greatest number of recent converts is Africa.

Some 87–90 percent of the world's Muslims are Sunni, and 10–13 percent are Shi'ite. Pakistan and India have considerable Shi'ite populations, but Iran has the largest concentration of Shi'ites, between 66 and 70 million, more than a third of the world's Shi'ite population.

Sunni or Shi'ite, all Muslims hope to go on the hajj at least once in their lifetime.

Sources: Nicolai Ouroussoff, "New Look for Mecca: Gargantuan and Gaudy," *The New York Times*, December 29, 2010; "Mapping the Global Muslim Population: A Report on the Size and Distribution of the World's Muslim Population" (Washington, D.C.: Pew Research Center, 2009), www.pewforum.org.

---

sequence of hajj observances that had been fixed by Muhammad; Muslims today continue to perform the same rituals (see Table 9.1, "The Nine Steps of the Hajj").

After thirty days' sail across the Mediterranean, Ibn Jubayr arrived in the port of Alexandria, Egypt, then under the rule of Saladin (1137/38–1193), the founder of the Ayyubid dynasty (1171–1250) in Egypt. Ibn Jubayr praised Saladin's generosity as a host but criticized the port officials for requiring the pilgrims to pay the zakat tax on the goods they carried. From Egypt, he traveled south with other pilgrims and crossed the Red Sea; on his arrival, he once again had to pay a tax. Before 945, all territory was under Abbasid rule and there were no border crossings; after 945, Muslim travelers, even those going on the hajj, had to pay the costs of leaving one country and entering another.

When Ibn Jubayr arrived at the outskirts of Mecca, he put on the two pieces of unsewn cloth permitted to the male pilgrim. (Because women pilgrims were obliged to cover all but their face, hands, and feet, they required more cloth.) While Sunni and Shi'ite rules differed slightly, all concurred that pilgrims should refrain from having sex, eating meat, and cutting their hair or nails during the hajj. Muslims could fulfill their obligation to go on the hajj only once a year: on the eighth, ninth, and tenth days of the twelfth month in the Islamic lunar calendar. After Ibn Jubayr had been in Mecca for some eight months, the month of the hajj arrived.

TABLE 9.1 The Nine Steps of the Hajj

1. To put on pilgrim's robes
2. To walk around the Kaaba seven times counterclockwise
3. To stand at Arafat on the ninth day of the twelfth month
4. To stay overnight near Arafat
5. To throw stones at three different locations where, Muslims believe, Satan tempted the prophet Ishmael
6. To sacrifice an animal at Mina
7. To repeat the circumambulation of the Kaaba (see step 2)
8. To drink water from the Zamzam well
9. To recite two sets of prayers at the Station of Abraham, where Abraham and Ishmael, Muslims believe, prayed together after the Kaaba was built

Source: Adapted from Vincent J. Cornell, "Fruit of the Tree of Knowledge: The Relationship Between Faith and Practice in Islam." From *Oxford History of Islam*, by John L. Esposito (1999) "The Nine Steps of Hajj" pp. 84–86 © 2000 by Oxford University Press, Inc. By permission of Oxford University Press, Inc.

The number of Muslims going on the hajj had increased dramatically over time. By 1184, Ibn Jubayr writes that the total number of pilgrims from Iraq alone *"formed a multitude whose number only God Most High could count."** The more unruly pilgrims (often from Yemen, in Ibn Jubayr's opinion) forced the Meccan authorities to replace the Kaaba's wooden covering with a strong iron dome.

Once pilgrims arrived in Mecca, they walked around the Kaaba seven times in a counterclockwise direction. On the eighth day of the month Ibn Jubayr and all the other pilgrims departed for Mina, which lay halfway to Mount Arafat. The hajj celebrated Abraham's release of his son Ishmael. The most important rite, **The Standing**, commemorated the last sermon given by the prophet Muhammad.

Fear of bandits prevented the pilgrims from spending the night at Arafat as was customary. When they arrived at Mount Arafat early in the morning of the ninth day, they first climbed the mountain and then descended to the plain, where they remained on their feet throughout the Standing:

> *When, on Friday, the midday and afternoon prayers were said together, the people stood contrite and in tears, humbly beseeching the mercy of Great and Glorious God. The cries of "God is Great" rose high, and loud were the voices of men in prayer. Never has there been seen a day of such weeping, such penitence of heart, and such bending of the neck in reverential submission and humility before God.**

As soon as the sun had set, the pilgrims proceeded quickly in the dark toward a mosque some three hours away for final prayers. They spent the rest of the night there.

When the pilgrims arrived at Mina the next day, their religious observance shifted suddenly from solemn piety to raucous celebration. They first threw stones at the wall where Muslims believe Satan tempted Ishmael, and they then slaughtered sheep to celebrate Abraham's substitution of a sacrificial ram for his son Ishmael. The

The Standing
The rite that marks the culmination of the hajj, when pilgrims meditate and pray (they are not required to stand) at the site where Muhammad gave his last sermon.

*The Travels of Ibn Jubayr, trans. R. J. C. Broadhurst (London: Jonathan Cape, 1952), pp. 191, 180.

change of pace was abrupt, and disturbances often broke out at Mina. Ibn Jubayr saw *"dissension and riot between the negro inhabitants of Mecca and the Turks of Iraq in which there were some hurts. Swords were drawn, arrow notches were put to the bow-string, and spears were thrown, while some of the goods of the merchants were plundered."*

After the religious observances were completed, giant bazaars sprang up in which Ibn Jubayr saw *"wares ranging from precious jewels to the cheapest strings of beads, together with other articles and various merchandises of the world."* The hajj may have been a religious duty, but it also had a distinctly commercial side: merchants from all over the Islamic world found a ready market among the pilgrims.

Finally, Ibn Jubayr, like almost all pilgrims, went to see Muhammad's tomb and mosque at Medina, even though this was not an obligatory part of the hajj. From Medina to Baghdad, Ibn Jubayr traveled along Zubaydah's Road, which he covered at a rapid 30 miles (50 km) per day: *"These tanks, pools, wells, and stations on the road from Baghdad to Mecca are monuments to Zubaydah. . . . But for her generous acts in this direction this road could not have been traversed."* Ibn Jubayr then traveled to Baghdad and visited the palace where the family members of the figurehead caliph *"live in sumptuous confinement in those palaces, neither going forth nor being seen."* Because of several months' delay caused by a shipwreck, Ibn Jubayr arrived back in Spain more than two years after his departure in 1185.

Ibn Jubayr's rihla offers a precious eyewitness account of the Islamic world in the late twelfth century, when the Abbasid caliphs continued as figureheads in Baghdad but all real power lay with different regional rulers. This arrangement came to an abrupt end in 1258, when the Mongols (see Chapter 14) invaded Baghdad and ended even that minimal symbolic role for the caliph.

The Travels of Ibn Jubayr, trans. R. J. C. Broadhurst (London: Jonathan Cape, 1952), pp. 184, 184–185, 216, 236.

CONTEXT AND CONNECTIONS

The Legacy of the Abbasid Empire

When Muhammad instructed his followers to perform the annual hajj pilgrimage, provided that they had the means to do so, the Islamic world was limited to the west coast of the Arabian peninsula. In the eighth century, after Islamic armies conquered much of western Asia and North Africa, Khaizuran was able to fulfill her hajj obligation by traveling from the palace in Baghdad for only a few weeks, while other pilgrims living at the edges of the Abbasid empire, whether in Central Asia or Africa, measured their journeys in years.

All Muslims, they were subjects of the Abbasid caliph, whom they recognized as both the political head of state and the religious head of the caliphate. No other head of a major state in the world at that time served concurrently as both religious and political leader. The Roman emperor headed the government based at Constantinople, while the church had different leaders in Rome, Constantinople, and other cities (see Chapter 10). Similarly, the Tang emperor led the government of China, and Buddhist abbots living in different monasteries throughout the empire headed their communities, as Ennin discovered on his pilgrimage from Japan (see Chapter 8).

The political structure holding the Abbasid empire together was fragile. Short of revenues, the Abbasid rulers made iqta grants to powerful men in the provinces who became more independent than either the satraps of the Achaemenid empire (see Chapter 6) or the provincial governors or tax farmers of the Roman empire (see Chapter 7). In 936 one iqta holder took all political power from the caliph and received the title *commander of commanders*. Nine years later the Buyids seized power from him, and the Abbasid empire fragmented into different regions bound by linguistic,

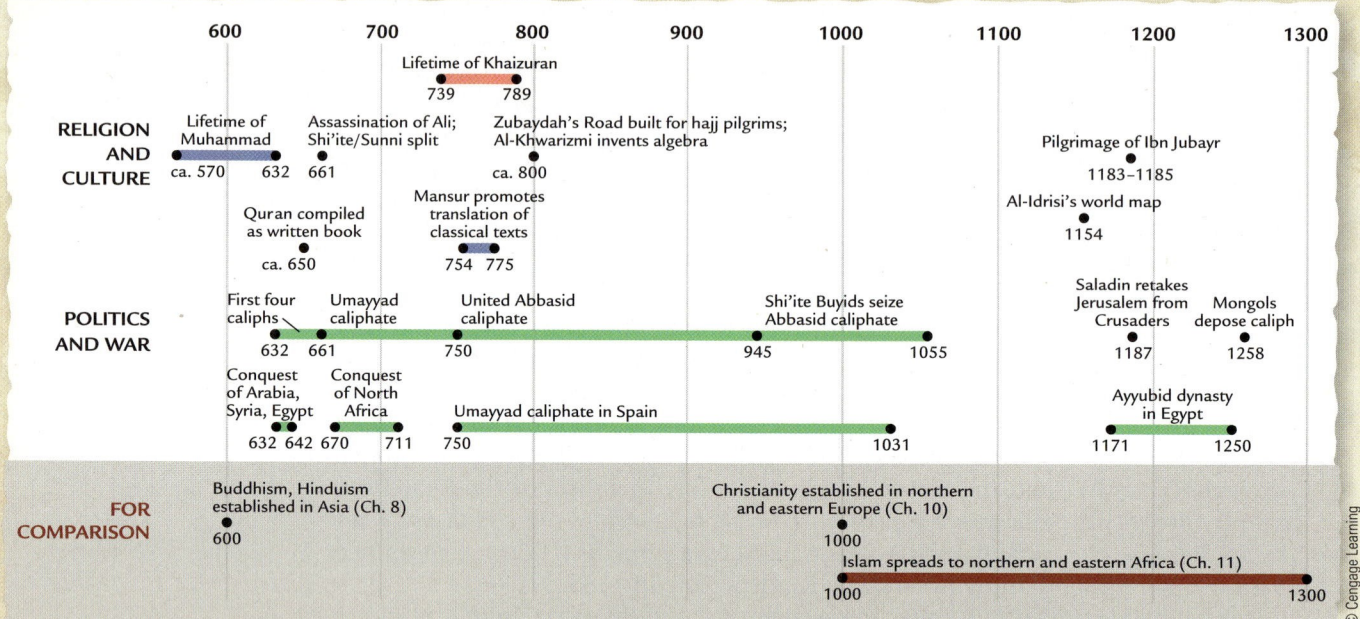

	600	700	800	900	1000	1100	1200	1300

Lifetime of Khaizuran
739 ● ━━━ ● 789

RELIGION AND CULTURE

Lifetime of Muhammad
ca. 570 ● ━━ ● 632

Assassination of Ali; Shi'ite/Sunni split
661 ●

Zubaydah's Road built for hajj pilgrims; Al-Khwarizmi invents algebra
ca. 800 ●

Pilgrimage of Ibn Jubayr
1183–1185 ●

Quran compiled as written book
ca. 650 ●

Mansur promotes translation of classical texts
754 ● ━ ● 775

Al-Idrisi's world map
1154 ●

POLITICS AND WAR

First four caliphs
632 ●

Umayyad caliphate
661 ●

United Abbasid caliphate
750 ●

Shi'ite Buyids seize Abbasid caliphate
945 ●

━━━━━━━━━━━━━━━━━━━━━━━━ ● 1055

Saladin retakes Jerusalem from Crusaders
1187 ●

Mongols depose caliph
1258 ●

Conquest of Arabia, Syria, Egypt
632 ● 642 ●

Conquest of North Africa
670 ● 711 ●

Umayyad caliphate in Spain
750 ● ━━━━━━━━━━━━━━━━━ ● 1031

Ayyubid dynasty in Egypt
1171 ● ━━━ ● 1250

FOR COMPARISON

Buddhism, Hinduism established in Asia (Ch. 8)
600 ●

Christianity established in northern and eastern Europe (Ch. 10)
1000 ●

Islam spreads to northern and eastern Africa (Ch. 11)
1000 ● ━━━━━━━━━━━━━━ ● 1300

© Cengage Learning

cultural, and religious ties. The Abbasids used two languages to govern: the Arabic of the heartland of Islam and the Persian of the Sasanians who preceded them in Iran (see Chapter 6). Because both languages continued to be spoken after 945, they enabled people to communicate across the Islamic world, just as Latin and Greek connected inhabitants of the Roman empire and Sanskrit and Chinese connected the Buddhists of Asia (see Chapters 7 and 8). The Abbasid caliphs continued as figureheads until 1258, when the Mongols invaded Baghdad (see Chapter 14).

Although primarily a religious obligation, the hajj had a profound effect on trade, navigation, and technology in the years after 945, as Ibn Jubayr discovered in the late 1100s. The hajj, and the resulting trade, pushed Muslims to adopt or to discover the fastest and most efficient means of transport from different places to Mecca and to equip their vessels with the best astronomical instruments, maps, and navigational devices. Despite the hardships, all Muslims viewed a trip to Mecca, no matter how distant, as an obligation to be fulfilled if at all possible. The result was clear: ordinary Muslims were far better traveled and more knowledgeable than their contemporaries in other parts of the world.

In the years after 945, multiple political and cultural centers arose that challenged Baghdad's position in the previously united Islamic world. As the next chapter will show, something similar happened in Europe as new political and cultural centers first appeared and then overtook the Byzantine capital at Constantinople.

VOYAGES ON THE WEB: Khaizuran

The Voyages Map App follows the traveler's journeys using interactive study tools, including 360-degree panoramic views of historic sites, zoomable maps, audio summaries, flash cards, and quizzes.

Key Terms

Khaizuran (228)
Muhammad (230)
caliph (230)
jihad (233)
hajj (233)
qadi (233)
Quran (233)

hadith (234)
Five Pillars of Islam (234)
Sunnis (234)
Shi'ites (234)
Maghrib (238)
Abbasid caliphate (239)
translation movement (239)

astrolabe (240)
ulama (241)
Zubaydah's Road (244)
iqta grant (244)
al-Bakri (248)
Ibn Jubayr (250)
The Standing (252)

For Further Reference

Abbott, Nabia. *Two Queens of Baghdad: Mother and Wife of Harun al-Rashid*. London: Al Saqi Books, 1986, reprint of 1946 original.

Allen, Roger. *An Introduction to Arabic Literature*. New York: Cambridge University Press, 2000.

Bennison, Amira K. *The Great Caliphs: The Golden Age of the 'Abbasid Empire*. New Haven: Yale University Press, 2009.

Berkey, Jonathan Porter. *Formation of Islam: Religion and Society in the Near East, 600–1800*. New York: Cambridge University Press, 2003.

Broadhurst, R. J. C., trans. *The Travels of Ibn Jubayr*. New Delhi, India: Goodword Books, 2004.

Burke III, Edmund. "Islam at the Center: Technological Complexes and Roots of Modernity." *Journal of World History* 20, no. 2 (June 2009): 165–186.

Clarence-Smith, William Gervase. *Islam and the Abolition of Slavery*. London: Hurst and Company, 2006.

Crone, Patricia. *Meccan Trade and the Rise of Islam*. Piscataway, N.J.: Gorgias Press, 2004.

Esposito, John L., ed. *The Oxford History of Islam*. New York: Oxford University Press, 1999.

Freeman-Grenville, G. S. P. *The East African Coast: Select Documents from the First to the Earlier Nineteenth Century*. Oxford, England: Clarendon Press, 1962.

Gutas, Dmitri. *Greek Thought, Arabic Culture: The Graeco-Arabic Translation Movement in Baghdad and Early 'Abbāsid Society (2nd–4th/8th–10th Centuries)*. New York: Routledge, 1998.

Hodgson, Marshall. *Venture of Islam*. Vols. 1–3. Chicago: University of Chicago Press, 1977.

Hourani, George F. *Arab Seafaring*. Exp. ed. Princeton: Princeton University Press, 1995.

Kennedy, Hugh. *The Prophet and the Age of the Caliphates*. 2d ed. London: Pearson Education Limited, 2004.

Levtzion, N., and J. F. P. Hopkins, eds. *Corpus of Early Arabic Sources for West African History*. New York: Cambridge University Press, 1981.

Lunde, Paul, and Caroline Stone, trans. *The Meadows of Gold: The Abbasids by Mas'udi*. New York: Kegan Paul International, 1989.

Turner, Howard R. *Science in Medieval Islam: An Illustrated Introduction*. Austin: University of Texas Press, 1995.

 Go to the CourseMate website at **www.cengagebrain.com** for additional study tools and review materials—including audio and video clips—for this chapter.

10

The Multiple Centers of Europe, 500–1000

Sometime around the year 1000, Leif Eriksson (LEAF ERIC-son) sailed with some forty companions from Greenland across the North Atlantic to Newfoundland in today's Canada. His former sister-in-law **Gudrid** and her second husband **Thorfinn Karlsefni** followed in a subsequent voyage. The travelers were originally from Norway in the Scandinavian region of Europe, which also includes Sweden, Finland, and Denmark. Europe in the year 1000 differed dramatically from Europe in 500. In 500, Europe contained only one major empire, Byzantium, with its capital at Constantinople (modern Istanbul, Turkey). Five hundred years later, Europe was home to multiple centers—modern-day France and Germany, Scandinavia, and Russia—that are still the most important European powers today.

Competition among these multiple centers provided a powerful stimulus, as the Scandinavian voyages to the Americas amply demonstrate. An account recorded several hundred years later, but based on oral history, reports that, after the Scandinavians arrived in the Americas, Karlsefni set off to explore with a man named Snorri:

Gudrid and Thorfinn Karlsefni

(Arni Magnusson Institute, Reykjavik, Iceland/The Bridgeman Art Library)

*K*arlsefni sailed south along the coast. . . . Karlsefni and his men sailed into the estuary and named the place Hope (Tidal Lake). Here they found wild wheat growing in fields on all the low ground and grape vines on all the higher ground. Every stream was teeming with fish. They dug trenches at the high-tide mark, and when the tide went out there were halibut trapped in all the trenches. In the woods there was a great number of animals of all kinds.*

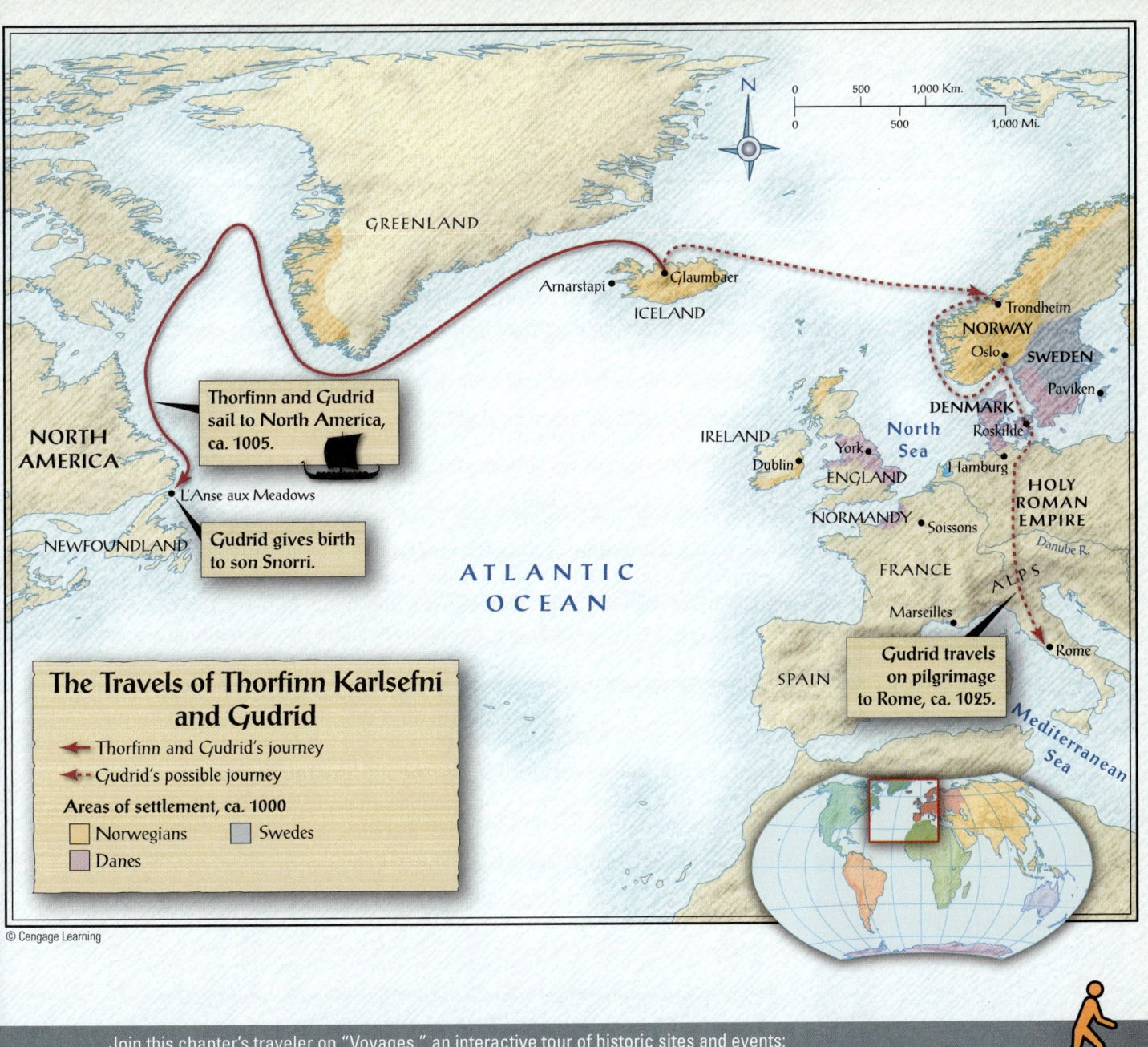

The Travels of Thorfinn Karlsefni and Gudrid

Thorfinn and Gudrid sail to North America, ca. 1005.

Gudrid gives birth to son Snorri.

Gudrid travels on pilgrimage to Rome, ca. 1025.

The Travels of Thorfinn Karlsefni and Gudrid

← Thorfinn and Gudrid's journey
◄- - Gudrid's possible journey

Areas of settlement, ca. 1000

☐ Norwegians   ☐ Swedes
☐ Danes

© Cengage Learning

Join this chapter's traveler on "Voyages," an interactive tour of historic sites and events:
www.cengagebrain.com

They stayed there for a fortnight [two weeks], enjoying themselves and noticing nothing untoward. They had their livestock with them. But early one morning as they looked around they caught sight of nine skin-boats; the men in them were waving sticks which made a noise like flails [tools used to thresh grain], and the motion was sunwise [clockwise].

Karlsefni said, "What can this signify?"

"It could well be a token of peace," said Snorri. "Let us take a white shield and go to meet them with it."

'From *The Vinland Sagas*, translated with an introduction by Magnus Magnusson and Hermann Pálsson (Penguin Classics, 1965). Copyright © Magnus Magnusson and Hermann Pálsson, 1965. Reprinted with permission of Penguin Group/UK.

Gudrid and Thorfinn Karlsefni
A couple originally from Iceland who settled in about 1000 in Greenland and then Canada and later returned to Iceland.

Karlsefni and Snorri went out to meet the men in boats, who stared at them and then left. Although this incident is recorded in a later source, archaeological evidence shows that the Scandinavians built at least one settlement at the Canadian town of L'Anse aux Meadows in today's Newfoundland.

Possessing faster and more maneuverable wooden boats than any of their contemporaries, the Scandinavians went as far as Russia, Greenland, Iceland, and Canada. Although we are accustomed to think of the distance between Europe and the Americas as enormous, the direct voyage from Greenland to the northeastern coast of Canada was only 1,350 miles (2,200 km). Hugging the coast of Greenland and Canada on a slightly longer route, a boat could remain within constant sight of land.

The Scandinavians were one of several different groups speaking Germanic languages who lived in western and northern Europe at the time the Western half of the Roman empire fell (see Chapter 7). Around 500, the residents of the Eastern Roman empire looked down on these peoples because they could not read and write, worshiped a variety of different deities rather than the Christian God, and lived in simple villages much smaller than Rome or the eastern capital of Constantinople. People of the Eastern empire saw these regions as uncivilized backwaters, good only as sources of raw materials and slaves. They did not recognize the vitality of these new centers.

By 1000, the situation had changed dramatically. The rise of regional states paralleled the rise of the Buddhist states of East Asia that borrowed the Tang dynasty blueprint for empire (see Chapter 8). These new European states, like Byzantium, were Christian, but their political structures differed from those of Rome because they were based on the war-band.

This chapter begins in Constantinople, the successor to the Roman empire. As the Byzantine empire contracted, new centers arose: first in Germany and France, then in Scandinavia, and finally in modern-day Russia.

Focus Questions

» *What events caused the urban society of the Byzantines to decline and resulted in the loss of so much territory to the Sasanian and Abbasid empires?*

» *What was the war-band of traditional Germanic-speaking society? How did the political structures of the Merovingians and the Carolingians reflect their origins in the war-band?*

» *When, where, how, and why did the Scandinavians go on their voyages, and what was the significance of those voyages?*

» *What were the earliest states to form in the area that is now Russia, and what role did religion play in their establishment and development?*

» *What did all the new states have in common?*

Byzantium, the Eastern Roman Empire, 476–1071

Byzantine empire
(476–1453) Eastern half of the Roman empire after the loss of the Western half in 476. Sometimes simply called Byzantium.

To distinguish it from the Western empire based in Rome, historians call the Eastern Roman empire, with its capital at Constantinople, the **Byzantine empire**, or simply Byzantium (see Map 10.1). The Byzantine empire lasted for over a thousand years after the Western empire ended, in spite of continuous

MAP 10.1 **The Byzantine Empire** The Byzantine empire grew dramatically during the reign of Justinian (r. 527–565), expanding its territory in North Africa, the Balkans, and Italy. Yet the plague struck for the first of at least fifteen times in 541–544, killing 7 million of his 26 million subjects. (© Cengage Learning)

pressure from surrounding peoples. Far worse than any attack by a foreign power, the bubonic plague struck the empire in 541 and then at regular intervals for two more centuries. The massive decline in population, coupled with the cutting off of shipping lines across the Mediterranean, resulted in a sharp economic downturn. Through all these events the empire's scholars continued to preserve Greek learning, systematize Roman law, and write new Christian texts. Over the centuries, however, the amount of territory under Byzantine rule shrank, providing an opportunity for other European centers to develop.

Justinian and the Legacy of Rome, 476–565

Constantinople, the city named for the emperor Constantine, had been a capital of the Eastern Roman empire since 330. Between 395 and 476 different rulers governed the Eastern and Western sections of the empire, but after 476 the Eastern emperor had no counterpart in Rome. The Christian church at this time had five major centers: Constantinople, Alexandria, Jerusalem, Antioch, and Rome. The top church bishops in the first four cities were called **patriarchs**. By 1000, the patriarch of Constantinople had become head of the Orthodox church of Byzantium. By the same year the highest-ranking bishop in Rome was called the **pope**.

Culturally the residents of the Eastern and Western halves of the empire had much in common: educated people often spoke both Greek and Latin, almost everyone was Christian, and citizens accepted Roman law. Sometimes people in the West referred to those living in the Eastern half as "Greeks" since nearly everyone there spoke Greek, not Latin, although not always as their mother tongue.

The first outbreak of plague in 541 occurred during the long reign of the emperor Justinian I (r. 527–565). A native of Thrace, the region north of Greece,

patriarch
In the 400s and 500s, the highest-ranking bishop of the four major Christian church centers at Constantinople, Alexandria, Jerusalem, and Antioch.

pope
In the 400s and 500s, the pope was the highest-ranking bishop in Rome, and by 1000, the pope was recognized as leader of the Catholic Church in Rome.

Justinian grew up speaking the local language and Latin. Like many Byzantine emperors, he was chosen by his predecessor, who had adopted him and raised him in Byzantium. In 520, Justinian met his future wife: an actress and circus performer named Theodora (497–548), who had already given birth to at least one child. She did not fulfill Byzantine ideals of modesty, yet Justinian married her, and the two ruled together for more than twenty years.

Early in their reign, a commission of legal scholars completed one of the most important legal works ever written: Justinian's Corpus of Civil Law. The corpus consists of three works: the Code (completed in 529), the Digest (533), and the Institutes (534). Working for three years, the commission gathered together all the valid laws of the Roman empire and reduced some 3 million laws, many no longer in effect, to a manageable body 1,500 pages long in its modern edition. The texts of the laws and the extensive legal commentary were written in Latin, still the official language of the central government, but the laws issued by Justinian himself were in Greek, which was rapidly becoming the administrative language of the empire. The Justinian Corpus preserved the core of Roman law not simply for sixth-century jurists but for all time.

Justinian and Theodora faced challenges to their rule, particularly from the residents of Constantinople who occasionally rioted against them. In 532, after suppressing one such outbreak, as an expression of gratitude, they sponsored an enormous church called Hagia Sophia, the Church of Holy Wisdom. Before the Hagia Sophia (hah-GHEE-ah so-FEE-ah), most Christian churches were built on a rectangular plan. This was the first Christian church built with a majestic dome: *"A spherical-shaped dome standing upon this circle makes it exceedingly beautiful,"* marveled the historian Procopius (pro-COE-pee-uhs); *"from the lightness of the building, it does not appear to rest upon a solid foundation, but to cover the place beneath as though it were suspended from heaven by the fabled golden chain."*

Justinian and Theodora managed the empire's relations with its neighbors with considerable success. Unlike his predecessors, Justinian challenged the Vandals, one of the peoples who led the conquest of North Africa in the fifth century (see Chapter 7). His successful military campaigns in Northwest Africa, coastal Spain, and Italy added territory to the empire. Yet on the eastern front, the armies of the Sasanian empire in Iran captured Antioch, the third-largest city in the Byzantine empire, revealing how vulnerable the Eastern empire was.

The Impact of the Plague and the Arab Conquests, 541–767

The fighting on both the Eastern and Western frontiers subsided immediately after the first recorded outbreak of the bubonic plague in 541. Many people, including Justinian himself, became terribly ill. In modern usage, the term **plague** refers to two distinct illnesses, bubonic plague and pneumonic plague, which form two phases of an outbreak. First, fleas that have drunk the blood of infected rodents transmit the bubonic plague to people. Lymph glands on the neck, under the arm, and on the groin swell up and turn black. Once part of the human population is infected with bubonic plague, the pneumonic plague spreads as one victim sneezes or coughs onto another. Pneumonic plague is almost always fatal.

One contemporary observer, Procopius, observed that the disease first appeared in towns along the coast and then moved inland, but he did not know why. Only in

plague
Refers to two distinct illnesses, bubonic plague and the almost always fatal pneumonic plague, forming two phases of an outbreak.

---

*Medieval Sourcebook (http://www.fordham.edu/halsall/source/procop-deaed1.html), trans. W. Lethaby and H. Swainson, from Procopius, *De Aedificiis*, in *The Church of St. Sophia Constantinople* (New York: 1894), pp. 24–28.

the late nineteenth century did scientists realize that black rats living on ships were the main agents responsible for spreading the disease.

The first outbreak hit the Egyptian port of Pelusium (pell-OOZE-ee-uhm) on the mouth of the Nile in 541 and spread across the Mediterranean to Constantinople in the following year. Ports such as Carthage, Rome, and Marseilles were affected in 543. At least fifteen outbreaks followed between 541 and 767, when the plague finally came to an end.

In the absence of accurate population statistics, historians have to estimate the deaths resulting from the plague. The deaths in the large cities were massive: some 230,000 out of 375,000 died in Constantinople alone.[1] High estimates put the death toll from the plague at one-quarter of the empire's population during Justinian's reign: of 26 million subjects, only 19 million survived.

Before the plague the Roman empire had been an urban society where powerful people met at the marketplace each day to discuss their affairs, enjoying theater and circus performances alongside their poorer neighbors. By 600 such an urban type of life had become a memory. Starting in 541 and continuing to sometime in the ninth century, the population declined, cities shrank, the economy contracted, and tax revenues plummeted. In these centuries of declining tax revenues, the government minted far fewer coins than earlier, and a barter economy replaced the partially monetized economy. Craftsmen and merchants gave up their occupations to become farmers.

Another consequence of these catastrophes was that the government could no longer afford to pay its soldiers. Instead, militias were formed by part-time soldiers who farmed the land during peacetime. When Islamic forces began to expand around 640 (see Chapter 9), the Byzantine empire ceded to the victorious Islamic armies large chunks of territory in Armenia and Africa.

In contrast to the multiple officials of Roman times, the basic administrative unit of the Byzantine empire during the seventh and eighth centuries was the *theme* (Greek plural: *themata*), headed by a single governor rather than the multiple officials of Roman times. This governor heard legal disputes, collected taxes, and commanded the local militia.

Society had also changed from Roman times. The high and low in rank led almost identical lives, and people no longer used a clan name and a personal name; a simple

The Striking Dome of Hagia Sophia Built in a mere five years, the dome of the Hagia Sophia cathedral in Constantinople (modern Istanbul, Turkey) is more than 100 feet (30 m) in diameter and over 180 feet (55 m) tall. Forty windows at the bottom of the dome give the impression that it floated in the air, and later observers believed that such a beautiful dome could only have been made with divine help.

Christian name (first name) sufficed. Fewer people knew Latin. Some people possessed more land than others, but they now worked the land alongside their poorer dependents. Slavery declined as well because no one could afford to feed slaves. Most of the people in the countryside were legally independent peasants who farmed the land intensively, often with two oxen and a plow, and grew only enough food for their own families.

The final outbreak of plague hit Constantinople in 747 and ended in 767. In the following years a slow revival began. The government minted more small coins, and trade and commerce increased slightly. The writing of manuscripts resumed, especially in monasteries, where scribes devised a new, smaller minuscule script that allowed them to write more words on a piece of parchment, the most common writing material at the time (see Chapter 7). Literacy was mainly concentrated among monks and nuns. Although monasteries had little land and not much wealth, like the monasteries of Egypt (see Chapter 7), they offered an appealing alternative to family life.

Religion and State, 767–1071

The Byzantine emperor ruled the empire, while the patriarch of Constantinople presided over the church, which held property throughout the empire. While the Christian emperors sometimes tried to impose their own views on the church, they also served as patrons, as Justinian's financing of the Hagia Sophia demonstrates.

Byzantine opinion during the eighth century was sharply divided over the use of images in Christian worship. The **iconoclasts**, literally "image-breakers," advocated the removal of all icons, or images, of Jesus, Mary, and any saints, yet permitted prayers directed to crosses. Like the Umayyads, who also banned images, the iconoclasts justified their position by citing the Second Commandment of the Hebrew Bible, forbidding the worship of graven images.

iconoclasts Members of a movement calling for the destruction of images of Jesus, Mary, and the saints because they were believed to violate the Second Commandment of the Hebrew Bible.

Iconoclasm was deeply controversial among Byzantines. When one Byzantine emperor ordered the removal of a statue of Jesus from the main entrance to his palace, an angry crowd of women killed the man who took the image down. The iconoclast movement also appalled many Christians in western Europe who frequently prayed to the statues of saints.

In 780, Irene, the widow of the emperor Leo IV, came to power in her mid-twenties and served as regent for her nine-year-old son. Few expected Irene to rule for long, but she surprised her opponents by tackling some of the major issues facing the empire. Hoping to work out a compromise to end the iconoclast controversy, Irene summoned a church council, a meeting that included the patriarch (the top-ranking cleric in Constantinople) and bishops from all over the Christian world. In 787, the Second Council of Nicaea met and condemned iconoclasm. Those at the meeting permitted all previous iconoclasts to repudiate their earlier positions against icons. Images that had been removed from different churches were returned.

During her reign, Irene, by agreeing to make various large payments of both books and money, managed to keep the Abbasid armies from taking the city of Constantinople. But she could not prevent the powerful Islamic forces from making incursions into the empire's shrunken territory.

Irene and her son did not share power easily. First he tried to seize power from her, then they ruled together, and then, in 797, she tried to overthrow him. Her allies blinded her son, possibly without her knowledge, and he died soon after. Irene then became the first woman to rule the Byzantine empire in her own right and called herself emperor (not empress).

Icon of Christ The iconoclasts opposed the use of icons like this intensely colored example, which shows Jesus holding the Gospel in his left hand and making a blessing with his right. The painter mixed his pigments in beeswax and then applied them to the wood to make a painting in encaustic. Coming to Byzantium from Egypt, this technique was prized for its lifelike eyes and skin tones. Jesus' face has two distinct halves: where the side on our right appears to judge the viewer, the side on our left is more compassionate. Was the artist trying to portray the human and divine sides of Jesus? (Jean-Luc Manaud/Getty Images)

In 802, the empress's courtiers deposed the elderly Irene and installed a general as her successor. The empire that Irene relinquished was less than a third the size it had been in the mid-sixth century. Justinian had ruled over an empire that controlled the eastern half of the Mediterranean, but Islamic forces had conquered large blocks of territory throughout the seventh century. The Byzantine empire had shrunk largely to the borders of modern-day Turkey, and its population was only 7 million. A new state outside the Byzantine empire, Charlemagne's Francia, had staked a claim as the legitimate heir to the Roman empire (as discussed later in this chapter).

In the centuries after 800, Byzantium, though small, continued to be an important intellectual center where scholars studied, copied, and preserved Greek texts from the past, analyzed Roman law, and studied Christian doctrine. In 1071, the Byzantines suffered a massive defeat at the battle of Manzikert (modern-day Malazgirt, Turkey) at the hands of the Seljuq Turks, who captured the emperor himself. After 1071, the Byzantine emperors continued to rule a much smaller empire from their capital at Constantinople with a much-weakened army.

The Germanic-Speaking Peoples of Western Europe, 481–1000

After the fall of the Western Roman empire, the Byzantines often referred to the peoples living in the north of Europe as *barbarians*, a Greek word meaning "uncivilized." The largest group was the Franks, who lived in the **Frankish kingdom**. Although uncivilized in Byzantine eyes, they commanded powerful armies who defeated the Byzantine armies in battle. The Franks were ruled first by the kings of the Merovingian dynasty (481–751) and then by the Carolingians (751–ca. 1000). And in 800, the pope crowned the king of the Franks, Charlemagne, the emperor of Rome. Unlike the Byzantine emperors, who governed an empire divided into regular administrative districts called *themata*, the Merovingian and Carolingian monarchs ruled as the leaders of war-bands, the most important unit of Frankish society.

Frankish kingdom The homeland of the Franks, including much of modern-day France, Germany, and the land in between.

Germanic-Speaking Europeans Before 500

Many different peoples lived in the regions of northern and central Europe and crowded the borders of the Western Roman empire before it fell in 476. They spoke a group of related languages now classed as Germanic, about which little is known because none was written down. Even so, analysts have been able to sketch some broad similarities among these peoples, usually on the basis of archaeological evidence. Those who lived near the Rhine Valley are called Franks.

The basic unit of society was the extended family, which was headed by the father, who might have more than one wife, as well as children and slaves. Since cattle herding was the basis of the economy, the more cattle an individual had, the higher his rank. Freemen looked down on slaves, who were usually war captives.

Beyond the immediate family were larger kinship groups consisting of several households bound by family ties on both the male and female sides. These groups feuded often and developed a complex set of rules for determining the correct handling of disputes. The best source for understanding the practices of these peoples is the Salic Law, a list of punishments for different crimes recorded early in the sixth century. Although written in Latin, the Salic Law shows little Roman influence.

One of the most important legal concepts was that of **wergeld** (literally "man-payment"), which set the monetary value of a human life. Wergeld (WEAR-geld) payments served to prevent an endless cycle of killing and counter-killing among feuding families. Different wergeld penalties were specified for men and women, both free and unfree. For example, the section of the Salic Law "On Killing Pregnant Women" says the following:

wergeld
Literally "man-payment," an important legal concept that set the monetary value of a human life. The function of wergeld payments was to prevent an endless cycle of killing and counter-killing among feuding families.

1. *He who kills a pregnant woman shall be liable to pay twenty-four thousand denarii [600 solidi, or 6 pounds, or 2.73 kg, of gold]. And if it is proved that the fetus was a boy, he shall also be liable to pay six hundred solidi for the child.*

2. *He who kills a girl less than twelve years old or up to the end of her twelfth year shall be liable to pay two hundred solidi [2 pounds, or .9 kg, of gold].*

3. *He who kills a woman of mature age up to her sixtieth year, as long as she is able to bear children, shall be liable to pay twenty-four thousand denarii [600 solidi, or 6 pounds, or 2.73 kg, of gold].*

4. *But if she is killed afterwards when she is no longer able to bear children he shall be liable to pay two hundred solidi [2 pounds, or .9 kg, of gold].[*]*

Penalties were levied in either silver denarius coins or gold solidus coins and varied depending on whether a woman had reached or passed childbearing age, and if pregnant, whether she was carrying a male or female child. These payments were the sole form of punishment: no one was imprisoned or banished.

In times of war, groups of warriors called **war-bands** gathered behind a leader, whose main claim to their allegiance was the distribution of plunder. A successful leader rewarded his men liberally with the spoils of victory, fed and clothed them, and provided them with horses, armor, and a place to live. His supporters, in turn, fought next to him in battles and banqueted with him when at peace.

war-band
The most important social unit among Germanic-speaking peoples. In times of war, warriors formed bands behind a leader, who gave them horses, armor, a place to live, and a share of plunder.

This society was extremely fluid, because war-bands could form rapidly and collapse equally quickly. Members of a war-band distinguished themselves from others by wearing a certain kind of clothing, having similar hairstyles, or carrying similar weapons. They often believed that they and the other members of the war-band had a common ancestor, sometimes a god, from whom they all claimed descent. According to custom, freemen were obliged to fight in wars while slaves were not. The freemen in these bands often gathered in assemblies, called Thing (TING), to settle internal disputes or to plan military campaigns.

---

*Katherine Fischer Drew, *The Laws of the Salian Franks* (Philadelphia: University of Pennsylvania Press, 1991), p. 127.

The Merovingians, 481–751

The most important leader to emerge from the constantly evolving alliances of Frankish society was Clovis (r. 481–511), who established the **Merovingian dynasty** that ruled what are now France and Germany from 481 to 751. He combined great military successes, such as defeating the Visigoths of Spain, with skillful marriage alliances to build a dynasty that lasted two centuries, far longer than any earlier dynasty in the region.

The Merovingian army consisted of different war-bands linked by their loyalty to Clovis. One incident, recounted by the chronicler Gregory of Tours (538/39–ca. 594), vividly illustrates the ties between Clovis and his followers. In 486, Clovis and his men removed many items from the treasuries of several churches, including a *"vase of marvelous size and beauty"* from Soissons. The bishop of the robbed church requested the vase's return. After Clovis and his followers had divided the goods they had stolen, Clovis addressed his men: *"I ask you, O most valiant warriors, not to refuse to me the vase in addition to my rightful part."* Most of his men agreed, but one man crushed the vase with his battle-ax because he felt that Clovis, although their leader, was not entitled to more than his fair share. The humiliated Clovis returned the pieces of the broken vase to the bishop.

One year later, Clovis summoned his troops for a review so that he could inspect their spears, swords, and axes, the iron weapons that helped to make his armies invincible. When he reached the man who had destroyed the vase, he threw the soldier's ax to the ground. As the soldier bent down to pick it up, Clovis grabbed his head and smashed it down on the weapon. *"Thus,"* he said, *"didst thou to the vase at Soissons."* This incident shows that, though called a king, Clovis was a war-band leader who ruled his men only as long as he commanded their respect, and he had to use brute strength coupled with rewards to do so.

One sign of the Merovingian king's role as a war-band leader was his hair, which only he was allowed to grow long. If someone challenged his hold on power and succeeded in overthrowing him, the challenger forced the king to shave off his hair—a visible reminder that he had lost leadership—and the challenger took power.

The Franks, a tiny minority of perhaps two hundred thousand people, lived among 7 million Gallo-Romans in modern-day France and Germany.[2] The Gallo-Romans were the Christian subjects of the fallen Roman empire who spoke Latin. Like many of his subjects, Clovis worshiped both Roman and local deities. However, as Gregory of Tours reports, when Clovis converted to Christianity a few years before his death in 511, he eliminated the largest cultural barrier between the Frankish peoples and the Gallo-Romans they governed.

Like the Roman emperor Constantine (see Chapter 7), Clovis promised to convert if Jesus Christ brought him victory in a battle; when his enemy surrendered, he was baptized, along with three thousand of his men. So few records about the early Merovingians survive that even the basic chronology of Clovis's reign is unknown. This battle may have occurred in 496, 498, or 506. When Clovis died, he had divided his realm among his four sons, according to Frankish custom, and they and their descendants continued to rule until the mid-eighth century.

Under the Romans, large landowners had lived with their slaves in widely dispersed estates. Under the Merovingians, the basic farming unit changed to the village. Former villa owners lived with others in small settlements near streams or forests and engaged in slash-and-burn agriculture, changing plots whenever a

Merovingian dynasty
A Frankish dynasty (481–751) in modern-day France and Germany whose founder, Clovis (r. 481–511), converted to Christianity and ruled as a war-band leader.

---

*Medieval Sourcebook (http://www.fordham.edu/halsall/source/gregtours1.html), "The Incident of the Vase at Soissons," in *Readings in European History*, ed. J. H. Robinson (Boston: Ginn, 1905), pp. 51–55.

field's productivity gave out. Ordinary people consumed a diet composed largely of hunted animals, fish caught in rivers, or plants foraged from the forest.

In the sixth century, monasteries—small communities under the supervision of the local bishop—gradually spread to western Europe from the eastern Mediterranean (see Chapter 7). Many were modeled on a monastery founded in 529 near Rome by Benedict of Nursia (ca. 480–545), who composed a concise set of practical rules for running a monastery. Benedictine monks devoted themselves full-time to manual labor and the worship of God, usually through public prayer conducted eight times each day. Unlike monks in more extreme monasteries, they ate an adequate diet and received enough sleep. The adult members of the community selected their leader, or abbot, who was to obey the local bishop.

In 590 an Irish monk named Saint Columbanus (543–615) arrived in the Merovingian kingdom and founded many monasteries that encouraged monks to be even more devout and disciplined. Columbanus (COH-luhm-bahn-us) taught that laypeople could contribute land and money to monasteries, read religious texts (or have them read aloud), and recite psalms from the Hebrew Bible. Irish monks copied, and so preserved, many manuscripts that would have otherwise been lost.

Bishops were among the few educated men in Merovingian society. They tended to have varied backgrounds. While some had served as priests, others had worked for the king; still others had been monks or abbots in monasteries, and some had no ties to the church but belonged to an important lay family, often one that controlled a fair amount of land. Many learned to read and write by studying with other bishops or in monasteries.

Most Merovingian bishops had married before assuming office. After they became bishops, their wives continued to assist them with their duties, but the popes in Rome frequently urged them to treat their wives as their sisters and stop sleeping with them. In some cases bishops slept surrounded by their male assistants so that everyone could see that they maintained their vows of celibacy.[3]

The head cleric of the Western church, the pope, was elected by the clergy in Rome. As Byzantine power declined, and the Byzantines lost control of northern and central Italy to a Germanic-speaking people called the Lombards in 568, the popes needed military protection because they had no armies of their own. Moreover, the Lombards were Arians, and the popes did not accept Arius's teachings (see Chapter 7). The popes eventually turned to the Carolingians, an important family living in the Merovingian realm, for help. In 753, the two formed an alliance against the Lombards.

Lindisfarne Gospel In 793, the Vikings raided the island of Lindisfarne, an important center of Christian learning famed for its illuminated manuscripts. Here, the artist monk portrays Matthew using a stylus to write the first page of the gospel named for him. One monk first made a sketch on the reverse side of an individual sheet of parchment, while a second monk turned it over and shone a candle through the animal skin so that he could see the outline, which he then filled with paint. Note the line of lowercase script on the top left of the page and the full-size letters below.

Charlemagne and the Carolingians, 751–ca. 1000

In 751, the **Carolingian dynasty**, from the eastern part of the Merovingian realm, overthrew the Merovingian rulers. The most powerful Carolingian ruler was Charles "the Great" ("le Magne" in old French), or Charlemagne (SHAHR-leh-maine). The events of his reign (768–814) demonstrated that the Carolingian realm exceeded Byzantium in importance. By 800, Europe had two powerful centers: Byzantium, which had inherited the legacy of Rome, and the new kingdom of the Franks.

Charlemagne became king of the Franks in 768 and then launched a series of wars against the neighboring Germanic-speaking peoples. The pope in Rome supported him against the Lombards, and Charlemagne rapidly conquered northern and central Italy, some parts of Spain, and much of Germany (see Map 10.2). In 800, during Irene's reign as Byzantine emperor, the pope crowned Charlemagne emperor of Rome. The pope used the pretext that Irene could not be emperor because she was female. The Byzantines were horrified. They thought of Charlemagne as the unlettered leader of primitive peoples, not as a monarch comparable to their own. By accepting the title, Charlemagne claimed that he, and not Irene, was the rightful successor of the emperors of Rome. In a great blow to the Byzantines, the Frankish kingdom styled itself the legitimate heir to the Roman empire.

Diverging from its roots in the war-band, Carolingian society was divided into two groups: the powerful (potentes) and the powerless (paupers), literally "the poor." The powerful owned their own land and could command others to obey them. Although some paupers owned land, they had no one to command. Among the powerless were slaves, a minority of the laborers in the countryside.

During Charlemagne's many conquests, his armies took vast numbers of prisoners from enemy forces; they sold these slaves to buyers, sometimes in distant lands. Writers in the eighth and ninth centuries used the word *captive*, not *slave*, for these prisoners of war. Charlemagne's Christian advisers urged him to stop the sale of Christian slaves to non-Christians, but he continued the practice. One of Europe's main exports to the Abbasids under Charlemagne and his successors was slaves.

Despite his title of emperor, Charlemagne was still very much a war-band leader. Although he had conquered more territory than any Germanic-speaking leader, he was much less educated than the Byzantine or Abbasid rulers of his day. His biographer, Einhard, reports that *"he also attempted to learn how to write, and, for this reason, used to place wax-tablets and notebooks under the pillows on his bed, so that, if he had any free time, he might accustom his hand to forming letters. But his effort came too late in life and achieved little success."** Unable to sign his name, Charlemagne liked having books read aloud to him.

Nevertheless, Charlemagne founded an academy where the sons of the powerful could be educated. He and his successors also established schools, one at the imperial court, others in monasteries. As in the Byzantine empire, a new script, Carolingian minuscule, came into use that fit more words on a page of parchment and eventually became the basis of today's lowercase Roman fonts. (See "World History in Today's World: The Origins of Lowercase Letters and Spaces.") During this revival of learning, monastic authors wrote Latin grammars, medical texts, and liturgies with detailed instructions for church ceremonies. However, literacy remained extremely restricted, with only a tiny number of officials able to read and write.

Carolingian dynasty
(751–ca. 1000) An important aristocratic family that overthrew the Merovingian rulers in 751. Their most powerful ruler was Charlemagne. After his death, the empire split into three sections, each under a different Carolingian ruler.

---

*Paul Edward Dutton, *Charlemagne's Courtier: The Complete Einhard* (Orchard Park, N.Y.: Broadview Press, 1998), II: 25.

MAP 10.2 The Carolingian Realms After coming to power in 768, Charlemagne continuously expanded the area under Carolingian rule. The unified empire did not last long. In 843, his grandsons divided his realm into three separate regions. The West Frankish kingdom eventually became modern-day France, while the East Frankish kingdom developed into modern Germany. The two states regularly vied for control of the territory between them. (© Cengage Learning)

The Origins of Lowercase Letters and Spaces

hey whats up?

Every time we text someone, we use two well-established conventions—lowercase letters and spaces—without ever considering their origins. Both Greek and Latin were written in all capital letters with no spaces; educated readers knew where one word ended and another began. Still, long strings of capital letters took up a lot of space, and it was time consuming to write out each letter.

As surviving papyrus manuscripts show, this practice began to change in the 300s in North Africa, and accelerated in the 500s, as increasing numbers of monks copied manuscripts on parchment. A division of labor existed in the monasteries: some monks prepared the skins for writing while others wrote the texts in ink, and still others painted the illustrations. Over time scribes experimented with half-size letters (the forerunners of lowercase letters) and with different forms of cursive writing. They added spaces to make it easier for the reader to distinguish the separate words.

Monasteries all over Europe developed their own distinctive scripts, whether for Latin in the West or Greek in Byzantium. One of the most popular was the Carolingian miniscule, which spread throughout Charlemagne's realm as monks from one monastery traveled to other monasteries and taught the script to other monks. The script first appeared at the end of the eighth century and remained in use for several hundred years. In the 1400s, when scribes wanted to revive the writing practices of the Romans, they erroneously revived the Carolingian script, which is the ancestor of all the lowercase fonts we use today.

Source: Dianne Tillotson, "Medieval Writing: History, Heritage, and Data Source," http://medievalwriting.50megs.com/writing.htm.

When Charlemagne died in 814, he left his empire intact to his son Louis the Pious (r. 814–840), but when Louis died in 840, his feuding sons divided the kingdom into thirds with the Treaty of Verdun (843). The West Frankish kingdom would eventually become modern France, and the East Frankish kingdom, modern Germany. The East and West kingdoms continuously fought over the territory of the Middle kingdom, which today contains portions of France, Germany, Italy, the Netherlands, and Switzerland. The Carolingians ruled until 911 in Germany and until 987 in the region of modern France, when they were succeeded by new dynasties.

Historians often describe the Carolingians as more centralized than the Merovingians, but in fact the two Frankish dynasties were more alike than different. Both dynasties were led by rulers who rewarded their followers with gifts and whose main source of revenue was plunder. The rulers of both dynasties were Christian, but many of their subjects did not observe basic Christian teachings.

By the tenth century, when Carolingian rule came to an end, the region of the Franks, sometimes called the Latin West, was no longer united. Its major sections—modern-day France and Germany—were beginning to become powerful centers in their own right. By 1000, Byzantium was no longer the only empire in Europe.

The Age of the Vikings, 793–1066

In 793, a group of **Viking** raiders came by boat and seized the valuables held in an island monastery off the English coast. The term *Viking* refers to those Scandinavians who left home to loot coastal towns. For the next three centuries the Vikings were the most successful plunderers in Europe, and no one could withstand their attacks. The peoples living in Scandinavia had many of the same

Viking
Term used for those Scandinavians who left home to loot coastal towns and who were most active between 793 and 1066.

customs as the Franks: their leaders commanded the loyalty of war-bands, plunder was their main source of income, and they gradually adopted Christianity and gave up their traditional gods. Some Scandinavian boatmen lived by stealing from coastal peoples, while others eventually settled in Iceland, Greenland, England, Scotland, Ireland, and Russia; ultimately, however, they decided not to stay on the Atlantic coast of Canada. Between 800 and 1000, Vikings formed several new states, creating still more centers in Europe (see Map 10.3).

MAP 10.3 **The Viking Raids, 793–1066**   From their homeland in Scandinavia, the Vikings launched their first raid on Lindisfarne on the North Sea in 793 and moved on to attack Iceland, Greenland, France, Spain, and Russia for more than two hundred years. They often settled in the lands they raided. In around 1000, they even reached North America. (© Cengage Learning)

Viking Raids on Great Britain, 793–1066

The Viking homeland was north of Charlemagne's realm, in Scandinavia, a region consisting of modern-day Norway, Sweden, and Denmark, whose residents spoke languages in the Germanic language family. The region had a cold climate with a short growing season, and many of its residents hunted walrus and whale for their meat or maintained herds on farms.

Since the Scandinavians conducted their raids by sea, the greatest difference between the Viking and the Frankish war-bands was the large wooden **longboat** held together by iron rivets and washers. These craft ranged between 50 and 100 feet (15 and 30 m) long, with most excavated examples around 75 feet (23 m) in length. The combination of oars and sails made these boats the fastest mode of transport in the world before 1000. Like the ancient Polynesians (see Chapter 5), the Scandinavian navigators recognized the shapes of different landmasses. No evidence of Scandinavian navigational instruments or maps survives. Unlike the Polynesians, the Scandinavians did not designate certain individuals as navigators; all men knew how to steer the longboats, and they announced their discoveries to everyone in their war-band. The first Viking targets were the monasteries of the British Isles in England, Ireland, and Scotland, which lay closest to the southwestern coast of Norway.

Before 500, Britain was home to a group of indigenous peoples whom the Romans had encountered, but after 500 these groups were absorbed by the Anglo-Saxons, a general term for the many groups speaking Germanic languages who migrated to Britain from present-day Denmark and northern Germany. Anglo-Saxon society resembled society on the continent: it, too, had a sharp distinction between free and unfree, with a legal system emphasizing the concept of wergeld.

longboat
Boat used by the Vikings to make raids; made of wood and equipped with both oars and sails, they were the fastest mode of transport before 1000.

The Longboats of the Scandinavians Sewn between 1066 and 1082, the Bayeux tapestry (held in northern France) is an embroidered piece of linen that stretches 231 feet (70 m). This detail shows the longboats in full sail. The boats are moving so quickly that the men seated in the first and third boats do not need to row. Notice that the leading and third boats are large enough to transport horses. (Musee de la Tapisserie, Bayeux/The Bridgeman Art Library)

The Anglo-Saxons converted to Christianity during the sixth and seventh centuries. Bede (ca. 672–735) became their most famous Christian thinker. He also wrote a history of the Anglo-Saxons that dated events before Christ's birth as B.C. and those after as A.D. This system is still in use in most of the world today, but historians prefer B.C.E. (Before the Common Era) and C.E. (Common Era) because they do not presume belief in the Christian God.

The English names for the days of the week also came into use at this time. Tuesday, Wednesday, Thursday, and Friday each combines the name of a Scandinavian god with the suffix *day*. Thursday, or Thor's day, is named for the vigorous god who ruled the sky and controlled thunder, wind, rain, and the harvest. Friday is named for Frey, the powerful god of fertility. Odin, the powerful god of war, was thought to have created the first man and the first woman; his name is also spelled Wodin, the root of the modern Wednesday. Odin's son Tiu gave his name to Tuesday. Sunday, Monday, and Saturday date to 321 C.E., when the Romans adopted the seven-day week, and Emperor Constantine named the days for different astronomical bodies: the sun, the moon, and the planet Saturn.

Anglo-Saxon monasteries made an appealing target for Viking raiders because they contained much detailed metalwork, whether reliquaries that held fragments of saints' bones or bejeweled gold and silver covers for illustrated manuscripts. The raiders also captured many slaves, keeping some for use in Scandinavia and selling others to the Byzantine and Abbasid empires.

In 866, a large Viking army arrived in England, just north of London, and established a long-term base camp. Between 866 and 954, the Scandinavians retained tenuous control of much of northern and eastern England, a region called the **Danelaw**. The residents paid an annual indemnity to their conquerors, and the Scandinavians settled throughout the Danelaw, Ireland, and Scotland. Alfred I (r. 871–899), who called himself "king of the Anglo-Saxons," managed to survive in the face of Viking attacks. After his death, various English, Anglo-Saxon, and Scandinavian leaders vied with each other for control of England, but no one succeeded for very long. In the tenth century, some Scandinavians settled in Normandy ("Northman's land") in northern France. From this base William the Conqueror launched a successful invasion of England in 1066, and his descendants ruled England for more than a hundred years.

Danelaw
Region including much of northern and eastern England, over which the Scandinavians maintained tenuous control between 866 and 954.

Scandinavian Society

Since the Scandinavians left only brief written texts, historians must draw on archaeological evidence and orally transmitted epics. Composed in Old Norse, a Germanic language, these epics were written down between 1200 and 1400. Two fascinating works entitled *Erik the Red's Saga* and *The Greenlanders' Saga*, together called **The Vinland Sagas**, recount events around the year 1000. The Scandinavians called the Americas Vinland, meaning either grape land or fertile land. Like all oral sources, these epics must be used cautiously; both glorify certain ancestors while denigrating others, and both exaggerate the extent of Christian belief while minimizing the extent of non-Christian practices.

The peoples of Scandinavia lived in communities of small farms in large, extended families of parents, children, grandchildren, unmarried siblings, and their servants. Women had considerable authority in Scandinavian society. They had property rights equal to those of their husbands and could institute divorce proceedings.

Leif Eriksson's sister-in-law Gudrid plays such a major role in *Erik the Red's Saga* that some have suggested it should have been named for her, and not for Leif's father Erik. She married three times, once to Leif Eriksson's brother, was widowed twice, and possibly went to Rome on a pilgrimage at the end of her life.

The Vinland Sagas
Term for *Erik the Red's Saga* and *The Greenlanders' Saga*, composed in Old Norse, that recount events around the year 1000. Both were written down between 1200 and 1400.

In the saga, whereas Gudrid is virtuous, Leif's illegitimate sister Freydis (FRY-duhs) is a murderer who will stop at nothing to get her way. Both women, however one-dimensional, are intelligent, strong leaders.

Like the Germanic-speaking peoples living on the European continent, the Scandinavians formed war-bands around leaders, receiving gifts and fighting for shares of plunder. In the years before 1000, new trade routes appeared linking Scandinavia with the Abbasid empire. Muslims bought slaves and furs from Scandinavians with silver dirham coins, over 130,000 of which have been found around the Baltic Sea.

At this time Scandinavian society produced a leader who played a role comparable to King Clovis of the Merovingians: Harald Bluetooth (r. 940–985) unified Denmark and conquered southern Norway. In 965 he became the first Scandinavian ruler to convert to Christianity, and the rulers of Norway and Sweden did so around 1030.

Scandinavian Religion

Women played an especially active role in pre-Christian religion because some served as seers who could predict the future. Once when famine hit a Greenland community, *Erik the Red's Saga* relates, a wealthy landowner hosted a feast to which he invited a prophetess. She asked the women of the community who among them knew *"the spells needed for performing the witchcraft, known as Warlock songs."* Gudrid reluctantly volunteered and *"sang the songs so well and beautifully that those present were sure they had never heard lovelier singing."* When she finished, the seer explained that the famine would end soon, since *"many spirits are now present which were charmed to hear the singing."*

The Scandinavians worshiped many gods. One traveler described a pre-Christian temple in Sweden that held three images. In the center was Thor, the most powerful deity who controlled the harvest. On either side of him stood the war-god Odin and the fertility goddess, Frey. Scandinavian burials often contain small metal items associated with Thor, such as hammers.

Burial customs varied. In some areas burials contained many grave goods, including full-size boats filled with clothing and tools, while in other areas the living cremated the dead and burned all their grave goods. (See the feature "Movement of Ideas Through Primary Sources: Ibn Fadlan's Description of a Rus Burial," page 280.) When people converted to Christianity, they were not supposed to bury grave goods, but many were reluctant to follow this prohibition for fear that the dead might starve or freeze as a result.

The Scandinavian Migrations to Iceland and Greenland, 870–980

As in Merovingian and Carolingian society, slaves and former slaves ranked at the bottom of society. In the saga, when a former slave proposes to Gudrid, her father is furious and rants at the suitor: *"I never expected to hear such a suggestion from you—that I should marry my daughter to the son of a slave! My lack of money must be very obvious to you!"* The proposal prompts him to give up his farm and leave for Greenland, where he hopes to find more fertile land. This was the impetus for migration: more fertile land than was available in Scandinavia, which was becoming increasingly crowded.

---

*From *The Vinland Sagas,* translated with an introduction by Magnus Magnusson and Hermann Pálsson (Penguin Classics, 1965). Copyright © Magnus Magnusson and Hermann Pálsson, 1965. Reprinted with permission of Penguin Group/UK.

In the first wave, between 870 and 930, Scandinavians went to Iceland. In 930 they established a Thing (assembly; see page 264), that had the power to pass laws and to hear disputes. Some have called Iceland's Thing the world's first legislature, but wealthy landowners had a greater say than the poor. Like the Polynesian explorers in the Pacific, the Scandinavian settlers had a huge impact on Iceland's environment. They brought pigs, horses, cattle, sheep, and goats with them, a combination that one historian likened to *"a bulldozer moving across this subarctic landscape."*[*]

The Vinland Sagas describe events occurring in Iceland sometime around 980, when Erik the Red was exiled by the Thing because he killed two men. Erik sailed west 200 miles (320 km) to Greenland and, after his term of exile ended, returned to recruit followers to go with him to Greenland. In 985 or 986, Erik led a fleet of fourteen boats to Greenland. His 400–500 followers included higher-ranking warband members as well as freemen, servants, and slaves.

The Scandinavians established two settlements on Greenland, the Eastern and Western Settlements. The settlers lived much as they had on Iceland, grazing animals on the narrow coast between the ocean and the interior ice, fishing for walrus, whales, and seals, and hunting polar bears and reindeer. They had to trade furs and walrus tusks to obtain the grain, wood, and iron they needed to survive. The Greenlanders established their own Thing assembly, which voted to adopt Christianity soon after 1000.

The Scandinavians in Vinland, ca. 1000

Around 1000, Leif Eriksson, the son of Erik the Red, decided to lead an exploratory voyage because he had heard of lands lying to the west of Greenland from a man named Bjarni Herjolfsson (bee-YARN-ee hair-YOLF-son). It is possible that others had preceded Bjarni to the Americas, but *The Vinland Sagas* do not give their names, so we should probably credit **Bjarni Herjolfsson**—and not Christopher Columbus—with being the first European to sail to the Americas. First Leif and then Thorfinn Karlsefni made several voyages to the Americas, landing in modern-day L'Anse aux Meadows, Newfoundland, Canada, and possibly going farther south to Maine. The Scandinavians arrived in North America after the end of the Maya classic era and before the great Mississippian cities of the Midwest were built (see Chapter 5). (See the feature "Visual Evidence in Primary Sources: The Scandinavian Settlement at L'Anse aux Meadows.")

The sagas report that Leif's brother-in-law, Thorfinn Karlsefni, decided to lead a group of sixty men and five women to settle in Vinland. Their first year went well because they found much wild game. Then *"they had their first encounter with Skraelings"*[†] (literally "wretches"), the term that the Scandinavians used for indigenous peoples. At first the Skraelings traded furs for cow's milk or scraps of red cloth, because Karlsefni would not allow his men to trade their iron weapons.

But relations soon deteriorated, and the Scandinavians and the Skraelings fought each other in several battles involving hand-to-hand combat. *Erik the Red's Saga* reports that the Skraelings *"were using catapults. Karlsefni and Snorri saw them hoist a large sphere on a pole; it was dark blue in color. It came flying in over the heads of Karlsefni's men and made an ugly din when it struck the ground."*[†]

The settlers in this story belonged to Karlsefni's war-band. Many had kin ties to him, whether direct or through marriage, and they probably gave him a share

Bjarni Herjolfsson The first European, according to *The Vinland Sagas*, to sail to the Americas, most likely sometime in the 990s.

Skraelings Term in *The Vinland Sagas* for the Amerindians living on the coast of Canada and possibly northern Maine, where the Scandinavians established temporary settlements.

---

[*]Thomas McGovern interview, *Nova: The Vikings,* 2000, transcript available at http://www.pbs.org/wgbh/nova/transcripts/2708vikings.html.

[†]From *The Vinland Sagas,* translated with an introduction by Magnus Magnusson and Hermann Pálsson (Penguin Classics, 1965). Copyright © Magnus Magnusson and Hermann Pálsson, 1965. Reprinted with permission of Penguin Group/UK.

of the lumber they shipped to Greenland, much as they would have given him a share of any loot they collected in battle. Whenever the Scandinavians went to a new place, they captured slaves, and North America was no exception. Karlsefni enslaved two Skraeling boys, who lived with the Scandinavians and later learned their language. The boys told them about their homeland: *"there were no houses there and that people lived in caves or holes in the ground. They said that there was a country across from their own land where the people went about in white clothing and uttered loud cries and carried poles with pieces of cloth attached."** This intriguing report is one of the earliest we have about Amerindians.

The Scandinavians, using metal knives and daggers, had a slight technological advantage over the Amerindians, who did not know how to work iron. But the newcomers could never have prevailed against a much larger force. The sagas succinctly explain why the Scandinavians decided to leave the Americas: *"Karlsefni and his men had realized by now that although the land was excellent they could never live there in safety or freedom from fear, because of the native inhabitants."**

In later centuries the Scandinavians sometimes returned to Canada to gather wood but never to settle. Sometime in the fifteenth century they also abandoned their settlements on Greenland because a drop in global temperature made life there much more difficult. These voyages are significant because the Scandinavians were the first Europeans to settle in the Americas. Their decision to leave resulted in no long-term consequences, a result utterly different from that of Columbus's voyages in the 1490s (see Chapter 15).

Russia, Land of the Rus, to 1054

Around 800, long before they set foot in Iceland, Greenland, or the Americas, early Scandinavians, mostly from Sweden, found that they could sail their longboats along the several major river courses, including the Volga and Dnieper Rivers, through the huge expanse of land lying to their east (see Map 10.4 on page 278). The peoples living in this region called themselves **Rus**, the root of the word *Russia*. This region offered many riches, primarily furs and slaves, to the raiders. Local rulers sometimes allied with a neighboring empire, such as Byzantium or the Abbasids, to enhance their power. When forming such an alliance the rulers had to choose among Judaism, Islam, or the Christianity of Rome or Constantinople, and the decisions they made had a lasting effect. The region of modern-day Russia also saw the rise of important centers before 1000, contributing to even more centers in Europe.

Rus
Name given to themselves by people who lived in the region stretching from the Arctic to the north shore of the Black Sea and from the Baltic Sea to the Caspian Sea.

The Peoples Living in Russia

The region of Russia (which was much larger than today's modern nation) housed different ecosystems and different peoples deriving their living from the land. To the north, peoples exploited the treeless tundra and the taiga (sub-Arctic coniferous forest) to fish and to hunt reindeer, bear, and walrus. On the steppe grasslands extending far to the west, nomadic peoples migrated with their herds in search of fertile pasture.

In the forests, where most people lived, they raised herds and grew crops on small family farms. Too poor to dedicate much land to raising hay, they had no draft animals and could clear the land only with fire and hand tools. The lack of natural fertilizer from draft animals forced them to clear new lands every few

*From *The Vinland Sagas,* translated with an introduction by Magnus Magnusson and Hermann Pálsson (Penguin Classics, 1965). Copyright © Magnus Magnusson and Hermann Pálsson, 1965. Reprinted with permission of Penguin Group/UK.

11

Expanding Trade Networks in Africa and India, 1000–1500

In 1325, a twenty-year-old legal scholar named **Ibn Battuta** (1304–1368/69[1]) set off on a hajj pilgrimage from his home in Tangier (tan-jeer), a Mediterranean port on the westernmost edge of the Islamic world (see Chapter 9). In Mecca, Ibn Battuta (IH-buhn bah-TOO-tuh) made a decision that changed his life: instead of returning home, he decided to keep going. A world traveler with no fixed destination and no set time of return, he followed trade routes that knitted the entire Islamic world together. These routes connected places like Mecca, which had been at the center of the Islamic world since Muhammad's first revelations, to others that had more recently joined that world, such as the sub-Saharan kingdom of Mali and the Delhi sultanate of north India. After his travels were over, Ibn Battuta dictated his adventures to a ghost writer. His account began:

Muslim Traveler, ca. 1300

(Bibliotheque Nationale, Paris, France/Superstock, Inc.)

H

My departure from Tangier, my birthplace, took place . . . in the year seven hundred and twenty-five [1325] with the object of making the Pilgrimage to the Holy House at Mecca and of visiting the tomb of the Prophet . . . at Medina. I set out alone, having neither fellow-traveller in whose companionship I might find cheer, nor caravan whose party I might join, but swayed by an over-mastering impulse within me, and a desire long-cherished in my bosom to visit these illustrious sanctuaries.[*]

———

[*]From H. A. R. Gibb, *The Travels of Ibn Battuta A.D. 1325–1354*, The Hakluyt Society, p. 8. Reprinted with permission. The Hakluyt Society was established in 1846 for the purpose of printing rare or unpublished Voyages and Travels. For further information please see their website at: www.hakluyt.com.

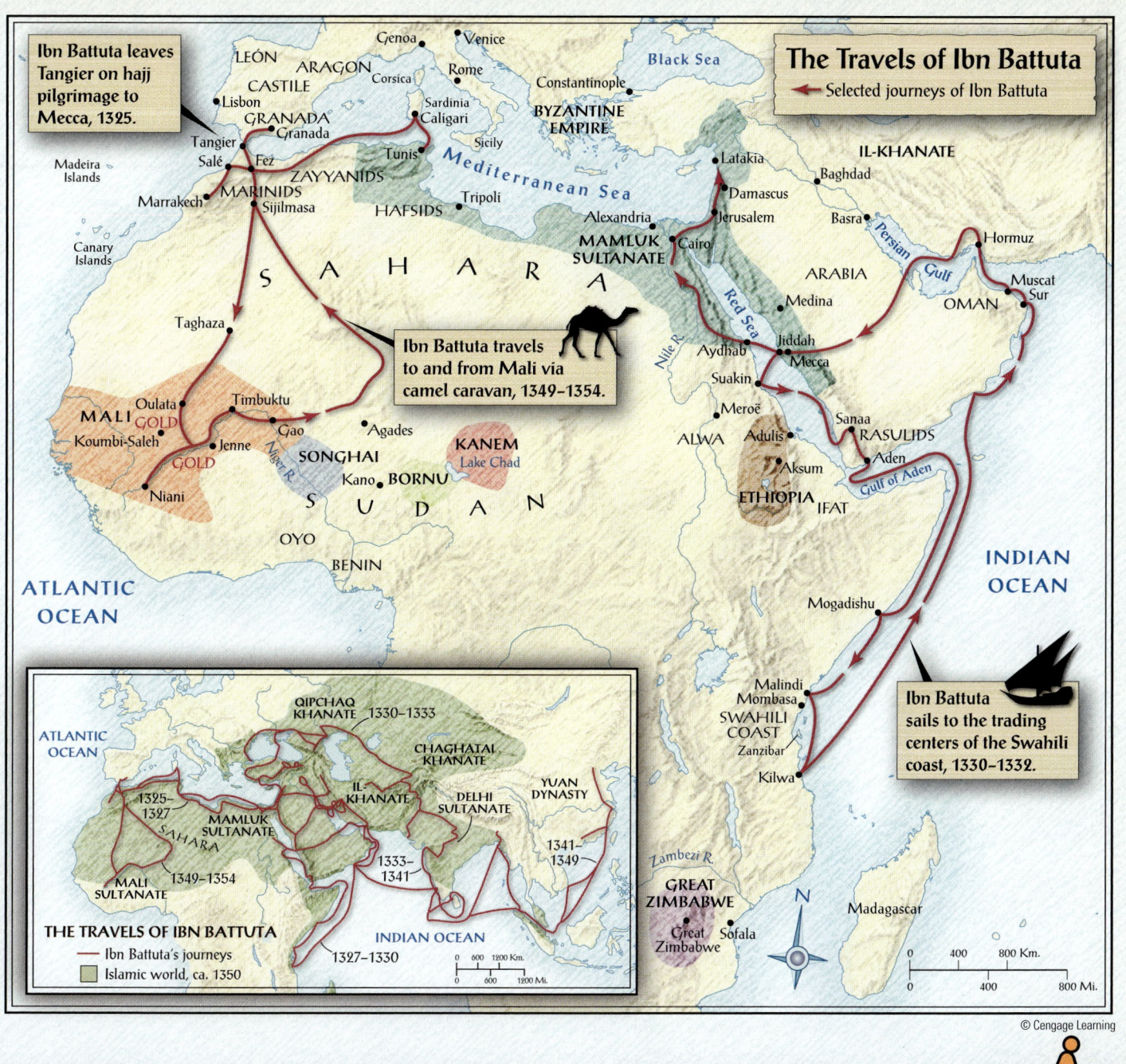

The Travels of Ibn Battuta

← Selected journeys of Ibn Battuta

Ibn Battuta leaves Tangier on hajj pilgrimage to Mecca, 1325.

Ibn Battuta travels to and from Mali via camel caravan, 1349–1354.

Ibn Battuta sails to the trading centers of the Swahili coast, 1330–1332.

THE TRAVELS OF IBN BATTUTA
— Ibn Battuta's journeys
Islamic world, ca. 1350

QIPCHAQ KHANATE 1330–1333
CHAGHATAI KHANATE
1325–1327
IL-KHANATE
MAMLUK SULTANATE
DELHI SULTANATE
YUAN DYNASTY
1341–1349
1333–1341
1327–1330
1349–1354
MALI SULTANATE

© Cengage Learning

Join this chapter's traveler on "Voyages," an interactive tour of historic sites and events: www.cengagebrain.com

So begins the account of the longest known journey taken by any single individual before 1500. Proceeding on foot, riding camels and donkeys, and sailing by boat, Ibn Battuta covered an estimated 75,000 miles (120,000 km)—an extraordinary distance in the preindustrial world. Because the Five Pillars of Islam obligated all Muslims to give alms, not just to the poor and the sick but also to travelers, Ibn Battuta was able to continue his travels even when his own funds were exhausted.

Ibn Battuta
(1304–1368/69) Legal scholar from Tangier, Morocco, who traveled throughout the Islamic world between 1325 and 1354 and wrote *The Travels*.

After setting out alone, Ibn Battuta soon fell in with a caravan of traders on their way to Cairo. Because he always traveled with Islamic merchants on established caravan routes, his itinerary provides ample evidence of the extensive trade networks connecting northern Africa, much of East and West Africa, and northern India. Many of the people he met accepted the teachings of the Quran, and he was able to communicate in Arabic everywhere he went. In each place he visited, he named the rulers, identified the highest-ranking judges, and then listed the important holy men of the town and their most important miracles. This narrow focus means that he rarely reported on some important topics, such as the local economy or the lives of women and non-Muslims.

Ibn Battuta was the first traveler to leave an eyewitness description of Africa south of the Sahara Desert, where he stayed in the kingdom of Mali. He visited Cairo—the capital city of the Mamluks (MAM-lukes) of Egypt, a powerful dynasty founded by military slaves—as well as several East African ports south of the equator. He remained for seven years in north India, then under Muslim rule, and visited many Indian Ocean ports. He did not, however, go to the interior of southern Africa or see the majestic site of Great Zimbabwe.

Many legs of Ibn Battuta's journey would not have been possible three hundred years earlier. In 1000 many parts of Africa were not connected to the broader Islamic world, including the rainforest of the West African coastlands and Central Africa, the densely populated Great Lakes region around Lake Victoria, and the southern African savanna. By 1450, however, expanding networks of trade had brought West and East Africa into increasing contact with the Islamic world of northern Africa and western Asia.

Focus Questions

» *How was sub-Saharan Africa settled before 1000? What techniques have historians used to reconstruct the past?*

» *What role did trade play in the emergence and subsequent history of the kingdoms of Ghana, Middle Niger, and Mali?*

» *How and why did the Mamluk empire based in Egypt become the leading center of the Islamic world after 1258?*

» *What was the nature of the Indian Ocean trade network that linked India, Arabia, and East Africa?*

Reconstructing the History of Sub-Saharan Africa Before 1000

The Sahara Desert divides the enormous continent of Africa into two halves: sub-Saharan Africa in contrast to North and East Africa. In the seventh century, Islamic armies conquered North Africa, and East Africans had much contact with Muslim traders throughout the Abbasid period (750–1258). We know much less about sub-Saharan Africa before 1000 because few Muslims, the source of so much of our information, traveled there. Apart from Arabic accounts, historians of Africa must draw on archaeological excavation, oral traditions, and analysis of languages to piece together sub-Saharan Africa's history before 1000.

The Geography and Languages of Sub-Saharan Africa

Africa is a large continent, with an area greater than that of the United States (including Alaska), Europe, and China combined. As we saw in Chapter 1, the first anatomically modern humans crossed the Sinai Peninsula from Africa into western Asia at least 150,000 years ago, possibly earlier. The Nile River Valley was the site of Africa's earliest complex societies, first in Egypt and then in Nubia (see Chapter 2). Rome's greatest rival, Carthage, operated from a base in North Africa, and after its defeat in 202 B.C.E., Romans bought much of their grain from Egypt. In the 300s, Christianity spread throughout the Mediterranean to Egypt, northern Africa, and Ethiopia (see Chapter 7). After 650, Islam replaced Christianity in much of northern Africa, but not in Ethiopia.

A glance at Map 11.1 shows why only North and East Africa had such close contacts with the larger world: 3,000 miles (4,800 km) across and around 1,000 miles (1,600 km) from north to south, the Sahara Desert posed a formidable barrier between the coast and the sub-Saharan regions. The first traders to cross the Sahara did so riding camels. The single-humped camel they used originated in Arabia and reached North Africa sometime in the first century B.C.E. Domesticated in the third or fourth centuries C.E., camels were much cheaper than human porters because they were hardier—capable of going for long periods without water and carrying much heavier loads. Camels did not need roads and crossed the desert along sandy tracks.

Immediately to the south of the Sahara is a semidesert region called the **Sahel** (meaning "shore" in Arabic). South of the Sahel (SAH-hel), sufficient rain fell to support the tall grasses of the dry savanna and a band of wooded savanna where many trees grew farther south. Rainfall was heaviest in Central Africa, and rainforest stretched from the Atlantic coast to the Great Lakes region. Differential rainfall caused the pattern to repeat itself south of the rainforest: first a band of woodland savanna, then dry savanna, and then the Kalahari Desert near the tip of southern Africa.

Africans today speak nearly two thousand different languages, one-third of the total number of languages spoken in the world (see Map 11.1). Several languages spoken in North Africa, including Egyptian, Nubian, Ethiopian, and Arabic, have had written forms for a thousand years or longer (see Chapters 2, 7, and 9). But none of those spoken south of the Sahara were written down before 1800. Today about five hundred of Africa's two thousand languages have written forms.

Sahel
Semidesert region south of the Sahara.

The Spread of Bantu Languages

Africa's languages cluster in several major groups. Arabic is spoken throughout the Islamic regions, while the **Bantu** languages of the Niger-Congo language family are widely distributed throughout sub-Saharan Africa. Since many of these languages show surprising uniformity over a wide area, earlier analysts posited that the migration of a single people, all speaking an earlier form of the Bantu language, accounted for the modern distribution.

More recently, however, African historians pioneered the use of a linguistic method called *glottochronology* to analyze the history of languages. By comparing vocabulary lists, linguists can count how many words in two languages are the same and how many have changed. The greater the number of shared words, the closer two languages are; the fewer the number, the more distant. Glottochronology can

Bantu
Name for the languages of the Niger-Congo language family and the speakers of those languages.

MAP 11.1 African Trade Routes Before 1500 The Sahara Desert forms a natural boundary between Saharan Africa and sub-Saharan Africa. Overland camel routes across the Sahara Desert linked Mali with the Mediterranean coast, while Indian Ocean sea routes connected the important center of Great Zimbabwe in East Africa to the Islamic world and Asia. (© Cengage Learning)

indicate which languages broke off from others and in what order but not always exactly when. Close analysis of the linguistic variation among modern Bantu languages suggests that multiple waves of change occurred. Accordingly, scholars today have discarded the theory of a single wave of Bantu migration.

A persuasive model for the spread of Bantu languages sees three different, and often overlapping, processes taking place over an extended period: the planting of the first crops, the development of metallurgy, and the spread of the Bantu languages. First, archaeological evidence shows that, sometime between 1000 and 500 B.C.E., different peoples began to cultivate crops. Those in the drier regions grew sorghum, millet, and rice, while those in the rainforest raised tubers such as yams. Like the Maya (see Chapter 5), many of these peoples engaged in slash-and-burn agriculture, with the result that they farmed the same place for only one or two seasons. As in other parts of the world, it took hundreds, possibly thousands, of years before people shifted to full-time agriculture.

During this transition to agriculture, different peoples learned how to work iron. Iron tools were much more effective than stone and wood tools in turning the earth and preparing it for seed. The first evidence of ironworking in Africa dates to about 600 B.C.E. Interestingly, people living north of the Sahara, along the Nile River in modern Sudan, and south of the Sahara in central Nigeria learned how to work iron at about the same time, but their differing metallurgical techniques indicate that they discovered how to work iron independently of each other.

Most sub-Saharan African peoples started to work iron without any previous experience in working copper. In contrast, in Eurasia the usual pattern was first to combine copper and tin into bronze and then, as the Hittites did in 2000 B.C.E., build on that expertise to smelt iron (see Chapter 2); the peoples of the Americas, though, never worked iron (see Chapter 5).

Africans built a greater variety of furnaces for smelting iron than people anywhere else in the world. Some furnaces had tall shafts; others used preheated air. These smelting techniques allowed Africans to make iron from much leaner ores than those used elsewhere. The technology for smelting iron spread throughout southern Africa by 300 C.E.

Although iron is an extremely useful metal that can be made into agricultural implements and military weapons, it is relatively soft and rusts. Steel is much stronger and more resistant to rusting. The difference between iron and steel is the amount of carbon in the metal: iron that has been worked by a blacksmith, or wrought iron, usually contains less than 0.2 percent carbon, while steel may contain up to 1.5 percent. African smelting furnaces often made iron with enough dissolved carbon to have the properties of steel.

In the same centuries that the sub-Saharan Africans were developing agriculture and refining their production of iron, the Bantu languages spread in a southward direction to the regions where rainfall was heavier. It is possible that different groups moved out from the heartland of the Bantu languages in modern-day Nigeria and Cameroon and that their ability to farm and to make iron tools enabled them to displace the indigenous populations, who hunted and gathered. Yet it is equally likely that indigenous peoples adopted the new farming and iron-smelting technologies and the Bantu languages at different times in different regions.

By 1000, agricultural peoples who used iron tools had settled throughout sub-Saharan Africa, many of them speaking Bantu languages. Their iron tools allowed them to move into and settle heavily forested areas such as the Great Lakes region.

Society and Family Life

The final centuries of these changes overlap with the first written records. As early as the eighth century, Arab geographers began to record some preliminary notes, often on the basis of hearsay, about sub-Saharan Africa, and Arabic sources dominate the historical record through the sixteenth century, particularly for North and East Africa. The lack of indigenous historical records means that, like

oral histories
Historical accounts passed from one generation to the next. Particularly important in societies where no written accounts survive.

griot/griotte
Royal storytellers who served as advisers to the rulers of Mali and other West African states. (A *griotte* is a female storyteller.)

lineage
Group of people claiming descent from the same ancestor, whether legendary or historical, who are not necessarily biologically related but consider themselves a family unit.

Mali
Kingdom founded ca. 1230 by Sundiata in West Africa. Generated revenue by taxing the caravans of the trans-Saharan trade.

their colleagues elsewhere, historians of sub-Saharan Africa must rely on **oral histories**. In Africa, royal storytellers, or **griots** (GREE-oh; a French word), often recited the events of the past to the monarchs they advised. Exciting breakthroughs in African history have come when historians have determined the exact date and location of a given event by linking events from oral histories with Arabic-language sources. Ibn Battuta's account occupies pride of place among these Arabic sources because he went to so many places and wrote at such great length. (The English translation of his account fills nearly a thousand pages in four volumes.)

Historians have been able to reconstruct the past by carefully examining historic accounts and judiciously considering which aspects of social and economic life were least likely to change. Jan Vansina, a prominent historian of Africa, coined the term *upstreaming* for their task because it resembles standing on a riverbank, observing what is happening, and making an intelligent guess about what occurred upstream.[2]

Upstreaming has led historians to concur that certain generalizations probably hold true for most of sub-Saharan Africa before 1000. While no estimates for Africa's overall population at this time exist, it is clear that people lived in villages of several hundred to several thousand residents and that fertile areas were more heavily populated than barren regions like the Sahara Desert. Often the people of one village claimed descent from the same ancestor, whether legendary or historical, and historians use the term **lineage** or *clan* for such family units. (Historians today avoid the word tribe because of its negative associations and condescending use in the past.)

Lineages and clans organized into villages were the bedrock of Africa's diverse societies. Men often dominated the tasks with the greatest prestige, like hunting or metallurgy, as well as anything requiring long-distance travel, such as military conquest, long-distance trade, and diplomatic negotiations. Women usually tilled the soil, gathered wild fruits and vegetables, made pottery, and prepared meals. Marriage patterns varied from village to village: a man might take a single wife or multiple wives, sometimes from within his own lineage, sometimes from other groups.

Men formed tight bonds with other men of the same age while undergoing initiations into adulthood. Younger men respected and obeyed more senior men. A man who fathered many children and attained great wealth was called a "great man." Great men earned their position at the top of village society, often by military prowess.

Great men led villages, and if continually successful in battle, they might form larger political units such as a chieftaincy or a kingdom. Historians usually describe villages as evolving into chieftaincies, and then chieftaincies into kingdoms or states, but the different stages were not sharply defined. During the lifetimes of the great men who led them, the villages they had conquered would submit gifts to them; after their deaths, however, the fragile political units they formed could easily break apart. In the course of his travels, Ibn Battuta met several great men who headed their own kingdoms, one of whom was the ruler of Mali.

The Kingdom of Mali and Its Precursors in Sub-Saharan Africa

The kingdom of **Mali**, centered on the Niger River basin, occupied much of West Africa south of the Sahara Desert. It straddled the Sahel and the vast savanna grasslands to the south. Because this territory included some of the world's biggest gold mines, merchants crossed the Sahara to this region perhaps as early as 500. Urbanization began in the West African Sahel with the development of the trans-Saharan trade. Ghana (ca. 700–1000) was the first kingdom to take advantage of its location at an important node of trade, and the kingdom of Mali built on these earlier achievements in taxing trans-Saharan trade as a pathway to power. Ibn Battuta offers a verbal snapshot of Mali's trade with the north in the 1350s: caravans brought slaves and gold from the south and exchanged them for cloth, pottery, and glass trinkets from the north.

The Kingdom of Ghana, ca. 700–1000

The Muslim geographer al-Bakri (d. 1094) provided the earliest and most detailed description of the kingdom of **Ghana** in his *Book of Routes and Realms* (see Chapter 9). Since al-Bakri never left his native Córdoba in Spain, he drew all of his information from earlier geographic accounts and from named informants who had been to the Sahara and the sub-Saharan trading kingdoms.

Ghana
The first empire in western Sudan. Prospered between 700 and 1000.

These kingdoms began as small settlements located at points where different routes crossed each other. Sijilmasa (sih-jil-MAHS-suh), located on the northern edge of the Sahara in modern Morocco, originated, al-Bakri reports, as a periodic market on a *"bare plain"* where local people came to buy and sell goods, like iron tools, only at certain times of year. He says the periodic market *"was the beginning of its being populated, then it became a town."** Sijilmasa grew into an important trade depot ruled by a royal lineage whose founder claimed descent from a family who sold iron tools at the earliest periodic market. Towns like Sijilmasa became city-states whose main source of revenue was the taxes their rulers collected from traders.

The kingdom of Ghana, which was the first empire in the region of the western Sudan, arose through a similar process. In the mid-1000s, al-Bakri reported that the kingdom contained two cities: preachers and scholars lived in the Islamic one, which had twelve mosques where Friday prayers were said; and *"six miles"* away, the king and his *"sorcerers"* lived in the other. Al-Bakri's informants drew a sharp line between Muslims and *"polytheists,"* whose *"religion is paganism and the worship of idols."** The king did not convert to Islam, but he welcomed Muslim visitors.

The king taxed the goods going in and out of the cities he ruled. Merchants paid a tax in gold on each donkey load of goods they brought in. The tax was higher for more valuable goods, like copper, and lower for cheaper commodities, like salt. These revenues financed the king's military campaigns. The king, al-Bakri wrote, could raise an army of 200,000 men, of whom 40,000 were archers. Since archaeologists have not found any sites that match al-Bakri's description, they have concluded that the kingdom did not have a fixed capital and that the king and his retinue regularly moved among different cities.

Jenne-jeno: A Different Path to Complex Society

Outside the kingdom of Ghana, 2 miles (3 km) southeast of Jenne, is the large urban site of Jenne-jeno (jen-NAY jenn-OH) in the **Middle Niger Valley** (see Map 11.1). Jenne-jeno's population in the 700s was between 15,000 and 27,000. Smaller surrounding towns of 500 to 1,500 people formed a nested hierarchy of villages, small towns, and medium-size towns.[3] Jenne-jeno, meaning "ancient Jenne" in the local Songhai language, is part of the city of Jenne, which is 220 miles (354 km) southwest of Timbuktu in Mali.

Middle Niger Valley
A recently discovered complex society, well established by the 700s, with large urban settlements but no distinct political center or full-time agriculture.

*Al-Bakri's *The Book of Routes and Realms,* as translated in *Corpus of Early Arabic Sources for West African History,* ed. N. Levtzion and J. F. P. Hopkins (New York: Cambridge University Press, 1981), pp. 65–66, 79–81.

In the years leading up to 1000, Jenne-jeno had a large population, but it did not resemble cities anywhere else in the world. For one thing, archaeologists have found no evidence of a clear political center. Nor did the city have any prominent buildings made of stone. For this reason archaeologists did not recognize the Middle Niger Valley as a complex society until the 1980s.

They changed their minds when they realized how big the settlement was; it covered over 80 acres (32 ha). Enormous mounds of debris standing over 26 feet (8 m) tall hold hundreds of thousands of broken pieces of dirt foundations and mud bricks, waste from ironworking, copper ornaments, clay figures used as toys, grinding stones, and fragments of pottery, all persuasive evidence of population density. The city's most prominent feature was its mud-brick wall 11.8 feet (3.6 m) across at the base.

The Middle Niger Valley society departs from the world's complex societies in other ways. The local people cultivated wet rice but never shifted to full-time agriculture; they continued to gather wild plants and to hunt wild animals. Archaeologists have yet to find evidence of social stratification, but they did detect occupational specialization: after 400 C.E., residents smelted iron outside the city and brought the partially worked metal to the city, where smiths worked it into tools.

As al-Bakri suggested, trade was crucial to the region. In the earliest centuries of occupation, the exchanges were largely local, with residents trading dried fish, fish oil, and rice for iron. Over time the city imported commodities from farther away, such as copper and salt from the Sahara. The city reached its greatest extent around the year 1000 and prospered for several hundred years.

Archaeologists are not certain why the city declined after 1300. The population dropped to one-tenth of its former size, and many of the surrounding satellite towns were abandoned. The ruler of Jenne-jeno converted to Islam sometime between 1200 and 1300, and he may have built a new city unspoiled by traces of local religion. It is also possible that the Black Death (discussed later in this chapter) reached the city and caused massive deaths. (See the feature "World History in Today's World: The High Price of Living in a World Heritage Site.")

Some states in pre-1500 Africa, like Ghana, controlled large amounts of territory, but usually they exercised direct political control over only a small core area. Even where such states existed, however, kings normally had little independent political power, usually serving as mediators and consensus builders for councils of elders. The lineage and clan elders made the most important decisions at the local level.

Unlike Mesopotamia, Egypt, India, China, or the Americas, where the first complex societies tapped agricultural surplus, most African states arose through control of strategic natural resources like water or gold. The loss of several key trading depots to a dynasty based in Spain drastically reduced the tax revenues paid to the kings of Ghana, and they lost their kingdom to a local lineage named the Sosso (SUE-sue) around 1150.

Sundiata and the Founding of the Mali Kingdom, ca. 1230

The best source about the rise of Mali is an oral epic, written down only in the twentieth century, that recounts the life and exploits of the founder of the Mali kingdom, Sundiata (soon-JAH-tuh) (r. ca. 1230). The peoples of West Africa spoke a group of related languages called Mande (MAHN-day), which included the Malinke (muh-LING-kay) language spoken in Mali. The Malinke version of the tale *Sundiata* tells how the son of a local ruler overthrew the Sosso king Soumaoro (sue-MAO-row) and united the different peoples of the region.

The High Price of Living in a World Heritage Site

The Great Mosque in the city of Jenne is the largest mud-brick structure in the world. It is also one of the world's most distinctive buildings. Rebuilt in 1906–1907 using traditional construction techniques, it is made from mud bricks between 16 and 24 inches (40 and 60 cm) thick. Supported by more than ninety wooden pillars, the prayer hall holds three thousand people; the roof has built-in ceramic caps that can be removed on hot days to introduce cool air. The mosque's unusual three minarets (normally mosques have four) each have an ostrich egg, a symbol of purity, suspended above the highest point. Rows of beams stick out from the mosque's walls but are not structural. They provide scaffolding for those who participate in an annual festival in which volunteers add a new mud layer to the building's exterior.

Regular maintenance is crucial to the survival of the building, but it is becoming more difficult to apply the mud. During a long drought in the 1970s, the Niger River dried up and later moved farther from the town, requiring the townspeople to walk longer distances to obtain mud. People started to manufacture mud bricks from a mix of dirt and garbage or garbage bags, perpetually giving the city a slight smell of garbage. Finally, the number of skilled masons has declined as modern building materials have become more popular.

In 1989, UNESCO named the Great Mosque and the surrounding old town of Jenne as a World Heritage Site. Such a designation ensures a steady stream of visitors and income, but in 2006 the city's residents rioted in response to the first survey of houses to be restored. They object to UNESCO's strict rules, which forbid any changes to the interior and the exterior of their traditional mud-brick homes. One city-dweller explained: "When a town is put on the heritage list, it means nothing should change, but we want development, more space, new appliances—things that are much more modern. We are angry about that." This provides a valuable reminder: modern homes offer many conveniences that preservationists often overlook in their enthusiasm to preserve the dwellings of the past.

Source: Neil MacFarquhar, "Mali City Rankled by Rules for Life in Spotlight," New York Times, January 8, 2011.

Each king of Mali had his own griot who had been taught the story of his dynastic predecessors and whose task was to compose new sections about the reigning king. The griots' extensive knowledge of the ancestral teachings granted them a prominent position in Mali society, and they often advised rulers on matters of state and accompanied them on diplomatic missions. Ibn Battuta's description is one of the earliest we have of the griots and their close relationship to the **sultan**. Ibn Battuta used the word *sultan*, meaning "ruler" in Arabic, for the Mali king because his predecessors had converted to Islam sometime around 1000.

Ibn Battuta described the Mali sultan's griots:

sultan
"Ruler" in Arabic. Any head of an Islamic state, often called *sultanates*.

Each of them is inside a costume made of feathers resembling the green woodpecker on which is a wooden head with a red beak. . . . They stand before the Sultan in this laughable get-up and recite their poems. . . . I have been told that their poetry is a sort of admonition. They say to the Sultan: "This platform, formerly such and such a king sat on it and performed noble actions, and so and so did such and such; do you do noble acts which will be recounted after you?"

*From H. A. R. Gibb, *The Travels of Ibn Battuta A.D. 1325–1354*, The Hakluyt Society, p. 962. Reprinted with permission. The Hakluyt Society was established in 1846 for the purpose of printing rare or unpublished Voyages and Travels. For further information please see their website at: www.hakluyt.com.

Once they were done reciting, the griots climbed up the platform on which the sultan was sitting and placed their head on his right shoulder, his left, and then his lap to show their respect.

The story of Sundiata remains our most detailed source about the early years of Mali. Sundiata was born to a king and his hump-backed wife, and he walked only at the age of seven. These traits indicated to the audience that both mother and son possessed unusual spiritual powers. In the hope that Sundiata would someday succeed to the throne, his father assigned him his own griot. One day, when his exasperated mother yelled at Sundiata because he was still entirely dependent on others for food, his griot sent word to the village blacksmith to send an iron bar so heavy that six men were needed to carry it. Sundiata easily picked up the bar with one hand and then stood up and walked. He grew into a strong and powerful warrior who was eventually forced into exile by one of his father's envious wives. After nearly ten years away, Sundiata returned to his kingdom and resolved to overthrow the oppressive rule of Soumaoro, the leader of the rival Sosso lineage.

The *Sundiata* epic reveals much about African religions. Sundiata's enemy Soumaoro is a sorcerer who knows how to make small figurines, or fetishes, and recite spells to wound his enemies. Still, Soumaoro is not invincible. He tells his wife that he must observe a taboo against touching a cock's spur, the sharp talon a rooster uses to attack his enemies. If he violates the taboo, he will lose the power granted to him by his ancestors. Sundiata's half-sister finds out the mysterious source of the sorcerer's power, or *jinn*. The Arabic word for a spirit or ghost (also the root of the English word *genie*), jinn is a key concept in Islam. Sundiata attaches a cock's spur to an arrow that hits Soumaoro on his shoulder.

A Modern Headdress from Mali When Ibn Battuta visited the sultan of Mali, he described griots who wore a feathered costume topped by a bird's head with a beak. Perhaps he saw something like this bird mask, made in the twentieth century out of feathers, porcupine quills, antelope horns, and mud, from the same region of Mali that he went to.

"The cock's spur no more than scratched him, but the effect was immediate and Sou-maoro felt his powers leave him."[*]

The epic illustrates how local African religion absorbed religious conceptions from Islam. Aside from the clue about jinn, *Sundiata* never explicitly mentions God or the power of Islam, even though al-Bakri's report about the Mali ruler's conversion to Islam dates to 1068, nearly two centuries before the events described in the epic occurred.

The *Sundiata* narrative sketches the process of state formation as a series of conquests, some within Mali, others beyond; some of human enemies, others of supernatural forces. By the end of the epic, Sundiata rules the kingdom of Mali.

How many of the events described in *Sundiata* can be confirmed by other sources? Arab chronicles confirm that the kingdom of Mali existed in the thirteenth century, and the great Arab historian **Ibn Khaldun** (1332–1406), a native of Tunis in North Africa, recorded the names of the Mali kings and the major events of their reigns. Ibn Khaldun (IH-buhn hal-DOON), perhaps the most important Muslim historian of all time, formulated an entirely original definition of history as the study of human society and its transformations. His painstaking work makes it possible to date Sundiata's reign to around 1230.

The process of state formation that the *Sundiata* narrative describes is plausible: armies several thousand strong did fight with iron-tipped bows and other metal weapons. The Mali army consisted of different independent armies, each led by a local leader who decided in each instance which higher leader he would support. At its largest point, reached some one hundred years after Sundiata's reign, the kingdom of Mali extended more than 1,000 miles (1,600 km) east to west and included the basins of both the Senegal and Niger Rivers.

The Mali government's primary source of revenue was taxing trade. One of Sundiata's most wealthy successors was Mansa Musa (r. 1307–1332), who visited Cairo on his way to Mecca in 1324. (*Mansa* is a word in the Malinke language meaning "supreme ruler," and *Musa* is Arabic for Moses; *Mansa Musa* means King Moses.) Five hundred servants, each carrying a staff of gold weighing 6 pounds (2.7 kg), walked in front of him. One hundred camels were required to carry his travel money, which was some 700 pounds (315 kg) of gold, making Mansa Musa one of the most talked-about and most welcome travelers of his day. A map of Afro-Eurasia made one hundred years after his death pictured Mansa Musa as a symbol of great wealth.[4]

Trans-Saharan Trade Networks

In 1352, twenty years after Mansa Musa's death, Ibn Battuta went to Mali. The only eyewitness description we have of the fabulously wealthy kingdom, his account provides our best source about the **trans-Saharan caravan trade network** connecting Mali with northern Africa. Traveling in caravans on well-established trade routes, Ibn Battuta witnessed the highly developed commercial network that traversed the sharply different geographic zones of the Sahara Desert, the Sahel, the grasslands, and the more heavily populated forests of Central Africa (see Map 11.1).

Those crossing the desert usually bought camels and provisions at towns like Sijilmasa, whose rise al-Bakri described. After twenty-five days crossing the desert, Ibn Battuta's exhausted caravan arrived in Taghaza, one of the major salt-producing

Ibn Khaldun (1332–1406) Prominent Muslim historian born in Tunis; he reported on the kings of Mali.

trans-Saharan caravan trade network A network of overland trade exchanging slaves and gold from sub-Saharan Africa for cloth, pottery, and glass trinkets from the Mediterranean.

[*]Excerpt from D. T. Niane, *Sundiata: An Epic of Old Mali*, trans. G. D. Pickett (London: Longman, 1965), p. 65.

Bibliotheque Nationale, Paris, France/Bridgeman Art Library

The Richest King in the Land? Mansa Musa of Mali In 1375, a European cartographer mapped Afro-Eurasia with unprecedented accuracy. This detail of the Catalan Atlas shows the blue Mediterranean Ocean, southern Spain, and North Africa. The mapmaker has also included written labels that identify the seated figure on the lower right as Mansa Musa, the richest king in the land because of the abundant gold in his country.

centers on the southern edge of the Sahara. *"It is a village with no attractions,"** remarks Ibn Battuta, who describes only dwellings and a mosque with walls of salt blocks and roofs of camel skins. Salt structures were long-lasting because there were less than 8 inches (200 mm) of rain each year. The slaves who mined the salt lived on a monotonous diet of camel meat, dates from North Africa, and millet from Mali, so even they were enmeshed in a trading economy.

Salt is an essential nutrient for all human beings, and it is even more important in hot areas because it allows the body to replace salt lost by sweating. Pure salt was so valuable that it was used as a currency. *"The Blacks,"* Ibn Battuta remarks, *"trade with salt as others trade with gold and silver; they cut it in pieces and buy and sell with these."** As Ibn Battuta made his way south of the Sahara, he learned that travelers did not have to carry either food or silver coins because they could trade small amounts of salt, small glass trinkets, or spices for whatever food and lodging they required.

---

*From H. A. R. Gibb, *The Travels of Ibn Battuta A.D. 1325–1354*, The Hakluyt Society, p. 947. Reprinted with permission. The Hakluyt Society was established in 1846 for the purpose of printing rare or unpublished Voyages and Travels. For further information please see their website at: www.hakluyt.com.

At the end of his stay in Mali, Ibn Battuta visited Timbuktu (tim-buk-TOO), a great trading city on the Niger River, whose ruler gave him a young male slave, a typical gift for an honored guest. The slave traders of Mali did not enslave people of their own country; they captured slaves in the forest belt to the south. When Ibn Battuta returned to Morocco, he traveled with a caravan carrying six hundred female slaves. One of the few reliable statistics available, Ibn Battuta's observation, combined with a handful of other sources, has led one historian to estimate that 5,500 slaves crossed the desert each year between 1100 and 1400.[5]

More women than men crossed the Sahara because more buyers wanted female slaves than male slaves. Once sold in the markets of Morocco, women slaves would work as servants and concubines for urban dwellers, or perhaps for the royal court. Since slave owners feared that male slaves might impregnate the female members of the household, they preferred castrated males, or eunuchs. In the premodern era, the operation to remove male slaves' genitals, whether partially or entirely, was perilous; only a lucky few survived.

Mali's other major export was gold. One historian has estimated that, in the thirteenth and fourteenth centuries, two-thirds of all the gold entering Europe passed through the North African cities of Tunis, Fez, and Cairo.[6] The gold originated in mines in Mali. Working conditions in the gold mines were grim: shafts could be over 60 feet (20 m) deep and frequently collapsed. Men dug out the ore while women extracted the gold. Both tasks were laborious, but the mining allowed subsistence farmers to augment their incomes.

Society in Mali

Ibn Battuta visited Mali because it was on an established caravan route and he was confident that he would be received there as he was throughout the Islamic world. The first ruler of Mali to convert to Islam did so around 1000, but his subjects, according to the geographer al-Bakri, did not. (See the feature "Movement of Ideas Through Primary Sources: Conversion to Islam in Fictional and Nonfictional Sources.")

By the time of Ibn Battuta's visit, Mali had become a Muslim kingdom, but people in Mali did not behave as Ibn Battuta felt observant Muslims should. Although he wrote as though there was a single standard of behavior that prevailed throughout the Islamic world, there was not. Within the structure of Islam, no supreme authority existed that could establish such a standard, which explains why Islamic religious and cultural practices were (and are) so diverse.

On his arrival in Mali, Ibn Battuta commented how unusual the kingdom was: *"No one takes his name from his father, but from his maternal uncle. Sons do not inherit, only sister's sons! This is something I have seen nowhere in the world except among the infidel Indians of al-Mulaibar [Malabar, on the east coast of India]."* In short, Mali society was matrilineal, with descent determined by the mother, not the father. Royal women had much more power than their North African counterparts, but the rulers were male.

Ibn Battuta disdainfully described the customs that did not seclude women. On one occasion he visited his caravan leader and his wife, who were hosting a male friend of the wife. Indignantly, Ibn Battuta inquired: *"Are you happy about this, you who have lived in our country and know the content of the religious law?"* His host defended himself, explaining that the local women *"are not like the women of your country,"* but the indignant Ibn Battuta refused to return to his host's house.

---

*From H. A. R. Gibb, *The Travels of Ibn Battuta* A.D. *1325–1354*, The Hakluyt Society, pp. 951, 952. Reprinted with permission. The Hakluyt Society was established in 1846 for the purpose of printing rare or unpublished Voyages and Travels. For further information please see their website at: www.hakluyt.com.

Conversion to Islam in Fictional and Nonfictional Sources

Even though they are experts in assessing reliability, most historians prefer nonfictional sources: why bother with a source that announces at the outset that the author is consciously altering what actually happened? Still, in fields for which primary evidence is scarce, historians sometimes find valuable information in fictional sources. Very few sources describe the Islamicization of sub-Saharan Africa before 1100. Here, we compare a fictional source with a nonfictional source on the same topic to see what we can learn about early conversions to Islam in Africa.

The first account is from a collection of sailor's fictional tales composed in the mid-900s in the port of Siraf on the Arabian Sea. The plot of the story is so intricate as to defy belief. Caught in a storm, an Arab slave ship from Oman is shipwrecked in an African kingdom, most likely in modern Somalia or Kenya. The ship's captain abducts the ruler and sells him as a slave at Oman. Several years later the same ship is again blown off course to the same locale; and when the traders go before the ruler, they are amazed to see the king they had kidnapped. The king explains that he got away and fled to Cairo and escaped being kidnapped by slave traders two more times. Finally, he reached his former kingdom, where his countrymen welcomed him back and he once again took the throne. Clearly, there are too many coincidences and narrow escapes for the storyteller's account to be strictly factual, but his account of the king's conversion to Islam is utterly plausible.

At first glance, the second account, from the Islamic geographer al-Bakri, writing in 1068, appears to be more straightforward. It describes how a Muslim teacher persuaded a king in Mali to convert to Islam. Recall, though, that al-Bakri lived in Spain his entire life and thus did not himself see the Mali king's conversion or the rainfall that followed it. Historians always prefer eyewitness accounts because details can be distorted in the retelling. This second account captures what an educated Muslim geographer writing in Córdoba heard about the conversion of a distant ruler to Islam. Not an eyewitness account, it is a just-so tale that explains why the king of Mali was called "the Muslim."

Sources: G. S. P. Freeman-Grenville, *The East African Coast: Select Documents from the First to the Earlier Nineteenth Century* (Oxford: Clarendon Press, 1962), excerpt 5, "Buzurg Ibn Shahriyar of Ramhormuz: A Tenth-Century Slaving Adventure," pp. 9–13. Reprinted by permission of the Estate of G. S. P. Freeman-Grenville; N. Levtzion and J. F. P. Hopkins, eds., *Corpus of Early Arabic Sources for West African History* (New York: Cambridge University Press, 1981), excerpt 22, "Al-Bakri," pp. 82–83.

From Buzurg's "A Tenth-Century Slaving Adventure"

He [the king] answered: "After you had sold me in Oman, my purchaser took me to a town called Basrah"—and he described it. "There I learnt to pray and to fast, and certain parts of the Quran. My master sold me to another man who took me to the country of the king of the Arabs, called Baghdad"—and he described Baghdad. "In this town I learnt to speak correctly. I completed my knowledge of the Quran and prayed with the men in the mosques. I saw the Caliph, who is called al-Muqtadir [r. 908–932]. I was in Baghdad for a year and more, when there came a party of men from Khorasan [west Iran, modern Turk-menistan] mounted on camels. Seeing a large crowd, I asked where all these people were going.

"I was told: 'To Mecca.'

"'What is Mecca?' I asked.

"'There,' I was answered, 'is the House of God to which Muslims make the Pilgrimage.' And I was told the history of the temple.

"I said to myself that I should do well to follow the caravan. My master, to whom I told all this, did not wish to go with them or to let me go. But I found a way to escape his watchfulness and to mix in the crowd of pilgrims. On the road I became a servant to them. They gave me food to eat and got for me the two cloths needed for the *ihram* [the ritual garments used for the pilgrimage]. Finally, they instructing me, I performed all the ceremonies of the pilgrimage. . . .

"And here I am, happy and satisfied with the grace God has given me and mine, of knowing the precepts of Islam, the true faith, prayers, fasting, the pilgrimage, and what is permitted and what is forbidden."

From al-Bakri's *The Book of Routes and Realms*, about the Malal region (modern-day Mali)

Beyond this country lies another called Malal, the king of which is known as al-musul-mani [the Muslim]. He is thus called because his country became afflicted with drought one year following another; the inhabitants prayed for rain, sacrificing cattle till they had exterminated almost all of them, but the drought and the misery only increased. The king had as his guest a Muslim who used to read the Quran and was acquainted with the Sunna [the model of behavior that all Muslims were expected to follow]. To this man the king complained of the calamities that assailed him and his people.

The man said: "O King, if you believed in God (who is exalted) and testified that He is One, and testified as to the prophetic mission of Muhammad (God bless him and give him peace), and if you accepted all the religious laws of Islam, I would pray for your deliverance from your plight and that God's mercy would envelop all the people of your country, and that your enemies and adversaries might envy you on that account."

Thus he continued to press the king until the latter accepted Islam and became a sincere Muslim. The man made him recite from the Quran some easy passages and taught him religious obligations and practices which no man be excused from knowing. Then the Muslim made him wait till the eve of the following Friday, when he ordered him to purify himself by a complete ablution, and clothed him in a cotton garment which he had.

The two of them came out towards a mound of earth, and there the Muslim stood praying while the king, standing at this right side, imitated him. Thus they prayed for a part of the night, the Muslim reciting invocations and the king saying "Amen."

The dawn had just started to break when God caused abundant rain to descend upon them. So the king ordered the idols to be broken and expelled the sorcerers from his country. He and his descendants after him as well as his nobles were sincerely attached to Islam, while the common people of his kingdom remained polytheists. Since then their rulers have been given the title of al-musulmani [the Muslim].

QUESTIONS FOR ANALYSIS

» *What specific actions did the two kings perform as they converted to Islam? Which of the Five Pillars described in Chapter 9 did each observe?*

» *Was it easier for people living closer to the Islamic heartland in Arabia to be observant Muslims? How so?*

» *Which account of conversion do you find more convincing? Why?*

Mali Horseman   This terracotta figurine of a mounted warrior dates to around 1200, the time of Sundiata's reign. Local rulers began to import horses from North Africa around 1000, but initially only the most important leaders, like the imposing man shown here, rode on horses. By 1400, the kings of the Mali regularly led armies of mounted warriors into battle. (Private Collection/Photo © Henri Schneebeli/Bridgeman Art Library)

Ibn Battuta concluded his discussion of Mali with an *"account of what I found good,"* namely, its secure roads, its high attendance at Friday services, and most of all, the *"great attention to memorizing the Holy Quran."** He was deeply impressed by the example of several different children who had been placed in shackles because they had failed to memorize assigned passages from the Quran.

The kings of Mali continued to govern after Ibn Battuta's departure in 1353, but they faced rival armies as cavalry warfare became more common around 1400. To fight these battles, they had to import large horses from the north because horses bred locally often died from sleeping sickness and other parasitic diseases. They also bought saddles, iron stirrups, and bits to control their mounts. By 1400, they had added helmets and chain mail armor to their equipment. The kings lost control of several major cities, such as Timbuktu in 1433, and around 1450 Songhai (SONG-high), a neighboring kingdom that similarly profited by controlling the trans-Saharan trade, conquered Mali and brought Sundiata's dynasty to an end.

Islamic North Africa and the Mamluk Empire

By the time of Ibn Battuta's travels, North Africa had split into three separate kingdoms, each ruled by a sultan. Each year these sultanates sent thousands of pilgrims, like Ibn Battuta, to Cairo, where they joined pilgrims coming from North and West Africa to form even larger caravans for the final trip to Mecca. Cairo had become the cultural capital of the Islamic world in 1261, when the rulers of the **Mamluk empire** announced the re-establishment of the caliphate after the fall of Baghdad in 1258 to the Mongols (see Chapter 9). Ibn Battuta traveled through Mamluk territory in Egypt, Syria, and Arabia and personally experienced the ravages of the plague, which struck Eurasia for the first time since the eighth-century outbreaks in Constantinople (see Chapter 10).

Mamluk empire (1250–1517) Dynasty founded by mamluk military slaves in Cairo that re-established the caliphate in 1261.

The Sultanates of North Africa

Three months after his departure from Tangier in 1325, Ibn Battuta arrived at the trading port of Tunis, the capital of one of the three sultanates in North Africa, with a population near one hundred thousand. Located on a point sticking out into the Mediterranean, it was ideally situated as a port for trade across the Strait of Gibraltar to southern Europe. European merchants traded

*From H. A. R. Gibb, *The Travels of Ibn Battuta A.D. 1325–1354*, The Hakluyt Society, p. 966. Reprinted with permission. The Hakluyt Society was established in 1846 for the purpose of printing rare or unpublished Voyages and Travels. For further information please see their website at: www.hakluyt.com.

fine textiles, weapons, and wine for animal hides and cloth from North Africa as well as gold and slaves transshipped from the interior.

In almost all of the North African states, a sultan headed the government. In exchange for taxes paid by the inhabitants (Muslims paid a lower rate than non-Muslims), the government provided military and police protection. In addition, the sultan appointed a **qadi**, or chief jurist, who was assisted by subordinate jurists in settling disputes in court. Anyone who, like Ibn Battuta, had studied law at Islamic schools was eligible to be appointed a qadi. These courts implemented Islamic law, called **sharia** (sha-REE-ah), which consisted of all the rules that Muslims were supposed to follow. Interpretation of certain points varied among the jurists belonging to different legal schools. Ibn Battuta had studied the legal interpretations of the Maliki school, one of the four major Sunni legal schools that interpreted the sharia.

The chief jurist in Tunis, Ibn Battuta informs us, heard disputes every Friday after prayers in the mosque: *"People came to ask him to give a decision on various questions. When he had stated his opinion on forty questions he ended that session."* The qadi's decision, called a *fatwa*, had the force of law and was enforced by the sultan's government.

Although Ibn Battuta had come to Tunis as an individual pilgrim, he left the city as the qadi for a caravan of Berber pilgrims going on the hajj. The caravan functioned like a small, mobile sultanate, with the caravan leader making all the important decisions about the route and Ibn Battuta serving as the traveling qadi. His new salary made it possible for him to marry the daughter of a fellow pilgrim, but the marriage did not last. *"I became involved in a dispute with my father-in-law which made it necessary for me to separate from his daughter,"* Ibn Battuta comments, without explaining further the reasons for the divorce (see Chapter 9).

The Mamluk Empire, 1250–1517

Sometime in the spring of 1326, not quite a year after his departure from Tangier, Ibn Battuta arrived in the port city of Alexandria and went immediately to see the city's most famous tourist attraction: the lighthouse overlooking the Mediterranean. Alexandria marked the westernmost point of the Mamluk empire, which ruled eastward all the way to Damascus.

The word ***mamluk*** originally referred to a type of non-Muslim slave used by Islamic states as warriors. In the ninth and tenth centuries, Islamic rulers in Afghanistan, North Africa, Spain, and Egypt, unable to recruit and train an efficient army from among their own populace, purchased large numbers of Turks from Central Asia to staff their armies. The number of slaves swelled in succeeding centuries.

Bought as children, the young mamluks studied Islam in preparation for their mandatory conversion. Living in isolation from the rest of the population, they continued to speak their own Turkic dialects and often could not read Arabic. They did no manual labor and could rise to high military rank. Once a mamluk soldier converted to Islam, he was freed, and his children would be born Muslim. This made his children ineligible for service as mamluks, a powerful check on the ability of any commander to develop his own power base.

Many of these mamluk slaves rose to high positions in the Ayyubid dynasty (1171–1250), which Saladin had founded and which Ibn Jubayr visited in 1183–1185 (see Chapter 9). Taking advantage of their growing power, the mamluk slave soldiers staged a coup in 1250 and founded the Mamluk dynasty. Only ten years

---

qadi
A Muslim jurist whose decisions were based on sharia.

sharia
Islamic law: all the rules that Muslims were supposed to follow, compiled on the basis of the Quran, the hadith, and earlier legal decisions.

mamluk
Non-Muslim slaves purchased by Islamic states in Afghanistan, North Africa, Spain, and Egypt and forced to convert to Islam before serving as warriors.

---

*From H. A. R. Gibb, *The Travels of Ibn Battuta* A.D. *1325–1354*, The Hakluyt Society, pp. 14, 18. Reprinted with permission. The Hakluyt Society was established in 1846 for the purpose of printing rare or unpublished Voyages and Travels. For further information please see their website at: www.hakluyt.com.

later, in 1260, Mamluk generals masterminded one of the greatest military victories in premodern times; 120,000 Mamluk troops defeated 10,000 Mongol archers at the battle of Ayn Jalut, north of Jerusalem in modern Israel (see Chapter 14). Hailing from the Central Asian grasslands and intimately familiar with horses, many Mamluk soldiers were skilled in the same fighting techniques used by the Mongols. Although the Mongols were often outnumbered, the Mamluk forces were one of the few armies in the world to defeat them in direct combat.

Cairo: Baghdad's Successor as the Cultural Capital of the Islamic World

Although the Mamluks were neither originally Muslim nor native speakers of Arabic, they positioned themselves as the protectors of the Islamic world. In 1261, they announced the re-establishment of the caliphate in Cairo, three years after its destruction by the Mongols in 1258. Thousands of refugees, particularly Islamic teachers, poured into Cairo, where they taught in the city's many colleges, called *madrasas* in Arabic. The high number of Islamic schools, many located in mosques, impressed Ibn Battuta.

The thirteenth and fourteenth centuries saw the rise throughout the Islamic world of a new type of Islamic mystic, or **Sufi**, who taught that the individual could experience God directly. Followers of individual Sufis believed that their teachers had *baraka*, or divine grace, and could help others gain direct access to God. When alive, these Sufi teachers usually formed their own lodges where they taught groups of disciples and hosted visitors. When they died, their tombs became pilgrimage sites because their devotees believed that they retained their occupant's *baraka*.

Ibn Battuta stayed three days with a Sufi teacher named Burhan al-Din the Lame, whom he described as *"learned, self-denying, pious and humble.""* Burhan al-Din urged Ibn Battuta to visit three teachers in India, Pakistan, and China. His advice is certain evidence of a Sufi network stretching all the way from Egypt to China, and Ibn Battuta eventually met all three men.

With a population between 500,000 and 600,000, Cairo was larger than most contemporary cities; only a few Chinese cities outranked it.[7] The city's population fell into distinct social groups. At the top were the Mamluk rulers, military commanders, and officials who kept records and supervised the tax system. Independent of the military were the Islamic notables, or *ulama* (see Chapter 9). Merchants, traders, and brokers formed a third influential group, who were often as wealthy and as respected as members of the Mamluk ruling class.

Below these elites were those who worked at respectable occupations: tradesmen, shopkeepers, and craftsmen. Farmers worked agricultural plots located in the center of Cairo and the outlying suburbs. At the bottom of society were the people whose occupations violated Islamic teachings, such as usurers (who lent money for interest) and slave dealers. Cairo residents looked down on their neighbors who sold wine or performed sex for a fee, and they shunned those whose occupations brought them into contact with human corpses or dead animals.

The Outbreak of Plague in Damascus, 1348

The sultan of the Mamluk empire provided camels, food, and water for the poorer hajj travelers and guaranteed the safety of the pilgrims who gathered in Cairo. Ibn Battuta was probably traveling in the company of

Sufi
An Islamic mystic who taught that the individual could experience God directly without the intercession of others.

---

*From H. A. R. Gibb, *The Travels of Ibn Battuta* A.D. *1325–1354*, The Hakluyt Society, p. 23. Reprinted with permission. The Hakluyt Society was established in 1846 for the purpose of printing rare or unpublished Voyages and Travels. For further information please see their website at: www.hakluyt.com.

some ten thousand pilgrims, who went overland to Damascus. Damascus was the second-largest city in the Mamluk empire and a great cultural center in its own right, having been the capital of the Umayyads in the seventh century.

In Damascus, Ibn Battuta's route converged with Ibn Jubayr's, and his account borrowed, often without acknowledgment, as much as one-seventh of Ibn Jubayr's twelfth-century narrative.[8] From Damascus, Ibn Battuta proceeded to Mecca. After some time there (scholars are not certain how long), he decided to continue east on his journey.

Some twenty years later, Ibn Battuta again passed through Damascus on his journey home. This time he was unwittingly traveling with the rats that transmitted one of the most destructive diseases to strike humankind: the plague. Historians reserve the term *Black Death* for the outbreak in the mid-1300s. Because Europe, the Middle East, and North Africa had experienced no major outbreaks of plague since the eighth century, the effects of the Black Death were immediate and devastating.

The first new outbreak in western Europe occurred in 1346 in the Black Sea port of Kaffa. From there the dreaded disease traveled to Italy and Egypt (see Map 13.2, page 365). In May or June 1348, Ibn Battuta first heard of the plague in Ghazza, Syria, where *"the number of dead there exceeded a thousand a day."** He returned to Damascus, where the city's residents stayed up all night praying at the Great Mosque, and then joined a barefoot march in hopes of lowering the death toll: *"The entire population of the city joined in the exodus, male and female, small and large; the Jews went out with their book of the Law and the Christians with their Gospel, their women and children with them; the whole concourse of them in tears and humble supplications, imploring the favour of God through His Books and His Prophets."** Damascus lost two thousand people *"in a single day,"* yet Ibn Battuta managed to stay well.

Modern historians estimate that the plague wiped out 33 to 40 percent of the population in Egypt and Syria alone.[9] By the beginning of 1349, daily losses began to diminish, but it would take two to three hundred years for the populations of Egypt and Syria to return to their pre-plague levels.

East Africa, India, and the Trade Networks of the Indian Ocean

The Indian Ocean touched three different regions, each with its own languages and political units: the East African coast, the southern edge of the Arabian peninsula, and the west coast of India. Much as the rulers of the trading posts on the Sahara survived by taxing overland trade, the sultans of the **Indian Ocean trade network**—the city-states and larger political units encircling the Indian Ocean—taxed the maritime trade. Some sultanates consisted of only a single port city like Kilwa in modern Tanzania, while others, like the Delhi sultanate, controlled as much Indian territory as the Mauryan and Gupta dynasties of the past (see Chapters 3 and 8).

Although politically decentralized, the Indian Ocean was bound together by frequent boat crossings to and from its different ports. Merchants who had grown

Indian Ocean trade network
Network traversed by dhows that connected the ports around the Indian Ocean in East Africa, Arabia, and western India.

*From H. A. R. Gibb, *The Travels of Ibn Battuta* A.D. *1325–1354*, The Hakluyt Society, pp. 918, 144. Reprinted with permission. The Hakluyt Society was established in 1846 for the purpose of printing rare or unpublished Voyages and Travels. For further information please see their website at: www.hakluyt.com.

up along the African coast had operations in Arabia or India, and much intermarriage among the residents of different coasts took place, contributing to a genuine mixing of cultures. Interior regions supplied goods to the coastal cities, but because so few outsiders visited them, we know much less about them.

The East African Coast

dhow
Main vessel used in the Indian Ocean trade, made from teak planks laid edge to edge, fastened together with coconut fiber twine, and caulked to prevent leaking.

In January 1329, after leaving Mecca, Ibn Battuta traveled south to the port of Aden, on the Arabian peninsula, and sailed to East Africa, most likely in a **dhow** (DOW). Among the earliest and most seaworthy vessels ever made, dhows served as the camels of the Indian Ocean trade. Boatmakers made dhows by sewing teak or coconut planks together with a cord and constructing a single triangular sail. Because dhows had no deck, passengers sat and slept next to the ship's cargo. Traders frequently piloted their dhows along the coastline of East Africa, the Arabian peninsula, and India's west coast. Their expenses were low: dhows required no fuel because they harnessed wind power, and traders and their family members could staff their own boats.

Everywhere Ibn Battuta traveled, he saw Indian, Persian, and Arabian ships and merchants. After leaving Aden, he sailed for fifteen days before he reached the port city of Mogadishu, Somalia, which exported woven cotton textiles to Egypt and other destinations. Mogadishu's political structure resembled that of other East African ports: headed by a sultan, the government maintained an army and administered justice through a network of qadi justices.

The sultan spoke his native Somali in addition to a little Arabic. The farther Ibn Battuta traveled from the Islamic heartland, the fewer people he would find who knew Arabic. Still, he could always be confident of finding an Arabic speaker. Because Ibn Battuta's stay in Mogadishu was brief, he did not go inland, where he would have seen villages growing the strange, colorful foodstuffs he ate, fewer people of Arabian descent, and more non-Islamic religious practices.

After a short stop in Mombasa, Ibn Battuta proceeded to Kilwa (modern Kilwa Kivinye), a small island off the coast of modern Tanzania; there he saw *"a large city on the seacoast, most of whose inhabitants are Zinj, jet-black in colour. They have tattoo marks on their faces."* Ibn Battuta used the word *zinj*, meaning black, to refer to the indigenous peoples of East Africa. The people he encountered may have already begun to speak the creole mixture that later came to be called Swahili (swah-HEE-lee), a Bantu language that incorporated many vocabulary words from Arabic. (*Swahili* means "of the coast" in Arabic.) Ibn Battuta arrived at Kilwa during a period of prosperity: a newly established dynasty had taken control of Sofala, a small port near the Zambezi River, which was a major entrepôt (trading center) for gold coming from the interior. Archaeological excavations have revealed that the city had a mosque and a palace built of stone, and its inhabitants lived in stone houses with indoor toilets, ate in kitchens equipped with Chinese porcelains, and wore imported silks and gold and silver ornaments.

We know more about the history of Kilwa than about many other East African ports because of the survival of *The Chronicle of the Kings of Kilwa* in both Portuguese and Arabic versions. This work gives the name of individual rulers but not their dates. By matching the names of rulers in *The Chronicle* with Ibn Battuta's detailed account, historians have concluded that the Kilwa dynasty began in the

---

*From H. A. R. Gibb, *The Travels of Ibn Battuta* A.D. *1325–1354*, The Hakluyt Society, pp. 379–380. Reprinted with permission. The Hakluyt Society was established in 1846 for the purpose of printing rare or unpublished Voyages and Travels. For further information please see their website at: www.hakluyt.com.

The Dhows of the Indian Ocean Unlike most other boats, the dhows of the Indian Ocean were sewn and not nailed together. Boatmakers sewed planks of teak or coconut trees together with a cord and added a single sail. This boat design was so practical that it is still in use today. (Hauke Dressler/LOOK Die Bildagentur der Fotografen GmbH/Alamy)

1200s. The kings of Kilwa were descended from Arabic-speaking settlers who came to the region from Yemen, further evidence of the ties linking the different societies on the Indian Ocean.

The sultan of Kilwa was a generous man, Ibn Battuta reports, who regularly gave gifts of slaves and ivory from elephant tusks, which he obtained in the interior: *"He used to engage frequently in expeditions to the land of the Zinj people, raiding them and taking booty."** Slaves and ivory, and less often gold, were Kilwa's main exports. Like the other East African ports, Kilwa imported high-fired ceramics from China, glass from Persia, and textiles from China and India.

Great Zimbabwe and Its Satellites, ca. 1275–1550

Although the interior of southern Africa supplied the Kilwa sultan with slaves and ivory, we know much less about it because Ibn Battuta and other travelers never described the region. There, on the high plateau south of the Zambezi River, stood a state that reached its greatest extent in the early 1300s. Its center was the imposing archaeological site of **Great Zimbabwe** (see Map 11.1).

Like other speakers of Bantu languages in sub-Saharan Africa, the people living on the Zimbabwe plateau cultivated sorghum with iron tools. Before 1000, most lived in small villages of houses made from wood beams held together by plaster. They traded ivory, animal skins, and gold.

Great Zimbabwe
Large city in Zimbabwe surrounded by smaller outlying settlements, all distinguished by stone enclosures called "zimbabwe" in the local Shona language. The location of the largest stone structure built in sub-Saharan Africa before 1500.

---

*From H. A. R. Gibb, *The Travels of Ibn Battuta A.D. 1325–1354,* The Hakluyt Society, pp. 379–380. Reprinted with permission. The Hakluyt Society was established in 1846 for the purpose of printing rare or unpublished Voyages and Travels. For further information please see their website at: www.hakluyt.com.

Sometime around 1000, some villagers became wealthy enough to build stone enclosures for themselves. By the thirteenth and fourteenth centuries, the population had reached ten thousand,[10] and they built three hundred small stone enclosures over a large area on the plateau. The word for these enclosures in the local Shona language is *zimbabwe*, which means "venerated houses" and is the name of the modern nation of Zimbabwe where they are located.

The Elliptical Building of Great Zimbabwe is the largest single stone structure in sub-Saharan Africa built before 1500. One estimate holds that four hundred laborers could have built the wall of this building during the slack period of the agricultural season over the course of four years.[11] Because the walls of Great Zimbabwe do not resemble any Islamic buildings along the coast, including those at nearby Kilwa, all analysts concur that Great Zimbabwe was built by the local people, not by the Arabic-speaking peoples of the coast.

Since the people who lived there did not keep written records, archaeological finds provide our only information about local religion. Nothing indicates Islamic beliefs. On the northern edge of the site, the Eastern Enclosure held six stylized birds carved from soapstone, which may depict ancestors or deities. The Zimbabwe people also made and probably worshiped phalluses and female torsos with breasts in the hope of increasing the number of children. (See the feature "Visual Evidence in Primary Sources: The Ruins of Great Zimbabwe.")

When excavated, the site contained a hoard that one archaeologist has called "a cache of the most extraordinary variegated and abundant indigenous and imported objects ever discovered at Great Zimbabwe or, indeed, anywhere else in the interior of south-central Africa." The hoard included pieces of broken, green, Chinese high-fired celadon ceramic pots and colorful Persian earthenware plates with script on them. The presence of a single coin at the site, embossed with the name of the king Ibn Battuta met at Kilwa, reveals that the site's residents traded with the coastal towns and were part of existing trade networks.

Kilwa was most prosperous at exactly the same time that Great Zimbabwe was—in the thirteenth and fourteenth centuries when Ibn Battuta visited the city. When the Portuguese arrived on the East African coast after 1500, both Kilwa and the Great Zimbabwe site had already declined dramatically from their earlier, glorious days, but we do not know why.

The Delhi Sultanate and the Hindu Kingdoms of Southern India

When Ibn Battuta sailed away from Kilwa, he embarked on a fifteen-year-long journey along the trade routes linking Africa with India and China. In Central Asia, he learned that a Muslim leader in India, Muhammad bin Tughluq (r. 1324–1351), had defeated his rivals to become the ruler of the powerful **Delhi sultanate** (1210–1526) and was deliberately staffing his government with foreign-born Muslims. Sensing a chance of employment, Ibn Battuta headed for Delhi.

The Delhi sultanate, like the Mamluk empire of Egypt and Syria, was founded by Turkish military slaves from Central Asia (see Map 11.2). It was not the first Islamic dynasty in South Asia. In the eighth century, conquering caliphate armies had established Islamic states in the Sind region of modern Pakistan, but no Muslim ruler managed to conquer land beyond the Sind. In 1210, however, a group of mamluks overthrew the reigning sultan, who was from Afghanistan, and conquered large sections of northern India, considerably expanding the territory under Muslim control. Southern India remained under the control of the Chola and other regional dynasties (see Chapter 8). Five different dynasties ruled between

Delhi sultanate (1206–1526) Islamic state led by former mamluk slaves originally from Afghanistan, who governed north India from their capital at Delhi. At their height, in the early 1300s, they controlled nearly all of the Indian subcontinent.

1210 and 1524, and since the capital was always at Delhi, these dynasties are collectively known as the Delhi sultanate. Delhi remained the capital of many later northern Indian dynasties and is still India's capital.

In addition to mamluk slaves, the Delhi sultans imported another important institution from the Islamic world: iqta grants, which had spread throughout the former Abbasid realm (see Chapter 9). Even in the late 1100s, the Afghani sultan who controlled Delhi asked the Abbasid caliphs to sign iqta grants giving him the right to tax and to govern the lands he had conquered, and he dedicated Friday prayers to the reigning caliph in Baghdad. Because the sultan, in turn, gave iqta grants to his main supporters, they had their own lands and armies, and his power was correspondingly diminished.

The people in the government believed that the most qualified person, even if not related to the sultan, should become sultan. The first mamluk to seize power killed the reigning king and then named himself sultan in 1210. Every time the sultan died, a free-for-all struggle broke out until a victor emerged as the new sultan. For this reason the Delhi sultanate witnessed many internal conflicts.

MAP 11.2 **The Delhi Sultanate** Starting in 1210, a Muslim dynasty based in Delhi gained control of northern India and established its capital in Delhi, a city from which a total of five different Muslim dynasties governed. Collectively known as the Delhi sultanate, none of these dynasties conquered the south, which continued to be governed by Hindu dynasties like the Chola dynasty. (© Cengage Learning)

The Ruins of Great Zimbabwe

Located near Masvingo, Zimbabwe, the Great Zimbabwe site contains several large ruins and many smaller stone structures whose original purpose is undocumented and therefore still not well understood. The ruins, covering almost 1,800 acres (7.2 sq km), fall into three groups: the Hill Complex, the Valley Complex, and the Great Enclosure. The site was first settled before 1000, when the first stone structures were built, and continued to grow through the 1300s. Little evidence of cereal agriculture survives, indicating that the city's population depended largely on cattle for their food supply.

Like other Bantu peoples, the Zimbabwe people living at the site knew how to work iron. Archaeologists have found nodules of iron ore from mines

The Hill Complex, a group of stone buildings forming a ritual space, stood above a granite cliff 330 feet (100 m) long and 100 feet (30 m) high on the northern edge of the site.

Area of detail

© Georg Gerster/Photo Researchers, Inc.

QUESTIONS FOR ANALYSIS

» *What methods have archaeologists used to analyze the function of the stone buildings at Great Zimbabwe?*

» *Whose analysis do you find more convincing?*

and alluvial gold collected from riverbeds. The site also contained a workshop where metalsmiths heated copper ingots in crucibles to make wire.

The Great Enclosure holds two large structures: the Elliptical Building and the solid Conical Tower inside it. The outer wall of the Elliptical Building is made of evenly cut granite blocks, fitted together without mortar, that are elegantly trimmed with an intricate (V-shaped) design on the top. What was the purpose of these two buildings? Two analysts, Peter S. Garlake and Thomas N. Huffman, have taken radically different approaches to the problem.

Garlake bases his analysis on close examination of the construction techniques used to make the different types of walls and the location of different artifacts. The sheer size of the Elliptical Building suggests to him that it was the palace of the ruler. Its walls, he contends, stood too high to be mere guard walls: they made a statement about the ruler's power to all his subjects.

Huffman, in contrast, examines the settlements of the Shona-speaking peoples who live near the site today. Since many of their houses are divided into areas for men to work and women to work, he wonders whether this might not be true of Great Zimbabwe as well. The one hundred smaller soapstone carvings of phalluses and female torsos with breasts found in the Elliptical Building resemble some figurines used in modern schools to teach adolescent girls about family life. The high walls of the Elliptical Building, Huffman believes, kept outsiders from observing the activities at a girls' initiation school.

Sources: P. S. Garlake, *Great Zimbabwe* (New York: Stein and Day, 1973); Thomas N. Huffman, "Where You Are the Girls Gather to Play: The Great Enclosure at Great Zimbabwe," in *Frontiers: Southern African Archaeology Today*, ed. M. Hall et al., *Cambridge Monographs in African Archaeology* 10 (Oxford: B. A. R., 1984), pp. 252–265.

The Eastern Enclosure contained six stone bird statues, suggesting that it was a ritual center.

Detail

© Georg Gerster/Photo Researchers, Inc.

In the Valley Complex, Enclosure 12 contained the largest hoard found on the site: over 220 pounds (100 kg) of iron hoes, 44 pounds (20 kg) of iron for wire, warthog and elephant tusks, thousands of Indian beads, and broken ceramic vessels from China and Iran.

With three entrances, the Great Enclosure contains the Elliptical Building, the Conical Tower, and mud and thatch huts where individual families lived.

The Conical Tower—possibly a symbolic granary—is a completely solid stone structure with an outer wall over 30 feet (9 m) high.

The Elliptical Building has an outer wall that runs 800 feet (250 m) long and contains 182,000 cubic feet (5,150 cubic m) of stone.

Qutb Minar One of Delhi's most recognizable landmarks, Qutb Minar is a high tower with inscriptions from the Quran written on the face of red and tan sandstone, measuring 237.8 feet (72.5 m) tall. Even before the founding of the first Delhi sultanate, a ruler based in Afghanistan initiated its construction, and the first Delhi sultan continued it. To the right stands a 23-foot (7 m) iron pillar, originally from the courtyard of a Jain temple, that dates to at least the 300s, if not earlier. As was common practice, the builders used pieces of destroyed Hindu and Jain temples to build both the tower and the nearby mosque. (© Atlantide Phototravel/Corbis)

Fueled by a desire for plunder, the armies of Muhammad bin Tughluq, the son of a Turkish slave and an Indian woman, succeeded in conquering almost all of India. To be closer to the lands he had conquered, in 1326 Muhammad bin Tughluq ordered his officials to move the capital 400 miles (650 km) south. This measure had disastrous consequences, including the loss of much territory; many of his subordinates turned against him because they lost their land.

In another departure from the practices of earlier rulers, Muhammad bin Tughluq decided to hire only foreigners to administer his empire. His goal was to build up an aristocracy born outside of India who would be loyal to him and protect him from any Indian Muslims who might overthrow him. He named Ibn Battuta to be the highest qadi in Delhi, a very high-ranking position, even though Ibn Battuta did not speak Persian, the language of the government. In fact, Ibn Battuta kept so busy attending court ceremonials and hunting expeditions that he heard no legal cases.

The Delhi sultanate granted Hindus the status of *dhimmi* ("protected subjects") even though they worshiped multiple gods. Hindus were obliged to pay the *jizya* tax, a head tax on non-Muslims, and they were not allowed to fight in the all-Muslim army. Their payment of taxes brought them some unusual rights: at least in some periods the Delhi sultanate repaired Hindu temples that had been damaged by Muslim troops in battle. They did not repair the temples of foreigners living in India, who did not pay the *jizya* tax. Muhammad bin Tughluq was infamous among Muslims for his support of Hinduism, and his successors did not grant Hindus all these benefits.

Throughout Muhammad bin Tughluq's reign, south India remained largely Hindu. After his government withdrew from the failed new capital, Hindu rulers gained control of urban centers in the south and established temple-centered kingdoms like that of the Cholas, who ruled until 1279 (see Chapter 8). The most important Hindu empire was based at **Vijayanagar** (vihj-eye-NUH-gah), in the modern Indian state of Karnataka. The Vijayanagar rulers (ca. 1336–1614) patronized Sanskrit learning and Hindu temples while creating a powerful army that enabled them to rule for more than two centuries.

Ibn Battuta remained in Delhi for seven years before the sultan named him his emissary to China. When he departed in August 1341, he was traveling with fifteen Chinese envoys, over two hundred slaves, one hundred horses, and various lavish gifts of textiles, dishes, and weapons—all intended for the Mongol rulers of China.

As Ibn Battuta made his way down the west coast of India, he visited towns that resembled the ports on the African side of the Indian Ocean. A sultan governed each port, where qadis administered justice, and each town had a bazaar and a mosque. Ibn Battuta arrived in Calicut at the head of a large embassy, carrying Muhammad bin Tughluq's gifts for the ruler of China and accompanied by several concubines, one pregnant with Ibn Battuta's child. At the time of his visit, thirteen Chinese-built vessels were in the port waiting for the winds to shift so they could return to China. *"On the sea of China,"* Ibn Battuta comments, *"traveling is done in Chinese ships only."**

The Chinese ships docked at Calicut differed markedly from dhows. The Chinese-built ships had wooden decks and multiple levels with compartments with doors. Some had up to twelve sails, made of *"bamboo rods plaited like mats."* These enormous ships, over 100 feet (30 m) long, carried six hundred sailors and four hundred armed men, convincing Ibn Battuta that their massive size was an indication of China's prosperity: *"There is no people in the world wealthier than the Chinese."**

Ibn Battuta much preferred the Chinese-built ships with their private cabins to the open dhows. On the day he sailed, he discovered that the best staterooms, those with lavatories, were taken by Chinese merchants. He indignantly transferred to a smaller vessel, where he could have a room big enough for him to stay with his female companions, *"for it is my habit,"* he said, *"never to travel without them."** Since it was a Friday, Ibn Battuta went to the mosque for prayers and arranged for his luggage to be transferred to the smaller boat, leaving his traveling companions on the larger vessel.

A violent storm broke out that night, and the captains of the two ships removed their vessels from the shallow harbor to the safety of the sea. The smaller boat survived, but the big ship was totally destroyed. Ibn Battuta stood horror-struck on the beach, watching floating corpses whose faces he recognized. Having utterly failed to protect the envoys he accompanied, Ibn Battuta fled. Eight years more in India, the Maldive Islands, and China passed before he returned home to Morocco.

Vijayanagar
(ca. 1336–1614) "City of victory" in Sanskrit. Important Hindu empire based in the modern Indian state of Karnataka. Vijayanagar rulers created a powerful army that enabled them to rule in central India for more than two centuries.

---

*From H. A. R. Gibb, *The Travels of Ibn Battuta A.D. 1325–1354*, The Hakluyt Society, pp. 813–814. Reprinted with permission. The Hakluyt Society was established in 1846 for the purpose of printing rare or unpublished Voyages and Travels. For further information please see their website at: www.hakluyt.com.

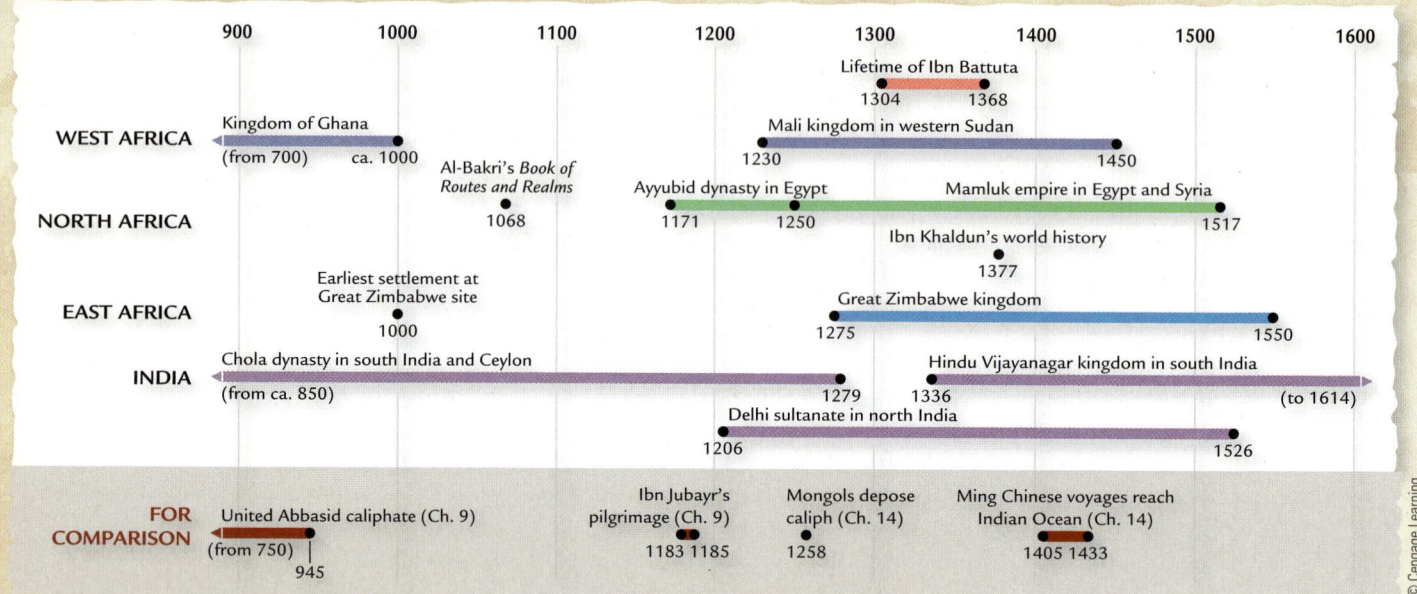

	900	1000	1100	1200	1300	1400	1500	1600

Lifetime of Ibn Battuta
1304 — 1368

WEST AFRICA
Kingdom of Ghana (from 700) — ca. 1000
Mali kingdom in western Sudan
1230 — 1450

Al-Bakri's *Book of Routes and Realms*
1068

NORTH AFRICA
Ayyubid dynasty in Egypt
1171 — 1250
Mamluk empire in Egypt and Syria
— 1517

Ibn Khaldun's world history
1377

EAST AFRICA
Earliest settlement at Great Zimbabwe site
1000
Great Zimbabwe kingdom
1275 — 1550

INDIA
Chola dynasty in south India and Ceylon (from ca. 850) — 1279
Hindu Vijayanagar kingdom in south India
1336 — (to 1614)
Delhi sultanate in north India
1206 — 1526

FOR COMPARISON
United Abbasid caliphate (Ch. 9) (from 750) — 945
Ibn Jubayr's pilgrimage (Ch. 9)
1183 1185
Mongols depose caliph (Ch. 14)
1258
Ming Chinese voyages reach Indian Ocean (Ch. 14)
1405 1433

© Cengage Learning

Africa's Many Ties to the Rest of the World

As Ibn Battuta discovered, many roads to Mecca went through Africa. His account of his travels is one of the most important sources for sub-Saharan African history. With no indigenous written sources before 1800, historians of Africa have exercised great ingenuity in reconstructing the past by drawing on oral histories (some transmitted over the centuries by griots), archaeology, glottochronology, and upstreaming.

Africa's path to complex society did not follow the agricultural surplus and river valley pattern of Mesopotamia, Egypt, India, or China (see Chapters 2–4). Residents of the Middle Niger Valley built huge urban complexes financed by trading dried fish, fish oil, and rice for iron; later they diversified and traded for copper and salt as well. Whereas the other peoples of Eurasia had worked bronze before iron, and the peoples of the Americas never worked iron at all (see Chapter 5), iron was the first metal that Africans smelted, sometime around 600 B.C.E. As elsewhere in Africa, the peoples of the Middle Niger cultivated wet rice but never shifted to full-time agriculture.

By Ibn Battuta's time, kingdoms like Mali were profitably engaged in the trans-Sahara trade in slaves and gold. Ibn Battuta's travels along this and other existing trade routes brought him to much of the recently Islamicized world of the 1300s: to the ports of northern and eastern Africa and around the Indian Ocean to the Delhi sultanate, as well as across the Sahara. He encountered Islamic practices everywhere he went: rulers and the well-off received him generously; students learned to recite the Quran in Arabic; Friday prayers were conducted in mosques; and he could always find companions, often hajj pilgrims or merchants, to accompany him on another leg of his journey. With the fall of Baghdad to the Mongols in 1258 (see Chapter 14), the center of the Islamic world shifted to Cairo, where the Mamluks founded a new caliphate in 1261 and welcomed Muslim students, teachers, and artists. At the second most important center in the Mamluk empire, Damascus, Ibn Battuta witnessed an outbreak of plague, which traveled across Eurasia along pathways opened by the Mongols and kept open by their successor states (see Chapter 14).

Dependent as he was on Muslims to give him alms, Ibn Battuta never ventured beyond the realm of Islam. He did not visit the inland stone city of Great Zimbabwe, travel south of Kilwa, Tanzania, on the East African coast, or travel to southern Africa. These places lay beyond the two trade networks that he traced in his travels through Africa: the trans-Saharan caravan trade network and the Indian Ocean trade network. In the Sahara he found that he could trade salt, glass trinkets, and spices to pay for meals and his lodging;

on the Indian Ocean, he traveled by dhow, the sea-going counterpart to the camels crossing the Sahara. Both networks provided channels for Africa's exports of slaves and gold to reach Europe and the Islamic world.

Ibn Battuta's account of his travels shows that, just as the Europeans sailed to Iceland, Greenland, and the Americas and so learned about a larger world (see Chapter 10), so too did Muslim geographers document more places in Afro-Eurasia. From Burhan al-Din the Lame in Cairo, Ibn Battuta learned of a Sufi network extending all the way to China, the farthest point he traveled in his lifetime. As we will see in the next chapter, during these same centuries, the Chinese were also learning about Africa and Europe.

Voyages on the Web: Ibn Battuta

The Voyages Map App follows the traveler's journeys using interactive study tools, including 360-degree panoramic views of historic sites, zoomable maps, audio summaries, flash cards, and quizzes.

Key Terms

Ibn Battuta (286)
Sahel (289)
Bantu (289)
oral histories (292)
griot/griotte (292)
lineage (292)
Mali (292)
Ghana (293)

Middle Niger Valley (293)
sultan (295)
Ibn Khaldun (297)
trans-Saharan caravan trade network (297)
Mamluk empire (302)
qadi (303)
sharia (303)

mamluk (303)
Sufi (304)
Indian Ocean trade network (305)
dhow (306)
Great Zimbabwe (307)
Delhi sultanate (308)
Vijayanagar (313)

For Further Reference

Childs, S. Terry, and David Killick. "Indigenous African Metallurgy: Nature and Culture." *Annual Reviews Anthropology* 1993 (22): 317–337.

Clarence-Smith, William Gervase. *Islam and the Abolition of Slavery*. London: Hurst and Company, 2006.

Dunn, Ross. *The Adventures of Ibn Battuta: A Muslim Traveler of the 14th Century*. Berkeley: University of California Press, 2005.

Garlake, P. S. *Great Zimbabwe*. New York: Stein and Day, 1973.

Hale, Thomas A. *Griots and Griottes: Masters of Words and Music*. Bloomington: Indiana University Press, 2007.

Hall, Martin. *Farmers, Kings, and Traders: The People of Southern Africa 200–1860*. Chicago: University of Chicago Press, 1990.

Hopkins, J. F. P. *Corpus of Early Arabic Sources for West African History*. New York: Cambridge University Press, 1981.

Huffman, Thomas N. "Where You Are the Girls Gather to Play: The Great Enclosure at Great Zimbabwe." In *Frontiers: Southern African Archaeology Today*, ed. M. Hall et al. *Cambridge Monographs in African Archaeology* 10. Oxford, England: B. A. R., 1984, pp. 252–265.

Irwin, Robert. *Mamlūks and Crusaders: Men of the Sword and Men of the Pen*. Burlington, Vt.: Variorum, 2010.

Irwin, Robert. *The Middle East in the Middle Ages: The Early Mamluk Sultanate 1250–1382*. London: Croom Helm, 1986.

Isichei, Elizabeth. *A History of African Societies to 1870*. Cambridge, England: Cambridge University Press, 1997.

Jackson, David. *The Delhi Sultanate: A Political and Military History*. New York: Cambridge University Press, 1999.

Lapidus, Ira M. *Muslim Cities in the Later Middle Ages*. Cambridge, Mass.: Harvard University Press, 1967.

Letzvion, Nehemia, and Randall L. Pouwels, eds. *The History of Islam in Africa*. Athens: Ohio University Press, 2000.

Lovejoy, Paul. *Transformations in Slavery: A History of Slavery in Africa*. 2d ed. New York: Cambridge University Press, 2000.

McIntosh, Roderick J. *Ancient Middle Niger: Urbanism and the Self-Organizing Landscape*. New York: Cambridge University Press, 2005.

Niane, D. T. *Sundiata: An Epic of Old Mali*. G. D. Pickett, trans. London: Longman, 2006.

Schoenbrun, David Lee. *A Green Place, A Good Place: Agrarian Change, Gender, and Social Identity in the Great Lakes Region to the 15th Century*. Portsmouth, N.H.: Heineman, 1998.

Vansina, J. "New Linguistic Evidence and 'The Bantu Expansion.'" *Journal of African History* 36 (1995): 173–195.

Vansina, J. *Paths in the Rainforest: Towards a History of Political Tradition in Equatorial Africa*. Madison: University of Wisconsin Press, 1990.

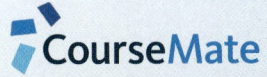 Go to the CourseMate website at **www.cengagebrain.com** for additional study tools and review materials—including audio and video clips—for this chapter.

12

China's Commercial Revolution, ca. 900–1276

In 1127, **Li Qingzhao** (LEE CHING-jow) (ca. 1084–ca. 1151) and her husband Zhao Mingcheng (JOW MING-chung) (1081–1129), a low-ranking Chinese official, abandoned their home in Shandong (SHAN-dong) province and joined half a million refugees fleeing to the south. After Zhao's death only two years later, Li recorded her memoir, which depicts the long-term economic changes of the Song (soong) dynasty (960–1276), when China's prosperity made it the world's most advanced economy, and the short-term consequences of military defeat, when the Song emperors were forced to surrender all of north China to a non-Chinese dynasty named the Jin (GIN) (1115–1234). As she explains, Li and Zhao fled from their home in north China and traveled 500 miles (800 km) to the Yangzi River:

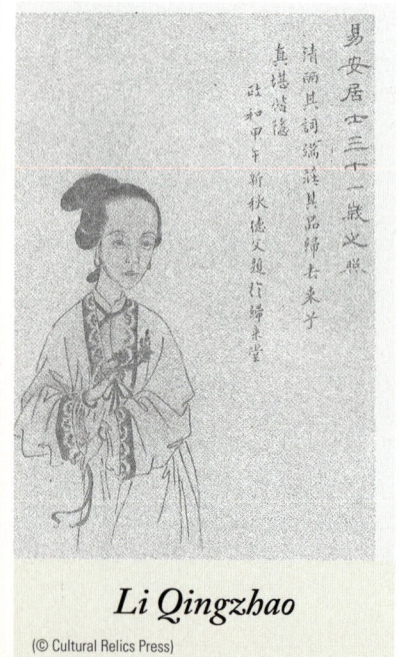

Li Qingzhao

(© Cultural Relics Press)

I n 1126, the first year of the Jingkang [JEENG-kong] Reign, my husband was governing Zichuan [DZE-chwan; in Shandong province] when we heard that the Jin Tartars were moving against the capital. He was in a daze, realizing that all those full trunks and overflowing chests, which he regarded so lovingly and mournfully, would surely soon be his possessions no longer. . . . Since we could not take the overabundance of our possessions with us, we first gave up the bulky printed volumes, the albums of paintings, and the most cumbersome of the vessels. Thus we reduced the size of the collection several times, and still we had fifteen cartloads of books. When we reached Donghai [DONG-high; Jiangsu], it

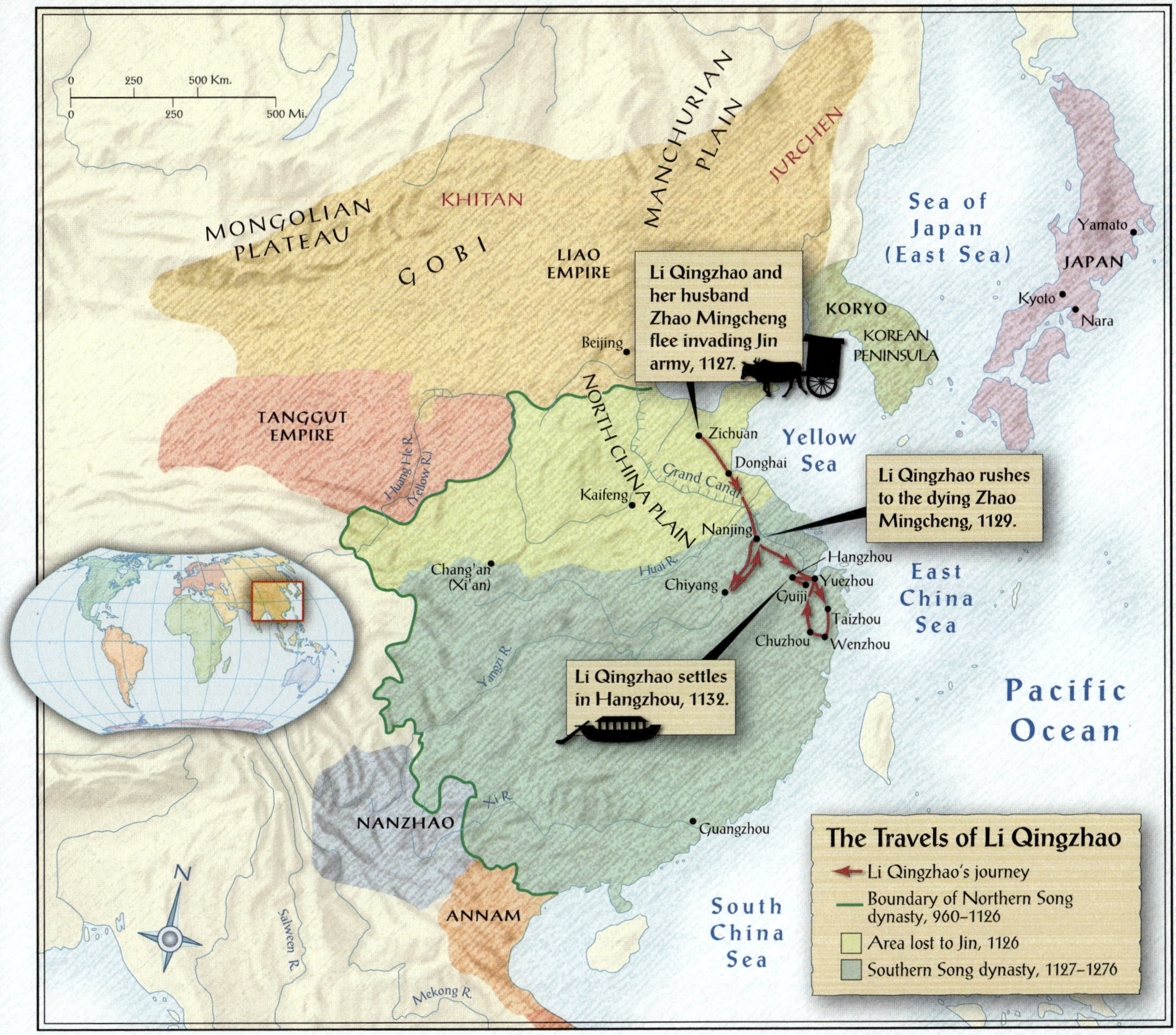

The Travels of Li Qingzhao map:

MONGOLIAN PLATEAU

KHITAN

GOBI

MANCHURIAN PLAIN

JURCHEN

LIAO EMPIRE

Sea of Japan (East Sea)

Yamato

JAPAN

Kyoto

Nara

KORYO KOREAN PENINSULA

Beijing

Li Qingzhao and her husband Zhao Mingcheng flee invading Jin army, 1127.

TANGGUT EMPIRE

Huang He R. (Yellow R.)

NORTH CHINA PLAIN

Grand Canal

Zichuan

Donghai

Yellow Sea

Kaifeng

Nanjing

Li Qingzhao rushes to the dying Zhao Mingcheng, 1129.

Chang'an (Xi'an)

Huai R.

Chiyang

Hangzhou

Yuezhou

Guiji

East China Sea

Taizhou

Chuzhou

Wenzhou

Yangzi R.

Li Qingzhao settles in Hangzhou, 1132.

Pacific Ocean

Xi R.

NANZHAO

Salween R.

Guangzhou

South China Sea

ANNAM

Mekong R.

N

The Travels of Li Qingzhao

← Li Qingzhao's journey

— Boundary of Northern Song dynasty, 960–1126

Area lost to Jin, 1126

Southern Song dynasty, 1127–1276

0 250 500 Km.
0 250 500 Mi.

© Cengage Learning

Join this chapter's traveler on "Voyages," an interactive tour of historic sites and events:
www.cengagebrain.com

took a string of boats to ferry them all across the Huai, and again across the Yangzi River to Jiank-ang [JI-AHN-kong; modern Nanjing, Jiangsu].

*Reprinted by permission of the publisher from *Remembrances: The Experience of the Past in Classical Chinese Literature* by Stephen Owen, p. 89, Cambridge, Mass.: Harvard University Press, Copyright © 1986 by the President and Fellows of Harvard College.

Li Qingzhao
(ca. 1084–ca. 1151)
Famous woman poet of the Song dynasty who wrote a first-person memoir about her marriage to Zhao Mingcheng.

After they reached Nanjing (NAHN-jeeng), Li explains, they had to abandon their last fifteen carts of books. Li was in her early forties at the time of her flight. She and her husband Zhao had been born into the top level of Song society, and their fathers had both served as high officials. The couple went by boat to south China, where they hoped they would be safe from the invading armies.

Li Qingzhao's memoir permits a glimpse of Chinese life at a time of wrenching political chaos. Seldom has the world seen such a mass panic as when the Jin armies defeated the Northern Song dynasty. While half a million other people made the same trip south as Li Qingzhao, her account stands out. For one thing, a woman wrote it. Highly educated in an age when the vast majority of women could not read, Li Qingzhao was the only woman of her time to achieve lasting fame as a poet. Even though only fifty of her poems survive today, many people consider her China's greatest woman poet, and she remains some people's favorite, male or female.

The fall of the Northern Song intensified a long-term migration from north to south China that had started centuries before Li Qingzhao's lifetime and continued centuries after it. Starting around 750, farmers realized they could grow more food in south China than in north China. In addition, during the years following the An Lushan rebellion of 755–763 (see Chapter 8), north China suffered continuous political instability that pushed people to migrate to the south.

These long-term migrations resulted in economic growth so dramatic that this period is called China's "commercial revolution." Before the revolution, most of China's farmers grew the food they ate. Largely self-sufficient, they bought little at markets. After the revolution, farmers and craftsmen produced full-time for the market, and China's economic growth affected its neighbors in Korea, Japan, and Vietnam as well. Advances in technology and navigation contributed significantly to Chinese knowledge of foreign peoples across Afro-Eurasia.

Focus Questions

» *What pushed people in north China to migrate south?*

» *What were the causes of the commercial revolution?*

» *How did the changes of the commercial revolution affect education—for men and for women—and religious life?*

» *How did China's economic growth influence its immediate neighbors of Japan, Korea, and Vietnam?*

The Five Dynasties Period and the Song Dynasty, 907–1276

The Tang dynasty (618–907), permanently weakened by the An Lushan rebellion of 755, came to an end in 907 (see Chapter 8). China then broke apart until 960, when the founder of the Song dynasty (960–1276) reunited the empire. The dramatic rise and fall of Chinese dynasties sometimes left the political structure basically unchanged, and this happened during the transition from the Tang dynasty to the Song. The new Song emperor presided over the central government. Almost all government officials were recruited by means of the civil service examinations, making the Song the world's first genuine bureaucracy. Despite the loss of north China to the Jin, Song officials successfully managed the transfer of the central government to a new capital in the south, where they presided over two centuries of unprecedented economic growth.

The Rise of the Northern Song Dynasty, 960–1126

The fifty-three years between the Tang and Song dynasties is known as the Five Dynasties period (907–960) because during this time China was ruled by different regional governments, of which five were most important. The Five Dynasties, in turn, came to an end when a powerful general overthrew a boy ruler of one of the regions and founded the **Song dynasty** in 960. By 976, he had united both north and south China and made his capital in Kaifeng (kie-fuhng), which, like China's earlier capitals, was in the Yellow River valley.

The Song founder kept in place the old political structure, with the emperor at the top of a central bureaucracy that oversaw local government. But there was one major difference. After unifying the empire in 976, the emperor summoned his most important generals and explained that the Tang dynasty had fallen apart because the regional governors, many of them also generals, exercised too much power. His generals agreed to retire, setting an important precedent. The Song initiated a period of greater civilian rule, as opposed to military rule, with genuine power remaining in the hands of bureaucrats, not generals.

Those officials stationed in the capital held the highest positions in the Song bureaucracy. The Song government referred all matters of state to the same six ministries as existed in the Tang: Revenue, Civil Appointments, Rites, Works, Punishments, and War. The heads of these six ministries all reported to the grand councilor, the highest official in the government, who was named to office by the emperor. If the emperor chose, he could, like the Song founder, be active in government matters.

The largest administrative districts during the Tang had been the prefectures. There were 220 such prefectures during the Song dynasty. Officials grouped these into more than twenty larger units called circuits. Each prefecture in a circuit was further divided into subprefectures headed by a magistrate, who was in charge of collecting taxes and implementing justice. Aided by two or three subordinate officials and a clerical staff, the magistrate depended on powerful local families to help him govern. At every level of the bureaucracy, officials were required to carry out the directives of the central government.

Song dynasty
(960–1276) Dynasty that ruled a united China from the northern capital of Kaifeng from 960–1126 and only the southern half of the empire from 1127–1276.

The Collapse of the Northern Song, 1126–1127

Since its founding, the Song dynasty had faced a problem common to earlier dynasties: keeping peace with the nomads to the north, in this case the Khitan (KEE-tan), a nomadic people living in modern-day Mongolia. To counter this threat, the Song formed an alliance with the Jurchen (JIR-chen), a forest-dwelling, fishing people based in Manchuria who proved to be skilled horsemen. They spoke Jurchen, an Altaic language similar in structure to Japanese. Originally a subject people of the Khitan, the Jurchen declared their independence by founding their own dynasty, the **Jin dynasty** ("gold" in Chinese), in 1115. The Song-Jurchen forces defeated the Khitan in 1125, yet as soon as victory was certain, the Jurchen leader ordered his

Jin dynasty
(1115–1234) Dynasty of the Jurchen people of Manchuria that ruled north China from 1127–1234, when the Mongols defeated their armies.

gunpowder
Mixture of potassium nitrate, sulfur, and charcoal used by the Chinese for fireworks and explosive weapons.

The Emperor as Painter Emperor Huizong (r. 1101–1125) is famous for his bird-and-flower paintings and his distinctive calligraphy, but recently art historians have carefully analyzed the brushstrokes in several paintings labeled "imperially brushed" and have discovered that they were made by different artists, probably those in the imperial workshop. They argue that Huizong's idiosyncratic calligraphy, in fact, lent itself to replication by others.

Palace Museum, Beijing, China/Cultural Relics Press

troops to attack the Song. The Jurchen army, with its superior horses, defeated the Song handily and conquered Kaifeng.

A powerful cavalry alone could not conquer the huge walled cities of north China like Kaifeng. For that, the Jurchen had to use weapons fueled by gunpowder, a Chinese invention. **Gunpowder** is an explosive material made with different ratios of potassium nitrate (also called saltpeter), sulfur, and charcoal. Before 900, the Chinese used gunpowder primarily for fireworks, but sometime around 900 they realized that they could use it as a weapon.

Chinese soldiers employed gunpowder in both simple and complex ways. In the most basic use, archers tied small bags of gunpowder onto their arrows, which then detonated on impact. One of the most complex and powerful weapons used in the siege of Kaifeng was the flame-thrower, which emitted a continuous stream of fire. The Jurchen also built siege towers, taller than the city's walls, from which they could shoot incendiary bombs made of bamboo shells containing gunpowder and fragments of porcelain that shot in all directions. Unable to devise an effective defense against this horrific new weapon, the residents of Kaifeng surrendered in January 1127.

The loss of the capital marked the end of the Northern Song dynasty (960–1126) and the beginning of the Southern Song dynasty (1127–1276). When the Jurchen captured Kaifeng, they took two emperors prisoner. One, Huizong (HWAY-dzong), had reigned from 1101 to 1125 and then abdicated in favor of his eldest son. The most artistically talented of China's emperors, Huizong did many paintings of birds and flowers and also perfected his own distinctive calligraphic style. His Jurchen captors gave Huizong the humiliating title *Marquis of Muddled Virtue*, and his son, *Doubly Muddled Marquis*.

Despite their success, Jurchen armies could not conquer the region south of the Huai River. One of Huizong's ten living sons managed to escape from Kaifeng and was named emperor in May of 1127. He did not realize it at the time, but both his father and his brother would die in captivity, making him the first emperor of the Southern Song dynasty. Hangzhou (HAHNG-jo), in Zhejiang province, became the capital of the Southern Song. This placed China's capital south of the Yangzi River for the first time in Chinese history and marked the new importance of southern China. Historians refer to the period when the capital of a united China was in Kaifeng as the Northern Song (960–1126) and the period when the capital was in Hangzhou as the Southern Song (1127–1276). Although China was not united after 1126, the period of the Song dynasty covers its founding in 960 to its collapse in 1276.

The military defeat of the Northern Song triggered one of the greatest migrations in human history. Most of the people who left Kaifeng worked for the Song government; they included 20,000 officials, 100,000 clerks, and 400,000 army soldiers and their families. In sum, more than 500,000 people, out of a population in north and south China of an estimated 100 million, crossed the Yangzi River in 1126 and 1127. Like Li Qingzhao, most never returned to north China.

China Divided: The Jin and the Southern Song, 1127–1234

Life in the south was extremely difficult for many northerners, who viewed the north and south as two distinct cultural regions. Northerners ate wheat and millet, often in the form of noodles or bread, while southerners ate rice. Worse, their spoken dialects were mutually incomprehensible. Hangzhou had been a small, regional city, and its population was hard-pressed to accept five hundred thousand new residents. Yet within a few years its 1 million residents had built it into a worthy successor to the Northern Song capital of Kaifeng.

Li Qingzhao's memoir provides a rare eyewitness account of the migration south. When she and her husband Zhao Mingcheng fled in 1127 to avoid the invading troops, they left behind belongings and artwork that filled ten rooms in their home, which was burnt to the ground by the Jurchen invaders a few months later. In the south, crisscrossed by many rivers and lakes, the couple moved more rapidly by boat.

The Southern Song emperor had taken temporary refuge in Nanjing, since there was no new capital yet. In the summer of 1129, when the emperor summoned Zhao Mingcheng to Nanjing for a personal audience, the couple was forced to separate, with Li Qingzhao remaining behind. Six weeks later, Li Qingzhao received a letter from her husband saying that he had contracted malaria. She frantically traveled the 100 miles (160 km) to Nanjing in twenty-four hours by boat, reaching his side just in time to watch him succumb to dysentery and die at the age of forty-nine.

Li Qingzhao closes her memoir with this sentence: *"From the time I was eighteen until now at the age of fifty-two—a span of thirty years—how much calamity, how much gain and loss I have witnessed!"* Alone and widowed, Li Qingzhao wrote some of her most moving poems:

> *The wind subsides—the dust carries a fragrance of fallen petals;*
> *It's late in the day—I'm too tired to comb my hair.*
> *Things remain but he is gone, and with him everything.*
> *On the verge of words, tears flow.*
>
> *I hear at Twin Creek spring's still lovely;*
> *How I long to float there on a small boat—*
> *But I fear that at Twin Creek my frail grasshopper boat*
> *Could not carry this load of grief.*[†]

---

*Stephen Owen, *An Anthology of Chinese Literature, Volume 1: Beginnings to 1911* (New York, N.Y.: W. W. Norton & Company, Inc., 1997).

[†]Excerpt from *Women Writers of Traditional China: An Anthology of Poetry and Criticism,* ed. Kang-i Sun Chang and Haun Saussy (Stanford, Calif.: Stanford University Press, 1999), p. 98.

Li Qingzhao gave voice to the losses suffered by the many people displaced by the Jurchen conquest. In the south, the Southern Song dynasty governed some 60 million people from the capital at Hangzhou, where Li Qingzhao settled and eventually remarried. For more than a century and a half after 1127, China was divided. With a government structure modeled after the Song dynasty, 1 million Jurchen ruled a population of some 40 million Chinese in the north until 1234.

After more fourteen years of fighting, the Southern Song and the Jurchen signed a peace treaty in 1142. But according to the humiliating terms of the treaty, the Southern Song, an *"insignificant state,"* agreed to pay the Jurchen, a *"superior state,"* tribute of 250,000 ounces of silver and 250,000 bolts of silk each year. This tribute was an enormous burden on the Song state and its people, who were well aware that earlier dynasties had received tribute from weaker neighbors, not paid it. The payments, however, stimulated trade and economic growth because the Jurchen used the money to buy Chinese goods as the people of south China rebuilt their economy and became one of the richest societies in the world.

The Commercial Revolution in China, ca. 900–1276

The expansion of markets throughout China between 900 and 1300 brought such rapid economic growth that scholars refer to these changes as a commercial revolution. We do not usually think of a change that takes place over more than four hundred years as revolutionary, and the commercial revolution affected different regions at different times. But for the people who personally experienced the expansion of markets, the changes were indeed dramatic.

Before the commercial revolution, farmers grew their own food in a largely self-sufficient barter economy and bought salt, if that, at the market. Officials strictly monitored all trade, and markets opened only at noon and closed promptly at dusk. As markets sprang up in different towns and more people went to them, these restrictions became increasingly difficult to enforce, and, by Li Qingzhao's day, such restrictions had long been forgotten. At the height of the commercial revolution in the Song dynasty, China's farmers sold cash crops such as tangerines and handicrafts such as pottery, baskets, and textiles at markets. They used their earnings to buy a variety of products, including food. Dependent on the marketplace for their incomes, they led totally different lives from those who had lived before the commercial revolution.

Changes in Agriculture and the Rise of the South

The origins of the commercial revolution go back centuries before Li Qingzhao's lifetime. In north China, where rainfall was lower (see Chapter 4), farmers planted wheat and millet; in south China, where rainfall was greater, farmers grew rice.

Before the commercial revolution, south China was universally viewed as a remote backwater whose many swamps provided a breeding ground for malaria and other diseases. When northerners moved south in search of more land, they settled in the highlands and drained the swamps. They used pumps to regulate the flow of water into walled fields for rice. After planting rice seeds in small gardens, they transplanted the rice plants into a field drained of water. Once the plants had taken root, they flooded the fields with water until the crop ripened.

Southern farmers experimented with different rice strains, and in the late tenth century they realized that a type of rice imported from Vietnam had a shorter growing season than indigenous rice, making it possible to harvest two crops a year rather than just one.

The shift from wheat and millet to rice had a dramatic impact on China's population. In 742, 60 percent of the population of 60 million lived in north China. By 980, 62 percent were living in south China, where they cultivated the higher-yielding rice. With more food available, the overall population increased to 100 million in the year 1000. The increasing surplus from higher-yield rice freed others to grow cash crops or to produce handicrafts. Thus one of the most important changes in China's history was this shift south. During the Song dynasty, for the first time, the majority of China's population lived in the south, a trend that continues today.

The Currency of the Song Dynasty

As more and more people began to produce for markets, they needed a way to pay for their purchases. In response, Song authorities greatly increased the money supply, which consisted of round bronze coins with square holes. By the eleventh century, the Song government was minting twenty times more coins than had the Tang dynasty at its height.[*]

Li Qingzhao's description of her husband's many shopping trips offers a rare glimpse into the new market economy under the Northern Song: *"On the first and fifteenth day of every month, my husband would get a short vacation from the Academy: he would 'pawn some clothes' for five hundred cash and go to the market at Xiangguo [SHE-AHNG-gwaw] Temple, where he would buy fruit and rubbings of inscriptions."*[†] Many people in the Song enjoyed tangerines and oranges, which were grown in south China but were available at reasonable cost at markets all over the empire. Zhao used bronze coins to purchase rubbings of inscriptions, art objects that only the richest people could afford.

Sometime near the year 1000, the government introduced the world's first **paper money**. Paper money's lighter weight was an advantage over bronze coins; a string of one thousand coins could weigh more than 8 pounds (4 kg). The new currency appeared at a time when China's paper-making technology was just reaching the Islamic world (see Chapter 9) and had not yet spread to Europe. While people continued to use coins, paper money expanded the money supply, further contributing to the economic growth of the commercial revolution.

Right from its start, the question of how much paper money to print was intensely controversial. Some wanted to print vast quantities of paper money; other officials urged caution. The debate came to a head in 1069, when the reigning emperor appointed a new grand councilor, named Wang Anshi (WAHNG AHN-shih), who held more radical views. He instituted the **New Policies**, which included paying all government salaries in money and extending low-interest loans to poor peasants. But peasants could not earn enough money to pay back their loans, and by 1086 the reforms had failed.

paper money
Money that could be used instead of bronze coins; issued around 1000 by the Song dynasty, the first government in world history to do so.

New Policies
Reforms, implemented between 1069 and 1086, that included paying all government salaries in money and extending low-interest loans to poor peasants.

Iron and Steel

The commercial revolution led to the increased production of all goods, not just of rice and fruit. Iron production boomed as entrepreneurs built large-scale workshops to make iron products in factory-like spaces with hundreds of workers. Song metallurgists made two kinds of iron: cast and wrought. Cast iron was poured

---

[*]Valerie Hansen, *The Open Empire: A History of China to 1600* (New York: W. W. Norton, 2000), p. 266.

[†]Reprinted by permission of the publisher from *Remembrances: The Experience of the Past in Classical Chinese Literature* by Stephen Owen, p. 82, Cambridge, Mass.: Harvard University Press, Copyright © 1986 by the President and Fellows of Harvard College.

into a mold and was so hard that it could not be worked with a hammer; wrought iron was malleable enough that blacksmiths could work it. The demand for both types of iron was considerable.

Soldiers needed iron armor and weapons, while government workshops produced iron tools and iron fittings, like nails and locks, for buildings and bridges. Although not mass-produced in the modern sense (that is, in factories using electric-powered machinery), iron goods were made in large quantities and at low prices. Song dynasty metalsmiths even crafted tall pagodas from iron.

The metalsmiths of the Song also learned how to produce steel, one of the strongest metals known. They heated sheets of iron together in a superheated furnace and then worked them by hand to make steel swords. After the forests around Kaifeng had been depleted for fuel and housing, Chinese metalsmiths learned to fire their smelters with coke, a fuel made from preheated coal that produced high temperatures.

The area around Kaifeng became the world's leading producer of iron. By 1078, China was producing 125,000 tons of iron, or 3.1 pounds per person, in the entire country. This ratio was matched in Europe only in 1700, on the eve of the Industrial Revolution, prompting historians to ask why, if the Song reached such an advanced stage of metal production, China did not experience a sustained industrial revolution. The answer most often given is that Britain's Industrial Revolution occurred under a unique set of circumstances. For example, the British invented machines to make up for a labor shortage, while the Song had no corresponding shortage of labor and therefore no need to develop labor-saving machinery.

Song-dynasty Cast-Iron Pagoda   For centuries Chinese metallurgists had used blast furnaces to make cast iron. By 1105 their technology was so advanced that they were able to cast this entire octagonal pagoda section by section. When completed, this pagoda, in Shandong province, stood 78 feet (24 m) high, evidence of the skill of Song metalworkers. Most pagodas are made from stone or brick, but several cast-iron examples survive in different parts of modern China. (New China Pictures Company/Visual Connection Archive)

Urban Life amid Commercial Prosperity

As newlyweds, Li Qingzhao and her husband had lived in Kaifeng, one of the world's most prosperous cities and possibly the largest, rivaled only by Cairo, with a population of five hundred thousand. (At that time London and Paris each had fewer than one hundred thousand residents.) Often, as they shared tea, Li and her husband played a drinking game that shows how close they were:

I happen to have an excellent memory, and every evening after we finished eating, we would sit in the hall called "Return Home" and make tea. Pointing to the heaps of books and histories, we would guess on which line of what page in which chapter of which book a certain passage could be found. Success in guessing determined who got to drink his or her tea first. Whenever I got it right, I would raise the teacup, laughing so hard that the tea would spill in my lap, and I would get up, not having been able to drink anything at all. I would have been glad to grow old in such a world.

*Reprinted by permission of the publisher from *Remembrances: The Experience of the Past in Classical Chinese Literature* by Stephen Owen, p. 85, Cambridge, Mass.: Harvard University Press, Copyright © 1986 by the President and Fellows of Harvard College.

Li Qingzhao and her husband clearly enjoyed each other's company, and he treated her as his intellectual equal. Urban prosperity gave them the leisure to share learning and leisure pursuits like this.

Kaifeng was a city with many sensual pleasures for those who could afford them, and the wealth from the commercial revolution meant that many people could. Kaifeng alone had seventy-two major restaurants, each standing three floors high and licensed by the government. Even working people could afford to eat noodles or a snack at the many stands dotting the city. (See the feature "Visual Evidence in Primary Sources: The Commercial Vitality of a Chinese City.")

Although Li Qingzhao does not write about crowding, Kaifeng's 1 million residents lived at a density of 32,000 people per square mile (2,000 per sq km). With people so crowded, sanitation posed a genuine problem, and disease must have spread quickly.

Footbinding

The southward migration eventually brought greater wealth to most people and eroded the distinctions among social groups. Although merchants continued to be at the bottom of the ideal social hierarchy—below scholars, peasants, and artisans—others envied their wealth. The continued expansion of the market turned many peasants into part-time and full-time artisans. Many of those making money selling goods at the market aspired to the high social position of the officials they saw above them.

Both in cities and the countryside, wealthy men sought second and third wives, called concubines, who they hoped would give them more children. Being able to support a large family including concubines and many children was a mark of prestige. Many observers complained about unscrupulous merchants who kidnapped women and sold them as concubines to newly wealthy men.

Brokers in women found that those with bound feet attracted a higher price than those with natural feet. Li Qingzhao's mother did not bind her daughter's feet, but by 1300 the wives and daughters of officials throughout south China did. The practice appeared first in the tenth century, when dancers at the imperial court, who were probably in their late teens, had begun to wrap their own feet to make them smaller. By the Southern Song, women from good families began to wrap their daughters' feet in the hopes of enhancing their chances of making a good match. The mothers started when the girls were young, around ten, so that their feet would never grow to their natural size.

In the Song period, feet were shortened only slightly, to around 7 or 8 inches (18 or 20 cm). The initial binding was very painful, but eventually girls could resume walking, though always with difficulty. Footbinding transformed a woman's foot into a sexual object that only her husband was supposed to see, wash, or fondle.

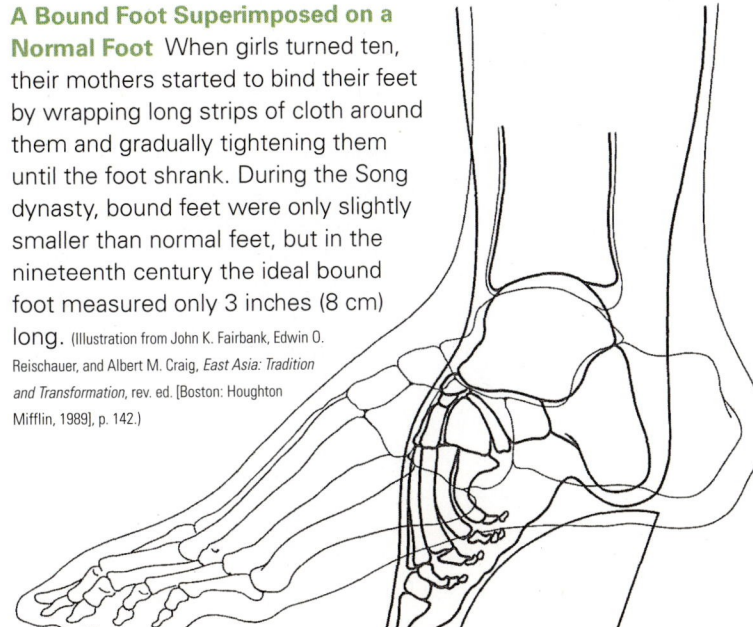

A Bound Foot Superimposed on a Normal Foot When girls turned ten, their mothers started to bind their feet by wrapping long strips of cloth around them and gradually tightening them until the foot shrank. During the Song dynasty, bound feet were only slightly smaller than normal feet, but in the nineteenth century the ideal bound foot measured only 3 inches (8 cm) long. (Illustration from John K. Fairbank, Edwin O. Reischauer, and Albert M. Craig, *East Asia: Tradition and Transformation*, rev. ed. [Boston: Houghton Mifflin, 1989], p. 142.)

The Commercial Vitality of a Chinese City

Li Qingzhao's memoir makes the reader wonder what the markets and cities of the Northern Song looked like. One of the masterpieces of Song painting, an extraordinary hand scroll sometimes called the *Mona Lisa* of China, depicts a city with many markets during the Northern Song. We are told in a brief biographical notice at the end of the painting that the scroll's painter—Zhang Zeduan (JAHNG zeh-dwon), who flourished around 1150—specialized in technical drawing: "He showed talent for fine-lined architectural drawing, and especially liked boats and carts, markets and bridges, moats and paths." The artist intended that viewers look at the hand scroll slowly, rolling it out inch by inch,

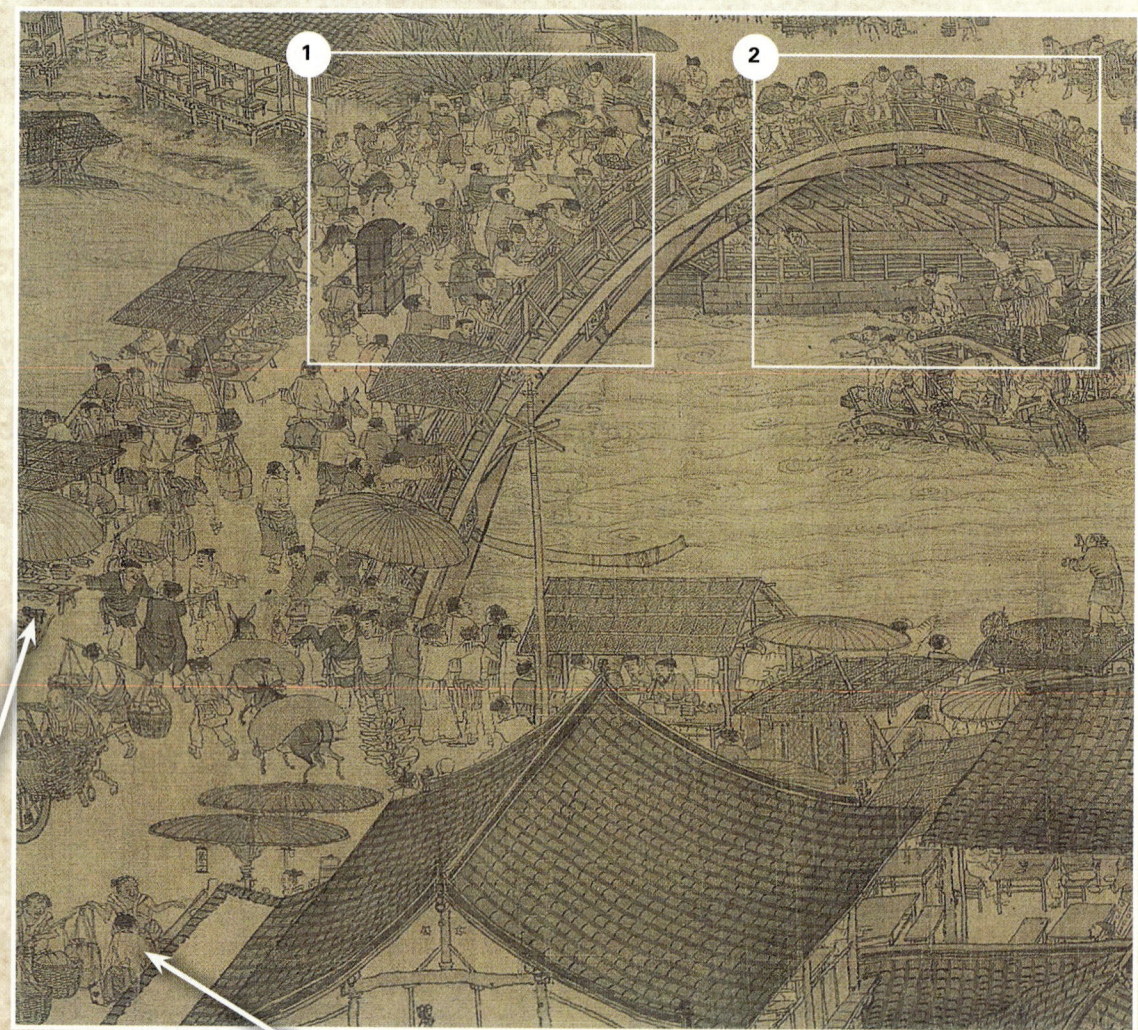

National Palace Museum, Beijing/Cultural Relics Press

This vendor has laid out his tools on a cloth for customers to see.

Three lightly clothed carriers put down their loaded baskets outside a stand serving drinks under two large umbrellas.

QUESTIONS FOR ANALYSIS

» *What are people buying and selling in the Qingming scroll?*

» *What do these transactions reveal about the commercial revolution of the Song dynasty?*

from right to left, and savoring the extraordinary detail that extends a full 17.25 feet (5.25 m) long. The painting, often referred to as the Qingming scroll, was completed sometime before 1186. Entitled *Peace Reigns over the River*, the scroll celebrates commercial life.

The dramatic high point of the painting comes right in the middle of the scroll. At first one views a boat with sailors hurriedly pulling the mast down. Then, as the scroll unfurls, the viewer understands why: the boat is going under the rainbow bridge, yet its towline has snapped. In his efforts to keep the boat from crashing, one sailor grabs a rope thrown by a passerby standing on the bridge, just as the men at the ship's bow gesture frantically to the oncoming boat to stay out of the way.

The bridge scene vividly illustrates the major change of the commercial revolution: commerce had exploded out of restricted market districts to blanket the cities of the twelfth century. Restaurants and food stands line the side of the river, and they have even crept up the bridge where passersby can eat a snack purchased from a seated baker or can buy ropes or scissors from vendors who have laid out their goods on the ground. As the scroll ends, when one goes through a large gate and finally enters the city proper, it dawns on the viewer that all the commercial activity seen so far has taken place outside the city walls—a location where all markets were banned during the Tang dynasty.

The detail of the scroll is so mesmerizing that one can easily forget that one is looking at a painting by an artist and not at a photograph. Zhang Zeduan has fit the city into an artfully constructed composition, complete with the rainbow bridge at the exact midpoint of the scroll, and has depicted a city without dirt, illness, or crowding. Curiously, Zhang has nearly omitted women from his cityscape. Of more than five hundred people in the scroll, only twenty or so are female. Surely a real city would have had more women outside, even if women from prestigious families, like Li Qingzhao, often remained indoors.

A collision is about to occur on top of the bridge: an official riding a horse confronts someone (a woman?) in a sedan chair. Several feisty servants gesture emphatically to the horseman to get out of the way.

1

2

A bystander on top of the bridge tosses a rope to the boat's frantic crew, who hope to avert a crash with a boat coming toward them from under the bridge.

The details of the bridge's construction—a round arch made from straight wooden beams wrapped together with iron—are clear from this angle. A wooden walkway at the water's edge allows pedestrians to pass underneath the bridge.

Book Publishing and the Education Boom

The commercial revolution brought an information revolution parallel to today's Internet boom, caused by a deceptively simple innovation, woodblock printing. Before 700, creating a book was a slow, laborious process, since all manuscript copies were done by hand. The introduction of woodblock printing sped up book publishing dramatically and significantly lowered the cost of books.

The effect on everyday life was profound, as many more men and women could afford books and learned to read. Because people had more disposable income, they could finance the education of their children. The rise in wealth and educational opportunity also prompted more people to take the government's civil service examination, the door to a job in the bureaucracy (see Chapters 4 and 8).

Woodblock Printing and the Invention of Movable Type

Using the same technique developed in the eighth century, Song dynasty printers used woodblocks to print individual sheets of paper (see Chapter 8). Printers could make hundreds of copies from the same block of wood. Folding each page in half, they sewed the sheets into bound chapters of thirty or so pages. Often people calculated the size of libraries in sewn chapters, which were stored in boxes.

Shortly after 1040, the Chinese bookmaker Bi Sheng (bee shung) invented **movable type**, in which each character is made separately and arranged on a frame to form a page. An eleventh-century description explains:

movable type
Printing method first developed in China after 1040 by printers who arranged reusable individual characters on the page.

> *Bi Sheng, a man of unofficial position, made moveable type. His method was as follows: he took sticky clay and cut in it characters as thin as the edge of a coin. . . . When he wished to print, he took an iron frame. . . . In this he placed the types, set close together. . . . If one were to print only two or three copies, this method would be neither simple nor easy. But for printing hundreds or thousands of copies, it was marvelously quick.*[*]

Since Chinese has thousands of different characters, making a different piece of type for each character was a slow and expensive process. For this reason, it was cheaper to carve woodblocks for smaller runs, such as a thousand books. Movable type made sense only for a few large-scale printing projects.

The low cost of books combined with sustained economic growth produced an education boom that intensified the competition for government jobs. More and more families hired scholars who had failed the civil service examinations to serve as tutors for their sons and daughters, buying books and study aids in large numbers. Though only a few passed the exams, many boys gained basic literacy.

The Education of Women

Some women began to enjoy increased educational opportunities in the twelfth and thirteenth centuries, exactly the time when footbinding began to spread. Although they were not allowed to take the civil service exams, many women learned to read and write and take care of their families' finances. We know a good deal about wealthy women in the Song dynasty from biographies, called epitaphs, that were placed in their tombs.

---

[*]Tsien Tsuen-hsuin, *Chemistry and Chemical Technology, Part I: Paper and Printing*, vol. 1 of *Science and Civilisation in China*, ed. Joseph Needham (New York: Cambridge University Press, 1985), pp. 201–202.

The epitaphs reveal what kind of woman was most admired in the twelfth and thirteenth centuries. Whereas Tang dynasty epitaphs emphasized women's physical appearance and ancestry, Song epitaphs frequently praised women for successfully managing their household finances, a skill requiring knowledge of math. In 1250, one official wrote an epitaph for Lady Fang, the wife of his younger brother:

My brother was untalented at making a living but loved antiques and would spend every cent to collect famous paintings and calligraphies. Lady Fang calmly made secret economies and never complained of lacking anything. . . .

Lady Fang was a widow for over ten years. During this time she arranged for her husband's tomb, completed marriage arrangements for her children, repaired the old house, and brought new fields into cultivation in order to continue the thread of our family and preserve the orphans. . . .*

---

*Patricia Buckley Ebrey, "The Women in Liu Kezhuang's Family," *Modern China* 10, no. 4 (1984), citation on 437.

The World's First Movable Type This model reconstructs the movable type Bi Sheng invented for printing in the 1040s. Because the printer had to cut out an individual clay type for each character, the cost of movable type was much higher than the traditional Chinese method of woodblock printing. For large print runs of over one hundred thousand, however, movable type made sense. The world's earliest surviving books printed with movable type were made in Korea around 1400, some fifty years before the German printer Johannes Gutenberg used movable type to print the Bible. (Ontario Science Centre, Toronto, Canada)

Note that the author commends her ability to manage her family's income after her husband's death. Funerary texts often praise widows for tutoring their young children at home and for making economies that allow their offspring to attend school when older. Some women did not remarry after their husband's deaths, but others did: Li Qingzhao remarried but soon divorced when her husband, an official, was found guilty of corruption. She spent the rest of her life in Hangzhou and the neighboring towns.

The Growth of Civil Service Examinations

The Song dynasty was the only government in the twelfth- and thirteenth-century world to recruit its bureaucrats via merit, as measured by a grueling series of examinations. At the time of the dynasty's founding in 960, civil service examinations had been in use for over a thousand years. But it was only in the Song era that the proportion of the civil officials in the bureaucracy who had passed the examinations reached nearly 90 percent (versus 5 percent for the Tang).[1] The tests were not always fair, but they were more equitable than the system of appointments by heredity or social position used elsewhere in the world. As a result, the Song era saw a decisive shift from government by aristocracy to government by merit-based bureaucracy.

During the Song dynasty, exam candidates took two rounds of exams, which were held every three years: the first in their home prefecture and the second in the capital. At the start of the dynasty, as in the Tang, examiners knew whose paper they were grading; after 1000, the candidates' names were covered up and the exam papers recopied so that examiners could not recognize anyone's handwriting. The emperor himself conducted the final stage, the palace examinations, in which those placing highest in the written exams were examined orally.

Success in the examinations brought a government-issued degree; each time the examinations were held during the Southern Song, some five hundred men received the highest rank of "**advanced scholar**." The degree did not guarantee employment. Those placing highest were given prestigious entry-level jobs, often drafting decrees for the emperor, but those with lower scores had to wait for a vacancy in the bureaucracy to open up, which could take years.

The government examiners devised different types of exams over the centuries. Successful candidates had to demonstrate mastery of a classic text, often within the Confucian tradition, by explaining from which text an unidentified passage had been taken. They were asked to compose poetry, or essays with a fixed number of lines and a set number of words per line (like a sonnet in English). The candidates also wrote essays about problems the central government might face, such as inflation or defeating border peoples. Many of these literary skills did not relate directly to what officials would do once in office. Still, those who wrote the questions were seeking to test a broad range of learning with the expectation that they could select the most educated, and so, they believed, the most virtuous, men to become officials. (See the feature "World History in Today's World: The College Entrance Examinations in China: How Best to Identify Talent?")

The examinations were not open to everyone. Local officials permitted only young men from well-established families to register for the first round of exams. Unlike farmers' sons, who were lucky to attend village school for a year or two, the sons of privileged families had the time and money to study for the exams, often at home with a tutor. Preparation required long years of study.

In the eleventh century, successful exam candidates tended to come from a small group of one hundred families living in the capital, Kaifeng. This was the

advanced scholar The highest degree given by the government to the top-scoring examination candidates.

The College Entrance Examinations in China: How Best to Identify Talent?

To gain admission to university in China, students have to score well on all parts of the college entrance examination, which emphasizes mathematics, the sciences, Chinese, and English. In 2011, 9.3 million students competed for 2.6 million spots in universities and another 3 million spots in technical institutes.

Today's examiners face a dilemma similar to that of the examiners of the Song dynasty. Song examiners hoped to select moral gentlemen solely on the basis of written examinations. Today's examiners must identify future scholars from standardized exams.

Some students try to distinguish themselves in creative ways. In 2011, one student wrote an entire answer using oracle-bone characters on the essay question, which, like the SAT, is designed to test writing ability. The examiners were torn: was this just a gimmick, or had the student really demonstrated mastery of the ancient writing system? When they consulted experts in ancient Chinese writing, they learned that the student had jumbled together different scripts and that the essay was comprehensible but not inspired. The student ultimately scored 6 out of 60 points for the essay, not enough for him to get into college.

Other students have more luck. One student received full points for a long poem in classical Chinese (the language in use before the twentieth century), with seven characters in each line. In this case the examiners consulted professors of literature, who agreed that the essay displayed genuine literary merit. But for this student, a perfect score on this part of the exam did not compensate for his poor performance on the math portion, and he, too, failed to gain admission to university.

In both instances, the examiners displayed a surprising degree of care: they did not immediately fail the unconventional answers but took the time to consult outside experts and followed their recommendations. In recent years, some university departments have requested a modification in the national examinations so that they can test students' knowledge of a single field and choose outstanding students in this way. Does it make sense, they wonder, for the universities to reject promising students in one field simply because of a low score in another?

Source: http://www.danwei.org/scholarship_and_education/oracle_bone_college_essay.php.

elite into which Li Qingzhao and Zhao Mingcheng were born, and both of their fathers had received the highest possible degree of advanced scholar.

As the population grew and printed books became more widely available, examinations became more competitive. By 1270, 1 out of every 250 people took the exams, and in some prefectures in southeast China (particularly in modern Fujian), as many as 700 men competed for a single place in the first round of the examinations. The high number of candidates increased the literacy rate: some historians believe that one in men, but many fewer women, could read.[*]

During the Song dynasty, children learned to read by using primers that taught a core vocabulary. One of the most popular, *The Three-Character Classic*, written circa 1200, consisted of rhyming lines of three Chinese characters each, which students had to learn by heart. The book reminded students of the five important Confucian relationships: father/son, husband/wife, elder brother/younger brother, friend/friend, ruler/subject:

[*]Valerie Hansen, *The Open Empire: A History of China to 1600* (New York: W. W. Norton, 2000), p. 295.

Father and son should live in love, in peace the married pair:
Kindness the elder brother's and respect the younger's care.
Let deference due to age be paid, comrades feel friendship's glow,
Princes treat well their minister—they loyalty should show.
These moral duties binding are on all men here below.[*]

Because almost everyone studied *The Three-Character Classic*, this version of Confucianism had great influence, not only in China but also all over East Asia, where many students used this primer to learn to read Chinese characters (even if they pronounced them in Japanese or Korean).

The most advanced students prepared for the examinations, which were outwardly fair. In fact, however, the sons and relatives of high officials were eligible to take a less competitive series of examinations, often with a pass rate of 50 percent, an advantage called the **shadow privilege**. Since Zhao Mingcheng's father was grand councilor, the highest official in the bureaucracy, his shadow privilege extended to his sons, grandsons, sons-in-law, brothers, cousins, and nephews. In the twelfth and thirteenth centuries, as more men became eligible for the shadow privilege, fewer candidates took the open examinations.

As competition increased, so did the pressure to cheat. Some candidates paid others to take the exams in their place, or they copied others' answers. In one scandal in Sichuan province, officials grading the exams took bribes, changed the names on the exams, and secretly marked the booklets to which they were supposed to give passing grades. Crafty students also bought commercial aids, like miniature books with tiny characters the size of a fly, that they could smuggle into the examination halls.

Cheating and heightened competition prompted many men to turn away from the examinations and government service altogether. In 1101, when Li Qingzhao married, she assumed that her husband would become an official, and he did. One hundred years later, many families of equally prominent rank chose instead to educate their sons at private academies and to keep them at home to run their family estates once their education was completed. As a book critical of the examination system explained:

If the sons of a gentleman have no hereditary stipend to maintain and no permanent holdings to depend on, and they wish to be filial to their parents and to support children, then nothing is as good as being a scholar. . . . For those who cannot be scholars, then medicine, Buddhism and Daoism, agriculture, trade, or crafts are all possible.[†]

This author uses the word *scholar* for everyone who earned a living by reading, writing, teaching, or editing. Many young men followed the book's advice. After studying at private academies, they returned to their family estates and pursued careers the author suggested.

shadow privilege
Privilege extended to sons and relatives of Song dynasty officials, allowing them to take a less competitive series of examinations.

Religious Life During the Song

Sustained economic growth allowed the Chinese to give money to practitioners of many different religions. Most Chinese did not adhere to a specific religion:

[*]*The Three-Character Classic,* Pei-yi Wu, "Education of Children in the Sung," in *Neo-Confucian Education: The Formative Stage,* ed. Wm. Theodore de Bary and John W. Chaffee (Berkeley: University of California Press, 1989), p. 323. Copyright © 1989, The Regents of the University of California.

[†]Valerie Hansen, *The Open Empire: A History of China to 1600* (New York: W. W. Norton, 2000), p. 294.

they worshiped the deities and consulted the religious specialists they thought most powerful.

Lay Chinese also made offerings to Buddhist and Daoist deities and to gods not associated with any organized religion. Many educated families were drawn to the teachings of Neo-Confucianism.

Neo-Confucian Teachings

The most influential private academy, the White Deer Academy, was founded in 1181 by the thinker **Zhu Xi** (1130–1200). Zhu Xi's curriculum emphasized moral cultivation. He wanted his students to become true Confucian gentlemen, not civil service officials, and he thought the best guidelines were the Confucian classics, in particular four texts: *The Analects* (which contained the conversations of Confucius with his students; see Chapter 4), *Mencius* (written by a follower of Confucius), and two chapters from a ritual manual. These writings are known collectively as *The Four Books*.

Zhu Xi (JOO she) criticized Buddhism as a non-Chinese religion and urged his followers to give up all Buddhist practices, yet Buddhist teachings about meditating and reaching enlightenment clearly influenced Zhu Xi's understanding of the transmission of the Way (see Chapter 4). He also claimed that studying and thinking on his own had allowed him to understand the Way as it had passed from Confucius to Mencius, from Mencius to a Tang dynasty thinker named Han Yu (768–824), and then to himself. He used the word *daotong*, or "transmission of the Way," for this process. Whereas earlier historians believed that Zhu Xi came up with this idea on his own, scholars have recently discovered other texts, not by members of Zhu Xi's school, that used the same word. Zhu Xi, then, adopted a word already in circulation for his own teaching. Similarly, he was not the first thinker to focus on the two chapters from the ritual manual included in *The Four Books*: Buddhist teachers in the early 1000s had noticed that these books contained ideas that overlapped with Buddhism, and the two chapters had already circulated in Buddhist monasteries as independent texts.

Because Zhu Xi's teachings were based on Confucianism but introduced major revisions, they are called **Neo-Confucianism**. Rather than focusing on ritual and inner humanity as Confucius had, Zhu Xi urged students to apprehend the principle in things. If students examined everything in the world around them (an all-inclusive concept that Zhu Xi called psychophysical stuff—*qi*—literally "air") and studied *The Four Books* carefully, Neo-Confucians believed that they could discern a coherent pattern underlying everything. Armed with that knowledge, an individual could attain sagehood, the goal of all Neo-Confucian education. (See the feature "Movement of Ideas Through Primary Sources: The Spread of Neo-Confucian Teachings.")

Zhu Xi did not attract a great following during his lifetime, and the government banned his teachings during the last years of his life, but they gained in popularity after his death. In the fourteenth century, his edition of *The Four Books* became the basis of the civil service examinations—an outcome Zhu Xi could never have anticipated. By the seventeenth century his teachings had also gained a wide following in Japan, Korea, and Vietnam.

Day-to-Day Religious Life

At the time that Zhu Xi and his followers were formulating their teachings, Neo-Confucian shrines spread throughout south China, and by the end of the Song dynasty, shrines to worthies had proliferated throughout the empire. A "worthy" was someone who embodied the Neo-Confucian virtues of being educated, honest, and concerned about his community's welfare. All worthies were male.

Zhu Xi
(1130–1200) The leading thinker of Neo-Confucianism, who wrote a commentary on *The Four Books*.

Neo-Confucianism
Teachings of the thinker Zhu Xi (1130–1200) and his followers that urged students to apprehend the principle in psychophysical stuff, or *qi*.

The Spread of Neo-Confucian Teachings

Zhu Xi and the other leading Neo-Confucian thinkers revived a literary genre called "records of conversations" to explain the most important concepts of their teaching. In form, the conversations between the teacher and student resembled the snippets of conversations between Confucius and his students captured in *The Analects*. Some twenty-five examples of Neo-Confucian records of conversations survive from the twelfth and thirteenth centuries.

This genre fit well with the Neo-Confucian conviction that everyone was born with a mind that could learn and recognize the truth, whether from reading a given text or from listening to a teacher. The main difference between students and a sage was that the sage had perfected his understanding of Neo-Confucian ideas, while students were still learning.

Records of conversations differed from other prose writings because they were in vernacular Chinese, a type of Chinese that sounded closer to speech than the traditional written language. The question-and-answer format allowed Neo-Confucians to employ colloquial expressions that added a conversational flavor. Still, the records of conversations were not transcripts of everything that was said in a conversation; they were carefully composed. In the first selection, for example, Zhu Xi explains two key concepts in his teaching: principle and psychophysical stuff. He also mentions the concepts of *yin* and *yang*, which refer, respectively, to "dark, passive" and "bright, active" qualities.

The records of conversations influenced how Neo-Confucian students expressed their ideas, particularly in the essays they wrote for the civil service examinations. The second selection presents criticisms of Neo-Confucian candidates' exam essays from three examiners who graded exams in 1187. The students ignored the usual rules of composition so that they could express their ideas as their teachers did; their decision appalled these examiners. Here they gave clear instructions for identifying Neo-Confucian–influenced essays, which would receive low scores.

The students' steadfast faith in the Neo-Confucian teachings, and their willingness to risk low scores, contributed to the spread of Neo-Confucian ideas throughout the empire. In the 1200s, as more and more people came to embrace Neo-Confucian thinking, examiners began to reward students for exactly this kind of writing, and in the 1240s and later, only students who wrote essays in the Neo-Confucian style could hope to do well on the civil service examinations.

Sources: [Selection 1] Daniel K. Gardner, trans., *Chu Hsi: Learning to Be a Sage: Selections from the Conversations of Master Chu, Arranged Topically* (Berkeley: University of California Press, 1990), pp. 90–92. [Selection 2] Hilde De Weerdt, *Competition over Content: Negotiating Standards for the Civil Service Examinations in Imperial China (1127–1279)* (Cambridge, Mass.: Harvard University Asia Center, 2007), p. 197.

From Zhu Xi's *Records of Conversations*

[Zhu:] "In the universe there has never been any psychophysical stuff without principle nor any principle without psychophysical stuff.

"Before the existence of heaven and earth, there was simply principle. As there was principle, there was heaven and earth. If there hadn't been principle, there'd be no heaven and earth, no people, no things. There'd be nothing at all to sustain them.

When there's principle, there's psychophysical stuff; it circulates everywhere, developing and nourishing the ten thousand things."

Someone said: "Is it principle that does the developing and nourishing?"

Zhu replied: "When there's this principle, there's this psychophysical stuff that circulates everywhere, developing and nourishing things. Principle has no physical form."

Someone asked if principle exists first or psychophysical stuff.

Zhu replied: "Principle has never been separate from psychophysical stuff. But principle is above form and psychophysical stuff is within form. From the point of view of what is above and what is within form, how can there possibly be no sequence? Principle has no form, while the psychophysical stuff is coarse and contains impurities."

Someone asked: "What about the statement that there must exist this principle and only then will there exist this psychophysical stuff?"

Zhu said: "Fundamentally, one can't speak of them in terms of first and later. But if we must trace their beginnings, we have to say that there first exists this principle. Still, principle is not a separate entity but exists in the midst of this psychophysical stuff. If there weren't this stuff, this principle would have nothing to adhere to. . . ."

There was a further inquiry: "What evidence is there that principle exists in the psychophysical stuff?"

Zhu replied: "For instance, that there is an order to the intermixing of the *yin* and *yang* and five elements is because of principle. If the psychophysical stuff doesn't coalesce, principle has nothing to adhere to."

Someone asked about the statement that first there exists principle and later there exists psychophysical stuff.

Zhu said: "There is no need to speak like this. Now we know that whether basically there first exists principle and later the psychophysical stuff, it's not open to investigation."

Recognizing the Examination Essays of the Neo-Confucians

According to the current regulations, a regulated prose-poem should be no longer than 360 characters; expositions should count 500 characters or less. Nowadays, in an essay on the meaning of the Classics, an exposition, or a policy response essay, some write up to 3,000 words. In the prose parts of the prose-poem they have sentences of up to fifteen or sixteen characters long, coming to a total of 500 to 600 characters per piece.

As for what we have called their eccentricities, expressions like "firm vision," "power," "to imagine," "to divide one's efforts," "comes from somebody's collected works," "determined direction," "view," "appearance," "air," "system," "closing off the mind," "every mind has a ruler, still there is a lot of noisy wrangling," and "with one trampling one can arrive; while washing the hands it can be accomplished"—all these are heterodox [nonstandard] and vulgar expressions.

QUESTIONS FOR ANALYSIS

» *Using modern standards for good writing, assess the strengths and weaknesses of Zhu Xi's writing style. Does he use the genre of records of conversation to good effect?*

» *Which aspects of the Neo-Confucian students' essays bothered the examiners? Did they object more to issues of form or of content?*

These shrines provided a physical reminder of Neo-Confucian teachers and teachings to ordinary people who might not otherwise have encountered them. They often housed a portrait of the person to be worshiped. Local people gathered at shrines on certain holidays, and a member of the community led a prayer asking the worthy to descend, listen to the prayer, and receive offerings: bolts of cloth, food, and drinks like wine or tea.[2]

Many other types of religion coexisted with the shrines to worthies. Li Qingzhao's account mentions ancestor worship in particular. When she and her husband parted, Zhao instructed her to *"carry the sacrificial vessels for the ancestral temple yourself; live or die with them; don't give them up."* Each household had an altar for ancestor worship. The wealthy put bronze vessels on their altars; ordinary people used pottery or wooden bowls and cups.

Much religious activity took place outside the home. Some religious practitioners going from market-town to market-town were associated with organized religions, like Daoism and Buddhism, while others, like the spirit mediums, tended to work on their own. Believing that evil spirits caused illness, many people consulted religious specialists, such as exorcists, in the hope of curing sick family members.

Buddhist monasteries offered many women a place where they could go unaccompanied by men and listen to Buddhist texts recited aloud (see Chapter 8). Thousands forswore marriage and became monks and nuns living in monasteries and nunneries. Male clerics outnumbered women six to one during the Song dynasty.

Vietnam, Korea, Japan, and the World Beyond

During the Song dynasty, as the commercial revolution led to technological breakthroughs, particularly in ocean exploration, the vastness of the larger world became apparent to educated Chinese. Chinese navigators continued to modify their designs for ships, whose large wooden construction profoundly impressed Ibn Battuta (see Chapter 11), and mapmaking also improved.

After the Song ruler signed the peace treaty of 1142 with the Jurchen, his dynasty entered a multistate world. The Southern Song was only one of several regional powers in East Asia at the time, of whom the Jurchen were the most powerful. Foreign trade with these powers played an important role in China's commercial revolution. Anyone traveling to Vietnam, Korea, or Japan in the thirteenth century would have seen signs of Chinese influence everywhere: people using chopsticks, Buddhist monasteries and Confucian schools, books printed in Chinese, and Chinese characters on all signposts and government documents. Chinese bronze coins, or local copies, circulated throughout the region, forming a Song dynasty currency sphere. But Vietnam, Korea, and Japan also had their own distinctive political structures and their own ways of modifying the collection of institutions, laws, education systems, and religions they had adopted from the Tang (see Chapter 8).

Technological Breakthroughs

Although Chinese ships traveled to Southeast Asia and India as early as the fifth century, they stayed close to the coastline because they did not have compasses. Already in the fourth century B.C.E. the Chinese had known that naturally magnetic lodestones would point north when placed on a board. The lodestones, however, eventually lost their magnetism and so were not suited to long sea voyages.

*Reprinted by permission of the publisher from *Remembrances: The Experience of the Past in Classical Chinese Literature* by Stephen Owen, p. 90, Cambridge, Mass.: Harvard University Press, Copyright © 1986 by the President and Fellows of Harvard College.

Sometime between 850 and 1050, Chinese metallurgists realized that, if they heated steel needles to a high temperature that we now call the Curie point and then cooled them rapidly, they could magnetize the needles. Placed in water on a float of some kind, the buoyant needles pointed north. In the twelfth and thirteenth centuries the use of a **steel-needle compass** made deep-water navigation possible, facilitating travel to distant places like Vietnam and Cambodia in Southeast Asia.

Although access to foreign lands improved, Song knowledge of the outside world grew only slowly. By the twelfth century, Chinese mapmakers had achieved the precision of grid maps with each square covering the same amount of territory. But their maps showed little beyond China's borders. One map describes foreign peoples, but it does so in words, without showing their geographic positions.

The Chinese tradition of writing about foreign peoples continued with the publication in 1225 of *The Description of Foreign Peoples* by **Zhao Rugua**. Zhao Rugua (JAO RUE-gwah) served as the director of the Department of Overseas Trade in Quanzhou, China's largest international trade port in Fujian province on the southeast coast (see Map 12.1). Not a traveler himself, he combined information from encyclopedias with what he learned from speaking with foreign and Chinese traders to describe the three states of East Asia most influenced by the Tang: Vietnam, Korea, and Japan.

> **steel-needle compass** A navigational instrument made by floating a steel needle that had been boiled to a high temperature in water: since the magnetized needle pointed north, sailors knew where to go.
>
> **Zhao Rugua** (fl. 1225) Author of *The Description of Foreign Peoples*, a compendium of information about China's closest trading partners in East Asia and distant places such as the east coasts of Africa and Spain.

Vietnam During the Song Dynasty

Since Vietnam directly bordered China on the south, it received the most extensive Chinese influence. Zhao did not consider it a separate country. Under direct Chinese rule during the Han and Tang dynasties, Vietnam, under the **Ly dynasty** (1009–1224), became independent. Because it was a tributary of China, its king acknowledged the superiority of the Chinese emperor and periodically sent delegations to the Chinese capital to present him with gifts. The Chinese emperor bestowed gifts on the emissaries in return.

The Chinese-educated scholars of the Ly (LEE) dynasty argued that their king, the southern emperor, ruled the southern kingdom of Vietnam because he, like the Chinese emperor, had the Mandate of Heaven (see Chapter 4). The Vietnamese kings credited local spirits with protecting the royal house and supported Buddhism. Since at least the fourth century, Buddhist monks had traveled back and forth between China and Vietnam, and Buddhist texts had circulated in both directions (see Chapter 8).

The Vietnamese king and his courtiers had received a Chinese-style education and could read and write Chinese. In 1042, the Ly emperor adopted a modified form of the *Tang Code* (see Chapter 8) so that his subjects would understand the laws of the kingdom, and in 1075 the government held the first civil service examinations. The dynasty's control beyond the major administrative centers was weak. In much of the kingdom's territory, largely independent chieftains ruled groups who lived in bands in

MAP 12.1 China's Trade Relations with the External World, 1225 In 1225, most of Song dynasty China's foreign trade was with Japan, Korea, and Vietnam. China exported silk and high-quality ceramics, while these different societies traded different minerals, raw materials, and foodstuffs in return. Chinese bronze coins circulated throughout the region, creating a currency sphere. (© Cengage Learning)

Ly dynasty
(1009–1224) The independent rulers of Vietnam who adopted the *Tang Code* in 1042.

Koryo dynasty
(936–1392) Dynasty that gave its name to the modern country of Korea, whose founder adopted Tang governing models.

the highlands and submitted valued items like rhinoceros horns and elephant tusks to the king. At the time of Zhao's writing, the Vietnamese exported to China the same unprocessed goods, including rhinoceros horn, elephant tusks, camphor, musk, and sandalwood, that they had for the previous thousand years (see Map 12.1).

Korea Under the Koryo Dynasty

Like Vietnam, Korea did not strike Zhao Rugua as foreign: *"Their houses, utensils and implements, their mode of dressing and their methods of administration are,"* Zhao remarked, *"more or less copies of what we have in China."**

In 936, the founder of the **Koryo dynasty** (936–1392) defeated his last rival and founded the dynasty that gave its name to the modern country of Korea. He modeled the structure of the central government on the Tang dynasty and divided the region into administrative districts like those in China.

The king used a Chinese-style exam to recruit officials and thereby reduce the influence of his main rivals, powerful families who formed a hereditary local aristocracy. This policy succeeded for over two hundred years until 1170, when aristocrats and their military supporters overthrew the Chinese-style administration. Military officers took over all government positions, and men of letters retreated to the countryside. Kings continued to rule as figureheads, but the top generals could and did replace them at will.

Trade with China persisted even during these politically unstable times. Korea exported precious metals like gold, silver, and copper and edible goods like ginseng and pine nuts in exchange for Chinese silks, books, and high-quality ceramics (see Map 12.1). Korean potters built high-firing kilns in which they made pale green, inlaid celadon pots even more beautiful than Chinese export ware.

Koreans also embraced woodblock printing. In 1251, Korean printers created a library of Buddhist texts that includes over eighty thousand pages and is universally acknowledged to be the highest-quality set made anywhere in East Asia. Much more so than their Chinese counterparts, Korean printers adopted the technology of movable type. The world's first surviving book printed with movable type was

Korean Celadon Vase Sometime after 1150, Korean potters introduced an important innovation to Chinese celadon wares, with their characteristic green-gray glaze colored by iron pigments. After the vessels had hardened to the consistency of cheese, the potters cut holes in the surface of thrown pots and then filled them with a mixture of water and different colors of clay. This is how they made the clouds and cranes flying on this vessel. The South Korean government has designated this vase, which stands 16.5 inches (42 cm) tall, as a national treasure because the inlay technique is so beautifully done. (Courtesy, Kansong Art Museum, Seoul)

*Frederick Hirth and W. W. Rockhill, *Chau Ju-kua: His Work on the Chinese and Arab Trade in the Twelfth and Thirteenth Centuries, Entitled Chu-fan-chï* (St. Petersburg: Imperial Academy of Sciences, 1911), p. 167.

made in Korea and dates to around 1400, some three centuries after the Chinese first invented movable type and half a century before the German Johannes Gutenberg printed the first Bible using movable type (see Chapter 15).

Transition to the Kamakura Shogunate in Japan

Zhao Rugua called Japan the *"Land of the Rising Sun,"* because *"this country is situated near the place where the sun rises."** The Japanese, Zhao reported, exported cedar from trees as tall as 15 yards (15 m). *"The natives split them into planks, which they transport in large junks to our port of Quanzhou for sale."** So many Song dynasty coins flowed into Japan that Chinese coins became the unofficial currency of Japan, which did not mint its own coins at the time.

Although the Japanese emperors had earlier looked to China as a model (see Chapter 8), after 900 certain warrior clans gradually gained power and forced the emperor to retire to Kyoto, abandon Chinese-style government, and remain as a figurehead. In 1185, the Minamoto (ME-nah-MOE-toe) clan defeated its rivals and established a new capital at Kamakura, a city just outside modern Tokyo.

During the Kamakura period (1185–1333), political power rested in the hands of the **shogun**, or general, who claimed to govern on behalf of the emperor. The shogun did not conduct Chinese-style civil service examinations but appointed members of powerful clans to office. Still, scholars continued to study both Buddhist and Confucian texts, many of them imported from China and written in Chinese characters; they also used the kana alphabet to represent the sounds of spoken Japanese (see Chapter 8).

The shogun patronized Buddhism, and the teachings of **Zen Buddhism** attracted many followers. Zen masters posed puzzling questions with no clear answer: for example, what is the sound of one hand clapping? As disciples meditated on these questions, their masters hoped that they would suddenly understand the teachings of the master and attain enlightenment.

shogun
"General" in Japanese; an all-powerful military leader governing on behalf of the emperor, who lived in Kyoto but exercised little actual power.

Zen Buddhism
A Japanese school of Buddhism that emphasized attaining enlightenment through meditation.

The World Beyond East Asia

Going beyond East Asia, Zhao Rugua's book covers the Islamic heartland of Arabia and Mecca and the Islamic periphery; the southern coast of Europe; and the northern and eastern coasts of Africa. Clearly dependent on Arab geographers for his knowledge of these places, Zhao's entries mix accurate information with sheer fantasy. For example, his description of Madagascar reports that a giant bird lives there that swallows camels whole.

But Zhao's information is not all myth. He was particularly knowledgeable about foreign products, such as dark-skinned African slaves, that he had seen with his own eyes in Quanzhou. *"In the West there is an island in the sea on which there are many savages, with bodies as black as lacquer and with frizzed hair. They are enticed by offers of food and then caught and carried off for slaves to the Arabian countries, where they fetch a high price."**

Zhao's knowledge of the non-Chinese was the product of the trading environment of Quanzhou. Almost every place on his list is located on a seacoast, and the goods he describes came to China on seagoing vessels. Knowing nothing of the nomadic peoples of the north, Zhao was completely unaware that as he was writing, a powerful confederation of Mongols was taking shape on the grasslands of Eurasia (see Chapter 14).

---

*Frederick Hirth and W. W. Rockhill, *Chau Ju-kua: His Work on the Chinese and Arab Trade in the Twelfth and Thirteenth Centuries, Entitled Chu-fan-chï* (St. Petersburg: Imperial Academy of Sciences, 1911), pp. 170, 171, 149.

13

Europe's Commercial Revolution, 1000–1400

Sometime around 1132, when he was in his early forties, **Peter Abelard** (1079–1142/44) wrote an account of his own life entitled *The Story of His Misfortunes*. The title was apt. Abelard wrote about his love affair with **Heloise** (ca. 1090–1163/64), a woman at least ten years younger than he was, and its disastrous outcome. No dry affadavit, the *Story* seeks both to defend Abelard's conduct and to document God's goodness.

Over the course of their eventful lives (they lived at exactly the same time as Li Qingzhao and Zhao Mingcheng), Heloise and Abelard personally experienced the changes occurring in Europe between 1000 and 1400. Like China of the Song dynasty (see Chapter 12), Europe underwent a dramatic commercial revolution, especially in agriculture. Most of the land in Europe was brought under cultivation in a process called *cerealization*. The economic surplus financed the first universities of Europe, new religious institutions, the Crusades, and trade with East Asia, all of which made the Europeans in 1400 richer and more knowledgeable about distant places than they had been in 1000.

Abelard, like many of his contemporaries, traveled so that he could study. He begins his *Story* with his childhood:

Abelard and Heloise
(Musée Condé, Chantilly, France/Giraudon/Art Resource, NY)

I was born on the borders of Brittany, about eight miles I think to the east of Nantes [NAHNT], in a town called Le Pallet [luh PAH-lay]. I owe my volatile temperament to my native soil and ancestry and also my natural ability for learning. My father had acquired some knowledge of letters before he was a knight, and later on his passion for learning was such that he intended all his sons to have instruction in letters before they were trained to arms. His purpose was fulfilled. I was his first-born, and being specially dear to him had the greatest care taken over my education. For my part, the more rapid and easy my progress

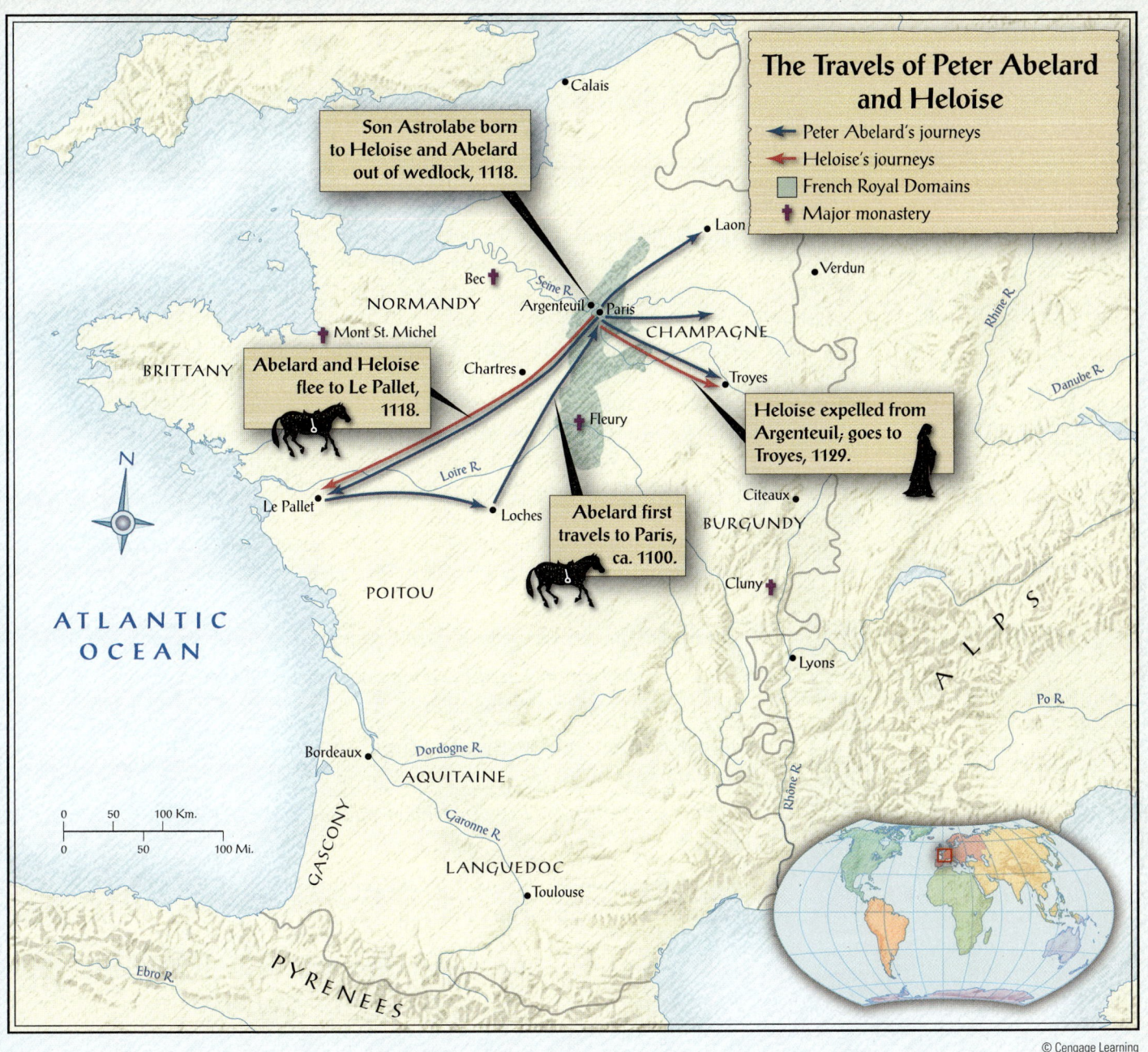

The Travels of Peter Abelard and Heloise

- ← Peter Abelard's journeys
- ← Heloise's journeys
- ▢ French Royal Domains
- ✝ Major monastery

Son Astrolabe born to Heloise and Abelard out of wedlock, 1118.

Abelard and Heloise flee to Le Pallet, 1118.

Abelard first travels to Paris, ca. 1100.

Heloise expelled from Argenteuil; goes to Troyes, 1129.

Calais

Bec ✝

NORMANDY

Seine R.

Argenteuil • Paris

Laon •

Verdun •

CHAMPAGNE

Rhine R.

Mont St. Michel ✝

Chartres

Troyes

Danube R.

BRITTANY

Fleury ✝

Loire R.

Citeaux •

Le Pallet •

Loches •

BURGUNDY

Po R.

ATLANTIC OCEAN

POITOU

Cluny ✝

Lyons •

A L P S

Rhône R.

Bordeaux •

Dordogne R.

AQUITAINE

Garonne R.

GASCONY

LANGUEDOC

Toulouse •

Ebro R.

P Y R E N E E S

0   50   100 Km.
0   50   100 Mi.

© Cengage Learning

Join this chapter's traveler on "Voyages," an interactive tour of historic sites and events: **www.cengagebrain.com**

in my studies, the more eagerly I applied myself, until I was so carried away by my love of learning that I renounced the glory of a military life. . . . I began to travel about in several provinces disputing, like a true peripatetic philosopher, wherever I had heard there was a keen interest in the art of dialectic.[*]

*From *The Letters of Abelard and Heloise,* translated and introduced by Betty Radice (Penguin Classics, 1974), p. 3. Copyright © Betty Radice, 1974. Reproduced by permission of Penguin Books Ltd.

Peter Abelard
(1079–1142/44) Prominent scholastic thinker who wrote about his affair with Heloise in his autobiography, *The Story of His Misfortunes.*

Heloise
(ca. 1090–1163/64) French nun who exchanged many letters with Peter Abelard, her former lover and the father of her child Astrolabe.

belard's speaking abilities and ferocious intelligence made him one of the best-known philosophers and most famous teachers in Europe. He traveled from one French town to another until he arrived in the great intellectual center of Paris, where one of the first universities in the world was taking shape. Students from all over Europe flocked to hear his lectures before returning home to serve their kings as officials or their churches as clergy. Heloise's uncle hired Abelard to tutor his brilliant niece, one of the few women in Europe who received the same education as her male peers.

During this time, new methods of farming produced much higher yields, and Europe's population increased as a result. Many landowning families initiated new inheritance practices that gave only the eldest sons the right to inherit their father's estates, forcing the other sons to go into education, as Abelard chose to do voluntarily, or the church, which after undergoing many different reforms, became one of the most vibrant institutions in medieval European society. Both Heloise and Abelard joined church orders after the discovery of their affair. The century from 1300 to 1400 saw a temporary halt in growth caused by a massive outbreak of plague but also changes that strengthened European monarchies.

Focus Questions

> » *What caused the cerealization of Europe, and what were its results?*
>
> » *What led to the foundation of Europe's universities? How did they gain the right to govern themselves?*
>
> » *How did economic prosperity affect the Christian church and different monastic orders?*
>
> » *What did the Crusaders hope to achieve outside Europe? Within Europe?*
>
> » *How did the major developments of the century from 1300 to 1400 strengthen European monarchies?*

The Cerealization and Urbanization of Europe

Europe experienced sustained economic prosperity between 1000 and 1300. The growth resulted not from migration to rice-growing regions as in China, but from the intensification of agriculture. Quite simply, Europeans reclaimed more land and farmed it more intensively than they had before. Europe's population grew dramatically as a result. As in China, the creation of a large agricultural surplus freed some people to pursue a variety of careers.

cerealization
Collective term for many agricultural practices that allowed Europeans between 1000 and 1300 to cultivate most of the land in Europe.

Agricultural Innovation

The agricultural innovations from 1000 to 1300 can be summed up in a single word: *cerealization.* Like the term *industrialization*, the word **cerealization** indicates a broad transformation that profoundly affected everyone who experienced it. Before cerealization, much of the land in Europe was not cultivated regularly; afterward, much of it was.

This transformation did not occur at the same time throughout Europe. Northern France and England were the most advanced regions. Farmers before

1000 realized that land became less fertile if they planted the same crop year after year, so each year they allowed one-third to one-half of their land to lie fallow. After 1000, a few farmers began to rotate their crops so that they could keep their land under continuous cultivation. One popular rotation of turnips, clover, and grain took advantage of different nutrients in the soil each year. This practice, so crucial to increasing agricultural yield, spread only slowly.

European farmers also began to exploit more sheep, horses, and cows in their farming. They raised sheep for their wool, while they could use both horses and oxen for transport. By 1200, horses, which worked harder and faster, gradually replaced oxen on European farms.

Before 1000, most of the plows used in Europe to prepare the earth for planting had wooden blades, which broke easily and could not penetrate far into the soil. Gradually farmers, particularly in northern France, added pieces of iron to their blades, which allowed them to dig deeper and increase productivity. In addition, iron horseshoes protected the hooves of the horses that pulled the plows. By 1200, many villages had their own blacksmiths who repaired horseshoes and plow blades.

The final innovation left the deepest imprint on the landscape. As early as 500, but particularly after 1000, farmers began to harness the water in flowing rivers to operate mills. Water mills were first used to grind grain and then were adapted to other uses, such as beating wool to make it thicker ("fulling" cloth), sawing wood, and sharpening or polishing iron. By 1100, records show that at least 5,600 water mills existed throughout England, or one mill for every thirty-five families.

Even more powerful than water mills were those powered by wind. The world's first windmills were built in Iran around 700; positioned on a vertical axis, the blades drove pumps that moved water from one irrigation channel to another. They came into use in Europe, often by the sea, just before 1200.

Each farming family performed a wide variety of tasks. Women tended to do the jobs closer to the home, like raising children, cooking food, tending the garden, milking cows, and caring for the other livestock. Men did the plowing and sowed seed, but both sexes helped to bring in the harvest. Many households hired temporary help, both male and female, at busy times of year to assist with shearing sheep, picking hops for beer, and mowing hay.

Population Growth and Urbanization

The clear result of Europe's cerealization was the marked population growth that occurred between 1000 and 1340. In 1000, Europe had a population of less than 40 million; by 1340 the population had nearly doubled to around 75 million. Even more significant was the geographic pattern of population growth. The number of people living in southern and eastern Europe—in Italy, Spain, and the Balkans—increased by 50 percent. But the population of northern Europe shot up by a factor of three, with the result that nearly half of Europe's people lived in northern Europe by 1340.[1]

The process of cerealization freed large numbers of people from working the land full-time. Individual households began to produce food products such as butter, cheese, and eggs or handicrafts like textiles and soap to sell at local markets. At first, people went to periodic markets to trade for the goods they needed. This began to change around 1000, when rulers minted the first coins since the fall of the Western Roman empire. With the new currency, many periodic markets gradually evolved into permanent markets that opened daily. Inside the walls of most European market towns were the marketplace, the lord's castle, and several churches.

Cutting-Edge Farming Techniques in Europe, 1300–1340 At first glance, the two men working the land may seem to be using traditional farming techniques. In fact, though, this detail from a manuscript illustrates two of the most important innovations in the cerealization of Europe: horse-drawn plowing equipment and the use of iron tools. The horse is pulling a harrow, a large rakelike tool with many teeth that broke up lumps of earth after the soil had been plowed. (British Library, London/HIP/Art Resource, NY)

These market towns arose first on the coasts of the Mediterranean, the English Channel, and the Baltic or along inland rivers like the Rhine. During the 1000s and 1100s, more and more people traveled from one market to another, sometimes going overland on new roads, to attend the fairs that occurred with increasing frequency.

Before 1000, only a handful of cities, all the sites of castles or church centers, existed north of the Alps. After 1000, the number of cities there increased sharply. European cities between 1000 and 1348 were not large. One of the largest, Paris, had a population of 80,000 in 1200, much less than the 450,000 people living in Islamic Córdoba and a mere fraction of Song dynasty Hangzhou's 1 million.

Yet the people who lived in Europe's cities had crossed an important divide: because they had stopped working the land, they were dependent on the city's markets for their food supply. Many urban artisans worked either in food preparation, like butchers and bakers, or in the field of apparel, like tailors and shoemakers. Because one-third to one-half of these artisans worked with no assistants, they depended on their wives and children to sell their goods. Some merchants specialized in transporting goods from one place to another; for example, a German woman in 1420 bought and sold *"crossbows, saddle bags, bridles, harnesses, halters, spurs, and stirrups, as well as . . . arrow quivers, soap, parchment, wax, paper, and spices."*

The people who lived in cities were intensely aware that they differed from those who worked the land and those who owned it. Tradesmen who worked in the same occupations and merchants who dealt in similar goods formed **guilds**

guilds
Associations formed by members of the same trade or merchant group that regulated prices and working hours.

*Claudia Opitz, "Life in the Late Middle Ages," in *A History of Women in the West,* vol. 2: *Silence of the Middle Ages,* ed. Chistiane Klapisch-Zuber (Cambridge, Mass.: Belknap Press of Harvard University Press, 1992), p. 296.

that regulated prices and working hours; they decided who could enter the guild and who could not; only those who belonged to the guild could engage in the business the guild regulated. One visible sign of the guilds' influence was the cathedrals they financed throughout Europe, sometimes with contributions from others.

After 1000, urban residents frequently petitioned their rulers for the right to pass regulations concerning trade and to mint coins. Local rulers often granted these rights in the hope that the guilds would support them against their rivals.

Land Use and Social Change, 1000–1350

The sharp increases in productivity brought dramatic changes throughout society. These changes did not occur everywhere at the same time, and in some areas they did not occur at all, but they definitely took place in northern France between 1000 and 1200.

One change was that slavery all but disappeared, while serfs did most of the work for those who owned land. Although their landlords did not own them, and they were not slaves, a series of obligations tied serfs to the land. Each year, their most important duty was to give their lord a fixed share of the crop and of their herds. Serfs were also obliged to build roads, give lodging to guests, and perform many other tasks for their lords. After 1000, a majority of those working the land became serfs.

Many serfs lived in settlements built around either the castles of lords or churches. (See the feature "Visual Evidence in Primary Sources: The Gothic Cathedral at Chartres.") The prevailing mental image of a medieval castle town is one in which a lord lives protected by his knights and surrounded by his serfs, who go outside the walls each day to work in the fields. Some use the term **feudal** for such a society. Yet historians today often avoid the word *feudal* because no one alive between 1000 and 1350 used such a word, and the term came into use only after 1600 as a legal concept.

The prominent French historian Georges Duby has described the social order of the eleventh and twelfth centuries in the following way. After 1000, the powerful comprised clearly defined social orders—lords, knights, clergy—who held specific rights over the serfs below them. Many lords also commanded the service of a group of warriors, or knights, who offered them military service in exchange for military protection from others.

Knights began their training as children, when they learned how to ride and to handle a dagger. At the age of fourteen, knights-in-training accompanied a mature knight into battle. They usually wore tunics made of metal loops, or chain mail, as well as headgear that could repel arrows. Their main weapons were iron and steel swords and crossbows that shot metal bolts.

One characteristic of the age was weak centralized rule. Although many countries, like England and France, continued to have monarchs, their power was severely limited because their armies were no stronger than those of the nobles who ranked below them. They controlled the lands immediately under them but little else. The king of France, for example, ruled the region in the immediate vicinity of Paris, but other nobles had authority over the rest of France. In other countries as well, kings vied with rival nobles to gain control of a given region, and they often lost.

In the eleventh and twelfth centuries, landowners frequently gave large tracts of land to various monasteries (discussed later in this chapter). The monasteries did not pay any taxes on this land, and no one dared to encroach on church-owned land for fear of the consequences from God. By the end of the twelfth century, the church owned one-third of the land in northern France and one-sixth of all the land in France and Italy combined.

feudal
A term that came into use after 1600 as a legal concept and refers to the legal and social system in Europe from 1000 to 1400, in which serfs worked the land and subordinates performed military service for their lords in return for protection.

The Gothic Cathedral at Chartres

Starting around 1150, people throughout Europe built cathedrals in the Gothic style, of which the Cathedral of Notre Dame at Chartres, France, is one of the best examples. The cathedral has an unusual front because the south tower (on the left) was built in 1160, while the much more opulent north tower was added in 1513 after a fire destroyed the original.

High, arched ceilings inspired awe in those who entered cathedrals, but medieval builders faced a major engineering challenge. Arches built in the traditional manner required thick walls to support them; otherwise the walls would buckle from the outward pressure. Two innovations allowed stoneworkers to deflect the pressure away from the walls and build taller structures: vaults with ribs inside the church and flying buttresses outside the walls. With the help of these supports, the ceiling of Chartres rises a glorious 121 feet (37 m) above the ground.

Since the walls did not bear the weight of the ceiling, they could be cut away to hold glass windows. Unlike many other cathedrals, Chartres preserves much of its original stained glass. Of 186

Sandro Vannini/Corbis

The north tower, completed in 1507, is so heavily decorated that architectural historians call its style "flamboyant style." It contrasts sharply with the original Gothic style of the south tower.

Half arches connect these flying buttresses outside to the cathedral wall, which they support, making it possible to build a high interior roof.

QUESTION FOR ANALYSIS

» *What does the Cathedral at Chartres reveal about the local economy in the 1100s, and how did it contribute to the local economy?*

original stained-glass windows, 152 have survived. Many windows were dedicated by guild members and portray biblical scenes above and scenes of that guild's work below.

The window shown here was dedicated to Saint Lubin (Saint Leobinus), the bishop of Chartres in 558, whose devotees believed that he performed miracles, including curing people afflicted with edema, an illness that caused excess swelling. Wine merchants and local innkeepers paid for the window, which was completed in 1210.

Chartres was both a religious and an economic center. Pilgrims flocked to the cathedral to worship Mary, the Virgin Mother of Jesus, and her robe, which they believed survived inside the cathedral. The pilgrims hoped that Mary would heal their illnesses and grant their prayers. Wealthy worshipers could afford to buy copies of her robe made for tourists, while others could purchase cheaper, lead figurines that they could pray to at home.

The young Lubin studies his alphabet while behind him his companion quaffs a glass of wine. All the round background windows portray scenes from the life of Saint Lubin.

His hand holding a whip, a wine merchant transports a cask of wine tied onto a donkey cart.

In each of the side panels, people wearing different-colored robes hold cups of wine.

A wine seller gives a goblet of wine to a seated traveler, while the young boy behind him announces that a new barrel of wine has been opened. Above his head is a barrel hoop, the sign of a tavern.

One of the most perplexing changes was the rise of primogeniture in northern France, England, Belgium, and the Netherlands. Before 1000, when the head of the family died, aristocratic families divided their property among their sons, and sometimes even granted their daughters a share of the estate. After 1000, they kept their estates intact by passing the property on to only one son. As Peter Abelard explained, he, the first-born son, was entitled to his father's lands but chose to give up his inheritance to pursue his studies.

He was an exception. Much more often first-born sons kept their family estates, and their brothers pursued other careers, whether as bureaucrats, churchmen, or knights in someone else's service. In many cases these second sons attended schools and universities before embarking on their chosen careers.

The Rise of the European Universities, 1100–1400

Although schools had existed in Europe at least since the time of the Roman empire, literacy rates remained low throughout the continent. Starting around 1100, groups of teachers gathered in two major centers—Paris, France, and Bologna, Italy—and began to attract large numbers of male students, many of them from well-off families who used their surplus wealth (the product of cerealization) to finance their sons' educations. In this early period, the universities were unregulated and free, as Peter Abelard experienced himself. Soon, however, the curriculum became more standardized. In a crucial development, cities, kings, and popes granted the universities a certain amount of self-rule and the right to grant degrees, rights that allowed universities to develop into independent centers of learning.

Education in Europe Before the Universities, ca. 1100

Latin remained the language of all educated people, the church, and administrative documents, and students had to learn to read and write Latin before they could advance to other subjects. The most basic schools also taught the simple mathematics needed by peddlers. Before 1100, most people who learned to read and write did so in local schools or at home with tutors or their parents. Some of these schools admitted girls, whether in separate classrooms or together with boys. Many schools were headed by a married couple so that the husband could teach the boys and the wife the girls. Often the schools were located close to the cathedrals that administered them.

While young, Heloise studied at a convent outside Paris. Many years later, the abbot Peter the Venerable recorded what he had heard about her when she was a school girl: *"I used to hear at that time of the woman who although still caught up in the obligations of the world, devoted all her application to knowledge of letters, something which is very rare, and to the pursuit of secular learning."* Few women equaled Heloise in her learning: thoroughly grounded in Latin, she also knew some Greek and Hebrew.

Peter Abelard has little to say about his early education except that he loved learning and that his favorite subject was "dialectic," by which he meant the study of logic. Dialectic was one of three subjects, along with grammar and rhetoric, that formed the trivium. The roots of the trivium curriculum lay in ancient Greece and Rome: one studied the structure of language in grammar, expression in rhetoric, and meaning in dialectic, the most advanced subject of the three. Then one advanced to the quadrivium, which included arithmetic, astronomy, geometry, and

*From *The Letters of Abelard and Heloise,* translated and introduced by Betty Radice (Penguin Classics, 1974), p. 217. Copyright © Betty Radice, 1974. Reproduced by permission of Penguin Books Ltd.

music theory. The trivium and quadrivium formed the basic core of the curriculum and together were known as the **liberal arts**. The highest-level subjects, beyond the trivium and the quadrivium, were theology, church law, and medicine.

Abelard wrote a treatise called *Sic et Non* (Yes and No) whose prologue explained his method of instruction:

> *to gather together the various sayings of the holy Fathers which have occurred to me as being surrounded by some degree of uncertainty because of their seeming incompatibility. These may encourage inexperienced readers to engage in that most important exercise, enquiry into truth. . . . For by doubting we come to inquiry, and by inquiry we perceive the truth.*[*]

Sic et Non poses a series of questions and then provides citations from classical sources and the Bible on 156 different topics without directly providing any solutions. If one posed the question correctly and considered the proper authorities, one could draw on the powers of reasoning to arrive at the correct answer, Abelard and his contemporaries believed. This optimism about the ability of human reason to resolve the long-standing debates of the past characterizes **scholasticism**, the prevailing method of instruction in Europe between 1100 and 1500.

In 1114, Abelard was named to his first teaching position in Paris as master of the cathedral school at Notre Dame. He became a canon, that is, a member of the small group of salaried clerics living close to the cathedral. When Peter Abelard began teaching, he focused on explicating the single book Ezekiel of the Hebrew Bible. The goal of most instructors was to cover an entire book in a year or two of instruction.

In the following year, Abelard, in his mid-thirties, met Heloise, who was in her teens or twenties (the exact year of her birth is unknown). Writing his *Story* fifteen years later, he explains:

> *There was in Paris at the time a young girl named Heloise, the niece of Fulbert, one of the canons, and so much loved by him that he had done everything in his power to advance her education in letters. In looks she did not rank lowest, while in the extent of her learning she stood supreme. A gift for letters is so rare in women that it added greatly to her charm and had made her most renowned throughout the realm.*[†]

Fulbert hired Abelard to be Heloise's tutor because of his reputation as a great scholar. The two fell in love almost immediately, as the *Story* continues: *"Need I say more? We were united, first under one roof, then in heart; and so with our lessons as a pretext we abandoned ourselves entirely to love. . . . My hands strayed oftener to her bosom than to the pages; love drew our eyes to look on each other more than reading kept them on our texts."*[†] Sometime in 1118, Heloise became pregnant.

Writing in 1131, Abelard claimed that he was willing to marry Heloise in secret. As a canon, he was allowed to marry, but in the 1100s more and more churchmen were celibate, especially high-ranking churchmen, and Abelard was nothing if not ambitious. Both Heloise and Abelard saw marriage as a sacrament

liberal arts
Basic core of the curriculum in Europe between 500 and 1500 that consisted of the trivium (logic, grammar, and rhetoric) and the quadrivium (arithmetic, astronomy, geometry, and music theory).

scholasticism
Prevailing method of instruction in Europe between 1100 and 1500 that held students could arrive at a correct answer if they used their powers of reasoning and consulted the appropriate sources.

---

[*]A. J. Minnis and A. B. Scott, *Medieval Literary Theory and Criticism, c. 1100–c. 1375* (Oxford: Clarendon Press, 1988), p. 99.

[†]From *The Letters of Abelard and Heloise,* translated and introduced by Betty Radice (Penguin Classics, 1974), pp. 217, 9–11. Copyright © Betty Radice, 1974. Reproduced by permission of Penguin Books Ltd.

that joined the property of two families together, not as an expression of love. We have no way of knowing whether Abelard actually proposed, but he was certainly secretive: he smuggled the pregnant Heloise out of Paris in nun's clothing even though she was not a nun.

Fulbert had no way of knowing about the marriage—if it ever took place—but he found out about the pregnancy. *The Story* explains what happened next: Fulbert's men discovered where Abelard was and *"punished me with a most cruel and shameful vengeance of such appalling barbarity as to shock the whole world; they cut off the parts of my body whereby I had committed the wrong of which they complained."* The couple then separated permanently. Leaving their child Astrolabe with Abelard's sister, Heloise entered the same nunnery at Argenteuil where she had studied as a child.

When the news of Abelard's affair broke, he left Paris and returned only in the 1130s, when he resumed teaching. In 1136, John of Salisbury arrived from England to study with Abelard, and he reported that Abelard *"was so eminent in logic that he alone [of those teaching] was thought to converse with Aristotle."*[†] Paris had become the most important center of learning in Europe because more people taught there than anywhere else.

Also during the early 1100s, the university at Bologna in Italy became a center for the study of law. Legal study flourished as people realized that law could be used to resolve the disputes that occurred constantly between kings and subjects, churches and nobles, and merchants and customers. All kinds of groups, whether in monasteries, guilds, or universities, began to write down previously unwritten laws. The Magna Carta, which formalized the relationships between the English king and his barons in 1215, is a good example.

The Import of Learning and Technology from the Islamic World, 1150–1250

From about 1150 to 1250, scholars recovered hundreds of Greek texts that had disappeared from Europe along with the Western Roman empire in 476 (see Chapter 10). Arabic versions of these texts had been preserved in the Islamic world, and their recovery fueled a period of great intellectual growth. Between 1160 and 1200, all of Aristotle's works were translated from Arabic into Latin. Like many of his contemporaries, Peter Abelard did not know more than a few words of Greek, so the translation of Greek texts into Latin had a direct impact on Europe's intellectual life. (See the feature "Movement of Ideas Through Primary Sources: Adelard of Bath.")

Along with learning, other technologies from the Islamic world, such as magnifying glasses and eyeglasses, entered Europe in the late 1200s. Eyeglasses were first made from transparent, naturally occurring quartz, and only later from glass. Europeans also profited from Islamic knowledge of medicine, which was much more advanced than European knowledge; students at European universities studied the works of the Greek doctor Galen (129–ca. 216), which had been updated by Islamic commentators.

Europeans also encountered paper, which the Chinese had first invented and which was transmitted to the Islamic world in the eighth century. Paper appeared first in Spain in the tenth century and then in Sicily in the eleventh, but parchment continued to be used in northern Europe. One copy of the Bible made in Winchester, England, was made from the skins of 250 calves selected from 2,500

---

[*]From *The Letters of Abelard and Heloise,* translated and introduced by Betty Radice (Penguin Classics, 1974), p. 17. Copyright © Betty Radice, 1974. Reproduced by permission of Penguin Books Ltd.
[†]Constant Mews, *Abelard and Heloise* (New York: Oxford University Press, 2005), pp. 11–12.

imperfect ones.[2] Paper won wide use only between 1250 and 1350 as Italian-made paper spread throughout Europe. In the era before printing, booksellers formed workshops in which literate craftsmen copied texts at maximum speed. Following the same route as paper, the ship's compass and the adjustable rudder originated in China and came to Europe via the Islamic world.

Some European scholars clearly admired Islamic learning. Among them were Peter Abelard and Heloise, who named their son Astrolabe (born in 1118, year of death unknown) after the Islamic navigation instrument (see Chapter 9). Others, however, remained suspicious of the Islamic world because it was not Christian, and the interest in Arab learning waned after 1250 once the works of important Greek thinkers had been translated into Latin.

The Universities Come of Age, 1150–1250

As contact with the Islamic world began to invigorate learning, the universities at Paris and Bologna gained significant independence in the century after Abelard's death in the 1140s. As trade guilds regulated their own membership, so too did students and instructors decide who could join the university.

Modern degrees have their origins in the different steps to full membership in the guild of university teachers. Starting students, like apprentices, paid fees, while more advanced bachelors, like journeymen, helped to instruct the starting students. Those who attained the level of masters were the equivalent of full members of the guild. In the 1170s, the masters of Paris gained the right to determine the composition of the assigned reading, the content of examinations, and the recipients for each degree, creating a more formalized structure than existed during Abelard's lifetime.

Most students came from well-off families and had ample spending money; therefore, they formed a large body of consumers whose business was crucial to local shopkeepers. Whenever students had a dispute with local authorities, whether with the city government or the church, they boycotted all local merchants.

The most dramatic conflicts occurred in Paris. In 1229, during the Mardi Gras season, a disturbance broke out, and the authorities killed several students in the confusion. The masters of the university demanded that city officials be punished and left the city for two years until the monarch gave in and agreed. The pope then issued an order recognizing the masters as a guild with the right to boycott. Thereafter, the papacy always supported university masters in disputes with French rulers.

By 1200, Paris and Bologna were firmly established as Europe's first universities, and other universities formed in England, France, and Italy and later in Germany and eastern Europe. Universities offered their home cities many advantages, all linked to the buying power of a large group of wealthy consumer-students.

As in both the Islamic world and Song China, young men came to large cities to study with teachers to prepare for careers in government, law, religious institutions, or education. The largest schools provided facilities for a wide variety of instructors to teach many different topics. Unlike either Islamic schools or Song dynasty schools, however, only European universities had the power to grant degrees independently.

Most students did not study long enough to get their first degree, which was the equivalent of a modern master's degree. Instead, many concentrated on improving their command of Latin, which remained the language of educated people and the church throughout Europe before 1500. Learning to take notes in Latin during a lecture greatly enhanced a young man's ability to draft a Latin document quickly. Some knowledge of mathematics was also useful.

Adelard of Bath

Adelard of Bath (ca. 1080–ca. 1152) is best known for his translation of Euclid's geometry into Latin from an Arabic translation of the original Greek text, which was written around 300 B.C.E. He also translated other works, including al-Khwarizmi's astronomical tables (see Chapter 9), and he is credited with introducing the use of the abacus, a Chinese mechanical calculator that uses beads, to the treasury officials of the English king Henry I. Most likely born in Bath, he studied first in France in Laôn and then went to Salerno, Italy, and Syracuse, Sicily, both centers of Islamic learning.

Adelard of Bath consistently praises Islamic learning, but scholars have not found any quotations from Arabic books in his writing. Although he studied in Italy, his transcriptions of Arabic words reflect Spanish pronunciation, not Italian as one would expect. It seems likely, therefore, that he spoke Arabic to an informant, probably from Spain, who explained Islamic books to him, and he then wrote down what he had been told. This kind of translation using native informants is exactly how the early Buddhist translators in China handled difficult Sanskrit texts (see Chapter 8).

The selections below are drawn from Adelard of Bath's *Questions on Natural Science*, a series of dialogues with his "nephew," who may have been a fictitious conversational partner like those appearing in the Neo-Confucian records of conversations (see Chapter 12). Their conversation illustrates how the great teachers of the twelfth century, including Peter Abelard, taught by using the Socratic method (see Chapter 6), in which they guided their students with pointed questions. The nephew's suspicion of Islamic learning was the typical European view. Few learned Arabic as Adelard of Bath had, and most saw Islam as the source of teachings that were contrary to Christianity. The uncle and nephew agree to accept reason as their guide, a conclusion that both the ancient Greeks and Peter Abelard would have applauded.

Source: From Charles Burnett, Italo Ronca, Pedro Mantas Espaa, and Baudouin van den Abeele, *Adelard of Bath, Conversations with His Nephew*, Cambridge University Press, 1998. Reprinted with permission of Cambridge University Press.

ADELARD: You remember, dear nephew, that, seven years ago, when I dismissed you (still almost a boy) with my other students in French studies at Laôn, we agreed amongst ourselves that I would investigate the studies of Arabs according to my ability, but you would become no less proficient in the insecurity of French opinions.

NEPHEW: I remember, and all the more so because when you left me you bound me with a promise on my word that I would apply myself to philosophy. I was always anxious to know why I should be more attentive to this subject. This is an excellent opportunity to test whether I have been successful by putting my study into practice, because since, as a listener only, I took note of you when often you explained the opinions of the Saracens [Muslims], and quite a few of them appeared to me to be quite useless. I shall for a brief while refuse to be patient and shall take you up as you expound these opinions, wherever it seems right to do so. For you both extol the Arabs shamelessly and invidiously accuse our people of ignorance in a disparaging way. It will therefore be worthwhile for you to reap the fruit of your labor, if you acquit yourself well, and likewise for me not to have been cheated in my promise, if I oppose you with probable arguments.

ADELARD: Perhaps you are being more bold in your presumption than you are capable. But because this disputation will be useful both to you and to many others, I shall put up with your impudence, as long as this inconvenience is avoided: that no one should think that when I am putting forward unknown ideas, I am doing this out of my own head, but that I am giving the views of the studies of the Arabs. For I do not want it to happen that, even though what I say may displease those who are less advanced, I myself should also displease them. For I know what those who profess the truth suffer at the hands of the vulgar crowd. Therefore, I shall defend the cause of the Arabs, not my own.

NEPHEW: Agreed, so that you may have no occasion for silence.

ADELARD: Well then, I think we should begin from the easier subjects. For if I speak sensibly about these, you may have the same hope concerning greater things. So let us start from the lowest objects and end with the highest.

(The two then discuss the sources of nourishment for plants, and then the nephew asks about animals.)

ADELARD: About animals my conversation with you is difficult. For I have learnt one thing from my Arab masters, with reason as guide, but you another: you follow a halter, being enthralled by the picture of authority. For what else can authority be called other than a halter? As brute animals are led wherever one pleases by a halter, but do not know where or why they are led, and only follow the rope by which they are held, so the authority of written words leads not a few of you into danger, since you are enthralled and bound by brutish credulity. Hence too, certain people, usurping the name of "an authority" for themselves, have used too great a license to write, to such an extent that they have not hesitated to trick brutish men with false words instead of true. For why should you not fill pages, why not write on the back too, when these days you generally have the kind of listeners that demand no argument based on judgment, but trust only in the name of an ancient authority? For they do not understand that reason has been given to each single individual in order to discern between true and false with reason as the prime judge. For unless it were the duty of reason to be everybody's judge, she would have been given to each person in vain. . . .

Rather I assert that first, reason should be sought, and when it is found, an authority, if one is at hand, should be added later. But authority alone cannot win credibility for a philosopher, nor should it be adduced for this purpose. Hence the logicians have agreed than an argument from authority is probable, not necessary. Therefore, if you wish to hear anything more from me, give and receive reason. . . .

NEPHEW: By all means let us do as you demand, since it is easy for me to oppose with reasonable arguments, nor is it safe to follow the authorities of your Arabs. Therefore, let us keep to this rule: between you and me reason alone should be the judge.

QUESTIONS FOR ANALYSIS

» *What does Islamic learning represent to Adelard of Bath? To his nephew?*

» *How do the two view European learning?*

» *On what basis will they decide if a given explanation is true or false?*

University studies, even short of a degree, prepared young men for careers in the church or in government administration, as did the civil service examinations in Song China. Many received employment as literate bureaucrats working for a noble or for members of the clergy, often near their hometown. Over time, as more and more families sent their sons to university, it became the norm for officials and clergy to be literate, and the proportion of students finishing their degrees consistently increased over time.

The Movement for Church Reform, 1000–1300

Although historians often speak of the church when talking about medieval Europe, Peter Abelard and Heloise's experiences make it clear that no single, unified entity called the church existed. The pope in Rome presided over many different local churches and monasteries, but he was not consistently able to enforce decisions. Below him, but not necessarily obedient to him, many churches and monasteries throughout Europe possessed their own lands and directly benefited from the greater yields of cerealization. In addition, devotees often gave a share of their increasing personal wealth to religious institutions. As a result, monastic leaders had sufficient income to act independently, whether or not they had higher approval.

Starting in 1000, different reformers tried to streamline the church and reform the clergy. Yet reform from within did not always succeed. The new begging orders founded in the thirteenth century, like the Franciscans and the Dominicans, explicitly rejected what they saw as lavish spending.

The Structure of the Church

By 1000, the European countryside was completely blanketed with churches, each one the center of a parish in which the clergy lived together with laypeople. Some churches were small shrines that had little land of their own, while others were magnificent cathedrals. The laity were expected to pay a tithe, or 10 percent, of their income to their local parish priest, and he in turn performed the sacraments for each individual as he or she passed through the major stages of life: baptism at birth, confirmation and marriage at young adulthood, and a funeral at death. The parish priest also gave communion to his congregation.

By the year 1000, this system had become so well established in western Europe that no one questioned it. Much as we agree to the obligation of all citizens to pay taxes, medieval Europeans accepted that all those born in a parish had to undergo baptism and the other sacraments and to pay the tithe.

The clergy fell into two categories: the secular clergy and the regular clergy. The secular clergy, like Abelard, worked with the laity as local priests or schoolmasters. Regular clergy lived in monasteries by the rule, or *regula* in Latin, of the church or monastic order.

Reform from Above

In 1046, one of three different Italian candidates vying for the position of pope had bought the position from an earlier pope who decided that he wanted to marry. Such **simony** was universally considered a sin. The ruler of Germany, Henry III (1039–1056), intervened in the dispute and named Leo IX pope (in office 1049–1056). Leo launched a reform campaign with the main goals of ending simony and enforcing celibacy.

Not everyone agreed that marriage of the clergy should be forbidden. Many priests' wives came from locally prominent families who felt strongly that their

simony
The sale of church office in Europe, considered a sin.

female kin had done nothing wrong in marrying a member of the clergy. Those who supported celibacy believed that childless clergy would have no incentive to divert church property toward their own family, and their view eventually prevailed.

Pope Gregory VII (in office 1073–1085) also sought to reform the papacy by drafting twenty-seven papal declarations asserting the independence of the church from secular powers. In his efforts to strengthen the papacy, he even claimed *"that the Roman Church has never erred, nor will it ever err, as the scripture testifies."* The separation of church and state did not occur in Gregory's lifetime, but he initiated the trend that culminated several hundred years later.

In 1215, Pope Innocent III (in office 1198–1216) presided over the fourth Lateran Council. More than twelve hundred bishops, abbots, and representatives of different European monarchs met in the Lateran Palace in Rome to pass decrees regulating Christian practice, some of which are in effect today. For example, they agreed that all Christians should receive communion at least once a year and should also confess their sins annually. The fourth Lateran Council marked the high point of the pope's political power; subsequent popes never commanded such power over secular leaders.

Reform Within the Established Monastic Orders

Abelard was condemned twice, once after his affair with Heloise and again near the end of his life for **heresy**, a grave charge. Historians may never fully understand the charges against Abelard because many of the original documents are lost. Though he was found guilty, powerful patrons protected him. In 1140, Peter the Venerable (abbot from 1122 to 1156) invited him to Cluny (CLUE-nee), the largest monastery in Europe, and refused to give him up. Peter's invitation quite possibly saved Abelard's life.

heresy
The offense of believing in teachings that the Roman Catholic Church condemned as incorrect.

Cluny's holdings in land and money were greater than those of the church in Rome, and the abbot there was more powerful than anyone in the church except for the pope. Founded in 910, the monastery at Cluny followed the rules of Saint Benedict (see Chapter 10). Three hundred monks, many from the most prominent families in France, lived at Cluny itself, and one thousand monasteries, home to twenty thousand monks, were associated with Cluny.

Since the abbot did not visit most of these monasteries, monastic discipline suffered. In 1098, several monks broke away from Cluny because they wanted reform. They began the Cistercian Order, which called for a return to the original rules of Saint Benedict. Unlike the Cluniac monasteries, each Cistercian monastery had its own abbot, and no one was admitted until he was over fifteen and had served a full year as a novice. All Cistercian abbots convened at regular intervals to ensure that everyone followed the same regulations. The Cistercians lived more austerely than the monks at Cluny, wearing simple clothes of undyed wool, eating only vegetarian food, and building undecorated churches. The Cistercian monasteries proved enormously popular, as did other movements for monastic reform. From 5 monasteries in 1119, the order mushroomed to 647 by 1250.

About half of the Cistercian monasteries were nunneries for women. After 1000, as Europe's population surged, many more women joined nunneries. But because their contemporaries did not think it appropriate for them to do the work monks did, a nunnery needed male staff to run its estates, farm the land, and perform religious services. The resulting chronic lack of revenue made the nunneries vulnerable to outside intervention, as Heloise's experience at Argenteuil shows.

---

*Joseph H. Lynch, *The Medieval Church: A Brief History* (London: Longman, 1992), p. 146.

Heloise and Abelard, Model Couple for the Twenty-first Century?

If you search the web for the ideal Valentine's Day gift, you will find several sites that suggest the letters of Heloise and Abelard—at least for women who like to read. The couple appear on multiple lists of famous lovers as well, and most sites give a short version of the couple's romance, recounting how they met, Heloise's disdain for marriage and love for Abelard, Abelard's castration, and the couple's burial together. Their love story has been made into a movie (*Stealing Heaven*), an opera (Stephen Paulus's *Heloise and Abelard*), and at least one novel, Antoine Audouard's *Farewell, My Only One*.

Many readers enjoy Abelard's *Story of His Misfortunes* and the seven letters the two exchanged after 1131 when they regained contact. These letters are genuine; historians are less certain about another set, published under the title *The Lost Letters of Heloise and Abelard:* *Perceptions of Dialogue in Twelfth-Century France*. Both sets provide multiple clues for readers trying to make sense of the couple's relationship.

Heloise has much to recommend her to modern feminist readers. Unusually well educated for her times, she challenged Abelard on multiple points when they debated theology as equals. Her frank avowal of love for Abelard also seems utterly modern. But what about her willingness to sacrifice everything—to give up Astrolabe to her sister-in-law, to enter a nunnery—for the sake of Abelard's future? Feminists find this side of her character less congenial. Astute readers also note that, in the letters after 1131, Abelard's ardor has cooled. Unlike Heloise, he has no interest in discussing their earlier romance; he is far more interested in theology.

In short, perhaps Heloise and Abelard are not the model couple for our times.

In the years after she entered the nunnery, Heloise rose to the rank of prioress, the second in command at the convent. When the king abruptly ordered the nuns to move elsewhere because he wanted their land, Heloise received a letter from Abelard for the first time since they had parted. He offered to her his own church, named the Paraclete, which had its own lands given by supporters. She accepted Abelard's invitation and served as abbess until her death in the 1160s. They were both buried in the graveyard at the Paraclete. (See the feature "World History in Today's World: Heloise and Abelard, Model Couple for the Twenty-first Century?")

Reform Outside the Established Orders

Although the Cistercians certainly thought of themselves as reformers, they still accepted the need for groups of men or women to live on landed monasteries or nunneries. But as the drive to reform continued, some asked members of religious orders to live exactly as Jesus and his followers had, not in monasteries with their own incomes but as beggars dependent on ordinary people for contributions. Between 1100 and 1200, reformers established at least nine different begging orders, the most important of which was the Franciscans founded by Saint Francis of Assisi (ca. 1181–1226). Members of these orders were called **friars**.

Francis was born to the well-off Italian family of a textile merchant, but while in his twenties he abandoned his family and began to live as a beggar. He attracted a small group of followers, and in 1209 the pope granted the Franciscans the right to preach on simple topics like the correct conduct of a Christian, but not to speak on complex theological issues.

friars
Members of the begging orders established in Europe between 1100 and 1200, of which the Franciscans were the best known.

The Franciscan movement grew rapidly even though Francis allowed none of his followers to keep any money, to own books or extra clothes, or to live in a permanent dwelling. In 1217, Francis had 5,000 followers; by 1326, some 28,000 Franciscans were active. Francis also created the order of Saint Clare for women, who lived in austere nunneries where they were not allowed to accumulate any property of their own.

In 1215, Saint Dominic (ca. 1170–1221) founded the order of Friars Preachers in Spain. Unlike Francis, he stressed education and sent some of his brightest followers to the new universities. **Thomas Aquinas** (1224/25–1274), one of the most famous scholastic thinkers, belonged to the Dominican order. Aquinas wrote *Summa Theologiae* (Summary of Theology), a book juxtaposing the teachings of various church authorities on a range of difficult questions, just as Abelard had; but where Abelard had trusted each reader to determine the correct interpretation, Aquinas wrote detailed explanations that remained definitive for centuries.

Thomas Aquinas (1224/25–1274) One of the most famous scholastic thinkers and a member of the Dominican order; author of *Summa Theologiae*, which interpreted difficult theological questions.

The Crusades, 1095–1291

The founding of the Franciscans and the Dominicans was only one aspect of a broader movement to spread Christianity that included Crusades. Some Crusades within Europe targeted Jews, Muslims, and members of other non-Christian groups. In addition, the economic surplus resulting from cerealization and urban growth financed a series of expeditions to the Holy Land to try to conquer Muslim-governed Jerusalem (the symbolic center of the Christian world because Jesus had preached and died there) and make it Christian again (see Map 13.1). The Crusaders succeeded in conquering Jerusalem, a pilgrimage center for all Christians, but held it for only eighty-eight years. During these years the Europeans who traveled to West Asia encountered new ideas and commodities that they introduced to Europe on their return home. The Crusades marked the first time since the Roman empire that European armies ventured beyond Europe; although unsuccessful in the long term, they established an important precedent for Europeans to establish colonies in distant foreign lands.

The Crusades to the Holy Land

Historians use the term *Crusades* to refer to military efforts in the name of Christianity between 1095, when the pope first called for Europeans to take back Jerusalem, and 1291, when the last European possession in Syria was lost. The word ***Crusader*** referred to anyone belonging to a large, volunteer force against Muslims, as indicated by a cross on Crusaders' clothing. In 1095, Pope Urban II (1088–1099) told a large meeting of church leaders that the Byzantine emperor requested help against the Seljuq Turks (see Chapters 9 and 10). He urged those assembled to recover Jerusalem:

Crusader Term that indicated anyone who attached a cross to his or her clothes as a sign of belonging to a large, volunteer force against Muslims between 1095 and 1291.

This royal city, therefore, situated at the center of the world, is now held captive by . . . His enemies, and is in subjection to those who do not know God . . . , to the worship of the heathens. She seeks therefore and [Jerusalem] desires to be liberated, and does not cease to implore you to come to her aid. . . . Accordingly undertake this journey for the remission of your sins, with the assurance of the imperishable glory of the kingdom of heaven.[*]

[*]Robert the Monk's account, James Harvey Robinson, ed., *Readings in European History: Vol. I* (Boston: Ginn and Co., 1904), 312–316.

MAP 13.1 **The Crusades** In response to the pope's request, thousands of Europeans walked more than 2,000 miles (3,200 km) overland through the Byzantine empire to reach Jerusalem, which the Europeans governed from 1099 to 1187. Others traveled to the Holy Land by sea. The Europeans who lived in Jerusalem for nearly a century developed their own hybrid culture that combined French, German, and Italian elements with the indigenous practices of the eastern Mediterranean. (© Cengage Learning)

If they died en route, the pope promised, they could be certain that God would forgive their sins because God forgave all pilgrims' sins. His audience cried, *"It is the will of God"* in response. This marked the beginning of the First Crusade.

An estimated 50,000 combatants responded to the pope's plea in 1095; of these, only 10,000 reached Jerusalem. Of those 10,000, some 1,500 were knights, the only fighters properly equipped for siege warfare. The Crusader forces consisted of self-financed individuals who, unlike soldiers in an army, did not receive pay and had no line of command. The problems of disorganization extended to the top ranks, which included some of France's and England's most prominent nobles. Rarely agreeing with each other about military strategy, they often could not even decide on their main commander. Nevertheless, the Crusaders succeeded in taking Jerusalem in 1099 from the rulers of Egypt, who controlled it at the time. After Jerusalem fell, the out-of-control troops massacred people still in the city.

As the city where Jesus died, Jerusalem had profound significance for Christians. European mapmakers often placed Jerusalem in the exact center of world maps that we now call **T-O maps** because they placed Afro-Eurasia inside a circle (the "O") divided by a T symbolizing rivers and the Mediterranean. Most often Asia occupied the top half of the circle, with Africa on the lower right and Europe on the lower left. T-O maps were stylized: European geographers realized that Jerusalem did not lie at the midpoint of the world. They knew, too, that the earth was sphere-shaped: the two-dimensional T-O maps depicted only the Northern Hemisphere because geographers believed a torrid zone, too hot for human habitation, separated the Northern and Southern Hemispheres (see Chapter 15). As the Crusaders reported what they saw of the Islamic world and what they learned from Islamic geographers about the world beyond (including Africa), T-O maps showed more and more places.

The Crusaders ruled Jerusalem as a kingdom for eighty-eight years, long enough that the first generation of Europeans died and were succeeded by generations who saw themselves as residents of Outremer (OU-truh-mare), the term the Crusaders used for the eastern edge of the Mediterranean. Even though Jerusalem was also a holy site for both Jews and Muslims, the Crusaders were convinced that the city belonged to them.

The Muslim ruler Saladin, however, disagreed. In 1169, Saladin overthrew the reigning Egyptian dynasty and in 1171 founded the Ayyubid dynasty (see Chapter 9). His biographer explained the extent of Saladin's commitment to jihad, or holy war against the Crusaders:

> *The Holy War and the suffering involved in it weighed heavily on his heart and his whole being in every limb: he spoke of nothing else, thought only about equipment for the fight, was interested only in those who had taken up arms.**

In 1176 Saladin married the widow of the Seljuq ruler of Central Asia, effectively allying the two great powers of the Islamic world. With this combined power, he devoted himself to raising an army strong enough to repulse the Crusaders.

After completing the hajj, on his way back to Spain in 1185, Ibn Jubayr traveled through Saladin's realm on his way to the Crusader-controlled port city of Acre, where he was able to go even

*Francesco Gabrieli, *Arab Historians of the Crusades,* trans. E. J. Costello (London: Routledge and Kegan Paul, 1969), p. 100.

T-O map
Stylized European maps of the world that showed Asia, Africa, and Europe with Jerusalem at the center.

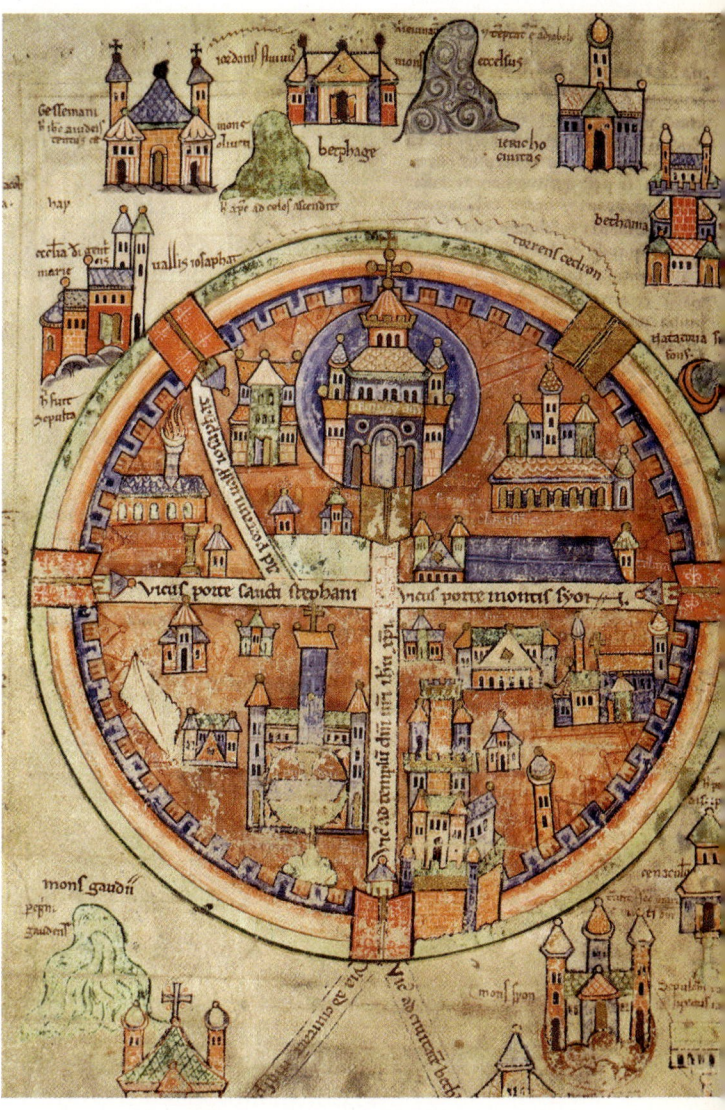

The Art Archive at Art Resource, NY

Jerusalem as Seen by a Crusader Although not a T-O map, this map shows the importance of Jerusalem to the Crusaders. It is from the *Chronicles of the Crusades* by Robert le Moine de Reims, French abbot of St. Remy, who was present at the conquest of the city in 1099. It depicts Christian churches topped by crosses as well as other buildings, possibly mosques or temples.

though Saladin was at war with the Crusaders. Ibn Jubayr saw hundreds of Christian prisoners taken captive by Saladin. Like all speakers of Arabic, he called the Crusaders *"Franks"* because there was no word *"crusader"* in Arabic; in fact, the Crusaders came from all over Europe, not just France and Germany. The incongruity of the situation struck him: *"One of the strangest things in the world is that Muslim caravans go forth to Frankish lands, while Frankish captives enter Muslim lands."*[*]

By 1187 Saladin had gathered an army of thirty thousand men on horseback carrying lances and swords like knights but without chain-mail armor. Half of his army consisted of light cavalry who could maneuver much more quickly than the twenty thousand Crusaders they faced. Saladin laid a trap for the Crusaders in an extinct Syrian volcano called the Horns of Hattin. The Crusader forces had no way to replenish their water supply, but the Muslim armies made sure that each camp had storage tanks supplied by camels carrying goat skins filled with water. On the day of the battle, Saladin's well-rested forces easily defeated the parched and exhausted Crusaders, baiting them by pouring fresh water out on the ground instead of giving it to them to drink. When Saladin's victorious troops took Jerusalem back, they restored the mosques as houses of worship and removed the crosses from all Christian churches, although they did allow Christians to visit the city.

Subsequent Crusades failed to recapture Jerusalem, but in 1201, the Europeans decided to make a further attempt in the Fourth Crusade. Because they did not have enough ships, they promised to pay the Venetian navy to transport them to the Holy Land. In June 1203, the Crusaders reached Constantinople and were astounded by its size: the ten biggest cities in Europe could easily fit within its imposing walls, and its population surpassed 1 million. One awe-struck soldier wrote home:

> If anyone should recount to you the hundredth part of the richness and the beauty and the nobility that was found in the abbeys and in the churches and in the palaces and in the city, it would seem like a lie and you would not believe it.[†]

When one of the claimants to the Byzantine throne refused to pay the Crusaders for their support, as promised, the commanders loosed their troops to attack the city in the hope that they could plunder what they needed to pay the Venetians to transport them to Jerusalem.

One of the most infamous atrocities in world history resulted: the Crusaders rampaged throughout the beautiful city, killing all who opposed them and raping thousands of women. They treated the Eastern Orthodox Christians of Constantinople precisely as if they were the Muslim enemy. The Crusaders' conduct in Constantinople turned the diplomatic dispute between the two churches, which had begun in 1054 (see Chapter 10), into a genuine and lasting schism between Roman Catholics and Eastern Orthodox adherents.

Europeans did not regain control of Jerusalem, but Cyprus remained in European hands until 1570. The Crusades provided an important precedent that the conquest and colonization of foreign territory for Christianity was acceptable.

---

[*]*The Travels of Ibn Jubayr,* trans. R. J. C. Broadhurst (London: Jonathan Cape, 1952), p. 313.

[†]Thomas F. Madden, ed., *The Crusades: The Essential Readings* (Oxford: Blackwell, 2002), p. 109, n4; citing Robert of Clari, *The Conquest of Constantinople,* trans. Edgar Holmes McNeal (New York: Columbia University Press, 1936), p. 112.

Europeans would follow this precedent when they went to new lands in Africa and the Americas (see Chapter 15).

The Crusades Within Europe

European Christians, convinced that they were right about the superiority of Christianity, also attacked enemies within Europe, sometimes on their own, sometimes in direct response to the pope's command.

Many European Christians looked down on Jews, who were banned from many occupations, could not marry Christians, and often lived in separate parts of cities, called *ghettos*. They also resented Jewish moneylenders (a profession that these different restrictions pushed Jews to do). But before 1095, Christians had largely respected the right of Jews to practice their own religion. This fragile coexistence fell apart in 1096, as the out-of-control crowds traveling through on the First Crusade attacked the Jews living in the three German towns of Mainz, Worms, and Speyer and killed all who did not convert to Christianity. Thousands died in the violence. Anti-Jewish prejudice worsened over the next two centuries; England expelled the Jews in 1290 and France in 1306.

These spontaneous attacks on Jews differed from two campaigns launched by the pope against enemies of the church. The first was against the Cathars, a group of Christian heretics who lived in the Languedoc region of southern France. Like the Zoroastrians of Iran (see Chapter 6), the Cathars believed that the forces of good in the spiritual world and of evil in the material world were engaged in a perpetual fight for dominance. In 1208, Pope Innocent III launched a crusade to Languedoc in which the pope's forces gradually killed many of the lords and bishops who supported Catharism.

In the early thirteenth century the pope established a special court, called the **inquisition**, to hear charges against accused heretics. Unlike other church courts, which operated according to established legal norms, the inquisition used anonymous informants, forced interrogations, and torture to identify heretics. One inquisitor in south France, active between 1308 and 1323, sentenced 633 offenders, many to life imprisonment.[3] The inquisition remained active in the region of the Cathars until 1330, and later popes established inquisition courts whenever they felt it necessary.

In 1212 the pope approved a crusade against non-Christians in Spain. Historians use the Spanish word *Reconquista* ("Reconquest") to refer to these and other military campaigns by Christians against the Muslims of Spain and Portugal. Before 1200, various Christian rulers had recovered isolated cities, such as Toledo, Spain, and Lisbon, Portugal, and the Crusader army won a decisive victory in 1212 and captured Córdoba and Seville in the following decades. After 1249, only the kingdom of Granada, on the southern tip of Spain, remained Muslim.

inquisition
Special court established by the pope to hear charges against those accused of heresy.

Disaster and Recovery, 1300–1400

The three centuries of prosperity and growth caused by cerealization and urbanization came to a sudden halt in the early 1300s, when first a series of food shortages and then the Black Death, which Ibn Battuta had seen in Damascus (see Chapter 11), rocked Europe. The fighting of the Hundred Years' War (1337–1453) between England and France caused additional deaths. In the long run, however, the economy and population recovered. The structure of European society also changed, and European kings, especially in France and England, emerged from this difficult century with more extensive powers than their predecessors.

Continuing Expansion of Trade Outside Europe

The Crusaders who returned from the Holy Land were one source of information for those seeking to learn about the world beyond Europe. Europeans gained access to other sources of information as trade networks linking Europe with Asia expanded. During the 1300s, merchants, usually from the Italian city-states of Venice or Genoa, traveled to West Asia, and sometimes to East Asia, to pursue trading opportunities (see Map 13.2).

In the twelfth and thirteenth centuries, Europeans consumed huge quantities of the new spices—such as pepper, cinnamon, ginger, cloves, and nutmeg—that entered Europe from Southeast Asia. Europeans used spices to enhance flavor and as medicines, not to preserve meat, as is often said. (Unpreserved meat spoiled and could not be salvaged; the wealthy ate freshly killed meat.) Surprisingly large quantities of spices went into a single meal: in 1319, the pope presided at a dinner for six guests in which he served lamb, pork, chicken, and partridges seasoned with 1 pound each of ginger and cloves.[4] To obtain spices, European merchants often traveled to Constantinople, the Black Sea, or Iran, where they established small commercial colonies with warehouses and homes. During the 1330s and 1340s, a small group of merchants even lived in the Mongols' capital at Beijing, China, where a bishop served the Christian congregation.

During these years, readers avidly devoured books about distant foreign places, especially those that purported to describe the actual travels of their authors. Marco Polo (1254–1324), a Venetian merchant who traveled to Asia, portrayed the wonders of the known world and painted China as especially wealthy. Even more popular was *The Travels of Sir John Mandeville*, published in the 1350s, which described a legendary Christian king named Prester John who ruled over a realm distant from Europe. Polo combined some firsthand knowledge with hearsay; Mandeville's writing was based on pure hearsay. Even so, both books created an optimistic impression of Asian wealth that inspired later explorers like Columbus to found overseas colonies (covered in Chapter 15).

Tombstone for an Italian Girl Who Died in China
In 1342, the daughter of a Venetian merchant died in Yangzhou, near the mouth of the Yangzi River, and her family commissioned a tombstone for her. The tombstone shows scenes from the life of a haloed figure, most likely Saint Catherine of Alexandria, for whom the deceased was named. To the left of the Latin text, four Chinese characters appear in a small rectangle; the artist's signature in stone is the equivalent of the red-colored seals Chinese painters stamped on their paintings. (Ricci Institute for Chinese-Western Cultural History, University of San Francisco)

Rural Famines and the Black Death

The first signs that three centuries of growth had come to an end were internal. The Great Famine of 1315–1322 affected all of northern Europe, and it was the first of repeated food shortages. Many starved to death, and thousands fled the barren countryside to beg in the cities.

These difficult times caused financial strains that, in turn, led to changes in rural society as rulers and feudal lords struggled to increase their tax revenues. Rulers found that they needed more money than they could obtain from the traditional obligations tying peasants to their lords. In 1315, therefore, the French king freed all the serfs on royal land so that he could charge them new and higher taxes.

MAP 13.2 **Movement of the Plague and Trade Routes** The complex network of trade routes linking Europe with Asia and Africa facilitated the movement of goods, like Asian spices, but also of disease, like the Black Death. Europeans learned about Asia from travelers like Marco Polo, who went to Mongolia and China, and John of Mandeville, who did not. Small communities of Europeans lived in the nodes of the network: in Constantinople, Kaffa, Khara Khorum, and the Chinese capital of Beijing. (© Cengage Learning)

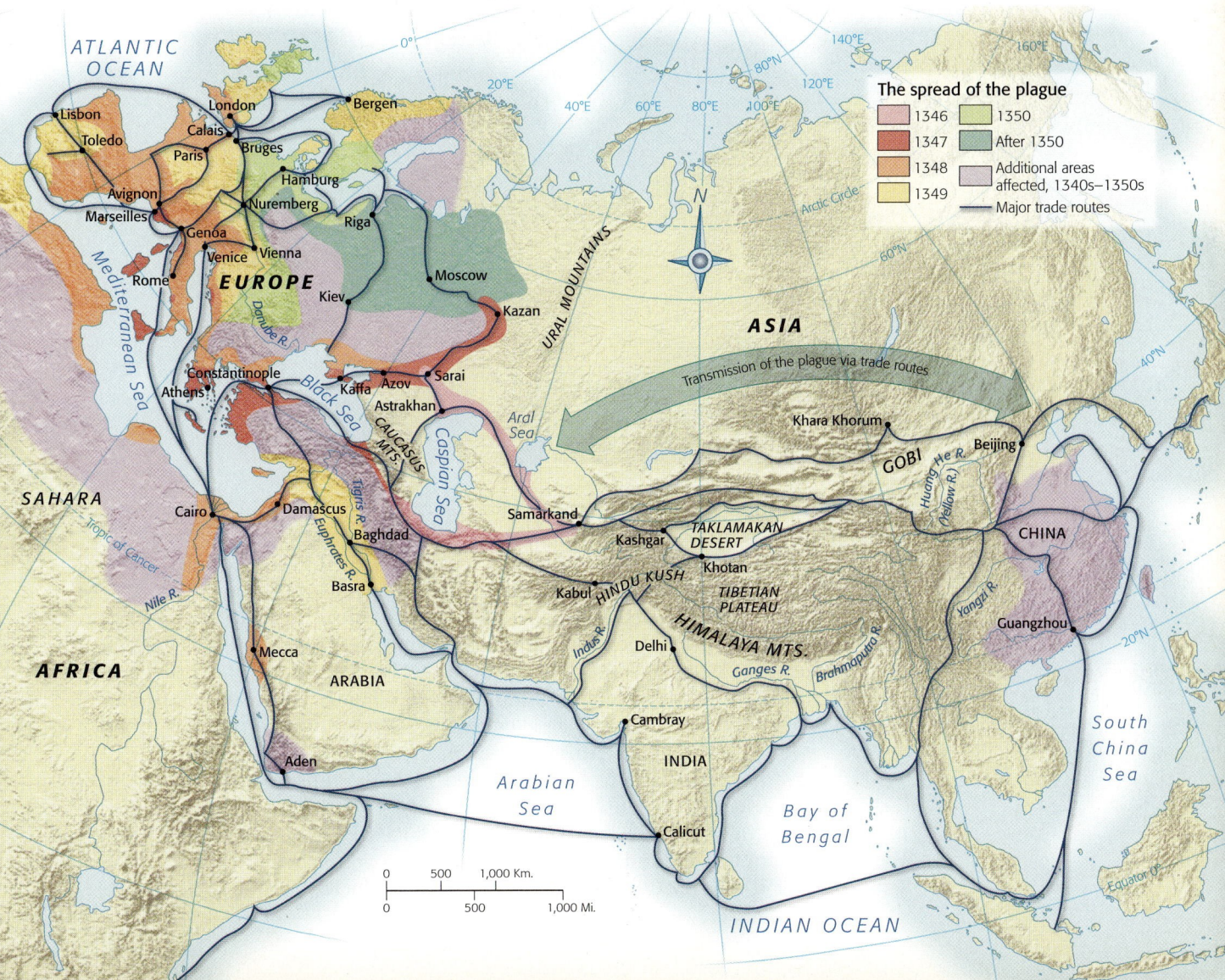

Portraying the Black Death

This painting, made more than a century after the Black Death struck Europe between 1346 and 1348, shows Saint Sebastian praying for those who had fallen ill with the plague. The artist depicts a plague victim wrapped in a white shroud, presumably because the black swellings on the bodies were too grisly to include in a painting displayed in a church.

Walters Art Museum, Baltimore/Bridgeman Art Library

Landlords in other places, like England and Germany, adopted short-term leases that replaced the lists of customary obligations and fixed rents at higher rates.

During these difficult decades, the Black Death came first to Europe's ports from somewhere in Asia, possibly north China (see Map 13.2). In 1346, the rats infected with the Black Death traveled by ship to the Genoese colony of Kaffa on the Black Sea. In 1348, the year in which Ibn Battuta observed the plague's toll in Damascus (see Chapter 11), the plague struck Italy, and then France and Germany one year later. Like the plague in sixth-century Byzantium (see Chapter 10), it had two phases: bubonic plague and pneumonic plague, which was almost always fatal. Historians reserve the term *Black Death* for this outbreak in the 1300s.

Since nearly six hundred years had passed since the most recent outbreak of 767, Europeans had lost whatever immunity they had developed, and the plague's initial toll was devastating. The Black Death reduced Europe's population from about 75 to about 55 million, and it only returned to pre-plague levels after 1500. The losses of the first outbreak were greatest. One doctor in Avignon, France, reported that, in 1349, two-thirds of the city's population fell ill, and almost all died. By the fourth outbreak, in 1382, only one-twentieth of the population was afflicted, and almost everyone survived.[5]

The Hundred Years' War and Monarchy in England and France

During this difficult century, the rulers of England and France engaged in a long series of battles now known as the **Hundred Years' War** (1337–1453). In 1337, Edward III of England (1327–1377) was next in line to the French throne, but the French nobles selected his cousin as king instead. Asserting his claim, Edward sent an army to France and launched a conflict that took more than a century to resolve.

France, with a population of some 15 million, was far richer than England, which had only around 4 million. The war was conducted entirely on French soil, and the opportunity to obtain plunder provided a strong incentive for the English troops.

The long conflict saw the end of battles fought by mounted knights. Early in the war, the English won significant victories because they used a new type of longbow 6 feet (1.8 m) tall that shot metal-tipped arrows farther and more accurately than the crossbows then in use. Knights donned even heavier armor to protect themselves, but they could not protect their horses. Moreover, the armor was so heavy that a knight who had fallen off his horse could not get up to fight an assailant armed with a staff. By the final years of the war, both sides were using gunpowder to shoot stones or cannonballs. Although difficult to aim accurately, these new weapons could destroy the walls surrounding a castle or town under siege and make it possible to take the city.

In 1429 a young illiterate peasant woman named Joan of Arc (1412–1431), who claimed divine guidance, succeeded in rallying the French forces and won a surprise victory. After capturing her in 1430, the English burned her as a heretic in 1431. In the years after her death, French forces won more victories. They defeated the English in 1453, when the French and the English signed a treaty marking the end of the war.

When they assess the significance of the Hundred Years' War, historians note how the political structure of France and England changed: at the beginning of the war, the two kingdoms consisted of patchworks of territory ruled by a king who shared power with his nobles. By the end of the war, the two countries had become centralized monarchies governed by kings with considerably more power.

This result had much to do with the changing nature of warfare. In conflicts during the early 1300s, the French and English kings summoned their nobles, who provided knights and soldiers. But the men best able to use first the longbow and then cannon were specialists who had to be paid. Over time, kings demanded money each year and so gained the right to tax the lords of their country.

In England, the king had summoned groups of advisers since the 1200s; contemporaries called these meetings "Parliament," which literally means "to talk." **Parliament** (PAR-la-ment) consisted of different groups, some nobles and some well-off city dwellers. It met whenever the English king convened his most powerful subordinates to explain why he needed new taxes. Most European rulers convened bodies similar to Parliament; the French equivalent, weaker than Parliament, was called the Estates General and included the nobles, clergy, and townsfolk.

The monarchies that evolved in France and England differed from earlier political structures. France and England were smaller than the earlier Roman and Byzantine empires, and their rulers consulted with their subordinates more often. The new monarchies, though, proved to be extremely effective, partially because they could command the allegiance of their subjects.

Hundred Years' War (1337–1453) War between the English and French fought entirely on French soil; it enhanced the powers of the kings of England and France to tax and to maintain a standing army.

Parliament (literally "to talk") Name for the different councils that advised the English kings and approved their requests for taxation.

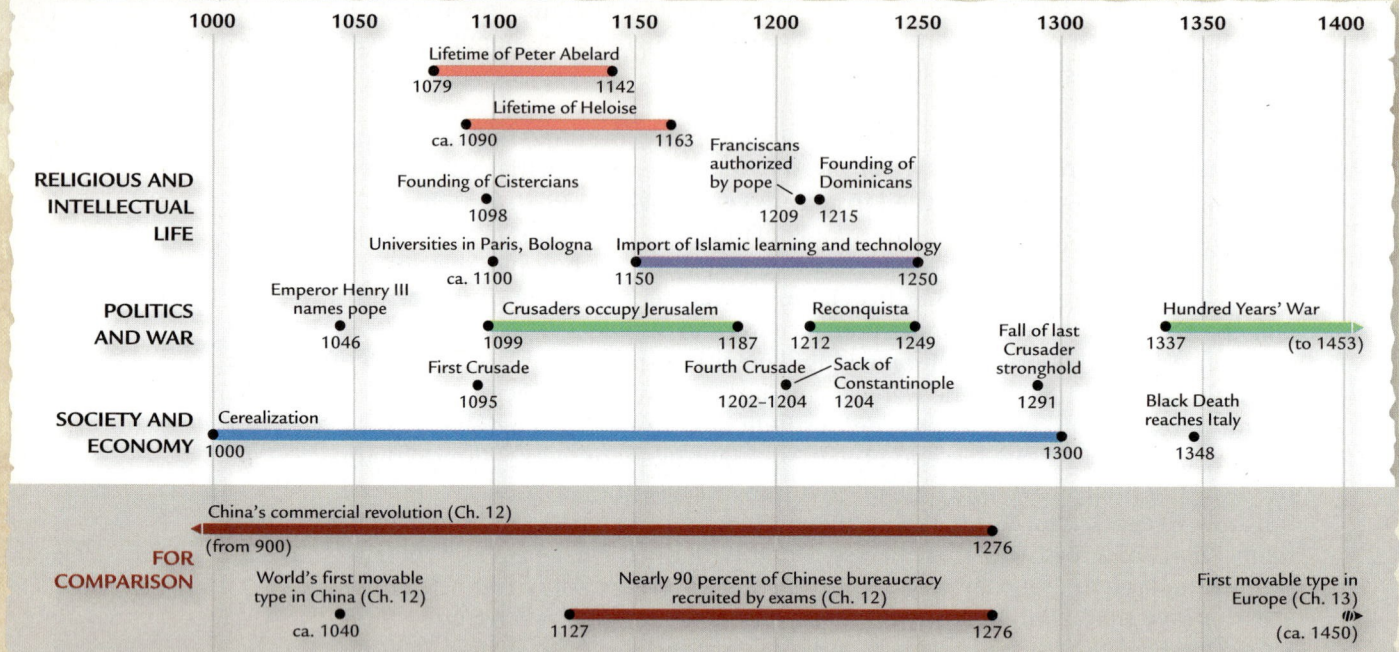

	1000	1050	1100	1150	1200	1250	1300	1350	1400

RELIGIOUS AND INTELLECTUAL LIFE

Lifetime of Peter Abelard
1079 — 1142

Lifetime of Heloise
ca. 1090 — 1163

Founding of Cistercians
1098

Franciscans authorized by pope
1209

Founding of Dominicans
1215

Universities in Paris, Bologna
ca. 1100

Import of Islamic learning and technology
1150 — 1250

POLITICS AND WAR

Emperor Henry III names pope
1046

Crusaders occupy Jerusalem
1099 — 1187

Reconquista
1212 — 1249

Fall of last Crusader stronghold
1291

Hundred Years' War
1337 (to 1453)

First Crusade
1095

Fourth Crusade
1202–1204

Sack of Constantinople
1204

SOCIETY AND ECONOMY

Cerealization
1000 — 1300

Black Death reaches Italy
1348

FOR COMPARISON

China's commercial revolution (Ch. 12)
(from 900) — 1276

World's first movable type in China (Ch. 12)
ca. 1040

Nearly 90 percent of Chinese bureaucracy recruited by exams (Ch. 12)
1127 — 1276

First movable type in Europe (Ch. 13)
(ca. 1450)

© Cengage Learning

The World of Europe's Commercial Revolution

Heloise and Abelard, the direct contemporaries of Li Qingzhao and Zhao Mingcheng (see Chapter 12), also experienced great prosperity, but on the western edge of Eurasia. As the shift to rice cultivation underpinned Chinese economic growth, cerealization sustained Europe's. Rotating crops and the use of horses and iron horseshoes, iron plow blades, and windmills allowed Europeans, particularly those living in France and England, to bring more land under cultivation. Between 1000 and 1340, Europe's population almost doubled to reach 75 million, making it the world region with the second-largest population, after China's 100 million.

As a young man Abelard started lecturing in Paris in 1114, when the cathedral there was in the early stages of becoming a university, and returned several times over the following decades. In Abelard's day Paris did not grant degrees, but by the 1170s instructors determined readings, the content of examinations, and degree recipients. The independent granting of degrees distinguished European universities from Islamic schools, which did not grant degrees (see Chapters 9 and 11), and Chinese academies, which also did not grant them but prepared students for civil service examinations that brought degrees from the central government (see Chapter 12).

Like Li Qingzhao, Heloise had received an excellent education. She could read Latin and some Greek and Hebrew, and like Zhao Mingcheng and Li Qingzhao, Heloise and Abelard delighted in learned conversation. Heloise's education made her unusual for her time, but many girls managed to attend village schools for at least a few years. Some also, like Heloise, joined Christian nunneries, which offered women an alternative to marriage, as did Buddhist nunneries in Asia.

The church was one of the most important institutions in Europe, although its titular heads, popes, continuously vied with monarchs to control church property, to choose bishops and other high-ranking clerics, and to decide legal disputes involving the church. In the late 1000s, Pope Gregory VII asserted the complete independence of the church; the actual separation of church and state was attained only several centuries later. This church-state division was not as sharp in the Islamic world or in China, where rulers often patronized religious institutions.

In 1095 Pope Urban II called for Christians to take Jerusalem back from Muslim control. We should not overestimate the impact of the Crusades: far more young men traveled within Europe to pursue their studies than joined the Crusades, and many fewer actually made it all the way to Jerusalem. Still, disorganized as they were, the Crusaders managed to gain control of Jerusalem for eighty-eight years.

The Crusades left a more important legacy: for the first time since the Roman empire, Europeans established colonies beyond Europe (Cyprus remained under European control until 1570). Some Crusaders found much to admire and copy in the Islamic world. Even the Europeans who stayed home were affected by imports from Muslim regions: Latin translations via Arabic of Greek thinkers, eyeglasses, and new medical ideas. Other imports to Europe that originated in China also came via the Islamic world: the adjustable rudder, the steel-needle compass, and, most influential of all, paper, which displaced parchment by 1350. The increasing complexity of T-O maps reflected the growing European curiosity about and knowledge of the outside world.

As European markets continued to expand, demand rose for different commodities, particularly those imported from Asia. The European appetite for spices was enormous. As we will learn in the next chapter, the most detailed account of the Mongol empire that survives today was written by a Franciscan friar sent by a French king, a clear indication of European interest in the world beyond Europe.

VOYAGES ON THE WEB: Peter Abelard and Heloise

The Voyages Map App follows the traveler's journeys using interactive study tools, including 360-degree panoramic views of historic sites, zoomable maps, audio summaries, flash cards, and quizzes.

KEY TERMS

Peter Abelard (342)
Heloise (342)
cerealization (344)
guilds (346)
feudal (347)
liberal arts (351)

scholasticism (351)
simony (356)
heresy (357)
friars (358)
Thomas Aquinas (359)
Crusader (359)

T-O map (361)
inquisition (363)
Hundred Years' War (367)
Parliament (367)

FOR FURTHER REFERENCE

Baldwin, John W. *The Scholastic Culture of the Middle Ages, 1000–1300*. Prospect Heights, Ill.: Waveland Press, 1971, 1997.

Cipolla, Carlo M. *Before the Industrial Revolution: European Society and Economy, 1000–1700*. New York: W. W. Norton, 1994.

Clanchy, M. T. *Abelard: A Medieval Life*. Malden, Mass.: Blackwell, 1997.

Lynch, Joseph H. *Early Christianity: A Brief History*. New York: Oxford University Press, 2010.

Madden, Thomas F. *The New Concise History of the Crusades*. Updated ed. New York: Rowman and Littlefield, 2005.

Mews, Constant. *Abelard and Heloise*. New York: Oxford University Press, 2005.

Moore, R. I. *The First European Revolution, c. 970–1215*. Malden, Mass.: Blackwell, 2000.

Opitz, Claudia. "Life in the Late Middle Ages." In *Silence of the Middle Ages*, ed. Chistiane Klapisch-Zuber, vol. 2 of *A History of Women in the West*. Cambridge, Mass.: Belknap Press of Harvard University Press, 1992, pp. 259–317.

Radice, Betty, trans. *The Letters of Abelard and Heloise*. Revised by M. T. Clanchy. New York: Penguin Books, 2003.

Rosenwein, Barbara. *A Short History of the Middle Ages*. Toronto: University of Toronto Press, 2009.

Spufford, Peter. *Power and Profit: The Merchant in Medieval Europe*. New York: Thames and Hudson, 2002.

Tyerman, Christopher. *God's War: A New History of the Crusades*. Cambridge, Mass.: Belknap Press, 2006.

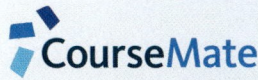
CourseMate Go to the CourseMate website at **www.cengagebrain.com** for additional study tools and review materials—including audio and video clips—for this chapter.

14

The Mongols and Their Successors, 1200–1500

In 1255, after his return from Mongolia, **William of Rubruck** (ca. 1215–ca. 1295) wrote a confidential report about his attempt to convert the Mongols to Christianity. He addressed it to his sponsor, the pious French king Louis IX (1214–1270). William's letter runs nearly three hundred pages long in translation and contains the most detailed, accurate, and penetrating description of the Mongols and their empire that exists today. In 1206, the Mongols exploded out of their homeland just north of China and conquered most of Eurasia by 1242. For the first time in world history, it became possible for individual travelers, like William, to move easily across a united Eurasia. Such movement prompted an unprecedented exchange of ideas, goods, and technologies. (The highly decorated capital letter below from a medieval manuscript shows two scenes from William's travels.) William's report is just one example of the different cultural exchanges that resulted and whose effects persisted long after different successor states replaced the Mongol empire. His account opens as follows:

William of Rubruck
(The Masters and Fellows of Corpus Christi College, Cambridge, MS 66A, f. 67r)

*W*e began our journey, then, around June 1, with our four covered wagons and two others which the Mongols had provided for us, in which was carried the bedding for sleeping on at night. They gave us five horses to ride, since we numbered five persons: I and my colleague, Friar Bartholomew of Cremona; Gosset, the bearer of this letter; the interpreter Homo Dei, and a boy, Nichols, whom I had bought at Constantinople with the alms you gave me. They supplied us in addition with two men who drove the wagons and tended the oxen and horses. . . .

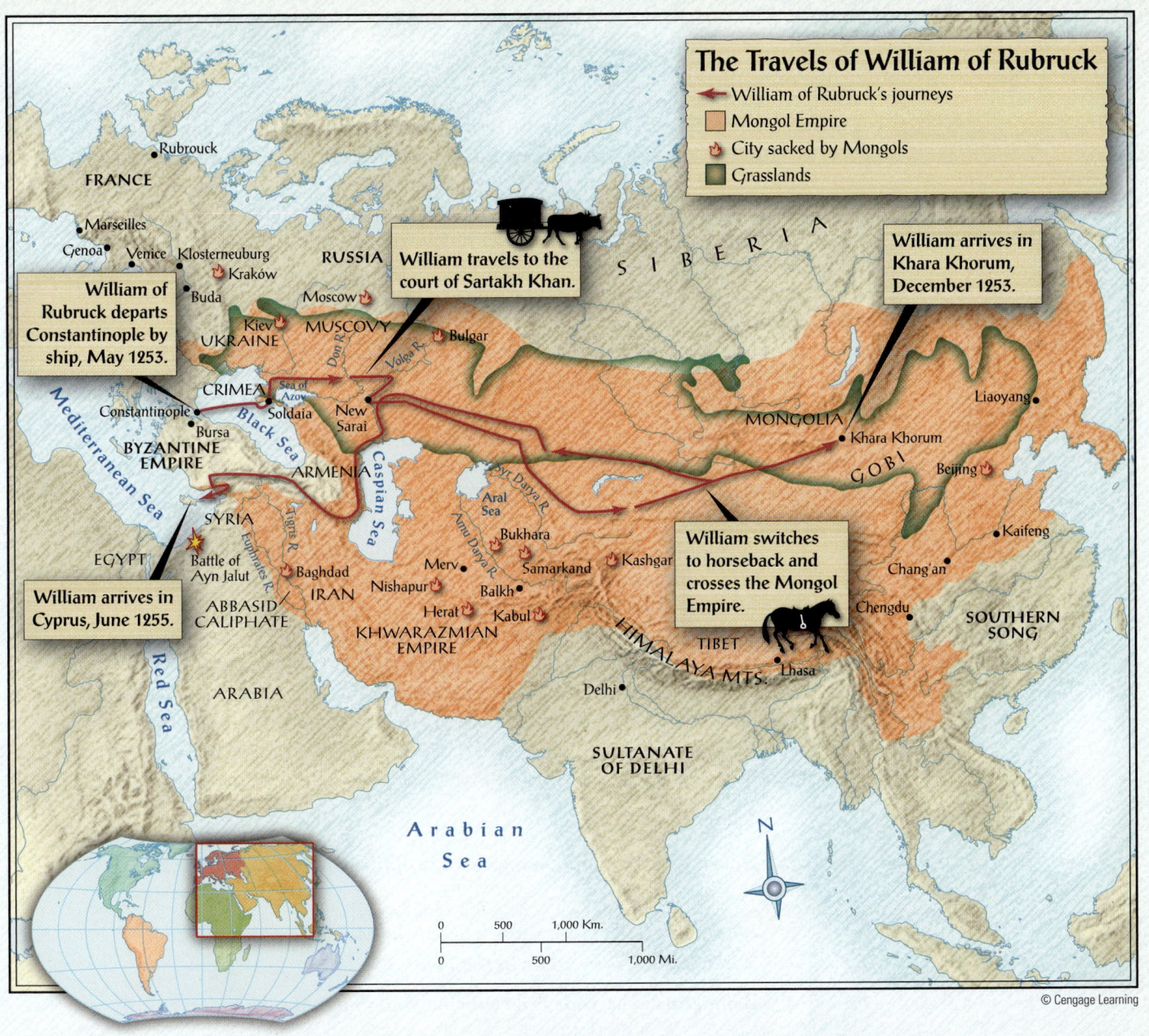

The Travels of William of Rubruck

- ← William of Rubruck's journeys
- ▨ Mongol Empire
- 🔥 City sacked by Mongols
- ▨ Grasslands

William of Rubruck departs Constantinople by ship, May 1253.

William travels to the court of Sartakh Khan.

William arrives in Khara Khorum, December 1253.

William arrives in Cyprus, June 1255.

William switches to horseback and crosses the Mongol Empire.

FRANCE — Rubrouck — Marseilles — Genoa — Venice — Klosterneuburg — Kraków — Buda — Moscow — Kiev — MUSCOVY — RUSSIA — SIBERIA — UKRAINE — Don R. — Volga R. — Bulgar — CRIMEA — Sea of Azov — New Sarai — Soldaia — Constantinople — Bursa — Black Sea — BYZANTINE EMPIRE — Mediterranean Sea — ARMENIA — Caspian Sea — MONGOLIA — Khara Khorum — GOBI — Liaoyang — Beijing — SYRIA — Tigris R. — Euphrates R. — Battle of Ayn Jalut — Baghdad — IRAN — ABBASID CALIPHATE — EGYPT — Red Sea — ARABIA — Nishapur — Merv — Herat — Balkh — Kabul — Syr Darya R. — Aral Sea — Amu Darya R. — Bukhara — Samarkand — Kashgar — Kaifeng — Chang'an — Chengdu — SOUTHERN SONG — KHWARAZMIAN EMPIRE — HIMALAYA MTS. — TIBET — Lhasa — Delhi — SULTANATE OF DELHI

Arabian Sea

0 500 1,000 Km.
0 500 1,000 Mi.

N

© Cengage Learning

Join this chapter's traveler on "Voyages," an interactive tour of historic sites and events: www.cengagebrain.com

Now on the third day after we left Soldaia, we encountered the Tartars [the Mongols]; and when I came among them, I really felt as if I were entering some other world. Their life and character I shall describe for you as best I can.[*]

---

[*]From Peter Jackson, *The Mission of Friar William Rubruck*, The Hakluyt Society, 1990, pp. 70–71. Reprinted with permission. The Hakluyt Society was established in 1846 for the purpose of printing rare or unpublished Voyages and Travels. For further information please see their website at: www.hakluyt.com.

William of Rubruck
(ca. 1215–ca. 1295)
Franciscan monk from
France who visited the
court of the Mongol
khan Möngke in 1253–
1254 and sent back
one of the most
detailed surviving
sources about the
Mongols.

In December 1253, after nine months of traveling—first by cart, then on horseback—through modern-day Turkey, Russia, the Ukraine, Siberia, and Mongolia, William arrived at the court of the Mongol leader Möngke (MUNG-keh) (d. 1259), the grandson of Chinggis Khan (the Mongolian spelling; Genghis Khan in Persian). His route through the grasslands ran several hundred miles north of the traditional Silk Routes linking China and Iran (see Chapter 8).

Called William of Rubruck because he was born sometime around 1215 in the village of Rubrouck, France, William was educated in Paris. A Franciscan friar, he went to Syria, then under the control of the Crusaders (see Chapter 13) in 1248, from where he departed for Mongolia.

As an outsider, William writes about the appearance of Mongol men and women, their process for making fermented horse's milk, and their worship of household spirits. No comparably detailed account by a Mongol survives. William visited the Mongols at the height of their power, during the years after Chinggis Khan had united the empire and before it broke apart.

William's gripping description allows us to understand how the Mongols created the largest contiguous land empire in world history, stretching from Hungary to the Pacific. Once they conquered a region or the local rulers surrendered, the Mongols placed a governor in charge and granted him considerable autonomy. Their loosely structured empire allowed many people, including William, to cross Eurasia and resulted in the interaction of societies and cultures that had been previously isolated. This chapter will also examine the states that succeeded the Mongols: the principality of Muscovy (Moscow) in Russia, the Ottomans in Turkey, the Yuan and Ming dynasties in China, and the successor states of Korea, Japan, and Vietnam.

Focus Questions

» *How did the Mongols' nomadic way of life contribute to their success as conquerors?*

» *What bound the different sectors of the Mongol empire together? What caused its breakup in the 1260s?*

» *What states succeeded the Qipchaq and Chaghatai khanates?*

» *What military innovations marked Ottoman expansion, and what cultural developments typified Ottoman rule?*

» *What was the legacy of Mongol rule in East and Southeast Asia?*

From Nomads to World Conquerors, 1200–1227

Chinggis Khan
(ca. 1167–1227)
Founder of the Mongol
empire who united the
different peoples living
in modern-day Mongo-
lia in 1206, when he
took the title Chinggis
Khan.

Founded by **Chinggis Khan** (ca. 1167–1227), the Mongol empire came into being between 1200 and 1250. At the time of Chinggis's birth around 1167, the Mongols lived in modern-day Mongolia with their herds of sheep, cattle, and horses and pursued a nomadic existence, trading with their sedentary neighbors primarily for grain, tea, textiles, and metal goods. After conquering the different peoples in Mongolia, Chinggis forged them into a fearsome fighting force that conquered gigantic sections of Europe, Central Asia, and China. The Mongols' skill with horses and systematic use of terror brought them unprecedented military success.

The Mongols' Nomadic Way of Life Before 1200

Nomadic peoples lived in the Mongolian grasslands even before the Mongols moved into Central Asia around 1000. The Mongols spoke Mongolian and different Turkic languages that are the basis of modern Turkish. The only source in Mongolian about the Mongols' early history is *The Origin of Chinggis Khan*, an anonymous oral epic that took shape in 1228 and was committed to writing a century or more later. (Many English translations are entitled *The Secret History of the Mongols*.) In 1206, Chinggis Khan ordered a Central Asian prisoner of war to record something he said in Mongolian. The prisoner wrote in his native Uighur, a Central Asian language spoken in Central Asia and in modern-day Xinjiang in west China. After this incident, the Mongols used the Uighur script to write the Mongolian language.

The Origin of Chinggis Khan gives a vivid sense of how the Mongols lived before they were unified. The Mongols' traditional homeland occupies much of the modern-day Mongolian People's Republic as well as the Inner Mongolian autonomous region just northwest of Beijing. This steppe region consists largely of grasslands, watered by a few rivers. Few trees grow there. While the soil and limited rainfall could not support a sedentary, farming population, the extensive grasslands perfectly suited pastoral nomads grazing their herds. (See the feature "World History in Today's World: Environmental Threats to the Grasslands of Mongolia and Inner Mongolia.")

After exhausting the available grass in a location, the Mongols moved to new pastures. Ranging from ten to several hundred people, an individual group, called a tribe by historians of Mongolia, might travel 100 miles (160 km) in its annual migration, usually on a fixed route. When the Mongols began their conquests, the fighters covered much larger distances and left their parents, wives, and children behind to tend their herds.

Religious Practices of the Mongols

The Mongols worshiped a variety of nature spirits. Each of the Mongols' tents, William noticed, contained several felt figurines representing protective spirits. The supreme deities of the Mongols were the sky-god Tengri and his counterpart, the earth-goddess Itügen. Certain people, called **shamans**, specialized in interceding with these gods, sometimes traveling to high mountains where the gods were thought to live. On other occasions, shamans burned bones and interpreted the cracks as indicators of the gods' wills, much like Shang dynasty diviners in ancient China (see Chapter 4).

The Mongols in central and western Mongolia had some contact with Christian missionaries from the Church of the East, which was based in Syria. These missionaries, the Christians most active in Central Asia, spoke the Turkic language Uighur when they preached among the Mongols. William called them Nestorians after Nestorius, a Syrian patriarch in Constantinople in 428, but in fact the Church of the East did not accept the teachings of Nestorius, whom successive church councils had declared a heretic.

Throughout his travels, William encountered Eastern Christians and acknowledged them as fellow Christians while profoundly disagreeing with them about their belief that Jesus had two distinct natures, one human, one divine. Like other Roman Catholics, and unlike Eastern Christians, William believed that Jesus had a single nature and that Mary was Jesus's mother. William gradually realized that the Mongols saw no contradiction between worshiping their traditional deities and praying to the Christian God.

shamans
Mongol religious specialists who contacted deities by burning bones and interpreting the cracks to determine the gods' wills.

Environmental Threats to the Grasslands of Mongolia and Inner Mongolia

Like many regions in the world, the original Mongol grasslands, now divided between Mongolia and Inner Mongolia, have experienced climate change in recent decades. In Mongolia, the winter of 2010 was particularly bad, with about 17 percent of all cattle, horses, goats, and sheep dying. From the 1920s to 1990, Mongolia, sometimes called Outer Mongolia, was a satellite state dependent on the Soviet Union, and the Communist government limited the size of herds. Since then, the democratic government has lifted all those restrictions, with the result that the number of animals has increased four times.

Until recently the average ratio in most herds was four sheep to one goat, but the demand for cashmere in recent years has reversed this, with goats now outnumbering sheep. Goats do great damage to the grasslands because they eat young shoots of grass before they can grow to maturity and their sharp hoofs tear the web of grasses keeping the topsoil in place. The result? The increasing desertification of the grasslands.

Mining, particularly strip mining, poses an equally real threat to the grasslands. Both Mongolia and Inner Mongolia, part of the People's Republic of China, have considerable coal reserves, which are of increasing importance as the world's demand for energy grows. Inner Mongolia is home to 24 million people, including 4.9 million Mongols, who do not always get along with the majority Chinese population. In May 2011, widespread protests broke out in Inner Mongolia when employees of Chinese state mining companies, in two separate and widely publicized incidents, killed two Mongol herdsmen. Both were protesting the destruction to the environment brought by strip mining.

In Mongolia, one-third of the population, or nearly 1 million Mongols, make their living by herding, yet mining occupies a growing share of the economy. The government retains a minority stake in each foreign-owned company. In 2011, the Mongolian government granted three foreign mining companies (from Russia, China, and the United States) the right to mine at Tavan Tolgoi, a mine estimated to hold 3 percent of the world's total coal reserves. In an effort to prevent conflict between Mongols and the mining companies, the government issued shares in Tavan Tolgoi to each of its citizens. An unintended result of shared ownership may be better protection for the environment.

Sources: Articles from different newspapers accessed via LexisNexis, particularly "Times Topics: Mongolia" in the *New York Times* database.

Mongol Society

Mongol society had two basic levels: ordinary Mongols and the families of the chiefs. The chief's sons and grandsons formed a privileged group from which all future rulers were chosen. Differences in wealth certainly existed, with some men having larger herds or better clothes than others, but no rigid social divisions or inherited ranks separated ordinary Mongols. Below them in rank, however, were slaves, who had often been captured in battle. The chiefs periodically collected a 1 percent tax simply by taking one of every hundred animals. Unlike sedentary peoples, who collected taxes once a year (usually in the fall after the harvest was in), Mongol chiefs imposed the tax whenever they chose.

The Mongols lived in felt tents that could be put up and dismantled rapidly. While the men led their herds to new grazing areas, the women packed up their households and organized the pitching of tents at the new campsite. William described the Mongols' traditional division of labor:

It is the women's task to drive the wagons, to load the dwellings on them and to unload again, to milk the cows, to make butter and curd cheese, and to dress the skins and stitch them together, which they do with a thread made from sinew. . . . They never wash clothes, for they claim that this makes God angry and that if they were hung out to dry it would thunder. . . .

The men make bows and arrows, manufacture stirrups and bits, fashion saddles, construct the dwellings and the wagons, tend the horses and milk the mares, churn the khumis (that is, the fermented mare's milk), produce the skins in which it is stored and tend and load the camels. Both sexes tend the sheep and goats, and they are milked on some occasions by the men, on others by the women.*

Because Mongol women ran their households when their menfolk were away and often sat at their husbands' side during meetings, they had much more decision-making power than women in sedentary societies, William realized. Living in close proximity to their animals, the Mongols used the products of their own herds whenever possible: they made their tents from felt, wore clothes of skins and wool, ate meat and cheese, and drank fermented horse's milk, or khumis. William describes his first reaction to this drink with unusual frankness: *"on swallowing it I broke out in a sweat all over from alarm and surprise, since I had never drunk it before. But for all that I found it very palatable, as indeed it is."*

The Mongols, however, could not obtain everything they needed from their herds and depended on their agricultural neighbors to provide grain, which they valued as a supplement to their monotonous diet. The Mongols also relied on settled peoples to obtain the silks and cottons that were so much softer and lighter than the Mongols' rough wool and felt. Although they could make do, if necessary, without grain, tea, or textiles, they required metal trade items like the knives, daggers, and spears used in hunting and war.

Before 1200, an uneasy peace prevailed among the Mongols and their neighbors. Individual Mongol groups might occasionally plunder a farming community, but they never expanded outside their traditional homelands. Under the powerful leadership of Chinggis Khan, all that changed.

The Rise of Chinggis Khan

Sometime around 1167, *The Origin of Chinggis Khan* reports, a chieftain of a small Mongol tribe and his wife gave birth to a son they named Temüjin, the future Chinggis Khan. When he was nine, a rival poisoned his father, and his widowed mother and her children were able to eke out a living only by grazing a small herd of nine horses and eating wild plants.

Difficult as it was for his mother, his father's untimely death brought Temüjin some advantages. Though only a teenager, Temüjin skillfully forged alliances with other leaders and began defeating other tribes. He eventually formed a confederation of all the peoples in the grasslands of modern Mongolia. In 1206, the Mongols awarded the thirty-nine-year-old Temüjin the title of universal ruler: Chinggis (literally "oceanic") Khan ("ruler").

*From Peter Jackson, *The Mission of Friar William Rubruck*, The Hakluyt Society, 1990, pp. 90–91, 99. Reprinted with permission. The Hakluyt Society was established in 1846 for the purpose of printing rare or unpublished Voyages and Travels. For further information please see their website at: www.hakluyt.com.

tanistry
Process the Mongols used to choose a new leader. Under tanistry, all contenders for power had to prove their ability to lead by defeating their rivals in battle.

khuriltai
Name of the Mongols' assembly that gathered to acclaim the new leader after he had defeated his rivals. Not an electoral body.

The Mongols used a political process called **tanistry** to choose a new leader. Its basic rule was that the most qualified member of the chief's family led the tribe.[1] In practice, each time a chief died or was killed by a challenger, all contenders for power fought to defeat their rivals in battle. When one warrior emerged victorious, the Mongols gathered at an assembly, or **khuriltai**, to acclaim the new leader. When this leader died, the destabilizing and bloody selection process began again.

Conquests Under Chinggis

Once he had united the Mongols, Chinggis weakened their group loyalties by dividing all his soldiers into units that crossed group lines. Each soldier belonged to four units: a unit of ten was part of a unit of one hundred, within a larger unit of one thousand, which finally belonged to one of ten thousand men. All able-bodied men between the ages of fifteen and seventy fought in the army, and women did so if necessary. Scholars estimate the total population of the Mongols at 1 million, far less than the populations of the lands they conquered and governed. Numbering only one hundred thousand in 1206, the Mongol forces reached several hundred thousand at the height of Chinggis's power in the 1220s.

The Mongols started with only one significant advantage over the European and Asian powers they conquered: horses. Their grassy homeland provided them with an unending supply of horses, and, because Mongol children were raised on

European Misconceptions about Cannibalism among the Mongols This marginal illustration in the writings of a European critic shows a seated Mongol roasting a human captive on a spit. To the left, one warrior chomps on a severed human leg as his comrade chops off a victim's head. This demonization of the Mongols as cannibals runs counter to the account of the most reliable eyewitnesses, including William of Rubruck, who saw no evidence "that the Mongols ate human flesh." What did William say about the Mongols' diet? (Masters and Fellows of Corpus Christi College, Cambridge, MS 16, fol. 166r)

horseback, they matured into highly skilled riders who could shoot from horseback with their compound bows of wood, horn, and sinew. The Mongols had so many horses that they could change their mounts three times a day, and they frequently put dummies on riderless horses to make their army look larger.

The overriding goal of the Mongol armies was to conquer territory as quickly as possible. It was much cheaper and faster, the Mongols realized, to take a city whose occupants surrendered without a fight than to lay siege to a walled, medieval settlement that could take months to fall. The Mongols placed captives on their front lines to be killed by their own countrymen, in the hope that the rulers of the cities on their path would surrender. If the enemy submitted voluntarily, the Mongols promised not to destroy their homes.

Mongol traditions held that Chinggis Khan could command the total obedience of his warriors in wartime but not in peacetime. Accordingly, he had good reason to keep conquering new territory. In war, the Mongols viewed all plunder as their due, but they limited their plunder to one-tenth of all the enemy's movable property if the enemy submitted voluntarily. Because the ruler shared the spoils with his men whenever he conquered a city, his followers had a strong incentive to follow him, and the ruler had no reason to stop fighting. Under Chinggis's leadership, the Mongols built one of the most effective fighting forces the world had ever seen.

At first Chinggis led his troops into north China, which was under the rule of the Jin dynasty (see Chapter 12), and conquered the important city of Beijing in 1215. In 1219, Chinggis turned his attention to Transoxiana, the region between the Amu Darya and Syr Darya Rivers, then under the rule of the Islamic Khwarazmian empire. In rapid succession the Mongols conquered the region's glorious cities (see the map on page 371). The Persian historian Juvaini (1226–1283) quotes an eyewitness: *"They came, they sapped, they burnt, they slew, they plundered, and they departed."*

Mongol Governance

After conquering Bukhara, Chinggis summoned all the local notables to explain how the new regime would work. He appointed one man, usually a Mongol, to be governor, or **darughachi** (dah-roo-GAH-chee), of the conquered region. The darughachi's main responsibility was to collect the required taxes. The darughachi were free to try different types of taxes in the various parts of the empire, as long as they produced sufficient revenue. The Mongols continued to levy irregular taxes, like their traditional 1 percent tax on herds, in addition to taxes on agriculture, and in many locations they also instituted a 5 percent tax on commercial transactions. Since the Mongols allowed the local governments to rule as they had before the conquest, the darughachi closely resembled the satraps of the Persian empire (see Chapter 6).

The Mongols reserved the highest positions in the occupying government, such as the darughachi, for Mongols. Above the darughachi were the khan and his kin, who did not hold official titles but made all the major decisions affecting the empire. Conquered peoples staffed the lower branches of government and were permitted to continue their own religious practices. Religious institutions did not have to pay taxes. The Mongols' willingness to leave much of the local government and customs intact meant that they could conquer enormous swaths of territory quickly without having to leave behind a large occupying force to rule the conquered lands.

darughachi
Regional governor appointed by the Mongols to administer the region and to collect taxes after they had conquered a new territory.

*Ata-Malik Juvaini, *Genghis Khan: The History of the World Conqueror,* trans. J. A. Boyle (Seattle: University of Washington Press, 1958), p. 107.

The United Mongol Empire After Chinggis, 1229–1260

When Chinggis Khan died in 1227, no one knew whether his empire would survive him. From 1229 to 1260, the Mongols remained united but were led by different rulers (see the chart "Mongol Rulers, 1206–1260"). They continued their conquests and took eastern Europe and northern China. During this time, they also introduced important innovations, such as the postal relay system, and began work on the Mongol capital at Khara Khorum. The postal relay system, the requirements for receiving envoys, and the court-financed merchant networks were the only institutions holding the different parts of the far-flung Mongol empire together, as William of Rubruck discovered when he traveled to Khara Khorum in the 1250s. His trip exemplifies the ease of movement across Eurasia and the cultural exchanges that resulted from the Mongol conquest.

The Reign of Ögödei, 1229–1241

Before he died, Chinggis had divided his entire realm into four sections, each for one of his sons. If the Mongols had followed the traditional election process, the succession dispute could have been protracted. Instead, at a khuriltai held two years after Chinggis's death, they acquiesced to Chinggis's request that his third son, Ögödei (r. 1229–1241), govern all four sections of the Mongols' realm.

In the 1230s, the Mongols attacked Russia repeatedly and subdued the Russian principalities (see Chapter 10). With nothing now standing between the Mongols and Europe, western European rulers, including the king of France and the pope, belatedly realized how vulnerable they were to Mongol attack. Until then, they had been preoccupied with taking back Jerusalem. Ignorantly assuming that any enemy of Islam had to be Christian and so a natural ally of theirs, the Europeans hoped to enlist the Mongols in the Crusades. Each European envoy returned with the same report: the Mongols demanded that the Europeans submit to them and give up one-tenth of all their wealth. The Europeans refused. In 1241–1242, the Mongols attacked Poland and crossed the Danube, advancing to within a few miles of Vienna, Austria.

There, on the brink of overrunning western Europe, the Mongols suddenly halted. News of Ögödei's death had reached the troops, and according to custom, all the warriors returned home to attend the khuriltai. Unable to choose a new leader quickly from among the brothers, sons, and nephews of Chinggis Khan, the Mongols never returned to eastern Europe, and the western European powers were spared invasion.

The Postal Relay System

postal relay system Mongol institution of fixed routes with regular stops where messengers could eat and get fresh mounts, which functioned as the central nervous system of the sprawling empire.

The warriors in Europe learned of Ögödei's death fairly quickly because of the **postal relay system**, which took shape during his reign and which allowed the ruler to communicate with officials in the furthest regions of the Mongol empire. The Mongols established fixed routes, with regular stops every 30 or so miles (50 km) at which messengers could eat and get fresh mounts. Official messengers carried a silver or bronze tablet of authority that entitled them to food and fresh horses. Because the riders could cover some 60 miles (100 km) a day, the relay system functioned as the central nervous system of the sprawling empire. The Mongols also used the postal relay stations to provide visiting envoys with escorts, food, and shelter and, most important, to guarantee their safe return.

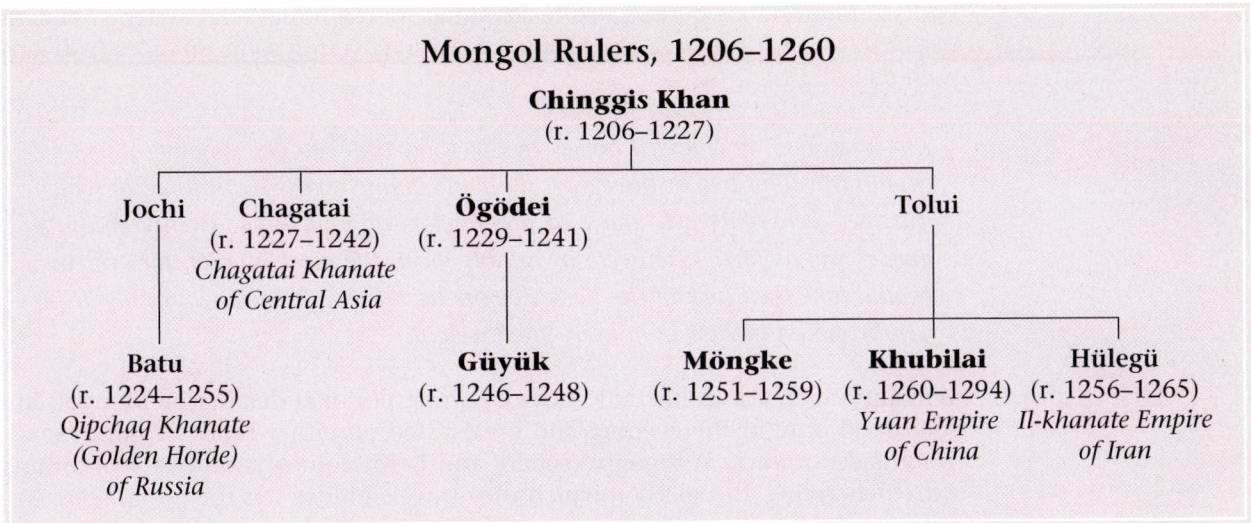

Mongol Rulers, 1206–1260

Chinggis Khan
(r. 1206–1227)

Jochi   **Chagatai**   **Ögödei**   Tolui
          (r. 1227–1242)   (r. 1229–1241)
          Chagatai Khanate
          of Central Asia

Batu   **Güyük**   **Möngke**   **Khubilai**   **Hülegü**
(r. 1224–1255)   (r. 1246–1248)   (r. 1251–1259)   (r. 1260–1294)   (r. 1256–1265)
Qipchaq Khanate   *Yuan Empire*   *Il-khanate Empire*
(Golden Horde)   *of China*   *of Iran*
of Russia

William of Rubruck began his journey in 1253, two years after the Mongols had finally settled on Möngke, one of Chinggis Khan's grandsons, as Ögödei's successor. William wore a brown robe and went barefoot because he was a Franciscan friar-missionary, not a diplomat. Just before he entered Mongol territory, however, he learned that if he denied he was an envoy, he might lose his safe-conduct guarantee and the right to provisions and travel assistance. He decided to accept the privileges granted to envoys.

The system for receiving envoys functioned well but not flawlessly, as William discovered. When he crossed the Don River, local people refused to help. To his dismay William found that the money he brought from Europe was useless: in one village, no one would sell him food or animals. After three difficult days, William's party once again received the mounts to which they were entitled. For two months, William reported, he and his compatriots *"never slept in a house or a tent, but always in the open air or underneath our wagons."*

On July 31, 1253, they arrived at the court of Sartakh, a great-grandson of Chinggis. Earlier envoys had reported that Sartakh was an observant Christian, and William hoped that Sartakh would permit him to stay. In his quest to obtain permission to preach, William personally experienced the decision-making structure of the Mongol government. Sartakh said that, to preach, William needed the approval of Sartakh's father, Batu, a grandson of Chinggis Khan who ruled the western section of the empire. When William asked Batu, Batu in turn decided that William needed the approval of the highest ruler of all, Möngke, before he could preach among the Mongols. Rather than write and ask permission, each ruler chose to send William in person to see his superior, a sign of the empire's decentralized nature.

William and his companion Bartholomew departed for Khara Khorum with a Mongol escort who told them: *"I am to take you to Möngke Khan. It is a four month journey, and the cold there is so intense that rocks and trees split apart with the frost: see whether you can bear it."* He provided them each with a sheepskin coat, trousers, felt

---

*From Peter Jackson, *The Mission of Friar William Rubruck*, The Hakluyt Society, 1990, pp. 99, 136. Reprinted with permission. The Hakluyt Society was established in 1846 for the purpose of printing rare or unpublished Voyages and Travels. For further information please see their website at: www.hakluyt.com.

boots, and fur hoods. At last, taking advantage of the postal relay system, William began to travel at the pace of a Mongol warrior, covering some 60 miles (100 km) each day:

> *On occasions we changed horses two or three times in one day; on others we would travel for two or three days without coming across habitation, in which case we were obliged to move at a gentler pace. Out of the twenty or thirty horses we, as foreigners, were invariably given the most inferior, for everyone would take their pick of the horses before us; though I was always provided a strong mount in view of my very great weight.*

William's reference to his bulk provides a rare personal detail. The Mongols ate solid food only in the evening and breakfasted on either broth or millet soup. They had no lunch. Although William and Bartholomew found the conditions extremely trying, the speed at which they traveled illustrates the postal relay system's crucial role in sending messages to officials and orders to the armies throughout the Mongol empire.

At Möngke's Court

On December 27, 1253, William arrived at the winter court of Möngke on the River Ongin in modern Mongolia, where the ruler and his retinue pitched their tents and where their herds stayed with them. On January 4, 1254, the two Franciscans entered Möngke's tent, whose interior was covered with gold cloth. Möngke *"was sitting on a couch, dressed in a fur which was spotted and very glossy like a sealskin. He is snub-nosed, a man of medium build, and aged about forty-five."* William asked Möngke for permission to preach in his territory. When his interpreter began to explain the khan's reply, William *"was unable to grasp a single complete sentence."* To his dismay, he realized that Möngke and the interpreter were both drunk.

His interpreter later informed him that he had been granted permission to stay two months, and William ended up staying three months at Möngke's court and another three at the capital of Khara Khorum, where he arrived in the spring of 1254. Khara Khorum was home to a small but genuinely international group of foreigners, who introduced important innovations from their home societies to the Mongols. There, William met a French goldsmith named William. Captured in Hungary and technically a slave, the goldsmith worked for Möngke, who paid him a large amount for each project he completed. The goldsmith made an elaborate drinking fountain that dispensed khumis, honey wine, grape wine, and rice ale. This fountain illustrates the many cultural exchanges of the time: the technology was French, while the drinks were both European and Mongol. Although they had originally come as captives and were not free to go home, these Europeans possessed valuable skills and enjoyed a much higher standard of living than the typical Mongol warrior.

Whenever the Mongols conquered a new city, they first identified all the skilled workers and divided them into two groups: siege-warfare engineers and skilled craftsmen. The engineers made catapults to propel large stones that cracked holes in city walls, and Chinese and Jurchen experts taught the Mongols how to

---

*From Peter Jackson, *The Mission of Friar William Rubruck*, The Hakluyt Society, 1990, pp. 140, 178, 180. Reprinted with permission. The Hakluyt Society was established in 1846 for the purpose of printing rare or unpublished Voyages and Travels. For further information please see their website at: www.hakluyt.com.

National Palace Museum, Taipei, Taiwan/The Bridgeman Art Library

A Mongol Hunting Party as Seen by a Chinese Artist In painting the hunting party of Khubilai Khan, the Chinese artist Liu Guandao rendered the horses' different stances and the varied facial features of the retainers in exquisite detail. Note the different animals the Mongols, but not the Chinese, used for hunting: a greyhound dog to the right of the khan and a cheetah, prized for its speed, on the saddle of the lowermost horse. The archer (*far left*) leans backward to shoot a bird flying high above in the sky; the skills the Mongols developed while hunting were directly transferable to warfare.

use gunpowder (see Chapter 12). Mongol commanders sent all the other skilled craftsmen to help build Khara Khorum. The Mongols' willingness to learn from their captives prompted extensive cultural exchange.

Some historians have coined the term *Pax Mongolica* (literally "Mongolian peace") for the period of Mongol unity; they are consciously invoking the precedent of Pax Romana, the peaceful first two centuries of the Roman Republic when travel throughout the Mediterranean facilitated the spread of Christianity (see Chapter 7). The period of Mongol unity differed in an important way, though. As the American historian of the Mongols, Thomas Allsen, has so aptly put it, "The peoples of the steppe were not a premodern equivalent of the United Parcel Service, disinterestedly conveying wares hither and yon between the centers of civilization."* Ideas, goods, and people did not flow freely across the grasslands: playing a crucial role as a filter, the Mongols determined what moved across the Eurasian steppe.

---

*Thomas Allsen, *Commodity and Exchange in the Mongol Empire: A Cultural History of Islamic Textiles* (New York: Cambridge University Press, 1997), p. 106.

Since the Mongols needed the help of siege engineers and metallurgists, they brought captives with those skills to their capital, where Rubruck met them. He also encountered astronomers who could *"foretell the eclipse of the sun and moon,"* a particularly valuable skill since the Mongols retreated indoors until an eclipse had ended. The Mongols also collected maps and geographic works about any of the places they conquered, because knowledge of local geography allowed them to obtain control faster.

The Mongol rulers designated a group of Central Asian merchants as their commercial agents, who would convert the Mongols' plunder into money and then travel caravan routes and buy goods the rulers desired. As a nomadic people, the Mongols particularly valued textiles because they could be transported easily. Instead of a fixed salary, rulers gave their followers suits of clothes at regular intervals. The Mongols had two types of tents: their traditional felt tents held up with poles on the interior and new-style tents with guy ropes on the outside. Both could be very large, holding as many as a thousand people, and could be lined with thousands of yards of lavishly patterned silks.

Illustrating the Mongols' tolerance for and interest in other religious beliefs, Möngke invited William to debate with Eastern Christian, Muslim, and Buddhist representatives at court. The French goldsmith generously offered his bilingual son as a replacement for William's incompetent interpreter. William accepted the invitation and so participated in a rare documented encounter among clergy of different faiths. Yet on the one occasion he had a competent interpreter, even William realized that he made no converts in the debate. (See the feature "Movement of Ideas Through Primary Sources: A Debate Among Christians, Buddhists, and Muslims at the Mongol Court.")

After his months in Khara Khorum, William returned to Acre, in the Holy Land, and then proceeded to France, where, in 1257, he met Roger Bacon (ca. 1214–1294), who preserved William's letter. After 1257, William disappears from the historical record, leaving the date of his death uncertain.

William's lack of success as a missionary is confirmed by one contemporary: in 1259, the king of Armenia, Hetum I (1226–1269), reported what the Mongols had told him about William. When William *"appeared before the great king of the Tartars [Batu], he began to press on him the Christian faith, saying that the Tartar—and every infidel—would perish eternally and be condemned to everlasting fire."*

William might have been more successful, the Mongol ruler Batu wryly commented, if he had tried to persuade the Mongols of the benefits of being a Christian, rather than threatening them with "everlasting punishment." The Armenian king's report provides crucial evidence confirming William's trip.

The Empire Comes Apart, 1259–1263

William's letter to his monarch reveals that only the postal relay stations bound the different parts of the Mongol empire together. The Mongols granted the darughachi governors wide latitude in governing, and they never developed an empire-wide bureaucracy. Officials from one part of the empire were not transferred to other regions, and they did not implement uniform standards and policies.

---

*From Peter Jackson, *The Mission of Friar William Rubruck*, The Hakluyt Society, 1990, p. 240 and Appendix V, p. 282. Reprinted with permission. The Hakluyt Society was established in 1846 for the purpose of printing rare or unpublished Voyages and Travels. For further information please see their website at: www.hakluyt.com.

Because the Mongols allowed the darughachi governors to use the local language for administration and the recruitment of local officials, Chinese, Persian, and Turkish continued to be spoken throughout the empire. The Mongols did not impose Mongolian as the language of administration. During William's trip, the different sections of the empire continued to forward some taxes to the center, but the empire broke apart after Möngke's death in 1259.

A year earlier, Möngke's brother Hülegü had led the Mongols on one of the bloodiest campaigns in their history, the conquest of Baghdad, in which some eight hundred thousand people died. Hülegü also ordered the execution of the caliph and so, in 1258, put a final end to the Abbasid caliphate, founded in 750 (see Chapter 9). In 1260, the Mamluk dynasty of Egypt defeated the remnants of Hülegü's army in Syria at the battle of Ayn Jalut (see Chapter 11).

This defeat was the first time the Mongols had lost a battle and also marked the end of a united Mongol empire. One khuriltai named Möngke's brother Khubilai (KOO-bih-leye) (d. 1294) the rightful successor, while a rival khuriltai named his brother Arigh Boke (d. 1264) the new khan. After 1260, it was impossible to maintain any pretense of imperial unity.

Another setback occurred in 1263, when the ruler of the Qipchaq (KIP-chack) khanate in Russia actively sought an alliance with the Mamluks against his cousin Hülegü in Iran. Never before had a Mongol allied with a non-Mongol force against another Mongol leader, and the alliance provides a clear date for the end of the unified Mongol empire.

Successor States in Western Asia, 1263–1500

After this breakup the Mongol empire divided into four sections, each ruled by a different Mongol prince (see Map 14.1 on page 386). The eastern sector consisted of the Mongolian heartland and China (discussed later in this chapter). In the western sectors, each time a ruler died his living sons divided his territory, and succession disputes were common. Three important realms dominated the western sector: the Il-khanate in Iran; the Qipchaq khanate or Golden Horde, north of the Black, Caspian, and Aral Seas; and the Chaghatai khanate in Central Asia. None of these khanates built an empire as large as the earlier Mongols had, and border disputes often prompted war among the three realms. The Mongol tradition of learning from other peoples continued as each of the three ruling families converted to Islam, the religion of their most educated subjects.

The Il-khanate, the Qipchaq Khanate, and the Rise of Moscow

Since the Mongols had conquered Iran in 1258, only two years before the empire broke apart in 1260, they were not well established there. Hülegü took the title *il-khan* ("subordinate khan" in Persian) to indicate that he was lower in rank than his brother Möngke; he ruled the **Il-khanate** (1256–1335). Like his brother Möngke, Hülegü was primarily a believer in shamanism. Five of Hülegü's sons and grandsons ruled Iran between 1265 and 1295. They allowed Muslims, Buddhists, and Eastern Christians to continue to worship their own belief systems. When Hülegü's great-grandson Ghazan (r. 1295–1304) took the throne in 1295, he announced his conversion to Islam, the religion of most of his subjects, and his fellow Mongols followed suit.

Il-khanate
Mongol government of the region of Iran (1256–1335), founded by Hülegü, who took the title *il-khan* ("subordinate khan" in Persian) to indicate that he was lower in rank than his brother Möngke.

A Debate Among Christians, Buddhists, and Muslims at the Mongol Court

In May 1254, Möngke sent word to William that, before departing, the Christians, Muslims, and Buddhists should meet and debate religious teachings, since Möngke hoped to "learn the truth." William agreed to participate, and he and the Eastern Christians, whom William called Nestorians, had a practice session in which he even took the part of an imaginary Buddhist opponent. On the appointed day, Möngke sent three of his secretaries—a Christian, a Muslim, and a Buddhist—to be the judges.

Since William's report is the only record that survives, historians cannot compare it with other descriptions of what happened. It is possible, for example, that he exaggerated his own role in the debate or misunderstood the arguments of his opponents.

The debate began with William arguing points with a Chinese Buddhist, whom William identifies by the Mongolian word *tuin* (TWUN). Like the Crusaders, William refers to the Muslims as Saracens and reports that they said little.

Source: From Peter Jackson, *The Mission of Friar William Rubruck*, The Hakluyt Society, 1990, pp. 231–235. Reprinted with permission. The Hakluyt Society was established in 1846 for the purpose of printing rare or unpublished Voyages and Travels. For further information please see their website at: *www.hakluyt.com*.

The Christians then placed me in the middle and told the *tuins* to address me; and the latter, who were there in considerable numbers, began to murmur against Möngke Khan, since no Khan had ever attempted to probe their secrets. They confronted me with someone who had come from Cataia [China]: he had his own interpreter, while I had Master William's son.

He began by saying to me, "Friend, if you are brought to a halt, you may look for a wiser man than yourself."

I did not reply.

Next he enquired what I wanted to debate first: either how the world had been made, or what becomes of souls after death.

"Friend," I answered, "that ought not to be the starting-point of our discussion. All things are from God, and He is the fountainhead of all. Therefore we should begin by speaking about God, for you hold a different view of Him from us and Möngke wishes to learn whose belief is superior." The umpires ruled that this was fair.

They wanted to begin with the issues I have mentioned because they regard them as more important. All of them belong to the Manichaean heresy, to the effect that one half of things is evil and the other half good, or at least that there are two principles; and as regards souls, they all believe that they pass from one body to another.

Even one of the wiser of the Nestorian priests asked me whether it was possible for the souls of animals to escape after death to any place where they would not be compelled to suffer. In support of this fallacy, moreover, so Master William told me, a boy was brought from Cataia [China], who to judge by his physical size was not three years old, yet was fully capable of rational thought: he said of himself that he was in his third incarnation, and he knew how to read and write.

I said, then, to the *tuin*: "We firmly believe in our hearts and acknowledge with our lips that God exists, that there is only one God, and that He is one in perfect unity. What do you believe?"

"It is fools," he said, "who claim there is only one God. Wise men say that there are several. Are there not great rulers in your country, and is not Möngke Khan the chief lord here? It is the same with gods, inasmuch as there are different gods in different regions."

"You choose a bad example," I told him, "in drawing a parallel between men and God: that way any powerful figure could be called a god in his own dominions."

But as I was seeking to demolish the analogy, he distracted me by asking, "What is your God like, of Whom you claim that there is no other?"

"Our God," I replied, "beside Whom there is no other, is all-powerful and therefore needs assistance from no one; in fact we all stand in need of His. With men it is not so: no man is capable of all things, and for this reason there have to be a number of rulers on earth, since no one has the power to undertake the whole. Again, He is all-knowing and therefore needs no one as counsellor: in fact all wisdom is from Him. And again He is the supreme Good and has no need of our goods: rather, 'in Him we live and move and are.' This is the nature of our God, and it is unnecessary, therefore, to postulate any other."

"That is not so," he declared. "On the contrary, there is one supreme god in Heaven, of whose origin we are still ignorant, with ten others under him and one of the lowest rank beneath them; while on earth they are without number."

As he was about to spin yet more yarns, I asked about this supreme god: did he believe he was all-powerful, or was some other god?

He was afraid to answer, and asked: "If your God is as you say, why has He made half of things evil?"

"That is an error," I said. "It is not God who created evil. Everything that exists is good." All the *tuins* were amazed at this statement and recorded it in writing as something erroneous and impossible. . . .

He sat for a long while reluctant to answer, with the result that the secretaries who were listening on the Khan's behalf had to order him to reply. Finally he gave the answer that no god was all-powerful, at which all the Saracens burst into loud laughter. When silence was restored I said: "So, then, not one of your gods is capable of rescuing you in every danger, inasmuch as a predicament may be met with where he does not have the power. Further, 'no man can serve two masters': so how is it that you can serve so many gods in Heaven and on earth?" The audience told him to reply; yet he remained speechless. But when I was seeking to put forward arguments for the unity of the Divine essence and for the Trinity while everyone was listening, the local Nestorians told me it was enough, as they wanted to speak themselves.

At this point I made way for them [the Eastern Christians]. But when they sought to argue with the Saracens, the latter replied: "We concede that your religion is true and that everything in the Gospel is true; and therefore we have no wish to debate any issue with you." And they admitted that in all their prayers they beg God that they may die a Christian death. . . .

Everybody listened without challenging a single word. But for all that no one said, "I believe, and wish to become a Christian." When it was all over, the Nestorians and Saracens alike sang in loud voices, while the *tuins* remained silent; and after that everyone drank heavily.

QUESTIONS FOR ANALYSIS

» *What is William's main point?*

» *How does William present the main teachings of Buddhism? Of Islam?*

» *In William's account of the debate, does anyone say anything that you think they probably did not? Support your position with specific examples.*

MAP 14.1 The Four Quadrants of the Mongol Empire After 1263 The first three Mongol rulers had governed the largest contiguous land empire in world history. But the Mongols were unable to choose a single successor to Möngke, the grandson of Chinggis Khan, who died in 1259. The empire broke into four quadrants, each governed by a different member of the founder's family. (© Cengage Learning)

Mongol domains, ca. 1300

- Qipchaq Khanate
- Vassal state of Qipchaq Khanate
- Il-Khanate
- Vassal state of Il-Khanate
- Chaghatai Khanate
- Vassal state of Chaghatai Khanate
- Yuan dynasty
- Vassal state of Yuan dynasty
- Mongol campaigns

The Il-khanate never succeeded in establishing an efficient way to tax Iran. Infamous for collecting taxes twenty or more times a year, officials frequently resorted to force to get Iran's cultivators to pay. The end result was severe impoverishment of the countryside, which had already been devastated in the 1250s during the Mongol invasions. The Il-khanate had regular contact with the Yuan dynasty in China (covered later in this chapter), and in the 1290s the government introduced paper money (using the Chinese word for it). The paper money failed completely, bringing commerce to a standstill, but the experiment testifies to the Il-khanate's willingness to borrow from neighboring peoples. The Il-khanate ended in 1335 when the last of Hülegü's descendants died, and Iran broke up into many small regions.

To the north, in the Qipchaq khanate, individual rulers converted to Islam as early as the 1250s, but Islam became the official religion only during the reign of Muhammad Özbeg (r. 1313–1341). The Qipchaq ruled the lower and middle Volga River Valley, the home of the Bulgars, who had converted to Islam in the tenth century. Many Qipchaq subjects in Russian cities to the north and west continued to belong to the Eastern Orthodox Church.

Before the Mongols conquered the region in the 1230s, the descendants of Prince Vladimir of Kiev had governed the various Rus principalities (see Chapter 10). Unable to mount a successful defense against the Mongols, the different Russian princes surrendered. At the beginning of the Mongol era, Kiev had been the most important city in Russia, but the conquests devastated the city, prompting many to move to other places.

The **principality of Muscovy** (Moscow) eventually emerged as Kiev's successor, partially because the rulers of Moscow were frequently better able to pay their share of tribute and so were favored by the Qipchaq khanate. **Ivan III** (r. 1462–1505) defeated other Russian families to become the undisputed leader of the region; in 1480 he stopped submitting tribute to the Qipchaq khanate, and in 1502 he brought the khanate to an end. Ivan III controlled large chunks of modern-day Russia: from the Black Sea in the south to Novgorod in the north and much of modern-day Poland.

principality of Muscovy
Successor to the Qipchaq khanate in modern-day Russia.

Ivan III
(r. 1462–1505) Muscovy's most important leader, who overthrew the Qipchaq khanate in 1502.

The Chaghatai Khanate and Timur the Lame

Straddling the Amu Darya and Syr Darya River Valleys, the Chaghatai khanate included the eastern grasslands in what is now modern Mongolia and a western half that included the great Silk Road cities of Bukhara and Samarkand. In the grasslands to the east, the Mongols could follow their traditional nomadic way of life, and different chieftains continued to rule this region after the breakup of the empire.

Starting around 1350, a Turkish-speaking leader of Mongol descent took power in Samarkand and the western section of the Chaghatai khanate. This leader, known to his Persian enemies as **Timur the Lame** (ca. 1336–1405), contracted to *Tamerlane* in English, succeeded in forming a powerful confederation and conquered much of modern Iran, Uzbekistan, Afghanistan, north India, and the Anatolian region of Turkey. He married a descendant of Chinggis Khan, so that he could claim to be his successor, and he too used terror to reduce resistance. Timur was famous for setting his enemies on fire or throwing them off cliffs.

Like the Mongols, Timur the Lame forcibly resettled artisans and architects from among the conquered townspeople of India, Iran, and Syria. In his capital of Samarkand, these craftspeople built foreign-influenced buildings with elaborate

Timur the Lame
(ca. 1336–1405) Also known in English as Tamerlane. Successor to the Chaghatai khanate, he conquered much of modern Iran, Uzbekistan, Afghanistan, and the Anatolian region of Turkey.

The Shah-i-Zinda Burial Complex at Samarkand This burial complex, within the city walls of Samarkand, contains structures, built from the 800s to the reign of Timur the Lame in the early 1400s, that show how the use of tiles changed over time. The earliest buildings display patterns made entirely with sand-colored brick. In the next phase, builders combined colored and uncolored bricks in complex mosaics. And in the final phase, the builders used tiles of a single hue to make the brilliantly blue roofs for which Samarkand is so famous. (Robert Harding World Imagery)

mosaic tilework that is still visible today. Samarkand became one of the most beautiful of all Central Asian cities.

Timur died in 1405 as he was preparing to lead his troops into China. Continuing the Mongol legacy of patronizing learning, Timur's grandson Ulugh Beg (1394–1449, r. 1447–1449) built an enormous astronomical observatory and compiled a star chart based on ancient Greek and Islamic learning. Ulugh Beg ruled for only two years before his son ordered him killed and took over as ruler, in keeping with the Mongol tradition of tanistry. Timur's empire soon fragmented because the different members of the royal house, unable to decide on a successor, simply divided it among themselves.

By 1500, almost all the Mongol successor states had ceased to exist in western Asia. The region of Iran had broken into smaller states, as had the territory of the former Chaghatai khanate. Muscovy emerged as the major power in the Volga region, leaving only a small Mongol successor state in the Crimea.

The Ottomans, 1300–1500

In the centuries that saw the fragmentation of the khanates in the west, a new power arose that initially replicated many elements of Mongol rule but then made crucial innovations that allowed it to build an empire that outlasted all the Mongol successor states. The **Ottomans**, a group of Turkic Muslim nomads, first gained control of Anatolia, in modern Turkey, which lay between the eastern edge of the Byzantine empire and the western edge of the Il-khanate. Over time, the Ottomans shifted from an army that fought for plunder to an army that received a fixed salary. Their conquest of Constantinople in 1453 marked the end of the Byzantine empire and the establishment of a major Islamic power in western Asia.

Ottomans
Group of Turkic Muslim nomads who gained control of the Anatolia region in modern Turkey around 1300. Their conquest of Constantinople in 1453 marked the end of the Byzantine empire.

The Rise of the Ottomans, 1300–1400

Even at the height of their power during the thirteenth century, the Mongols sent few troops to Anatolia, which lay on the western edge of their empire. Around 1300 a man named Osman (the origin of the name *Ottoman*) emerged as the leader of a group of nomads who successfully conquered different sections of the Anatolian peninsula.

Few documents survive from this early period, and one of the most important sources about the Ottomans' own religion is Ibn Battuta's journal (see Chapter 11). In 1331, he visited the port city of Bursa, which lay across the Sea of Marmora from Constantinople, on his way to India. Referring to the Ottoman leader Orhan (Osman's son) as "sultan," Ibn Battuta reported that he *"fights the infidels [Byzantium] continually and keeps them under siege."*[*] This is one of the earliest reports of the Muslim beliefs of the Ottomans. Although continuously at war with the Byzantine empire, the Ottomans welcomed local Christians to join them in their fight and did not force them to convert to Islam.

In the 1300s, the Ottomans continued to conquer chunks of the weakened Byzantine empire in Greece, Bulgaria, and the Balkans, but they bypassed Constantinople. By 1400, they became the most powerful group professing loyalty to the Byzantine ruler, who controlled only the city of Constantinople and its immediate environs. The Ottomans could not stand up to the armies of Timur the Lame, but they resumed their conquests after his death in 1405.

As the Ottoman realm expanded, Ottoman rulers began to see themselves as protectors of local society, with Islamic law as their main tool. They paid mosque officials salaries and included them as part of their government bureaucracy. Agriculture thrived under their rule, and they were able to collect high revenues from their agricultural taxes, which they used to build roads for foot soldiers.

The Ottomans enjoyed unusual military success because of their innovative policies. Unlike their enemies, they paid market prices for food and did not simply steal supplies from the local people. As a result, farmers willingly brought their produce to market to sell to the Ottomans.

When the Ottomans captured Christian soldiers, they forced these enslaved prisoners of war to join the army. Called **Janissaries**, many eventually converted to Islam. To prevent the Janissaries from building up large private estates, the Ottomans required them to be celibate so that they would not have descendants. Even so, many local people volunteered their sons for Janissary units because the boys could rise to a much higher position than if they remained on family farms.

Janissaries
(Turkish word meaning "new soldiers") Soldiers of the Ottomans, recruited from conquered Christians and required to be celibate.

[*]H. A. R. Gibb, trans., *The Travels of Ibn Battuta A.D. 1325–1354*, vol. 2 (London: Hakluyt Society, 1958–1994), p. 452.

The Ottomans also took advantage of new weapons using gunpowder. Although the Mongols had used some gunpowder, their most effective troops were mounted cavalry with bows and arrows. Around 1400, however, gunpowder weapons improved noticeably, and the Ottomans demonstrated their command of the new gunpowder technology in the 1453 conquest of Constantinople.

The Ottoman Conquest of Constantinople, 1453

When the Byzantine emperor requested the doubling of an annual subsidy from the Turks, the young Ottoman emperor Mehmed II (r. 1451–1481) decided to end the fiction of Byzantine rule. Mehmed, who is known as **Mehmed the Conqueror**, began construction of a large fort on the western shore of the Bosphorus, just across from Constantinople, and positioned three cannon on the fort's walls where they could hit all ships that entered the harbor to provision the Byzantine troops. (See the feature "Visual Evidence in Primary Sources: The Siege of Constantinople, 1453.")

Eight thousand men on the Byzantine side faced an Ottoman force of some eighty thousand, assisted by a navy of over one hundred ships and armed with powerful cannon that could shoot a ball weighing 1,340 pounds (607 kg). Even so, the walls of Constantinople were so strong that it took two long months before the Ottomans took the city. On the day the city fell, Mehmed II led a small group of guards and advisers to the Hagia Sophia (see page 261), the largest and most striking church in the city, and explained his plans to convert the church into a mosque. Turning many churches into mosques, the Ottomans transformed Constantinople from a Christian into a Muslim city. The official name of the city was Qustantiniyya, "city of Constantine," but its residents referred to it as Istanbul, meaning simply "the city" in Greek.

Under Ottoman rule, the Greek, Slavic, and Turkic peoples living in the region moved to the city, bringing great prosperity. Priding himself on his patronage of learning and art, Mehmed commissioned scholars to copy the ancient Greek classics, to write epic poetry in Italian, and to produce scholarly works in other languages, like Arabic and Persian. Realizing that the state needed educated officials, he established Islamic schools in the different cities of the realm.

The Ottomans consolidated their control of the former Byzantine lands. Although they had started in 1300 as nomadic warriors, by 1500 they had become the undisputed rulers of western Asia, and the salaried Janissary army was much more stable than the Mongol army, which had been propelled by the desire for plunder. Like the Mongols, the Ottomans adopted new technologies from the peoples they conquered.

Mehmed the Conqueror (r. 1451–1481) Leader of the Ottomans who conquered Constantinople in 1453 and patronized scholars from different countries.

East Asia During and After Mongol Rule, 1263–1500

At the time the Mongol empire broke apart in 1260, Chinggis's grandson Khubilai Khan (r. 1260–1294) controlled the traditional homeland of Mongolia as well as north China. Conquering south China, where the wet terrain proved extremely difficult for the Mongol horsemen to traverse, posed a genuine challenge. Only after building a Chinese-style navy did the Mongols succeed in taking south China, but they never conquered Japan or Southeast Asia. The Mongols ruled China for nearly one hundred years until, in 1368, a peasant uprising overthrew them. The cultural exchanges of the Mongols continued to influence Ming dynasty (1368–1644) China, most clearly in the sea voyages of the 1400s.

Converting a Church into a Mosque The Ottomans transformed Hagia Sophia into a mosque by adding four minarets outside the original church building and by clearing a giant hall for prayer inside. They also constructed a traditional Islamic garden, complete with fountain, behind the mosque. (Steve McCurry/Magnum Photos)

The Conquests of Khubilai Khan and Their Limits

Of the Mongol rulers who took over after 1260, **Khubilai Khan** (1215–1294) lived the longest and is the most famous. Suspicious of classical Chinese learning, Khubilai learned to speak some Chinese but not to read Chinese characters. During his administration in China, the Mongols suspended the civil service examinations (see Chapter 12); preferring to appoint officials, they tried to pair a non-Chinese official, either a Mongol or a Central Asian, with each Chinese appointee, though the small number of Mongol officials available made it difficult to do so. In any case, the Mongol administration in China absorbed many local customs. For example, in 1271 Khubilai adopted a Chinese name for his dynasty, the Yuan, meaning "origin."

Khubilai Khan's most significant accomplishment was the conquest of south China, resulting in the unification of north and south China for the first time since the tenth century. Demonstrating a genuine willingness to learn from other peoples, Khubilai Khan commissioned a giant Chinese-style navy that conquered all of south China by 1276. The Mongols became the first non-Chinese people in history to conquer and unify north and south China.

Khubilai Khan (1215–1294) Grandson of Chinggis Khan who became ruler of Mongolia and north China in 1260 and who succeeded in conquering south China in 1276, but not Japan or Vietnam.

The Siege of Constantinople, 1453

Although the fall of Constantinople was one of the major turning points in world history, surprisingly few portrayals of the event survive. One of the most detailed illustrations is from a manuscript describing the travels of Bertrandon de la Broquière (BEAR-trahn-dohn duh lah BROKE-ee-air) (d. 1459) from Dijon, France, to the Ottoman empire in 1432–1433. Traveling on a mission for a French nobleman, Bertrandon hoped to find out whether it was feasible to launch a new crusade to free the Holy Land from Muslim rule. Although he visited Constantinople twenty years before 1453, his book included a picture of the fall, which he must have learned about after his return to France and before his death in 1459.

Bertrandon's *Voyage d'Outremer*, or *Voyage to Outremer*, offered European readers an eyewitness description of the Ottomans' power during the reign of Murad II (r. 1421–1451). The sultan's army impressed Bertrandon because his men ate only small amounts when traveling and rode strong horses. The soldiers' armor was lighter than the armor of the French, and their level of discipline seemed high to Bertrandon.

Bertrandon visited Adrianople (modern-day Edirne, Turkey), where the ambassador of Milan hosted him and took him to court. Here he saw the Ottoman sultan, who, he reported, had four major advisers who had to approve anyone's request to speak in person to the ruler. The painting shows several advisers standing in an ornate tent in the foreground.

Bibliotheque Nationale, Paris/Bridgeman Art Library

This label in medieval French reads, "The headquarters of the Grand Turk with two of his principal advisers; The headquarters of the captain-general of the Turks."

QUESTION FOR ANALYSIS

» *Which different weapons and fighting techniques does the painting portray?*

The artist painted a view of Constantinople, the peninsula of the Golden Horn, from the western shore of the Bosphorus. To protect the city, the Byzantines connected a giant chain (not shown in the painting) across the entrance to the Golden Horn to block the Ottoman warships, but the Ottomans simply transported their ships overland in wooden cradles along metal tracks to just outside the city, where they could fire on the walls. They carried a total of seventy ships, of which the artist shows only a handful, over the 200 foot (61 m) tall hill on the left of the painting. Outside the city the Ottomans arrayed a force of eighty thousand to lay siege; inside the city, a combined force of eight thousand Byzantines and their non-Byzantine allies succeeded in defending the city for two months before it fell.

This painting, though based on secondhand information, is surprisingly accurate. The artist captures the city's vulnerability: on all sides the Ottoman forces gather, while the Byzantines are concentrated in the central walled triangle extending into the Bosphorus. The painting does not convey the noise and confusion of cannon warfare; the scene is sunny and the setting idyllic. But one can easily imagine that all the forces arrayed outside the walls will soon be able to conquer the city.

1

These men are pulling the Ottoman boats on wooden carriages along a metal track to get around the chain blocking water access.

The Byzantines had triremes, or boats with three tiers of rowers, which could row faster than the one- or two-tiered Ottoman boats, but the Ottomans commanded many more ships than the Byzantines.

Bibliotheque Nationale, Paris/Bridgeman Art Library

Ottoman engineers constructed this pontoon bridge so that their armies could get closer to the city walls, where their artillery was more effective.

2

Bibliotheque Nationale, Paris/Bridgeman Art Library

A fishmonger offers fish for sale, a reminder that daily life continued in the city during the two-month-long siege.

3

Bibliotheque Nationale, Paris/Bridgeman Art Library

The headquarters of the Ottomans. An elderly prisoner kneels before an officer.

Like all Mongol armies, Khubilai's generals and soldiers wanted to keep conquering to obtain even more plunder. The Mongols made forays into Korea, Japan, and Vietnam even before 1260, and they continued their attacks under Khubilai's rule.

Of these three places, Korea, under the rule of the Koryo dynasty (936–1392), was the only one to come under direct Mongol rule. In 1231, a Mongol force active in north China invaded, prompting the Korean ruler to surrender. He agreed to disband his army, made heavy payments to the Mongols, and sent five hundred young men, including the crown prince, and five hundred young women as hostages to the Mongol court. Sporadic fighting continued, and the Mongols gained firm control only in 1273. Acknowledging the Mongols as their overlords, the Koryo rulers continued on the throne, but the Mongols forced them to intermarry with Mongol princesses, and the Koreans adopted many Mongol customs.

Once they had subdued Korea and gained control of north and south China, the Mongols tried to invade Japan, then under the rule of the Kamakura (see Chapter 12), in 1274 and 1281. To this end the Mongols forced the Koreans to provide nine hundred ships as well as many soldiers and supplies. Later sources report that a powerful wind destroyed the Mongol ships, an event described to this day by Japanese as *kamikaze* or "divine wind." (In World War II, Japanese fliers who went on suicide missions were called kamikaze pilots.) Contemporary sources do not mention the weather but describe a Mongol force of no more than ten thousand on either occasion being turned back by the fortifications the Japanese had built on their coastline. The costs of repelling the invasion weakened the Kamakura government, which fell in 1333, and Japan began three centuries of divided political rule that would end only in 1600 when the country was reunified.

The Mongols also proved unable to conquer Vietnam, then under the rule of the Tran dynasty (1225–1400). Mongol armies sacked the capital city at Hanoi three times (in 1257, 1284, and 1287), but on each occasion an army staffed by local peoples regained the city and promised to pay tribute to the Mongols, who then retreated.

When Khubilai Khan died in 1294, a new generation of leaders took over, who had grown up in China, spoke and wrote Chinese, and knew little of life on the steppes. The fourth emperor in the Yuan dynasty, Renzong (r. 1312–1321), received the classical education of a Chinese scholar and reinstated the civil service exams in 1315. Under his direction, the Mongols introduced a new Neo-Confucian examination curriculum that tested the candidates' knowledge of Zhu Xi's commentary on *The Four Books* (see Chapter 12) and remained in use until 1905.

After Emperor Renzong's death, the Yuan government entered several decades of decline. The 1330s and 1340s saw outbreaks of disease that caused mass deaths; a single epidemic in 1331 killed one-tenth of the people living in one province. Scholars suspect the Black Death that hit Europe in 1348 may have been responsible, but the Chinese sources do not describe the symptoms of those who died.

Faced with a sharp drop in population and a corresponding decline in revenue, the Yuan dynasty raised taxes, causing a series of peasant rebellions. In 1368, a peasant who had been briefly educated in a monastery led a peasant revolt that succeeded in overthrowing the Yuan dynasty and driving the Mongols back to their homeland, from which they continued to launch attacks on the Chinese. He named his dynasty the Ming, meaning "light" or "bright" (1368–1644).

The First Ming Emperors, 1368–1405

The founder of the **Ming dynasty**, Ming Taizu, prided himself on founding a native Chinese dynasty but in fact continued many Mongol practices. In addition to the core areas ruled earlier by the Northern Song dynasty, the Ming realm included Manchuria, Inner Mongolia, Xinjiang in the northwest, and Tibet, which had all been conquered by the Mongols. The Ming also took over the provincial administrative districts established by the Mongols, which still define modern China.

> **Ming dynasty**
> (1368–1644) A native Chinese dynasty that overthrew the Mongols but continued many of their practices.

When the Ming founder assumed office, he appointed all new officials and suspended the civil service examinations because he was suspicious of Confucian learning. In 1381, realizing how difficult it was to staff the entire central government, he reinstated the examinations with a Confucian curriculum identical to that of the Mongols. Competition for the exams intensified in succeeding centuries, and the ruling elite remained Confucian because of this decision.

Oddly, the Ming founder, the one emperor in Chinese history who was born a peasant, had a conservative vision of China's society and believed that no one could change his or her social position. On conquering China he ordered his officials to survey all the land and record how much each household owned; this was the first complete empire-wide survey since the Tang dynasty. Ming officials assigned each household a category of labor such as agriculture, military service, or salt mining and required that each household contribute a fixed number of days of that type of labor annually. In fact, many people paid others to fulfill their labor obligations.

When the Ming founder died in 1398, he hoped that his grandson would succeed him, but one of the emperor's brothers led an army to the capital and set the imperial palace on fire. The unfortunate new emperor, only twenty-one at the time, probably died in the fire, making it possible for his uncle to name himself the third emperor of the Ming dynasty, or the Yongle emperor (r. 1403–1424).

The Chinese Voyages to South and Southeast Asia and Africa, 1405–1433

Viewed as a usurper his entire life, the Yongle emperor pursued several policies to show that he was the equal of the Ming founder. For example, he ordered all written materials to be copied into a single, enormous set of books called *The Yongle Encyclopedia*. He moved the capital from Nanjing, where many remained sympathetic to the deposed emperor, to Beijing, the former capital of the Mongols. He sent five military expeditions to Mongolia in the hope of vanquishing the Mongols, but none succeeded. The Yongle emperor also launched a series of imperially sponsored voyages to demonstrate the strength of his dynasty to all of China's trading partners.

Chinese geographical knowledge of the world had grown considerably since the mid-twelfth century (see Chapter 12). No maps made under the Mongols survive today, but a Korean map copied around 1470, the Kangnido map, showing heavy Islamic influence, was based on several earlier maps that cartographers combined without paying attention to scale. As a result, Korea is too big, Africa is tiny, and India is missing altogether. Still, this is one of the earliest surviving Chinese maps portraying the world outside China. It includes both the Islamic world

Christopher Columbus

(1451–1506) Explorer who visited European colonies in the Mediterranean, the Atlantic Ocean, and the west coast of Africa before voyaging to the island of Hispaniola in 1492.

At the time of his first voyage to the Americas, Columbus was in his early forties. Born in Genoa, Italy, as a teenager he had sailed on wooden boats to the different settlements of Genoese and Venetian merchants in the Mediterranean. Later, in his thirties, he lived for three years in the Madeira Islands, a Portuguese possession off the African coast in the Atlantic, and visited the Portuguese slave-trading fort at São Jorge da Mina on the west coast of Africa. Madeira, the world's largest sugar producer in 1492, used indigenous peoples from the nearby Canary Islands and African slaves to work on its plantations. While in the Canary Islands, Columbus heard that one could sail west, and, assuming he could reach Asia by doing so, he persuaded the rulers of Spain to finance a trial voyage across the Atlantic in search of the Indies, the source of so many valuable spices. After the first voyage in 1492, he made three more trips to the Americas before his death in 1506.

Unlike voyages the Vikings made to Newfoundland around 1000 and Ming Chinese voyages to East Africa in the 1400s, the Spanish and Portuguese voyages had far-reaching consequences. After 1300, while the Mexica (or Aztec) in Mexico and the Inca in Peru were creating powerful expansionist empires, on the opposite side of the Atlantic Europeans were learning about geography as part of their humanistic studies. Spanish and Portuguese explorers traveled farther and farther, first to the islands of the Mediterranean and the Atlantic, then to the west coast of Africa, and finally to the Americas, always claiming colonies for their monarchs. The Europeans transported plants, animals, and people (often against their will) to entirely new environments on the other side of the Atlantic. Within one hundred years of Columbus's first voyage, millions of Amerindians had perished (the death toll reached 95 percent in some areas), victims of European diseases that no one understood.

Focus Questions

» *How did the Aztec form their empire? How did the Inca form theirs? How did each hold their empire together, and what was each empire's major weakness?*

» *How did humanist scholarship encourage oceanic exploration? What motivated the Portuguese, particularly Prince Henry the Navigator, to explore West Africa?*

» *How did the Spanish and the Portuguese establish their empires in the Americas so quickly?*

» *What was the Columbian exchange? Which elements of the exchange had the greatest impact on the Americas? On Afro-Eurasia?*

The Aztec Empire of Mexico, 1325–1519

Starting sometime around 1325, the Mexica (meh-SHE-kah), a people based in western Mexico, moved into central Mexico to Tenochtitlan (some 30 miles [50 km] northeast of modern-day Mexico City). The Mexica were one of many Nahua (NAH-wah) peoples who spoke the Nahuatl (NAH-waht) language. Like the Maya, the Nahua peoples had a complex calendrical system, built large stone monuments, and played a ritual ball game. The Mexica believed in a pantheon of gods headed by the sun that demanded blood sacrifices from their devotees. To sustain these gods, they continually went to war, gradually conquering many of the city-states in central Mexico to form the **Aztec empire**.

The Mexica Settlement of Tenochtitlan

Though each people tells the story of its past differently, disparate accounts agree that around the 1200s various groups migrated to central Mexico. The heart of this area is the Valley of Mexico, 10,000 feet (3,000 m) above sea level and surrounded by volcanoes. The Valley of Mexico contains many shallow lakes and much fertile land.

The last Nahua groups to arrive referred to themselves as "Mexica" (meh-SHE-kah), the origin of the word *Mexico*, but many historians call them by the modern word *Aztec*. Although *Aztec* is a term that no one at the time used, this text uses it to refer to the empire the Mexica built. Linguistic analysis of the Nahuatl language indicates that its speakers originated somewhere in the southwest United States or northern Mexico.

By the 1300s, some fifty city-states, called **altepetl** (al-TEH-peh-tuhl), occupied central Mexico, each with its own leader, or "speaker," and its own government. Each altepetl had a palace for its ruler, a pyramid-shaped temple, and a market. The Mexica migrated to the region around the historic urban center of Teotihuacan, a large city with many lakes. Since this region was already home to several rival altepetl, the Aztec were forced to settle in a swampland called **Tenochtitlan** (teh-noch-TIT-lan). The Mexica gradually reclaimed large areas of the swamps and on the drier, more stable areas erected stone buildings held together with mortar. They planted flowers everywhere and walked on planks or traveled by canoe from one reclaimed area to another.

Traditional accounts say the Mexica people arrived at Tenochtitlan in 1325, a date confirmed by archaeological excavation. At its height, Tenochtitlan contained sixty thousand dwellings, home to perhaps two hundred thousand people in an area of 5 square miles (13 sq km). The central marketplace offered cooked and uncooked food, slaves, tobacco products, and luxury goods made from gold, silver, and feathers. Consumers used cotton cloaks, cacao beans, and feather quills filled with gold dust as media of exchange, since the Mexica had no coins.

Nahua Religion and Writing

The Mexica believed that their patron god was Huitzilopochtli (wheat-zeel-oh-POSHT-lee), whose name meant "the hummingbird of the south." Also the warrior god of the sun, Huitzilopochtli played a key role in the Mexica origin legend. On the long migration from their original homeland in Aztlan, the Mexica arrived at a mountain where an elderly priestess guarded a temple. A ball of feathers fell from the sky, and she became pregnant with a young male fetus, the future Huitzilopochtli. Ashamed by the news of her mother's pregnancy, her daughter organized an army to kill her mother. When a soldier warned Huitzilopochtli, still in the womb, of the impending attack, he emerged as a full-grown warrior, killed the priestess's daughter, and rolled her body parts down the hill as his army defeated the attackers.

This legend provides a rationale for the massive Mexica blood sacrifices, many of which occurred in the Great Temple in Tenochtitlan. The Nahuatl term for human blood was "precious water." The most important Nahua deity, the sun, controlled agriculture and crops, primarily the corn, beans, and peppers that were the main source of food. Ranking just under the sun-god were the gods of rain and

Mexica Skull-Mask Worshipers used deerskin straps to tie this skull-mask around their waists in a display of fearsomeness. The mask was made by applying small fragments of turquoise, black lignite coal, and white conch to the front half of a skull (the human teeth are original). The highly polished pyrite eyes glisten in the light, and the red mollusk shell nose inlays replicate the color of flayed human tissue. The mask vividly captures the importance of human offerings to the Mexica deities.

agriculture. In addition, each altepetl had several deities associated with its native place. The deities, the Mexica believed, needed to drink much human blood so that they would keep the soil fertile, the harvest plentiful, and the succession of seasons regular. Most of the sacrificial victims were drawn from prisoners of war.

While many societies engaged in human sacrifice, the Mexica killed unusually high numbers of people at one time: eighty thousand, according to one Spanish source.[1] The Spanish may have exaggerated the death toll to discredit their predecessors, but they gave much lower numbers of sacrificial victims for other Amerindian peoples, suggesting that the Mexica indeed performed more sacrifices.

The Mexica credited the creator god Quetzalcoatl (kate-zahl-CO-ah-tal) with devising the Nahua method of writing. The Nahua wrote on bark paper or deerskin covered with a thin white layer of limestone plaster. Their way of writing functioned quite differently from Mayan. Nahuatl texts combine pictures with rebus writing, which uses images to represent something with the same sound; in English, for example, a picture of an eye functions as a rebus for the word *I*. The Nahua's writing served as a trigger to memory; people who had been trained to tell a certain story could look at a Nahua manuscript and be reminded of the details. But if one did not know the original story beforehand, it was impossible to know what the pictures said, meaning that it was not a true writing system.

Nahua Society

The Nahua peoples treated certain human beings like gods. The leader of the Mexica, their Great Speaker, was carried in a feathered chair. His advisers never looked at the Great Speaker or addressed him directly: a screen always separated them from him. The Great Speaker was in charge of all external matters, including war, the receipt of gifts, and relations with other altepetl. A group of nobles, priests, and successful warriors chose the new Great Speaker, and although they treated him as their ritual superior, they could depose him if they did not approve of his rule. The second-highest leader, a man called the Female Snake, took charge of all internal affairs. Usually a close relative of the Great Speaker, he consulted with him frequently. All the top officials came from the royal family and had large private estates.

Most of the Nahuas were commoners, each of whom belonged to a "big house," a group who believed they were descended from a common ancestor. Each big-house group had their own lands, and some had schools for warriors. The Mexica capital contained some twenty big-house groups, and more lived in other regions. The lowest-ranking people in Nahua society were slaves, often the original residents of the Valley of Mexico.

Ordinary people and slaves farmed the land and generated the surplus that underpinned the expansion of the Mexica altepetl. The Nahua planted bean and pepper seeds in the same holes as corn seeds. Because they had no draft animals, metal tools, or wheels, everything had to be carried and cultivated by hand.

Corn ripened in only fifty days, providing sufficient food for a family as well as a surplus. Grinding corn was exclusively women's work; for fear that they might antagonize the gods, men were forbidden to help. Ordinary people were required to pay tribute to their Mexica overlords by contributing a share of the crop, performing labor service, paying other goods, and most onerous of all, providing victims for human sacrifice.

The Military and the Conquests of the Mexica

If successful in battle, warriors could rise in Mexica society to a high position. They then received lands of their own and were not required to pay taxes on them. Conversely, the best human sacrifice one could offer to the gods, the Nahua believed, was a warrior taken captive in battle. In their system of thirteen heavens and eight underworlds, the highest heaven, the Paradise of the Sun-God, was for men who had killed the enemy in battle and for women who had died in childbirth, a type of battle in its own right.

The Mexica troops fitted their clubs, spears, and darts with blades made from obsidian, a volcanic glass that was sharp and easy to work but dulled easily. They protected themselves with thick cotton armor. Hand-to-hand combat was considered the most honorable form of warfare.

In 1428, the Mexica formed the Triple Alliance with two other peoples and launched a series of conquests that led to the creation of an empire. By 1500, they had conquered 450 altepetl in modern Mexico, extending all the way to Guatemala, and ruled over a subject population estimated at between 4 and 6 million (see Map 15.1).[2]

The Aztec empire, though large and with a beautiful capital, had one major weakness. Once the Mexica conquered a given people, they demanded tribute and took sacrificial victims from them, yet they did nothing to incorporate them further into their empire.

The Inca Empire, 1400–1532

The **Inca empire**, 2,500 miles (4,000 km) to the south in the highlands of the Andes, was structured differently. Each time the Inca conquered a new group, they integrated them into the empire, requiring them to perform labor and military service and resettling some groups to minimize the chances of revolt. Like the Mexica, the Inca worshiped deities that demanded human sacrifices, but never as many as in Mexico. Although the Inca successfully integrated subject peoples into their empire, they did not have an orderly system of succession. Each time their ruler died, everyone who hoped to succeed him plunged into full-time conflict until a new leader emerged victorious.

Inca Religion and Andean Society

The ordinary people of the Andes lived in kin groups called **ayllu** (aye-YOU) that worked the land in several adjacent ecological zones so they could maximize their yield should the crops in one zone fail. Some

Inca empire
Andean empire founded in 1438 by Pachakuti (d. 1471), which ruled over a peak population of 10 to 12 million.

ayllu
Andean kin groups of the Inca empire that worked the land in several adjacent ecological zones as a hedge against crop failure in any one zone.

MAP 15.1 The Aztec Empire Starting from their capital at Tenochtitlan (modern Mexico City), the Mexica conquered different neighboring peoples living between the Gulf of Mexico and the Pacific Ocean. The Aztec empire's rulers required the conquered peoples to pay taxes and submit tribute, but gave few benefits in return. When Cortés landed on the coast of Mexico, he quickly found allies among the conquered peoples, particularly the Tlaxcalans. (© Cengage Learning)

crops, like quinoa (KEEN-wah), grew in several different zones. (See the feature "World History in Today's World: Quinoa Goes Global.")

Most ayllu were divided into smaller subgroups, and men tended to marry women from another subgroup. All the people in a given ayllu recognized one person as a common ancestor. Ordinary people believed that, in addition to their ancestors, hundreds of spirits (*wak'a*) inhabited places in the landscape such as streams, caves, rocks, and hills.

The Inca believed that some deities ranked far above these local spirits. The most important Inca deities were the Creator, the Creator's child the Sun, and the Thunder gods. By 1500, the sun-god had become the most important deity, probably because the Inca ruler, the Sapa Inca, or "Unique Inca," claimed descent from the sun-god. The priest of the sun-god was the highest-ranking priest in Inca society and the second most powerful person in the Inca empire.

Both the Sapa Inca and the sun-god priest belonged to the aristocracy, which was divided into three tiers: the close relatives of the ruler and previous rulers, more distant relatives, and then the leaders of the groups who had been conquered by the Inca. Although most Inca traced their ancestry through their father's line, the ruler's mother's family played a central role in court politics because the ruler took his wives from his mother's family.

The Inca had no orderly system of succession. Each time the Inca ruler died, all contestants for the position from among his male kin launched an all-out war until a single man emerged victorious, much like the system of tanistry prevalent among the Mongols (covered in Chapter 14 of Volume 1). The new ruler was then installed in an elaborate coronation honoring the sun-god. During his reign the

Quinoa Goes Global

Quinoa—you may have noticed it in the grocery store or in soups and salads on menus. This species of goosefoot is related to spinach, Swiss chard, beets, and lamb's-quarters; its seeds make a translucent grainlike starch once they have been washed clean of their bitter saponin coating. NASA identified quinoa as one of the world's most nutritious plants, particularly suitable for long space voyages, because it contains nine amino acids, including lysine, which few other plants do.

First cultivated around 5000 B.C.E., quinoa is indigenous to the Lake Titicaca region of Bolivia. Valuing quinoa, the Incans offered the crop to the sun-god and each spring used a gold tool to dig the first furrow for quinoa seeds. But the Spanish looked down on quinoa as indigenous and therefore low-class, and under Spanish rule European grains gradually displaced quinoa in the local diet.

Today, Bolivians toast quinoa flour or boil it with sugar and sometimes add apple and cinnamon to make a nutritious breakfast drink. In the past five years, as foreign demand has increased, the price has tripled, bringing new prosperity to quinoa growers. Fewer people from southern Bolivia leave home in search of jobs, and living standards have risen in one of the world's poorest countries.

But prosperity for the farmers has made it more difficult for ordinary Bolivians to afford quinoa. A 2.2-pound (1-kg) bag of quinoa costs the equivalent of $4.85, versus $1.20 for a bag of noodles and $1 for a bag of rice. Opting for pasta over quinoa, young Bolivians also prefer bottled cola drinks to homemade quinoa drinks. Domestic consumption of quinoa has declined one-third since the price went up.

Concerned by the declining consumption of quinoa domestically, nutritionists are calling for government measures to encourage Bolivians to continue to eat quinoa. The government is giving loans to quinoa farmers to increase production, and they plan to distribute the plant to pregnant and nursing women. As long as the global price stays high, production should eventually catch up with demand, bringing the domestic price down.

Source: Simon Romero and Sara Shahriari, "Quinoa's Global Success Creates Quandary at Home," *New York Times*, March 19, 2011.

Sapa Inca lived as a deity among his subjects, eating special foods and wearing unusual clothing. Even so, he had to keep the support of the aristocracy, which could easily overthrow him at any time.

Like the ayllu ancestors, the ruler was believed to continue to live even after death. The Inca mummified the bodies of deceased rulers and other high-ranking family members. They placed the mummies in houses around the main square of Cuzco, their capital city high in the Andes at an elevation of 11,300 feet (3,450 m). One Spanish observer described their interaction with these mummies:

> Most of the people of Cuzco served the dead, I have heard it said, who they daily brought out to the main square, setting them down in a ring, each one according to his age, and there the male and female attendants ate and drank. . . . The mummies toasted each other and the living, and the living toasted the dead.*

He did not explain how the living communicated with the dead, but it seems likely that priests intervened.

---

*Terence d'Altroy, *The Incas* (Malden, Mass.: Blackwell, 2002), p. 97 (citing Pedro Pizarro).

The Marvels of Incan Engineering at Machu Picchu The settlement at Machu Picchu, which stands 8,000 feet (2,400 m) above sea level, embodies the Incan talent for engineering in its even stone houses arrayed on multiple levels, connected by manmade waterways and more than one hundred stairways. Built around 1450 as a summer palace for the ruler Pachakuti, the site was abandoned after the collapse of the Incan empire and rediscovered by outsiders only in the early 1900s. Today it is one of the world's most visited sites and the most famous of all the Inca ruins. (Robert Harding World Imagery)

The Inca organized the worship of local spirits who inhabited places in the landscape, ancestors of the rulers, and deities into a complex ritual calendar specifying which one was to be worshiped on a given day. Of 332 shrines in Cuzco, 31 received human sacrifices, in many cases a young boy and a young girl, a symbolic married couple. These usually occurred in times of hardship, like an epidemic, or during unusual astronomical events, like eclipses. Occasionally, larger sacrifices occurred, such as when a ruler died, but the largest number of sacrificial victims killed at a single time was four thousand.

The Inca Expansion

As the Aztec believed their history began with their occupation of Tenochtitlan, the Incas traced their beginnings to their settlement in Cuzco. Archaeological evidence suggests that the Inca moved to Cuzco sometime around 1400. Although oral accounts conflict, most accept the date of 1438 as the year Pachakuti (patch-ah-KOO-tee) (d. 1471), the first great Inca ruler, seized the throne from his brother in a coup and launched the military campaigns outward from Cuzco. The Inca conquered neighboring lands because they desired the goods produced in each ecological zone: the herds of llamas and alpaca, crops like grain and potatoes, and the gold, feathers, shells, and minerals from the jungle lowlands and the shore.

Much of Inca warfare consisted of storming enemy forts with a large infantry, often after cutting off access to food and water. For several days enemy forces traded insults and sang hostile songs such as this: *"We will drink from the skull of the traitor, we will adorn ourselves with a necklace of his teeth, . . . we play the melody of the pinkullu [a musical instrument resembling a flute] with flutes made from his bones, we will beat the drum made from his skin, and thus we will dance."** Attackers in quilted cotton launched arrows, stones from slingshots, and stone spears, and in hand-to-hand combat used spears and clubs, some topped with stone or with bronze stars.

Like other Andean peoples, the Inca knew how to extract metallic ore from rocks and how to heat different metals to form alloys. They made bronze and copper, but they did not develop their metallurgical expertise beyond making club heads, decorative masks, and ear spools for the nobility.

At its height, the Inca army could field as many as one hundred thousand men in a single battle, most of the rank-and-file drawn from subject peoples who were required to serve in the army. Although soldiers fought only seasonally and returned home at harvesttime, the rate of Inca expansion was breathtaking. Starting from a single location, Cuzco, the Inca conquered large chunks of southern, central, and coastal Peru, Ecuador, the eastern lowlands of Peru and Bolivia, and the mountains of Argentina and Chile (see Map 15.2). By 1532 they ruled over a population estimated at 10 to 12 million.

MAP 15.2 The Inca Empire In 1438, the Inca ruler Pachakuti took power in the capital at Cuzco and led his armies to conquer large chunks of territory along the Andes. Two north-south trunk routes, with subsidiary east-west routes, formed a system of over 25,000 miles (40,000 km) of roads. By 1532, the Inca ruled 10 to 12 million people in an empire of 1,500 square miles (4,000 sq km). (© Cengage Learning)

Inca Rule of Subject Populations

Unique among the Andean peoples, the Inca incorporated each conquered land and its occupants into their kingdom. They resettled thousands of people, forcing them to move to regions far from their original homes. The Inca also brought many images of subjects' ancestral deities to Cuzco, holding the images hostage so that their devotees would not rise up against their Inca overlords.

---

*Terence d'Altroy, *The Incas* (Malden, Mass.: Blackwell, 2002), pp. 226–227.

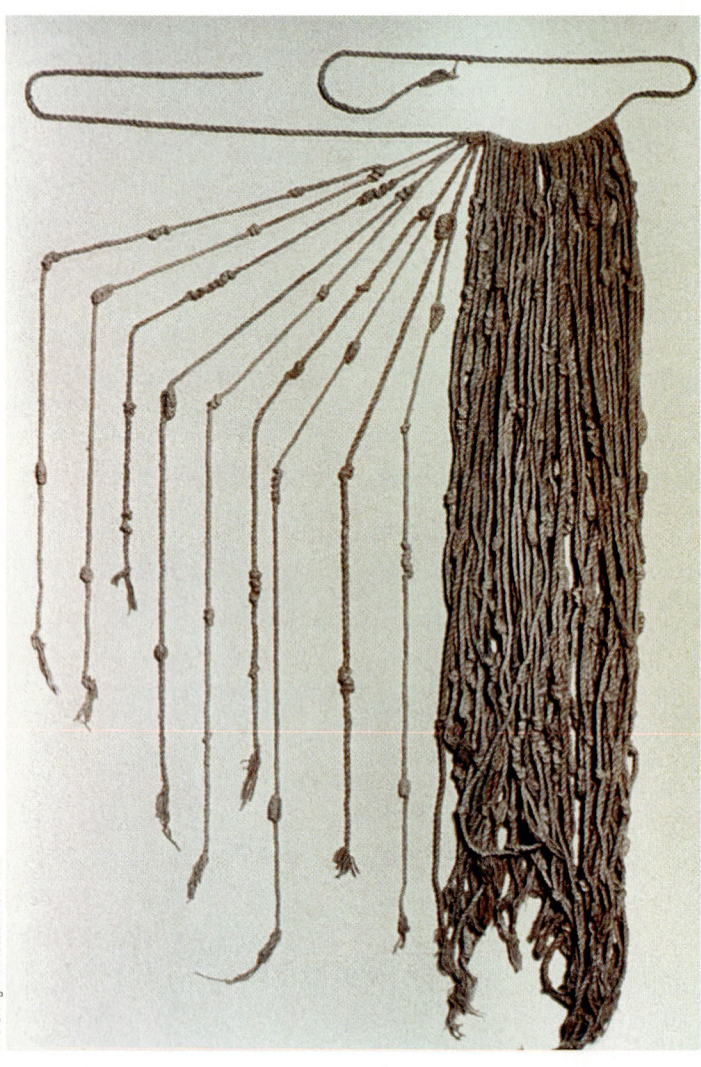

The Granger Collection New York

Keeping Records with Knots The Inca kept all their records by using knotted strings, called quipu, attaching subsidiary cords, sometimes in several tiers, to a main cord. Different types of knots represented different numeric units; skipped knots indicated a zero; the color of the string indicated the item being counted.

quipu
Inca system of record keeping that used knots on strings to record the population.

The Inca, like the Mongols, encouraged different peoples to submit to them by treating those who surrendered gently. They allowed local leaders to continue to serve but required everyone to swear loyalty to the Inca ruler, to grant him all rights to their lands, and to perform labor service as the Inca state required.

Inca officials also delegated power to indigenous leaders. Those of high birth could serve in the Inca government as long as they learned Quechua (KETCH-wah), the language of the Inca. Each official was in charge of a certain number of households: top officials supervised ten thousand households, while the lowest functionaries watched over ten. Each year Inca officials counted the population, not with a written script but by using a system of knotted strings, called **quipu** (key-POOH). Since no one can understand the quipu records, the population of the Inca empire remains unknown. Each town had a knot keeper who maintained and interpreted the knot records, which were updated annually.

To fulfill the Inca's main service tax, male household heads between twenty-five and fifty had to perform two to three months' labor each year. Once assigned a task, a man could get as much help as he liked from his children or wife, a practice that favored families with many children.

The Inca did not treat all subject peoples alike. From some resettled peoples they exacted months of labor, and many subject groups who possessed a specific skill, such as carving stones or making spears, performed that skill for the state. Others did far less. For example, many Inca looked down on a people they called Uru, literally meaning "worm," who lived on the southern edge of Lake Titicaca. The Uru were supposed to catch fish, gather grasses, and weave textiles, but they performed no other labor service. An even more despised group was required each year to submit a single basket filled with lice, not because the Inca wanted the lice, but because they hoped to teach this group the nature of their tax obligations.

Each household also contributed certain goods, such as food, blankets, textiles, and tools, that were kept in thousands of storehouses throughout the empire. One Spaniard described a storehouse in Cuzco that particularly impressed him: *"There is a house in which are kept more than 100,000 dried birds, for from their feathers articles of clothing are made."* This system functioned so well that the corn and potatoes in the storehouses could support an army for months.

*Terence d'Altroy, *The Incas* (Malden, Mass.: Blackwell, 2002), p. 281.

One lasting product of the Inca labor system was over 25,000 miles (40,000 km) of magnificent roads (see Map 15.2). While some of these routes predated the Inca conquest, the Inca linked them together into an overall system. Since the Inca did not have the wheel, most of the traffic was by foot, and llamas could carry small loads. With no surveying instruments, the Inca constructed these roads across deserts, yawning chasms, and mountains over 16,000 feet (5,000 m) high. Individual messengers working in shifts could move at an estimated rate of 150 miles (240 km) per day, but troops moved much more slowly, covering perhaps 7–9 miles (12–15 km) per day.

Despite its extent, the Inca empire appeared stronger than it was. Many of the subject peoples resented their heavy labor obligations, and each time an Inca ruler died, the ensuing succession disputes threatened to tear the empire apart.

Intellectual and Geographic Exploration in Europe, 1300–1500

Between 1300 and 1500, as the Mexica and Inca were expanding their empires overland in the Americas, Portuguese and Spanish ships colonized lands farther and farther away, ultimately reaching the Americas. European scholars extended their fields of study to include many new topics. Meanwhile, new printing technology made books more available and affordable, enabling people like Christopher Columbus to read and compare many different books.

During the same period, European navigators between 1350 and 1492 began to venture into previously unexplored waters and sailed past the Strait of Gibraltar into the Atlantic. Portuguese and Spanish voyagers founded colonies on the Canary Islands, which were inhabited by an indigenous Stone Age people, and on the uninhabited Madeira Islands. The pace of European exploration hastened, especially after 1450, when many different explorers, of whom Columbus is only the most famous, crossed the Atlantic.

The Rise of Humanism

Since the founding of universities in Europe around 1200, students had read Greek and Latin texts and the Bible. Instructors like Peter Abelard used an approach called scholasticism, in which the main goal was to reconcile the many differences among ancient authorities to form a logical system of thought. Around 1350, a group of Italian scholars pioneered a new intellectual movement called **humanism**. Humanists studied many of the same texts as before, but they tried to impart a more general understanding of them to their students in the hope that students would improve morally and be able to help others do the same.

One of the earliest humanist writers was the Italian poet Petrarch (1304–1374). Scholasticism, Petrarch felt, was too abstract. It did not teach people how to live and how to obtain salvation. Although he composed much poetry in Latin, he is remembered for the poetry he composed in Italian, one of several European vernacular languages that came into written use in the fourteenth and fifteenth centuries.

In 1487, a Venetian woman named Cassandra Fedele (fay-DAY-lay) (1465–1558) addressed the students and faculty of the University of Padua in a public oration that set out her own understanding of humanism. Having studied Greek

humanism
Intellectual movement begun around 1350 in Italy by scholars who opposed scholasticism. Emphasized the study of the humanities, which included traditional fields like logic, grammar, arithmetic, and music and newer fields like language, history, literature, and philosophy.

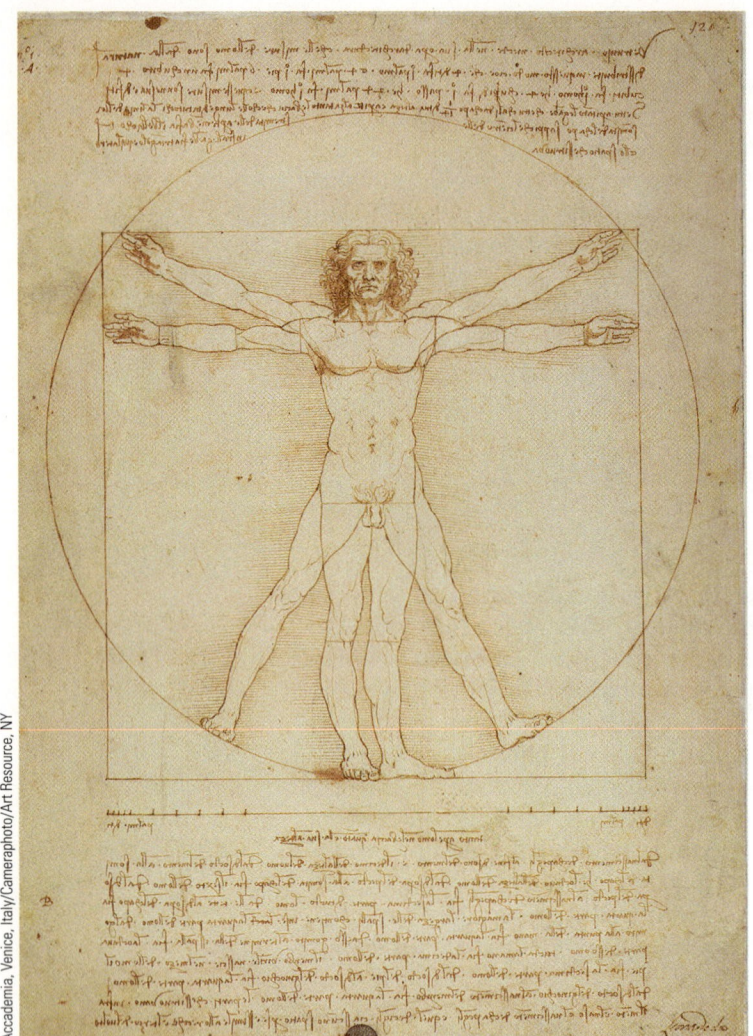

Accademia, Venice, Italy/Cameraphoto/Art Resource, NY

The Art of Humanism In 1487, the scientist, artist, and engineer Leonardo da Vinci portrayed man, not God, as the center of the universe. Above and below the ink drawing, the left-handed da Vinci wrote notes in mirror writing to explain that his drawing illustrated a text about proportions by the Roman architect Vitruvius (ca. 75–ca. 15 B.C.E.). Unlike earlier artists, da Vinci personally dissected corpses so that he could portray the structure of human muscles as accurately as possible.

and Latin with a tutor, Fedele urged her audience to devote themselves to studying Cicero, Plato, and Aristotle because, she maintained, while wealth and physical strength cannot last, *"those things which are produced by virtue and intelligence are useful to those who follow."* She continued: *"And how much more humane, praiseworthy and noble do those states and princes become who support and cultivate these studies! Certainly for this reason this part of philosophy has laid claim for itself to the name of 'humanity,' since those who are rough by nature become by these studies more civil and mild-mannered."* She eloquently expressed the major tenet of humanism: studying the humanities made students, whether from noble or low-born families, more refined and better people.*

Rather than treat Latin translations as flawless, the humanists checked them against texts in the original languages, including the Greek of the Bible. When they did, they found that many of the most difficult-to-understand passages were corrupted by translation errors. One product of humanist scholarship was multilingual editions of the Bible that printed the Latin, Greek, Hebrew, and Aramaic texts on the same page so that scholars could compare them.

Historians call this period of humanist revival the Renaissance, which means "rebirth," to contrast it with the earlier centuries. Most historians no longer see the Renaissance as a sharp departure from earlier periods; they recognize that the intellectual advances of the twelfth and thirteenth centuries underpinned those of the humanist era.

Europe's First Movable Type

The introduction of printing in Europe contributed greatly to the humanist movement because movable type made books cheaper, enabling scholars to more easily compare different versions of the same text. Johannes Gutenberg (ca. 1400–1468) printed the first European book, a Bible, using movable type sometime before 1454. This was not the first book in the

*Cassandra Fedele, "Oration to the University of Padua (1487)," in *The Renaissance in Europe: An Anthology,* ed. Peter Elmer et al. (New Haven: Yale University Press, in association with the Open University, 2000), pp. 52–56.

world made using movable type; the Chinese knew about movable type as early as the eleventh century, and the world's earliest surviving book using movable type was made in Korea in 1403. We should remember, too, that Gutenberg could not have printed the Bible if paper, a Chinese invention, had not come into widespread use in Europe between 1250 and 1350.

Movable type, however cumbersome for Chinese with its thousands of characters, functioned beautifully for alphabetic languages like Latin. Gutenberg made several crucial innovations: a mold with rows in which different letters could be placed, an oil-based ink, and the type itself. Close analysis of Gutenberg's earliest books shows variation among individual letters, suggesting that he may have made hundreds of the same letter by hand, maybe even from wood, and did not cast them from a metal mold as is often supposed.

Within fifty years of its introduction, printing had transformed the European book. Although European readers had once prized illuminated manuscripts prepared by hand, with beautiful illustrations and exquisite lettering, now typesetters streamlined texts so that they could be printed more easily. Some of the most popular books described marvels from around the world. The Latin translation of the Greek geographer Ptolemy and the travel account of Marco Polo, a Venetian who traveled in Asia, were both in Columbus's personal library, and he carefully wrote long notes in the margins of the passages that interested him.

Early European Exploration in the Mediterranean and the Atlantic, 1350–1440

Widely read travel accounts whetted the appetite for trade and exploration. European merchants, primarily from the Italian city-states of Venice and Genoa, maintained settlements in certain locations far from Europe, such as Constantinople, the island of Cyprus, and other smaller islands in the Mediterranean (see Map 15.3). These communities, which existed primarily for the convenience of the merchants, had walled enclosures called *factories* that held warehouses, a place for ships to refit, and houses for short- and long-term stays. The Ottoman conquest of Constantinople in 1453 would encourage many of these merchants to go west instead.

Starting around 1350, European navigators began to sail past the Strait of Gibraltar into the Atlantic Ocean. In 1350, two Italian explorers wrote the first book about the Canary Islands and their non-Christian inhabitants. The Europeans captured some of these Canary Islanders and sold them in the slave markets of Europe, where they were much in demand. Also around 1350, the Portuguese reached the Azores, which lie one-third of the distance from Europe to the Americas. After 1350, cartographers began to show the various Atlantic islands off the coast of Africa on their maps.

One motivation for exploring these unknown islands was religious. As the Catholic rulers of Spain and Portugal regained different Islamic cities in Iberia during the thirteenth and fourteenth centuries in a campaign called the *Reconquista*, they hoped to expand Christian territory into North Africa. At the time, Spain itself contained several distinct kingdoms. In 1415, a Portuguese prince named Henry, now known as **Henry the Navigator** (1394–1460), led a force of several thousand men that captured the Moroccan fortress of Ceuta (say-OO-tuh). Using the rhetoric of the Crusades and armed with an order from the pope, his goal was to convert the inhabitants to Christianity.

Henry tried to take the Canary Islands for Christianity in 1424, but the inhabitants, armed only with stone tools, repelled the invaders; nevertheless, the Portuguese continued to capture and enslave Canary Islanders on a regular basis. The

Henry the Navigator (1394–1460) Portuguese prince who supported Portuguese explorations in the Mediterranean, Atlantic, and along the West African coast.

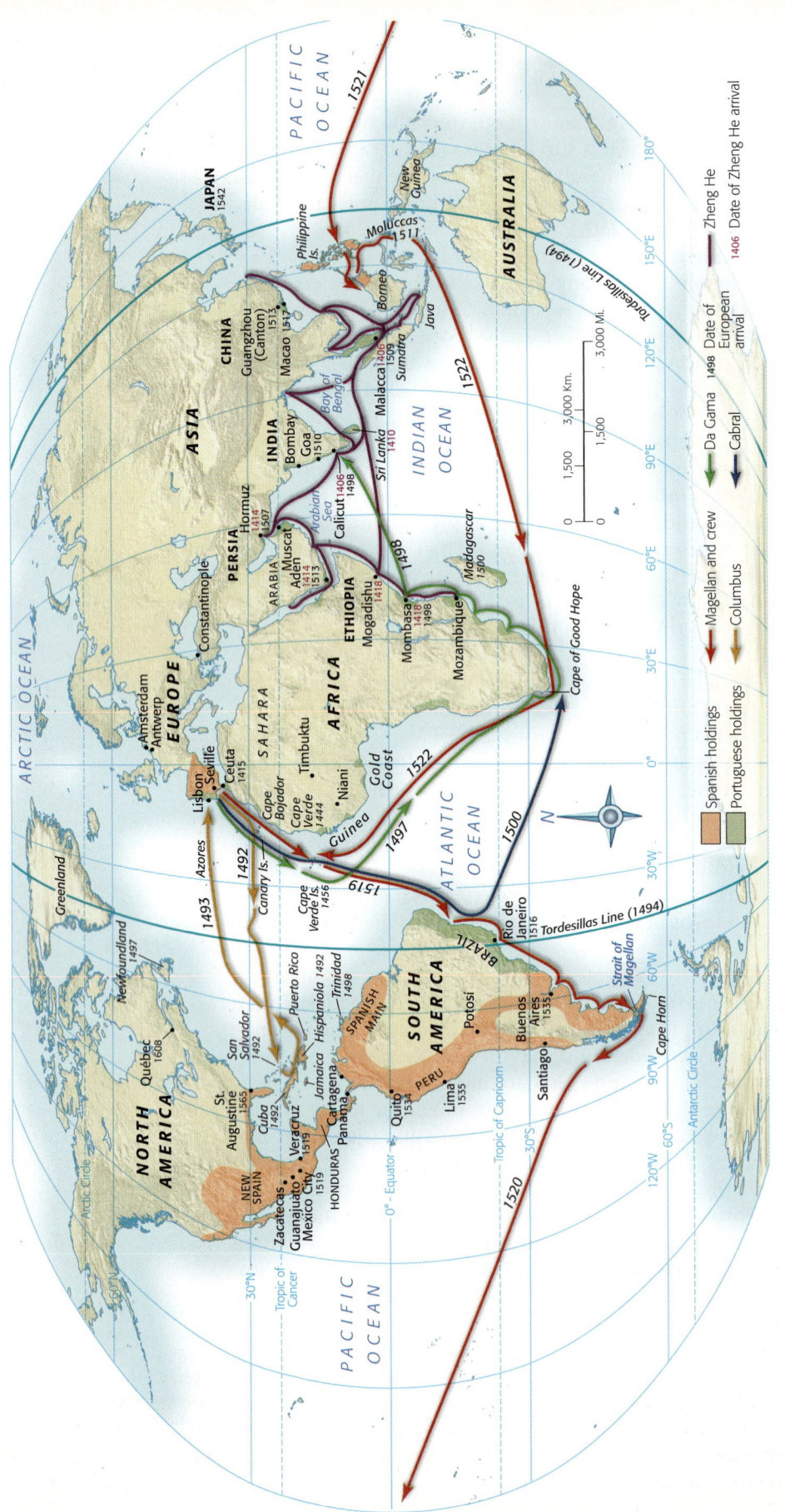

MAP 15.3 The Age of Maritime Expansion, 1400–1600 Between 1400 and 1600, maritime explorers pioneered three major new routes: (1) across the Atlantic Ocean from Europe to the Americas, (2) across the Pacific from the Americas to Asia, and (3) south along the west coast of Africa to the Cape of Good Hope. Once the Portuguese explorer Vasco da Gama rounded the Cape in 1498, he connected with the well-traveled hajj route linking East Africa with China that Zheng He's ships had taken in the early 1400s (see page 420). (© Cengage Learning)

Portuguese occupied the island of Madeira, and in 1454 they established plantations there, which soon exported large amounts of sugar.

Many navigators were afraid to venture past the Madeira Islands because of the dreaded torrid zone. Greek and Roman geographers had posited that the northern temperate zone, where people lived, was bordered by an uninhabitable frigid zone to the north and a torrid zone to the south, whose scorching heat made it impossible to cross. Following the revival of interest in Greek and Roman geography in the twelfth century, all informed people realized, as the ancients had, that the globe was round. (The American writer Washington Irving invented the myth that everyone before Columbus thought the world was flat.)

Many Europeans had assumed that Cape Bojador, just south of the Canary Islands in modern Morocco, marked the beginning of the impenetrable torrid zone (see Map 15.3). But in 1434 the Portuguese successfully sailed past the cape and reported that no torrid zone existed.

The Portuguese Slave Trade After 1444

Since no torrid zone existed, Henry realized, the Portuguese could transport slaves from the west coast of Africa and sell them in Europe. Portuguese vessels had already brought back thirty-eight African slaves from West Africa. In 1444, Henry dispatched six caravels to bring back slaves from the Arguin bank, south of Cape Bojador in modern-day Mauritania. The caravel was a small sailing ship, usually about 75 feet (23 m) long, that had two or three masts with square sails.

In 1444, Henry staged a huge public reception of the slaves for his subjects. The ships' captains presented one slave each to a church and to a Franciscan convent to demonstrate their intention to convert the slaves to Christianity. An eyewitness description captures the scene:

> These people, assembled together on that open space, were an astonishing sight to behold. . . . Among them were some who were quite white-skinned, handsome and of good appearance; others were less white, seeming more like brown men; others still were as black as Ethiopians, so deformed of face and body that, to those who stared at them, it almost seemed that they were looking at spirits from the lowest hemisphere. But what heart, however hardened it might be, could not be pierced by a feeling of pity at the sight of that company?*

This may seem to be an early critique of slavery, but in fact, the author, like many of his contemporaries, saw the trade in slaves as a Christian act: the Africans, as non-Christians, were doomed to suffer in the afterlife, but if they converted, they could attain salvation. From its very beginnings, the European slave trade combined the profit motive with a missionary impulse.

Within ten years the Portuguese slave traders had reached agreements with two rulers in northern Senegal to trade horses for slaves each year. The price of a horse varied from nine to fourteen slaves. Horses did not live long in sub-Saharan Africa's tropical climate, but because rulers liked them as a symbol of power and a war tool, the demand never flagged. By the time of Henry's death in 1460, Portuguese ships had transported about 1,000 slaves a year, fewer than the 4,300 slaves

*Peter Russell, *Prince Henry "the Navigator": A Life* (New Haven: Yale University Press, 2000), pp. 242–243, n8, citing *Crónica dos Feitos na Conquista de Guiné,* II: 145–148.

who crossed the Sahara overland in Muslim caravans each year at the time. After 1460, the oceanic trade continued to grow. Many of the African slaves worked on sugar plantations, either in the Canary Islands or on Madeira.

The Portuguese continued their explorations along the African coast, and in 1487, a Portuguese ship commanded by Bartholomew Dias rounded the Cape of Good Hope at Africa's southern tip. The Portuguese became convinced that the quickest way to Asia and the riches of the spice trade was around Africa, as Chapter 16 will show.

The Iberian Conquest of Mexico, Peru, and Brazil, 1492–1580

Columbus's landfall in the Caribbean had immediate and long-lasting consequences. Representatives of the Spanish and Portuguese crowns conquered most of Mexico and Latin America with breathtaking speed. In 1517, the Spanish landed for the first time on the Aztec mainland; by 1540, they controlled all of Mexico, Central America, and the northern sections of South America. Portugal controlled Brazil by 1550. By 1580, Spain had subdued the peoples of the southern regions of South America. Given that the residents of the Canary Islands, armed only with stone tools, managed to repel all attempts to conquer them for 150 years, how did the Spanish and Portuguese move into the Americas and conquer two sophisticated empires so quickly?

The subject peoples of the Aztec empire, who had not been integrated into the empire, welcomed the Spanish as an ally who might help them overthrow their overlords. Moreover, the Spanish arrived in Peru just after the installation of a new Sapa Inca, whose opponents still hoped to wrest power from him. The Europeans had other advantages, like guns and horses, which the Amerindians lacked, but the newcomers were completely unaware of their most powerful weapon: the disease pools of Europe.

Columbus's First Voyage to the Americas, 1492

In 1479, Isabella (1451–1504) ascended to the throne of Castile and married Ferdinand of Aragon, unifying the two major kingdoms of Spain. Throughout the 1480s, Columbus approached both the Spanish and the Portuguese monarchs to request funds for a voyage to the Indies by sailing west from the Canary Islands.

In keeping with the scholastic and humanist traditions, Columbus cited several authorities in support of the new route he proposed. One passage in the Bible (II Esdras 6:42) stated that the world was six parts land, one part water. Columbus interpreted this to mean that the distance from the Iberian Peninsula to the western edge of Asia in Japan was only 2,700 miles (4,445 km). In actuality, the distance is over 6,000 miles (10,000 km), and the world is about 70 percent water and 30 percent land, but no one at the time knew this.

In rejecting his proposal, the scholars advising the Portuguese and Spanish monarchs held that the distance from Spain to Japan was far greater than Columbus realized. The men on board a ship carrying its own provisions on the proposed route, they reasoned, would die of starvation before reaching Asia. Although right about the distance from Iberia to Japan, these advisers did not realize that the Americas lay in between.

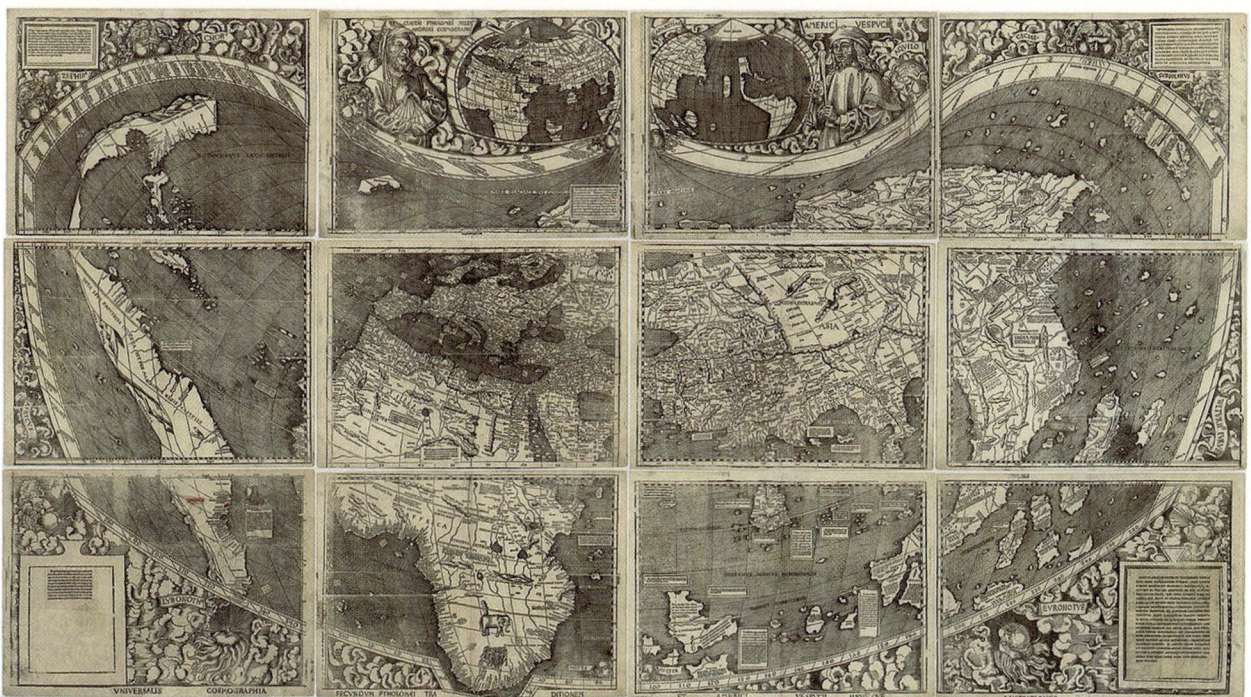

The First Map to Show the Americas In 1507, a German mapmaker named Martin Waldseemüller published one hundred copies of this printed map of the world, in twelve sections, each measuring 18 by 24.5 inches (46 by 62 cm). When the Library of Congress purchased this map from a German library in 2001, it paid $10 million for it. Expanding the ancient geographer Ptolemy's seven climatic zones, this map depicts the Americas as a continent separate from Asia, a fact Columbus never realized. Waldseemüller named the new landmass "America," for Amerigo Vespucci, a navigator whose writings deeply influenced the mapmaker. The word "America" appears halfway down the continent of South America, to the left of Africa. (Martin Waldseemüller (1470–1521) Universalis Cosmographia Secundum Ptholomaei Traditionem et Americi Vespucii Alioru[m]que Lustrationes, [St. Dié], 1507. One map on 12 sheets, made from original woodcut, Geography and Map Division, Library of Congress)

Several developments in 1492 prompted Isabella and Ferdinand to overturn their earlier decision. Granada, the last Muslim outpost, fell in 1492, and all of Spain came under Catholic rule. In that same year the rulers of Aragon and Castile expelled all Jews from Spain, a measure that had been enacted by France and England centuries earlier. Delighted with these developments, Ferdinand and Isabella decided to fund Columbus, primarily because they did not want the Portuguese to do so, and also because he was asking for only a small amount of money, enough to host a foreign prince for a week.

Isabella and Ferdinand gave Columbus two titles: *admiral of the ocean sea* and *viceroy*. An admiral commanded a fleet, but *viceroy* was a new title indicating a representative of the monarch who would govern any lands to which he sailed. Columbus was entitled to one-tenth of any precious metals or spices he found, with the remaining nine-tenths going to Isabella and Ferdinand. No provision was made for his men.

Columbus departed with three ships from Granada on August 3, 1492, and on October 12 (celebrated in the United States as Columbus Day) of the same year arrived in the Bahamas. He soon proceeded to Hispaniola, a Caribbean island occupied by the modern nations of Haiti and the Dominican Republic. Although

Europeans knew about Islamic astrolabes and sextants, Columbus did not use them. He sailed primarily by dead reckoning: he used a compass to stay on a westerly course. By dropping a float from the ship's bow and counting the seconds until the stern passed the float, he estimated his speed and so the approximate distance he traveled in a day. From his travels to the Canary Islands and the Azores, Columbus knew when the prevailing wind across the Atlantic blew east and when west and timed his trips accordingly.

His first encounter with the people on Hispaniola was peaceful: *"In order to win their friendship,"* Columbus wrote in his logbook, *"I gave some of them red caps and glass beads which they hung round their necks, and also other trifles. These things pleased them greatly and they became marvelously friendly to us."** The two sides exchanged gifts and tried to make sense of each other's languages. The island's residents spoke **Arawak**. *"They are the color of Canary Islanders (neither black nor white),"* Columbus noted, an indication that he thought of the Arawak as potential slaves.

In keeping with his humanistic background, Columbus revised Ptolemy to fit with his own experience. He explained in a letter addressed to the Spanish monarchs that *"Ptolemy and the other geographers believed that the world was spherical."* Columbus believed this until his third voyage, when he came *"to the following conclusions concerning the world: that it is not round as they describe it, but the shape of a pear, which is round everywhere except at the stalk, where it juts out a long way; or that it is like a round ball on part of which is something like a woman's nipple."** Columbus's eyes were troubling him, but the ocean seemed to tilt upward, and this was the only way he could explain it. Columbus always thought that he was in Japan; he had no idea that he had landed on a continent unknown to the ancients. The first map to use the word *America* on a new continent (much smaller than reality) appeared in 1507 (see page 419); before then everyone assumed that Columbus and all the other explorers immediately after him were somewhere in the Indies.

Arawak
General name for a family of languages spoken in the 1500s over a large region spanning from modern Venezuela to Florida. Also refers to speakers of these languages.

A Comparison of Columbus's and Zheng He's Voyages

Many people have wondered why the Spanish and the Portuguese, and not the Chinese of the Ming dynasty, established the first overseas empires. The Chinese, who first set off in 1405, had almost a century's head start on the Europeans. (See the feature "Visual Evidence in Primary Sources: Comparing Zheng He's and Columbus's Ships.")

China was richer than either Spain or Portugal. It was arguably the most prosperous country in the world in the early fifteenth century, while Spain and Portugal were far smaller. Yet their small size gave both the Portuguese and the Spanish powerful motivation to seek new lands.

Columbus's voyages differed from the Chinese voyages in another critical sense. The navigators on the Chinese treasure ships knew each destination because they followed the best-traveled oceanic route in the world before 1500. Muslim pilgrims from East Africa traveled up the East African coast to reach their holy city of Mecca, and Chinese pilgrims sailed around Southeast Asia and India to reach the Arabian peninsula. The Zheng He voyages simply linked the two hajj routes together. In contrast, when Columbus and other later explorers set off, they were consciously exploring, looking for new places to colonize and going where no one else (or at least no one else that anyone remembered) had gone before.

*J. M. Cohen, trans., *The Four Voyages of Christopher Columbus* (New York: Penguin, 1969), pp. 35, 218.

Moreover, the Chinese had no concept of a "colony"—no colonies comparable to Madeira or the Canary Islands. The Ming dynasty governed a huge empire, and there is no indication that the Yongle emperor (r. 1403–1424) wanted to make it bigger by using the voyages. He simply hoped that the various nations of the world would acknowledge him as the rightful ruler of the Chinese. Rulers of earlier Chinese dynasties had sometimes conquered other peoples, but always in contiguous neighboring lands, never overseas.

The Ming government ordered an end to the voyages in 1433 because they brought no financial benefit to the Chinese. In contrast, the Spanish and Portuguese voyages brought their countries immediate returns in gold and slaves and the promise of long-term profits if settlers could establish enterprises such as sugar plantations.

Spanish Exploration After Columbus's First Voyage, 1493–1517

From the beginning Columbus did not exercise tight control over his ships, the *Niña*, the *Pinta*, and the *Santa Maria*. When he first reached the Americas, the ship *Niña* set off on its own to search for gold, and Columbus had no choice but to welcome it back. The *Santa Maria* had already run aground and been dismantled to make a fort, and Columbus needed both remaining ships to return home. With only two ships, he was forced to leave thirty-nine men behind in the fort, but when he returned on his second voyage in 1493, he found that all had been killed, presumably in disputes with the Arawak over women. Relations between the Arawak and the Spanish worsened, and skirmishes regularly occurred.

Once the Spanish realized that Columbus had discovered a new landmass, they negotiated the **Treaty of Tordesillas** (tor-day-SEE-yuhs) with the Portuguese in 1494, while Columbus was away on his second voyage. The treaty established a dividing line: all newly discovered territory west of the line belonged to Castile, while all the lands to the east were reserved for Portugal. Lands already ruled by a Christian monarch were unaffected by the agreement. Portugal gained Africa, the route to India, and eventually Brazil.

Columbus never solved the problem of how to compensate his men. When recruiting sailors in Spain he spoke of great riches, but the agreement he had signed with Ferdinand and Isabella gave his men nothing. On his first voyage, his men expected to sail with him to Asia and return, but on subsequent voyages many joined him expressly so that they could settle in the Americas, where they hoped to make fortunes. In 1497, the settlers revolted against Columbus, and he agreed to allow them to use Indians as agricultural laborers. Because Columbus was unpopular with the settlers, in 1499 the Crown removed him from office and replaced him with a new viceroy.

Spanish and Portuguese navigators continued to land in new places after 1503. The Spanish crossed 120 miles (193 km) from Cuba to the Yucatán Peninsula in 1508–1509 and reached Florida in 1510. In 1513, Vasco Núñez de Balboa (bal-BOH-uh) crossed through Panama to see the Pacific, and by 1522 the Portuguese navigator Magellan had circumnavigated the globe, although he died before his ship returned home.

The Conquest of Mexico, 1517–1540

One of the early Spanish **conquistadors**, Hernán Cortés (hare-NAN kor-TES), who led the conquest of Mexico, came first to Hispaniola in 1506 and moved to Cuba in 1509. Like many of the other Spanish

Treaty of Tordesillas Treaty signed by the Portuguese and the Spanish in 1494 that established a dividing line: all newly discovered territory west of the line belonged to Castile, while all of the islands to the east were reserved for Portugal.

conquistadors Literally "conquerors," the term for the Spaniards who conquered Mexico, Peru, and Central America in the 1500s.

Comparing Zheng He's and Columbus's Ships

What did Columbus's and Zheng He's ships look like? Since no drawings of any of their boats survive, nautical historians must compare multiple images of boats from the period to reconstruct what these vessels looked like. Even then, crucial information is still missing: the actual length of Columbus's main ship, the *Santa Maria*, ranged anywhere from 80–120 feet (24–37 m). A small wooden boat left as an offering in a church near Barcelona reveals the most about the construction of the *Santa Maria*. In the 1440s or 1450s, a sailor crafted it to give thanks for surviving a storm. Since he was not a shipbuilder, it may not be entirely accurate. But it has much more information about construction than do many drawings.[*]

We know even less about the Zheng He ships, since no contemporary models exist. Dimensions written in Chinese units survive, but scholars disagree about what they mean. Earlier studies used one value to arrive at a mind-boggling length of 400 feet (122 m), but a recent study, using a new value, has halved that to 200 feet (61 m), which naval historians agree is the longest possible length for an entirely wooden ship. Otherwise it would simply snap into pieces.[**]

These estimates mean that the Zheng He vessels were between 166 and 250 percent bigger than Columbus's.

The full fleet of 317 Chinese treasure ships, led by Admiral Zheng He, carried 28,000 men; the doctors on board outnumbered Columbus's entire crew. The Chinese ships were technologically more advanced, too. The ships had watertight compartments that could contain a leak. If Columbus's sailors could not plug a leak, the entire ship would fill with water and sink. The Chinese sailors feasted on fresh fish that thrived in their watertight compartments, while Columbus's men had to make do with hardtack, or dried biscuits.

Yet the size of the treasure ships was also a drawback. At 200 feet (61 m), they were simply too big to sail into unknown waters. One of Columbus's original three ships ran aground during the first voyage, and he complained that his ships were too large for successful exploration.

[*]Franceo Gay and Cesare Ciano, *The Ships of Christopher Columbus* (Roma: Libreria dello Stato, 1996).

[**]André Wegener Sleeswyk, "The Liao and the Displacement of Ships in the Ming Navy," *The Mariner's Mirror* 82, no. 1 (1996): 3–13.

Comparison of Columbus's and Zheng He's Fleets

	Distance Traveled	Length of Ships	Number of Ships	Size of Crew	Number of Voyages
Columbus's ships	4,000 miles (6,400 km)	80–120 feet (24–37 m)	3	87	4
Zheng He's ships	7,000 miles (11,000 km)	200 feet (61 m)	317	28,000	7

QUESTIONS FOR ANALYSIS

» *Is bigger always better? Why or why not?*

» *If you were a Spanish shipbuilder, which feature of the Chinese ships would you most want to adopt? Why?*

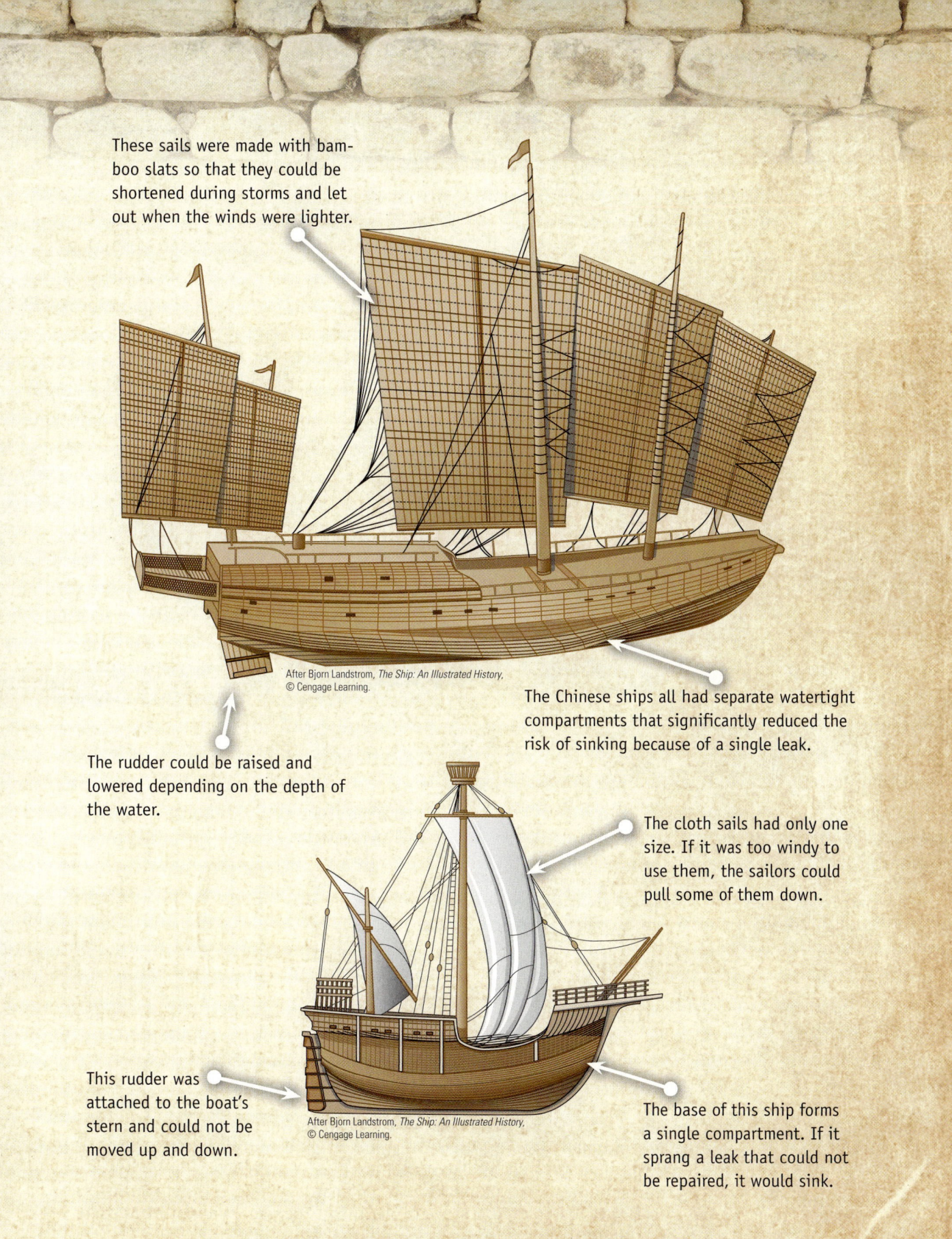

These sails were made with bamboo slats so that they could be shortened during storms and let out when the winds were lighter.

After Bjørn Landstrom, *The Ship: An Illustrated History*, © Cengage Learning.

The Chinese ships all had separate watertight compartments that significantly reduced the risk of sinking because of a single leak.

The rudder could be raised and lowered depending on the depth of the water.

The cloth sails had only one size. If it was too windy to use them, the sailors could pull some of them down.

This rudder was attached to the boat's stern and could not be moved up and down.

After Bjørn Landstrom, *The Ship: An Illustrated History*, © Cengage Learning.

The base of this ship forms a single compartment. If it sprang a leak that could not be repaired, it would sink.

Cortés's Interpreter, Malinche This image, created by a local artist, dates to the 1500s and shows what Cortés's army looked like when it first landed in Mexico. The Spaniards, with their heavy armor and a single horse, contrast sharply with the local peoples, who use bands tied around their foreheads to bear the weight of food in containers as well as to carry a small child (*far left*). The army was a mixed force. Malinche, who was Cortés's mistress and interpreter, stands at the far right, with the bearded Cortés on her left. (Bibliotheque Nationale, Paris, France/Snark/Art Resource, NY)

conquistadors ("conquerors"), he came from a family of middling social influence and made his fortune in the Americas. Cortés, in Cuba, heard that the Maya peoples of the Yucatán talked about a larger, richer empire to the north. He sought to launch an expedition and within two weeks had recruited 530 men to travel with him.

When Cortés landed on the coast of Mexico in early 1519, he immediately met a woman who helped him penetrate the Spanish-Nahuatl language barrier: a Nahua noblewoman named **Malinche** (mah-LEEN-chay) who had grown up among the Maya and could speak both Nahuatl and Mayan. Given to Cortés as a gift, Malinche learned Spanish quickly. The Spaniards called her Doña Marina. As adviser to Cortés, she played a crucial role in the Spanish conquest of Mexico, partly because she commanded the respect of the Nahua peoples.

Malinche
A Nahua noblewoman, trilingual in Spanish, Nahuatl, and Mayan, who served as translator for and adviser to Cortés.

Cortés landed on April 20, 1519, and slightly over two years later the Aztec had surrendered their capital and their empire to him (see Map 15.1). Yet this outcome was far from certain. The Spanish had only 1,500 men.

The encounter between the Nahua and the Spaniards is unusual because we have surviving sources from both sides—the European colonizers and the indigenous peoples. One of Cortés's foot soldiers, Bernal Díaz del Castillo, wrote the most detailed account from the Spanish point of view. On the Nahua side, a Franciscan missionary named Fray Bernardino de Sahagún (FRAY burr-nar-DEE-noh day sah-hah-GUHN) compiled the **Florentine Codex** in the 1550s on the basis of interviews he and his research assistants conducted and recorded in an alphabet for Nahuatl developed by Spanish missionaries. This account is not the same as a first-person contemporary account, yet since Sahagún and his team systematically crosschecked what their informants reported, it is the best Nahuatl-language account we have.

The *Florentine Codex* records the response of the reigning Great Speaker Moctezuma (also spelled Montezuma) to the first envoy from the Spanish:

> It especially made him faint when he heard how the guns went off at the Spaniards' command, sounding like thunder. . . . And when it went off, something like a ball came out from inside, and fire went showering and spitting out. . . . And if they shot at a hill, it seemed to crumble and come apart. . . . Their war gear was all iron. They clothed their bodies in iron, they put iron on their heads, their swords were iron. . . .
>
>   And their deer that carried them were as tall as the roof.[*]

The Spaniards' "deer" were horses, an animal not native to the Americas, whose size greatly impressed the Mexica.

On their way to Tenochtitlan, the Spaniards fought a major battle lasting nearly three weeks with the people of Tlaxcala (tlash-CAH-lah). After their defeat, the Tlaxcalans became the Spaniards' most important allies against the hated Mexica overlords. When, in November 1519, the Spaniards first arrived at the capital city of Tenochtitlan, the Great Speaker Moctezuma allowed them to come in unharmed. The Spaniards could not believe how beautiful the city was. Bernal Díaz described this event:

> Gazing on such wonderful sights, we did not know what to say, or whether what appeared before us was real, for on one side, on the land, there were great cities, and in the lake ever so many more, and the lake itself was crowded with canoes, and in the Causeway were many bridges at intervals, and in front of us stood the great City of Mexico.[*]

For one week the Spaniards and the Mexica coexisted uneasily, until the Spanish placed Moctezuma under house arrest. Then, in the spring of 1520, while Cortés was away, one of his subordinates ordered his men to massacre the city's inhabitants, and prolonged battles resulted. The Spaniards killed Moctezuma and, after suffering hundreds of casualties, retreated to Tlaxcala, the city of their allies. At this point, it seemed that the Mexica would win.

Florentine Codex
The main source in Nahuatl about the events of the Spanish conquest, compiled by a Franciscan missionary in the 1550s based on interviews with native witnesses.

---

[*]Stuart B. Schwartz, *Victors and Vanquished: Spanish and Nahua Views of the Conquest of Mexico* (New York: Bedford/St. Martin's, 2000), pp. 97, 133.

But by then smallpox had reached the Americas. The native peoples of America had little or no resistance to European smallpox, measles, malaria, sexually transmitted diseases, or even the common cold. Beginning in December 1518, disease ravaged Hispaniola and then Puerto Rico, Jamaica, and Cuba, and in the spring of 1520, smallpox crossed into the Yucatán and soon arrived in Tenochtitlan. Moctezuma's successor died of smallpox in early December, and the mass deaths threw the entire city into disarray.

Even so, the Spaniards had great difficulty conquering the Aztec empire. They laid siege to Tenochtitlan for eighty days of sustained fighting before the city surrendered in August of 1521. Spanish guns and cannon were not decisive. Some one hundred thousand troops and a portable fleet of boats supplied by the Tlaxcalans enabled the Spaniards to win.

In 1524, twelve Franciscan friars arrived in Mexico, where they were welcomed by Cortés. The Franciscans became the most important missionary order among the Nahuatl speakers. They searched for parallels between native beliefs and Christian teachings at the same time that they suppressed practices, like human sacrifice and polygamy, that they saw as un-Christian. (See the feature "Movement of Ideas Through Primary Sources: *The Sacrifice of Isaac*: A Sixteenth-Century Nahuatl Play.") The Spanish gradually imposed a more regular administration over Mexico under the governance of a viceroy.

The Spanish Conquest of Peru, 1532–1550

The order of events in the Spanish conquest of Peru differed from that in Mexico, where Cortés had arrived before smallpox. The smallpox virus traveled overland from Mexico and, in 1528, caused an epidemic in which many Inca, including the Sapa Inca, died. War among the contenders to the throne broke out. In November 1532, when the Spanish forces arrived, led by Francisco Pizarro (pih-ZAHR-oh) (1475–1541), they happened upon the moment of greatest instability in the Inca kingdom: when the newly enthroned Sapa Inca had not yet completely subdued his main rival. Atahualpa (ah-tuh-WAHL-puh; also spelled Atawallpa) had become ruler only after defeating his older half-brother, whom he still held in captivity. Atahualpa had taken severe countermeasures against his brother's supporters, many of whom sided immediately with the Spaniards.

When Pizarro and his 168 men arrived at Cajamarca, an important city in the Peruvian highlands where Atahualpa was living, Atahualpa initially received the Spanish peacefully. Then, on their second day in Cajamarca, the Spanish attacked unexpectedly. Their guns, armor, and horses gave them an initial advantage. An estimated seven thousand Inca, yet not a single Spaniard, died in the carnage.

Pizarro himself captured Atahualpa, who offered to pay an enormous ransom for his release: the Inca filled a room 2,600 cubic feet (74 cubic m) half with gold and half with silver, which the Spaniards melted down and divided among Pizarro's troops. Those with horses received 90 pounds (41 kg), equivalent today to perhaps $500,000, and those on foot half that amount. Then the Spanish reneged on their agreement and killed Atahualpa.

It took twenty more years for the Spanish to gain control of Peru. In 1551, they named the first viceroy for Peru and gradually established a more stable administration. The first Spanish census, taken in the 1570s, showed that half the population had died from European disease, with the toll in some places reaching as high as 95 percent. The Amerindians who lived at high altitudes suffered much fewer losses than those living on the coast.

The Portuguese Settlement of Brazil, 1500–1580

In 1500, Pedro Álvares Cabral (kah-BRAHL) (1467/68–1520) landed in Brazil. Although the Portuguese claimed Brazil following Cabral's voyage, few of them came to this resource-poor country. Most Portuguese sought their wealth in Asia, as discussed in the next chapter. In 1533 the Portuguese monarch John III (r. 1521–1557) made a systematic effort to encourage the settlement of Brazil by dividing it into fifteen slices, each occupying 160 miles (260 km) of the coastline and extending inland indefinitely. He granted these territories to Portuguese nobles, many of them his courtiers.

John III also authorized the Jesuits, a new order of Catholic priests founded in 1540, to preach in Brazil. Many Jesuits traveled to the interior, converted the indigenous peoples, and then resettled them in villages. The settlers searched for gold throughout the sixteenth century but never found significant amounts.

Instead, the Portuguese began to build sugar plantations, with the guidance of technicians brought from the Canary Islands. Since so many of the indigenous Amerindians had died, the plantation owners imported slaves from Africa, who had learned how to cultivate sugar in the Canary Islands and the Madeiras.

The Structure of Empire and the Encomienda System

In 1580 Philip II succeeded to the throne of both Spain and Portugal, and the two countries remained under a single king until 1640. The Portuguese and Spanish empires had evolved parallel structures independently. The highest colonial official, the viceroy, presided over a royal colony and governed in concert with an advisory council who could appeal any decisions to the king.

Both empires had the **encomienda system**, first established by the Spanish in 1503. Life under the Aztec and the Inca empires had accustomed the peoples of Mexico and Peru to shipping large quantities of goods, especially precious metals, to their rulers, and the encomienda system continued to collect resources and send them on to the center. Under this system, the monarchs "entrusted" (the literal meaning of *encomienda*) a specified number of Amerindians to a settler, who gained the right to extract labor, gold, or other goods from them in exchange for teaching them about Christianity. The monarchs took as their model the governmental structure used to administer lands newly recovered from Muslim kingdoms in the Reconquista (see page 415).

At first the Spaniards who received encomienda grants had much more power than the immigrants who had not, but over time their advantage lessened. The encomienda recipients had easy access to unskilled labor and could collect tribute from the locals, but ordinary Spaniards could obtain a land grant and hire labor to build estates of their own. Although designed to protect the indigenous peoples, the encomienda system often resulted in even greater exploitation.

The social structure in the colonies was basically the same throughout Latin America. At the top of society were those born in Europe, who served as military leaders, royal officials, or high church figures. Below them were creoles, those with two European parents but born in the Americas. Those of mixed descent (mestizos in Spanish-speaking regions, memlucos in Brazil) ranked even lower, with only Amerindians and African slaves below them. By 1600, one hundred thousand Africans lived in Brazil, many working in the hundreds of sugar mills all over the colony.

encomienda system
(Literally "entrusted") System established in 1503 by the Spanish in the hope of clarifying arrangements with the colonists and of ending the abuse of indigenous peoples of the Americas.

The Sacrifice of Isaac: A Sixteenth-Century Nahuatl Play

The members of the Catholic orders who lived in Mexico used different approaches to teach the Nahua peoples about Christianity. In addition to printing bilingual catechisms in Spanish and Nahuatl, they sponsored the composition of plays in Nahuatl on religious themes. Since these plays were not published but only circulated in hand-written manuscripts, very few survive. The short play *The Sacrifice of Isaac* recounts the story from the Hebrew Bible of Abraham and Isaac, which addresses a topic of great interest to the Nahua peoples: human sacrifice.

God the Father appears in the play to ask Abraham to sacrifice his son Isaac, but he later sends an angel to instruct Abraham to offer a lamb instead. Abraham, his first wife, and Isaac all embody obedience, a virtue prized both by the ancient Hebrews and the Nahua peoples. Abraham's slave Hagar and her son Ishmael urge Isaac to disobey his father; both still worship the sun (not God), a sure clue to the audience that they are evil.

Corresponding faithfully to the version in the Hebrew Bible, the play shows an obedient Isaac offering himself for sacrifice until the moment the angel instructs Abraham to free him and sacrifice a lamb instead. The lively quality of the Nahuatl language suggests that it was written sometime after the Spanish conquest, probably by a native speaker who converted to Christianity.

Source: Excerpt from Marilyn Ekdahl Ravicz, *Early Colonial Religious Drama in Mexico: From Tzompantli to Golgotha*, The Catholic University of America Press, 1970, pp. 87–90 and 95–96. Reprinted with permission of The Catholic University of America Press.

The Devil, Ishmael, and Hagar Trick Isaac

(A demon enters, dressed either as an angel or as an old man.)

DEMON: What are you doing, young man? For I see your affliction is very great.

ISHMAEL: Most certainly my affliction is great! But how is it that you know if I have pain? Who told you this?

DEMON: Do you not see that I am a messenger from heaven? I was sent here from there in order to tell you what you are to do here on earth.

ISHMAEL: Then I wait to hear your command.

DEMON: Hear then why it is that you are troubled. Do I astound you? Truly it is because of the beloved child, Isaac! Because he is a person of a good life, and because he always has confidence in the commands of his father. So you contrive and wish with all your energy that he not be obedient to his father and mother. Most assuredly I can tell you what you must do to accomplish this.

ISHMAEL: Oh how you comfort me when I hear your advice. Nor do I merit your aid. You are most truly a dweller in heaven and my protector!

DEMON: Open your heart wide to my command! Look now—his father and mother have invited many others to a banquet; they are relaxing and greatly enjoying themselves. Now is the time to give Isaac bad advice so that he might forget his father and his mother and go with you to amuse himself in some other place. And if he should obey you, they will certainly punish their son for this, however well they love him.

ISHMAEL: I shall do just as you command.

DEMON: Then, indeed, I am going to return to heaven. For I came only to console you and tell you what you must do. . . .

(Hagar the slave and her son Ishmael enter.)

HAGAR: Now while the great lord Abraham once again entertains many for the sake of his son whom he so greatly loves, we are only servants. He values us but little. And you, my son, merit nothing, are worthy of nothing. Oh that I might placate myself through you, and that you might calm all my torment upon earth! But so it is; your birth and its reward are eternal tears.

(Here they both weep—also the son.)

ISHMAEL: Oh you sun! You who are so high! Warm us even here with your great splendor as well as in every part of the world, and—in the way which you are able—prosper all the peoples of the earth! And to us, yes, even to us two poor ones— who merit nothing and who are worthy of nothing! Know now, oh my mother, what I shall do: later, when they are all feasting, perhaps I shall be able to lead Isaac away with some deceit, so that we might go to divert ourselves in some other quarter. With this action he will violate the precept of his father, who will not then love him with all of his heart.

HAGAR: What you are thinking is very good. Do it in that way.

Abraham and Isaac on the Mountain

ABRAHAM: Now hear me, my beloved son! Truly this is what the almighty God has commanded me in order that His loving and divine precept might be fulfilled; and so that He might see whether we—the inhabitants of the earth—love Him and execute His Divine Will. For He is the Lord of the living and of the dead. Now with great humility, accept death! For assuredly He says this: "Truly I shall be able to raise the dead back to life, I who am the Life Eternal." Then let His will be done in every part of the earth.

(Here Abraham weeps. The Music of the "Misericordia" is heard.)

ISAAC: Do not weep, my beloved and honored father! For truly I accept death with great happiness. May the precious will of God be done as He has commanded you. . . .

ANGEL: Abraham! Abraham!

(Here an angel appears and seizes Abraham's hand so that he is unable to kill his son.)

ABRAHAM: Who are you, you who speak to me?

ANGEL: Now know the following by the authority and word of God. For He has seen how much you love Him; that you fulfill His divine precept; that you do not infringe it; that you brought your cherished son—he whom you love so much— here to the peak of the mountain; and that you have come to offer him here as a burnt sacrifice to God the almighty Father. Now truly for all this, by His loving Will, I have come to tell you to desist, for your cherished son Isaac does not have to die.

ABRAHAM: May His adored will be done as He wishes it. Come here, oh my beloved son! Truly you have now been saved from death by His hand.

(Here he [Abraham or Isaac] unties the cloth with which he was blindfolded, and loosens the ropes with which his hands were bound.)

ANGEL: Then understand this: as a substitute for your beloved son, you shall prepare a lamb as God wishes it. Go, for I shall accompany you and leave you at your house.

QUESTIONS FOR ANALYSIS

» *What information does the author include to make the audience think Ishmael is bad and Isaac good?*

» *What does the text propose as an appropriate substitute for human sacrifice?*

The Columbian Exchange

At the same time that European diseases like smallpox devastated the peoples living in America, European animals like the horse, cow, and sheep came to the Americas and flourished. In the other direction came plant foods indigenous to the Americas like tomatoes, potatoes, peanuts, and chili peppers. This transfer is referred to as the **Columbian exchange**.

Columbian exchange
All the plants, animals, goods, and diseases that crossed the Atlantic, and sometimes the Pacific, after 1492.

Of all the European imports, smallpox had the most devastating effect on the Americas. Only someone suffering an outbreak can transmit smallpox, which is contagious for about a month: after two weeks of incubation, fever and vomiting strike; the ill person's skin then breaks out with the pox, small pustules that dry up after about ten days. Either the victim dies during those ten days or survives, typically with a pock-marked face and body.

One Nahuatl description captures the extent of the suffering:

Sores erupted on our faces, our breasts, our bellies. . . . The sick were so utterly help-less that they could only lie on their beds like corpses, unable to move their limbs or even their heads. . . . If they did move their bodies, they screamed with pain.[*]

Although no plants or animals had an effect as immediate as smallpox, the long-term effects of the Columbian exchange in plants and animals indelibly altered the landscape, diets, and population histories of both the Americas and Europe. When Columbus landed on Hispaniola, he immediately realized how different the plants were: *"All the trees were as different from ours as day from night, and so the fruits, the herbage, the rocks, and all things."* He also remarked on the absence of livestock: *"I saw neither sheep nor goats nor any other beast."*[†]

On his second voyage in 1493, Columbus carried cuttings of European plants, including wheat, melons, sugar cane, and other fruits and vegetables. He also brought pigs, horses, sheep, goats, and cattle. More like wild boars than modern hogs, pigs were the first to adapt to the Americas, eating wild grasses, reproducing in large numbers, and moving into many areas emptied of humans by the depredations of smallpox.

While smallpox traveled from Europe to the Americas, there is evidence that syphilis traveled in the other direction. The first well-documented outbreaks of syphilis in Europe occurred around 1495, and one physician claimed that Columbus's men brought it to Madrid soon after 1492. No European skeletons with signs of syphilis before 1500 have been found, but an Amerindian skeleton with syphilis has, suggesting that the disease did indeed move from the Americas to Europe. Causing severe pain, syphilis could be passed to the next generation and was fatal for about one-quarter of those who contracted it, but it did not cause mass deaths.

Assessing the loss of Amerindian life from smallpox and the other European diseases has caused much debate among historians because no population statistics exist for the Americas before 1492. Different historians have come up with estimates for the regions with the heaviest populations—Mexico, between 4 and

---

*Michael Wood, *Conquistadors* (Berkeley: University of California Press, 2000), p. 81, citing the *Florentine Codex*.

†Alfred W. Crosby, *The Columbian Exchange: Biological and Cultural Consequences of 1492* (Westport, Conn.: Greenwood Press, 1972), p. 4, n2, citing Christopher Columbus, *Journals and Other Documents on the Life and Voyages of Christopher Columbus,* trans. Samuel Eliot Morison (New York: The Heritage Press, 1963), pp. 72–73, 84.

6 million, and Peru, between 10 and 12 million—but even these numbers are controversial. Figures for the precontact population can be little more than guesswork. The first reliable figures for Amerindian populations came with Spanish colonization. In 1568, Spanish authorities counted 970,000 non-Spanish living in Mexico and 1.2 million living in Peru.[3] For the entire period of European colonization in all parts of the Americas, guesses at the total death toll from European diseases, based on controversial estimates of precontact populations, range from a low of 10 million to a high of over 100 million.

By 1600, two extremely successful agricultural enterprises had spread through the Americas. One was sugar, and the other was cattle raising. The Americas contained huge expanses of grasslands in Venezuela and Colombia, from Mexico north to Canada, and in Argentina and Uruguay. In each case the Spaniards began on the coastal edge of a grassland and followed their rapidly multiplying herds of cattle to the interior.

As European food crops transformed the diet of those living in the Americas, so too did American food crops transform the eating habits of people in Afro-Eurasia. American food crops moved into West Africa, particularly modern Nigeria, where even today people eat corn, peanuts, squash, manioc (cassava), and sweet potatoes.

Two crops in particular played an important role throughout Afro-Eurasia: corn (maize) and potatoes (including sweet potatoes). Both produced higher yields than wheat and grew in less desirable fields, such as on the slopes of hills. Although few people anywhere in the world preferred corn or potatoes to their original wheat-based or rice-based diet, if the main crop failed, hungry people gratefully ate the American transplants. By the eighteenth century corn and potatoes had reached as far as India and China, and the population in both places increased markedly.

CONTEXT AND CONNECTIONS

1492: The Break Between the Premodern and Modern Worlds

History departments offer many yearlong survey classes, and individual instructors often choose midway points for their classes. Not so for world history, which almost always breaks at 1500 (or 1492). Christopher Columbus's landing on the island of Hispaniola changed the world permanently.

Many claims have been made about voyagers who reached the Americas before Columbus. Some of these voyages have left convincing evidence, like the Viking settlement at L'Anse aux Meadows on Canada's Atlantic coast in about 1000 or the chicken bones showing contact between Polynesia and the west coast of South America in the 1350s. Some of the claims have no basis at all: absolutely no evidence suggests that Zheng He's ships reached the Americas, as has been proposed. Some theories are possible without being certain: English fishing boats that sailed from Bristol to Iceland in 1480 and 1481 to seek new fishing grounds for cod might have made

it all the way to the Americas, but they left no traces there. Whatever the credibility of these claims—and new evidence is emerging all the time—none of these voyages did more than touch down in the Americas, and they left no lasting impact. Columbus's voyages were utterly different.

After Columbus's landfall in 1492, the pace of events accelerated. Spain conquered Mexico in 1521 and Peru in 1551. The once-powerful Aztec and Inca empires collapsed quickly. They both had internal weaknesses; the many subject peoples of the Mexica resented their overlords, and the Inca were right in the middle of a protracted succession struggle.

The Europeans also had superior weapons made from metal. The Mexica and the Inca knew how to work different metals, including gold and silver, but they could not work iron, and they had no metal weapons. Theirs were all made from stone and wood. Recall the eyewitness description from the *Florentine*

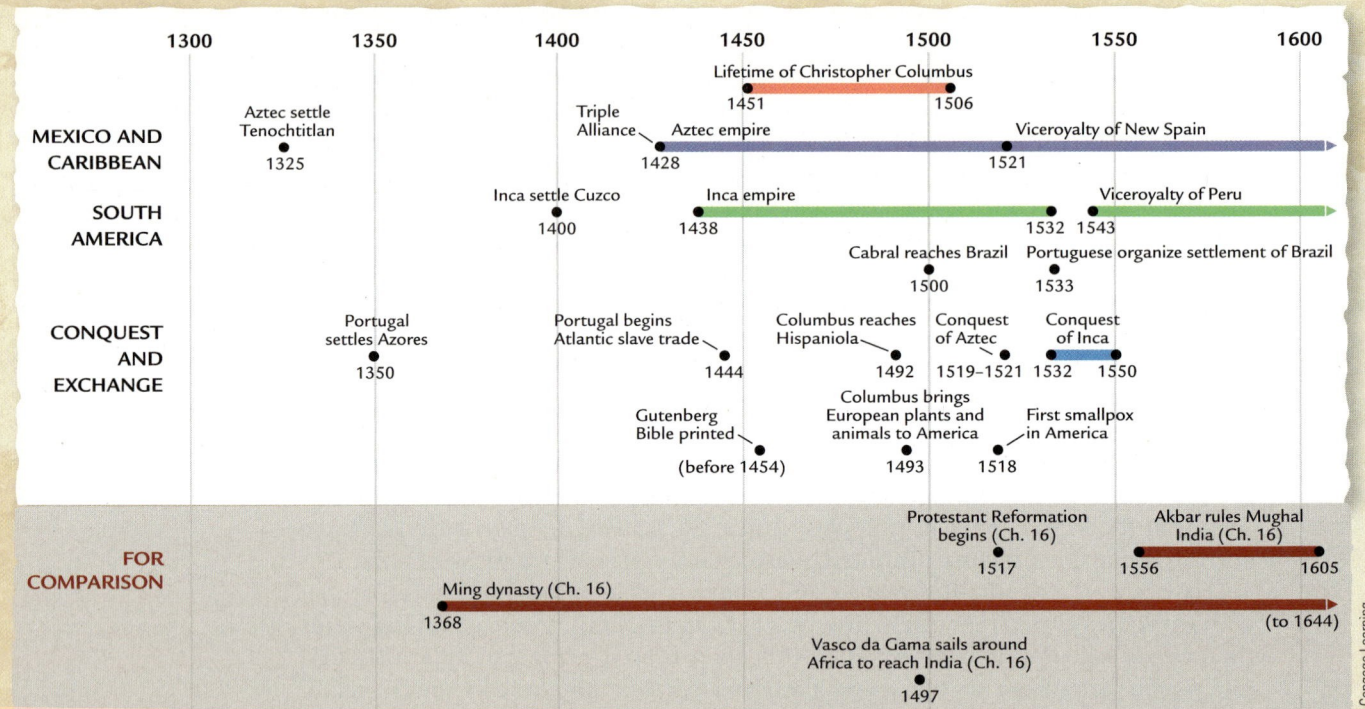

MEXICO AND CARIBBEAN

Aztec settle Tenochtitlan
1325

Triple Alliance

Lifetime of Christopher Columbus
1451 — 1506

Aztec empire
1428

Viceroyalty of New Spain
1521

SOUTH AMERICA

Inca settle Cuzco
1400

Inca empire
1438 — 1532

Viceroyalty of Peru
1543

Cabral reaches Brazil
1500

Portuguese organize settlement of Brazil
1533

CONQUEST AND EXCHANGE

Portugal settles Azores
1350

Portugal begins Atlantic slave trade
1444

Columbus reaches Hispaniola
1492

Conquest of Aztec
1519–1521

Conquest of Inca
1532 — 1550

Gutenberg Bible printed
(before 1454)

Columbus brings European plants and animals to America
1493

First smallpox in America
1518

FOR COMPARISON

Protestant Reformation begins (Ch. 16)
1517

Akbar rules Mughal India (Ch. 16)
1556 — 1605

Ming dynasty (Ch. 16)
1368 (to 1644)

Vasco da Gama sails around Africa to reach India (Ch. 16)
1497

© Cengage Learning

Codex of the Spanish army: their guns produced "thunder," they were clothed head to toe in iron, and their "deer" (read: horses) "were as tall as the roof."

European horses were only one example of the unfamiliar plants and animals that flowed from Europe to the Americas and from the Americas to Africa and Eurasia in the Columbian exchange. Cows, sheep, and pigs came to the Americas and altered the American landscape; tomatoes, potatoes, corn, and chili peppers traveled the other way, transforming first the European and then the African and Asian diets.

As discussed in Chapter 16, silver from Spanish mines in the Americas had an equally dramatic effect on the European economy. After 1550, when the Spanish mastered the technique of using mercury to separate silver from ore, they began to ship large quantities of silver home via the Philippines. The silver brought great prosperity to the Spanish empire and financed European purchases in Asia.

The diseases that came to the Americas from Europe devastated native peoples: smallpox killed so many that one can trace its deadly route from Hispaniola to Puerto Rico, Jamaica, and Cuba and then on to Mexico and Peru. Because no population figures predate Columbus, it is impossible to know how many perished, but estimates range between 10 and 100 million. In 1568, the Spanish counted 2,170,000 non-Spanish survivors in Mexico and Peru, the two areas with the heaviest indigenous populations. Everyone else had died.

The mass deaths of the Amerindians preceded the large-scale movement of Europeans and Africans to the Americas. The migrations in the first hundred years after Columbus's arrival in Hispaniola produced the mixed population of the Americas today.

Before 1492 world history often concerns individual regions and the intermittent contacts among them. After 1492, Europe, the Americas, and Africa were so tightly connected that events in one place always affected the others. In the next chapter we will learn what happened when Europeans traveled to Asia.

Voyages on the Web: Christopher Columbus

The Voyages Map App follows the traveler's journeys using interactive study tools, including 360-degree panoramic views of historic sites, zoomable maps, audio summaries, flash cards, and quizzes.

Key Terms

Christopher Columbus (402)
Aztec empire (405)
altepetl (405)
Tenochtitlan (405)
Inca empire (407)
ayllu (407)

quipu (412)
humanism (413)
Henry the Navigator (415)
Arawak (420)
Treaty of Tordesillas (421)
conquistadors (421)

Malinche (424)
Florentine Codex (425)
encomienda system (427)
Columbian exchange (430)

For Further Reference

Coe, Michael, and Rex Koontz. *Mexico: From Olmecs to the Aztecs*. London: Thames and Hudson, 2008.

Cohen, J. M., trans. *The Four Voyages of Christopher Columbus*. New York: Penguin, 1969.

D'Altroy, Terence. *The Incas*. Malden, Mass.: Blackwell Publishing, 2002.

Flint, Valerie I. J. *The Imaginative Landscape of Christopher Columbus*. Princeton: Princeton University Press, 1992.

Grafton, Anthony, et al. *New Worlds, Ancient Texts: The Power of Tradition and the Shock of Discovery*. Cambridge, Mass.: The Belknap Press of Harvard University Press, 1992.

Lockhart, James. *The Nahuas After the Conquest: A Social and Cultural History of the Indians of Central Mexico, Sixteenth Through Eighteenth Centuries*. Stanford: Stanford University Press, 1992.

Lockhart, James, and Stuart Schwartz. *Early Latin America: A History of Colonial Spanish America and Brazil*. New York: Cambridge University Press, 1983.

McEwan, Colin, and Leonardo López Luján. *Moctezuma Aztec Ruler*. London: British Museum Press, 2009.

Quinn, David B. "Columbus and the North: England, Iceland, and Ireland." *William and Mary Quarterly*, 3d series, 49, no. 2 (1992): 278–297.

Russell, Peter. *Prince Henry "the Navigator": A Life*. New Haven: Yale University Press, 2000.

Schwartz, Stuart B. *The Iberian Mediterranean and Atlantic Traditions in the Formation of Columbus as a Colonizer*. Minneapolis: The Associates of the James Ford Bell Library, University of Minnesota, 1986.

Schwartz, Stuart B. *Victors and Vanquished: Spanish and Nahua Views of the Conquest of Mexico*. New York: Bedford/St. Martin's, 2000.

Smith, Michael E. *The Aztecs*. Malden, Mass.: Blackwell Publishing, 2003.

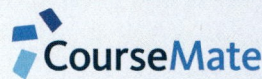 Go to the CourseMate website at **www.cengagebrain.com** for additional study tools and review materials—including audio and video clips—for this chapter.

16

Maritime Expansion in Afro-Eurasia, 1500–1700

The Italian priest **Matteo Ricci** (1552–1610) knew more about China than any other European of his time. Though frustrated by the small number of converts he made to Christianity during his two decades as a missionary, Ricci (REE-chee) described Chinese political and social life in positive terms. While Ricci was sometimes less complimentary, in the following passage his idealized view of China was meant as a criticism of his own society. Ricci was correct in his assessment that China was more populous, more prosperous, and more stable than Europe in the first decade of the seventeenth century:

Matteo Ricci

(Ricci Institute for Chinese-Western Cultural History, University of San Francisco)

I *t seems to be quite remarkable . . . that in a kingdom of almost limitless expanse and innumerable population, and abounding in copious supplies of every description, though they have a well-equipped army and navy that could easily conquer the neighboring nations, neither the King nor his people ever think of waging a war of aggression. . . . In this respect they are much different from the people of Europe, who are frequently discontent with their own governments and covetous of what others enjoy. . . . Another remarkable fact and . . . marking a difference from the West, is that the entire kingdom is administered by . . . Philosophers. The responsibility for orderly management of the entire realm is wholly*

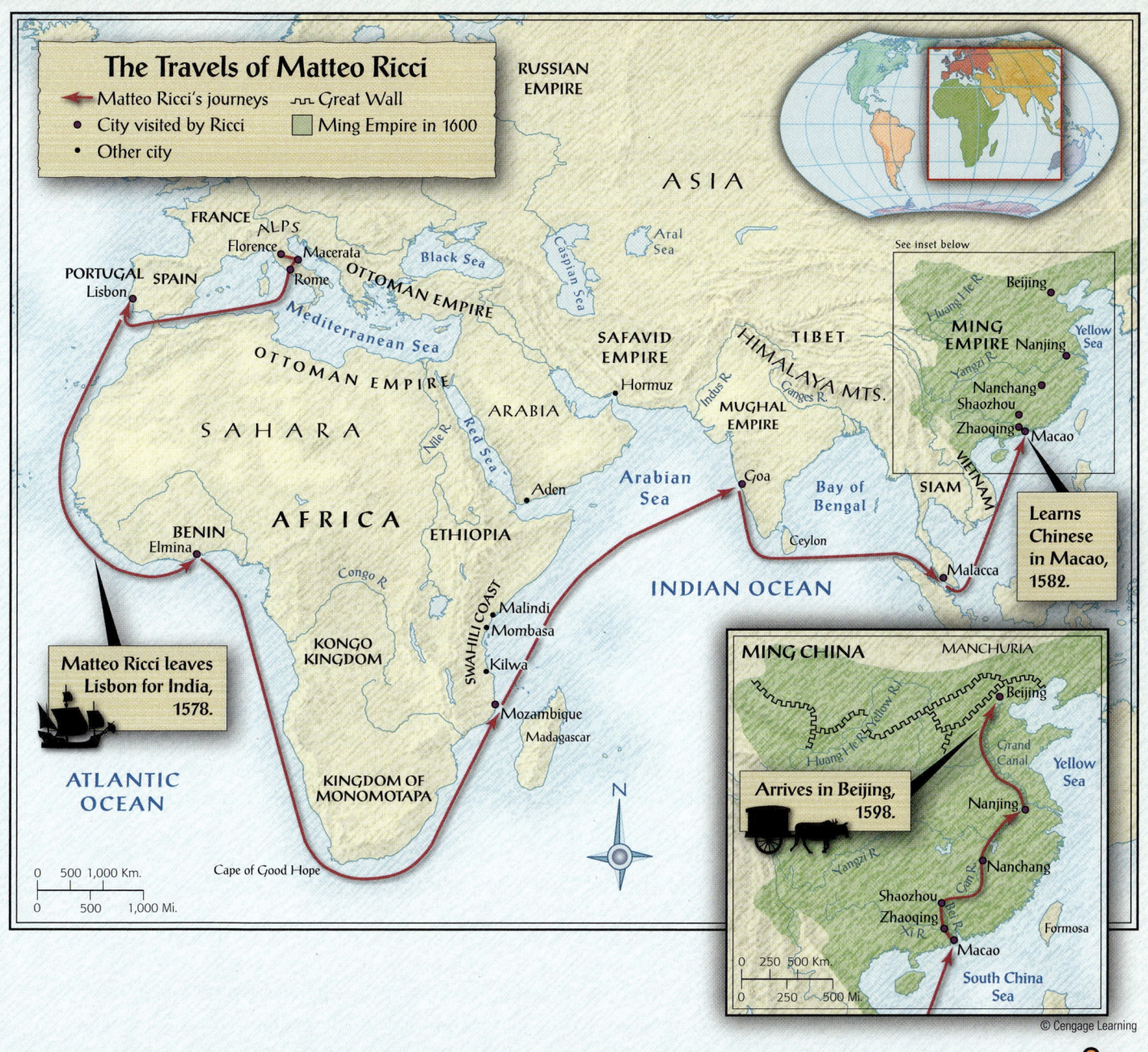

The Travels of Matteo Ricci

← Matteo Ricci's journeys   〰 Great Wall
● City visited by Ricci   ■ Ming Empire in 1600
● Other city

RUSSIAN EMPIRE

ASIA

Aral Sea

FRANCE
ALPS
Florence   Macerata
PORTUGAL   SPAIN   Rome
Lisbon

Black Sea

Caspian Sea

OTTOMAN EMPIRE

Mediterranean Sea

OTTOMAN EMPIRE

SAFAVID EMPIRE

Hormuz

TIBET

HIMALAYA MTS.

Indus R.

Ganges R.

MUGHAL EMPIRE

Nile R.

Red Sea

ARABIA

SAHARA

AFRICA

Congo R.

BENIN
Elmina

ETHIOPIA

Aden

Arabian Sea

Goa

Bay of Bengal

Ceylon

INDIAN OCEAN

SIAM

VIETNAM

Malacca

Matteo Ricci leaves Lisbon for India, 1578.

SWAHILI COAST

Malindi
Mombasa
Kilwa

KONGO KINGDOM

Mozambique
Madagascar

ATLANTIC OCEAN

KINGDOM OF MONOMOTAPA

Cape of Good Hope

N

0   500   1,000 Km.
0   500   1,000 Mi.

See inset below

MING EMPIRE

Huang He R.

Beijing

Nanjing

Yellow Sea

Nanchang
Shaozhou

Zhaoqing
Macao

Yangzi R.

Learns Chinese in Macao, 1582.

MING CHINA

MANCHURIA

Huang He R. / Yellow R.

Beijing

Grand Canal

Yellow Sea

Arrives in Beijing, 1598.

Nanjing

Yangzi R.

Nanchang

Gan R.

Shaozhou
Zhaoqing
Xi R.

Red R.

Macao

Formosa

South China Sea

0   250   500 Km.
0   250   500 Mi.

© Cengage Learning

Join this chapter's traveler on "Voyages," an interactive tour of historic sites and events:
www.cengagebrain.com

*and completely committed to their charge and care. . . . Fighting and violence among the people are practically unheard of. . . . On the contrary, one who will not fight and restrains himself from returning a blow is praised for his prudence and bravery.**

___

*"The Diary of Matthew Ricci," in *Matthew Ricci, China in the Sixteenth Century*, trans. Louis Gallagher (New York: Random House, 1942, 1970), pp. 54–55.

From Ricci's point of view, all that China lacked was religious truth. He understood that to communicate his Christian ideas he had to conform to the expectations of the "Philosophers," the scholar-officials who staffed the enormous imperial bureaucracy of Ming China. To this end, he learned Mandarin Chinese, studied Confucian texts, and dressed in silk garments to show a social status "equal of a Magistrate."

Italian by birth, Ricci joined the Jesuits, a Catholic religious order dedicated to "conversion of the Infidels." Because it was the Portuguese who pioneered the direct oceanic route from Europe to Asia, Ricci traveled from Rome to Lisbon to learn Portuguese and prepare for his mission. He then spent four years in India before traveling to China, where he lived from 1582 until his death in 1610. Meanwhile, other Jesuits were traveling to Japan, Brazil, Quebec, West Africa, and the Mississippi River Valley. The Jesuits were taking advantage of the new maritime connections established in the sixteenth century by the navigators who pioneered direct routes from Europe to the Americas, West Africa, the Indian Ocean, and East Asia.

While European mariners were a new presence in the Indian Ocean, they traveled on routes that had long been used by Asian and African merchants. In fact, the new maritime routes from Europe to Africa, the Indian Ocean, and East Asia first developed by Portuguese sailors were far less revolutionary than the connections between Europe, Africa, and the Americas that followed from the voyages of Christopher Columbus (see Chapter 15). Moreover, the dominant powers in Asia remained land-based empires, such as Mughal (MOO-gahl) India and Ming China, rather than European overseas colonies. As Matteo Ricci's story shows, Europeans who traveled the maritime routes often operated on the margins of these powerful Asian empires.

At the same time, the creation of more direct and sustained networks accelerated commercial and cultural interaction among Europe, Africa, and South and East Asia in the sixteenth and early seventeenth centuries, especially after the Dutch displaced the Portuguese as the main European players in the Indian Ocean. Following the maritime trade routes to China, Matteo Ricci became part of an ongoing "great encounter" between Europe and China.[1] Between 1400 and 1600, new and deepening economic linkages developed in the Indian Ocean, even as the Asian empires, such as India and China, became larger and more ambitious. In both Europe and Asia, major cultural and intellectual developments accompanied these new encounters and connections.

Focus Questions

» *What changes and continuities were associated with Portuguese and Dutch involvement in the Indian Ocean trade?*

» *What were the main political characteristics of the major South Asian and East Asian states? How was their development influenced by the new maritime connections of the sixteenth and early seventeenth centuries?*

» *How did the religious and intellectual traditions of Eurasia change during this period, and what were the effects of encounters between them?*

Maritime Trade Connections: Europe, the Indian Ocean, and Africa, 1500–1660

Unlike the Atlantic, the Indian Ocean had long served to connect rather than divide, facilitating trade among East Africa, the Persian Gulf, India, Southeast Asia, and China along a maritime Silk Road that complemented the one that had long connected eastern and western Eurasia by land. The Portuguese added a new element to these networks when their ships appeared in Indian Ocean waters in the early 1500s. Though their intention was to create an empire like that being constructed by Spain in the Americas, their political and military ambitions went largely unmet. The Dutch followed the Portuguese, bringing with them innovations in naval technology and business organization that stimulated the older oceanic trade networks while also building new ones.

Africa was connected to both the Atlantic and Indian Ocean systems. In East Africa the Portuguese merely inserted themselves into an existing commercial network. In West Africa, however, an entirely new oceanic trade began: the Atlantic slave trade.

Portugal's Entry into the Indian Ocean, 1498–1600

Henry the Navigator's exploration of the Atlantic Ocean culminated in 1488 when Bartholomew Dias and his crew rounded the southern tip of Africa at the Cape of Good Hope (see Map 15.3, page 416). These journeys had both economic and religious motives: in seeking an oceanic trade link with Asia, the Portuguese were trying to outflank Muslim intermediaries who controlled the land routes through western Asia and North Africa. They were also keenly aware of the West African gold that was enriching their Muslim enemies in Morocco, and by sailing south they hoped to divert those riches to their own treasuries.

In 1497 the Portuguese explorer **Vasco da Gama** (1460–1524) sailed for India. The trip was not an easy one. After reaching the Cape of Good Hope, most of the crew wanted to return home and nearly mutinied. Sailing up the East African coast, da Gama hired a local pilot who used Arabic-language charts and navigational guides to lead the Portuguese from Africa to western India. One of these books boasted of the superiority of Arab knowledge: *"We possess scientific books that give stellar altitudes. . . . [Europeans] have no science and no books, only the compass. . . . They admit we have a better knowledge of the sea and navigation and the wisdom of the stars."*[*] The Portuguese were sailing into well-charted waters, the same ones visited by Zheng He one hundred years earlier (see Chapter 15).

When they reached India, the Portuguese anchored their ships in cosmopolitan ports that were at the center of the world's most extensive maritime trading system. In the western Indian Ocean, merchants transported East African gold, ivory, slaves, and timber to markets in southern Arabia, the Persian Gulf, and western India. Among the many goods exported from India along the same routes was highly valuable cotton cloth, often dyed by Indian craftsmen specifically to appeal to customers in distant markets across the ocean.

On the east coast of India another set of maritime networks connected the Bay of Bengal and the markets of Southeast Asia with Ming China. Muslim-ruled

Vasco da Gama (1460–1524) Portuguese explorer who in 1497–1498 led the first European naval expedition to reach India by sailing around the Cape of Good Hope, laying the foundation for the Portuguese presence in the Indian Ocean in the century.

[*]Ahmad ibn Majid, *Book of Useful Information on the Principles and Rules of Navigation*, cited in *Saudi Aramco World*, July/August 2005, p. 46.

Malacca (mah-LAK-eh), which controlled trade through the straits between Sumatra and the Malaya Peninsula, had a population of over fifteen thousand traders from all over the Indian Ocean world. Here silk and sugar joined the long list of traded commodities. Cinnamon from the fabled "spice islands" was particularly precious, and since the Middle Ages the European market for pepper had grown exponentially. Whoever controlled the narrow straits at Malacca would profit handsomely from all this commercial activity.

Economically, the Portuguese had almost nothing to offer: the first Indian king with whom they negotiated was insulted by the poor quality of their gifts. It was a long-standing problem: Europe produced nothing that was valued in Asian markets. But the Portuguese made up for their economic weakness with military technology: with their ship-mounted cannon, they could blow their competitors out of the water and destroy the coastal defenses of political rivals. Seizing important trading centers from East Africa to Malacca, the Portuguese controlled a huge area after 1582. Their aggressive behavior earned them a widespread reputation as rough, greedy, and uncivilized.

In some cases the Portuguese redirected trade to profit themselves at the expense of previous merchant groups, such as the Swahili (swah-HEE-lee). For centuries the East African gold trade had been dominated by Swahili merchants, African Muslims who lived on the coast. The Swahili town of Kilwa, one of a series of commercially powerful city-states along the coast, was ideally suited for this trade, since it was the furthest point south that mariners from India, Persia, and Arabia could safely reach and return in the same year using the monsoon winds. The Portuguese used their cannon to destroy the sea walls of Kilwa and tried to divert the gold southward through their settlement in Mozambique. That they did so while flying militant Crusader crosses on their sails did not endear them to local Muslim merchants and rulers.

But the degree of disruption the Portuguese caused at Kilwa was exceptional. More often they simply inserted themselves into existing commercial networks and used military force to extort payments from Asian and African rulers and traders. "What they set up was not an empire," argues one historian, "but a vast protection racket." Portuguese officials required that all ships trading in the ocean purchase a license, and if an Indian Ocean captain was found trading without one he risked Portuguese cannon fire: "the Portuguese were selling protection from violence which they themselves had created."[*]

Siam (later known as Thailand) is a good barometer of both the extent and limitations of Portuguese power. In the 1500s Siam was a rising kingdom struggling to establish its independence from Burma. The Portuguese were welcomed as trading partners and military allies. Access to European cannon and local adaptation of Portuguese styles of military fortification helped Siamese leaders centralize power and establish their independence. Siam later remained open to the Dutch and French and benefited greatly from the expansion of Indian Ocean trade. There were limits on European influence, however. Popular culture remained rooted in Siamese adaptations of Hinduism and Buddhism. Asian traders, including Japanese, Chinese, and Malays, far outnumbered European ones. And trade with China, not with Europe, was central to Siam's commercial life. The country remained free from European colonial control even into the twentieth century (see Chapter 26).

The biggest gap between Portuguese ambition and achievement was in religion. While the Portuguese made few converts to Christianity, Islam continued to spread. Initially, the Portuguese had been hopeful that they would locate the kingdom of

---

[*]Michael Pearson, *The Indian Ocean* (London: Routledge, 2003), p. 121.

Fort Jesus, Mombasa Still standing on the Kenyan coast today, Fort Jesus was built by the Portuguese in 1593. The fort was built not only to protect Portuguese trade interests in the Indian Ocean, but also to assert the Christian conquest of the Swahili-speaking Muslims of Mombasa. The Swahili word for a jail, *gereza*, derives from the Portuguese word for a church, *igreja*, indicating how the residents of Mombasa themselves saw Fort Jesus. (© Adriane Van Zandbergen/Alamy)

Prester John, a mythical Christian African ruler. While Prester John did not exist, the Portuguese did form an alliance with the kingdom of Ethiopia, whose leaders had converted to Christianity a thousand years earlier. In 1542 Cristovão da Gama, son of the navigator, died while leading Portuguese forces against a Muslim enemy of the Ethiopian king. But the Ethiopians, with rituals and beliefs in common with the Egyptian church, resisted Catholic missionaries. The Portuguese/Ethiopian alliance fell apart, and in eastern Africa and across the Indian Ocean world it was Islam rather than Christianity that proved most attractive to new converts.

By the early seventeenth century, other powers, both European and Asian, were using ship-based cannon to challenge Portuguese fortifications. In 1622, for example, the British allied themselves with Safavid Iran to take the strategic port of Hormuz, at the mouth of the Persian Gulf, from the Portuguese, and in 1631 a local uprising drove the Portuguese from their strategic East African fortification of Fort Jesus.

The Dutch East India Company, 1600–1660

The most potent challenge to Portuguese commercial profit came from Dutch merchants, who were, by the early seventeenth century, developing both more efficient business systems and more advanced shipping technologies. Early Dutch trading ventures in Europe and the Atlantic were often very profitable, but merchants could be financially ruined if violent storms sank their ships or pirates stole their cargo. To spread the risk they developed **joint-stock companies**, a new form of business enterprise based on the sale of

joint-stock companies
Business organizations in which shares are sold to multiple stockholders to raise funds for trading ventures, while spreading both risk and profit; often backed by government charters granting monopolies of trade in particular goods or with specific regions.

The Dutch in Java The city of Bantam on the island of Java was strategically important for control of maritime trade. The English, Portuguese, and Dutch vied for control of that trade, with the Dutch East India Company dominating after they secured control over nearby Batavia (today's Jakarta, Indonesia) in 1619. As this seventeenth-century Dutch engraving shows, the bustling port city of Bantam was crowded with people and goods, and with buildings that show a mix of European, Islamic, and Javanese architectural styles. (Bibliotheque nationale de France/Archives Charmet/Bridgeman Art Library)

bourgeoisie
The French term for urban middle-class society—people with education and property but without aristocratic titles.

Dutch East India Company
Founded in 1602 in Amsterdam, a merchant company chartered to exercise a monopoly on all Dutch trade in Asia. The company was the effective ruler of Dutch colonial possessions in the East Indies.

shares to multiple owners. The joint-stock system allowed men and women of small means to buy a few shares and potentially reap a modest profit with little risk, since investors shared losses as well as profits.

These joint-stock companies put the Dutch at the forefront of early modern commercial capitalism. The development of financial institutions such as banks, stock exchanges, and insurance companies increased the efficiency with which capital could be accumulated and invested. Rather than seeking a single big windfall, investors now looked for more modest but regular gain through shrewd reinvestment of their profits. This dynamic was at the core of the new capitalist ethos associated with the **bourgeoisie**, the rising social group in Amsterdam and other urban areas of western Europe in the seventeenth century. The bourgeoisie based their social and economic power, and their political ambitions, on ownership of property rather than inherited titles.

Dutch culture reflected the rise of this commercially dynamic bourgeoisie. In many cultures trade was a low-status activity, it being assumed that a merchant could only be rich if he had made someone else poor. Seeking higher social status for their families, successful merchants in cultures as diverse as Spain and China would often use their assets to educate their sons to be "gentlemen" (in Spain) or members of the "literati" (in China). In Holland, by contrast, the leading citizens were all involved in trade, and commerce was seen as a noble calling.

The greatest of the joint-stock companies, and the largest commercial enterprise of the seventeenth century, was the **Dutch East India Company**, founded by a group of Amsterdam merchants in 1602. The government of the Netherlands granted a charter to the company giving it a monopoly on Dutch trade with Asia, with administrative and military responsibilities overseen from company head-quarters in Batavia in what became the Dutch East Indies (today's Indonesia). In the coming centuries other European powers would copy the Dutch model and use chartered companies to extend their own national interests.

Dutch capitalism was not based on free-market principles. The Dutch East India Company was a heavily armed corporate entity that maintained its monopoly through force. *"Trade cannot be maintained without war,"* said one governor of the East India Company, *"nor war without trade."*[*] The Dutch thus repeated the Portuguese pattern of using military force in the Indian Ocean to secure commercial profit, while at the same time introducing modern business and administrative techniques that made them more efficient and effective. In addition to their commercial innovations, the Dutch had made major advances in ship design and construction.

In 1641 they took Malacca from the Portuguese, and after 1658 they ruled the island of Sri Lanka (south of India). The Dutch presence in Africa focused on Cape Town, established at the southern tip of the continent in 1652 to provision Dutch ships en route to the Indian Ocean. Of course, the Dutch faced the same problem that the Portuguese and other European traders had earlier faced: what goods could they offer Asian merchants? One solution was to engage in inter-Asian trade, carrying Indian cottons further east, for example, while supplying spices for South Asian markets. Another solution was silver.

The Dutch were lucky that at this time the entire Indian Ocean economy was being stimulated by the introduction of large quantities of American silver mined by the Spanish in South America and shipped across the Pacific (see Map 16.1, page 448). In the seventeenth century, increased access to silver finally gave European traders bargaining power in Asia. The Spanish city of Manila in the Philippines became the destination for the Manila Galleons, an annual shipment of silver from Mexico. Thus, silver was central to an emerging trans-Pacific trade, which was from the beginning connected to the Indian Ocean network. In the late sixteenth century, this flow of silver between the Americas and Asia was helping to lay the foundation of a global economy, and the Dutch were perfectly positioned to benefit.

The Dutch East India Company made huge profits, especially from the spice trade. To do so, they sometimes violently intervened in local affairs to increase production, as on the Bandas Islands, where they killed or exiled most of the local population and replaced them with slaves drawn from East Africa, Japan, and India to grow nutmeg. The rate of profit on the spice trade ranged from several hundred to several thousand percent. Investors back in Holland were delighted, as were European consumers, who, thanks to the efficiency of Dutch methods, could now enjoy Asian spices at cheaper prices. According to one historian, seventeenth-century Holland was so prosperous the country enjoyed an *"embarrassment of riches."*[2]

Africa and the Atlantic Ocean, 1483–1660

While the East African coast had oceanic links connecting the Swahili city-states with the wider world, West Africa's international networks were traditionally land-based, across the Sahara. When the Portuguese sailed down the West African coast in the fifteenth century, therefore, these were the first significant coastal contacts that West Africans had experienced. Portugal's initial goals were the discovery of gold and transit to the East, as well as trade in commodities such as pepper and ivory. A new source of profit developed

*James D. Tracy, *The Political Economy of Merchant Empires* (New York: Cambridge University Press, 1991), p. 1.

after they settled Madeira in 1454 and began growing sugar, already part of the Mediterranean economy, on Atlantic islands (see Chapter 15). Production, and demand for slaves, boomed when plantations were developed on the Brazilian coast, and by the early seventeenth century sugar plantations in Brazil and the Caribbean were proliferating.

Kongo kingdom
West-central African kingdom whose king converted to Christianity in the early sixteenth century and established diplomatic relations with the Portuguese. Became an early source of slaves for the new Atlantic slave trade.

The **Kongo kingdom** was one of the earliest African societies to be destabilized by the new Atlantic slave trade. When the Portuguese arrived at the capital city of Mbanza Kongo in 1483, they found a prosperous, well-organized kingdom with extensive markets in cloth and iron goods. King Afonso Mvemba a Nzinga (uh-fahn-so mm-VEM-bah ah nn-ZING-ah) (r. 1506–1543), converted to Christianity, renamed his capital San Salvador, sent his son Enrique to study in Lisbon, and exchanged diplomatic envoys with both Portugal and the Vatican. (See the feature "Visual Evidence in Primary Sources: An Ivory Mask from Benin, West Africa.")

Aided by the Portuguese, Afonso undertook wars of conquest that added additional territory to the Kongo kingdom. As elsewhere in Africa, Afonso's wars were about power, not profit: slaves were a byproduct of the fighting, not its purpose. Still, these battles did have the side effect of further stimulating the slave trade. In West Africa, as in many parts of the world, captives taken during war might simply be killed, but more often they were exchanged, redeemed for a ransom, or kept as dependent workers. Into this traditional system came the new labor demands of the Atlantic plantation system. Portuguese merchants were anxious to purchase war captives. As demand for slaves increased, tragically so did the supply. Alarmed at the escalation in slave trading, King Afonso complained to his "*brother king*" in Portugal:

> *Many of our people, keenly desirous as they are of the wares and things of your Kingdoms, . . . seize many of our people, freed and exempt men . . . and so great, Sir, is the corruption and licentiousness that our country is being completely depopulated. . . . That is why we beg of your Highness to help and assist us in this matter . . . because it is our will that in these Kingdoms there should not be any trade of slaves nor outlet for them.*[*]

Foreign goods and foreign traders had distorted the traditional market in slaves, which had previously been an incidental byproduct of warfare, into an economic activity in its own right. Afonso's complaints fell on deaf ears.

As other European nations including Holland, France, and Britain became involved in slave trading and sugar production on the islands of the Caribbean, the demand for slaves increased decade by decade. Only African societies closest to the western coasts were immediately affected, yet by the eighteenth century the rise of the Atlantic slave trade would fundamentally alter the terms of Africans' interactions with the wider world (see Chapter 19).

Empires of Southern and Eastern Asia, 1500–1660

In the course of Matteo Ricci's long journey he came in contact with a great variety of cultural and political systems. By far the largest and most powerful of these societies were Mughal India and Ming China.

---

[*]Cited in John Reader, *Africa: A Biography of the Continent* (New York: Vintage, 1999), pp. 374–375.

Mughal India was a young and rising state in sixteenth-century South Asia with an economy stimulated by internal trade and expanding Indian Ocean commerce. Keeping the vast Mughal realms at peace, however, required India's Muslim rulers to maintain a stable political structure in the midst of great religious and ethnic diversity.

In the sixteenth century Ming China was the most populous and most productive society in the world. We have seen that Matteo Ricci was impressed with its order and good governance. But even while the Ming dynasty earned Ricci's admiration in the early seventeenth century, it was about to begin a downward spiral that would end in loss of power and a change of dynasty in 1644.

Since political leaders in the neighboring East Asian states of Vietnam and Korea had long emulated Chinese systems and philosophies of statecraft, Ming officials recognized these states as "civilized." Japan, while also influenced by China in many ways, was by Ming standards disordered and militaristic in this period, though it did achieve a more stable political system in the seventeenth century.

The Rise of Mughal India, 1526–1627

During Matteo Ricci's four-year stay in western India, the **Mughal dynasty**, the dominant power in South Asia, was at the height of its glory under its greatest leader, **Emperor Akbar** (r. 1556–1605). Building on the military achievements of his grandfather, who had swept into northern India from Afghanistan in the early sixteenth century, Akbar's armies controlled most of the Indian subcontinent. Ruling 100 million subjects from his northern capital of Delhi, the "Great Mughal" was one of the most powerful men in the world.

The Mughal state was well positioned to take advantage of expanding Indian Ocean trade. It licensed imperial mints that struck hundreds of millions of gold, silver, and copper coins of uniform value and trusted purity. Dyed cotton textiles were a major export, along with sugar, pepper, diamonds, and other luxury goods.

State investment in roads helped traders move goods to market. The Mughals also supported movement of populations into previously underutilized lands by granting tax-exempt status to new settlements. The eastern half of Bengal (today's Bangladesh) was transformed from tropical forest land into a densely populated rice-producing region.

Agriculture was the ultimate basis of Mughal wealth and power, providing 90 percent of the tax income that paid for Mughal armies and the ceremonial pomp of the court at Delhi. The Mughals sent tax clerks out to the provinces, who surveyed the lands and diverted much of the revenue to Delhi. In those parts of India where a pre-Mughal aristocracy was used to collect and retain these taxes, the Mughals confirmed the old rulers' rights to 10 percent of the local revenue, and thus ensured their loyalty. This revenue system, controlled from the top but with recognition of the prerogatives of local rulers, was part of a broader Mughal attempt to integrate existing Indian authorities into their government.

People may be conquered by the sword, but more stable forms of administration are necessary if conquest is to turn into long-term rule. A principal political challenge the Mughal rulers faced was that their Islamic faith differed from the Hindu beliefs of most of their subjects. Akbar's policy was one of toleration and inclusion. He canceled the special tax that Islamic law allows Muslim rulers to collect from nonbelievers and granted Hindu communities the right to follow their own social and legal customs. Hindu *maharajahs* were incorporated into the Mughal administrative system at the regional level, just as rural aristocrats were at the local level. Since the Hindu population was accustomed to a social system

Mughal dynasty
(1526–1857) Mughal emperors who controlled most of the Indian subcontinent from their capital at Delhi during the height of their power in the sixteenth and seventeenth centuries.

Emperor Akbar
(r. 1556–1605) The most powerful of the Mughal emperors, who pursued a policy of toleration toward the Hindu majority and presided over a cosmopolitan court.

An Ivory Mask from Benin, West Africa

The kingdom of Benin already had a long history of political and cultural achievement before the arrival of the first Europeans in the sixteenth century. Believed to be descendants of Oduduwa (oh-doo-doo-wah), ancestor of all Yoruba kings, Benin's rulers, the *obas*, were associated with great spiritual powers. Starting in the fourteenth century, Beninese artists, organized into a guild by the king, began producing magnificent brass sculptures of royalty. Using a sophisticated "lost-wax" technique, they made a beeswax model, covered it with clay, fired the sculpture to melt the wax inside, poured molten bronze into the clay form, and then broke off the outer clay layer. Their achievement was not only technical but also artistic. The Benin bronzes are known for their naturalism, a quality that made them highly attractive to European collectors. In fact, in 1897 the British colonial government looted over a thousand of these invaluable pieces, and the fight to return them to West Africa continues.

The bronze used in these sculptures, however, was imported from the Mediterranean and was therefore extremely expensive. Beninese artists more often carved masks and wall decorations directly from wood and ivory, sometimes incorporating cowrie shells imported from the Indian Ocean. This ivory mask, made around 1520, depicts Idia (ee-DEE-ah), the Queen Mother of Oba Esigie (eh-see-GEE-ay). Like the Benin bronzes, it conveys a powerful sense of the individuality of its subject. The Portuguese were present in West Africa by this time and had allied with King Esigie and helped him fight off an enemy invasion. Their role in West African politics was still quite marginal, however, as indicated by the minor representation of European figures at the top.

A century and a half after this mask was made, a Dutch visitor was impressed with the capital city:

> The houses in this town stand in good order, one close and evenly placed with its neighbor, just as the houses in Holland stand. . . . The king's court is very great. It is built around many square-shaped yards. These yards have surrounding galleries where guards are always placed. I myself went into the court far enough to pass through four great yards like this, and yet wherever I looked I could still see gate after gate which opened into other yards.[*]

Earlier, in the sixteenth century, the pepper trade was so profitable that Benin's obas had closed the slave market. By the time the Dutch visitor came to Benin in 1688, however, slavery had become a major item of commerce, as elsewhere in West Africa. Nevertheless, Benin's artistic tradition continues today.

[*]Olfert Dapper, *Description of Benin* (Madison: University of Wisconsin Press, 1998), p. 40.

» *From the way they are represented on this mask, what might we infer about the extent of Portuguese influence on the artists of Benin?*

In Benin, as in many African societies, the Queen Mother was a pivotal figure in the king's council, and he often relied on her to gain a consensus of opinion among clan leaders.

The Queen Mother had a special role in representing the interests and opinions of women.

The oba of Benin, King Esigie, is said to have worn this mask on his hip at a commemoration ceremony for Queen Idia.

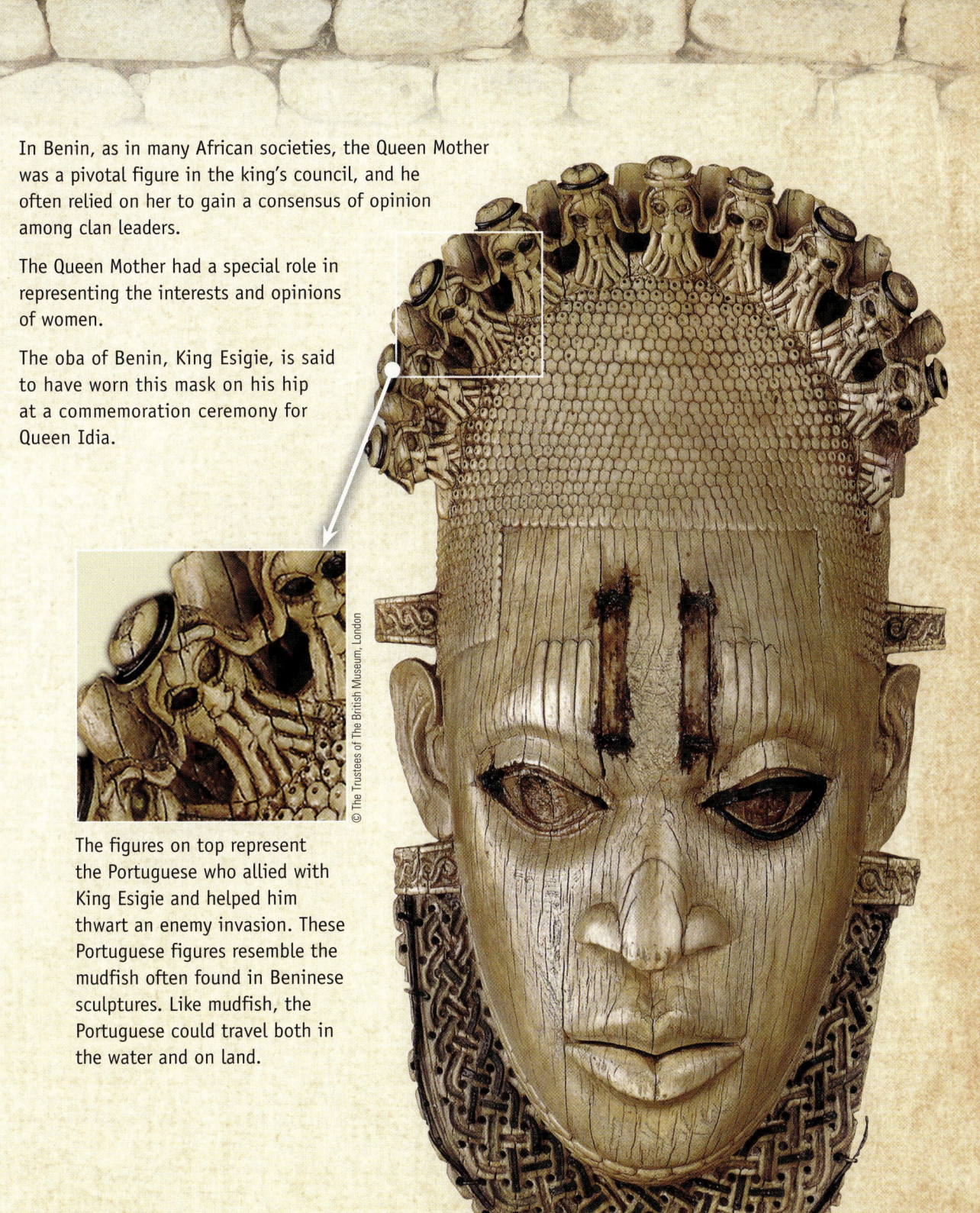

The figures on top represent the Portuguese who allied with King Esigie and helped him thwart an enemy invasion. These Portuguese figures resemble the mudfish often found in Beninese sculptures. Like mudfish, the Portuguese could travel both in the water and on land.

Religious Tensions in India

Contemporary India is a democratic, secular state with full constitutional guarantees of freedom of religion. Still, tensions between majority Hindus and minority Muslims remain.

Muslims form a distinct subclass in Indian society, where they account for about 14 percent of the population: they have lower levels of education, lower incomes, and shorter life expectancies than national averages. Notwithstanding a number of Muslim success stories, the boom in the Indian economy over the past two decades has widened those gaps and increased Muslims' sense of exclusion, as has the development of Hindu nationalism over that same period.

In spite of the secular constitution adopted upon achieving independence in 1947, some have always regarded the country as a Hindu one, including members of the large and influential Bharatiya Janata Party (BJP). The BJP has been implicated in several incidents that have sharpened tensions. One occurred in 1992 when a group of militant Hindu nationalists destroyed the Babri Mosque in Ayodhya, which, they claimed, had been built on the site of the Hindu god Rama's birthplace. Another came in 2002, when violence between Hindus and Muslims broke out in the western state of Gujarat amid accusations that the state government, then under BJP rule, had looked the other way when Hindu mobs attacked Muslims. Over one thousand people were killed, mosques were destroyed, and businesses torched.

Then in November 2008 came the worst terrorist attacks in Indian history, when Muslim gunmen killed 164 people and wounded hundreds of others after seizing control of Mumbai's main train station and a Jewish community center and laying siege to several hotels. That the attackers arrived by boat from Pakistan, possibly with support from members of Pakistani intelligence, did not assuage the suspicion of many Hindus that the Muslim community, despite their widespread denunciations of the attack and protestations of loyalty, could not be trusted. In fact, troubled relations with Pakistan, a neighboring Muslim nation, increases the isolation of India's own Muslims. The trend toward residential and educational segregation continues.

India, however, has several towering historical figures who serve as examples of how religious diversity can be met with toleration and mutual respect, among them the Mughal emperor Akbar and the nationalist leader Mahatma Gandhi. That India has moved beyond the terrorist attacks of 2008 without reprisals or significant communal violence offers hope that their legacy will endure.

---

in which people paid little attention to matters outside their own caste groups, they might have viewed the ruling Muslims as simply another caste with their own rituals and beliefs. (See the feature "World History in Today's World: Religious Tensions in India.")

Akbar's policy of religious tolerance was continued by his successor Jahangir (r. 1605–1627) and his remarkable wife **Nur Jahan** (1577–1645). Jahangir himself was a weak ruler, addicted as he was to opium and alcohol. When faced with regional rebellions, therefore, it was Nur Jahan (noor ja-HAN), an intelligent and skilled politician, who took charge and kept Mughal power intact. Since women were secluded in the *zezana*, or women's quarters, she could not appear at court in person. Instead she issued government decrees through trusted family members. Taking special interest in women's affairs, she donated land and dowries for orphan girls. From an Iranian family, Nur Jahan also had a great cultural influence through her patronage of Persian-influenced art and architecture. She built many of the most beautiful mosques and gardens in north India. So great was his admiration of Nur Jahan that Jahangir had coins struck with her image, a privilege usually reserved for the emperor himself.

Nur Jahan
(1577–1645) Mughal empress who dominated politics during the reign of her husband Jahangir. By patronizing the arts and architecture and by favoring Persian styles, she had a lasting cultural influence on north India.

Nur Jahan was also interested in commerce and owned a fleet of ships that took religious pilgrims and trade goods to Mecca. Even more than Akbar's, her policies facilitated both domestic and foreign trade. Though she dictated policy from behind the closed doors of the zezana, Nur Jahan's favorable attitude toward trade and entrepreneurship had a strong influence on the wider world. Indian merchants, sailors, bankers, and shipbuilders were important participants in Indian Ocean markets, and the cosmopolitan ports of Mughal India teemed with visitors from Europe, Africa, Arabia, and Southeast Asia (see Map 16.1). But there was little Chinese presence, and no attempt to follow up the fifteenth-century voyages of Zheng He. Unlike the Mughal rulers of India, the leaders of Ming China saw maritime trade more as a threat than as an opportunity.

The Apogee and Decline of Ming China, 1500–1644

By 1500 the **Ming dynasty** in China was at the height of its power and prestige. In 1368 the Ming had replaced the Mongol Yuan dynasty, and the early Ming rulers were highly conscious of the need to restore Confucian virtue after years of what they saw as "barbarian" rule. Like earlier Chinese dynasties, the Ming defined their country as the "Middle Kingdom" and called the emperor the "Son of Heaven." China was at the center of the world, and the emperor ruled with the "Mandate of Heaven."

The emperor's residence in the Forbidden City in Beijing (bay-JING), constructed during the early Ming period and still standing today, was at the center of a Confucian social order based on strict hierarchical relationships. The emperor stood at the top of a social hierarchy in which everyone owed him unquestioning obedience, while the emperor was expected to emulate the benevolent behavior of the greatest Confucian sages, seeking the best interests of those below him. Likewise, junior officials owed obeisance to senior ones, younger brothers to older ones, wives to husbands, and children to parents. Hierarchy governed foreign relations as well. Ming officials respected those societies that had most successfully emulated Chinese models, such as Korea and Vietnam. Japan and the societies of Inner Asia were usually thought of as "inner barbarians," peoples touched by Chinese civilization but still uncouth. All the rest of the world's peoples were regarded as "outer barbarians." From a Ming standpoint, the only conceivable relationship between any of these other kingdoms and China was a tributary one. Foreign kings were expected to send annual missions bearing tribute in acknowledgment of China's preeminent position.

Confucians believed that if such stable hierarchies of obeisance and benevolence were maintained, then the people would prosper. And in the early sixteenth century peace and prosperity were indeed the norm in Ming China. The networks of canals and irrigation works on which so much of the empire's trade and agriculture depended were refurbished and extended. Most important for trade and governance was the Grand Canal connecting the political and military capital Beijing with the productive Yangzi River Valley and fertile rice-producing regions further south. Public granaries were maintained as a hedge against famine. New food crops, including maize, peanuts, and potatoes from the Americas, helped improve nutrition: the population had reached about 120 million people by the time of Matteo Ricci's arrival in 1582.

The **examination system**, based on the Confucian classics and requiring years of study, helped ensure that the extensive Ming bureaucracy was staffed by competent officials at the local, county, and imperial levels. With a hierarchy of well-educated officials supervised by dynamic emperors, the early Ming efficiently carried out essential tasks of government, such as the maintenance of the irrigation

Ming dynasty (1368–1644) Chinese imperial dynasty in power during the travels of Matteo Ricci. It was at its height during the fifteenth century, but by 1610 the Ming dynasty was showing signs of the troubles that would lead to its overthrow.

examination system Chinese system for choosing officials for positions in the Ming imperial bureaucracy. Candidates needed to pass one or more examinations that increased in difficulty for higher positions.

MAP 16.1 Maritime Trade in the Eastern Indian Ocean and East Asia By 1630 the Dutch had overtaken the Portuguese in Indian Ocean trade, the French and English were becoming more active, and Spanish silver from American mines was stimulating trade across South, Southeast, and East Asia. Dutch ships passed through Cape Town in South Africa bearing Asian and African cargo, such as valuable spices, for European markets. Still, the dominant powers in Asia remained land-based empires such as the Mughal empire in India and the Ming empire in China. Traditional trade routes controlled by local sailors and merchants—between Japan and China, between the South China Sea and the Bay of Bengal, and between western India, the Persian Gulf, and East Africa—were also growing in volume in the seventeenth century. (© Cengage Learning)

systems and canals so essential to Chinese prosperity. At the height of the Ming, the roads were kept safe and ordinary people could find justice in the courts.

The elaborate and expensive Ming bureaucracy required an efficient system of tax collection. In 1571 Ming officials decided that only payments in silver would be acceptable, generating a surge in global demand for silver. While Japan was the traditional source of silver for China, its mines could not keep up with demand. But the shortfall was met by the massive new silver mines being opened in the Spanish Americas. Much of that silver flowed into China, stimulating the Ming economy and increasing tax collections.

Despite such benefits, Ming officials had a negative view of seaborne trade, which they saw as the unpredictable realm of pirates like the Japanese. Their efforts to control such trade met with only limited success, however, and in the emerging world economy reliance on foreign silver supplies made the Ming economy vulnerable to distant economic shocks. While the influx of silver stimulated growth, it also caused inflation, and rising prices particularly distressed the less well-off. Even more destabilizing for the Chinese imperial state was the effect of declining silver supplies on the world market after 1620. By that date economic contraction was contributing to an accelerating crisis in Ming governance.

The decline of the Ming is associated with the **Wanli Emperor** (r. 1573–1620). His apathetic attitude toward his duties allowed personalities and petty jealousies to influence the imperial court. Uneducated eunuchs, whose traditional role was limited to caring for the imperial household, rose in influence at the expense of scholar-officials. Without imperial oversight, corruption increased: gifts could determine the outcome of court cases, grain intended for famine relief was sold on the market, and irrigation works went untended. Bandits vexed merchants on the roads, and local peasant uprisings became more common. When Matteo Ricci was finally granted permission to enter the Forbidden City and performed the ritual *kowtow*, prostrating himself with his forehead on the ground, he did so before a vacant Dragon Throne. The Wanli Emperor was inaccessible, remaining deep in the recesses of the Forbidden City.

Matteo Ricci, in his tribute to Ming governance cited in the chapter opening, appears to have failed to notice the decay that was setting in below the impressive façade of the Wanli Emperor's court. In 1644, northern invaders from Manchuria breached the walls of Beijing and drove the Ming from power (see Chapter 20).

Tradition and Innovation: Korea, Vietnam, and Japan, 1500–1650

The societies most strongly connected to Chinese civilization in the early modern period were Korea, Vietnam, and, more loosely, Japan. The Choson (choh-SAN) dynasty of Korea, which closely followed the Ming imperial model, established one of the world's most stable political systems, ruling the Korean peninsula from 1392 until the early twentieth century. The capital at Seoul (sole) was home to a Confucian academy where young men trained for examinations that led to social prominence and political power.

While early modern Korea was not as commercially dynamic as Ming China, it did benefit from a remarkable series of innovations undertaken by the **Emperor Sejong** (r. 1418–1450). Before his time, learning to read and write required years of training in the complexities of Chinese script. Then in 1446, Sejong (SAY-jung) brought together a group of scholars to devise a new phonetic script based on the Korean language. This distinctive han'gul (HAHN-goor) writing system, still in use today, enabled many more Koreans to read and write. Emperor Sejong supported projects to write the history of the country in the new Korean script and to translate

Wanli Emperor (r. 1573–1620) Ming emperor at the time of Matteo Ricci's mission to China. Vain and extravagant, he hastened the decline of the Ming dynasty through lack of attention to policy and the promotion of incompetent officials.

Emperor Sejong (r. 1418–1450) Korean emperor of the Choson dynasty, credited with the creation of the han'gul script for the Korean language.

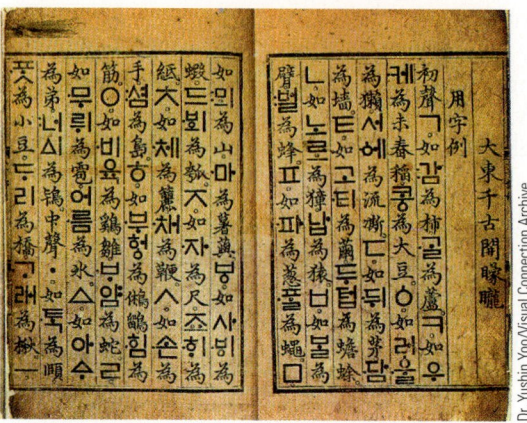

King Sejong and the Korean Alphabet   *Hunminjeongeum* ("The Correct Sounds for the Instruction of the People") was a project sponsored by King Sejong to extend literacy by creating an alphabet based on spoken Korean. The text shown here (along with Sejong's statue in Seoul) is from 1446. Written in a mixture of Chinese and hang'ul characters, it was used as a primer by those who could already read Chinese characters to learn the new phonetic script.

key Buddhist texts. He also supported printers in producing large books more cheaply. Korea became one of the world's most literate societies.

Vietnamese leaders copied Chinese imperial models while at the same time jealously guarding their independence. After 1428, the general who took power in Vietnam after defeating a Ming army gave his name to the new **Lê dynasty**. One story relates that General Lê (lee) sent a gift of cattle to his retreating Ming counterpart, as if to say that the invasion would not stop Vietnam from pursuing positive relations with China. Indeed, Confucian scholar-officials gained greater influence at court in traditionally Buddhist Vietnam. Military expeditions expanded the size and strength of the Vietnamese state, and agrarian reforms led to greater equality in landholding and greater productivity in agriculture.

Japan lay further outside the orbit of Chinese civilization than either Korea or Vietnam. Political power was decentralized during Japan's Ashikaga (ah-shee-KAH-gah) shogunate (1336–1568), and the Japanese emperor, unlike his Chinese, Korean, and Vietnamese counterparts, was a ritual figure with no real authority. The greatest political power was the *shogun*, a supreme military ruler who acted independently of the imperial court. But the Ashikaga shoguns themselves had little control over the *daimyo* (DIE-mee-oh), lords who ruled their own rural domains. As each daimyo had an army of *samurai* (SAH-moo-rye) military retainers, incessant warfare spread chaos through the islands.

Ashikaga Japan was a land of contrasts. While the daimyo lords engaged in violent competition for land and power, they also acted as benefactors of Buddhist monasteries, which promoted spiritual reflection. The samurai warriors, with their strict *bushido* code of honor and loyalty, were also practitioners of the Zen school of Buddhism, with its emphasis on mental discipline and acute awareness. Flower arranging and the intricate refinement of the tea ceremony were also highly developed, peaceful counterpoints to the ceaseless military competition of the daimyo.

In the late sixteenth century several Japanese lords aspired to replace the Ashikaga family; the most ambitious was **Toyotomi Hideyoshi** (r. 1585–1598),

Lê dynasty
(1428–1788) The longest-ruling Vietnamese dynasty. Drawing on Confucian principles, its rulers increased the size and strength of the Vietnamese state and promoted agricultural productivity.

Toyotomi Hideyoshi
(r. 1585–1598) A daimyo (lord) who aspired to unify Japan under his own rule. His attempts to conquer Korea and China failed, and members of the competing Tokugawa family became shoguns and unified the islands.

Himeji Castle Incessant warfare during the Ashikaga period led the Japanese daimyo lords to build well-fortified stone castles. The introduction of cannon in the sixteenth century made the need for such fortifications even greater. Himeji Castle was begun in 1346; Toyotomi Hideyoshi greatly expanded and beautified it in the late sixteenth century. Now a UNESCO World Cultural and Heritage Site, Himeji is the best-preserved castle in all of Japan. (© Jon Arnold Images Ltd/Alamy)

whose plans included not only the consolidation of power on the Japanese islands but also conquest of the Ming empire. In 1592, as Matteo Ricci was journeying in southern China, Hideyoshi's forces attacked the Korean peninsula with an army of two hundred thousand soldiers. A statue of Admiral Yi in central Seoul still commemorates his use of heavily fortified "turtle ships," armed with multiple cannon and wooden planks shielding their decks, to defend Korea against the Japanese attack.

In a power struggle following Hideyoshi's death, the Tokugawa (TOH-koo-GAH-wah) clan emerged victorious. After 1603, the **Tokugawa shogunate** centralized power by restraining the independence of the daimyo, forcing them to spend half the year in the shogun's new capital of Edo (today's Tokyo). Compared with the highly centralized imperial model of Korea, political power in Japan was still diffuse, with many daimyo still controlling their own domains. But the Tokugawa system brought a long-term stability that made possible economic and demographic growth. In the seventeenth century, as market exchanges became central to the Japanese economy, Japanese cities such as Osaka and Nagasaki emerged as vibrant commercial centers.

Tokugawa shogunate
(1603–1868) The dynasty of shoguns, paramount military leaders of Japan. From their capital at Edo (now Tokyo), Tokugawa rulers brought political stability by restraining the power of the daimyo lords.

Despite this increased unity, some daimyo formed diplomatic and trade alliances with Jesuit missionaries, undercutting the centralizing ambitions of the Tokugawa court at Edo. As a result, Jesuit missionaries attracted many converts, and the shoguns became deeply suspicious of both European and Japanese Christians. After 1614 they outlawed the foreign faith; hundreds of Japanese Christians were killed, some by crucifixion, when they refused to recant their Christian beliefs. Apart from an annual Dutch trade mission confined to an island in the port of Nagasaki, no Christians were allowed to enter the country. Japanese trade with China and Korea, however, continued to flourish.

Eurasian Intellectual and Religious Encounters, 1500–1620

In the early modern Afro-Eurasian world, intellectual ferment was often associated with new religious ideas. In western Europe the Protestant Reformation divided Christians over basic matters of faith. Matteo Ricci himself was a representative of the Catholic Reformation, which sought to re-energize Roman Catholicism. In Mughal India, many people converted to Islam, and the new faith of Sikhism was founded. In China, Matteo Ricci attempted to convince Ming scholar-officials that Christianity was compatible with the oldest and purest versions of Confucianism. (See the feature "Movement of Ideas Through Primary Sources: Chinese and Japanese Views of Christianity" on page 456.)

Challenges to Catholicism, 1517–1620

While Renaissance humanism had led to significant artistic and intellectual achievement in western Europe (see Chapter 15), it coincided with increasing corruption in the Catholic Church. For example, popes and bishops raised money for prestigious building projects, such as Saint Peter's Basilica in Rome, by selling "indulgences," which church authorities said could liberate souls from purgatory and allow them to enter into heaven. Thus the cultural richness of the Roman church was underwritten by practices that some European Christians viewed as corrupt and worldly.

One infuriated critic, a cleric named **Martin Luther** (1483–1546), argued that salvation could not be purchased; only God could determine the spiritual condition of a human soul. Luther made his challenge public in 1517 and was called before church authorities, who viewed Luther's preaching as a direct assault on the authority of priests, bishops, and the papacy itself. When he refused to recant, he was excommunicated by the church. Luther then began to lead his own religious services, initiating the Protestant Reformation. The Christian church, already divided since the eleventh century between its Eastern Orthodox and Roman Catholic branches, was now divided within western Europe itself (as further discussed in Chapter 17 of Volume 2).

As a significant minority of sixteenth-century western Europeans left Catholicism, they developed a variety of alternative church structures, rituals, and beliefs. Lutherans, as the followers of Martin Luther were called, downgraded the importance of intermediaries between the individual and God and therefore challenged the whole edifice of the Catholic priestly hierarchy. Taking advantage of increased literacy and the wider availability of printed Bibles after the fifteenth-century introduction of movable-type printing in Europe (see Chapter 15), Luther argued that individuals should read their own Bibles and not rely on priests to interpret God's word for them. He translated the Bible into the German language, making

Martin Luther
(1483–1546) German theologian who in 1517 launched the Protestant Reformation in reaction to corruption in the Catholic Church. His followers, called Lutherans, rejected the priestly hierarchy of Catholicism, emphasizing that believers should themselves look for truth in the Bible.

the Scriptures available for the first time to the many who could read German but not Latin. In the seventeenth century, the number of Protestant churches multiplied, further challenging Catholic authority and leading to significant political violence as European kings and princes chose sides (as those reading Volume 2 will learn in the next chapter). Much of Europe, like the region of Matteo Ricci's hometown in central Italy, remained securely Catholic. Even here the impact of the Protestant Reformation was profound, however, for the Catholic Church was shaken out of its complacency and launched a response known as the **Catholic Reformation**, or Counter-Reformation. A major focus of the Catholic Reformation was more rigorous training of priests to avoid the abuses that had left the church open to Protestant criticism. As a member of the Jesuit order, or Society of Jesus, Ricci was especially trained in the debating skills needed to fend off Protestant theological challenges. The Jesuits were one of several new Catholic orders developed to confront the Protestant challenge and to take advantage of the new maritime routes to spread their faith around the world.

Another challenge to Catholic belief that developed during Ricci's lifetime was the "new science" associated with his fellow Italian **Galileo Galilei** (1564–1642). Catholic theologians had reconciled faith and reason by incorporating classical Greek thinkers, especially Aristotle, into church teachings. Galileo (gal-uh-LAY-oh) struck at the heart of that intellectual system by challenging both the authority of Aristotle and Catholic assumptions about the natural world. He contradicted Aristotle by showing that a body in motion would stay in motion unless acted upon by an external force, an insight that would later prove essential to new understandings of planetary motion. Pointing his telescope toward the heavens, Galileo discovered spots on the sun, craters on the moon, and other indications that the heavens were not a place of absolute, unchanging perfection as the church had said.

Galileo also affirmed the heliocentric theory, first proposed in 1543 by the Polish astronomer Nicolaus Copernicus, which placed the sun rather than the earth at the center of the solar system. Further support for the Copernican system, a theory contrary to both classical tradition and church teachings, was offered by the German mathematician Johannes Kepler, who argued that elliptical rather than circular orbits best explained planetary motion. Church authorities argued that the heliocentric theory contradicted the book of Genesis by displacing the earth from its central place in God's creation. The inquisition, a church bureaucracy devoted to the suppression of heresy, tried Galileo and forced him to recant his support for the heliocentric theory. But the "scientific revolution" that Galileo had helped to launch could not be so easily suppressed (as those who read Volume 2 will learn).

The ferment of the new ideas arising from the Protestant Reformation and the "new science" helped sharpen Matteo Ricci's intellectual training and prepare him for his travels. In India he took part in lively religious and philosophical debates that were valuable preparation for his missionary work in China.

Islam, Sikhism, and Akbar's "Divine Faith," 1500–1605

In the Mughal capital of Delhi, Akbar, in addition to bringing Hindus and Muslims together, attracted to his court scholars, artists, and officials from Iran, Afghanistan, and Central Asia. Mughal India proved a fertile environment for artistic growth as Persian, Turkish, and Indian influences flowed together. The Taj Mahal, a "love poem in marble" built by Akbar's grandson as a memorial to his wife, is the best-known example of the Persian-influenced architecture inspired by Nur Jahan and other Mughal leaders.

Akbar was keenly interested in religion, and he routinely invited leaders from various religious traditions to debate at his court. In 1579, the year after Ricci

Catholic Reformation
Reform movement in the Catholic Church, also called the Counter-Reformation, that developed in response to the Protestant Reformation. The church clarified church doctrines and instituted a program for better training of priests.

Galileo Galilei
(1564–1642) Italian scientist who provided evidence to support the heliocentric theory, challenging church doctrine and the authority of Aristotle. He was forced to recant his position by the inquisition, but his theories were vindicated during the scientific revolution.

Akbar with Representatives of Various Religions at His Court For years, the Mughal emperor Akbar hosted weekly conversations among scholars and priests of numerous religions, including the Jesuits seen here on the left. Akbar sponsored the translation of varied religious texts, including the Christian Bible, into Persian, even though he himself was illiterate. When criticized by some Muslim scholars for his patronage of Hindu arts and his openness to other religious traditions, Akbar is said to have replied, "God loves beauty." (Reproduction by kind permission of the Chester Beatty Library, Dublin, CBL In 03.264b)

arrived at Goa, a diplomatic embassy arrived from the Great Mughal requesting that Catholic missionaries come to Delhi. *"We hope for nothing less than the conversion of all India,"** wrote Ricci. Two missionaries went to Delhi, bringing a richly produced, lavishly illustrated, and very costly Bible as a gift for the emperor. Although the emperor did not convert, his interest in the Jesuit mission characterized his open-mindedness.

During this time Sufism was also attracting new converts. In addition to obeying the Muslim laws of submission, Sufis were mystics who used special rituals and prayers meant to bring them closer to God. The mystical Sufis often used rhythmic motion and special chants to create a meditative state in which they could feel God's presence, and they showed great devotion to spiritual leaders who guided them in these practices, often venerating these teachers' tombs and treating them as places of pilgrimage. Some Muslim scholars, especially those who stressed the more legalistic aspects of Islam, looked with suspicion on the emotional Sufi forms of religious devotion. Akbar brought both the legal scholars and the Sufi mystics to his court and listened intently to their debates.

Akbar also brought Jews, Hindus, and representatives of other faiths, such as Sikhs (sicks), to Delhi. Sikhism was a new faith whose followers rejected the caste system while striving to reconcile Islamic and Hindu beliefs. Akbar extended to the Sikhs the same tolerance he had granted more established religions (though that policy of tolerance would be reversed later in the Mughal period; see Chapter 20). Having encountered so many different spiritual traditions, he announced his own adherence to a "Divine Faith" that he said both included and transcended them all:

O God, in every temple I see people that seek Thee; in every language I hear spoken, people praise Thee; if it be a mosque, people murmur in prayer; if it be a Christian church they ring the bell for love of Thee . . . it is Thou whom I seek from temple to temple.[†]

Akbar's "Divine Faith" never spread beyond the Mughal court and disappeared after his own death.

---

*"The Diary of Matthew Ricci," in *Matthew Ricci, China in the Sixteenth Century,* trans. Louis Gallagher (New York: Random House, 1942, 1970), p. 114.

[†]Steven Warshaw and C. David Bromwell with A. J. Tudisco, *India Emerges* (Berkeley: Diablo Press, 1974), p. 60.

Meanwhile, Hinduism was undergoing important changes and reforms. The epic story of the *Ramayana*, formerly read only by priests trained in the ancient Sanskrit language, was retold in 1575 by a prominent poet using the commonly spoken Hindi language, making this story of the ancient king, a manifestation of the god Vishnu, more accessible. This development added to the importance of forms of Hindu devotion that de-emphasized the role of Brahmin priests. Like the translation of the Bible into languages such as English and German and the new availability of Buddhist texts in the Korean han'gul script, the Hindi *Ramayana* promoted religious inquiry at all levels of society, not just among kings, priests, and philosophers.

Ricci in China: Catholicism Meets Neo-Confucianism, 1582–1610

Ming China was less religiously diverse than Mughal India, with Buddhism as the empire's majority faith. In fact, when Ricci first arrived in Ming China, he adopted the dress of a Buddhist priest, with a shaved head, a beard, and flowing robes. Soon he came to understand, however, that affiliating himself with Buddhism would not carry much weight with the Confucian scholar-officials who manifested the power of the emperor. Many of these literati looked down on the poorly educated Buddhist clergy. Ricci subsequently changed his appearance and habits to appeal to this prestigious class of individuals. His plan was to convert China from the top down.

Confucian scholars emphasized education as the main route to self-cultivation. While most of the emperor's subjects remained nonliterate peasant cultivators, children from more privileged households were taught to read from a young age, often by memorizing a list of one thousand characters that taught Confucian virtues like hard work and respect for elders and teachers. After they had mastered the basics, boys had to memorize the classic texts of Confucianism, collections of poems, and histories of past times that usually focused on the virtues of ancient sages.

In theory, any young man could take the annual examinations and, if successful, become an imperial official. In reality, only the elite could afford the private tutors needed for success. Still, the Ming system was based on merit: wealth and status could not purchase high office, and even the privileged had to undergo years of intensive study.

Though women were barred from taking the examinations, the Ming emphasis on education did contribute to the spread of female literacy. Foreign observers noted how many girls were able to read and write. However, education for girls reinforced Confucian views of gender. Rather than reading histories of sages and virtuous officials, girls usually read stories about women who submitted to their parents when they were young, obeyed their husbands once they were married, and listened to their sons when they became widowed. Singled out for special praise were widows who demonstrated eternal loyalty to their husbands by declining to be remarried. Chinese girls were thereby indoctrinated into the Confucian ideal of strict gender hierarchy.

Matteo Ricci paid careful attention to debates between advocates of various schools of Confucianism as he built up an argument for the compatibility of Confucianism and Christianity. At this time the Neo-Confucian philosophy of Wang Yangming (1472–1529) was especially influential. While other Confucians had emphasized close observation of the external world, Wang stressed self-reflection, arguing that *"everybody, from the infant in swaddling clothes to the old, is in full possession of . . . innate knowledge."** Ricci accused Wang's Neo-Confucian followers of

---

*Valerie Hansen, *The Open Empire: A History of China to 1600* (New York: W. W. Norton, 2000), p. 391.

Chinese and Japanese Views of Christianity

In China and Japan, the political and social structures of the two empires led to quite different outcomes when Jesuit missionaries tried to convert social and political elites to Christianity.

In China, where the number of converts was quite small, Ming officials were tolerant of the foreign faith in spite of criticisms such as those expressed by Confucian intellectuals in the first document below. Such toleration of Christianity lasted into the Qing period until 1715, when the church reversed Matteo Ricci's policy by declaring that Confucian rites were incompatible with Christianity. Emperor Kangxi was furious: "To judge from this proclamation, their religion is no different from other small, bigoted sects of Buddhism." In 1721 he banned Christians from preaching in his empire.

In Japan, the less centralized political structure at first worked to the Jesuits' advantage. They converted a number of daimyo, and the numbers of Japanese *Kirishitan* (i.e., "Christians") grew. At the same time, however, the ambitious general Toyotomi Hideyoshi, aspiring to the unification of Japan, regarded the Japanese Christians and their missionary sponsors as a threat. In 1587 he issued the edicts reproduced here restricting conversion activities and banning foreign missionaries. While Hideyoshi put no constraints on European trade, Tokugawa shoguns later severely restricted Europeans of all backgrounds from entering the country.

Sources: Excerpt from Jacques Gernet, *China and the Christian Impact: A Conflict of Cultures*, Cambridge University Press, 1986, pp. 39–40, 53, 82, 107, 108, 120, 159, 1691. Reprinted with permission of Cambridge University Press; English translation copyright © 1997 by David J. Lu. From *Japan: A Documentary History*, ed. David J. Lu (Armonk, N.Y.: M. E. Sharpe, 1997), pp. 196–197. Used with permission of M. E. Sharpe, Inc. All Rights Reserved. Not for reproduction.

Chinese Commentaries on Christianity

1) [The Jesuits] are extremely intelligent. Their studies concern astronomy, the calendar, medicine and mathematics. . . . Truly they have the means to win minds. . . . The only trouble is that it is a pity that they speak of a Master of Heaven, an incorrect and distasteful term which leads them into nonsense. . . . Our Confucianism has never held that Heaven had a mother or a bodily form, and it has never spoken of events that are supposed to have occurred before and after his birth. Is it not true that herein lies the difference between our Confucianism and their doctrine?

2) The superiority of Western teaching lies in their calculations; their inferiority lies in their veneration of a Master of Heaven of a kind to upset men's minds. . . . When they require people to consider the Master of Heaven as their closest relative and to abandon their fathers and mothers and place their sovereign [king] in second place, giving the direction of the state to those who spread the doctrine of the Master of Heaven, this entails an unprecedented infringement on the most constant rules. How could their doctrine possibly be admissible in China? . . .

3) [The Ming emperor] sacrifices to Heaven and to Earth; the princes sacrifice to the mountains and rivers within the domains; holders of high office sacrifice to the ancestral temple of the founder of their lineage; gentlemen and ordinary individuals sacrifice to the tables of their own [immediate] ancestors. . . . In this way . . . there is an order in the sacrifices that cannot be upset. To suggest that each person should revere a single Master of Heaven and represent Heaven by means of statues before which one prays each day . . . is it not to profane Heaven by making unseemly requests?

4) In their kingdom they recognize two sovereigns. One is the political sovereign [the king,] the other is the doctrinal sovereign [the pope]. . . . It comes down to having two suns in the sky, two masters in a single kingdom. . . . What audacity it is on the part of these calamitous Barbarians who would like to upset the [political and moral] unity of China by introducing the Barbarian concept of the two sovereigns!

5) We Confucians follow a level and unified path. . . . To abandon all this in order to rally to this Jesus who died nailed to a cross . . . to prostrate oneself before him and pray with zeal, imploring his supernatural aid, that would be madness. And to go so far as to enter darkened halls, wash oneself with holy water and wear

amulets about one's person, all that resembles the vicious practices of witchcraft. . . .

6) Our father is the one who engendered us, our mother the one who raised us. Filial piety consists solely in loving our parents. . . . Even when one of our parents behaves in a tyrannical fashion, we must try to reason with him or her. Even if a sovereign behaves in an unjust way, we must try to get him to return to human sentiments. How could one justify criticizing one's parents or resisting one's sovereign on the grounds of filial piety toward the Master of Heaven?

Edicts of Toyotomi Hideyoshi (1587)

I. Limitations on the Propagation of Christianity

1. Whether one desires to become a follower of the padre [Catholic priest] is up to that person's own conscience.
2. If one receives a province, a district, or a village as his fief, and forces farmers in his domain who are properly registered under certain temples to become followers of the padre against their wishes, then he has committed a most unreasonable illegal act. . . .
4. Anyone whose fief is over 200 chō* and who can expect two to three thousand kan* of rice harvest each year must receive permission from the authorities before becoming a follower of the padre.
5. Anyone whose fief is smaller than the one described above may, as his conscience dictates, select for himself from between eight or nine religions. . . .
8. If a daimyō who has a fief over a province, a district, or a village, forces his retainers to become followers of the padre, he is committing a [great] crime. . . . This will have an adverse effect on [the welfare of] the nation. Anyone who cannot use good judgment in this matter will be punished. . . .

II. Expulsion of Missionaries

1. Japan is the country of gods, but has been receiving false teachings from Christian countries. This cannot be tolerated any further.
2. The [missionaries] approach people in provinces and districts to make them their followers, and let them destroy shrines and temples. This is an unheard of outrage. When a vassal receives a province, a district, a village, or another form of a fief, he must consider it as a property entrusted to him on a temporary basis. He must follow the laws of this country, and abide by their intent. However, some vassals illegally [donate part of their fiefs to the church]. This is a culpable offense.
3. The padres, by their special knowledge [in the sciences and medicine], feel that they can at will entice people to become their believers. In doing so they commit the illegal act of destroying the teachings of Buddha prevailing in Japan. These padres cannot be permitted to remain in Japan. They must prepare to leave the country within twenty days of the issuance of this notice.
4. The black [Portuguese and Spanish] ships come to Japan to engage in trade. Thus the matter is a separate one. They can continue to engage in trade.
5. Hereafter, anyone who does not hinder the teachings of the Buddha, whether he be a merchant or not, may come and go freely from Christian countries to Japan.

*chō 2.45 acres (1 ha).
*kan 8.2 pounds (3.75 kg).

QUESTIONS FOR ANALYSIS

» *In the Chinese documents, how is Christianity judged to be incompatible with China's social and political traditions? How is that incompatibility described?*

» *In the Japanese documents, how does Toyotomi Hideyoshi differentiate between acceptable and unacceptable means of spreading and practicing Christianity?*

» *In the two sets of documents, what do the commentators regard as strengths of the missionaries in gaining converts, and the greatest dangers if they succeed?*

distorting Confucianism. By returning to the original works of the ancient sages, Ricci said, the Chinese literati would discover that one could convert to Christianity while retaining the ethical and philosophical traditions of Confucius.

Once his language skills were sufficiently developed, Ricci took advantage of a favorite Ming pastime to share his views. Scholar-officials would often invite interesting speakers to a banquet and, after dinner, hold philosophical debates. For many in the audience Ricci's well-known ability to instantly memorize and repeat long lists of information, and even repeat them backward, would have been of greater interest than his views on Confucian philosophy and Christian theology. It was a highly relevant skill in a society where difficult exams were the main path to power and status. While his hosts might have been entertained by his arguments, few were persuaded by them.

Ricci also impressed his hosts with examples of European art and technology, especially printed books, paintings, clocks, and maps. Lavishly illustrated and beautifully bound books contrasted with the austerity of Chinese woodblock prints. Chinese artists adapted European techniques of landscape painting, and Ming astronomers were impressed by European telescopes and the precision with which the Jesuits could predict such events as eclipses. Late-sixteenth-century European clocks, while not very reliable by later standards, were much more accurate than the water clocks used by the Chinese. Ricci's world map, locating the "western barbarians" for the first time in relation to the "Middle Kingdom," was such a success that Chinese artisans were employed to print reproductions.

For Ricci, however, mnemonic tricks, maps, and clocks were only a means to convert his audience to Christianity. Criticizing both Buddhism and Neo-Confucianism, Ricci emphasized those aspects of the Western tradition that appealed most to Confucian intellectuals: its moral and ethical dimensions rather than its character as a revealed religion. For example, after learning that Chinese scholars were usually upset to hear about the suffering and death of Jesus, he largely avoided that central aspect of Christianity.

Ricci's most influential work published in Chinese was *The True Meaning of the Lord of Heaven*. Composed with the aid of the small number of Chinese Christian converts, it is a dialogue between a "Chinese Scholar" and a "Western Scholar." In the following passage Ricci criticizes Buddhism and argues for the compatibility of Confucianism and Christianity:

Chinese Scholar: *The Buddha taught that the visible world emerges from "voidness" and made "voidness" the end of all effort. The Confucians say: "In the processes of Yi there exists the Supreme Ultimate" and therefore make "existence" the basic principle [of all things] and "sincerity" the subject of the study of self-cultivation. I wonder who, in your revered view, is correct?*

Western Scholar: *The "voidness" taught by the Buddha [is] totally at variance with the doctrine concerning the Lord of Heaven [i.e., Christianity], and it is therefore abundantly clear that [it does] not merit esteem. When it comes to the "existence" and "sincerity" of the Confucians, however . . . they would seem to be close to the truth.*[*]

---

[*]Matteo Ricci, *The True Meaning of the Lord of Heaven,* trans. Douglas Lancashire and Peter Hu Kuo-chen, S.J. (Paris: Institut Ricci-Centre d'études chinoises, 1985), p. 99.

Such arguments did not convince many, but at least the Jesuits in China, unlike their brethren in Japan, were accepted as representatives of a legitimate school of philosophy.

Some Catholics, especially members of the competing Dominican and Franciscan religious orders, felt that attempts by Ricci and the Jesuits to reconcile Christianity and Confucianism went too far. For example, Ricci argued that veneration of ancestors was compatible with Christianity and the biblical command to "honor your father and your mother." Less flexible church authorities felt that Chinese ancestor rites were pagan and should be rejected. Ricci knew that such a rigid interpretation of cultural practice would limit the appeal of Christianity among potential converts, who would be ostracized by family and friends if they abandoned their household shrines. In fact, after an eighteenth-century pope reversed Ricci's approach, declaring that ancestor worship was idolatrous, Catholicism lost its status as a legitimate faith in China. Nevertheless, by debating these issues, Ricci helped lay the foundation of an ongoing "great encounter" between Europe and China.

CONTEXT AND CONNECTIONS

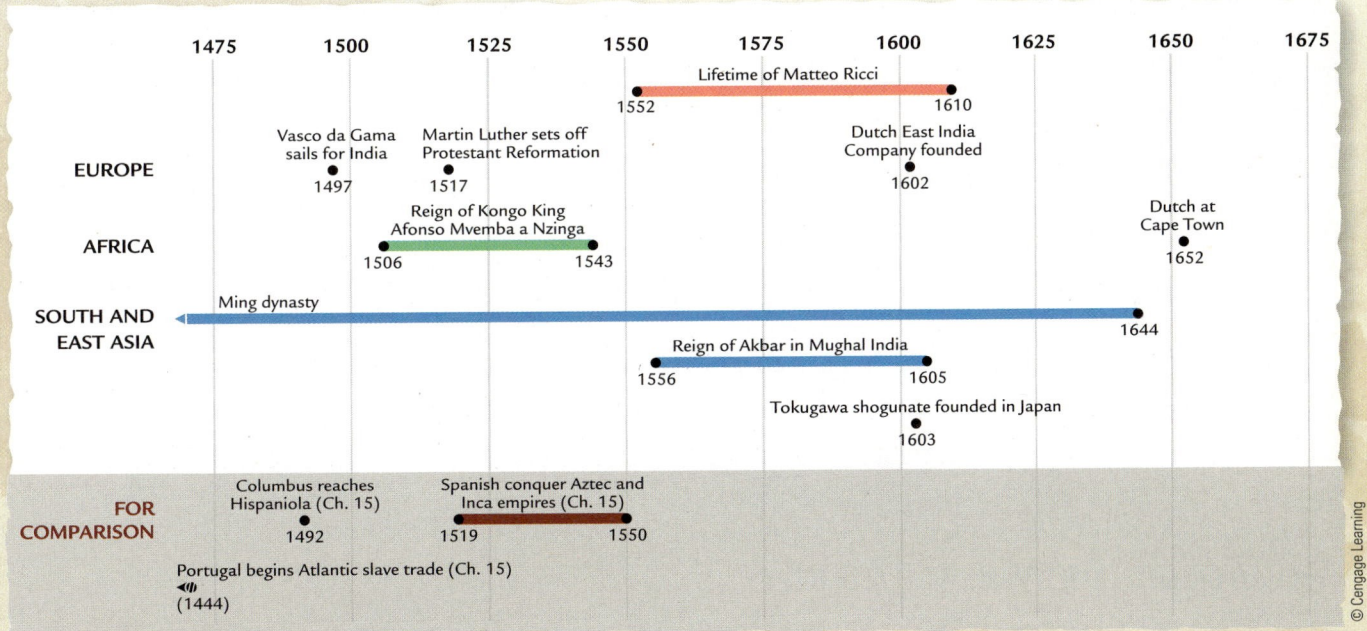

© Cengage Learning

Empires of Land and Sea

When Christopher Columbus sailed west to reach the "Indies," he greatly underestimated the circumference of the globe. The better-informed Portuguese, whose route Matteo Ricci followed to China, succeeded where Columbus failed by establishing a direct oceanic link to the riches of the Indian Ocean and South China Sea. Nevertheless, the biologic, demographic, political, and economic consequences of Columbus's journeys were more dramatic. The "Columbian encounter," which brought the Eastern and Western Hemispheres into systematic contact for the first time, was in many ways the starting point of modern world history.

Prior to 1500 the Indian Ocean, in contrast to the Atlantic, was already interconnected, although those connections were commercial and cultural rather than political or military, and largely remained so. Ming emperors had proven uninterested in pursuing political dominance across the ocean at the time of Zheng He in the fifteenth century (see Chapter 15), while the Portuguese and other European powers tried but failed. The story of maritime expansion in Asia is therefore as much one of continuity as of change. Massive land-based empires, especially the Mughal dynasty in India and the Ming dynasty in China, remained the dominant powers. Inter-Asian trade remained the key to commercial profit, even as the Portuguese and later the Dutch inserted themselves into these markets. In Africa the Atlantic slave trade was new and an ominous sign for the future, but at first it affected only a few coastal West African societies; East African city-states continued their traditional orientation toward commerce with India and the Persian Gulf.

However, there were also important changes in the Indian Ocean world in the sixteenth and seventeenth centuries. The destructive power of ship-based cannon allowed the Portuguese to seize crucial transit points such as Malacca, setting an example that would later be followed by the Dutch, British, and French. The innovative ship designs and commercial practices of the Dutch further stimulated trade and made the competition between European chartered companies a new feature of Asian politics. The influx of American silver was crucial. Increased availability of silver coins facilitated trade and gave European merchants the wherewithal to compete more effectively in Asian markets. The implications were not yet clear to Asian rulers, but the foundations had been laid for a new global market controlled from Europe.

Christian missionaries like Matteo Ricci played only a small part during this time of intellectual ferment across Afro-Eurasia. Whereas in some areas of the Americas, such as the Andes and Mesoamerica, conversions to Catholicism quickly followed Spanish conquest, in Africa and Asia it was Islam that expanded during this period. While the Protestant Reformation played a role in propelling the Jesuits and other Catholic orders out into the world to expand the pope's religious domain, and while "new science" forced the Catholic Church to respond to new intellectual challenges, neither European science nor religious reform had a significant impact in Asia before the end of the seventeenth century. Instead, existing religious and intellectual modes of discourse—between Muslims and Hindus in India, and between Buddhists and Confucians in China—remained the norm. In some places Christian missionaries contributed to the debate, but only in rare cases did they have a significant influence; in this regard, Japan and Kongo were exceptional.

Meanwhile, religious divisions were deepening in western Eurasia, where in both Christian and Muslim lands religion and politics formed a combustible mixture in the seventeenth and eighteenth centuries. The struggle for religious ascendency in western Europe divided the continent between warring Catholic and Protestant powers, while the old rivalry between the Sunni and Shi'ite branches of Islam magnified the struggle between the Iranian Safavid and Turkish Ottoman empires for regional predominance. In the new age of gunpowder weapons, the stakes of such conflicts were higher than ever before.

Voyages on the Web: Matteo Ricci

The Voyages Map App follows the traveler's journeys using interactive study tools, including 360-degree panoramic views of historic sites, zoomable maps, audio summaries, flash cards, and quizzes.

Key Terms

Matteo Ricci (434)
Vasco da Gama (437)
joint-stock companies (439)
bourgeoisie (440)
Dutch East India Company (440)
Kongo kingdom (442)

Mughal dynasty (443)
Emperor Akbar (443)
Nur Jahan (446)
Ming dynasty (447)
examination system (447)
Wanli Emperor (449)
Emperor Sejong (449)

Lê dynasty (450)
Toyotomi Hideyoshi (450)
Tokugawa shogunate (451)
Martin Luther (452)
Catholic Reformation (453)
Galileo Galilei (453)

For Further Reference

Brook, Timothy. *The Troubled Empire: China in the Yuan and Ming Dynasties*. Cambridge, Mass.: Belknap, 2010.

Cameron, Euan. *The Sixteenth Century (Short Oxford History of Europe)*. New York: Oxford University Press, 2006.

Chaudhuri, K. N. *Asia Before Europe: Economy and Civilization of the Indian Ocean from the Rise of Islam to 1750*. Cambridge, England: Cambridge University Press, 1990.

Cook, Harold J. *Matters of Exchange: Commerce, Medicine, and Science in the Dutch Golden Age*. New Haven: Yale University Press, 2008.

Dale, Stephen Frederick. *Indian Merchants and Eurasian Trade, 1600–1750*. Cambridge, England: Cambridge University Press, 1994.

Eraly, Abraham. *The Mughal World: India's Tainted Paradise*. London: Phoenix, 2007.

Findly, Ellison Banks. *Nur Jahan: Empress of Mughal India*. New York: Oxford University Press, 1993.

Green, Toby. *The Rise of the Trans-Atlantic Slave Trade in Western Africa, 1300–1589*. New York: Cambridge University Press, 2011.

Laven, Mary. *Mission to China: Matteo Ricci and the Jesuit Encounter with the East*. London: Faber & Faber, 2011.

Pearson, Michael. *The Indian Ocean*. New York: Routledge, 2007.

Pearson, Michael. *Port Cities and Intruders: The Swahili Coast, India, and Portugal in the Early Modern Era*. Baltimore: Johns Hopkins University Press, 2002.

Sherif, Abdul. *Dhow Cultures and the Indian Ocean: Cosmopolitanism, Commerce, and Islam*. New York: Columbia University Press, 2010.

Spence, Jonathan. *The Memory Palace of Matteo Ricci*. New York: Viking Penguin, 1984.

Subrahmanyam, Sanjay. *The Portuguese Empire in Asia, 1500–1700*. 2d ed. London: Wiley-Blackwell, 2012.

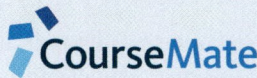 Go to the CourseMate website at **www.cengagebrain.com** for additional study tools and review materials—including audio and video clips—for this chapter.

The adventures of **Evliya Çelebi** (ev-lee-yah che-LEH-bee; 1610–1683) began with a dream. Son of the chief goldsmith to the powerful sultan of the Ottoman empire, at eighteen years old Çelebi was already highly gifted in the art of religious recitation (he would recite the entire Quran over one thousand times in his lifetime). In 1628 he dreamt of a visit from the Prophet Muhammad himself, who told him, *"You will be a world traveler and unique among men."** This nocturnal blessing was welcome, since Çelebi already had a great curiosity about the world around him. *"I longed,"* he wrote, *"to set out for the Holy Land, towards Baghdad and Mecca and Medina and Cairo and Damascus."** Visiting those places and many more, he became the greatest of all Ottoman voyagers: even today in the Turkish language you say of someone who feels a constant urge to travel: "Evliya Çelebi gibi," "He is like Evliya Çelebi."

Çelebi traveled from his birthplace of Constantinople (today's Istanbul) across the vast Ottoman empire. His most memorable journey came when he performed the hajj, visiting the holy sites of Mecca, Medina, and Jerusalem, before settling in Cairo, the great commercial and intellectual center of early modern Islam. He also went beyond the empire, to Europe and Iran. In Europe he witnessed and participated in the wars fought between the sultan's forces and those of the Holy Roman empire, while in Iran he described the tense relations between its Safavid dynasty and his own Ottoman rulers.

Though both the Ottomans and Safavids were Muslim societies, religious differences amplified their political and military competition. The Ottomans, controlling the most holy sites of Islam in Arabia, were defenders of the dominant Sunni branch of Islam, while the Safavids promoted the competing Shi'ite interpretation of the faith. Çelebi encapsulated the competition between them in an account where, with characteristic humor, he described the building of the extraordinary Sûleymaniye Mosque in Constantinople:

*Robert Dankoff and Sooyong Kim, translation and commentary, An Ottoman Traveller: Selections from the Book of Travels of Evliya Çelebi (London: Eland Publishing, 2010), pp. 7, 36.

Evliya Çelebi
(Topkapi Palace Museum/The Bridgeman Art Library)

The minaret on the left with the three galleries is called the Jewel Minaret. . . . The reason is that, in order for the foundation to settle, Sûleyman Khan

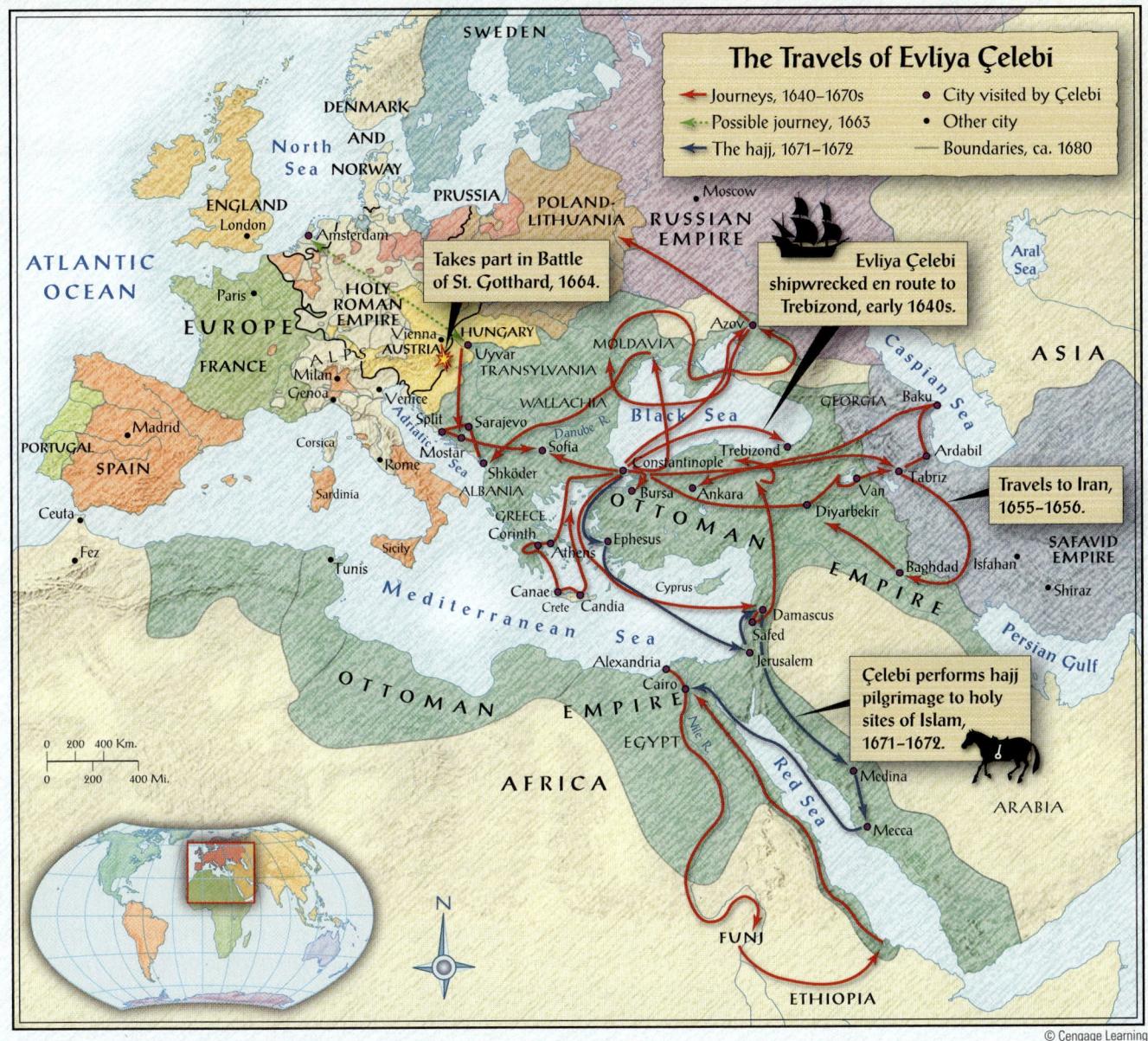

The Travels of Evliya Çelebi

Legend:
- → Journeys, 1640–1670s
- ← → Possible journey, 1663
- → The hajj, 1671–1672
- • City visited by Çelebi
- • Other city
- — Boundaries, ca. 1680

Takes part in Battle of St. Gotthard, 1664.

Evliya Çelebi shipwrecked en route to Trebizond, early 1640s.

Travels to Iran, 1655–1656.

Çelebi performs hajj pilgrimage to holy sites of Islam, 1671–1672.

© Cengage Learning

Join this chapter's traveler on "Voyages," an interactive tour of historic sites and events:
www.cengagebrain.com

had the building of this mosque stop for a year. . . . Shah Thamasp, the King of Persia [Iran] when he heard of the halt to construction, dispatched a great embassy with 1000 purses of money and a box of all kinds of valuable jewels. In his letter he wrote, "I heard that you did not have enough money to complete the mosque. . . . I have sent you this amount of money from the treasury and these jewels. Sell them and spend the money, and take pains to finish the mosque. Let us have a share in your pious works. . . ." Sûleyman Khan was incensed by the letter. In the presence of the [Safavid] emissary he distributed the 1000 purses of money to the Jews in Constantinople . . . then he gave the architect

Sinan the box of jewels while the emissary was still present and said to him: "The so-called precious stones he sent are worthless beside the stones of my mosque. So put them with the rest and use them in the construction." When the emissary understood the situation, he was dumbstruck. . . . Meanwhile, the chief architect used the jewels to decorate the grooves of that minaret with artistry of all sorts . . . that is why it is called the "Jewel Minaret."*

*Robert Dankoff and Sooyong Kim, translation and commentary, An Ottoman Traveller: Selections from the Book of Travels of Evliya Çelebi (London: Eland Publishing, 2010), pp. 13–14.

Evliya Çelebi
(1610–1683) The most famous of Ottoman travelers; his writings contain rich portraits of his own society as well as those he visited in Europe, Iran, Arabia, and North Africa.

This exchange of insults between the Ottoman sultan and the Iranian shah was part of an ongoing struggle between the two empires for control of the geographic heart of the Islamic world.

In seventeenth-century Europe as well, religious divisions fueled competition for wealth and power. The Protestant Reformation was opposed by the Habsburg dynasty, which, with its rich capital at Madrid funded by the wealth of the Americas, took up the Catholic cause. Çelebi's travels took him to the Habsburg-ruled city of Vienna, from which Catholic emperors struggled not only to fend off Ottoman offensives into central Europe—Çelebi himself participated in one of these campaigns in 1664—but also to suppress the theological and political challenge of the Protestant Reformation. From the early sixteenth until the late seventeenth century, warfare between Catholics and Protestants was a constant of European life, and Catholic–Protestant rivalry strongly influenced the political development of states such as England and France. In both Christendom and the lands of Islam, religion and politics often formed a deadly combination: the refinement of gunpowder technologies was making warfare ever more lethal.

Since the interconnected societies of western Eurasia, from England in the northwest to Iran in the southeast, were at the center of emerging world systems of trade and empire, these early modern struggles between religiously divided states had a lasting influence on the global balance of power. By the mid-eighteenth century, the Safavid empire had collapsed and Iran would no longer be a major political player. The Ottoman empire, while still a significant presence, had lost the initiative to rising European states, including a newly expansive Russian empire and Prussia, the strongest of numerous German kingdoms. The balance of power in western Eurasia now favored France, Britain, Austria, Prussia, and Russia, and by 1750 national competition had largely replaced religious rivalries. The building blocks for a European-dominated global order were in place.

Focus Questions

» *What were the main features of the kingdoms and empires of western Eurasia in the seventeenth century?*

» *When, where, and how were religion and politics most closely intertwined in western Eurasian societies? When and why did religion come to play a less prominent political role?*

» *How did the balance of power between the dominant states of western Eurasia shift during this period?*

Land Empires of Western Eurasia and North Africa, 1500–1685

Unlike the maritime empires described in the last two chapters, the Ottoman, Safavid, and Russian empires were land-based, created by the overland expansion of political and military power into neighboring territories. Facing outward toward central Eurasia, the origins of these land-based empires lay in the relationship between steppe nomads and settled agricultural peoples.

The rulers of the Ottoman empire, already well established in the fifteenth century when their power was magnified by their seizure of Constantinople in 1453, were the most successful of the Turkic-speaking peoples who had migrated westward from the steppes to conquer sedentary agricultural societies. The Safavids were also Turkic-speaking and nomadic in origin. Both societies adopted Islamic law and tradition, although the Sunni (SOO-nee) Ottomans and the Shi'ite (SHEE-ite) Safavids had different, often conflicting, interpretations of Islam.

The rulers of Russia, in contrast, were products of a settled agrarian society, although their southern frontier had long had contact with steppe nomads. Starting in the mid-fifteenth century, the Russians turned the tables on the Mongols and conquered parts of the steppe that had once been ruled by the Golden Horde. By the mid-seventeenth century, under the Romanov dynasty, the Russian empire was moving westward toward Poland, eastward into Siberia, and southward toward the edges of Ottoman and Safavid power. The influence of the Russian Orthodox Church spread along with the empire.

The Ottoman Empire, 1500–1650

The splendor of the Sublime Porte, center of Ottoman power in Constantinople, was legendary. The sultan's palace defined the city as a center of political power, while other monumental buildings expressed its religious focus—for example, the Hagia Sophia, an ancient Christian church converted into a mosque after the Ottoman capture of the city in 1453, and the sixteenth-century Sûleymaniye Mosque. European visitors of the time were awestruck by the Ottoman capital. Çelebi describes one such group of *"Frankish [European] infidels"*: *"Wherever they looked, they put finger to mouth and bit it in astonishment. . . . They threw off their Frankish hats and cried out in awe, 'Maria, Maria!'"**

The people of Constantinople fully mirrored the ethnic and religious diversity of the empire. In the neighborhood of Galata, for example, Çelebi found *"eighteen Muslim quarters, seventy quarters of Greek infidels, three of cranky Franks, one of Jews, and two of Armenians."* Çelebi noted that one neighborhood was full of *"grief-stricken Mudejars [Muslims] who came from Spain, driven out by the infidels"** after the Christian reconquest of Iberia was completed in 1492 (see Chapter 15). Although this diverse population was residentially segregated, and each community was substantially responsible for its own internal affairs, they shared common public spaces such as markets, gardens, and public baths. Constantinople was one of the world's most cosmopolitan cities.

---

*Robert Dankoff and Sooyong Kim, translation and commentary, *An Ottoman Traveller: Selections from the* Book of Travels *of Evliya Çelebi* (London: Eland Publishing, 2010), pp. 16, 18–19.

The glories of their capital reflected the successes of Ottoman governments and military elites in effectively administering and taxing the peasants, craftsmen, and merchants of their sprawling and productive domains. From their Anatolian heartland, where Turkish peasants predominated, the Ottomans added Palestine, Syria, Arabia, Iraq, and much of Hungary to the sultan's domains in the sixteenth century.

Ottoman fleets came to dominate the Black Sea and the eastern and southern shores of the Mediterranean, and the Ottoman navy defeated Christian fleets in the Red Sea, Persian Gulf, and Indian Ocean. From southeastern Europe Ottoman armies marched into the German-speaking lands of central Europe. The Ottomans also ruled Greece and conquered all of the Mediterranean coast of North Africa except Morocco, which remained the only significant Arab-ruled kingdom. In Egypt, Arabia, and Syria, Arabs were ruled by Turkish-speaking Ottoman administrators.

In the fifteenth century the Ottomans' military strength had derived from their cavalry, which included soldiers known as *ghazis* (GAH-zeez), horsemen of nomadic origin who were ambitious to conquer the Christian infidels of Byzantium for Islam. But the increasing scale of Ottoman military operations and the organization necessary to use gunpowder weapons such as muskets and cannon led to greater military professionalism. An old saying has it that peoples who are "conquered on horseback" cannot be "governed on horseback," meaning that more stable forms of administration are needed for long-term rule. Ghazis were therefore given land grants in conquered territories with responsibilities for maintaining order and collecting taxes; they became administrators rather than fighters.

At the same time, slaves became more important in the Ottoman military and in the central administration of the empire: Evliya Çelebi frequently and casually described the slaves that he personally accumulated as part of his share of the spoils of military campaigns. Apart from the common use of slaves as domestic servants, the Ottomans had begun to rely on **Janissaries**, slave soldiers who were recruited from conquered Christian lands and trained as professional soldiers. Janissaries trained year-round and became skilled at using gunpowder weapons. As the need for such soldiers increased, the Ottomans regularly enslaved Christian youth in the Balkan and Caucasus Mountains to meet the demand, leaving a simmering sense of grievance among the communities that were forced to give up children to their conquerors.

The concept of "elite slaves" sounds strange to modern ears, but reliance on slaves as soldiers and administrators was an old tradition. A sultan might not be able to trust his own brothers or sons because they were vying for power of their own, but the loyalty of a slave general was absolute. If he disobeyed he could simply be killed: he had no family ties to protect him. By the sixteenth century, Janissaries played a central role in administration as well as in the military. Even the sultan's chief minister was a slave.

After conquering Arabia and Palestine, the Ottomans controlled Mecca, Medina, and Jerusalem, the three holiest cities for Muslims. Since these were the holy pilgrimage sites to which Muslims like Evliya Çelebi hoped to travel, their supervision was a great responsibility, and the Ottomans were therefore able to emphasize their role as guardians of Islam. The question, however, was how to reconcile protection of Islam with the extraordinary diversity of the sultan's subjects. Just as Akbar in Mughal India had to devise a strategy to stabilize Islamic rule over a Hindu majority (see Chapter 16), so also Ottoman rulers needed to incorporate dozens of different communities with diverse religious and legal traditions.

The master strategist who reconciled central authority with local autonomy was Sultan **Süleyman** (r. 1520–1566). A strong military leader who greatly expanded

Janissaries
An elite corps of slaves trained as professional soldiers in the Ottoman military. Janissary soldiers were Christian youths from the Balkans who were pressed into service and forced to convert to Islam.

Süleyman
(r. 1520–1566) Credited with the development of literature, art, architecture, and law and for inclusive policies toward religious minorities, Süleyman extended the Ottoman empire while maintaining economic and political stability.

the empire, Süleyman (soo-lay-MAHN) also devised an administrative system that regularized relations between the government and its population. His court reflected the ethnic diversity of his empire. Turkish was the language of administration and military command, Arabic the language of theology and philosophy, and Persian the language of poetry and the arts. Europeans called him "Süleyman the Magnificent" for the dazzling opulence and splendor of his court. But within the empire he became known as "Süleyman the Lawgiver" for bringing peace and stability to the realm. The sultan's officials gained power through merit rather than family lineage. As an Austrian ambassador reported, *"Those who are dishonest, lazy and slothful never attain to distinction, but remain in obscurity and contempt. That is why they succeed in all they attempt . . . and daily extend the bounds of their rule."*[*]

Süleyman centralized religious authority and sponsored the building of mosques and religious schools, partly to combat the intermixture of pagan practices with Islam. For example, Süleyman sent religious experts to rural Anatolia to promote Islamic orthodoxy among Muslim peasants who still embraced folk beliefs, deities, and rituals.

Nevertheless, the Ottomans did not impose a single legal system on existing cultural and religious traditions. Instead, they allowed local Christian and Jewish populations to govern their own affairs and maintain their own courts as long as they remained loyal to the sultan and paid their taxes promptly.

This relative tolerance is demonstrated by the experiences of many of the Iberian Jews who were driven from Catholic Spain in 1492. Along with the Spanish Muslim refugees Çelebi encountered, these Jews found safe haven in Ottoman-ruled North Africa. In fact, when Çelebi presents a version of the "Jewish language," he starts with "un, dos, tire, korta"; he was describing not Hebrew but Ladino, the language based on medieval Spanish spoken by the Iberian Jews known as the Sephardim. Just as they had in medieval Spain, Ladino-speaking Jews made significant contributions to the intellectual and commercial life of the Ottoman empire. Of course, even while allowed to pursue their professions and regulate their own community affairs, Jews faced persistent popular prejudice. Çelebi referred to them as *"an ancient and accursed people."*[†]

In foreign affairs, Süleyman was aggressively expansionistic. The Ottoman siege of Vienna in 1529 was turned back by the city's defenders, and in the Mediterranean a combined European fleet under Spanish command defeated the Ottoman navy in the Battle of Lepanto in 1571. Still, the Ottomans stayed on the offensive in southeastern Europe into the later seventeenth century. Çelebi crafted an inventive

British Library, London/Art Resource, NY

Süleyman the Magnificent This portrait of Süleyman the Magnificent, also known as "the Lawgiver," shows the influence of Persian miniature painting on the arts of the Ottoman empire. Though most Muslim scholars rejected the practice of representing the human form in paintings and illuminated book manuscripts, fearing the sin of idol worship, the Ottomans borrowed these old artistic practices from their Iranian rivals.

[*]*The Turkish Letters of Ogier Ghiselin de Busbecq, Imperial Ambassador at Constantinople, 1554–1562,* trans. Edward S. Foster (New York: Oxford University Press), p. 66.

[†]Robert Dankoff and Sooyong Kim, translation and commentary, *An Ottoman Traveller: Selections from the* Book of Travels *of Evliya Çelebi* (London: Eland Publishing, 2010), pp. 93–94.

description of a massive Muslim expedition looting and plundering its way across western Europe to Amsterdam. The passage was pure fantasy (perhaps a satire on the tall tales of travelers). Quite realistic, however, was his description of a Habsburg victory over Ottoman forces in Austria in 1664 and his own participation the following year in a diplomatic mission to Vienna. With firm control over the Balkans, Greece, and much of Hungary, and with a large and well-equipped army, the Ottomans were a major player in the European balance of power.

Against the persistent Ottoman threat, the Europeans sought an ally in the Persian shah of Safavid Iran. As the Austrian ambassador noted:

> *On [the Ottoman] side are the resources of a mighty empire, strength unimpaired, experience and practice in fighting . . . endurance of toil, unity, discipline, frugality and watchfulness. . . . [W]orst of all, the enemy is accustomed to victory, and we to defeat. . . . Persia alone interposes in our favor; for the enemy, as he hastens to attack, must keep an eye on this menace to his rear.*[*]

For all their religious and cultural divergences, the Europeans and the Safavids found that mutual antipathy to the Ottomans gave them a starting point for cooperation.

The Shi'ite Challenge: Foundations of Safavid Iran, 1500–1629

Iran (referred to by Çelebi and others at the time as Persia) is a rich and productive land with a long history of influence in western and southern Asia. With Mesopotamia and the Mediterranean to the west and the Indus Valley and India to the south and east, Persia benefited from contacts with other civilizations. Its agricultural wealth and its location as a commercial crossroads also attracted invaders. In the early sixteenth century, some of these invaders founded the **Safavid dynasty** (1501–1722) and challenged the power of the Ottoman empire.

Like the Ottoman ghazis, the Safavid invaders had a religious motivation. Known as *kizilbash* ("redheads") because of the color of their turbans, they were members of an unorthodox Islamic sect led by a man named **Ismail** (r. 1501–1524). The "redheads" swept down from Azerbaijan, conquered the Persian-speaking lands, and drove west, capturing the important cities of Baghdad and Basra. Ismail then adopted mainstream Shi'ite beliefs and imposed them on his conquered subjects, including both Sunni Muslims and followers of the ancient Zoroastrian faith, some of whom fled to India to avoid persecution. In the history of Islam, Ismail's policy was a rare example of the forced imposition of faith.

Shi'ites believe that when Muhammad died, religious and political authority should have passed through his son-in-law Ali to Ali's son Hussein. Sunni Muslims, in contrast, argue that the Prophet's successors could be chosen freely from among Muhammad's close companions. In the seventh century the two sides came to blows. First Ali was killed, and then his son Hussein fell to the Sunni caliph. Shi'ites still visit the tomb of Hussein in Karbala (in today's Iraq), and every year an elaborate festival of mourning is held to commemorate his death.

To ensure the religious and political loyalty of their subjects, the Safavids decreed that the names of the Sunni caliphs, the first successors to the Prophet, should be publicly cursed. That was a problem for Evliya Çelebi: when he first heard the public cursing of a leader that he, as a Sunni, venerated, he recounted,

Safavid dynasty
(1501–1722) Dynasty that established Shi'ite Islam as the state religion in Iran and challenged the powerful Ottoman empire. The Safavids fell to invaders from Central Asia in the early eighteenth century.

Ismail
(r. 1501–1524) Founder of the Safavid dynasty in Iran who forced his subjects to adopt Shi'ite Islam. Came into military and religious conflict with the Ottoman empire, which was Sunni.

The Turkish Letters of Ogier Ghiselin de Busbecq, Imperial Ambassador at Constantinople, 1554–1562, trans. Edward S. Foster (New York: Oxford University Press), p. 66.

"I nearly went out of my mind."[*] Since he was on a diplomatic mission (as they did with the Habsburgs, the Ottomans alternated between warfare and diplomacy with Iran), the local governor decreed that there was to be no public cursing of Sunni caliphs, upon pain of death, while the Ottoman officials were present.

The Shi'ites, long a suppressed minority, now controlled a major Islamic state. Later, the Ottoman army retook the Tigris-Euphrates River Valley, including Baghdad and Basra, where the cultural boundary between Arabic- and Persian-speaking populations and the religious boundary between Sunni and Shi'ite majorities were located.

Although the shift toward Shi'ism in Iran was permanent, over time the religious passions that drove initial Safavid policies died down. The greatest Safavid ruler, Shah **Abbas I** (r. 1587–1629), built a new capital at Isfahan (is-fah-HAHN), which was a city of half a million residents when a European visitor commented on *"the great number of magnificent palaces, the agreeable and pleasant houses . . . the really fine bazaars, the water channels and the streets of which the sides were covered with tall plane trees."*[†] The gardens of Isfahan were legendary, and under Abbas Persian culture spread both east and west. Persian verse was widely admired, influencing Swahili poets in East Africa as well as Urdu poets in India. Isfahan, a showcase for Persian architecture and engineering, influenced the graceful silhouette of the Taj Mahal in India. In addition to creating beautiful abstract patterns on rich carpets, Persian artists were famous for miniature paintings depicting scenes from everyday life.

The economy also blossomed under Abbas's long and stable rule, with new irrigation works supporting agriculture, new markets for handicrafts, and a pilgrim trade bringing visitors to the holy sites of Shi'ite Islam. Iranian silks, carpets, and ceramics were traded on overland markets to the east and west and also into Indian Ocean circuits. Armenian merchants, many of whom had been forcibly relocated to Isfahan during Abbas's wars, played a crucial role in Iranian trade. As minorities in the lands where they traded, from the Mediterranean to Southeast Asia, Armenian traders relied on their shared linguistic and Christian religious heritage for social support while at the same time adjusting to the legal and cultural environment in which they worked.

In addition, Shah Abbas invited other European merchants and diplomatic representatives to Isfahan. Abbas was anxious to acquire guns and cannon and to train professional soldiers who could use them efficiently. The antagonism of many Iranian leaders to all things Christian and European was offset by the Safavid need to cultivate European alliances in their struggle with the Ottomans. The Safavid rulers abided by the old adage that "the enemy of my enemy is my friend" to seek European alliances against Constantinople. (See the feature "Movement of Ideas Through Primary Sources: A French View of the Iranians.")

Observing the jockeying for position among the Europeans at the Safavid court, one French visitor to Isfahan noticed that the Russian ambassador was given precedence. *"The Muscovite [Russian] is our neighbor and our friend,"* the chief minister told the Frenchman, *"and the commerce has been a long time settled between us, and without interruption. We send ambassadors to each other reciprocally almost every year, but we hardly know the other [Europeans]."*[‡] As the Russian empire expanded to the south, commercial and diplomatic relations between the two powers intensified.

Abbas I
(r. 1587–1629) Safavid ruler who created a long and stable reign, beautified the capital city of Isfahan, promoted foreign trade, and repelled Ottoman invaders.

---

[*]Robert Dankoff and Sooyong Kim, translation and commentary, *An Ottoman Traveller: Selections from the Book of Travels of Evliya Çelebi* (London: Eland Publishing, 2010), p. 56.

[†]Cited in Ronald W. Ferrier, *A Journey to Persia: Jean Chardin's Portrait of a Seventeenth Century Empire* (London: I. B. Tauris, 1996), p. 44.

[‡]Sir John Chardin, *Travels in Persia, 1673–1677,* an abridged English version of *Voyages du chevalier Chardin en Perse, et autres lieux de l'Orient* (London, Argonaut Press, 1927), p. 8.

A French View of the Iranians

Jean de Chardin (1643–1713) was a French-man who traveled twice to the Safavid empire in Iran (or Persia, as Europeans then called it), learning the language and forming strong opinions about the inhabitants. His *Travels in Persia* is a valuable primary source on European-Iranian relations in the late seventeenth century.

Still, as with all such travel accounts, we must be cautious about accepting his portrait at face value. It is important to consider the author's own point of view. For one thing, Chardin was a jeweler, and he was frustrated by what he saw as "deceits" and "tricks" in his business dealings, experiences that may have colored his perspective. Even more important to remember is that Chardin was a Protestant member of the bourgeoisie, the emerging French middle class. Therefore, as much as the following document is a comment on Iranians, it can be used to reveal Chardin's own worldview through the contrasts he draws with his hosts, highlighting his own values of thrift, foresight, plain speaking, hard work, and detached curiosity.

Source: Sir John Chardin, *Travels in Persia, 1673–1677*, an abridged English version of *Voyages du chevalier Chardin en Perse, et autres lieux de l'Orient* (London, Argonaut Press, 1927), p. 70. Spelling and usage have been modernized.

From *Travels in Persia*

They [Iranians] are true philosophers on the account of [their] . . . hope and fear of a future state; they are little guilty of covetousness, and are only desirous of getting, that they may spend it; they love to enjoy the present, and deny themselves nothing that they are able to procure, taking no thought for the morrow, and relying wholly on providence, and their own fate; they firmly believe it to be sure and unalterable . . . so when any misfortune happens to them, they are not cast down, as most men are, they only say quietly [so] it is ordained. . . .

The most commendable property of the manners of the Persians, is their kindness to strangers; the reception and protection they afford them, and their universal hospitality, and toleration, in regard to religion, except the clergy of the country, who, as in all other places, hate to a furious degree, all those that differ from their opinions. The Persians are very civil, and very honest in matters of religion; so far that they allow those who have embraced theirs, to recant, and resume their former opinion. . . . They believe that all men's prayers are good and prevalent; therefore, in their illnesses, and in other wants, they admit of, and even desire the prayers of different religions. . . . This is not to be imputed to their religious principles . . . but I impute it to the sweet temper of that nation, who are naturally averse to contest and cruelty. . . .

Two opposite customs are commonly practiced by the Persians; that of praising God continually, and talking of his attributes, and that of uttering curses, and obscene talk. Whether you see them at home, or meet them in the streets, going about business or walking; you still hear them uttering some blessing or prayer. . . . The least thing they set their hand to do, they say, "In the Name of God"; and they never speak of doing anything, without adding, "If it pleases God. . . ." [At] the same time, come out of the same men's mouths a thousand obscene expressions. All ranks of men are infected with this odious vice. Their bawdy talk is taken from Arse, and C——t, which modesty forbids one to name. . . . [W]hen they have spent their Stock of bawdy names, they begin to call one another Atheists, Idolaters, Jews, Christians; and to say to one another, "The Christians Dogs are better than thou. . . ."

The Eastern People are not near so restless, and so uneasy as we; they sit gravely and soberly, make no motion with their body . . . for they don't believe that a man that is in his wits, can be so full of action as we are . . . I'll repeat it once more: The Persians are the most kind people in the world; they have the most moving and the most engaging ways, the most complying tempers, the smoothest and the most flattering tongues, avoiding in their conversation, relations or expressions which may occasion melancholy thoughts. . . .

As civil as that nation is, they never act out of generosity. . . . They do nothing but out of a principle of interest, that is to say, out of hope or fear: And they cannot conceive that there should be such a country where people will do their duty from a motive of virtue only, without any other recompense. It is quite the contrary with them; they are paid for everything, and beforehand too. One can ask nothing of them, but with a present in one's hand. . . . The poorest and most miserable people never appear before a great man, or one from whom they would ask some favor, but at the same time they offer a present, which

is never refused, even by the greatest lords of the kingdom. . . .

As for what relates to travelling, those journeys that are made out of pure curiosity are . . . inconceivable to the Persians. . . . They have no taste of the pleasure we enjoy in seeing different manners from ours, and hearing of a language which we do not understand. . . . They asked me if it was possible that there should be such people amongst us, who would travel two or three thousand leagues with so much danger, and inconveniency, only to see how they were made, and what they did in Persia, and upon no other design. These people are of the opinion, as I have observed, that one cannot better attain to virtue, nor have a fuller taste of pleasure than by resting and dwelling at home, and that it is not good to travel, but to acquire riches. . . . It is from this spirit of theirs no doubt, that the Persians are so grossly ignorant of the present state of other nations of the world, and that they do not so much as understand geography, and have no maps; which comes from this, that having no curiosity to see other countries. . . . The Ministers of State generally speaking, know no more what passes in Europe, than in the world of the moon. The greatest part, even have but a confused idea of Europe, which they look upon to be some little island in the North Seas, where there is nothing to be found that is either good or handsome; from whence it comes, say they, that the Europeans go all over the world, in search of fine things, and of those which are necessary, as being destitute of them.

QUESTIONS FOR ANALYSIS

» *In Chardin's view, what are the most positive and negative attributes of the Persians?*

» *What passages in the document best reveal Chardin's own middle-class value system?*

Origins of the Russian Empire, 1500–1685

Before the sixteenth century, the Slavic-speaking Russian people had been deeply influenced by Greek-speaking Byzantium. Medieval Russian princes and merchants cultivated relations with Constantinople, and the Russian city of Kiev became a central point for the diffusion of literacy and Orthodox Christianity. The monastic tradition of Orthodox Christianity took deep root.

The early consolidation of a Russian state is largely the story of two Ivans, Ivan III (r. 1440–1505) and Ivan IV (r. 1533–1584). Ivan III ruled Muscovy from his capital at Moscow, drove the weakened Mongols out of the other Russian states, and asserted his authority over them. He made an explicit connection between his own power and the Byzantine legacy, calling himself *tsar* ("caesar") and declaring that Russia would defend the Orthodox Christian heritage after the fall of its traditional center of Constantinople to the Ottomans. Ivan's strategy of maintaining a large territorial buffer around the core Russian lands to protect them from invasion would become a perennial element of Russian imperial policy.

A generation later Tsar Ivan IV centralized royal authority even further and extended Russian power to the west, east, and south, earning the nickname "Ivan the Terrible" for the random cruelty of his later years. His armies engaged Catholic Poland and Protestant Sweden to the west, conquered Muslim populations in the rich steppe grasslands to the south, and began to drive into the Caucasus Mountains between the Black and Caspian Seas. Defense and expansion of the Orthodox faith inspired Ivan's conquests.

To the east, across the Ural Mountains, lay the forbidding lands of Siberia. The quest for animal furs lured the first Russian frontiersmen to these lands, and state power followed later (see Chapter 20). Already in the seventeenth century, Russians were trading furs on a substantial scale, meeting the demand for exotic and elegant furs among kings and aristocrats from England to Iran. In fact, Evliya Çelebi described a specialized Ottoman guild of furriers whose goods included *"furs of sable, ermin, Russian silver fox"* and *"outlandish bearskin caps."* * Furs were the most valuable of the commodities that linked the economy of Russia southward across the Black and Caspian Seas.

Long-term political stability came with the rise of Russia's Romanov dynasty (1613–1917). Following the death of Ivan the Terrible came a "time of troubles" with no clear successor to the title of tsar. That period of uncertainty ended in 1613 when the Russian nobles offered royal power to Mikhail Romanov. The Romanovs further centralized state power and continued Russia's imperial expansion (see Chapters 20 and 27). Russia, along with the Ottoman empire, became the most enduring of land-based empires in the modern era: both Romanov tsars and Ottoman sultans ruled into the early twentieth century.

The main sources of revenue for the tsars and the nobility were agricultural surpluses. Village-based farming was the foundation of all the land-based empires, not only Russia but also the Ottoman and Safavid empires, Mughal India, and Ming China (see Chapter 16). What was distinctive about Russia was the persistence of serfdom. Russian peasants were tightly bound to their villages, and the tsars and aristocracy increasingly saw these "souls," as they called the

---

*Robert Dankoff and Sooyong Kim, translation and commentary, *An Ottoman Traveller: Selections from the* Book of Travels *of Evliya Çelebi* (London: Eland Publishing, 2010), p. 27.

peasants, as property that could be bought and sold. The oppressive conditions of serfdom in Russia contrasted with developments in western Europe, where serfdom had either disappeared altogether or where peasant obligations were becoming less burdensome.

The Struggle for Stability in Western Europe, 1500–1715

The sixteenth century and the first half of the seventeenth century were a time of turmoil in western Europe. As religious strife became entangled with the ambitions of emperors, kings, and princes, warfare became more common. The social conflict that came with urbanization and commercialization also heightened tensions, and attempts at political centralization often met with resistance.

The Habsburgs were the most powerful family in Europe at the beginning of this period. Originally from central Europe, through marriages and diplomatic maneuvers the **Habsburg dynasty** came to rule Spain, the Netherlands, parts of Italy, and much of German-speaking Europe. Also commanding the vast resources of Spain's American empire, the Habsburgs aspired to control a pan-European Catholic empire. Conflict with the Ottoman empire, including the need to protect Vienna from Ottoman attack, was one check on Habsburg power. Another was the rising power of England and France. Queen Elizabeth I (r. 1558–1603) of England was solidly Protestant and stridently anti-Spanish, while the Catholic monarchs of France competed with the Spanish Habsburgs for power and influence. The rebellious provinces of the Netherlands were another major distraction and expense.

By the mid-seventeenth century the Habsburgs had declined in power relative to their rivals, as religious and dynastic conflict brought civil war to England and France and devastating violence to central Europe, where decades of religiously driven warfare laid the countryside to waste. By the early eighteenth century, however, stability had returned. Catholic France and Protestant England had established stable constitutional orders (France with absolute royal power and England with a balance between king and Parliament) that allowed their leaders to focus on international expansion. In central and eastern Europe the strongest military powers were Austria—though the Habsburgs no longer controlled Spain or the Netherlands, they were still a formidable force—and Prussia, the rising power among the politically fractured German-speaking lands.

Habsburg dynasty
Powerful ruling house that expanded from Austria to Spain, the Netherlands, and the Spanish empire, as well as throughout the German-speaking world when Charles V (r. 1516–1556) was elected Holy Roman emperor.

The Habsburgs: Imperial Ambitions and Political Realities, 1519–1648

The greatest of the Habsburg monarchs was Charles I, who ruled Spain from 1516 to 1556. Educated in the Netherlands, he inherited both the Spanish crown at Madrid and the Habsburg domains in central Europe. His Dutch experience tied him to one of the most dynamic commercial economies in the world. The central European territories dominated from Vienna were crucial in the European military balance, and his Spanish possessions included all the riches of the Americas. His family connections also made him king of Naples, controlling the southern part of Italy.

Martin Luther Preaching Martin Luther was known as a powerful preacher, as seen in this contemporary depiction. The rapid spread of his Protestant ideas, however, resulted from the printing press as well. In 1455 the first metal movable type outside of Asia was invented by a German goldsmith; one hundred years later that invention allowed Martin Luther's ideas to spread far and wide.

British Library, London/HIP/Art Resource, NY

In 1520, Charles was crowned as Holy Roman emperor with the title Charles V, having defeated the French king to win that position. The Holy Roman empire was a vestige of a much earlier attempt to recreate Roman unity in Europe in collaboration with the Catholic Church, though by the sixteenth century the "emperor," elected by seven of the many archbishops and princes who ruled over German-speaking lands, had little real power. However, it was a prestigious position, and having been crowned emperor by the pope, Charles became the principal defender of the Catholic faith.

With extensive territorial possessions in Europe and all the wealth of the Americas at their disposal, it seemed that the Habsburgs might be able to create a political unity in western Europe. But for all the military campaigns undertaken by Charles V during his long reign, it was not to be. The French were too powerful a rival in the west, while the Ottoman Turks challenged Habsburg supremacy in eastern Europe and the Mediterranean. Equally significant were the violent repercussions from the Protestant Reformation that began to appear in the mid-sixteenth century (see Map 17.1).

Charles V became Holy Roman emperor just as Martin Luther was challenging church authority (see Chapter 16). In 1521 Charles V presided over a meeting intended to bring Luther back under papal authority. Luther refused to back down and was declared an outlaw. The German princes chose sides, some declaring themselves "Lutherans," others remaining loyal to the pope and Holy Roman emperor. Decades of inconclusive warfare followed, and religious division became a permanent part of the western European scene. Exhausted, in 1555 Charles agreed to a peace that recognized the principle that princes could impose either Catholicism or Lutheranism within their own territories. He then abdicated his throne, retired to a monastery, and split his inheritance between his brother Ferdinand, who took control of the Habsburgs' central European domains, and his son Philip, who became king of Spain.

Philip II (r. 1556–1598) Son of Charles V and king of Spain. Considering himself a defender of Catholicism, Philip launched attacks on Protestants in England and the Netherlands.

While **Philip II** (r. 1556–1598) ruled over a magnificent court at Madrid, the viceroyalties of New Spain were established, the Ottomans were defeated in a great naval battle at Lepanto (1571), and the Philippines (named for Philip himself) were brought under Spanish control. However, even with the vast riches of New Spain, wars severely strained the treasury, and increased taxes led to unrest. Philip's militancy in attempting to impose Catholic orthodoxy on his subjects made religious divisions even more acute.

One example is the rebellion in 1568 of the Spanish *moriscos* (mohr-EES-kos), Arabic-speaking Iberians who stayed in Spain after 1492. Though forced to convert

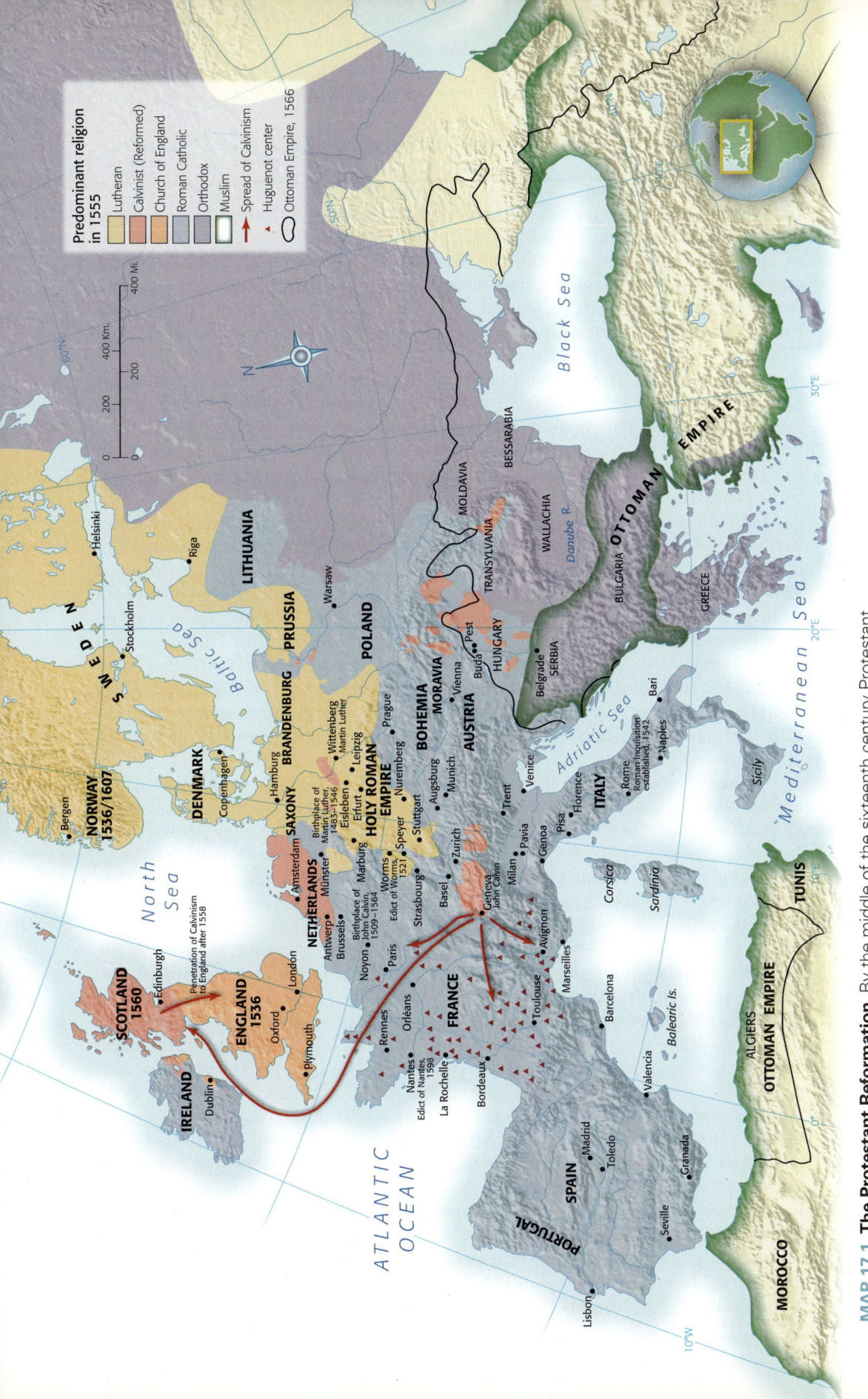

MAP 17.1 The Protestant Reformation By the middle of the sixteenth century Protestant churches were dominant in England, Scotland, the Netherlands, Switzerland, and Scandinavia. German principalities were divided between Protestants and Catholics. Catholicism remained dominant across most of southern Europe, though Protestants formed a significant minority in France. The religious landscape was especially complex in southeastern Europe, where, under Ottoman authority, there were substantial communities of Catholics, Protestants, Orthodox Christians, and Muslims. (© Cengage Learning)

Predominant religion in 1555

Lutheran
Calvinist (Reformed)
Church of England
Roman Catholic
Orthodox
Muslim
Spread of Calvinism
Huguenot center
Ottoman Empire, 1566

to Christianity, many morisco families continued to practice Islam in private. When the church tried to impose Catholic orthodoxy on them, the resulting rebellion took two years to suppress; Philip later ordered the expulsion of all remaining Iberian Muslims. Among their descendants were the Spanish Muslims Çelebi encountered in Constantinople.

Philip also struggled with the Calvinists in his Dutch provinces. **John Calvin** was a Protestant theologian whose Reformed Church emphasized the absolute power of God over weak and sinful humanity. The possibility of salvation for human souls lay entirely with God, Calvin argued: *"eternal life is foreordained for some, eternal damnation for others."*

Philip regarded these Calvinists as heretics, and when he tried to seize their property they armed themselves in self-defense. Attempts to put down the rebellion only stiffened Dutch resistance. The struggle was never resolved in Philip's lifetime, but in 1609 a treaty was signed that led to the effective independence of the Dutch United Provinces. It was in this political context that the Dutch East India Company emerged as a powerful trading company (see Chapter 16).

England was another constant source of concern to Philip. Its Protestant rulers harassed the Spanish at every turn, such as by supporting the privateers who plundered Spanish treasure ships in the Caribbean. In 1588, Philip sent a great naval armada to invade England, but poor weather combined with clever English naval strategy to defeat the attempt. By the early seventeenth century, the Habsburg empire was reeling from these religious conflicts and the expense of fighting on so many fronts. At this same time, silver imports from the New World began to decline. Like the rulers of Ming China, another great empire for which expanding supplies of silver were a necessity, the Spanish Habsburgs found themselves in a difficult financial position. By midcentury, their Italian possessions, though Catholic, were also in revolt.

Things were no better in the eastern Habsburg domains. The peace of 1555 had broken down, and warfare continued to rock central Europe. Unrest between Catholic and Lutheran rulers finally led to the catastrophic **Thirty Years' War** (1618–1648). As armies rampaged through the countryside, up to 30 percent of the rural population died from famine and disease, a loss of population almost as great as that brought by the Black Death three hundred years earlier. Finally, the Peace of Westphalia (1648) recognized a permanent division between Catholic and Protestant Germany. The ideal of a single overarching imperial structure was gone, replaced by the concept of separate national states that, though often in conflict, recognized one another's sovereignty and agreed to abide by rules governing war and diplomacy. By 1648 the era of Habsburg dominance of western Europe was over.

Evliya Çelebi's first diplomatic mission to Vienna came just a few years earlier, and his views on Austria were mixed. As a Sunni Muslim, he saw the prolific use of religious statues and paintings in Viennese Catholic churches as idolatrous. (Calvinist Protestants had a similar reaction, as they also frowned on the veneration of images.) Nevertheless, he gives space in his *Book of Travels* to how Catholic priests explained their rationale to his Ottoman audience: *"When the priests harangue the people, just as your sheikhs do, they have difficulty conveying their message with fine words alone. So we convey the message through images of the prophets and saints and paradise, depictions of divine glory. . . . But we do not worship them in any way."** Çelebi was very impressed, especially by the paintings he saw. *"When one sees the depiction of paradise,"* he wrote of one painting, *"one wishes to die and go to heaven. . . . Truly, when it comes to painting, the Franks prevail over the Indians and Persians."**

John Calvin
(1509–1564) A Protestant leader whose followers emphasized individual scriptural study and the absolute sovereignty of God.

Thirty Years' War
(1618–1648) Series of wars fought by various European powers on German-speaking lands. Began as a competition between Catholic and Lutheran rulers and was complicated by the dynastic and strategic interests of Europe's major powers.

---

*Robert Dankoff and Sooyong Kim, translation and commentary, *An Ottoman Traveller: Selections from the* Book of Travels *of Evliya Çelebi* (London: Eland Publishing, 2010), pp. 240–241, 241.

la fin ces Voleurs infames et perdus ,   Monstrent bien que le crime (horrible et noire engeance)   Et que cest le Destin des hommes vicieux
mme fruits malheureux a cet arbre pendus   Est luy mesme instrument de honte et de vengeance ,   Desprouuer tost ou tard la iustice des Cieux .

The Hanging Tree This French engraving from 1633 shows the awful violence that ravaged Europe during the Thirty Years' War. The victims, says the text, "hang from the tree like unfortunate fruit." (Erich Lessing/Art Resource, NY)

He was also impressed by the status and skills of Vienna's men of learning, comparing Austrian doctors and scholars favorably to ancient Greek and medieval Muslim models. *"In the city of Vienna,"* he wrote, *"there are perfect masters of surgery . . . and scholars of such wisdom and skill the equal of Ibn Sinā and Pythagoras together."** He was equally impressed by their libraries, complaining that Muslims did far less to preserve their ancient texts. Vienna's commercial life, too, brought praise from Çelebi. Of the numerous shops, he wrote, *"so prosperous and well stocked are they that each shop is worth an Egyptian treasure."†*

On the other hand, as we might expect given that the Ottomans and Austrians had recently fought a bitter war, he was also critical of Habsburg society, particularly in military affairs. He contrasted the Austrians unfavorably to the Hungarians:

> *The Austrians . . . have no stomach for a fight and are not swordsmen and horsemen. Their infantry musketeers, to be sure, are real fire-shooters; but . . . they can't shoot from the shoulder as Ottoman soldiers do. Also, they shut their eyes and fire at random. . . . The Hungarians on the other hand, though they have lost their power, still have fine tables, are hospitable to guests, and are . . . true warriors. . . . They do not torture their prisoners as the Austrians do. . . . In short, though both of them are unbelievers without faith, the Hungarians are the more honorable and cleaner infidels.†*

---

*J. W. Livingstone, "Evliya Çelebi on Surgical Procedures in Vienna," *Al-Abath* 23 (1970): 232.

†Robert Dankoff and Sooyong Kim, translation and commentary, *An Ottoman Traveller: Selections from the* Book of Travels *of Evliya Çelebi* (London: Eland Publishing, 2010), pp. 232, 230–231.

The military balance between Austrians and Ottomans in southeastern Europe seesawed for another century. Though horsemanship, as Çelebi indicated, still had strong cultural and military value in the seventeenth century, it was the effective use of gunpowder weapons that was fast becoming crucial to success. After 1648 the Habsburgs, now limited to Austria and central Europe, managed to hold their own and remain one of the great powers of western Eurasia.

Religious Conflict and Political Control in France and England, 1500–1715

In France and England, more centralized monarchical governments developed in the early modern period, in both cases influenced by the need to counter Habsburg aspirations to a broader empire. In both countries, however, internal divisions of several kinds stood in the way of national success, most notably religious differences and conflicts between kings and aristocrats over the relative weight of their power. In both France and England centralizing forces overcame such divisions, though with great violence and with very different political outcomes.

In France, Protestants were a minority to be reckoned with (see Map 17.1). As French Calvinists, known as Huguenots (HEW-guh-noh), faced increasing persecution, religious warfare began. In 1572, after ten years of constant conflict, a mass slaughter of Huguenots started in Paris and soon spread to other French cities. In 1589, the Protestant Henry of Navarre took the throne as Henry IV. Facing Catholic armies and a largely hostile Catholic population, Henry publicly converted to Catholicism and then, in 1598, issued the Edict of Nantes granting limited toleration of Protestant worship. Still, Catholic-Protestant tensions persisted.

The dominant French political figure of the time was **Cardinal Richelieu** (1585–1642). Although Richelieu (RISH-el-yeuh) was a Catholic church official, his policies were guided by the interests of the French monarchy rather than by religious affiliation. He was willing, for example, to ally France with German Protestants against the Spanish Habsburgs, whom he saw as the main rivals to French power. Richelieu's attempt to amass greater power for the king and his ministers alienated the French nobility, and the common people resented increased taxes to pay for military campaigns.

When the king and Cardinal Richelieu both died within a few months of each other and a child-king, **Louis XIV** (r. 1643–1715), came to the throne, revolts broke out. From 1648 to 1653, France was wracked by civil war between the monarchy and those who were fed up with high taxes and the centralization of authority at court. But the French monarchy survived, and when Louis XIV came of age, he created a court of legendary power, with his Versailles Palace rivaling Constantinople's Sublime Porte in splendor and luxury.

At the time that Louis XIV became king, the nobility still dominated the countryside, and they remained jealous of their prerogatives. Both lords and peasants lived in a world where local affiliations and obligations were more important than national ones. As during medieval times, peasants labored on their lords' estates and were subject to manorial courts. They spoke local dialects, lived by local customs, and viewed the royal court as distant. Roads were poor, local tolls hampered trade, and even weights and measures varied in different parts of the country.

Cardinal Richelieu
(1585–1642) Influential adviser to French kings who centralized the administrative system of the French state and positioned the Bourbon rulers of France to replace the Habsburgs as the dominant Catholic force in Europe.

Louis XIV
(r. 1643–1715) Known as the "Sun King," Louis epitomized royal absolutism and established firm control over the French state. Aggressively pursued military domination of Europe while patronizing French arts from his court at Versailles.

Louis XIV at Court King Louis XIV was an active patron of new science. It was his finance minister, Jean-Baptiste Colbert, who suggested that the king form the Royal Academy of Sciences in 1666. Here Colbert is shown presenting members of the Academy to the king; two globes and a large map indicate that the French monarch saw the development of science as a means of expanding his empire. (Réunion des Musées Nationaux/Art Resource, NY)

To assert his power, Louis increased the use of officials known as *intendants*, often from the middle class or the lower ranks of the nobility, who depended on royal patronage and owed their loyalty to the king. Dispatched across the country, they enforced royal edicts that cut into the power of the landed nobility. As nobles lost local power, they too sought royal patronage and gravitated toward the lavish banquets, plays, operas, and ballets the court provided for their entertainment at Versailles.

Louis XIV also definitively resolved France's religious divisions by emphasizing the Catholic nature of the state. Although a minority, Protestants had an influence on French life and politics beyond their numbers. In 1685, Louis formally revoked the Edict of Nantes, realigning the French state with Catholicism. Soon hundreds of thousands of French Protestants fled to England, Switzerland, the Netherlands, and the Dutch East India Company settlement at Cape Town in South Africa. Adopting the motto *"One King, One Law, One Faith,"* Louis was determined to weaken Spain and Austria and position France as the world's dominant Catholic power.

In 1713, after years of French conflict with Spain, the Netherlands, and the Austrian Habsburgs, a settlement was finally reached that brought order to the dynastic politics of Europe. Faced with the possibility that the Habsburgs might reunify Madrid and Vienna under a single ruler, the European powers supported a plan to put a member of Louis XIV's Bourbon family on the Spanish throne, with the stipulation that the French and Spanish crowns could never be united. Now Louis and his successors could put even more energy into challenging England in a global competition for empire.

Louis XIV's form of government has been termed "royal absolutism." *"I am the state,"* he said, implying that all of public life should be directed by his own will. The French "Sun King" was the envy of all who aspired to absolute power, including contemporary English monarchs who also aspired to magnified royal power. However, in this case religious divisions and the tradition of parliamentary power checked royal absolutism and led to the execution of one king and limitations on the authority of all later ones.

Under Queen Elizabeth, English society had entered the seventeenth century in relative tranquility and with increasing national confidence. In religious matters, Elizabeth followed the Anglican Church of England tradition established by her father, King Henry VIII. Although Catholicism was made illegal, Henry actually retained many Catholic rites and traditions, including a hierarchy of powerful bishops. Many English Protestants wanted further reform to purge Catholic influences like the emphasis on saints, statues, and elaborate rituals. Among them were the English Calvinists, Protestant reformers known as **Puritans**, who grew discontented with the Stuart kings who came to power after Elizabeth. They scorned the opulence of court life and the culture of luxury of Anglican bishops. Increased taxes and assertions of centralized royal power were additional causes of complaint.

Under King **Charles I** (r. 1625–1649), tensions exploded. Charles pursued war with Spain and supported Huguenot rebels in France, but he could not raise taxes to finance his policies without the approval of Parliament. In 1628, when Parliament presented a petition of protest against the king, he disbanded it and did not call another session for eleven years. By then Charles was so desperate for money that he had no choice but to reconvene Parliament. Reformers in Parliament tried to use the occasion to compel the abolition of the Anglican ecclesiastical hierarchy in favor of a more decentralized church organization. When Charles arrested several parliamentary leaders on charges of treason, the people of London reacted with violence. The king fled London, and the English Civil War (1642–1649) began.

Opposition to the king's forces was organized by the Puritan leader Oliver Cromwell (1599–1658). Puritan soldiers showed their disdain by stabling their horses inside Anglican churches, smashing statues, and knocking out stained-glass windows. After seven years of fighting, Cromwell prevailed. The king was captured and, in 1649, beheaded.

Oliver Cromwell became Lord Protector of the English Commonwealth and instituted a series of radical reforms. But the Commonwealth was held together by

Puritans
Seventeenth-century reformers of the Church of England who attempted to purge the church of all Catholic influences. They were Calvinists who emphasized Bible reading, simplicity and modesty, and the rejection of priestly authority and elaborate rituals.

Charles I
(r. 1625–1649) King of England whose attempts to centralize royal power led to conflict with Parliament, where some members also resented the influence of his Catholic wife. His execution marked the end of the English Civil War.

little other than his own will and his control of the army, and some of his policies were highly unpopular. Puritan suppression of the theaters, for example, while in keeping with strict Calvinist ideals, was resented by many. When Cromwell died in 1658, the Commonwealth went with him, and in 1660 Parliament invited Charles's son home from exile to reestablish the monarchy.

When Charles II returned to England, absolute power was not an option. He could only raise funds with the approval of Parliament. Charles himself preferred relatively tolerant policies, but Parliament imposed restrictions on Catholics and Protestant "dissenters" who rejected the Anglican Church in favor of a more thoroughly reformed Protestantism: only Anglicans were allowed to hold public office.

With the death of Charles II, religious tension rose to the point of crisis when his Catholic brother came to the throne as King James II (r. 1685–1689). While James II did not try to impose Catholicism on the largely Protestant kingdom, he did seek greater tolerance for his own faith. In response, in 1688 Parliament invited Charles's reliably Protestant daughter Mary, together with her Dutch husband William of Orange, to take the throne. James II raised an army but was defeated by Protestant forces. The accession of William and Mary, known as the Glorious Revolution, made permanent the Protestant character of the English monarchy.

Since they had been invited to rule by Parliament, William and Mary were required to accept the principle of annual parliamentary meetings. They also approved a **Bill of Rights**. While restrictions on individual liberty remained and most people had no real voice in governance, the English Bill of Rights established important precedents for the future—freedom of speech in Parliament, for example, and the right to trial by jury—for England and for the world.

Bill of Rights
In 1689, King William and Queen Mary of England recognized a Bill of Rights that protected their subjects against arbitrary seizure of person or property and that required annual meetings of Parliament.

English governance thus differed from French absolutism. By the eighteenth century the balance between king and Parliament gave English society a stable foundation. English commerce thrived, both domestically and across the world, and the English navy became dominant. Rising from religious strife and civil war, England became a great power, and the nation became "British" after unification with Scotland in 1707. The French and the British, with their very different political cultures and religious foundations, would soon be engaged in a global contest that brought war to both the Americas and Asia (see Chapter 19).

The Shifting Balance of Power in Western Eurasia and the Mediterranean, 1650–1750

The religious divisions that inflamed most of Europe during the sixteenth and seventeenth centuries eventually abated. By the middle of the eighteenth century the situation stabilized as Catholic and Protestant rulers increasingly pursued policies on the basis of dynastic and national interests rather than religious ones.

New powers were emerging to displace old empires. In the later seventeenth century, Russia, England, and France each arose as great powers and were joined by Austria, still ruled by the Habsburg family, and Prussia, a rising German-speaking kingdom. As these five great powers jockeyed for advantage, others saw their power decline. Formerly powerful Poland was divided. Safavid Iran was invaded and conquered. The Ottomans remained powerful, but by the eighteenth century their days of expansion were over (see Map 17.2).

MAP 17.2 Western Eurasia in 1715 By the early eighteenth century the Habsburg attempt to unify western Europe had failed, and the continent was permanently divided between Catholic and Protestant powers. In 1715 the dominant powers in the west were France, Britain, Austria, and Prussia. The Russian and Ottoman empires to the east were formidable military powers, but the golden age of Spain had ended. (© Cengage Learning)

Legend:
- French Bourbon lands
- Spanish Bourbon lands
- Austrian Habsburg lands
- Prussian lands
- Great Britain
- Boundary of the Holy Roman Empire
- Russian Empire
- Russian gains, by 1725
- Ottoman Empire, 1722

Safavid Court This painting shows the court of Shah Suleyman II in the late seventeenth century. The shah is entertained by musicians, while his retainers prepare for an evening hunt, with a European visitor looking on. The style is Iranian, although European influence can be seen in the use of perspective to create a pastoral background. Suleyman II was an ineffective ruler who enjoyed these luxuries as his empire declined in power. (Institute of Oriental Studies, St. Petersburg, Russia/The Bridgeman Art Library)

Between 1650 and 1750, power shifted north and west, toward western Europe. Even the rulers of imperial Russia, whose empire continued to expand to the south and east, looked to the west for models of strength and innovation.

Safavid Collapse and Ottoman Persistence, 1650–1750

By the late seventeenth century corruption and poor leadership were already weakening the Safavids. Shah Abbas had neglected to groom a successor. The next shah, pampered in the seclusion of the royal harem his whole life, had little education and no experience in government or administration. The new shah's courtiers followed his example of debauchery and corruption. Shi'ite clerics, who had been principal supporters of the Safavid dynasty in its earliest days, were appalled.

The last Safavid shah attempted to reverse these trends and regain the support of the clergy by imposing harsh conditions of public morality. He banned music, coffee, and public entertainments, restricted women to the home, and even destroyed

The Coffeehouse in World History

One of the most enduring institutions arising from the early modern Islamic world is that of the coffeehouse. Coffee is of African origin and spread to southern Arabia, where it was used by Sufi mystics to fuel their nighttime rituals. By the mid-sixteenth century the habit of coffee drinking had spread to the major cities of Islam, where coffeehouses were popular with men from all social positions as places for leisure, discussion, and games such as chess and backgammon. Women, barred from coffeehouses, drank coffee at public baths, which served a similar social function. By 1650 there were over six hundred coffeehouses in Constantinople alone.

From here coffee and coffeehouses spread to both Europe and India. Legend has it that European coffee drinking began after the Turks left bags of coffee behind when they lifted their siege of Vienna in 1683. In reality, Armenian merchants had already brought coffee to Italy and France, and it was the university town of Oxford in England that was probably the site of the first European coffeehouse. As mass printing spread, cheap newspapers became available to fuel argumentation and debate, and men from the emerging English middle class found the coffeehouse a respectable, convivial, and inexpensive place to spend an evening.

Because of this connection with political and intellectual debate, authorities in Europe, as well as in the Islamic world, associated coffeehouses with radical and subversive ideas. In 1656 the Ottoman sultan tried to shut down Constantinople's coffeehouses, but all such attempts to limit their appeal proved futile.

In the nineteenth and twentieth centuries many European coffeehouses became more genteel, attracting a bourgeois clientele and serving chocolates and cakes. But the grittier, smoke-filled tradition of the coffeehouse as a place of independent thought and discussion endured. In the 1950s, American coffeehouses were associated with artistic forms such as free jazz and countercultural poetry. In the 1960s this association with youth culture continued, as coffeehouses became centers of protest music in the folk tradition.

More recently, coffeehouses in the United States have become the domain of large corporations. In many places, corporate homogenization now threatens the individuality and eccentricity of older coffeehouses. However, there are still many coffeehouses in Europe, in the Middle East, and in American university towns that carry on the old traditions of free thinking, argumentation, and debate.

---

the imperial wine cellar. (See the feature "World History in Today's World: The Coffeehouse in World History.") Though popular with some clerics, such actions were insufficient to revive the empire. As in Puritan-ruled England under Cromwell, people soon tired of such heavy-handed moral impositions.

Weakness at the top was a recipe for disaster. Lacking strong direction, the bureaucracy became a drain on productivity. Bribery was constant, and provincial governors raised taxes for their own account. The Safavid empire was easy pickings by 1722, when Afghan invaders descended on the capital of Isfahan and left it in ruins. By 1747, the political legacy of the Safavid empire was gone (although the dominance in Iran of Shi'ite Islam remained, as did the widespread influence of Iranian cultural influences across the region).

The Ottomans, in contrast, persisted as a significant political and military power into the mid-eighteenth century, with an empire that still included much of southeastern Europe (see Map 17.2). Unlike Safavid Iran, where the quality of the shah's character was a determining factor, Ottoman administrative reforms created stronger institutional leadership in both civilian and military affairs. As a sign of continuing vigor on the international scene, Ottoman armies laid siege to Vienna once again in 1683, threatening to expand even further into central Europe, and as late as 1739 Ottoman forces defeated the Austrians, who ceded Balkan territory to Constantinople. In general, however, the Ottomans' place in the great power balance was now defensive rather than expansionistic, with eighteenth-century military leaders defending the empire's borders against rising powers, especially Russia.

As the "gunpowder revolution" continued to make warfare more deadly, it also made defending an empire with expansive frontiers more expensive. While Ottoman agricultural and commercial production was still substantial, economic expansion was no longer keeping up with population growth or with the rapid pace being set by the dynamic commercial economies of western Europe. Thus, while the Ottoman empire's eighteenth-century fiscal decline was only relative, it made it difficult to keep up with Russia and the rising Western powers. In spite of such longer-term problems, however, the Ottomans persisted, and in the eighteenth century their realm remained one of the world's great land-based empires.

Political Consolidation and the Changing Balance of Power in Europe, 1650–1750

In the later seventeenth century stability returned to Europe. With the Habsburgs' failure to create a united Catholic empire, permanent political and religious divisions in western Europe became accepted. Like the rulers of France and England, those in Prussia, Austria, and Russia each consolidated their power internally while competing for national advantage.

Austria, Prussia, and Russia all followed the French example of royal absolutism. The Habsburgs still controlled an expansive empire from their capital at Vienna, and they were secure in their core territories after the second Ottoman siege of Vienna was lifted. The Austrian Habsburgs ruled over an ethnically and religiously diverse population. Facing the same challenge as the Ottomans—how to assert a single royal authority over a diverse population—the Habsburgs generally pursued a similar policy: as long as the authority of the king was acknowledged and taxes were paid, local autonomy would be accepted. Thus after a Hungarian rebellion was suppressed, the privileges of the Hungarian nobility and many traditional Hungarian legal customs were retained. The diversity of the empire's peoples and the resources they contributed to trade and manufacturing provided a solid foundation, and in the mid-eighteenth century Habsburg Austria was a formidable power.

In Protestant-dominated northern Germany, Prussia was the rising power in the aftermath of the Thirty Years' War. Although the German-speaking lands were still divided into numerous territories, Prussia, from its capital at Berlin, emerged as the strongest German state. Under King Frederick William I (r. 1713–1740), Prussia became a pioneer in military technology and organization, using the latest cannon and muskets and developing a professional standing army of well-trained and disciplined troops. Many features of modern military life, such as precision marching, were pioneered under Frederick William. The Prussian middle class had little political influence. Instead, the traditional rural aristocracy, accepting and

European and Asian Influences in Russian Architecture

Architecture reflects the diverse cultural influences on a people who straddle the geography of Europe and Asia. Russia's cultural exceptionality within the history of European Christianity traces back to the tenth century, when Prince Vladimir chose to affiliate the Principality of Kiev with the Greek-speaking Byzantine Church, headquartered in Constantinople, rather than with the Latin-speaking Catholic Church centered in Rome (or with the Muslims of the Volga River). Apart from strong Byzantine influence in religion, art, and architecture, early Russians also had long-term cultural exchanges with the nomadic peoples of the Eurasian steppe, a cultural factor that was greatly enhanced when Russia was absorbed into the Mongol empire in the fourteenth century. In the early modern period, as the Russian empire expanded south and east, interactions with Iranian and Turkish peoples also left their cultural mark.

Russia's cultural orientation shifted westward, however, under Peter the Great and his successors. As a young monarch, Peter traveled west to France, the Netherlands, and Russia, hoping, among other goals, to find allies for his wars with the Ottoman

St. Basil's Cathedral was built by Ivan the Terrible in the 1550s to commemorate his conquest of the khanate of Kazan centered on the Volga River, whose rulers were Muslim descendants of Mongolian conquerors. The church's bright colors were added later, in the seventeenth and eighteenth centuries.

Some scholars theorize that the "onion dome" architecture was inspired by the central mosque at Kazan (destroyed by Ivan's army), combined with Greek Byzantine influences and Renaissance styles from Italy.

The official name of the church is the "Cathedral of the Protection of Most Holy Theotokos on the Moat." Theotokos is the Greek name for Mary, the mother of Jesus.

The close proximity of St. Basil's to Red Square in Moscow, near the Kremlin, the heart of Russia's political establishment, shows the traditionally close connection between tsarist rule and Russia's Orthodox Christian Church.

© Steve Vidler/Superstock

In 1929, under the officially atheistic communist government of the Soviet Union, the church was secularized and turned into a museum. Currently, one church service a year is held at St. Basil's, which has been a UNESCO World Heritage Site since 1990.

empire. In the process he became aware of the great advances taking place in Western shipbuilding and resolved to create a Baltic fleet along modern lines. Similarly, he built the city of St. Petersburg in emulation of the latest architectural styles and employing Western construction techniques. From the eighteenth century onward, then, Russia's cultural legacy has included a broad range of European and Asian features in music, religious life, dance, and architecture.

The Winter Palace building was originally planned as the main residence of the Romanov family and as the focal point for the new city of St. Petersburg, begun in 1703 after Peter the Great returned from his tour of western Europe. It took hundreds of thousands of conscripted laborers more than two decades to complete the city.

Later Romanovs moved the capital back to Moscow, though they returned to the milder climate of St. Petersburg during the winter; hence the name "Winter Palace." Continual additions eventually led to a palace with over fifteen hundred rooms.

Peter Christopher/Masterfile

The palace complex was greatly expanded and thoroughly redecorated in the elaborate Baroque style during the reign of Empress Catherine the Great (r. 1762–1796; see Chapter 20) under a French architect.

Catherine began the art collection that today forms the core of the Hermitage Museum, one of the world's great art galleries. Today, the Hermitage Museum attracts over 3 million visitors each year.

The Winter Palace played a central role in later Russian history. In 1905, revolution erupted when the tsar's guard massacred protesters in its courtyard. In 1917, after the abdication of the last tsar, the building was temporarily the seat of the Russian government once again, until the communists moved the capital back to the Kremlin in Moscow.

QUESTION FOR ANALYSIS

» *What are the main differences in architectural form between St. Basil's Church and the Winter Palace?*

benefiting from the Prussian kings' innovations, were the bedrock of royal absolutism. Their cooperation in taxing and controlling the peasants gave Frederick William and his successors resources to expand the military and make Prussia a force to be reckoned with.

Russian culture and the Russian state had developed in interaction not with western Europe but with steppe nomads, Byzantine Christians, and Asian powers such as the Safavid empire. However, a major shift came with Tsar **Peter the Great** (r. 1685–1725). After visiting the Netherlands as a young man, Peter came back urgently aware of Russia's backwardness and undertook reforms designed to put Russia on par with the rising Western states. He built the new city of St. Petersburg on the Baltic Sea as Russia's "window on the West." Its elegant baroque buildings, emulating those of Rome and Vienna, stood in contrast to the churches and palaces of Moscow, which reflected Central Asian architecture. (See the feature "Visual Evidence in Primary Sources: European and Asian Influences in Russian Architecture.") Peter also tightened the dependence of the nobility on the Russian state. In a move that symbolized his desire to bring the country in line with Western models, he ordered Russian nobles to shave off their luxurious beards. From now on they would dress according to the latest European fashions.

Peter's ultimate goal, however, was power, and that meant focusing on the military. He established a regular standing army larger than any in Europe and bought the latest military technology from the West while working toward Russian self-sufficiency in the production of modern guns, cannon, and ships for his Baltic fleet. He also sponsored a new educational system to train more efficient civilian and military bureaucrats. But the middle class remained small, weak, and dependent on state patronage. The situation of the serfs was worse than ever. It was their heavy taxes that paid for the grandeur of St. Petersburg and the power of the Russian military, and it was their sons who fought Peter's wars.

Peter won victories against Poland, Sweden, and the Ottoman empire, pushing Russia's imperial frontiers from the Baltic Sea in the north to the Black Sea in the south. The Siberian and Central Asian frontiers of the Russian empire also continued to expand, in the latter case bringing more Muslims under Russian rule. Pragmatism dictated that there would be no systematic attempt to convert subject peoples to Orthodox Christianity.

From a global perspective, the political evolution and rising power of France and Britain were even more important than the achievements of Austria, Prussia, and Russia. Even during the sixteenth and seventeenth centuries, when both kingdoms faced severe internal turmoil over religion and political power, they were asserting themselves as colonial powers (see Chapter 18). In the eighteenth century, with their religious and political divisions largely resolved, and with Spain and Portugal now diminished as imperial rivals, France and Britain each became formidable global powers in the Americas and in Asia.

The struggle between France and Britain had economic and military components. In the seventeenth century both countries had adopted **mercantilism**, a policy that put national economic interests at the forefront of foreign policy. Through the use of monopolistic chartered companies, Louis XIV's government sought to control foreign trade by directing colonial resources for the sole benefit of the French nation while restricting the access of others to French colonial markets. The British also adopted mercantilist policies to protect their colonial

Peter the Great
(r. 1685–1725) Powerful Romanov tsar who built a new Russian capital at St. Petersburg, emulated Western advances in military technology, and extended the Russian empire further into Asia.

mercantilism
Dominant economic theory in seventeenth- and eighteenth-century Europe that emphasized the role of international economics in interstate competition. Under mercantilism, restrictive tariffs were placed on imports to raise their prices, maximize the country's exports, and build up supplies of gold and silver bullion for military investment.

holdings and to develop their markets in North America and South Asia. By 1750, Britain was by far the world's greatest sea power.

By that time the roster of great powers that would compete for European and global supremacy—France, Britain, Austria, Prussia, and Russia—was in place. After the fall of Safavid Iran in 1722, the remaining Islamic powers, Mughal India and the Ottoman empire, would not be able to keep pace (see Chapter 20).

CONTEXT AND CONNECTIONS

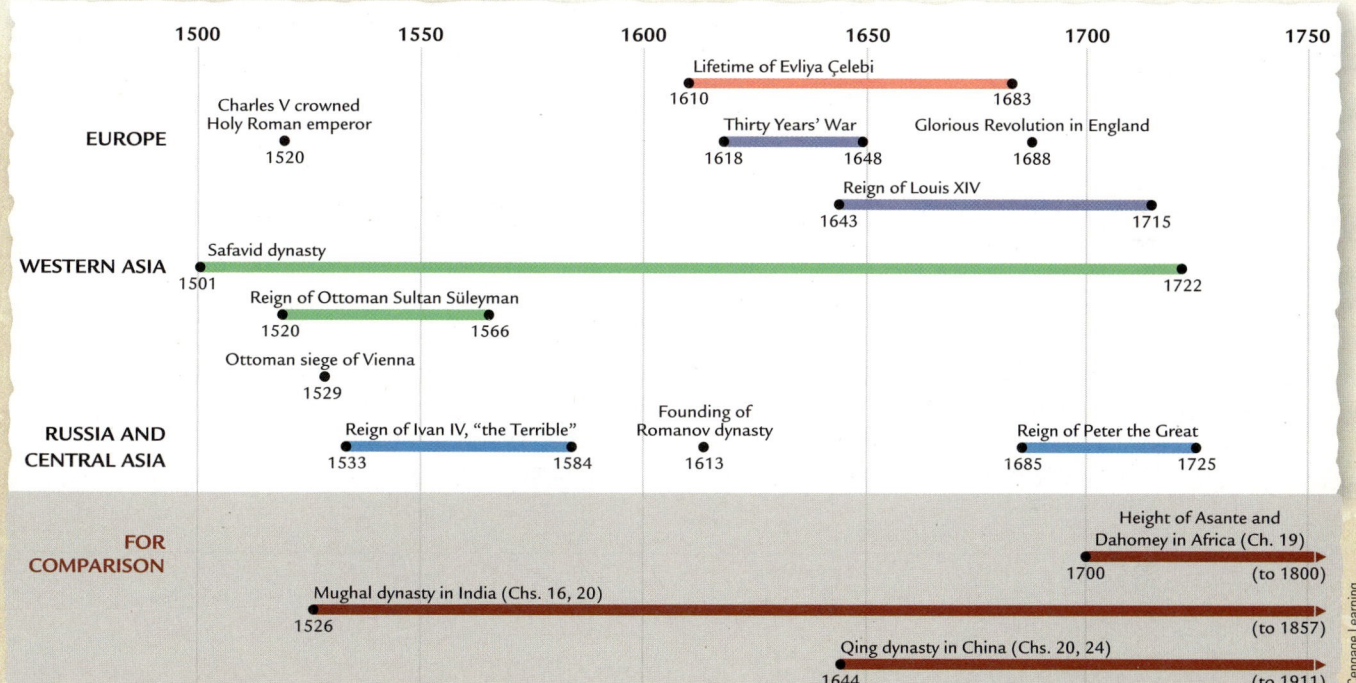

Early Modern Eurasia and the Rise of the West

Evliya Çelebi wrote in a confident, sometimes even arrogant, tone of superiority about the varied Christian and Muslim lands he visited. Indeed, from his mid-seventeenth-century perspective the Ottoman empire had significant advantages over its rivals. By the time of his death in 1683, however, the balance of power had begun to shift toward Europe. The age of land-based empires was far from over, as the persistence of the Ottomans and Austrian Habsburgs and the rapid growth of the Russian empire all made clear. But amid the commercial growth that followed from early modern maritime expansion, the biggest winners in the race for

supremacy in western Eurasia would be those who controlled strong navies and overseas colonies, especially France and Britain.

Another key to the rising power of Europe was the effective centralization of state power. In the early modern period, local interests were increasingly subsumed by national and dynastic ones, usually through the successes of ambitious monarchs like Louis XIV in France and Peter the Great in Russia (though in Britain's case this occurred after 1688 through a stable balance of authority between king and Parliament). In turn, increased consolidation of state power aided in the coordination and financing of increasingly expensive and sophisticated military organizations.

Part of the reason for increased authority of European monarchies was a rebalancing of the relationship between church and state in the aftermath of the Protestant Reformation. The end of the Habsburg attempt at pan-European Catholic supremacy meant that Catholic rulers were able to show less deference to church authorities than they had in the past. In Protestant-dominated states like Britain and Prussia, the close identification between church and state bolstered the authority of civil leadership even more dramatically, while in Russia the tsars were able to assert their authority over the Orthodox Church and use it to help promote their policies. The end of the religious wars of the seventeenth century was a precondition for the future global advance of the Christian nations of the West.

From a Muslim perspective, the seventeenth century can be viewed as the beginning of a long-term decline in economic, political, and even cultural prestige on the world stage. The rift between Sunnis and Shi'ites continued, as did the subservience of the Arab peoples to Ottoman rule. While Islam continued to spread across Africa, South Asia, and the Indian Ocean world, it no longer had an effective political champion after the eighteenth-century Ottoman empire declined in military power relative to rising European states and the British displaced the Mughal empire as the dominant force in India (see Chapter 20). The consequent loss of initiative to European Christians was an outcome that certainly would have surprised and saddened Evliya Çelebi.

As late as 1750 no one world region could be identified as central to a single global political system. True, the Western Hemisphere was divided and occupied by European powers, as we will see in the next chapter, and international maritime trade was increasingly under Western control. However, in 1750 the Chinese empire was still the most populous and productive in the world, while the Ottomans and Mughals remained forces to be reckoned with. As Chapter 20 will show, by 1850 all that had changed: China had been invaded by European powers, the Mughals had lost control of India to the British, and the Ottomans needed to be propped up by Western military forces to stave off Russian advances. Ultimately it was the Industrial Revolution of the nineteenth century (see Chapter 23) that put Europe firmly at the center of a single global system of political and economic power.

Voyages on the Web: Evliya Çelebi

The Voyages Map App follows the traveler's journeys using interactive study tools, including 360-degree panoramic views of historic sites, zoomable maps, audio summaries, flash cards, and quizzes.

KEY TERMS

Evliya Çelebi (462)
Janissaries (466)
Süleyman (466)
Safavid dynasty (468)
Ismail (468)
Abbas I (469)

Habsburg dynasty (473)
Philip II (474)
John Calvin (476)
Thirty Years' War (476)
Cardinal Richelieu (478)
Louis XIV (478)

Puritans (480)
Charles I (480)
Bill of Rights (481)
Peter the Great (488)
mercantilism (488)

FOR FURTHER REFERENCE

Beik, William. *Louis XIV and Absolutism: A Brief Study with Documents.* New York: Bedford/St. Martin's, 2000.

Bergin, Joseph. *The Seventeenth Century: Europe 1598–1715.* New York: Oxford University Press, 2001.

Braudel, Fernand. *The Mediterranean and the Mediterranean World in the Age of Philip II.* Sian Reynolds, trans. New York: Harper and Row, 1972.

Chardin, Jean de. *A Journey to Persia: Jean Chardin's Portrait of a Seventeenth Century Empire.* Ronald W. Ferrier, trans. and ed. London: I. B. Tauris, 1996.

Clot, Andre. *Suleiman the Magnificent.* London: Saqi Books, 2004.

Coward, Barry. *The Stuart Age: England, 1603–1714.* 3d ed. New York: Longman, 2003.

Dankoff, Robert, and Sooyong Kim. *An Ottoman Traveller: Selections from the* Book of Travels *of Evliya Çelebi.* London: Eland Publishing, 2010.

Fichtner, Paula Sutter. *Terror and Toleration: The Habsburg Empire Confronts Islam, 1526–1850.* New York: Reaktion Books, 2008.

Hughes, Lindsay. *Russia in the Age of Peter the Great.* New Haven: Yale University Press, 2000.

Savory, Roger. *Iran Under the Safavids.* New York: Cambridge University Press, 2007.

Tezcan, Baki. *The Second Ottoman Empire: Political and Social Transformation in the Early Modern World.* New York: Cambridge University Press, 2010.

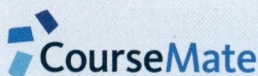 Go to the CourseMate website at **www.cengagebrain.com** for additional study tools and review materials—including audio and video clips—for this chapter.

18

Empires, Colonies, and Peoples of the Americas, 1600–1750

By the early 1600s, the Spanish had conquered the once-mighty Aztec and Inca and were secure in their American empire. But some areas had not been effectively occupied, and some Amerindian peoples held on to their independence. A battle-hardened young soldier, **Catalina de Erauso** (1585–1650), described an encounter with one such group in South America:

Catalina de Erauso

(From Francisco Pacheco, *El Alferez Dona Cataline de Erauso,* 1630. Jacket art courtesy of Beacon Press. Translation copyright © 1996 by Michele Stepto and Gabriel Stepto)

On the third day we came to an Indian village whose inhabitants immediately laid hold of their weapons, and as we drew nearer scattered at the sound of our guns, leaving behind some dead. . . . [A soldier] took off his helmet to mop his brow, and a devil of a boy about twelve years old fired an arrow at him from where he was perched in a tree beside the road. . . . The arrow lodged in the [soldier's] eye. . . . We carved the boy into a thousand pieces. Meanwhile, the Indians had returned to the village more than ten thousand strong. We fell at them again with such spirit, and butchered so many of them, that blood ran like a river across the plaza. . . . The men had found more than sixty thousand pesos' worth of gold dust in the huts of the village, and an infinity more of it along the banks of the river, and they filled their helmets with it. [*]

---

[*]Excerpt from Catalina de Erauso, *Lieutenant Nun: Memoir of a Basque Transvestite in the New World,* trans. Michele Stepto and Gabriel Stepto (Boston: Beacon Press, 1996), pp. 33–34.

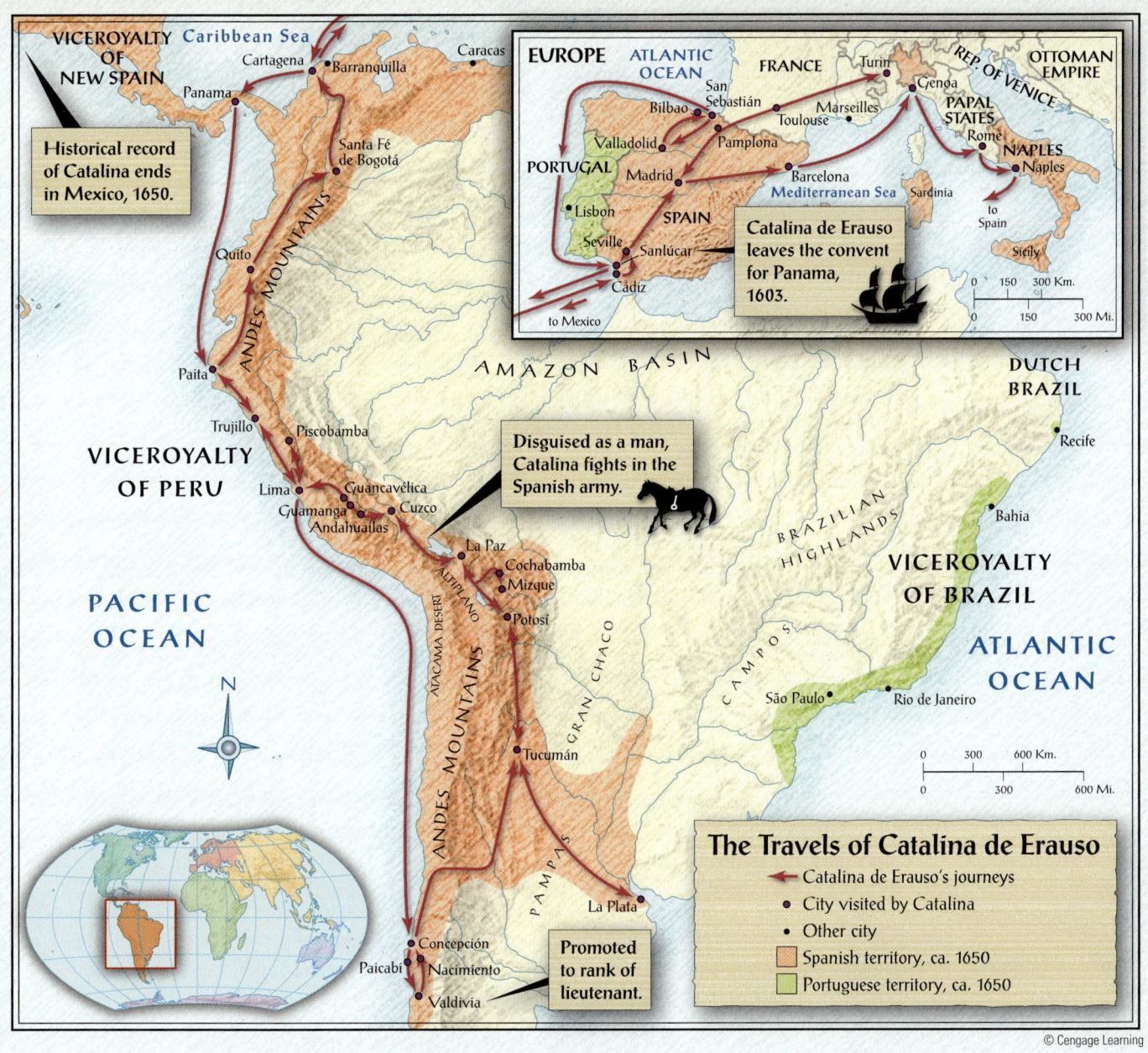

VICEROYALTY OF NEW SPAIN

Caribbean Sea

Cartagena
Barranquilla
Caracas
Panama

Historical record of Catalina ends in Mexico, 1650.

Santa Fé de Bogotá

Quito

ANDES MOUNTAINS

Paita

Trujillo
Piscobamba

VICEROYALTY OF PERU

Lima
Guancavélica
Cuzco
Guamanga
Andahuailas

La Paz
Cochabamba
Mizque
Potosí

Disguised as a man, Catalina fights in the Spanish army.

PACIFIC OCEAN

ALTIPLANO

ATACAMA DESERT

ANDES MOUNTAINS

GRAN CHACO

Tucumán

PAMPAS

La Plata

Concepción
Paicabí
Nacimiento
Valdivia

Promoted to rank of lieutenant.

N

AMAZON BASIN

BRAZILIAN HIGHLANDS

CAMPOS

DUTCH BRAZIL

Recife

Bahia

VICEROYALTY OF BRAZIL

ATLANTIC OCEAN

São Paulo
Rio de Janeiro

EUROPE ATLANTIC OCEAN FRANCE Turin REP. OF VENICE OTTOMAN EMPIRE

San Sebastián
Bilbao
Marseilles
Toulouse
Genoa
PAPAL STATES
Rome
NAPLES
Naples

Valladolid
Pamplona

PORTUGAL
Madrid
Barcelona
Mediterranean Sea
Sardinia

Lisbon
Seville
Sanlúcar
SPAIN

Catalina de Erauso leaves the convent for Panama, 1603.

Cádiz

to Mexico

to Spain

Sicily

0   150   300 Km.
0   150   300 Mi.

0   300   600 Km.
0   300   600 Mi.

The Travels of Catalina de Erauso
— Catalina de Erauso's journeys
• City visited by Catalina
• Other city
▢ Spanish territory, ca. 1650
▢ Portuguese territory, ca. 1650

© Cengage Learning

Join this chapter's traveler on "Voyages," an interactive tour of historic sites and events:
www.cengagebrain.com

Surprisingly, it was a woman who painted this matter-of-fact picture of slaughter. Catalina de Erauso (kat-ah-LEE-nah day eh-rah-OO-so), one of the most remarkable figures of the seventeenth century, was born in northeastern Spain and was placed in a convent by her family at the age of four. At the age of fifteen, when she was about to take the permanent vows that would confine her for a lifetime, she

Catalina de Erauso
(1585–1650) Female Basque/Spanish explorer who, dressed as a man, lived the life of a soldier and adventurer in the Spanish colonial Americas.

stole the keys and escaped: *"I shook off my veil and went out into a street I had never seen. . . . I holed up for three days, planning and re-planning and cutting myself out a suit of clothes. . . . I cut my hair and set off without knowing where I was going."**

Disguised as a boy, Erauso found employment as a personal assistant for a local nobleman, but she left when he *"finally went so far as to lay hands on me."* She stole some money, boarded a ship for Panama, and joined the Spanish army. For the next twenty years, Erauso traveled in the Spanish Americas, disguised as a man. A member of Spain's ethnically distinct Basque (bask) community, Erauso often teamed up with fellow Basques as she soldiered her way across Panama, Peru, Chile, Bolivia, and Argentina. According to her own story, her violent streak kept getting her into trouble. Card games often ended with insults and drawn swords, and more than once she had to run from the law after killing a man.

Erauso's exploits have become part of Latin American folklore, where she is known as *la monja alférez* (la mon-ha al-FAIR-ez), "the lieutenant nun." Her story is exceptional. But her deception was made easier by the frontier conditions. New arrivals from Europe and Africa increased decade by decade, interacting with indigenous inhabitants in a fluidly changing cultural landscape. It was literally a "new world"—new for European officials, settlers, and adventurers; new for African slaves who did much to build the new American societies; and new for America's indigenous peoples, who saw their ways of life undermined as they came under the control of Spain, Portugal, France, and England. The interaction of peoples from Europe, Africa, and the Americas was the foundation upon which colonial American societies would be built.

This chapter examines the political, economic, social, and cultural life of colonial America in the seventeenth and early eighteenth centuries, focusing especially on gender and race relations, the role of the Americas in the global economy, and the differences between the various European colonial ventures.

Focus Questions

» *What were the principal forms of political and economic organization in the Americas in this period, and how were they linked with global developments?*

» *What were the key demographic and cultural outcomes of the interaction of European, African, and Amerindian peoples in various regions of the Americas?*

» *What connections and comparisons can we draw between the different European colonial ventures in the Americas?*

The Americas in Global Context: The Spanish Empire, 1600–1700

In a remarkably short time the Spanish laid waste to the Aztec and Inca empires (see Chapter 15) and established a firm foothold in much of the region we now call Latin America. To rule their vast new territories, they immediately set up a

---

*Excerpt from Catalina de Erauso, *Lieutenant Nun: Memoir of a Basque Transvestite in the New World*, trans. Michele Stepto and Gabriel Stepto (Boston: Beacon Press, 1996), p. 4.

highly centralized government that relied on close cooperation between crown and church. It was a strictly hierarchical power structure, with officials from Spain and locally born Spaniards at the top, the increasing number of people of mixed descent in the middle, and Indians and African slaves at the bottom. As Erauso's story shows, however, the farther one went from centers of authority the more fluid relations of gender and race became, giving at least some people with modest backgrounds new possibilities in life.

From Conquest to Control

When Erauso arrived in Panama in 1603, the Spanish empire was the most powerful European colonial venture in the Americas and a rising maritime power in the world, having established a base of power at Manila in the Philippines. True, a Spanish armada had been repulsed by England in 1588, and the Dutch, still under Spanish rule, were laying the foundations for their own global enterprise. But Philip II of Spain could count on American resources, especially silver, as a foundation of his power (see Chapter 17). The Spanish continued to subjugate Amerindian peoples even while in some remote regions indigenous societies remained independent into the eighteenth century.

During the sixteenth century, the Spanish Habsburgs asserted increasing authority through a centralized bureaucracy headed by the Council of the Indies. In 1535, they sent the first viceroy to Mexico City, and in 1542 a second was dispatched to Lima. From that time forward, the emperor in Madrid sent officials to America as representatives of royal power. Eventually four **viceroyalties** were created: New Spain (with a capital at Mexico City), New Granada (Bogotá), Peru (Lima), and La Plata (Buenos Aires; see Map 18.1). Below the viceroys were presidencies, captaincy-generals, governors, and municipal authorities.

viceroyalties
Seats of power of the Spanish officials representing the king in the new world.

The other great institution of Spanish rule was the Catholic Church. The pope granted the Spanish crown the right to exercise power over the church in the Americas in all but purely spiritual affairs. Civil authorities appointed and dismissed bishops, while church leaders often served as top government officials. In the early colonial period, bishops sent directly from Spain occupied the higher church positions. In frontier areas, where missionaries brought Catholicism, they also brought Spanish rule.

At the same time that their missionary work extended the zone of Spanish control, many representatives of Catholic religious orders positioned themselves as protectors of indigenous peoples against more rapacious Spanish settlers. The most prominent of these was the Dominican friar **Bartolomé de las Casas**, who argued for humane treatment of Amerindians as he criticized *"the outrageous acts of violence and the bloody tyranny"* of Spaniards who had *"lost all fear of God, all love of their sovereign, and all sense of self-respect."* While missionaries played an integral role in the extension of colonial authority, therefore, they also criticized the appalling conditions that followed.

Bartolomé de las Casas
(ca. 1484–1566) A Spanish Dominican friar who argued for the humanity of Amerindians and criticized Spanish mistreatment of them.

As more Iberians crossed the ocean, American-born Spaniards grew in number. Known as *criollos* (kree-OY-os) ("creoles" in English), by the seventeenth century they were participating in government. Although the top positions continued to be held by officials from Spain, criollos became a social and economic elite, often by seizing Amerindian land and exploiting Amerindian labor.

Although lust for gold had been a principal motive of the early conquistadors, it was silver that filled the Spanish treasury and transformed the world

*Bartolomé de las Casas, *A Short Account of the Destruction of the Indies,* trans. Nigel Griffin (London: Penguin, 2004), p. 42.

NEW FRANCE
(Conquered by England, 1760)

ENGLISH COLONIES
(Independence declared, 1776)

ATLANTIC OCEAN

40°W

40°N

Mississippi R.

Colorado R.

Effective frontier of Spanish settlement

Silver
Silver
COAHUILA

Rio Grande

FLORIDA
(Ceded to England, 1763–1783)

Gulf of Mexico

VICEROYALTY OF NEW SPAIN
BAJIO LEÓN (1535)

Guadalajara ✕ Zacatecas
✕ Guanajuato

Havana

Sugar cane
Beef
Tobacco

HAITI [SAINT-DOMINGUE]
(Ceded to France, 1697)

20°N

Mexico City Veracruz

Silver

Sugar cane
Indigo

Beef

Sugar cane

PUERTO RICO

Cacao

Sugar cane
Cochineal

BRITISH HONDURAS

Sugar cane

JAMAICA
(Conquered by England, 1655)

SANTO DOMINGO

Guatemala Silver

Caribbean Sea

Sugar cane

Cochineal
Cacao
Indigo

Sugar cane

Pearls

Caracas

Cacao

Gold

Orinoco R.

Magdalena R.

Bogotá

GUIANA

N

PACIFIC OCEAN

VICEROYALTY OF NEW GRANADA
(Separated from Viceroyalty of Peru, 1717, 1739)

Quito

Equator 0°

Amazon R.

Forest products

VICEROYALTY OF PERU
(1590s)

Sugar cane

Lima Cuzco

VICEROYALTY OF BRAZIL
(1720)

Sugar cane Pernambuco

Sugar cane Salvador

Cacao

Sugar cane

La Paz

Chuquisaca
(La Plata; Sucre)

Potosí

Diamonds
Gold

Rio de Janeiro
(Capital, 1763)

A N D E S

Paraná R.

São Paulo

20°S

Yerba
Tobacco

VICEROYALTY OF LA PLATA
(Separated from Viceroyalty of Peru, 1776)

Wheat

Beef and hides

AUDIENCIA OF CHILE
(Retained by Viceroyalty of Peru, 1776)

Santiago

Buenos Aires Montevideo

Beef and hides

Claimed but not settled by Spain

| 0 | 500 | 1,000 Km. |
| 0 | 500 | 1,000 Mi. |

Territories claimed by Spain
Viceroyalty of New Spain
Viceroyalty of New Granada
Viceroyalty of Peru and Audiencia of Chile
Viceroyalty of Rio de la Plata

Territories claimed by Portugal
Viceroyalty of Brazil

✕ Silver mine

Islas Malvinas
(Falkland Islands)

Cape Horn
80°W 60°W

MAP 18.1 **The Spanish Empire in the Americas** This map of the early-eighteenth-century Americas shows the territorial dominance of the Spanish empire and its four viceroyalties. Though Portuguese Brazil was also large and rich, English and French colonial possessions were small and poor in resources by comparison. We should remember that this map shows European *claims* to territory. Some Amerindian societies remained autonomous and unconquered, especially in more remote regions of mountains, forests, and deserts. (© Cengage Learning)

economy. In 1545, shortly after silver deposits were found in Mexico, the greatest discovery in world history was made high in the Andes at **Potosí** (poh-toh-SEE), where the Spanish found a whole mountain of silver. Andean silver enabled European trade with Asia, and much of the silver extracted from Potosí ended up in China. The exploitation of American silver and Amerindian labor, therefore, stimulated the development of a more integrated early modern world economy (see Chapter 16).

Silver mining and the trade it made possible generated huge profits, but not for the workers who dug open the mountain. Mining has always been difficult and

Potosí
Location high in the Andes in modern Bolivia where the Spanish found huge quantities of silver. Silver exports from Potosí and other American mines helped finance development of the early modern world economy.

The Silver Mine at Potosí The silver mines of Spanish America, of which Potosí was the greatest, enriched the Spanish treasury and facilitated the expansion of global trade. As this engraving from 1590 shows, however, it was the heavy toil of Amerindian workers on Potosí's mountain of silver that made it all possible. Spanish mine operators used the mercury amalgamation process to increase the yield of silver from ore, resulting in the frequently lethal mercury poisoning of workers such as those seen here. (The Granger Collection New York)

dangerous work. With the technology available in the sixteenth century, conditions were so brutal that force was needed to get workers for the mines. Though the crown had placed restrictions on *encomienda* (in-coh-mee-EN-dah) holders (see Chapter 15), a new legal system called the *repartimiento* (reh-par-TEE-me-en-toh) gave Spaniards the right to coerce Amerindian labor for specific tasks. Although the intent of reforming the encomienda system had been to limit abuses, most Spaniards still casually assumed they retained a right to enslave Amerindians. Erauso, for example, commented that during one of her trading ventures a civic leader *"gave me ten thousand head of llama to drive and a hundred-some-odd Indians."* Apparently, these Amerindians had no say in the matter.

Although the Spanish called their Andean labor system *mita* (mee-tah)—the same name used by the Inca for their system of labor tribute—the Spanish mita differed greatly from the Inca one. Under the Inca, mita required every household to contribute labor for tasks such as military service, road construction, and the maintenance of irrigation works. Exemptions were granted for families in difficult circumstances, and workers were fed, clothed, and well treated. By contrast, the voracious Spanish appetite for silver meant that little attention was paid to the well-being of local communities or individual laborers. Under the Spanish mita system, every adult male had to spend one full year out of every seven working in the mines at wages that were not sufficient for his own support, let alone for his family. After 1554, when the discovery of the **mercury amalgamation process** increased the efficiency of silver extraction from ore, profits soared while working conditions worsened. Mercury poisoning led to sickness and death for many Amerindian miners. In addition, women, children, and the elderly back in their villages had to work harder to compensate for the absence of adult males from their communities, leading to further hardships. The silver economy predicated the wealth of some on the suffering of many: that was to be a recurring theme in Latin American history. (See the feature "World History in Today's World: Restoring the Great Inca Road.")

By 1600 Potosí, with a population over one hundred thousand, was a major market for foodstuffs and other supplies. When Erauso set off with her llamas and one hundred Indians, she intended to exploit this market: *"[The official] also gave me a great deal of money to buy wheat in the Cochabamba plains. My job was to grind it and get it to Potosí, where the scarcity of wheat made for high prices. I went and bought eight thousand bushels . . . hauled them by llama to the mills . . . and took them to Potosí. I then sold them all . . . and brought the cash back to my master."* The llamas she used as transport were indigenous, but the wheat grew from seeds brought from Europe, an example of the ongoing Columbian exchange (see Chapter 15).

Expanding markets accompanied the growth of administrative centers such as Mexico City, Lima, and Buenos Aires, which stimulated local and regional trade in foodstuffs. In colonial Latin America market-based agriculture took place on large estates known as **haciendas** (ha-cee-EN-das). While many Amerindian communities remained largely self-sufficient by farming small village plots, the Spanish hacienda owners focused on meeting the rising demand for agricultural produce. In addition to growing crops for sale, many grazed vast herds of cattle.

The hacienda owners were closely integrated into the larger networks of church, state, and market. But within the boundaries of their own large estates,

mercury amalgamation process
A process used to increase the efficiency with which silver could be extracted from ore. The use of mercury was highly toxic and led to the death of many Amerindian mine workers.

haciendas
Large estates characteristic of colonial agriculture in Latin America.

---

*Excerpt from Catalina de Erauso, *Lieutenant Nun: Memoir of a Basque Transvestite in the New World*, trans. Michele Stepto and Gabriel Stepto (Boston: Beacon Press, 1996), pp. 6, 16.

Restoring the Great Inca Road

A wonder of premodern engineering, the *Capaq Ñan* (in the Quechua language) or Great Inca Road once covered 4,500 miles (7,000 km; see Chapter 15 and Map 15.2), with some stretches over 40 feet (12 m) wide, ascending to altitudes of over 13,000 feet (4,000 m) above sea level. Now, with the assistance of the World Conservation Union, the Great Inca Road is being restored with the goals of boosting income from ecotourism, providing an impetus for sustainable development in one of the poorest regions of the Americas, and giving the indigenous people of the Andes opportunities to reconnect with their traditions of conservation and their ancient holy sites. Support for the restoration project has come from the governments of Argentina, Bolivia, Chile, Ecuador, and Peru.

The project has been championed by Ricardo Espinosa, who in 1999 hiked nearly 2,000 miles (3,000 km) from Quito, Peru, to La Paz, Bolivia, and then published a photographic journal of his travels, *All Inca Roads*. "The Incas did not have draught animals, so wheeled carriages were not possible or necessary," says Espinosa. "Their roads were designed for a world of people on foot. To once again walk those routes brings us closer to their creators. It permits us to see what they saw."[*]

Though the road has been obliterated where it passes through cities and towns, for most of its length it is remarkably well preserved, a tribute to the talents of the Inca who designed and built it over five centuries ago. Far and away the most traveled section of the Great Inca Road today is the stretch approaching the magnificent site of Machu Picchu, which many intrepid tourists prefer to reach by foot rather than by train. It is hoped that by opening other sections of the route to trekkers, congestion along the Machu Picchu route can be relieved.

Espinosa emphasizes that the success of the Great Inca Road project depends on the level of participation of indigenous communities, to ensure that they will benefit from it. "The communities united by each section," he says, "would work in partnership to manage tourism activities and preservation of the route." Given the long history of exploitation of indigenous peoples in the Andean region and their long-held suspicion of outside intervention, development and conservation that include and benefit Quechua-speaking communities would indeed be a great step forward.

---

[*]Abraham Lama, "Resurrection of the Great Inca Route," *Tierraamérica: Environment and Development*, January 7, 2012; http://www.tierramerica.info/nota.php?lang=eng&idnews=2124.

---

hacienda owners had almost total control, governing their lands and the people who lived on them without reference to outside authority. Spanish landowners used debt peonage as a means of control, making loans to "their" Indians that were to be repaid in labor. But wages were never enough to repay the debt. In fact, descendants of the original borrowers often inherited these obligations and became legally and permanently bound to a single estate, unable to seek higher wages or better working conditions elsewhere. Debt peonage, like much of the hacienda system, would long persist in Latin America.

African labor supplemented that of Amerindians in some parts of Spain's American empire, most notably in Peru and Mexico. In the early conquest period, African slaves played a variety of roles, including fighting alongside the Spanish conquerors of the Andes and engaging in skilled crafts they brought with them from Africa, such as goldsmithing. As the mixed Spanish/Amerindian population grew, however, Afro-Peruvians began to lose their status as intermediaries between the Spanish and Amerindians, and by the eighteenth century they had become a despised subclass of manual laborers. Still, Afro-Peruvians made important cultural contributions to colonial society. For example, in coastal Peru, as in the Mexican coastal state of Guerrero where Africans also lived in large numbers, African musical instruments and rhythms are still found today.

Spain's main goal was to extract minerals and other raw materials from America. Although it imported from the Americas such goods as dyes, cotton, and livestock hides for the manufacture of leather, no product came close in value to the tons of silver bullion sent in the annual armadas both directly to Spain and via the Manila galleons from Mexico to the Spanish Philippines (see Chapter 16). Taking much from its American empire but investing little, Spain failed to lay the foundations for long-term economic growth. While other European nations were developing innovative commercial organizations (see Chapter 17), the Spanish crown and nobility were overly reliant on mineral wealth. As a consequence, the Dutch, English, and French effectively challenged stagnant Spain for American preeminence during the seventeenth and eighteenth centuries.

And while the Spanish had set the early pace for the incorporation of the Americas into the global economy, they did not advance the process nearly as far as the rising northern European commercial powers. The extraction of gold and silver had immense consequences for international trade, of course, stimulating economies from Europe to South and East Asia (see Chapter 17). But the Spanish crown and Spanish nobility remained largely aloof from commercial life, unlike in the Netherlands, where merchant capitalists dominated, or in England, where traders and trading companies were to be patronized by the crown (and, especially in England, by the landed gentry).

Colonial Society: Gender and Race on the Margins of Empire

Within the Western Hemisphere, the basic patterns of life in Spanish-speaking America had been established by 1750. The process of subjugating and incorporating indigenous societies into the Spanish empire was well advanced. Large-scale haciendas and mining operations were the foundation of commercial economies based on exploitation of the labor of Amerindians and African slaves. Officials from Spain dominated the upper ranks of both church and state, while criollos became local officials, hacienda landowners, and merchants.

The small Spanish elite occupied the top of the social hierarchy, and the Amerindians who continued to speak indigenous languages and practice ancient cultural traditions remained at the bottom. Between the two groups a complex mix of peoples and cultures emerged. Ingredients of this mix included European immigration, the forced migration of African slaves, and the continuing decline of indigenous American populations owing to disease and deprivation.

The Spanish elite imported their cultural models into the new context of the Americas and were especially concerned with enforcing strict hierarchies of caste, gender, and religious and ethnic identity. Men were guided by a code of family honor, responsible for the virginity of their daughters and the fidelity of their wives. At the same time, they did not hold themselves to the same standards, often boasting of their multiple sexual conquests.

The fixation of the Spanish elite with "purity of blood" went back to the Reconquista (see Chapter 15), when reserving public office for men of pure Spanish descent was instituted to keep converted Jews and Muslims out of positions of power. This policy was transferred to the Americas: the king's subjects of non-Spanish and non-Catholic origin were expected to defer to their social superiors.

It was easy for the Spanish officials to maintain such elitist hierarchies in the courts, schools, and urban spaces of Mexico City, Lima, and other bastions of Spanish authority. Outside the cities, however, the social environment was much more fluid. Spanish men rarely brought their wives and families to the Americas, and liaisons between Spanish men and indigenous women made "purity of blood" impossible to maintain. By the seventeenth century, a distinct **mestizo** (mes-TEE-zoh), or mixed Spanish/Amerindian, category had emerged that led to the biological and cultural blending that came to characterize Mexican society.

Also difficult to maintain under frontier conditions was the power of the Catholic bishops to impose religious orthodoxy. In Spain itself, the inquisition (the Catholic bureaucracy devoted to suppressing heresy) strictly monitored the beliefs and behavior of the population. Families of *conversos* and *moriscos* (mohr-EES-koz), who had been forcibly converted from Judaism and Islam, were subjected to special scrutiny. On the colonial frontier, however, such groups were sometimes able to retain elements of their old faith. Even today some Mexican families incorporate Jewish elements in their family traditions.

Converted Amerindians were the largest group of Catholics deviating from the church's theology and rituals, especially in Mexico and Peru, where missionaries had baptized many descendants of the Aztec and Inca. Many Amerindians embraced Catholicism as a way to adapt to their new world, perhaps feeling that their old gods had abandoned them. At the same time, these converts adapted Christianity to maintain their own spiritual, ritual, and aesthetic traditions. Unlike in China, where Matteo Ricci had adapted Christianity to the traditions of his intended converts (see Chapter 16), in Spanish America it was not the missionaries but the colonized peoples themselves who blended their cosmologies into Catholicism. While some church leaders campaigned against the continuation of "idol worship" among baptized Amerindians, more often Spanish missionaries tolerated such practices. Amerindian populations gradually stabilized after the great losses of the sixteenth century, and where they formed a majority, as in the Andes, missionaries had little choice but to work through indigenous cultures.

This process of **syncretism**, the blending of existing and imported religious ideas, is an important theme in world history that is also seen, for example, when Islam spread to Africa and Buddhism to China. A thousand years before the conquest of the Americas, European converts to Christianity had themselves adapted some of their pagan ideas to the new faith. For both ancient Europeans and colonized Amerindians, former gods reappeared as Christian saints. And while the Christian God might be male, worship of Mary as the Virgin Mother allowed Catholic Aztecs to retain the female presence in their religious worship previously represented by the fertility goddess Tonantzin.

The centrality of the female principle in Mexican worship crystallized in the cult of the **Virgin of Guadalupe**. In 1531 a peasant named Juan Diego reported to a Spanish bishop that the Virgin Mary had appeared to him. The bishop was initially doubtful, but the cult of the Virgin of Guadalupe proved remarkably popular. Though apparitions of the Virgin Mary were relatively common in Spain, the Virgin of Guadalupe had a special appeal in Mesoamerica, helping to fill the gap left as worship of goddesses like Tonantzin declined. Represented as dark in complexion, like most of her devotees, she remains a symbol of Mexican identity and an embodiment of religious syncretism.

---

mestizo
Offspring of an Amerindian and Spanish union. Cultural and biologic blending became characteristic of Mexican society, marked by a complex racial hierarchy, the casta system, in which people were carefully categorized into dozens of categories of racial descent.

syncretism
The fusion of cultural elements from more than one tradition. In colonial Latin America religious syncretism was common, with both Amerindians and Africans blending their existing beliefs and rituals with Catholicism.

Virgin of Guadalupe
An apparition of the Virgin Mary, with a dark complexion, said to have appeared to a Mexican farmer in 1531. The cult of the Virgin of Guadalupe exerted a powerful attraction to Mesoamerica's surviving Amerindians. She remains a symbol of Mexican identity.

In Catalina de Erauso's story the Catholic Church plays a more practical role. Once after she had stabbed a man in a fight she sought refuge in a church, where the civil authorities could not pursue her without the bishop's permission. In tough spots such as these she also relied on fellow members of the Basque-speaking minority for protection. Facing discrimination in Iberia, many Basques joined the Spanish army in the Americas. Erauso was exceptionally proud of her Basque heritage, but when dealing with Italians or Portuguese she was always quick to identify herself with Spain and assert Spanish superiority. Her multiple identities are another example of the fluidity of frontier life.

Erauso's autobiography also gives us fascinating insights into race and gender in frontier Spanish America. Once in Peru, she deserted the army and wandered alone into the mountains, where she nearly died but was rescued by two men who took her to their mistress's ranch:

> *The lady was a half-breed, the daughter of a Spaniard and an Indian woman, a widow and a good woman. . . . The next morning she fed me well, and seeing that I was so entirely destitute she gave me a decent cloth suit. . . . The lady was well-off, with a good deal of livestock and cattle, and it seems that, since Spaniards were scarce in those parts, she began to fancy me as a husband for her daughter . . . a girl as black and ugly as the devil himself, quite the opposite of my taste, which has always run to pretty faces.*[*]

Never intending to marry the girl but merely to receive the widow's gifts, Erauso went along with this plan. She then writes, *"In the two months I was putting off the Indian woman, I struck up a friendship with the Bishop's secretary,"* who introduced Erauso to his niece with the indication that they might get married. Again, Erauso accepted gifts from this potential in-law, but then *"saddled up and vanished."*

We cannot know how much of this story is embellished. But apart from the twist of wooing other women in the guise of a man, it suggests how Iberian men (as Erauso presented herself to be) were highly desirable marriage partners for families wishing to sustain or improve their social status. Marriage to a Spaniard could "improve" the family bloodline. Spanish men were in such short supply that Erauso could, by her own account at least, contract multiple engagements with ease. Of course, Spanish women were even less available as marriage partners. Most Spanish men could not afford to "import" wives from Iberia, so they made the best unions they could, usually fathering mixed-race children.

Erauso's narrative also shows the complex racial mixture in the Spanish empire. She describes the widow as a "half-breed" who is "good" and "well-off." The daughter, on the other hand, is described as "black" and "ugly," though that was not enough to stop Erauso from wooing the young woman. Here we see the two fundamental racial realities of the Spanish Americas. On the one hand, racial mixing was accepted as a part of life. On the other hand, whiteness was always linked with higher status, wealth, and beauty. So even in the many places where mestizos or mulattos (of mixed Spanish/African descent) formed the majority, the ideal was Spanish "pure blood." Perhaps the widow thought marriage to a white soldier like Erauso could improve the color and status of her "ugly" daughter's children. (See the feature "Visual Evidence in Primary Sources: Representing the Casta System.")

Gender relations and the social roles of women varied by social class. As in many societies, including the North African ones that had strongly influenced

---

[*]Excerpt from Catalina de Erauso, *Lieutenant Nun: Memoir of a Basque Transvestite in the New World,* trans. Michele Stepto and Gabriel Stepto (Boston: Beacon Press, 1996), pp. 28–29.

medieval Iberia, Spanish men demonstrated their wealth and status by keeping women away from the public realm. Elite parents, preoccupied with protecting the family honor, arranged unions for adolescent daughters who would, upon marriage, lead restricted lives. Those for whom no acceptable marriage could be found were sent to convents. Poorer families in which women played vital economic roles as farmers and artisans could not imitate such behavior; their darker skin and ruddy complexions resulting from outdoor work marked their lowly status.

At the same time, elite women sometimes had access to education, and those in convents might rise to power and authority within the confines of their all-female communities. **Sor Juana Inés de la Cruz** (1648–1695) was the most famous of such women. Born into a modest family, she was a child prodigy who learned to read Latin before the age of ten. She became a lady-in-waiting for the viceroy's wife in Mexico City and a popular figure at court. But after her application to the University of Mexico was denied, she entered the convent. In contrast to Catalina de Erauso, who saw convent life as a prison, Sor Juana recognized that only by restricting herself to an all-female community would she be able to develop her remarkable literary and intellectual skills.

Sor Juana's writings cover many topics, and her poetry is still taught to Mexican schoolchildren. She is best known for her passionate defense of the spiritual and intellectual equality of women with men: *"There is no obstacle to love / in gender or in absence, / for souls, as you are well aware, / transcend both sex and distance."** After years of correspondence and debate with church leaders who denounced her work, she saw the futility of trying to change their minds and stopped publishing altogether. In 1694, church officials forced her to sell her library of four thousand books, and the next year the plague took her life, silencing one of the finest minds in the Spanish-speaking world.

Sor Juana's story illustrates the degree to which New Spain duplicated the Spanish social order. But Erauso's narrative reminds us that the "new world" could also mean new possibilities. Would she have been able to carry on her deception for so long had she remained in Spain? In frontier conditions the watchfulness of church and state was not as strong as it was in Europe or in Mexico City, giving Erauso a chance to carve out a life appropriate for her personality and ambition.

> **Sor Juana Inés de la Cruz**
> One of the great literary figures of colonial New Spain. Wrote poetry, prose, and philosophy despite having been denied a university education. Best known for her defense of the intellectual equality of men and women.

Brazil, the Dutch, New France, and England's Mainland Colonies

Throughout the sixteenth century and into the seventeenth century, Spain remained the dominant imperial force in the Americas. But it was not the only European kingdom using American resources to advance its place in the world. Portugal, though it placed a greater emphasis on its Asian empire, controlled Brazil, with its vast economic potential. Likewise the Dutch focused on Asia during the height of their world power in the seventeenth century, but they also harassed the Spanish and Portuguese in the Western Hemisphere. The French and English were latecomers to the American colonial game, starting their settlements in North America only after the Spanish had created their great empire to the south. Here as well, diverse demographic and cultural patterns arose from the interactions of Europeans, Africans, and indigenous peoples, and the farther one moved from European-dominated centers toward the frontier, the more fluid those interactions were.

---

*Quoted in Octavio Paz, *Sor Juana*, trans. Margaret Sayers Peden (Cambridge: Harvard University Press, 1988), p. 219.

Representing the Casta System

In New Spain, a complex racial hierarchy, known as the *casta* system, involved the use of dozens of terms to describe various racial mixtures and skin tones. Brothers and sisters of mixed ancestry might themselves vary in skin tones, facial structure, hair quality, eye color, and other markers of descent. Still, the way an individual was classified and observed would affect his or her chances in life: marriage and inheritance, education, access to the royal bureaucracy, or leadership roles in the church. Judgments of character, honor, and morality were linked to one's rank on the ladder of the castas. This meant that individuals of mixed background would usually do their best to emphasize their Spanish heritage in appearance, culture, and language.

In eighteenth-century Mexico, casta paintings were a well-developed tradition. These paintings represented racial and ethnic mixture by portraying a father and mother of different backgrounds and at least one of their children. These two works by Miguel Cabrera are part of a larger series of casta portraits of remarkable sensitivity and beauty.

De Español y Mestiza, Castiza.

It seems as if this Spaniard's mixed-race wife and child share in his prestige and prosperity. He has respectfully removed his hat, and looks at them with obvious affection.

The fine silk for their clothing was likely imported from China: the trans-Pacific trade in Mexican silver for such Chinese luxury goods was common in the colonial era.

Museo de America, Madrid, Spain/The Bridgeman Art Library

In the first example, Cabrera shows a Spanish man, a mestiza woman, and their daughter, labeled castiza. The second illustrates a mestizo husband, his Indian wife, and their sons, labeled coyotes. Cabrera's other portraits are labeled as follows:

- From a Black and an Indian, *China Cambuja*
- From a *China Cambujo* and a Indian, *Loba*
- From a *Lobo* and an Indian, *Albarazado*
- From an *Albrazado* and a *Mestiza*, *Barcino*

- From a Spaniard and a Negro, *Mulata*
- From a Spaniard and a *Mulata*, *Morisca*

This complex list is only a small sample of the names and combinations of racial and ethnic mixtures found in Mexican casta paintings. In many of these works, African and Amerindian backgrounds are associated with poverty and degradation. In this more humanistic example from Cabrera, however, the "coyotes" are rendered in a strongly sympathetic manner.

De Meſtizo y d India, Coyote

© Elisabeth Waldo-Dentzel

Note how the figures touch and/or look at each other. What impression do we get of the relationship between husbands and wives and between parents and children?

The child's cap stands out against the group's otherwise drab apparel. How might we determine its significance?

The couple seems poor, but the burro indicates that the man has work and the vegetables indicate that they have enough to eat.

QUESTION FOR ANALYSIS

» *What do these paintings tell us about the relationship among social status, clothing, and physical appearance in eighteenth-century New Spain?*

505

The Portuguese and Brazil

In the sixteenth century, Portugal's overseas efforts focused on the Indian Ocean (see Chapter 16). Brazil, discovered by accident and acquired by treaty, was an afterthought, with no large cities to conquer and no empires to plunder. Portuguese settlement was initially limited to the coast, and apart from a lucrative trade in precious types of wood, Brazil initially offered little promise.

This situation changed dramatically in the later sixteenth century with the expansion of sugar plantations in northeastern Brazil. By the end of the seventeenth century, 150,000 African slaves made up about half of the colony's population. Meanwhile, Portuguese adventurers pushed into the interior seeking slaves, gold, and exotic goods such as brightly colored feathers from the Amazon. In 1695, gold was discovered in the southern interior in a region that thereby gained the name *Minas Gerais*, "General Mines." European prospectors brought African slaves to exploit the gold deposits, displacing the local Amerindians in the process. By the early eighteenth century, profits from sugar and gold had turned Brazil into Portugal's most important overseas colony, and for hundreds of years, until today, the settlement of the interior of Brazil by a predominantly Euro-African population has continued.

Missionaries were powerful players in Brazil. Jesuits operated large cattle ranches and sugar mills to raise funds for church construction and missions to the interior. As in the Spanish Americas, while many missionaries tried to stop the worst abuses of colonization and often sought to protect Indian interests, they unwittingly introduced epidemic diseases that devastated Amerindian populations; inevitably, they undercut indigenous life by extending imperial borders into the interior.

As soon as the sugar plantation economy was established in the northeast, slaves began to run away into the interior. Some of the runaways, called maroons, assimilated into Amerindian groups (see Chapter 19). Others formed their own runaway communities known as *quilombos* (key-LOM-boz). Since the members of quilombos were born and raised in different African societies, their political and religious practices combined various African traditions and gods. The largest and most powerful of the quilombos was **Palmares** (pal-MAHR-es), founded in the early seventeenth century. The people at Palmares adapted the Central African institution of *kilombo*, a merit-based league of warriors that cut across family ties, ruled by their elected *Ganga Zumba* (Great Lord). Their religious life was syncretic, combining traditions of the Kongo kingdom (see Chapter 16) with other African traditions and Catholicism. With a population in the tens of thousands, Palmares defended itself against decades of Portuguese military assaults until it was finally defeated in 1694. However, the adaptation of African religion and culture to the American environment continued in Brazil and other parts of the Americas long after the fall of Palmares.

By 1750, Brazil had an exceptionally diverse culture. The Brazilian elite remained white, and dominated laborers who were, in this case, primarily African rather than Amerindian. As in Spanish America, a large mixed-race group emerged, along with a similarly complex hierarchy that paralleled the Spanish castas, while Brazilian Catholicism also underwent a process of religious syncretism.

In Brazil, "black" and "African" were associated with slavery, the lowest condition of all. But like the Spanish casta system, the social and racial hierarchy in Brazil was flexible enough that individuals or families might try to improve their standing. Dress, speech, education, marital status, and above all, economic success were means

Palmares The largest and most powerful maroon community (1630–1694) established by escaped slaves in the colonial Americas. Using military and diplomatic means, their leaders retained autonomy from Portuguese Brazil for over half a century.

by which colonial Brazilians of mixed descent might try to negotiate higher status. Still, the basic polarities remained clear: white at the top, black at the bottom.

The Dutch in the Americas

Like the Portuguese, the Dutch were initially focused on Indian Ocean trade. However, from 1630 to 1654, they seized control of the northeastern coast of Brazil as part of their larger global offensive against the Catholic empires of Spain and Portugal.

After an extremely violent conflict, in 1619 the Protestant Dutch had won their independence from Catholic Spain, which at that time also ruled over Portugal and therefore Brazil. Following the model of the successful Dutch East India Company, a group of merchants formed the Dutch West India Company in 1621 to penetrate markets and challenge the Spanish in the Americas. Their main advantage was an aggressive form of capitalism in which they constantly reinvested their profits in faster ships and larger ventures. In Brazil, the most important of these were the sugar plantations, to which the Dutch brought more capital investment and a larger supply of slaves.

Ousted from Brazil by the Portuguese in 1654, some Dutch planters transferred their business techniques and more advanced sugar-processing technology to the Caribbean. The following explosion of sugar production transformed Spanish-ruled islands like Cuba and Puerto Rico, as well as English ones like Jamaica and Barbados and French ones like Martinique and Saint-Domingue, and had dramatic consequences for Africa and the world economy (see Chapter 19).

Farther north, the Dutch West India Company founded the colony of New Netherland in 1624 and traded up the Hudson River Valley, allying with the powerful Iroquois Confederacy to tap into the lucrative fur trade. A small number of Dutch immigrants came as settlers to farm these rich and well-watered lands. But overall, Dutch commercial goals were still focused on Southeast Asia. In 1664, the Dutch surrendered New Netherland to the English without a fight. Their largest outpost, New Amsterdam, was renamed New York, and henceforth it was the French and English who would compete for dominance in North America.

New France, 1608–1754

Since the days of Columbus, European navigators had sought a western route to Asia. In the second half of the sixteenth century, French mariners sailed up the St. Lawrence River looking for a "northwest passage" to Chinese markets. What they found instead was the world's largest concentration of freshwater lakes and a land teeming with wildlife. In 1608, Samuel de Champlain founded the colony of New France with its capital at **Québec** (keh-BEC). In the later seventeenth century, French expeditions on the Mississippi and Ohio Rivers also added vast territories to the domains of French kings, although there were fewer Europeans and less immediate economic impact. The abundance of valuable furs farther north, in today's Canada, was what most attracted French attention.

Even prior to the establishment of Québec, French fur traders had made their way up the St. Lawrence and into the Great Lakes. Like the Russians, who were expanding fur markets into Siberia at the same time (see Chapter 17), French fur traders went far beyond the frontiers of formal colonial control, driven by lucrative European, Ottoman, and Safavid markets. Their indigenous trading partners did the actual work of trapping beavers and bringing the pelts to French trading posts. The yield of the Amerindian trappers increased with the use of iron tools from Europe, driving the quest for fur ever deeper into the interior.

Québec
(est. 1608) Founded by Samuel de Champlain as the capital of New France (in modern Canada); became a hub for the French fur trade and the center from which French settlement in the Americas first began to expand.

French Fur Trader French traders ventured far beyond the borders of European colonial society in their quest for valuable furs such as beaver pelts. They frequently adopted the technologies, languages, and customs of Amerindian peoples, and they sometimes married into Amerindian societies. At the same time, on the other side of the world, the global fur market was also driving Russian traders deep into the forests of Siberia. (Timewatch Images/Alamy)

Living far from other Europeans, French fur traders adapted to the customs of the First Nations peoples (as they are called in Canada). For example, tobacco smoking was an important ritual that cemented trade and diplomatic alliances. Sometimes traders assimilated deeply into First Nations communities and bore children who were Amerindian in language and culture. More often French trappers and traders visited only seasonally; their children, known in French as *métis* (may-TEE), learned both French and indigenous languages such as Cree and served as cultural and commercial intermediaries between First Nations and European societies.

The fur trade had complex environmental and political effects. Once their traditional hunting grounds were exhausted, Amerindians had to venture farther to lay their traps. The competition for beaver pelts put them increasingly in conflict with each other, while the guns for which furs were traded made the ensuing warfare more lethal. New technologies and the desire for new commodities (iron tools and alcohol, as well as firearms) affected indigenous life well beyond the areas of European colonial control. On the Great Plains, for example, the introduction of firearms from New France and horses from New Spain enabled a new and more efficient style of buffalo hunting and mobile warfare among groups like the Sioux.

In the St. Lawrence region, the French were allied with the **Huron** people, who were receptive to the Jesuit missionaries who came up the river. French traders established residence in Huron country and negotiated with local chiefs to supply them with furs. Division of labor by gender facilitated the process. Since Huron men worked in agriculture only when clearing fields in early spring, they were available for hunting and trading parties during the rest of the year, while the women stayed behind to tend the fields. The political power and economic

---

métis
In colonial New France, the offspring of a European and Amerindian union.

Huron
A matriarchal, Iroquoian-speaking Amerindian group in the St. Lawrence region that was devastated by the smallpox brought by French fur traders and missionaries in the mid-seventeenth century.

resources that came from the fur trade therefore went mainly to men, a development that undercut the traditional power of Huron women: male chiefs became more powerful at the expense of the matriarchs chosen by their clans to represent them on the Huron confederacy council.

While some Huron chiefs and hunters became powerful from fur trading, the overall effects of contact with the French were disastrous. By 1641, half of the Huron population had been killed by disease. Many Huron sought baptism, praying that the priests' holy water would save them from the smallpox that the missionaries themselves had unwittingly introduced.

Meanwhile, French settlers were attracted to the farmlands surrounding the city of Québec, where some fifty thousand French men and women lived by 1750. These farmers, and the small urban population they supported, represented the beginnings of quite a different European presence in what would later become Canada. While the fur traders and missionaries sought to integrate themselves into indigenous societies in their search for pelts to sell or souls to save, settlers were driven by the search for cheap land and lumber. In later years, as their numbers swelled and the frontier advanced, settlers would increasingly displace First Nations peoples (see Chapter 25).

In the first half of the eighteenth century, however, the most valuable French possessions in the Americas were not vast North American territories but relatively small Caribbean islands. Using African slave labor, French plantations in the West Indies made huge profits producing sugar for European markets. The same was true for England.

Mainland English Colonies in North America

For the English, as for the French, the Caribbean islands and sugar were the economic focal points of their American venture (see Chapter 19). On the mainland, again like the French, the English were relative newcomers to American settlement in the first half of the seventeenth century, with initial settlements in what Europeans considered less desirable northern areas such as Virginia and Massachusetts.

Jamestown, founded in 1607 and the first permanent English settlement in **Virginia**, was nearly wiped out in its early years, but by the 1630s the colony was thriving. The soil was rich, and the Virginia colonists discovered a lucrative Atlantic market for tobacco. Long used by Amerindian peoples for social and ritual purposes, tobacco became the foundation of Virginia's prosperity and generated a strong demand for labor.

Virginia (est. 1607) English colony in North America with an export economy based on tobacco production. The use of European indentured servants gave way to dependence on slave labor.

English attitudes excluded Amerindians from participation in the evolving economy of Virginia, even as laborers. (In any event, woodland Amerindian men looked down on agricultural work; moreover, imported diseases were soon decimating their population.) Unlike the French, who cooperated with Amerindian societies, the English drove indigenous peoples out, replacing them with "civilized" English farmers. Sir Walter Raleigh, a major investor in Virginia settlement, had taken this approach when he was sent to put down a late-sixteenth-century Irish rebellion, creating settlements where the "savage Irish" were to be replaced by more dependable English farmers. In Virginia, the "savages" to be brought under control were Amerindian rather than Irish, but Raleigh's strategy remained the same.

However, plantations required more work than free settlers could provide. One solution was indentured labor. In this system, employers paid for the transportation costs of poor English and Irish peasants in return for four to seven years of work, after which time they received either a return passage or a small plot of land. Cheap as this labor was, tobacco planters needed a labor force even cheaper and more servile. In

1619, when the first shipment of captive Africans arrived at Jamestown, they were treated as indentured servants. By the 1650s, however, a racial distinction between white servants and African slaves had become the rule. By the late seventeenth century, planters were buying larger numbers of African slaves in Virginia markets.

Virginia's population developed, therefore, through exclusion of Amerindian peoples, free immigration of English settlers, and forced immigration of African slaves. Colonial authorities worried about contact between Europeans and Africans; as early as 1630, one Hugh Davis was whipped *"for abusing himself to the dishonor of God and the shame of Christians, by defiling his body in lying with a Negro."*[*] By the later seventeenth century, Virginia law prohibited interracial unions, though such liaisons continued nevertheless. Mixed-race Virginians were discriminated against both legally and socially. Though terms such as *mulatto* were commonly used for a person of mixed race, by the eighteenth century the English generally viewed anyone with any sign of African parentage as "black," a status closely associated with that of "slave." Those relatively few blacks who were legally free, as well as free mulattos who came from mixed unions, thus found themselves closely associated with slavery by the social norms and legal statutes of colonial society.

Even as the importance of slave bondage increased, Virginia's institutions evolved toward a system in which free, propertied white men had a voice in their own governance. Virginia became a royal colony in 1624, with a governor-general appointed by the king. However, the English Civil War that raged from 1642 to 1649 impeded direct colonial rule from London, and by the 1660s Virginia's assembly, the House of Burgesses, was acting as an independent deliberative body. By the eighteenth century, Virginia's ruling class of planters were accustomed to running their own affairs and would resist renewed attempts by the English monarchy to impose central control (see Chapter 22).

Carolina
(est. 1663) English colony that was patterned after West Indian social and economic patterns, with large plantations growing rice and indigo with slave labor. Unlike in Virginia, Africans were a majority of the seventeenth-century population.

Farther south, the English colony of **Carolina** more closely resembled the colonies of the West Indies, especially on the coast and the coastal islands. Carolina's plantations were generally much larger than Virginia's and their use of slaves more intensive. Rice and indigo (used to produce a rich blue dye) were the main crops. Because Africans greatly outnumbered the few English settlers, they retained more of their own culture. West African words, language patterns, stories, and crafts persisted into the twentieth century among African Americans along Carolina's coast and offshore islands.

Slavery was less important in the middle colonies, where New York City and Philadelphia emerged as vibrant political and economic centers. The twenty thousand German settlers who had arrived in Pennsylvania by 1700 added an ethnic variable, but the European immigrant population was still primarily English and Scottish.

New England
Colony that began with the arrival of English Calvinists in 1620s, and characterized by homogeneous, self-sufficient farming communities.

The settlement of **New England** began with the arrival in the 1620s and 1630s of religious dissenters from the established Church of England. More English settlers soon came for economic reasons: land was cheap, and wages were relatively high. Entire families migrated to New England intending to recreate the best features of the rural life they knew in England and combine them with American economic opportunity.

New England farming communities were self-sufficient both economically and demographically. Whereas elsewhere European men outnumbered European immigrant women, in New England their numbers were equally balanced, making cultural and racial mixture much less common. Since families did their own farm

*Quoted in George Fredrickson, *White Supremacy: A Comparative Study in American and South African History* (New York: Oxford University Press, 1981), p. 100.

work, there was little call for slave labor. Regarding indigenous peoples as competitors for land and water resources, the settlers drove them out, beyond the colonial boundaries. With a population composed predominantly of English settlers, colonial New England was an exceptionally homogeneous place.

Boston was the commercial center of New England, its merchants oriented not to the farming settlements of the interior but to the maritime trade of the Atlantic. The cod fisheries of the North Atlantic provided the original foundation of Boston's wealth. Dried and salted, cod was an important source of protein and improved health throughout the Atlantic region. The highest-quality fish was consumed locally or exported to Europe. Cheaper, lower-quality fish was sent to the Caribbean as inexpensive food for plantation slaves.

The colonial population of New England was troublesome for English authorities almost from the start. Because most of the early settlers were dissenting Protestants, the Church of England did not have the same authority as the Catholic Church in the Spanish colonies. And, as in Virginia, the English Civil War meant that there was little imperial oversight of colonial affairs during the middle of the seventeenth century. When British monarchs in the eighteenth century tried to impose a more centralized administrative system, they found that New Englanders would not willingly give up the voice in public affairs to which they had become accustomed (see Chapter 22).

In the seventeenth and early eighteenth centuries, then, England's mainland colonies were of limited economic and strategic importance. The silver of New Spain and the sugar of the West Indies generated profits on a much greater scale than Carolina's rice, Virginia's tobacco, or New England's fish. Faced with a hostile alliance of French and Indian societies to the north and west, the potential for expansion beyond the Atlantic seaboard seemed uncertain. These tensions were not confined to North America. By 1750, England and France were poised to battle for control of such diverse colonial territories as the Ohio River Valley, plantation colonies in the Caribbean, and trade settlements in South Asia (see Chapters 19 and 20). By that time the significance of Britain's mainland American colonies had grown substantially.

Comparisons Across the Colonial Americas

By 1750, Europe's impact on the Americas was profound. While different geographical conditions led to diverse economic and demographic outcomes, the various political, religious, and cultural traditions of the European colonial powers also left deep marks.

Throughout the Americas, one common feature was the continuing effects of the Columbian exchange. Horses and cattle, both introduced by the Spanish, flourished on the grasses of the wide-open South American plains (and, somewhat later, on the North American plains). It was the iron tools and large domesticated animals brought from Europe that allowed colonists to convert these rich grasses into protein by grazing herds of cattle in a way never before possible, also supplying an export industry in hides. In other regions, such as Virginia, hogs brought from Europe thrived. European food crops like wheat and barley were planted along with native American crops like maize, potatoes, squash, and tomatoes to increase agricultural productivity.

However, few Amerindians shared in the bounty. Contagious disease continued to cause high mortality among Amerindians, even beyond the formal boundaries of

European empires. The decimation of Amerindian populations transformed the landscape. In Mexico, for example, Amerindian farmlands were converted to grazing for European livestock; in the Chesapeake area, tobacco plantations replaced the more varied Amerindian agricultural and hunting landscapes.

All European powers exploited their colonies according to mercantilist economic principles (see Chapter 17), harnessing American profits to augment the wealth and power of their monarchs. The Spanish and Portuguese in particular benefited from the supplies of gold and silver flowing from American mines, which lubricated their own trade with the dynamic economies of Asia. Actual imperial control of commerce was never as great in practice as it was in theory, however. In the seventeenth century, smuggling and piracy were common, and colonists were frequently able to evade laws that required them to trade only with their home countries. In the middle and late eighteenth century, when European states attempted to apply mercantilist regulations in the Americas more strictly, tensions with colonists in both Spanish and British America resulted (see Chapter 22).

Within the various colonies, quite different economic regimes took hold. Some enterprises were merely extractive: mines in Spanish America or furs in New France, for instance. Here indigenous people formed the workforce (usually by compulsion in New Spain and often voluntarily in Canada). In New Spain, large mining operations and expanding urban centers offered growing markets for hacienda owners, exceptionally powerful men who commanded the labor and obedience of dependent workforces on their large estates, usually Indians or mixed-race mestizos.

Lacking minerals to exploit, the economies of the English colonies all relied on agriculture (and, in New England, fishing), though their agricultural regimes and settlement patterns differed. In temperate New England, independent farmers worked small but productive plots, largely with family labor, and provided most of their own sustenance. In contrast, large plantations were the characteristic form of landholding in colonial Carolina. In the coastal lowlands and offshore islands, Carolina resembled the West Indian pattern of settlement, exploiting massed African slave labor to produce great quantities of high-value commodities for export. In Virginia, a mixed pattern emerged. Slave labor was central to the Virginian economy, but the plantations were smaller than in Carolina. Here European settlers generally worked relatively small farms using a few slaves to supplement family and indentured labor.

Religious traditions shaped the development of all of the colonial American cultures. Not surprisingly, the religious rivalries of the Reformation were exported to the Americas. The Catholic kings of France, Portugal, and Spain, seeing themselves as defenders of a single universal church, incorporated church officials in the administration of their territories. The politics of the Reformation magnified territorial and commercial competition between the Catholic Spanish and Protestant English, as well as between the Catholic Portuguese and Protestant Dutch. These politics also affected French settlement. After 1627 the French monarchy, doubtful of Huguenot loyalty, banned Protestant emigration to New France.

In some English colonies, specific Protestant groups were dominant. The Church of England was the established church of Virginia and Carolina, while the Congregationalist Church, emphasizing the autonomy of individual congregations, was dominant in Massachusetts and Connecticut. Rhode Island, Maryland (after 1700), and Pennsylvania were the only colonies that guaranteed freedom of

© Robert Frerck/Odyssey Productions, Inc.

© David Lyons/Alamy

Catholic and Protestant Churches in the Americas There is a sharp contrast between the interior of the Spanish colonial church of Santa Maria Tonantzintla (*left*) in Puebla, Mexico, and that of the Old Whaler's Church (*right*) in Martha's Vineyard, Massachusetts. The Spanish church embodies the Catholic preference for richly embellished church interiors associated with elaborate rituals and incorporates indigenous Amerindian themes. The New England church reflects the asceticism and simplicity of the Calvinist tradition, and bears no trace of Amerindian influence.

religious worship, accommodating Catholic settlers who were not welcome in New England or Virginia.

As part of the religious divide of the early modern period, the English developed a strongly negative view of the Spanish and their empire. Associating Spain with religious intolerance and violent treatment of native peoples, the "black legend" of Spanish barbarism and cruelty infused English literature and philosophy. In the twentieth century the Mexican poet Octavio Paz turned the "black legend" on its head, arguing that the English were exceptionally harsh in their exclusion of Amerindians from colonial life, while the Spanish church at least allowed them *"to form a part of one social order and one religion."* The chance to be an accepted part of colonial society, *"even if it was at the bottom of the social pyramid,"* Paz wrote, *"was cruelly denied to the Indians by the Protestants of New England."** (See the feature "Movement of Ideas Through Primary Sources: Prospero and Caliban.")

*Octavio Paz, *The Labyrinth of Solitude* (New York: Grove Press, 1961), pp. 101–102.

Prospero and Caliban

When Catalina de Erauso arrived in New Spain, William Shakespeare was the leading playwright in the English-speaking world. Shakespeare's imagination, like that of many Europeans in the early seventeenth century, was stimulated by tales of exotic adventure in what one of Shakespeare's characters referred to as "this brave new world." That line comes from *The Tempest* (1611), a drama that reflects European fascination with new discoveries in the Americas. Shakespeare used reports from Virginia settlers who had survived a shipwreck to weave a fantastic tale of magic, revenge, and the triumph of justice.

The great magician named Prospero and his daughter, Miranda, are stranded on an island. In the scene below, Prospero speaks with a misshapen monster named Caliban, the only native inhabitant of the island. From Prospero's perspective, Caliban deserves harsh treatment. In spite of the kindness shown by the magician, the monster attempts to rape Miranda. Things look very different from Caliban's viewpoint. The powers he inherited from his mother, Sycorax, cannot counter Prospero's magic, and he has no choice but to serve as the magician's slave while plotting his vengeance. Their unequal positions are even reflected in their names, which might be translated as "Prosperity" and "Cannibal." Though Shakespeare presents Prospero as having justice on his side, he also allows Caliban to voice his complaints as an abused native imprisoned by a colonial master.

Source: Excerpt from William Shakespeare, *Tempest.* http://the-tech .mit.edu/Shakespeare/tempest/index.html. The glossary is original.

The Tempest, Act I, Scene 2

PROSPERO: Thou poisonous slave, got[•] by the
  devil himself
  Upon thy wicked dam,[•] come forth!

CALIBAN: As wicked dew as e'er my mother
  brush'd
  With raven's feather from unwholesome fen
  Drop on you! a south-west blow on ye
  And blister you all o'er!

PROSPERO: For this, be sure, tonight thou shalt
  have cramps,
  Side-stitches that shall pen thy breath up;
  urchins[•]
  Shall, for that vast of night that they may
  work,
  All exercise on thee;[•] thou shalt be
  pinch'd

As thick as honeycomb, each pinch more
  stinging
  Than bees that made 'em.

CALIBAN: This island's mine, by Sycorax my
  mother,
  Which thou takest from me. When thou
  camest first,
  Thou strokedst me and madest much of
  me, wouldst give me
  Water with berries in't, and teach me how
  To name the bigger light, and how the less,
  That burn by day and night:[•] and then I
  loved thee
  And show'd thee all the qualities o' the
  isle,
  The fresh springs, brine-pits, barren place
  and fertile:
  Cursed be I that did so! All the charms
  Of Sycorax, toads, beetles, bats, light on
  you!

[•] **got** Begotten.
[•] **dam** Mother.
[•] **urchins** Goblins.
[•] **exercise on thee** Torment you.

[•] **day and night** The sun and moon.

For I am all the subjects that you have,
Which first was mine own king: and here
    you sty° me
In this hard rock, whiles you do keep
    from me
The rest o' the island.

PROSPERO: Thou most lying slave,
Whom stripes° may move, not kindness! I
    have used° thee,
Filth as thou art, with human care, and
    lodged thee
In mine own cell, till thou didst seek to
    violate
The honour of my child.

CALIBAN: O ho, O ho! would't had been done!
Thou didst prevent me; I had peopled else°
This isle with Calibans.

PROSPERO: Abhorred slave,
Which any print of goodness wilt not
    take,
Being capable of all ill! I pitied thee,
Took pains to make thee speak, taught
    thee each hour
One thing or other: when thou didst not,
    savage,
Know thine own meaning, but wouldst
    gabble like
A thing most brutish, I endow'd thy
    purposes
With words that made them known. But
    thy vile race,

Though thou didst learn, had that in't
    which good natures
Could not abide to be with; therefore wast
    thou
Deservedly confined into this rock,
Who hadst deserved more than a prison.

CALIBAN: You taught me language; and my
    profit on't
Is, I know how to curse. The red plague
    rid you
For learning me your language!

PROSPERO: Hag-seed,° hence!
Fetch us in fuel; and be quick, thou'rt
    best,
To answer other business. Shrug'st thou,
    malice?
If thou neglect'st or dost unwillingly
What I command, I'll rack thee with old
    cramps,
Fill all thy bones with aches, make thee
    roar
That beasts shall tremble at thy din.

CALIBAN: No, pray thee.
    Aside
I must obey: his art is of such power,
It would control my dam's god, Setebos,
    and make a vassal of him.

PROSPERO:
So, slave; hence!

° **sty** Imprison.
° **stripes** Whippings.
° **used** Treated.
° **else** Otherwise.

° **hag-seed** Child of a witch.

QUESTIONS FOR ANALYSIS

» *To what extent does Shakespeare encourage us to empathize with Caliban?*

» *Is Caliban's situation in any way analogous to that of conquered Amerindian peoples?*

Paz underestimated the missionary impulse among Protestant settlers in North America, some of whom made a strong effort toward converting Amerindians. He was correct, however, in pointing out the difference between the casta hierarchy of the Spanish empire and the forms of racial discrimination that developed in English North America. The Spanish system, though based on hierarchy and inequality, was flexible, allowing for gradations of identification and classification among people of mixed European, African, and Amerindian backgrounds. The English system of racial classification was more sharply segregated. Though substantial intermixing occurred among the three main population groups in the early colonial period, English authorities made little accommodation for mixed-race identities.

Gender identities were strongly fixed in every colonial society. As in Europe at that time, even modes of dress were regulated by law: no one was allowed to dress above his or her station, and mixing of clothing by gender was not permitted. However, as we have seen, social realities could be more fluid on the frontier, as when French fur traders interacted with matrilineal First Nations peoples and adopted their customary respect for female authority.

Catalina de Erauso was, of course, most exceptional. Badly wounded in a fight, and thinking she had better confess her sins before she died, Erauso told a priest about her deception. He did not believe her, but the nuns sent to discover the truth confirmed that she was actually a woman. After she recovered, Erauso went to Spain to seek a pension from the king for her service as a soldier, and to Rome to meet the pope. News of her strange story spread across Europe, and as Erauso journeyed by horseback across France on her way to Italy, people came out to the road to see the famous woman warrior in a man's uniform. During her papal audience at the Vatican, she was admonished to restrain herself from violent behavior, but then the pope gave her formal permission to dress as a man for the rest of her life.

While in Rome, Erauso narrated her story to an unknown scribe, ending with the following anecdote:

> *And one day in Naples, as I was strolling about the wharves, I was struck by the tittering laughter of two ladies, who leaned against a wall making conversation with two young men. They looked at me, and I looked at them, and one said, "Señora Catalina, where are you going all by your lonesome?" "My dear harlots," I replied, "I have come to deliver one hundred strokes to your pretty little necks, and a hundred gashes with this blade to the fool who would defend your honor." The women fell dead silent, and they hurried off.*[*]

How did Erauso see herself? Did she resent having to act as a man in order to live her own life as she pleased? Or was her cross-dressing more than a masquerade? History provides no additional evidence.

It seems that Erauso preferred the life of the colonial frontier. According to legend, she returned to Mexico, disappeared into the mountains with a pack of burros, and was never heard from again. She was one of many European immigrants for whom the Americas represented new possibilities.

---

[*]Excerpt from Catalina de Erauso, *Lieutenant Nun: Memoir of a Basque Transvestite in the New World*, trans. Michele Stepto and Gabriel Stepto (Boston: Beacon Press, 1996), p. 39.

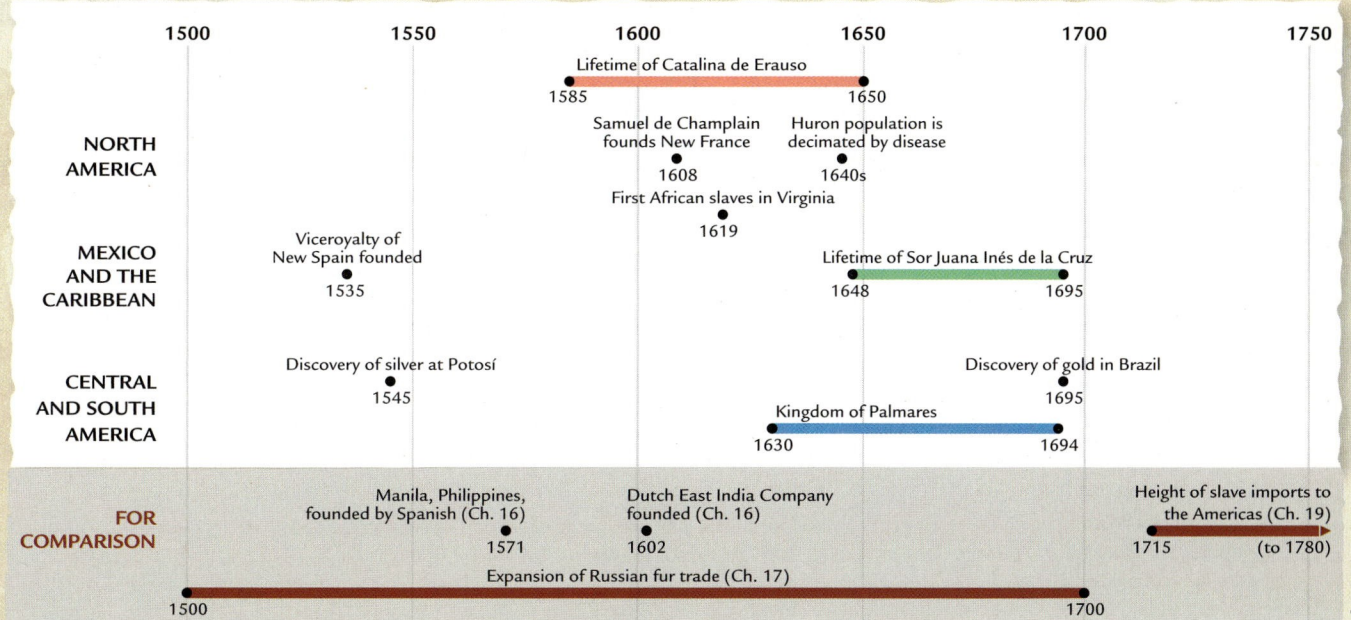

NORTH AMERICA

Lifetime of Catalina de Erauso
1585 — 1650

Samuel de Champlain founds New France
1608

Huron population is decimated by disease
1640s

First African slaves in Virginia
1619

MEXICO AND THE CARIBBEAN

Viceroyalty of New Spain founded
1535

Lifetime of Sor Juana Inés de la Cruz
1648 — 1695

CENTRAL AND SOUTH AMERICA

Discovery of silver at Potosí
1545

Discovery of gold in Brazil
1695

Kingdom of Palmares
1630 — 1694

FOR COMPARISON

Manila, Philippines, founded by Spanish (Ch. 16)
1571

Dutch East India Company founded (Ch. 16)
1602

Height of slave imports to the Americas (Ch. 19)
1715 (to 1780)

Expansion of Russian fur trade (Ch. 17)
1500 — 1700

© Cengage Learning

Spain, the Americas, and the World

That the Habsburg dynasty won the sixteenth-century silver and gold lottery was significant for world history. American mineral wealth, combined with extensive Habsburg territorial control in Europe, elevated the court of Madrid to the top rank in an interconnected world where European dynastic rivalries had gone global. The political and military impulses of the *reconquista* (the Christian reconquest of Iberia, completed in 1492) were then transferred to the international stage, as Catalina de Erauso's narrative shows. The Spanish emphasis on "purity of blood" once directed at Jews and Muslims was one such continuity (even as, ironically, racial mixture was common in the Spanish Americas); the admixture of militarism and Catholicism was another.

Spain's leading role would not long endure, however: even the fabulous riches flowing from Potosí and other American mines were not sufficient to enable the Spanish to turn back the challenge of the Protestant Reformation (see Chapter 17) or to maintain their lead in imperial affairs. Following the Spanish head start, the English, French, and Dutch were left to vie for marginal American territories to

the north. Though less well endowed with resources and population, the colonial economies they developed were more dynamic.

The Dutch were pioneers in the development of the tools of merchant capitalism, including joint-stock companies and chartered monopolies to develop new markets (see Chapter 16). The English, who had begun their American venture as little more than pirates, built on and further developed these tools of mercantile capitalism to become the greatest naval force in the world by the eighteenth century, further expanding their empire in both Asia and the Americas. By then, with Spain reduced to a minor power, it was the British and the French who would compete for European supremacy on the global stage (see Chapters 19 and 20).

We should not, however, make the common mistake of overstating the global role of the West in the period from 1500 to 1750. The Americas were unique in the degree to which society was transformed environmentally, politically, and culturally by the Western impact. Even here, some indigenous

517

societies still remained outside the orbit of colonial empires, and through cultural mixing and merging, indigenous traditions continued.

In Afro-Eurasia, European ascendency was less assured in the early eighteenth century. Land-based empires remained more important in Asia, for example, than maritime ones. As we shall see in upcoming chapters, European global dominance was not fully secured until the nineteenth century, in the wake of the Industrial Revolution.

Although Europeans had only a tiny footprint on the African continent by 1750, millions of African lives had been utterly transformed by the Atlantic slave trade. Their experiences in the Americas varied, with some finding opportunities in the new world, much as Catalina de Erauso did, but the most common story by far was the hardship of brutal plantation work. On the sugar islands of the West Indies, Africans slaved to harvest the sugar and other crops that would enrich and empower their European masters. The trade in slaves brought untold misery to both those Africans forced into exile and to the continent of Africa itself, as we will see in the next chapter.

Voyages on the Web: Catalina de Erauso

The Voyages Map App follows the traveler's journeys using interactive study tools, including 360-degree panoramic views of historic sites, zoomable maps, audio summaries, flash cards, and quizzes.

Key Terms

Catalina de Erauso (492)
viceroyalties (495)
Bartolomé de las Casas (495)
Potosí (497)
mercury amalgamation
    process (498)

haciendas (498)
mestizo (501)
syncretism (501)
Virgin of Guadalupe (501)
Sor Juana Inés de la Cruz (503)
Palmares (506)

Québec (507)
métis (508)
Huron (508)
Virginia (509)
Carolina (510)
New England (510)

FOR FURTHER REFERENCE

Benton, Lauren A. *Law and Colonial Cultures: Legal Regimes in World History, 1400–1900*. New York: Cambridge University Press, 2002.

Burns, Kathryn. *Colonial Habits: Convents and the Spiritual Economy of Cuzco, Peru*. Durham: Duke University Press, 1999.

Eccles, William J. *The French in North America, 1500–1783*. Rev. ed. Lansing: Michigan State University Press, 1998.

Erauso, Catalina de. *Lieutenant Nun: Memoir of a Basque Transvestite in the New World*. Michele Stepto and Gabriel Stepto, trans. Boston: Beacon Press, 1996.

Fernandez-Armesto, Felipe. *The Americas: The History of a Hemisphere*. London: George Weidenfeld and Nicholson, 2003.

Kamen, Henry. *Empire: How Spain Became a World Power, 1492–1763*. New York: HarperCollins, 2003.

Lavrin, Asunción. *Sexuality and Marriage in Colonial Latin America*. Lincoln: University of Nebraska Press, 1992.

Nash, Gary. *Red, White and Black: The Peoples of Early North America*. 5th ed. New York: Prentice Hall, 2005.

Nellis, Eric. *An Empire of Regions: A Brief History of British Colonial America*. Toronto: University of Toronto Press, 2010.

Paz, Octavio. *Sor Juana*. Margaret Sayers Peden, trans. Cambridge, Mass.: Harvard University Press, 1988.

Restall, Matthew. *Seven Myths of the Spanish Conquest*. New York: Oxford University Press, 2004.

Sweet, James H. *Recreating Africa: Culture, Kinship, and Religion in the African-Portuguese World, 1441–1770*. Durham: University of North Carolina Press, 2006.

Taylor, William. *Magistrates of the Sacred: Priests and Parishioners in Eighteenth Century Mexico*. Stanford: Stanford University Press, 1996.

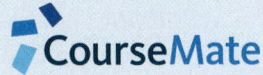

Go to the CourseMate website at **www.cengagebrain.com** for additional study tools and review materials—including audio and video clips—for this chapter.

19

The Atlantic System: Africa, the Americas, and Europe, 1550–1807

In 1789, members of England's growing abolitionist movement, campaigning against the slave trade, provided an eager audience for a new publication, *The Interesting Narrative of the Life of Olaudah Equiano, or Gustavus Vassa, the African.* For many, it was the first time they heard an African voice narrate the horrors of slavery. **Olaudah Equiano** (ca. 1745–1797) purchased his own freedom at the age of twenty-one, pursued a career as a sailor, and became a leader of the black community in Britain and an important contributor to the abolitionist movement. His story shows how he suffered as a slave, but also how he beat the odds. Equiano's readers learned of the horrors of the infamous Middle Passage across the Atlantic:

Olaudah Equiano

(Royal Albert Memorial Museum, Exeter, Devon, UK/The Bridgeman Art Library)

*T*he first object which saluted my eyes when I arrived on the coast was the sea, and a slave-ship. . . . These filled me with astonishment, which was soon converted into terror. . . . I was now persuaded that I had gotten into a world of bad spirits, and that they were going to kill me. . . . [T]hey made ready with many fearful noises, and we were all put under deck . . . now that the whole ship's cargo was confined together [the stench of the hold] was absolutely pestilential. The closeness of the place, and the heat of the climate, added to the number in the ship, which was so crowded that each had scarcely room to turn himself, almost suffocated us. . . . This wretched situation

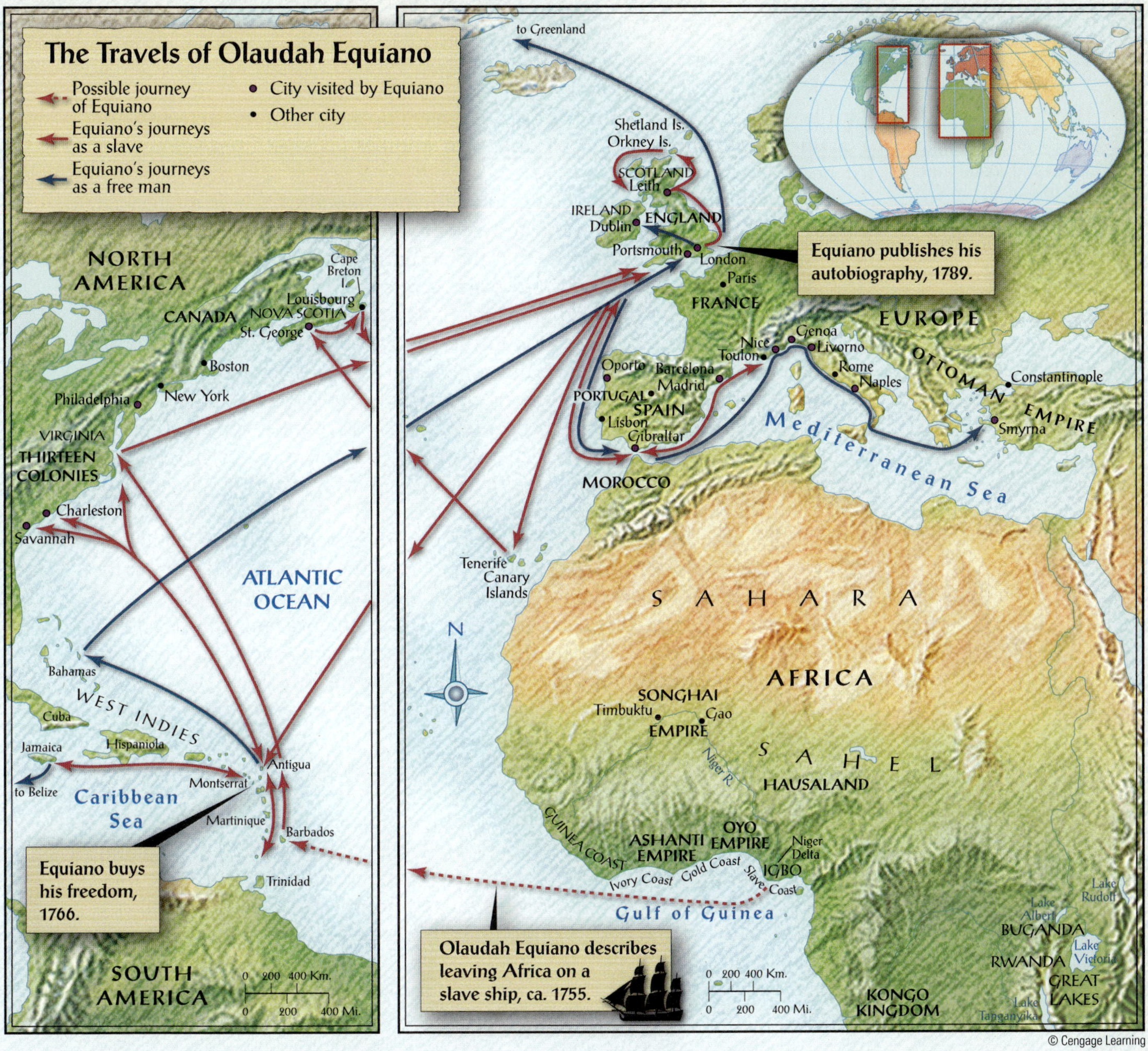

The Travels of Olaudah Equiano

Legend:
- Possible journey of Equiano
- Equiano's journeys as a slave
- Equiano's journeys as a free man
- City visited by Equiano
- Other city

to Greenland

Shetland Is.
Orkney Is.

SCOTLAND
Leith

IRELAND
Dublin
ENGLAND
Portsmouth
London
Paris

Equiano publishes his autobiography, 1789.

FRANCE

EUROPE

Genoa
Nice · Livorno
Toulon · Rome
Oporto · Naples
Barcelona
Madrid

OTTOMAN EMPIRE

Constantinople
Smyrna

PORTUGAL
Lisbon
SPAIN
Gibraltar

Mediterranean Sea

MOROCCO

NORTH AMERICA

Cape Breton I.
Louisbourg
CANADA
St. George
NOVA SCOTIA

Boston

Philadelphia
New York

VIRGINIA
THIRTEEN COLONIES

Charleston
Savannah

ATLANTIC OCEAN

Tenerife
Canary Islands

Bahamas

WEST INDIES

Cuba
Jamaica
Hispaniola
to Belize
Montserrat
Antigua
Caribbean Sea
Martinique
Barbados
Trinidad

Equiano buys his freedom, 1766.

SOUTH AMERICA

N

0 200 400 Km.
0 200 400 Mi.

AFRICA

SAHARA

SONGHAI EMPIRE
Timbuktu
Gao

SAHEL
HAUSALAND

Niger R.

GUINEA COAST
ASHANTI EMPIRE
OYO EMPIRE
Niger Delta
IGBO
Ivory Coast Gold Coast Slave Coast

Gulf of Guinea

Olaudah Equiano describes leaving Africa on a slave ship, ca. 1755.

Lake Rudolf
Lake Albert
BUGANDA
Lake Victoria
RWANDA
GREAT LAKES
KONGO KINGDOM
Lake Tanganyika

0 200 400 Km.
0 200 400 Mi.

© Cengage Learning

Join this chapter's traveler on "Voyages," an interactive tour of historic sites and events:
www.cengagebrain.com

was again aggravated by the galling of the chains, now become insupportable; and the filth of the [latrines], into which the children often fell, and were almost suffocated. The shrieks of the women, and the groans of the dying, rendered the whole a scene of horror almost inconceivable.[*]

[*]Olaudah Equiano, *The Interesting Narrative of the Life of Olaudah Equiano, or Gustavus Vassa, the African,* ed. Vincent Carretta, 2d ed. (New York: Penguin, 2003), p. 55.

Olaudah Equiano
(1745–1797) Afro-British author and abolitionist who told of his enslavement as a child in Africa, his purchase of his own freedom in the West Indies, his move to England, and his wide travels as a sailor.

At least 12 million Africans had similar experiences between the sixteenth and nineteenth centuries, and an unknown number perished even before they reached the slave ports on the coast.

The historical importance of Equiano's *Interesting Narrative* has been established, though some scholars question the authenticity of its earliest passages. Some evidence, albeit inconclusive, suggests that the author was born in the Americas and created his account of Africa and the voyage across the Atlantic by retelling other slaves' stories. Whether Olaudah Equiano (oh-lah-OO-dah ek-wee-AHN-oh) actually experienced the terror he reports in the passage above or based the story on other accounts, few other sources bring us closer to the reality faced by millions of Africans in this period or offer a more eloquent critique of slavery.

By 1745, when Equiano's life began, the Atlantic slave trade was at its height. Hundreds of thousands of Africans crossed the Atlantic every year. They lived in diverse environments—the Brazilian tropics, the temperate lands of Virginia, the rocky shores of Nova Scotia—and performed a great variety of tasks. The fate of most of the 12 million Africans sent to the Americas in the seventeenth and eighteenth centuries, however, was tied to the sugar plantations of the West Indies. Sugar was the foundation of the Atlantic economy, a source of immense profit and great suffering.

A complex set of interconnections among Africa, America, and Europe characterized the Atlantic system. The so-called triangular trade sent Africans to the Americas as slaves; sugar, tobacco, and natural resources from the Americas to Europe; and manufactured goods from Europe to both Africa and the Americas. Africans labored on American plantations financed and managed by Europeans. The planters sent their profits back to Europe, stimulating economic growth, while in those parts of Africa affected by the Atlantic slave trade life became much less secure.

The Atlantic system fostered political competition. Warfare among West Africans increased, while European powers vied for Atlantic supremacy; Equiano himself participated in naval clashes between the French and British. The slave trade also had cultural repercussions. Africans arrived not merely as slaves but also as carriers of traditions that were to profoundly influence the development of American societies (see also Chapter 18).

Finally, the abolition of slavery was itself a complex process involving actors from different parts of the Atlantic, including plantation slaves who resisted bondage and Europeans who grew uncomfortable with the contradiction between the dictates of Christian charity—the admonition to treat others as you would be treated yourself—and the inhumanity of plantation slavery. It was to his readership of fellow Christians that Olaudah Equiano especially appealed with his *Interesting Narrative*.

Focus Questions

» *How were existing African economic and political systems integrated into the Atlantic plantation system? What were the effects of this interaction on Africans and African societies?*

» *What were the major social and economic features of the plantation complex in the West Indies and on the American mainland? What cultural patterns were associated with forced African migration to the Americas?*

» *How did the plantation complex affect political and economic developments in Europe in the eighteenth century? What led to the abolition of the British slave trade in the early nineteenth century?*

African History and Afro-Eurasian Connections, 1550–1700

The impact of the Atlantic slave trade on African societies, and its overall importance in African history, cannot be judged outside of Africa's cultural and geographic context. Contrary to common assumptions, Africa had not been an isolated continent; it had ancient connections to Europe and Asia across the Mediterranean, the Red Sea, and the Indian Ocean. It was therefore fitting for Equiano's tale to begin in Africa.

Africa's diverse deserts, grasslands, and rainforests produced a variety of political systems. Some Africans lived in small bands of hunter-gatherers, while others were subjects of powerful monarchs. Equiano described the Igbo-speaking villages in the Niger Delta region of West Africa as productive communities where yam-based agriculture supported a dense population. Other nearby societies had more centralized and hierarchical political structures, but in Igbo (ee-BWOH) society, men and women accumulated titles and authority on the basis of achievements rather than birth. As was nearly universal in Africa, clan elders played a crucial role in negotiating the consensus needed for group decisions. Even when owing tribute or obeisance to a more distant chief or king, African villages retained their own mechanisms for keeping peace and administering justice.

Much of the cultural and economic energy of the continent came from interaction among African peoples themselves. For example, in the **Great Lakes region** of east-central Africa, migration led to fruitful encounters between Africans of different linguistic and cultural backgrounds. Bantu-speaking migrants from the west brought knowledge of grain agriculture, as well as their sophisticated iron technology. In return, these farmers gained access to cattle from their pastoralist neighbors, descendants of migrants from the upper Nile River Valley. In the societies that resulted from this mixing of peoples, farming provided the bulk of calories and was the focus of work, while cattle represented wealth and prestige. No proper marriage contract could be negotiated unless the groom's family gave cattle to the family of his intended. Agriculture in the Great Lakes region was also stimulated by the introduction of plantains (bananas), a Southeast Asian fruit that had first been brought from across the Indian Ocean by Indonesian voyagers to the island of Madagascar. Supported by agricultural surpluses and dominated by clans wealthy in cattle, a number of powerful kingdoms such as Rwanda and Buganda emerged in the seventeenth-century Great Lakes region.

While societies in the Great Lakes region developed without direct contact beyond the continent, other African societies had formative contacts with external political systems, commercial markets, and religious traditions. For example, Ethiopia, Kongo, and South Africa all had connections to the wider Christian world. The Ethiopian Church was already over a thousand years old when the Portuguese attempted a military alliance in the sixteenth century.

In the Kongo kingdom (see Chapter 16), civil war and invasion by outside forces led to disintegration of the monarchy and the abandonment of the Kongo capital of San Salvador in the seventeenth century. Into this political vacuum stepped **Kimpa Vita** (ca. 1680–1706), also known as Dona Beatriz. In a powerful example of religious syncretism that blended existing and imported religious ideas, Kimpa Vita declared that she had been visited by Saint Anthony. It was said that she died each Friday, only to arise each Sunday after having conversed with God, who told her that the people of Kongo must unite under a new king. She taught that Christ

Great Lakes region
A temperate highland region in and around the Great Rift Valley in east-central Africa, characterized by agriculture and cattle pastoralism, a substantial iron industry, and dense populations.

Kimpa Vita
(ca. 1680–1706) Christian reformer in the Kongo kingdom, also known as Dona Beatriz. She preached that Jesus Christ was an African, blending Kongo beliefs with Catholic ones, before being executed as a heretic by a leader vying for the Kongo throne.

and the apostles were black men who had lived and died in Kongo. Portuguese missionaries regarded her beliefs as heresy. Nevertheless, her doctrine was popular, and her followers repopulated the old capital city. She was captured by one of the contestants for the Kongo throne, tried for witchcraft and heresy, and burned at the stake. But the Kongo tradition of depicting Jesus as an African endured.

The ascetic Calvinist version of Christianity, so different from both the mysticism of Ethiopia's Coptic Christianity and the syncretism of African and Christian beliefs in Kongo, was brought to South Africa by Dutch and French Huguenot immigrants in the late seventeenth century. In the southeastern tip of Africa, where Cape Town was founded in 1652, the indigenous Khoisan (KOI-sahn)-speaking peoples were few in number, had no metal weapons, and most fatally, no resistance to diseases such as smallpox. Within a hundred years, white settlers had enslaved them or driven them beyond the expanding colonial border.

Islam provided another avenue for Africa's global interconnection. On the East African coast, African Muslims had long plied maritime trade routes even while political circumstances changed. The sultan of Oman (oh-MAAN), at the entrance to the Persian Gulf, wrested control of the Swahili coast from the Portuguese and evicted them from Fort Jesus in Mombasa in 1696 (see Chapter 16). Thereafter, Swahili princes and aristocrats ruled over their own local affairs, while generally acknowledging the Omani sultan as their overlord. Traditional Swahili arts and crafts—poetry, jewelry, and the carving of elaborate wooden doors for the houses of the rulers and wealthy merchants—continued through such political transitions, combining Islamic and African motifs.

The other center of African Islam was the **Sahel**, the arid region south of the Sahara Desert. Here urban civilization developed around trade between grain farmers and cattle pastoralists of the grassland savanna and between the Sahel and the rainforest further south. Fishermen drew on the resources of the great Niger River. Flowing from the mountains of the west, through the savanna to the desert's edge, and on through the rainforests of the Niger Delta—where Equiano placed his childhood home—the river was a highway of trade; West Africa's most important cities clustered on its banks. Stimulated as well by the trans-Saharan trade, cities like Timbuktu were southern destinations for camel caravans from North Africa.

The **Songhai empire**, with its capital at Gao along the Niger River, arose from a thousand-year-old tradition of large-scale states in this region (see Map 19.1). In addition to leading armies of conquest, the *askias* (emperors) of Songhai (song-GAH-ee) were patrons of Islamic arts and sciences. The Sankore Mosque in Timbuktu, with its impressive library, became a center of intellectual debate, drawing scholars from far and wide. Timbuktu was famous for its gold trade as well as its book market, where finely-bound editions were eagerly sought by Muslim scholars, both Arab and African. When rulers, traders, and intellectuals from Songhai went on the hajj (pilgrimage) to Arabia, they amplified the empire's connections with the broader world.

Even within the mighty Songhai empire, however, most Africans lived in small agricultural villages far from the urban, Islamic world of kings, cavalry, and long-distance trade. In the rural societies of the Sahel, Islam spread slowly. Here older gods and ritual practices endured, sometimes incorporated with elements of Islam. Even in cities like Timbuktu and at the court of powerful Songhai kings, syncretism was characteristic of West African Islam, for example, when African customs regarding marriage and inheritance were blended with the influence of Islamic law.

The success of the askias (AH-skee-as) of Songhai in enlarging their territory and expanding their trade ultimately proved their undoing because it attracted the

Sahel
Arid region south of the Sahara Desert that played an important historic role as a West African center of trade and urbanization. Islam traveled with the caravans across the Sahara, making the Sahel a diffusion point for Islam in West Africa.

Songhai empire
(1464–1591) Important Islamic empire with prosperity based on both interregional and trans-Saharan trade. Stretched from the Atlantic into present-day Nigeria, reaching its height in the sixteenth century before being invaded by Morocco.

Caravan Approaching Timbuktu The city of Timbuktu was an important terminus of the trans-Saharan trade dating back to the thirteenth century, its strategic location on the Niger River making it central to the wealth and power of the Songhai empire. Under the patronage of Songhai's rulers, Timbuktu became an important center of Islamic scholarship as well: the library at the Sankore Mosque attracted both African and Arab scholars. Today, Timbuktu is a UNESCO World Heritage Site. (Bibliotheque nationale de France, Paris/Archives Charmet/The Bridgeman Art Library)

attention of neighbors to the north. Morocco's leaders had remained independent of the Ottoman empire and had successfully driven off the Portuguese. Envious of Songhai's gold and salt mines, the Moroccan sultan decided on conquest, and in 1591 the army he sent out from Marrakesh conquered Songhai. But the Moroccans were unable to sustain direct rule over such a long distance as the once mighty Songhai empire splintered into numerous smaller kingdoms, chiefdoms, and sultanates. Never again would a large-scale African state rise to such dominance in the Sahel.

While Songhai was at its height in the sixteenth century, Europeans were constructing fortifications along the West African coast. The major centers of population and prosperity lay in the African interior, connected to the wider world across the Sahara, but the Portuguese, French, English, and others were finding a way to redirect West African trade to the coast, focusing on the commodity in which they were soon most interested: slaves. By the eighteenth century, Africans from the Sahel who may once have crossed the Sahara to Morocco might be enslaved and sent in ships to Jamaica. While connections to the Islamic world across the Sahara Desert and the Indian Ocean continued, Africa's international connection was now turning toward the Atlantic Ocean and beyond, to the Americas.

MAP 19.1 Major African States and Trade Routes, ca. 1500 In the sixteenth century, Africa's primary global connections were across the Sahara Desert, up the Nile, across the Red Sea, and into the Indian Ocean. Large kingdoms and empires such as those of Songhai in the west and Ethiopia in the northeast benefited from participation in world trade, as did the Swahili city-states in the east. The arrival of Europeans added a new set of interconnections along the West African coast, but only in South Africa did Europeans come as settlers. Large states were the exception in Africa; societies smaller in scale populated vast regions of the continent. (© Cengage Learning)

Africa and the Americas: The Plantation Complex

European occupation of the Americas, the continuing decline of Amerindian populations, and new trade links with West Africa set the stage for the rise of the **Atlantic plantation system**, in which the use of slaves to grow crops like sugar led to a new set of interchanges among Europe, Africa, and the Americas. The lives of at least 12 million Africans were utterly transformed when they experienced the horrors of the voyage from Africa to the Americas, called the Middle Passage. The enslavement and forced emigration of millions of Africans to the Americas reaped huge fortunes for the British, French, Dutch, Spanish, and Portuguese who controlled the system. On the islands of the Caribbean, where the plantation complex was centered, landscapes changed dramatically as imported plants and animals replaced indigenous ones and Africans became the predominant population. Sugar planters exploited their labor to supply expanding global markets for sugar and related products like molasses and rum.

As Equiano's story illustrates, Africans were more than passive victims of the Atlantic slave trade and plantation system. Many resisted. And though mortality rates among slaves were high and survivors were often deprived of the use of their own languages, many managed to retain much of their culture and contributed it to the new American societies (see also Chapter 18). Meanwhile, the social and political systems of many West African societies were disrupted by their integration into the Atlantic system.

Atlantic plantation system
The focal point in the new set of interchanges among Africa, Europe, and the Americas that peaked in the eighteenth century. Utilized African slave labor to produce large quantities of agricultural products, particularly sugar, for international markets.

The Ecology and Economics of Plantation Production

European conquest of the Americas and the continuing outcomes of the Columbian exchange, along with the Portuguese opening of new trade links with West Africa, set the stage for the rise of the Atlantic plantation system (see Chapters 16 and 18). A newly interconnected Atlantic world combined the financial, political, and military power of Europe, American land and natural resources, and African labor.

When the Spanish first conquered the islands of the Caribbean, they were unable to effectively exploit the labor of the indigenous Amerindian inhabitants, who could stand neither the strain of European rule nor the deadly effects of diseases to which they had no immunity. European indentured servants were later imported, for example, to work on tobacco plantations on the island of Barbados in the 1620s, but they were vulnerable to the tropical diseases such as yellow fever and malaria that had been brought across the ocean from Africa. Starting in the mid-seventeenth century, when sugar became virtually the sole focus of West Indian agriculture, neither Europeans nor Amerindians could provide sufficient labor.

Enslaved Africans filled the void. They were expensive, and became more so over time. But from a sugar planter's perspective they were worth the investment because they could survive in the now more dangerous Caribbean disease environment. Through migration and trade contacts, West Africans had long been exposed to Afro-Eurasian diseases and had developed resistance to the same endemic diseases as had Europeans. In addition, through genetic adaptation and childhood exposure, Africans were also more likely to survive malaria and yellow fever. Ironically, what should have been a great advantage in life, the ability to survive in difficult disease environments, proved to be a tragic disadvantage to the Africans hauled across the ocean to toil on sugar plantations.

Slavery had been common in history, but the scale and commercial orientation of the sugar industry were something new. Many societies have allowed for slavery, but such "societies with slaves" differ from "slave societies," where slaveholding is the heart of social and economic life. "Societies with slaves" were common in the Islamic world and in Africa itself. Equiano described a mild form of servitude in the Niger Delta region, where the slaves had a lower place in society but retained legal rights. Slavery was also commonplace in the Ottoman empire, as we saw in the tale of Evliya Çelebi (see Chapter 17). Here slaves played important roles as soldiers and household servants, but since the basic agricultural work of Ottoman society was performed by freemen, we can classify this as a "society with slaves" rather than a "slave society." Genuine "slave societies" developed in northeastern Brazil and the Caribbean, where 80 percent of enslaved Africans were sent and where slavery was central to every facet of life. Coastal Carolina was also a "slave society," while in Virginia the intensive use of slaves on tobacco plantations took place within a mixed economy (see Chapter 18).

Purchasing and provisioning a sugar plantation, and buying the slaves needed to work it, took substantial capital. Sugar planters were usually men of property, either nobles with estates and aristocratic titles or middle-class entrepreneurs. For the latter, profits from sugar could improve not only their finances but also their social standing. Some of the great estates and chateaux of eighteenth-century France and Britain were built on the financial foundation of slave labor in the Caribbean. More broadly, the need to provision the sugar islands with food, clothing, iron goods, machinery, and other commodities not produced locally stimulated economic development in eighteenth-century North America and western Europe, providing many Europeans with jobs and markets for their goods.

On a typical Caribbean plantation, the owner and his family occupied a "great house." As absentee ownership became more common, especially on British islands such as Jamaica, the master's house might stand empty for long periods waiting for his occasional arrival from Europe. The work of overseeing slave labor was performed by lower-status European immigrants, legendary for their harshness, or by men of mixed race (though mulattos did not automatically have higher status on a plantation). Equiano told of a French sugar planter on Martinique with *"many mulattoes working in the fields [who] were all the produce of his own loins!"*[*]

Slaves performed all the backbreaking work of planting, weeding, harvesting, and turning the raw cane into a semiprocessed product for export. Because raw sugar is bulky, the juice had to be squeezed out of the cane and boiled down for shipment. Sugar production was an agro-industrial enterprise, organized like a factory, where profitable operation requires that the assembly line is always rolling, with raw materials always at hand. Sugarcane was planted year round so that it could be cut and processed year round, with full-time use of the machinery that crushed the juice from the cane and the large copper kettles that boiled down the juice. The entire process was physically strenuous, and the kettles sometimes exploded, taking lives in the process.

Under such harsh conditions, plantation overseers worked many Africans to death. Barbados is representative. In 1680, fifty thousand African slaves toiled on the island. Over the next forty years planters imported another fifty thousand slaves, but the total black population actually *dropped* to forty-five thousand. Slave

---

[*]Olaudah Equiano, *The Interesting Narrative of the Life of Olaudah Equiano, or Gustavus Vassa, the African,* ed. Vincent Carretta, 2d ed. (New York: Penguin, 2003), pp. 105–109.

Caribbean Sugar Mill   Sugar production was an industrial as well as agricultural enterprise. Here wind power is used to crush the sugarcane; the rising smoke indicates the intense heat of the furnaces used to boil down the juice. The slaves' work was hard, dangerous, and unceasing: such machinery was usually operated six days a week, year-round.

populations were not self-sustaining. The mortality rate was high, and the birthrate was low because the harsh working conditions and poor diet adversely affected the fertility of slave women. As Equiano noted, the overseers, *"human butchers"* left in charge by their absentee masters, *"pay no regard to the situation of pregnant women. The neglect certainly conspires with many others to cause a decrease in the births, as well as in the lives of the grown negroes."* In the late eighteenth century Equiano calculated that Barbados, not the worst island in terms of African mortality, required a thousand fresh imports annually just to maintain a level population.

Equiano himself escaped the harsh fate of working on a Caribbean sugar plantation. While still a boy he was sold to a British naval officer; he spent much of his early life aboard ships and developed a lifelong fondness for London, where he was baptized as a teenager. He was then sold to a Philadelphia merchant with business interests in the West Indies. Literate in English, and with a good head for numbers, Equiano was well treated and had significant freedom while tending to his master's business, which sometimes included trading in slaves. Of course, he witnessed many cruelties:

---

*Olaudah Equiano, *The Interesting Narrative of the Life of Olaudah Equiano, or Gustavus Vassa, the African,* ed. Vincent Carretta, 2d ed. (New York: Penguin, 2003), pp. 105–109.

It was very common in several of the islands, particularly in St. Kitt's, for the slaves to be branded with the initial letters of their master's name, and a load of heavy iron hooks hung around their necks. . . . I have seen a negro beaten till some of his bones were broken, for only letting a pot boil over. It is not uncommon, after a flogging, to make slaves go on their knees and thank their owners and . . . say "God Bless You."[*]

While distressed by his own bondage, Equiano was keenly aware of the even worse fate he could have faced as a field slave.

Of course, sugar was not the only slave-produced plantation crop in the Americas. Slaves also labored on the tobacco plantations of Virginia and the rice and indigo plantations of Carolina (see Chapter 18). But while Carolina plantations were organized much like those of the West Indies, the British colonies of the Chesapeake were further at the margins of the plantation complex. Here male and female slaves were more balanced in numbers. Better diet and higher fertility made the slave population self-reproducing in British North America by 1720, though here as elsewhere African resistance to enslavement was endemic.

African Culture and Resistance to Slavery

Previously some historians argued that the process of being uprooted and enslaved overwhelmed Africans, who—deprived of any connection with home—became psychologically dependent on their masters and lost their will to resist. More recent historical research has revealed the inaccuracy of this image of passivity. Resistance to slavery was widespread.

Slaves were constantly looking for ways to escape their bondage and, failing that, to resist their captivity in large or small ways. Slave traders, owners, and overseers were ever vigilant, and the penalties for open insubordination were gruesome. Slaves often found safer, more subtle ways to assert their humanity and express their defiance. Songs and stories derived from African cultural traditions might be used to ridicule a master using coded language he could not understand. Religious rites—African, Christian, or a synthesis of multiple belief systems and rituals—might serve as assertions of dignity and spiritual resilience. External appearances of deference to the slave master could be deceiving.

Resistance to slavery sometimes began even before the slave ships arrived in America. Equiano describes the nets that were used to keep Africans from jumping overboard and relates that *"one day . . . two of my wearied countrymen, who were chained together . . . preferring death to such a life of misery, somehow made through the nettings and jumped into the sea."*[*] Insurrections aboard slave ships were also common, as this dramatic description from 1673 attests:

A master of a ship . . . did not, as the manner is, shackle [the slaves] one to another . . . and they being double the number of those in the ship found their advantages, got weapons in their hands, and fell upon the sailors, knocking them on the heads, and cutting their throats so fast as the master found they were all lost . . . and so went down into the hold and blew up all with himself.[†]

---

[*]Olaudah Equiano, *The Interesting Narrative of the Life of Olaudah Equiano, or Gustavus Vassa, the African*, ed. Vincent Carretta, 2d ed. (New York: Penguin, 2003), pp. 105–109, 59.

[†]Richard Ligon, *A True and Exact History of the Island of Barbadoes* (London: Parker and Guy, 1673), p. 47.

Equiano tells of a slave trader who had once cut off the leg of a slave for running away. When Equiano asked how such an action could be squared with the man's Christian conscience, he was simply told *"that his scheme had the desired effect—it cured that man and some others of running away."*[*]

Some Africans were freed by their masters, but many others simply escaped. Yet if an individual or a small group escaped, where would they go, and how would they live? Options for escaped slaves included joining pirate communities in the Caribbean (which in spite of their reputation for brutality were relatively egalitarian), forming autonomous communities of runaway slaves, or settling among Amerindian populations.

Already in the sixteenth century Africans were banding together to form **maroon communities**, societies formed by escaped slaves. Perhaps the best known was Palmares in northeastern Brazil (see Chapter 18). Palmares was unique in scale, but smaller maroon communities were common in the eighteenth-century Caribbean. Some of the islands were too small for maroons to successfully avoid recapture, but the interior mountains of Jamaica were perfect for that purpose.

When the Spanish fled Jamaica in 1655 during a British attack, they left behind hundreds of African slaves who headed for the hills. Now free, these maroons farmed, fished, and occasionally pillaged British sugar plantations on the coasts. Their threat to the British came not so much from raiding but from the sanctuary that they could provide to other escaped slaves. After several slave uprisings in the early eighteenth century, the British increased their attacks on the maroons. The British and maroons fought to a stalemate, leading to a treaty that allowed the maroons autonomy in exchange for the promise that they would hunt, capture, and return future runaways.

In some places runaway slaves formed alliances with Amerindians. Sometimes individual escaped slaves, or small groups, would become assimilated into indigenous societies. Sometimes larger-scale cooperation between maroons and Amerindians occurred. In Florida, Africans who escaped from slavery in Carolina and Georgia formed an alliance with Creek Indians, and the cultural interaction between the two groups led the "Black Seminoles" to adopt many elements of Creek culture.

Of course, slaves who escaped could be recaptured and face terrible punishments, or they could find survival in an unknown environment to be extremely difficult. Even when Africans had to resign themselves to their fate as plantation slaves, covert resistance was possible. Slowing down and subverting the work process was a common form of defiance, even where the risk of the whip was ever present.

Religion is perhaps the area where Africans could best resist the psychological and spiritual torments of enslavement without risking flight or outright rebellion. Where Africans were greatest in number, their religious practices showed the strongest continuity. In both Brazil and Cuba, for example, Africans merged their existing beliefs with Christianity. In both colonies the *orisas* (or-EE-shahs), gods of the Yoruba (yaw-roo-bah) people (of present-day western Nigeria), were transformed into Catholic saints. Xàngó, the Yoruba deity of fire, thunder, and lightning, is still venerated today in the Cuban and Brazilian syntheses of Catholicism and African

Private Collection/The Bridgeman Art Library

A Jamaican Maroon In Jamaica and elsewhere in the Caribbean escaped slaves banded together to form maroon communities. This man's gun and sword show that the maroons organized themselves to protect their independence from European colonialists. While some joined maroon communities, other escaped slaves joined Amerindian societies or the crews of pirate ships.

maroon communities Self-governing communities of escaped slaves common in the early modern Caribbean and in coastal areas of Central and South America.

---

[*]Olaudah Equiano, *The Interesting Narrative of the Life of Olaudah Equiano, or Gustavus Vassa, the African,* ed. Vincent Carretta, 2d ed. (New York: Penguin, 2003), p. 59.

participation in the slave trade began to transform African social, economic, and military institutions.

The **Asante kingdom** was an expanding power in the forest region of eighteenth-century West Africa. As the ruling kings, the *Asantehenes*, pursued their ambitions for greater power through military expansion, they took many prisoners. Before the rise of the Atlantic slave trade, these war captives might be traded in prisoner exchanges, redeemed for ransom, or kept as household servants. Where war captives had once been a mere byproduct of wars fought for other purposes, now Asante (uh-SHAN-tee) generals had a new motive for military expansion: the Atlantic slave trade. British slave traders sailed to Cape Coast Castle, one of many coastal fortifications built to facilitate the slave trade, to pay with currency, rum, cloth, and guns for these unfortunate captives.

The kingdom of **Dahomey** (dah-HOH-mee) was even more proactive than Asante in using the slave trade to advance state interests. Its kings traded slaves for guns to build a military advantage over their neighbors. As the prices for slaves rose during the eighteenth century, more and more guns were imported into West Africa. Faced with aggressive neighbors like Dahomey, other African rulers found they too needed to enter the slaves-for-guns trade, out of self-defense. Keeping your own people from being enslaved could mean selling people from neighboring societies to protect your own. It was a vicious cycle.

Indigenous African slavery was transformed by the Atlantic slave trade. Before the Atlantic system developed, an African parent in difficult circumstances might "pawn" a child to someone with sufficient resources to keep him or her alive. It was a desperate move, but sometimes necessary. A child thus enslaved was not viewed as mere property of his or her master. Rather, the chances were good that the child would be incorporated into the social networks of the master's village.

In Africa, where land was usually plentiful and people were the scarce (and therefore valuable) resource, this process of incorporation sometimes took the form of "fictive kinship." Descendants of captive outsiders (such as pawned children or war captives) would come to be identified with local lineages. Though the stigma of slave origins might never be completely forgotten, their descendants would gradually become recognized as members of the community. Female slaves, who were preferred for both their productive and reproductive capabilities, helped further this process of assimilation. In patrilineal societies, where descent is traced through the father's line, children of a free man and a slave woman had rights in their father's lineage.

African practice stood in contrast to the situation in the Americas, where European masters seldom acknowledged responsibility for their own slave-borne offspring. African slave raiders profited from the complementary preference of African masters for female slaves and European plantation owners for male ones. Male slaves could be exported, while female captives were more likely to be sold within West Africa's own slave markets. In each case, the fates of their children were likely to be quite different. In Africa the women's offspring would often be assimilated into the host community; in the Americas assimilation into European society was hardly an option.

As an antislavery activist, Equiano perhaps had an interest in downplaying the negative aspects of indigenous slavery. But he addresses the issue of slavery in Africa in a forthright way, whether the account is based on his own childhood memories or on accounts he had heard from other slaves:

Asante kingdom
(ca. 1700–1896) A rising state in eighteenth-century West Africa in the rainforest region of what is now Ghana. Asante's wars of expansion produced prisoners who were often sold into the Atlantic slave circuit.

Dahomey
(ca. 1650–1894) African kingdom in present-day southern Benin, reaching its height of influence in the eighteenth century. Its leaders sought regional power by raiding for slaves in other kingdoms and selling them for firearms and European goods.

Armed Dahomey Female Warriors Dahomey was a rising West African power in the eighteenth century, infamous for its militarism and systematic use of the slave trade to secure the weapons needed to expand its power. Dahomey was also known for its battalion of fierce and well-trained women soldiers, called *Mino* ("our mothers") in the Fon language, and "Amazons" by Europeans. The *Mino* were accorded high status. Led by female officers, they took on some of the social attributes of men, and were not allowed to marry or bear children during their term of service. (Private Collection/The Stapleton Collection/The Bridgeman Art Library)

Each master of a family has a large square of ground. . . . Within this are his houses to accommodate his family and slaves; which, if numerous, frequently cause these tenements to present the appearance of a village. In the middle stands the principal building, appropriated to the sole use of the master. . . . On each side are the apartments of his wives. . . . The habituations of the slaves and the rest of his family are distributed throughout the rest of the enclosure.

---

*Olaudah Equiano, *The Interesting Narrative of the Life of Olaudah Equiano, or Gustavus Vassa, the African,* ed. Vincent Carretta, 2d ed. (New York: Penguin, 2003), p. 36.

In such a village, where there was so little physical distance between master and slave, where conditions of housing and diet were relatively equal, and where the ability to exploit the labor of slaves carried with it a responsibility to protect them, there was little chance that the type of chattel slavery characteristic of the American plantation could ever develop. But the transformation of West African systems of slavery under the impact of the Atlantic trade is suggested by a passage from the *Interesting Narrative* where Equiano, being taken to the coast, is purchased by an African master. Equiano first sketches the traditional practice of incorporating outsiders:

> *A wealthy widow . . . saw me; and having taken a fancy to me, I was bought off the merchant, and went home with them. Her house and premises . . . were the finest I ever saw in Africa: they were very extensive, and she had a number of slaves to attend her. The next day I was washed and perfumed, and when mealtime came, I was led into the presence of my mistress, and ate and drank before her with her son. That filled me with astonishment; and I could scarcely avoid expressing my surprise that the young gentleman should suffer me, who was bound, to eat with him who was free. . . . Indeed everything here, and their treatment of me, made me forget that I was a slave. The language of these people resembled ours so nearly, that we understood each other perfectly. They had also the very same customs as we. . . . In this resemblance to my former happy state, I passed about two months; and now I began to think I was to be adopted into the family. . . .*[*]

As in times past, his new mistress could have kept the young man, and by marriage he and his descendants would likely have become integrated into that society. However, by this time traditional systems had been transformed under the influence of the Atlantic trade. His new mistress now had the option of selling him for cash; in Equiano's account she sold him back into the slave export channel that led to the coast.

In such ways, on scales large and small, the Atlantic market transformed traditional institutions. Warfare increased, and the climate of insecurity often led to more centralized political structures. African merchants and political leaders who traded in slaves gained power and status. By the later eighteenth century, as more African states came to rely on slaves not just as commodities for export but also to play essential domestic roles as soldiers and laborers, some African "societies with slaves" started to become "slave societies." This transformation of slavery under the influence of the Atlantic trade meant that there were now kingdoms in Africa itself wherein conditions of servitude became essential to the functioning of state and society. While the power of a few Africans was enhanced, by far the biggest political and economic advantages went to European slave traders and plantation owners.

Some historians have warned that we should not exaggerate the impact of the Atlantic slave trade on continental Africa. It is true that many African societies had no connection with external slave markets and that others were part of Muslim

---

[*]Olaudah Equiano, *The Interesting Narrative of the Life of Olaudah Equiano, or Gustavus Vassa, the African,* ed. Vincent Carretta, 2d ed. (New York: Penguin, 2003), pp. 52–53.

commercial networks that included slave markets of long standing. Despite the slave trade, farming and herding remained the principal economic activities in Africa. But it is hard not to conclude that the Atlantic slave trade had sharply negative effects, not only for those taken captive and shipped to the Americas but also for the continent they were forced to leave behind. In a continent where land was plentiful but people were scarce, the loss of population through the export of slaves harmed economic growth. Europe and Asia experienced surges in population during the eighteenth century, due in large part to the introduction of productive new food crops from the Americas. While such crops were introduced in Africa as well, the total population of the African continent nevertheless remained stagnant, strongly suggesting that the large-scale export of slaves had a deeply damaging effect on Africa's overall economic productivity.

Europe and the Atlantic World, 1650–1807

By the eighteenth century the Atlantic Ocean was a dense network for the exchange of people, goods, plants, animals, diseases, religious and political ideas, and cultural forms such as music and storytelling traditions, all circulating freely among Europe, Africa, and the Americas. Meanwhile, Britain and France—now surpassing the Spanish, Portuguese, and Dutch as the world's dominant naval powers—were locked in nearly constant conflict. In spite of great profits from sugar plantations and other commercial enterprises, war costs strained both countries. Mercantilist policies, intended to generate the funds to fight these wars (see Chapter 17), created incentives for smuggling by respectable New England merchants as well as less reputable pirates of the Caribbean. As a result, the Atlantic world emerged as a transcultural zone where enterprising adventurers, sometimes even former slaves like Olaudah Equiano, sought their fortunes.

Economic and Military Competition in the Atlantic Ocean, 1650–1763

The economic exchange among Europe, Africa, and the Americas is often called the **triangular trade**, which refers to the movement of manufactured goods from Europe to Africa, of African humanity to the Americas, and of colonial products, such as sugar, tobacco, and timber, back to Europe.

triangular trade
The network of interchange among Europe, Africa, and the colonial Americas. Consisted of raw materials and agricultural produce sent from the Americas to Europe; manufactures sent to Africa and used for the purchase of slaves; and slaves exported from Africa to the Americas.

The image of triangular trade is convenient, but it simplifies the realities of world trade in this period. For example, Indian Ocean trade networks connected to Atlantic networks whenever they brought cotton textiles from India to West African consumers (see Map 19.2). Paid for in American silver, Indian textiles were then exported to Africa, Europe, and the Americas. During this era, European traders imported huge quantities of cowrie shells, harvested from the Indian Ocean, into West Africa, where they were used as currency. Global trade links were not simply triangular but interoceanic; the Atlantic system was part of an emerging global economy.

European mercantilist policies that sought to monopolize colonial markets in both the Indian and Atlantic Oceans resulted in political and military conflict. While the Portuguese, Spanish, and Dutch still profited from their American and Asian possessions, none of them could compete with the growing military strength of France and England. The War of Jenkins's Ear (1739–1742) was symptomatic of Spain's slow decline (see Chapter 17). The Spanish, after asserting that only their own ships could trade among their own American colonies, caught the English captain Robert Jenkins smuggling goods to and from their territory. When he got

From 1518 to 1850 approximately 11,000,000 slaves were shipped from Africa to the Western Hemisphere; of these about 500,000, or 5 percent, were imported into areas now part of the United States.

Main sources of African slaves

Main slave-trade routes from Africa

Main areas of slave importation in the Western Hemisphere

MAP 19.2 The Atlantic Slave Trade The Middle Passage from Africa to the Americas was the greatest forced migration in human history. The vast majority of the Africans who lived through it were put to work on Caribbean islands or coastal plantations. The Arab trade in African slaves, across the Sahara Desert and the Indian Ocean, was much older, but at no time matched the scale of the Atlantic trade. (© Cengage Learning)

back to Britain, Jenkins claimed the Spaniards had tortured him and cut off his ear, and he held it up in Parliament demanding revenge.

The outbreak of the War of Jenkins's Ear between the British and the Spanish in the Caribbean paralleled competition and conflict in Europe. The great powers—Britain, France, Prussia, Russia, and Austria—were still jockeying for position (see Chapter 18). When the Prussian army invaded Austrian territory, the resulting War of the Austrian Succession (1740–1748) soon involved all the major European powers. France allied with Prussia, and Britain with Austria. While the British dominated the French in naval battles, the French were dominant on the continent, producing a stalemate in Europe with no immediate effect on possessions in the Americas, though the conflict did focus British and French attention on the economic and strategic value of their American colonies, especially the sugar islands. In this age of mercantilism, economic competition was a zero-sum game where one nation could only benefit at the expense of another, a commercial equivalent to warfare. (See the feature "Movement of Ideas Through Primary Sources: Sugar in British Politics.")

With such economic competition fueling political and military tensions, the French and British were soon back at war. Skirmishes that began in the Ohio River Valley in North America led to the outbreak of the **Seven Years' War** (1756–1763). Fought simultaneously in Europe, the West Indies, India, and North America (in the

Seven Years' War (1756–1763) Fought simultaneously in Europe, the West Indies, North America, and South Asia, this war shifted the balance of power between Britain and France in favor of the British, making their influence paramount in India and Canada.

British colonies it was known as the "French and Indian War"), this tri-continental conflict may be thought of as the first "world war." Victories over France secured British predominance in India and in Canada, where, while still the property of a Royal Navy officer, Olaudah Equiano saw action as a combatant at the British siege of Louisbourg in 1758:

> *The engagement now commenced with great fury on both sides: [the French ship] immediately returned our fire and we continued engaged with each other for some time; during which I was frequently stunned with the thundering of the great guns, whose dreadful contents burned many of my companions into eternity.*[*]

The British victory in this engagement at the gateway to the St. Lawrence River soon led to the conquest of Québec and New France and positioned the British for eventual mastery over India (see Chapter 20).

Like the Spanish and French, the British pursued mercantilist policies that were never entirely effective in controlling trade in North America and the Caribbean. For example, the sugar and molasses produced on islands in the British West Indies were supposed to be sent directly to England. However, New England merchants defied such strictures and traded directly with the Caribbean, exchanging North American products such as timber, cattle, horses, and foodstuffs for sugar. They then refined the sugar into molasses or rum to trade directly for slaves on the West African coast, contrary to mercantilist regulations.

Although American merchants found ways to evade mercantilist restrictions on trade, they deeply resented them. The anger of colonial traders was strongest in commercial cities such as Boston, Philadelphia, and New York. The Seven Years' War added to the tensions between the British crown and its American colonies. Having spent a huge sum to defend the American colonies from France, the British thought it fair that Americans help pay for their own protection. But new taxes and restrictions on trade soon prompted colonists to rally to the slogan "no taxation without representation." The Boston Tea Party (1773), during which merchants dressed as Amerindians threw bricks of tea into Boston Harbor, arose from resentment at the monopoly on tea imports granted to the British East India Company (see Chapters 20 and 22).

The eighteenth-century Atlantic was therefore the scene of increasing tensions between European powers and colonial societies, and frustrated merchants were not the only source of trouble. Rimming the Atlantic, and manning the ships that transported goods and people around it, was a multitude of uprooted people whose story should also be told.

Life on the Eighteenth-Century Atlantic Ocean

Olaudah Equiano, who spent almost half his life aboard ship, was familiar with the turbulent mass of humanity that made its living from the sea: slave traders, cod fishermen, pirates, and officers and crew fighting for king and country. Violence was common. Press gangs stalked the English coast looking for a chance to seize the able-bodied and force them onto British

---

[*]Olaudah Equiano, *The Interesting Narrative of the Life of Olaudah Equiano, or Gustavus Vassa, the African,* ed. Vincent Carretta, 2d ed. (New York: Penguin, 2003), p. 83.

Sugar in British Politics

In the mid-eighteenth century West Indian sugar was the most profitable resource in the British empire, with small islands like Jamaica and Barbados generating huge revenues. Plantation owners were not the only beneficiaries, as we see in this *Letter to a Member of Parliament* from 1745. The question had to do with how much the British government should tax sugar at the point of its arrival in England, that is, how high the "duty" should be. The huge profits that the sugar industry generated made a tempting target for a government trying to raise revenue to fight its increasingly expensive wars with France. The letter was published anonymously, meaning that the publisher was most likely trying to influence public opinion against a rise in the sugar tax, which the author warns would do more harm than good. His argument shows how closely sugar had become tied up with British economic, political, and military policies by the mid-eighteenth century.

Source: A Letter to a Member of Parliament, Concerning the Importance of our Sugar-Colonies to Great Britain, by a Gentleman, who resided many Years in the Island of Jamaica (London: J. Taylor, 1745). Spelling modernized.

From *A Letter to a Member of Parliament, Concerning the Importance of our Sugar-Colonies*

In the first place, I will endeavor to convince you, that whatever additional duty shall be laid on sugar, it will be at the cost of the sugar planter. . . .

Secondly, I shall show, that such an additional duty will be an oppression and discouragement and an unequal load upon our sugar colonies at this juncture especially, and will render abortive the very scheme itself which is intended by it, of advancing the revenue. And,

Thirdly, I shall set forth the great advantages that this nation receives from the sugar colonies, and especially from the island of Jamaica, and the great advantages that it will continue to receive, if due encouragement be given to the sugar planter. . . .

Now the case of the sugar planter is, that he is at a prodigious distance from the market . . . and being already in debt, as the greatest number of the sugar planters are, and having already established his sugar works . . . he must be ruined if those are not kept employed. . . .

We have no foreign market worth notice, but Holland and Hamburg, and . . . the Dutch will buy the French sugar, at the French colonies at a low price, and carry it securely to Holland in their own ships. And it is well known that the French at their colonies can and do sell their sugar much cheaper than we can in our colonies, because they have better sugar land in their islands, and nearer the seaside than we have. . . .

[T]he sugar planter is [now] at a vast deal greater expense to make sugar. . . . His Negro slaves . . . were sold at Jamaica at £35 per head [but now cost] £50 per head. . . . The sugar planter pays double the freight for his sugar home than he did before . . . and double the freight out for all his utensils for making sugar, and all his furniture for his house use and family, and slaves. . . .

[U]nless the price of sugar here at market do advance very considerably, the sugar planter can't go on, but will be ruined. If the planter, to all his other advanced charges, hath a further duty laid upon his commodity, he will be disabled from purchasing every year a fresh supply of Negroes, mules, and cattle; and as his present stock drops off, he will disabled from making the quantity of sugar he does at present . . . by which means the scheme for raising more money upon that commodity, by advancing the duty, will be rendered abortive. . . .

The principal charge which the sugar planter is at, to raise and carry on his work, is Negroes; and those are purchased in Africa by the English merchants, chiefly with the produce and manufactures of this nation, such as woolen goods. . . . At the same time that they are purchasing the Negroes on the coast of Africa, with those cargoes of British manufactures, they purchase also a great deal of gold, elephants' teeth, and some very valuable dying woods. . . .

For strength to carry on his sugar work, next to the negroes, the planter must be furnished with mules, cattle, horses, etc. Of cattle the most part are raised in the colonies; some horses are raised in the colonies and some are supplied from North America. . . . [His equipment] . . . will cost him at least 500 pounds. Add to this, the great quantity of nails, locks, hinges, bolts, and other sorts of iron ware; and lead that he must have for his buildings. And for his field work he must have great quantities of bills, hoes, axes, iron chains; also gear for his mill and his cattle . . . and all this of English manufacture. . . .

Besides this extraordinary expense . . . he must have a house to live in, and furniture, and clothes, and other necessaries for himself and family, servants and slaves. To build his house he must have materials from England . . . and his furniture and clothing entirely from England. . . .

And for their food, they have a great deal, as cheese, bacon, pickles, some flour and biscuits, when cheap, and beer, ale and cider, in great quantities from England; salted beef and butter from Ireland; and salted fish, flour, biscuits and sundry other kinds of provisions for their negroes from North America.

There are in the island of Jamaica only, a hundred thousand negros, a few more or less; every one of these . . . do make use of the value of twenty shillings a year, in goods from England. In clothing they make use of a vast quantity of Manchester goods . . . and many other implements, all of British manufacture. I believe . . . it amounts to a hundred thousand pounds a year in British manufactures, consumed by the negros in Jamaica only.

And now, Sir, if you'll be pleased to take a view of the whole process of the sugar manufacture, from the beginning to the time of delivering the commodity into the hands of the consumer; that is to say, from purchasing the negroes on the coast of Africa, and transporting them to the West Indies . . . I am sure that you will be amazed to consider, what a prodigious number of ships, of sailors, of merchants, of tradesmen, manufacturers, mechanics, and laborers, are continually employed, and reap a profit thereby. . . .

And should the sugar colonies be so much discouraged, by the laying on of an additional duty . . . you see plainly how very much our trade and navigation, and how many of our manufactures would be affected by it, and that would not be the worst of it [because] in proportion as our sugar colonies should decline, those of our neighbors, our enemies and rivals in trade and navigation would advance.

QUESTIONS FOR ANALYSIS

» *What are the main arguments the author provides against an increase in the sugar duty?*

» *How does this document inform us about the relationship of colonies to the political, military, and economic affairs of British society at the time?*

ships chronically short of sailors, a situation that Equiano and many others saw as akin to slavery. English peasants, driven from the countryside by land enclosures that favored the landed gentry, often ended up as sailors, as did Irishmen forced off their lands by English settlement. If some were forced aboard ship, the sea was also often a voluntary refuge for the desperate.

Life aboard ship was rough, nearly as much like a prison for the sailors above as for the slaves who might be in the hold below. Sailors had no privacy and were closely controlled. Captains had to be alert to any signs of indiscipline or they might lose command of their crews. Sometimes disgruntled sailors felt they had nothing more to lose and risked their lives in mutiny. The great lexicographer Samuel Johnson commented: *"A ship is worse than a jail. There is, in a jail, better air, better company, better convenience of every kind; and a ship has the additional disadvantage of being in danger."*

Johnson went on to say that once men became accustomed to life at sea they no longer could adjust to any other. That seemed to fit Equiano, who *"being still of a roving disposition"* after he gained his liberty, never stayed for more than a few years on dry land. Contrary to Johnson's grim view, however, life at sea offered opportunity for an ambitious soul from a poor background. Military prowess, acumen in trade, seamanship—all required competence. Life at sea rewarded ability, in contrast to most of British life, where ancestry and social class held sway. Even as a young slave, Equiano was able to earn a promotion to the rank of "able seaman" for his service during the Seven Years' War. He equated that promotion with status as a freeman, and it made him eligible for a payment from the crown at war's end. He was bitterly disappointed when his owner, who was also his commanding officer, not only pocketed his pension but also sold him to a new master. Still, life at sea gave Equiano his greatest opportunities.

It was also at this time that Captain James Cook (1728–1779) was rising to prominence in the British Navy. The son of a farmer, Cook rose through the ranks on the basis of his leadership abilities and navigational expertise to become one of the most famous men in the British empire (see Chapter 21).

The Atlantic Ocean also represented opportunities for fishermen. Enormous hauls of cod were pulled from the **Grand Banks**, off the coast of Newfoundland. Basque fisherman had first discovered this area in medieval times, and salted cod became a staple of the Mediterranean diet. By the eighteenth century, ships from Britain, Spain, France, Iceland, Portugal, and Massachusetts were exploiting this rich source of protein, which once cured was easily stored and transported.

In New England, the codfish became a symbol of prosperity. In the early eighteenth century the Boston Town Hall had a gilded cod hanging from its ceiling. The fishing communities of the North Atlantic provided an alternative to the slave-based plantation model that was dominant to the south:

Grand Banks
Fishing area located south and southeast of present-day Newfoundland, Canada. Noted for its immense quantities of cod, a source of protein for the residents in and around the Atlantic and of large profits for British colonial traders.

New Englanders were becoming a commercial people, independent and prosperous and resentful of monopolies. While the West Indies sugar planters were thriving on their protected markets, New Englanders were growing rich on free-trade capitalism. . . . Even the fishermen were independent entrepreneurs, working not on salary but, as they still do in much of the world, for a share of the catch.[*]

---

[*]Mark Kurlansky, *Cod: A Biography of the Fish That Changed the World* (New York: Penguin, 1997), p. 75.

Some participants in the Boston Tea Party were involved in trading salt cod to the West Indies for molasses to be refined and sold in Africa for slaves. Thus, while cod fishing might instill an independent spirit in New England, it also provided plantation owners with a cheap way to feed captives in the West Indies. In the Atlantic world, slavery and freedom were two sides of the same coin.

Abolition of the British Slave Trade, 1772–1807

In 1775, now a free man, Olaudah Equiano took a job working as a plantation supervisor on the Central American coast. Equiano did not seem to mind, and when the job was over he even congratulated himself on a job well done: *"All my poor countrymen, the slaves, when they heard of my leaving them were very sorry, as I had always treated them with care and affection, and did everything I could to comfort the poor creatures."* In this passage from the *Interesting Narrative* Equiano seems to imply that slavery could be made humane.

Over the next decade, however, Equiano came to believe that slavery was inherently evil and needed to be abolished. His change in thinking was partly an outcome of deepening religious conviction. After surviving a shipwreck, Equiano joined the Methodist movement, whose founder had argued that slavery was incompatible with Christian morality. In that vein, Equiano wrote, *"O, ye nominal Christians! Might not an African ask you, 'learned you this from your God, who says unto you, Do unto all men as you would men should do unto you.'"* In his increasing consciousness of the incompatibility of Christianity and slavery, Equiano was a man of his times. Throughout the 1780s more and more British Christians raised their voices in opposition to slavery. Though the slave owners and slave traders formed a powerful lobby in the British Parliament, public opinion was turning against them. (See the feature "Visual Evidence in Primary Sources: The Horrors of the Middle Passage.")

Apart from Christian conscience, other factors aided the antislavery **abolitionist** cause. In 1772 a judge had ruled that no slave, once he or she reached England, could be compelled to return to a colony where slavery was practiced. Essentially, this meant that the condition of slavery had no legal basis in British law. National pride was a stimulus to abolitionism. Britons were proud of their tradition of "liberty," constitutionally guaranteed by the Bill of Rights of 1689. But the British constitution was also based on the protection of rights of property. Which rights were paramount: those of slaves to their own liberty, or those of slave owners to the use and disposition of their property?

One strategy of the British abolitionists was to show the link between British sugar consumption, by far the highest in the world, and the evils of slavery. In his poem "Poor Africans," William Cowper wrote:

> *I pity them greatly, but I must be mum,*
> *For how could we do without sugar and rum?*
> *Especially sugar, so needful we see,*
> *What, give up our desserts, our coffee and tea?*

abolitionist
A man or woman who advocated an end to the practice of slavery. In the late eighteenth century a powerful abolitionist movement grew in England.

---

*Olaudah Equiano, *The Interesting Narrative of the Life of Olaudah Equiano, or Gustavus Vassa, the African,* ed. Vincent Carretta, 2d ed. (New York: Penguin, 2003), pp. 211, 61.

The Horrors of the Middle Passage

British abolitionists were well aware of the power of visual images to advance their cause, anticipating that a shocked public would pressure Parliament to end the trade in slaves. Political cartoons were one way to both express and influence public opinion. The cartoon below refers to the case of a slave trader, Captain John Kimber, who was accused in 1792 of torturing a fifteen-year-old African girl to death when she refused to "dance" for him. ("Dancing" was a required physical activity for slaves when

The ABOLITION of the SLAVE TRADE.
Or the Inhumanity of Dealers in human flesh exemplified in Capt. Kimbers treatment of a young Negro Girl of 15 for her Virgin Modesty

Captain Kimber is clearly depicted as being responsible for the abuse of the African girl. He seems to be enjoying himself.

For his portrayal of the victim the artist chose to use dark ink, obscuring her features. What effect does this technique have on the viewer?

The sailor pulling the rope says: "Damn me if I like it I have a good mind to let go." The other two sailors say: "My Eyes Jack our Girls at Wapping are never flogged for their modesty," and "By G-d that's too bad if he had taken her to bed to him it would be well enough. Split me, I'm almost sick of this Black Business."

QUESTION FOR ANALYSIS

» *Of these two images, which gave the more powerful indictment of the slave trade?*

they were brought up to the ship's deck for exercise; slave captains routinely enforced that rule with the lash.) Kimber was acquitted, and the sailors who gave evidence against him were convicted of perjury. Abolitionists were outraged and their opponents encouraged by this legal ruling. The title of the illustration reads: "The Abolition of the Slave Trade, or the inhumanity of the dealers in human flesh exemplified in Captn Kimbers treatment of a Young Negro Girl of 15 for her virgin modesty."

The image below, the slave ship *Brooks*, was widely circulated by abolitionists to show (in the words of a modern historian) "that the slaver itself was a place of barbarity, indeed a huge, complex technologically sophisticated instrument of torture."* First circulated by the Society for Effecting

the Abolition of the Slave Trade in 1788, this engraving was widely known across Britain and the United States. Its depiction of a "close packed" slave ship made "an instantaneous impression of horror upon all who saw it," according to Thomas Clarkson, a prominent abolitionist who wrote the text that accompanied this image. Clarkson interviewed British sailors in slave ports like Bristol and Liverpool, who told him bloodcurdling stories of inhumanity on ships like the *Brooks*, where, another abolitionist wrote, "human creatures [were] reduced nearly to the state of being buried alive." The *Brooks* made ten voyages to Africa between 1781 and 1804, its captains purchasing 5,163 slaves, of whom 4,559 survived the Atlantic crossing. This image of the *Brooks* undoubtedly contributed to the abolition of the British slave trade in 1807.

*Marcus Rediker, *The Slave Ship: A Human History* (New York: Viking, 2007), p. 309.

Each adult African man aboard the *Brooks* was allocated a plank 6 feet by 16 inches with no more than 2 feet 6 inches of vertical space, too little to allow him to sit up. Not shown are the tubs of excrement that fouled the air in the slave hold.

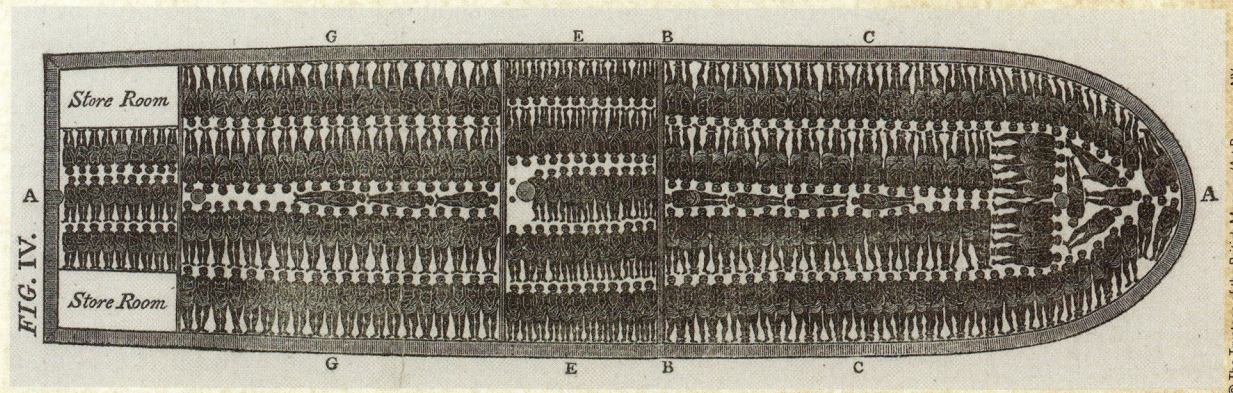

The artist who produced this engraving carefully drew every individual African on board, showing each wearing only a loincloth. Shown here are 482 slaves. On an earlier voyage, before a 1788 law that regulated the slave trade, one *Brooks* captain had crammed 609 Africans in this same space: 351 men, 127 women, 90 boys, and 41 girls.

Abolitionist boycotts helped win the debate at the breakfast table, as more Britons came to see slavery not as something distant and abstract, but as an evil in which they personally participated by consuming slave-grown sugar.

Equiano intended his *Interesting Narrative* to be part of the accelerating abolitionist campaign. Like many authors at this time, he advertised for subscribers who would pay in advance and receive their copies once the book was written and printed. Subscriptions were a way for propertied men and women to support causes they believed in. The subscribers to Equiano's book included major antislavery campaigners such as Thomas Clarkson and Josiah Wedgwood. As a university student, Clarkson had been assigned the topic: "Is enslaving others against their will ever justified?" Clarkson decided the answer was "no" and devoted himself to the abolitionist cause. Wedgwood, the highly successful ceramics entrepreneur, made his antislavery position widely known when he designed a best-selling plate featuring the image of an African in chains saying "Am I Not a Man and a Brother?" Even William Wilberforce, the member of Parliament who took the abolitionist cause to the House of Commons, was among Equiano's subscribers.

After the publication of the *Interesting Narrative* in 1789, Equiano spent three years touring England, Scotland, and Ireland speaking at antislavery meetings. He was hugely successful in advancing the cause of abolitionism while doing well for himself financially. Book royalties made him the wealthiest black man in England, and his property was moderately increased by the family income of the English wife he married in 1792. Proud of his new status as a married man, he announced the marriage in the new edition of his *Interesting Narrative*.

As he began an English family, Equiano remained politically active. Wilberforce had decided to press only for the abolition of the slave trade, not of the condition of slavery itself. This more limited agenda had a better chance in Parliament. Many members thought it was permissible to stop slaves from being seized and transported but did not think it proper for the state to interfere in existing property relations, even when the property consisted of human beings. Despite this more limited agenda, the abolition of the slave trade took much longer than its proponents had hoped. Equiano was still waiting when he passed away prematurely at the age fifty-two (leaving behind his wife Susanna and daughter Joanna, who inherited his substantial estate). The delay came from the conservative British reaction to the excesses of the French Revolution, whose leaders so loudly proclaimed the cause of liberty (see Chapter 22).

The British abolitionist cause, while largely religiously inspired, had been stimulated by eighteenth-century Enlightenment philosophies stressing rational thought and the quest for human liberty (see Chapter 21). The Scottish free-market economist Adam Smith, for example, had argued that slavery, by preventing the negotiation of free labor contracts, distorted economies and undermined growth. And it was French thinkers who were most influential in developing the concept of "liberty, equality, and fraternity" as a universally applicable ideal. The radicalism of the French Revolution, however, led the British government to look on political reform with deep suspicion. Equiano even removed the names of some of his more radical subscribers from the *Interesting Narrative* to avoid guilt by association.

It was not until 1807 that Parliament finally passed the **Act for the Abolition of the Slave Trade**, ending the trade in slaves among British subjects. Another whole generation of Africans had to wait before slavery itself was abolished in the British empire, an advance that did not help slaves in non-British territories such as Cuba, Brazil, and the southern United States. Meanwhile, the British government, with the full backing of public opinion, pursued a global campaign to eliminate slave markets. That was a significant turnabout, considering that Britain had perhaps benefited more than any other nation from four centuries of the Atlantic slave trade.

> **Act for the Abolition of the Slave Trade**
> Law passed in 1807 by the British Parliament ending the trade in slaves among British subjects. The British government then used the Royal Navy to suppress the slave trade internationally.

CONTEXT AND CONNECTIONS

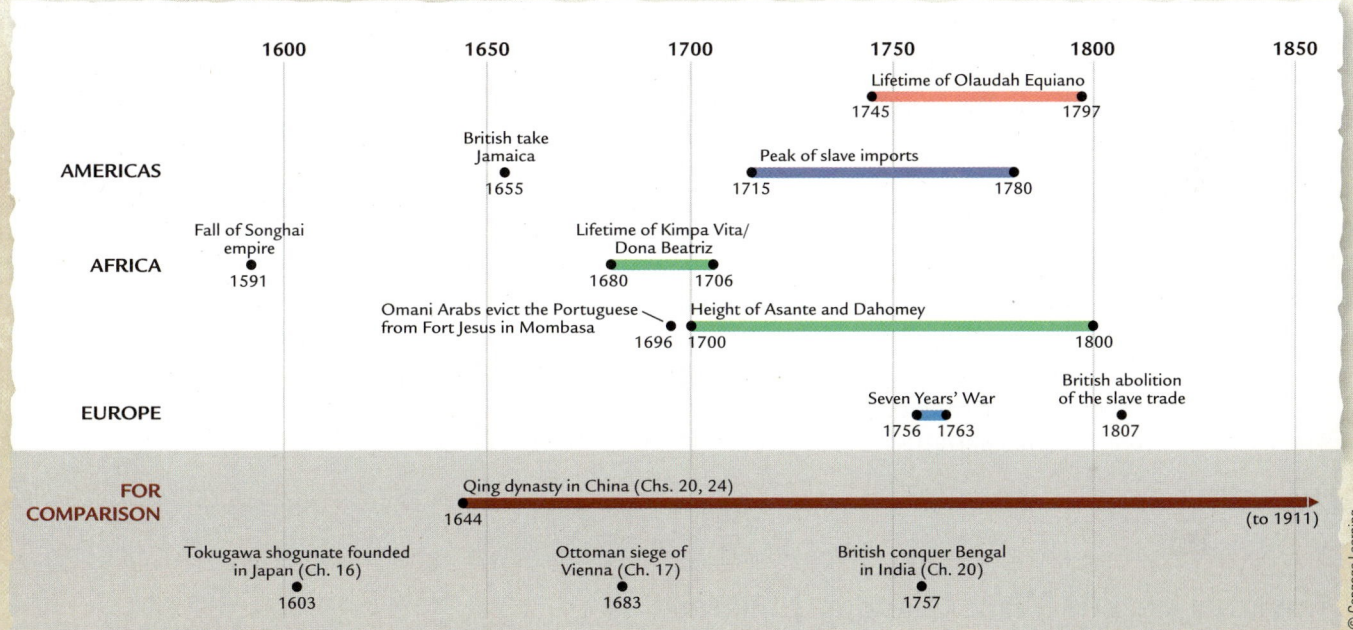

Atlantic Slavery and the Plantation Complex in World History

The use of massed slave labor on agricultural plantations was part of world history from ancient times until the late nineteenth century, from the Roman empire through the final abolition of slavery in Brazil in 1888. Still, the type of slavery Olaudah Equiano experienced, witnessed, and fought against was exceptional in scale: the largest, most intensive, and most profitable plantation slave system ever.

Not all societies treated slaves simply as brute labor. In the Ottoman empire, slaves could rise to positions of significant power even as they suffered constraints on their freedom of movement or

endeavor (see Chapter 17). In Africa, as Equiano described it, slaves were often incorporated into the communities of which they became a part, and they tended to lose their disabilities over time. Such "societies with slaves" were quite different from the "slave societies" that had long been associated with sugar.

Sugar plantations had relied on massed slave labor even before the rise of the Atlantic slave trade. From ninth-century Arab origins, the plantation complex moved westward into the Mediterranean, fed by slave-trading circuits that extended south into Africa and east toward the Black Sea. (In fact, the word *slaves* is derived from *Slavs*, the name of the eastern European people traded into the Mediterranean.) The Portuguese then transferred the sugar plantation system to islands offshore of western Africa, across the Atlantic to Brazil, and then into what became the world's most intensive center of production, the West Indies (see Chapter 16).

It was ironic that Europeans were the ones who created the harsher forms of modern slavery associated with brutal plantation work in the Americas. Slavery had virtually disappeared from western Europe itself, while the upsurge in Christian religious conviction following the Reformation (see Chapter 17) was making it more difficult to reconcile faith with slavery. And it was during the height of the Atlantic slave trade, in the eighteenth century, when Enlightenment ideas of rationality, freedom, and liberty were being developed (see Chapter 21).

Of course, the vast profits to be made by cheaply producing commodities like sugar provided individuals and nations with powerful motives for involvement in the plantation system. From the seventeenth century on, increasingly sophisticated financial mechanisms and maritime technologies had made possible the concentration of resources and the development of global markets necessary for such large-scale agro-industrial business operations. At the same time, competition between European states, especially France and Britain, made sustaining plantation profits a matter of great national interest (see Chapter 17).

Then, in the late eighteenth century, the beginnings of the Industrial Revolution, the independence of the United States, and a shift in British priorities toward India all lessened the importance of West Indian sugar (see Chapters 20, 22, and 23). The British, after ending the slave trade in 1807 and outlawing slavery within the British empire in 1834, became global abolitionist campaigners. In some parts of the world, slavery continued into the twentieth century, but the plantation complex was at an end. Brazilian and Caribbean industries declined and new centers of sugar production, such as Hawai'i and Fiji, relied on indentured contract laborers rather than slaves.

For Africa, however, the story was not over, for those who had remained behind had suffered as well. In the short run, African life had become more dangerous and insecure, and in the long run the continent suffered from the lost vitality and productivity of millions of its sons and daughters.

VOYAGES ON THE WEB: Olaudah Equiano

The Voyages Map App follows the traveler's journeys using interactive study tools, including 360-degree panoramic views of historic sites, zoomable maps, audio summaries, flash cards, and quizzes.

KEY TERMS

Olaudah Equiano (520)
Great Lakes region (523)
Kimpa Vita (523)
Sahel (524)
Songhai empire (524)

Atlantic plantation system (527)
maroon communities (531)
manumission (532)
Asante kingdom (534)
Dahomey (534)

triangular trade (537)
Seven Years' War (538)
Grand Banks (542)
abolitionist (543)
Act for the Abolition of the Slave Trade (547)

FOR FURTHER REFERENCE

Anstey, Roger. *The Atlantic Slave Trade and British Abolition, 1760–1810.* New York: Macmillan, 1975.

Carretta, Vincent. *Equiano, the African: Biography of a Self-Made Man.* New York: Penguin Books, 2007.

Curtin, Philip. *Africa Remembered: Narratives by West Africans from the Era of the Slave Trade.* 2d ed. Long Grove, Ill.: Waveland Press, 1997.

Curtin, Philip. *The Rise and Fall of the Plantation Complex: Essays in Atlantic History.* 2d ed. New York: Cambridge University Press, 1998.

Eltis, David. *Economic Growth and the Ending of the Trans-Atlantic Slave Trade.* New York: Oxford University Press, 1987.

Equiano, Olaudah. *The Interesting Narrative of the Life of Olaudah Equiano, or Gustavus Vassa, the African.* 2d ed. Vincent Carretta, ed. New York: Penguin Putnam, 2003.

Gomez, Michael A. *Exchanging Our Country Marks: The Transformation of African Identities in the Colonial and Antebellum South.* Chapel Hill: University of North Carolina Press, 1998.

Lovejoy, Paul. *Transformations in Slavery: A History of Slavery in Africa.* 3d ed. New York: Cambridge University Press, 2011.

Mintz, Sidney. *Sweetness and Power: The Place of Sugar in Modern History.* New York: Penguin Books, 1985.

Northrup, David. *Africa's Discovery of Europe, 1450–1850.* New York: Oxford University Press, 2002.

Omari-Tunkara, Mikelle Smith. *Manipulating the Sacred: Yoruba Art, Ritual, and Resistance in Brazilian Candomblé.* Detroit: Wayne State University Press, 2006.

Patterson, Orlando. *Slavery and Social Death: A Comparative Study.* Cambridge, Mass.: Harvard University Press, 1985.

Rediker, Marcus. *The Slave Ship: A Human History.* New York: Viking, 2007.

Sparks, Randy J. *The Two Princes of Calabar: An Eighteenth-Century Atlantic Odyssey.* Cambridge, Mass.: Harvard University Press, 2004.

Thornton, John. *Africa and Africans in the Making of the Atlantic World, 1400–1800.* 2d ed. New York: Cambridge University Press, 1998.

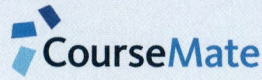 **CourseMate**

Go to the CourseMate website at **www.cengagebrain.com** for additional study tools and review materials—including audio and video clips—for this chapter.

20

Empires in Early Modern Asia, 1650–1818

The British were just consolidating their power in northeastern India in the late 1780s when a young Chinese sailor named **Xie Qinggao** (ca. 1765–1821) visited Calcutta (Kolkata), India. Xie had been born in the Guangdong province of south China, a region with a long history of commercial interaction with foreign ships. His life was transformed when, at the age of eighteen, he was involved in a shipwreck and rescued by a Portuguese vessel. His subsequent travels extended beyond coastal China, the Japanese islands, the Korean peninsula, and Southeast Asia to include the entire Indian Ocean commercial world and Europe itself. Years later, he recalled his impressions of British rule in India:

Southern Chinese Sailor in Local Attire, 1800s
(© North Wind Picture Archives)

Bengal is governed by the British. The military governor, who is named "La" ["Lord"] rules from Calcutta. There is a small walled city inside of which live officials and the military while merchants reside outside the wall in the surrounding district. . . . The buildings and towers form cloud-like clusters, the gardens and pavilions are strange and beautiful. . . . More than 10,000 English live there with fifty to sixty thousand soldiers from the local people. . . . When the top officials go out on parade it is particularly impressive. In the front are six men on horseback . . . all wearing big red robes. The two men on the left

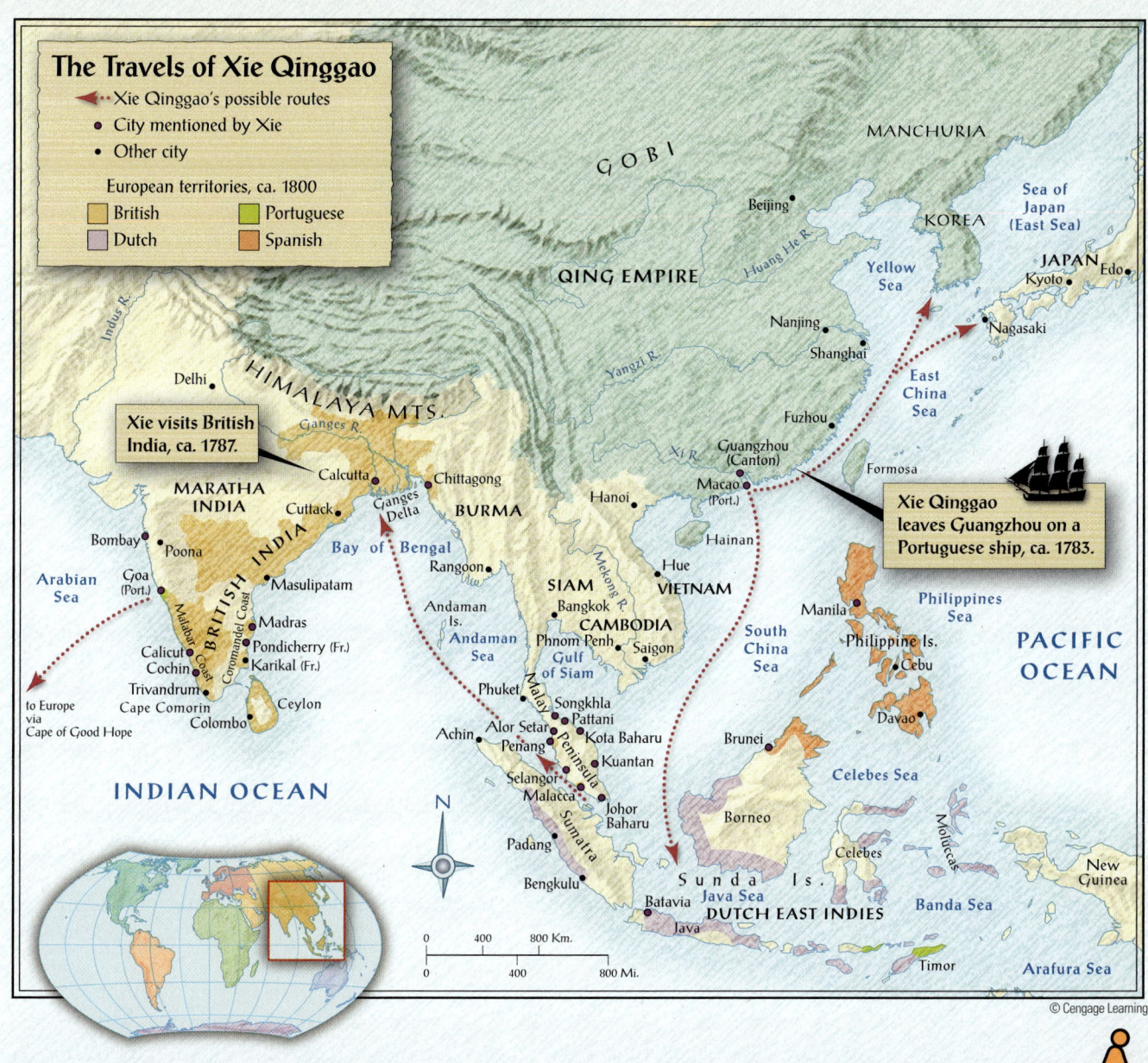

The Travels of Xie Qinggao

- ◄···· Xie Qinggao's possible routes
- • City mentioned by Xie
- • Other city

European territories, ca. 1800

- British
- Dutch
- Portuguese
- Spanish

GOBI

MANCHURIA

Beijing

KOREA

Sea of Japan (East Sea)

JAPAN

Kyoto

Edo

QING EMPIRE

Yellow Sea

Nanjing

Shanghai

Nagasaki

HIMALAYA MTS.

Ganges R.

Delhi

Fuzhou

East China Sea

Xie visits British India, ca. 1787.

MARATHA INDIA

Calcutta

Cuttack

Ganges Delta

Chittagong

BURMA

Hanoi

Yangzi R.

Xi R.

Guangzhou (Canton)

Macao (Port.)

Formosa

Xie Qinggao leaves Guangzhou on a Portuguese ship, ca. 1783.

Bombay

Poona

Masulipatam

Rangoon

SIAM

Bangkok

Hue

VIETNAM

Hainan

Arabian Sea

Goa (Port.)

Bay of Bengal

Andaman Is.

CAMBODIA

South China Sea

Manila

Philippines Sea

Madras

Pondicherry (Fr.)

Karikal (Fr.)

Andaman Sea

Phnom Penh

Saigon

Philippine Is.

Calicut

Cochin

Trivandrum

Cape Comorin

Colombo

Ceylon

Gulf of Siam

Phuket

Songkhla

Pattani

Kota Baharu

Kuantan

Cebu

Davao

to Europe via Cape of Good Hope

Achin

Alor Setar

Penang

Selangor

Malacca

Johor Baharu

Brunei

Celebes Sea

INDIAN OCEAN

Padang

Sumatra

Borneo

Moluccas

New Guinea

N

Bengkulu

Sunda Is.

Batavia

Java

Java Sea

DUTCH EAST INDIES

Celebes

Banda Sea

0   400   800 Km.

0   400   800 Mi.

Timor

Arafura Sea

PACIFIC OCEAN

Malay Peninsula

Mekong R.

© Cengage Learning

Join this chapter's traveler on "Voyages," an interactive tour of historic sites and events:
www.cengagebrain.com

and the right are dressed just like the "La," but his chest is covered with strange embroidery that looks like a fortunetelling sign. . . . The local people are of several types. The Bengalis are relatively numerous, and the Brahmin caste is particularly well off. . . . The rich among them have clothing, food and dwellings like those of the English that are beautiful and impressive. The poor are almost naked . . . taking cloth several inches wide to wrap around their waists to cover their lower halves.[*]

---

[*]Xie Qinggao, *Hailu jiaoyi,* ed. An Jing (Beijing: Shangwu yingshugan, 2002), translation courtesy of Valerie Hansen, personal communication (2009).

Xie Qinggao
(ca. 1765–1821) Sailor from southern China who traveled across the Indian Ocean and throughout Europe. After becoming blind, Xie retired from sailing and dictated his story, published as *Hai-Lu*, or *Record of Sea Journeys*.

Xie Qinggao (shee-ay ching-GOW) was living in the Portuguese settlement of Macao, working as a translator because blindness had ended his career as a sailor, when a visitor from a neighboring Chinese province, fascinated by Xie's stories of his adventurous sailor's life, decided to write them down. If not for the visitor's curiosity, Xie's story, like that of most ordinary people throughout history, would never have been documented. By 1820, when Xie recorded this story in his *Record of Sea Journeys*, the British had conquered all of South Asia.

Xie's presence in Calcutta was part of an age-old trading network that connected the South China Sea with ports in Southeast Asia, India, the Persian Gulf, and East Africa. That network existed before the arrival of Portuguese ships in the sixteenth century and continued to exist even as the Dutch, British, and French developed more aggressive and heavily armed commercial organizations (see Chapter 16). But the officials of the British East India Company described by Xie Qinggao (called "Company men") were representative of an important new phase of this history. In their conquest of Bengal the British were striking at the authority of the Mughal empire and so, for the first time, directly challenging one of the major Asian land-based empires.

Indeed, the creation and maintenance of empire were a consistent political theme in early modern South and East Asia. The Manchu emperors of the Qing (ching) dynasty, ruling not just China but also extensive Central Asian territories, controlled the greatest land-based empire of the age. As Qing armies and diplomats extended their influence to the east, they came into increasing contact with emissaries of the Russian empire, which was expanding into Central Asia from the west. Meanwhile, the British were moving to supplant the Mughals as the major power of South Asia. Taken together, the expansion of the British and Russian empires showed the increasing influence of Europe in Asian affairs. Japanese rulers, however, resisted these eighteenth-century trends, consolidating power on their own islands rather than seeking further territory, and rejecting European influence as a matter of state policy.

This chapter focuses on the expansion of empires in the late seventeenth and eighteenth centuries in East, South, and Central Asia. In the process we will see how imperial leaders had to contend with factors such as changing military technologies, commercial growth, increasing social and religious interactions, and population growth and ecological change, all of which might affect the success or failure of their policies.

Focus Questions

» *How did the Qing emperors build and maintain their empire in East and Central Asia?*

» *What factors drove Russian imperial expansion in the eighteenth century?*

» *What were the principal causes of the decline of Mughal power, and how were the British able to replace the Mughals as the dominant power in South Asia?*

» *In comparison with the Qing, Russian, and British empires, what were some unique features of early modern Japanese history?*

The Power of the Qing Dynasty, 1644–1796

By the early seventeenth century underlying weaknesses made the Ming dynasty in China vulnerable to invasion and conquest (see Chapter 16). In 1644 armies from Manchuria overran Beijing, deposed the Ming dynasty, and established the Qing dynasty. From 1683 to 1796, just three long-ruling emperors ruled Qing China, bringing remarkable political stability to the empire. It was a time of explosive population growth, economic expansion, and intellectual and artistic dynamism. It was also at this time that imperial China expanded to its greatest extent, encompassing parts of Central Asia, Tibet, and the island of Taiwan. Qing emperors ruled China until 1911.

Establishment of Qing Rule, 1636–1661

The Manchu had been nomads who lived on the steppe to the northeast of China beyond the Great Wall (see Map 20.1). By the sixteenth century, under Chinese influence, some Manchu had taken up agriculture; literacy and Confucian philosophy were influencing Manchu society as well.

Earlier Ming officials, using a time-honored strategy for maintaining peace along the borders, had bestowed favors on Manchu leaders, such as the right to wear elaborate dragon-patterned robes of silk. The Manchu in turn emulated Chinese-style governance, while maintaining their own language and nomadic traditions such as fighting on horseback and a love of hunting. In the 1590s Ming generals called on the Manchu to help resist a Japanese invasion. Unfortunately for the Ming, the previously divided Manchu armies united under a single ruler, who declared himself leader of the **Qing dynasty** and organized his fighters into eight "banners," named for the color of the flags that the different regiments carried in battle. As the Manchu army grew in strength and the Ming declined, Mongol and Chinese generals allied with the Qing (meaning "brilliant"), while maintaining their units under their own regimental banners.

In 1644, after one of China's own rebel armies stormed the capital and the last Ming emperor committed suicide, the Manchu established their power over Beijing and the north. However, Ming holdouts waged fierce battles against Qing forces in the south for four decades. The Qing used diplomacy as well as force in dealing with the resistance: adversaries who surrendered were well treated and were incorporated into the Qing military under the banner system. The Manchu, earlier regarded by the Chinese as "barbarians," were now masters of China itself.

To legitimize the new dynasty and to attract Chinese scholar-officials into the imperial bureaucracy, Qing rulers maintained Confucianism as the official state ideology. They also retained the examination system and the Chinese system of ministries, assigning one Chinese and one Manchu official to each. The Chinese scholar-officials had the requisite knowledge and experience, but the Manchu officials, thought to be more loyal, were there to supervise the work.

Even while Qing rulers made political adjustments as part of their new government, they carefully guarded their Manchu culture and identity. Intermarriage between Manchu and Han Chinese was forbidden. (The term *Han Chinese*, which derives from an early Chinese dynasty, is used to differentiate Chinese people from other ethnic groups in China.) Though fluent in Chinese, the Manchu elite continued to speak their own language and to practice their own form of Buddhism. Qing emperors spent their summers at the great palace of Chengde

Qing dynasty (1644–1911) Sometimes called the Manchu dynasty after the Manchurian origins of its rulers. The Qing (meaning "brilliant") extended their rule from Beijing as far as Mongolia and Tibet.

(chungh-deh), beyond the Great Wall, where horsemanship, hunting, and camping were reminders of nomadic life.

While the Manchu made few efforts to impose their culture on Chinese subjects, the Qing did decree that all men had to cut their hair in the Manchu style, called a *queue* (kyoo), with a shaved forehead and a single long braid in back. Chinese men reluctantly complied, saying it was either "lose your hair or lose your head."

> **Emperor Kangxi** (r. 1662–1722) One of the most powerful and long-ruling emperors in Chinese imperial history, who extended the Qing empire, expanded the economy, and cultivated an image as a Confucian scholar and sage.

The Age of Three Emperors, 1661–1796

The success of the Qing emperors in retaining their own culture while earning the cooperation and loyalty of Han Chinese subjects found expression in the social, economic, and intellectual achievements of the late seventeenth and eighteenth centuries. When **Emperor Kangxi** (r. 1662–1722) ascended the Dragon Throne in 1662, the fate of the Qing was still in doubt. However, by 1683, he had successfully suppressed Ming resistance and annexed their last redoubt, the island of Taiwan. Six decades of Kangxi's rule established the

MAP 20.1 **The Qing Empire, 1644–1783** Beginning from their homeland in the north, the Manchu rulers of the Qing dynasty not only conquered China but also built an empire stretching far into Central Asia, matching the contemporary expansion of the Russian empire. The Qing empire grew to more than twice the size of its Ming predecessor. Tibetans, Mongols, and other subject peoples were ruled indirectly through local authorities loyal to the Qing emperors. (© Cengage Learning)

The Qing Empire
- Qing homeland
- Dominant by 1644
- Dominant by 1659
- Acquired from Russia, 1689
- Dominant by 1783
- Principal tributary states
- Great Wall

Qing as masters of one of the greatest empires the world had ever known. His successors Yongzheng (r. 1723–1735) and Qianlong (r. 1736–1796) consolidated that achievement. Together, these three emperors ruled for more than 130 years.

Because the Manchu were of "barbarian" origin, it was important for Kangxi (kang-shee) to convince his Chinese subjects, especially the scholar-officials, that his rule was soundly based on Confucian principles. He studied the Confucian classics and modeled himself on the "sage rulers" of the Chinese past. At the pinnacle of the imperial bureaucracy, he oversaw tremendous economic expansion. Confucians believed that land and agriculture are the source of wealth and that a large population is a sign of prosperity. Farmers improved agricultural productivity by planting American crops like peanuts, sweet potatoes, and maize in previously marginal areas, and China's population boomed, growing from about 100 million in 1500 to about 250 million by 1750. Population growth in China was therefore another important outcome of the Columbian exchange (see Chapter 15). The cities of Beijing, Nanjing (nahn-JING), and Guangzhou (gwahng-jo) each grew to over a million residents. By Confucian standards, Qing China was prosperous indeed.

Kangxi's successor, the emperor Yongzheng, promoted an empirical form of Confucianism, encouraging scholars to gather data in minute detail from across the empire, and compiled an 800,000-page encyclopedia to guide imperial administration. By ordering a thorough census of landholdings and basing rural taxation on updated land registers, Yongzheng both increased state revenue through more efficient tax collection and spread the tax burden more equitably between commoners and gentry.

Kangxi: Emperor and Scholar The Emperor Kangxi was careful to model his image on that of China's Confucian "sage rulers" to secure the loyalty of Han Chinese scholar-officials. Kangxi was in fact a dedicated scholar with deep knowledge of the Confucian classics.

Palace Museum, Beijing

During the reign of **Qianlong** the power of Qing China reached its height. Coming to the throne as a young man, Qianlong (chee-YEN-loong) ruled for sixty years before abdicating: true to Confucian ideals of filial piety, he did not want his reign to exceed that of his grandfather, Kangxi. During these six decades the commercial economy became even more dynamic. Mainstays of production were luxury goods for export, especially silk and porcelain. Vast quantities of silver from Japan and Spanish America continued to flow into Qing China, financing public works as well as private investment. Some Chinese farmers found that tobacco, another American crop, was a profitable addition to their fields. Artisans and small-scale entrepreneurs expanded the glass-making, brewing, and coal-mining industries. Thus eighteenth-century China retained its long-established position as the largest industrial economy in the world.

Qianlong (r. 1736–1796) Qing emperor who ruled during the empire's greatest territorial expansion and prosperity. Late in his reign, corruption began to infect the state bureaucracy. Rejected an English attempt to establish diplomatic relations.

The World of Women in Qing China

Yangzi River Valley
Agriculturally productive region with the important urban center of Nanjing. The Yangzi River Delta was the site of strong industrial and commercial growth in the eighteenth century.

Cotton textile production emerged as a major commercial industry around the city of Nanjing in the lower **Yangzi River Valley**. Unlike silk, cotton cloth was inexpensive, affordable to all but the poorest Chinese consumers, and had the advantages of being comfortable, durable, and easy to clean. Traditionally, women produced textiles in China; the expansion of the cotton industry reinforced those traditions.

All Chinese women were expected to work with their hands. Wealthy women, who were not expected to make a financial contribution to the household, often produced beautiful embroideries. For rural women, tending silkworms and spinning silk thread were admired as accomplishments that had the additional virtue of providing income. A traditional adage summed up the division of labor: "Men plow, women weave."[1] Spinning and weaving cotton within the household meshed neatly with traditions, and in commercialized regions such as the Yangzi (yang-zuh) delta, these activities drove economic growth. Chinese women did not receive much benefit from this work. Upon marriage young women left their own families to join their husband's household, where they were subject to their husband's authority and often at the mercy of demanding mothers-in-law.

In fact, their role in textile production may have made women's situation worse, since more time working at home may have increased the practice of footbinding, which reshaped young girls' feet into small points. Originally bound feet were a distinction signifying wealth and leisure, but the fashion spread throughout the Han Chinese population. Young girls' feet were broken and compressed into 3-inch balls by binding the four smaller toes under the sole of the foot and forcing the big toe and heel together. With bound feet, women suffered constant pain, limited mobility, and frequent infections. However, the old practice of female infanticide did decline during this period, perhaps because the improved financial prospects of women in textile production softened the attitude that boys were a blessing while girls were a burden.

Coming from the steppes, where mobility was key, the Manchu had never bound their own daughters' feet. Indeed, the practice disgusted Qing officials. The cultural traditions of the steppes required that women be able to ride horses and perform other strenuous physical tasks. But footbinding was so well established among the Han Chinese that Qing officials did not try to abolish it.

While most Chinese women lived lives of constant toil, elite women had opportunities for education and artistic expression. Unlike the sons of elite households, who were prepared by tutors for the state examinations, girls were educated to be refined in language and behavior and to bring honor to their husbands and their household. Educated to be sensitive and cultured, these women wrote many of the greatest poems from Qing times. Often they expressed deep emotional attachment to the other women in their lives, as in these lines from Wang Duan in tribute to the aunt who had mentored her:

> *Holding my hand, you lead me to the west garden*
> *Where, I still remember, I used to read.*
> *With deep emotion I recall your kindness in educating and cultivating me.*
> *For a long time, your love fills my heart.*[*]

---

[*]Wang Duan, "Xinwei chunri fanzhao Wulin fucheng Chusheng yimu ji yong ci ti Minghu yinjian tu yuanyun," trans. Haihong Yang, "'Hoisting one's own banner': Self-inscription in lyric poetry by three women writers of late imperial China," 2010, http://ir.uiowa.edu/etd/766, p. 219.

Stapleton Collection/The Bridgeman Art Library

The Weaving of Flower'd Silks, two Women at Work.

Silk Weaving Silk weaving was a highly profitable enterprise in eighteenth-century China. Women played a central role in all stages of silk production, operating large and complex looms such as the one pictured here. The spinning of cotton thread and weaving of cotton cloth were also increasingly important at this time, and women dominated production in the cotton industry as well.

The Qing Empire and Its Borderlands

Territorial expansion, by both force and diplomacy, was one of the greatest Qing achievements. The advances of the "gunpowder revolution" (see Chapter 17) were complemented by the use of the banner system to incorporate frontier peoples into the imperial armies, extending Qing power far to the west.

During the century after the Manchu secured southern China and Taiwan, the Qing empire doubled in size. The Manchu then had to deal with the age-old Chinese problem of bringing stability to the unsettled western and northern fringes of their empire. That meant asserting their control over Mongolian nomads and Turkic-speaking Muslim peoples to their west, stationing soldiers as far away as Tibet. Meanwhile, the Russians were also extending their empire into Central Asia (as discussed later in this chapter), creating the possibility of border conflict.

As in the past, the main threat came from steppe nomads, of which the most formidable were the Zunghars, Central Asian Mongols devoted to Tibetan Buddhism. The spiritual leader of the Tibetans and of the Zunghar Mongols was the Dalai Lama (DAH-lie LAH-mah). The Manchu used both force and subterfuge against the Zunghars, sending an army to Tibet but also supporting one of the rival contenders for the title of Dalai Lama, correctly assuming that their support would win his loyalty. Tibet began paying tribute to Beijing, which weakened the Zunghars. Finally in 1757, Qianlong issued a genocide order: the Zunghar men were slaughtered (a few survived by crossing into Russian territory), the women and children enslaved, and the lands repopulated with sedentary minorities, such as the Muslims still found in today's Xinjiang (shin-jyahng) province. Qing authority now extended far beyond the Great Wall; after 1757, the Qing were never again threatened by steppe nomads. (See the feature "World History in Today's World: Ethnic and Religious Conflict in Western China.")

Elsewhere, Qing officials relied on diplomacy, much like the Ming exacted tribute from societies outside their direct control. Annual tribute missions to Beijing symbolized the fealty even of powerful leaders, such as the emperors of Korea and Vietnam, who preserved their own political autonomy through ritual recognition of the Qing as overlords. Tribute was also sent by non-Han peoples living on the margins of Chinese society in the hills, jungles, and steppes.

Though Tibet and the western Xinjiang had been brought under Qing rule, these areas were not, like Chinese provinces, administered directly by scholar-officials. Rather, local political authorities were allowed to continue under Manchu supervision as long as they ensured that taxes were paid, kept order, and maintained loyalty to the Qing. For example, the Qing appointed a Tibetan official to report on Tibetan affairs but otherwise did nothing to supplant the power and influence of Buddhist monks. Tibetan and Mongol emissaries were often received at Chengde, the Manchu summer palace, rather than in the Forbidden City in Beijing.

Unlike the Ming, the Qing were not interested in asserting cultural superiority over tributary societies. The Ming had actively assimilated linguistically and culturally foreign peoples into Han Chinese language and culture. But the Qing viewed China as just one part of a wider Manchu empire. Eighteenth-century Qing maps had Chinese labels for Chinese provinces and Manchu labels for non-Chinese areas, illustrating how Qianlong saw himself as a Chinese emperor over the core of his empire, but as a Manchu emperor when dealing with peoples to the west.

Qing Trade and Foreign Relations

Not all of the Qing empire's external relations took place within the tributary system. A growing Russian presence challenged traditional forms of diplomacy, and the British sent emissaries to Beijing. Though the Qing treated the Russians on equal terms, they were reluctant to grant diplomatic equality to other European powers.

As the Russian empire expanded eastward, Kangxi was concerned that the Russians might ally with the steppe nomads. After some skirmishes, the Russians and the Chinese agreed to the **Treaty of Nerchinsk** in 1689, according to which the Qing recognized Russian claims west of Mongolia, while the Russians agreed to disband settlements to the east. Yongzheng and Qianlong continued this policy of avoiding conflict with the Russians through treaties that fixed the boundary between the two empires. The few Jesuit priests remaining in Beijing were now joined by a handful of Russian Orthodox ones. Converts to Christianity remained very few (see Chapter 16).

While the Russians came overland, other Europeans came by sea. European trade focused on south China, especially Guangzhou (called Canton by the Europeans), which had remained loyal to the Ming in the period after the fall of Beijing. Like their late Ming predecessors, Qing emperors regarded oceanic trade with suspicion. They associated Guangzhou with "greedy" traders rather than sober

Treaty of Nerchinsk 1689 treaty between Romanov Russia and Qing China that fixed their Central Asian border.

Ethnic and Religious Conflict in Western China

The official report from China's restive western province of Xinjiang in late 2011 was that after an exchange of gunfire the police had apprehended a group of Muslim "terrorists" attempting to cross into Pakistan for "jihadist training." That account was disputed by observers, who suspected that the incident was part of a broader security crackdown on the Uighurs (WEE-gerz), the Turkic-speaking Muslims of Xinjiang.

The Uighurs are deeply concerned that Han Chinese immigration, propelled by economic growth and encouraged by the communist government, is turning them into outsiders in their own homeland. Ethnically as well as religiously distinct, the Uighurs face deep prejudice in education and employment. As in neighboring Tibet, some believe the only solution is the creation of a separate Uighur nation, or at least greater provincial autonomy. The Chinese government, as in neighboring Tibet, tolerates no discussion of independence or autonomy for Xinjiang. Instead, it has put in place tight restrictions on public assembly and Muslim religious practice.

The secretary of the Xinjiang Communist Party set the tone in 2008 when he declared that "the field of religion has become an increasingly important battlefield against enemies."* Regulations restricted Friday sermons

---

*"Wary of Islam, China Tightens a Vise of Rules," *The New York Times*, October 18, 2008.

to one half-hour, forbade private study of the Quran and of Arabic, and allowed Uighur pilgrimages to the holy sites in Arabia only under strict government control. Government employees and students in state schools are not allowed to attend mosques or to fast during the month of Ramadan as required by Islam, meaning that Uighurs must often choose between practicing their religion and participating in public life.

In the summer of 2009, mounting tensions led to bloodshed when clashes between Uighurs and Han Chinese in the provincial capital of Urumqi led to 156 deaths, thousands of injuries, and the destruction of property. Since that time the government has kept an even stronger security presence in Xinjiang, a traditionally underdeveloped region far from Beijing and from the economic dynamism of the east and south, but now the focal point of investment in the development of its rich mineral, coal, and oil resources. Moreover, Xinjiang borders several Central Asian nations, including Russia, Afghanistan, Pakistan, and India. Xinjiang's resources and strategic location mean that the government is unlikely to make concessions to Uighur demands for protection of their language, culture, religion, and economic rights or for limitations on Han Chinese immigration.

---

scholar-officials, and with adventurous sailors like Xie Qinggao (who was born and raised in this area) rather than dependable village-bound farmers. Accordingly, the Qing restricted European trade to this single port and required European traders to deal only with state-approved firms known as *cohongs*. Since cohong merchants had a monopoly on trade with Europeans, they found it easy to fix prices and amass huge profits.

The structure of the China trade frustrated the British in particular. Having little to trade for Chinese goods but silver, they saw the continued outflow of money toward Asia as a fiscal problem. As conflicts between British merchants and sailors and Chinese officials and residents of Guangzhou increased, tensions mounted. Britain, the greatest maritime commercial power of the time, rankled at its lack of open access to the vast Chinese market.

As a result, the British government, responding to complaints from trading companies, sought to establish formal diplomatic relations. In 1792 King George III

Macartney Mission
The 1792–1793 mission in which Lord Macartney was sent by King George III of England to establish permanent diplomatic relations with the Qing empire. Because he could not accept the British king as his equal, the Qianlong emperor politely refused.

sent the **Macartney Mission** to negotiate an exchange of ambassadors. Qing officials allowed Macartney to travel from Guangzhou to Beijing, but the negotiations were unsuccessful. The Qing expected this representative of a "barbarian" king to recognize the superiority of the Qianlong emperor. However, Macartney refused to perform the ritual *kowtow* of full prostration before the emperor, consenting only to drop to one knee, as he would before his own king. Macartney asked that more ports be opened to foreign trade and that restrictions on trade be removed. Qianlong's response to King George III was unequivocal: *"We have never valued ingenious articles, nor do we have the slightest need of your country's manufactures. Therefore, O King, as regards your request to send someone to remain at the capital, while it is not in harmony with the regulations of the Celestial Empire we also feel very much that it is of no advantage to your country."* Qianlong saw China as the center of the civilized world, and he insisted that the British should appear before him only if bearing tribute in recognition of his superior position.

Qianlong's attitude was understandable. The Qing controlled the largest and wealthiest empire on earth and had no need to look beyond their borders for resources. But all was not well. As in late Ming times, inefficiency and corruption were creeping into the system. As Qianlong grew old and more apt to delegate his immense authority to others, the power of eunuchs once again increased at court, their petty rivalries frustrating the efforts of Confucian scholar-officials to maintain a vigorous administration. The absence of technological improvements in farming put pressure on the food supply. As more marginal lands were cleared for cultivation, deforestation led to the silting up of rivers, and floods resulted. As the situation worsened, some Chinese peasants rebeled, dreaming of restoring the Ming dynasty while viewing the non-Chinese Manchu as illegitimate, lacking the "Mandate of Heaven" (see Chapter 16).

When Qianlong abdicated the Dragon Throne in 1796, the gravity of these internal challenges was not yet clear. Nor could he foresee how powerful the British would be in fifty years when they returned to impose their demands by force (see Chapter 24). As the nineteenth century began, Qing officials still believed that the old ways sufficed to meet current challenges. But the threat to imperial China no longer came by land; as the nineteenth century unfolded, no Great Wall could keep out the new invaders from the sea.

The Russian Empire, 1725–1800

Like the Chinese, the Russian people had long experience with steppe nomads. The Russian state had been founded as part of the dissolution of the Mongol empire, and Russian leaders viewed control of the steppes as necessary for the security of their heartland. Peter the Great had added momentum to that tradition by pushing Russia's borders further west, east, and south, making the empire a great power on two continents (see Chapter 17). Yet for all the splendor of the Romanov court, conditions for the majority of Russians, serfs living in rural villages, remained grim.

Russian Imperial Expansion, 1725–1800

In the west, Russia dominated the Baltic Sea region after Peter's army decisively defeated the Swedes in 1721. When the Polish kingdom collapsed after the

---

*J. L. Cranmer-Byng, ed., *An Embassy to China: Lord Macartney's Journal, 1793–1794* (Hamden, Conn.: Archon Books, 1963), p. 340.

1770s, Russia, along with Prussia and Austria, shared in its partition. Russian power thrust to the south as well, largely at the expense of the Ottoman empire. The great prize was the Crimean peninsula on the northern shore of the Black Sea, annexed by Russia in 1783. A major trade emporium since ancient times, the Crimea brought both strategic and economic benefits. Russia made its first inroads into the difficult mountainous terrain of the Caucasus Mountains at this time as well (see Map 20.2).

In the Caucasus, Russian penetration was not carried out by imperial forces but by mercenary soldiers called **Cossacks** (from the Turkish word *kazakh*, meaning "free man"). The Cossacks originated as fiercely independent horsemen, Slavic-speakers who had assimilated the ways of their nomadic Mongol and Turkish neighbors on the steppes. The Cossack code of honor was based on marksmanship, horsemanship, and group spirit. Russian soldiers and administrators subsequently followed fur traders and Cossacks into the Siberian frontier, taking formal control to make sure the tsars got their share.

As Russia expanded to the east across Siberia, Cossacks were at first hired by private traders who were extending the lucrative fur-trapping frontier (see Chapter 17). As in New France at the same time (see Chapter 18), the fur trade exploited the expertise and labor of indigenous Siberians, whom the Russians called the "small people of the north." These people were vulnerable to the military technology and diseases brought from the west. If a community did not deliver its quota of furs, Cossacks might attack, carrying women and children off into slavery. Though trappers and traders might profit, Russian merchants and the Russian treasury reaped the lion's share. Once the fur-bearing animals of a given area had been slaughtered to clothe the fashionable in Moscow, Paris, or Constantinople, the frontier moved on to virgin terrain. Thus the eastern frontier of the Russian empire extended to Alaska, which the Bering Expedition claimed for the tsar in 1741 (see Map 20.2).

The Russian empire also established influence over parts of Asia south of Siberia. In hopes of establishing direct trade links with India, Peter the Great maintained armed control over the steppes on Russia's borders while pursuing a diplomatic strategy on the Central Asian frontier. He ordered that young men be taught Mongolian, Turkic, and Persian languages and sent them to the many small principalities of Central Asia as diplomatic representatives. The empire maintained this approach, relying on negotiation rather than force, until later Russian leaders adopted a more militarized policy in the nineteenth century. Meanwhile, as we have seen, Russia's eastward expansion brought it into contact with the Qing frontier, where skirmishes between Russian and Manchu soldiers led to the Treaty of Nerchinsk.

Reform and Repression, 1750–1796

Much of the new imperial territory was acquired during the reign of **Catherine the Great** (r. 1762–1796), one of the dominating figures of eighteenth-century Eurasian politics. A German princess who married into the Romanov family, Catherine brought cultural and intellectual influences from western Europe to the tsarist court at St. Petersburg. Exciting new ideas were energizing reform and revolution in the West (see Chapter 22). However, while Catherine brought the latest in art, architecture, and fashion to Russia, she adamantly ruled out political reform. Instead, she consolidated ever more power to herself.

Cossacks Horsemen of the steppes who helped Russian rulers protect and extend their frontier into Central Asia and Siberia.

Catherine the Great (r. 1762–1796) German princess who married into the Romanov family and became empress of Russia. Brought western European cultural and intellectual influences to the Russian elite. Her troops crushed a major peasant uprising.

The Russian Empire

- Russia in 1533
- Added by 1598
- Added by 1721
- Added by 1796
- ✕ Fort

PACIFIC OCEAN

BRITISH NORTH AMERICA (CANADA)

✕ Novo Arkhangelsk (Sitka)
TLINGIT

ALEUTS

RUSSIAN AMERICA (ALASKA)

Border set in 1826

INUIT

INUIT

INUIT

CHUKCHI

Bering Strait

50°N

60°N

70°N

Bering Sea

KORYAKS

Kolyma R.

Petropavlovsk
ALEUTS

Kamchatka Peninsula

Zashiversk

Okhotsk
Sea of Okhotsk

Sakhalin I.

GREENLAND

ARCTIC OCEAN

100°W *120°W* *140°W* *80°N* *160°W* *180°* *160°E* *140°E* *60°W* *40°W* *20°W* *0°* *20°E* *40°E* *60°E* *80°E* *100°E* *120°E*

Iceland

70°N

Arctic Circle

Yana R.

Zhigansk

Olenek R.

Vilyuy R.

Yakutsk

YAKUTS

LAMUTS

Kara Sea

Barents Sea

S I B E R I A

Khatanga R.

EVENKI

Amur R.

MANCHURIA

SWEDEN

GREAT BRITAIN

NORWAY

FINLAND

Arkhangelsk

Obdorsk
SAMOYEDS

OSTYAKS

Ob R.

TARTARS

Verkhoturye

Surgut

Lower Tunguska R.

TUNGUSY

Yenisey R.

OSTYAKS

EVENKI

Nerchinsk ✕

Baltic Sea

St. Petersburg

Novgorod

Tula R.

Kem R.

Bratsk ✕

Krasnoyarsk ✕

Irkutsk ✕

HOLY ROMAN EMPIRE

PRUSSIA

Riga

Moscow

Smolensk

Nizhni Novgorod

Kama R.

Samara

Omsk ✕

Biysk ✕

MONGOLIA

URAL MOUNTAINS

Tobol R.

Ishim R.

Irtysh R.

Q I N G
E M P I R E

POLAND

AUSTRIA

HUNGARY

Kiev
UKRAINIANS

Dnieper R.

Saratov

COSSACKS

COSSACKS

Ural R.

Volga R.

KAZAKS

Dniester R.

COSSACKS

GEORGIA

Black Sea

Caspian Sea

Aral Sea

OTTOMAN EMPIRE

TIBET

BHUTAN

NEPAL

BURMA

IRAN

AFGHANISTAN

INDIA

MAP 20.2 The Expansion of Russia, 1500–1800 By the end of the eighteenth century the Russian empire extended westward into Europe, southward toward the Black Sea and Caspian Sea, and most dramatically, eastward into Central Asia, Siberia, and the Americas. (© Cengage Learning)

The Russian nobility benefited from Catherine's authoritarianism. In return for their loyalty and service in the bureaucracy and the military, Catherine gave the nobles more power over the serfs who farmed their estates. At the same time, the profitable market for grain in western Europe gave them incentive to make increasingly harsh demands on their serfs. In their elegant townhouses and country estates, the Russian aristocracy saw Western luxuries as essential to their lifestyle and thought little of those who toiled for them like slaves.

As the situation of the serfs deteriorated, unrest led to rebellion. In the 1770s a Cossack chieftain named Yemelyan Pugachev gained a huge following after claiming that he was the legitimate tsar. Pugachev promised the abolition of serfdom and an end to taxation and military conscription. After several years of rebellion, Pugachev was captured, brought back to Moscow, and sliced to pieces in a public square. Catherine became even less tolerant of talk of reform.

Catherine's imperial policies were pragmatic. Though herself a convert to the Orthodox faith, she restrained the church from attempting to convert non-Russian peoples. In the case of Siberia, the reason was financial: converts to Orthodoxy had tax protections that indigenous people lacked. In the cases of the steppes and the Central Asian frontier, Catherine saw that working with local Muslim leaders was the best way to maintain stability. In the Crimea, for example, she protected the rights of the local Muslim nobility, declaring, *"It is Our desire that without regard to his nationality or faith, each [nobleman] shall have the personal right to these lands and any advantages that will accrue from their use."* (See the feature "Movement of Ideas Through Primary Sources: Petitioning Catherine the Great.")

Thus while conditions for Russian serfs might deteriorate and force might prevail on the Siberian frontier, imperial Russian interactions with Asian societies were flexible. As in the Qing empire, Catherine brought people of the Central Asian steppes within the Russian imperial orbit without requiring cultural assimilation or a complete break with their traditions.

Musée des Beaux-Arts, Chartres, France/Erich Lessing/Art Resource, NY

Catherine the Great Equestrian portraits of monarchs on white horses were common in eighteenth-century Europe, though rarely were women represented this way. Catherine, a German princess who married into the Russian royal family, removed her husband from the throne in 1762 in a bloodless coup. Tough and brilliant, she ruled under her own authority for over three decades.

Petitioning Catherine the Great

One of Catherine the Great's innovations was to invite petitions from her subjects. Often people felt that oppression resulted from the misuse of power by local and provincial officials: if only the tsarina herself knew of these abuses, they thought, surely she would correct them. Catherine the Great encouraged this attitude and invited her subjects (other than the serfs, who had no right to address her) to submit their petitions to her. Such a flood of petitions flowed to St. Petersburg, however, that it is unlikely that she even saw most of them, and once the French Revolution showed the dangers of stirring up public opinion (see Chapter 22), the freedom to petition the tsarina was revoked.

The first of the two petitions below was submitted by a group of Tartar nobles, that is, by the Muslim, Turkic-speaking elite of an area incorporated into the Russian empire. The Kazan Tartars had ruled the Volga River region in the fourteenth century, but in the fifteenth century this region was conquered by the Russian tsar Ivan the Terrible. Ivan slaughtered much of the Muslim population and forcibly converted many of the survivors to Orthodox Christianity. Not until the reign of Catherine did the tsars allow new mosques to be built again in Kazan.

The second petition to Catherine was submitted by a group of Jewish leaders in Belarus. The majority of the population of Belarus (meaning "white Russia") consisted of Slavic speakers closely related to Russians in language and culture. Belarus was ruled from Poland/Lithuania until the eighteenth century, after which it was incorporated into the Russian empire. The Jews of this region were known as *Ashkenazim*. Their liturgical language was a form of Hebrew, but their everyday language was Yiddish, a dialect of German infused with Hebrew vocabulary that was unintelligible to Russian speakers. To the greatest extent possible, the Ashkenazim took care of their own community affairs.

Source: David G. Rowley, *Exploring Russia's Past: Narratives, Sources, Images*, vol. I, To 1850 (New York: Pearson, 2006), pp. 208–209.

Petition from Tartar Nobles in Kazan Province, 1767

12. We the under-signed believe that nothing is more offensive to a person, regardless of his faith and rank, than to suffer disrespect and insults toward his religion. This makes one extremely agitated and provokes unnecessary words of abuse. But it often happens that people of various ranks say extremely contemptuous things about our religion and our Prophet . . . and this is a great affront for us. Therefore we request a law that anyone who curses our religion be held legally accountable. . . . [We further ask that] we Tartars and nobles not be forced to convert to Orthodoxy, but that only those who so wish . . . be baptized. . . .

15. If any of our people are voluntarily baptized into the faith of the Greek confession [i.e., into the Orthodox Church] they should be ordered to move to settlements with Russians the very same year in which the conversion takes place. . . . We ask that, under no circumstances, are converts to be permitted to sell their houses, garden plots, and pastures to Russians or people of other ranks, but are to sell only to us Tartars; they must sell either to unconverted kinsmen or other Tartars. . . . Also, without a special personal order from Her Imperial Majesty, no churches should be built in our localities and thereby put pressure upon us. . . .

Petition from Belarussian Jews, 1784

1. Some [Belarussian Jews] who live in towns engage in trade and, especially, in the distillation of spirits, beer and mead [honey beer], which they sell wholesale and retail. This privilege was extended to them when Belarus joined the Russian Empire. Hence everyone active in this business used all their resources to construct buildings suitable for distillation. . . . After the Belarussian region joined the Russian Empire, the Jews in some towns constructed more of these in the same fashion and at great expense. The imperial monarchical decree [on Jews] emboldens them to request tearfully some monarchical mercy.

2. According to an ancient custom, when the squires built a new village, they summoned the Jews to reside there and gave them certain privileges for several years and the permanent liberty to distill spirits, brew beer and mead, and sell these drinks. On this basis the Jews built houses and distillation plants at considerable expense. . . . But a decree of the governor-general of Belarus has now forbidden the squires to farm our distillation in their villages to Jews, even if the squires want to do this. As a result [these] poor Jews [have been left] completely impoverished. . . . They therefore request an imperial decree authorizing the squire, if he wishes, to farm out distillation to Jews in rural areas.

3. . . . Jews have no one to defend them in courts and find themselves in a desperate situation—given their fear, and ignorance of Russian—in case of misfortune, even if innocent. . . . To consummate all the good already bestowed, Jews dare to petition that . . . in matters involving Jews and non-Jews . . . a representative from the Jewish community . . . be present to accompany Jews in court and attend the interrogation of Jews. But cases involving only Jews . . . should be handled solely in Jewish courts, because Jews assume obligations among themselves, make agreements and conclude all kinds of deals in the Jewish language and in accordance with Jewish rites and law (which are not known to others). Moreover, those who transgress their laws and order should be judged in Jewish courts. Similarly, preserve intact all their customs and holidays in the spirit of their faith, as is mercifully assured in the imperial manifesto. . . .

QUESTIONS FOR ANALYSIS

» *What attitude did the writers of these petitions express toward Catherine's imperial authority?*

» *What do these documents tell us about the relationship of religion to empire in eighteenth-century Russia?*

India: From Mughal Empire to British Rule, 1650–1800

In the later seventeenth century, the Mughal empire was at its zenith when the emperor **Aurangzeb** (ow-rang-ZEB) completed a series of conquests that extended his power throughout south India. Proud of his accomplishments, he took the title Alamgir, "World Seizer." A hundred years later, however, Mughal power was in retreat as the British East India Company established its political and military dominance in the region.

Even during Aurangzeb's long rule (1658–1707), ambitious regional leaders resisted the central power of Delhi. Although Aurangzeb successfully reasserted and even extended imperial power, after his death the Mughal empire began to fragment, leading to invasions from Iran and Afghanistan and the emergence of autonomous regional states. As in the past history of India and other land-based empires in Eurasia, the wealth of empire attracted invaders from the mountains and steppes who were strong enough to destabilize the existing order, but not to replace it. Arriving by sea, however, the British represented something entirely new. Starting from their base in Bengal, they would fill the power vacuum left by Mughal decline.

Aurangzeb and the Decline of Mughal Authority, 1658–1757

Aurangzeb was an energetic, capable, and determined ruler who presided over a stable and prosperous realm. The wealth he controlled was staggering. Some came from territorial conquests that brought treasure flowing back to Delhi. But agriculture, trade, and industry were the true foundations of India's prosperity.

Mughal officials encouraged the commercial farming of sugarcane, indigo, and cotton to enhance the tax base, and many peasants benefited from the focus on marketable crops. American crops like maize and tobacco were another stimulus to growth. The population did not increase as rapidly as China's in the same period: disease and periodic famine following the failure of monsoon rains kept mortality rates high. Still, the population of India rose from about 150 million in 1600 to about 200 million in 1800. As in other land-based empires, taxes on peasant agriculture were the principal source of government revenue.

The stability of the Mughal heartland in north India was good for trade and industry. Participation in the expanding Indian Ocean economy brought in gold and silver that financed not only Aurangzeb's military adventures but also entrepreneurial activity. Silk and opium were produced for Southeast Asian markets, but the principal source of prosperity was the textile sector. The European market for cotton cloth was a new and profitable one. Consumers in the Netherlands, France, and England found Indian cotton cloth cheaper, more comfortable, and more easily washed than domestic woolens or linens. South Asians were among the most powerful commercial agents in the world, using the silver that flowed in through Indian Ocean trade to pay cash advances to weavers, who then contracted lower-caste women to spin cotton yarn.

For Mughal rulers, commercial wealth was a mixed blessing, however. Prosperity afforded provincial leaders the cash and incentive to build up their own military forces as well as an incentive to try to keep their own wealth rather than pass it along to Delhi. Aurangzeb's constant military campaigns were largely driven by the need to assert central control over such restive provinces.

V&A Images, London/Art Resource, NY

V&A Images, London/Art Resource, NY

Mughals at War   Mughal control of South Asia was based on military supremacy, from early-sixteenth-century conquest through the reign of Aurangzeb. As this Mughal painting (in the Persian style) shows, cavalry played a central role, but the use of gunpowder weapons was also crucial to Mughal strategy.

In the process Aurangzeb reversed Akbar's earlier policy of religious tolerance (see Chapter 16). While many Muslims lived in major cities and in the northeast and northwest of the empire, most Mughal subjects were Hindus. Whereas Akbar had courted allies among Hindus and other communities, Aurangzeb stressed the Islamic nature of his state, imposing on nonbelievers the special tax that the Quran allows but that Akbar had suspended. The tax caused great resentment.

Mughal relations with the Sikhs deteriorated when Aurangzeb tried to interfere in the selection of their new *guru* (spiritual leader). Sikhism was a new religion that emphasized equality before God, rejecting the caste system of Hinduism but incorporating other elements of Hindu belief and ritual. Aurangzeb's heavy-handed intervention in Sikh affairs, including the execution of one of their leaders, led to a full-scale uprising in the northeastern Punjab region. Sikhism, formerly pacifistic, became more militant in the process: to this day, ceremonial knives are part of the daily attire of Sikh men.

Maratha kingdoms
Loosely bound, west-central Indian confederacy that established its autonomy from Mughal rule in the eighteenth century and challenged the invading British in the nineteenth.

Nader Shah
(1688–1747) Iranian ruler who invaded India from the north in 1739, defeating the Mughal army and capturing the Mughal emperor, who handed over the keys to his treasury before Nader Shah agreed to withdraw. Mughal power went into permanent decline.

Joseph Francois Dupleix
(1697–1764) Governor-general in charge of all French establishments in India. Dupleix used diplomacy to forge alliances with local rulers and with their help defeated a much larger British force in the 1740s.

Hindus trying to wrest free of central control also rebelled, such as in the **Maratha kingdoms** in western and central India, motivated by religious resentments as well as political and economic ambitions. Aurangzeb had fairly easily subdued other regions, but Maratha leaders used guerilla tactics, well suited to the region's tough terrain, to keep the Mughal armies at bay. From 1695 to 1700, Aurangzeb left Delhi to live in military encampments. Vast sums were spent on his campaigns, and as the emperor was preoccupied with military affairs, corruption and incompetence crept into the government.

By the time of his death in 1707, Aurangzeb was full of despair. From his deathbed he wrote his son: *"I have not done well to the country or to the people, and of the future there is no hope."* A prolonged succession struggle ensued, regional leaders ignored Delhi, tax collectors withheld government funds, and the empire became vulnerable to invasion.

The initial threat came from Iran. After the fall of the Safavid dynasty (see Chapter 17), **Nader Shah** (1688–1747) had rallied Iranian forces to defend the country from Afghan invaders. Turning the tables, in 1739 the Iranians seized key political and commercial centers in Afghanistan, then entered northern India, defeated the Mughal army, and captured the emperor. Begging for mercy, the Mughal emperor handed over the keys to his treasury, and even the fabled Peacock Throne, before Nader Shah agreed to withdraw.

Nader Shah's invasion of India marked the death knell of Mughal authority. The Marathas tried to march on Delhi but were decisively defeated by Afghani invaders in 1761. With Maratha expansion checked, India seemed ready to break apart. Instead, the British took the mantle of Mughal imperial power.

Foundations of British Rule, 1739–1818

The seaborne European empires in Asia were originally geared toward commercial profit rather than territorial control. Mughal rulers paid little attention to the Dutch, British, and French East India Companies operating on the fringes of their empire. In Amsterdam, Paris, and London, Company home offices handled shipping schedules, insurance, and warehousing. In Asia, Company agents identified profitable opportunities and negotiated with local political and commercial elites. The usual pattern was for Europeans to directly control only their own "factories," fortified outposts where they lived and kept their trade goods, and perhaps a bit of adjacent territory (see Chapter 17).

Cotton cloth was a major trade item, as were opium (first destined for Indonesian markets, and later for China), raw silk (exported to both Europe and Japan), and pepper. Saltpeter, a key ingredient in gunpowder, was another important European import from Asia. European rulers, following the theory of mercantilism, believed that their own economies were damaged by the high silver exports needed to finance this trade. But the commerce was so profitable that silver exports continued.

With the decline of Mughal power after 1739, some Company employees were tempted to join in the general scramble to gain greater freedom from imperial authority. It was such "men on the spot," rather than policymakers in distant European capitals, who laid the foundations for further European expansion. One of the first and most brilliant of these was the French Company's commander **Joseph Francois Dupleix** (1697–1764). During the 1740s he seized the British factory at Madras in south India, only to be attacked in turn by a local Indian ruler who wanted the wealth of Madras (today called Chennai) for himself. Dupleix (doo-PLAY) commanded just 230 French troops plus some 700 *sepoys* (SEE-poyz), Indian soldiers employed and trained by the Europeans. Nevertheless, superior French firepower and organization enabled the defeat of a force of nearly ten thousand men. Dupleix then became an Indian ruler himself by taking the title of his defeated Indian enemy. For diplomatic reasons, however, Paris ordered Dupleix to return Madras to the British, who would soon follow Dupleix's example with more lasting effect.

The British East India Company factory at Calcutta tapped into the rich trade of the populous Mughal province of Bengal. The *nawab* (ruler) of Bengal, Siraj ud-Daulah (suh-RAJ uhd-duh-OO-lah), saw the British as a threat after they fortified their Calcutta factory against French attack, and in 1756 his soldiers seized Calcutta. But Robert Clive, a British soldier of fortune, cleverly outmaneuvered him. First, Clive secured backing from Hindu commercial and banking interests in Bengal who preferred to deal with the commercially-minded British. Second, Clive made an alliance with the nawab's own uncle, who hoped to use this alliance to become nawab himself. In 1757, at the **Battle of Plassey**, the nawab's fifty thousand troops faced only eight hundred Englishmen, plus about two thousand sepoys. But some of Siraj ud-Daulah's troops had been secretly paid not to fight by Clive's moneylender friends, while the forces controlled by his uncle switched to the British side. Afterwards, Siraj's uncle was duly installed as nawab, but the British plundered his treasury, as Company officials drained fortunes from north India to build stately London residences and palatial country houses in England. The chests full of silver they sent back home reversed, for the first time, the flow of bullion back toward Europe and away from the Indian Ocean economies.

From Bengal, the British could perhaps have marched on Delhi and ended the Mughal era once and for all. But Clive decided on a more subtle policy of recognizing the weakened Mughal emperor while insinuating the Company into existing Mughal institutions. The East India Company became the official revenue collector of the rich northeastern provinces of Bengal, Bihar (bee-HAHR) and Oudh (OW-ad). Clive used the threat of military force to divide and conquer, extorting alliances from various nawabs, maharajahs, and sultans by offering them "protection."

In Parliament, some doubted whether Clive and the Company were serving Britain's interests, horrified by the famine following the failure of the monsoon rains in 1769 during which one-third of Bengal's population perished. Although the Company fed its own employees and soldiers, it did nothing for Bengalis while continuing to extract its revenue. One member of Parliament complained: *"We have outdone the Spaniards in Peru. They were at least butchers on a religious principle, however diabolical their zeal. We have murdered, deposed, plundered, usurped—nay, what think you of the famine in Bengal being caused by a monopoly of the servants of the East India Company?"*[*]

The India Act in 1784 attempted to redress such abuses. **Lord Charles Cornwallis** was dispatched as governor-general and commander of British forces in India. Unlike Clive, Cornwallis was an aristocrat and a member of the British establishment. His assignment was to draw a strict line between administration and trade by implementing a policy whereby Company employees might serve as either officials or traders, but not as both. Cornwallis believed that British colonial rule could be fair and just. As his successor declared: *"No greater benefit can be bestowed on the inhabitants of India than the extension of British authority."*[†] That idea would long endure as a justification for British colonial rule.

Battle of Plassey 1757 battle that gave the British East India Company control of the rich eastern Mughal province of Bengal. Sir Robert Clive used alliances with Indian rulers to defeat the larger forces of Siraj ud-Daulah, the nawab of Bengal.

Lord Charles Cornwallis (1738–1795) British general who surrendered to American forces at Yorktown and later served as governor-general of India and Ireland.

---

[*]Horace Walpole, speech quoted in *Cambridge History of India,* vol. 5 (Cambridge: Cambridge University Press, 1929), p. 187.

[†]Quoted in Francis Watson, *A Concise History of India* (London: Thames and Hudson, 1979), p. 131.

British influence spread through negotiation as well as force. Provincial rulers looked to the British as patrons and protectors in the anarchy that accompanied Mughal decline. The British also absorbed Indian influences, learning Indian languages and adopting Mughal styles of dress and behavior. Because there were no English women in India, Company employees frequently associated with local consorts and even took Indian wives, who provided a cultural and linguistic bridge to Indian society.

In the field of law we see one example of the complex intercultural processes that developed. Xie Qinggao's account of a Company court proceeding at Calcutta provides a snapshot of British influence:

> *The head judge sits, and ten guest judges [the jury] sit on his side. The head guest judge is the elder of the guest merchants. . . . On the day they consider the suit and then decide the outcome, if one of the guest judges does not agree they must hear the case again. Even if this happens two or three times, no one views this as inconvenient.*[*]

But while the Company men used British-style jurisprudence among themselves, they did not choose to displace South Asian legal traditions. Instead, a situation of legal pluralism developed. Indian litigants could pursue their cases in local courts or in British ones. They might choose British courts because of corruption in the Mughal ones; however, they would still expect their own customs to be respected. The British East India Company therefore employed Muslim and Hindu legal advisers to help implement a multilayered intercultural judicial system.

Another adaptation of a Mughal institution to British purposes was the revenue system that Cornwallis designed. The main tax collectors for the Mughal empire had been *zamindars*, men with appointed positions but no permanent title over the lands from which they gathered revenue. However, the British regarded landed property and security of title as foundations of a stable rural order and granted the zamindars more permanent rights over the lands they tax-farmed. In return, the zamindars were to pay the British a fixed annual rent. The zamindars then became some of the wealthiest men in South Asia, and strong allies of the British.

In the 1770s the top Company official declared: *"The dominion of all India is what I never wish to see."* But in the unsettled conditions of the late eighteenth century, it was difficult to avoid greater involvement in the subcontinent's political and military affairs. In the west, when Maratha armies threatened the British East India Company's factory at Bombay (today's Mumbai), the British engaged in a series of alliances and interventions in that region. Finally, in 1818 they defeated the Marathas in battle and established control over South Asia. Without central planning or foresight, the British had gone from maritime prowess to mastery over one of the world's most populous and productive regions.

Like the Qing and the Russians in Central Asia, the British initially adapted themselves to local circumstances, relying on powerful regional allies like the zamindars to collect revenue and administer justice. Later in the nineteenth century, however, empowered by industrial growth and technological change, British officials would become more distant from their Indian subjects. Then the gradual displacement of Mughal by British authority would give way to a much more intrusive presence (see Chapter 24).

---

[*]Xie Qinggao, *Hailu jiaoyi*, ed. An Jing (Beijing: Shangwu yingshugan, 2002), translation courtesy of Valerie Hansen, personal communication (2009).

A British East India Company Official Eighteenth-century Englishmen adopted many features of Mughal court life: dressing in Mughal fashion, smoking from a hookah, enjoying the entertainment of Indian musicians and dancers, and taking up the Mughal sport of polo. Many of these Mughal cultural practices, including the game of polo, had themselves been imported from Persia; this portrait bears comparison with that of the Safavid shah Suleyman II (see page 483). (British Library, London/Werner Forman/Art Resource, NY)

Tokugawa Japan, 1630–1790

After Hideyoshi's adventurous attempt to invade China at the end of the sixteenth century (see Chapter 16), early modern Japan remained largely aloof from empires and empire building. Unlike Korea and Vietnam, Japan was not part of the tributary system tying the local elite to the Chinese emperor. Unlike other islands like the Spanish Philippines, the Dutch East Indies, or Qing-controlled Taiwan, it was subject to no foreign power. Instead, Japan followed its own distinctive political, economic, and cultural dynamic. In spite of this relative isolation, these two centuries were a period of tremendous vitality in Japanese history. The Tokugawa (toe-koo-GAH-wah) shoguns and daimyo lords ruled over a rapidly growing society with a flourishing economy. Tokugawa Japan had a rich cultural and intellectual life, with major accomplishments in fields such as poetry, theater, and architecture.

The story of early modern Japan divides roughly into two periods. From 1630 to 1710, the Tokugawa system was at its height of affluence and creativity. But from 1710 to 1800, a series of financial and environmental problems stymied the Tokugawa. Population growth stalled, and a widening gap between rich and poor led to increasing social tension.

Stability and Prosperity in Early Tokugawa Japan, 1630–1710

While the Japanese emperor remained a shadowy figure secluded in the ritual center of Kyoto, real political power rested with the Tokugawa shoguns in the political capital at Edo (Tokyo). The shoguns, literally "commanders of force," successfully brought peace and stability to the Japanese islands, even while the provincial lords, the daimyo, retained substantial authority within their own domains (see Chapter 16). With stability enforced, seventeenth-century Japan reaped the fruits of peace.

The nation brought back into production valuable resources that had been neglected during the violence and insecurity of the sixteenth century. Farmers devoted much time and labor to improving irrigation, and yields increased as rice paddies replaced dry field agriculture. After the most easily accessible lands were developed, Japanese farmers cleared forests and terraced hillsides to bring more fields into production, while fishermen took greater advantage of the bounty of the surrounding seas.

The shoguns and daimyo tapped into this productive wealth through an efficient tax system based on precise surveys of land and population. Farmers, no longer subject to arbitrary taxes, had an incentive to boost production knowing that they could keep the surpluses. At the same time, Chinese demand for silver and copper stimulated mining. The administrative elite siphoned off some of the new wealth, but some of it also went toward the improvement of roads and irrigation works, further stimulating economic growth. An increase in coinage made possible a shift from local and regional self-sufficiency to a truly national economy.

The expansion of Japanese cities was one of the most notable features of the period. Many castle towns, originally civil war strongholds, developed into cultural and commercial centers. The most spectacular example was the capital of Edo (ED-doe), which grew from a small village to a city of more than a million people by 1720.

A pressing social question of the early Tokugawa period was to define a peacetime role for the samurai warriors. Accordingly, the samurai code, or *bushido* ("the way of the warrior"), instructed samurai to cultivate both the military and civil arts, and in times of peace to emphasize the latter: *"Within his heart [the samurai] keeps to the ways of peace, but . . . keeps his weapons ready for use. The . . . common people make him their teacher and respect him. . . . Herein lies the Way of the* samurai, *the means by which he earns his clothing, food and shelter."** The samurai therefore positioned themselves as the intellectual and cultural leaders of Tokugawa Japan. They established schools, wrote Confucian treatises, and patronized the arts. But they maintained absolute allegiance to their daimyo lords, for whom they were ever ready to die.

The dynamism of the times tested boundaries. Regulations requiring rural families to be self-sufficient were widely ignored as farm families increasingly

---

*Quoted in Ryusaku Tsunoda et al., *Sources of the Japanese Tradition* (New York: Columbia University Press, 1958), pp. 399–400.

geared their production toward urban markets. In gender relations as well, the social dynamism of the period contradicted the Tokugawa theory of strict Confucian hierarchy. Elite women made prominent literary contributions, and women of other social classes claimed some mobility and economic opportunity. While women in samurai households were most subject to tight patriarchal control, urban merchant and artisan families were less restrictive. Thus women participated as performers as well as audience members in some of the new forms of dance and theater. (See the feature "Visual Evidence in Primary Sources: The 'Floating World' of Tokugawa Japan.")

Tokugawa Japan and the Outside World

Even as Japanese society was rapidly changing, the shoguns pursued conservative policies, most evidently in foreign affairs. Alarmed by the early success of Christian missionaries (see Chapter 16), Tokugawa leaders promulgated a series of **Seclusion Edicts** that strictly limited contact with Europeans. After the 1630s, only a single annual Dutch trading mission was allowed, with the stipulation that no Bibles or other Christian texts were to enter the country. Japanese were forbidden to practice Christianity or even to risk exposure to that religion through travel overseas.

But even in foreign relations, reality sometimes contradicted these policies of isolation. For one thing, Japanese seclusion applied only to Europeans. Trade with Chinese and Korean merchants grew even as that with the Europeans declined, and as a result Japanese foreign trade increased throughout this period. Xie Qinggao, who visited Nagasaki as a sailor, noted the high volume of Japanese exports in silver, porcelain, paper and brushes, and flower vases, much of it destined for Chinese markets. And while contact with Europeans was limited, the scientific and philosophical books that reached Japan through the annual Dutch trade missions found an eager audience, especially among samurai. In fact, for centuries Western knowledge was called **Dutch learning**, and the ability to read Dutch became a sign of worldly sophistication.

While Dutch learning was new and exotic, Chinese influence on Japanese intellectual life was deep and well established. Xie noted that *"the king wears Chinese clothes"* and that *"the country uses Chinese writing."** He overstated the degree of Chinese cultural influence on Japan, where both clothing styles and the writing system were unique Japanese adaptations of Chinese models, rather than mere copies. Some Tokugawa thinkers, many of them samurai, were anxious to downplay China's influence. They exalted Japan's indigenous Shinto religion and its emphasis on the spiritual forces of the natural and ancestral worlds, at the same time attacking Buddhism. Buddhism, some argued, led to empty abstract thoughts, while Shinto connected believers to a tangible spirit of shared national feeling. Others further argued that Japan, not China, should be regarded as the "Middle Kingdom" because of the greater purity of its Confucian traditions.

This sense of intellectual competition was not connected to empire building. The only territorial expansion of the Tokugawa shogunate was to the lightly populated northern islands, especially Hokkaido (ho-KIE-do), whose indigenous Ainu people lived by hunting, gathering, and fishing and were no match for Japanese weapons. After losing several battles, the Ainu were gradually disenfranchised by Japanese settlers and fishermen.

Seclusion Edicts
Series of edicts issued by the Tokugawa shoguns that, beginning in the 1630s, outlawed Christianity and strictly limited Japanese contact with Europeans.

Dutch learning
Traditional Japanese title for Western knowledge. Knowledge of Dutch in Tokugawa Japan was a sign of worldliness and sophistication.

---

*Xie Qinggao, *Hailu jiaoyi,* ed. An Jing (Beijing: Shangwu yingshugan, 2002), translation courtesy of Valerie Hansen, personal communication (2009).

The "Floating World" of Tokugawa Japan

Three important cities played different roles in seventeenth-century Japan. Kyoto was the imperial capital, a city of temples and palaces. Here the emperor, his courtiers, and Buddhist monks and nuns kept alive ancient Japanese arts, such as the tea ceremony and the traditions of Zen Buddhism, including meditative gardens. Edo was the dynamic administrative center. Here daimyo kept palaces to remain close to the heart of political power, and many samurai turned themselves from warriors into scholars. Osaka was the country's commercial capital, the focal point of enlarged and intensified trade networks. New artistic forms accompanied social change in these cities. Poets experimented with a simple new form called *haiku*, and urban audiences patronized the new *kabuki* (ka-BOO-ki) theater, more realistic and emotive than previous forms of Japanese drama.

The shoguns favored a strictly hierarchical society along Confucian lines and preferred that

Courtesy, Hikone Castle Museum

This screen was owned by a noble daimyo family, but Tokugawa merchants were also important patrons of ukiyoe artists.

» *The word* ukiyoe *had earlier been written with characters meaning "sorrowful world," with a Buddhist emphasis on impermanence. Do the figures on this screen seem to live in a "sorrowful world," or in a "floating world" as described by Ryōi?*

everyone keep in his or her place. Their constant edicts ordering people to dress in clothes and live in houses appropriate to their social status indicate that many people were *not* doing so. As in early modern western Europe, where the urban merchant class was also increasing its wealth and cultural influence, Japanese merchants ignored the laws that restricted the clothes they could wear: when they could afford it, they wore the fine silk robes presumably reserved for the daimyo.

The arts of the Tokugawa period demonstrate the cultural fluidity of seventeenth-century Japanese culture. The image here is a painting from Hishikawa Mononobu (1625–1694), one of the most prominent Tokugawa artists who depicted the *ukiyoe*, or "floating world," of languid pleasures. As described by his contemporary Asai Ryōi, the floating world meant "living only for the moment, turning our full attention to the pleasures of the moon, the snow, the cherry blossoms, and the maple leaves; singing songs, drinking wine, diverting ourselves in just floating, floating; caring not a whit for the pauperism staring us in the face, refusing to be disheartened, like a gourd floating along with the river current; this is what we call the *floating world*."* A major artistic theme of the movement was the portrayal of bordellos, which, as in this painting, were as much about refined pastimes such as music and literature as about sexual gratification.

*Quoted in Richard Lane, *Images from the Floating World* (New York: Putnam, 1978), p. 11.

Area of detail

Courtesy, Hikone Castle Museum

Earlier Japanese decorative artists emphasized calm landscapes and nature subjects. This screen-within-a-screen shows that older style in juxtaposition with the new Tokugawa ukiyoe theme.

One art critic writes: "A strong visual contrast is established between the ethereal realm of the monochrome landscape in a meticulously brushed Chinese style and the worldly ambiance of the bordello pursuits in the foreground."[†]

This is a scene from a brothel, but do the characters exhibit sexual tension?

Urban Tokugawa culture is known for its emphasis on refinements in recreation and leisure activities such as music, backgammon, calligraphy, and painting.

[†] John T. Carpenter, "The Human Figure in the Playground of Edo Artistic Imagination," in *Edo: Art in Japan, 1615–1868*, ed. Robert T. Singer et al. (Washington, D.C.: National Gallery of Art, 1998), p. 378.

Eventually tensions would result when the Russians also extended their imperial frontier to the islands north of Japan. But in the eighteenth century Hokkaido was still very remote, and the increased Japanese presence was not an exception to the usual Tokugawa practice of seclusion and isolation. For several hundred years, Japanese rulers, in stark contrast to Qing, Russian, and British activities in Asia, simply opted out of the empire-building game.

Challenges, Reform, and Decline, 1710–1790

In 1710 Japan was rich, populous, and united. But the eighteenth century brought new challenges. The main problem was ecological. During the seventeenth century the population of Japan had doubled to over 30 million people. Farms became smaller and smaller, and without improvements in technology or sources of energy, Japan had nearly reached its limit in food production. As in China, the spread of irrigation had led to silting up of rivers and increased danger of floods. In addition, population growth and the building of larger cities had depleted Japan's timber resources. Wood became more expensive, and excessive logging led to soil erosion and a further decline in productivity.

In the 1720s and 1730s, **Yoshimune** (r. 1716–1745), one of the greatest Tokugawa shoguns, launched a program of reform. Through constant edicts he urged frugality and curtailment of unnecessary consumption. He told the samurai to give up the ease of urban life and return to the countryside. True to the Confucian tradition, Yoshimune interpreted social problems as resulting from moral lapses. But his edicts were no more successful in changing people's behavior than those of previous shoguns.

Nevertheless, Yoshimune did sponsor some successful reforms. Most importantly, he tried to make life easier for increasingly hard-pressed farmers. He reformed tax collections to eliminate the corruption that local officials had allowed to creep into the system, and he set strict limits on interest rates to relieve indebted farmers. He also sponsored the cultivation of sugar and ginseng to replace imports from Korea and Southeast Asia and promoted planting sweet potatoes on marginal land to increase the food supply. Support for increased fishing, also, resulted in greater supplies of seafood and fertilizer to refresh the exhausted soil.

Yoshimune, thinking that merchants were responsible for many of Japan's problems, sought to bring them under control. Increased government involvement in commerce especially suited larger trading houses that were anxious to secure government-backed monopolies. But these policies tended to undermine entrepreneurialism, and they gradually made Japanese business more regulated and monopolistic and less dynamic and inventive.

For all his effort and energy, Yoshimune's reforms were mainly a matter of "struggling to stand still."[2] After 1750, the social problems arising from the ecological and economic crisis increased: incidents of rural unrest nearly doubled. Peasants particularly resented policies forcing them to toil on public works projects without pay. Tensions also grew in rural communities as families competed for scarce water and timber.

It is a testament to the solidity and effectiveness of Tokugawa institutions that such crises did not lead to a breakdown of the political order, as was occurring in Mughal India. The political, economic, and cultural legacies of the Tokugawa endured far into the nineteenth century, until outside powers finally dispelled Japan's isolation and awakened its ambitions for empire (see Chapter 24).

Yoshimune (1738–1795) Eighth Tokugawa ruler to hold the title of shogun. A conservative but capable leader under whose rule Japan saw advances in agricultural productivity.

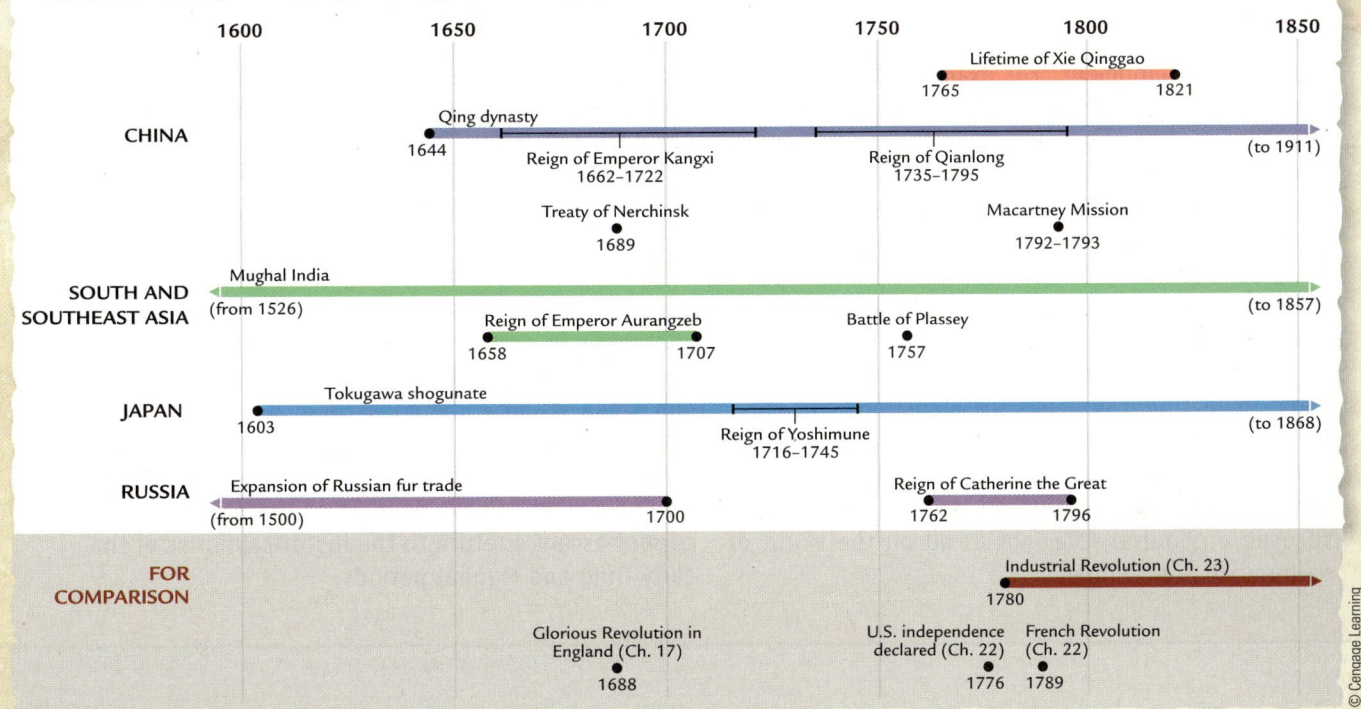

World Economies and the Great Divergence

As our own times change, so often do our views of the past. The recent economic successes of China and India have led some historians to reconsider Asia's place in the development of the modern world economy.

In the late seventeenth century, Mughal India was one of the world's most prosperous empires; Tokugawa Japan was urbanizing and commercializing; and the rulers of Qing China were cultivating the continuing expansion of the world's largest economy. By the early nineteenth century, however, the Industrial Revolution in Europe was rapidly shifting the global balance of economic power westward (see Chapter 23), ensuring the military and technological supremacy of Europe. The relationship between Britain and China shows just how suddenly and dramatically the change occurred. In 1793 the emperor Qianlong easily rebuffed British emissaries seeking stronger commercial and diplomatic ties; in 1839 ironclad British steamships destroyed China's coastal defenses and imposed

their own terms of trade on humiliated Qing rulers (see Chapter 24).

In the past, many historians assumed that a bundle of specifically European characteristics paved the way for industrial modernity. These factors included an early lead in scientific inquiry (see Chapter 21); the development of commercial capitalism and the relatively high status of merchants; competition between nations for economic and military advantage; and higher labor costs leading to increased innovation in manufacturing (see Chapters 16 and 17). In this view, Europe's early modern commercial empires translated smoothly into global economic dominance in the industrial age. Those assumptions have now been critiqued by historians who insist on a more global perspective, arguing that, prior to 1800, Europe's industrial potential was not unique.

That is the argument of historian Kenneth Pomeranz in his comparative study of what he calls

577

When the young botanist **Joseph Banks** (1743–1820) sailed aboard the *Endeavour* as part of a British expedition across the Pacific Ocean, his interest went beyond flora and fauna to include the people he encountered on the voyage. From the Amerindians of Tierra del Fuego (the southern tip of South America), to the Polynesians of the Pacific, to the Aboriginal peoples of Australia, Banks kept careful notes of his interactions with peoples of whom Europeans had little previous knowledge. His concern with these cultures went beyond mere curiosity. He was interested in understanding the relationships *between* societies. For example, when Banks learned that Tahitians understood the speech of the Maori (MAO-ree) of New Zealand, he recognized that there was a family connection between the two peoples. Banks was a pioneer of *ethnography*, the study of the linguistic and cultural relationships between peoples. However, he was mystified by the behavior of the Polynesian people he and his shipmates met when they stepped ashore on the island of Tahiti:

Joseph Banks

(Private Collection/Photo © Agnew's, London/The Bridgeman Art Library)

Though at first they hardly dared approach us, after a little time they became very familiar. The first who approached us came crawling almost on his hands and knees and gave us a green bough. . . . This we received and immediately each of us gathered a green bough and carried it in our hands. They marched with us about 1/2 a mile and then made a general stop and, scraping the ground clean . . . every one of them threw

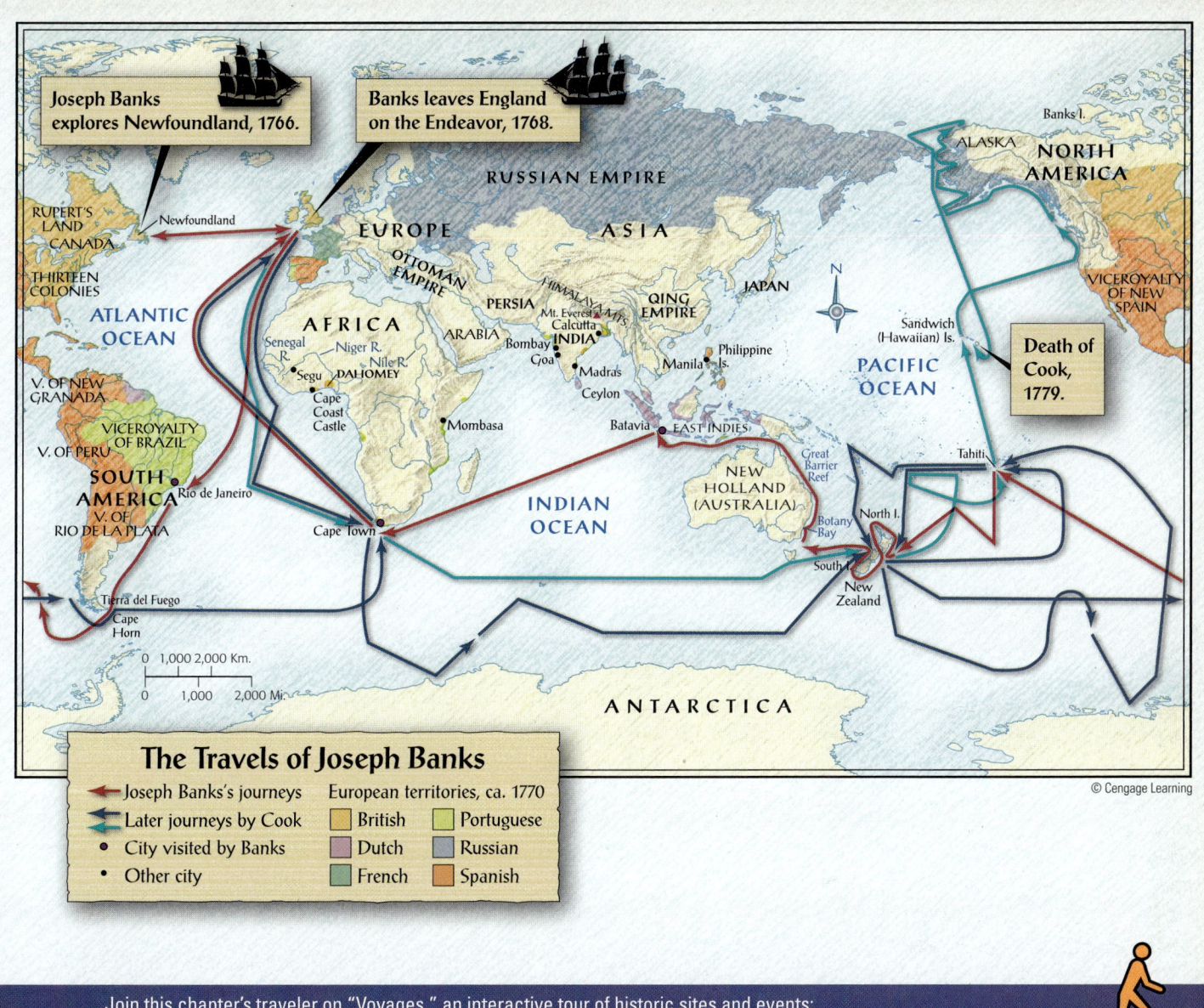

The Travels of Joseph Banks

Joseph Banks explores Newfoundland, 1766.

Banks leaves England on the Endeavor, 1768.

Death of Cook, 1779.

RUSSIAN EMPIRE

EUROPE

ASIA

JAPAN

OTTOMAN EMPIRE

PERSIA

HIMALAYA MTS.

QING EMPIRE

Mt. Everest

Calcutta

INDIA

ARABIA

Bombay

Goa

Madras

Manila

Philippine Is.

Ceylon

AFRICA

Senegal R.

Niger R.

Nile R.

Segu

DAHOMEY

Cape Coast Castle

Mombasa

Batavia

EAST INDIES

NEW HOLLAND (AUSTRALIA)

Great Barrier Reef

Botany Bay

North I.

South I.

New Zealand

Tahiti

Banks I.

ALASKA

NORTH AMERICA

VICEROYALTY OF NEW SPAIN

Sandwich (Hawaiian) Is.

PACIFIC OCEAN

RUPERT'S LAND CANADA

Newfoundland

THIRTEEN COLONIES

ATLANTIC OCEAN

V. OF NEW GRANADA

VICEROYALTY OF BRAZIL

V. OF PERU

SOUTH AMERICA

V. OF RIO DE LA PLATA

Rio de Janeiro

Cape Town

INDIAN OCEAN

Tierra del Fuego

Cape Horn

ANTARCTICA

0   1,000 2,000 Km.

0   1,000   2,000 Mi.

© Cengage Learning

The Travels of Joseph Banks

→ Joseph Banks's journeys

→ Later journeys by Cook

• City visited by Banks

• Other city

European territories, ca. 1770

British   Portuguese

Dutch   Russian

French   Spanish

his bough down upon the bare place and made signs that we should do the same. . . . Each of us dropped a bough upon those that the Indians had laid down, we all followed their example and thus peace was concluded.[*]

[*]J. C. Beaglehole, ed., *The Endeavour Journal of Joseph Banks*, 2d ed., vol. 1 (Sydney: Halsted Press, 1962), p. 252. Here as elsewhere, some revisions of Banks's punctuation and usage have been made.

Joseph Banks
(1743–1820) English
botanist on Captain
James Cook's first
voyage in the Pacific,
who categorized differ-
ent species of plants
and brought them back
to England. Also estab-
lished the Royal Botanic
Gardens at Kew.

James Cook
(1728–1779) British sea
captain whose three
voyages to the Pacific
Ocean greatly expanded
European knowledge of
the region. Regarded as
a great national hero by
the British public, he
was killed in an altera-
tion with Hawai'ian
islanders in 1779.

S uch ceremonies became a bit less mysterious to Banks after he began to learn the Tahitian language and made friends with a high priest who helped him understand Polynesian customs. Still, even after years of contact, the cultural gulf between the Tahitians and the Englishmen remained.

Banks returned to England in 1771 after a three-year journey. The crewmen who had survived the *Endeavour*'s three years at sea were among the few at that time who had sailed around the entire world. Their captain, **James Cook** (1728–1779), became an instant celebrity. He had accomplished his mission of charting the Pacific Ocean, thus facilitating future European voyages to such places as Hawai'i, New Zea-land, and Australia. He had also carried out important astronomical observations.

In fact, scientific inquiry was central to the *Endeavour*'s mission. The drawings and specimens of plant and animal life Banks brought back greatly expanded European knowledge of the natural world. He was interested not merely in collect-ing exotic flora and fauna but also in systematically classifying and cataloging his findings. While Cook was using his mathematical and navigational skills to chart the oceans, Banks was developing a system for naming and describing natural phenomena to clarify familial relationships in nature.

Why was Banks taken on board the *Endeavour* in the first place? There was no immediate, tangible benefit from his work. But science now enjoyed considerable social and political support. Especially in Britain and France, leaders understood the connection between science and empire. Banks's reconnaissance of the natu-ral world, like that of the physical world undertaken by Cook, was a prelude to the more assertive European imperialism of the nineteenth century. While Polyne-sians were struggling to understand what they saw as the strange behavior of their British visitors, Cook was claiming their islands *"for the use of his Brittanick maj-esty."* Banks came home dreaming of *"future dominions,"* an influential advocate of British settlement in Australia.* Science and empire would remain companions throughout the nineteenth century.

After the return of the *Endeavour* Banks never again traveled outside Europe. But from 1778 to 1820, as president of the Royal Society, the most prestigious scientific establishment in Europe, he focused on fields such as "economic bot-any," which linked science to technological and economic development. At the same time, men and women more philosophically inclined than Banks were extending the scientific model of inquiry, with its emphasis on reason, to human society, creating what is called the European Enlightenment.

Focus Questions

» *When and how did Europe's scientific revolution begin to have practical applications?*

» *How did Enlightenment thought derive from the scientific revolu-tion, and how did it differ from previous European thought systems?*

» *How did systematic classification and measurement support European imperialism in the late eighteenth and early nine-teenth centuries?*

» *How did the societies of Oceania and Australia experience encoun-ters with Europeans in this period?*

*Quoted in Patrick O'Brien, *Joseph Banks: A Life* (Chicago: University of Chicago Press, 1987), pp. 105, 264.

From Scientific Revolution to Practical Science, 1600–1800

Joseph Banks was heir to a tradition that stretched back to the sixteenth century, when Nicolaus Copernicus first published his theory of a heliocentric solar system and Galileo Galilei upset church authorities by providing strong evidence that the earth rotates around the sun (see Chapter 16). For most eighteenth-century Europeans the Christian faith, in both its Catholic and various Protestant forms, still held most of the answers to basic questions about relationships between God, humanity, and the natural world. By then, however, especially among the elites of northern Europe, an increasingly prominent group of men and women had embraced the "new science," with its emphasis on rational inquiry. Aided by the patronage of European monarchs, more members of the aristocracy and of the rising middle class began to pursue science as a vocation.

The development of science in eighteenth-century Europe was important from a purely intellectual standpoint. But Western science became "revolutionary" in global terms only when practical applications of science increased the political and military power of Europeans on the world stage. Joseph Banks himself played a leading role in promoting the practical applications of science, both on his own English estate and more broadly in the British empire. During his lifetime scientific inquiry became progressively more linked to real-world applications and economic purposes.

The Development of the Scientific Method

In seventeenth-century western Europe, a sharp intellectual debate divided thinkers into two basic camps: the "ancients" and the "moderns." The "ancients," who carried forward the scholarly traditions of the humanists (see Chapter 15), continued to emphasize the authority of Aristotle and other classical authors as the foundation on which knowledge in fields such as medicine, mathematics, and astronomy should be built. The "moderns" had a bolder idea. Rejecting the belief that deference should always be given to classical authorities (or Christian theology), they argued that the unfettered application of human reason provided the key to knowledge.

It was an optimistic viewpoint that contradicted the traditional Christian conception of humanity as "fallen" from God's grace, tainted by original sin, and capable of salvation only through God's mercy. The "moderns" believed instead that humankind was endowed by God with reason, and through that reason could apprehend and accurately describe God's creation. *"All our knowledge begins with the senses, proceeds then to the understanding, and ends with reason. There is nothing higher than reason,"* wrote the eighteenth-century German philosopher Immanuel Kant (1724–1804).[*]

One seventeenth-century thinker who used a *deductive* approach to truth was the Frenchman **René Descartes** (1596–1650). Descartes (DAY-cart) argued that the axioms of true philosophy had to be rigorously grounded in the human capacity to reason. He associated rationality with mathematics and thought the rigorous application of logic could result in a unified system of truth. Emphasizing systematic doubt as a key to knowledge, he questioned even his own existence. His solution to that question, *"I think, therefore I am,"* demonstrated that his ability to perceive the rational order of creation was at the core of his own existence. Descartes also had to

René Descartes (1596–1650) French scientist, mathematician, and philosopher who developed the deductive method of reasoning (moving from general principles to particular facts).

---

[*]Immanuel Kant, *Critique of Pure Reason,* ed. and trans. Wolgang Schwarz (Berlin: Scientia Verlag Aalen, 1982), p. 217.

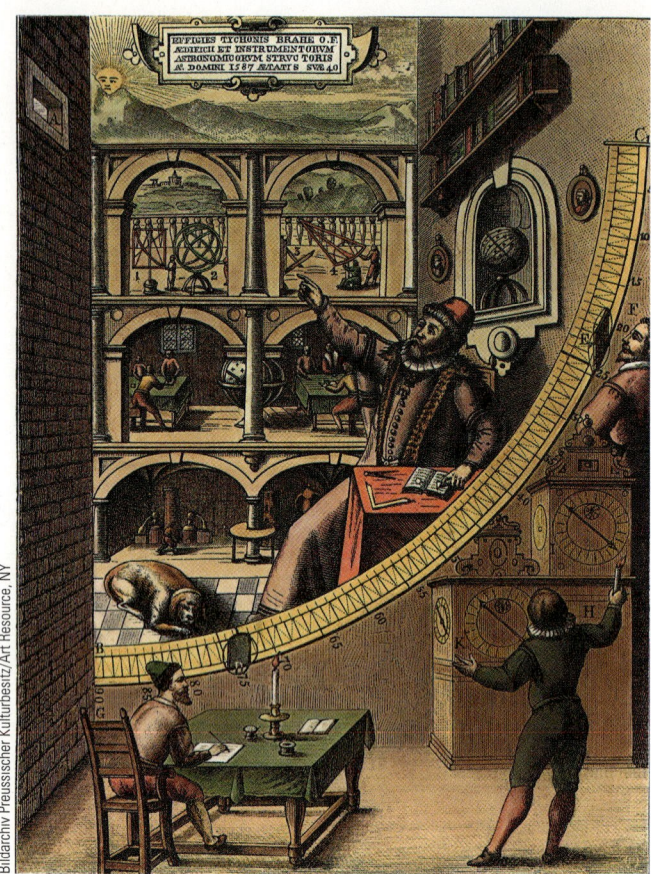

Bildarchiv Preussischer Kulturbesitz/Art Resource, NY

Advances in Astronomy Apart from Galileo and Newton, many other European scientists were involved in the quest for astronomical knowledge. Here the Danish astronomer Tycho Brahe is depicted in the observatory from which he made the most detailed stellar observations since ancient Greek times. The German mathematician Johannes Kepler used Brahe's data to support the Copernican view of a sun-centered universe.

Sir Francis Bacon (1561–1626) English politician, essayist, and philosopher. Known for his *Novum Organum* (1620), in which he argues for inductive reasoning and the rejection of *a priori* hypotheses. His science was based on close observation of natural phenomena.

doubt the existence of God before he could prove to his own satisfaction that God did, in fact, exist. Proof came from rational thought rather than inherited wisdom or sacred texts.

While Descartes' philosophy was based on introspection, others were laying the foundations for modern science based on experimentation and careful observation of the natural world. The Englishman **Sir Francis Bacon** (1561–1626) was one of the main proponents of an *inductive* approach to science: working from modest, carefully controlled observations toward larger truths. Like Descartes, Bacon believed that doubt produced knowledge. *"If a man will begin with certainties,"* he wrote, *"he shall end in doubts; but if he will be content to begin with doubts he shall end in certainties."** (See the feature "Movement of Ideas Through Primary Sources: A Japanese View of European Science.")

Both Descartes, using reason to deduce truths about existence, and Bacon, using an inductive approach that emphasized close observation and careful record keeping, were part of the intellectual trend in western Europe that increasingly emphasized human possibilities. In spite of our sinful natures, they argued, our ability to reason gives the means to comprehend the brilliance of God's creation, to strive toward truth on the basis of science. Such beliefs, controversial in Protestant England and Catholic France, were, as we have seen, actively repressed in seventeenth-century Italy at the time of Galileo, and religious critiques of science continued into the modern era (see Chapter 23). Still, by the eighteenth century the prestige of science was on the rise, often under the protection of political authorities.

Isaac Newton (1642–1727), born the same year that Galileo died, did more than anyone to create a systematic new architecture for science. Newton described a predictable natural world in which all matter exerts gravitational attraction in inverse proportion to mass and distance: the universal law of gravitation. Newton was a skilled experimental scientist in Bacon's inductive tradition. His work in optics, for example, led to the development of much more powerful telescopes. But he was preeminently a theorist who followed Descartes' lead in using reasoned, deductive thinking to establish general principles that tied together his own findings and those of other scientists. To achieve the mathematical rigor necessary to describe the acceleration and deceleration of bodies in motion, Newton became one of the inventors of differential calculus.

Western Europe's educated elite were ready for Newton's worldview. Whereas the new science had earlier caused anxiety by calling faith into question, by the

---

*Sir Francis Bacon, *Advancement of Learning,* with a preface by Thomas Case (London: Oxford University Press, 1906), p. 35.

early eighteenth century an English poet could write: *"Nature and Nature's laws lay hid in night; God said Let Newton Be! and all was light."** The association between God and Newton in this poem shows that the tension between science and faith was beginning to ease. Newton himself was a devout Christian. While many Christians continued to believe that God actively intervened in nature, those who adopted Newton's outlook tended to see the universe as a self-functioning outcome of God's perfect act of creation. He had embedded perfect proportionality and balance in nature, which was comprehensible to humanity through our ability to reason. God was like a master clock maker who, having set his elegant machine in motion, did not need to interfere further with its functioning.

Newton confidently declared that he could use mathematics to *"demonstrate the frame of the system of the world."* Joseph Banks inherited not only Newton's optimism but also his position as president of the Royal Society, an assembly of leading thinkers. Starting with Newton and continuing with Banks, the Royal Society served as a nerve center for European science.

Practical Science: Economic Botany, Agriculture, and Empire

The close study of plant life is characteristic of all cultures. Reliant on the natural world for medicine as well as for food, people have always sought an intimate knowledge of their environment. But it was only with the rise of modern botany that scientists began to systematically collect and organize a global catalogue of the world's flora.

Carl Linnaeus (1707–1778) was the pioneering figure in this area. As a medical student, Linnaeus first studied plants for their medicinal properties, but as his enthusiasm for plant collecting grew, he enlarged his focus. He traveled across Sweden gathering plant specimens, restored the botanical gardens at his university, and eventually sent nineteen of his students on voyages of trade and exploration around the world to increase the range of specimens available for scientific study. Two of Linnaeus's students were aboard the *Endeavour* with Joseph Banks.

As with Newton, the greatest scientists were those who combined experimentation and observation with theoretical system building. In 1735 Linnaeus published his classification of living things, *Systema Naturae*, laying out a scheme of classification for naming and categorizing plant life. His system classified species into hierarchical categories still in use today: genus/order/class/kingdom. Thus, any new plant from anywhere in the world could be classified in a well-ordered system that, to Linnaeus, demonstrated the beauty and orderliness of God's creation.

Linnaeus also developed the binomial ("two name") system for giving organisms consistent Latin names, the first name indicating the genus and the second the species. The world's plants were, of course, already named by the local people who were familiar with them. Now, as Linnaeus's students brought more and more specimens back to Europe, they received new names that made them, for the first time, part of a single knowledge system.

Linnaeus knew of Banks, and after the return of the *Endeavour* sent him a letter of congratulations. Though a more brilliant theoretician and original thinker than Banks, Linnaeus had failed in his attempts to derive practical, economic lessons from his botany. But economic botany was precisely the area in which Banks excelled.

Banks was a leading figure in the drive for "improvement," which in agriculture meant using scientific methods to increase the productivity of existing land and bring new land under cultivation. Both Banks and King George III (r. 1760–1820),

*Alexander Pope, "Epitaph Intended for Sir Isaac Newton," in *Pope: Selected Works,* ed. Herbert Davis (London: Oxford University Press, 1966), p. 651.

in Calcutta, that economic botany *"would help to banish famine in India and win the love of the Asiatics for their British conquerors."** The connection between science and empire was explicit.

The European Enlightenment, 1700–1800

Enlightenment
European philosophical movement of the late seventeenth and eighteenth centuries that stressed the use of reason, rather than the authority of ancient philosophers or religious leaders, in descriptions of society and the natural world.

The optimism characteristic of the new science influenced European views on society as well. During the eighteenth century, **Enlightenment** thinkers argued that the same capacity for reason that allowed scientists to unlock the secrets of the natural world could also be applied to social, political, and economic questions. Just as the inner workings of nature could be understood by human reason and described with mathematical precision, so Enlightenment philosophers saw rational, critical thinking as the best means of understanding and improving society. By the late eighteenth century, some thought that progress in human affairs was not only possible, but inevitable.

For such lofty ideals to find application in society, they need to influence those in power, and Enlightenment philosophy did impress Europe's kings, queens, and aristocracies. But there were limits to how far "enlightened" rulers would follow through on reform. Few rulers were willing to apply reason and critical thought in a way that undermined the traditions that gave them power.

"Enlightened" Ideas: Politics, Economics, and Society

The contrast between two English political philosophers, Thomas Hobbes (1588–1679) and John Locke (1632–1704), demonstrates the growing optimism of the Enlightenment. A friend of René Descartes, Hobbes applied the Frenchman's method of deductive reasoning to the question of how best to sustain political order in human society. His answer was deeply pessimistic. In the state of nature, he argued, anarchy prevails, and life is *"nasty, brutish, and short."†* Social and political order become possible only when individuals relinquish their autonomy to a despotic ruler. Hobbes rejected the "divine right of kings," the idea that royal authority came directly from God. Instead, he used reasoned arguments to support his advocacy for absolute monarchy as the best form of government.

John Locke
(1632–1704) Philosopher who applied Bacon's inductive reasoning to the study of politics and argued that a stable social order is based on a contract between rulers and ruled and requires the safeguarding of "life, liberty and property."

John Locke (1632–1704), a medical doctor who preferred Bacon's inductive approach, starting with experience and observation, reached very different conclusions. In his *Essay Concerning Human Understanding* (1690), Locke argued that political order derives from a contract in which individuals receive protection of their basic rights, "life, liberty and property," while they voluntarily give up some of their autonomy to the state, which was itself balanced between executive and legislative authorities. What Locke described was not a democracy: in his view only propertied males were capable of participating in government. But the rights of all would be protected regardless of gender or social class.

Hobbes's pessimism derived from witnessing the anarchy of the English Civil War, while Locke's optimism was connected to the role he played as an adviser to King William and Queen Mary during the Glorious Revolution (see Chapter 17). The balance between the powers of king and Parliament, and the protection of individual liberties through a Bill of Rights, were real-world applications of Locke's theories.

---

*Quoted in Richard Drayton, *Nature's Government: Science, Imperial Britain, and the 'Improvement' of the World* (New Haven: Yale University Press, 2000), p. 118.

†Thomas Hobbes, *The Leviathan.*

A French thinker who was influenced by English constitutional thought was the Baron de Montesquieu (1689–1755), who traveled to England to observe its very different constitutional system. This experience greatly influenced his book *The Spirit of the Laws* (1748), in which he argued for limitations on the power of government and a rational distribution of power between different social classes. Montesquieu (maw-tuh-SKYOO) believed that, as societies became more advanced, their political systems would become more liberal and their people more free. Following Locke, who argued that executive and legislative powers should be separate and balanced, Montesquieu maintained that judicial functions should also be protected from executive interference.

The most original economic thinker of the Enlightenment was Adam Smith, whose *Wealth of Nations* (1776) emphasizes the self-regulating power of markets. Smith argued for the encouragement of free markets and unfettered economic interchange within and between nations. The French term **laissez faire** (lay-say FAIR) has often been applied to Smith's vision of free-market capitalism. He argued that economic productivity is based on a division of labor. An individual who performed all the processes necessary to make a pin would be hard pressed to produce one a day. But if the work process is subdivided among workers, each specializing in one aspect of production, Smith argued, thousands could be produced in a day. He applied the same principle to international trade. If each nation specializes in the production of what it is best fit to produce, and trades with other nations specializing in products best fitted to their economic potential, everyone gains through mutual exchange. Smith was opposed to slavery because he thought that labor contracts negotiated in a free market lead to more efficient production. He believed that the "invisible hand" of the market functioned like Isaac Newton's laws of gravitational attraction, maintaining balance and harmony in economic affairs. Like Locke, he believed that protection of private property was a core function of government.

Smith's advocacy of the free market contradicted existing European economic policies based on monopoly and mercantilism (see Chapter 17). Like other Enlightenment thinkers, Smith was using reason to challenge existing traditions and assumptions. And whereas mercantilism had been based on a zero-sum view of economics, in which one nation could advance only at another's expense, Smith held the more optimistic view that freer international trade would lead to more wealth for all.

While philosophers across Europe aspired to the title "enlightened," it was through Paris that the intellectual currents of the Western world flowed. Indeed, we still use the French word for philosophers, **philosophes** (fill-uh-SOHF), to describe these intellectuals today. The most important of them was François-Marie Arouet, better known as **Voltaire** (1694–1778). Voltaire (vawl-TARE) was most famous as a satirist who used his reason like a searchlight to illuminate all the superstitions, prejudices, and follies of eighteenth-century European society. In his great novel *Candide* (1759), Voltaire mocked the corruption and injustice of the world around him. He believed that reason makes all phenomena and situations intelligible to the human intellect. He also thought that relativism, the ability to see yourself and your own social circumstances in a wider context, is a necessary component of enlightened thinking, since tolerance toward and understanding of others is a precondition for self-knowledge. Voltaire incurred the displeasure of religious authorities by arguing that organized religion is always and everywhere a hindrance to free and rational inquiry.

Enlightenment ideas were discussed passionately in the *salons* (drawing rooms) of Paris. Often hosted by women of means and education, these salons brought philosophical and artistic discussions into the homes of the elite; Voltaire and other notable philosophers were highly sought-after guests. But though women

laissez faire
(French, "leave to do") Economic philosophy attributed to Scottish Enlightenment thinker Adam Smith, who argued that businesses and nations benefit from a free market where each party seeks to maximize its comparative economic advantage.

philosophes
French intellectuals who promoted Enlightenment principles.

Voltaire
(1694–1778) The pen name of François-Marie Arouet, one of the most prominent Enlightenment writers, who used satire to critique the irrationality of French society.

A Parisian Salon Mid-eighteenth-century Paris was the center of European intellectual life. *Salons* were gatherings at private homes at which entertainment was combined with intellectual edification, including poetry readings and discussion of the latest Enlightenment philosophies. Wealthy women often hosted these lively events, competing to attract prestigious guests and distinguished authors. Polite and erudite conversation was the main purpose of a salon, though the card table in this drawing indicates that other amusements might be on the agenda as well. (Louvre, Paris/Reunion des Musées Nationaux/Art Resource, NY)

were often hostesses for these gatherings and participated in the lively discussions, few Enlightenment thinkers were willing to consider that restrictions on the role of women in society were a matter of prejudice and tradition, not reason.

Some women protested their exclusion from full participation in intellectual life. At the same time that Sor Juana was meeting resistance from Catholic Church authorities in New Spain because of her writings (see Chapter 18), a seventeenth-century English scientist, Margaret Cavendish, noted that restrictions on women's roles resulted from nothing more than *"the over-weening conceit men have of themselves."*[*] Another Englishwoman, Mary Astell, challenged John Locke's idea that absolute authority, while unacceptable in the state, was appropriate within the family. Late in the eighteenth century, **Mary Wollstonecraft** went even further in her *Vindication of the Rights of Women* (1792), asking: *"How many women waste life away . . . who might have practiced as physicians, regulated a farm, managed a shop, and stood erect, supported by their own industry?"*[†] Only through equal access to

Mary Wollstonecraft (1759–1797) An English author and reformer who advocated equality of rights for women.

---

[*]Quoted in Moira Ferguson, ed., *First Feminists: British Women Writers, 1578–1799* (Bloomington: Indiana University Press, 1985), p. 86.

[†]Mary Wollstonecraft, *A Vindication of the Rights of Women* (Boston: Peter Edes, 1792; New York: Bartleby.com, 1999), chapter 9.

education, full citizenship, and financial autonomy, Wollstonecraft said, could women's full potential as individuals and as wives and mothers be achieved.

For the elite who attended salons, arguing about daring ideas was mostly a matter of fashion. At the other end of society, Enlightenment ideas were of little concern to tradesmen and farmers, people who Voltaire and most other philosophes considered irrational and tradition-bound. Of all the social classes in France, Enlightenment thought had the greatest impact on the *bourgeoisie*, or middle class.

The French bourgeoisie were economically successful but lacked the social status and political rights of aristocrats. Skepticism toward religious and civil authority thus came naturally to many of these educated, middle-class men and women. Expanding literacy meant that even those who did not travel in the refined circles of royal and aristocratic patronage, and who might never be invited to a salon, nevertheless had access to Enlightenment ideas. The most important publishing project of the age was the **Encyclopedia,** or *Rational Dictionary of the Arts, Sciences and Crafts*, a collection of all the great Enlightenment works that was compiled in Paris between 1751 and 1776. More powerfully than any other work, this encyclopedia made the case for a new form of universal knowledge based on reason and the critical use of human intellect. The growth of the printing and publishing industries facilitated the dissemination of the *Encyclopedia*, and translation into English, Spanish, and German gave it international impact.

The German philosopher Kant emphasized that cowardice stood in the way of enlightenment. Unquestioned tradition and blind faith, *"man's inability to make use of his understanding without direction from another,"* hinders our progress. *"Have courage to use your own reason,"* Kant concluded; *"that is the motto of enlightenment."*[*] But translating that motto into political reality meant confronting powerful vested interests, with radical, and ultimately revolutionary, implications.

"Enlightened Despots" in Eighteenth-Century Europe

Voltaire and most other philosophes thought that if society were to become enlightened, the change would have to come from above. That provided some European monarchs, so-called **enlightened despots**, with a new rationale for absolute power. Rather than simply claiming "divine right," they portrayed themselves as bringing order, harmony, and reason to their domains. In the late seventeenth century, Louis XIV of France is supposed to have said, *"I am the state."* Now in the eighteenth century, the Prussian leader Frederick the Great defined himself as *"first servant of the state,"* implying that the kingdom was greater than the king, who needed to demonstrate his competence in action.

Frederick the Great (r. 1740–1786) was perhaps the most "enlightened" of the great monarchs of the eighteenth century. As a young man, Frederick studied music and literature. He became a first-rate flute player, and his patronage made Prussia, previously considered only a military power, a center for the arts. Frederick absorbed French literature and the ideas of the philosophes. After meeting in 1750, he and Voltaire maintained a correspondence, trading philosophical ideas. Frederick reformed the Prussian legal system to emphasize reason and justice over tradition, advocated freedom of conscience, and allowed some freedom of the press. However, Prussia's military ethic continued, and it remained a tightly regimented society. Prussian territory doubled in size as Frederick's army became one of the largest and strongest in Europe.

Encyclopedia (1751–1776) A collection of the works of all the great Enlightenment thinkers that promoted a new form of universal knowledge based on reason and the critical use of human intellect.

enlightened despots Eighteenth-century European rulers who sought to systematically apply Enlightenment ideals to the administration of government.

---

*Immanuel Kant, *What Is Enlightenment?* ed. and trans. Lewis White Beck (Indianapolis: Bobs-Merrill, 1959), p. 85.

Joseph Banks did not accompany Cook's later journeys. But from England he played a major role in the settlement of Australia. By 1820 the foundation had been laid for a British colony of settlement on a continent that had been virtually unknown to Europeans before Cook's voyage.

Captain Cook in Polynesia, 1769–1779

Tupaia
(ca. 1725–1770) A Polynesian high priest who contributed his expert navigational skills to Captain James Cook's first Pacific voyage.

On the first voyage, Cook and Banks were aided by a Tahitian high priest named **Tupaia** (ca. 1725–1770). Tupaia (too-PUH-ee-uh) knew several Polynesian languages and, coming from a family of navigators, was able to supplement Cook's instruments and charts with a local understanding of winds and currents. He also helped Banks understand Polynesian cultural practices, such as the meaning of the peace ritual that had so mystified the Englishman when he first set foot on the island.

In spite of Tupaia's help, miscommunications between Europeans and Polynesians persisted. In his journals, Banks noted with frustration *"how much these people are given to thieving."* *"All are of the opinion,"* he writes, *"that if they can once get possession of anything it immediately becomes their own."* Usually it was small items that went missing, but when some of their important astronomical devices disappeared, Cook was worried. Banks, with his developing knowledge of Tahitian society, was able to work with local people to get the equipment back.

Theft among the British was a problem as well. Sailors kept stealing nails from the ship to trade with the islanders, for whom iron was new and valuable. However, one day when a Tahitian woman refused to sell her stone axe for an iron nail, a sailor took it anyway, and Cook decided to make an example of him. He ordered a flogging for the man and invited some Tahitian chiefs to witness the punishment. Banks describes the scene:

> [The chiefs] stood quietly and saw him stripped and fastened to the rigging, but as soon as the first blow was given they interfered with many tears, begging the punishment might cease, a request which the Captain would not comply with.*

The Tahitians' views of property and punishment were quite different from those of the English; they were much less focused on exclusive ownership of material goods and would never use corporal punishment in a simple case of theft. Unlike Banks, who made a genuine attempt to understand the people of the island and to mediate such disputes while deepening his understanding of their culture, Cook had a strictly utilitarian attitude: he wanted to make his astronomical and navigational observations, get fresh supplies of food and water, and move on.

Cultural and political misunderstanding led to the death of Captain Cook on a Hawai'ian beach in 1779. When Cook and his men first arrived, they received a joyous and generous reception. Nevertheless, there were tensions. His men were exhausted from a futile trip to the Arctic in search of a "northwest passage" linking Asia and Europe, and they resented Cook's attempts to stop them from their usual practice of trading iron nails for sex. Cook was trying to protect the Hawai'ians from the venereal diseases he knew were rampant on his ship. After departing Hawai'i, storm damage forced Cook to return. This time there was no

*Quoted in Patrick O'Brien, *Joseph Banks: A Life* (Chicago: University of Chicago Press, 1987), pp. 94, 95.

joyous greeting. Instead, an argument escalated into violence, and an islander stabbed Cook to death. (See the feature "Visual Evidence in Primary Sources: The Death of Captain Cook.")

For all the power of predictability and prediction afforded by modern science, the death of Captain Cook shows the limitations of reason in governing human interactions. There were no chronometers, no astronomical sightings, no surveys or charts with which to safely navigate the waters of cross-cultural communication. The challenge for Polynesians came when they were drawn into a European-dominated global system that brought new economic relations, new technologies, and new belief systems that undermined the existing order of Oceanic societies. Many Polynesians would be killed by new diseases brought by the Europeans, including Tupaia, who died of dysentery within two years of his first encounter with them.

Joseph Banks and the Settlement of Australia

The impact of Joseph Banks on the history of Australia is inscribed on one of its most famous geographic features, Botany Bay, where Banks undertook an intensive reconnaissance of eastern Australia's unique plant life. He is sometimes called "the Father of Australia" for the role he played in the foundation of the colony of New South Wales in 1788 with its capital at Sydney.

New South Wales began as a penal colony, its overwhelmingly male population consisting of prisoners, many of them Irish, who had little to lose from taking a chance on resettlement halfway around the world. The colony got off to a rocky start. Few of the convicts knew how to survive in this foreign terrain. Nor could they rely on the local Koori population of Aboriginal Australians, which initially kept its distance and then launched a series of attacks.

The colonial economy of New South Wales strengthened with the introduction of merino sheep in 1805, descendants of the same sheep that Joseph Banks had imported from Spain to Kew Gardens for the king's flock. The grasslands of New South Wales proved to be ideal grazing grounds, and wool exports financed the development of colonial society. By the early nineteenth century, most settlers were free immigrants rather than convicts, the cities of Sydney and Melbourne were on paths to prosperity, and new British colonies were founded across the continent. After 1817, the name *Australia* was used to refer to this collection of colonies.

Joseph Banks regarded those developments as "improvement," another successful outcome of the application of practical science. But British settlement had a devastating impact on the original inhabitants of the continent. Aboriginal Australians had rich and complex religious and artistic traditions, as well as keen knowledge of the local environment from which, as hunter-gatherers whose ancestors had lived on the continent for tens of thousands of years, they derived all the necessities of life. But they had no metal tools, no hierarchical political organization, and, like the Polynesians, no immunity to Afro-Eurasian diseases like smallpox. As in the Americas in previous centuries, the Aborigines experienced the European territorial advance as a plague: more than half died in the nineteenth century. The survivors fled to remote deserts and mountains, worked for Europeans on their commercial ranches, or moved to cities, where they formed a socially and economically disenfranchised subclass.

The Death of Captain Cook

James Cook had been sent off in royal fashion when his ships departed the Hawai'ian islands in the summer of 1779. When they returned to mend a broken mast, however, the Hawai'ians seemed disappointed and confused at their return. Tensions ran high, especially after a high chief was flogged for stealing a pair of iron tongs. Cook's crew noticed that some men were piling stones on the beach, as if getting ready for an attack. Cook invited one of the chiefs with whom he had been friends to come aboard his ship, but the *kahuna* (kah-HOO-nuh) was prevented by his own people

© Dixson Galleries, State Library of New South Wales, Sydney, Australia. Pxd59, f.1/The Bridgeman Art Library

The anger of the Hawai'ians that led to this incident, Obeyesekere argues, came from Cook's unwillingness to help them in their war with Maui and his increasingly belligerent demands for food and supplies.

Obeyesekere notes that as soon as news of Cook's death reached England, his status as a Hawai'ian god became a subject of music, art, and theater. Cook's godlike status, he argues, came about not from Hawai'ian beliefs but from European myths of "conquest, imperialism, and civilization."[*]

---

[*]Gananath Obeyesekere, *The Apotheosis of Captain Cook: European Mythmaking in the Pacific* (Princeton: Princeton University Press, 1997), p. 3.

from doing so. A warrior then threatened Cook with an iron dagger. Cook shot at him, and a melee broke out. On that morning, July 14, 1779, on a beach at Kealakekua Bay, Captain James Cook was stabbed to death. That fact is certain. But the cause and context of Cook's death are controversial. The engraving reproduced here, made by John Webber, the officially appointed artist of the expedition, provides some evidence but does not resolve scholarly differences in the interpretation of Cook's death.

Anthropologist Marshall Sahlins argues that Cook had first arrived during the Makahiki (ma-kah-HEE-kee) festival dedicated to the fertility god Lono. His appearance at that precise time, and his landing near the god's main temple, caused the Hawai'ians to identify him with Lono. When Cook later returned to repair a broken mast, however, the Makahiki cycle had ended. Now it was time for Lono to be symbolically defeated, Sahlins explains,

and replaced by the war god Ku. In conformity with the ritual cycle, Lono-Cook was killed.

Nonsense, says Gananath Obeyesekere, who maintains that Sahlins is guilty of typical European arrogance in saying that the Hawai'ians saw Cook as a god. In fact, Obeyesekere argues, the Hawai'ians were guided by "practical rationality," a universal common sense that would make it impossible for them to mistake a man for a god. Sahlins responds that he is the one interpreting events from within the logic of traditional Hawai'ian beliefs, while it is actually Obeyesekere who is imposing foreign beliefs on the Hawai'ians by ignoring their own cosmology and value structures. In Hawai'ian belief, he notes, there was a strong equation between status as a powerful chief and affiliation with a god like Lono.

There is no clear conclusion to this debate, as Sahlins and Obeyesekere offer differing interpretations of this image.

Area of detail

© Dixson Galleries, State Library of New South Wales, Sydney, Australia. Pxd59. f.1./The Bridgeman Art Library

Sahlins claims that he can identify the actual killer of Cook in this image: Nuha, a powerful warrior who was "an ideal champion for the aging king in the ritualistic murder of Lono-Cook."[1]

Accepting the overall accuracy of this image, Sahlins even claims to be able to identify the murder weapon: "an iron spike manufactured at [a] factory in Birmingham, requisitioned by Cook 'to be distributed to them as presents toward obtaining their friendship.'"[2]

---

[1] Dan Lynch, "Gananath Obeyesekere v. Marshall Sahlins: Did Hawaiians Consider Captain Cook as a God?" Unpublished paper, California State University Long Beach, 2006.
[2] Marshall Sahlins, *Islands of History* (Chicago: University of Chicago Press, 1985), p. 131.

QUESTION FOR ANALYSIS

» *Though John Webber was at the scene, he could not possibly have had the perspective on events that is shown in this drawing. Does the change in perspective from what he actually saw to how he represented the event diminish the reliability of the image as a historical source?*

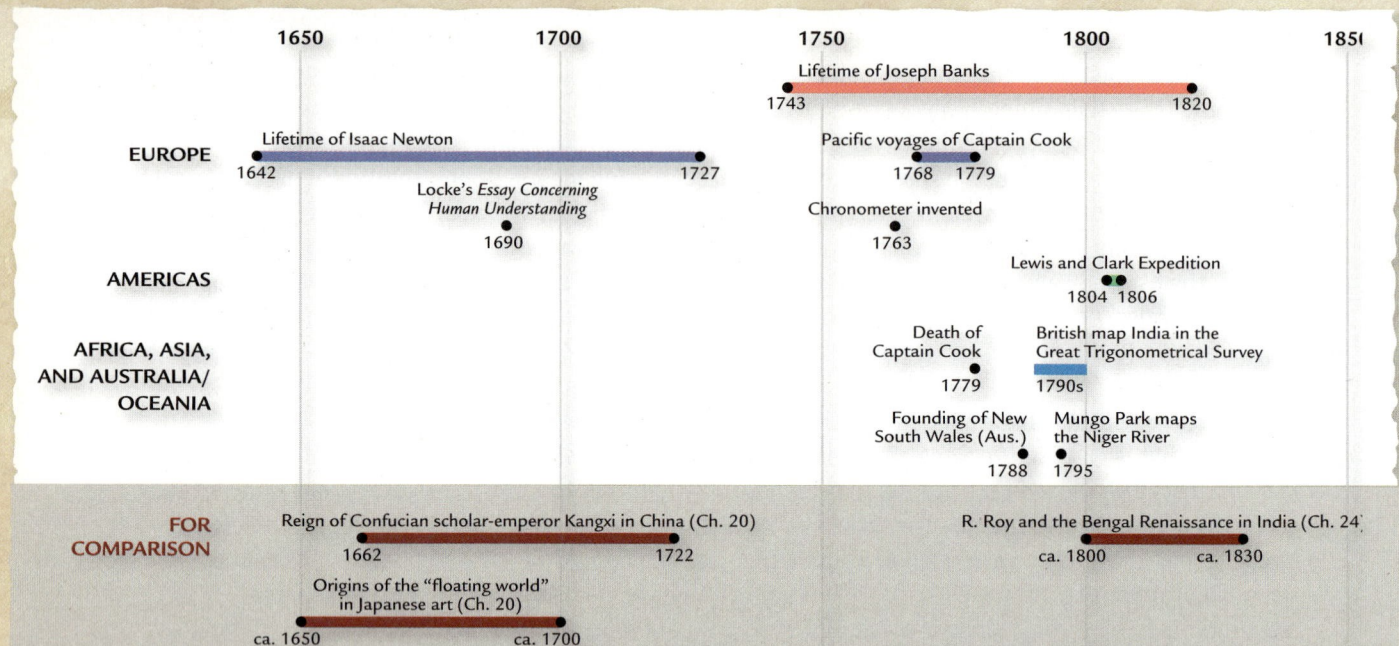

Science, Technology, and Revolution in World History

Initially, Europe's scientific revolution had only limited global effects. While many Asian and African producers and consumers felt the impact of Europe's involvement in the expanding early modern economy of the sixteenth and seventeenth centuries, they largely retained their own cultural and intellectual traditions. True, "Dutch learning" had entered Japan, European cartography had influenced the Qing empire (see Chapter 20), and some Iranian and Chinese artists had borrowed Western artistic techniques. But outside those areas where European dominance had been asserted earlier (as in the colonial Americas or those parts of Africa most affected by the Atlantic slave trade), European ideas, both religious and scientific, were only marginal, if present at all.

The "practical science" advocated by Joseph Banks helped bring more and more of the world under European sway, if not always direct control, and the Industrial Revolution would magnify Europe's cultural and intellectual influence even further (see Chapter 23). Already during Banks's lifetime new technologies like the steam engine and new forms of factory organization were revolutionizing the British economy. By the late nineteenth century a flood of new technologies—railroads, steamships, telegraph lines—were boosting the productivity of industrial societies and propelling change around the world (see Chapters 24–26).

When confronted with the overwhelming material outcomes of European science and technology, people across the world would be forced to call their own beliefs and traditions into question. Should they adopt the new ideas as superior to their own, like Sugita Gempaku? Should they resist them as undermining their own established way of life, as conservatives in the Russian, Ottoman, and Qing empires would advocate during the nineteenth century? Or maybe, like Japanese society, seek out a middle ground, synthesizing their own traditions with Western science and the insights of the Enlightenment (see Chapters 23 and 24)?

Many peoples across the world would have to struggle to find the freedom to even be able to make their own choices about how to adapt to the power of Western science and technology. In colonial Africa, for example, Western conquest was so rapid and comprehensive in the decades before 1900 that people had little time to adjust (see Chapter 26). Here, as in Polynesia and Oceania, Joseph Banks's idea of "improvement," that progress need take no account of indigenous interests, would long prevail. Ideas of European racial superiority reinforced such attitudes.

Within Europe, science had challenged the intellectual monopoly of religious authorities, a tension that would continue into modern times with the development of evolutionary biology (see Chapter 23). Enlightenment philosophy, while it attracted the interest of kings, queens, and aristocrats, would also prove problematic for the status quo once members of the middle class began to push for reform—and revolution when necessary—in support of ideas that undercut traditional authority. The "age of reason" promised "improvement," a better future, while challenging much that people had long held to be tried and true. Both the promise of a better future and the more unsettling consequences—questions of the relationship between rulers and those they rule, between faith and science, between individuals and communities—would become part of the human condition over the next two centuries. First, Westerners had to deal with such issues themselves, as they did in revolutions in the United States, France, and Latin America, the topics of the next chapter.

Voyages on the Web: Joseph Banks

The Voyages Map App follows the traveler's journeys using interactive study tools, including 360-degree panoramic views of historic sites, zoomable maps, audio summaries, flash cards, and quizzes.

Key Terms

Joseph Banks (580)
James Cook (582)
René Descartes (583)
Sir Francis Bacon (584)
Isaac Newton (584)
Carl Linnaeus (585)
Enlightenment (590)

John Locke (590)
laissez faire (591)
philosophes (591)
Voltaire (591)
Mary Wollstonecraft (592)
Encyclopedia (593)
enlightened despots (593)

problem of longitude (596)
African Association (598)
Great Trigonometrical Survey (598)
Lewis and Clark Expedition (600)
Tupaia (602)

For Further Reference

Crosby, Alfred. *The Measure of Reality: Quantification in Western Europe, 1250–1600*. New York: Cambridge University Press, 1997.

Desmond, Ray. *The History of the Royal Botanic Gardens at Kew*. 2d rev. ed. Edinburgh: Royal Botanic Gardens Press, 2007.

Drayton, Richard. *Nature's Government: Science, Imperial Britain, and the "Improvement" of the World*. New Haven: Yale University Press, 2000.

Edney, Matthew H. *Mapping an Empire: The Geographical Construction of British India, 1765–1843*. Chicago: University of Chicago Press, 1990.

Fara, Patricia. *Sex, Botany and Empire: The Story of Carl Linnaeus and Joseph Banks*. New York: Columbia University Press, 2004.

Fernandez-Armesto, Felipe. *Pathfinders: A Global History of Exploration*. New York: W. W. Norton, 2007.

Gascoigne, John. *Joseph Banks and the English Enlightenment: Useful Knowledge and Polite Culture*. New York: Cambridge University Press, 2003.

Henry, John. *The Scientific Revolution and the Origins of Modern Science*. 3d ed. New York: Palgrave, 2008.

Hooper, Steven. *Pacific Encounters: Art and Divinity in Polynesia, 1760–1860*. Honolulu: University of Hawai'i Press, 2006.

Israel, Jonathan. *Radical Enlightenment: Philosophy and the Making of Modernity, 1650–1750*. New York: Oxford University Press, 2002.

Jacob, Margaret. *The Cultural Meaning of the Scientific Revolution*. New York: McGraw-Hill, 1988.

Principle, Lawrence. *Scientific Revolution: A Very Short Introduction*. New York: Oxford University Press, 2011.

Salmond, Anne. *The Trial of the Cannibal Dog: The Remarkable Story of Captain Cook's Encounter in the South Seas*. New Haven: Yale University Press, 2003.

Sorbel, Dava, and William J. H. Andrews. *The Illustrated Longitude: The True Story of a Lone Genius Who Solved the Greatest Scientific Problem of His Time*. New York: Walker & Co., 1998.

Veth, Peter, ed. *Strangers on the Shore: Early Coastal Contact in Australia*. Canberra: National Museum of Australia Press, 2008.

 Go to the CourseMate website at **www.cengagebrain.com** for additional study tools and review materials—including audio and video clips—for this chapter.

22

Revolutions in the West, 1750–1830

In the summer of 1805 a young South American traveled to Madrid, Rome, and Paris. Eager to expand his horizons after his tutor had required him to study the great texts of the Enlightenment, **Simón Bolívar** (1783–1830) witnessed firsthand the excitement and the fear caused by the rising empire of Napoleon Bonaparte in the aftermath of the French Revolution.

One day Bolívar climbed one of the famous hills of Rome to gain a panoramic view of the "eternal city." He was awestruck by the echoes of the city's great imperial past, which, he thought, summed up all that was great and all that was tragic in history. But he saw the destiny of the Americas as greater still. Inspired by the French example, he pledged to play his part to liberate South America from the Spanish empire and thus advance the cause of liberty for all mankind:

Simón Bolívar

(© Mireille Vautier)

Here every manner of grandeur has had its type, all miseries their cradle. . . .

[Rome] has examples for everything, except the cause of humanity: . . . heroic warriors, rapacious consuls . . . golden virtues, and sordid crimes; but for the emancipation of the spirit . . . the exaltation of man, and the final perfectibility of reason, little or nothing. . . . The resolution of the great problem of man set free seems to have been something . . . that would only be made clear in the New World. . . . I swear before you, I swear

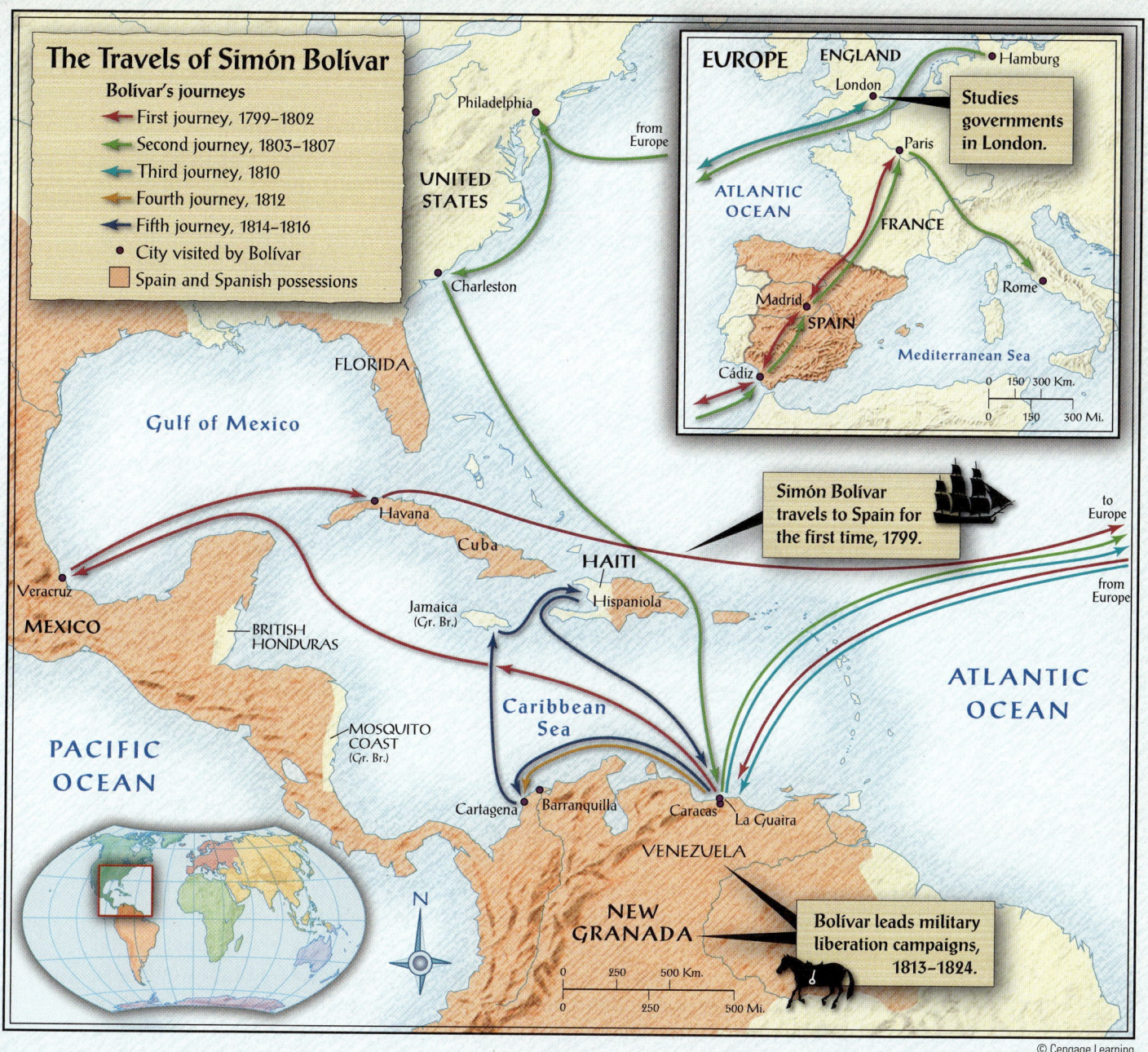

The Travels of Simón Bolívar

Bolívar's journeys

— First journey, 1799–1802
— Second journey, 1803–1807
— Third journey, 1810
— Fourth journey, 1812
— Fifth journey, 1814–1816
● City visited by Bolívar
▢ Spain and Spanish possessions

EUROPE ENGLAND · Hamburg

London

Studies governments in London.

from Europe

ATLANTIC OCEAN

Paris

FRANCE

Rome

Madrid

SPAIN

Cádiz

Mediterranean Sea

| 0 | 150 | 300 Km. |
| 0 | 150 | 300 Mi. |

Philadelphia

UNITED STATES

Charleston

FLORIDA

Gulf of Mexico

Havana

Cuba

HAITI

Hispaniola

Jamaica (Gr. Br.)

Simón Bolívar travels to Spain for the first time, 1799.

to Europe

from Europe

ATLANTIC OCEAN

Veracruz

MEXICO

BRITISH HONDURAS

MOSQUITO COAST (Gr. Br.)

PACIFIC OCEAN

Caribbean Sea

Cartagena Barranquilla

Caracas La Guaira

VENEZUELA

NEW GRANADA

Bolívar leads military liberation campaigns, 1813–1824.

| 0 | 250 | 500 Km. |
| 0 | 250 | 500 Mi. |

N

© Cengage Learning

Join this chapter's traveler on "Voyages," an interactive tour of historic sites and events:
www.cengagebrain.com

by the God of my fathers, I swear on their graves, I swear by my Country that I will not rest body or soul until I have broken the chains binding us to the will of Spanish might![*]

[*]Excerpt from Simón Bolívar, "Oath Taken at Rome, 15 August 1805," trans. Frederick H. Fornoff, in *El Libertador: Writings of Simón Bolívar,* ed. David Bushnell (New York: Oxford University Press, 2003), pp. 113–144.

Simón Bolívar's (see-MOAN bow-LEE-var) oath changed not only his own life but also the course of Latin American history. Over the next two decades he led the drive for the independence of Spain's South American colonies. In Latin America he is known simply as *El Libertador* (el lee-bare-TAH-door), "the Liberator."

Having grown up in one of the richest households in Venezuela, Bolívar first went to Europe in 1799, when he was only sixteen, to visit an uncle in Madrid. There he spent his money freely while enjoying the life of the Spanish court. He fell in love and, in spite of his youth, married and returned with his bride to Caracas. Sadly, she died just eight months later. Now in his early twenties, inspired by the examples of revolution in North America and France, he returned to Europe to visit a former teacher, a revolutionary who had been driven out of Venezuela by the Spanish authorities.

Apart from visiting Rome, he spent most of this trip in Paris, the intellectual center of the Enlightenment and the political center of revolution. In the previous decade the French monarchy had been overthrown and replaced by a republic. Now the republic was being superseded by the dictatorship of Napoleon Bonaparte. Bolívar's worldview was greatly affected by his experience of postrevolutionary French politics. The French Revolution, like ancient Rome, had brought forth both *"golden virtues"* and *"sordid crimes."* Only in the Americas, thought Bolívar, could the full liberation of the human spirit be achieved.

Bolívar proved himself a brilliant military leader. Between 1813, when he entered his native Caracas at the head of a liberation army, and 1824, when he drove the Spanish army from Peru, he fulfilled the oath he had taken in Rome. Like other revolutionaries of the late eighteenth and early nineteenth centuries, Bolívar started out with high hopes founded in Enlightenment optimism. But turning independence from Spanish rule into true liberty for the people of South America proved difficult. By the time of Bolívar's death in 1830, many South Americans had become concerned about his dictatorial tendencies. His story, as one biographer has emphasized, is one of "liberation and disappointment."[*]

Elsewhere in Latin America and the Caribbean, and in North America and France, other revolutionaries also believed that prejudice and tradition would give way to rationality and enlightenment and that new political and social systems would both guarantee liberty and provide order and security. In 1776, Britain's North American colonists had broken free and founded a democratic republic that seemed to combine liberty with moderation. A more volatile historical precedent was the French Revolution, which swung violently from constitutional monarchy to radical republic to military dictatorship. In the Caribbean, the Republic of Haiti was created following one of the largest slave uprisings in world history.

The issue of slavery was very much on Bolívar's mind. Like his North American counterpart George Washington, Bolívar was a slave owner. Could the dream of liberty be compatible with the reality of slavery? Such discrepancies between dreams and harsher realities were, in fact, a central theme of the age. Reconciling the twin mandates of liberty and equality, and securing both within a stable and well-ordered state, was a tremendous challenge for revolutionaries across North and South America, the Caribbean, and France.

---

[*]David Bushnell, *Simón Bolívar: Liberation and Disappointment* (New York: Pearson Longman, 2004).

Focus Questions

» *What political compromises were made in establishing the new United States of America?*

» *What were the major phases of the French Revolution?*

» *How were the revolutions in Latin America and the Caribbean influenced by the history of colonialism?*

» *How much did the outcomes of these revolutions in western Europe and the Americas represent a thorough transformation of existing political and social structures?*

Rebellion and Independence in America, 1763–1797

On April 19, 1775, after British soldiers marched on the town of Concord to seize and destroy arms secretly stockpiled there by the Massachusetts militia, the two sides exchanged gunfire at Concord's North Bridge. Surprised by the colonials' steadfast resistance and confused by their irregular tactics, the British beat a retreat back to Boston, harassed along their flanks all the way.

To say the shots fired at Concord, products of a skirmish in a small corner of the British empire, were "heard 'round the world" is an overstatement. Even the term *American Revolution* is misleading, since these events initially involved only a small part of the vast American landmass. Yet over time these events would have a powerful global impact. The Declaration of Independence (1776), justifying the rebellion, is one of the most influential political statements in world history, while the Constitution of the United States of America (1787) has, through recurrent crises, provided a model of limited yet effective government. The founding of the United States was a powerful testament to the principles of the Enlightenment. Nevertheless, compromises made during the nation-building process, especially bargains about slavery, undermined the Enlightenment's highest aspirations of universal liberty and equality.

Rebellion and War, 1763–1783

A key turning point in the relations between Britain and the colonists was the British victory in the French and Indian War. That particular North American conflict was only one theater of the Seven Years' War (1756–1763) that pitted the British against French imperial forces (see Chapter 19). Victory gave the British control of Canada and new territories in India, while opening new possibilities for expansion on the western frontier of Britain's North American colonies. Many colonists were anxious to expand into the Ohio River Valley and other areas west of the Appalachian Mountains. But British leaders were cautious. No sooner had they defeated the French than they were faced with a Native American uprising. European settlements on the frontier would generate more conflict, inevitably requiring more British troops and resources. Britain's Proclamation of 1763 established a fixed westward limit to colonial expansion, much to the disgust of colonists.

Not only were the British restraining colonial expansion, but they also required the colonists to bear the cost of their own defense. Colonists bitterly resented both the new taxes, such as the Stamp Act of 1765, and attempts to restrict colonial trade

Library of Congress LC-USZC4-4600

The Boston Massacre On March 5, 1770, British soldiers shot and killed five Boston men, galvanizing public opinion against the colonial authorities. This image of the scene, published by radical activist Paul Revere just three weeks later, magnified those feelings of resentment. It should not be taken, however, as an accurate view of the event. Rather than lining up to fire, as shown here, the British soldiers were engulfed in a riotous crowd. Crispus Attucks, an African American who was one of the first to die, is depicted at the soldiers' feet as a white man.

George Washington (1732–1799) Commander of the Continental Army in the American War of Independence from Britain; also the first president of the United States of America.

Declaration of Independence (1776) Document written by Thomas Jefferson justifying the separation of Britain's North American colonies, declaring them free and independent states.

with the West Indies. New England merchants were aggrieved by the monopoly granted to the British East India Company for the supply of tea to the colonies. Resistance to that law took the form of illegal smuggling and, more dramatically, the Boston Tea Party, where colonists dressed as Amerindians tossed a boatload of East India Company tea into Boston Harbor. Lacking representation in Parliament, colonials had no direct way to influence British government policy. *"No taxation without representation!"* became their rallying cry.

British policies led many settlers to conclude that their rights as freeborn British subjects were being assailed. By forcibly repressing boycotts and urban demonstrations, British authorities increased the number of colonists whose self-identity was shifting from "British" to "American." The final straw was suspending the charter of the Massachusetts Bay Company in 1775, disbanding the colonial legislature, and imposing a British governor. By this time the colonists had formed militias for self-defense, setting the stage for the confrontation at Concord.

A Continental Congress convened in 1775 that brought together representatives from each of the thirteen colonies. **George Washington** (1732–1799) was appointed commander of its army. Washington, a Virginian, had served as an officer during British military campaigns in the Ohio River Valley.

On July 4, 1776, Congress approved Thomas Jefferson's **Declaration of Independence**, which not only detailed the colonists' grievances but also made a stirring announcement of universal political values:

We hold these truths to be self-evident, that all men are created equal, that they are endowed by their Creator with certain inalienable Rights, that among these are Life, Liberty and the pursuit of Happiness.—That to secure these rights, Governments are instituted among Men, deriving their just powers from the consent of the governed.

The phrase "consent of the governed" built on John Locke's theory of government as based on a contract in which individuals receive protection of their basic rights by voluntarily submitting to a legitimate government (see Chapter 21). Jefferson went even further: legitimacy derives directly from the "consent of the governed." When such legitimacy was lacking, rebellion was justified: *"When a long train of abuses and usurpations . . . evinces a design to reduce them under absolute Despotism, it is their right, it is their duty, to throw off such Government, and to provide new Guards for their future security."*

The British had some advantages in the war that began in 1776. The tens of thousands of "redcoat" soldiers in North America were well equipped and well trained. Moreover, many Loyalists in the colonies argued against rebellion. For inventor, diplomat, and continental congressman Benjamin Franklin, this was a family affair. Franklin himself exchanged his British identity for an American one reluctantly, and his son William, the royally appointed governor of New Jersey, refused to do so. Many free blacks, aware that slavery had already been eliminated in Britain and that prominent leaders of the rebellion included slave owners like Washington and Jefferson, were Loyalist as well. Likewise, Amerindians who had earlier fought with the British against the French, such as the Mohawk nation under their leader Joseph Brant (Thayendanegea), stood with the British. (For later developments in Brant's family and their loyalty to the British empire, see Chapter 25.)

In 1777, however, colonists defeated a British force at Saratoga in New York (see Map 22.1). Not only did that surprise victory give the colonists a forward base against the Mohawk, but it also persuaded the French that the American rebellion might succeed. Early in 1778 a Franco-American treaty was signed, with France hoping to weaken its main global rival. The French supplied the rebel army with weapons and harried the British fleet in the Atlantic and Caribbean.

Apart from the French alliance, the rebellious colonists had several advantages. The rural population supported the Continental Army with supplies, information on British movements, and knowledge of the local terrain. Women played a notable role. They did extra work, including blacksmithing and other "male" jobs, in the absence of their soldier-husbands, and they also produced shoes, clothes, and munitions for the Continental Army. Finally, since British soldiers were reluctant to search them, women made excellent spies and carriers of communication.

Another advantage was the leadership ability of General Washington, who managed to maintain the morale of his troops through the harsh winter at Valley Forge in 1777–1778 and to outmaneuver the British commander Lord Cornwallis at the siege of Yorktown in 1781. After Washington's army surrounded the British, French ships cut off Cornwallis's route of retreat, and the war was over. In the Treaty of Paris (1783), the British government acknowledged the independence of the new United States of America.

The loss of the thirteen North American colonies after 1781 caused the British government to reconsider its global priorities and place a greater emphasis on Asia. In fact, after his surrender at Yorktown, Lord Cornwallis retained his high political standing and was appointed governor-general of British India (see Chapter 20). Subsequent British expansion in India laid the foundation for what historians call "the second British empire."

Creating a Nation, 1783–1797

An early motto of the new republic was *Novus Ordo Secolorum*: "A New Order of the Ages." The founders saw the birth of their nation as an event that would usher in a new era, *"an epoch,"* as Washington put it, *"when the rights of mankind were better understood and more clearly defined, than at any former period."* Nevertheless, in the new nation social continuities accompanied political change.

Under British rule each of the thirteen colonies had developed a distinct political culture. In spite of another new motto, *E Pluribus Unum*, "Out of Many, One," representatives of the individual states proved reluctant to sacrifice local sovereignty to create a more unified nation. The first constitution, the Articles of

MAP 22.1 The American Revolutionary War In terms of military firepower, the British empire far outmatched the American Continental Army. The British could deploy an almost unlimited number of well-armed professional soldiers, and their navy was able to enforce a blockade of American ports. As would happen so often in modern world history, however, fighters who were highly motivated to throw off the imperial yoke managed to overcome the odds and win their independence. (© Cengage Learning)

Confederation, required that the federal government request funds from the individual states. Lacking its own tax-raising power, however, the Confederation government had no army and therefore no effective power.

Though the British had left, the problem of taxation remained. Under the Articles of Confederation, the states were responsible for debts remaining from the war, and they levied taxes to meet those obligations. These taxes forced poorer farmers, who lived primarily through barter, to sell land to raise the necessary cash. Such farmers also stood to lose their right to vote, which was accorded only to property owners. Incensed that land speculators were profiting at their expense in this way, Massachusetts war veterans rose up in an armed rebellion, strengthening arguments for a stronger federal government with powers of taxation and the ability to take responsibility for war debts. Debates over the degree to which a central government should have license to tax and borrow would continue far into the future.

Mercy Otis Warren, one of the most prolific writers of her time, put it this way: *"Our situation is truly delicate and critical. On the one hand we are in need of a strong federal government founded on principles that will support the prosperity and union of the colonies. On the other we have struggled for liberty . . . [and will not relinquish] the rights of man for the dignity of government."** In addition to balancing the powers of government with the rights of individuals, delegates from the thirteen states met at the Constitutional Convention in 1787 to face the central issue of how to rebalance the relative power of the state and federal governments.

Compromise was the hallmark of the new **Constitution of the United States of America** (1787). While granting to the federal government the powers of taxation, judicial oversight, banking, international diplomacy, and national defense, specific powers, such as determining the voting franchise, were left to the states. A system of checks and balances, as earlier proposed by the French philosophe Montesquieu, ensured the separation of executive, legislative, and judicial authority. The convention struck a balance between the interests of large and small states by creating a two-house legislature. A House of Representatives allocated each state a number of seats based on its population, and a Senate gave each state equal representation by two senators.

Equally important was the balance struck between the power of majorities and the rights of minorities. Congress amended the Constitution in 1791 with a Bill of Rights to ensure that specific civil liberties would be guaranteed even in the face of majority opinion. For example, the Bill of Rights made the establishment of a state church impossible, protecting the rights of religious minorities. It also guaranteed freedom of the press, freedom of assembly, the right to bear arms as part of "well-regulated militias," and other fundamental freedoms. The original Constitution was not very democratic, however. Most states restricted the vote to property owners, and women were not enfranchised (except briefly in New Jersey, owing to an oversight in the original state constitution that was "corrected" thirty-one years later). The president and senators were elected indirectly rather than by popular vote. No political agency was given to Native Americans, slaves, or even most free blacks.

George Washington was the unanimous choice of the state electors as president. Washington, like Simón Bolívar on his European sojourn, looked to ancient Rome for inspiration. Importantly, his model was the general Cincinnatus, who, after leading Roman armies to victory, left the political stage to live as a simple citizen. In 1797, after two terms as president, Washington refused a third term and retired to his plantation. Washington's example of voluntarily leaving office when he felt his public service was completed powerfully reinforced constitutional limitations on executive power. (However, Napoleon Bonaparte in France, discussed later in this chapter, and leaders of many other new nations in later years did not follow that example; see the feature "Visual Evidence in Primary Sources: Portraits of Power: George Washington and Napoleon Bonaparte.") Washington's Farewell Address, warning against any *"permanent alliances with any portion of the foreign world,"* would have a lasting influence on United States foreign policy.

Neither Washington nor the other leaders of the Constitutional Convention, however, could resolve the fundamental dichotomy between liberty and slavery. Southern delegates had no intention of applying the principle that "all men are created equal" to the 40 percent of Southerners who were slaves. Though the

> **Constitution of the United States of America**
> (1787) Agreement that created a more unified national structure for the United States, providing for a bicameral national legislature and independent executive and judicial authority, and incorporating a Bill of Rights.

*Mercy Otis Warren, Letter of September 17, 1787 to Catherine Macauley, Gilda Lehrman Collection, GLC 1800.3, pp. 1–2. The reference is to the original document, available online through the Gilda Lehrman Collection and the Digital History Library: http://www.digitalhistory.uh.edu/exhibits/dearmadam/letter4.html.

Portraits of Power: George Washington and Napoleon Bonaparte

During the eighteenth and nineteenth centuries in Europe and the Americas, political leaders commissioned paintings of themselves to project images of power. Portraits such as those reproduced here could inform people not merely of the fact of power but also of the particular type of power leaders were associated with. President George Washington of the United States (in office 1789–1797) and Emperor Napoleon Bonaparte of France (r. 1799–1814) were keenly aware of classical Greek and Roman models in projecting images of power, as were their portraitists Gilbert Stuart (1796) and

The stormy sky in the background might illustrate the difficult times that Washington and his comrades passed through, while the rainbow just above his upper arm might symbolize their ultimate victory.

The inkstand on the table and the books below show his importance in crafting the nation's foundational documents.

Washington wears no signs of military rank, holds a sheathed sword with its point down, and offers his open hand. The impression is one of peace.

White House Historical Association (White House Collection) (21)

Jean-Auguste-Dominique Ingres (1806). Washington identified himself with the democratic tradition of Athens and the republican period of Rome; Napoleon, in contrast, emphasized the imperial Roman tradition. Simón Bolívar, whose portrait at the beginning of the chapter can be compared with those here, was also keenly aware of both the republican and imperial traditions of ancient Rome.

Napoleon holds a scepter topped by a figure of Charlemagne, the early medieval king whose empire was one of his models.

Unlike Washington's open right hand, Napoleon's right fist is clenched high on his scepter, adding to the contrast between the two portraits.

At his coronation in 1804, Napoleon wore two different crowns, first a laurel crown like the one shown here and then a bejeweled reproduction of Charlemagne's crown. New rulers often seek legitimacy by associating themselves with older symbols of power.

What different reactions might Napoleon's supporters and detractors have had in viewing this portrait? Napoleon did not commission this painting, and we do not know what he himself thought of it.

QUESTION FOR ANALYSIS

» *In these portraits, what is similar or different about how Napoleon Bonaparte and George Washington are represented? Compare each with the portrait of Simón Bolívar at the beginning of the chapter with the same question in mind.*

abolitionist movement was gaining momentum at this time (*The Interesting Life of Olaudah Equiano* was published in 1789; see Chapter 19), plantation owners prevailed. Adding insult to injury, the Constitution defined each slave as three-fifths of a person for the purpose of calculating the size of congressional delegations and allowed the states to define slaves as nonpersons for all other purposes.

The issue of slavery shows that the new United States did not start with a blank slate. Both before 1776 and after Washington's resignation in 1797, Northern merchants and Southern slaveholders dominated the social and economic order. For this reason, historians continue to debate whether the "war for independence" should really be considered a "revolution." Here the American experience was similar to that of the English, who in 1689 altered the balance of power between monarch and Parliament and instituted a Bill of Rights (see Chapter 17) while retaining the previous social order, in that case dominated by a landed aristocracy. French republicans, on the other hand, experimented with a more truly "revolutionary" transformation of their society—killing their king, stripping their nobles of titles, abolishing slavery—thinking that society could be transformed from bottom to top and a fresh page in history turned.

The French Revolution, 1789–1815

The attempt by French revolutionaries to turn the noblest words of the Enlightenment into action was strongly opposed by the monarchy, the nobility, the church, and neighboring kingdoms, as well as by many French themselves who thought the revolutionaries were going too far. Significant numbers in the provinces resented the primacy of Paris as the revolutionary center. In the resulting disorder compromise would prove impossible.

The Revolution moved through three stages. The first focused on the relatively moderate goal of constitutional monarchy. The second phase of the Revolution was led by the Jacobins, who sought a radical transformation of French society. But Jacobin rule soon degenerated into a bloody Reign of Terror. Finally, amid the turmoil emerged a military genius, Napoleon Bonaparte, who not only restored order but also extended French power across Europe. Thus, as in ancient Rome, though all in the course of a single decade, monarchy was replaced by a republic and then the republic by empire.

Louis XVI and the Early Revolution, 1789–1792

The complex causes of the French Revolution are still debated by historians. The heightened ambitions of the French middle class certainly must be taken into account: many members of the bourgeoisie detested the inherited privileges of the king and nobility. Most still took the idea of monarchy for granted, but a minority, aware of the example of the new United States, became republicans, arguing that the people themselves should be sovereign. These lawyers, doctors, teachers, merchants—with property and education but no titles—drew from Enlightenment ideas to promote reform and, failing that, revolution.

The vast majority of French men and women were farmers whose resentment over the feudal obligations they still owed their aristocratic overlords intensified when bad harvests in the 1780s caused hunger and hardship. Many fled to the cities, especially Paris, where overcrowding and unemployment added fuel to the revolutionary fire. Ruling over 24 million subjects from a fabulous palace at Versailles,

Louis XVI (r. 1774–1793) was one of the wealthiest and most powerful people in the world, but he proved incapable of uniting his deeply divided people.

The most immediate cause of the revolt of 1789 was the precarious state of French finances. When Louis XVI took the throne, the French treasury was nearly empty. The loss of the Seven Years' War (1756–1763) had cost the French territory in the Americas and Asia, leaving a pile of debt, and they had received no economic benefit from their backing of the American rebels. The common people were crushed by taxes, while the nobility, who enjoyed the luxurious entertainments of Versailles as guests of the king, paid none at all.

The economic crisis led to a political one when Louis and his ministers decided they had no choice but to convene an Estates-General in Paris to which each of the three Orders of French society would send representatives. The First Estate consisted of the Catholic Church, the Second Estate consisted of the nobility, and the Third Estate comprised everyone else, that is, the vast majority of French men and women. It was an extreme measure. Unlike Britain with its annual Parliament, no French king had called a meeting of the Estates-General since 1614.

In the provinces, elections were held for **Third Estate** delegates, many of whom were middle-class professionals. Inspired by the American Revolution, they demanded fundamental reforms, such as the creation of a representative legislative body. They collected notebooks of grievances in the French provinces to bring to Paris a catalogue of complaints and ideas for change.

Many members of the First Estate were also members of the nobility, and the Catholic Church, by far the biggest landowner in France, was, like the aristocratic members of the Second Estate, exempted from direct taxation. Since each estate had only one vote, Louis anticipated that the privileged members of the First and Second Estates would vote together, canceling out any more radical proposals that came from the Third Estate.

Rather than accept this situation, delegates from the Third Estate took matters into their own hands. When Louis had them locked out of the assembly hall where they planned to meet, the delegates reacted with furor. They met on a tennis court instead, declared themselves to be a **National Assembly**, and took an oath not to disband until a constitutional monarchy had been established. It was a clear signal that the leaders of the Third Estate believed that sovereignty lay with the people and their representatives, and not with the king. Reacting with fear, Louis XVI summoned eighteen thousand troops to defend his palace at Versailles, 12 miles (19.3 km) outside of Paris. It was the summer of 1789, and the French Revolution had begun.

Thus far the contest was between the men of power—the king and his nobles—and the relatively wealthy and well-educated delegates of the Third Estate, who *aspired* to power and influence. But the actions of the common people pushed events in a new direction. Parisians stormed the Bastille (bass-TEEL), a building that served as both a jail and an armory. They freed prisoners, armed themselves from the arsenal's stockpile, and killed the mayor of Paris. The people of Paris were earning their reputation as a radical force of revolution.

Louis decided he had better compromise with the Third Estate after all. He recognized the National Assembly, which promptly declared the principle of equality before the law, eliminated the special prerogatives of the nobility, and abolished serfdom and all the remaining feudal obligations of the peasantry. In the "Declaration of the Rights of Man and the Citizen," the National Assembly declared that *"men are born and remain free and equal in rights,"* that *"the natural and inalienable rights of man"* are *"liberty, property, security, and resistance to oppression,"* that all

Louis XVI (r. 1774–1793) King of France whose inability to adequately reform the French fiscal system laid the foundation for the French Revolution. After showing reluctance to rule as a constitutional monarch, Louis was arrested and beheaded by republican revolutionaries.

Third Estate Before the French Revolution, the order of French society that included the most common people (the First Estate was the clergy, the Second the aristocracy, and the Third everyone else).

National Assembly (1789) Assembly that launched the French Revolution, formed by members of the Third Estate after the failure of the Estates-General. They agreed on the "Declaration of the Rights of Man and of the Citizen," forcing the king to sign the assembly's constitution.

citizens are eligible for government positions *"without other distinctions than that of virtues and talents,"* and that necessary taxation *"must be assessed equally on all citizens in proportion to their means."* Freedom of thought and religion were established, and mandatory payments to the Catholic Church were eliminated. The ideas of the philosophes were thus articulated as political principles.

In spite of this radical agenda, the National Assembly was otherwise quite conservative. For example, in spite of lobbying by middle-class Parisian women affiliated with groups like the *Cercle sociale* (Social Club), the assembly extended no rights to women. In her *Declaration of the Rights of Women*, the author Olympe de Gouges (oh-limp duh GOOJ) protested: *"The exercise of the natural rights of women has only been limited by the perpetual tyranny that man opposes to them; these limits should be reformed by the laws of nature and reason."*[*] Such appeals were ignored.

Within the National Assembly, revolutionary zeal was secondary to cooperating with Louis XVI in establishing a new constitutional monarchy. But neither the king nor the assembly could control the pace of change. In the fall of 1789, in both urban and rural areas, the poor took direct action. Angered by the high price of bread and distrustful of the intentions of the king, twenty thousand Parisians marched to Versailles in what was called the "March of the Women" because of the preponderance of housewives and market women in its ranks. The marchers forced the king and his family to leave Versailles and return to his palace in the heart of Paris, where they could keep a closer eye on him.

Despite the political centrality of Paris, the vast majority of French men and women were village-based peasants. Their "justice" came from courts presided over by their lord. They had to donate free labor cultivating his estates and were often forced to grind their wheat into flour at the lord's mill, where lack of competition allowed him to charge whatever he liked. While the National Assembly deliberated the elimination of feudal practices, French farmers took matters into their own hands, sometimes burning only the manorial rolls that listed their feudal obligations, and sometimes burning the estates themselves to the ground.

In this tense atmosphere the National Assembly organized a Legislative Assembly to draft a new set of basic laws, following the United States's example of a written constitution and the British example of sharing power between the king and representatives of the people. But the plan could not work without the king's cooperation. In the summer of 1791, Louis tried to escape from France, hoping to rally support from other European monarchs for his return as an absolute ruler, but he was captured and held a virtual prisoner in his palace.

Meanwhile, many members of the nobility had fled to other capitals, hoping to convince Europe's kings and aristocrats, with whom many of them had family connections, to help overthrow the Legislative Assembly and bring back royal absolutism. The defeat of French forces by Habsburg regiments in the Netherlands in 1792 led to fears of an Austrian invasion and the restoration of the monarchy. As counterrevolution became a real threat, a severe grain shortage following the previous year's poor harvest further increased tensions. The people of Paris staged demonstrations and then attacked the royal palace. Hundreds of citizens and soldiers died.

The time when compromise was possible was at an end. While some in the Legislative Assembly were disappointed that the king and his followers refused to play by the new rules of constitutional monarchy, others were happy that the experiment had not worked. They were republicans, who believed that any form of monarchy undermined liberty. The next phase of the French Revolution would belong to them.

---

[*]Olympe de Gouges, *Écrits politiques, 1788–1791,* trans. Tracey Rizzo (Paris: Côtes Femmes, 1993), p. 209. Reprinted in Tracy Rizzo and Laura Mason, eds., *The French Revolution: A Document Collection* (Boston: Houghton Mifflin, 1999), p. 111.

Parisian Women March to Versailles Women played a distinctive role in the French Revolution. Elite women sponsored the gatherings that spread Enlightenment and revolutionary ideals in their *salons*, while the common women engaged in direct action, as here in 1789, where they are shown marching to Versailles to force the king to return to Paris. (The Granger Collection, New York)

The Jacobins and the Reign of Terror, 1793–1795

Under pressure from the people of Paris, the Legislative Assembly declared a republic and instituted universal manhood suffrage. The National Assembly dissolved itself in favor of a National Convention, which immediately declared the end of the monarchy and began writing a republican constitution for France. They found Louis XVI guilty of treason and beheaded him in January 1793.

Under the **Jacobins**, the radical republican faction led by Maximilien Robespierre (ROBES-pee-air), the French Revolution passed through its most idealist and most violent phase. Robespierre had been deeply influenced by the philosophy of Jean-Jacques Rousseau, who had argued that the only legitimate state was one that expressed the "general will" of the people. Rousseau envisioned a form of direct democracy practiced by enlightened citizens, but he rejected the checks on government power proposed by Montesquieu and implemented in the Constitution of the United States. Instead Rousseau talked of constructing a "Republic of Virtue."

In the name of "liberty, equality, and fraternity," the republic confiscated lands belonging to the church and to the nobility and abolished slavery in the French empire. The absolute equality of the French was demonstrated by their new salutation: everyone, rich and poor alike, was addressed as "Citizen." The Jacobins would try to wipe the slate clean: they symbolized the beginning of a new age by decreeing that the year 1793 would be "Year One" of a new calendar, marking the victory of reason over the old Christian faith. The months were divided

Jacobins
The most radical republican faction in the National Convention. They organized a military force that saved the republic, but their leader Maximilien Robespierre, head of the Committee of Public Safety, ruled by decree and set in motion the Reign of Terror.

621

into three weeks of ten days each, following the logic of the new metric system. The old names of the days of the week, irrationally based on pagan traditions, were replaced. Time itself would have a revolutionary new beginning.

But no fresh start was really possible; the past could not be so easily erased. The Jacobins regarded the Catholic Church as an outmoded den of superstition and corruption: they moved to confiscate its land and curtail its privileges. Devout Catholics, especially in the provinces, deeply resented these attacks on the church. Meanwhile the Jacobins, fighting to save the Revolution from its domestic and foreign enemies, seized private property for state purposes. The bourgeoisie were shocked when it became clear that their property was no longer secure. (See the feature "Movement of Ideas Through Primary Sources: Edmund Burke's Reflections on the French Revolution.")

After the kings of Prussia and Austria, alarmed by the execution of the king, declared war on France to end the Revolution and restore the monarchy, Robespierre imposed a harsh dictatorship. Not for the last time in world history, a revolutionary leader declared that to save the revolution from its enemies, its most cherished principle, liberty, would have to be sacrificed. A dictatorial Committee of Public Safety replaced democratic institutions.

The committee quashed its enemies with a so-called Reign of Terror in which forty thousand people were beheaded. The symbol of the Revolution now became the guillotine (gee-yuh-TEEN), in which the condemned had their heads removed by the swift fall of a sharp, heavy blade. That the guillotine became a symbol of revolutionary violence is ironic. The philosophes were horrified by grisly public executions, with the executioner often needing several swings of his heavy axe to fully decapitate the condemned or where screaming victims were taunted as they slowly burned to death at the stake. Dr. Joseph Guillotin had intended his invention as an enlightened means of execution, clean and swift. Now his attempt at humane reform had been transformed into an efficient means of terror.

Though their methods were harsh, the Jacobins were successful in securing the republic against Austrian and Prussian invaders. They ordered a mass levy of conscripts and fielded an enormous army. The consequences of this mass conscription were cultural and political as well as military. Most of the soldiers were peasants who had never before traveled far from home, where they practiced local customs and spoke regional dialects distinct from Parisian French. Once trained for defense of the republic, many developed a stronger sense of national identity, transformed from peasants into Frenchmen.

Military success, however, only emboldened the Jacobins' domestic enemies. People in the provinces were angry at the radicalism they associated with Paris, and many members of the middle class favored a more moderate republic. A further irony was added to the story of the guillotine: those who had used it to execute their enemies often ended with their own heads in a basket. Robespierre himself was beheaded before the end of 1794.

Napoleon Bonaparte (1769–1821) Military commander who gained control of France after the French Revolution. He declared himself emperor in 1804 and attempted to expand French territory, but failed to defeat Great Britain and abdicated in 1814. He died in exile after a brief return to power in 1815.

The Age of Napoleon, 1795–1815

The National Convention reasserted power and created a new constitution with a more limited electorate and a separation of powers. From 1795 to 1799, however, the country remained sharply divided. The Directory, which formed the executive branch of the new government, faced conspiracies both by the Jacobins trying to return to power and by monarchists trying to restore the Bourbon dynasty. Meanwhile, the French armies continued to gain victories as a young general named **Napoleon Bonaparte** (1769–1821) took

MAP 22.2 **Napoleonic Europe in 1810** Although the enlargement of France by 1810 was only temporary, Napoleon's campaigns had lasting effects on the map of Europe. By consolidating territory in German- and Italian-speaking areas, challenging the power of traditional aristocracies, and exemplifying the power of nationalism, Napoleon helped lay the foundations for the later emergence of new nation-states (see Chapter 23). (© Cengage Learning)

northern Italy from the Austrians. In 1799 two members of the Directory plotted with Napoleon to launch a coup d'état and form a new government.

Like George Washington, Napoleon looked to ancient Rome for inspiration. But unlike the American general, Napoleon followed Rome's imperial example, transforming a republic into an empire (see Map 22.2). In a series of plebiscites the French people voted their approval for Napoleon's enhanced power, tired of chaos and the bickering of politicians, and proud of the successes of Napoleon's armies. He neutralized political opposition by bringing all but the most fervent monarchists into his administration. In 1801 he reached a compromise with the pope that allowed Catholic worship and restored government support for the clergy, healing the deep rift that the radical republicans had opened. Then, in 1804, he crowned himself Emperor Napoleon I, though only after securing the approval of the legislature and ratifying the move through a national referendum.

Edmund Burke's Reflections on the French Revolution

British parliamentarian Edmund Burke (1729–1797) has been called "the father of conservatism," a reputation that came mostly from his denunciation of the excesses of the French Revolution in a letter he wrote to a French aristocrat, published as *Essays on the French Revolution*. In fact, Burke's politics were generally liberal: he upheld the rights of Parliament and limitations on those of the king; supported the American Revolution, Catholic rights in his native Ireland, and the abolition of the slave trade; and spoke strongly against the corruption of the British East India Company (see Chapter 20).

In the *Essays*—written in 1790 before the execution of Louis XVI, the bloodshed of the Reign of Terror, and the dictatorship of the Jacobins—Burke argued that the French had been mistaken in basing their case for liberty on abstract ideals such as "the rights of man." Instead, he explained how liberty was better protected with a constitution grounded on inherited cultural and political institutions. Using abstract ideas to overrule custom and tradition pushed the revolutionaries, he said, toward corruption and dictatorship. Critics of Burke, defenders of Enlightenment thinking such as Thomas Paine (*The Rights of Man*) and Mary Wollstonecraft (*A Vindication of the Rights of Women*), rejected his arguments, though it was not long before the violence unleashed by the Jacobins and the tyranny imposed by Napoleon seemed to vindicate Burke's position.

Source: Edmund Burke, *Works* (London: 1867).

From *Essays on the French Revolution*

The question of dethroning [a king] will always be, as it has always been, an extraordinary question of state. . . . As it was not made for common abuses, so it is not to be agitated by common minds. The speculative line of demarcation, where obedience ought to end, and resistance must begin, is faint, obscure, and not easily definable. It is not a single act, or a single event, which determines it. Governments must be abused and deranged indeed, before it can be thought of; and the prospect of the future must be as bad as the experience of the past. . . . The wise will determine from the gravity of the case . . . but, with or without right, a revolution will be the very last resource of the thinking and the good. . . .

The [British] parliament says to the king, "Your subjects have inherited this freedom," claiming their franchises not on abstract principles "as the rights of men," but as the rights of Englishmen, and as a patrimony derived from their forefathers. You will observe that from Magna Carta [onward] it has been the uniform policy of our constitution to claim and assert our liberties as an entailed inheritance derived to us from our forefathers, and to be transmitted to our posterity . . . without any reference whatever to any other more general or prior right. . . . Thus . . . in what we improve, we are never wholly new; in what we retain, we are never wholly obsolete. . . .

You [in France] chose to act as if you . . . had everything to begin anew. You began ill, because you began by despising everything that belonged to you. . . . Respecting your forefathers, you would have been taught to respect yourselves. You would not have chosen to consider the French as a . . . nation of low-born servile wretches until the emancipating year of 1789. . . . You would not have been content to be . . . a gang of Maroon slaves, suddenly broke loose from the house of bondage, and therefore to be pardoned for your abuse of the liberty to which you were not accustomed. . . .

Compute your gains: see what is got by those extravagant and presumptuous speculations which have taught your leaders to despise all their predecessors, and all their contemporaries, and even to despise themselves, until the moment in which they became truly despicable. . . . France, when she let loose the reins of regal authority, doubled the license of a ferocious dissoluteness in manners, and of an insolent irreligion in opinions and practices; and has extended through all ranks of life, as if she were communicating some privilege, or laying open some secluded benefit, all the unhappy corruptions that usually were the disease of wealth and power. This is one of the new principles of equality in France. . . .

Remember that your parliament of Paris told your king, that, in calling the states together, he had nothing to fear. . . . It is right that these men should [now] hide their heads. . . . They have seen the French rebel against a mild and lawful monarch, with more fury, outrage, and insult, than ever any people has been known to rise against the most illegal usurper, or the most [bloody] tyrant. Their resistance was made to concession; their revolt was from protection; their blow was aimed at a hand holding out graces, favors, and immunities. . . .

They have found their punishment in their success. Laws overturned; tribunals subverted; industry without vigor; commerce expiring, the revenue unpaid, yet the people impoverished; a church pillaged, and a state not relieved; civil and military anarchy made the constitution of the kingdom; everything human and divine sacrificed to the idol of public credit, and national bankruptcy the consequence. . . . The principle of property, whose creatures and representatives they are, was systematically subverted. . . .

After I have read over the list of the persons and descriptions elected into the Third Estate, nothing which they afterwards did could appear astonishing. Among them, indeed, I saw some of known rank; some of shining talents; but of any practical experience in the state, not one man was to be found. The best were only men of theory. . . . Nothing can secure a steady and moderate conduct in such assemblies, but that the body of them should be respectably composed, in point of condition in life, of permanent property, of education, and of such habits as enlarge and liberalize the understanding. . . .

Judge, Sir, of my surprise, when I found that a very great proportion of the assembly (a majority, I believe) was composed of practitioners in the law. It was composed, not of distinguished magistrates . . . but . . . of obscure provincial advocates . . . the fomenters and conductors of the petty war of village vexation. . . . To these were joined men of other descriptions, from whom as little knowledge of, or attention to, the interests of a great state was to be expected, and as little regard to the stability of any institution; men formed to be instruments, not controls. Such in general was the composition of the Third Estate in the National Assembly; in which was scarcely to be perceived the slightest traces of what we call the natural landed interest of the country.

QUESTION FOR ANALYSIS

» *What were the main arguments Burke used to criticize the French Revolution, and how did he assert the superiority of British constitutional development? (To answer this question, you may want to review England's "Glorious Revolution," Chapter 17, page 481, and compare it to the French Revolution.)*

By the orderliness and rationality of his administration, Napoleon seemed an "enlightened despot," fulfilling the hopes of the eighteenth-century philosophes. He sponsored the creation of the Bank of France to stabilize finances, enforced use of the metric system of weights and measures to rationalize trade and accounting, and initiated a new system of laws, the Napoleonic Code, recognizing the legal equality of all French citizens. The eminent jurists who created the Napoleonic Code used the deductive Cartesian approach (that is, after the manner of Descartes; see Chapter 21). Starting from general principles (rather than inherited custom), they constructed a reasoned system of civil law. The Code became highly influential across Europe and, exported with the French overseas empire, worldwide.

nationalism
The defining ideology of the nation-state, emphasizing the rights and responsibilities of citizens toward the nation as superior to those based on regional, religious, familial, or other identities. Nationalism often asserts a common ethnic and linguistic heritage in legitimizing state power.

In the results of Napoleon's campaigns, historians have also seen the origins of modern **nationalism**, the belief that individuals are bound together in a common purpose and a common destiny by ties of language, culture, and history. National identity was not entirely new, but in France in the wake of the Revolution and Napoleonic campaigns, the nation became a much stronger focal point of identity. Earlier, for example, members of the nobility were strongly tied by marriage to aristocracies in other countries and had much more in common with them than with their own countrymen. French peasants were tied more strongly to their local communities and provincial cultures than to the French state in Paris. Now the French saw themselves as citizens of a nation rather than subjects of a king, and Napoleon cultivated their sense of patriotism and national pride, promising them not liberty but glory.

French nationalism grew in parallel with Napoleon's military achievements. Though the emperor abandoned his planned invasion of England after the 1805 victory of Lord Nelson's fleet at Trafalgar, a testament to Britain's continuing naval superiority, Napoleon's forces were unstoppable on the continent of Europe. In some cases the French were greeted as liberators. The German composer Ludwig van Beethoven, for example, initially dedicated his "Heroic" symphony to Napoleon. When he realized that personal ambition and the quest for French glory were the emperor's true motivations, he scratched that dedication from the title page. Simón Bolívar, living in Paris after his visit to Rome, was likewise disappointed by Napoleon's imperial pretensions, but like others, he still admired Bonaparte's political and military skills.

French armies swept through Iberia and Italy and asserted control over the Netherlands, Poland, and the western half of Germany. The Austrians and Prussians suffered embarrassing losses to the French troops, who were commanded by the greatest general of the age and by a new breed of military officers chosen for their talent rather than their aristocratic connections.

But Napoleon's ambition caused him to overreach and bring about his own downfall. In 1812 he mounted a massive attack on Russia. The Russian army could in no way prevent this assault, but they used their vast spaces to military advantage. When Napoleon reached Moscow, he found that the city had been abandoned and largely burned to the ground by its own people. Napoleon had nothing to claim as a prize. The French army, retreating through the harsh Russian winter, was decimated. Of the 700,000 troops that had invaded Russia, fewer than 100,000 returned.

A broad coalition of anti-French forces then went on the offensive, invaded France, forced Napoleon to abdicate in 1814, and restored the Bourbon monarchy by placing Louis XVIII (r. 1814–1824) on the throne. Dramatically, Napoleon then escaped his exile, returned to Paris, and reformed his army before finally being defeated by British and Prussian forces at the Battle of Waterloo in 1815. By this roundabout route, France finally became a constitutional monarchy. Napoleon died in exile on a remote South Atlantic island.

Napoleon's impact beyond France itself was substantial. Napoleon's amalgamation of small western German states into the Confederation of the Rhine set the stage for the development first of German nationalism—the idea that the politically fragmented Germans should be bound together in a single state reflecting their unity of language and culture—and later of a centralized German nation-state. Similarly, on the Italian peninsula, it was in the wake of Napoleon's conquest that modern Italian nationalism, and the quest for a unified Italian nation, began. As far away as Egypt, invaded by the French in 1798, Napoleon destroyed the status quo, stimulating Egyptians' own national consciousness and setting the stage for the emergence of a more powerful Egyptian state (see Chapter 23).

More relevant to Simón Bolívar, by overthrowing the Spanish monarchy Napoleon gave an opening to the forces of South American liberation. Within France's own overseas empire, the most dramatic developments took place on the Caribbean island of Saint-Domingue (san-doe-MANG).

The Haitian Revolution, 1791–1804

The colony of Saint-Domingue was by far France's richest overseas possession. Occupying the western half of the island of Hispaniola, Saint-Domingue accounted for as much as a third of French foreign trade. Half a million African slaves toiled on the colony's plantations, and the number who died of maltreatment and disease was so great that the planters had to constantly import more and more Africans to keep enough slaves working in the fields.

As the reverberations of 1789 reached Saint-Domingue, revolution in Haiti also moved through several stages. Initially the central conflict was between the whites who dominated the plantation economy and the *gens de couleur* (zhahn deh koo-LUHR), free men and women of mixed race, who about equaled the whites in number. They were artisans and small farmers who supplied food and other goods to the large plantations; some were even prosperous enough to own a few slaves themselves. Many were literate, and having followed the events of the American and French Revolutions, they demanded liberty and equality for themselves. By 1791, civil war broke out between the planters and the gens de couleur.

While neither of these groups had any intention of ending slavery, the civil war that broke out between them made an opening for a vast slave uprising organized by a *Voudun* (voh-doon) priest called Boukman (because he was literate). Voudun beliefs and rituals derived from West and Central Africa, and as a religious leader Boukman had great authority among African slaves, while his position as a field manager and coach driver for his master gave him wide-ranging connections in the slave community. He secretly organized thousands of slaves to rise up at his signal. When they did so, in the summer of 1791, they were spontaneously joined by tens of thousands of other slaves from across the island, as well as by maroons, runaway slaves who lived in the mountains.

Just as French peasants had burned the manor houses of their aristocratic overlords, now Boukman's slave army attacked the planters' estates in Saint-Domingue. Forty thousand marched on the city of Le Cap, where whites and gens de couleur had taken refuge. The slaughter lasted for weeks. When planter forces finally captured and executed the rebel leader, they fixed his head to a pole with a sign that read: *"This is the head of Boukman, chief of the rebels."*

Bibliothèque Nationale, Paris, France/Archives Charmet/The Bridgeman Art Library

Toussaint L'Ouverture   This contemporary engraving shows the Haitian revolutionary leader Toussaint L'Ouverture in an equestrian pose associated with civil and military power. Toussaint brought Enlightenment ideals to the elemental struggle of Haiti's slaves for liberation. His leadership was sorely missed in Haiti after he was tricked into negotiations with France and died in a French prison.

In 1792 the French government sent an army to restore order. But then a new commander emerged. François-Dominique Toussaint was born a slave but had been educated by a priest and had worked in his master's house rather than in the fields. The name by which he is remembered, **Toussaint L'Ouverture** (1744–1803), reflects his military skill: *l'ouverture* refers to the "opening" he would make in the enemy lines. But Toussaint's political, intellectual, and diplomatic strengths were equally important in turning the raw material of a slave uprising into an independent nation freed from the savage inequalities of slavery.

Like Olaudah Equiano, who was touring England in support of his abolitionist writing at this time, Toussaint L'Ouverture (too-SAN loo-ver-CHUR) could bridge the worlds of slave and master. He could organize the slaves to fight while forging alliances with whites, gens de couleur, and the foreign forces that intervened in the conflict. By 1801 his army controlled most of the island. Toussaint supported the creation of a new constitution that granted equality to all and that declared him governor-general for life.

Toussaint L'Ouverture
(1744–1803) Leader of the Haitian revolution. Under his military and political leadership, Haiti gained independence and abolished slavery, becoming the first black-ruled republic in the Americas. He died in exile in France.

Initially some radical French revolutionaries supported the rebels, but Napoleon had other ideas, and in 1802 he sent an expedition to crush Toussaint's new state. Although Toussaint was open to compromise as long as slavery would not be restored, he was arrested and sent to France, where, harshly treated, he died in prison in 1803.

Meanwhile, as Haitian rebels kept up the fight, Napoleon's soldiers, lacking immunity to tropical diseases, succumbed to malaria and yellow fever. Just as the Russian winter defeated him to the east, so too the West Indies climate undid his forces on Saint-Domingue. His troops withdrew, and in 1804 the independent nation of Haiti was born.

The independence of Haiti had ramifications throughout the Atlantic world. Slave owners in the United States were terrified by Haiti's example. Some plantations stepped up security measures, placing even tighter limits on slaves' movements, while the U.S. government at first refused to grant Haiti diplomatic recognition.

Venezuela was even more directly affected. In 1795 a Venezuelan who returned from Haiti, a free *zombo* (of mixed African-Amerindian ancestry), led a rebellion of slaves and free persons of color, sending the elite of Caracas into a panic. Simón Bolívar was just twelve at that time, but later he would seek the support of the Haitian government in his own fight for freedom and would argue for the abolition of slavery.

The Latin American Wars of Independence, 1800–1824

Simón Bolívar and other Latin American revolutionaries looked to the ideals of the Enlightenment and the examples of the United States, France, and Haiti in charting their own wars of independence. At the same time, events in Mexico and South America reflected the unique experiences with the social, cultural, demographic, and economic conditions of Spanish rule (see Chapter 18). Relations between *criollos* (American-born Spaniards) and people of African, Amerindian, or mixed descent shaped the course of revolution. Beyond widespread agreement on the need to expel the Spanish, the divergent interests of these groups made it difficult to establish common political ground.

In Mexico as in South America, a major question was whether the revolutionaries would be content fighting for independence from Spain or would also want more substantial social and economic reforms. Frightened by the bloodshed in France and the slave uprising in Haiti, elites were cautious. But in Mexico, Bolivia, Venezuela, and elsewhere, many Amerindians and slaves sought a complete transformation of society, aided by some establishment figures who took seriously such revolutionary mottoes as "liberty," "equality," and "brotherhood."

Simón Bolívar and South American Independence

The conditions for Latin American independence were closely connected to events in Europe. In 1808 Napoleon put his own brother on the Spanish throne, forcing the Spanish king to abdicate. (The king of Portugal, in contrast, fled to Brazil, which was ruled as a monarchy throughout this period.) In the Spanish-speaking Americas, loyalty to the king meant opposition to the French-imposed regime in Madrid, and local elites created *juntas* (ruling groups) to assert local rule. But were these juntas (HUN-tahs) temporary organizations to be disbanded when the legitimate king returned to power, or precursors of a permanent transfer of power from Madrid to the Americas? Loyalists made the former argument, while republicans like Bolívar and his Argentinean counterpart José de San Martín (1778–1850) saw the chance to win complete independence. This division of opinion meant that republicans would have to fight against powerful local loyalists as well as Spanish troops.

A principal grievance was the power of the direct representatives of royal authority in Spanish America. These *peninsulares* dominated the affairs of church and state, much to the frustration of ambitious criollos, who felt that the existing system was an impediment to their rightful place as leading members of their communities. Criollo merchants, for example, were continually frustrated by restrictions on trade imposed by the peninsulares.

But the struggle involved more than just imperial representatives and local elites. In most places, building a popular base of support for independence required appealing to Indians, Africans, mestizos, and other people of mixed descent, who together made up the vast majority of the population.

For example, Bolívar's home city of Caracas, facing the sea, was culturally and economically connected to the Caribbean. Slave plantations were an important part of its economy, and Bolívar spent part of his childhood on a plantation worked by slaves. In addition, Caracas had a large community of *pardos*, free men and women of mixed African-Spanish-Native American ancestry. As in Haiti, unity across lines of class and race was hard to achieve.

In the Venezuelan interior Bolívar would need the cooperation of *llaneros* (yah-NEYR-ohs), tough frontier cowboys of mixed Spanish-Amerindian descent (like the *gauchos* of Argentina and the *vaqueros* of Mexico). Farther south, Bolívar's armies eventually entered the Viceroyalty of Peru, where the social divide was between the Spanish-speaking colonists of the coastal areas and the still considerable Amerindian population of the Andes. Bolívar was constantly tested by the necessity of forging alliances among such disparate groups.

As elsewhere in Spanish America, a junta composed of local elites took power in Caracas following Napoleon's removal of the Spanish king. These leaders saw their power as temporary until the rightful monarchy was restored. The conservative junta sent the well-traveled Bolívar on diplomatic missions to London and Washington in 1810, but he betrayed them by lobbying the British to support his plan for independence. Upon his return, Bolívar attended the first Congress of Venezuela, which on July 3, 1811, became the first such body in Latin America to declare independence from Spain.

Racial, ethnic, and regional divisions inhibited any strong sense of "Venezuelan" identity upon which a new nation could be founded. The constitution restricted voting rights to a small minority of overwhelmingly white property owners and did nothing to abolish slavery. In addition, the llaneros of the interior felt threatened by a constitutional provision that extended private property ownership to the previously uncharted plains. If wealthy ranchers fenced off the lands where they herded wild cattle, the cowboys might lose their livelihood and their independence.

A huge earthquake in the spring of 1812 compounded the instability of the new Venezuelan republic. Soon forces loyal to Spain were on the offensive. The young republic collapsed, and Bolívar set out on the military path he would pursue for the next twelve years, proclaiming a *"war to the death"* (see Map 22.3). Captured Spaniards would be executed, he declared, while American-born Spanish loyalists would be given a chance to mend their ways.

In the summer of 1813 Bolívar's army entered Caracas, but the divisions within society worked against him. To broaden his movement's appeal, Bolívar had forged alliances with groups that had been excluded from the first congress and constitution. He sought out the cooperation of the llaneros and promised to abolish slavery. But many criollos in the capital regarded the cowboys as bandits and, haunted by memories of the violent Haitian Revolution, reacted with suspicion.

In addition to such internal dissension, the cause of independence suffered a setback in 1815 after Napoleon's defeat at Waterloo and the restoration of the Spanish monarchy. The Madrid government dispatched fifty ships and over ten thousand soldiers to restore imperial authority in South America. Bolívar retreated to the island of Jamaica, where he once again sought British help. He also traveled to Haiti, pursuing support from its government with a pledge to seek *"the absolute liberty of the slaves who have groaned beneath the Spanish yoke in the past three centuries."* Most importantly from a military standpoint, he recruited battle-hardened British mercenaries to serve as his elite force.

---

*Excerpt from Simón Bolívar, "Oath Taken at Rome, 15 August 1805," trans. Frederick H. Fornoff, in *El Libertador: Writings of Simón Bolívar,* ed. David Bushnell (New York: Oxford University Press, 2003), p. 77.

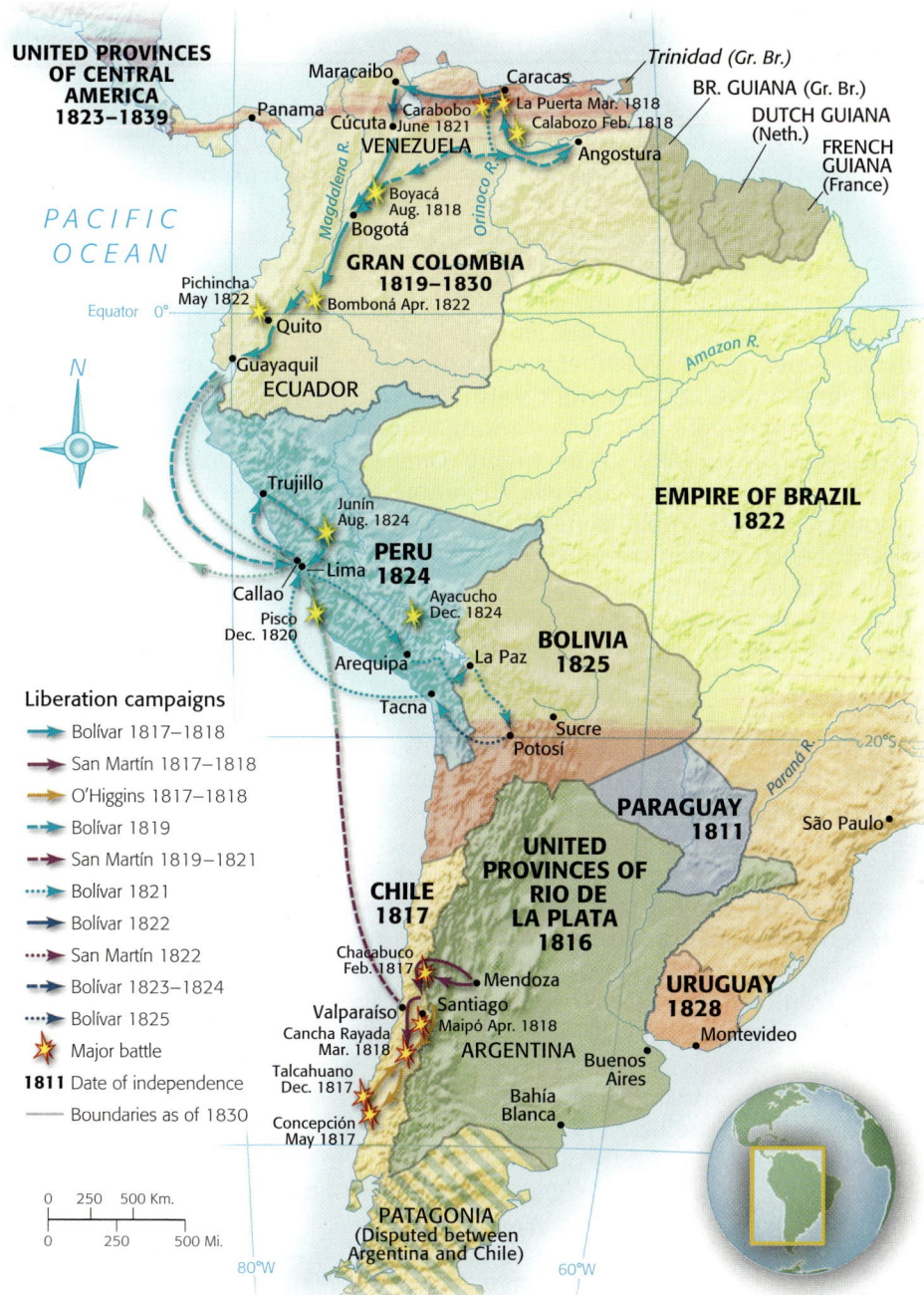

UNITED PROVINCES OF CENTRAL AMERICA 1823–1839

Panama

Maracaibo

Trinidad (Gr. Br.)

Caracas
La Puerta Mar. 1818
Calabozo Feb. 1818

BR. GUIANA (Gr. Br.)

DUTCH GUIANA (Neth.)

FRENCH GUIANA (France)

Cúcuta   Carabobo
June 1821

VENEZUELA

Angostura

PACIFIC OCEAN

Boyacá
Aug. 1818

Bogotá

GRAN COLOMBIA 1819–1830

Equator 0°

Pichincha
May 1822

Bombóna Apr. 1822

Amazon R.

Quito

Guayaquil

ECUADOR

Trujillo

Junín
Aug. 1824

EMPIRE OF BRAZIL 1822

PERU 1824

Lima

Callao

Pisco
Dec. 1820

Ayacucho
Dec. 1824

Arequipa

La Paz

BOLIVIA 1825

Tacna

Sucre
Potosí

Liberation campaigns

- Bolívar 1817–1818
- San Martín 1817–1818
- O'Higgins 1817–1818
- Bolívar 1819
- San Martín 1819–1821
- Bolívar 1821
- Bolívar 1822
- San Martín 1822
- Bolívar 1823–1824
- Bolívar 1825
- ✶ Major battle
- **1811** Date of independence
- Boundaries as of 1830

PARAGUAY 1811

São Paulo

CHILE 1817

UNITED PROVINCES OF RIO DE LA PLATA 1816

Chacabuco
Feb. 1817

Mendoza

Valparaíso   Santiago

Cancha Rayada
Mar. 1818

Maipó Apr. 1818

URUGUAY 1828

Montevideo

Talcahuano
Dec. 1817

ARGENTINA

Buenos
Aires

Concepción
May 1817

Bahía
Blanca

0   250   500 Km.
0   250   500 Mi.

PATAGONIA
(Disputed between
Argentina and Chile)

80°W   60°W

MAP 22.3 Independence in Latin America Paraguay led the way toward Latin American independence in 1811, followed by rebels in Buenos Aires who declared the independence of the United Provinces of Rio de la Plata (the core of today's Argentina) in 1816. The next year forces led by José de San Martín crossed the Andes, linked with the rebel army of Bernardo O'Higgins, and secured Chilean independence. The Chilean rebels then traveled north by sea to attack Spanish positions at Lima, with inconclusive results. By that time, however, Simón Bolívar had secured the independence of Venezuela and Ecuador, uniting them into the independent state of *Gran Colombia*. Combined Chilean and Colombian forces defeated the Spanish at Ayacucho in 1824, finalizing the independence of Spanish Latin America. (© Cengage Learning)

Returning to Venezuela in 1817, Bolívar established himself in the interior and was recognized as the supreme commander of the various patriotic forces that were contesting Spain's effort to re-establish control. He offered freedom to slaves who joined his army, and he revived his alliance with the llaneros of the plains. Bolívar's toughness in battle and his willingness to share the privations of his men—once spending a whole night immersed in a lake to avoid Spanish forces—won him their loyalty.

In 1819, even while the Spanish still held Caracas and other important cities, delegates to the **Congress of Angostura** planned for the resuscitation of independent Venezuela. Bolívar argued for a strong central government with effective executive powers, fearing that a federal system with a strong legislature would lead to division and instability. Rather than stay in his native country to see these plans carried out, however, Bolívar went south and west to confront imperial forces in the Spanish stronghold of Bogotá. Seeking a broader foundation for Latin American liberty, he began his fight for *Gran Colombia*, a political union he envisioned would encompass today's Venezuela, Colombia, Panama, Ecuador, and Peru.

Bolívar and his troops suffered greatly on their campaign into the frigid Andes, but their morale remained high. The Spanish forces, on the other hand, became demoralized. Led by generals who could not match Bolívar's strategic brilliance, they quickly gave way, first in Bogotá and then in Ecuador. Meanwhile, further south, other liberators were scoring equivalent successes. José de San Martín (hoe-SAY deh san mar-TEEN) took the region of Rio de la Plata (today's Argentina), while Chile's successful republican forces were led by Bernardo O'Higgins (the Spanish-speaking son of an Irish immigrant). Together San Martín and O'Higgins had occupied the coastal regions of Peru, leaving only its Andean region in loyalist hands.

The situation in the Andes had been tense since an Amerindian uprising in 1780 led by **Tupac Amaru II** (1741–1781), a descendant of the last Inca ruler. Tupac Amaru (TOO-pack ah-MAR-oo) had been educated by Jesuit priests and for a time served the Spanish government. But the poverty, illiteracy, and oppression faced by his own people caused him first to petition for reform and then, when his pleas were ignored, to change his name, adopt indigenous dress, and organize a rebellion. It was the first uprising against Spanish rule in the highlands for over two hundred years.

Spanish authorities savagely suppressed Tupac Amaru's revolt, forcing him to witness the torture and death of his own wife and family members before his own execution. The Spanish government then banned the wearing of indigenous cloth and the use of the indigenous Quechua (KEH-chwah) language. These Spanish attempts at cultural assimilation were not successful, however, as local Amerindians avoided contact with Spanish officials whenever they could. Though highland Amerindians were potential allies of Bolívar, they remained aloof, more concerned with the autonomy of their own communities than the independence of nations.

Nevertheless, Bolívar's troops engaged the Spanish in the Andes in 1824 at the Battle of Ayacucho. Their victory was complete, and South America was free from Spanish control. Still unanswered, however, was how independence from Spain would translate into liberty for the diverse peoples of South America.

Congress of Angostura
(1819) Congress that declared Venezuelan independence after Simón Bolívar gave an opening address arguing for a strong central government with effective executive powers.

Tupac Amaru II
(1741–1781) José Gabriel Condorcanqui Noguera, a descendant of the last Inca ruler; called himself Tupac Amaru II while leading a large-scale rebellion in the Andes against Spanish rule. He was defeated and executed.

Mexico and Brazil, 1810–1831

Mexico's path to independence had a different starting point. Whereas the initial struggle in Venezuela was led by socially conservative criollos, in Mexico the deposition of the Spanish king quickly led to a popular uprising of mestizos and Indians. Parish priest **Miguel de Hidalgo y Costilla** (1753–1811) rallied the poor in the name of justice for the oppressed. From his pulpit in the town of Dolores, he issued his famous *Grito* ("cry"): *"Long live Our Lady of Guadalupe! Long live the Americas and death to the corrupt government!"* His appeal to the Virgin of Guadalupe, a dark-skinned representation of the Virgin Mary as she had appeared to a lowly peasant (see Chapter 18), symbolized Hidalgo's appeal to Indians and mestizos. Hidalgo called for the creation of a Mexican nation with the words *"¡Mexicanos, Viva México!"*

While this was shocking to Spanish officials, Hidalgo also alarmed Mexico's criollos, who flocked to the loyalist banner. His forces scattered, and Hidalgo was excommunicated and then captured and executed. The Spanish publicly displayed his severed and mutilated head as a warning to other rebels. As late as 1820, Spanish authority seemed secure.

When independence did come in 1821, it resulted not from a popular insurgency but from a conservative backlash against changes emanating from Madrid. Threatened by liberal reforms in Spain, elite conservatives supported Mexican military officers who turned on their former Spanish allies. Contrary to Father Hildago's vision, Mexican independence brought neither social nor economic reform. Nevertheless, Hidalgo still symbolizes Mexican independence, and the anniversary of the *Grito de Dolores*, September 16, is still celebrated as Mexico's national day.

Brazil followed its own distinct path toward independence. In 1808 the Portuguese royal family fled Napoleon's invasion, seeking refuge in Brazil. In 1821 the king returned to Portugal, leaving his son Pedro behind as his representative. Pedro, however, declared himself sympathetic to the cause of independence, and in 1824 Pedro I (r. 1824–1831) became the constitutional monarch of an independent Brazil. Although unpopular with some people, such as sugar planters who disapproved of an 1830 treaty with Britain to abolish the slave trade, the constitutional monarchy lasted until 1889 (see Chapter 25).

Museo Nacional de Historia, Castillo de Chapultepec, Mexico City, D.F./Schaalkwijk/Art Resource, NY

Father Hidalgo In 1810 Father Hidalgo rallied the common people of Mexico, especially mestizos and Indians, under the banner of the Virgin of Guadalupe for independence from Spain. Mexican elites opposed him, however, and cooperated with Spanish authorities to crush the uprising. Hidalgo was executed. When Mexican independence was achieved in 1821, the criollo elite were firmly in charge of the new nation.

Miguel de Hidalgo y Costilla
(1753–1811) Mexican priest who launched the first stage of the Mexican war for independence. Hidalgo appealed to Indians and mestizos and was thus viewed with suspicion by Mexican criollos. In 1811, he was captured and executed.

Revolutionary Outcomes and Comparisons, to 1830

In the first half of the nineteenth century the United States of America established itself as a vigorous republic. By 1830 there were twenty-four states; settlers moved to new territories; and high wages and cheap land attracted swelling numbers of European immigrants.

Americans pursued what they considered their "manifest destiny," a clear and divinely approved mission to settle the continent. The vast Louisiana Purchase (purchased in 1803 from Napoleon, who, having lost Haiti, needed a quick source of funds) gave the new republic room to grow, and Lewis and Clark's expedition pointed the way west (see Chapter 21). These lands were not, however, empty. Over the course of the nineteenth century, U.S. westward expansion would be marked by blood and violence. And since the issue of slavery remained unresolved, regional tensions increased. As new states entered the Union, would they be free states or would they be slave states? It would take a violent civil war to solve that question (see Chapter 25).

In Europe, conservative elites used the defeat of Napoleon to suppress reform. The Bourbon dynasty was restored in France, and Prince Metternich of Austria orchestrated the **Congress of Vienna** (1815), which reinstated the balance of power among Britain, France, Austria, Prussia, and Russia (see Map 22.4). Aristocrats once again flaunted their wealth in the capitals of Europe, no longer afraid of revolutionary violence.

However, the spread of nationalism and the association of that idea with progressive reform proved a constant challenge to European rulers. When Greek nationalists won their independence from the Ottoman empire in 1829, the event did not at first appear to threaten the European status quo. But it was not long before ethnic minorities in the Austrian and Russian empires began organizing along national lines, while the idea of a single, powerful German nation began to spread as well. Other ideals of the French Revolution also remained alive, such as the idea that equality could only be achieved through a more equitable distribution of wealth. Though basic liberal concepts such as the equality of all citizens before the law still had not been achieved by 1830, a rising generation of revolutionaries would soon try once again to overturn Europe's status quo (see Chapter 23).

In Haiti, the transition from slave colony to free republic proved difficult. Freed slaves fled the plantations to establish their own farms on small plots of land, an improvement in their way of life but one that led to a massive decline in overall production. The sharp decline in plantation exports robbed the new government of its tax base. The political transition to independence proved equally difficult. The personal ambitions of early Haitian rulers, fueled by tensions between the mixed-race gens de couleur and Haitians of African/slave descent, created a long-standing culture of corruption and dictatorship in Haitian politics.

In Latin America, Simón Bolívar's vision of a state of *Gran Colombia* was never achieved. Military commanders preferred to take power over their own separate republics, and South America became a patchwork of separate, often squabbling, nations. (See the feature "World History in Today's World: Venezuela and Colombia: Uncomfortable Neighbors.") Lacking strong traditions of

Congress of Vienna (1815) Conference at which the balance of power among European states was restored after the defeat of Napoleon Bonaparte.

Kingdom of Prussia
Austrian Empire
— Boundary of German Confederation

MAP 22.4 Europe in 1815 After the disruptions to the political map of Europe caused by the French Revolution and the expansion of Napoleon's empire (see Map 22.2), in 1815 European diplomats restored earlier boundaries and established a conservative status quo at the Congress of Vienna. One important change was the appearance of the Austrian-led German Confederation and of a Prussian-dominated tariff union, both of which helped lay the foundation for the later unification of Germany (see Chapter 23). (© Cengage Learning)

local governance, these new republics were dominated by a small number of wealthy landowners. Concentrated wealth provided no foundation on which to build democracy, and as Bolívar foresaw, the fragmentation of *Gran Colombia* left South America vulnerable to external powers such as Great Britain and the United States.

One of Bolívar's top commanders, José Antonio Páez, declared Venezuela a separate republic in 1830, repudiating the connection with *Gran Colombia*, while establishing an authoritarian style of rule that would have ominous implications

Venezuela and Colombia: Uncomfortable Neighbors

Had Simón Bolívar been successful in creating a unified *Gran Colombia*, the separate nations of Venezuela and Colombia would not even exist. Instead, these nations have a long history of tension, including border disputes, that has continued into the twenty-first century.

The situation has worsened in the past twenty years, with large numbers of Colombian military forces stationed near the border fighting Marxist guerrillas. In 1998, when Colombian rebels crossed into Venezuela, the country responded with its own military incursion into Colombia. Since then, the two sides have alternated between diplomacy and saber rattling, moving close to war in 2008 when the Colombian government accused Venezuela of actively aiding the Marxist rebels and Venezuela broke off diplomatic relations.

Drug trafficking has made the border problems even tougher to resolve. Apart from Marxist guerrillas, members of the well-organized Colombian drug cartels also frequently cross over into Venezuela, seeking to establish transit points for the export of cocaine to Europe and North America. They bring with them, of course, stockpiles of arms. One clash between rival Colombian gangs again led to bloodshed inside Venezuela early in 2012.

The vastly different ideologies of the two governments exacerbated such tensions in the first decade of the new century. President Álvaro Uribe of Colombia (in office 2002–2008) cultivated a close relationship with the United States, seeking military aid in the suppression of the drug trade and guerrilla activity. Uribe was a business-oriented leader who laid the foundations for a free-trade agreement with the United States, cementing even deeper ties. In stark contrast, Hugo Chávez, president of Venezuela since 1999, is a left-wing populist, a dedicated supporter of Fidel Castro and the Cuban revolution, and a sworn enemy of "American imperialism." Chávez also controls billions of dollars a year in oil revenue, making him a formidable regional leader. He idolizes Simón Bolívar, dreaming of a wide South American federation to be organized, he asserts, along socialist lines.

More recently, the distraction of President Chávez's cancer treatments and the more moderate tone of the new Colombian president, Juan Santos, led to a mild thaw in relations. Still, there is little prospect of a warm relationship between the two neighbors, and a grand federation between Venezuela and Colombia is even more remote now than it was in Bolívar's day.

---

caudillos
Latin American military men who gained power through violence during the early nineteenth and twentieth centuries.

for all of Latin America. He was one of the ***caudillos*** (cow-DEE-yos), dictatorial rulers who looked after their own interests and those of the military above all else. If Napoleon had been something of an "enlightened despot," the same could rarely be said of the caudillos who seized power in many of the new South American nations.

Although Africans, Amerindians, and people of mixed descent played important roles in the Latin American wars of independence, their efforts were not to be rewarded with power or privilege, even where slavery was abolished. Benefiting most from independence were the criollos, who consolidated their political and economic dominance by assuming positions of authority vacated by departing peninsulares. As for the church, while individual priests might side with the downtrodden, the Catholic hierarchy still allied itself with the wealthy and powerful.

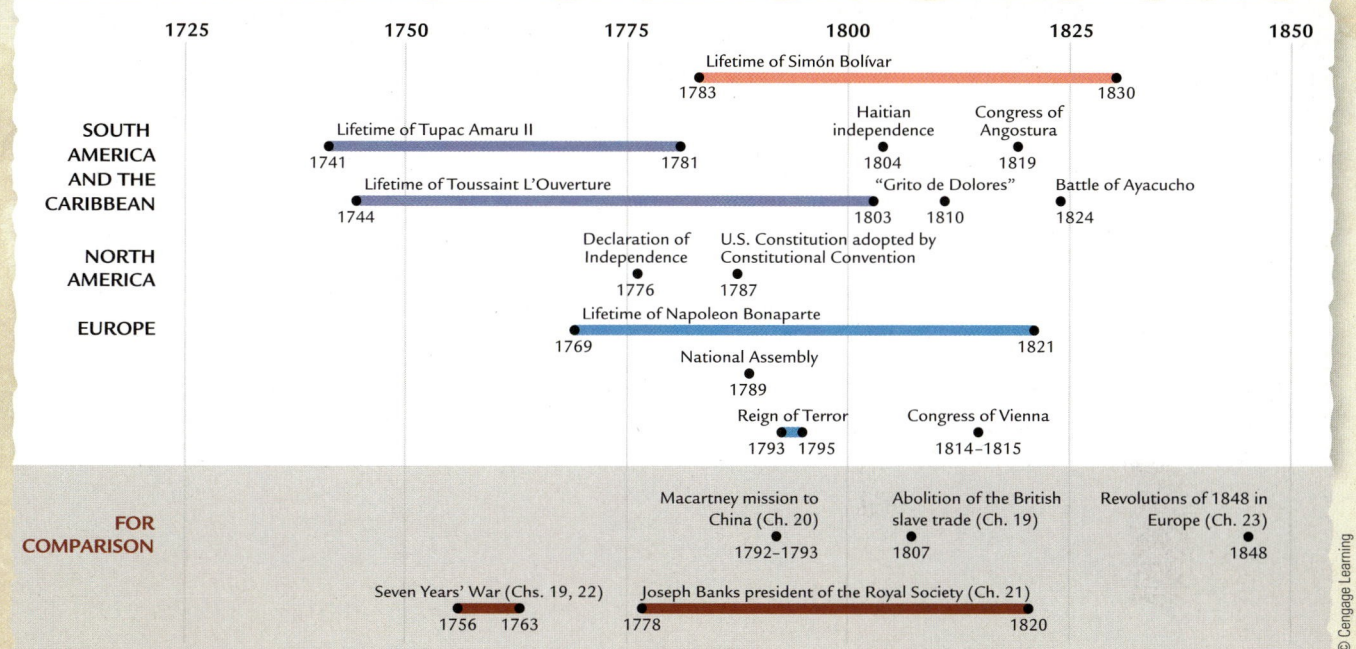

| | 1725 | 1750 | 1775 | 1800 | 1825 | 1850 |

SOUTH AMERICA AND THE CARIBBEAN

Lifetime of Simón Bolívar
1783 — 1830

Lifetime of Tupac Amaru II
1741 — 1781

Haitian independence
1804

Congress of Angostura
1819

Lifetime of Toussaint L'Ouverture
1744 — 1803

"Grito de Dolores"
1810

Battle of Ayacucho
1824

NORTH AMERICA

Declaration of Independence
1776

U.S. Constitution adopted by Constitutional Convention
1787

EUROPE

Lifetime of Napoleon Bonaparte
1769 — 1821

National Assembly
1789

Reign of Terror
1793 — 1795

Congress of Vienna
1814–1815

FOR COMPARISON

Macartney mission to China (Ch. 20)
1792–1793

Abolition of the British slave trade (Ch. 19)
1807

Revolutions of 1848 in Europe (Ch. 23)
1848

Seven Years' War (Chs. 19, 22)
1756 — 1763

Joseph Banks president of the Royal Society (Ch. 21)
1778 — 1820

© Cengage Learning

The Global Legacies of Revolution

How much change does it take to make a revolution? To go through a "complete revolution" means to experience a bottom-to-top transformation, a thorough reordering of society at every level. Of the cases considered in this chapter, only the brief period of extreme republicanism in France under the Jacobins approaches that definition. In every other case—in the United States, in France under the National Convention and Napoleon, in Haiti and Latin America—in spite of significant political change, notable continuities with prerevolutionary societies remained.

Enlightenment philosophers were, of course, the ones who suggested that custom and tradition should be tossed aside if and when they stood in the way of a rationally ordered society. They were more conservative on the question of how to achieve that end, however, generally trusting that sophisticated, cosmopolitan elites would lead the way. In Britain's North American colonies, it was indeed the more privileged and well educated who led the war of independence and the creation of

the new republic. Even so, the doctrine of popular sovereignty required them to look beyond their own self-interest as planters, merchants, and professionals and take seriously the aspirations of the broader society (if not of blacks, Amerindians, or women).

In every other case, however, the old order's resistance to change required revolutionaries to mobilize excluded members of society to generate the power they needed, as when Simón Bolívar assembled his coalition of elite criollos, cowboys, and slaves to throw off Spanish rule. Even if, as in France and Haiti, revolutionaries did not originally plan it that way, those at the bottom usually rose up demanding to be heard (peasants burning manor houses in France, Parisians seizing the Bastille, Haitian slaves organizing themselves to attack the sugar plantations and their owners, mestizos and Indians rallying to the banner of Father Hidalgo in Mexico).

Once the genie of mass agitation was out of the bottle, middle-class revolutionaries were generally anxious to put it back: to define liberty in a way that protected property, and to limit voting rights to those "responsible" enough to use them wisely. That was the path advocated by philosopher John Locke and reflected in the constitutions of both Great Britain and the United States. In contrast, the more radical restructuring of society in France led to the Jacobin dictatorship and ultimately to Napoleon's empire, precedents that both historians and aspiring revolutionaries would closely investigate for centuries to come.

As we will see, the eighteenth-century revolutions left enduring global legacies. Participants in the 1848 uprisings in western Europe, and later revolutionary leaders in Russia and China, found inspiration in the events of 1789 (see Chapters 23 and 27). And later, anticolonial nationalists in Asia and Africa would look to North and South America in their quest for independence from European empires (see Chapter 30). The French and Haitian examples were especially inspiring to revolutionaries intent on mobilizing masses of people to achieve wholesale change. For conservatives, on the other hand, the dangers of mass mobilization outweighed the benefits: they recalled Edmund Burke's warning that radical revolution leads to dictatorship.

In the 1950s, when Chinese communist leader Chou En-Lai was asked the lessons of the French Revolution, he said, "It is too soon to tell."

Voyages on the Web: Simón Bolívar

The Voyages Map App follows the traveler's journeys using interactive study tools, including 360-degree panoramic views of historic sites, zoomable maps, audio summaries, flash cards, and quizzes.

Key Terms

Simón Bolívar (608)
George Washington (612)
Declaration of Independence (612)
Constitution of the United States of America (615)
Louis XVI (619)

Third Estate (619)
National Assembly (619)
Jacobins (621)
Napoleon Bonaparte (622)
nationalism (626)
Toussaint L'Ouverture (628)
Congress of Angostura (632)

Tupac Amaru II (632)
Miguel de Hidalgo y Costilla (633)
Congress of Vienna (634)
caudillos (636)

638

FOR FURTHER REFERENCE

Allison, Robert. *The American Revolution: A Concise History*. New York: Oxford University Press, 2011.

Bailyn, Bernard. *The Ideological Origins of the American Revolution*. Cambridge, Mass.: Belknap, 1992.

Bell, Madison Smartt. *Toussaint Louverture: A Biography*. New York: Pantheon, 2007.

Brown, Howard G. *Ending the French Revolution: Violence, Justice, and Repression from the Terror to Napoleon*. Charlottesville: University of Virginia Press, 2007.

Bushnell, David. *Simón Bolívar: Liberation and Disappointment*. New York: Pearson Longman, 2004.

Bushnell, David, and Neill MacAuley. *The Emergence of Latin America in the Nineteenth Century*. New York: Oxford University Press, 1994.

Doyle, William. *Origins of the French Revolution*. New York: Oxford University Press, 1999.

Englund, Steven. *Napoleon: A Political Life*. New York: Scribner's, 2004.

Geggus, David P. *The Impact of the Haitian Revolution in the Atlantic World*. Columbia: University of South Carolina Press, 2002.

McNeill, J. R. *Mosquito Empires: Ecology and War in the Greater Caribbean, 1620–1914*. New York: Cambridge University Press, 2010.

Rowe, Michael, ed. *Collaboration and Resistance in Napoleonic Europe: State Formation in an Age of Upheaval*. New York: Palgrave Macmillan, 2003.

Van Young, Eric. *The Other Rebellion: Popular Violence, Ideology, and the Mexican Struggle for Independence, 1810–1821*. Stanford: Stanford University Press, 2001.

Wood, Gordon S. *The American Revolution*. New York: Modern Library, 2002.

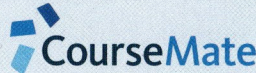

Go to the CourseMate website at **www.cengagebrain.com** for additional study tools and review materials—including audio and video clips—for this chapter.

23

The Industrial Revolution and European Politics, 1765–1880

In the summer of 1848, the young Russian émigré **Mikhail Bakunin** (1814–1876) rushed to Paris as revolution once again engulfed the French capital. The fire of revolt quickly spread to Berlin, Vienna, Budapest, Rome, Milan, and all across Europe. History was on the revolutionaries' side, Bakunin thought. Freedom was coming: kings, princes, and popes would be tossed on the rubbish heap of history.

Those were distant memories by the summer of 1851, as Bakunin sat in solitary confinement in a St. Petersburg prison. Captured by Austrian forces while raising a failed rebellion in Prague, he was sentenced to death and then turned over to Russian authorities, who gave him the chance to write a "confession" to the tsar. *"There was in my character,"* he wrote, *"a radical defect: Love for the fantastic, for out-of-the-way, unheard of adventures, for undertakings which open up an infinite horizon and whose end no man can foresee."*[*]

Though Bakunin was dispirited and in poor health, with little chance of ever seeing his family or the light of day again, his message to Tsar Nicholas still conveyed the optimism of the heady days of 1848:

[*]Cited in E. H. Carr, *Mikhail Bakunin* (New York: Vintage, 1937), p. 1.

Mikhail Bakunin
(Private Collection/The Stapleton Collection/The Bridgeman Art Library)

Now what shall I say to you, Sire, of the impression produced on me by Paris! This huge city, the center of European enlightenment, had suddenly been turned into the wild Caucasus: on every street, almost everywhere, barricades had been piled up like mountains. . . . NOBLE WORKERS in rejoicing, exulting crowds, with red banners and patriotic songs [were] reveling in their victory! And in the midst of this unlimited freedom, this

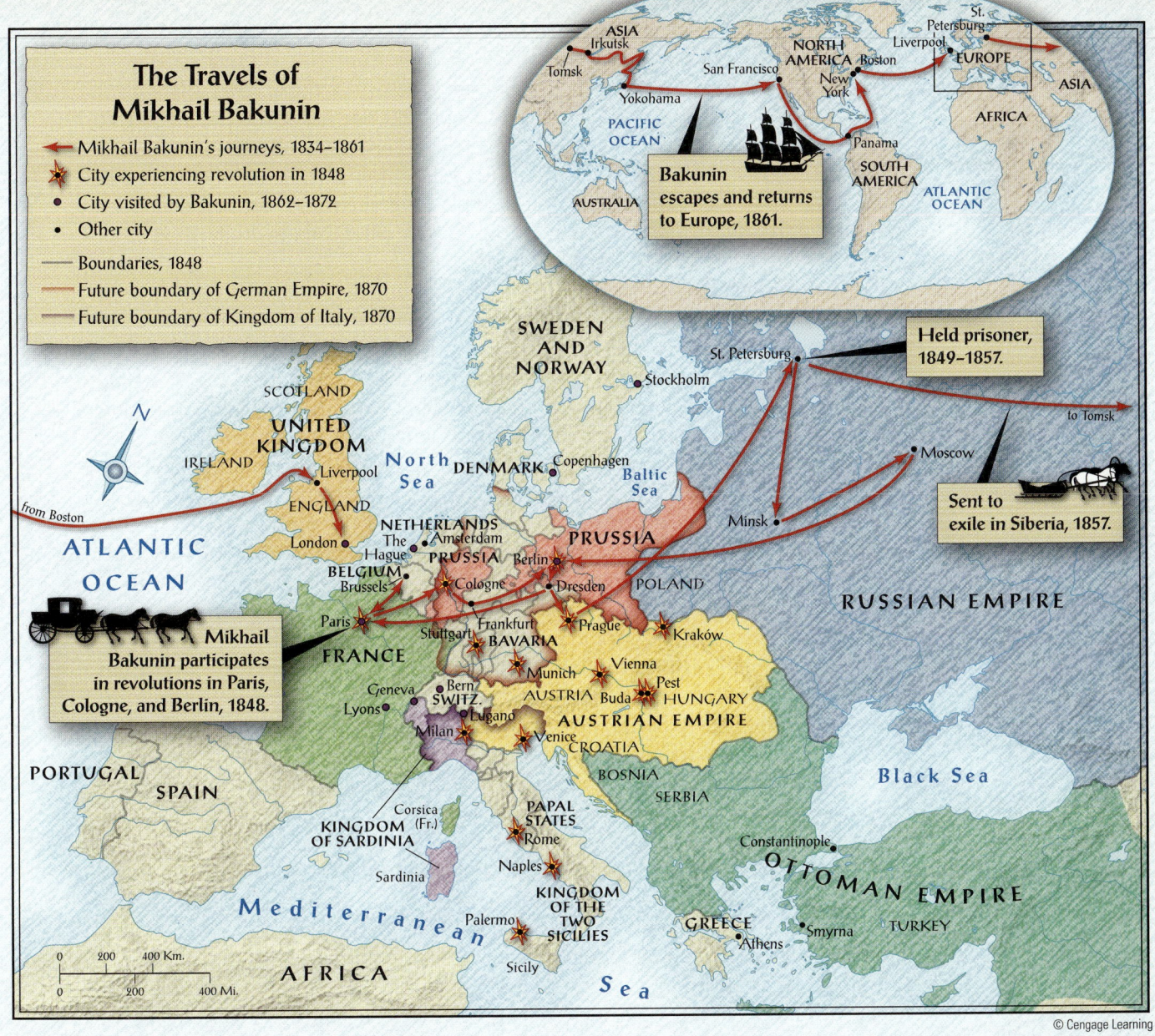

The Travels of Mikhail Bakunin

- → Mikhail Bakunin's journeys, 1834–1861
- ✦ City experiencing revolution in 1848
- • City visited by Bakunin, 1862–1872
- • Other city
- Boundaries, 1848
- Future boundary of German Empire, 1870
- Future boundary of Kingdom of Italy, 1870

Bakunin escapes and returns to Europe, 1861.

Held prisoner, 1849–1857.

Sent to exile in Siberia, 1857.

Mikhail Bakunin participates in revolutions in Paris, Cologne, and Berlin, 1848.

© Cengage Learning

Join this chapter's traveler on "Voyages," an interactive tour of historic sites and events:
www.cengagebrain.com

*mad rapture, all were so forgiving, sympathetic, loving of their fellow man. . . . [N]owhere have I found so much noble selflessness, so much truly touching integrity . . . with such heroism as I found in these simple, uneducated people, who always were and always will be a thousand times better than their leaders! . . . It seemed that the whole world had been turned upside down.**

*The Confession of Mikhail Bakunin, trans. Robert C. Howes (Ithaca: Cornell University Press, 1977), pp. 54–55.

Mikhail Bakunin
(1814–1876) A Russian
anarchist and revolu-
tionary imprisoned for
his role in the revolu-
tions of 1848. He
escaped from Siberian
exile, circled the world,
and returned to Europe
to continue his cam-
paign for liberty.

Bakunin's celebration of the common people did not move the tsar to forgive him. He was stripped of the aristocratic title inherited from his father and sent on a long journey by sleigh over frozen roads to enforced exile in Siberia. (It was 1857; the Trans-Siberian Railway, the world's longest, would not be opened for another thirty-five years.) Meanwhile, conservative rulers had re-established order in all the European capitals.

Bakunin, a fiery advocate of freedom, was not deterred, planning instead another *"unheard of adventure."* In 1861 he escaped, crossed the vast expanses of Siberia by steamboat to the Pacific Ocean, avoided a Russian naval patrol by boarding an American ship to Japan, and then sailed to San Francisco, Panama, New York, and finally London. On board he sang Russian songs, discussed religion with a young English clergyman (from whom he managed to borrow 250 dollars), and spread the words *freedom* and *revolution* wherever he traveled. Bakunin circled the world to return to Europe, the epicenter, he thought, of humankind's quest to overthrow the dead weight of the past and build a truly democratic future. He traveled restlessly, to France, Italy, Poland, Germany, Switzerland, and Sweden, his fame growing as one of the leading revolutionaries of Europe's industrial age.

Mikhail Bakunin's tumultuous life encompassed one of the most eventful periods of human history: the Industrial Revolution. Coal-driven steam engines unleashed the power of fossil fuels in the industrializing economies of western Europe and the United States, driving the machinery of new factories and propelling steamships and locomotives. More efficient transportation bound the entire world's people more tightly in networks of trade and communication. Bakunin's own early travels were by cart, sleigh, and wind-driven sailing ships, his later ones by railroad and steamship.

As more people moved to cities, often living in squalid conditions, rapid social change further stimulated debates among European reformers and revolutionaries: between liberals, who emphasized individual liberty; socialists, who stressed the collective good; and nationalists, who gave more thought to the advancement of their own group and less to the fate of humanity as a whole. And as the Industrial Revolution put Europe firmly at the center of a rapidly expanding world economy, reformers in other parts of the world learned about and were inspired by the ideals of 1848: liberalism, socialism, and nationalism.

Mikhail Bakunin's anarchism—his belief that states are inherently oppressive—stood in contrast with the communism of his archrival, Karl Marx, whom he accused of attempting to replace one form of government oppression with another. Marx was ultimately more influential. His writings, along with the very different ones of the English evolutionary biologist Charles Darwin, contributed to the widespread belief that the industrial age was a time of progress. But western Europe's rapid industrial growth posed particular challenges to its closest neighbors, the Russian and Ottoman empires. Political elites in these old land-based empires, now on the fringe of industrializing Europe, were torn between policies of reform, including the adaptation to Western models of law and governance, and conservative policies that stressed continuity over change.

» *What were the most important outcomes of the Industrial Revolution?*

» *What were the main features of European political development during and after the revolutions of 1848?*

» *Why were the ideas of Karl Marx and Charles Darwin of such great significance for world history?*

» *How did the leaders of the Russian and Ottoman empires respond to the challenge of an industrializing western Europe?*

The Industrial Revolution: Origins and Global Consequences, 1765–1870

It would be difficult to exaggerate the consequences of the **Industrial Revolution**. The productive capacity of human societies, and the ability of *Homo sapiens* to dominate the planet, had not received such a boost since the emergence of agriculture eleven thousand years earlier, and that breakthrough paled by comparison with the industrial one. The unlocking of fossil fuels as the key source of energy—first coal, then petroleum—literally changed the planet's atmosphere. Total global output of manufacturing rose over 400 percent between 1750 and 1900. The same period also saw a massive shift of production from East to West: India and China accounted for over half of the world's manufacturing production in 1750, but Europe and the United States accounted for nearly three-quarters by 1900 (see Table 23.1). Global population doubled in the same period.

Innovations—new forms of energy, new inventions, new ways of organizing human labor—were the foundation of the Industrial Revolution. By burning coal to

Industrial Revolution
Changes that began in late eighteenth-century Britain and transformed the global economy by creating new markets for raw materials and finished goods; accompanied by technological changes that revolutionized production processes, living and working conditions, and the environment.

TABLE 23.1 **Manufacturing Production of Selected Countries, 1750–1900, as Percentage of Global Total**

	1750	1800	1830	1860	1880	1900
China	33.1	33.3	29.9	19.5	12.5	6.3
India/Pakistan	24.4	19.7	17.9	8.4	2.8	1.7
Russia	4.7	5.4	5.4	7.1	7.8	8.9
France	3.9	4.1	5.4	8.0	7.8	6.8
Japan	3.9	3.4	2.7	2.7	2.5	2.4
Germany	3.2	3.4	3.8	4.9	8.4	13.1
Italy	2.4	2.7	2.2	2.7	2.5	2.6
Great Britain	1.6	4.1	9.8	19.9	22.8	18.5
United States	—	0.7	2.7	7.1	14.7	23.7
World	100	100	100	100	100	100

Adapted with permission from David Christian, *Maps of Time: An Introduction to Big History* (Berkeley: University of California Press, 2004), p. 408, Table 13.1.

drive steam engines, applying those steam engines to power machinery, and organizing mechanical processes in factories to centralize and rationalize the division of labor, industrial societies achieved unprecedented economic growth. Britain took the lead, soon followed by continental Europe and the United States. By the middle of the nineteenth century, industrialized societies were poised to translate economic power into military and political predominance on the world stage.

The Industrial Revolution was a global process. Improvements in transportation and communications—the steamship, railroad, and telegraph—created a worldwide market for raw materials. At the same time, as industrial production outstripped domestic demand, industrialists sought world markets to expand production even further.

Origins of the Industrial Revolution, 1765–1850

The British empire stimulated Britain's early modern economy. Timber and furs from Canada, sugar from the Caribbean, cotton textiles from India, and tea from China were part of a global trade network dominated by British shipping. Trade profits generated investment capital that could be applied to industrial production, and Britain's well-established trade and communications infrastructure would prove an immense advantage as the Industrial Revolution propelled British merchants to seek out expanded global markets and sources of raw materials.

The fluidity of the British elite spurred economic innovation. Whereas elsewhere in Europe the titled nobility remained aloof from commerce, in Britain less rigid lines divided aristocrats, members of the gentry, and merchant families. And while continental European philosophers usually concerned themselves with more abstract questions, the "practical science" advocated by leaders like Joseph Banks and inventors like John Harrison (see Chapter 21) created a British culture open to experimentation and innovation.

James Watt
(1736–1819) Scottish inventor who developed the world's first powerful and cost-effective steam engine; one of the most important contributors to Britain's Industrial Revolution.

A key date was the year 1765, when **James Watt** (1736–1819) unveiled the first workable steam engine. Just as Harrison had solved the problem of longitude by perfecting earlier chronometer designs, Watt tinkered with existing mechanisms until he found a way to generate considerably more power than ever before. Coal, long used as one of several sources of energy, now took center stage as the force behind the steam engine. British coal production increased tenfold between 1750 and 1850. Watt's steam engine realized the full potential of this energy revolution: for the first time it became possible to turn coal into cheap power.

Most importantly, the Industrial Revolution was unleashed by improvements in the production of iron. Iron smelters worldwide had long used wood charcoal to fuel their furnaces, but doing so limited production amounts to small batches, and increased demand for iron drove wood prices ever higher. While coal was plentiful in Britain, much of it contained too many impurities to burn at the high temperatures necessary for iron production. Then in the early eighteenth century an English inventor discovered a means of purifying coal to make a more concentrated product called coke. In the 1760s, after another innovator devised a way to remove impurities from the coke-iron product, coal could be used to make low-cost, high-quality iron in plentiful amounts.

Meanwhile, other entrepreneurs were focusing on the social organization of production. In his *Wealth of Nations*, Adam Smith had argued that division of labor was a key to increased productivity (see Chapter 21). Smith used the example of pins. A single person making a pin from start to finish, Smith explained, would be much less productive than a group of artisans who each focused on a single step in the process, an insight that paved the way for the factory system of production.

In the 1760s, entrepreneur and abolitionist **Josiah Wedgwood** began to experiment with a more complex division of labor in his ceramics factory. By breaking the production process down into specialized tasks, his factory produced greater quantities of uniform dinnerware at less expense. The days when a master potter and a few apprentices painstakingly produced pottery by hand were coming to an end. Wedgwood advanced the factory system of production even further when, in 1782, he was the first to install a steam engine, combining Smith's division of labor and Watt's steam power. The age of mass production had begun.

Wedgwood modeled his designs on those found on imported Chinese porcelain, the finest in the world and avidly collected by the British elite. Once Wedgwood brought the price down, even the less affluent could afford a few pieces of "china" for their cupboard. The middle-class consumer (then and now) played a key role in the expansion of industrial markets.

But it was in the textile industry where division of labor and steam power combined to reach full potential. At that time, India was by far the world's largest producer of cotton textiles, and Indian calico cloth flooded the British market. Unhappy with the competition, British wool producers convinced Parliament to impose high tariffs on Indian calicoes, making them less affordable.

However, the tariffs did not apply to rising imports of raw cotton. At first, British entrepreneurs used a decentralized "putting-out" system to produce cotton textiles, where they would provide raw materials to a rural family who would manufacture the cloth. The family used a traditional gender division of labor, the women first spinning the cotton into thread that the men then wove into cloth. Since spinning took more time than weaving, men were frequently idled while they waited for their wives to catch up.

British inventors solved the problem by mechanizing the spinning process, making it possible to produce much greater quantities of high-quality cotton thread. But with spinning now more efficient, it was the old methods of weaving that held back production, giving industrialists an incentive to mechanize the entire process. Experiments with steam-driven power looms took several decades, but by the 1830s the manufacture of cloth had been mechanized and consolidated into factories.

Of course, inexpensive labor was needed to make the factories profitable, and Britain's agricultural revolution helped create such a workforce (see Chapter 21). As "improving farmers" drove the rural poor out of their villages and off the land, many English peasants, desperate for work, moved to the mines and emerging factory towns. Their lives were no longer governed by the seasons and the constraints of muscle power, but dominated by the relentless power of steam and the factory clock.

On a global level, growth in textile production increased the demand for raw cotton, which could not be grown in Europe. After 1793 new production in the United States augmented supplies from India. In that year, American inventor Eli Whitney created the cotton gin, which efficiently separated seeds from cotton. Whitney's machine stimulated cotton production in the United States, which soon became the world's biggest supplier.

The energy revolution of coal and steam, together with the more efficient social organization of the factory system, transformed virtually every field of manufacture. Britain's early lead

Josiah Wedgwood (1730–1795) English ceramics manufacturer who combined the use of steam power with factory organization to greatly increase the output and lower the cost of his products. He was a prominent supporter of the abolition of slavery.

Mary Evans Picture Library/The Image Works

British Coal Miner Coal provided the energy that almost miraculously increased productivity during the early Industrial Revolution. But getting it out of the ground was difficult, dirty, and dangerous. Children and teenagers played an important role. Young workers like the boy pictured here suffered from stunted growth and short life expectancy.

in industrialization combined with its strength in international commerce to make it a dominant global power. Following Britain's lead, coal-rich Belgium also developed a substantial network of steam-fired factories, followed by France and Germany. Industrial production was also increasing in the United States, particularly in northern states like Massachusetts (see Chapter 25).

Global Dimensions of the Industrial Revolution, 1820–1880

The Industrial Revolution was a global process. The revolution in transportation and communications dramatically increased the pace of global interactions, and people around the world consumed inexpensive, factory-produced goods. By the end of the nineteenth century, most of humankind participated in the global commodity markets of industrial capitalism. *Globalization* is the term we now use to refer to the shrinking of the world—what some have called the "annihilation of time and space"—by rapid transport and communications; in the late nineteenth century, railroads, steamships, and telegraphs were making the world a much smaller place.

Early industrial Britain had benefited from its transportation network. The country's coastal shipping, combined with river and canal transport, stimulated domestic markets. Water transport had always been more efficient than transport by land, but as the price of iron dropped, railroads became a viable alternative. By midcentury a dense network of railroads covered western Europe (see Map 23.1), increasing both urbanization and mobility. Railroads were not only an efficient and inexpensive means of transporting freight; they could also transport people more cheaply and comfortably than by stagecoach. In North America, transcontinental railroads in the United States and Canada speeded European settlers west. In fact, if Mikhail Bakunin had arrived in San Francisco just ten years later on his round-the-world voyage, in 1871 rather than 1861, he would likely have used the transcontinental railroad himself to cross from the Pacific to the Atlantic, and would have learned more about the United States as a result. By 1880 railroad construction had also begun in Russia, British India, and Mexico.

By 1850 steamships, another product of "the age of steam and iron," had improved transportation in industrial nations. The United States benefited most from steamboats. Large waterways like the Mississippi River conveyed people and goods over great distances and helped integrate the young country economically as well as culturally. With steamships and railroads supporting access to markets, inexpensive iron plows imported from Europe (and later manufactured in the United States itself) made possible the agricultural settlement of the Great Plains.

The international influence of steamships was even more revolutionary. The first steam-powered crossing of the Atlantic took place in 1838 and of the Pacific in 1853. Though sailing ships remained common, by the 1870s steamships were dramatically reducing transportation times and shipping costs, as well as enhancing the military advantage of Western nations around the world. The completion of the Suez Canal in 1869 (linking the Mediterranean and Red Seas), combined with the power of steamships, cut transportation time from Europe to South Asia from months to weeks. Such advances enabled the expansion of European imperialism in Africa and Southeast Asia and the tightening of control over existing colonies, like British India (see Chapters 24 and 26).

The invention of the telegraph meant that information could move even more quickly than people and goods. The first long-range telegraph message was sent in 1844. In 1869 a submarine cable was laid beneath the Atlantic Ocean, allowing for instantaneous transcontinental communication. Telegraphs brought an information revolution to world markets, which became more integrated than

MAP 23.1 Continental Industrialization, ca. 1850 Ease of access to iron and coal spurred industrialization in parts of Europe, such as northeastern France, Belgium, and northwestern regions of the German Confederation. By 1850 railroad connections supplemented rivers and canals as means of transport with an efficiency that lowered the cost of both raw materials and finished products. By the end of the century every nation in Europe was tightly integrated by rail, facilitating the movement of people and goods across the continent. (© Cengage Learning)

ever before when traders could compare prices much more quickly and accurately across continents. Shipping companies used the telegraph to lower their costs and increase global trade. Military officers with telegraphic information had a powerful tactical advantage, as well.

Industrialization expanded the need for raw materials, especially cotton. After the British gained control of India (see Chapter 20), the export of raw Indian cotton replaced the export of finished cloth. Partly because of the lower cost of factory-made textiles, and partly because of the tariffs aiding British industry, India actually suffered a process of deindustrialization during the early mid-nineteenth century, as unemployed Indian spinners, weavers, and dyers fled to the countryside (see Chapter 24). Such were the complex and uneven outcomes of industrialization: British villagers were forced off the land and into the cities while Indian artisans had no choice but to leave the towns for the villages.

Muhammad Ali
(r. 1808–1848) Egyptian ruler who attempted to modernize his country's economy by promoting cotton cultivation and textile manufacturing and by sending young Egyptians to study in Europe.

Another supplier of cotton was Egypt. After Napoleon's invasion of Egypt in 1798 (see Chapter 22), an ambitious Ottoman military commander seized power. **Muhammad Ali** (r. 1808–1848) had witnessed firsthand the superiority of European weaponry and knew that his regime needed to keep up with the latest advances. Muhammad Ali (moo-HAH-muhd AH-lee) encouraged cotton production to pay for railroads, factories, and guns, while sending science and engineering students to study in France. Egyptian peasants, however, saw little benefit from global markets.

There was even less benefit from industrialization for slaves picking cotton in the United States. Growth in British textile manufacturing in the first half of the nineteenth century, which increased the demand for cheap cotton, actually intensified slavery in southern American states such as Alabama and Mississippi and stimulated expansion of slave production to new territories like Texas. For many in India, Egypt, and North America, the Industrial Revolution's appetite for cotton was a curse, not a blessing.

The web of industry drew in commodities from around the world. Palm oil and peanuts from West Africa helped lubricate industrial machinery. Cattle hides from the *pampas* (PAHM-pahs) grasslands of Argentina spurred a proliferation of leather goods. Mexican plantations exported sisal for making rope. Africans and Latin Americans participated in the Industrial Revolution primarily as suppliers of raw materials.

As we will see in the following three chapters, the Industrial Revolution challenged ways of life in the Americas, Africa, Asia, and the Pacific. In fact, similar challenges faced the peoples of Europe. In England in the 1810s, for example, skilled artisans known as Luddites broke into factories and smashed the machinery, seeing mechanization as a threat to their livelihoods. New urban residents lost their bonds of community; once having known virtually everyone around them, they now found themselves living in urban anonymity. Kings, aristocrats, and religious leaders often saw growing cities as breeding grounds for moral decay and social disorder. But there were many Europeans, Mikhail Bakunin among them, who emphasized the possibilities of the new age for the liberation of the human spirit.

Reform and Revolution in Nineteenth-Century Europe, 1815–1880

In 1815 the great powers of Europe banded together to quell the fires of the French Revolution and its aftermath (see Chapter 22). Their success did not last long. Monarchy and aristocratic prerogative no longer sat well with the rising urban middle class and Europe's new industrial working class.

The rising social classes strove for greater liberty, augmenting the ideals they inherited from the Enlightenment and French Revolution with new ideologies. Liberals, most influential in Britain, emphasized the freedom of the individual and the sanctity of private property. Socialists, growing in numbers and influence, stressed their belief in collective organization for the betterment of society. Anarchists like Bakunin thought that all communities, including workers in factories, should be free to regulate their own affairs and choose their own leaders, without the interference of rulers and governments. The romantic movement, especially strong among Germans, increasingly emphasized depth of feeling over the cool rationality of the Enlightenment. The passion of romanticism became linked with nationalism, the belief that individuals are bound together in a common purpose and a common destiny by ties of language, culture, and history (see Chapter 22).

Nationalism became the strongest of the ideologies swirling first through industrial Europe and then across the world.

Tensions rising from industrial change reached a crescendo in 1848, when revolutions spread across Europe and seemed ready to sweep the old order away. But the fire of revolution soon died down. Revolutionaries like Mikhail Bakunin were shocked and disappointed when conservative, authoritarian leaders re-established control.

Nineteenth-Century Ideologies: Liberalism, Socialism, Anarchism, Romanticism, and Nationalism

Mikhail Bakunin embodied the new sensibilities. His writings show the influence of five different, sometimes contradictory, ideas: liberalism, socialism, romanticism, anarchism, and nationalism.

Liberalism implied open-mindedness and the need for social and political reform. In the nineteenth century, Britain was most strongly associated with liberal tendencies, while European monarchs and their supporters resisted reform. Liberals favored freedom of conscience, freedom of trade, the protection of property rights, and limitations on the political power of religious authorities. While liberals approved of the extension of voting rights to men with property and education, only late in the century did liberalism become associated with universal male suffrage.

Socialism was better developed in France and Germany. Some socialists favored the overthrow of the state as a precondition for the collectivization of property and the realization of social equality. Other socialists thought their cause could be advanced by working within existing institutions, while advocates of yet another strand of socialism created utopian communities outside the state. In France and Germany revolutionary and reformist socialists vied for influence; in liberal Britain, democracy and socialism developed together. In Russia, on the other hand, with its more authoritarian government, the revolutionary strand of socialism predominated.

Romanticism prioritized emotional intensity and authenticity over the rationalism and formality of the Enlightenment, and a focus on nature as a reaction against the gritty, crowded conditions of cities and factories. In poetry, the expression of deep feeling took precedence over formality of construction. Romantic painters were sensitive to the evocative power of nature, focusing on forests, mountains, and moonlight, or emphasizing the exotic in their depictions of distant cultures, especially those of Asia. Starting with Ludwig van Beethoven, German composers developed themes of musical romanticism culminating in the long, complex, and powerful operas of Richard Wagner (1813–1883).

Romanticism was strongly connected to *nationalism*, the most powerful political ideology of the industrial age. Nationalists, like Wagner, sought to develop cultural and historical pedigrees for peoples who did not yet have nation-states to represent them. Some nationalists worked to bring together members of language groups, such as Italians who spoke a wide variety of related dialects and who, like Germans, were divided by what nationalists saw as artificial political boundaries. Others sought to separate their group from multinational empires: Poles from Russia, Greeks from the Ottoman empire, and Hungarians from Austria. Unlike the concern showed by liberals and socialists for humanity as a whole, nationalists focused on the interests of their particular group.

Mikhail Bakunin debated adherents of each of these positions while promoting his own brand of *anarchism*. Liberals, he thought, were on the right track in their advocacy of individual freedom. However, he sharply criticized them for favoring such rights only for the middle class, not for disenfranchised workers. Though their philosophy favored small government, he said, *"when the masses are restless, even the most enthusiastic liberals immediately reverse themselves and become the most fanatical champions of the State."*[*] In this critique of liberalism Bakunin agreed with the socialists, who also saw the liberal defense of property rights as a way for the middle class to protect its interests against working people. Bakunin criticized the socialists, however, for thinking that they could take over the state (through revolution) or influence it (through elections) to promote workers' interests. Where Bakunin differed with the socialists was in his belief that governments are by nature repressive: the leaders of a socialist state would look after their own interests, not those of the masses.

Though Bakunin was a romantic figure himself—passionate, fearless, and unconventional—he saw romanticized nationalism as an increasing threat when conservative leaders used patriotic appeals to gain the support of the very workers who should, he thought, oppose them. His goal, sincere if perhaps naïve, was a world where people have *"what they really want, the free self-organization and administration of their own affairs from the bottom upward, without any interference or violence from above."*[†] Instead of seizing state power, Bakunin thought, revolutionaries should destroy it. Except in small or remote communities, such as utopian settlements established along communal lines, Bakunin's anarchist vision has never been effectively put into practice.

Victorian Britain, 1815–1867

In 1815, when Bakunin was an infant and while European leaders restored order in the wake of Napoleon, Britain was dominated by those who associated change with the excesses of the French Revolution. The landed classes who controlled Parliament imposed tariffs on imported grain, raising the price of bread. Unemployment was high among returning soldiers. The enclosure movement and the new factory system were driving many out of villages and into urban slums.

Conditions in cities were appalling. Wages were low, and many employers preferred children, especially girls, as factory workers because they were nimble, could fit into tight spaces, and were easy to control. Industrial cities were unhealthy places. The lack of sanitation was noted by Friedrich Engels, a German socialist leader, during his visit to Manchester in 1844:

> *Right and left a multitude of covered passages lead from the main street into numerous courts, and he who turns in thither gets into a filth and disgusting grime, the equal of which is not to be found. . . . Inhabitants can pass into and out of the court only by passing through foul pools of stagnant urine and excrement. . . . At the bottom flows, or rather stagnates, the Irk, a narrow, coal-black, foul-smelling stream, full of debris and refuse, which it deposits on the shallower right bank. In dry weather, a long string of the most disgusting, blackish-green, slime pools are left standing on this bank, from the depths of which bubbles of miasmatic gas constantly arise and give forth a stench unendurable even on the bridge forty or fifty feet above the surface of the stream.*[‡]

[*]Mikhail Bakunin, "God and the State," in *Bakunin on Anarchy*, ed. Sam Dolgoff (New York: Knopf, 1972), p. 234.

[†]Mikhail Bakunin, "Some Preconditions for a Social Revolution," in *Bakunin on Anarchy*, ed. Sam Dolgoff (New York: Knopf, 1972), p. 338.

[‡]Excerpt from *The Marx-Engels Reader*, Second Edition, edited by Robert C. Tucker. Copyright © 1978, 1972 by W. W. Norton & Company, Inc. Used by permission of W. W. Norton & Company, Inc.

Disease spread rapidly in such neighborhoods, becoming even more deadly after increased contact with India brought cholera to England. In London, thousands died from infected water supplies.

Better-off families moved to pleasant suburbs, isolated from filth, disease, and the pollution spewed by what poet William Blake called England's *"dark, satanic mills."* The prevailing view of the upper class was that the poor were responsible for their own fate, an attitude satirized by novelist Charles Dickens in *A Christmas Carol*, when Ebenezer Scrooge says that if people are so poor that they are likely to die, *"they should do so and decrease the surplus population."*

The British middle and lower classes had no right to vote and thus no direct means of influencing policy. Attempts by industrial workers to form unions were outlawed by Parliament as dangerous "combinations." Factory workers might find solidarity in churches: Methodism's egalitarian ethos allowed workers to assert spiritual, if not social and political, equality. Others sought solace in gin and opium.

By the time of Queen Victoria (r. 1837–1901), however, the reform impulse animated British politics. Charitable organizations grew in size, their leaders arguing that the poor could improve their lot if only they would adopt middle-class values like thrift and sobriety. Many saw that the government also had a role to play, especially in improving health and sanitation.

Early Victorian reform was guided by a philosophy called *utilitarianism*. Jeremy Bentham, utilitarianism's leading proponent, argued that political and social policies needed to be judged by their utility in light of present-day circumstances. In 1840 the government built a model prison based on Bentham's designs in which each prisoner had a separate cell with more light and air than in the notoriously dark and dank prisons of the previous age. Following utilitarian philosophy, the number of crimes for which the death penalty could be applied was radically reduced.

Animated by British "practical science," the government sponsored scientific studies to improve urban planning, water supplies, and hygiene. Investigations of child labor led to public outcry and legislation that regulated abhorrent labor conditions. Restrictions on the activities of Catholics were lifted. And by the 1850s wages increased: even less-skilled workers were beginning to benefit from British pre-eminence in industry and trade.

The conservatism of the post-Napoleonic period was giving way to a more liberal political environment. Middle-class liberals, believers in free trade and individual autonomy, were frustrated by their lack of political representation and by policies that favored landed interests over urban ones. Most did not, however, believe in democracy: education and property were still preconditions for political participation.

The **Reform Bill of 1832** brought Parliament into closer accord with the social changes brought on by industrialization. First, seats in Parliament were redistributed to take account of the growth of cities. Second, the bill lowered the property requirements for voting so that better-off members of the middle class, such as male shopkeepers, could vote. This new Parliament better reflected the interests of industrialists and the urban middle class.

Economic policies began to shift toward free trade. As improvements in transportation made grain from the Americas and eastern Europe less expensive, factory owners lobbied for an end to agricultural tariffs, arguing that cheaper bread would help keep wages down. In 1846 Parliament opened British markets to foreign grain, showing the new power of urban interests versus the interests of the rural gentry.

John Stuart Mill (1806–1873), who Mikhail Bakunin admiringly called an *"apostle of idealism,"*[*] was a powerful voice of British liberalism. In his book *On*

---

[*]Paul McLaughlin, *Mikhail Bakunin: The Philosophical Basis of His Theory of Anarchism* (New York: Algora Publishing, 2002), p. 113.

Reform Bill of 1832 Bill that significantly reformed the British House of Commons by lowering property qualifications for the vote. Still, only wealthier middle-class men were enfranchised.

John Stuart Mill (1806–1873) English philosopher and economist who argued for the paramount importance of individual liberty and supported greater rights for women.

Liberty (1859), Mill argued that liberty involved freedom not only from arbitrary government interference but also from *"the tendency of society to impose, by other means than civil penalties, its own ideas and practices as rules of conduct on those who dissent from them."*[1] His emphasis on freedom from both political oppression and social conformity led Mill to conclusions that were radical for the time: he thought the vote should be extended not only to working men but also to women.

By the 1860s, social change again necessitated political reform. The Reform Bill of 1867 nearly doubled the number of voters, though women and those without property were still excluded. The easing of restrictions on trade unions increased their power, and at the end of the 1880s another reform bill gave most British men the vote.

The combination of economic success and relatively peaceful political reform made many mid-Victorians supremely confident of their nation and optimistic about its future. (See the feature "Visual Evidence in Primary Sources: The Great Exhibition and the Crystal Palace.") Naval superiority in the Mediterranean Sea and Indian Ocean, and imperial successes such as the conquest of India, reinforced that sense of self-satisfaction.

The British constitution was evolving to suit new circumstances, just as Edmund Burke had predicted. (See the feature "Movement of Ideas Through Primary Sources" in Chapter 22.) On the European continent, by contrast, many societies were rocked by revolution and unsettled by the redrawing of national borders.

France: Revolution, Republic, and Empire

In 1815, diplomats at the Congress of Vienna restored the Bourbon dynasty to power in France (see Chapter 22). After the revolutionary and Napoleonic years, however, it was impossible to return to the past, and in 1830 a popular uprising overthrew the unpopular Bourbon monarch.

Some of those who organized street protests against the king clamored for a return to republican government. Many middle-class liberals, however, feared that a republic would favor working-class opinion at the expense of private property. Their leaders advocated a constitutional monarchy and invited Louis Philippe, a nobleman with moderate views, to take the throne. More interested in business than in royal protocol, King Louis Philippe was called the "bourgeois king." His regime was certainly more open than that of the Bourbons, though voting was restricted to a small minority of property-owning men. Republicans despised him.

In early 1848, police in Paris fired on a crowd of demonstrators, and 1,500 barricades went up around the city. Louis Philippe abdicated and fled the country. *"No sooner had I learned that they were fighting in Paris,"* Bakunin wrote in his confession to the tsar, *"than . . . I set out again for France."*[*] For the first time in fifty years, France was a republic in which the people themselves were sovereign. The change was so sudden that men meeting in a newspaper office to plan the country's future were divided on how to proceed. An influential socialist, Louis Blanc (loo-EE blawnk), argued that private ownership of industry was inefficient, leaving many unemployed, and unfair, giving workers no say in how the factories were run. He called for cooperative workshops to be set up by the government and run by the workers. Employment would be guaranteed for all. Bakunin strongly disagreed with Blanc's approach, which *"advised the people to rely in all things upon the State."*[†] Instead, he

---

[*]*The Confession of Mikhail Bakunin,* trans. Robert C. Howes (Ithaca: Cornell University Press, 1977), p. 56.

[†]Mikhail Bakunin, "Socialism," in *Bakunin on Anarchy,* ed. Sam Dolgoff (New York: Knopf, 1972), p. 121.

thought, workers should seize the factories and run them cooperatively, with no interference from Blanc or the republican government.

Blanc's plan was even more strongly opposed by middle-class defenders of property rights. Heeding liberal criticism, the republic implemented only a weakened version of his vision for public employment. Some public works projects were funded, such as planting trees, and those who could not find work were guaranteed enough money to live on. Almost all this money was spent in Paris, a fact resented by the rural majority, who largely backed the presidential candidacy of **Louis Napoleon** (1808–1873), the nephew of Napoleon Bonaparte.

Louis Napoleon represented, in his own words, *"order, authority, religion, popular welfare at home, national dignity abroad."* Liberals fearful of socialism and the many French peasants who resented the preferential treatment of Parisian workers also, of course, recalled the glorious days of Napoleon Bonaparte. After being elected president, Louis Napoleon declared himself Napoleon III, emperor of France. As in the 1790s, France went swiftly from constitutional monarchy to republic to empire.

Napoleon III presided over the Second Empire (1852–1870), a period of stability, prosperity, and expanding French power. As president, Louis Napoleon eliminated Blanc's socialist program and sought to stimulate the economy by selling government bonds to finance railway construction and by backing semipublic financial institutions to provide capital for commerce and industry. Although Napoleon III was authoritarian, he respected the rule of law and basic civil liberties. Like Napoleon Bonaparte, he gained support by appealing to French nationalism and by expanding the overseas French empire, sending armies to Mexico and Vietnam (see Chapters 25 and 26).

Eventually, however, Napoleon III was unable to cope with the rising threat of Prussia. In 1870 German armies invaded France and drove him from power, to be replaced in 1871 by the Third Republic. Leaders of the Third Republic would change many of Napoleon III's policies but would retain his emphasis on overseas imperial expansion.

Louis Napoleon (1808–1873) Conservative nephew of Napoleon Bonaparte who was elected president of the Second Republic before declaring himself emperor in 1852. Was forced to abdicate in 1870 after losing the Franco-Prussian War.

The Habsburg Monarchy, 1848–1870

News of the 1848 uprising in Paris spread like wildfire across Europe. The dominant power in central Europe was the Austrian empire, still ruled by the Habsburg family. Protestors, university students prominent among them, took to the streets of Vienna in early 1848 demanding new rights. The befuddled emperor reportedly asked, *"Are they allowed to do that?"* Prince Metternich, the conservative architect of the Congress of Vienna, resigned his position as chancellor and fled to England.

While nationalism held nations like France together, it had the potential to tear multiethnic empires like Austria apart, as Italian, Hungarian, Czech, Croatian, and other Habsburg subjects agitated for national rights. In Budapest a Hungarian assembly created a new constitution ratifying religious freedom, equality before the law, and an end to the privileges of the old feudal nobility. Revolution also swept Milan, the chief city of Austria's northern Italian possessions, and Prague, the mixed German-Czech city where Bakunin was captured by Austrian forces, leading to his imprisonment and deportation.

The young Emperor Franz Joseph II (r. 1848–1916) sought the support of the rural majority. As in France, peasants were shocked by the radicalism of university students and urban workers, and their support helped Habsburg authorities re-establish control within their German-speaking territories. But Franz Joseph's success was far from complete. By 1859 Italian rebels won independence from Austria, and in 1866 Prussian forces defeated the Habsburg army. The discontent of subject

The Great Exhibition and the Crystal Palace

London's Hyde Park was the site of mid-Victorian Britain's monument to industrial, technological, and commercial progress: the Great Exhibition of the Works of Industry of All Nations. Queen Victoria herself opened the Exhibition to great public acclaim in 1851. Her husband, Prince Albert, one of the principal planners, was at her side. The Great Exhibition received over 6 million visitors, some traveling from continental Europe and the United States, and raised enough money through admission fees to endow the great Victoria and Albert Museum and the Natural History Museum, both of which still stand near Hyde Park today. The Crystal Palace, an imposing glass and iron structure built to enclose the Exhibition and protect attendees from the weather, was itself a wonder of industrial technology.

Over half the exhibit space was devoted to the tools and products of British manufacturers, and great attention was paid to colonial contributions to the country's wealth and power. Collecting Indian artifacts and containing them within the exhibition hall, for example, was an implicit

The Crystal Palace, completed in time for the opening of the Great Exhibition in 1851, was 1,851 feet (564 m) long, with an interior height of 128 feet (39 m). It used more than a million square feet of glass, more than any other building up to that time.

Recent innovations in glass manufacturing provided the architects with the large panes necessary to give the building the "crystal" effect of clear walls and ceilings. Queen Victoria bestowed a knighthood on creator Joseph Paxton, who designed the building in just ten days, for his achievement.

Another innovation was the provision of public toilets, first just for men and later for women as well. Visitors paid a penny to use the facilities, hence the term "to spend a penny" in British English for making a lavatory trip.

© Science Museum/Science & Society

The huge central transept was the site of concerts, circuses, and tightrope walking; music was provided by the world's largest organ.

When the Great Exhibition ended, the Crystal Palace was taken apart and re-erected in a South London suburb. The Crystal Palace Football Club is a reminder of the role the surrounding grounds then played in sporting life, even after the building was finally destroyed by fire in 1936.

assertion of the legitimacy of Britain's imperial claim over South Asia and another expression of the ongoing relationship between science and empire (see Chapter 21).

The Great Exhibition had an enduring global influence. Later, other nations would also erect monumental buildings and put their achievements on display, inviting all nations to participate in "world's fairs" such as those held in Paris (1878), Chicago (with the Columbian Exposition of 1893), and, most recently, Shanghai, at China's World Expo (2010).

Visitors to the Great Exhibition passed through a series of courts focused on the history of art and architecture (from ancient Egypt through the Renaissance) and natural wonders of the world. The main attractions, however, were exhibits of the latest industrial technology: "every conceivable invention," as Queen Victoria noted in her diary.

Some one hundred thousand objects were spread over 10 miles (16 km) of viewing space.

Prince Albert emphasized that the Great Exhibition demonstrated the orderly progress of British society. "We have no fear here either of an uprising or an assassination," he bragged to his cousin, King William of Prussia, who had survived a revolutionary uprising just three years earlier, in 1848.

V & A Images, London/Art Resource, NY

Visitors gasped in amazement at the Koh-I-Noor diamond, the largest cut diamond in the world at that time; took their first ever look at photographs at the display of the recently invented daguerreotype; witnessed the powerful and fast-loading revolving pistol of Samuel Colt; and wondered at the latest ingenuities of industrial machinery and design.

The largest exhibit was a huge hydraulic press used for bridge building, with a series of metal tubes, each weighing well over 1,000 tons.

An even more popular display was a simple statue of a female Greek slave, demurely hidden in a small red tent and wearing only a simple chain. Exoticism and sexual allure, it seems, were just as interesting to the Victorians as mechanical might.

QUESTION FOR ANALYSIS

» *How would the wonders of technology displayed in London in 1851 compare with those that might be assembled for a similar "Great Exhibition" today?*

nationalities continued. With crises looming, the emperor proclaimed the Dual Monarchy in 1867, creating a federal structure for the empire. He would be simultaneously emperor of Austria and king of Hungary, allowing each state its own separate institutions.

Through this compromise Austria retained its great power status and settled the long struggle between German rulers and Hungarian subjects. However, it did nothing to address the grievances of Czechs or Croats. Failure to resolve the empire's regional, ethnic, and class divisions would help spark world war in the next century (see Chapter 27).

The Unification of Italy, 1848–1870

In 1848 Italian liberals dreamt of a new political order based on ties of language, culture, and history. But they would have to overcome significant regional differences and the long-standing division of the Italian peninsula into numerous states. The north was subject to the same forces of industrialization and urbanization as western Europe, while the south was still largely peasant and traditional in its Catholicism. Differences in dialect made it difficult for Italians from various parts of the peninsula to understand one another. Such divisions had enabled conservatives to stifle liberal reforms and attempts at unification.

Giuseppe Garibaldi
(1807–1882) Italian nationalist revolutionary who unified Italy in 1860 by conquering Sicily and Naples. Though he advocated an Italian Republic, the new country became a constitutional monarchy instead.

Like other Italian idealists of the time, **Giuseppe Garibaldi** (jew-SEP-pay gar-uh-BAWL-dee) (1807–1882) believed in the need for a *risorgimento*, a political and cultural renewal of Italy that would restore its historic greatness. Condemned to death for leading an uprising in Genoa, he fled to South America, where he took part in a Brazilian uprising. In 1848 he returned to Italy, defending the newly declared Roman republic against a French force sent to restore the pope's authority over the city, as well as fighting in the northern wars against Austria.

Then in 1860 a rebellion broke out in southern Italy. With the kingdom of Naples tottering, Garibaldi landed on the island of Sicily with a thousand poorly trained troops, overthrew its corrupt ruler, and crossed to the mainland. Joined by other enthusiastic rebels, his army marched north, bringing Naples and Sicily into a new, united Italy in 1861. Garibaldi's exploits stirred Mikhail Bakunin, and when the two finally met in 1867, their warm embrace was cheered by an enthusiastic crowd.

Garibaldi's victory was not complete, however, as Italy became not a republic but a constitutional monarchy. Once the revolutionaries had paved the way, the process of Italian unification was commandeered by conservative political leaders, especially the Count of Cavour, prime minister of the Piedmont kingdom in the northwest. Cavour successfully promoted the claim of his own sovereign to be king of all Italy. By 1870 the Papal States were incorporated into the kingdom, and the process of unification was complete, adding Italy to the list of great powers in Europe with an eye toward empire.

Sharp divisions remained, however. For many, the concept of being "Italian" was something entirely new. Especially in the south, church and family retained their traditional importance, and local traditions—in food, clothing, and speech—predominated over the much newer national ideals. Many in the north felt more comfortable with European culture, with life in Paris or Vienna, than with the Mediterranean lifestyle of their new countrymen. In France, in contrast, revolution and empire had melded the French people into what one historian has called an "imagined community"; that is, they felt a common sense of citizenship and identity with all other Frenchmen, however different their circumstances. Italians had a much longer road in forging a common national identity.

Germany: Nationalism and Unification, 1848–1871

From the standpoint of world history, the most important European political development of the nineteenth century was the creation, in 1871, of a unified Germany. Almost immediately, Germany became the world's second-ranking industrial nation and a significant new economic and military force in world affairs.

The process of German political consolidation began with Napoleon: many of the hundreds of small states that existed before his empire were not restored after 1815. Instead, the Congress of Vienna recognized a German Confederation of forty-two separate polities, including the large kingdoms of Austria, Prussia, Saxony, and Bavaria. Of these, Prussia, with its capital in Berlin, was the most powerful. Austria, as a multiethnic empire, was a poor fit. When Prussia sponsored the expansion of a German customs union from the 1820s onward to increase trade among German states, it excluded Austria, its main rival for supremacy within the Confederation.

Another and even more potent legacy of the Napoleonic era, beyond political consolidation, was the very *idea* of German nationhood. France had demonstrated the power of national unity, and now more Germans aspired to go beyond confederation to nationhood of their own. But would the process of nation building be controlled by liberals, strongest in the west, or by monarchical conservatives, represented by Prussia?

That was the key question when the revolutionary flame of 1848 swept across the German states. Having left Paris for Prague, Bakunin found himself in Dresden, the capital of the kingdom of Saxony, when an insurrection broke out. He threw himself into the fray as a leader of the democratic forces, until Prussian soldiers came to the rescue of the Saxon army. As Bakunin fled to Prague, it was clear that the Prussian government would oppose unification based on a popular uprising.

Indeed, Friedrich Wilhelm IV of Prussia (r. 1840–1857) took a hard line, using military force to crush demonstrators who stormed an arsenal and seized a royal palace in Berlin. Although the king did grant Prussia a constitution with a representative assembly elected through universal manhood suffrage, he and his ministers remained free to ignore it and rule as they liked. Friedrich Wilhelm saw the constitution as an expression of royal beneficence, not as a matter of rights.

The Prussian government in 1848, like that of Austria, feared that German political unification would undermine its power. In other German states, however, significant support existed for a unified Germany under a liberal constitution. A committee of prominent liberals organized an election, and in 1848 the **Frankfurt Assembly** met to write a constitution. The delegates drafted a Declaration of Fundamental Rights that embodied the best of liberal political principles, including freedom of assembly and freedom of speech. Seeking a symbol of unity, they offered the crown to Friedrich Wilhelm as constitutional monarch of a democratic German state. But the Prussian king refused to accept what he called *"a crown from the gutter,"* rejecting the principle of popular sovereignty upon which the proposed constitution was based.

Friedrich Wilhelm's refusal killed any hope of unifying Germany under a liberal constitution. But the forces of industrialization, the building of railroads, and rapid urbanization were creating conditions in which a unified Germany seemed more desirable than ever. In the 1860s, under the initiative of its chancellor, **Otto von Bismarck** (1815–1898), Prussia started to create a new German nation. "Germany" became a reality in 1871 after a coalition of armies led by Prussia defeated Napoleon III and occupied Paris. The Prussian king Kaiser Wilhelm II was then crowned emperor of Germany in the Hall of Mirrors in the grand Versailles

Frankfurt Assembly Assembly held in 1848 to create a constitution for a united German Confederation; elected Friedrich Wilhelm IV as constitutional monarch, but Wilhelm refused the offer on the principle that people did not have the right to choose their own king.

Otto von Bismarck (1815–1898) Unified Germany in 1871 and became its first chancellor. Previously, as chancellor of Prussia, he led his state to victories against Austria and France.

German Industrialization The Krupp family had been important innovators and manufacturers of armaments since the period of the Thirty Years' War (1630–1648). In the nineteenth century, with the foundations of the Krupp Steelworks, they became the most important of German industrialists, their field cannon playing an important role in securing victory in the Franco-Prussian War (1870–1871). Here the sprawling Krupp steel factory in the town of Essen shows that fields and factories could still be found close in late-nineteenth-century Europe. (Ullstein Bilderdienst/The Granger Collection New York)

Palace, a tremendous blow to French national pride and a signal that militarism and territorial expansion would be the foundation of the new German state. Bismarck, Prussia's "iron chancellor," was, in Bakunin's words, *"an out-and-out aristocratic, monarchical"* Prussian conservative *"with a militarist and bigoted bugbear of an emperor as chief."*[*] Bismarck had told a committee of the German Confederation in 1862: *"Not through speeches and majority decisions are the great questions of the day decided—that was the mistake of 1848—but by iron and blood."*[†] Bismarck's victories over Denmark, Austria, and most especially France sparked German national pride, inspiring many with a romantic vision of a grand German state fulfilling the people's destiny as a great world power.

Events confirmed that vision. Berlin became a great world capital, its population doubling to over 1.5 million in the two decades after unification; German manufacturing boomed as large companies plowed massive sums into research and development; the gross national product doubled between 1870 and 1890. But the German achievement had unsettling implications for the other great powers, which now faced an invigorated competitor for markets and empire.

---

[*]Mikhail Bakunin, "Critique of Economic Determinism and Historical Materialism," in *Bakunin on Anarchy,* ed. Sam Dolgoff (New York: Knopf, 1972), p. 315.

[†]Quoted in Otto Pflanze, *Bismarck and the Development of Germany,* vol. 1 (Princeton: Princeton University Press, 1990), p. 184.

New Paradigms of the Industrial Age: Marx and Darwin

Europeans in this era believed that science could reveal the secrets of the natural world and that human society could be improved through rational inquiry. Of the many scientists and social theorists of Europe's industrial age, Karl Marx and Charles Darwin stand out for the enduring global influence of their work. Marx, in his dissection of capitalism and explanation of the inevitability of socialist revolution, developed a systematic framework for the analysis of human history. Darwin, in describing how natural selection drives the process of evolution, developed an original framework for understanding natural history. Both developed new ways of ordering knowledge that substantially altered previous modes of thought.

Karl Marx, Socialism, and Communism

The Manifesto of the Communist Party, published during the revolutionary year of 1848 by **Karl Marx** (1818–1883) and Friedrich Engels, directly challenged the status quo:

> *The Communists . . . openly declare that their ends can only be attained by the forceful overthrow of all existing social conditions. Let the ruling classes tremble at a Communistic revolution. The proletarians have nothing to lose but their chains. They have a world to win. WORKING MEN OF ALL COUNTRIES UNITE!*[*]

Karl Marx (1818–1883) German author and philosopher who founded the Marxist branch of socialism; wrote *The Manifesto of the Communist Party* (1848) and *Das Kapital* (1867).

Even though conservatives retook control after 1849, Marx believed that socialist revolution in Europe was not only possible but inevitable.

Marx was a brilliant student who had earned a doctoral degree in philosophy. He absorbed much from the works of the dominant German philosopher of the early nineteenth century, Georg Hegel. Hegel had argued that the human mind progresses through stages toward absolute knowledge. Marx accepted this theory of progress, but rejected the idea that it takes place primarily at the level of consciousness. Instead he developed a materialist view that saw history propelled by changes in "modes of production." To greatly simplify Marx's concept of scientific materialism, he held that economic forces—the way things are produced—generate the social, political, and ideological characteristics of a given society.

Hegel's dialectic described a process in which a dominant idea, called a thesis, generates a contending idea called an antithesis. These two ideas come into conflict until they generate a new, superior idea called a synthesis. Marx interpreted the dialectic in terms of material relations rather than abstract ideas. Changing modes of production produce antagonistic social classes. These social classes come into conflict in the political arena, generating ideologies that match their class interests.

As Marx analyzed the original French Revolution, for example, he explained that the rise of capitalism challenged the old feudal system of production, leading to the rise of the bourgeoisie (the propertied middle class that stood between the aristocracy and the mass of French society) and its overthrow of the monarchy and aristocracy. Whereas the aristocracy had promoted an ideology of power that emphasized family lineage, the bourgeoisie emphasized rights of property. Liberal philosophers such as John Stuart Mill, with their emphasis on individual rights, Marx argued, simply expressed the interests of the property-owning bourgeoisie.

[*]Excerpt from *The Marx-Engels Reader*, Second Edition, edited by Robert C. Tucker. Copyright © 1978, 1972 by W. W. Norton & Company, Inc. Used by permission of W. W. Norton & Company, Inc.

Marx recognized that the bourgeoisie, *"during its rule of scarce one hundred years, has created more massive and more colossal productive forces than have all preceding generations together."* But he argued that capitalism contains a fatal flaw. The very efficiency of capitalism causes recurrent crises when more goods are produced than the market can absorb. Wages are slashed and factories are closed. Then the economy recovers, but with each crash the division between the property owners and the workers increases: *"Society as a whole,"* Marx wrote, *"is more and more splitting up into two great hostile camps, into two classes directly facing each other: Bourgeoisie and Proletariat."* The struggle between these two classes, the propertied middle class and the industrial working class, was made inevitable by the capitalist mode of production, and the victory of the working class, Marx argued, would lead to the realization of socialism. The full establishment of socialism, though it might take a long time, would be the *final* stage in human progress, after which there would be no further class conflict.

From a global perspective, Marx explained the link between industrial capitalism and European imperialism:

> *The need of a constantly expanding market for its products chases the bourgeoisie over the whole surface of the globe. . . . It has drawn from under the feet of industry the national ground on which it stood. . . . In place of the old local and national seclusion and self-sufficiency, we have intercourse in every direction, universal inter-dependence of nations. . . . The bourgeoisie, by the rapid improvement of all instruments of production and by the immensely facilitated means of communication draws all . . . nations into civilization.*

Global expansion, however, can only delay the collapse of capitalism, not prevent it.

Marx's internationalist philosophy challenged the idea of nationalism. Nationalists argued that bonds of culture and history unified a people across lines of social class. To them, a German was a German, whether she was a princess or a chambermaid, whether she lived in Prussia or in Austria. To Marx, such romanticized notions merely distracted proletarians from recognizing that their true interests lay not with the rich and powerful who spoke the same language, but with workers across the world. The Socialist International, which Marx helped to organize, was dedicated to fostering such working-class solidarity. But despite Marx's arguments, nationalism exerted an increasingly powerful influence among all social classes.

Marx was hated and feared not only by conservatives and liberals, but also by many fellow socialists. Some thought that liberalism, protecting individual rights, and socialism, stressing the interests of workers and the common good, were compatible, and that through the extension of voting rights to working people socialism could develop through democratic rather than revolutionary means.

Bakunin, while he agreed with Marx that revolution would be necessary, saw dangerous seeds of dictatorship in his German competitor's philosophy. A government founded on Marxist principles, Bakunin warned, *"will not content itself with . . . governing the masses politically . . . it will also administer the masses economically, concentrating in the State the production and division of wealth. . . . It will be the reign of scientific intelligence, the most aristocratic, despotic, arrogant, and elitist of regimes."*†

*Excerpts from *The Marx-Engels Reader*, Second Edition, edited by Robert C. Tucker. Copyright © 1978, 1972 by W. W. Norton & Company, Inc. Used by permission of W. W. Norton & Company, Inc.

†Mikhail Bakunin, "Critique of Economic Determinism and Historical Materialism," in *Bakunin on Anarchy,* Sam Dolgoff ed. (New York: Knopf, 1972), p. 319.

As we will see when examining communist regimes of the twentieth century (Chapters 27–30), Bakunin's prophecy was perfectly accurate. Though by the time of Marx's death in 1883 there had been no socialist revolutions, his ideas were spreading and his followers were increasing.

Charles Darwin, Evolution, and Social Darwinism

Prior to publishing his groundbreaking book *On the Origin of Species by Means of Natural Selection* in 1859, the British scientist **Charles Darwin** (1809–1882) had spent many years gathering evidence. Geologists had already determined that the earth was millions of years old and that its surface features had changed greatly over time. Darwin believed that long-term biologic change, or evolution, also characterized natural history. His search was for the mechanism of the evolutionary process.

Charles Darwin (1809–1882) English natural historian, geologist, and proponent of the theory of evolution.

In the Galápagos Islands off the coast of South America, Darwin observed that finches and turtles differed from those on the mainland and even in other areas of the islands. He theorized that the variations resulted not from separate acts of creation but from the adaptation of species to different environments. His principal contribution was the idea that natural selection drove this process.

Darwin explained that the origins of all life on earth resulted from competition for survival. Organisms with traits that gave them a better chance of survival passed those traits along to their offspring. Over time, the accumulation of diverse traits led to the appearance of new species, while failure in the struggle for existence led to the extinction of unsuccessful ones. Like Newton's theory of gravitation, Darwin's evolutionary theory was elegant, universally applicable, and a substantial advance in understanding.

In *The Descent of Man* (1871), Darwin made it clear that human beings had also undergone natural selection in their evolution as a species, an idea that generated considerable controversy by contradicting traditional accounts of human creation. Some European religious leaders denounced his work as an example of the immorality of modern life and thought. Religious objections to the theory of evolution were even stronger and more persistent in the United States and in the Islamic world.

Religious ideas themselves were not standing still. In Europe and the United States, for example, evangelical Protestantism, with an emphasis on a more personal and emotionally intense relationship with the divine, inspired many toward action, seeking out converts in the slums of burgeoning cities or around the world through missionary activities. In the Islamic world, an important nineteenth-century development was the emergence of the Wahhabis, who emphasized a return to the purity of early Islam and a rejection of outside influences. Across religions, a major theme was a sharp reaction against crass *materialism*—the focus on the production and consumption of material goods—to the exclusion of ethical and spiritual concerns. (See the feature "Movement of Ideas Through Primary Sources: Religious Leaders Comment on Science and Progress.")

Yet Darwin's insights were accepted by virtually all natural scientists. His ideas reflected broader intellectual trends beyond the domain of natural science. The great upsurge in economic productivity was inspiring a belief that human history is a story of progress. Karl Marx had absorbed this idea as a student and saw Darwin's theory of evolution as reinforcing his own view that human history proceeds through stages (feudalism, capitalism, socialism). Marx was just one of many observers who thought that Darwin's work supported an optimistic view of human history.

Religious Leaders Comment on Science and Progress

While the nineteenth century saw the rise of secular ideologies such as liberalism, socialism, and nationalism, religion continued to shape the views of most people around the world. The excerpts below illustrate the implications of modern industrial ideologies for religious faith as interpreted by a Sunni Muslim scholar and a Roman Catholic pope.

The first selection comes from Sayyid Jamāl ad-dīn al-Afghani (1838–1897). He was educated in Islamic schools in Afghanistan and Iran and then spent twenty years in British-ruled India, also traveling to western Europe and the Ottoman empire. Al-Afghani saw pan-Islamic unity as necessary for effective resistance to European dominance and worked to heal divisions between the Sunni and Shi'ite Muslim communities. His efforts did not, of course, go unchallenged. Sufi mystics and Wahhabi purists, for example, had little use for his attempt to reconcile Islam with Western science.

The second passage is by Pope Pius IX (r. 1846–1878), who became a staunch conservative when Roman revolutionaries forced him to temporarily flee the Vatican in 1848. Pius IX greatly increased papal authority when he proclaimed the doctrine of papal infallibility, which stated that the pope's statements on central issues of faith were to be regarded as coming directly from God and could not be challenged. His criticism of the loss of spiritual focus in the face of materialism has been a consistent theme of the Roman Catholic Church ever since.

Sources: Excerpt cited and translated in Nikki Keddie, *Sayyid Jamāl ad-dīn "al-Afghani": A political biography* (Berkeley: University of California Press, 1972), pp. 161, 186. Reprinted by permission; excerpt, Pope Pius IX, *Quanta Cura (Condemning Current Errors)*, from www.ewtn.com.

Sayyid Jamāl ad-dīn al-Afghani

1. "Lecture on Teaching and Learning" (1882)

If someone looks deeply into the question, he will see that science rules the world. There was, is, and will be no other ruler in the world but science. . . . In reality, sovereignty has never left the abode of science. However, this true ruler, which is science, is continually changing capitals. Sometimes it has moved from East to West, and other times from West to East. . . . The acquisitions of men for themselves and their governments are proportional to their science. Thus, every government for its own benefit must strive to lay the foundation of the sciences and to disseminate knowledge. . . .

The strangest thing of all is that our *ulama* [scholarly community] these days have divided science into two parts. One they call Muslim science, and one European science. Because of this they forbid others to teach some of the useful sciences. They have not understood that science is that noble thing that has no connection with any nation, and is not distinguished by anything but itself. Rather, everything that is known is known by science, and every nation that becomes renowned becomes renowned through science. . . .

How very strange it is that the Muslims study those sciences that are ascribed to Aristotle with the greatest delight, as if Aristotle were one of the pillars of the Muslims. However, if the discussion relates to Galileo, Newton and Kepler, they consider them infidels. The father and mother of science is proof, and proof is neither Aristotle nor Galileo. The truth is where there is proof, and those who forbid science and knowledge in the belief that they are safeguarding the Islamic religion are really enemies of that religion. The Islamic religion is the closest of religions to science and knowledge, and there is no incompatibility between science and knowledge and the foundation of the Islamic faith. . . .

2. "Answer of Jamāl ad-dīn to Renan" (1883)

All religions are intolerant, each one in its way. The Christian religion, I mean the society that follows its inspirations and its teachings . . . seems to advance rapidly on the road of progress and science, whereas Muslim society has not yet freed itself from the tutelage of religion. . . . I cannot keep from hoping that Muslim society will succeed someday in breaking its bonds and marching resolutely in the path of civilization after the manner of Western society. . . . No I cannot admit that this hope be denied to Islam.

Pope Pius IX

Quanta Cura (Condemning Current Errors), 1864

For well you know, my brothers, that at this time there are many men who applying to civil society the impious and absurd principle of "naturalism," dare to teach that "the best constitution of public society . . . requires that human society be conducted and governed without regard being had to religion any more than if it did not exist; or, at least, without any distinction between true religion and false one." From which false idea . . . they foster the erroneous opinion . . . that "liberty of conscience and worship is each man's personal right, which ought to be legally proclaimed and asserted in every rightly constituted society; and that a right resides in the citizens to an absolute liberty, which should be restrained by no authority whether ecclesiastical or civil, whereby they may be able openly and publicly to manifest and declare any of their ideas whatever, either by word of mouth, by the press, or in any other way." Whereas we know, from the very teaching of our Lord Jesus Christ, how carefully Christian faith and wisdom should avoid this most injurious babbling.

And, since where religion has been removed from civil society, and the doctrine and authority of divine revelation repudiated, the genuine notion itself of justice and human right is darkened and lost, and the place of true justice and legitimate right is supplied by material force . . . [then] human society, when set loose from the bonds of religion and true justice, can have, in truth, no other end than the purpose of obtaining and amassing wealth, and . . . follows no other law . . . except . . . ministering to its own pleasure and interests.

Amidst, therefore, such great perversity of depraved opinions . . . and (solicitous also) for the welfare of human society itself, [we] have thought it right again to raise up our Apostolic voice.

QUESTIONS FOR ANALYSIS

» *How do Pius IX and al-Afghani differ in their views of the relationship between religion and the ideas and ideals of industrial modernity?*

» *Are there any connections between these nineteenth-century debates and current controversies concerning science and faith in the Christian and Islamic worlds?*

But Darwin's concept of adaptation and survival in the natural world had dangerous implications when applied to human society. *Social Darwinism* was the idea that differences in status could be explained by the superiority of some and the inferiority of others. Social Darwinists argued that wealth and power were the proper reward for superior talent, while the poor were those with inferior traits. Analogies from nature were thus used to justify social inequality. Social Darwinism was also used to explain Europe's increasing global dominance: European imperialism was simply natural selection at work. "Inferior peoples" would be displaced as part of an inevitable natural process—the "survival of the fittest." As a scientist, Darwin himself never drew such social and political corollaries from his work.

Reform and Reaction: Russia and the Ottoman Empire, 1825–1881

In 1798 Napoleon invaded Ottoman Egypt. Then in 1812 he marched on Moscow. Though the French retreated in both cases, the invasions put Russians and Ottomans on notice: the West was advancing. For both empires, the question became: was it better to emulate the legal, economic, educational, social, and political reforms of western Europe, or to follow conservative policies that emphasized continuity with the past?

Emancipation and Reaction in Russia

Mikhail Bakunin was from a generation of educated Russians inspired by the revolutionary changes that had taken place to the west and anxious to bring change to their homeland. *"Russia figures as a synonym for brutal repression,"* he said; *"thanks to the execrable [policies] of our sovereigns, the name 'Russian' . . . stands for 'slave and executioner.'"*[*] While that very state of oppression had forced him into exile, Bakunin still held high hopes for Russia. The history of peasant uprisings in Russia, such as Pugachev's rebellion (see Chapter 20), assured him that Russians would not *"patiently resign themselves to their misery"* forever, and he saw the Russian *mir*, or village, with its collective decision making and community ownership of land, as a foundation on which an anarchist future could be built.

In the short term, the prospects for a Russian revolution, or even for liberal reform, were bleak. After 1815, Russian tsars commanded the world's largest army and an empire that spread from Poland to Alaska. But their imperial power was not reflected in social conditions. Russia was overwhelmingly rural. It had a powerful aristocracy but a weak middle class and almost no modern industry. With neither a strong bourgeoisie nor a growing proletariat, Russian society was divided between a landowning nobility and serfs so poor, illiterate, and lacking in rights that aristocrats could win or lose these "souls" (as they called their serfs) in a game of cards. The nobility profited from this system, as did the government, which depended on serf conscripts for its huge army. Change was not likely to come from above, nor from below, as the tsar's secret police sent Mikhail Bakunin and hundreds of other dissenters into exile.

Crimean War
(1853–1856) War fought in the Crimean peninsula between the Russian and Ottoman empires. France and Britain sent troops to aid the Ottomans and prevent Russian expansion.

[*]Mikhail Bakunin, "On the 17th Anniversary of the Polish Insurrection," in *Bakunin on Anarchy*, ed. Sam Dolgoff (New York: Knopf, 1972), p. 59.

Emancipated Serfs As with freed slaves in the U.S. South during the late nineteenth century, living conditions for most Russian serfs were not immediately transformed by emancipation in 1861. Most were illiterate and, like the wheat threshers shown here, had to rely on their own labor power. (Adoc-Photos/Art Resource, NY)

Still, with the advent of modern industry, the gap between Russia and the other great powers widened, as demonstrated by the **Crimean War** (1853–1856). Having already taken control of the Crimean peninsula on the northern shore of the Black Sea, the Russians sought to expand even further along the Ottoman frontier. Fearing that Russian success would upset the balance of power in Europe, the British and the French came to the Ottomans' defense. Poorly trained Russian conscripts used badly outdated rifles, while modern British and French naval vessels dominated the Black Sea. Unable to make up in numbers what they lacked in equipment and organization, the Russians were defeated. The lesson was clear: modern wars could not be won without an industrial foundation.

Tsar Alexander II (r. 1855–1881), who succeeded to the throne near the end of the Crimean conflict, recognized that Russia's social structure, based on serfdom, could not support a powerful modern state. In 1861 Alexander II issued his **Emancipation Edict**. Increased labor mobility was one rationale for emancipation, since industrial development would require the movement of peasants into cities. However, to avoid antagonizing the nobility, the edict required that

Tsar Alexander II (r. 1855–1881) Also known as Alexander the Liberator; best known for his emancipation of the serfs.

Emancipation Edict 1861 edict by Tsar Alexander II that freed the Russian serfs. However, serfs had to pay their former owners for their freedom, and the land they were allocated was often insufficient to produce the money needed to meet that cost for freedom.

serfs pay for their own emancipation, although the amount of land they were allocated was often insufficient to meet that cost.

At the same time, the tsar's government began taking action in support of industrialization. During the 1870s government support led to a boom in railroad construction, stimulating the coal and iron industries. High tariffs on foreign goods promoted the development of Russian factories, although they continued to lag well behind the pace of western European growth. While by 1880 British, French, and German workers were enjoying some benefits of increased productivity, such as better clothing and housing, Russian workers were still suffering from the dangerous and squalid conditions that had marked the first phase of industrialization in the West.

Another challenge for Alexander's government was the question of nationalities. In Germany, nationalism might overcome regional and class differences to serve as the ideological foundation of a modern state. In multiethnic Russia, such use of nationalism to bolster the power of conservative elites was impossible: over half the people in the empire were not Russian. Russia was more like multiethnic Austria, where nationalism was also a divisive force. The tsars harshly suppressed nationalist uprisings, such as an 1863 rebellion in Poland.

By that time Bakunin's generation was losing influence to a younger group of Russian revolutionaries with little patience for philosophical debate. The secret police were everywhere, forcing Russian rebels to conspire in secret. Russian anarchists, agreeing with Bakunin that freedom could be achieved only through the abolition of the state, its bureaucracy, and its army, despaired of doing so through a popular uprising. Some anarchists accepted the need for violence and even terrorism to achieve their ends: a bomb killed Tsar Alexander II in 1881, causing a further crackdown on dissidence. A link between anarchism, violence, and assassination—foreign to Bakunin's thinking—was now established.

With the stifling of liberal, socialist, and even nationalist thought, Russian intellectuals and artists instead focused on the question of whether and to what degree Russia should learn from and adopt western European cultural and constitutional models. "Westernizers" answered in the affirmative, while "Slavophiles" declared that Russia should stand by her Slavic traditions, Orthodox Christianity, and tsarist state.

Such debates would be repeated around the world in the coming years as the rising Western industrial powers put more and more pressure on other peoples. For the Ottomans living, like the Russians, in close proximity to rising European nations, these questions were of immediate relevance.

Reform and Reaction in the Ottoman Empire

Tanzimat reforms 1839–1876) Restructuring of the Ottoman empire; control over civil law was taken away from religious authorities, while the military and government bureaucracies were reorganized to gain efficiency.

Though still large and powerful, the Ottoman empire was under increasing pressure in the early nineteenth century. Having lost control of Egypt to the independent regime of Muhammad Ali, Greece to an independence movement in 1829, and Algeria to French invaders in 1830, the Ottomans were also slipping in the Balkans, the mountainous region of southeastern Europe they had controlled since the days of Süleyman the Magnificent.

After the loss of Greece, Ottoman leaders launched the **Tanzimat** (TAHNZ-ee-MAT) **reforms**, an attempt by civilian bureaucrats to break the power of the elite Janissary corps (see Chapter 17) and to reorganize the army along modern lines. The Ottoman government established new types of schools within the

Turkish Factory Nineteenth-century industrialization was a global process, with many world regions tied to industrial processes solely as suppliers of raw materials and consumers of finished products. Here we see that in the western Ottoman empire, factory production itself became a part of economic life. In this factory girls and women are weaving silk thread into cloth; the factory supervisor, however, is a man. In Japan as well (see Chapter 24), early textile production relied primarily on women's labor. (© Roger-Viollet/The Image Works)

empire, such as colleges of military science and medicine, and sponsored student travel and study in western Europe. A new system of primary and secondary schools following a European-style curriculum supplemented the existing *madrasas*, or religious schools. The urban elite began to travel more widely and to read French, Armenian, and Turkish newspapers, and European-style buildings were erected in Istanbul to modernize the capital. The legal system was revamped so that the same civil code applied to everyone, Muslim and non-Muslim alike, with full equality before the law. Finally, to facilitate trade with the West, the Tanzimat reformers introduced a new commercial code modeled on European rather than Islamic principles.

Some Muslim religious leaders worried that by borrowing so many ideas from the West the government was undercutting the traditional religious and cultural

The Jasmine Revolution and the Arab Spring

The rapid spread of revolts in the Arab world in 2011 brought to mind 1848 in Europe: in both cases rulers suddenly faced the wrath of their people. Beginning in December 2010, when a young street vendor named Mohamed Bouazizi set himself on fire on a Tunis street to protest the corruption and incompetence of the country's leaders, massive street demonstrations spread across North Africa and the Middle East.

The Tunisians were successful in ousting their president and demanding genuinely free elections. Suddenly, street protests made other Arab authorities, who had held power through force and fear, look vulnerable. New technologies—mobile phones, blogs, Twitter, social media websites—meant that protesters were able to bypass government control of information through traditional channels such as newspapers and television. That was indeed the lesson learned by Wael Ghonim, an Egyptian marketing manager for Google who, in February 2011, set up a Facebook page that would propel Egypt's own successful overthrow of the long-standing regime of President Hosni Mubarak.

The Mubarak regime, with a strong political base in the military and an extensive and intrusive security service, was not easily intimidated by the surging protests. Mubarak claimed that true democracy in Egypt would empower religious parties like the Muslim Brotherhood, an argument meant to secure support internally as well as from Western leaders. It did not work.

Wave after wave of demonstrations, centered in Cairo's Tahrir Square, culminated in the resignation of Mubarak. Then, when the military tried to control the pace and direction of political reform, the protesters returned to insist on honest elections, and then again to protest what they saw as a weak verdict in Mubarak's trial. As Mubarak lay near death in the summer of 2012, Muhammad Morsi, a Muslim Brotherhood leader and Egypt's newly elected president, took up the challenge of uniting the divided nation.

The bloodiest outcome came in Libya, where the megalomaniac Muammar Gaddafi had imposed his eccentric ideas on the country since 1969. Willing to take his whole country down with him, Gaddafi responded to the uprising against him with appalling brutality. Aided by Western nations, however, the revolt succeeded: Gaddafi himself was captured and summarily executed.

In some countries leaders offered to compromise with protesters; in others, such as Syria and Bahrain, demonstrators faced brutal crackdowns. The eventual outcome of the Arab Spring is still impossible to predict. As in Europe in 1848, the old order will perhaps be able to maintain control in some places, and the most idealistic visions of protesters will likely be dashed. Still, just as European politics were never the same again after 1848, so it is likely that the Arab Spring marked a permanent shift in the politics of North Africa and the Middle East.

foundations of their society. They resented their loss of control over the educational and legal systems that had been a principal source of their power and prestige. On the other hand, progressive Ottoman officials were dissatisfied with the centralized and bureaucratic nature of the Tanzimat program and argued for a constitutional monarchy guided by the principles of liberalism. But unlike in nineteenth-century western Europe, where masses of people had been engaged in the dramatic events of 1848, the talk of reform remained limited to Ottoman elites. (See the feature "World History in Today's World: The Jasmine Revolution and the Arab Spring.")

When Sultan Abd al-Hamid (AHB-dahl-ha-med) III came to power in 1876, he at first agreed to create a representative government. With the backing of conservatives, however, he suspended the constitution a year after its creation and ruled as dictator. Vacillating between reform and reaction, Ottoman authorities proved unable to strike a stable balance. As in Russia, reactionary policies triumphed over reformist ones.

CONTEXT AND CONNECTIONS

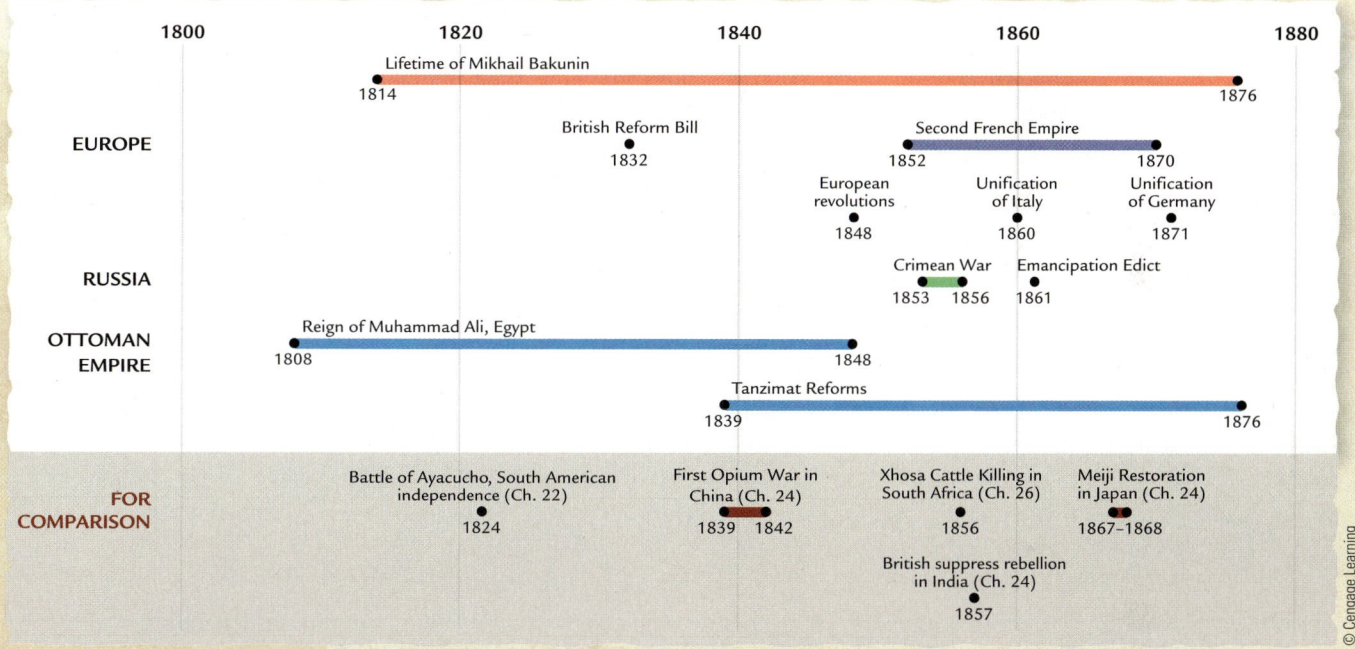

© Cengage Learning

Global Repercussions of the Industrial Revolution

Europe's prominent place in world affairs was not, of course, something that began with the Industrial Revolution. As described in Chapters 15–18, maritime expansion and access to American resources, especially silver, had enriched European societies in the early modern period. But in the late eighteenth century, much of the world's population—most notably in China—was only marginally affected (see Chapter 20).

It was the Industrial Revolution that placed western Europe firmly at the center of world power. Economically, that meant heightened competition for the raw materials necessary for factory production, many of which (cotton and rubber, for example) were available only outside of Europe itself. As other European states, especially Germany, caught up with Britain's early lead, competition for such resources, as well as for markets for industrial products, intensified. By the late nineteenth century, heightened economic competition would drive a "New Imperialism" that led to direct European control over hundreds of societies (see Chapters 24–26).

Militarily, the Industrial Revolution changed the global balance of power dramatically. Earlier maritime and gunpowder technologies were not a European monopoly, as their effective use by the Ottoman empire demonstrated (see Chapter 17). Now, with steam-powered battleships, more powerful field artillery, and rapidly repeating rifles, the technological and financial costs of keeping up with the rising industrial powers of the West escalated decade by decade. Of the old land-based empires, only Mikhail Bakunin's native Russia was able to keep pace.

The global tensions that resulted from European industrial supremacy had social, cultural, and political implications as well. As we have seen, in both the Russian and Ottoman empires, nineteenth-century elites debated whether to assimilate western European cultural traits as a spur to modernization or to abide by their established cultural and religious traditions. By the late nineteenth century, such debates resonated around the world. For example, while Chinese leaders vacillated on whether and how they might meet the Western challenge by borrowing Western ideas, Japanese reformers won a decisive victory with the Meiji Restoration in 1868 (see Chapter 24). By 1880 the Japanese government had learned, like the Russians and Ottomans before them, that industry was key to success, perhaps even survival, in the harshly competitive Western-dominated world order.

The social consequences of the Industrial Revolution, including the movement of many more people to cities, were also global. Social change led to intellectual ferment. Latin Americans, Africans, and Asians, as well as Europeans, were soon discussing the merits of the key ideas—nationalism, socialism, liberalism—that had formed the background for Mikhail Bakunin's political activism and anarchist philosophy. The revolutionaries of 1848 took aim at the traditional foundations of European social and political authority, attacking the inherited position of kings, landed aristocrats, and religious leaders. Such tensions appeared elsewhere in the world as well whenever new conditions and new ideas undermined customary authority. Faced with aggressive European expansion and a resulting social and political disequilibrium, Africans, Asians, Arabs, Native Americans, and others began to question how they might best adapt (see Chapters 24–26). In the industrial age, the mandate for change became insistent.

Meanwhile, within Europe, the rise of a unified Germany significantly altered the balance of power, removing Britain from its previous pinnacle of supremacy and alarming the French and the Russians as well. After 1890, Germany would become more aggressive in challenging the British empire, helping propel a scramble for colonies in Africa and Asia (see Chapter 26), and in the twentieth century the aggressive militarism present at the birth of Germany in 1871 would lead to two devastating world wars (see Chapters 27–29). Industrial progress was a mixed blessing.

Voyages on the Web: Mikhail Bakunin

The Voyages Map App follows the traveler's journeys using interactive study tools, including 360-degree panoramic views of historic sites, zoomable maps, audio summaries, flash cards, and quizzes.

Key Terms

Mikhail Bakunin (640)
Industrial Revolution (643)
James Watt (644)
Josiah Wedgwood (645)
Muhammad Ali (648)
Reform Bill of 1832 (651)

John Stuart Mill (651)
Louis Napoleon (653)
Giuseppe Garibaldi (656)
Frankfurt Assembly (657)
Otto von Bismarck (657)
Karl Marx (659)

Charles Darwin (661)
Crimean War (665)
Tsar Alexander II (665)
Emancipation Edict (665)
Tanzimat reforms (666)

For Further Reference

Allen, Robert C. *The British Industrial Revolution in Global Perspective.* New York: Cambridge University Press, 2009.

Anderson, Benedict. *Imagined Communities: Reflections on the Origin and Spread of Nationalism.* London: Verso, 1991.

Auerbach, Jeffrey. *The Great Exhibition of 1851: A Nation on Display.* New Haven: Yale University Press, 1999.

Bakunin, Mikhail. *Bakunin on Anarchy: Selected Works by the Activist-Founder of World Anarchism.* Sam Dolgoff, ed. and trans. New York: Knopf, 1972.

Goodwin, Jason. *Lords of the Horizons: A History of the Ottoman Empire.* New York: Picador, 2003.

Hobsbawm, Eric. *The Age of Capital, 1848–1875.* New York: Simon and Schuster, 1975.

Mayr, Ernst. *One Long Argument: Charles Darwin and the Genesis of Modern Evolutionary Thought.* Cambridge, Mass.: Harvard University Press, 1993.

Mokyr, Joel. *The Lever of Riches: Technological Creativity and Economic Progress.* New York: Oxford University Press, 1992.

Randolph, John. *The House in the Garden: The Bakunin Family and the Romance of Russian Idealism.* Ithaca, N.Y.: Cornell University Press, 2007.

Rosen, William. *The Most Powerful Idea in the World: A Story of Steam, Industry, and Invention.* New York: Random House, 2010.

Tilly, Louise. *Industrialization and Gender Inequality.* Washington, D.C.: American Historical Association, 1993.

Wheen, Francis. *Karl Marx: A Life.* New York: W. W. Norton, 2000.

24

The Challenge of Modernity in China, Japan, and India, 1800–1910

In 1859 the government of Japan sent its first delegation to visit the United States. On the crossing **Fukuzawa Yûkichi** (foo-koo-ZAH-wah yoo-KEE-chee) (1835–1901), a twenty-four-year-old samurai, studied *Webster's Dictionary*, but it did not prepare him very well for his experiences in San Francisco. *"There were many confusing and embarrassing moments,"* he later wrote, *"for we were quite ignorant of the customs of American life."* At his hotel he was amazed when his hosts walked across expensive carpets with their shoes on. Fukuzawa attended a dance wearing the outfit of a samurai, with two swords and hemp sandals:

Fukuzawa Yûkichi

(Fukuzawa Memorial Center for Modern Japanese Studies, Keio University)

To our dismay we could not make out what they were doing. The ladies and gentlemen seemed to be hopping around the room together. As funny as it was, we knew it would be rude to laugh, and we controlled our expressions with difficulty as the dancing went on. . . . Things social, political, and economic proved most inexplicable. . . . I asked a gentleman where the descendants of George Washington might be. . . . His answer was so very casual that it shocked me. Of course, I know that America is a republic with a new president every four years, but I could not help feeling that the family of Washington would be revered above all other families. My reasoning was based on the reverence in Japan for the founders of the great lines of rulers—like that for Ieyasu of the Tokugawa family of Shoguns.

*From *The Autobiography of Yukichi Fukuzawa*, by Eiichi Kiyooka, 1960, pp. 114–116. Copyright © 1960 Columbia University Press. Reprinted with permission of the publisher.

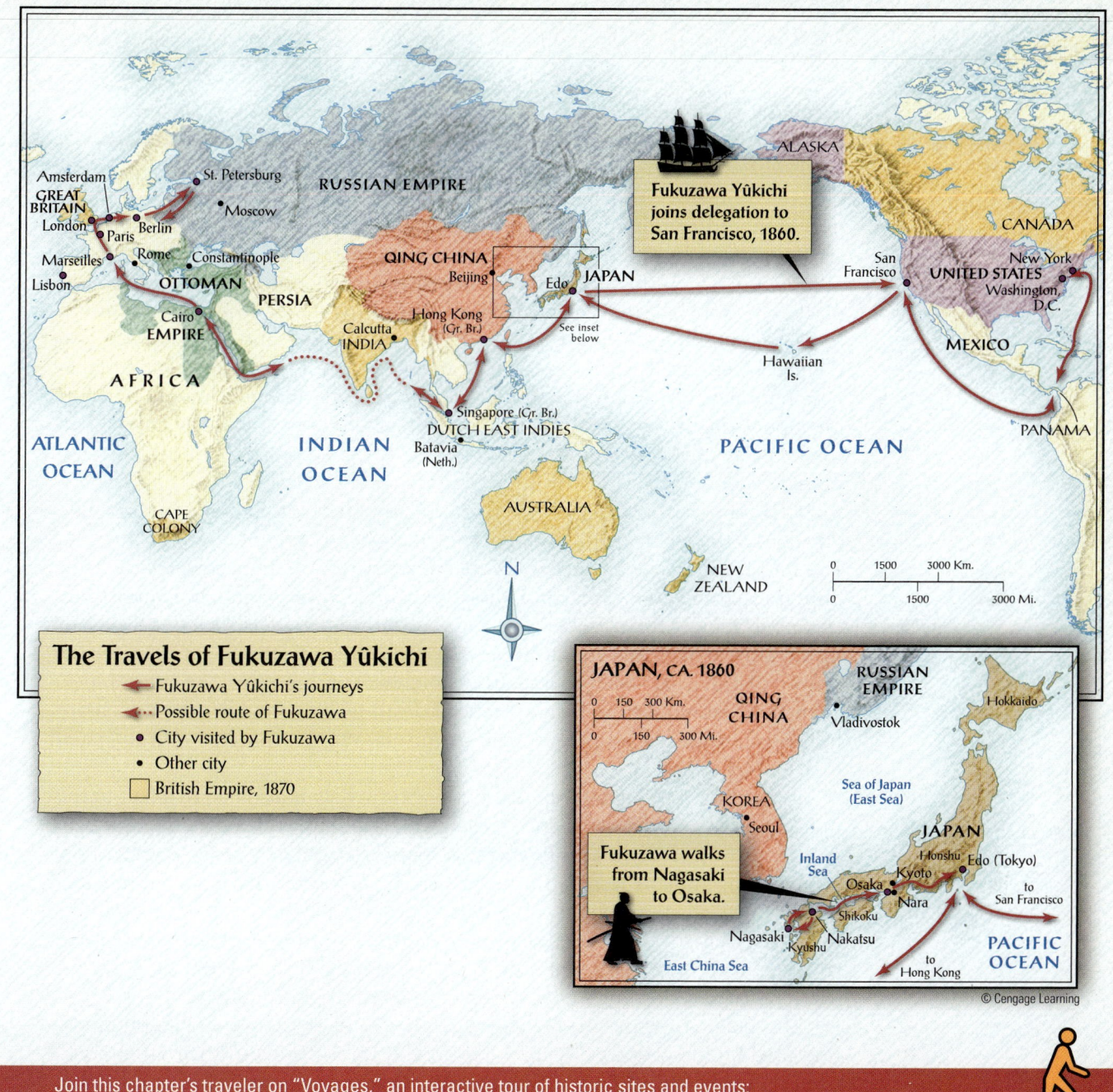

The Travels of Fukuzawa Yûkichi

← Fukuzawa Yûkichi's journeys
◀······ Possible route of Fukuzawa
• City visited by Fukuzawa
• Other city
☐ British Empire, 1870

Fukuzawa Yûkichi joins delegation to San Francisco, 1860.

JAPAN, CA. 1860

Fukuzawa walks from Nagasaki to Osaka.

© Cengage Learning

Join this chapter's traveler on "Voyages," an interactive tour of historic sites and events: **www.cengagebrain.com**

T
hough he was much more knowledgeable about the Western world than most Japanese, Fukuzawa said of himself and his American hosts, *"neither of us really knew much about the other at all."**

Fukuzawa had grown up in a low-ranking samurai family that was expected to give unconditional support and service to their lord, but he was an ambitious nonconformist. As a young man he dedicated himself to "Dutch learning," and

---

*From *The Autobiography of Yukichi Fukuzawa*, by Eiichi Kiyooka, 1960, p. 115. Copyright © 1960 Columbia University Press. Reprinted with permission of the publisher.

Fukuzawa Yûkichi
(1835–1901) Japanese writer, teacher, political theorist, and founder of Keio Academy (now Keio University). His ideas about learning, government, and society greatly influenced the Meiji Restoration. Considered one of the founders of modern Japan.

becoming convinced of the merits of Western science, he developed a philosophy that emphasized independence over subservience and science over tradition.

Fukuzawa's lifetime was one of remarkable change. All across the world, societies struggled to adapt to the new industrial age with its advances in transportation and communications technologies, the spread of new religious and secular ideologies, and the dynamics of a changing global economy. In western Europe, rulers, reformers, and rebels all struggled for control over the direction of change. Russian and Ottoman elites debated whether to emulate Western models (see Chapter 23). In East Asia, Japanese, Chinese, and Koreans were also divided when faced with increasingly aggressive Western powers. While Japanese reformers like Fukuzawa embraced change along Western lines as a means of empowerment, conservatives here and elsewhere in East Asia saw Europe and the United States as hostile threats to their established social, political, and economic systems.

Fukuzawa was a leader of the Westernizing faction that came to dominate Japan after the overthrow in 1868 of the Tokugawa shogunate (see Chapter 20). The new Japanese government was able to resist the Western powers and, with military victories over China and Russia, expand its own empire. In contrast, the leaders of Qing China proved incapable of reforming their society quickly or thoroughly enough to turn aside the Western challenge. By the late nineteenth century, China had been carved into spheres of influence by Britain, France, Germany, Japan, and the United States. Korean leaders were also slow to adapt to the industrial age, and the Korean peninsula was incorporated into the Japanese empire.

In meeting the challenge of modernity, South Asians also had to adapt to the industrial age, as well as balance their own traditions with powerful new economic forces and cultural influences. A major rebellion in 1857 signaled how deeply many Indians resented British rule. The failure of that revolt stimulated Indian intellectuals and political leaders to develop new ideas and organizations to achieve self-government. Indian nationalists, like those in Japan and China, struggled with the question of how to deal with the power of Western models in everything from clothing to house design to political philosophy.

This chapter focuses on the various strategies of resistance and accommodation used by the peoples of China, Japan, and British India in their attempts to come to terms with the industrial age. All these societies had to respond to the rising challenge from the West. Fukuzawa Yûkichi's proposal that Japan should emulate the West to become strengthened and modernized was just one of the solutions put forward in nineteenth-century East and South Asia.

Focus Questions

» *What were the main forces that undermined the power of the Qing dynasty in the nineteenth century?*

» *What made it possible for Japan to be transformed from a relatively isolated society to a major world power in less than half a century?*

» *What were the principal ways that British-ruled Indians responded to imperialism?*

» *How and why did Chinese, Japanese, and Indian societies respond differently to the challenges of industrial modernity?*

China's World Inverted, 1800–1906

Four decades after China's emperor dismissed Britain's diplomatic advances (see Chapter 20), the British returned with firepower to forcibly open Chinese markets. Suddenly faced with Europe's industrial might, Qing officials agreed to a series of unequal treaties. Soon after, a major rebellion shook the Qing dynasty to its foundations. While some officials, humiliated by the decline in imperial prestige, entertained reform, as in the Russian and Ottoman empires they were outmaneuvered by conservatives who opposed adopting Western political, educational, and economic models. By the end of the nineteenth century, soldiers from Britain, France, the United States, and Japan had occupied the Forbidden City. Imperial China had lost its ancient status as the "Middle Kingdom" and become a chessboard on which the great powers moved their pieces, dividing China into their own "spheres of influence."

The conservatives' policies were a disaster. Fukuzawa Yûkichi, who had successfully helped implement reforms based on Western models in Japan, observed in 1899: *"I am sure that it is impossible to lead [the Chinese] people to civilization so long as the old government is left to stand as it is."*[*] Seven years later the last Manchu emperor abdicated, and so ended the last of China's millennia-old imperial dynasties. China's dominant role in East Asia had been usurped by Japan.

Qing China Confronts the Industrial World, 1800–1850

In the late eighteenth century the British East India Company faced an old problem for Western traders in China: apart from silver, they had no goods that were of much value in Chinese markets. Their solution was to develop poppy plantations in South Asia, refine the poppy seeds into opium, and smuggle the narcotic into China. The strategy was commercially brilliant, since narcotics create their own demand through the spiral of drug addiction. But it was ethically problematic and even hypocritical. As Victorian reformers sought to stamp out opium addiction in Britain, the East India Company was promoting opium smuggling to China.

Highly addictive, opium is a strong painkiller that also induces lethargy and a sense of hopelessness. Addicts neglect their own health and the care of their dependents. Opium smugglers conducted their illegal trade in open disregard for Chinese governmental authority. Moreover, the lucrative opium trade drained silver out of China, thus jeopardizing China's silver-based fiscal system and undermining its economy (see Chapter 16).

By 1839 Sino-British relations were in crisis. The Qing government declared that drug traders would be beheaded and sent a scholar-official named Lin Zezu (lin say-SHOE) to Guangzhou to suppress the opium trade. In a letter to Queen Victoria, Lin made his government's position clear:

> *[By] introducing opium by stealth [the British] have seduced our Chinese people, and caused every province in the land to overflow with that poison. They know merely how to advantage themselves; they care not about injuring others! . . . Therefore those foreigners who now import opium into the Central Land are condemned to be beheaded and strangled.*[†]

---

[*]From *The Autobiography of Yukichi Fukuzawa*, by Eiichi Kiyooka, 1960, p. 277. Copyright © 1960 Columbia University Press. Reprinted with permission of the publisher.

[†]Mark A. Kishlansky, ed., *Sources of World History*, vol. 2 (New York: HarperCollins College Publishers, 1995), p. 268.

To the British government, however, the issue was not opium but free trade. Commercial interests were lobbying the British government for more open access in general to Chinese markets, which had traditionally been highly regulated. According to liberal economic theory, free trade is always and everywhere best for everyone. If the Chinese could not understand this simple idea, then they would have to be *forced* to open their markets. The British responded to Lin's appeal with war.

The first **Opium War** (1839–1842) was a severe shock to the Qing government. The British used their iron-clad gunboats to blockade the Chinese coast and bombard coastal cities such as Guangzhou and Shanghai. Being so easily defeated by "Western barbarians," many Qing commanders committed suicide in disgrace. In 1842, as the British sailed up the Yangzi River and prepared to blast apart the walls of Nanjing, Qing officials realized that they would have to negotiate.

With no bargaining power, the Qing felt compelled to agree to the humiliating terms of the **Treaty of Nanjing**, the first of a series of unequal treaties that eroded Chinese sovereignty in the coming decades. The agreement opened five "treaty ports" to unrestricted foreign trade and gave possession of Hong Kong, upriver from the great port of Guangzhou, to the British. The treaty's provision of extraterritoriality, through which British subjects were governed by British rather than Chinese law at the treaty ports, was a crushing blow to Chinese pride.

The Treaty of Nanjing left the British and other European nations eager for even greater power over China. Using supposed Qing violations of the Nanjing treaty as a pretext, in the second Opium War of 1856 the British and French invaded and marched toward Beijing. They burned Qianlong's magnificent summer palace to the ground and briefly occupied the Forbidden City. In 1860, the Qing agreed to another, even more unequal treaty that opened more ports to Western trade and allowed "international settlements" in key Chinese cities such as Shanghai and Guangzhou. These settlements, where only Europeans were allowed to live, were foreign enclaves on Chinese soil. The British also mandated that imperial documents were no longer to use the Chinese character for "barbarian" to describe the British.

The Taiping Rebellion, 1850–1864

The Opium Wars and the unequal treaties that followed had exposed Qing weakness, leading some Chinese to conclude that the Manchu had lost the "Mandate of Heaven." Behind the political chaos of nineteenth-century China was a startling fact: the population had grown by over 100 million between 1800 and 1850; people were suffering from neglect, misrule, and hunger. Farmers brought more marginal lands into production; agricultural yields declined; villages were repeatedly flooded. Although imperial governments had long been responsible for flood control and famine relief, the Qing bureaucracy, fighting foreign invaders, raised taxes for its military in the midst of the people's suffering.

In the mid-nineteenth century China was shaken by revolts, including a major Muslim uprising in the northwest. The situation was especially desperate in Guangdong province, where the **Taiping Rebellion** (1850–1864) began, and then spread throughout southern China, sending the empire into chaos. The leader of the Taiping (tie-PING) was Hong Xiuquan (1813–1864). After traveling to Guangzhou and failing the imperial examinations several times (see Chapter 16), Hong Xiuquan (hoong shee-OH-chew-an) studied with some Western missionaries, adding his own interpretation to their message.

Opium Wars In the first Opium War (1839–1842), Britain invaded the Qing empire to force China to open to trade. In the second Opium War (1856–1860), an Anglo-French force once again invaded to enforce the unequal treaties that resulted from the first war and extract further concessions.

Treaty of Nanjing (1842) One-sided treaty that concluded the first Opium War. Britain was allowed to trade in additional Chinese ports and took control of Hong Kong. The provision for extraterritoriality meant that Britons were subject to British rather than Chinese law.

Taiping Rebellion (1850–1864) Massive rebellion against the Qing led by Hong Xiuquan, who claimed to be the younger brother of Jesus Christ come to earth to create a "Heavenly Kingdom of Great Peace." The imperial system was greatly weakened as a result of the uprising.

Hong claimed to be the younger brother of Jesus Christ, come to earth to establish a "Heavenly Kingdom of Great Peace." Mixing Christianity with peasant yearnings for fairness and justice, Hong attracted hundreds of thousands of followers to his vision of reform. In their Heavenly Kingdom, the Taiping proclaimed, *"inequality [will not] exist, and [everyone will] be well fed and clothed."*

At the core of the Taiping movement were committed followers who practiced severe self-discipline. Many of these initiates were, like Hong, from the Hakka ethnic group. The Hakka were only brought under imperial control during Ming times and had never fully assimilated Confucian ideas of hierarchy. Women had relatively independent roles, and their feet were never bound. Hong's "long-haired rebels" refused to wear the long, braided ponytail (or *queue*) mandated by Manchu authorities as a sign of subservience. *"Ever since the Manchus poisoned China,"* he said, *"the influence of demons has distressed the empire while the Chinese with bowed heads and dejected spirits willingly became subjects and servants."*[†]

Hong and his original converts attracted a mass following. In late 1850 some twenty thousand Taiping rebels defeated an imperial army sent to crush them; they then went on the offensive and began a long northward march that ended in 1853 with an invasion of Nanjing. Of the tens of thousands of Manchu living within the city walls, those who did not die in battle were systematically slaughtered. Hong moved into a former Ming imperial palace and declared Nanjing the capital of his Heavenly Kingdom of Great Peace.

After 1853, however, the Taiping rebels gained no more great victories. Their rhetoric of equality alienated the educated elite, and influential members of the gentry organized militias to fight them when Qing defenses proved inadequate. As the Taiping movement grew in wealth and power, some leaders abandoned the plain living advocated by Hong and indulged in expensive clothing, fine food, and elaborate rituals. In addition, the Taiping were unable to recruit experienced administrators because their religious beliefs were at odds with the Confucian ideals of scholar-officials. Perhaps most important, the unsophisticated Taiping leaders did nothing to form foreign alliances that might have altered the balance of power in their favor.

In the early 1860s, the British and French, who had done so much to undercut the Qing, now rallied to the dynasty's defense. From their base at Nanjing, the Taiping threatened Shanghai and the European interests that were rapidly developing there. In 1864, Qing forces, supported by European soldiers and armaments, stormed Nanjing. A Manchu official reported: *"Not one of the 100,000 rebels in Nanjing surrendered themselves when the city was taken but in many cases gathered together and burned themselves and passed away without repentance."* By that time as many as 30 million people had been killed, and China's rulers were more beholden to European powers than ever before. The principal question facing China's government and intellectual elite became even more insistent: how to respond to the Western challenge?

"Self-Strengthening" and the Boxer Rebellion, 1842–1901

In the wake of the Opium War, some educated Chinese began arguing that only fundamental change would enable the empire to meet the rising Western challenge. Those calls became louder after the debacle

---

[*]Franz Michael and Chang Chung-li, *The Taiping Rebellion: History and Documents* (Seattle: University of Washington Press, 1971), vol. 2, p. 314; vol. 3, p. 767.

[†]Jen Yu-Wen, *The Taiping Revolutionary Moment* (New Haven: Yale University Press, 1973), pp. 93–94.

of the Taiping Rebellion. The drug trade was no longer the issue. Now representatives of industrial capitalism arrived by steamship looking for markets and cheap labor, while an increasing number of missionaries sought the salvation of Chinese souls. The educated reform faction joined together in the **Self-Strengthening Movement**, with the motto *"Confucian ethics, Western science."* China, these reformers said, could acquire modern technology, and the scientific knowledge underlying it, without sacrificing the ethical superiority of its Confucian tradition. As one of their leaders stated, *"What we have to learn from the barbarians is only one thing, solid ships and effective guns."*[*]

The reformers established government institutions for the translation of Western scientific texts, the first since the days of Jesuit influence in the seventeenth century. Members of the gentry established new educational institutions that merged the study of Confucian classics with coursework in geography and science. And for the first time some young Manchu and Chinese men ventured to Europe and the United States to study Western achievements firsthand.

Conservatives scoffed at the Self-Strengthening Movement. A prominent Neo-Confucian commented that since the most ancient times no one *"could use mathematics to raise a nation from a state of decline or to strengthen it in times of weakness."*[†]

Self-Strengthening Movement
Nineteenth-century Chinese reform movement with the motto "Confucian ethics, Western science." Advocates of Self-Strengthening sought a way to reconcile Western and Chinese systems of thought.

---

[*]Teng Ssu-yü and John K. Fairbank, *China's Response to the West: A Documentary Survey, 1839–1923* (Cambridge, Mass.: Harvard University Press, 1954), pp. 53–54.

[†]Quoted in Patricia Buckley Ebrey, *Cambridge Illustrated History of China* (London: Cambridge University Press, 1996), p. 245.

A Qing Arsenal A major focus of the Self-Strengthening Movement was military modernization. Here Qing officials survey cannon at an arsenal built in 1865, after the suppression of the Taiping Rebellion. The reformers hoped to achieve self-sufficiency in military infrastructure with the aid of foreign advisers; however, the corruption and inefficiency of the imperial bureaucracy prevented them from achieving that goal, a great contrast to Japanese achievements in military production in the following decades.

Wellcome Library, London

Like Muslim scholars in the Ottoman empire, Chinese scholar-officials derived their power and prestige from training in a long-standing and historically successful body of knowledge. To accept foreign principles in education would undercut the influence of the scholarly elite, and to emphasize military over scholarly pursuits would go against Confucianism. "One does not waste good sons by making them soldiers," went an old saying; it was a disparaging view of the military that Matteo Ricci had noted centuries earlier (see Chapter 16).

Conservative attitudes coalesced at the top of the imperial hierarchy. During the reign of two child emperors, real power lay in the hands of a conservative regent, the **Empress Ci Xi** (1835–1908), an intelligent and ambitious concubine who came to dominate the highest reaches of the Qing bureaucracy. Conservatives rallied around Ci Xi (kee SHEE). She discouraged talk of reform and diverted funds for modernization, such as programs to build railways and strengthen the military, to prestige projects, such as rebuilding the ruined summer palace. Instead of building real warships, she ordered an ornamental marble boat to decorate the palace lake.

Ci Xi's power was checked by the unequal treaties with Western nations, whose arrogance toward the Celestial Empire infuriated the "Dowager Empress." In spite of limited beginnings of industrialization and the acquisition of some modern armaments, the Qing military was no match for its rivals. In 1884, during a dispute over rights to Vietnam, French gunboats obliterated the Qing southern fleet within an hour. Southeast Asia, no longer tributary to the Qing, would now belong to France. (For more discussion on imperialism in Southeast Asia, see Chapter 26.)

The European powers were not the only ones threatening the integrity of the Qing empire: by this time Japan was also aggressively pursuing a policy of industrialization and militarization. Japan and Qing China came into conflict in Korea, where an uprising against the Chosôn dynasty drew in both Japanese and Chinese military forces, resulting in the Sino-Japanese War of 1894–1895. The Qing, having lost their southern fleet to France, now lost almost their entire northern fleet to Japan. The treaty that ended the war gave Japan possession not only of Korea but also of the island of Taiwan.

After these military defeats, Chinese reformers finally won official support when the young Guangxu (gwahng-SHOO) emperor (r. 1875–1908) issued a series of edicts in the summer of 1898 that came to be called the Hundred Days' Reforms. Guangxu was inspired by a group of young scholars who had traveled to Beijing to present a petition urging the founding of a state bank, the raising of government bonds for large-scale building of railroads, and the creation of a modern postal system. The most fundamental of the Hundred Days' Reforms concerned education. Expertise in poetry and calligraphy would no longer be required. Instead, the examination essays would focus on practical issues of governance and administration. Beijing College was to add a medical school, and all the Confucian academies were to add Western learning to their curricula.

Ci Xi ended the Hundred Days' Reforms by proclaiming that Guangxu had asked her to rule in his name and confining him, along with his most progressive advisers, in the palace. Some advocates of Self-Strengthening were charged with conspiracy and executed; others left the country or lapsed into silence.

Meanwhile the aggression of external powers intensified. Germans seized the port city of Qingdao (ching-DOW) and claimed mineral and railway rights on the Shandong peninsula; the British expanded their holdings from Hong Kong; and the Russians increased their presence in Manchuria (see Map 24.1). Public anger grew, directed at the Manchu for letting the empire slip so dramatically.

During the nineteenth century, many Chinese sought security by joining secret societies. One of these, the "Society of Righteous and Harmonious Fists," also known

Empress Ci Xi
(1835–1908) The "Dowager Empress" who dominated Qing politics in the late nineteenth century, ruling as regent for the emperor Guangxu. She blocked the Hundred Days' Reforms and other "Self-Strengthening" measures.

MAP 24.1 Asia in 1910 By 1910, empire was the status quo across Asia. In addition to the established British, French, and Dutch possessions, the United States (Philippines) and Japan (Korea and Taiwan) were new imperial players. The Russian empire was also a powerful presence, expanding at the expense of Iran, though its defeat by Japan in 1905 showed the limits of its influence in East Asia. Qing China was still technically a sovereign state; however, with the "concessions" controlled by Western powers after the imposition of unequal treaties, important coastal regions were under de facto European colonial control. (© Cengage Learning)

as the Boxers because of their emphasis on martial arts, now rose to prominence. The Boxers were virulently antiforeign. In 1898 they attacked European missionaries and Chinese Christian converts, thus beginning the **Boxer Rebellion**. Empress Ci Xi, having resisted progressive reforms, decided to side with the rebels and declared the Boxers a patriotic group, proclaiming, *"The foreigners have been aggressive towards us, infringed upon our territorial integrity, trampled our people under their feet. . . . They oppress our people and blaspheme our gods."* (See the feature "Visual Evidence in Primary Sources: The Boxer Rebellion: American and French Views.")

Imperial support for the Boxers proved disastrous. In the summer of 1900, on the grounds that foreigners in China had to be protected, twenty thousand troops from over a dozen different nations marched on Beijing and occupied the Forbidden City. Another humiliating treaty followed. The Qing were required to pay 450 million ounces of silver (twice the country's annual revenue) to the occupying forces. Like the Taiping, the Boxer Rebellion left China weaker and more beholden to foreigners than ever before.

Finally, after the disaster of the Boxer Rebellion, Ci Xi's government implemented the Hundred Days' Reforms, abolishing the examination system and making plans for a constitutional order with some degree of popular representation. An imperial decree finally abolished the cruel practice of footbinding. But it was too late for the Manchu leadership to usher China into modernity. In 1912, the first revolution in twentieth-century China thrust the Qing dynasty into historical oblivion (see Chapter 27).

> **Boxer Rebellion**
> (1898) Chinese uprising triggered by a secret society called the Society of Righteous and Harmonious Fists, a fiercely anti-Western group. Intended to drive out Westerners, it resulted instead in foreign occupation of Beijing.

The Rise of Modern Japan, 1830–1905

When Fukuzawa Yûkichi wrote that China could never move forward under Qing leadership, he was in a good position to judge. He had been instrumental in Japan's own transformation from weakness and isolation to industrialization, centralized state power, and imperialism. After the Meiji (MAY-jee) Restoration of 1868, Japan adapted to the new industrial age by looking to the West not just for its technology but also for its principles of education, economic organization, and state building. Yet socially, culturally, and spiritually, the Japanese retained their ancient traditions. By borrowing foreign ideas and adapting them to Japanese culture, Japanese society actually achieved the "self-strengthening" that had been desired by Chinese reformers.

The turning point came in 1853. After the arrival of a U.S. fleet, isolation from the West was no longer possible. Having observed the devastating aftereffects of the Opium Wars for China, Fukuzawa and others advocated radical reform based on the rapid acquisition of Western knowledge and technology. As in China (as indeed in western Europe and the Russian and Ottoman empires), the reform was opposed by defenders of the status quo. But in Meiji Japan, reformers took charge of imperial policy, laying the foundations of military and industrial modernization. Military victories over China in 1895 and Russia in 1905 confirmed their success and fulfilled Fukuzawa's dream that his country would be recognized as equal to the Europeans and Americans in Asian affairs.

Late Tokugawa Society, 1830–1867

Growing up in the busy commercial center of Osaka, where his father had been sent to look after his daimyo lord's affairs, Fukuzawa was highly conscious

---

*Victor Purcell, *The Boxer Uprising: A Background Study* (New York: Cambridge University Press, 1963), p. 224.

The Boxer Rebellion: American and French Views

The Boxer Rebellion (1898–1901) marked the death throes of the Qing dynasty. The decision of the Dowager Empress, Ci Xi, to support the "Righteous Society of Harmonious Fists" against the "Western barbarians," despite their anti-Manchu rhetoric, was calamitous. The Qing had to pay huge reparations, and though they did finally institute real political and social reforms, it was too late. In 1912 a new Republic of China marked the final end of China's long imperial history.

One of the Boxers' principal grievances was against Christian missionaries, who came to China in increasing numbers in the second half of the nineteenth century. Unlike Matteo Ricci (see Chapter 16), who had adapted his Christian message to the Confucian tradition and Chinese cultural norms, the European and American missionaries who arrived in the 1800s expected converts not only to accept Christianity, but also to conform to Western family models, styles of dress and housing, medical systems, and other cultural practices.

As with the Indian rebels of 1857 (discussed later in this chapter), who were driven in part by their belief that the British planned to use Christianity to subvert local cultures and traditions, so too the Boxers singled out missionaries as particular enemies. In the summer of 1900, 239 foreign Christians were killed by the Boxers across north China; Chinese converts and sympathizers were murdered as well. As the Boxers marched on Beijing, foreigners took refuge in a walled compound. Although the Qing commander acted to protect them, twenty thousand foreign soldiers (from Britain, France, Russia, Japan, and the United States) also arrived to occupy the capital and rescue the besieged.

President William McKinley (in office 1897–1901) wields a sword, while the figure of Uncle Sam attacks with a bayonet at the end of his rifle. The two figures represent the five thousand American soldiers sent as part of the China Relief Operation in 1900 to break the Boxer siege of Western delegations in Beijing.

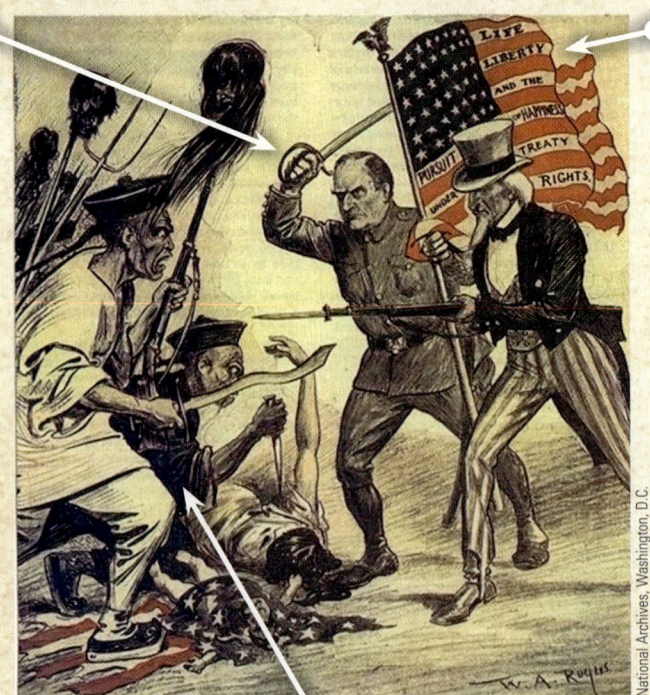

National Archives, Washington, D.C.

"Life, Liberty, and the Pursuit of Happiness under Treaty Rights," inscribed on the American flag, justifies their actions in defense of the unequal treaties which, since the Treaty of Nanjing in 1842, had made it impossible for the Qing rulers of China to regulate international trade.

In spite of the United States's participation in the occupation of the Forbidden City, McKinley's Open Door Policy advocated free trade with China without territorial annexation.

The Boxer rebels are shown as savages, with frenzied expressions. They march with heads on pikes, reach to stab a prostrate woman, and have murdered the child at their feet. The baby is wrapped in a tattered American flag, an image that would arouse strong emotions.

Another principal grievance of the Boxers was the partition of China into Western "spheres of influence." Because of their defeat, their attempt to end such meddling actually added to the danger that foreign interference would increase. Though the United States, with its Open Door Policy, proclaimed its opposition to the further partition of China, the division of the world's oldest and most populous empire continued unabated.

The political cartoons here, one from the United States and the other from France, are both from the period of the Boxer Rebellion but demonstrate different attitudes toward the conflict. In neither case does it seem that the Chinese will have much to say about the outcome.

Queen Victoria of Great Britain (left) seems shocked as Kaiser Wilhelm of Germany aggressively takes the first slice of the Chinese "pizza."

China leaps up in alarm, shown here in the stereotypical late-nineteenth-century Western fashion, with exceptionally long fingernails and a long flowing queue of braided hair.

Tsar Nicholas of Russia eyes Wilhelm's action and seems to be ready to join in; looking over Nicholas's shoulder, France is unarmed and, while she seems interested, appears less engaged.

The United States is missing from this scene.

Gianni Dagli Orti/The Art Archive at Art Resource, NY

The Japanese figure on the right studies the "pizza" as if he is planning a chess move. He holds no weapon, but his menacing sword lies on the table ready for action.

QUESTIONS FOR ANALYSIS

» *Compare the Chinese characters in the two cartoons. Both are caricatures, but is one more sympathetic to the Chinese predicament than the other? How so?*

» *Compare the Western figures in the two cartoons. What arguments for or against the Western invasion of China might the two artists be making?*

of the gap between his family's samurai status and its low income. Samurai were not supposed to deal with mundane affairs such as shopping and handling money. But since they could not afford servants, lower samurai like the Fukuzawa family had no choice but to do so. Fukuzawa remembered how they would do their shopping at night, with towels over their faces to hide their shame. Even worse was the scornful treatment they met when they returned to their home village: *"Children of lower samurai families like ours were obliged to use a respectful manner of address in speaking to the children of high samurai families, while these children invariably used an arrogant form of address to us. Then what fun was there in playing together?"* Although Fukuzawa's father was an educated man and well versed in the Chinese classics, no achievement on his part could raise his family's status.

While at the bottom of the samurai hierarchy, the Fukuzawa family had higher status than most people. Below them were the farmers, then the artisans, then the merchants, and lowest of all, the outcasts who performed such unsavory tasks as working in leather and handling the bodies of executed criminals.

As a young man Fukuzawa tested the attitude of the peasants by addressing them first in the haughty tones of the samurai and then speaking to them in the dialect of an Osaka merchant. The peasants abased themselves with humility when Fukuzawa spoke as a samurai, but they treated him with scorn when he imitated the speech of a merchant.

The young Fukuzawa longed to escape the social strictures that limited his ambitions. Education proved the key. Fukuzawa received no formal education until he was fourteen, and then it was the traditional curriculum of Confucian classics taught in Chinese. Frustrated, he sought his family's permission to travel to the port city of Nagasaki, the site of the annual Dutch trade mission. This was the only opening the Tokugawa government allowed to Europeans, and it was therefore also the center of "Dutch learning" (see Chapter 20). Fukuzawa's study of Western medical and scientific texts convinced him of the superiority of Western over Chinese styles of education.

Commodore Matthew Perry (1794–1858) American naval officer and diplomat whose 1853 visit to Japan opened that country's trade to the United States and other Western countries.

In 1853, after Fukuzawa began his Western studies, American **Commodore Matthew Perry** (1794–1858) sailed into Edo harbor, his steam-powered "black ships" sending shock waves through Japanese society. Perry's mission was to impress on the Tokugawa government the power of Western military technology and force it to establish diplomatic relations with the United States and open Japanese ports to foreign trade. Fearing that the Americans and Europeans might unleash a destructive barrage to open Japan to the outside world, the Tokugawa government submitted and, in 1858, signed an unequal treaty with the United States and five European powers granting access to treaty ports and rights of extraterritoriality.

Among those who accused the shogun of having humiliated the nation by signing this treaty were some daimyo who hoped to use the crisis to increase their independent power. Some even acquired modern weapons to fire at passing European ships. In the early 1860s, it was not clear whether the Tokugawa government still possessed enough authority to enforce its edicts. Seeking some breathing space, in 1862 the shogun sent a delegation to Europe hoping to delay further unequal treaties. Fukuzawa, who was part of this delegation, later published his observations of European life in a widely read book called *Western Ways*.

By the time of his return to Japan in 1863, things were becoming more and more dangerous. Apart from the rebellious lords, another rising source of anti-Tokugawa

---

*From *The Autobiography of Yukichi Fukuzawa*, by Eiichi Kiyooka, 1960, p. 18. Copyright © 1960 Columbia University Press. Reprinted with permission of the publisher.

Commodore Perry's Arrival in Japan   This Japanese print shows the arrival of Commodore Matthew Perry's steam-powered "black ships" near Edo (modern Tokyo) in 1853. After Perry's return to Japan in 1854, demanding that Japan be opened to Western trade, Japanese leaders debated how best to respond. The 1859 Tokugawa mission to San Francisco, on which Fukuzawa Yûkichi served, was an attempt to discover more about the U.S. government and its motives in East Asia.

pressure was coming from a group of *rônin* (ROH-neen), samurai without masters. The rônin were a floating population of proud men of limited means, many of whom were nostalgic for a glorious past when their military skills were highly prized. *"The whole spirit,"* Fukuzawa said, *"was one of war and worship of ancient warriors."** These rônin were stridently antiforeign. Fukuzawa, who had now learned English and was working as a government translator, was a potential target for their anger. For years he never left his home at night, fearful of being assaulted by anti-Western thugs.

The Meiji Restoration, 1867–1890

The challenge of the West required a coordinated national response, and neither the weakened Tokugawa government nor the rebellious daimyo could provide one. But there was another possible source of national unity: the imperial court at Kyoto. Some rebels against Tokugawa rule flocked to the banner of the child emperor under the slogans *Revere the Emperor!* and *Expel the Barbarians!*

---

*From *The Autobiography of Yukichi Fukuzawa*, by Eiichi Kiyooka, 1960, p. 164. Copyright © 1960 Columbia University Press. Reprinted with permission of the publisher.

In 1867 supporters of the emperor clashed with the shogun's forces. Fukuzawa was now a teacher, and when the fighting came to Edo he was lecturing on economics from an American textbook: *"Once in a while . . . my pupils would amuse themselves by bringing out a ladder and climbing up on the roof to gaze at the smoke overhanging the attack."*[*] He remained neutral, for his own safety and that of his students, fearing that the imperial forces would prove to be just as antiforeign as those of the shogun. Through the Keio Academy he had founded in 1858, Fukuzawa was a highly visible potential target of conservatives. Not only had he instituted a Western curriculum at Keio, but he also welcomed the addition of foreign sports to the academy's programs. (See the feature "World History in Today's World: Baseball in Asia.")

The armies of the imperial party were successful. In 1868 the **Meiji Restoration** brought a new government to power at Edo, now renamed Tokyo. Fukuzawa was delighted to discover that the administration of the newly restored Meiji ("enlightened") emperor, then only a child, was dominated by reformers who began to utterly transform the closed, conservative society that Fukuzawa had known as a child. Most were, like Fukuzawa himself, men from middle and lower samurai families that placed a strong emphasis on scholarship.

The Meiji reforms replaced the feudal domains of daimyo with regional prefectures under the control of the central government. Tax collection was centralized to solidify the government's economic control. For the first time commoners were allowed to carry arms, as the Meiji government created a national conscript army equipped with the latest weapons and led by officers trained in modern military organization. All the old distinctions between samurai and commoners were erased: *"The samurai abandoned their swords,"* Fukuzawa noted, and *"non-samurai were allowed to have surnames and ride horses."*[†] The rice allowances on which samurai families had lived were replaced by modest cash stipends. Many former samurai had to face the indignity of looking for work.

Fukuzawa coined two of the Meiji reform's most popular slogans: *"Civilization and Enlightenment"* and *"Rich Nation, Strong Army."* Viewing education as the key to progress, the government set up a national system of compulsory schooling and invited Fukuzawa to head the Education Ministry, but he preferred to keep his independence, founding both a university and a newspaper.

The policy of the Meiji oligarchs was to strengthen Japan so it could resist Western intrusion and engage the world as an equal by adopting Western methods. In 1873 a mission to Europe was stunned by the West's industrial and technological development. The participants were particularly impressed with the newly unified Germany and the politics of its chancellor, Otto von Bismarck, finding these to be a model combination of nationalism and military-industrial power (see Chapter 23).

Many at home, however, were critical of this new direction. Some samurai took up arms against the Meiji regime, most notably the forty-two thousand who participated in the Satsuma Rebellion of 1877. Their leader, Saigō Takamori, ritually disemboweled himself when the battle turned against his men, and he later became a hero to the conservatives. But the Meiji reformers countered by creating their own cult of Saigō and turning him into a romantic hero. As they had used the phrase "Revere the Emperor" to modernize Japan, so again they appealed to tradition to support policies of change.

Meiji Restoration (1868) A dramatic revolution in Japan that overthrew the Tokugawa, restored national authority to the emperor, and put the country on a path of political and economic reform under the slogans "Revere the Emperor" and "Expel the Barbarians." Meiji industrialization turned Japan into a major world power.

---

[*]From *The Autobiography of Yukichi Fukuzawa*, by Eiichi Kiyooka, 1960, p. 210. Copyright © 1960 Columbia University Press. Reprinted with permission of the publisher.

[†]Fukuzawa Yûkichi, *The Speeches of Fukuzawa: A Translation and Critical Study,* ed. Wayne Oxford (Tokyo: Hokuseido House, 1973), p. 93.

Baseball in Asia

When fans in the United States celebrate their national championship as a "World Series," they ignore the popularity of the sport in other countries. Latin America, the Caribbean, and East Asia are also important global centers of baseball.

Japan is at the forefront of Asian baseball. The sport arrived during the Meiji period and immediately became popular at high schools and universities, including Fukuzawa Yûkichi's Keio Academy. Japan's annexation of Taiwan (1895) and Korea (1910) led to the development of baseball traditions in those two countries as well.

In Korea, as in Japan, professional baseball has proven a commercial success, while in Taiwan the emphasis has remained on the amateur youth game. Between 1971 and 1991, Taiwanese teams won an amazing fourteen Little League world championships. Meanwhile, Japanese and Korean players are actively recruited by American teams. Ichiro Suzuki is widely considered the greatest Japanese player in American baseball history.

Though the Asian and American versions of baseball have the same rules, there are significant cultural differences. For example, in Japan, unlike the United States, the authority of the coaches and the decisions of the umpires are unquestioned, and players are expected to practice with single-minded dedication to refine their skills and build team spirit. American players who have gone to Japan are often seen as too individualistic, resisting the orders of their managers, arguing with umpires, and following their own training regimen rather than that of the team.

Perhaps no one knows more about these cultural differences than Bobby Valentine, who, after an extensive American professional career, successfully managed Japan's Chiba Lotte Marines for nine years. Hired to coach the Boston Red Sox starting with their 2012 season, Valentine knows that baseball's future will be global. In 2005, he offered a challenge to the Major League Baseball champion Chicago White Sox to play a seven-game series against the Marines, his own Japanese national championship team. That never happened, but perhaps the day will come when professional teams from the United States, Japan, South Korea, Taiwan, Cuba, Mexico, Australia, the Dominican Republic, the Netherlands, and other baseball-loving countries will compete in a genuinely *World* Series.

As in Europe, the rewards of increased industrial productivity were unequally distributed in Meiji Japan. Landowners benefited the most from advances in agriculture, such as the importation of new seeds and fertilizer and the government creation of agricultural colleges to improve methods of cultivation. Rice output increased 30 percent between 1870 and 1895, but peasants often paid half their crop in land rent and had to pay taxes now as well. To make ends meet, many rural families sent their daughters to work in factories the government was setting up. Poorly paid and strictly supervised, young girls and women lived in factory dormitories, their dexterity and docility exploited for the benefit of others.

Meiji Japan went further than Germany in giving the state control of industrial development. The government constructed railroads, harbors, and telegraph lines and made direct investments in industry. Meiji ministers and the oligarchs behind them did not leave economic development to market forces. They viewed economic planning as more conducive to social harmony than market competition.

In fact, Fukuzawa discovered how ignorant some were of the most basic principles of market economies when he showed one official his translation of an American economics textbook. Since there was no Japanese word for *competition*, he had substituted a word of his own invention, *kyōsō*, literally, "race-fight."

When a treasury official objected to the use of the term, Fukuzawa explained that the concept was fundamental to the world of commerce. *"I understand the idea,"* said the official, *"but that word 'fight' is not conducive to peace. I could not take the paper with that word to the chancellor."*[*]

The industrial economy was based on a tight connection between state and industry that continued even after the government sold its industrial assets to private interests. After 1880, Japanese industry was controlled by **zaibatsu** (zye-BOT-soo), large industrial cartels that collaborated closely with the civil service. Some of the nineteenth-century zaibatsu, like Mitsubishi, still exist today. Liberal, free-trade economic notions were never as strong in Japan as in Britain and the United States.

Similarly, nationalism was more powerful than liberalism in late-nineteenth-century Japanese politics, though Fukuzawa did plant the seed of liberal thinking with an influential essay on John Stuart Mill's *On Liberty* (see Chapter 23). Like Mill, Fukuzawa addressed issues of gender, writing that *"the position of women must be raised at once"* and that education should be the first step toward greater gender equality.[†] A twenty-year-old woman named **Toshiko Kishida** (toe-she-ko KEE-she-dah) went even further, speaking eloquently for women's rights in meetings across the country, even adding a little humor: *"If it is true that men are better than women because they are stronger, why aren't our sumo wrestlers in the government?"*[‡]

One of Fukuzawa's greatest contributions in resolving the strains of the early Meiji period was in creating a space for "public opinion" in Japanese politics. Even if he disagreed with what Toshiko said, when she traveled the country arguing for women's rights she embodied Fukuzawa's principle of *enzetsu*, a word he created to describe something that had never existed in Japan before: "public speaking." In becoming a modern nation, Japan was also becoming a mass society where rulers had to take account of popular feelings and opinions. Since he was a newspaper editor, Fukuzawa's views were widely discussed, and as a writer and publisher, he was the principal source of the Japanese public's view of the Western world. In fact, *all* Western books in Japan came to be known as *Fukuzawa-bon*.

Fukuzawa was particularly proud of his part in using public opinion to pressure the Meiji oligarchs for a formal constitution that provided for a popularly elected legislature. After years of debate, in 1889 Japan became a constitutional empire, with a legislature elected by propertied male voters. The Japanese constitution was based on the German one, where the emperor rather than elected representatives controlled the real levers of power. Like Germany under Bismarck, Meiji Japan achieved unification through conservative nationalism rather than a broader liberalism based on individual rights. The slogan *"for the sake of the country"* encapsulated the idea that individuals were to sacrifice for the larger good. And as in Germany, militarism in Japan combined with nationalism to make the country more aggressively imperialistic.

zaibatsu
Large corporations that developed the Japanese industrial economy in close cooperation with the imperial government.

Toshiko Kishida
(1863–1901) An early Japanese feminist who urged that as part of the Meiji reforms, women should have equal access to modern education and be allowed to take part in public affairs.

Japanese Imperialism, 1890–1910

The idea that Japanese national prestige required the acquisition of an empire was reinforced by global trends. The last two decades of the nineteenth century saw a spurt of imperialist activity by the Europeans and the United States around the world (see also Chapter 26). Doctrines of Social Darwinism were increasingly popular, portraying international relations as

---

[*]From *The Autobiography of Yukichi Fukuzawa*, by Eiichi Kiyooka, 1960, p. 190. Copyright © 1960 Columbia University Press. Reprinted with permission of the publisher.

[†]Fukuzawa Yûkichi, *Fukuzawa Yukichi on Japanese Women: Selected Works* (Tokyo: University of Tokyo Press, 1988), p. 138.

[‡]http://womenshistory.about.com/library/qu/blqutosh.htm?pid=2765&cob=home.

Peace Negotiations This print by Kiyochika Kobayashi shows Japanese and Chinese negotiations at the end of the Sino-Japanese War. By the terms of the Treaty of Shimono-seki (1895), the Qing empire ceded the island of Taiwan to Japan, recognized Japanese rights over Korea, and agreed to make substantial reparation payments. The Qing and Meiji diplomats in this portrait are clearly differentiated by their clothing. (Musée des Arts Asiatiques-Guimet, Paris, France/Réunion des Musées Nationaux/Art Resource, NY)

a "struggle for existence." Fukuzawa, who had earlier held more liberal and idealistic views, also adopted this harder-edged attitude, saying: *"There are only two ways in international relations: to destroy, or to be destroyed."** His opinion mattered, not only because of his books and his newspaper, but also because graduates of his own Keio Academy were now rising to power in the Meiji bureaucracy.

Japan flexed its imperial muscles first in Korea, where its forces confronted those of China while both were responding to an uprising in 1894. Japanese victory in the consequent **Sino-Japanese War** (1894–1895) caused a wave of national pride. In addition to acquiring control over Korea and Taiwan, the Meiji government forced Qing China to grant it access to treaty ports and rights of extraterritoriality similar to those enjoyed by European powers. At the same time, Japan renegotiated its own treaties with Europe, this time on a basis of equality.

Japan pressured Korea to adopt reforms that paralleled its own of the early Meiji period. At first the Korean king allied himself with the Japanese, but in 1896 he sought protection from the Russians. For the next eight years, Korean reformers allied themselves with Japan while the king and other conservatives promoted Russian interests on the peninsula. Meanwhile, Meiji rulers saw the presence of Russian troops in the Qing province of Manchuria as a direct threat to their own "sphere of influence" in northeastern Asia.

The result was the **Russo-Japanese War** of 1904–1905. Just as the Japanese Navy had decimated the northern Qing fleet ten years earlier, now it scored a major naval victory over Russia. The Japanese Navy, led by its impressive flagship *Mikasa*, destroyed or disabled most of Russia's Pacific fleet. While the United States brokered peace negotiations, the Japanese government posted advisers to all the important Korean ministries. In 1910, after a Korean nationalist assassinated the Japanese prime minister, the Meiji government annexed Korea.

Sino-Japanese War (1894–1895) A war caused by a rivalry over the Korean peninsula; ended with a one-sided treaty that favored Japan, which obtained treaty rights in China as well as control of Korea and Taiwan.

Russo-Japanese War (1904–1905) War caused by territorial disputes in Manchuria and Korea. Japan's defeat of Russia was the first victory by an Asian military power over a European one in the industrial age.

*Quoted in Helen M. Hopper, *Fukuzawa Yûkichi: From Samurai to Capitalist* (New York: Pearson Longman, 2005), p. 120.

Japan's victory in the Russo-Japanese War had global consequences. Russia was a traditional European great power, and the tsar commanded the world's largest military. There was now no question that Japan must be counted among the great powers of the world. And there was also the question of race. The defeat of a European power by an Asian one inspired nationalists across Asia and Africa: European superiority was not inevitable after all.

As Japanese imperial ambitions grew in Asia and the Pacific, the Germans, French, and British were also expanding their presence in the region, while the United States annexed Hawai'i and took over the Philippines. The world was becoming a smaller place, and the imperial aspirations of the great powers, now including Japan, would become a touchstone of conflict in the twentieth century.

British India, 1818–1905

By the early nineteenth century, the British were the "new Mughals," the dominant political force on the Indian subcontinent (see Chapter 20). The effects were felt by hundreds of millions of artisans and farmers whose livelihoods were deeply affected when the British used that political power to drain India of raw materials for Britain's own industrialization. And unlike the rulers of Qing China and Tokugawa Japan, who initially retained their authority as they struggled to adapt to industrial modernity, Indian elites were subject to more direct colonial control.

Even under foreign rule, however, South Asians carried on the same type of debate that could be heard in China and Japan, as well as in Russia and the Ottoman empire: whether to adjust to the new circumstances by rejecting Western cultural models, by embracing them, or by finding a way to balance them with indigenous cultural traditions. The first of those choices inspired a major rebellion in 1857, but after the British had suppressed the revolt and consolidated their rule even further, the option of holding onto the past was no longer viable. Indian nationalists then began developing new ideas and organizations in response to the problem of British rule, and by the beginning of the twentieth century they had laid the foundations of modern Indian nationalism.

India Under Company Rule, 1800–1857

There was no exact date on which the British took control of India. The Battle of Plassey in 1757, which laid the riches of Bengal in the northeast open to the British East India Company, was certainly a turning point (see Chapter 20). The defeat of the Maratha confederacy in 1818 added the rich and populous territories in the hinterland of Bombay (today's Mumbai) to British control. By the time the Sikhs of the Punjab succumbed in 1849, the British East India Company controlled virtually the entire subcontinent. By 1850 the British "Raj" was one of the great empires of world history.

Britain could not control so much territory and so many people without the participation of indigenous allies. Much of the subcontinent was ruled through a "princely state" system whereby traditional rulers were kept in nominal charge with the guidance of British advisers. These princely rulers became part of the British East India Company's administrative machinery, helping them in such crucial areas as tax collection while maintaining an appearance of continuity with the past.

There was no mistaking the economic changes that came to India with British rule. Whereas early Mughal rulers had stimulated the South Asian commercial economy by promoting its connection with Indian Ocean markets, the British yoked the Indian economy to British interests. As a result, deindustrialization became a major problem (see Chapter 23). By 1830, unemployment among India's textile workers was reaching a critical level, leaving India "to fall backward in time . . . losing most of its artisan manufacturing abilities, forcing millions of unemployed craftsmen to return to the soil to scratch meager livelihoods directly from crowded land."* In India, the rural-to-urban migration of the European Industrial Revolution was reversed.

Technological and social changes caused shifts in Anglo-Indian social and cultural interactions as well. In the eighteenth century, almost all the Europeans in India had been men. They often spoke Indian languages, wore Indian clothing, established relationships with Indian women, and played Mughal games like polo. But in the age of steamships and the telegraph, British officials became more aloof from the Indians among whom they lived. As more officials brought British wives with them, gender played an important role in this progressive distancing of British rulers from Indian subjects. No longer would long-term relationships with local women help British men bridge the cultural gap. Segregated official towns strictly limited Indian access and allowed British men to live with their families and fellow countrymen rather than within Indian society. Behind these official lines they carefully followed the rituals of Victorian social life, such as dressing formally for dinner no matter what the temperature and replacing local curries with tinned meats and other reminders of home. The British constructed "hill stations" in the Himalayas where officials and their families could retreat from the terrible heat of the plains below, literally looking down on the Indians they ruled.

Now it was Indians who tried to adjust to English language and culture. In the northeastern city of Calcutta (today's Kolkata), Britain's main commercial center, young Indians like **Rammohun Roy** (1772–1833) explored ways to assimilate European cultural influences. A native speaker of Bengali, Roy studied Sanskrit so he could read ancient Vedic texts in their original language, and he also wrote in Arabic, Persian, and English. Businessman as well as scholar, Roy gleaned liberal ideas from contact with British traders and officials. He used those ideas to promote a reformed Hinduism that combined both a return to the religion's most ancient philosophical principles and a series of reforms in the liberal spirit, such as an end to child marriage.

Roy became the leader of an intellectual movement called the Bengal Renaissance, an important influence on later Indians who absorbed Western culture and thought into their own traditions. He was also politically active, lobbying the

Image credit: © Bristol City Museum and Art Gallery, U.K./The Bridgeman Art Gallery

Rammohun Roy   Rammohun Roy was the leading thinker of the Bengal Renaissance, striving to reconcile liberal ideas from the West with Bengali, Persian, Mughal, and Hindu cultural and intellectual traditions. Himself a Hindu, Roy advocated reform of the caste system and restrictions on child marriage, while promoting the idea that Hinduism could be reformed from within by returning to the original principles of its ancient sacred texts.

Rammohun Roy (1772–1833) Bengali reformer and religious philosopher who opposed the caste system, polygamy, the prohibition of widow remarriage, the lack of education for common people, and discrimination against women.

*Stanley Wolpert, *India* (Berkeley: University of California Press, 1991), p. 51.

British government for changes to policies that favored British business interests at the expense of Indian ones. In 1830, Roy traveled to England as an ambassador of the Mughal emperor, now a mere figurehead, to lobby for Indian interests and in opposition to the predatory nature of East India Company rule. Inspired by the revolutionary ideals of "liberty, equality, and brotherhood," he chose a French vessel to make the trip. Roy's attitude toward Britain, like that of many later Indian leaders, was a complex mixture of admiration and resentment.

The British believed that they could show India the path to progress, defining "progress" as the replacement of Indian culture by British culture. In the 1830s, one East India Company official declared that British education should create a *"class of persons Indian in blood and color, but English in taste, in opinions, in morals, and in intellect."* Roy and his successors rejected that approach, believing instead that they could use European ideas to reinvigorate Indian traditions.

However, as a reformer Roy firmly agreed with one British policy: the decision to abolish the practice of *sati,* which encouraged high-caste Indian widows to throw themselves on the funeral pyres of their deceased husbands. To the British, sati was the cruel outcome of ancient superstition, an offense to universal morality that no Christian ruler could tolerate. To Roy and other Indian reformers, sati was a perversion of Hindu ethics that would fade away if Hindus returned to the ancient texts and achieved a deeper understanding of their own faith.

The abolition of sati was just one example of the increasing British intrusion on Indian customs and ways of life in the mid-nineteenth century, which combined with more aggressive Company policies toward Indian rulers to provoke a powerful counter-reaction. An increase in British missionaries traveling to India was adding to the wider concern that the British had come not just to rule but also to overturn Indians' cultural traditions and convert them to a foreign religion. When combined with a loss of support from some of India's traditional elites for the British presence and with the economic strains that were appearing in the countryside, the missionary presence created a volatile situation.

Indian Revolt of 1857
Revolt of Indian soldiers against British officers when they were required to use greased ammunition cartridges they suspected were being used to pollute them and cause them to convert to Christianity. The revolt spread across north India.

The Indian Revolt of 1857 and Its Aftermath

The **Indian Revolt of 1857** began with a mutiny among the *sepoys* (SEE-poyz), the two hundred thousand Indian soldiers commanded by British officers. The sepoys were essential to British rule, and their revolt sent shock waves across north India.

The immediate cause of the Indian Revolt was Britain's introduction of a new, faster-loading rifle for its troops. The loading procedure required soldiers to bite off the ends of the guns' ammunition cartridge casings, which were greased. The rumor spread among Muslim troops that the cartridges had been greased with pig fat; many Hindus believed that fat from cattle had been used. Both groups suspected that the British were trying to pollute them, since contact with pork was forbidden to Muslims and cattle were sacred to Hindus. The rebellious soldiers saw the new cartridges as part of a plot to convert them to Christianity. (See the feature "Movement of Ideas Through Primary Sources: Religion and Rebellion: India in 1858.")

Outraged that some sepoys had been imprisoned for refusing to use the greased cartridges, a group of soldiers killed their British officers, marched to Delhi, and rallied support for the restoration of the aging Mughal emperor. The revolt quickly spread across northern and western India. The rani (queen) of Jhansi (JAN-see), one of the Maratha kingdoms, rallied her troops and rode into battle.

---

*Bureau of Education, *Selections from Educational Records,* Part I (1781–1839), ed. H. Sharp (Calcutta: Superintendent, Government Printing, 1920), p. 34.

Violence was terrible on both sides, the rebels sometimes killing British women and children, and the British strapping rebels to cannon and blowing them to pieces. Even after order was restored, bitterness caused by such violence was an enduring tension underlying race relations in the British Raj, further accelerating the process of segregation between the rulers and the ruled.

British observers believed that the cause of the rebellion was simply the backwardness of the Indian people. Prior to 1857, many had held the liberal belief that Indians were perfectly capable of "becoming English" through education and assimilation. After 1857, racial stereotypes became much more powerful, with many in Britain believing that Indians (like Africans) were naturally and permanently inferior. Social Darwinism reinforced this emerging belief in race as the physical manifestation of not just cultural but also biologic inferiority.

The Indian rebels knew what they were fighting against but were less unified about what they were fighting for. Loyalty to an aged and obscure Mughal emperor was not enough to build a broad sense of Indian unity. In South Asia the cultural, linguistic, and religious landscape was exceptionally diverse, making it all the more necessary to develop a sense of identity embracing all the peoples under British rule. Failure to do so and the lack of coordination among regional rebellions made it easy for the British to retake control.

By 1858 the revolt was over, and the British government responded by disbanding the East India Company and abolishing the last vestiges of Mughal authority. In 1876, Queen Victoria added "Empress of India" to her titles. Direct control was extended over many of the princely states. Still, alliances were maintained with many traditional rulers, who were pampered financially even if they had no real political power. The British colonial administration was centralized and given enhanced fiscal responsibilities. At the top of that system stood the Indian Civil Service, elite government officials selected on the basis of a rigorous examination. In theory, anyone who passed the examination could join the Indian Civil Service. Since the exams were only administered in England, however, Indian candidates did not have a realistic chance.

The general trend was toward a much harsher racial division in colonial society. When a British viceroy ruled that an Indian could testify against a British subject in court, he was widely attacked by the British community. Westernized Indians were disheartened when the British turned to the remnants of the old aristocracy for allies, and dismayed when the British mocked them for trying to assimilate elements of English culture. In 1885 they organized a new political movement called the Indian National Congress.

The Origins of Indian Nationalism, 1885–1906

Amidst all the political and social tensions, the Indian economy continued to grow. As in Europe, railroads played a major role (see Map 24.2 on page 696). Tracks and engines were imported from Britain, creating profits for English manufacturers and employment for British workers, while Indian taxpayers financed the 50,000 miles (80,500 km) of rail constructed under British rule. The primary economic purpose of the railways was to speed the export of Indian raw materials, such as cotton, in support of British industry, as well as the import of British manufactured goods, such as the iron goods and finished textiles that were displacing India's own manufactures. But there were benefits to Indians as well. The railroads, along with telegraphs and a postal service, created a communications infrastructure that put India's diverse peoples and regions in closer contact with one another than ever before.

Religion and Rebellion: India in 1858

The following passage was written in the Urdu language in 1858 by an Indian Muslim, Maulvi Syed Kutb Shah Sahib. Maulvi Syed saw the Indian Revolt as a chance to drive the British out of India. In this letter to Hindu leaders, he urged Hindu-Muslim cooperation to accomplish that goal, arguing that the British were consciously defiling both religions in an attempt to force conversions to Christianity.

One of the grievances Maulvi Syed mentions is British laws concerning widows. Islamic law encourages the remarriage of widows, following the example of Muhammad, whose wife Khadijah was a widow. Among Hindus, however, patriarchal beliefs dictated that a wife's life was essentially over once her husband died. Thus the custom of sati encouraged widows to throw themselves on the fire when their husbands were cremated to demonstrate their devotion and to allow them to be reunited in the next life. In fact, relatively few Hindu women, usually from the highest castes, actually did so. In 1829 the British abolished sati and issued another order that widows should be allowed to remarry.

Another controversy to which the author refers is the "doctrine of lapse," a colonial ruling that if an Indian prince died without a male heir, direct control over his territory would go to the British. In 1856, the city of Lucknow and the rich province of Oudh had been taken over by the British through this device. The author's references to tainted bread may refer to the widespread suspicion that the British were forcing Indians under their control (such as sepoy soldiers and prisoners) into contact with forbidden animal fats as a step toward converting them to Christianity.

Source: *Records of the Government of the Punjab and Its Dependencies,* New Series, No. VII (Lahore: Punjab Printing Company, 1870), pp. 173–175.

Maulvi Syed on British Christians

The English are people who overthrow all religions. You should understand well the object of destroying the religions of Hindustan [India]; they have for a long time been causing books to be written and circulated throughout the country by the hands of their priests, and, exercising their authority, have brought out numbers of preachers to spread their own tenets. . . .

Consider, then, what systematic contrivances they have adopted to destroy our religions. For instance, first, when a woman became a widow they ordered her to make a second marriage. Secondly, the self-immolation of wives [sati] on the funeral pyres of their deceased husbands was an ancient religious custom; the English . . . enacted their own regulations prohibiting it. Thirdly, they told people it was their wish that they . . . should adopt their faith, promising that if they did so they would be respected by Government; and further required them to attend churches, and hear the tenets preached there.

Moreover, they decided and told the rajahs that such only as were born of their wives would inherit the government and property, and that adopted heirs would not be allowed to succeed, although, according to your [Hindu] Scriptures, ten different sorts of heirs are allowed to share in the inheritance. By this contrivance they will rob you of your governments and possessions, as they have already done with Nagpur and Lucknow.

Consider now another of their designing plans: they resolved on compelling prisoners, with the forcible exercise of their authority, to eat their bread. Numbers died of starvation, but did not eat it, others ate it, and sacrificed their faith. They now perceived that this expedient did not succeed well, and accordingly determined on having bones ground and mixed with flour and sugar, so that people might unsuspectingly eat them in this way. They had, moreover, bones and flesh broken small and mixed with rice, which they caused to be placed in the markets for sale, and tried, besides, every other possible plan to destroy our religions.

They accordingly now ordered the Brahmins and others of their army to bite cartridges, in the making of which fat had been used. The Muslim soldiers perceived that by this expedient the religion of the Brahmans and Hindus only was in danger, but nevertheless they also refused to bite them. On this the British resolved on ruining the faith of both, and [lashed to the cannons] all those soldiers who persisted in their refusal [and blew them to pieces]. Seeing this excessive tyranny, the soldiery now, in self-preservation, began killing the English, and slew them wherever they were found, and are now considering means for slaying the few still alive here and there. It is now my firm conviction that if these English continue in Hindustan they will kill everyone in the country, and will utterly overthrow our religions; but there are some of my countrymen who have joined the English, and are fighting on their side. . . .

Under these circumstances, I would ask, what course have you decided on to protect your lives and faith? Were your views and mine the same we might destroy them entirely with a very little trouble; and if we do so, we shall protect our religions and save the country. . . .

All you Hindus are hereby solemnly adjured, by your faith in Ganges; and all you Muslims, by your belief in God and the Koran, as these English are the common enemy of both, to unite in considering their slaughter extremely expedient, for by this alone will the lives and faith of both be saved. . . .

The slaughter of cows is regarded by the Hindus as a great insult to their religion. To prevent this a solemn compact and agreement has been entered into by all the Muslim chiefs of Hindustan, binding themselves, that if the Hindus will come forward to slay the English, the Muslims will from that very day put a stop to the slaughter of cows, and those of them who will not do so will be considered to have abjured the Koran, and such of them as will eat beef will be regarded as though they had eaten pork. . . .

The English are always deceitful. Once their ends are gained they will infringe their engagements, for deception has ever been habitual with them, and the treachery they have always practiced on the people of Hindustan is known to rich and poor. Do not therefore give heed to what they say. Be well assured you will never have such an opportunity again. We all know that writing a letter is an advance halfway towards fellowship. I trust you will all write letters approving of what has been proposed herein.

QUESTIONS FOR ANALYSIS

» *What reasons does Maulvi Syed give to justify the rebellion? Which of those reasons does he feel are most important?*

» *What actions does he think are necessary for the rebellion to succeed? Given what you know about Indian history (see also Chapters 16 and 20), what might have prevented such actions from being taken?*

MAP 24.2 Indian Railroads, 1893 After the Indian Revolt of 1857, the British stabilized their rule by allying themselves more strongly with traditional Indian rulers. Some of the "princely states" were very extensive and their rulers, such as the Nizams of Hyderabad, were quite wealthy. Even in the princely states, however, the British were clearly predominant. After 1857, the British built an extensive railroad and telegraph network to tighten their control, though improved transport and communications had the unintended consequence of helping bring Indians together from across the subcontinent, fueling the growth of Indian nationalism. (© Cengage Learning)

India's emerging middle class, often educated in India in the English language following a British school curriculum, had the clearest vision of "India" as a single political space that, under proper leadership, could come together and speak with one voice. In the beginning, however, the **Indian National Congress** was composed of relatively advantaged men who cared most about the interests of their own social class. For example, it campaigned to have the examination for the elite Indian Civil Service administered in India so that Indians would have a better opportunity to compete.

Since they were in closer personal contact with whites than most Indians, the congress members were sensitive to the racism that permeated British India. Every

British outpost had a "club" where British officials and merchants gathered to gossip, drink, play billiards and tennis, and talk of home. Indians—no matter how accomplished, how fluent in English, or how well educated—were excluded from these racially segregated centers of power, except as servants. Rudyard Kipling, the Bombay-born poet of empire, captured the British attitude of absolute and essential difference between themselves and their subjects: *"East is East, and West is West, and never the twain shall meet."*[*]

Following in the tradition of Rammohun Roy, young congress members like **Gopal K. Gokhale** (1866–1915) tried to reconcile the British and Indian values they had absorbed through upbringing and education. They challenged their rulers to live up to the high ideal enunciated by Queen Victoria in 1858: *"And it is our further will that, so far as may be, our subjects, of whatever race or creed, be freely and impartially admitted to offices in our service, the duties of which they may be qualified, by their education, ability and integrity."* At the beginning, Gokhale (go-KAHL-ee) and the Indian National Congress were fighting not to change the system but to find a place within it, believing that slow reform was better than revolutionary change. They did not seek independence, but self-rule for India within the British empire. And self-rule could not be achieved, they acknowledged, until its people learned to respect one another more fully across lines of religion, caste, language, and gender.

Other Indian nationalists, such as **Bal Gangadhar Tilak** (1856–1920), took a more confrontational approach. They questioned why the British had any right to be in India at all. Tilak (TIH-lak) declared: *"Swaraj ['self-rule'] is my birthright, and I must have it!"*[†] Tilak's appeal was more emotional, and his plan much simpler than that of the congress: organize the masses to pressure the British, and they will leave. Tilak's radicalism was both a threat to the British and a challenge to the Indian National Congress. Because he used Hindu symbols to rally support, his movement also alarmed the country's large Muslim minority. While Indian nationalists accused the British of using "divide and rule" tactics, the British justified their rule by claiming that only they could be neutral among the subcontinent's diverse cultural and religious groups.

The British promise of "good government" was tested during the failure of the monsoon rains in 1896–1897. With its command of railroads and telegraphs, the British government could be expected to move food from regions with a surplus to those in need. As during the tragic Irish famines of the 1840s, the British government decided to leave matters to the market rather than relieve their subjects' suffering: grain prices climbed as merchants stockpiled food, and millions starved to death. To Indians, British lack of action in the crisis seemed to indicate cruelty rather than competency.

The government meanwhile continued to use spectacular public rituals to display its power and legitimize its rule. The most impressive was the "durbar" procession, a combination of circus, parade, and political theater held at Delhi in 1903. Organized to celebrate the coronation of the new British king, it featured maharajahs in ceremonial garb, hundreds of parading elephants, tens of thousands of marching soldiers, and elaborate salutes to India's new emperor.

But grand political theater was not enough to smooth over increasing tensions as British India entered the twentieth century. A flashpoint of conflict arose in

---

[*]Rudyard Kipling, "The Ballad of East and West," cited in Kingsley Amis, *Rudyard Kipling and His World* (London: Thames and Hudson, 1975), p. 54.

[†]Quoted in Stanley A. Wolpert, *Tilak and Gokhale: Revolution and Reform in the Making of Modern India* (Berkeley: University of California Press, 1991), p. 191.

Indian National Congress
(1885) Formed by wealthy, Western-educated Indians to advance the cause of Indian involvement in their own governance. In the twentieth century, it would become the vehicle for India's independence under the leadership of Mohandas K. Gandhi.

Gopal K. Gokhale
(1866–1915) Indian political leader, social reformer, and advocate of Indian self-government achieved through negotiation.

Bal Gangadhar Tilak
(1856–1920) Indian nationalist who demanded immediate independence from Britain, mobilizing Hindu religious symbolism to develop a mass following and arguing that violence was an acceptable tactic for anticolonial partisans.

Delhi Durbar of 1903 The British rulers of India used lavish political ceremonies to awe their subjects. Never was the pomp and circumstance greater than at the durbar held in Delhi in 1903 to celebrate the coronation of King Edward VII as emperor of India. Representing the absent king was his viceroy, Lord Curzon, who accepted the congratulations of the Indian princes, seen here riding on magnificently outfitted elephants in procession before the Mughal-era Red Fort. *(© Christie's Images/Corbis)*

1905 when British bureaucrats, for no reason other than administrative expediency, decided to split in two the culturally and economically integrated northeastern province of Bengal. No Indians were consulted about the **Partition of Bengal**, which created a predominantly Muslim province in the east. Nationalists again accused the British of using "divide and rule" tactics to reinforce their power by dividing Hindus from Muslims.

In protest, the Indian National Congress organized a boycott of British goods. Bengali activists made huge bonfires of English cloth across the province, showing the connection between their economic and political grievances. Conditions were now ripe for the development of mass nationalism, bringing together the Western-educated elite of the congress and the millions of urban and rural Indians struggling toward a better future.

In 1906, the same year of the anti-Partition protests, the man who would be most responsible for forging that alliance between leaders and people returned to India. Mohandas K. Gandhi (1869–1948) was then a little-known lawyer coming home from South Africa, where he had led that country's Indian community in protests against racial discrimination. Gandhi (GAHN-dee) would come to symbolize a new India in the twentieth century.

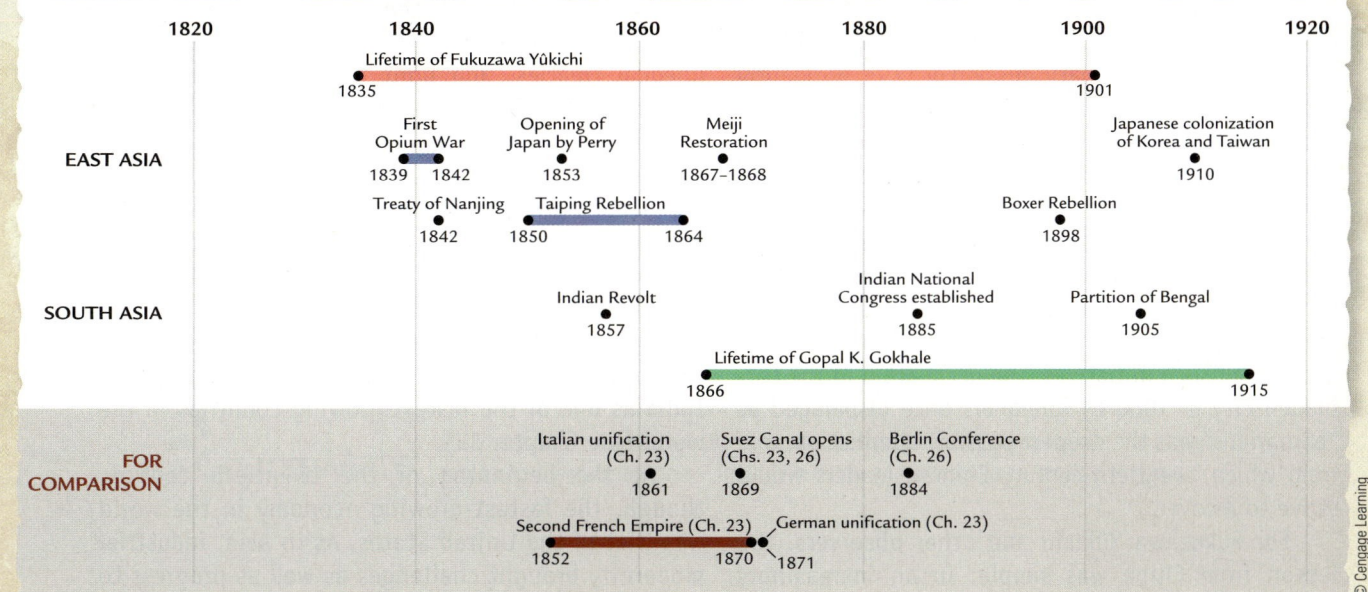

Timeline:

| | 1820 | 1840 | 1860 | 1880 | 1900 | 1920 |

EAST ASIA

Lifetime of Fukuzawa Yūkichi — 1835 to 1901

First Opium War — 1839–1842
Opening of Japan by Perry — 1853
Meiji Restoration — 1867–1868
Japanese colonization of Korea and Taiwan — 1910

Treaty of Nanjing — 1842
Taiping Rebellion — 1850–1864
Boxer Rebellion — 1898

SOUTH ASIA

Indian Revolt — 1857
Indian National Congress established — 1885
Partition of Bengal — 1905

Lifetime of Gopal K. Gokhale — 1866 to 1915

FOR COMPARISON

Italian unification (Ch. 23) — 1861
Suez Canal opens (Chs. 23, 26) — 1869
Berlin Conference (Ch. 26) — 1884

Second French Empire (Ch. 23) — 1852–1870
German unification (Ch. 23) — 1871

© Cengage Learning

Asia in the Modern World

Even prior to 1800, Asian societies were contending with the challenges of modernity. Commercial expansion and the growth of cities in the seventeenth and eighteenth centuries were signs of economic and social dynamism but strained the cultural traditions and political institutions in Mughal India, Qing China, and Tokugawa Japan (see Chapter 20). This was the world of Fukuzawa Yūkichi's childhood, one in which his family's samurai traditions were no longer in sync with the evolution of Japanese society.

Rapid population growth was an even greater modern challenge: China's population grew from about 110 million in 1600 to 330 million in 1800, India's from approximately 100 million to 225 million, and Japan's from 12 million to 30 million. During the eighteenth-century agricultural revolution in Britain, innovators like Joseph Banks brought greater productivity to rural areas (while displacing many farmers in the process; see Chapter 21). In contrast, the growth of food production in Asia was largely *extensive* rather than *intensive*, requiring peasant communities to bring marginal lands under cultivation to keep pace with population growth. In manufacturing as well, Asian growth was based on the abundance of cheap labor rather than on innovations leading to higher productivity per worker.

By the early nineteenth century, the Industrial Revolution in the West had greatly magnified the difference in economic productivity between western Europe and South and East Asia (see Chapter 23). By the mid-nineteenth century, industrialization and its new technologies gave European nations both the motive and the means to intervene more forcefully in Asian affairs.

India was already feeling the impact in the late eighteenth century (see Chapter 20). In gradually expanding British East India Company authority at the expense of the Mughal empire, the British took advantage of the centrifugal force of Indian regionalism. At first the British largely accommodated themselves to Indian languages and cultures, but after 1800, and especially after the rebellion of 1857, they formed a tightly bound ruling clique. In responding to British rule, Indian reformers faced

699

Pauline Johnson-Tekahionwake (1861–1913) watched nervously as several older male poets recited their verse. It was the winter of 1892, and the hall in Toronto was packed for an "Evening with Canadian Authors." Her ambition was to be a well-known, financially independent poet, and here was her chance to make an impression. She chose to recite "A Cry from an Indian Wife," a poem that focused on her concern with Canada's First Nations, its indigenous inhabitants:

Pauline Johnson-Tekahionwake

(Vancouver Public Library, Special Collections, 9429. Photographer: Cochran Brantford, Ontario)

They but forget we Indians owned the land
     From ocean unto ocean; that they stand
Upon a soil that centuries agone
Was our sole kingdom and our right alone.
They never think how they would feel today,
If some great nation came from far away,
Wresting their country from their hapless braves,
Giving what they gave us—but war and graves . . .
Go forth, nor bend to greed of white man's hands,
By right, by birth we Indians own these lands,
Though starved, crushed, plundered, lies our nation low . . .
Perhaps the white man's God has willed it so.[*]

---

[*]Excerpt from *Flint and Feather: The Complete Poems of E. Pauline Johnson (Tekahionwake)*. Copyright © 1969 Hodder and Stoughton, pp. 17–20.

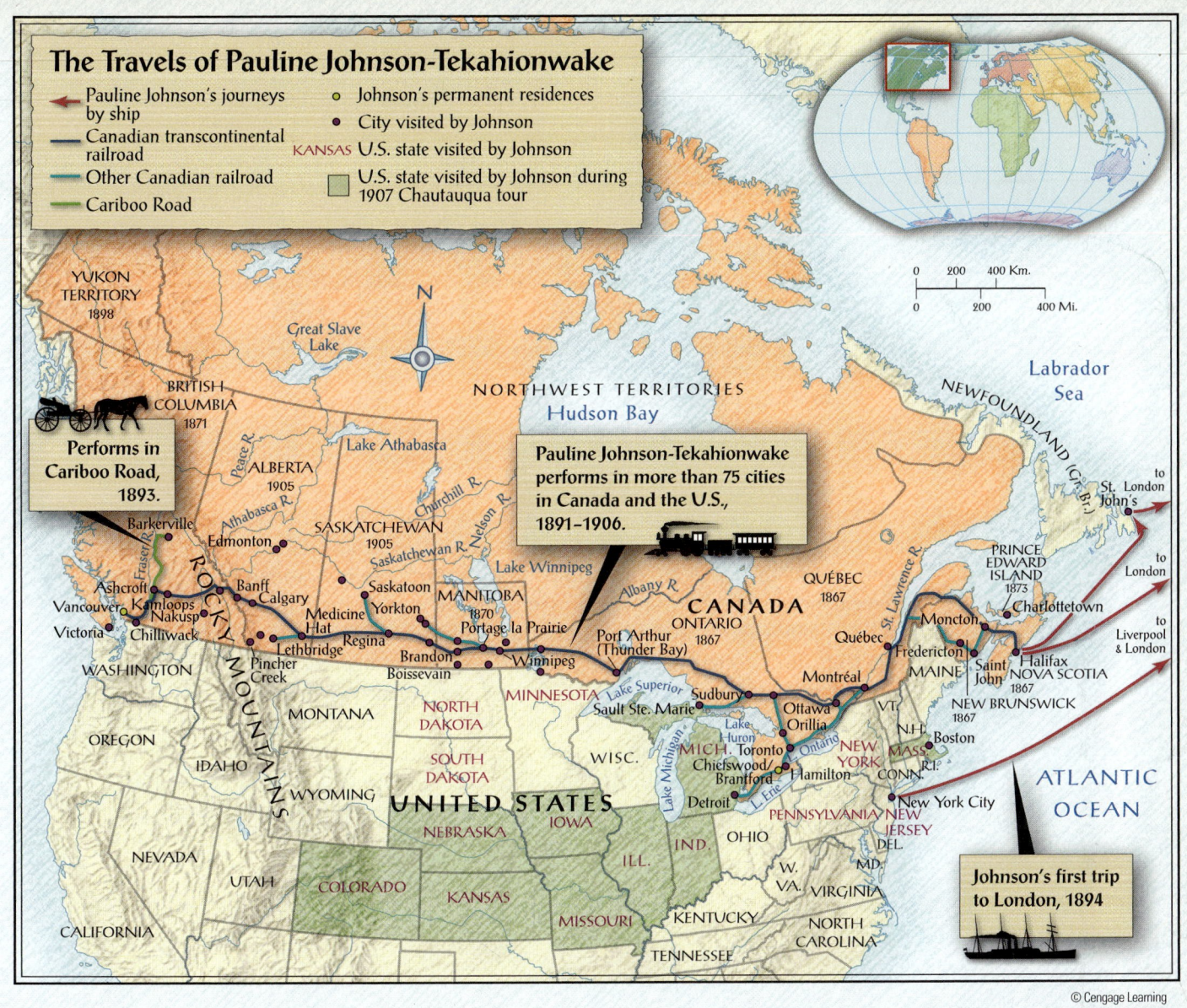

The Travels of Pauline Johnson-Tekahionwake

Legend:
- ← Pauline Johnson's journeys by ship
- Canadian transcontinental railroad
- Other Canadian railroad
- Cariboo Road
- ○ Johnson's permanent residences
- ● City visited by Johnson
- KANSAS U.S. state visited by Johnson
- U.S. state visited by Johnson during 1907 Chautauqua tour

Performs in Cariboo Road, 1893.

Pauline Johnson-Tekahionwake performs in more than 75 cities in Canada and the U.S., 1891–1906.

Johnson's first trip to London, 1894

© Cengage Learning

Join this chapter's traveler on "Voyages," an interactive tour of historic sites and events: **www.cengagebrain.com**

Patriotic Canadians might have heard these as dissonant words; nevertheless, they gave Johnson's powerful performance loud applause.

"A Cry from an Indian Wife" reflected Johnson's own mixed ancestry. Her father's family was Mohawk, an Iroquois (IR-uh-kwoi) band that had established a close alliance with the British during the colonial period. As a child, Pauline would listen to Mohawk legends and tales of a family history that included Joseph Brant, the Mohawk leader who had fought with the British in the American War of Independence (see Chapter 22). The British family connection went deeper when Pauline's father married an Englishwoman. Their wedding photograph shows optimism toward this cultural mixture: the groom wears both British medals and an Iroquois wampum belt, while the English bride's stiff Victorian attire is offset by the ceremonial tomahawk she holds in her lap.

Pauline Johnson-Tekahionwake (1861–1913) Canadian poet of mixed English and Mohawk ancestry.

703

Pauline's father balanced two worlds, serving as both a Canadian government employee and a respected member of the Six Nations Band Council. Her mother instilled strict Victorian values in her children on the Six Nations Reserve in Ontario. Johnson-Tekahionwake (da-geh-eeon-WA-geh) would have a lifelong challenge trying to balance her Mohawk heritage with her English ancestry. Though she grew up on the Iroquois reserve, she spoke only English, and though fascinated by Mohawk tales, she was most influenced by British literature. She was a loyal and patriotic Canadian, yet she spoke out against her country's policies toward indigenous First Nations societies.

As an adult, Pauline Johnson began to use her father's Mohawk family name, Tekahionwake ("double life"), in advertisements for a new career: traveling across Canada performing her poetry. Before radio and movies, there was a big audience for traveling artists, and Pauline Johnson-Tekahionwake became one of the nation's best-known entertainers. Her performances drew attention to her dual heritage. She appeared on stage in a dramatic buckskin outfit to perform poems such as "A Cry from an Indian Wife," after intermission reappearing in a Victorian evening gown to recite poems of nature and love. Having found a way to earn a living through her art—a challenge for a woman of her time—Johnson-Tekahionwake crossed Canada nineteen times, often performing in the United States as well, before retiring to Vancouver on the Pacific coast, where she collected native stories.

But the late nineteenth century was a difficult time for a mixed-race person. Racial divisions were becoming more and more sharply drawn in Canada, where the white majority thought that Amerindian peoples were doomed to disappear in the face of industrial and commercial progress. The engine of progress, symbolized by the very railroad that Johnson used to reach her audience, threatened to over-run anyone who stood in its way.

Indeed, the nineteenth century was a time of relentless change across the Western Hemisphere. In 1830, much of North and South America still lay outside the control of European-derived governments. By 1895, revolutionary changes in transportation and communications technologies, along with the arrival of many new European immigrants, had changed the balance of power. The frontiers of modern nations expanded at the expense of indigenous peoples. Industrialization, mining, and commercial forestry and agriculture became the keys to wealth and power in the Americas.

Perhaps the most striking feature of this period was the rise of the United States as both the dominant hemispheric power and a global force. Canada was also a growing economic power, where many shared in rising prosperity. In Latin America, where industrialization lagged behind, only privileged elites enjoyed the benefits of state building.

Telegraphs, steamships and railroads, massive new cities, and enormous industrial fortunes helped consolidate the power of national states, while posing challenges to many older ways of life. Social readjustments in the nineteenth-century Americas included the abolition of slavery, the arrival of new immigrants, changing gender relations, and, as Johnson-Tekahionwake's story indicates, difficult times for indigenous peoples.

Focus Questions

» What challenges did Canada and the United States need to over-come in establishing themselves as transcontinental powers?

» What factors help explain conditions of inequality in nineteenth-century Latin America?

» Across the Americas, did nineteenth-century developments repre-sent progress for indigenous peoples, ethnic and racial minorities, and women?

Political Consolidation in Canada and the United States

Consolidation of state power was a major feature of the nineteenth century in North America. Canada overcame deep regional divisions to become a nation, while the United States emerged from the Civil War with a more powerful and ambitious federal government than ever before. In both cases, governments extended their authority more deeply into society and more broadly across expanded territories as increased immigration from Europe brought the Great Plains and the Pacific coast under the control of Ottawa and Washington.

Confederation in Canada

Canada was a product of slow evolution rather than revolutionary transformation. In 1830, British North America consisted of more than half a dozen discon-nected colonies. Yet by 1892, when Pauline Johnson-Tekahionwake made her debut on a Toronto stage, Canadians possessed a national identity even while affiliating themselves with the British empire. Like many, Johnson-Tekahionwake was proud of being both Canadian and British: *"And we, the men of Canada, can face the world and brag/That we were born in Canada beneath the British flag."*[*]

In 1830, British North America contained a diversity of peoples and land-scapes. Upper Canada, with its capital at Toronto on the northern shore of Lake Ontario, was the fastest-growing region, where cheap land attracted English, Irish, and Scottish immigrants. Lower Canada, the lands along the St. Lawrence River now known as Québec, retained its French-speaking Catholic majority, the *Québe-cois* (kay-bek-KWAH). The Atlantic colonies were primarily populated by seafaring people dependent on the bounty of the Atlantic Ocean. And at the opposite end was British Columbia, its Pacific capital of Victoria more accessible to San Fran-cisco than to Toronto. Far from the main population centers lay trading posts that brought commercial opportunity to the frontier, but also guns, alcohol, and vio-lence to indigenous communities (see Chapter 18).

Several First Nations, such as the Cree, Ojibwa (oh-JIB-wuh), Sioux (soo), and Squamish (SKWAW-mish), lived on the Great Plains and remained indepen-dent in the early nineteenth century. Mingled among them were communities

[*]Excerpt from *Flint and Feather: The Complete Poems of E. Pauline Johnson (Tekahionwake)*. Copyright © 1969 Hodder and Stoughton, pp. 81–83.

Library and Archive of Canada. acc. 1973-84-1

A Métis Man and His Wives The métis of the Canadian frontier were culturally and biologically mixed descendants of French traders and First Nations women. Protective of their independence, many métis resisted incorporation into the Canadian confederation, often in alliance with First Nations communities. These rebellions were defeated by Canadian forces in 1869 and 1885.

responsible government
Nineteenth-century constitutional arrangement in North America that allowed colonies to achieve dominion status within the British empire and elect parliaments responsible for internal affairs. The British appointed governors as their sovereign's representative and retained control of foreign policy.

of French-speaking *métis* (may-TEE), frontiersmen of mixed European-Amerindian descent. Farther from the main areas of European settlement and British control were the Inuit hunters of the far north.

Having learned from the American War of Independence to accommodate settlers' political ambitions, the British government offered Britons who emigrated to British North America (or to Australia, New Zealand, or South Africa) limited participation in government, while still appointing a governor from London to watch out for British imperial interests. By 1830, however, this compromise had not achieved stability. British North Americans called for **responsible government**, an elected parliamentary government in which the leader of the majority party would become prime minister. By the 1840s, as the climate for reform increased in Britain, an official report recommended responsible government for Canada, while new policies cut British tariffs on North American goods, such as timber, fish, and grain, flowing to British markets. Previously, the mercantilist logic of direct imperial control had limited economic growth; now the removal of the old restrictions led to a boom in trade, especially with the United States.

In this atmosphere of reform, even French Canadians favored continued association with the British empire. As far back as 1763 the British Parliament had guaranteed equal rights for French-speaking Catholics. Though the influx of British settlers alarmed the Québecois, most trusted that British constitutional models would protect their linguistic, religious, and cultural traditions. Likewise, many First Nations peoples in Canada favored continuing association with the British empire. For the Johnson family, whose ancestors had fought alongside the British for generations, the beneficence of Britain and of Queen Victoria was unquestioned.

Meanwhile, the American Civil War (1861–1865; discussed in the next section) gave the British a further incentive to settle the constitutional status of Canada. While most British subjects in North America were antislavery, and while Canada served as a terminus for the underground railway of escaped slaves, others were sympathetic to the Confederate cause, prompting fears of invasion by Union forces. With American interests already prominent in the Canadian economy, the British were now even more anxious to retain their political predominance.

In 1867 the British Parliament passed the British North America Act, creating the **Confederation of Canada** with a federal capital at Ottawa. Though only four of the current Canadian provinces were included in the original confederation, a legal framework for its further evolution was established. Canada was now a "dominion" within the British empire in which local affairs, including economic and taxation policy, were in the hands of the Canadian and provincial governments. However, Queen Victoria appointed a governor-general to represent the Crown, and Britain continued to control Canada's foreign relations.

Political consolidation and economic growth went hand in hand after 1867, facilitated by the building of the **Canadian Pacific Railway** (1867–1884). The railway led to the incorporation of new provinces (Manitoba, the Northwest Territories, and British Columbia), while utterly transforming Canada's Great Plains.

Before the Industrial Revolution, only buffalo and, later, horses and cattle could convert the tough grasses of the plains into nutrients for human populations. Now, with the advent of cheap steel plows and the inexpensive transport provided by the Canadian Pacific Railway and the local railway routes feeding into it, grain production boomed. Canadian wheat exports rose from 10 million bushels in 1896 to 145 million bushels in 1914. Over a million farmers and their families took advantage of free land and the cheap agricultural implements churned out by the new industrial plants and moved out onto the prairie. They were the audience for Pauline Johnson-Tekahionwake as she took her act to the town halls and opera houses springing up in farming centers and mining camps. Marking the rise of the Canadian west, Alberta and Saskatchewan (sa-SKACH-uh-won) entered the confederation in 1905.

Economic growth was promoted by a stable and effective federal government. Twenty-five years of Conservative Party dominance ended in 1896, followed by four consecutive elections won by the Liberals, with a strong centrist base. The Liberal Party emphasized "race fusion," acknowledging Canada as a bicultural land where English and French, Protestant and Catholic, could live in peace, forging a Canadian identity based on mutual tolerance. Canadians did not always live up to that ideal: Amerindians and Asian immigrants were subject to sometimes brutal racism. Still, at least for racially and economically dominant Canadians, a unique nationalism accommodating Canada's affiliation with the British empire was taking shape.

Confederation of Canada
(1867) Confederation of former British colonies united under a single federal constitution. Recognized under the British North America Act, the confederation was a dominion within the British empire.

Canadian Pacific Railway
(1881–1885) The railway's completion led to the transcontinental integration of Canada and opened Canada's Great Plains to European settlement.

Sectionalism and Civil War in the United States

Unlike Canada, the United States entered the nineteenth century with a strong constitution and a lively sense of national identity. (See the feature "Movement of Ideas Through Primary Sources: Alexis de Tocqueville's *Democracy in America*.") The Louisiana Purchase of 1803 gave the young country a sense of unbounded opportunity (see Map 25.1). The way was open as never before for the westward expansion of the United States. But westward expansion also provoked crisis. As new states entered the Union, would they be slave states or free? Could balance between the North and South be maintained in the scramble for new territory? Would American nationalism prove stronger than American sectionalism?

An important context for those questions was the massive economic expansion of the United States in the first half of the nineteenth century, what historians have called a "market revolution." The agrarian republic foreseen by Thomas Jefferson was made obsolete by the technological advances of the Industrial Revolution, which led to an economy focused on factories, cities, and market-oriented farming in the North and, in the South, the massive expansion of cotton production to meet the demands of the booming textile industry in Britain (see Chapter 23).

Better roads and, especially, canals and railways linked producers with markets in ways never before possible. The completion in 1825 of the 363-mile Erie Canal, for example, connected the Great Lakes with New York City, drastically lowering the transportation costs of grain exports to eastern cities and across the Atlantic. The Southern economy was also booming: by 1803 cotton had already become the largest U.S. export; by 1860 cotton made up more than half the value of exports. But the economies of North and South were diverging further as a result. Debates over federal government tariff policies on imported manufactured goods, intended to promote Northern industry but resisted by Southern cotton planters, heightened sectional political tensions.

Andrew Jackson
(in office 1829–1837)
The seventh president of the United States after first serving in the military as general and in Congress as senator; a symbol of the expansion of voting rights and an aggressive advocate of westward expansion.

Populism and expanded democracy marked the presidency of **Andrew Jackson** (in office 1829–1837). Unlike previous American presidents from elite New England or Virginia families, Jackson presented himself as representing the common man, emphasizing his humble roots rather than his experiences as a slaveholder and plantation owner. His followers also made much of his military leadership in the War of 1812. Jackson's emphasis on populist democracy was symbolized by his inauguration party: he threw the doors of the White House open to one and all, and a riot nearly broke out. Indeed, politics in the United States was becoming more fractious in the 1820s as the nation became more democratic. Expanded voting rights brought popular passions to the political stage as new states entering the Union allowed all free men to vote and the established eastern states reduced or eliminated property qualifications.

Jackson was an advocate of limited central government, as shown by his battle to eliminate the federally chartered Bank of the United States and leave banking to the states. Still, Jackson was sometimes forced to defend the prerogatives of Washington, as he did effectively when the legislature of South Carolina attempted to unilaterally nullify the congressional tariff legislation of 1828. The question of how best to balance federal and state power was still unresolved when Jackson left office, feeding further the sectional division between the North, where many supported an enhanced federal role, and the South, where states' rights advocates were dominant.

Westward expansion exacerbated the conflict. Already in 1820, the question of whether the new state of Missouri would allow slavery had bitterly divided the

American Congress and the American people. The question intensified after 1848 with the U.S. victory in the Mexican-American War (discussed in the next section), when huge territories—Texas, California, the Great Plains, the desert Southwest, and the Rocky Mountains—were added to the United States. Would those vast spaces be settled by free white homesteaders or by plantation owners and black slaves?

The Democratic Party, which had become identified with Southern planter interests, declared that the issue should be decided by "popular sovereignty," meaning by the voters within the new states, a principle that had been accepted when Missouri entered the Union as a slave state. **Abraham Lincoln** (in office

Abraham Lincoln (in office 1861–1865) Sixteenth president of the United States and the country's first Republican president. His election on an antislavery platform led eleven states to secede from the Union, plunging the country into the American Civil War.

MAP 25.1 **U.S. Expansion, 1783–1867** The United States expanded dramatically during the decades after independence. Vast territories were purchased from France (the Louisiana Purchase) and Russia (Alaska), acquired by treaty with Great Britain (the Pacific Northwest) and Spain (Florida), and annexed from Mexico after its defeat in the Mexican-American War (the desert Southwest). Contemporary observers regarded the growth of the United States into a transcontinental power as such an inevitability that they called the process one of "manifest destiny." (© Cengage Learning)

Alexis de Tocqueville's *Democracy in America*

The French historian Alexis de Tocqueville first traveled to the United States in 1831 at the age of twenty-six, and at age thirty he published the original French version of *Democracy in America*. Later, as a deputy in the French National Assembly, he was a political moderate and opposed both the Socialists and Louis Napoleon (see Chapter 23). Based on extensive travels and personal observations, *Democracy in America* is still regarded as one of the most insightful analyses of the "American character" ever written.

Source: Alexis de Tocqueville, *Democracy in America*, http://xroads .virginia.edu/~HYPER/DETOC/toc_indx.html.

Author's Introduction

Among the novel objects that attracted my attention during my stay in the United States, nothing struck me more forcibly than the general equality of condition among the people. . . . The more I advanced in the study of American society, the more I perceived that this equality of condition is the fundamental fact from which all others seem to be derived and the central point at which all my observations constantly terminated.

On Patriotism

As the American participates in all that is done in his country, he thinks himself obliged to defend whatever may be censured in it; for it is not only his country that is then attacked, it is himself. . . . Nothing is more embarrassing in the ordinary intercourse of life than this irritable patriotism of the Americans. A stranger may be well inclined to praise many of the institutions of their country, but he begs permission to blame some things in it, a permission that is inexorably refused.

Geography and Democracy

The chief circumstance which has favored the establishment and the maintenance of a democratic republic in the United States is the nature of the territory that the Americans inhabit. Their ancestors gave them the love of equality and of freedom; but God himself gave them the means of remaining equal and free, by placing them upon a boundless continent. General prosperity is favorable to the stability of all governments, but more particularly of a democratic one, which depends upon the will of the majority, and especially upon the will of that portion of the community which is most exposed to want. . . . In the United States not only is legislation democratic, but Nature herself favors the cause of the people.

In what part of human history can be found anything similar to what is passing before our eyes in North America? The celebrated communities of antiquity were all founded in the midst of hostile nations, which they were obliged to subjugate before they could flourish in their place. Even the moderns have found, in some parts of South America, vast regions inhabited by a people of inferior civilization, who nevertheless had already occupied and cultivated the soil. To found their new states it was necessary to extirpate or subdue a numerous population. . . . But North

America was inhabited only by wandering tribes, who had no thought of profiting by the natural riches of the soil; that vast country was still, properly speaking, an empty continent, a desert land awaiting its inhabitants. . . .

Three or four thousand soldiers drive before them the wandering races of the aborigines; these are followed by the pioneers, who pierce the woods, scare off the beasts of prey, explore the courses of the inland streams, and make ready the triumphal march of civilization across the desert. . . . Millions of men are marching at once towards the same horizon; their language, their religion, their manners differ; their object is the same. Fortune has been promised to them somewhere in the West, and to the West they go to find it. . . .

Religion and Democracy

The Americans combine the notions of Christianity and of liberty so intimately in their minds that it is impossible to make them conceive the one without the other. . . .

In France I had almost always seen the spirit of religion and the spirit of freedom marching in opposite directions. . . .

[American Catholics] attributed the peaceful dominion of religion in their country mainly to the separation of church and state. I do not hesitate to affirm that during my stay in America I did not meet a single individual, of the clergy or the laity, who was not of the same opinion on this point. . . .

Associations and Civil Society

In no country in the world has the principle of association been more successfully used or applied to a greater multitude of objects than in America. . . . The citizen of the United States is taught from infancy to rely upon his own exertions in order to resist the evils and the difficulties of life; he looks upon the social authority with an eye of mistrust and anxiety, and he claims its assistance only when he is unable to do without it. . . . If some public pleasure is concerned, an association is formed to give more splendor and regularity to the entertainment. Societies are formed to resist evils that are exclusively of a moral nature. . . . In the United States associations are established to promote the public safety, commerce, industry, morality, and religion. There is no end which the human will despairs of attaining through the combined power of individuals united into a society.

Tyranny of the Majority

I know of no country in which there is so little independence of mind and real freedom of discussion as in America. In any constitutional state in Europe every sort of religious and political theory may be freely preached and disseminated. . . . In America the majority raises formidable barriers around the liberty of opinion; within these barriers an author may write what he pleases, but woe to him if he goes beyond them.

QUESTIONS FOR ANALYSIS

» What does de Tocqueville see as the most essential features of American civilization, and what does he identify as its strengths and weaknesses?

» Are the Frenchman's observations still relevant to an understanding of the United States today?

1861–1865), a leader of the new Republican Party founded by antislavery activists in 1854, disagreed. To put the issue in the hands of territorial voters, Lincoln declared, would be little more than giving them *"the liberty of making a slave of other people."* More than most Northern politicians, Lincoln stressed the moral dimension of the question. He was opposed to the westward spread of slavery *"because of the monstrous injustice of slavery itself."*[1] Other Republicans opposed slavery not because it was wrong but because they thought that slavery was incompatible with the spread of the free, independent farmers they saw as the bedrock of society.

For many white Southerners, Lincoln and the Republican Party were a threat to freedoms long protected by the sovereignty of the states. Republicans represented a hard-edged industrialism that contrasted with the gracious Southern way of life based on virtues like valor and honor. After all, some argued, sick or elderly slaves were cared for by their masters, while industrial workers injured on the job were thrown into the street.

After Lincoln's election in 1860, these divisions could no longer be bridged: *"A house divided against itself,"* he said, *"cannot stand."* Eleven Southern states declared their independence as the Confederate States of America, plunging the country into civil war (1861–1865). Some people, thinking the war would soon be over, brought picnics to witness the first battles. They did not account for the technological changes that made modern warfare more deadly. Increasingly precise weapons and powerful explosives, combined with tactics that threw masses of uniformed soldiers in waves upon each other, led to suffering on an unimagined scale. Over six hundred thousand people died, the most in any American armed conflict.

The fight between Union and Confederate forces was an unequal one in terms of resources. The North had a clear superiority in industrial infrastructure: railroads for moving men and material, iron foundries to produce guns and munitions, and textile factories to produce uniforms. The Confederates had several less tangible advantages: superior military leadership and soldiers who believed deeply in their cause and were fighting to defend their homes. However, the South's export-oriented agricultural economy left it vulnerable to a Union naval blockade. The Confederate states were highly dependent on British markets for tobacco and cotton and British factories for arms and ammunition. Unable to match the productivity of Northern farms and factories, by 1865 Southern resistance was overwhelmed.

In 1863 Lincoln had issued the Emancipation Proclamation, making the abolition of slavery, rather than the mere preservation of the Union, a goal of the war. After the Union victory in 1865, the federal government was in a position to finally settle the question that had been left unresolved at the Constitutional Convention: how could the principle of liberty be reconciled with the reality of slavery? More immediately, how should the Northern victors treat their vanquished foes? The assassination of Abraham Lincoln in 1865 meant that the most able American politician would not be there to help resolve such issues.

Reconstruction
(1865–1877) Period immediately after the American Civil War during which the federal government took control of the former Confederate states and oversaw enforcement of constitutional provisions guaranteeing civil rights for freed slaves.

Federal troops occupied the South to ensure that federal law was observed as part of a process known as **Reconstruction**. White Southerners resented the occupation and the assertions of Republicans that the South should be remade in a Northern image. In spite of new constitutional amendments intended to protect the civil and voting rights of freed slaves, Southern politicians in the Democratic Party sought to end Reconstruction and restore a race-based system of governance. The presidential election of 1876 was a major turning point. The Democratic candidate won a narrow majority of the popular vote, but the results in several states were disputed. An electoral commission gave all the disputed states to the Republican candidate, Rutherford B. Hayes. Southern Democrats were convinced to accept this outcome when Hayes agreed to withdraw federal troops from the former Confederacy and to put an end to Reconstruction.

For some, the end of Reconstruction was a positive development; they felt Reconstruction had unconstitutionally magnified the power of the federal government at the expense of the states. But for Southern blacks, "states' rights" was a disaster. Vigilante violence against blacks increased dramatically, and Southern state legislatures enacted segregationist policies that came to be known as Jim Crow laws. Like Russian serfs, who were emancipated at about the same time (see Chapter 23), freed American slaves discovered that their freedom was far from complete.

The American Civil War had several important global implications. First, the conflict showed the more tightly interconnected nature of the global economy in the age of industry. When the fighting disrupted cotton exports from the American South, a surge in the price of raw cotton on global markets resulted. British textile manufacturers were hard hit, while alternative cotton producers benefited (such as those in Egypt; see Chapter 26). Other globally relevant lessons of the American Civil War were the pivotal role of industry in determining its outcome, and the degree of civilian mobilization required to keep large armies in the field for such an extended period. Not until the world wars of the twentieth century, however, would the terrible cost of industrialized conflict be fully realized.

The Gilded Age

After the Union victory the United States experienced a spurt of population growth and productivity. As in Canada, the opening of the Great Plains to European settlement and agriculture brought huge economic dividends. As the price of steel fell, even farmers of modest means could afford steel plows to cut the prairie soils as the spread of railroads and steamships lowered transport costs and made commercial agriculture possible in more regions. Increased agricultural production led to falling grain prices in the cities, where industrial employment surged. Silver and gold booms hastened the opening of the American West and brought a flood of investment capital to the nation's banks.

Urbanization was a key development, as the percentage of Americans living in cities rose from roughly 10 percent in 1850 to over 30 percent by 1890, by which time Philadelphia had over a million residents and New York nearly 2 million. Most dramatic was the growth of Chicago: the "city with broad shoulders" served as the principal hub for the processing and transport of agricultural goods from the West, growing from merely thirty thousand citizens in 1850 to over a million by 1890. Further west, St. Louis served as a gateway to expanding western settlement.

During the last two decades of the nineteenth century, the United States took a leadership position in the Second Industrial Revolution, when electricity and steel supplemented steam and iron and when huge steel firms and railroads exceeded any level of economic organization the world had ever seen. Mark Twain, the great American author and humorist, called it a **Gilded Age**. (A gilded object is covered with gold on the outside, concealing base metal within.) Yet beyond the fortunes of the most privileged were a host of problems: grinding rural poverty across the South; an urban working class crammed into dirty and unsafe tenements in the industrial North; and political favors for sale to the highest bidder. Exuberant growth created deep inequalities: by 1890 less than 1 percent of the U.S. population controlled 90 percent of the nation's wealth.

Gilded Age
Period of economic prosperity in the United States in the last two decades of the nineteenth century, when the opulence displayed by the wealthy masked the poverty, political corruption, and unsafe living and occupational conditions for the working class.

Orphans of the Gilded Age This image of street children in New York was captured in the 1880s by Jacob Riis, a Danish-American social reformer who used such photographs to bring the middle class's attention to the distress of those left behind by surging American economic growth.

In reaction to the inequalities of the Gilded Age, small farmers in the Midwest and Plains states organized a movement against corporate interests that controlled the storing and shipping of grain. At the same time, industrial workers began to form unions to fight for better pay and working conditions. Some Americans advocated socialism, thinking that capitalism would never serve the greater good. But they remained a minority. When most Americans demanded equality, what they really meant was opportunity.

In 1893 the nation celebrated its self-confidence at the World's Columbian Exposition held in Chicago, designed to surpass the world's fair held the previous year in Paris. Chicago, the most rapidly growing city in the Americas, sponsored the construction of a dazzling model city, featuring the world's first Ferris Wheel as a response to the Eiffel Tower of Paris. It was the first time that many arriving from farms and small towns had ever seen electric lights. The Columbian Exposition was a monument to "progress."

Attending the fair was Frederick Jackson Turner, a historian from the University of Wisconsin and author of the paper "The Significance of the Frontier in American History." Turner noted that the cultural and political development of the United States had been predicated on the availability of an open frontier. The lack of class enmity in American life, compared with the harsher social conflict in Europe, had everything to do with the frontier mentality. American democracy itself was a product of the frontier, Turner argued (ignoring the people who had lived there prior to white settlement). Now, however, the frontier was closing. How would Americans deal with these changed circumstances?

There were indeed signs that American society was in trouble. Economic boom turned to bust in 1873 as overproduction led to a business slump, not just in the United States but in Europe as well. Thousands lost their jobs; farmers could not sell their grain or milk. The crisis was temporary, but the historian's question still deserved an answer. At century's end the United States was clearly no longer a frontier society but a modern industrial state. In the three decades following the Civil War, it had become the world's leading industrial *and* agricultural producer. In the twentieth century, the country would trade continental frontiers for global ones and make its influence felt among all the world's peoples.

Reform and Reaction in Latin America

Consolidation of state power also characterized nation-states in Latin America. As in Canada and the United States, Latin Americans had to overcome regional and sectional differences to develop effective national institutions. They also faced external challenges. In the middle of the nineteenth century, Mexico lost northern territory to the United States and then suffered a decade of French occupation. Domination by Europe and the United States skewed Latin American economic production toward foreign markets: overreliance on exports of agricultural produce and natural resources and imports of industrial goods and technologies hindered the development of integrated national economies.

Conservatives, Liberals, and the Struggle for Stability in Mexico

In 1821 Mexico won its independence from Spain under conservative ideas and leaders (see Chapter 22). Afterward, the government fell into the hands of ineffective soldier-politicians, the *caudillos* (cow-DEE-yos), of whom General Antonio Lopez de Santa Ana (1794–1876) was the most notorious. After independence, authorities proved incapable of dealing with the challenges that lay before them.

One major problem arose when Mexico's territorial integrity was challenged in its northern state of Texas. Traditionally, Mexico's wealth in people, resources, settled agriculture, and culture was in its central and southern parts. Texas, in contrast, was an untamed frontier with only a few officials and missionaries mixed in with the *vaquero* (vah-KAIR-oh) cowboys, Amerindians such as Apache and Comanche, and the occasional American adventurer. None of them paid much attention to Mexican authorities.

In the 1820s, Mexico attempted to stabilize this distant frontier by inviting English-speaking settlers into Texas. Most were Americans who planned to use slave labor to produce cotton. But since Mexico had already abolished slavery, the importation of slaves was illegal. President Santa Ana would either have to enforce that law or allow the Texans to flout his authority.

By 1836, when Santa Ana came north with his troops, there were thirty thousand American settlers in Texas. Unhappy with Mexican rule, these settlers allied with discontented Spanish-speaking Texans to fight for independence. Despite his victory at the Alamo, Santa Ana lost Texas to the better-organized and well-armed rebels. Initially, the rebels declared a republic, but a referendum in 1845 prepared the way for the U.S. annexation of Texas.

Mexico's loss of territory to the United States did not stop there. President James Polk, a Southern Democrat, pursued an aggressive policy toward Mexico, provoking war in 1846. U.S. forces penetrated to Mexico City, and the Treaty of Guadalupe Hidalgo (1848) gave the United States the northern half of Mexico.

Alta California entered the Union in 1850 as the state of California, adding its mineral wealth and fertile farmland to the United States. The desert Southwest and mountain West were open for white settlement. Mexico's "*Norte*" had become the American Southwest.

Responding to this humiliating loss and inspired by the European revolutions of 1848 (see Chapter 23), **Benito Juárez** (beh-NEE-toh WAH-rez) (1806–1872) and other middle-class Mexicans supported *La Reforma*, a movement to get rid of caudillo rule and create a more progressive Mexican nation. A Zapotec Amerindian, Juárez had struggled to advance in a society monopolized by the criollo elite (see Chapter 18). Nevertheless, he worked his way through law school and in 1848 was elected governor of the southern state of Oaxaca.

> **Benito Juárez** (1806–1872) Mexican statesman and politician who was intermittently president of Mexico during the 1860s and 1870s and leader of *La Reforma*. His liberal principles were enshrined in the Constitution of 1857.

Juárez and the liberals succeeded against conservative resistance, and the principles of *La Reforma* were enshrined in the Mexican Constitution of 1857. The new constitution restricted the privileges of the Catholic clergy and the military. Most liberals saw the church as restricting individualism and progress while upholding the power of the large landowners. The constitution also contained a Bill of Rights and established a strong unicameral legislature to offset executive power. The old caste system was eliminated: everyone was now equal before the law.

Conservatives, however, reacted angrily to such reforms, especially limitations on the church's power and the seizure of its land. While some in the church followed the earlier example of Father Hidalgo in supporting the rights of the majority (see Chapter 22), most priests allied with the conservative elites.

Contention between liberals and conservatives created an opening for the French emperor Napoleon III (see Chapter 23), who sent troops to Mexico in 1861. His stated intention was to force payments of Mexican debt, but his real motive was to resurrect a French empire in the Americas. The liberal government fought back. In 1862, on the fifth of May (*Cinco de Mayo*), a small army of Mexicans defeated a much larger French force at the Battle of Puebla. But Mexico lost the war after conservatives helped the French invaders take Mexico City. While pressure from Europe and the United States eventually forced the French to withdraw, the struggle between liberals and conservatives for control of Mexico continued until the death of Juárez in 1872.

The coming to power of **Porfirio Díaz** (1830–1915) in 1876 altered the balance in Mexican politics, since he himself was a political conservative but an economic liberal. Like the old caudillos, he ruled as dictator, and during his long tenure as president (1876–1880 and 1884–1911) he ignored the ideals of *La Reforma*, such as freedom of speech and assembly. He was, however, a firm believer in free trade and foreign investment. Mexico actively sought investments from Britain

The Granger Collection New York

Porfirio Díaz During his long rule Porfirio Díaz improved Mexico's transportation infrastructure and invited foreign investment. He did nothing, however, to address the country's deep social and economic inequalities, or to respond to the demands of liberal Mexicans for democratic reforms. Like many dictators in world history, he was fond of bestowing medals and honors on himself.

and the United States to help stimulate its economy. Economic development had political implications: the power of the state expanded, for example, as improved rail transportation gave the government greater access to the entire country.

Apart from railroads and mining, most new investment was in agriculture. Mexico had inherited from the colonial period a system of large landholdings known as *haciendas*. In the colonial era these large estates were only weakly connected to international markets; now, in response to the expansion of those markets, their owners intensively planted export crops like cotton, sugar, and hemp. Commercial agriculture brought great wealth to Mexico's landowners, its urban commercial class, and foreign investors. Many formerly self-sufficient peasants, however, were driven by poverty to work on these commercial plantations for very low wages.

Nineteenth-century liberals believed that social, political, and economic freedoms all progressed as part of the same package. But the late-nineteenth-century Mexican economy showed the limitations of that theory. The Díaz regime demonstrated to the world that the open markets espoused by classical liberalism could be combined with authoritarian political rule.

Spanish-Speaking South America

Simón Bolívar's vision of a great South American confederation had failed against regional diversities and the ambitions of politician-soldiers (see Chapter 22). By the 1830s, there were nine separate nations where the Spanish empire in South America had once been. As in Mexico, their economies were largely geared toward exporting raw materials for industrial processes completed elsewhere and then importing the finished products. Plantation owners, commercial intermediaries, political elites, and foreign investors all prospered, but farmers and laborers were left behind.

The story of Venezuela was fairly typical. The president, José Antonio Páez (1790–1873), was a self-made military leader for whom the liberation campaigns had been a personal opportunity as well as a political cause. Páez (PAH-ays) consolidated his power in typical caudillo fashion by forging an alliance with the old criollo aristocracy. While the president was a man of rough manners, fond of attending cockfights, the snobbish oligarchs were willing to overlook such behavior because Páez was able to control the common people.

Nevertheless, in the 1860s, after a brief civil war, Venezuelan reformers took charge and established a more liberal regime. Slavery was finally abolished, and the government borrowed money to build railroads and expand school facilities. Still, little changed: the export-oriented agricultural sector was controlled by an economic oligarchy with close ties to foreign investors.

Argentina was more economically successful. Railroads made it easier to get Argentine cattle to market, and the development of refrigerated steamship compartments in the 1860s brought European consumers Argentine beef. As the economy boomed, the capital, Buenos Aires, became one of the world's great cities. Cosmopolitan politicians, merchants, and lawyers enjoyed the city's broad boulevards, elegant plazas, and pleasant cafés. A growing working class, many of them recent immigrants from Italy, worked in meatpacking plants and other export-oriented industries. From their neighborhood cafés arose the sensual *tango*, Argentina's gift to musical culture.

Apart from Argentina, the most successful South American republic was Chile. As elsewhere in Latin America, conservatives and liberals, centralizers, and believers in provincial autonomy squared off for influence in Chilean politics, but here

Porfirio Díaz (1830–1915) President of Mexico during much of the last half of the nineteenth century and during the first decade of the twentieth century. While he ignored Mexican civil liberties, Díaz developed infrastructure and provided much-needed stability.

Library of Congress

Buenos Aires The Argentine capital of Buenos Aires was an exceptionally prosperous city in the first decade of the twentieth century. As in Paris, New York, and Berlin, automobiles were beginning to compete with horse-drawn carriages along its spacious boulevards.

War of the Pacific
(1879) War among Bolivia, Peru, and Chile over the natural resources of the Pacific coast. Chile emerged victorious, gaining international prestige, while Bolivia's loss made it a poor, landlocked country.

a conservative consensus emerged early on. The Catholic Church was especially powerful in Chile.

Political consensus may have been easier to achieve in Chile because of its success in competing with its neighbors, Peru and Bolivia. Starting in the 1840s, the three countries greatly benefited from *guano* (GWA-noh), or bird droppings, a valuable natural resource available along the Pacific coast: guano makes an excellent fertilizer, and the global expansion of commercial agriculture brought high prices for it. Of course, shoveling guano was not pleasant. When Chileans showed little interest, tens of thousands of Chinese laborers were transported to South America to do the job.

As guano deposits declined, Peru, Bolivia, and Chile began to develop nitrate mines in the same region as an alternative source of fertilizer. The intensifying competition among them led to the **War of the Pacific** in 1879. Chile's victory strongly enhanced its reputation: its political institutions strengthened, its economic situation improved, and Chileans developed a stronger sense of national identity. The war was disastrous for Bolivia, which became a land-locked country and one of the poorest societies in the Americas (see Map 25.2).

Still, even in Chile and Argentina, the most economically successful South American societies of the late nineteenth century, industrialization and urbanization lagged far behind the pace set by the United States and Canada. Production of raw materials and importation of manufactured goods remained the norm, as did foreign investors' hold on much of the profit from growth.

From Empire to Republic in Brazil

The largest country in South America, Brazil, followed a unique path, hardly surprising given its distinct ecology, demography, size, and relationship to Portugal. After Brazilian liberals declared the country's independence from Portugal in 1822, the heir to the Portuguese throne, already living in Brazil, agreed to serve as the new nation's constitutional monarch. Brazil therefore achieved independence much more quickly, and with less bloodshed, than other South American nations. (see Chapter 22).

Still, Brazil's principal political tensions were quite similar to those of its republican neighbors. Brazil's liberals, including its urban middle class, responded to progressive European trends, such as free trade and the protection of civil liberties, while the country's conservatives, large estate owners and military men,

MAP 25.2 **Latin America, ca. 1895** By 1895 all of the nations of South America and Central America were independent except for British, French, and Dutch Guyana. Bolivia became landlocked after losing the War of the Pacific in 1879 and ceding coastal territory to Chile. Panama seceded from Colombia in 1903 with military backing from the United States, which was anxious to protect its canal zone interests. Many Caribbean islands remained British, French, and Dutch colonies. However, Cuba was freed from Spanish rule in 1898, the same year the United States took control over Puerto Rico. Dense railroad networks were a sign of foreign investment in exports like minerals and livestock products, as seen here in Mexico, Chile, Argentina, Uruguay, and southern Brazil. (© Cengage Learning)

stressed traditional values such as the authority of the Catholic Church. The abolition of slavery, although a major liberal priority, was not achieved until 1888, later than anywhere else in the Americas.

In the nineteenth century, coffee replaced sugar as Brazil's primary export, a response to rising demand among newly affluent middle-class consumers in Europe and the United States. Plantations expanded inland from initial bases in the south, and by 1880 Brazil was the world's largest coffee producer. Rubber, another important Brazilian export, was closely tied to industrialization. The Brazilian government stimulated a rubber boom by granting gigantic land concessions, while improved transportation and communications technologies allowed Brazilian entrepreneurs, backed by foreign capital, to exploit the Amazon basin on a large scale. The Amazonian city of Manaus grew as fast as the mining towns of the western United States, its opulent opera house a symbol of the excesses that came with quick money. (See the feature "World History in Today's World: Agriculture and Amazonian Ecology.")

The rubber boom went bust, however, when production spread to Central Africa and Southeast Asia, while overexploitation led to declines in Amazonian yields (see Chapter 26). The rubber bust was matched by a sharp decline in coffee exports during a global economic slump in the 1890s. Brazil found itself in the same dependency trap as other South American nations: too reliant on exports of agricultural products and raw materials and on imports of industrial goods and technologies from Europe, and thus strongly exposed to downward trends in global markets.

At least the Brazilian economy finally became less reliant on slave labor. In the second half of the nineteenth century a surge of immigration provided Brazil with an alternative. The northeastern plantation regions, where the slave-plantation economy was centered, became less important as coffee, cattle, and grain production surged in the south. Abolitionist sentiment grew, the emperor was deposed, and in 1889 Brazil finally became a republic, with the motto *"Order and Progress"* proudly displayed on its new green and gold flag. Slavery was finally purged from the Western Hemisphere.

The Nineteenth-Century Americas in Perspective

All across the Americas, changes resulted from integration into global markets and consolidation of state power. One general result was the elimination of Amerindian sovereignty. In 1830, many indigenous societies still governed their own affairs; by 1895 such independence remained only in the most remote regions. As ever larger numbers of European immigrants crossed the Atlantic and slavery ended, racial demographics changed in diverse ways. Just as important were changes in gender roles. Pauline Johnson-Tekahionwake was not the only woman seeking greater autonomy in late-nineteenth-century society, when an increasingly organized women's movement was articulating a platform of voting rights and social equality.

The Fates of Indigenous Societies

The nineteenth century was decisive for America's indigenous peoples. Before the Industrial Revolution, Amerindian societies in regions as diverse as the Andes, the Arctic, Amazonia, and the Great Plains retained control over their own political, social, and cultural lives. Some, like the Johnson family and other Iroquois on the Six Nations Reserve, maintained connections with settler societies while balancing old traditions and new influences. But by the end of the century Amerindian sovereignty had disappeared.

Agriculture and Amazonian Ecology

The Amazonian rainforest appears so lush that we might assume its soils to be almost endlessly fertile. That is not the case. Fertility in the Brazilian Amazon is concentrated in the multiple layers of forest canopy, not at the ground level, where nutrients are quickly recycled by plant life rather than stored in the soil. The ecology of the rainforest is more fragile than it appears.

The explosion of agriculture in today's Brazilian Amazon threatens that delicate balance. The cycle begins with illegal roads cut into the forest by loggers anxious to reach mahogany trees that fetch a high price on world markets. Then farmers use those roads to gain access to the deeper interior for their fields. Their activities are often illegal, contravening Brazil's environmental laws and the legal rights of Amerindian peoples. Still, the culture of land grabbing, facilitated by official corruption and negligence, continues.

Farmers' use of the slash-and-burn technique magnifies the problem. Burning the forest canopy releases nutrients into the soil, resulting in bumper crops in the initial harvest. After a season or two, however, that fertility is exhausted and there is no way to replenish it. Then farmers leave the blighted land, move on to even more remote locations, and repeat the process.

Scientists fear the arrival of an ecological tipping point at which the forest will be damaged beyond any hope of recovery. At least 40 percent of the Amazonian forest cover has disappeared in the past four decades, and the rate of depletion is accelerating. Since the Amazon creates half of its own rainfall through the moisture released by its plant life, recent periodic droughts may become permanent in the next few decades.

There is no question that Brazil needs to harness the resources of the Amazon in its quest to remain one of the world's fastest-growing economies (see Chapter 32). In the past decade Brazil has surpassed the United States as the world's leading soybean producer, for example, and the Amazon has played a major role. In 2011, the country signed a long-term agreement to export soybeans to China, projecting years of increased output. And most of the Amazon's soybeans are used not as human food but as feed for chickens, cattle, and, especially in China, pigs. It is a very inefficient and environmentally damaging process, taking 16 pounds of grain to produce just 1 pound of meat.

If sustainability is not achieved in Amazonian agriculture, however, not only will Brazil face a steep loss in productivity, but the whole world will suffer. Currently, photosynthesis in the Amazon converts carbon dioxide into 20 percent of all the oxygen in the earth's atmosphere. Can future generations live without it?

In Mexico, for example, following independence in 1821, Mayan-speaking villagers on the Yucatán (yoo-kah-TAHN) peninsula continued to live much as before, with little reference to Spanish-speaking government officials. They grew maize, beans, and other staple crops, in communities deeply rooted in the pre-Columbian past. Although Christians, their Catholicism was a mixture of local and imported beliefs. Now part of a wider network as both producers and consumers, their self-sufficiency nevertheless allowed them to choose their own terms of contact with the outside world.

By the 1840s, commercial agriculture in the Yucatán was booming. At first, planters of sugar and *henequen* (a fibrous plant used for rope making) could not attract Amerindian workers at the wages they were willing to offer. Just at this time, however, Mexican tax collectors were becoming more visible and aggressive because of the expensive wars with Texas. Forced, in many cases for the first time, to produce cash to pay their taxes, peasants resorted to debt peonage (see Chapter 18). Formerly independent peasants were becoming almost like slave laborers on large estates.

Meanwhile, the Spanish-speaking elite of the Yucatán revolted against the authority of Mexico City and declared the peninsula's independence. Taking advantage of the disarray, a small group of Maya militants began a guerrilla campaign in 1847 known as the **Yucatán Rebellion**, attacking both Mexican government officials and local oligarchs, the owners of the large commercial haciendas. Since the Mexican army was occupied with war against the United States, the rebels soon controlled over half of the Yucatán peninsula. Once the war in the north was over, however, Mexican officials redeployed their forces against the Maya rebels.

Mexican liberals, under the Zapotec leader Benito Juárez, saw the Maya as primitive folk standing in the way of "progress." Nation building and market economics were engines of progress, and the Yucatán rebels were attacking both. Although government authority had largely been reasserted by the 1850s, scattered fighting in defense of Maya sovereignty continued until 1895. By then the economic autonomy of the Yucatán Maya had been broken: the need for cash to pay their taxes had driven them to low-wage peonage on plantations producing agricultural commodities for export.

In the United States, the dominant society had no use for Amerindians even as subservient laborers. Driven primarily by the discovery of gold in Georgia and insistent pressure for fresh land on which to grow slave-produced cotton, the U.S. Congress passed the **Indian Removal Act** in 1830. President Jackson supported and oversaw the forced migration of southeastern Amerindians such as the Creek and Cherokee to a specially designated "Indian Territory" in today's Oklahoma. Ironically, before the act, the Cherokee had tried to preserve their sovereignty and hold on to their land by adopting a constitution that melded traditional Cherokee ways with the American political model. That experiment ended tragically with a forced march west that killed over four thousand on what the Cherokee call the *Nunna daul Tsuny*, the *"Trail Where They Cried"* or the *"Trail of Tears."*

The life and customs of the indigenous communities of the Great Plains were quite different from those of the agricultural Maya and Cherokee. Plains Amerindians lived in mobile bands and depended on buffalo hunting for both food and a source of trade goods. The ancient buffalo-hunting culture of the Plains had been given a new stimulus by the arrival of horses in the sixteenth and seventeenth centuries. Formerly agricultural people, like the Lakota (luh-KOH-tuh) Sioux and the Cheyenne, moved onto the Plains and used horses and rifles to develop an efficient hunting culture. Then the earlier trickle of Europeans passing through turned into a flood. After 1846, when Great Britain ceded Oregon to the United States, large numbers of settlers sought their fortune on the "Oregon Trail." By the time of the American Civil War, the Dakota Territory was strung with a series of forts to protect settlers in transit from Amerindian attacks.

For a time it seemed that negotiations between the Sioux and the U.S. government might preserve stability. An 1868 treaty, for example, forbade white settlement for all time in the Black Hills, sacred to the Sioux and other Plains societies. Four years later, however, gold was discovered, and waves of white prospectors descended on mining camps in the heart of sacred Sioux land. It seemed to Sioux leaders like **Sitting Bull** (ca. 1831–1890) that treaties with the U.S. government were worth less than the paper they were written on.

The Sioux prepared for war, and in the summer of 1876 they defeated Lieutenant Colonel George Custer and his unit of the Seventh United States Cavalry at the Battle of Little Bighorn, killing Custer and over half of his men. Although Custer's demise was the outcome of a military blunder, the American press portrayed it as a heroic "last stand" against "savages." Amid calls for swift vengeance, some advocated not just the defeat of the Sioux but also the total annihilation of Amerindians.

The spread of railroads, starting in the 1870s, notched up tensions as European immigrants and American settlers began arriving in the Dakota Territory as permanent homesteaders. In 1890 the U.S. government abrogated its treaty with the Sioux to open lands for these settlers. Now confined to reservations, the Lakota, who had depended on open lands where buffalo grazed, found their whole way of life imperiled.

Despairing of a political or military solution to their crisis, some Plains Amerindians were attracted to the teachings of a mystic named Wovoka (wuh-VOH-kuh), leader of the Ghost Dance Movement, which combined indigenous beliefs and imported Christian ones. Wovoka's followers believed that he was a messiah sent to liberate them and that by dancing the Ghost Dance they would hasten a millennium in which earthquakes would drive the invaders from the earth and leave the native peoples in peace and prosperity.

The U.S. government regarded the Ghost Dance Movement as subversive and ordered the arrest of Sitting Bull in the mistaken belief that he was a leader of the movement. Early in 1890, Sitting Bull was killed in a skirmish; two weeks later, at the Wounded Knee Massacre, the Seventh Cavalry fired into a group of Sioux captives, killing between 150 and 300 people, nearly half of whom were unarmed women and children. An editorial writer at a South Dakota newspaper had this to say:

The Whites, by law of conquest, by justice of civilization, are masters of the American continent, and the best safety of the frontier settlements will be secured by the total annihilation of the few remaining Indians. Why not annihilation? Their glory has fled, their spirit broken, their manhood effaced; better that they die than live the miserable wretches that they are.[*]

Such violent racism in support of a policy of genocide was not uncommon. (The author of this editorial was L. Frank Baum, who ten years later would write the beloved children's story *The Wonderful Wizard of Oz*.)

Rather than outright annihilation, however, the federal Bureau of Indian Affairs separated Amerindian children from their parents to prevent them from learning the language, culture, and rituals of their own people—a form of cultural genocide. The Ghost Dance and other ceremonies were forbidden and could be practiced only in secret. Amerindian armed resistance was over. The frontier wars persisted only in entertainment, courtesy of Buffalo Bill Cody's tremendously popular Wild West shows, where Americans flocked to be thrilled by stylized reenactments of the frontier wars.

When she began to travel across Canada in the 1890s, Pauline Johnson-Tekahionwake saw firsthand the tragedy of the Plains Amerindians. She witnessed the sad spectacle of *"a sort of miniature Buffalo Bill's Wild West"*[†] in which Blackfoot warriors caricatured their old war maneuvers. Some might have been veterans of the **Métis Rebellions**, the uprisings of mixed-race and First Nations peoples that had inspired Johnson to write "A Cry from an Indian Wife."

The métis settlement in the Red River Valley of what is now the Canadian province of Manitoba represented the older form of European-First Nations interaction.

Chief Joseph Chief Joseph (hin-MAH-too-yah-LAT-kekt, "Thunder Rolling Down the Mountain") was a Nez Perce Amerindian leader and a famous man of peace. The discovery of gold led the U.S. government to renege on its treaty with the Nez Perce, shrinking their reservation to a tenth of its former size. In 1877, Chief Joseph led his people, pursued by U.S. cavalry, in a desperate attempt to reach Canada. He was captured and exiled to Oklahoma. Only in 1885 were Joseph and his remaining followers allowed to return to their homes in the Pacific Northwest.

Métis Rebellions (1867 and 1885) Rebellions by the métis of the Red River Valley settlement in Manitoba, a group with mixed French-Amerindian ancestry that resisted incorporation into the Canadian Confederation. In 1885 their leader, Louis Riel, again led them in rebellion against Canadian authority.

[*]L. Frank Baum, *Aberdeen Saturday Pioneer*, December 20, 1890.

[†]Pauline Johnson-Tekahionwake, cited in Betty Keller, *Pauline: A Biography of Pauline Johnson* (Toronto: Douglas and Macintyre, 1981), p. 94.

During the heyday of the fur trade, when French trappers and traders relied on native communities for both profit and survival, mixed-race families were not uncommon. Sometimes Europeans were absorbed into indigenous communities, and sometimes, as with the métis, the offspring of mixed unions established their own communities.

The first of two Métis Rebellions came immediately after Canadian confederation in 1867. London had transferred authority over the vast territories of the Hudson's Bay Company to the Canadian government without consulting the people who lived there. The métis leader Louis Riel organized his community to resist incorporation into Canada, which they feared would lead to loss of their lands and the erosion of their French language. Riel declared a provisional government and soon secured guarantees that Canada would protect the language and Catholic religion of the métis. Negotiations led to the incorporation of Manitoba into Canada in 1870.

At the same time, Canadian policies assumed that First Nations peoples would disappear as a distinct population. Plains dwellers were increasingly desperate. The buffalo were dwindling; alcohol was becoming a scourge. The railroad brought settlers and commerce, but for Amerindians hunting traditions and their lack of capital made a transition to farming almost impossible. In exchange for exclusive reserves and small annuities, band after band gave up claim to the lands of their forebears.

The Indian Act of 1876 asserted the authority of the Canadian state over First Nations communities. Children were separated from their families and sent to "industrial schools," given English names, and forbidden to speak their own languages. (See the feature "Visual Evidence in Primary Sources: The Residential School System for First Nations Children.") The Indian Act also allowed Canadian officials to ban traditional rituals, such as the *potlatch*, in which men held enormous feasts to give away all the wealth they had accumulated in the previous years. This ceremony expressed the core cultural values of the peoples of the Pacific West. The idea of giving away all your wealth to solidify your social standing could not have stood in greater contrast to the ethos of industrial and commercial capitalism on which Canada was being built.

Meanwhile, government surveyors were dividing the prairie into 640-acre (259-ha) lots. The arrival of a flood of settlers would make the métis a minority in their own land, and in 1885 Louis Riel once again organized resistance, this time forging alliances with disaffected Cree, Assiniboine, and other First Nations peoples. Métis partisans attacked a government outpost as Riel's indigenous allies burned down white homesteads. But they were no match for three thousand troops sent west on the Canadian Pacific Railway. Riel was arrested, convicted of high treason, and hanged. When Pauline Johnson-Tekahionwake recited "A Cry from an Indian Wife" in 1892, these events were still fresh in the minds of her audience.

If we compare the Yucatán Rebellion, the struggles of the Lakota Sioux, and the Métis Rebellions, we might first be struck by this difference: whereas the Mexican government and economic oligarchy wanted to incorporate the Maya peasantry as laborers in the commercial plantation system, the United States and Canada had no use for Amerindians even as workers, instead driving them into reservations to make room for settlers.

But the three cases have this in common: in the Yucatán, the Black Hills, and Manitoba, people rose up to defend their long-established cultures against foreign intrusion and commercial agriculture. All three societies had creatively merged indigenous and imported ideas: Maya beliefs and Catholicism, Sioux traditions with horse-based buffalo hunting, French and First Nations cultures in the days of the fur trade. Now all these peoples lost their ability to control their interactions with the national societies being constructed around them.

Abolition, Immigration, and Race

Race was a major issue during Pauline Johnson-Tekahionwake's lifetime. During her childhood the dividing lines were fairly simple: British (mostly Protestants), French and Irish (mostly Catholics), First Nations peoples (themselves quite diverse), and mixtures between them such as the métis. By the time of her adult travels, that picture had been complicated by the arrival of new immigrants: Chinese, Italians, Russians, and others. Early in the twentieth century, half of the population on the prairies was born outside of Canada. The same was true throughout the Americas. The United States was the most favored destination, but Argentina and Brazil also attracted many European immigrants.

In Brazil and the Caribbean, the abolition of slavery was connected to immigration patterns and policies. Slavery was abolished in the British West Indies in 1833 and on the French islands fifteen years later. Unable to keep the former slaves as poorly paid wage earners, landowners turned to indentured workers. In the English-speaking Caribbean, indentured laborers came largely from British India, part of a broader South Asian diaspora (scattering) that also took contract workers to South Africa, Malaya, and Fiji. In Cuba, where slavery was not abolished until 1878, the sugar plantations required so much labor that over a hundred thousand Chinese workers came to the island as indentured workers to supplement slave labor.

Like Cuba, Brazil was bringing in new migrants even before slavery was abolished in 1888. Brazilian employers brought contract laborers from Japan to work on coffee farms. In fact, the largest group of Japanese-descended persons outside Japan is found in Brazil. Much larger and more influential in Brazilian culture, however, was the Afro-Brazilian population with its origins in the old sugar plantation system. Brazilian art, music, dance, and religious worship all show a deep African influence.

Reflecting the racism so characteristic of the age, the rulers of republican Brazil were embarrassed by the country's African heritage. The words of their motto were "order" and "progress," and in their minds black people represented neither. To "improve" the country racially, the government recruited immigrants from Europe. Germans, Italians, and others were given incentives to relocate to the economically dynamic southern part of the country. The northeast, the base of the old plantation system, remained more African in population and culture. Even so, Brazil retained the traditional flexibility and ambiguity in race relations inherited from the colonial period. While the elite class was predominantly white and the poorest class predominantly black, a vast intermediate stratum of mixed descent existed. A complex terminology of racial designations classified people by speech, education, style of clothing, and other factors in addition to color. Racial classification, therefore, could be a matter of negotiation rather than simple appearance: as they say in Brazil, "Money whitens."

Racism was also evident in immigration to the United States. For example, the Anglo-Protestant majority portrayed Irish Catholics as drunk, violent, and lazy. Demeaning stereotypes also greeted new immigrants from southern and eastern Europe, such as Italian Catholics and Russian Jews. Prejudice against Chinese and Japanese immigrants on the west coast was even more intense, and Congress banned Chinese immigration altogether in 1882. Still, in 1890 fully 14.8 percent of the population had been born outside the United States. Some doubted whether these new arrivals, with their unfamiliar foods, languages, and customs, could ever be assimilated.

Racism continued to drive policy toward Americans of African descent, where the "one drop rule," in contrast with Brazil's more complex race-status hierarchy, classified all individuals with any appearance of African descent as black. In 1896 the Supreme Court upheld the legality of racial segregation in the South. In

The Residential School System for First Nations Children

After the conquest of Amerindian communities, nineteenth-century governments in both the United States and Canada implemented residential school systems designed to separate Amerindian children from their families and thus from the culture of their people. Children in these often church-run schools were given new names, converted to Christianity, forced to speak only English, and punished for speaking the language of their own people. Physical and sexual abuse were common, and rates of infectious disease, especially tuberculosis, were high. In Canada, attendance by First Nations children at residential schools was compulsory until 1948.

Finally, in 1998 the Canadian government formed the Aboriginal Healing Foundation to support community projects in reparation for the damage done by this attempted cultural genocide of First Nations peoples. In 2008, the Canadian prime minister made a formal statement of

In this photograph, "Thomas" wears long braided hair and leans against a large fur robe. He holds what appears to be a toy gun, perhaps given to him as a prop by the photographer.

Assuming the photographer posed the boy, what impression does he seem to have wanted the photograph to have on its viewers?

One writer says that this image shows "the disorder and violence of warfare and of the cross-cultural partnerships of the fur trade . . . that had dominated life in Canada since the late sixteenth century."* How does the image show that?

Saskatchewan Archives Board, Regina

*John S. Milloy, *A National Crime: The Canadian Government and the Residential School System, 1879 to 1906* (Winnipeg: University of Manitoba Press, 1999), p. 4.

apology, recognizing that "the consequences of the Indian residential schools policy were profoundly negative and that this policy has had a lasting and damaging impact on aboriginal culture, heritage, and language." The statement highlighted the "tragic accounts of the emotional, physical, and sexual abuse and neglect of helpless children, and their separation from powerless families and communities."

These two photographs were taken at the Regina Industrial School in the Canadian province of Saskatchewan and published in the *Annual Report* of the Canadian Department of Indian Affairs in 1904. They record the appearance of a First Nations child identified only as "Thomas Moore" (his true name was not recorded), supposedly upon his first arrival and again a few years later.

Saskatchewan Archives Board, Regina

Apart from his hair and clothing, what is different and meaningful about Thomas's facial expression and posture in the second photograph?

The wall against which Thomas is leaning in this photograph seems much more solid and permanent than the fur robe in the earlier picture, perhaps symbolizing the superior strength of Christian Canadian society.

The goal of the Canadian government was to replace buffalo hunting with settled agriculture, a transformation perhaps symbolized by the potted plant included in this photograph.

In Australia as well, aboriginal children were taken from their parents, forced into residential schools, and denied the chance of learning their own language and culture.

QUESTION FOR ANALYSIS

» *Taken together, what do these two photographs tell us about the ideology behind the residential school system in turn-of-the-century Canada?*

Northern cities recent immigrants, in spite of prejudices against them, often fared better than African Americans; many Irish Americans, for example, found good work as police officers and firemen, jobs that were closed to blacks. The cruel irony was that African Americans, most of whose ancestors had witnessed the birth of the republic, now watched as new arrivals from Europe leaped ahead of them.

The late nineteenth century was a time of harsh racial rhetoric and even harsher racial realities in the United States and across the Americas. Encounters among Amerindians, Africans, Asians, and Europeans seemed to have been resolved decisively in favor of the latter. For all the variation among the nations of North and South America, they had one thing in common: light-skinned men were in charge.

Gender and Women's Rights

In 1848, the Seneca Falls Convention was held in upstate New York. Sometimes seen as the beginning of the modern women's movement, the meeting was inspired by the abolitionist movement and the revolutions of 1848 in Europe (see Chapter 23). The women met to proclaim universal freedom and gender equality, declaring:

> Now, in view of this entire disfranchisement of one-half the people of this country, their social and religious degradation . . . and because women do feel themselves aggrieved, oppressed, and fraudulently deprived of their most sacred rights, we insist that they have immediate admission to all the rights and privileges which belong to them as citizens of these United States.

Such proclamations would eventually transform gender relations in the United States, Canada, and the world. In the short run, however, most women, like Pauline Johnson-Tekahionwake, had to explore their own possibilities without much external support. Just as she investigated her own complex identity through life and art, her public performances also explored her identity as a woman. The costume change she made halfway through her recitals—from buckskin to evening gown, from Tekahionwake to Pauline Johnson—transformed her from a passionate and even erotic persona to a distant and ethereal one.

For middle-class women in the United States and Canada, the bicycle became a symbol of a new mobility and new kind of freedom. For Pauline Johnson-Tekahionwake, the canoe played this role. Some of her nature poems, such as "The Song My Paddle Sings," were based on canoe trips she took as a young woman on the Six Nations Reserve:

> . . . The river rolls in its rocky bed;
> My paddle is plying its way ahead . . .
> And up on the hills against the sky,
> A fir tree rocking its lullaby,
> Swings, swings,
> Its emerald wings,
> Swelling the song that my paddle sings.*

---

*Excerpt from *Flint and Feather: The Complete Poems of E. Pauline Johnson (Tekahionwake)*. Copyright © 1969 Hodder and Stoughton, pp. 31–33.

In her canoe poems, Johnson-Tekahionwake is always in control, even when, as is often the case, she has a male companion. The independence asserted in her poetry was reflected in her personal life as well. She had several significant relationships but no marriage, and though money was a constant worry, she was financially independent. Perhaps Johnson-Tekahionwake's autonomy arose from her mixed heritage, deriving from both the matriarchal tradition of the Mohawk and the new possibilities for women proclaimed at Seneca Falls.

How exceptional were Pauline Johnson-Tekahionwake's attitudes and experiences for a woman of her time? The answer would depend on geographic location and class standing. Wealthier women in major commercial cities like Toronto, Chicago, or Buenos Aires had much in common. Some were politically active, seeking legal equality and the vote for women. Some organized campaigns for social improvement, working to limit abuses of child labor, to improve sanitary conditions, or to fight the evils of alcohol. Some daughters of the middle class took advantage of new educational opportunities. There were only a few female doctors, lawyers, and university professors in the Americas by the end of the nineteenth century, but there were many new openings for schoolteachers and nurses. Lower down the social order, the invention of the typewriter and the emergence of large corporations also created a vast new job market for female secretaries.

Often young women from the lower or middle classes took temporary positions as teachers, nurses, or secretaries until they married. Such behavior was acceptable as long as they abandoned employment when they married and started families. According to the "cult of true womanhood" dominant at the time, woman's role was in a "separate sphere," where she would maintain a refined home environment as a sanctuary from the brutal and competitive "men's world" of business and industry. Even though women like Johnson-Tekahionwake might reject the "cult of true womanhood," it was a powerful idea embraced by many urban middle-class women and by poorer women who aspired to be middle class.

Women's progress toward equality and autonomy depended partly on where they lived, varying tremendously according to their nation, culture, race, and social class. A middle-class homemaker in Buenos Aires had a more comfortable life than a Swedish pioneer getting her family through winter on the Canadian prairie. Likewise, an Irish nun teaching immigrant children in Chicago would be difficult to compare with a Maya mother sending her sons off to work on a Yucatán plantation. For her part, Pauline Johnson-Tekahionwake possessed a life of mobility and autonomy that would have been unimaginable to her foremothers.

Bicycle Advertisement This advertisement from 1896 associates the bicycle with the newfound mobility and independence of the "new woman." In the poems of Pauline Johnson-Tekahionwake, it was often a canoe that allowed women to "be content."

The Granger Collection New York

King Khama III
(ca. 1837–1923) King of the Bangwato, a Tswana-speaking southern African group. His successful diplomacy helped establish the Bechuanaland protectorate, putting the Bangwato and other kingdoms under British rather than South African rule.

own affairs. The British public responded positively to their appeals, the colonial secretary argued in their favor, and they even had an audience with Queen Victoria. Thanks in great part to their effort and skill, the people of Botswana were later spared the agonies of *apartheid* ("separateness") as practiced in twentieth-century South Africa (see Chapter 30).

Still, Khama's success was only partial. Individual African societies might make better or worse deals with the forces of imperialism, but none could escape them. The late nineteenth century was the time of the New Imperialism, when powerful industrial nations vied for control of colonial territories and resources all across the globe. In Southeast Asia as well, Europeans were competing for colonies, while American, French, German, and British flags went up over scattered Polynesian islands, Meiji Japan took control over Korea and Taiwan, and the last sovereign Amerindian societies were defeated in the United States and Canada (see Chapters 24 and 25).

Applied science and industrial productivity generated the technological, military, and economic advances that powered the New Imperialism. Those societies in possession of the tools of empire—modern firearms, telegraphs, and steamships—were able to assert their power as never before. In Africa and Southeast Asia, local leaders were able to resist only by manipulating European rivalries for their own ends. Even such independent states as Siam and Ethiopia were incorporated into the unequal global system based on empire. Indigenous leaders around the world could relate to King Khama's predicament.

Focus Questions

» *What were the main causes of the New Imperialism?*

» *In what different ways did Africans respond to European imperialism?*

» *What were the main outcomes of the New Imperialism in Southeast Asia?*

» *What connections and comparisons can be made between Africa and Southeast Asia in the late nineteenth century?*

The New Imperialism

Europeans and Africans had interacted long before the Industrial Revolution. After the sixteenth century, especially in western Africa, their relationship increasingly focused on the slave trade, though direct European involvement was limited to collecting and transporting slaves from coastal fortifications (see Chapter 19). Until the late nineteenth century, Europeans in Africa's interior included only a small group of settlers moving out from Cape Town and a few intrepid explorers.

The Industrial Revolution altered this pattern. By 1808, when the British Parliament abolished the slave trade, the economic needs of European economies were shifting: the slave-based West Indian sugar plantations were declining in importance, while factory owners sought inexpensive sources of raw materials and new export markets for their manufactures. In the mid-1800s European explorers fanned out across the continent to assess its cultural and physical geography, identify its resources, and evaluate the transportation potential of its rivers. Pressed on by evangelical Christians who had been involved in the abolitionist movement, the British government took an active role in stamping out the slave trade.

For most of the nineteenth century, African merchants and African political authorities facilitated the new trade connections as Europeans still largely remained at the coasts. Then something dramatic happened. As King Khama noted, suddenly after 1870 Africans confronted *"a multitude of white men."* The era of **New Imperialism** had begun. Heightened competition among industrial states for African raw materials and markets was one motive for European colonial expansion; personal ambition and religious conviction were others.

These motivations developed at the same time as the means to make conquest possible. The "tools of empire" included more than just accurate rifles and rapid-fire machine guns. Steamships and telegraphs shrank the distance between European centers of command and European officials on the ground, allowing for quicker coordination. Because African rivers drop sharply from highlands to the sea, sailing ships could not penetrate far inland. But steam-powered ships could readily penetrate the continent's interior, and beginning in the 1890s, railroads too conveyed troops and colonial administrators. Advances in medical technology were also vital: in the 1840s it was discovered that quinine, from the bark of a South American tree, provided protection against malaria. Routes to the interior of Africa, once known as "the white man's graveyard," were now open.

New Imperialism
An increase in European imperial activity during the late nineteenth century, caused primarily by increased competition between industrial states for raw materials and markets and by the rise of a unified Germany as a threat to the British empire.

Political and Economic Motives

Though the French and Portuguese had long-standing coastal enclaves, it was the British who dominated European-African interactions for the first two-thirds of the nineteenth century. Already the world's most important maritime power, by this time the British had taken the lead in industrialization as well (see Chapter 23) and were aggressively pursuing new sources of raw materials and markets across the globe. Before 1870, however, it seemed that they had little appetite for adding vast new holdings to their formal empire. In Latin America and in China, the British had asserted their economic dominance without the expense of direct colonial occupation, an approach supported by free-trade ideology. It seemed that relations with Africa would follow that pattern of "informal empire."

The global dynamic of European imperialism changed after 1871 with the unification of Germany, the fastest-growing industrial economy in the second half of the nineteenth century. Having defeated the French (see Chapter 23), the Germans wanted to show that they were the equals of the British by acquiring an empire of their own.

For the French as well, the quest for prestige underlay efforts to restore the country's international standing after its humiliating defeat by the Germans. Imperial expansion in Africa and Southeast Asia accomplished that goal and gave legitimacy to the government of the Third Republic.

With the United States and Japan also asserting themselves as military powers in Asia, by the 1880s the whole international system was becoming much more competitive than it had been in the earlier period of British dominance, and the liberal belief that every nation's economic needs could be met through free trade in open markets was starting to dim. Secure and protected colonial markets were now more often seen as essential to further industrialization.

Within Europe, domestic politics spurred more active imperialism as well when politicians used patriotic appeals to cultivate popularity with newly enlarged electorates in France, Britain, and Germany. Leaders of the Third Republic appealed to "national honor" in extending their colonial frontiers. In Britain, a new generation of Tories (members of the Conservative Party), led by Benjamin Disraeli (1804–1881), sought to broaden their base of support beyond the rural gentry by becoming the party of empire, using appeals to patriotism and national glory to win elections. In Germany, Otto von Bismarck recognized that rapid industrialization and urbanization were having destabilizing social effects and that the German working class was becoming organized. If the public's attention could be focused on military glory and imperial expansion, then nationalism would strengthen German unity and weaken the appeal of socialism.

Imperial expansion in the age of the New Imperialism was closely tied to industrial capitalism, coinciding with the **Second Industrial Revolution** in the latter half of the nineteenth century. A rapid acceleration in industrial technology meant that electricity, steel, and petroleum superseded coal and iron. Large corporations were now investing huge sums in the chemical and metal industries, which required secure access to natural resources like tin, oil, and rubber from around the world. Believing free markets were not adequate to their needs, nationalistic policymakers reintroduced mercantilist economic strategies. Chartered companies—state-backed monopolies like those that had dominated Europe's earlier colonial enterprises (see Chapter 16)—were once again used to secure markets, sources of raw materials, and overseas investment opportunities.

Second Industrial Revolution
The more technologically sophisticated and capital intensive industrialism of the later nineteenth century. Electricity, steel, and petroleum superseded coal and iron, and large corporations now required secure access to natural resources from around the world.

Ideology and Personal Ambition

In each case, by the late nineteenth century, the idea of a "civilizing mission," that the "natives" needed European stewardship for their own improvement, gave a humanitarian justification for the pursuit of national self-interest. Earlier, however, the French and mid-Victorian Britons had approached Africa with liberal ideas that emphasized the possibilities of human improvement and the potential for human equality. Of course, their concept of "civilization" was ethnocentric, based on the idea that Africans and other "natives" could be raised to the superior European level. Still, they placed no limit on what Africans with proper education and social circumstances, rescued from the ravages of the slave trade, might achieve.

In the early nineteenth century, missionaries inspired by the abolitionist movement had dedicated themselves to the salvation of African souls and the redemption of the continent from spiritual practices that they regarded as primitive superstition. The career of **David Livingstone** (1813–1873), the great Scottish missionary and explorer, shows that in the period prior to the "scramble for Africa" such missionaries, in spite of cultural prejudices, believed in the intellectual and spiritual capacities of African peoples.

Livingstone spent the better part of his life exploring the continent and preaching Christianity to its people, often far beyond the borders of European control and therefore relying on African hospitality and protection. Livingstone saw Africans as fully capable in every way; his dream was eventually to have African Christians in positions of church leadership. In pursuit of this goal, he spent time among the Bangwato, serving as a tutor to one of the kings who accompanied Khama to London.

Livingstone's goal was achieved by Samuel Ajayi Crowther, the first African bishop of the Church of England. Born in what is now western Nigeria, Crowther was sold into slavery in 1821. By then the British were committed to abolition,

David Livingstone (1813–1873) Scottish missionary and explorer idolized in Britain for his commitment to the spiritual and moral salvation of Africans.

and the Royal Navy seized the Portuguese ship on which he was held captive along with his mother and brother. The British dropped the twelve-year-old off at Freetown in Sierra Leone, earlier established as a home for such "re-captives." After education in Sierra Leone and England, and having served on a mission to the Niger River, Crowther was ordained as an Anglican priest. One of his enduring contributions to African Christianity was his translation of the Christian texts into his own native Yoruba and other African languages.

In 1864, Crowther became the Anglican bishop of West Africa. But he was disappointed to find that some white missionaries resented his appointment and refused to follow his directives. Unlike Livingstone, they viewed blacks as permanent children, incapable of handling high office. Such racism forced Crowther into retirement, and an English bishop replaced him. (See the feature "Movement of Ideas Through Primary Sources: Bishop Turner's View of Africa.")

Crowther's story shows that by the later nineteenth century, liberal optimism in African capacities was fading, replaced by the idea that humanity consists of a set of clearly demarcated racial groups arranged along a hierarchy of ability. The shock of the Indian Mutiny of 1857 and the publication of Charles Darwin's *On the Origin of Species* in 1859 (see Chapters 23 and 24) contributed to this hardening of racial attitudes. By the end of the century, Social Darwinism, the application of Darwin's idea of the "struggle for existence" to national and racial groups, had become the conventional wisdom of the West. Now most white people saw themselves as sitting atop an unchangeable hierarchy of races, a belief that justified colonial expansion as part of the natural order of things.

The hardening of racial attitudes found expression in the contrast between David Livingstone and the young American journalist Henry Morton Stanley (1841–1904), who set off to find Livingstone in Central Africa when he was feared lost late in his career. Unlike Livingstone, who lived peacefully among Africans and acknowledged their help and hospitality, Stanley organized his expedition along military lines. A man of strong determination forged by a difficult Welsh childhood, Stanley's treatment of Africans was so harsh that the British government insisted he stop flying the Union Jack. Stanley later traced the great Congo River from its source deep in Central Africa to its outlet on the Atlantic and, having been rebuffed by Britain, formed an alliance with the ambitious **King Leopold II of Belgium** (r. 1865–1909) to profit from his discoveries.

Belgium was a small kingdom that had become independent from the Netherlands only in 1830. Leopold envied Queen Victoria's vast empire and, convinced that great wealth could be gained in Africa, declared, *"I must have my share of this magnificent African cake!"* Against a background of intensified competition for markets and raw materials for industry and the surging nationalism of European politics, Leopold's initiative to use the Congo River as a gateway to a vast Central African empire was the spark that set off a mad rush for African territory.

Concerned that Leopold's imperialism might destabilize the balance of power in Europe, Otto von Bismarck brought together representatives of the European colonial powers at the **Berlin Conference** in 1884 to establish rules for the partition of Africa. No Africans were present. The European delegates declared that the boundaries of the French, British, Belgian, German, Portuguese, Italian, and Spanish possessions in Africa would be recognized only where those powers established "effective occupation" of the territories ceded to them in Berlin. For Africans, this meant twenty years of constant warfare and instability as European governments launched a wave of invasions to secure the effective occupation of the territories they claimed. Millions of Africans would die.

King Leopold II of Belgium
(r. 1865–1909) Ignited a "scramble for Africa" when he claimed the large area of Central Africa he called the Congo Free State. The ruthless exploitation of Congolese rubber by Leopold's agents led to millions of deaths.

Berlin Conference
(1884) Conference organized by the German chancellor Otto von Bismarck in which representatives of the major European states divided Africa among themselves.

Bishop Turner's View of Africa

While the "scramble for Africa" was taking place, some people of African descent in the Americas began to develop a "Pan-African" perspective that stressed the common circumstances and aspirations of black people around the world. One strand of Pan-Africanism focused on the possible emigration of American blacks back to Africa. Here a major figure was Henry McNeal Turner (1834–1915). Born free but poor in South Carolina, Turner learned to read and write while working as a janitor at a law firm. After becoming a preacher, in 1857 he joined the African Methodist Episcopal Church (AME), an entirely black-run denomination, and during the American Civil War served as the first black chaplain in the U.S. Army. After the war he was elected to the Georgia assembly but was prevented from taking his seat on racial grounds. That he was of mixed race and fair skinned made no difference.

The failure of Reconstruction (see Chapter 25) to bring true liberty to black Americans left Turner bitter. As lynching and legalized segregation became the norm, he argued that it was foolish to suppose that blacks would ever be allowed to prosper in the United States, and he became a strong advocate for emigration to Africa. His first interest was Liberia, an independent nation founded by freed African Americans. He then became aware of South Africa, where black Christians were interested in affiliating themselves with the AME Church to escape the control of white missionaries. In the 1890s he traveled to both countries and ordained a number of South African bishops.

Source: From Edwin S. Redkey, *Respect Black: The Writings and Speeches of Henry McNeal Turner* (New York: Arno Press). Copyright © 1971, pp. 42–44, 52–55, 83, 143–144.

1883

There is no more doubt in my mind that we have ultimately to return to Africa than there is of the existence of a God; and the sooner we begin to recognize that fact and prepare for it, the better it will be for us as a people. We have there a country unsurpassed in productive and mineral resources, and we have some two hundred millions of our kindred there in moral and spiritual blindness. The four millions of us in this country are at school, learning the doctrines of Christianity and the elements of civil government. As soon as we are educated sufficiently to assume control of our vast ancestral domain, we will hear the voice of a mysterious Providence, saying, *"Return to the land of your fathers. . . ."*

Nothing less than nationality will bring large prosperity and acknowledged manhood to us as a people. How can we do this? Not by constantly complaining of bad treatment; by holding conventions and passing resolutions; by voting for white men for office; by serving as caterers and barbers, and by having our wives and daughters continue as washerwomen and servants to the whites. No—a government and nationality of our own can alone cure the evils under which we now labor, and are likely yet the more to suffer in this country.

It may be asked, where can we build up a respectable government? Certainly not in the United States. . . . I am sure there is no region so full of promise and where the probabilities of success are so great as the land of our ancestors. The continent appears to be kept by Providence in reserve for the Negro. There everything seems ready to raise him to deserved distinction, comfort and wealth. . . . And the time is near when the American people of color will . . . erect the UNITED STATES OF AFRICA.

The murders and outrages perpetrated upon our people, . . . since 1867 [are] . . . an orgy of blood and death. . . . I know we are Americans to all intents and purposes. We were born here, raised here, fought, bled and died here, and have a thousand times more right here than hundreds of thousands of those who help to snub, proscribe and persecute us, and that is one of the reasons I almost despise the land of my birth. . . .

1891

You can ridicule it if you like, but Africa will be the thermometer that will determine the status of the Negro the world over. . . . The elevation of the Negro in this and all other countries is indissolubly connected with the enlightenment of Africa. . . .

1893

These black [Muslim] priests . . . walking around here with so much dignity, majesty and consciousness of their worth are driving me into respect for them. Some come from hundreds of miles from the country—out of the bush—better scholars than any in America. What fools we are to suppose these Africans are fools! . . . Since I reached here, I see native Africans running engines, manning oar and steamboats, and . . . two black ocean pilots and another black man measuring the depth of the ocean and guiding the ship amid the dangerous points. Poor black man, how the world tells lies about you!. . . .

I have found out another thing since I have come to Africa, gone scores of miles through the interior and noted the tact, taste, genius and manly bearing of the higher grade of the natives. . . . Those who think the receding forehead, the flat nose, the proboscidated mouth and the big flat-bottom foot are natural to the African are mistaken. There are heads here by the millions, as vertical or perpendicular as any white man's head God ever made. . . .

I have long ago learned that the rich Negro, the ignorant Negro . . . and the would-be white Negro care nothing for African redemption, or the honor and dignity of the race . . . I have never advocated all the colored people going to Africa, for I am well aware that the bulk of them are lacking in common sense and are too fond of worshiping white gods. . . . [E]very man who has a drop of African blood in his veins should be interested in the civilization, if not the salvation, of her millions, and how any black man can speak in contemptuous language of that great continent and her millions, when they gave him existence . . . is a mystery to me.

QUESTIONS FOR ANALYSIS

» *How did Turner think Africa could be useful to African Americans, and vice versa?*

» *How were his ideas about Africans in particular, and race issues in general, similar to or different from those of Social Darwinists?*

Africa and the New Imperialism

As late as 1878, Europe's colonial presence was almost entirely restricted to the African coast (see Map 26.1). The all-out scramble for control of African territory was therefore something new. In contrast to India, where British power had been expanding since the eighteenth century (see Chapter 24), most Africans confronted European power *after* the development of industrial technology like machine guns, field cannon, telegraphs, and steamships. The suddenness of the onslaught, aided by such technologies, caught Africans off guard. Should they fight back? Seek diplomatic options? Ally themselves with the new intruders? African leaders tried all of these options, with little success.

Although European imperialists reduced Africa to a set of simple stereotypes, in which "tribal Africa" represented the "heart of darkness," in reality it was a continent of immense cultural and geographic complexity. Africa's own historical dynamics, including the rise of Muslim states in West Africa, the creation of the Zulu empire in the far south, and the expanding nineteenth-century trade in ivory and slaves in East Africa, are an essential context for understanding Europe's partition of the continent.

Western and Eastern Africa

As the Industrial Revolution changed the economic relationship between Europe and West Africa, European merchants shifted their business from the purchase of human beings to the search for commodities needed to supply expanding factories at home. While Egypt became a major source of raw cotton for British industry (see Chapter 23), the most important product coming from sub-Saharan Africa was palm oil for use as an industrial lubricant. Responding to a growing demand starting in the 1820s, African farmers planted and processed oil products for the export market, and many West Africans became wealthy in this trade. Factory-produced cloth and iron goods were becoming cheaper at the same time as higher demand was increasing the price Europeans would pay for palm oil. At least in some regions, Africans found the terms of trade moving in their favor.

Initially, as West African economies became more integrated into world markets, political power remained with African kingdoms and chiefdoms. In an influential essay in 1868, a British-educated African surgeon named John Africanus Horton called for African kingdoms to reform themselves by incorporating Western constitutional practices, as their contemporaries were doing in Japan (see Chapter 24). Like Bishop Crowther, Dr. Horton

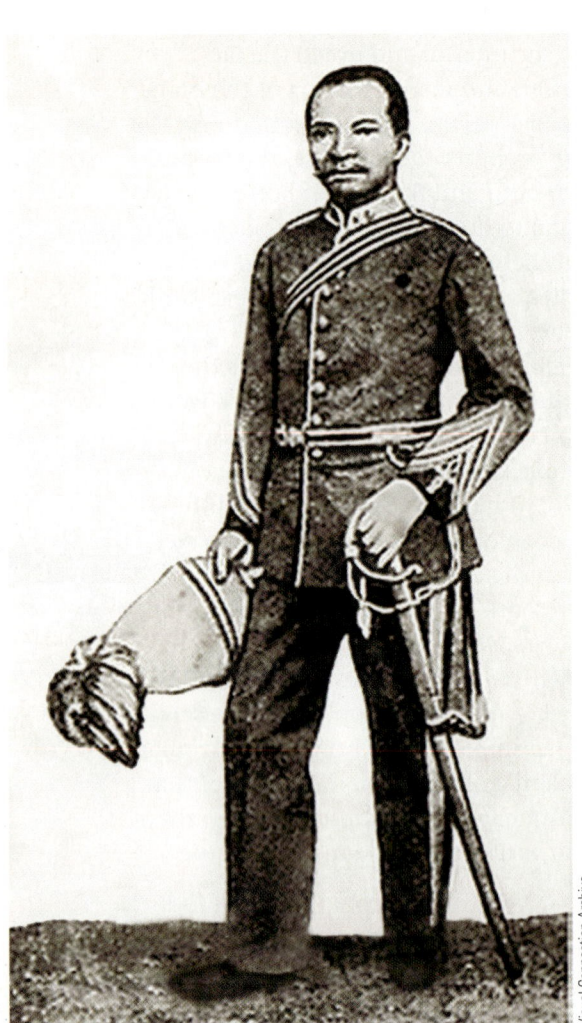

Visual Connection Archive

John Africanus Horton John Africanus Horton (1835–1883) was born and raised in Freetown, Sierra Leone, after his father had been liberated from a slave ship by the British navy. Horton studied medicine in Scotland, served as an officer in the British army, advocated self-determination under British guidance for West African peoples, and established a bank in Freetown to aid aspiring African entrepreneurs.

MAP 26.1 Africa, 1878 and 1914 The dramatic expansion of European imperialism in Africa is seen in the comparison of maps from 1878 and 1914. Before the "scramble for Africa" the European colonial presence was largely limited to small coastal enclaves. At that time frontiers of European settlement were found only in Algeria and in the Cape Colony. By 1914, Europeans dominated the entire continent, with only Liberia and Ethiopia retaining their independence. The British were the main power in eastern and southern Africa, the French in western and northern Africa, and the Belgians in Central Africa. (© Cengage Learning)

had been trained by the British for a position of responsibility at a time when it was thought that the future lay with European-educated Africans. Now, as the forces of conquest gathered, Horton's idea that African traditions might be merged with Western models to secure the continent's progress quickly became obsolete.

Asante kingdom
Dominant power in the West African forest in the eighteenth and early nineteenth centuries. The Asante capital was sacked by British forces in 1874 and again in 1896. In 1900, Yaa Asantewa's War represented a final attempt to expel the British.

For example, in 1874 Britain reversed its policy of noninvolvement in Africa's interior by attacking the **Asante kingdom**, the dominant power in the West African forest in the eighteenth and nineteenth centuries. In the 1820s, Asante armies had held their own in a skirmish with the British, but now they were badly outgunned. Moreover, some coastal chiefdoms, regarding the Asante as a threat to their independence, had allied themselves with the British. As in Mesoamerica in the 1520s, indigenous rivalries facilitated European conquest.

Further north, in the grasslands of the West African interior, Islamic reformers had created a string of new states by the early 1800s, after the demise of the Songhai empire (see Chapter 19). The seeds of Islamic reform were planted by Sufi brotherhoods, whose initiates practiced a mystical form of Islam by mastering complex prayers and rituals. The origins of the jihad movements of nineteenth-century West Africa lay in their criticism of political leaders who tolerated the mixing of Islamic and traditional African practices and beliefs.

One of the most important West African jihad leaders was Usuman dan Fodio (1754–1817). In what is now northern Nigeria, dan Fodio called for the local emir to put his government in line with Islamic law. When the emir tried to assassinate him, Usuman dan Fodio (OO-soo-mahn dahn FOH-dee-oh) and his followers went on the offensive. They built a large army and consolidated several small emirates into the new Sokoto (SOH-kuh-toh) caliphate. From here the jihadist impulse spread both east and west. Throughout the nineteenth century, West African Muslim populations became stricter in their practice, and Islam gained large numbers of new adherents.

At first, the leaders of Sokoto and other jihadist movements focused on reforming their own Muslim societies and paid little attention to Europeans, as long as the French presence remained limited to the coast. In the 1870s, however, the French began to move up the Senegal River, and conflict with the Muslim states of the interior followed. The West African Muslim who organized the most sustained resistance to the French invasion was **Samori Toure** (ca. 1830–1900).

Samori Toure
(ca. 1830–1900)
Founder of a major state in West Africa who adopted the pose of a jihadist leader in competition with neighboring kingdoms. After being forced into confrontation by the French, he launched a long but unsuccessful guerrilla campaign against them.

Samori Toure (sam-or-REE too-RAY), from a relatively humble merchant background, built a new state on the upper Niger by training soldiers to use imported rifles. At first his ambitions were merely political, but in 1884 he declared himself to be *"commander of the faithful,"* leader of a jihad against lax Muslims and unbelievers. Even then, Samori avoided confronting the French, focusing instead on controlling trade routes in slaves, salt, and gold. But once the French had conquered his neighbors, they turned their attention to Samori.

Unable to prevail in conventional warfare, in 1891 Samori retreated to the east with his army and launched a guerrilla campaign. Cut off from access to imported ammunition and gunpowder, Samori's soldiers learned to manufacture their own from local materials. But they could not hold out for long. Because his soldiers oppressed the local people, Samori had no local base of support, and the French were relentless in their attacks. After Samori was captured and exiled in 1893, the French were masters from the Senegal to the Niger Rivers.

The French march to the east threatened British control of Egypt and the Nile Valley. To head off the French advance, British forces moved to stake a claim of "effective occupation" over the savanna region still dominated by the Sokoto caliphate. After Usuman dan Fodio's death, the caliphate became decentralized, with individual emirs controlling walled city-states and the surrounding countryside. Thus the British did not face the combined armies of a unified caliphate and were able to attack each city-state separately. The traditional tactics of savanna warfare, where peasants retreated into walled cities while warriors mounted cavalry charges, were no match for rifles and machine guns; British field cannon easily blew breaches in the city walls. Some emirs fought, some fled, and some surrendered, as British forces took control of what is now northern Nigeria.

In West Africa, the lack of alliances among African peoples facilitated the process of European imperialism. Lacking organizational or ideological foundations for a broader unity, African leaders dealt only with the local manifestations of the scramble for Africa. Even as they vied with one another, the Europeans possessed a broader overview of African developments, and they used their superior communications technology and geographical knowledge to great advantage.

In eastern Africa, the Swahili city-states had long focused outward, on Indian Ocean trade (see Chapter 16). In the early nineteenth century, however, interior peoples began to bring increased supplies of ivory to the coast in response to rising demand in the West for billiard balls, piano keys, combs, and other products manufactured from expensive elephant tusks. That trade caught the attention of the sultans of Oman, who strengthened their claim to Zanzibar and moved their capital to the island in the 1830s.

Soon well-armed caravans were marching into the interior, decimating elephant herds and, even more tragically, intensifying the East African slave trade just as the Atlantic one was being abolished. David Livingstone and other European observers were appalled, and their appeals to end the Arab-dominated trade provided a strong humanitarian argument for greater British involvement in the interior of East Africa.

By the 1880s, the British and the Germans were scrambling for East African territory, with the British especially concerned to control Lake Victoria (as they renamed it), which explorers had identified as the headwaters of the Nile River. Already devastated by the slave trade, East Africans were unable to stop them.

Southern Africa

In southern Africa as well, the dynamics of African history intersected with European imperialism. Long before the Dutch established their settlement at Cape Town (see Chapter 16), the ancestors of King Khama and his people, Bantu-speaking farmers, herders, and ironworkers, had populated the land.

In the late eighteenth century, drought led small chiefdoms in the region to band together to secure permanent water sources. The most successful of the new states was the Zulu empire of **Shaka** (r. 1820–1828). He formed a standing army of soldiers from different clans, emphasizing their loyalty to him and to the Zulu state rather than to their own chiefdoms, and chose his generals on the basis of merit rather than chiefly status. Young women were organized into agricultural regiments, and no one was allowed to marry without Shaka's permission.

The conquests of Shaka's armies were known as the *mfecane* (mm-fuh-KAHN-ay), "the crushing." Many chiefdoms were violently absorbed into the Zulu empire, though some neighboring chiefs submitted voluntarily. In either case, conquered peoples were taken into Zulu society and became Zulu. What had been one of many small, clan-based chiefdoms was becoming a powerful nation. The mfecane set in motion a chain reaction as other leaders copied Zulu military tactics and carried the frontier of warfare a thousand miles north. The Bangwato and other societies in the interior fled, abandoning much of their land.

At the same time that the mfecane was disrupting southern African societies, white settlers known as Boers, descendants of earlier Dutch and French colonists, were seeking land for further expansion. The Boers moved into territories temporarily depopulated in the wake of Zulu warfare, causing frontier conflicts that alarmed British authorities.

Shaka
(r. 1820–1828) Founder and ruler of the Zulu empire. Zulu military tactics revolutionized warfare in southern Africa. Through the *mfecane*, or "crushing," Shaka violently absorbed many surrounding societies into his empire.

The British were a new factor in southern Africa, having taken Cape Town from the Dutch during the Napoleonic Wars. Though their main concern was the security of Cape Town and the maritime route to India, they now became embroiled in the affairs of the interior, attempting to control African societies on their borders as well as the Boers, who resented British interference.

While the Boers had never been able to subdue African resistance to their encroachment, British firepower now overwhelmed some Xhosa (KOH-suh) chiefdoms, which lost rich grazing lands to the colonists. Neither negotiation nor military resistance could stem the European tide. Contact with colonial society also created deep divisions within Xhosa society. Traditionalists saw those Xhosa who converted to Christianity and grew crops for colonial markets as having abandoned their own people and traditions.

Then another disaster struck. A cattle disease, inadvertently introduced by the Europeans in the 1850s, wiped out large numbers of Xhosa cattle. Facing starvation as well as invasion, some Xhosa turned to the prophecies of a young woman, Nongqawuse (nawng-ka-WOO-say) (ca. 1840–1898), who said the ancestors told her that evil would be driven from the land if the people slaughtered their remaining cattle. Ancestral warriors would return, she said, and new cattle herds would emerge from the ground to replace those that were diseased and killed.

Belief in the power of ancestors, and that women often had the power to communicate with them, was traditional to the Xhosa. But the idea that the raising of the dead would accompany a new era of peace was borrowed from Methodist missionaries. Like the doctrines of Hong Xiuquan in China (see Chapter 24) and Wovoka on the Great Plains (see Chapter 25), Nongqawuse's message was an example of syncretism, a combination of indigenous beliefs with the Christian concept of the "millennium," a period of perfect peace that awaits believers at the end of time. Seeing no other way out of their predicament, many Xhosa followed Nongqawuse's prophecy and killed their cattle. When the departed warriors failed to return and hunger spread throughout the land, the **Xhosa Cattle Killing** of 1856–1857 ensured the success of British conquest. Over one hundred thousand African lives were lost, while the survivors were incorporated into Britain's Cape Colony.

Unlike the Xhosa, the Zulu and most other southern African societies retained their sovereignty into the 1870s. Their colonial fate was not determined until mineral discoveries—diamonds in 1868 and gold in 1884—combined with New Imperialism to finally motivate the British to conquer the rest of the South African interior. The Boers, proud of their independence, created several republics in the northern interior of South Africa and then sought a German alliance to further protect themselves against British imperialism. Africans in the interior, including Khama's Bangwato, found themselves facing the full brunt of European military technology for the first time.

In 1879, British authorities issued an ultimatum demanding that the Zulu king Cetshwayo disband his regiments. Cetshwayo (chet-SWAY-yoh) refused to comply. Zulu warriors did defeat the British at the major Battle of Isandhlwana (ee-san-DLWAH-nah), but like the Battle of Little Bighorn (see Chapter 25), this defeat only made the invaders more determined. Zulu warriors, who had been trained to rush the enemy in dense regimental ranks, were slaughtered by British cannon and machine guns. In 1880 the British sacked the Zulu capital and sent Cetshwayo into exile.

The main figure of the New Imperialism in southern Africa was **Cecil Rhodes** (1853–1902), a mining magnate (and founder of the De Beers diamond syndicate) who advocated a British empire *"from Cape to Cairo."* His British South Africa Company (BSAC) was a chartered company with its own army and ambitions for

Xhosa Cattle Killing (1856–1857) A large cattle die-off in Africa caused by a European disease. Some Xhosa accepted Nongqawuse's prophecies that if the people cleansed themselves and killed their cattle their ancestors would return and bring peace and prosperity. The result was famine and Xhosa subjection to the British.

Cecil Rhodes (1853–1902) British entrepreneur, mining magnate, head of the British South Africa Company, and prime minister of the Cape Colony; played a major role in the expansion of British territory in southern Africa.

conquest. It was to avoid annexation by the BSAC that Khama traveled to London, even as Rhodes was planning an invasion of the Boer republics, on whose land the great gold strikes were located.

After the failure of Rhodes's BSAC invasion, the British government resorted to war. The South African War (1899–1902) that followed was a preview of twentieth-century warfare. The British had no trouble taking control of the towns and railway lines, but they were frustrated by the tactics of the Boer combatants, who blended into the civilian population and launched guerrilla attacks in the countryside. To separate civilians from soldiers, the British put Boer women and children into "concentration camps" (the first use of that term). Over twenty thousand Boer civilians, many of them women and children, died of illness. Though the South African War was between the British and the Boers, some twenty thousand Africans, enlisted to fight by both sides, were also killed.

The British won the war but then compromised with their defeated foes. The **Union of South Africa** (1910) was created by joining British colonies with former Boer republics under a single constitution, creating, as in Canada (see Chapter 25), a self-governing dominion within the British empire. The union has been called "an alliance of gold and maize," combining British mining and Boer agriculture. Both needed African labor. In 1913 the Native Land Act, passed by the new, all-white South African parliament, limited Africans to "native reserves" that included only a tiny proportion of their traditional landholdings. The goal was to drive Africans to work in mines and on white farms at the lowest possible pay, laying the economic foundations for what would later be called apartheid.

Because of King Khama's negotiations with the British government, his people were not part of this new South Africa and were ruled instead by the British Colonial Office. The Zulu and the Xhosa, meanwhile, like other Africans incorporated into the Union of South Africa, experienced the harshest form of colonial racism. As mineworkers and low-wage laborers on settler farms, they struggled at the lowest level of the global economy.

Meanwhile, in neighboring German Southwest Africa (today's Namibia), another chilling precedent was being set for the twentieth century. In 1904, after a Herero rebellion was put down by superior European firepower, the German commander ordered that they be driven into the Kalahari Desert and prevented from returning. Tens of thousands of Herero died in what some historians consider the century's first genocide.

The Granger Collection New York

THE RHODES COLOSSUS
STRIDING FROM CAPE TOWN TO CAIRO.

Cecil Rhodes The most important of Victorian imperialists, Cecil Rhodes dreamed of British imperial control of eastern and southern Africa "from Cape to Cairo." Combining political and economic clout, Rhodes was prime minister of the Cape Colony, founder of the De Beers diamond syndicate, owner of some of the world's richest gold mines, and head of the British South Africa Company. He later endowed the Rhodes Scholarship program to bring elite Americans of British descent to Oxford University in England so that the United States might share Britain's imperial purpose.

Union of South Africa
Self-governing dominion within the British empire created in 1910 from a number of British colonies and Boer republics after the South African War. This compromise protected both British mining and Boer agriculture at the expense of African interests.

African Resistance to Conquest

Between 1880 and 1900, European powers occupied and partitioned Africa. France and Britain held the largest African empires; Portugal and Germany each had substantial territories in the east and south; Italy and Spain were relatively minor players; and King Leopold of Belgium claimed the vast Congo in the center of the continent.

In spite of European technological superiority, Africans fought back. The Nile Valley was one arena of resistance to British imperialism. Its strategic value increased with the construction of the **Suez Canal** between the Mediterranean and the Red Sea in 1869. Built by a French engineer and financed by French and English capital, the canal became the main shipping route between Europe and Asia.

The Egyptian *khedive*, who inherited his position as Egyptian ruler from Muhammad Ali (see Chapter 23), thought that revenue from the canal would allow Egypt to maintain its independence. But a fall in cotton prices after 1865, when the end of the American Civil War brought U.S. cotton back onto the world market, reduced Egyptian government revenues. Unable to pay the country's debts, the khedive was forced to sell Egypt's shares in the Suez Canal to the British and to accept European oversight of government finances. European officers were imposed on the Egyptian military, which was reorganized as an Anglo-Egyptian force.

In 1882, nationalist Egyptian military officers rebelled against the khedive and his European backers but were quickly suppressed by the British, who then forced the khedive to accept a governor-general to oversee the Egyptian government. The British thus came to dominate Egypt, much as they dominated the "princely states" in India (see Chapter 24), keeping real power in their own hands while allowing indigenous rulers to retain their titles and their luxurious lifestyles.

Once in control of Egypt, the British, as we have seen, needed to secure the Upper Nile Valley as well. Here they faced resistance from a jihadist state in Sudan, where a cleric named **Muhammad Ahmad** (1844–1885) proclaimed himself to be **the Mahdi** (MAH-dee), the "guided one" that some Muslims believe will come to announce the end of days and the final judgment of humankind. In 1881, he declared a holy war against Egypt, which also brought him into conflict with Britain. The Mahdi's forces took the strategic city of Khartoum from the British in 1884, while killing the British commander of a combined Anglo-Egyptian force. When Muhammad Ahmad died of typhus a few months later, however, his movement lost central direction.

The jihadist movement regained momentum in the 1890s under the *khalifa* ("successor") to the Mahdi. Conflict with the Europeans could not be avoided: to answer French and German colonial claims, the British became intent on establishing "effective occupation" over the entire Nile Valley. The Battle of Omdurman (1898) was the bloodiest battle between European and African forces during the entire period. Though outnumbered two to one, Anglo-Egyptian forces used their Maxim guns to terrible effect. The British lost forty-seven soldiers that day; among the khalifa's forces over ten thousand were killed. British soldiers took vengeance for the commander killed at Khartoum, reportedly slaying Sudanese soldiers as they lay wounded on the field.

Elsewhere African resistance to colonial occupation was smaller in scale, as in the Asante kingdom. The British had sacked the Asante capital of Kumasi in 1874, but then withdrew. In the 1890s, however, with the Germans and French now active in the region, British forces once again moved toward Kumasi. The Asante reluctantly accepted a British protectorate, but they rebelled after the new British governor demanded that the "golden stool" be brought before him. The golden stool was the sacred symbol of Asante kingship; according to legend, it had descended from the heavens to confirm the sovereignty of the first Asante king. The governor's request was intolerable.

As they prepared for war, some Asante doubted whether they could succeed. A queen mother from one of the confederated chiefdoms, Yaa Asantewa (YAH

Suez Canal
(1869) French-designed canal built between the Mediterranean and the Red Seas that greatly shortened shipping times between Europe and Asia; dominated by European economic interests.

Muhammad Ahmad, the Mahdi
(1844–1885) *Mahdi* is the term some Muslims use for the "guided one" expected to appear before the end of days. Muhammad Ahmad took this title in Sudan and called for a jihad against British-dominated Egypt.

ah-san-TAY-wuh), stood forward and spoke: *"[If] you the men of Asante will not go forward, then we will. We the women will. I shall call upon my fellow women. We will fight the white men. We will fight till the last of us falls in the battlefields."** The Yaa Asantewa War of 1900 was a military defeat for the Asante, but it caused later British governors to treat the Asante royal family with greater respect and to acknowledge Asante legal traditions when codifying colonial laws.

The British also faced stiff resistance in the southern African kingdom of the Ndebele (nn-day-BEH-lay) people. Descendants of a Zulu regiment that had moved northward, the Ndebele were militarily formidable, but no match for the British South Africa Company of Cecil Rhodes. Lobengula, their king, tried to negotiate for the security of his people by signing a treaty granting the British mineral rights below the soil while retaining his own authority on the land. Even so, Lobengula, like some Amerindian leaders in the same period (see Chapter 25), recognized that the invaders were unlikely to keep their promises. *"Did you ever see a chameleon catch a fly?"* he asked a missionary. *"The chameleon gets behind the fly and remains motionless for some time, then he advances very slowly and gently . . . [then] he darts his tongue and the fly disappears. England is the chameleon and I am that fly."*† Sure enough, the Ndebele were absorbed into the British colony of Rhodesia after the loss of two wars of resistance in the 1890s. (See the feature "World History in Today's World: Who Owns Zimbabwe's Land?")

Coordinating resistance was even more difficult in regions where traditional political organization was less centralized. The Maji Maji (MAH-jee MAH-jee) Revolt in German East Africa was led by a religious prophet, Kinjekitile, who attempted to forge an alliance between numerous small chiefdoms. In the 1890s, German military conquest had met little opposition. By 1905, however, people in the region grew angry after the Germans forced them to grow cotton. African farmers had little time to tend their own food crops while enduring the hard labor of planting, weeding, and harvesting cotton. The payment they received was barely enough to pay colonial taxes, and cotton robbed their fields of fertility.

Maji Maji meant "powerful water," a reference to a sacred pool that attracted pilgrims from across a wide area. Kinjekitile used this sacred shrine as a rallying point. He promised his followers that bathing in the sacred stream would make them immune to German bullets. Of course, this did not happen, and the Germans suppressed the Maji Maji revolt ruthlessly. But they also learned not to press their advantage too far, and they no longer enforced mandatory cotton growing.

The aftermath of both the Asante and Maji Maji revolts shows that Africans' willingness to fight could force the Europeans to adjust their policies. Throughout the colonial period, Africans also used more subtle forms of resistance, such as songs and dances that criticized their European rulers, as a way to preserve their culture and express their humanity. (African slaves in the Americas had adopted similar strategies; see Chapter 19.)

Africans were, nonetheless, consistently demeaned by the imperial powers. A new fad at Western expositions was to display "natives" as a curiosity for the amusement of Western audiences. King Khama and his colleagues were taken to see a "Somali village" on display at London's Crystal Palace. One wonders what the southern African kings, dressed in formal Victorian attire, and the Somalis, presented to the public in their "primitive" state, thought of one another. The worst excess came in 1906, when a Central African named Ota Benga was

---

*Yaa Asantewa, cited in David Sweetman, *Women Leaders in African History* (London: Heinemann, 1984), pp. 34–35.

†Neil Parsons, *A New History of Southern Africa*, 2d ed. (London: Macmillan, 1993).

Who Owns Zimbabwe's Land?

The southern African nation of Zimbabwe is blessed with some of the most productive agricultural land on the continent, along with significant mineral riches. Still, compared to its potential, and also to its former economic strength, the Zimbabwean economy today is in trouble. Formal employment occupies only about 10 percent of the population; tens of thousands of Zimbabweans have crossed into Botswana and South Africa looking for work. Hyperinflation made the currency so worthless that it was replaced in 2009 by the U.S. dollar. The government is crippled by external debt obligations. Meanwhile, political conditions over the past decade and recent droughts have led to a decline in agricultural production.

The blame for Zimbabwe's tough economic times falls on President Robert Mugabe, leader of the country since it achieved African majority rule in 1980. Once known as Rhodesia, the country emerged from a difficult colonial history. As in neighboring South Africa, white Rhodesians took the best land for themselves and forced rural Africans onto inadequate "native reserves" to farm overworked lands. Nevertheless, Mugabe initially promised to respect the citizenship and property rights of white Zimbabweans. Land would be redistributed only with the consent of white farmers, who would be fairly compensated (with financial support from Britain, the former colonial power).

Then in 2000, facing political opposition, Mugabe found a populist campaign strategy in the land issue. Why should black Zimbabweans, whose great-grandparents had been ruthlessly dispossessed and whose elders had fought a tough guerrilla war to gain majority rule, be land-poor in their own country? He announced a fast-track land reform program and backed a grassroots war veterans' organization that marched onto white farms, threatening violence unless properties were immediately handed over. Mugabe's family and high-ranking military officers took over some of the farms; others were subdivided into hundreds of small farms to provide peasant subsistence. Agricultural production fell off sharply.

Given the appalling human rights record of the Mugabe regime, many foreign observers decried the injustice and economic irrationality of Zimbabwe's hasty land redistribution, though Chinese political and economic support has allowed Mugabe to weather the storm. But the leaders of South Africa reacted cautiously, given the sensitivity of the land issue in their own country. The question for both countries is: can the redress of colonial injustices be squared with the need for stability and economic development?

displayed in a cage at the Bronx Zoo in New York. He later committed suicide. The disrespect and cruelty fostered by racist ideas such as Social Darwinism endured into the twentieth century.

The New Imperialism in Southeast Asia, Austronesia, and the Pacific

As in Africa, Europeans had long competed for access to trade in Southeast Asia and had established some imperial bases, but here as well it was only in the late nineteenth century that the New Imperialism led to nearly complete Western domination. In mainland Southeast Asia, the French allied with Vietnamese emperors to extend their power over what became French Indochina. The British expanded from India into Burma and used the commercial city of Singapore to extend their empire into Malaya. On the thousands of islands that make up insular Southeast Asia, the Dutch were the dominant Western power; the United States joined the imperial club when it took the Philippines from Spain (see Map 26.2). Meanwhile, the British consolidated their control over Australia and New Zealand, and Europeans, Americans, and Japanese hoisted their flags in displays of conquest across the islands of the Pacific.

Mainland Southeast Asia

Vietnam's imperial structure was declining in the late eighteenth century. With the country wracked by rebellion, the Nguyen (noo-WEN) family allied with French missionaries and in 1802 established the new Nguyen dynasty, with Catholic missionaries representing French influence at the Vietnamese court.

The French moved from indirect influence to direct imperial control when Emperor Napoleon III, anxious to expand his country's global empire, sent an army of occupation to Vietnam in 1858 (and to Mexico a few years later; see Chapter 25). In 1862 the Nguyen ruler ceded control of the Mekong (MAY-kong) Delta and the commercial center of Saigon to France, opened three "treaty ports" to European trade, and gave the French free passage up the Mekong River. That was not enough to satisfy the French government, which after 1871, here as in Africa, pursued an even bolder imperial strategy. By 1884 the French were in control of all of Vietnam but still faced guerrilla resistance. The French army of conquest killed thousands of rebels and civilians before establishing firm control. French authorities called the violence inflicted on the Vietnamese a campaign of "pacification."

By then French forces had conquered the neighboring kingdom of Cambodia and had taken Laos by agreement with the kingdom of Siam (discussed in the next section). In 1897, they combined these territories into the **Federation of Indochina**, or simply French Indochina. French colonial authorities took over vast estates on which to grow rubber and turned rice into a major export crop. The profits went almost entirely to French traders and planters, though some Chinese and Vietnamese merchants in Saigon also benefited from the increase in commerce that came with the tighter integration of Southeast Asia into global markets.

Federation of Indochina
(1897) Federation created by the French after having conquered Vietnam, Cambodia, and Laos—an administrative convenience, as the societies that made up the federation had little in common.

Burma was likewise incorporated into the British empire in stages. By the 1870s, Britain controlled the south, while in the north a reformist Burmese king attempted to modernize the country under indigenous rule. British representatives had no patience for these experiments. They refused to take off their shoes in the king's presence, a terrible affront to court protocol. Finally, in 1886 British forces invaded from India and took the capital of Mandalay. While suppressing a number of regional rebellions, they brought administrators from India and began building railroads to the rich timber resources of the Burmese jungles.

The trading city of Singapore had been Britain's most valuable possession in Southeast Asia since 1819. It attracted many Chinese immigrants and became the center of the Chinese merchant diaspora in the region, while Indians arrived as clerks and officeworkers. Initially, the British were content to control the main ports and grow rich on the trade between the Indian Ocean and the South China Sea, leaving politics to the dozens of Muslim sultanates of Malaya. But in the 1870s economic and strategic interests led to a more active imperialism. The completion of the Suez Canal in 1869 shortened the shipping routes from Europe to

MAP 26.2 **The New Imperialism in Southeast Asia, 1910** European nations had controlled parts of Southeast Asia, such as the Dutch East Indies and the Spanish Philippines, since the sixteenth and seventeenth centuries. The New Imperialism of the nineteenth century strengthened European control over those societies while bringing the entire region, with the exception of Siam (Thailand), under Western colonial rule. In remote regions, such as the highlands of central Borneo, the process of conquest was not complete until the early twentieth century. (© Cengage Learning)

the Indian Ocean, and British merchants were particularly anxious to exploit the rich tin resources of the Malay Peninsula, for which the Second Industrial Revolution had dramatically increased demand.

As in Africa, local rivalries supported a policy of "divide and conquer." British "residents" gave local rulers "advice" on the governance of their sultanates; if a sultan refused, they would simply recognize another ambitious man as ruler and work through him. As in Egypt and the princely states of India, indigenous rulers remained in place but power was squarely in the hands of Europeans. The British prided themselves on having brought efficient administration to yet another corner of the globe. Meanwhile, they expanded plantations of commercial crops such as pepper, palm oil, and rubber.

Courtesy of Francois Denis Fievez

Rubber in French Indochina After 1875, the Second Industrial Revolution caused a sharp rise in global demand for rubber, leading to the creation of large plantations in French Indochina and British Malaya. As this image from a Vietnamese plantation indicates, first-stage processing took place on site, making rubber plantations "agro-industrial enterprises" similar to the old sugar plantations of the West Indies (see Chapter 19), with labor conditions that could be equally harsh.

Insular Southeast Asia, Austronesia, and the Pacific

The Dutch had been the dominant European presence in the islands of Southeast Asia since the seventeenth century (see Chapter 16). After the Dutch East India Company was disbanded in 1799, colonial authorities imposed even harsher economic conditions on the Dutch East Indies. In 1830, for example, Dutch authorities forced rice farmers on the island of Java to convert to sugar production. One Dutch official declared that *"they must be taught to work, and if they were unwilling out of ignorance, they must be ordered to work."** Through coercion the Dutch could buy sugar at low prices and then sell it for a great profit on world markets.

Dutch authorities asserted more and more formal administrative control over Java and Sumatra, where individual sultans had previously been left in charge of local affairs. At the same time, the increasing presence of other European powers motivated the Dutch to seek control of hundreds of other islands. Those who resisted, such as rebels on the Hindu-ruled island of Bali, were slaughtered. The New Imperialism significantly deepened Dutch power over the Indonesian archipelago.

The United States was the new presence in Asia and the Pacific. The arrival of Admiral Perry in Japan in 1853 (see Chapter 24) significantly expanded American influence in Asia, and the United States claimed a direct territorial stake in the Pacific when it annexed the Hawai'ian Islands in 1898.

*Cited in D. R. SarDesai, *Southeast Asia Past and Present,* 4th ed. (Boulder: Westview, 1997), p. 92.

The extension of American imperialism to the Philippines came as a result of the Spanish-American War of 1898–1900. That conflict, initially centered on the Caribbean island of Cuba, spread to include the Philippines, where Spain had been in power since the foundation of Manila in 1571.

In the 1880s Filipino nationalists began resisting Spanish authority, and in 1896 they revolted to gain independence. In 1899, the Spanish handed the islands over to the Americans by secret treaty. Some Americans protested that it was contrary to American principles to become a colonial power. The writer Mark Twain joined the Anti-Imperialist League, declaring that American motives in the Philippines were no more pure than those of European imperialists and just as driven by economics.

The Filipino revolutionaries continued to struggle for independence, now against an American army of occupation. Four years of fighting left five thousand U.S. soldiers and over sixteen thousand Filipino combatants dead. As in South Africa at the same time, thousands of civilians perished in concentration camps used to separate them from the guerrillas. While the Anti-Imperialist League continued its protests, President William McKinley declared that *"it is our duty to uplift and civilize and Christianize"* the Filipinos, making Social Darwinism a driving idea in U.S. foreign policy.

Observing the debate in American public opinion, British poet of empire Rudyard Kipling urged Americans to take on imperial responsibilities:

Take up the White Man's burden—
Send forth the best ye breed—
Go bind your sons to exile
To serve your captives' need;
To wait in heavy harness,
On fluttered folk and wild—
Your new-caught, sullen peoples,
Half-devil and half-child.[*]

Kipling worried that the British empire was in decline and that only an imperialistic United States could save the world for "Anglo-Saxon civilization." Americans needed to *"take up the White Man's burden,"* Kipling argued, for the benefit of the Filipinos themselves. A differing view of such events was offered by the African American writer W. E. B. Du Bois (doo BOYZ), who, noting that the New Imperialism had led to white domination across the world, predicted in 1903 that *"the problem of the twentieth century is the problem of the color-line."*[†] His statement was as true for Southeast Asia as it was for Africa or the United States, and throughout the Pacific Ocean as well.

Because Australia and New Zealand were settlement colonies, British motivation for expansion there predated the Second Industrial Revolution and the New Imperialism. By the time the scramble for Africa began in the 1870s, in fact, Australian Aborigines had already been reduced to a defeated and subservient people as the continent's economy, fueled by wool exports and gold discoveries, boomed. In New Zealand, however, British settlers had faced tougher resistance from the Polynesian-speaking Maori people. Though an 1840 treaty had created the framework for

---

[*]Verse from "The White Man's Burden" by Rudyard Kipling, from *Rudyard Kipling's Verse Definitive Edition* by Rudyard Kipling, 1920, Doubleday.

[†]W. E. B. Du Bois, *The Souls of Black Folk* (New York: Vintage, 1990).

British-Maori coexistence, guaranteeing the Maori land rights and giving them the status of British subjects, by the 1860s warfare had broken out. British victory was followed by new legislation that eased the way for European purchase of Maori land: by 1890 indigenous New Zealanders had lost nearly 95 percent of their holdings.

Okinawa was annexed by Japan in 1879. French Polynesia, with its capital on Tahiti, was established in 1889. New Guinea was taken by Germany in 1884; in 1899, Samoa was divided between Germany and the United States. The process of the New Imperialism was complete: by century's end, empires blanketed the globe.

Imperial Comparisons Through Case Studies

Case studies from Africa and Southeast Asia demonstrate both the economic and the political implications of the New Imperialism. The history of rubber shows how industrial and technological developments led to imperialism as a form of economic domination. Politically, a comparison of how the rulers of Siam (Thailand) and Ethiopia retained their independence shows how these exceptions prove the rule of Western dominance. (See the feature "Visual Evidence in Primary Sources: National Flags.")

A Case Study of the New Imperialism: Rubber

During the Second Industrial Revolution, inventors found new applications for rubber in such products as waterproof clothing and factory conveyor belts. The spread of telephones, electrical lines, and bicycles generated a booming trade in rubber. At first the only source was the Brazilian Amazon (see Chapter 25), where "rubber barons" built palatial homes while indigenous Amerindian peoples suffered from the introduction of diseases to which they had no resistance.

Even Brazil's extensive rubber reserves were not enough to meet demand. To maintain their country's monopoly, Brazilians tried to prevent the export of rubber seeds, but a British agent managed to smuggle some to a specially built hothouse at Kew Gardens outside London (see Chapter 21). From there, rubber seedlings were sent to British colonies in Asia. Plantings in Singapore were successful, and from there rubber was taken to Malaya, Thailand, Vietnam, and the Dutch East Indies. As in Brazil, great fortunes were made at the expense of local farmers, and rainforests were felled to make room for large rubber plantations. European traders secured access to an essential commodity and reaped the lion's share of profits, as colonial taxation drove local peasants to work for low wages under harsh conditions.

The most notorious abuses took place in the Congo Free State, the personal domain of Leopold II, where wild rubber grew in abundance. The Belgian king ordered his agents to use whatever means necessary to maximize the harvest from Central African forests and paid them bonuses based on the amount of rubber they delivered. The result was a reign of terror. Sometimes the agents kept women in cages, promising to release them only after their husbands had delivered enough rubber. Like the farmers forced to grow cotton in East Africa, the families of rubber collectors went hungry because they could not tend their own fields.

When the unreasonable rubber quotas were still not met, the killing began. Belgian officers and agents paid Free State soldiers to bring back the hands of those they killed. These soldiers would sometimes chop off the hands of the living and bring them back to the Belgian trade stations for a cash reward. Eventually 10 million people died, mostly from hunger.

National Flags

Banners and flags have a long history as markers of individual and group identity. Flags took on even more important symbolic power in the nineteenth century with the rise of European nation-states and the spread of their empires. In the West, where flags had earlier been closely associated with royal families, they now became the symbols of entire nations. The imposition of a nation's flag beyond the nation's frontier became a defining symbol of imperialism.

Here are nineteenth-century flags from societies that struggled to retain their independence: Liberia (West Africa), Ethiopia (East Africa), Siam (or Thailand, Southeast Asia), the Hawai'ian kingdom, and the Cherokee nation (United States). Creating these flags and preserving the right to fly them were important expressions of resistance to colonialism.

Courtesy Rick Wyatt, www.crwflags.com

The West African Republic of Liberia was founded in 1847 by freed American slaves. An earlier version of the flag had a cross rather than a star in the upper left. When the flag was first presented, "many eyes were suffused with tears. . . . Who that looked back to America and remembered what he saw and felt there, could be otherwise than agitated?"[*]

Courtesy Rick Wyatt, www.crwflags.com

This flag, first used in 1897, features the "Lion of Judah" as a symbol for Ethiopia. Red stands for power and faith; yellow for peace, wealth, and love; and green for land and hope. These became the colors of global African nationalism, and they can now be found on the flags of nations such as Ghana, Zimbabwe, Guyana, and Grenada. The flag has deep religious symbolism for Jamaican Rastafarians.

---

[*]Cited in Carl Patrick Burrowes, *Power and Press Freedom in Liberia, 1830–1970* (Trenton: Africa World Press, 2004), p. 60.

This flag dates from 1891. One of several different flags from Siam, it was flown above the palace only when the king was present. At the center is the royal coat of arms, with a trident and golden crown above. Later, the flag of Thailand evolved to emphasize national rather than royal identity, with horizontal stripes of red, white, and blue.

This flag was commissioned by Kamehameha the Great, the first Hawai'ian to unify the islands, in 1816, and it flew until 1893. The eight bars represent the major Hawai'ian Islands, and the British Union Jack reflects the attempts of Hawai'ian monarchs to use an alliance with Britain as protection against the United States and other imperialist powers. This is the current state flag of Hawai'i.

After the U.S. government forcibly moved the Cherokee people to Oklahoma (see Chapter 25), the nation adopted a constitution to mark their quest for sovereignty in their new home. The date on this flag (currently in use) commemorates that constitution. Each of the seven yellow stars represents one of the original Cherokee clans; the black star represents those who lost their lives on the "Trail of Tears."

QUESTION FOR ANALYSIS

» *How do these flags combine indigenous and imported design elements?*

Torture in King Leopold's Congo Here two victims of King Leopold's policies, Mola and Yoka, display their mutilated limbs. The hands of Mola were eaten by gangrene after his hands were tied too tightly by Leopold's agents. Yoka's right hand was cut off by soldiers who planned to receive a bounty at headquarters by using the hand as proof of a kill. Once the world learned about this extreme violence, humanitarian voices were raised against Leopold. (Courtesy, Anti-Slavery International, London)

Leopold claimed to be a great humanitarian, but by the late 1890s stories of violence from the Congo began to reach home. A clerk in Brussels noticed that ships arriving full of rubber and ivory were returning to the Congo with only guns and ammunition in their holds. His further investigation revealed the full horror of Leopold's crimes, and he helped form the Congo Reform Association to demand that they be ended. Finally, in 1908 King Leopold sold his African empire to the Belgian government, reaping a huge profit on the sale. A heritage of violence still affects the Congo today, while Brussels is filled with the many grand monuments that Leopold built with the fortune he made in the rubber trade.

Enduring Monarchies: Ethiopia and Siam

Given the overwhelming strength of European domination in the age of the New Imperialism, it seems surprising that Ethiopia and Siam (present-day Thailand) managed to retain their independence. A comparison between them shows that while factors such as competent leadership were important, the continuing independence of these two states merely confirmed overwhelming European domination in Africa and Southeast Asia.

The ancient Christian kingdom of Ethiopia first met modern European firepower in 1868 when a British relief column was sent to rescue several British subjects held hostage by the Ethiopian king. The British easily crushed the African army they encountered. Though the Ethiopian leader had killed himself on the field of battle, leaving the kingdom defenseless, the British then withdrew.

When **Menelik II** (r. 1889–1913) became emperor, he was determined to strengthen his state against further assault. Ethiopia, like Tokugawa Japan, had long had a decentralized political structure in which rural lords, commanding their own armies, were as powerful as the emperor himself. Menelik (MEN-uh-lik) consolidated power at the imperial court and created his own standing army, equipped with the latest repeating rifles. He also used his credentials as a Christian to enhance his diplomatic influence in Europe, where his ambassadors played the European powers against one another to Ethiopia's advantage.

Menelik was also fortunate that the European assault on Ethiopia came from Italy, the weakest of the European imperial powers. At the Battle of Adowa (1896) the Ethiopians were victorious, though Italy did take the strategically important region of Eritrea on the Red Sea. Britain, by then dominant in northeastern

Menelik II
(r. 1889–1913) Emperor who used diplomacy and military reorganization to retain Ethiopian independence, defeating an Italian army of invasion at Adowa in 1896.

Africa, was convinced that Menelik would be able to maintain security on the Egyptian frontier and allow European traders free access to his kingdom. Since this was a cheaper solution than occupying the country by force, the British sponsored the development of modern infrastructure, such as banks and railroads, during Menelik's reign. The benefits, as usual, went to Ethiopian elites and European investors. The Ethiopian majority continued to scratch a meager living from the soil.

Simultaneously, the kings of Siam also faced the danger of absorption into European empires, with the British expanding from India in the west and the French threatening from Indochina in the east. Two long-ruling kings, Mongkut (r. 1851–1868) and Chulalongkorn (r. 1868–1910), transformed the ancient kingdom into a sovereign nation. Both used internal reform and diplomatic engagement to deal with the threats of the New Imperialism.

As a young man Mongkut (MANG-koot) lived in a Buddhist monastery. When he emerged to become king in 1851, he found that his monastic experience, where he had interacted with men from all social classes, prepared him to become a popular leader. Having learned English, mathematics, and astronomy from Western missionaries, he could interact effectively with Europeans as well.

Observing China's fate after the Opium Wars (see Chapter 24), Mongkut was determined to meet the Western challenge. Conservatives at court opposed his reforms, arguing that they would undermine Buddhist traditions. Nevertheless, Mongkut invited Western emissaries to his capital, installed them as advisers, and exempted them from the usual court protocols, such as crawling on their knees before the king. Though Mongkut favored the British, he balanced their influence with French and Dutch advisers. He also opened Siam to foreign trade, giving merchants from various countries a stake in his system.

Most importantly, Mongkut chose an English tutor for his son and heir, **Chulalongkorn**. After Chulalongkorn (CHOO-luh-AWHN-korn) came to power in 1868, he appointed an able set of Siamese advisers who understood that their traditions and sovereignty could be preserved only through reform. Chulalongkorn altered the legal system to protect private property, abolished slavery and debt peonage, expanded access to education, and encouraged the introduction of telegraphs and railroads. Moreover, he centralized governmental power through a streamlined bureaucracy that reached from the capital into the smallest villages.

Like his father, Chulalongkorn was an able diplomat who played Europeans off one another. Lacking a strong army, he gave up claims to parts of his empire, such as Laos, to protect the core of his kingdom. Not only did this appease the French and the British, but it also gave his kingdom a more ethnically Thai character.

Chulalongkorn was fortunate that the British and the French were anxious to avoid conflict between their Indian and Indochinese empires. Because their traders and missionaries were allowed to establish themselves in the kingdom, and because the Siamese leader was able to ensure peace and stability in his domain, the French and British agreed in 1896 to recognize the independence of the kingdom of Siam as a buffer between their empires (see Map 26.2).

As with Ethiopia, the independence of Siam was secured by internal reform, centralization of government power, and deft diplomatic maneuvering, all outcomes of effective political leadership. Nevertheless, had the British or French wished to conquer Ethiopia or Siam, they could have done so. The achievement of Menelik and Chulalongkorn in the 1890s was to position their countries to take advantage of inter-European rivalries.

Chulalongkorn
(r. 1868–1910) King of Siam (Thailand) who modernized his country through legal and constitutional reforms. Through successful diplomacy he ensured Siam's continued independence while neighboring societies were absorbed into European empires.

Photo by W. & D. Downey/Getty Images

King Chulalongkorn of Siam   This photograph from 1890 shows King Chulalongkorn of Siam with his son, the Crown Prince Vajiravudh Rama, who was studying in Britain. Chulalongkorn used deft diplomacy to maintain the independence of Siam (Thailand) during the height of the European scramble for colonial territory. Father and son are dressed in European style, but the warm embrace of their hands was a Southeast Asian touch. British males rarely showed such affection in Victorian portraits.

In the age of the New Imperialism, it was only under unusual circumstances that African and Southeast Asian societies could retain their sovereignty. King Khama's situation was much more common. He did his best with the diplomatic resources at his disposal, but his kingdom was too small and too poorly armed to survive as an independent state. Unlike Menelik and Chulalongkorn, most African and Southeast Asian rulers did not command sufficient resources to protect themselves from the New Imperialism. Even in Ethiopia and Siam, the economic impact of Western industrial capitalism brought new and difficult challenges to rural peoples, who were now bound, like their counterparts in colonial empires, to a global economy to which they contributed much more than they received.

CONTEXT AND CONNECTIONS

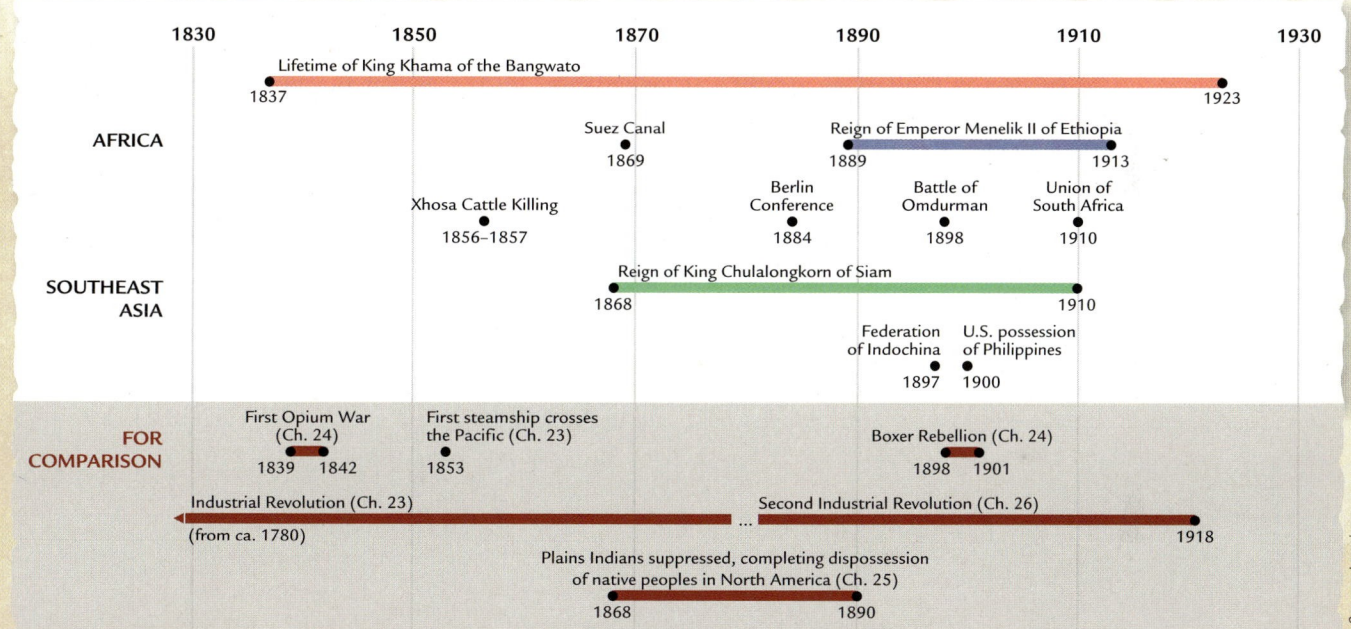

© Cengage Learning

The New Imperialism in World History

In the second half of the nineteenth century many small-scale societies and kingdoms that had maintained their autonomy could no longer resist the imperial ambitions of aggressive European nation-states. The story of their often spirited resistance and ultimate defeat was a global one: from the Great Plains of Canada and the United States, to the Yucatán of Mexico (see Chapter 25), to small Pacific islands, to the interior of the African continent. If even a mighty empire like Qing China succumbed (see Chapter 24), smaller states like King Khama's Bangwato could not hope to defend themselves.

When King Khama and his colleagues traveled to London in 1895, they were visiting the epicenter of global financial and military power. By then, however, the British could no longer be complacent. They had lost their early industrial lead to emerging economies in Germany and the United States, and the British empire, while still by far the world's largest, faced challenges from its newly ambitious competitors in the age of the New Imperialism.

Before 1850, European maritime prowess had only intermittently been translated into political domination, though British control over India set a precedent (see Chapter 20). It was the Industrial Revolution that provided the means and motivation for further imperial expansion (see Chapter 23). Initially, though, it seemed that the British would be content with "informal empire" rather than more direct forms of administrative domination: in China and Latin America that policy was generating great profit without the expense of conquest and control. By the late nineteenth century, however, refinements in chemical and metallurgical processes—the Second Industrial Revolution—led to more sophisticated production techniques, much larger industrial corporations, and intensified competition for raw materials and markets. As Britain's new competitors developed newer and more efficient industrial infrastructure, such competition unleashed the rapid expansion of empires in the last quarter of the century. The "scramble for Africa" was the most dramatic example of the new global quest for imperial dominion.

By 1900, when foreign troops occupied the Forbidden City in Beijing (see Chapter 24) and the process of partition and conquest in Africa, Southeast Asia, and the Pacific neared completion, the organizing principle of a world unified by industrial markets was clear. Western Europe and the United States stood astride the globe, seemingly reinforcing the Social Darwinist claim of their natural superiority,

with only Japan offering a clear example of non-European achievement in the race to industrialized military power.

Africa, Southeast Asia, and the Pacific offered a safety valve for European and Japanese competition in the late nineteenth century, but entering the twentieth century the flags of empire crowded against each other across the world, and European conflicts would turn inward during two great world wars (see Chapters 27 and 29). The First and Second World Wars would draw the world's peoples into devastating conflict arising from inter-European competition, but would ultimately undercut Western domination. By mid-century, anticolonial nationalists would effectively organize themselves to campaign for national independence. By the end of the twentieth century, the West's global dominance, which had seemed so natural in 1900, would come to appear a relatively brief episode in world history.

Meanwhile, King Khama's mission to London had important long-term consequences. Because of his efforts, the Bangwato and the other peoples of Botswana entered the British empire as a protectorate and avoided incorporation into apartheid South Africa (see Chapter 31). It was perhaps a small victory when measured against the great events of the time, but one of which Khama's descendants are justifiably proud.

VOYAGES ON THE WEB: King Khama III

The Voyages Map App follows the traveler's journeys using interactive study tools, including 360-degree panoramic views of historic sites, zoomable maps, audio summaries, flash cards, and quizzes.

Key Terms

King Khama III (732)
New Imperialism (735)
Second Industrial Revolution (736)
David Livingstone (736)
King Leopold II of Belgium (737)

Berlin Conference (737)
Asante kingdom (742)
Samori Toure (742)
Shaka (743)
Xhosa Cattle Killing (744)
Cecil Rhodes (744)
Union of South Africa (745)

Suez Canal (746)
Muhammad Ahmad, the Mahdi (746)
Federation of Indochina (749)
Menelik II (756)
Chulalongkorn (757)

For Further Reference

Headrick, Daniel. *The Tools of Empire: Technology and European Imperialism in the Nineteenth Century*. New York: Oxford University Press, 1981.

Hochschild, Adam. *King Leopold's Ghost: A Story of Greed, Terror and Heroism in Colonial Africa*. Boston: Houghton Mifflin, 1999.

Lockard, Craig. *Southeast Asia in World History*. New York: Oxford University Press, 2009.

Markus, Harold G. *The Life and Times of Menelik II: Ethiopia 1844–1913*. New York: Oxford University Press, 1975.

Martin, B. G., ed. *Muslim Brotherhoods in Nineteenth Century Africa*. New York: Cambridge University Press, 2003.

Owen, Norman G., ed. *The Emergence of Modern Southeast Asia*. Honolulu: University of Hawai'i Press, 2004.

Packenham, Thomas. *The Scramble for Africa, 1976–1912*. 2d ed. London: Longman, 1999.

Parsons, Neil. *King Khama, Emperor Joe and the Great White Queen: Victorian Britain Through African Eyes*. Chicago: University of Chicago Press, 1998.

Peiers, J. B. *The Dead Will Arise: Nongqawuse and the Great Xhosa Cattle Killing Movement of 1856–1857*. London: James Currey, 1989.

Reid, Richard. *A History of Modern Africa: 1800 to the Present*. 2d ed. London: Wiley-Blackwell, 2011.

Wyatt, David K. *A Short History of Thailand*. 2d ed. New Haven: Yale University Press, 2003.

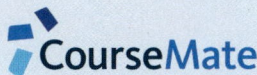 **CourseMate** Go to the CourseMate website at **www.cengagebrain.com** for additional study tools and review materials—including audio and video clips—for this chapter.

27

War, Revolution, and Global Uncertainty, 1905–1928

The violence and brutality of the First World War (1914–1918) made a mockery of the nineteenth-century idea of progress. The carnage left many people with doubt and pessimism about the future. Others, inspired by the revolutionary changes that accompanied the war, saw a brighter day dawning. Having witnessed the Russian Revolution of 1917 firsthand and interviewed many world leaders, the American journalist **Louise Bryant** (1885–1936) was in a good position to gauge the high stakes of the postwar world. She was entering the period of world history that one historian later called "the age of extremes." Bryant believed that the world was, for better or for worse, at a turning point:

Louise Bryant

(Hulton-Deutsch Collection/Corbis)

On the grey horizon of human existence looms a great giant called Working Class Consciousness. He treads with thunderous step through all the countries of the world. There is no escape, we must go out and meet him. It all depends on us whether he will turn into a loathsome, ugly monster demanding human sacrifices or whether he shall be the savior of mankind.[*]

[*]Quotes from Louise Bryant, *Six Red Months in Moscow* (New York: George H. Doren, 1919), p. xx.

The Travels of Louise Bryant

→ Louise Bryant's journeys
→ Louise Bryant's 1919 speaking tour
• City visited by Bryant
• Other city

Louise Bryant and John Reed witness Russian Revolution, 1917.

Bryant visits Central Asia, 1920.

Bryant goes on speaking tour across the U.S., 1919.

© Cengage Learning

Join this chapter's traveler on "Voyages," an interactive tour of historic sites and events:
www.cengagebrain.com

Bryant was an exceptional woman for her times. Impatient with restrictive conventions and an ardent feminist, she was described as someone who *"refuses to be bound . . . an artist, a joyous, rampant individualist, a poet and a revolutionary."* She was a child of the American West, born in San Francisco and then, after her father's premature death, raised on a remote ranch in Nevada with only her grandfather, a Chinese cook, and her imagination for company. After graduating from the University of Oregon, Bryant wanted to be a serious journalist, but the only job she could get was as a "society" writer for a Portland newspaper. It was 1909, and women were not expected to be involved with "hard" news. She married a dentist but felt increasingly hemmed in by her middle-class surroundings.

Louise Bryant
(1885–1936) American journalist, traveler, feminist, and author of several books on the Russian Revolution.

John Reed, cited in Mary Anne Dearborn, "Reviving Louise Bryant," Oregon Cultural Heritage Commission, http://www.ochcom.org/bryant/.

Then a young journalist named John Reed swept into her life. She left with him for New York, experiencing the cultural and intellectual dynamism of Greenwich Village. This was the life she craved, full of adventure and purpose. After a series of stormy love affairs that nearly tore their relationship apart, Bryant and Reed were married, and together they traveled to Russia in the summer of 1917. Both left important records of that experience, but Reed overshadowed Bryant in historical memory. Given the gender perceptions of the time, Bryant's journalism was never taken as seriously as that of her husband.

During her lifetime Bryant witnessed remarkable changes. In the industrialized world telephones and electricity became commonplace, and the automobile and airplane were invented; Bryant saw the great aviator Amelia Earhart, a symbol of female emancipation, as a role model. In some places, women fought for and won the right to vote. The creativity of African American musicians led to the creation of jazz music, the first significant influence of the United States on global culture. Scientific advances continued, as physicists such as Albert Einstein made huge strides toward understanding nature at both cosmic and atomic levels, while Sigmund Freud, whom Bryant once interviewed, plumbed the depths of the human psyche.

But a shadow of uncertainty hung over these accomplishments. The industrially driven devastation of the First World War in Europe caused immense suffering not only for soldiers but also for civilians. In mobilizing their empires for the war effort, the European powers made their local conflict a genuinely global one, severely disrupting the lives of many Africans, Asians, and peoples of the Pacific. While the president of the United States, Woodrow Wilson, confidently proclaimed that this was *"the war to end all wars,"* one that would *"make the world safe for democracy,"* competing national interests destabilized the postwar world.

Meanwhile, both before and during the war, major world societies—Mexico, China, and Russia—were rocked by revolution. Louise Bryant, a socialist, saw hope in uncertainty, applauding downtrodden people who rose up against local oppressors or imperial masters. But she recognized as well the dangers that war and revolution had unleashed.

Focus Questions

» *How can the First World War be regarded as a "total war," both for the domestic populations of the main combatants and for the entire world?*

» *How did the postwar settlements fail to resolve global political tensions?*

» *How did the outcomes of revolutions in Mexico, China, and Russia add to the uncertainty of the postwar world?*

World War I as Global "Total" War

World War I (1914–1918) represented a radical change in warfare. Conditions of "total war" meant that the fight engaged masses of civilians and required the complete mobilization of economic and human resources. Governments assumed unprecedented powers to regulate social, political, and economic life. For each of the main combatants—Germany, Austria, Britain, France, Russia, and the United States—the war strained traditional social and political systems. Nothing would remain the same. The British called it simply the Great War.

The war can also be called "total" because it was a truly global conflict, involving not just Europeans but also Americans, Indians, Chinese, Australians, Japanese, Vietnamese, Arabs, Turks, Armenians, Africans, and others. While colonial peoples had been caught up in earlier European conflicts, the global involvement of World War I was unprecedented. Young men from the United States shipped out to Europe, Indian soldiers marched to Baghdad, Southeast Asians worked behind the lines on the western front, West Africans fought in the trenches: all had life-changing experiences.

Causes of World War I, 1890–1914

On June 28, 1914, in the Balkan city of Sarajevo, a Serbian nationalist assassinated Archduke Franz Ferdinand, heir to the Austrian throne. The Balkan region had long been an unstable zone between the Austrian and Ottoman empires (see Map 27.1). As the Ottomans declined, Austrians were asserting themselves, in the process provoking local nationalists who did not want to escape one empire only to be dominated by another (see Chapter 23).

Despite their cultural similarities as Slavs and their long history of coexistence, the inhabitants of the Balkans vied with one another over religious differences. Serbian nationalists, members of the Orthodox Christian faith, looked to their coreligionists in Russia for support; Croatian nationalists allied themselves with Catholic Austria; Bosnian Muslims sided with the Ottoman empire.

These local Balkan tensions led to mobilization for full-scale war between the great powers because of the rising militarism, aggressive nationalism, and intense imperial competition that had preoccupied the leading industrial nations since the age of the New Imperialism (see Chapter 26). In the late nineteenth century, tensions between the great powers, now including Japan and the United States, had found an outlet in colonial rivalries outside of Europe. By 1900, however, there were no African, Asian, or Pacific lands left to conquer. The assassination of Archduke Franz Ferdinand was therefore like a spark that set alight the dry tinder of heavily militarized national competition.

After dismissing Otto von Bismarck in 1890 (see Chapter 23), **Kaiser Wilhelm II** (r. 1888–1918) abandoned careful diplomacy for a more aggressive foreign policy. His naval buildup caused Britain to reverse its practice of avoiding commitments on the continent. Likewise the French and Russian governments, alarmed by German ambitions, overcame their long-standing mutual distrust. A series of treaties produced a combination of alliances that divided Europe into two opposing blocs: the Triple Entente (ahn-TAHNT) of France, Britain, and Russia against the Triple Alliance of Germany, Austria, and Italy. The alliance system gave diplomats few options for the resolution of any crisis.

Thus the Balkan crisis led to an explosive confrontation between two hostile and heavily armed camps. The Austrian government threatened Serbia with war if it did not comply with a set of humiliating demands. The Serbs appealed to Russia, while the Germans backed up the Austrians. The Ottoman empire, fearful of Russian and British designs, allied itself with Germany. After a period of indecision, Italy joined with Britain, France, and Russia.

Kaiser Wilhelm II (r. 1888–1918) German emperor whose foreign policy and military buildup changed the European balance of power and laid the foundation for the Triple Alliance and the Triple Entente.

MAP 27.1 **World War I, 1914–1918** By the end of World War I, horrific violence along the western front in Belgium, Luxembourg, and northeastern France, and on the eastern front in the Russian empire and eastern Europe, had led to the deaths of over 8 million soldiers, with 20 million wounded. On the southern front, defeat led to the dissolution of the Ottoman empire. While these three theaters saw the fiercest fighting, the global effects of the conflict made this truly a world war. (© Cengage Learning)

Public opinion compounded the war atmosphere. In urbanized, industrial societies, foreign affairs were no longer the exclusive purview of diplomatic elites. Expanding electorates had involved broader segments of European populations in politics at a time when inexpensive daily newspapers struck a nationalistic tone. Declarations of war were therefore met with popular excitement and patriotic demonstrations. Only in Russia, where the tsar and his ministers generally ignored public opinion, did the government act without a popular mandate. With remarkable naïveté, Europeans believed the war would be quick and conclusive, and that their side would win. (See the feature "Movement of Ideas Through Primary Sources: Emma Goldman's Critique of Militarism.")

Louise Bryant was cynical about the war, seeing it as nothing but a capitalist tactic to increase profits. It seemed clear to her and to other socialists that French and German workers shared common cause against their bosses; for them to fight each other under the banner of patriotism went against their own best interests. Nevertheless, even the German Social Democratic Party, which had long urged *"workers of the world unite!"*, now voted in favor of war.

Total War in Europe: The Western and Eastern Fronts

German war planners had hoped that Britain might remain neutral, but the British had pledged to defend neutral Belgium. When the Germans attacked Belgium en route to France, war with Britain became inevitable. Unlike 1870, when the Prussians quickly took Paris, in 1914 the German advance was stopped 20 miles (32.2 km) short (see Map 27.1). The ensuing stalemate on the **western front** resulted in a new tactic: trench warfare. On one side, French and British soldiers fortified entrenched positions with razor wire; on the other side, Germans did the same. Miserable in the muddy trenches, soldiers were called on to charge "over the top," braving harrowing gunfire in desperate attempts to overrun enemy positions. With bombs bursting around them, or choking on poisonous mustard gas, they had little chance of survival, let alone victory. Immobilized, battle lines established early in Belgium and northern France hardly shifted as the trenches were reinforced and connected with tunnels in elaborate underground networks for supplies and communications.

western front
During World War I, the line separating the elaborate trenches of German and Allied positions, which soon became almost immobile. Trench warfare was characteristic of the western front.

The casualties of trench warfare were horrific as the two sides fought year after year over the same small stretches of territory. At the Battle of Verdun in 1916, more than half a million French and German troops lost their lives. The same year, the Battle of the Somme killed nearly a million British and German soldiers. The slaughter brought no advantage to either side. Often, young men from the same neighborhood, school, or village volunteered to join the same regiment, trained and shipped out together, then received the same order to go over the top—they might all be killed in a few minutes.

Many young men had married as they headed off to war: for decades afterward, millions of war widows lived lives of regret for their lost youth. The survivors of trench warfare lost not only their companions but also their physical and mental health. The constant barrage of artillery shells meant that many suffered for the rest of their lives from "shell shock," the trauma of their ordeal in the trenches returning with every loud sound. "Lost generation" was the term used to refer to the young adults who came of age during the Great War, not just those who died, but also those who lost their hopes and dreams.

Civilians also suffered. Before 1914, despite their increasing rivalry, Germany and Britain had been major trade partners. Now, to undermine the German war

Emma Goldman's Critique of Militarism

"Preparedness, the Road to Universal Slaughter" was written by the anarchist Emma Goldman and published in New York in 1915. Emma Goldman (1869–1940) was born into a Jewish family in Lithuania, then part of the Russian empire. As a teenager she moved to St. Petersburg, where she was first exposed to radical politics, and at sixteen she moved to New York. As a young woman she advocated violence and assassination, tactics that were deeply rooted in Russia's anarchist and revolutionary traditions (see Chapter 23). Later she became a pacifist, preferring mass organization as a means of countering the economic and political oppression of industrial capitalism. Louise Bryant, who attended a speech by Goldman in Portland in 1914, was just one of many young Americans stirred to radical political action by her oratory. The two became well acquainted, and Goldman attended the funeral of Bryant's husband John Reed in Moscow in 1921.

Goldman was arrested several times, once for heading an anticonscription campaign in the leadup to the First World War. After the Alien Act of 1918 allowed the deportation of "undesirable" immigrants without a trial, in 1919 the U.S. government deported her back to Russia. She left after two years, profoundly disappointed at the suppression of civil rights by Vladimir Lenin and the Bolsheviks. Goldman then settled in Canada, traveling frequently to France and England, and continued to write and speak in defense of individual liberty.

Source: Mother Earth 10, no. 10 (December 1915).

Preparedness, the Road to Universal Slaughter

"Ammunition! Ammunition! O, Lord, thou who rulest heaven and earth, thou God of love, of mercy and of justice, provide us with enough ammunition to destroy our enemy." Such is the prayer which is ascending daily to the Christian heaven. . . . [All] of the European people have fallen over each other into the devouring flames of the furies of war, and America, pushed to the very brink by unscrupulous politicians, by ranting demagogues, and by military sharks, is preparing for the same terrible feat. In the face of this approaching disaster, it behooves men and women not yet overcome by the war madness to raise their voice of protest, to call the attention of the people to the crime and outrage which are about to be perpetrated upon them.

America is essentially the melting pot. No national unit composing it is in a position to boast of superior race purity, particular historic mission, or higher culture. Yet the jingoes and war speculators are filling the air with the sentimental slogan of hypocritical nationalism, "America for Americans," "America first, last, and all the time." This cry has caught the popular fancy from one end of the country to another. In order to maintain America, military preparedness must be engaged in at once. A billion dollars of the people's sweat and blood is to be expended for dreadnaughts and submarines for the army. The pathos of it all is that the America which is to be protected by a huge military force is not the America of the people, but that of the privileged class; the class which robs and exploits the masses, and controls their lives from the cradle to the grave. No less pathetic is it that so few people realize that preparedness never leads to peace, but that it is indeed the road to universal slaughter. . . .

Forty years ago Germany proclaimed the slogan: "Germany above everything. Germany for the Germans, first, last and always. We want peace; therefore we must prepare for war. Only a well armed and thoroughly prepared nation can maintain peace, can command respect, can be sure of its national integrity." And Germany continued to prepare, thereby forcing the other nations to do the same. The terrible European war is only the culminating fruition of the hydra-headed gospel, military preparedness. . . .

But though America grows fat on the manufacture of munitions and war loans to the Allies to help crush Prussians the same cry is now being raised in America which, if carried into national action, would build up an American militarism far more terrible than German or Prussian militarism could ever be, and that because nowhere in the world has capitalism become so brazen in its greed and nowhere is the state so ready to kneel at the feet of capital.

"Americanization" societies with well known liberals as members, they who but yesterday decried the patriotic clap-trap of today, are now lending themselves to befog the minds of the people and to help build up the same destructive institutions in America which they are directly and indirectly helping to pull down in Germany—militarism, the destroyer of youth, the raper of women, the annihilator of the best in the race, the very mower of life. . . .

The very proclaimers of "America first" have long before this betrayed the fundamental principles of real Americanism, of the kind of Americanism that Jefferson had in mind when he said that the best government is that which governs least; the kind of America that David Thoreau worked for when he proclaimed that the best government is the one that doesn't govern at all; or the other truly great Americans who aimed to make of this country a haven of refuge, who hoped that all the disinherited and oppressed people in coming to these shores would give character, quality and meaning to the country. That is not the America of the politician and munition speculators. . . .

Supposedly, America is to prepare for peace; but in reality it will be the cause of war. It always has been thus—all through bloodstained history, and it will continue until nation will refuse to fight against nation, and until the people of the world will stop preparing for slaughter. Preparedness is like the seed of a poisonous plant; placed in the soil, it will bear poisonous fruit. The European mass destruction is the fruit of that poisonous seed. It is imperative that the American workers realize this before they are driven by the jingoes into the madness that is forever haunted by the specter of danger and invasion; they must know that to prepare for peace means to invite war, means to unloose the furies of death.

QUESTIONS FOR ANALYSIS

» *Based on these arguments, how would Goldman have responded to the criticism that as a Lithuanian Jew she had no right to question American patriotism?*

» *If we consider the actual experience of the United States during and after the war, were Goldman's warnings justified?*

The Western Front Trench warfare on the western front was a harrowing experience. When officers called for the troops to "go over the top," the men had to navigate a gauntlet of razor wire while facing exploding shells, constant gunfire, and sometimes poison gas. There were more than 1.5 million casualties in the Battle of the Somme alone, including, undoubtedly, some of the British soldiers shown here. (Popperfoto/Getty Images)

effort, the British navy blockaded Germany's seaports, and in response German submarines targeted British shipping in the Atlantic Ocean. International trade came to a standstill. European prosperity had been based on an interlinked world economy, and its collapse led to an extreme shortage of consumer goods, especially when domestic industries shifted toward the production of war materiel.

Protracted total war transformed European government and society. Because all of a nation's energies had to be tapped in the interests of survival, governmental power expanded. The transition to a more planned economy was least revolutionary in Germany, where the state and large corporations were already in close cooperation before the war. In Britain, however, national economic planning represented a major shift away from economic liberalism. Everywhere, the First World War began a long-term trend toward greater government involvement in economies.

Government bureaucracies of all kinds expanded dramatically. Unions lost the right to strike. Traditional liberties—freedom of speech, freedom of assembly—were curtailed. The British Parliament even began to regulate the hours of the nation's pubs, where working men and women sought relief from wartime drudgery. Less time spent drinking, it was thought, would improve industrial efficiency.

For women, the war brought opportunities as well as costs. The nursing profession expanded, and with so many men absent, women became more important in factories as well. In France, many women ran family farms. Such circumstances undermined the idea that the woman's place was in the home, while men dominated the public sphere. Before the war, British suffragists, campaigners for women's voting rights, used hunger strikes and public demonstrations to press their cause. The wartime contributions of British women helped swing public opinion, and in 1918 women over thirty possessing property and education were granted the right to vote.

In eastern Europe total war extracted a higher price than in the West. The original conflict between the Austrian empire and Serbia escalated when the Russian army entered the Balkan conflict, spreading warfare as far as Romania and Bulgaria. But the main battle line between German and Russian forces was the **eastern front**. Having only recently begun to industrialize, Russia was still a primarily rural empire, a fatal weakness under conditions of industrialized total war. German invaders took hundreds of thousands of Russian prisoners, whom they treated with extreme harshness. Morale among peasant conscripts was poor to begin with and deteriorated rapidly. Mutinies were common: soldiers and sailors, mostly descendants of serfs, felt little loyalty toward their aristocratic officers. Sometimes they killed their own commanders rather than head into futile battles; frequently they simply abandoned their weapons and walked home. Louise Bryant noticed them as she entered Russia, *"great giants of men, mostly workers and peasants, in old, dirt-colored uniforms from which every emblem of Tsardom had been carefully removed."*[*]

Famine stalked the Russian countryside as war disrupted food production. Factories closed when industrialists lost access to the Western capital on which Russian industrialization depended. Despite deteriorating circumstances, Tsar Nicholas II refused to consider the humiliating conditions of surrender offered by the Germans. By 1917, the Russian people were demoralized and exhausted.

Total War: Global Dimensions

Apart from the mobilization of civilian life in Europe, total war also required access to global resources such as petroleum, now essential for the maintenance of supply lines. Battles were fought in Africa and the Middle East; Japan declared war on Germany to seize German concessions in China; Britain and France depended on their Asian and African empires for manpower and materiel. With the entrance of the United States, by 1917 the Great War had truly become a world war.

The decision by the Ottoman empire to side with Germany opened a **southern front** that extended the war to the Middle East and North Africa. During the late nineteenth century, German banks, commercial houses, and manufacturers had invested heavily in the Ottoman economy, and the Ottomans saw a German alliance as protection against the French, British, and Russians. The most important strategic Ottoman position was the Dardanelles, a narrow strait connecting the Black Sea with the Mediterranean. In 1915, British forces, including many

eastern front
The front in Russia during World War I. The German army moved quickly across eastern Europe into Russia; low morale plagued the poorly equipped Russian army in the face of superior German technology.

southern front
The front in World War I caused by the Ottoman empire's decision to ally with the German army. Britain mobilized colonial forces from India, Egypt, and Australia to engage Ottoman forces at Gallipoli; British forces also occupied Mesopotamia and Palestine.

---

*Quotes from Louise Bryant, *Six Red Months in Moscow* (New York: George H. Doren, 1919), p. 21.

Gloire à la plus grande France
9387

Private Collection/Archives Charmet/The Bridgeman Art Library

Franco-African Soldier Total war meant the mobilization of African and Asian colonial subjects. This young man, fighting for "the greater glory of France," is a Senegalese Sharpshooter, most likely a West African Muslim. He stands proudly, with German helmets perched atop his head. Perhaps the helmets were captured in fighting; more likely, they were placed on his head for dramatic effect by a studio photographer.

Senegalese Sharpshooters
Mostly Muslim soldiers from French West Africa who were conscripted by the French empire in World War I and developed a reputation as fearsome fighters.

Australians, attacked the heavily fortified Ottoman position at Gallipoli. In a scene reminiscent of the carnage on the western front, thousands of Australian soldiers were mowed down. After a quarter of a million casualties, the British withdrew from Gallipoli.

In the wake of Gallipoli, the British could spare neither men nor materiel from their home islands to fight on the southern front, so they mobilized regiments from their African and Asian colonies. A force made up primarily of Egyptian soldiers under British command moved toward Ottoman-controlled Palestine, while Indian soldiers engaged Ottoman forces in Mesopotamia. Knowing that many Arab subjects of the Ottoman empire were unhappy with Turkish rule, the British also forged an alliance with Arab leaders.

Though the French did little fighting outside Europe, they also looked to their empire for support. They had long recruited indigenous soldiers from their imperial possessions, but the number of volunteers was not enough to meet wartime demand. French colonial officials pressured local African leaders in their colonial territories to supply, by force if necessary, more conscripts for the French army. The most famous regiment of colonial recruits was the **Senegalese Sharpshooters**, young Muslims from French West Africa who developed a reputation as fearsome fighters. They suffered cruelly from the harsh winters of northern France, however, and many died or were maimed on the western front.

Most of the Arab, Indian, and African soldiers mobilized by the British and the French during the war were Muslims, creating a potential condition of divided loyalty as they fought for Christian empires, especially since the Ottoman sultan was widely regarded as the *caliph*, or successor to the political powers of the Prophet Muhammad. The British commander of the Palestinian campaign was therefore careful when entering Jerusalem—holy to Islam as well as to Christianity and Judaism—to assure his Indian troops as well as the city's residents that all their holy sites would be respected.

Battles between German East Africa and British-controlled Kenya also demonstrated the scope of total war in East Africa. On one side were African soldiers led by German officers, and on the other a largely Indian army commanded by the British. The German commander's only goal was to tie down the Anglo-Indian forces to keep them from being redeployed to the Middle East. He therefore repeatedly struck and then retreated, requisitioning local food reserves for his army and destroying what was left to deny sustenance to his opponents. Famine and disease stalked the land; total war reached even the remote interior of East Africa.

In Southeast Asia, the main consequence of the war was French recruitment of young Vietnamese men for the Indochinese Labor Corps. The French needed laborers behind their lines on the western front and preferred to relieve French soldiers of hard work such as digging fortifications and maintaining roads. Those jobs were given to Vietnamese conscripts, allowing the French to concentrate more troops on the front line. At the same time Indochinese rice and rubber were directed to support the French war effort.

The Indians, West Africans, and Vietnamese conscripted by the British and French, as well as the civilians in colonial territories who produced coffee, rubber, tin, and other goods for imperial forces, contributed much to the war effort but received little in return. Later, anticolonial nationalist leaders would base their claims to greater self-government or independence on the sacrifices they had made during the war.

The Role of the United States

The United States's entrance into the war was a major turning point, again highlighting the global nature of total war. In 1914, the country had a small army, and Americans were still inclined to follow George Washington's advice that the republic should not *"entangle our peace and prosperity in the toils of European ambition."* Initially, President **Woodrow Wilson** (in office 1913–1921) kept the United States out of the war, but true neutrality proved impossible. With Germany's trade blocked by the British navy, America supplied industrial and military provisions to France and Britain. Between 1914 and 1916 American exports to these two countries grew from $824 million to $3.2 billion, bringing industrial expansion to the United States without any military cost.

America's entry into the war was largely in response to Germany's use of submarine warfare, itself a reaction to the British embargo on Germany. In 1915, the Germans sank the *Lusitania*, a civilian passenger ship with many Americans on board. After President Wilson protested, the Germans promised to stop attacking ships without warning. Meanwhile, business interests in the United States urged a rapid military buildup. While citing national security reasons, they were also aware, as critics like Louise Bryant pointed out, that military spending was highly profitable.

Early in 1917 the Germans, aiming to stop American arms shipments to Britain, resumed submarine attacks. By that time Wilson had decided on war, but he still had to convince Congress and the American people. Americans, it seemed, could be persuaded to overcome their hesitation to fight only if they were offered some great moral purpose. *"The world must be made safe for democracy,"* Wilson told Congress. *"Its peace must be planted upon the tested foundations of political liberty."*

Wilson's idealism swung public opinion in favor of war, and a draft was instituted. Now the United States faced the same mandates of total war as the other combatants. Mobilization gave the government unprecedented power. Economic and political life became more centralized while restrictions were placed on free speech, the right of workers to strike, and freedom of the press.

Though the Americans did not experience the worst of trench warfare, the timing of their arrival was critical. The Germans had imposed a humiliating peace on Russia (covered later in this chapter) and were speeding troops west to try to break the gridlock on the western front. The arrival of a million-strong American force turned the tide in favor of the British and the French; on November 11, 1918, the Germans agreed to an armistice ending hostilities, and the war was over. The United States was now in a position to influence the peace talks that followed, taking a place alongside the major European powers. Germany was excluded from the bargaining table, as were the Asians and Africans, whose fates were also to be determined.

Woodrow Wilson (in office 1913–1921) President of the United States during and after World War I. Wilson's idealistic view, enshrined in his Fourteen Points, was that Allied success in the war would lead to the spread of peace and democracy.

The Postwar Settlements

As diplomats headed to France to prepare the peace terms, an outbreak of influenza raced around the world, killing tens of millions. Wartime violence and dislocation had paved the way for an epidemic that further deepened the world's distress. Between 1918 and 1920 as many as 50 million people died, far more than had lost their lives during the war itself. The influenza epidemic contributed to the sense that the world had changed in some fundamental way and that the future was uncertain.

In this atmosphere, representatives of the Allied powers—Britain, France, Italy, and the United States—gathered at the **Paris Peace Conference** in 1919. In retrospect, the settlements negotiated in Paris seem clearly wrongheaded. France was intent on punishing Germany for the war, undermining the liberal political order created after Kaiser Wilhelm II abdicated in 1918. New national boundaries drawn in eastern Europe and the Mediterranean generated violence, instability, and dictatorships. Britain and France confiscated German colonies and Ottoman provinces for their own empires, thus stoking the flames of nationalism in Africa, the Middle East, and Asia. And the U.S. Senate voted against joining the new League of Nations that Woodrow Wilson had proposed precisely to avoid a catastrophic recurrence of total war.

Paris Peace Conference
(1919) Conference that resulted in the Versailles treaty, which added to post–World War I tensions. A war-guilt clause and reparations payments destabilized Germany, and efforts to create stable nations from former imperial provinces in eastern Europe were problematic.

The Paris Peace Conference

The principal leaders at the Paris Peace Conference—Woodrow Wilson of the United States, Georges Clemenceau of France, and David Lloyd George of Britain—faced an enormous task. Germany had to somehow be reincorporated into Europe. The Austrian and Ottoman empires were in ruins, requiring the construction of entirely new political systems in central Europe and western Asia (see Map 27.2). Moreover, Germany had to relinquish its colonies in Africa and the Pacific. The world's map had to be redrawn.

Wilson brought to Paris the same high-minded attitude with which he earlier urged America's entry into the war. His "Fourteen Points" contained specific recommendations based on a few clear principles. Wilson stressed the importance of free trade, the right of peoples to national self-determination, and the creation of a permanent international assembly to provide safeguards against future wars. The British goal, on the other hand, was to safeguard Britain's imperial interests, while Clemenceau demanded that Germany pay reparations as punishment for the war.

As the Allies negotiated, others sought to influence the outcome. At a Pan-African Congress also held in Paris in 1919, black leaders from Africa, the West Indies, and the United States spoke for the interests of Africans and peoples of African descent. A delegation of Egyptians also planned to attend the conference to represent Arab and Muslim interests, but the British government refused them permission to travel. The Chinese delegation, upset by concessions made to Japan, angrily returned home. Also in Paris was a young Vietnamese man named Ho Chi Minh (hoh chee MIN), who petitioned the Western powers to apply the principle of self-determination to the Vietnamese people in French Indochina. Rebuffed, Ho became a member of the French Communist Party and later the leader of a Vietnamese insurgency against the French (see Chapter 29). Lacking a voice at the Paris Peace Conference, many of the world's people could only wait to see what the great powers would decide for them.

MAP 27.2 **Territorial Changes in Europe After World War I** The Versailles treaty altered the map of Europe dramatically through the application of Woodrow Wilson's policy of "national self-determination." New nations appeared in central and eastern Europe, carved from the former Russian, Austro-Hungarian, and Ottoman empires, though the complex ethnic composition of the region often made it impossible to draw clear lines between "peoples" and "states." The handover of the key regions of Alsace and Lorraine from Germany to France caused much bitterness among German nationalists. (© Cengage Learning)

In the end, the Versailles treaty that resulted from the Paris Peace Conference fell far short of Wilson's goals. The Allies did agree to Wilson's plan for a **League of Nations** that would provide a permanent diplomatic forum in the hopes of avoiding future conflict. But tensions resulted from French insistence on punishment for Germany; from the difficulty in creating coherent states in eastern Europe; from the imperial ambitions of Britain and France; and from the lack of participation in the League of Nations by both Russia, embroiled in revolution, and the United States, retreating into isolationism. The First World War was not a war to end all wars, and the world had not been made safe for democracy.

League of Nations
Assembly of sovereign states, advocated by Woodrow Wilson, that was intended to provide a permanent diplomatic forum in the hopes of avoiding future conflict.

The Weimar Republic and Nation Building in Europe

Weimar Republic (1919–1933) The government of Germany created after World War I, based on a liberal democratic constitution. The new republic was immediately faced with huge war debts, political turmoil, and rising inflation.

After surrender and the kaiser's abdication, German liberals and socialists cooperated in the creation of the new **Weimar Republic**. Many years after the revolutions of 1848, Germany finally had a liberal, democratic constitution. But cultivating a liberal political culture was still difficult. A communist uprising in 1919 challenged the Weimar (VAHY-mahr) leaders from the left, while on the right angry veterans blamed liberal weakness for the nation's defeat. At war's end, many Germans were hungry, cold, and dispirited.

The harsh peace terms insisted upon by France made recovery more difficult than it had to be. The French insisted on huge reparation payments that crippled the German financial system. As one British economist immediately warned, the economic punishment of Germany was simply foolish in an era of economic interdependence: everyone stood to lose. The treaty also called for the complete demilitarization of the Rhineland, the German province bordering France, and severe restrictions on German rearmament.

By 1923 the new Weimar Republic was foundering. It was unable to meet its reparation obligations, and the French occupied the Ruhr Valley, Germany's industrial heartland, in lieu of payment. As the government printed more money to make up for the shortfall in its treasury, inflation spiraled out of control. People needed a wheelbarrow full of bank notes to buy a loaf of bread, and the savings of the middle class were wiped out. Although an attempt by right-wing military forces to seize power from elected politicians was thwarted, the rebellious officers had a good deal of public support.

Then signs of recovery appeared. In 1925 international agreements eased Germany's reparation payments and ended the occupation of the Ruhr Valley. The German economy finally came back to prewar levels, and Berlin regained its status as a major cultural, intellectual, and artistic center. In just a few years, however, another economic crisis would drive many Germans toward the political extremes of left and right, undermining the Weimar Republic's fragile liberalism (see Chapter 28).

In the meantime, postwar reconstruction was transforming eastern, central, and southeastern Europe, where competitive nationalist sentiments led to conflict. The complex cultural geography of the region meant that ethnic, linguistic, and religious groups lived scattered among each other in many places, making it impossible to delineate neat boundaries between them.

Along the German-Polish cultural frontier, for example, German-speakers and Polish-speakers often lived side by side in the same towns and villages, along with a substantial Jewish population. Poland, which had disappeared from the map of Europe in the eighteenth century (see Chapter 20), was now restored as a nation-state. Polish nationalists felt that Germans who found themselves living in the new Poland had to either accept second-class status or move west to Germany, where they "belonged." The repression of Polish Jews was even more extreme. In this tense atmosphere it proved impossible for Poland to develop a liberal, democratic political culture. In 1926, tired of the endless squabbling of politicians, conservative army officers seized power and imposed restrictions on free speech and political organization. Likewise, the new Balkan state of Yugoslavia, where Croatian Catholics and Bosnian Muslims resented the political dominance of Orthodox Serbs, emerged as an authoritarian state.

The slide toward dictatorship in eastern, central, and southern Europe arose from a contradiction that Wilson had not recognized: that nationalism is based on the rights of *groups*, while liberalism focuses on the rights of *individuals*. Nationalists, with an "us versus them" mentality, were prone to restrict the rights of minority groups rather than follow the liberal philosophy of protecting individual rights regardless of ethnic background. The problem was particularly acute for peoples with no state to protect them, such as Europe's Jews and the Roma (Gypsies). As a basis for political reconstruction, nationalism caused as many problems as it solved.

The Mandate System in Africa and the Middle East

The fate of former German colonies and Ottoman provinces was another issue to be determined in the postwar settlements. In Africa and the Middle East, French and British colonial interests took priority. The great powers paid only token attention to the concept that rights of national self-determination should be granted to African and Arab peoples. Instead, the Allies devised the **Mandate System**, which assumed that since not all the world's people were ready for self-governance, the great powers should rule over them under League of Nations auspices until they were "prepared." Race was the unspoken determinant of who was deemed capable of self-rule.

In Africa, the Mandate System allowed the French, British, Belgian, and South African governments to take over former German colonies. With the addition of German East Africa (today's Tanzania) to its empire, Britain finally achieved Cecil Rhodes's dream of controlling a continuous stretch "from Cape to Cairo" (see Chapter 26). The French expanded their West African holdings, and the Belgians enlarged their Central African empire. While the Mandate System required reports to the League of Nations showing that they were looking out for "native rights," the Europeans ruled the mandated territories just like their other African colonies, doing little or nothing to prepare them for eventual self-determination.

Still, African experiences during the war and the Mandate System's long-term goal of national self-determination for former German colonies inspired a new generation of African nationalists. In South Africa, for example, leaders of the African National Congress called for greater rights, including an extension of the right to vote to Western-educated African property owners and an end to residential segregation. In West Africa, consciousness of the continent's place in the wider world also increased. More African students studied in Europe and the United States and came back questioning the legitimacy of colonial rule. Thus, the seeds of African nationalism began to sprout in the wake of World War I.

The most complex application of the Mandate System came in the Middle East, where the collapse of Ottoman authority created a power vacuum. While the French and British wanted control of such rich and strategic areas as Turkey, Mesopotamia, Syria, and Palestine, they had to contend with well-organized forces of Turkish, Arab, and Jewish nationalism.

As the Ottoman empire collapsed, some of its subject peoples sought to liberate themselves. Hoping for an independent state, some Armenians had supported Russia during the war. Ottoman officials responded by relocating millions of Armenians in a forced march west. As many as 1.5 million Armenians perished in what most historians call the Armenian Genocide, an attempt to destroy the people and their culture.

The surviving Armenians did finally gain a state of their own in the postwar settlements, though other peoples in the region, such as the Kurdish-speaking population of the former Ottoman empire, did not. The great powers rejected their proposal for a new state of "Kurdistan," and the Kurdish people were scattered across the new postwar states of Turkey, Iraq, Syria, and Iran.

Mandate System
System by which former Ottoman provinces and German colonies were redistributed; based on the idea that some societies were not ready for national self-determination, it expanded the empires of Britain, France, Belgium, and Japan while angering African, Arab, and Chinese nationalists.

In the Middle East the postwar situation was complicated by three contradictory promises made by the British during the war: the first to the Arabs, the second to the French, and the third to Zionists, Jewish nationalists who hoped to establish a Jewish state in Palestine.

In 1915, to gain Arab support against the Ottoman empire, the British had promised the prominent Hashemite family to *"recognize and support the independence of the Arabs"* after the war. Contradicting that agreement, the British then signed a secret treaty with the French arranging to divide Ottoman provinces between themselves. A third agreement, difficult to reconcile with the previous two, was the **Balfour Declaration** of 1917, which committed the British government to support the creation of a "national home" for the Jewish people in Palestine. The British government was seeking additional support for the war effort from Zionists.

Balfour Declaration (1917) Declaration that committed the British government to help create "a national home for the Jewish people" in Palestine. Britain made this declaration to gain support from Zionists during World War I.

Zionism had originated in the late nineteenth century among European Jews who were alarmed at persistent anti-Semitism. After nearly two millennia of Jewish exile from their original home, Zionists argued, a nation-state was necessary to represent Jewish interests in the world and give Jews a place of refuge in times of crisis. They had advocated Jewish emigration to Ottoman Palestine before the war. However, most Zionists had never been to the Middle East, and most of the people actually living in Palestine in 1917 were Arab.

After the war, the British tried to use the Mandate System to reconcile these contradictory promises. True to their 1916 secret agreement, the British and the French divided the Middle East region between them. The French received a League of Nations mandate over Syria and Lebanon, and the British stitched together three Ottoman provinces centered on the cities of Mosul, Baghdad, and Basra into a new entity they called Iraq. Members of the Hashemite family were installed in Syria and Iraq as political leaders, though the French and British retained control over military, security, and economic issues.

The French were not able to impose their authority on Syria without a fight. Faisal al-Hashemi had been declared king of an independent Arab state by the Syrian National Congress and had traveled to Paris as head of an Arab delegation in 1919. When the French tried to impose their authority, Faisal and his supporters resisted. Defeated by the French, Faisal then fled to Baghdad, where the British agreed to install him as king of Iraq. Lacking a base of support in Iraq, Faisal proved compliant with British authorities, who were looking for a way to balance Arab demands with their own strategic and economic interests.

Instability in Iraq could have been anticipated. An artificial creation, it was divided between a Shi'ite Arab majority in the south, a Sunni minority in the center, and a Kurdish-dominated region in the north. The choice of Faisal as king showed British favoritism toward the Sunni Arabs. Gertrude Bell, the British diplomat most responsible for the creation of modern Iraq, wrote in 1920: *"I don't for a moment doubt that the final authority must be in the hands of the Sunnis, in spite of their numerical inferiority. . . . Otherwise you will have a theocratic state, which is the very devil."* Shi'ite Iraqis resented Sunni political ascendancy, which would last until the American invasion of 2003 (see Chapter 32). The British also drew a new line on the map at the Jordan River, separating Palestine, which they ruled directly, from the new kingdom of Jordan, where they installed yet another Hashemite ruler as king.

Arab nationalists complained vigorously about the Mandate System, saying that Arabs *"are not naturally less than other more advanced races"* and that they

---

*Gertrude Bell, "Letter to Her Father," October 3, 1920; cited in Scott Horton, "Bell on the Shi'a in Iraq," *Harpers Magazine*, March 19, 2008.

did *"not stand in need of a mandatory power."* Still, the lack of Arab unity gave Europeans the upper hand. The French remained dominant in Syria, and the British in Iraq, even after they later accelerated the transition from mandate status to fuller sovereignty.

The situation was even more complicated in Palestine. Wartime anti-Semitism had increased the popularity of Zionism among American and European Jews, and even many who had no plans to emigrate to Palestine contributed money to purchase land for those who did decide to move. Arab leaders were alarmed. While still the majority in Palestine, Arabs there feared a future in which they would become a minority in the land where many of their families had lived for over a thousand years.

It was impossible for the British to please both Zionists and Arab nationalists. The Balfour Declaration's support for a "national home" for Jews in Palestine fell short of support for a Jewish state, as the British asserted their own authority over the mandated territory. Arab nationalists viewed any immigration of Jews into Palestine with suspicion. When the British allowed such immigration in large numbers in the early 1920s, massive Arab demonstrations erupted. When the British curtailed Jewish immigration in response, Zionist leaders were furious. The British were determined to keep Palestine because of its strategic location in the eastern Mediterranean region, but the political price for doing so was exceptionally high. (See the feature "World History in Today's World: Israel, Palestine, and the Right of Return.")

British and French leaders viewed the enlargement of their empires in Africa and the

Gertrude Bell Gertrude Bell (astride a camel in the center of this photograph) was an English traveler, writer, and archaeologist who played a central role in shaping Britain's Middle East policy during and after the Great War. Fluent in Arabic, Bell helped organize the anti-Ottoman Arab uprising of 1916–1917. She was influential in the creation of the new kingdoms of Jordan and Iraq after the war; some have criticized the imperial arrogance with which she drew their boundaries. The most powerful woman in Britain's foreign service, though herself opposed to women's suffrage, Bell died and was buried in Baghdad.

Middle East as spoils of war that augmented their existing global reach. They anticipated that they would retain their traditional global dominance, especially with the Russians distracted by revolution, the Germans desperate and disarmed, and the Americans returning to isolationism. But the world had changed. The British had liquidated many foreign investments to fight the war and slipped from being the world's largest creditor to facing significant debts, especially to the United States. Western European economic supremacy was on the wane. The belief that future control of the world system lay with Europe was therefore an illusion. The forces of anticolonial nationalism were gathering throughout Africa and Asia. Just two generations later, the British and French empires were being supplanted by independent African and Asian nations, and European hegemony was replaced by the rising power of the United States and the new Soviet Union (see Chapter 29).

Israel, Palestine, and the Right of Return

Jewish Zionists and Palestinian Arabs both claim a "right of return" to the same small country, incompatible visions that have been a major factor in stalling the Middle East peace process. Without agreement on the core question of who has a right to immigrate to Israel, no lasting peace will be possible.

For Israelis, the right of all Jews to relocate to Israel is a fundamental principle. In 1950, the Israeli parliament, the Knesset, passed a law stating firmly that "every Jew has the right to come to this country." That law applies across the entire Jewish diaspora, meaning that all Jews from anywhere in the world have, as a matter of ancient heritage, automatic immigration rights.

Two traditional paths to Jewish status—maternal ancestry and conversion—are both recognized. However, ultraorthodox rabbis have discriminated against converts to less stringent Reform and Conservative versions of Judaism and sometimes against secular Jews as well. In a 2011 case, a gay couple came to Israel and applied for citizenship. It was quickly granted to the Jewish man, but initially denied to his non-Jewish partner, even though the rights of "spouses" are guaranteed under the law. Israelis continue to disagree on the basic question: "who is a Jew?"

For Palestinians, the phrase "right of return" means something altogether different. Their assertion is that Arab refugees who fled Palestine in the 1948 war that followed the creation of Israel (see Chapter 30) should be allowed to return to their ancestral homes. Hundreds of thousands of Palestinian families have lived in exile in surrounding Arab countries, and across the world, since that time. Some still hold title deeds for the properties that their grandparents and great-grandparents abandoned, and sometimes even the keys to their old houses.

For Israel, the question involves its very survival as a Jewish state. If a large number of the millions of Palestinians were to return, the percentage of Arab citizens in Israel could rise from the current 20 percent to over half the population. Given that arithmetic, Israeli leaders have refused to compromise on the issue, while Palestinian leaders have been equally adamant that they will not give up their historical claims.

Pioneers of Global Revolution: Mexico, China, and Russia

In the twentieth century the revolutionary traditions of Europe and the Atlantic world (see Chapters 22 and 23) would spread across the globe. First in China, Mexico, and Russia and later in societies across Asia, Africa, and Latin America, masses of common people mobilized to topple existing elites and to usher in new political systems (see Chapter 29). As Louise Bryant had suspected, socialism would now play a much greater role. While nineteenth-century revolutionaries had struggled to balance nationalism with liberalism, now the mixture of nationalism and socialism proved most potent, much to the horror of conservatives everywhere.

The Mexican Revolution, 1910–1920

In 1915, when Louise Bryant first met her future husband and journalistic ally John Reed, he had just returned from Mexico, where he had accompanied the rebel leader Pancho Villa into battle. Reed's enthusiasm for the revolutionary cause was contagious, inspiring Bryant with exhilarating tales of downtrodden Mexican cowboys fighting for liberation against corrupt politicians, landowners, and priests.

Before 1910, Porfirio Diáz ruled Mexico as an elected dictator, winning rigged elections ever since 1880. Under Diáz's economic liberalism and political authoritarianism, foreign investors had financed the development of many large-scale plantations producing crops for export (see Chapter 25). The benefits of growth were, however, monopolized by foreigners and the small group of oligarchs with connections to the Diáz regime. The new and increasingly important petroleum sector, for example, was almost entirely under foreign, largely American, control.

A dissatisfied younger generation of Mexicans demanded reform. Among their leaders was Francisco Madero, educated at the University of California in the United States, who ran for the presidency in 1910 against the old dictator. When Diáz claimed victory, Madero refused to concede, rallying supporters under the slogan *"Effective Suffrage and No Reelection."* Madero's message resonated across Mexico; the aged Diáz fled to Europe.

Removing a dictator is often an easier task that creating a stable new political order, however: the overthrow of Diáz was only the beginning of the Mexican Revolution. In 1913, Madero was assassinated by one of his military officers, who was in turn deposed by the liberal leader Venustiano Carranza, who then had to fight to assert his government's authority. Though Carranza held power in Mexico City and controlled the federal army, two former partners in his revolutionary coalition, **Emiliano Zapata** (1879–1919) and Pancho Villa, now turned against him. As many as 2 million people were killed in the chaos of the civil war that engulfed Mexico between 1913 and 1920.

Rallying support with the cry *¡Justicia, Tierra, y Liberdad!* ("Justice, Land, and Liberty!"), Zapata followed in the tradition of Father Hidalgo in his passionate embrace of the rights of the poor (see Chapter 22). His followers, mostly landless Indian peasants from southern Mexico, wanted to redistribute the large plantations to the landless. Carranza, a middle-class moderate like Madero before him, saw that as an unacceptable intrusion on the rights of property owners. In 1919, Carranza's agents assassinated Zapata, and the southern rebel army fell apart.

In the north Pancho Villa, praised by John Reed for his *"reckless and romantic bravery,"* led the fight against Carranza's government. His army of small ranchers and cowboys (*vaqueros*) resented the elite who controlled the best grazing lands and water sources. Villa was angered when the United States officially recognized the Carranza government: his downfall came after he crossed the border to attack a town in New Mexico. The U.S. army counterattacked, Villa went into hiding, and in 1923 he was assassinated. His exploits made him an enduring folk hero, and together Villa and Zapata personified the aspirations of millions of the poorest Mexicans.

Carranza's government instituted a new constitution in 1917, trying to balance the different interests that had emerged during the revolution. While the Constitution of 1917 protected the rights of property owners, it also declared that *"private property is a privilege created by the Nation,"* opening the path for land reforms benefiting peasants. The constitution also promised to protect working

Emiliano Zapata (1879–1919) Leader of a popular uprising during the Mexican Revolution; mobilized the poor in southern and central Mexico to demand "justice, land, and liberty."

Villa and Zapata This photograph from 1915 shows Pancho Villa (*center*, sitting on the presidential throne in the National Palace) with Emiliano Zapata (*right*) at his side, his trademark hat on his knee. The two revolutionaries were soon chased from Mexico City, however, by forces loyal to Venustiano Carranza. Zapata was assassinated by Carranza's men in 1919, Villa by unknown assailants in 1923. (© Underwood & Underwood/Corbis)

conditions, for example, by enforcing the eight-hour workday. The mineral resources of the country, including oil, were declared property of the nation as a whole, and not of any individual, local or foreign, a provision that would allow future Mexican governments to nationalize the energy sector of the economy (see Chapter 28).

These promises of land reform, workers' rights, and the use of oil resources for the good of the nation were not immediately implemented, however, and remained points of contention far into the future. Moreover, the revolution did not lay the foundation of a truly liberal political culture. Though Mexico avoided the replacement of one dictator by another, a single political party established a monopoly on power. After 1920, leaders of the National Revolutionary Party used patronage, corruption, and backroom deals to try to reconcile the interests of the rich and the poor, the needs of the nation and the influence of foreign investors, and rural and urban populations. Mostly, however, party leaders acted to extend their own wealth and power. The revolution that had begun with such excitement sank into corruption and bureaucratic stasis.

The Chinese Revolution

After the humiliations of the Boxer Rebellion (see Chapter 24), China entered the twentieth century in desperate need of a new government to unify its people and defend itself against foreign encroachment. In 1911, the last Qing emperor, a boy at the time, abdicated when Yuan Shikai (yoo-ahn shee-KI), the most capable of the Qing generals, refused to come to the dynasty's defense. Nationalists led by Sun Zhongshan, better known as **Sun Yat-sen** (1866–1925), declared a new Republic of China. Lacking an army, Sun was dependent on Yuan's support. In 1912, after serving as president for only a few weeks, he stepped aside, and delegates to the new national assembly elected Yuan as president.

Sun Yat-sen (soon yot-SEN) grew up near Guangzhou, the center of European influence in south China. He earned a medical degree in Hong Kong in 1892 and then moved to Hawai'i, where he started the political organizing that would put him at the head of the Guomindang (gwo-min-DAHNG), or Nationalist, Party. Sun envisioned a stable, modernized China, with a liberal legal system and a just distribution of resources, taking its rightful place among the world's great powers.

The new Republic of China faced daunting challenges. Japanese imperialists were already in formal control of Taiwan and exercised great power in Manchuria. In 1919, Western diplomats gave Japan control over Chinese territory on the Shandong peninsula formerly controlled by Germany, in acknowledgment of its wartime alliance with France and Britain. On May 4, 1919, Chinese university students staged an unprecedented public demonstration in Tiananmen Square in Beijing, appealing to the government to restore Chinese dignity in the face of Japanese aggression. Their **May Fourth Movement** led to strikes, mass meetings, and a boycott of Japanese goods. Chinese nationalism was on the rise, but the republican government was powerless to respond to the students' appeals.

The domestic military situation was another challenge for Sun and the Guomindang. In 1916 Yuan broke with the Nationalists and declared the foundation of a new imperial dynasty. When regional generals rejected Yuan's imperial pretensions, formed their own armies, and began to act as warlords, the country descended into a decade of chaos. The only stable and prosperous parts of China were the foreign enclaves. Sun retreated to Guangzhou, where the Guomindang was rebuilt by his brother-in-law and successor Jiang Jieshi, known in the West as Chiang Kai-shek (1887–1975). Chiang was a tough military man who defeated the warlords and finally established central authority over most of the country by 1927. Under Chiang's authoritarian command, however, Sun's idealistic emphasis on reform was supplanted by a growing culture of militarism and corruption.

Meanwhile, in 1921, in the wake of the May Fourth Movement, the Chinese Communist Party was formed in Shanghai. Seeking support from the new communist

Sun Yat-sen
(1866–1925) The founding father of the Republic of China after the revolution of 1911; established the Guomindang, or Nationalist Party.

May Fourth Movement
(1919) A student-led protest in Beijing's Tiananmen Square against the failure of the Versailles treaty to end Japanese occupation of Chinese territory. Such anti-Japanese protests spread across China, and focused on a boycott of Japanese goods.

May Fourth Movement May 4, 1919, was an important day in the development of Chinese nationalism. Hundreds of thousands of protesters gathered in Tiananmen Square in Beijing, angered by the Versailles treaty, which had given Chinese territory to Japan. Demonstrations were held across the country, with students playing a large role. The protests lasted for months as supporters of the movement boycotted Japanese goods. The demonstration in this photograph took place in November 1919 in the city of Fuzou. (Sidney Gamble Photographs, Manuscripts Division, Department of Rare Books and Special Collections, Princeton University Library)

government in Russia, Chiang Kai-shek made a tactical alliance with the Communists. But in 1927, when he felt more secure in power, Chiang turned against them. Guomindang soldiers and street thugs killed thousands of Communists in the coastal cities, and those remaining fled to the countryside.

One Chinese Communist, Mao Zedong (1893–1976), argued that there was an advantage in this forced retreat into the countryside, since it would be the peasants who would lead the way to socialism. Rejecting the traditional Marxist emphasis on the leading role of the industrial workers, Mao wrote: *"In a very short time . . . several hundred million peasants will rise like a tornado . . . and rush forward along the road to liberation. They will send all imperialists, warlords, corrupt officials, local bullies, and bad gentry to their graves."* By allying with this elemental peasant force, Mao believed, the Communists could drive Chiang from power and bring about true revolution.

While Chiang and the Guomindang controlled the cities, Mao and the Communists established rural bases (see Map 28.1 on page 818). It would be two decades before the contest of power between the Nationalists and the Communists would finally be resolved (see Chapter 30).

Russia's October Revolution

Even more than the Mexican and Chinese Revolutions, the Russian Revolution had a profound impact on world history. Both those who were sympathetic to the revolution, like Louise Bryant, and those who saw the emergence of "godless communism" as a threat to freedom and decency agreed that a fundamental historical change had occurred. Indeed, the Bolsheviks and their leader Vladimir Lenin saw themselves as fighting not just to control one country but also to change the destiny of all humanity.

Russia's first revolutionary crisis had occurred in 1905, after Russia's defeat in the Russo-Japanese War (see Chapter 24). Protesters converged on the Winter Palace in St. Petersburg to petition the tsar for reform, carrying holy icons and petitions addressing the tsar respectfully as "our father." Mounted on horseback, the tsar's private guards rode the marchers down, killing many and shattering old bonds of trust.

In the ensuing crisis, Tsar Nicholas II (r. 1894–1917) conceded a series of reforms, including, for the first time, a representative assembly, called the Duma. He also approved a crash program of industrialization that, though it achieved substantial progress by 1913, also created further social instability. The money for industrialization came largely from higher taxes on already miserable peasants, and the new industrial workers labored under much worse conditions and at much lower pay than their Western counterparts.

Although representatives of the Russian middle class could now express their desire for greater reform through the Duma, real power still lay with aristocrats, army officials, and the tsarist bureaucracy. While some reformers argued that the powers of the Duma could be expanded, others argued that nothing would change until the old order was entirely swept away. One of these revolutionary groups was the Social Democratic Party, communist followers of the Marxist tradition.

After 1903, the Social Democrats split into two factions. One group, the Mensheviks, adhered to the traditional Marxist belief that socialism could only be built on the foundation of capitalism. Before Russia's workers could seize power for themselves, a modern industrial economy would have to be built. The Mensheviks therefore favored an alliance with the Russian middle class and supported a revolution that would lead to a liberal, multiparty constitutional republic.

Vladimir Lenin (1870–1924), the leader of the opposing Bolshevik faction, had a different vision. Lenin's radicalism started in childhood, when his elder brother was hanged for plotting to assassinate the tsar. Lenin himself was exiled first to Siberia and then to western Europe. There he developed his theory that a "revolutionary vanguard," a small, dedicated group of professional revolutionists,

Vladimir Lenin (1870–1924) Born Vladimir Ilyich Ulyanov, Lenin led the Bolsheviks to power during the Russian Revolution of 1917. Leader of the Communist Party until his death in 1924.

could represent the interests of the industrial proletariat. Rather than waiting for Russia's industrial workers to increase in numbers and in political consciousness, Lenin argued, the Bolshevik vanguard could seize power and rule in the name of the working class. Dictatorship rather than democracy was implicit in Lenin's concept of the revolutionary vanguard, with self-appointed leaders speaking for the masses rather than the masses speaking for themselves.

Lenin's opportunity to implement his ideas came as a result of World War I. Many blamed the tsar for the huge human and economic costs of war. Faced with mutiny in the army and near anarchy across the country, Tsar Nicholas abdicated in February 1917. When Louise Bryant arrived in the summer of 1917, the Provisional Government that had replaced him was also losing legitimacy when it decided to continue to fight Germany, hoping to maintain access to foreign loans and to share in the division of Ottoman lands if the Allies won. The German military, hoping that Lenin's presence would undermine the pro-war provisional government in St. Petersburg, gave him transport on a sealed train car from Switzerland back to Russia.

By then the Russian people were simply sick and tired of war. Louise Bryant described the passionate appeal of one veteran for peace at a public meeting: *"Comrades! I come from the place where men are digging their graves and calling them trenches! I tell you the army can't fight much longer!"* A peasant delegate said that if they were not given sufficient land *"they would go out and take it."* *"Over and over like the beat of the surf came the cry of all starving Russia,"* Bryant wrote, *"'Peace, land and bread!'"* The Provisional Government was unable to deliver on any of these demands.

After the tsarist bureaucracy collapsed, a new form of social and political organization emerged: the *soviets* (Russian for "committees") of workers in factories, of residents in urban neighborhoods, of railway workers, and even of soldiers and sailors in the military. It was a radical form of democracy in which participants in a common enterprise had the right to speak and be represented, with decisions made through public discussion and consensus. This model of direct popular control was quite popular with Russia's anarchists, who followed in the tradition of Mikhail Bakunin (see Chapter 23).

In this atmosphere, Lenin returned from exile. As Russian society slid from dictatorship to near anarchy, his clear vision and organizational abilities put the Bolsheviks in a position to make a play for power. In Bryant's words, *"Lenin is a master propagandist. . . . He possesses all the qualities of a 'chief,' including the absolute moral indifference which is so necessary to such a part."* Though a sophisticated intellectual who wrote complex books on Marxist theory, in the summer of 1917 Lenin reduced the Bolshevik program to two simple slogans: *"Peace, Land, and Bread!"* and *"All Power to the Soviets!"* The fiery speeches and tireless organizing of another prominent Bolshevik, Leon Trotsky (1879–1940), did much to advance the communist cause that summer. (See the feature "Visual Evidence in Primary Sources: History, Photography, and Power.")

In the fall, Lenin and the Bolsheviks planned and executed a coup d'état that later communists would celebrate as the October Revolution. Hardly a shot was fired in the Provisional Government's defense. Lenin disbanded the Constituent Assembly recently elected to write a new constitution. As Bryant wrote, *"A big sailor marched into the elaborate red and gold assembly chamber and announced in a loud voice: 'Go along home!'"* Russia's brief experiment with multiparty representative democracy had ended.

---

*Quotes from Louise Bryant, *Six Red Months in Moscow* (New York: George H. Doren, 1919), pp. 48–49, 138–139, 78.

Civil War and the New Economic Policy, 1917–1924

The Communist Party, as the Bolsheviks were now called, considered the Constituent Assembly irrelevant. Defending the revolution was the first order of the day. To fulfill their promise to bring peace, they signed a treaty in 1918 ceding to Germany rich Ukrainian and Belarusian lands. The Communists saw this unequal treaty as only a temporary setback, being certain that workers in Germany would soon rise up, overthrow their government, and establish a true and equitable peace with Russia. Their self-assurance in such dangerous circumstances was remarkable.

The Communists also contended with powerful counter-revolutionary forces, as aristocratic generals turned their attention from the Germans to undoing the revolution. The Russian Civil War of 1919–1921 pitted the Communist Red Army, commanded by Leon Trotsky, against the "White Armies" organized by former tsarist generals with the help of the United States and Great Britain. The Communists murdered the tsar and his family and organized a secret police service even more terrifying than the old tsarist one.

By 1921, when the civil war ended, Lenin was securely in control and ruling with an iron hand. The anarchic democracy of freely elected soviets was replaced by strict party discipline in all facets of life. Even within the Communist Party Central Committee, dominated by Lenin, only limited debate was permitted. All other political organizations were banned.

Bryant believed that circumstances pushed the Communists toward dictatorship. *"In the beginning,"* she wrote of Lenin, *"he imagined he could maintain a free press, free speech and be liberal toward his enemies. But he found himself faced by a situation where iron discipline was the only method capable of carrying the day."* Perhaps that was a naïve judgment: the free play of ideas and organizations was never part of Lenin's plan. The emerging communist dictatorship of the Bolsheviks was not just a product of the difficult circumstances faced by postwar Russia but, as Mikhail Bakunin had warned half a century earlier, a logical outcome of Karl Marx's political philosophy.

It was of great import for world history that Lenin and the Bolsheviks were able to assert their claim to power not only in Russia, but also across most of the old Russian empire. Though they lost lands in the west (such as Poland, Finland, and Lithuania), they retained the rich lands of the Ukraine, the vastness of Siberia, Central Asia with its potential for agricultural development, and the strategic Caucasus Mountains in the south. These regions were brought together in 1922 in the Union of Soviet Socialist Republics (U.S.S.R.). Allegedly a federal republic, in reality the Soviet Union was a top-down dictatorship dominated by Moscow.

After the civil war ended, Lenin instituted the New Economic Policy (1921–1924). Peasants were allowed to keep the land they had recently won and to farm it as they saw fit. Restrictions on private business were lifted for all but the largest enterprises, such as transportation and heavy industry. Under the New Economic Policy, the country experienced a brief respite of relative peace and the beginnings of economic recovery. But it was also during this time that, in an ominous preview of the future, the first of the Soviet labor camps was established, with the motto *"With an Iron Hand, Mankind Will Be Driven to Happiness!"*

Stalin and "Socialism in One Country"

Louise Bryant never returned to Russia after Lenin's death in 1924, perhaps because she did not want to see how little her hopes for socialism were being

---

*Louise Bryant, *Mirrors of Moscow* (New York: Thomas Seltzer, 1923), pp. 11–12.

History, Photography, and Power

As Joseph Stalin consolidated his power over the Soviet Union beginning in the late 1920s, he ordered that the history of the Russian Revolution be altered to magnify his own role. Stalin's propagandists portrayed him as having been exceptionally close to Vladimir Lenin, his close confidant and handpicked successor. In fact, while Lenin appreciated Stalin's discipline and loyalty, he regarded the younger man as of limited intelligence. In the 1930s, when Stalin began purging many of Lenin's closest allies from the Communist Party and executing many of the

Though Lenin is shown here as a passionate orator, in fact he was not a good public speaker. To stir the masses with oratory the Bolsheviks relied on Leon Trotsky, who, as described by Louise Bryant, "swayed the assembly as a strong wind stirs the long grass."

David King Collection

During the revolution, Lev Kamenev served as editor of the communist daily newspaper *Pravda* ("Truth"). He traveled to London to explain communist policies to the British government but was deported after one week.

Although the Bolsheviks fought against Russia's deeply rooted anti-Semitism, it returned under Stalin's rule. Trotsky, born Lev Bronstein, was the most prominent of the Jewish Bolsheviks.

"Old Bolsheviks" who knew Lenin personally (see Chapter 28), the historical record was "adjusted" to remove many prominent revolutionists from the story.

Stalin's propagandists altered the photographic as well as the historical record of the revolution. This picture of Lenin speaking in Moscow in 1920 (left) is an iconographic image that was reproduced around the world. From the later 1920s, when the retouched version (below) was first produced, until the 1990s, Soviet citizens saw only the altered image in which two prominent Communists, Leon Trotsky and Lev Kamenev, had been erased and replaced with a set of wooden steps.

Stalin resented the leading role that Trotsky played as commander of the Red Army during the Russian Civil War of 1919–1921, and Trotsky was airbrushed out of all photographs from that period. In 1936 Kamenev was accused of plotting against Stalin and executed. Trotsky, exiled from Russia, died in Mexico in 1940 when one of Stalin's agents plunged an ice pick into his skull.

David King Collection

» *With today's widespread knowledge about digital editing, is it more or less likely that viewers would be fooled by such brazen alterations as seen in these photographs?*

realized after Joseph Stalin (r. 1926–1953) succeeded Lenin. Expelled from the seminary where he briefly studied, Stalin lacked Lenin's intellectual brilliance. While the exiled Lenin associated with European intellectuals, Stalin was robbing banks to raise funds for the party. Having spent time in jail, he knew the ways of the tsarist secret police from personal experience. *Stalin*, his chosen revolutionary name, means "man of steel."

From 1919 to 1924, Stalin was absolutely loyal to Lenin, who entrusted him with secret and sensitive tasks. He stayed in the background while other Communists argued about policies and sought positions of authority, serving on all the important committees but joining no faction. When Lenin died, Stalin exploited divisions within the Central Committee to position himself as a safe and neutral choice for leadership. But by 1926, Stalin had consolidated his authority and established a personal dictatorship, driving Leon Trotsky, his main competitor for the role of heir to Lenin, into exile.

More than personal ambition was at stake. Stalin had a clear vision of how to move the Soviet Union forward, a vision encapsulated by the slogan "**Socialism in One Country**." Some Communists, like Trotsky, who thought socialism could be built in Russia only with the help of revolutions in advanced industrial nations, advocated a policy of fomenting proletarian uprisings in the West. Other Communists, acknowledging the weak development of Russian capitalism and the small size of the Russian proletariat, thought that the mixed approach of the New Economic Policy, with scope for private enterprise, was the correct course. Stalin rejected both ideas. Instead, socialism would be built through top-down government control of every aspect of economic, political, and social life.

In 1928, Stalin launched the first of his Five-Year Plans. The entire economy was nationalized in a crash policy of industrialization. Noting that Russia was far behind more advanced economies, Stalin said, *"We must make good this lag in ten years . . . or we will be crushed."* After the Soviet Union cut all ties with foreign economies, there was only one way Stalin could raise the capital needed for industrialization: by squeezing it out of the Soviet people. Low wages and harsh working conditions characterized new factories built to produce steel, electricity, chemicals, tractors, and other vital foundations of industrial growth. Especially productive workers received medals rather than higher wages, while poor performance could result in exile to a Siberian labor camp.

Faced with Stalin's brutal policies, people could no longer even turn to religion for solace. Denouncing the Orthodox Church as a foundation of the old, tsarist regime, Stalin turned churches into municipal buildings and heavily regulated the few remaining monasteries. In the world's first atheistic state, communist theory, stripped of complexity and vitality, was the new orthodoxy. Russia's rich cultural traditions now atrophied under Stalin's dictatorship, with artists required to produce simple propaganda in line with state policy or face severe consequences.

Still, within ten years the successes of "Socialism in One Country" were notable. The Soviet Union had the fastest-growing industrial economy in the world, with production increasing as much as 14 percent a year. But the harshly repressive society Stalin created bore little resemblance to the hopeful scenario portrayed by Louise Bryant in the books she wrote during the early years of the revolution. Stalin's version of socialism was indeed a *"loathsome, ugly monster demanding human sacrifices."*

"Socialism in One Country"
Joseph Stalin's slogan declaring that Soviet socialism could be achieved without passing through a capitalist phase or revolutions in industrial societies. This policy led to an economy based on central planning for industrial growth and collectivization of agriculture.

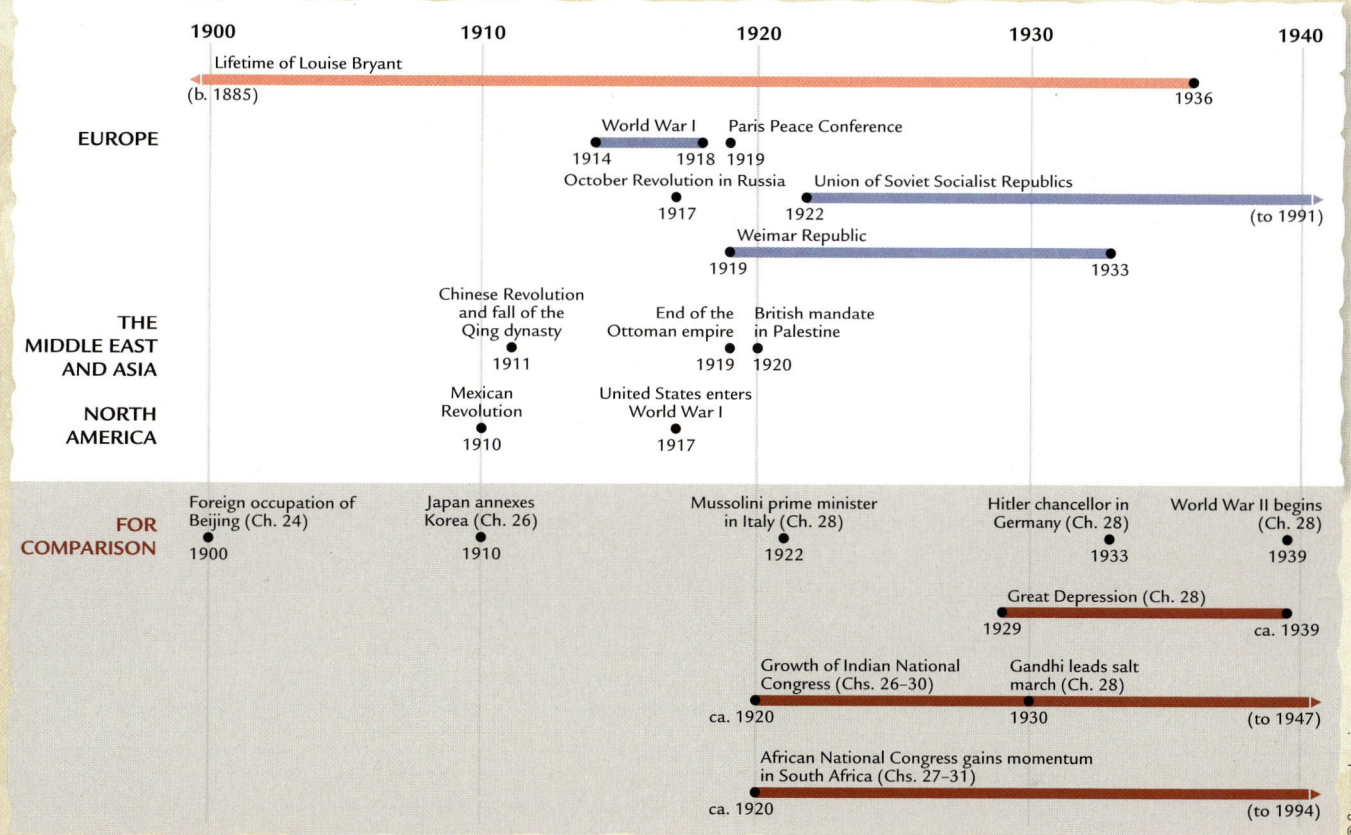

Timeline:

| | 1900 | 1910 | 1920 | 1930 | 1940 |

Lifetime of Louise Bryant (b. 1885) — 1936

EUROPE

World War I 1914–1918
Paris Peace Conference 1919
October Revolution in Russia 1917
Union of Soviet Socialist Republics 1922 (to 1991)
Weimar Republic 1919–1933

THE MIDDLE EAST AND ASIA

Chinese Revolution and fall of the Qing dynasty 1911
End of the Ottoman empire 1919
British mandate in Palestine 1920

NORTH AMERICA

Mexican Revolution 1910
United States enters World War I 1917

FOR COMPARISON

Foreign occupation of Beijing (Ch. 24) 1900
Japan annexes Korea (Ch. 26) 1910
Mussolini prime minister in Italy (Ch. 28) 1922
Hitler chancellor in Germany (Ch. 28) 1933
World War II begins (Ch. 28) 1939
Great Depression (Ch. 28) 1929–ca. 1939
Growth of Indian National Congress (Chs. 26–30) ca. 1920 (to 1947)
Gandhi leads salt march (Ch. 28) 1930
African National Congress gains momentum in South Africa (Chs. 27–31) ca. 1920 (to 1994)

© Cengage Learning

Entering the "Age of Extremes"

Over the past century we have become accustomed to the drastic changes set in motion by the First World War. It is hard for us to imagine a world where political and economic power was so highly concentrated in Europe; where women were politically voiceless; where despite industrialization, the power of human and animal muscles was still the main energy source for farming; where ancient empires endured; and where a naïve belief in limitless progress was widely shared. War and revolution shattered such complacency.

The industrialized nature of total war came as a shock. Going into the war, cavalry regiments were essential to European war planning. But the entire cavalry system was rendered anachronistic by the savage firepower of shells and machine guns. Hundreds of thousands of horses were killed, and the whole culture of "civilized" warfare between mounted "gentlemen"

disappeared. Strafing aircraft and poison gas pointed to a more violent future when the lines between soldiers and civilians would blur even further. Just a generation later, during the Second World War, the targeting of civilian populations for aerial bombardment became common (see Chapter 29).

In cultural terms, total war accelerated the existing trend toward "mass societies" in which common people played a much larger role. Posters and newspapers were the principal media used to galvanize public support for war, but already radio was supplementing telegraphy and new film industries had been born. By 1920, commercial radio broadcasts and the growth of cinema had created a broad platform for such dynamic cultural developments as the new African American art form of jazz music, which spread across the globe to enrich the lives of millions. Radio and film, however, also provided elites with new means to sway public opinion and could also be used as mechanisms of propaganda and control, a trend that would serve authoritarian regimes in Italy and Germany in the 1920s and 1930s (see Chapter 28).

To Louise Bryant and other idealists, the rise of mass societies was a sign of human liberation. Revolutions in Mexico, China, and Russia showed that ruling elites could no longer take the obedience of common men and women for granted. The same was true in Europe's overseas empires, where the war had caused many Africans and Asians to question the impregnability of their rulers and to aspire to nations of their own (see Chapters 28 and 30). It seemed, however, that the political activation of peasants and workers had a dark side as well, creating conditions of anarchy in which dictatorship could flourish, as in the absolute control established by the Communist Party in the Soviet Union under Vladimir Lenin and Joseph Stalin.

From today's perspective, communism seems to have been a historical dead end. The Soviet Union no longer exists, and the People's Republic of China, while retaining communist political control, has thrown in its lot with market economics (see Chapters 31 and 32). In the immediate postwar era, however, there were many who logically questioned whether it was liberal capitalism that might be destined for historical obsolescence. Many on the conservative right and on the communist left felt empowered by the uncertainty of the war's aftermath, an antiliberal trend that would be greatly magnified by the Great Depression yet to come.

In 1914, secret alliances had propelled the world to war. Woodrow Wilson then offered the League of Nations as a solution, a body where regular and open discussion could head off conflicts before they led to bloodshed. Wilson's vision would eventually be realized, but not until after another world war and the founding of the United Nations in 1945 (see Chapter 29). In the meantime, the League of Nations proved ineffective, crippled by the lack of participation by the United States and the Soviet Union. As it turned out, the crisis-filled decades of the 1920s and 1930s were merely an interlude between two world wars. The next would dwarf the first in intensity and global impact.

Voyages on the Web: Louise Bryant

The Voyages Map App follows the traveler's journeys using interactive study tools, including 360-degree panoramic views of historic sites, zoomable maps, audio summaries, flash cards, and quizzes.

Key Terms

Louise Bryant (762)
Kaiser Wilhelm II (765)
western front (767)
eastern front (771)
southern front (771)
Senegalese Sharpshooters (772)

Woodrow Wilson (773)
Paris Peace Conference (774)
League of Nations (775)
Weimar Republic (776)
Mandate System (777)
Balfour Declaration (778)

Emiliano Zapata (781)
Sun Yat-sen (783)
May Fourth Movement (783)
Vladimir Lenin (785)
"Socialism in One Country" (790)

For Further Reference

Bryant, Louise. *Six Red Months in Russia*. Portland, Ore.: Powells, 2002.

Dearborn, Mary V. *Queen of Bohemia: The Life of Louise Bryant*. Bridgewater, N.J.: Replica, 1996.

Fitzpatrick, Sheila. *The Russian Revolution*. 3d ed. New York: Oxford University Press, 2008.

Fromkin, David. *A Peace to End All Peace: The Fall of the Ottoman Empire and the Rise of the Modern Middle East*. New York: Holt, 2001.

Goldstone, Jack. *Revolutions: Theoretical, Comparative and Historical Studies*. Belmont, Calif.: Wadsworth, 2002.

Hart, John Mason. *Revolutionary Mexico*. Berkeley: University of California Press, 1997.

Keegan, John. *The First World War*. New York: Vintage, 2000.

Macmillan, Margaret. *Paris 1919: Six Months That Changed the World*. New York: Random House, 2003.

Meyer, G. J. *A World Undone: The Story of the Great War, 1914–1918*. New York: Delacorte, 2007.

Neiberg, Michael S. *Fighting the Great War: A Global History*. New York: Cambridge University Press, 2005.

Reed, John. *Ten Days That Shook the World*. New York: Penguin, 2007.

Schiffrin, Harold. *Sun Yat-Sen and the Origins of the Chinese Revolution*. Berkeley: University of California Press, 2010.

Service, Robert. *The Russian Revolution, 1900–1927*. 3d ed. New York: Palgrave Macmillan, 2007.

Strachan, Hew. *The First World War in Africa*. New York: Oxford University Press, 2004.

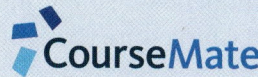 **CourseMate** Go to the CourseMate website at **www.cengagebrain.com** for additional study tools and review materials—including audio and video clips—for this chapter.

28

Responses to Global Crisis, 1920–1939

After she had participated in the struggle for the creation of the new Turkey following the First World War, the novelist **Halide Edib** (1884–1964) was forced into exile in 1926 after falling out of favor with the country's president. For the next thirteen years she traveled to France, Britain, and the United States, writing books and lecturing at universities. In 1935 she went to India, a trip that resulted in the book *Inside India* and speculation about the future direction of the world. From her own experience in Turkey she understood the struggle of formerly powerful societies to overcome more recent Western domination and the difficulties in reconciling ancient cultures with modern influences. Edib's musings about the future importance of India and China were far-sighted:

Halide Edib

(From *Memoirs of Halide Edib* by Halide Adivar Edib [N.J.: Gorgias Press]. Reprinted by permission of Gorgias Press)

India seemed to me like Allah's workshop: gods, men and nature abounded in their most beautiful and most hideous; ideas and all the arts in their ancient and most modern styles lay about pell-mell. Once I used to think that first-hand knowledge of Russia and America would enable one to sense the direction which the world was taking; but this India must certainly have its share in shaping the future. Not because of its immemorial age, but because of the new life throbbing in it! Perhaps the same is true of China. . . . How much must one see and understand before being able to have any idea of the working of history?[*]

[*]Halide Edib, *Inside India* (London: Allen and Unwin, 1937), p. 29.

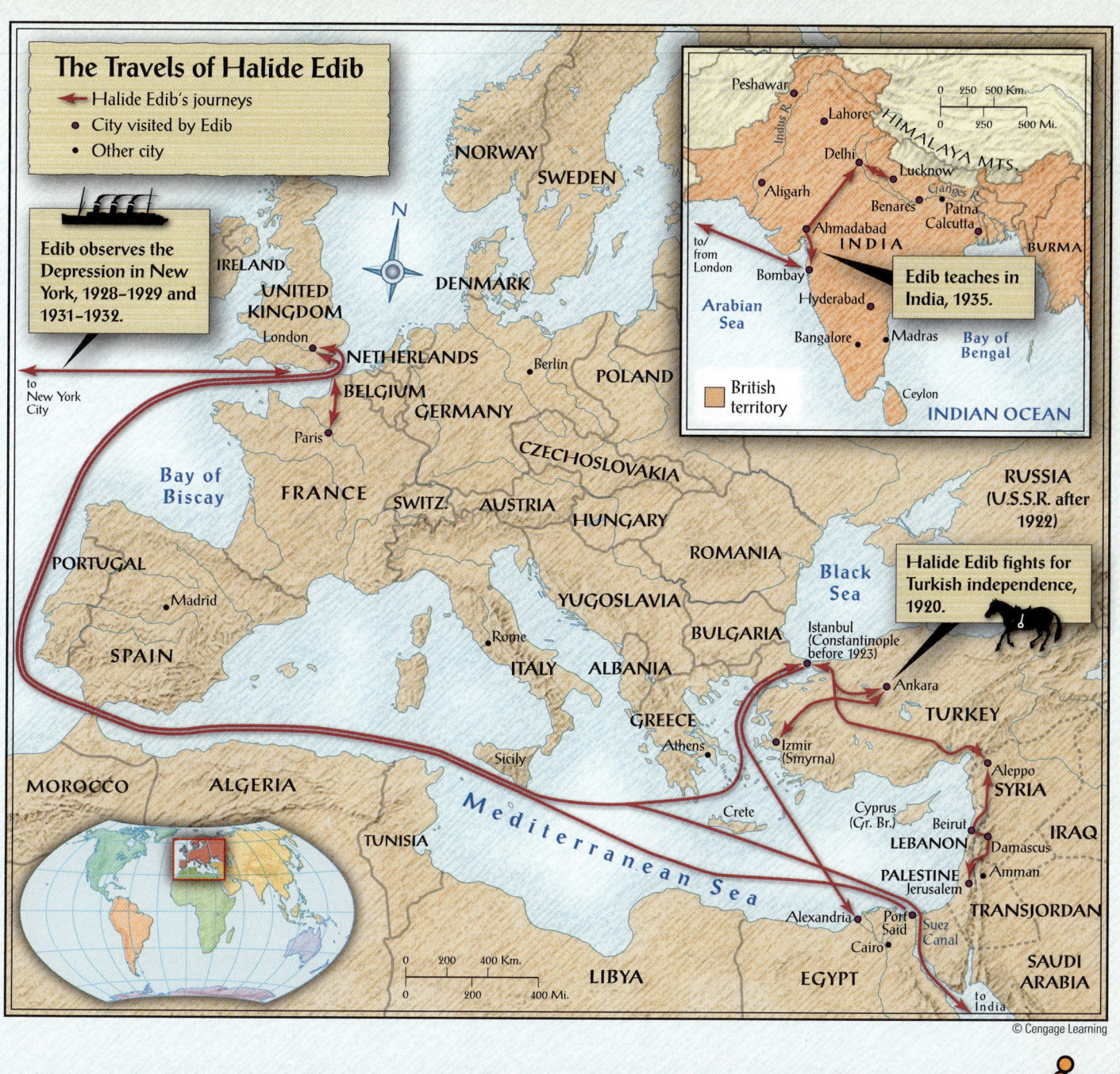

The Travels of Halide Edib

← Halide Edib's journeys
● City visited by Edib
● Other city

Edib observes the Depression in New York, 1928–1929 and 1931–1932.

Edib teaches in India, 1935.

British territory

Halide Edib fights for Turkish independence, 1920.

Halide Edib (hall-ee-DEH eh-DEEP) was the daughter of a progressive Ottoman official who made sure she learned Arabic and studied the Quran but also had her tutored by an English governess and sent her to a Greek-run school. In 1901, fluent in Turkish, English, Greek, and Arabic, Edib was the first Muslim girl to graduate from the American College for Girls in Istanbul. As a child of privilege,

795

Halide Edib
(1884–1964) Turkish nationalist best known for her many popular works of fiction featuring female protagonists. She was part of the army that formed the Turkish nation and later served as a member of the Turkish parliament and as a professor of English literature.

she had the luxury of exploring many different ideas and forming her identity in a safe and secure environment. She remained a practicing Muslim.

After graduation Edib married and had two children: *"My life was confined within the walls of my apartment. I led the life of an old-fashioned Turkish woman."* But over the next two decades she grew beyond traditional gender roles, publishing her first novel in 1908 and helping to found the Society for the Elevation of Women. In 1910 she left her husband after he married a second wife, in conformity with Islamic law but against her wishes. After her divorce Edib became even more active in public affairs. In 1912 she was involved with the Turkish Hearth Club, where, for the first time, men and women attended public lectures together. It was the outbreak of war in 1914, however, that thoroughly transformed her life.

The Ottoman government sent Edib west to Damascus and Beirut to organize schools and orphanages for girls. Before long, however, the Ottoman armies were in retreat, and she returned to Istanbul with her second husband, a medical doctor. After British forces occupied Istanbul, she fled east in disguise, wearing a veil and carefully concealing her manicured fingernails as she and her husband rode on horseback to join the Turkish nationalist army headquartered at Ankara. She was given official rank and served the cause as a translator and press officer.

Though the nationalists were victorious—Turkey was recognized internationally in 1923—Edib's voyages were not over. During her years of exile, from 1926 to 1939, the uncertainties of the postwar world were turning into genuine global crises. When she came to New York as a visiting professor of literature at Columbia University in 1931–1932, the United States was suffering from the economic collapse that became known as the Great Depression. She witnessed the global effects of that economic downturn in Britain and France, from where she also viewed the emergence of fascism with the rise to power of Benito Mussolini in Italy and Adolf Hitler in Germany. These fascist regimes represented an assault on the liberal tradition, with state power growing at the expense of individual liberties. In the Soviet Union, Joseph Stalin was further consolidating his communist dictatorship.

With the global economy in crisis and political tensions on the rise, fewer people defended liberal ideals such as free trade and free political association. Ideologies that magnified the role of the state grew in popularity, while extreme nationalism allowed authoritarian rulers in many parts of the world to concentrate ever greater power. Even the liberal institutions of democratic states were sorely tested by the challenges of the 1930s. Authoritarian tendencies gained momentum wherever liberalism was weak or absent, such as in Russia, the European colonial empires, and the new nation of Turkey.

Nationalism could also be a positive force, however, providing a source of hope for many colonized Africans and Asians. The great Indian nationalist leader Mohandas K. Gandhi personified these hopes, while giving the entire world a model of peaceful political change. Like Halide Edib, Gandhi saw the fight for national independence as inseparable from the fight for justice, including equality for women, who had few rights under colonialism. Gandhi's peaceful philosophy, a source of inspiration to many, stood in sharp contrast to the renewed militarism that would soon lead to another world war.

---

*Halide Edib, *Inside India* (London: Allen and Unwin, 1937), p. 207.

Focus Questions

» *How did governments in different parts of the world respond to the crisis of the Great Depression?*

» *Why did liberal democracy decline in influence as fascism, communism, and other authoritarian regimes rose in power and popularity?*

» *How successful were anticolonial nationalists in Asia and Africa during this period?*

» *What major events led to the outbreak of the Second World War?*

The Great Depression, 1929–1939

In October 1929 prices on the New York Stock Exchange plunged; within two months, stocks lost half their value. The next year a string of bank failures across Europe and the Americas spread economic turmoil around the world, bringing the **Great Depression**. Unemployment surged; agricultural prices plummeted. In spite of various government policies intended to correct the problem, by 1939 global markets still had not recovered.

> **Great Depression**
> Economic depression beginning in 1929 with the crash of stock prices in New York followed by a series of bank failures in Europe; marked by sustained deflation, unemployment in industrial nations, and depressed crop prices.

The Great Depression in the Industrialized World

The Great Depression revealed the central role the United States now played in the global economy, as well as the degree to which finance and trade integrated nearly all the world's people into a single economic system. Historians continue to debate the causes of the Great Depression, but two factors clearly stand out: the speculative excesses of the American stock market, and the international debt structure that emerged after the First World War.

By the later 1920s the global economy had recovered from postwar malaise, and even Germany, in spite of the punishing reparations it still owed to France, seemed back on the road to recovery (see Chapter 27). In the United States, financial markets reflected the frenetic pace of life during the "jazz age" of the 1920s, with its glamorous movie stars, mass-produced automobiles, and sensational gangsters. Speculators bought stock on borrowed money and, trusting that markets would endlessly increase in value, used paper profits to extend themselves even further. Then on October 24, 1929, the bubble burst. When the stock market collapsed, investors and the bankers who had lent them money were ruined. As capital investment dried up, the stock market collapse turned into a general economic crisis.

A sharp division between rich and poor magnified the problem. By 1929, only 1 percent of the U.S. population controlled 20 percent of its wealth. Since ordinary workers could no longer afford the products being churned out by American manufacturers, many plants went out of business. More and more workers found themselves staring at locked factory gates. By 1932, one-fourth of workers in the United States were unemployed.

The vulnerability of the international financial system was revealed when the stock market crash led to a general run on banks in both the United States and Europe. During World War I the United States had replaced Great Britain as the

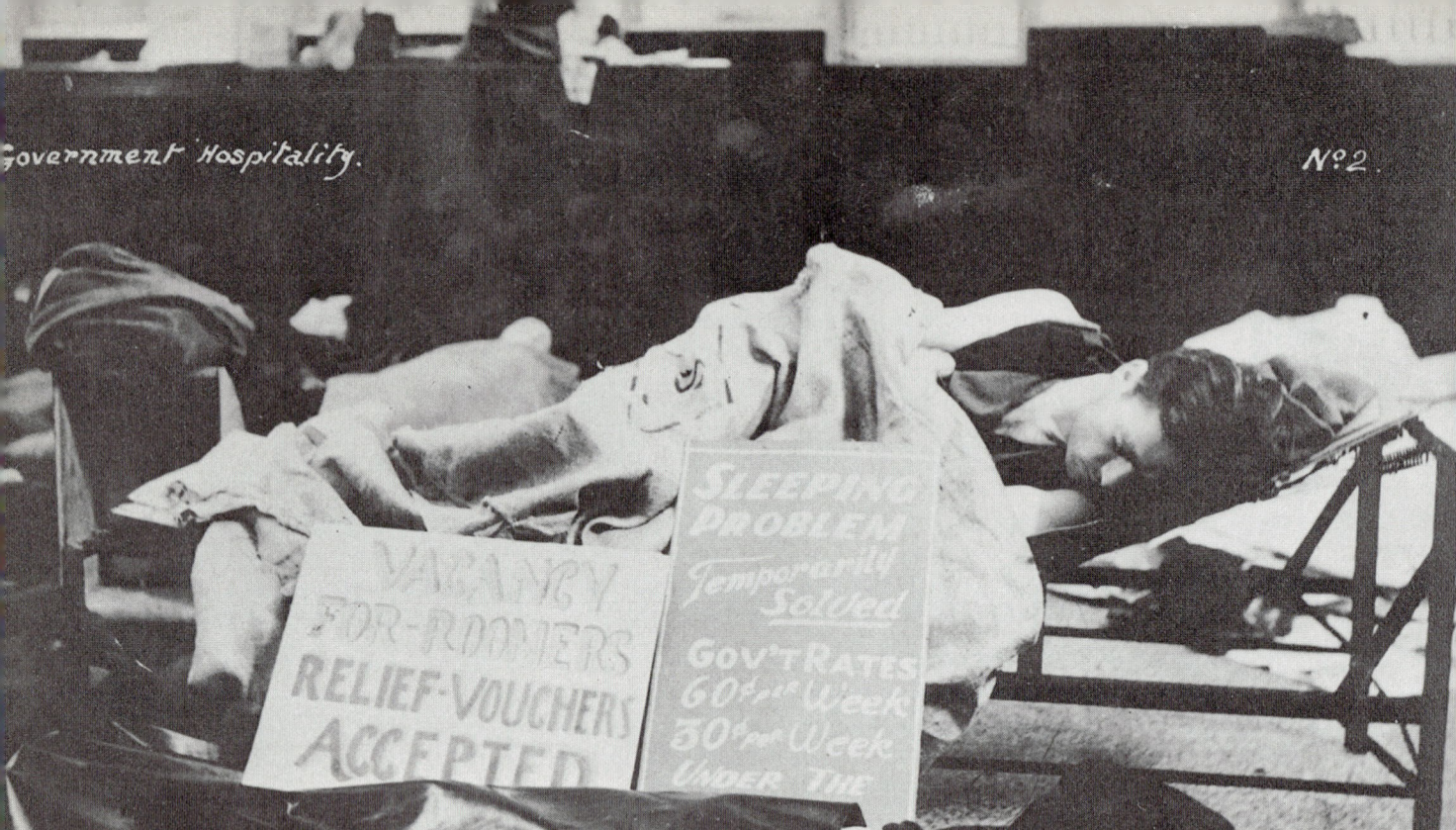

The Great Depression Those left unemployed by the Great Depression often became homeless. Here a Canadian man takes shelter on a cot in an office, his plight seemingly left unsolved by his government's efforts to provide relief vouchers to "temporarily solve" the problem. (Library and Archives of Canada)

world's leading source of investment capital, and European governments were deeply in debt to American banks. The banking crisis was particularly acute in Germany, where the Weimar government was forced to borrow heavily to make the huge payments to France required by the Versailles treaty. Financiers in the United States lent Germans money, which they then paid to France, which then sent the money back to the United States as French payments on American loans. After the stock market collapse, American investors called in their loans to German banks, and the system collapsed. In the spring of 1931 the largest bank in Vienna declared bankruptcy as the Great Depression became global. By 1933, German factories produced only half the goods they had manufactured in 1929, and half the workforce was idle.

The policies of Western politicians exacerbated the crisis. In 1930, the United States imposed high tariffs to protect American manufacturing from foreign imports. Great Britain followed suit in 1932, increasing interchange within its empire instead of participating in global free trade. Though intended to save jobs, protectionist measures caused steep declines in international trade and further loss of employment. By the early 1930s the world was trapped in a deflationary spiral, as wages and prices descended in a vicious cycle.

In these circumstances, there was little faith that free markets could solve the problem. As during World War I, governments in France, Britain, and the United States again took a much more active role in domestic economies. In the United States, President **Franklin Delano Roosevelt** (in office 1933–1945) implemented his New Deal programs. Social Security created a "safety net" for many of the nation's elderly, and the Works Progress Administration put the unemployed

Franklin Delano Roosevelt (in office 1933–1945) President of the United States during the Great Depression and World War II. Created the New Deal, intended to stimulate the economy through government spending, financial sector reform, and a safety net for those most in need.

to work on public infrastructure. Price subsidies helped stabilize farm prices while legislation strengthened workers' rights to unionize and strike. Government protection of depositors' accounts restored faith in the banking system. Although the New Deal was quite popular, it did not get at the root of the economic problem, and in 1939 unemployment in the United States still stood at 16 percent.

The same pattern of government intervention unfolded in France and Britain, although the economic role of the state was more strongly developed in Sweden, Norway, and Denmark. Here, Social Democrats pledged to construct a "welfare state" that would protect their citizens through comprehensive education, health care, housing subsidies, and unemployment insurance. But while such measures reduced suffering, they did not resolve underlying economic issues any more than Roosevelt's policies. No merely national solution could possibly solve the problem of depressed global markets caused by a shortage of credit.

The Great Depression in Global Perspective

Depressed agricultural prices hit farmers hard everywhere, including hundreds of millions of peasant farmers in Africa, Asia, and Latin America. In very remote areas peasants might have the option of withdrawing from market production and focusing on their own family and village subsistence. But by the 1930s the vast majority had become so enmeshed in global markets that withdrawal was not an option.

Most Africans, for example, were connected to the world economy either as workers for European-owned mines and plantations or as peasant producers of commodities for export. Small-scale family farms grew cash crops like cocoa, cotton, and coffee not only to get the cash for imported goods like cloth, kerosene lamps, and bicycles, but also to pay the taxes demanded by European colonial governments. Parents with extra money often invested in school fees for their children. Thus in some areas, access to Western education was another stimulus for rural families to grow commercial crops.

When coffee and cocoa prices fell by over half in early 1930, many Africans were suddenly unable to meet their tax obligations or pay their debts. Since Western manufactures had increasingly displaced indigenous industries, they had come to depend on imported goods like iron hoes and cotton clothing, which they could no longer afford. Years of hardship followed during which school attendance declined as young people were sometimes forced to leave their villages in search of work.

Conditions were equally bleak where export commodities were produced on plantations. Brazil, the world's largest coffee producer, also experienced the steep fall in prices when coffee consumption in the United States and Europe declined. Exporters destroyed huge stockpiles of Brazilian coffee, hoping that decreasing the supply would increase global prices. Agricultural workers left the plantations to scratch a living out of the soil or to join the destitute in the burgeoning *favelas*, or urban slums. The situation was similar in Southeast Asia, after a global decline in automobile and bicycle production caused rubber prices to crash. In Vietnam, as in Brazil, unemployed plantation workers were left destitute.

In the villages of India, the drop in crop prices further squeezed farmers who were already, in the words of Halide Edib, *"at the mercy of rain, moneylender, and tax-gatherer."*[*] By 1932 peasant incomes had fallen by half. To avoid losing their land, many families sold the gold jewelry they were saving for their daughters' dowries. In the 1930s, billions of rupees worth of such "distress gold" were sold, and many couples delayed or canceled marriage. At the same time, many South

---

[*]Halide Edib, *Inside India* (London: Allen and Unwin, 1937), p. 170.

Asian Muslims had to cancel plans to perform the hajj, the pilgrimage to Mecca and Medina that could take a lifetime of planning. As cotton prices plunged and textile factories in Europe and the United States cut production or closed, Egyptian farmers were struck equally hard. Whereas over 16,000 people a year traveled from Egypt to Arabia before 1929, only about 1,700 made the pilgrimage in 1933.

In Latin America, economic nationalism was a common response to the crisis. In Mexico, for example, President Lázaro Cárdenas nationalized the country's petroleum industry, arguing that the profits should be used to help the Mexican people rather than enrich foreign companies. To aid rural Mexicans, he redistributed large amounts of land to peasant communities, finally fulfilling the promise of the Mexican Revolution (see Chapter 27). In Brazil, Getúlio Vargas, after seizing dictatorial power in a 1930 coup, began a program of infrastructural and industrial development based on state monopolies intended to end the country's dependence on foreign markets and industrial imports. Cárdenas and Vargas both went even further than leaders in the United States and western Europe in asserting state economic power as a response to the Great Depression.

These were also troubled times in Halide Edib's native Turkey. Mustafa Kemal, like the Latin American leaders, was determined to build up Turkey's own industrial base and make the country less dependent on foreign imports. Kemal's government followed a policy of "import substitution," which used high tariffs to shield local producers from global competition. Though import substitution did create some new industrial jobs, the policy was, in global terms, economically dysfunctional. As with the protective tariffs imposed by the leading industrialized nations, the effect was to decrease international trade even further, hampering global economic recovery.

Fascism, Communism, and Authoritarianism

Even in the most liberal societies, where private enterprise and individual liberty were well established, both World War I and the global depression brought greater government economic intervention. In Italy, Germany, and the Soviet Union, where liberalism had much shallower roots, the challenges of the early twentieth century created a climate in which explicitly antiliberal, authoritarian political ideologies—**fascism** and communism—flourished. Fascists, most notably Benito Mussolini in Italy and Adolf Hitler in Germany, were contemptuous of representative government. Weak, vain, and vacillating politicians should be replaced by strong leaders who represented not self-interested factions but the people as a whole. Only then, they promised, could national greatness be achieved. Unity of purpose and the role of the state in organizing the collective will were more important in fascist thinking than individual rights. Fascists were extreme nationalists, and while racism was strongly present across the world—from the segregated cities and schools of the United States to the racially based empires of Britain and France—the German Nazis imposed racial policies of unprecedented severity. Germany's Jews were the principal target.

fascism
Authoritarian political doctrine based on extreme nationalism, elevation of the state at the expense of the individual, and replacement of independent social organizations in civil society with state organizations.

Communists also had no use for liberal democracy, following Karl Marx's idea that representative governments were merely committees for managing the affairs of the property-owning bourgeoisie (see Chapter 23). But in opposing the liberal emphasis on individual rights, communists underplayed national unity while emphasizing class solidarity. The workers of each nation, after uniting to overthrow their oppressors, would unite to create global socialism. In reality, the Soviet

Union was the only existing communist society in the 1930s. As Stalin collectivized agriculture, oversaw rapid industrialization, and purged the state of his perceived enemies, the Soviet people lived in perpetual fear and deprivation.

Although fascists and communists hated each other passionately, they shared a common loathing for liberal democracy. Following the Great Depression, with the democratic nations struggling to restore their vitality without much success, many came to believe that fascism or communism was the cure.

Mussolini and the Rise of Fascism

For **Benito Mussolini** (1883–1945), the state bound the people together: *"Everything for the state, nothing against the state, no one outside the state."* Mussolini was bitterly disappointed by the performance of the Italian government and military during World War I. In the postwar period he organized quasi-military groups made up largely of former soldiers, called Blackshirts, who assaulted socialists and communists in the streets. Their belligerence intimidated middle-class politicians, whose weakness, Mussolini thought, could allow Bolshevism to spread to Italy. Mussolini's supporters called him *Il Duce* (ill DOO-chey), "the leader."

It was true that disunity made the country vulnerable to both outside powers and internal dissension. After all, the Italian nation was only six decades old: for many, local dialects and cultural traditions were still more relevant than national ones. Social tensions accompanied industrialization in the north, while the south was still mired in the poverty that had driven many to emigrate to the United States and Argentina. The existing constitutional monarchy seemed unable to reconcile regional and class divisions. The Catholic Church, although it dominated the lives of most Italians, was also powerless to bridge such divides. Extreme nationalism was Mussolini's answer. (See the feature "World History in Today's World: Europe's Far Right.")

Mussolini stepped in with supreme confidence and determination, offering order, discipline, and unity. His passionate speeches contrasted sharply with the bland style of most politicians. Landowners and industrialists, favoring Mussolini's call to unity and order as a means of suppressing anarchism and communism, financed the fascists as the Blackshirts harassed union leaders, broke strikes, and kept potentially rebellious farm laborers and tenants in line.

In 1922, Mussolini organized disaffected war veterans in a march on Rome. Though the elected government declared a state of siege to rebuff Mussolini's play for power, the king and the military refused to enforce it. With their support Mussolini maneuvered his way into the prime minister's position. It seemed for a time that the fascists would be willing to work within the framework of Italy's constitution. As the violence of fascist thugs continued, however, many members of the Italian middle class who had been attracted by Mussolini's youth and vigor began to turn against him. Mussolini responded by consolidating his power, arresting opponents, and outlawing their political parties. After 1926 Mussolini ruled as dictator.

Mussolini's definition of fascism was explicitly antiliberal, focusing on the power of the state over the rights of individuals: *"Liberalism denied the State in the name of the individual; Fascism reasserts the rights of the State as expressing the real essence of the individual."* The foundation of liberty in liberal societies is free

Benito Mussolini (1883–1945) Prime minister of Italy and the world's first fascist leader. Also known as Il Duce, he founded the Italian Fascist Party and formed an alliance with Hitler's Germany.

'From *Fascism Doctrine and Institutions*, 1935, pp. 7–42. http://www.worldfuturefund.org/wffmaster/Reading/Germany/mussolini.htm.

Europe's Far Right

In the summer of 2011, hours after the usually placid Norwegian capital of Oslo was rocked by a deadly explosion, a lone gunman went on a rampage at a summer camp for youth volunteers of the country's ruling Labor Party, killing sixty-nine teenagers and young adults and wounding many others. The killer, Anders Breivik, justified his actions by stating that leftist politicians had sponsored the "Islamic colonization" of his country, leading to the "deconstruction of Norwegian culture."[*]

Later that same year, German authorities announced that a Neo-Nazi cell had been responsible for a spate of murders and beatings in the past decade, targeting Turkish immigrants. The eastern part of Germany, where high unemployment among young men has provided a fertile recruiting ground for the far-right National Democratic Party, was at the center of the investigation. Meanwhile, liberal and leftist organizations accused German intelligence agencies of focusing on Muslim extremists while ignoring a growing threat from far-right terror groups.

Very few condone such violent, extralegal behavior, of course, and moderate conservative and social democratic parties continue to represent the views of most Europeans. Still, the emotional fuel of the immigration issue is pushing more voters to support extreme right-wing parties in several countries. In some, they have recently received enough votes to form significant parliamentary minorities for the first time, as in Finland and Denmark. Far-right appeals to social conservatism and ethnic solidarity found a wider audience after the recent economic downturn led to higher unemployment and cuts in government spending.

Once it seemed that western Europe had left behind religious divisiveness and national chauvinism. The fall of fascism, postwar economic resurgence, and the creation of the European Union led to a culture of tolerance, secularism, and cosmopolitanism. Now that consensus is threatened as many Europeans worry that immigrants, rather than adapting to the languages and cultures of their new homes, will instead remain unassimilated outsiders, threatening their own cultural integrity and national identity.

On the other side of the issue are many who regard far-right voters as racists willing to scapegoat marginalized outsiders, raising the specter of a twenty-first-century fascist resurgence. Meanwhile, events in Norway and Germany have focused greater attention on the need for security services to pay close attention to terrorist organizations of all kinds, domestic as well as international.

[*]"Norwegian Terror Suspect Breivik Tells Court Today He Deserves a Medal," *The Christian Science Monitor*, February 6, 2012.

association: organizations formed voluntarily by people with similar regional, class, or political interests. Mussolini had no sympathy with this idea. Instead, he installed a system of "corporations" by which all citizens involved in a common undertaking would be organized by the state. "Corporatism" replaced independent unions with state-sanctioned ones and took over the nation's youth organizations. In theory, fascist government controlled the activities of everyone, though the fascists never actually achieved that level of intrusion in the lives of individuals.

For the dull compromises of parliamentary democracy Mussolini substituted a theatrical politics that involved singing, flag waving, marching, and stirring oratory. He often invoked Rome's imperial past and promised to make it once again the center of a mighty empire. In 1935, in defiance of the League of Nations, he invaded Ethiopia to avenge Italy's humiliating defeat at the Battle of Adowa by King Menelik's army in 1896 (see Chapter 26). Fervent patriotism in the cause of empire proved another effective way to bind together the young Italian nation.

Some Italians were active supporters of Mussolini's regime, willing to trade liberty for security and a renewed sense of national pride. Others, usually Italian communists, paid for opposition to Mussolini with their lives. Most Italians did not care too much one way or the other. Rather than actively supporting the fascist cause or risking a fight against it, they simply went on with their daily lives. As the Italian Marxist Antonio Gramsci wrote, before spending years in a fascist prison: *"Indifference is actually the mainspring of history. . . . What comes to pass does so not so much because a few people want it to happen, as because the mass of citizens abdicate their responsibility and let things be."**

Hitler and National Socialism in Germany

After World War I, Germany was both humiliated and financially devastated by the war and the punitive Versailles treaty (see Chapter 27). Although the Weimar Republic had brought liberal democracy to Germany in the 1920s, progress ended with the onset of the Great Depression. Germans were desperate for solutions. By the early 1930s the center was falling out of German politics, as communists on the far left and fascists on the extreme right gained popularity.

The German liberals and socialists who had overseen the creation of the Weimar Republic were all heirs to the Enlightenment tradition, believing that the use of reason was key to the achievement of a just and stable social order. For many Germans, however, the war had called into question belief in reason. During what some historians have called an "age of anxiety" in the West, expressionist artists probed darker emotions. The psychological theories of Sigmund Freud, emphasizing the power of unconscious impulses, gained in popularity. Even scientific advances were deeply unsettling, as when Albert Einstein's theory of relativity challenged Newtonian physics, removing time as an independent variable by positing a four-dimensional space-time in which observation itself depends on the speed and location of the observer. These cultural and intellectual trends reinforced the general state of overall uncertainty in which the Weimar Republic had been born.

Into this anxious environment stepped **Adolf Hitler** (1889–1945) and his National Socialist Party, promising to restore greatness, confidence, and order. Hitler had a very different idea than did liberals or socialists of what "the people" meant. Socialists believed that "the people" meant the masses of workers, and liberals believed that each individual was autonomous and that "the people" was simply the sum of those individuals. For Hitler, however, *das Volk* (das FOHLK), "the people," was a single organism bound by history, tradition, and race. Just as no cell is independent from the others in a living organism, so all Germans were connected by their racial destiny. Hitler defined Germans as an "Aryan" race superior to all others.

According to Nazism, any German who did not live up to the ideal of racial pride and racial purity was like a cancerous growth that needed to be excised. Nazi targets included communists, with their internationalist doctrine; homosexuals, with their supposed rejection of traditional family values; and the handicapped, considered physically inferior. Proponents of the racist pseudo-science of eugenics (also popular in the United States in the 1930s) argued that selective breeding could lead to superior human beings. If the smartest "Aryan" men and women married and had children, they could produce a "master race." Eugenic medical practices led to the sterilization of many girls from poor families to stop their "genetic defects" from being passed on to another generation.

Adolf Hitler
(1889–1945) Leader of the National Socialist Party who became chancellor of Germany and dismantled the Weimar constitution. His ultranationalist policies led to persecution of communists and Jews, and his aggressive foreign policies started World War II.

*Antonio Gramsci, from *Avanti!*, in *Selections from Political Writings 1910–1920* (London: Lawrence and Wishart, 1977), p. 17.

Bauf
Jugendherbergen
und Heime

Mary Evans Picture Library/The Image Works

National Socialist Propaganda The Nazi Party often used images of healthy blond children to emphasize German vitality and racial superiority and organized young people into party-based boys' and girls' clubs. This poster for the "League of German Girls" solicits donations to a fund to "Build Youth Hostels and Homes." In spite of her smile, and the flowers on the swastika-labeled collection tin, all of the money collected actually went into weapons production.

But Hitler was even more concerned with racial mixing. Looking for a scapegoat on whom to blame the country's problems, he tapped into the centuries-old tradition of anti-Semitism. Although German Jews were thoroughly assimilated into national life, he identified them as the main threat: *"The personification of the devil as the symbol of all evil assumes the living shape of the Jew."* For the Nazis, the supposed racial characteristics of Jews contrasted with, and thereby illuminated, the virtues of the German *Volk*. Only by isolating the Jews, and ultimately eliminating them, could the goal of racial purity be achieved.

In the late 1920s such ideas were on the far fringe. But after the Great Depression revealed the weakness of the Weimar political system, voters increasingly abandoned the parties of the center-right and the center-left for the communists and the fascists. Between 1928 and 1932, the National Socialist share of the vote jumped from 2.6 to 37.3 percent of the national total, and Hitler's deputies controlled more than a third of the seats in the Reichstag. Many of his early supporters came from the lower middle class, people who did not have savings or job security, although some more affluent Germans were also attracted to National Socialism as a bulwark against communism. Young people were especially caught up in Hitler's emotional, patriotic appeals. Almost half the party members were under thirty.

The German Communist Party also gained strong support in the elections of 1932. Alarmed by the communist threat, German business leaders increased their support for the ardently anticommunist National Socialists. Despite their distaste for Hitler, whom most educated Germans saw as wild and unrefined, conservatives thought they would be able to control him from behind the scenes as he rallied the public against communism. While President Paul von Hindenburg was reluctant to elevate Hitler, he needed Hitler's support to form a governing coalition, which Hitler would join only if he was made chancellor. In 1933, Hindenburg announced a new government with Hitler at its head.

A month after he took office, a fire broke out in the Reichstag (the German parliament). The arson was likely the work of a single individual, but Hitler accused the Communist Party of treason and had all Communist members of the Reichstag arrested. The remaining representatives then passed a law that suspended constitutional protections of civil liberties for four years and allowed Hitler to rule as a dictator. The emergency powers granted to Hitler became permanent.

Hitler dismantled the Weimar institutions and became the *Führer* (leader) of an industrial state of huge potential power. Changes to German society were sudden and extreme. The Nazis abolished all political parties other than the National

Socialists and replaced Germany's federal structure with a centralized dictatorship emanating from Berlin. Like the fascists in Italy, they took over or replaced independent organizations in civil society such as labor unions. Hitler Youth replaced the Boy Scouts and church-sponsored youth groups as part of a plan, reinforced by a new school curriculum, to teach fascism to the next generation. Artists, architects, writers, and filmmakers who did not conform to the National Socialist vision of a strictly regimented society were censored, harassed, and often driven into exile. (See the feature "Visual Evidence in Primary Sources: Angst and Order in German Cinema.") Hitler promised a Third Reich ("Third Empire") that would last a thousand years.

The Nazis also restricted the authority of German religious leaders. Protestant churches came under tight state control. Though the Catholic Church had reached an understanding with Mussolini, Hitler was less accommodating. The Nazi state seized church properties and imprisoned priests who resisted totalitarianism. Many Catholics joined the National Socialist Party all the same. Christian leaders would later be criticized for not having done enough to prevent Hitler's rise to power.

Having already sent the communists off to prison camps, the Führer (FYUR-ruhr) turned to the "Jewish problem." In 1935, the Nazis imposed the Nuremberg Laws, which deprived Jews of all civil rights and forbade intermarriage between Jews and other Germans. Some Jews emigrated, but most German Jews were deeply assimilated into the country's cultural and social life and could not imagine that Germans would further persecute them. In 1938, however, the Nazis launched coordinated attacks against Jews throughout Germany and Austria. After this "Kristallnacht" ("Crystal Night")—named for the smashing of the windows in Jewish homes, synagogues, and stores—more Jews fled. Those who remained were forced into segregated ghettos. After 1938, it was no longer possible to suppose that Hitler's anti-Semitic tirades were merely political rhetoric: the machinery for the destruction of European Jews was being set in motion (see Chapter 29).

Hitler's dictatorship, like Mussolini's, relied on either active support or passive consent from the majority of the population. Part of his appeal was negative: at a time of fear and insecurity, Hitler identified enemies, such as communists and Jews, who could be blamed for the country's problems. But Hitler's economic successes also help explain his popularity. While workers in the Western democracies vainly struggled to find jobs, German unemployment dropped from over 6 million people to under two hundred thousand between 1932 and 1938. It seemed that government economic intervention was key. German ministries fixed prices and allocated resources in close coordination with the country's largest corporations. Massive public works projects, such as the world's first superhighways and a large military buildup, put millions of Germans back to work.

With communists and Jews out of the way, Hitler promised, traditional values of courage, order, and discipline would once again inspire and empower the German people. Women's highest calling was to stay in the home and nurture pure-bred Aryan children. The Nazis' massive rallies, with their precision marching, flag waving, and spellbinding speeches by the Führer himself, turned politics into theater and gave people a sense of being part of something much larger than themselves. Radio broadcasts and expertly-made propaganda films such as *Triumph of the Will*, Leni Riefenstahl's infamous depiction of a Nazi rally, spread the excitement throughout the land.

Of course, not everyone was taken in. But outspoken opposition to Hitler meant imprisonment or death. Most Germans were content to go about their daily lives, appreciative of the relative order and prosperity.

Angst and Order in German Cinema

Expressionism was one response to the horrific experience of war. Strongly emotive, expressionism captured the angst of a postwar generation torn from the securities of a world seemingly changed forever. Many expressionists challenged the viewer with strong colors, primitive outlines, violent emotion, rapid movement, and heightened sexual energy. It was art for an age of anxiety. In film, the most famous expressionist work is *The Cabinet of Dr. Caligari*, a 1920 horror film that plumbs the darkness of the human psyche; an advertising poster for the film is reproduced here.

Neoclassicism was a different response to postwar uncertainty, with the goal of restoring a sense of order by returning to the calm harmony associated with Greek art. The second image here exemplifies the neoclassical style. *Olympia*, directed by the great German film artist Leni Riefenstahl, was a tribute to the Berlin Olympics of 1936. While her technical brilliance is widely

The sets for this silent film featured jagged, canvas-painted backgrounds, with few right angles or settled spaces. The expressionistic look of the film, including sharp contrasts between light and dark, reinforced its theme of disorder and violence in the human psyche.

The film's emphasis on dark, uncontrollable urges reflected the increasing influence of Sigmund Freud, the great Austrian psychologist who emphasized the power of the unconscious mind.

Photofest, Inc.

The story features the evil Dr. Caligari, who controls a sleepwalking man, Cesare. Caligari displays Cesare at carnivals, claiming he can predict the future. At night, Cesare performs murder on Caligari's behalf. Or does he?

The film leaves the viewer to doubt: who is the doctor and who is the patient? Who is sane and who is deranged? What is reality and what is fantasy? Such unsettling, unanswered questions were new to film when *Dr. Caligari* was premiered in Berlin in 1920, but in later decades they would become common in the genre of psychologically-driven horror films.

acknowledged, Riefenstahl's work has also been judged by its propaganda value for the Nazi regime. Neoclassicism was the style preferred by Adolf Hitler.

The National Socialists denounced expressionism as a perverse form of modernism created by Jews and subversives to undermine the confidence and willpower of the German people. In 1937, Joseph Goebbels (Hitler's minister of propaganda) organized an exhibition of so-called "degenerate art" in Munich to rally the public against artistic modernism. Many "degenerate"

painters, architects, designers, and filmmakers were driven into exile.

Germany's loss was America's gain. Hollywood benefited enormously from the influx of émigré film talent in the 1930s. Erich Pommer (the producer of *Dr. Caligari*) and Billy Wilder (one of the most productive and popular Hollywood directors) were Jewish refugees from fascism who significantly influenced film in the United States. Along with Jews from Poland, Russia, Lithuania, and elsewhere, they made enduring contributions to American culture.

The look of *Olympia* could not possibly be more different than that of *Dr. Caligari*. Here all is rational and orderly; right angles, classical harmony, and idealized depictions of the human body dominate.

After silently and reverently panning across the ruins of the Parthenon, Riefenstahl's camera shows a Greek statue of a discus thrower slowly fading into the statuesque figure of a modern athlete, who gracefully completes the throw. The continuity between classical and modern is immediately asserted.

Photo Leni Riefenstahl, All Rights Reserved, Archiv LRP

As a photographer and cinematographer, director Leni Riefenstahl (1902–2003) was one of the most influential visual artists of the twentieth century. Yet the fact that her art was placed at the service of Adolf Hitler has long clouded her reputation as a pioneering female artist.

The propaganda value of *Olympia* for Nazi racism was somewhat undermined by Riefenstahl's necessary inclusion of the victories of African American athlete Jesse Owens in the 1936 Summer Olympics; his world record-setting long jump is beautifully rendered.

QUESTION FOR ANALYSIS

» *From what you know of fascism, why were the Nazis so opposed to expressionist works like* Dr. Caligari *and so strongly in favor of neoclassical works like* Olympia? *(Try to watch clips of* Dr. Caligari *and* Olympia *online before you answer.)*

Stalin: Collectivization and the Great Purges

For all the ambition of Mussolini and Hitler, neither could match the total control of society achieved by Joseph Stalin (1879–1953). While Stalin's totalitarian control predated the global depression and was independent of it (see Chapter 27), the Soviet Union also saw an escalation of state power in the 1930s.

Starting in 1928, Stalin launched the U.S.S.R. on a path of rapid industrialization based on centralized Five-Year Plans. Since most of the country was still agricultural, Stalin needed to find a way to apply his policy of "Socialism in One Country" to rural areas as well. Lenin had promised the peasants land in return for political support, and his New Economic Policy allowed small-scale private ownership in the countryside. But for many communists this policy was an aberration, since private ownership would lead to agrarian capitalism. Instead, Stalin ordered the **collectivization** of the rural sector and suddenly moved millions of peasants into barracks on collective farms.

collectivization
Stalin's replacement of peasant villages with large, state-run collective farms, following the idea of "Socialism in One Country." Millions died in famines and as a result of state terror campaigns.

There was substantial resistance to collectivization, which Stalin attributed to the *kulaks* (koo-LAHKS), more prosperous peasants who, he said, were out to exploit their fellow villagers. When Stalin sent the Red Army into the countryside, he said it was to help the masses defeat these kulaks. In reality, the Soviet state was waging war on its own people. The result, in 1932–1933, was famine. Ukrainians suffered the most, victims of Stalin's brutal punishment for their attempt to establish an independent republic after the First World War.

But the industrial sector continued to expand rapidly. The Communist Party bureaucracy treated the non-Russian parts of the Soviet Union, especially those of Central Asia, in colonial fashion, as sources of raw materials for industrial growth in the Russian heartland. In contrast with other industrial societies, the Soviet Union allowed no unemployment. But Soviet workers received almost no material benefit; wages were kept low to generate investment for further industrial expansion. Rapid industrialization also poisoned the air and water.

In the later 1930s Stalin, always paranoid about plots against him, stepped up his repression of the Old Bolsheviks (see the feature "Visual Evidence in Primary Sources" in Chapter 27). During the **Great Purges**, Stalin ordered his secret police to arrest many former colleagues of Lenin and forced them to confess to supposed crimes. Movie cameras recorded their statements admitting to trumped-up charges of treason before they were taken out and shot. In 1937 alone, Stalin had half of the army's officer corps imprisoned or executed. The decimation of his own military leadership was an irrational move given that Hitler's rise to power was a direct threat. Even as he killed and imprisoned his generals, Stalin ordered a massive military buildup to protect the Soviet Union from the likelihood of yet another German invasion.

Great Purges
The execution by Stalin in the late 1930s of many "Old Bolsheviks" he regarded as competitors for power. Public trials and forced confessions marked the Great Purges.

Soviet citizens lived in a nearly constant state of terror. "Fear by night, and a feverish effort by day to pretend enthusiasm for a system of lies," writes one historian, "was the permanent condition."* A single wrong word or glance could lead to a knock on the door and exile to Stalin's gulags, the vast system of slave-labor camps that embodied Stalin's dictum: *The easiest way to gain control of the population is to carry out acts of terror.*

Authoritarian Regimes in Asia

The challenge to liberalism was not limited to Europe and the Soviet Union. In many other parts of the world where liberal traditions were absent or only weakly

---

*Robert Conquest, *The Great Terror: A Reassessment* (New York: Oxford University Press, 1997), p. 252.

developed, the uncertainty of the postwar period and the economic crisis of the Great Depression strengthened authoritarianism. In both Japan and Turkey, state intervention in economic and political life increased through the inter-war years.

Ultranationalism in Japan

Although the Versailles treaty had rewarded Japan with territorial concessions at China's expense (see Chapter 27), nationalists remained dissatisfied:

We are like a great crowd of people packed into a small and narrow room, and there are only three doors through which we might escape, namely, emigration, advance into world markets, and expansion of territory. The first door has been barred to us by the anti-Japanese immigration policies of other countries. The second is being pushed shut by tariff barriers. . . . It is quite natural that Japan should rush upon the last remaining door . . . of territorial expansion.[*]

The Great Depression strengthened the arguments of nationalists and militarists for a more aggressive foreign and imperial policy.

In the 1920s, the country had shown signs of heading in a more democratic direction. Japan was a constitutional monarchy, with an emperor whose role was ceremonial. Though still quite limited, voting rights were extended to more Japanese men, and the cabinet was no longer chosen by imperial advisers but by the party that gained the most votes in elections.

Other factors, however, limited liberal democracy in Japan. One was the power of civil service bureaucrats, who controlled policy together with the *zaibatsu*, Japan's large industrial conglomerates. In 1926, when the new emperor Hirohito came to the throne, ultranationalists saw an opportunity to expand their influence. A new requirement stipulated that the minister of defense be an active military officer with power nearly equal to that of the prime minister. Even Fukuzawa Yûkichi, back at the turn of the century, had begun to emphasize national glory over individual liberty (see Chapter 24). Militaristic sentiment emphasizing that attitude had grown during the 1920s. After the market collapse of 1930 led to falling farm prices and tough times for the farm families whose sons made up most of the soldiers in the army, the military role in government became even greater.

Ultranationalists in Japan envisioned a new Asian economic system that would combine Japanese management and capital with the resources and cheap labor of East and Southeast Asia. The turning point came with the **invasion of Manchuria**, in which the Japanese seized northeastern China in the name of their emperor. As part of the Versailles settlement, the Japanese had been allowed to keep soldiers in the Manchurian capital, although Manchuria was still formally a province of China. Then, in 1931, Japanese military commanders there, in defiance of civilian politicians in Tokyo, ordered their soldiers to leave their barracks and occupy the main population centers and the transportation infrastructure. Brought to trial, the disobedient officers denounced the government and used the courtroom to whip up public support for the army's ambitions. As imperial fever grew, civilian politicians lost what little control they had over the military.

As in Italy and Germany, militarization brought Japanese corporations lucrative government contracts. And as in the fascist countries, Japan's economic policies seemed successful. Military spending, even if it required government borrowing, boosted the economy, as did the occupation of Manchuria. After 1932,

invasion of Manchuria (1931) Invasion that occurred when Japanese military officers defied the civilian government and League of Nations by occupying this northeastern Chinese province, leading to the further militarization of the Japanese government.

[*]Hashimoto Kingoro, "Address to Young Men," in *Sources of Japanese Tradition,* ed. William Theodore de Bary, vol. 2 (New York: Columbia University Press, 1958), p. 289.

expanding employment opportunities that benefited the Japanese working class further solidified the ultranationalists' political support.

The Rise of Modern Turkey

The new nation of Turkey emerged from the violent collapse of the Ottoman empire in an exceptionally hostile environment. Without the skillful military and political leadership of **Mustafa Kemal** (1881–1938), a former Ottoman officer, Turkey may well have been partitioned by the victorious Allies. For his role, Kemal earned the name Atatürk, "Father Turk." With the success of Kemal's armies, by 1923 the great powers agreed to recognize a sovereign Turkish republic that retained the core territories and population of the old empire.

Halide Edib played an important role in the creation of the new Turkish nation. In 1919, as the Ottoman empire crumbled before British and Greek invaders, she stood in front of a crowd of thousands and rallied them to the cause of Turkish nationalism. Her heart, she later wrote, *"was beating in response to all Turkish hearts, warning of approaching disaster. . . . I was part of this sublime national madness. . . . Nothing else mattered for me in life at all."*[*] She and her husband then went to join Kemal's forces in Ankara, where she became one of the nationalist leader's closest confidantes. After independence was secured, however, they had a falling out. Whereas Edib and her husband led a party that favored the expansion of liberal democracy, Kemal intended to be the unchallenged leader of an absolutist state. *"What I mean is this,"* he told her. *"I want everyone to do as I wish. . . . I do not want any criticism or advice. I will have only my own way. All shall do as I command."* According to her memoirs Edib responded, *"I will obey you and do as you wish as long as I believe you are serving the cause."* But Kemal ignored her and said, *"You shall obey me and do as I wish."*[†] Shortly thereafter he banned her political party and she went into exile.

Kemal's authoritarian tendencies were not without precedent. Earlier Ottoman reformers had also taken a paternalistic view, regarding their subjects like children who needed guidance but also stern discipline. Such attitudes were also common during this era of postwar uncertainty and global economic crisis. Having forged a new country through war, Mustafa Kemal put his personal stamp on the ideas that would guide Turkey for decades to come. His goal was to put Turkey on an equal economic and military footing with the European powers, and he ordered rapid modernization to achieve that end. In the nineteenth century, the Ottoman empire had vacillated about how much it should adopt Western models (see Chapter 23). Kemal had no second thoughts in imposing a secular constitution with a strict line between mosque and state.

Kemal's drive to separate religion from politics included laws to improve the status of women. His regime gave girls and young women increased access to education, a move Edib strongly supported. Not surprisingly, after the emotional pain she suffered when her first husband took a second wife, she also favored the Turkish law abolishing polygamy.

Mustafa Kemal (1881–1938) Also known as Atatürk, an Ottoman officer who led the nationalist army that established the Republic of Turkey in 1923. A reformer who established the secular traditions of the modern Turkish state, he served as its leader until his death.

Turkey's New Alphabet The Turkish leader Mustafa Kemal instituted a top-down program of modernization and westernization in the new nation of Turkey. In 1928, he declared that Turkish would no longer be written in Arabic script and that Latin characters would henceforth be used for all purposes, public and private. Here Kemal himself demonstrates the new alphabet.

© Photo12/The Image Works

---

[*]Halide Edib, http://gvcommunity.tripod.com/ladies/haide.htm.

[†]Halide Edib, *The Turkish Ordeal* (New York: Century, 1926), p. 128.

Edib applauded when, in 1930, Turkey became the first predominantly Muslim country in which women had the right to vote.

On the other hand, she critiqued the authoritarian means by which these reforms were attained. When Kemal banned women from wearing veils in all government buildings, schools, and public spaces, for example, Edib argued that while the veil should never be imposed on women, neither should it be banned by governments. *"Wherever religion is interfered with by governments, it becomes a barrier, and an unremovable one, to peace and understanding."* Education and freedom to choose were the keys to reform, she thought. Too impatient for gradual reform, however, Kemal simply imposed his own will on the nation.

Following the general trend of the times, Mustafa Kemal's modernization policies depended on centralized state power. After export prices fell in 1930, his government taxed the countryside heavily to finance state-sponsored industrialization. Along with imposing high tariffs on foreign products, this industrial policy of import substitution sought to replace imported goods with domestic manufactures. Turkey joined the many nations seeking a merely domestic solution to a global problem. As long as trade was inhibited and the global economy remained stagnant, the shadow of the Great Depression would remain. When Mustafa Kemal died in 1938 and Halide Edib returned home the next year to become a professor of English at the University of Istanbul, the problem remained unresolved.

Anticolonial Nationalism in Asia and Africa

Colonial governments are, by their nature, autocratic: racially based authoritarianism was thus the political status quo across Africa, South Asia, and Southeast Asia in the 1920s. The economic crisis of the Great Depression, however, led European powers to exploit their colonies even more. Harsh policies, such as the use of forced labor, combined with the general decline in the global economy to spread distress throughout Africa and Asia. As a result, movements of anticolonial nationalism gathered strength.

These forces were strongest in India, where **Mohandas K. Gandhi** (1869–1948) and the Indian National Congress organized mass resistance to British rule. In Africa and most of Southeast Asia, mass nationalism was in an earlier stage of development. Nevertheless, by the 1930s a new generation of Western-educated leaders was forging links with mass supporters in both Africa and Asia.

Mohandas K. Gandhi
(1869–1948) Indian political leader who organized mass support for the Indian National Congress against British rule. His political philosophy of nonviolent resistance had worldwide influence.

Gandhi and the Indian National Congress

Halide Edib, in exile from Turkey, traveled to India in 1935. Speaking before an audience at the National Muslim University, her thoughts were more on someone in the audience than on her own speech. Looking out at the *"fragile figure"* before her, she wrote in her book *Inside India*, *"I was thinking about the quality of Mahatma Gandhi's greatness."* Gandhi had turned the Indian National Congress into the voice of India.

Before 1914, the Indian National Congress had been a reformist organization, seeking greater participation of Indians in their own governance but accepting the basic outlines of British rule (see Chapter 24). Given the contribution Indians had made to the British war effort, they expected to be rewarded with substantial political reform. But the British offered only modest proposals for a gradual increase in Indian participation.

---

*Halide Edib, *Inside India* (London: Allen and Unwin, 1937), pp. 231, 81.

Amritsar Massacre
(1919) A turning point in Anglo-Indian relations, when a British officer ordered his troops to fire directly into a peaceful crowd in the city of Amritsar. Following this event, in 1920 the Indian National Congress, led by Mohandas K. Gandhi, began its first mass campaign for Indian self-rule.

Then in 1919 the **Amritsar Massacre** shocked the nation. Although the British had banned public meetings, the peaceful, unarmed crowd that gathered for a religious ceremony was unaware of that order. In a horrible display of the violence on which colonial authority was based, a British officer ordered his Indian troops to fire directly into the crowd, which was confined in a garden area. The soldiers fired 1,650 rounds of ammunition, leaving 400 dead and 1,200 wounded. Cooperation turned to confrontation, and in 1920 the Indian National Congress launched its first mass public protest to gain *Hind Swaraj*, Indian self-rule.

By then Gandhi, a Western-educated lawyer, had discarded European dress for the spare clothing of an ascetic Hindu holy man. His philosophy was in fact influenced by both traditions. Western ideals of equality informed his insistence that the so-called Untouchables, those considered outside and beneath the Hindu caste hierarchy, be given full rights and recognition as human beings. But his two main principles were from the South Asian tradition. *Ahimsa* (uh-HIM-sah), or absolute nonviolence, was at the center of Gandhi's moral philosophy. *Satyagraha* (SUHT-yuh-gruh-huh), or "soul force," was the application of that philosophy to politics. Gandhi believed that it is self-defeating to use violence to counter violence, no matter how just the cause. The moral force of his arguments earned him the title *Mahatma*, "Great Soul."

But in 1920, after the British threw Gandhi and other Congress leaders in jail, depriving the movement of disciplined leadership, violence did accompany the first mass campaigns of civil disobedience. Deciding that the Indian people were not ready to achieve self-rule through satyagraha, Gandhi retreated to his *ashram* (AHSH-ruhm), a communal rural home, and spun cotton on a simple spinning wheel for hours at a time. The gentle clicking of the wheel stimulated meditation, and Gandhi stressed that Indians should produce their own simple cloth at home rather than import the British textiles that had, since the nineteenth century, represented imperial economic exploitation (see Chapter 23 and the feature "Movement of Ideas Through Primary Sources: Gandhi and Nehru on Progress and Civilization.")

In 1930 Gandhi re-emerged to lead another campaign of mass civil disobedience. In his Salt March, he walked hundreds of miles to the sea to defy a British law that forbade Indians from using ocean water to make their own salt. While the Salt March galvanized his supporters and received international press coverage, the British responded with a combination of repression and concessions. After initially jailing Congress leaders, they then compromised with the Government of India Act of 1935, which called for elections of semi-representative regional assemblies. The Indian National Congress won huge victories in ensuing elections, which still fell far short of achieving Indian self-government.

While Gandhi remained the symbol of Indian nationalism, other strong political actors emerged. In 1928 Jawaharlal Nehru (1889–1964), a British-educated son of a wealthy Congress leader, was elected president of the party. Although a follower of Gandhi, he did not think the moral transformation of Indian society was a necessary prerequisite for self-rule. Also, he was a socialist who believed in industrialization (see Chapter 30). Whereas Gandhi idealized the simplicity of village life, Nehru saw the "backwardness" of village life as an obstacle to progress.

Though Gandhi used Hindu symbols to rally mass support, he and Nehru agreed that the Indian National Congress should be open to members of all faiths. That did not mollify leaders of the new **Muslim League**, who feared that under self-rule they would be oppressed by the Hindu majority.

Gandhi did his best to reassure the Muslim community, and Nehru's vision was of a secular state in which religion would play no part. Based on her visit to India, Halide Edib was confident that nationalist unity could transcend religious

Muslim League
Political party founded in British India to represent the interests of the Muslim minority. The party eventually advocated a separate nation for Indian Muslims: Pakistan.

Gandhi's Salt March In 1930 Mohandas K. Gandhi received significant international press coverage when he and his followers marched 240 miles (386 km) from his ashram to the sea to make salt. It was a perfect example of nonviolent civil disobedience, since the manufacture of salt was a legal monopoly of the British Indian government. (© Dinodia Images/Alamy)

differences. Nevertheless, distrust between the two communities increased. During the 1930s, Muslim League members conceived of a separate state for Muslim-majority areas (a goal that was achieved in 1947 with the creation of Pakistan; see Chapter 30). But in 1939 state power still rested with the British, who insisted that their presence as a neutral arbiter between India's diverse peoples would be necessary far into the future.

Colonialism and Resistance in Africa and Southeast Asia

Nationalist movements were also developing in Africa and Southeast Asia during this period. As in India, Western-educated leaders were beginning to create political structures that could mobilize large numbers of people to challenge European authority. However, since such movements were not nearly as well developed as in India, European powers continued to rule Africa and most of Southeast Asia with great confidence.

One feature of colonialism is that the ruling powers must find indigenous allies to help them control and administer their territories. While the British, French, Dutch, Belgians, and Portuguese each developed particular modes of colonial rule, similar features prevailed. For example, it was too expensive to staff colonial administrations solely with European personnel. While the top positions were always reserved for Europeans, it made sense to educate members of the colonized society as clerks, nurses, and primary school teachers. However, in the process of being educated, young Africans and Southeast Asians also learned about the French Revolution and the traditional liberties of British subjects. They could not help but reflect on their own situations and aspire for greater freedom for themselves and for their people.

813

Gandhi and Nehru on Progress and Civilization

The two most influential Indian leaders of the twentieth century were Mohandas K. Gandhi and Jawaharlal Nehru, representing different generations in the Indian National Congress. Gandhi, born in 1869, was the inspirational force behind Indian resistance to British colonialism in the 1920s and 1930s. Nehru, twenty years younger, participated in that resistance and later led the independent Indian republic as its first prime minister, from 1947 to 1964 (see Chapter 30).

Both men were influenced by the time they spent in Great Britain. Gandhi sailed to Britain in 1888 to pursue a law degree, and while in London he was strongly influenced by cultural trends and by philosophers who called into question the relentless materialism of late Victorian society. Among them were vegetarians and Theosophists, who emphasized intuition and mysticism over rationalism and formal theology. He was also influenced by the American writer Henry David Thoreau and the Russian novelist Leo Tolstoy, both of whom celebrated the simplicity of rural life.

Nehru's British experience was quite different. His father, a famous lawyer and a man of great wealth, sent him to study at two of the world's most famous educational institutions, Harrow School and then Cambridge University. Interacting with England's elite, the young Nehru was strongly influenced by the reformist socialism fashionable with the younger generation at the start of the twentieth century. Such socialists accepted the need for the economic development that came with capitalist industrialism but argued for a more equitable distribution of its proceeds.

Gandhi and Nehru, therefore, though close friends as well as political allies, had very different visions of India's future. While many Indians have been strongly influenced by Gandhi's philosophy over the decades, Nehru's attitude has been much more evident in Indian government policy since the country achieved independence in 1947.

Sources: M. K. Gandhi, *Hind Swaraj* (Ahmedabad, India: Navajivan, 1938 [1908]), pp. 31–33; Jawaharlal Nehru, *An Autobiography* (New Delhi: Allied, 1942), pp. 510–511.

Mohandas K. Gandhi, *Hind Swaraj* (1909)

Let us first consider what state of things is described by the word "civilization." Its true test lies in the fact that people living in it make bodily welfare the object of life. We will take some examples. The people of Europe today live in better-built houses than they did a hundred years ago. This is considered an emblem of civilization, and this is also a matter to promote bodily happiness. Formerly, they wore skins, and used spears as their weapons. Now, they wear long trousers, and, for embellishing their bodies, they wear a variety of clothing, and, instead of spears, they carry with them revolvers containing five or more chambers. If people of a certain country, who have hitherto not been in the habit of wearing much clothing, boots, etc., adopt European clothing, they are supposed to have become civilized out of savagery.

Formerly, in Europe, people ploughed their lands mainly by manual labor. Now, one man can plough a vast tract by means of steam engines and can thus amass great wealth. This is called a sign of civilization. Formerly, only a few men wrote valuable books. Now, anybody writes and prints anything he likes and poisons people's minds. Formerly, men traveled in wagons. Now, they fly through the air in trains at the rate of four hundred and more miles per day. This is considered the height of civilization. . . . Formerly, when people wanted to fight with one another, they measured between them their bodily strength; now it is possible to take away thousands of lives by one man working behind a gun from a hill. This is civilization. Formerly, men worked in the open air only as much as they liked. Now thousands of workmen meet together and for the sake of maintenance work in factories or mines. Their condition is worse than that of beasts. They are obliged to work, at the risk of their lives, at most dangerous occupations, for the sake of millionaires. Formerly, men were made slaves under physical compulsion. Now they are enslaved by temptation of money and of the luxuries that money can buy. . . . Formerly, people had two or three meals consisting of home-made bread and vegetables; now, they require something to eat every two hours so that they have hardly leisure for anything else. . . . This civilization takes note neither of morality nor of religion. . . . Civilization seeks to increase bodily comforts, and it fails miserably even in doing so.

This civilization is irreligion, and it has taken such a hold on the people in Europe that those who are in it appear to be half mad. They lack real physical strength or courage. They keep up their energy by intoxication. They can hardly be happy in solitude. Women, who should be the queens of households, wander in the streets or they slave away in factories. For the sake of a pittance, half a million women in England alone are laboring under trying circumstances in factories or similar institutions. This awful act is one of the causes of the daily growing suffragette movement.

[The English] are a shrewd nation and I therefore believe that they will cast off this evil. They are enterprising and industrious, and their mode of thought is not inherently immoral. Neither are they bad at heart. I therefore respect them. Civilization is not an incurable disease, but it should never be forgotten that the English are at present afflicted by it.

Jawaharlal Nehru, "Gandhi" (1936)

I imagine that [Gandhi] is not so vague about the objective as he sometimes appears to be. . . . "India's salvation consists," he wrote in 1909, "in unlearning what she has learned during the last fifty years. The railways, telegraphs, hospitals, lawyers, doctors, and suchlike all have to go. . . ."

All this seems to me utterly wrong and harmful doctrine, and impossible of achievement. Behind it lies Gandhi's love and praise of poverty and suffering and the ascetic life. . . . Personally I dislike the praise of poverty and suffering. . . . Nor do I appreciate in the least the idealization of the "simple peasant life." I have almost a horror of it, and instead of submitting to it myself I want to drag out even the peasantry from it. . . . What is there in "The Man with the Hoe" to idealize over? Crushed and exploited for innumerable generations, he is only little removed from the animals who keep him company. . . .

The desire to get away from the mind of man to primitive conditions where mind does not count, seems to me quite incomprehensible. The very thing that is the glory and triumph of man is decried and discouraged, and a physical environment which will oppress the mind and prevent its growth is considered desirable. Present-day civilization is full of evils, but it is also full of good; and it has the capacity in it to rid itself of those evils. To destroy it root and branch is to remove that capacity from it and revert to a dull, senseless, and miserable existence. But even if that were desirable it is an impossible undertaking. We cannot stop the river of change or cut ourselves adrift from it, and psychologically we who have eaten of the apple of Eden cannot forget that taste and go back to primitiveness.

QUESTION FOR ANALYSIS

» *How do Gandhi and Nehru define and evaluate the concept of "civilization"? Might it be possible to find a compromise between their two perspectives?*

The gap between aspirations and realities for Western-educated members of colonized societies was stark. The French, for example, had developed a model of assimilation holding the promise that Asians and Africans could "become" French in language and culture, and thereby aspire to French citizenship. However, most Africans who pursued this path—studying French history, speaking perfect French, and immersing themselves in French culture—found that the colonialists still saw them through a racist lens as *indigenes* (ihn-deh-JEN), "natives" who were automatically inferior. The same deeply frustrating dynamic held sway in the Dutch East Indies, where people of mixed race, educated in Dutch schools, could never be social equals of the colonizers. The British also relied on Western-educated youth in places like Nigeria and Burma to carry out essential administrative tasks, yet there was no concept of assimilation, no idea that Nigerians or Burmese could ever "become English." Still, Africans and Asians educated in English often emulated British cultural models, despite being rejected as equals.

The European policy of relying on indigenous figureheads spurred additional resentments driving nationalist feelings among Western-educated Africans and Asians. In Southeast Asia, for example, the Vietnamese emperors of the Nguyen dynasty continued in office. Malaysian sultans were also given privileged positions. In West Africa, the British brought the king of Asante back from exile (see Chapter 26). They were integrating such leaders into an administrative structure they called "indirect rule," priding themselves on the respect they showed to local customs. In reality, European colonists forged alliances with "traditional" ruling elites to use them in maintaining order and collecting taxes. By the 1930s impatient nationalists increasingly saw such figures as hindrances to self-rule.

"Indirect rule" promoted local ethnic affiliations while forestalling the emergence of broader national identities. The British, in particular, divided Africans into discrete "tribes" and played their leaders against one another to secure continued control. One of the nationalists who deplored this policy was the Nigerian **Nnamdi Azikiwe** (NAHM-dee ah-zee-KEE-way) (1904–1996). From the largely Christian southeast region of Nigeria, Azikiwe argued that only when all Nigerians identified themselves with the nation as a whole, whatever their ethnic and religious backgrounds, would they be able to struggle effectively for self-rule. Having stowed away on a ship to the United States in 1925 and then graduated from the University of Pennsylvania, Azikiwe returned to West Africa in 1937 and founded the Nigerian Youth Movement while editing the *West African Pilot*, a newspaper dedicated to inspiring Africans to challenge British colonial policies. Azikiwe created a sports association focused on the increasing popularity of soccer in Nigeria to galvanize popular support for his nationalist cause.

During the 1930s sporadic popular uprisings in Africa and Southeast Asia arose in response to colonial tax, trade, and land policies, but they had only limited and localized effects because they were not connected to larger political organizations. In the **Igbo Women's War** of 1929, for example, women in southeastern Nigeria rebelled against what they felt to be an intrusion on their family privacy when the British insisted on counting every person in their household for tax purposes. Using traditional Igbo (ee-BWOH) means of protesting male abuse of authority, the women dressed up in special costumes, gathered in large numbers, and sang songs of derision to shame the African chiefs who acted as tax collectors. The British modified their tax system slightly in response, but there were no wider reforms. The women lacked a broader organization to connect their local efforts with a wider anticolonial struggle.

Colonial tensions were strongest where Europeans came not just as rulers but also as settlers, as in South Africa and Kenya. Here Africans had lost not only their

Nnamdi Azikiwe (1904–1996) Pioneering Nigerian nationalist who, after gaining higher education in the United States, edited a newspaper and formed cultural and political organizations to unite West Africans against British colonialism.

Igbo Women's War (1929) Rebellion led by women in colonial Nigeria who used traditional cultural practices to protest British taxation policies.

sovereignty but also much of their best farming and herding land. The British colony of Kenya in East Africa saw the rise of a mass protest movement in the 1920s. Anticolonial feelings were strongest among Kikuyu-speaking Kenyans who lost their land to white settlers. As in the Igbo Women's War, however, merely local protest was not enough to gain substantial reform. Meanwhile, a young leader named Jomo Kenyatta (1895–1978) was earning a doctorate in anthropology from the London School of Economics. Only later, after the Second World War, would he return and lead a nationalist movement that connected Western-educated Africans with peasants and workers.

Across Africa and Southeast Asia, the Great Depression made the already difficult conditions of colonialism even worse. In spite of a drop in world cotton prices that made their crops virtually worthless, for example, farmers in equatorial Africa were forced to plant, weed, and harvest cotton because the French needed cheap supplies from the colonies to keep French textile factories open. Likewise, in East Africa a "grow more crops" campaign required African farmers to dedicate land and labor to export crops that were basically worthless. Hunger resulted when farmers' energy was diverted away from subsistence crops. Unemployment rose in Malaya, Vietnam, and the Dutch East Indies after 1929, when the drop in automobile manufacturing depressed the world market for rubber, a major plantation crop in these British, French, and Dutch colonies. Small-scale farmers sometimes stopped growing export crops and focused on food crops for their own consumption to lessen their exposure to world markets. However, colonial governments still required cash payment of taxes and were willing to use force to compel those payments. The French penalized Vietnamese peasants who did not pay taxes with forced labor on government projects and French-owned plantations. As in Africa, however, the peoples of French Indochina still lacked the organizational and ideological means for effective resistance.

Africa and Southeast Asia have been called the "quiescent colonies" during this period. But in larger historical perspective, the 1930s were merely a pause in the resistance to colonial occupation that began in the late nineteenth century. Nationalist leaders during this time were laying the foundations for the large-scale movements of mass nationalism that would emerge at the end of the new worldwide military conflict that was about to erupt.

The Road to War

World War II did not sneak up on anyone. In the 1930s numerous events in Europe, Asia, and Africa heralded a coming conflict. After the trauma of 1914–1918, the world's people barely had a chance to catch their breath before confronting another total war, even more global and more violent.

Not content with the occupation of Manchuria, Japanese militarists sought a greater Asian empire. Having already left the League of Nations, they launched a savage attack on coastal China in 1937, in defiance of international law. Fighting between the Guomindang government of Chiang Kai-shek and Communist revolutionaries led by Mao Zedong had made China particularly vulnerable (see Chapter 27). Attacked in 1927 by their former Guomindang allies, the Communists had retreated to the interior. During the Long March of 1934–1936, the Communists walked some 7,500 miles (12,000 km) to consolidate a base in the northeast. After the Japanese invaded, Chiang and Mao agreed to cease their hostilities and fight the common Japanese enemy, but they never combined forces or coordinated their efforts (see Map 28.1).

MAP 28.1 The Japanese Invasion of China Six years after the invasion of Manchuria (see Chapter 27), Japanese forces began the conquest of coastal China in 1937, quickly taking Beijing, Shanghai, and other major cities. Chinese resistance, though extensive, was limited by divisions between the Guomindang government of Chiang Kai-shek and the Communists, led by Mao Zedong. Expelled from coastal cities by the Guomindang after 1927, the Communists relocated first to the southern interior and then, after their dramatic Long March, established a new base in the northeastern Shaanxi province. (© Cengage Learning)

Rape of Nanjing Slaughter in 1937 by the Japanese army of hundreds of thousands of Chinese civilians during their occupation of the city. The soldiers used tactics such as gang rape and child mutilation to spread terror among the Chinese population.

Convinced of their racial superiority, the Japanese invaders treated Chinese soldiers and civilians alike with callous brutality. During the **Rape of Nanjing**, Japanese soldiers killed hundreds of thousands of Chinese civilians, using tactics

Bettmann/Corbis

The Rape of Nanjing One of the most brutal episodes during the Japanese invasion of China was the Rape of Nanjing. Here Japanese soldiers are seen using live captives for bayonet practice, with fellow soldiers and future victims looking on. Though the Chinese have long remembered such atrocities, until recently Japanese schoolchildren learned nothing about them.

such as gang rape and mutilation of children to spread terror among the population. Total war, with its disregard of the distinction between soldiers and civilians, was being taken to a new level.

The inability of international institutions to counter military aggression was similarly demonstrated by the Italian occupation of Ethiopia in 1935, an attack that featured airplanes dropping poison gas on both civilians and soldiers. The Ethiopian emperor Hailie Selassie (1892–1975) went to the League of Nations for help:

> *I ask the fifty-two nations, who have given the Ethiopian people a promise to help them in their resistance to the aggressor, what are they willing to do for Ethiopia? And the great Powers who have promised the guarantee of collective security to small States on whom weighs the threat that they may one day suffer the fate of Ethiopia, I ask what measures do you intend to take? Representatives of the world, I have come to Geneva to discharge in your midst the most painful of the duties of the head of a State. What reply shall I have to take back to my people?*

The emperor warned that if the international community did not take effective action, no small nation would ever be safe. The League of Nations placed economic sanctions on Mussolini but would go no further. With Italy having access to colonial resources, such as Libyan oil, and receiving aid from the German government, the sanctions had little effect.

Meanwhile, German and Italian fascists saw their movement gaining ground in Spain. In 1936, a democratically elected Spanish government was implementing socialist policies to deal with the crisis of the Great Depression. In reaction, Spanish conservatives took up arms under the leadership of General Francisco Franco (1892–1975) to overthrow the Republicans, who fought to defend the liberal constitution. During the **Spanish Civil War** (1936–1939) the Soviet Union supported the Republicans, while the Nazis supported Franco and his quasi-fascist movement. The liberal democracies of France, Britain, and the United States remained neutral. Mired in their own domestic concerns, they missed this chance to support democracy against fascism, although some young people in the Western democracies did form volunteer brigades to fight with the Spanish Republicans, such as the Abraham Lincoln Brigade from the United States. Nevertheless, aided by the German air force and Italian troops, by 1939 Franco was victorious. The Spanish Civil War was a harbinger of greater conflict, with Stalin and Hitler both noting Western unwillingness to take a forceful stand for democracy.

France, Britain, and the United States were equally slow to respond to Hitler's imperial ambitions. He had declared that the Germans needed *lebensraum* (LEY-buhns-rowm), "living space," in which to pursue their racial destiny. Taking the Social Darwinist idea of a racial "struggle for existence" to its extreme conclusion, Hitler declared that Jews had no role in this future, while the Slavic peoples of eastern Europe and Russia were racial inferiors who would provide manual labor under German management. Hitler declared that the ethnic Germans scattered across eastern Europe needed to be reunited with the homeland. While Stalin took this threat seriously, most Western leaders thought that Hitler could be contained. In fact, some Westerners sympathized with Hitler's anti-Semitism and anticommunism.

Still, Nazi aggression required a response. In 1936, German military forces moved into the Rhineland region bordering France, in violation of the Versailles treaty. Next, Hitler asserted the right to annex the Sudetenland, a province of Czechoslovakia where, he claimed, the German minority was facing discrimination (see Map 28.2). One Conservative member of the British Parliament, Winston Churchill, recommended an Anglo-French initiative through the League of Nations to head off Hitler's military expansionism. But Churchill, who would be Britain's great wartime leader (see Chapter 29), was unable to convince either his party or the British public to take a firm stand and risk war.

Instead, Prime Minister Neville Chamberlain flew to Munich in 1937 to deal directly with the German dictator. Chamberlain's policy of *"active appeasement"* was based on the premise that Hitler would be content with minor concessions, and that diplomacy could prevent a major European war. The British public, still scarred by the trauma of the Great War, largely supported Chamberlain's quest for *"peace in our time."* Germany occupied the Sudetenland unchecked, and the next year Hitler annexed Austria as well. Ever since, the term *appeasement* has meant the failure to stop an aggressor in time.

The lack of Western resolve alarmed Joseph Stalin, who feared that his army would be unable to withstand a German invasion, a problem partly of his own creation since many Russian military officers had been killed during the Great Purges. Much as they hated and mistrusted each other, in the summer of 1939

Spanish Civil War
(1936–1939) Conflict between conservative nationalist forces, led by General Francisco Franco and backed by Germany, and Republican forces, backed by the Soviet Union. The Spanish Civil War was seen by many as a prelude to renewed world war.

MAP 28.2 The Growth of Nazi Germany, 1933–1939 The major turning point in the expansion of Nazi Germany was the annexation of the Sudetenland from Czechoslovakia in 1938. Joseph Stalin interpreted British diplomatic efforts to avoid renewed world war with alarm, and he agreed to a secret treaty to divide Poland between Hitler's Germany and his own Soviet Union. The German invasion of Poland from the west in 1939 therefore triggered the annexation of eastern Poland by the Soviet Union. (© Cengage Learning)

Hitler and Stalin signed a nonaggression pact, secretly dividing Poland between them. Hitler was merely delaying his planned attack on Russia, while Stalin was playing for time to ready his country for war.

When Hitler invaded Poland on September 1, 1939, Britain and France immediately declared war on Germany but took no active military steps to confront the German army. Meanwhile, in the United States public opinion was largely opposed to another intervention in European politics. Soon, however, peoples across Europe, Africa, Asia, and the Americas would be embroiled in a total war the likes of which humanity had never seen.

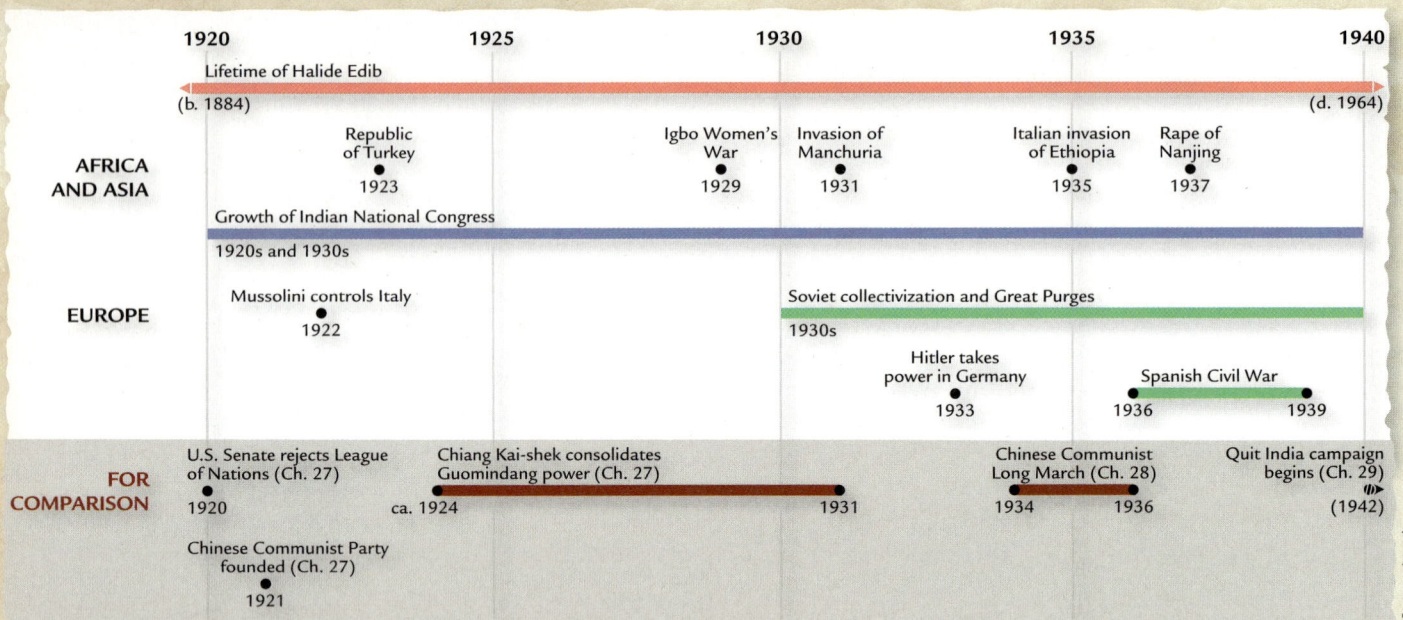

	1920	1925	1930	1935	1940

Lifetime of Halide Edib (b. 1884) — (d. 1964)

AFRICA AND ASIA

Republic of Turkey 1923 • Igbo Women's War 1929 • Invasion of Manchuria 1931 • Italian invasion of Ethiopia 1935 • Rape of Nanjing 1937

Growth of Indian National Congress 1920s and 1930s

EUROPE

Mussolini controls Italy 1922 • Soviet collectivization and Great Purges 1930s • Hitler takes power in Germany 1933 • Spanish Civil War 1936–1939

FOR COMPARISON

U.S. Senate rejects League of Nations (Ch. 27) 1920 • Chiang Kai-shek consolidates Guomindang power (Ch. 27) ca. 1924–1931 • Chinese Communist Long March (Ch. 28) 1934–1936 • Quit India campaign begins (Ch. 29) (1942)

Chinese Communist Party founded (Ch. 27) 1921

© Cengage Learning

Suspended Between Two World Wars

By the summer of 1940, German, Italian, and Japanese aggression and the death of democracy in Spain had sounded a warning bell that tolled across the world. Like France and Britain before, the United States was slow to take heed, avoiding involvement in the Spanish Civil War and remaining neutral even as the Germans overran France and began an aerial bombardment of Britain. By then the catastrophe of another world war was inevitable.

It is understandable that the interwar generation valued peace so highly. For those who had experienced the ravages of the Great War two decades earlier, the thought of another total war was terrible indeed. Yet even before the Great Depression, global tensions ran high, aggravated by the long list of national grievances that remained after the Paris Peace Conference (see Chapter 27). As the 1930s progressed, international institutions such as the League of Nations proved ineffective in dealing with national aggression. The emergence of Halide Edib's own Turkey through military mobilization showed that national rights were best secured not with talk, but with action.

With the Great Depression, liberal democracy and free-market capitalism lost much of their allure. Responses from the far right and the far left—fascism, communism, and ultranationalism—offered alternatives that, whatever their cruelties, reinvigorated the Italian, German, and Soviet economies and emboldened Japan. Across the world, in nations as diverse as Brazil and Turkey, authoritarian leaders magnified the role of the state in social and economic affairs, suppressing the more democratic programs of dissidents like Halide Edib.

It seemed that the French and British had come out of the Paris Peace Conference with their status strengthened. They not only retained their global empires, but with the addition of former German colonies and Ottoman provinces, expanded them. Under the exigencies of total war, however, they had expended vast sums of financial capital. The British, the dominant source of global capital investment before the war, were now in debt to American financial institutions (see Chapter 27). How could they sustain a world-embracing empire when their relative global financial standing had slipped? It was only after the Second World War that the British and French discovered that the costs of empire exceeded the benefits, when decolonization led to a cascade of new Asian and African nations (see Chapter 30).

Meanwhile, the United States and the new Soviet Union stood on the sidelines. The Americans, having put a toe in the cold waters of international engagement during World War I, pulled back, demilitarized, and with the U.S. Senate's failure to ratify the League of Nations treaty, minded their own business. The Soviet Union, industrializing under Stalin's brutal dictatorship, was cut off from global economic and cultural developments. But as the French traveler Alexis de Tocqueville had predicted as early as the 1830s (see Chapter 25), the huge populations and vast resources of Russia and the United States were bound to put these two nations at the forefront of global affairs. When, in the aftermath of the Second World War, the global order based on European colonialism shattered, the United States and the Soviet Union would come to dominate the Cold War world (see Chapters 29–31). Fascism would be defeated by 1945, but the communist challenge to capitalism and liberal democracy would endure.

VOYAGES ON THE WEB: Halide Edib

The Voyages Map App follows the traveler's journeys using interactive study tools, including 360-degree panoramic views of historic sites, zoomable maps, audio summaries, flash cards, and quizzes.

KEY TERMS

Halide Edib (794)
Great Depression (797)
Franklin Delano Roosevelt (798)
fascism (800)
Benito Mussolini (801)

Adolf Hitler (803)
collectivization (808)
Great Purges (808)
invasion of Manchuria (809)
Mustafa Kemal (810)
Mohandas K. Gandhi (811)

Amritsar Massacre (812)
Muslim League (812)
Nnamdi Azikiwe (816)
Igbo Women's War (816)
Rape of Nanjing (818)
Spanish Civil War (820)

FOR FURTHER REFERENCE

Chang, Iris. *The Rape of Nanjing: The Forgotten Holocaust of World War II.* New York: Penguin, 1998.

Crozier, Andrew. *The Causes of the Second World War.* Malden, Mass.: Wiley-Blackwell, 1997.

Dalton, Dennis. *Mahatma Gandhi: Non-Violent Power in Action.* New York: Columbia University Press, 1993.

Edib, Halide. *House with Wisteria: Memoirs of Halide Edib.* Charlottesville, Va.: Leopolis Press, 2003.

Fitzpatrick, Sheila. *Stalin's Peasants: Resistance and Survival in the Russian Village After Collectivization.* New York: Oxford University Press, 1996.

Gellner, Ernest. *Nations and Nationalism.* Malden, Mass.: Wiley-Blackwell, 2006.

Griffin, Roger. *Modernism and Fascism: The Sense of Beginning Under Mussolini and Hitler.* New York: Palgrave Macmillan, 2010.

Hobsbawm, Eric. *The Age of Extremes: A History of the World, 1914–1991.* New York: Vintage, 1996.

Mango, Andrew. *Atatürk: The Biography of the Founder of Modern Turkey.* New York: Overlook, 2002.

Paxton, Robert. *The Anatomy of Fascism.* New York: Vintage, 2005.

Payne, Stanley. *Civil War in Europe, 1905–1949.* New York: Cambridge University Press, 2011.

Rothermund, Dietmar. *The Global Impact of the Great Depression, 1929–1939.* New York: Routledge, 1996.

Snyder, Timothy. *Bloodlands: Europe Between Hitler and Stalin.* New York: Basic Books, 2010.

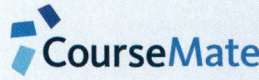

Go to the CourseMate website at **www.cengagebrain.com** for additional study tools and review materials—including audio and video clips—for this chapter.

29 The Second World War and the Origins of the Cold War, 1939–1949

By the spring of 1944, Nazi Germany had occupied France for nearly four years. In preparation for a British and American invasion at the Normandy coast, underground resistance fighters were being parachuted into the French countryside. **Nancy Wake** (1912–2011), a young Australian, was the only woman in her group. War can produce unlikely heroes, and Nancy Wake was one. While she had traveled to Paris in the 1930s looking for adventure, fun, and romance, now she was risking her life in the fight against Nazi Germany:

Nancy Wake
(Australian War Memorial, Negative Number P00885.001)

*A*s the Liberator bomber circled over the dropping zone in France I could see lights flashing and huge bonfires burning. I hoped the field was manned by the Resistance and not by German ambushers. Huddled in the belly of the bomber, airsick and vomiting, I was hardly Hollywood's idea of a glamorous spy. I probably looked grotesque. Over civilian clothes, silk-stockinged and high-heeled, I wore overalls, [and] carried revolvers in the pockets. . . . Even more incongruous was the matronly handbag, full of cash and secret instructions for D-Day. . . . But I'd spent years in France working as an escape courier . . . and I was desperate to return to France and continue working against Hitler. Neither airsickness nor looking like a clumsily wrapped parcel was going to deter me.*

*Excerpt from Nancy Wake, *The Autobiography of the Woman the Gestapo Called the White Mouse*, p. v. Copyright © 1985 Pan Publishing.

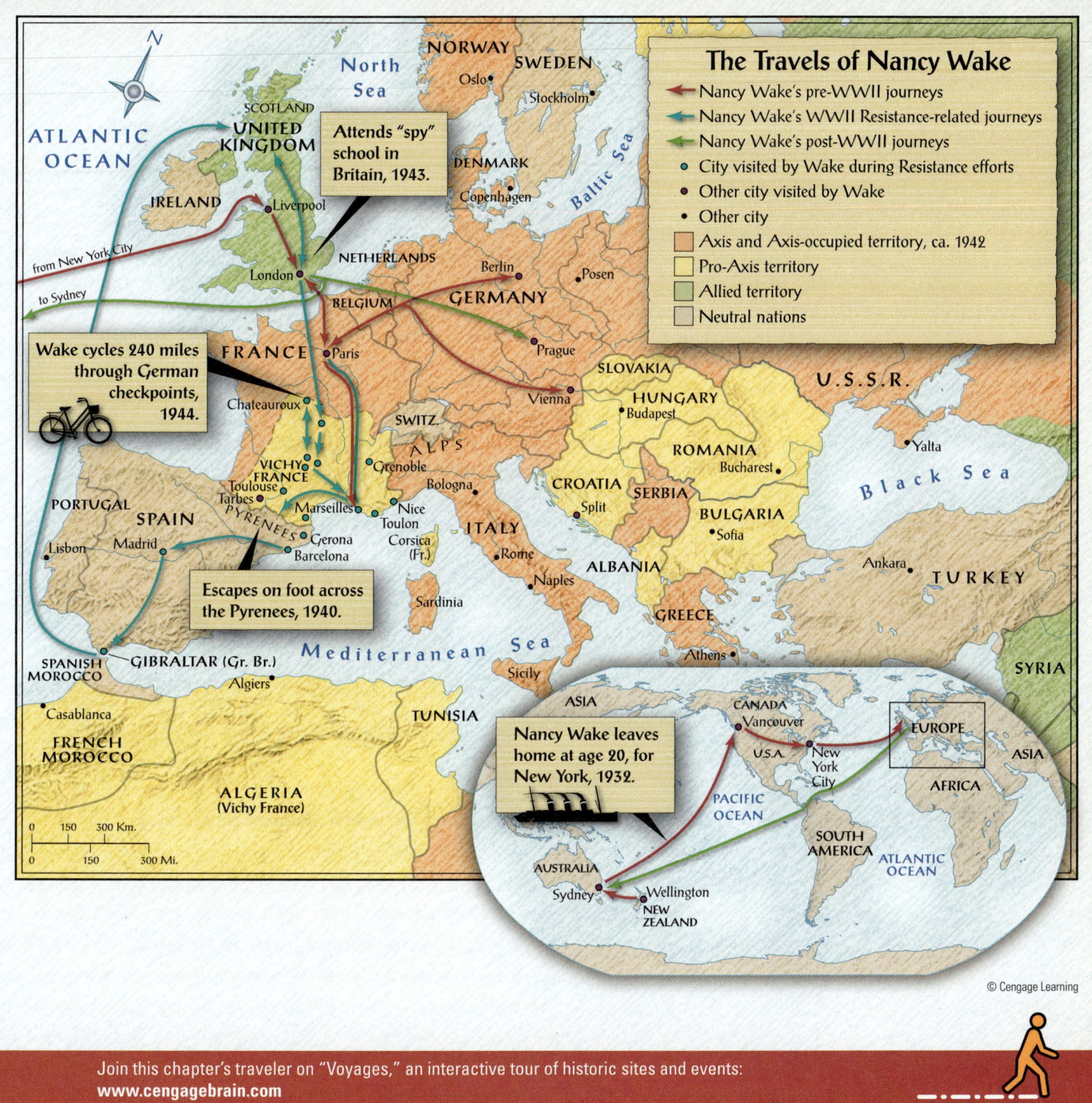

The Travels of Nancy Wake

- → Nancy Wake's pre-WWII journeys
- → Nancy Wake's WWII Resistance-related journeys
- → Nancy Wake's post-WWII journeys
- • City visited by Wake during Resistance efforts
- • Other city visited by Wake
- • Other city
- Axis and Axis-occupied territory, ca. 1942
- Pro-Axis territory
- Allied territory
- Neutral nations

Attends "spy" school in Britain, 1943.

Wake cycles 240 miles through German checkpoints, 1944.

Escapes on foot across the Pyrenees, 1940.

Nancy Wake leaves home at age 20, for New York, 1932.

© Cengage Learning

Join this chapter's traveler on "Voyages," an interactive tour of historic sites and events:
www.cengagebrain.com

The German secret police, the Gestapo, called her "the White Mouse" and put her at the top of their "most wanted" list. But Wake evaded capture and went on to become the most highly decorated female veteran of the war.

Born in a family that was originally from New Zealand, Wake had both English and Polynesian ancestry. Even as a child she *"dreamt of seeing the world,"* and at the age of twenty she sailed from Australia to Canada and traveled by train to New York; in 1934 she settled in Paris. At that time, Wake was more interested in parties than

Nancy Wake
(1912–2011) Highly
decorated Australian
veteran of the Second
World War. After
serving as a courier for
the French under-
ground resistance early
in the war, she traveled
to England for training
and parachuted into
central France in 1944
during the Allied
reoccupation.

in politics, but she had an awakening when she traveled to Vienna, where she witnessed Jews being publicly humiliated: *"The Nazis had the Jews on a big wheel going around . . . maybe a dozen of them, and they were whipping them."*[*] Later she wrote, *"I resolved then and there that if I ever had the chance I would do anything, however big or small, stupid or dangerous, to try and make things more difficult for their rotten party."*[†]

Wake became engaged to a wealthy French industrialist and lived an exciting life, with a wide circle of Parisian friends and frequent vacations to the Alps. But there was an undercurrent of tension. *"In common with many others I feared war was inevitable and then where would we all be? When would laughter end and the tears begin?"*[†] By 1937, civil war was raging in neighboring Spain and the threat of Hitler's Germany was growing.

After Hitler attacked Poland in 1939, there was an ominous pause before Germany opened a western front against France. After that invasion came in 1940, Wake served as a courier for the underground resistance, passing messages and helping the *maquis* (mah-KEE)—the antifascist fighters—escape from both the Gestapo and collaborating French authorities. Soon there was too much heat on the "White Mouse"; she hiked to Spain over difficult and dangerous mountain passes, and from there went to England. After training in Britain, she parachuted into central France, joined the maquis, and witnessed the liberation of Paris.

Wake's story puts a human face on the concept of total war. The military mobilization, civilian involvement, and global reach of this conflict were even greater than that of the First World War and had unprecedented global effects. The war deeply affected the world's peoples, and with its end came the rise of the United States and the Soviet Union as global superpowers and the beginning of their Cold War rivalry.

Focus Questions

» *What factors contributed to early German and Japanese successes and later Allied ones?*

» *How did civilians in various parts of the world experience the Second World War as a total war?*

» *How did the outcome of the war affect the global balance of political and military power?*

The Second World War: Battlefields, 1939–1945

The Second World War (1939–1945) reached the entire world. Japan's expansion into China made Asia and the Pacific a full-scale theater of war (see Chapter 28). As during the First World War (see Chapter 27), African and Arab societies became involved, this time through the desert war fought in North Africa. But control of Europe remained central, with Britain and the Soviet Union allied against Germany (see Map 29.1). As during World War I, the United States made a delayed but decisive commitment to the war, this time fighting in both Asia and Europe.

[*]This is found online in multiple sources, including http://www.abc.net.au/schoolstv/australians/wake.htm.

[†]Excerpt from Nancy Wake, *The Autobiography of the Woman the Gestapo Called the White Mouse*, pp. 7, 42. Copyright © 1985 Pan Publishing.

Legend:
- Hitler's Greater Germany
- Allied with Germany
- Occupied by Germany and its allies
- Grand Alliance
- Neutral nations
- ★ Major battle

NORWAY — Oslo
SWEDEN — Stockholm
FINLAND — Helsinki
Siege of Leningrad, Sept. 1941–Jan. 1944
Leningrad
SOVIET UNION — Moscow
Riga
Smolensk
Tula
Siege of Stalingrad, Aug. 21, 1942–Jan. 31, 1943
Stalingrad
Russian front, spring 1944
Russian front, Nov. 1942
Russian front, Dec. 1941
Volga R.
Don R.
Dnieper R.
Dniester R.

NORTH Sea
DENMARK — Copenhagen
German surrender: Reims, May 7, 1945 Berlin, May 8, 1945
Baltic Sea
Pinsk
Kiev
UKRAINE

NORTHERN IRELAND
IRELAND
UNITED KINGDOM — London
Battle of Britain, fall 1940
NETHERLANDS
Dunkirk
BELGIUM
Battle of the Bulge, Dec. 1944
Western front, Feb. 1945
Rhine R.
Elbe R.
GERMANY — Berlin
Rhine Crossing, March 7, 1945
Russian front, Feb. 1945
Posen
Warsaw
Vistula R.
Kraków
SLOVAKIA
HUNGARY — Budapest
ROMANIA — Bucharest
Yalta
Black Sea

ATLANTIC OCEAN
Invasion of Normandy, June 6, 1944
Paris
FRANCE
Vichy
VICHY FRANCE (Occupied Nov. 1942)
Axis troops occupy Vichy France, Nov. 10 and 11, 1942
SWITZERLAND
Vienna
Danube R.
Po R.
Bologna
Italian front, Feb. 1945
ITALY
Rome (Liberated June 1944)
Monte Cassino, May 1944
Salerno, Sept. 1943
Allies land in Provence, Aug. 15, 1944
Allies invade Sicily and Italy, July–Sept. 1943
Sicily, July 1943
CROATIA
SERBIA
BULGARIA — Sofia
ALBANIA
GREECE — Athens
Danube R.

PORTUGAL — Lisbon
SPAIN — Madrid
Ebro R.
SPANISH MOROCCO
GIBRALTAR (Gr. Br.)
Casablanca, Nov. 1942
FRENCH MOROCCO
ALGERIA (Vichy France)
Rommel defeated in Tunisia; Axis troops evacuated, May 1943
TUNISIA
LIBYA
MALTA (Gr. Br.)
Crete (Gr.)
Mediterranean Sea
El Alamein, summer 1942
Cairo
EGYPT
Nile R.
Suez Canal
Ankara
TURKEY
Cyprus (Gr. Br.)
SYRIA
PALESTINE (Br. Mandate)
TRANS-JORDAN (Br. Mandate)

0   150   300 Km.
0   150   300 Mi.

MAP 29.1 World War II in Europe and North Africa Through the summer of 1941 the Axis powers, led by Germany and Italy, held the momentum in the European theater of war, with Paris occupied, Britain isolated, the Soviet Union invaded, and eastern Europe and the Balkans under fascist domination. An important Allied triumph came with British victory at El Alamein in Egypt in 1942, but the real turning point was Soviet success in turning back the Germans at Stalingrad. After the United States entered the war, Allied invasions of Italy (1943) and of occupied France at Normandy (1944) turned the tide. (© Cengage Learning)

After the German invasion of Poland in 1939, the Second World War proceeded in two phases. From 1940 to 1942, initiative and success lay with the **Axis powers**: Germany, Italy, and Japan. While the Germans and Italians advanced across continental Europe and the Mediterranean, Japanese armies were on the offensive in East and Southeast Asia. But after Germany invaded the Soviet Union in June 1941 and Japan attacked the United States in December of that same year, the momentum shifted as the Soviet Union and the United States mobilized their considerable resources. In 1943 the Soviet, British, and American Allies turned the tide, and by 1944, aided by resistance movements in France, Vietnam, the Philippines, and elsewhere, the Allies were on the offensive.

Axis powers
Alliance of Germany, Italy, and Japan during the Second World War.

German *Blitzkrieg* and the Rising Sun of Japan, 1939–1942

When the German army invaded Poland, it unleashed a new form of warfare: the *blitzkrieg* (BLITS-kreeg) or "lightning war," which combined the rapid mobility of tanks and mechanized infantry with massive air power. As western Poland was quickly overrun, Stalin made use of his secret agreement with Hitler to occupy the eastern part of the country. In the German zone, true to Hitler's racial policies, the process of segregating Polish Jews began immediately, while ethnic Poles were forced into labor camps to serve German war industries. On the Soviet side, Stalin ordered the execution of the Polish officer corps, most notoriously carried out at the Massacre at Katyn Forest in 1940, where tens of thousands of Poles were killed.

While Hitler and Stalin crushed Poland, France and Britain declared war on Germany but took no military steps. Instead, during the so-called Phony War of 1939–1940, they shored up their own defenses. Nancy Wake and her fiancé moved south from Paris to Marseilles (mahr-SEY), trying to distance themselves from the anticipated German invasion.

In the spring of 1940, the Germans invaded Denmark and Norway and soon controlled Belgium, the Netherlands, and northern France. In the 1930s the French had planned for a repetition of trench warfare by building an elaborate series of concrete bunkers, the Maginot Line. It was an outmoded strategy based on memories of the previous war: the Germans used their new blitzkrieg tactics and their control of Belgium to bypass the Maginot Line, and in 1940, they occupied Paris. British forces evacuated France, while during the Battle of Britain the *Luftwaffe* (the German Air Force) pummeled the island in preparation for a seaborne invasion.

The victory of the Royal Air Force in the Battle of Britain ensured that the planned invasion would never happen. Unable to destroy Britain's air defenses, gain air superiority, or force a surrender, the Germans bombarded London to terrorize its citizens and sap their morale. During this "blitz," when Londoners crowded into underground train stations to escape the bombing, Britain held together under the firm leadership of Prime Minister **Winston Churchill** (1874–1965): *"Hitler knows that he will have to break us in this Island or lose the war. . . . Let us therefore brace ourselves to our duties, and so bear ourselves that, if the British Empire and its Commonwealth last for a thousand years, men will still say, 'This was their finest hour.'"* Londoners took heart from the fact that the massive Cathedral of St. Paul's in the heart of their city, though surrounded by burning rubble, stood unscathed.

German officials found local collaborators to aid in the conquest and control of Europe. The word *quisling* entered the language to refer to such collaborators, after Vidkun Quisling, the Norwegian fascist who betrayed his country while running a German puppet regime. In France, while the German army occupied and

Winston Churchill
(1874–1965) British prime minister during the Second World War who rallied his people to stand firm during the war's dark early days. A staunch anti-communist, he coined the term *iron curtain* after the war to describe Stalin's domination of eastern Europe.

Bettmann/Corbis

Blitzkrieg German *blitzkrieg* ("lightning war") tactics, based on rapid movement of mechanized forces, contrasted sharply with the immobility of trench warfare during World War I. The German forces seen here moved quickly across Belgium in 1940 and then over-ran French defenses en route to the occupation of Paris.

directly administered northern France, the south with its capital at Vichy (VEE-shee) came under the authority of a French regime that cooperated with the Nazis. Some officials in Vichy France sought wealth and power, while others were fascist sympathizers who held anti-Semitic and anticommunist views and favored "order" over democracy. The Axis powers found collaborators in other countries as well. In the Balkans, Croatian nationalists in the Ustase Party forged an alliance with the Germans to gain the upper hand over Serbian rivals. In Asia, the kingdom of Thailand cooperated with the Japanese in exchange for Laos and half of Cambo-dia. The collaboration of Vichy France with Nazi Germany also had global impli-cations: all but one of the French colonial governors in Africa and Southeast Asia acknowledged Vichy authority.

At the same time, men and women in France, Norway, Ethiopia, Italy, Yugosla-via, Vietnam, the Philippines, and elsewhere organized underground resistance cells to defeat fascist invaders and their local allies. Polish leaders gathered in Lon-don and formed a government-in-exile. In 1940 Nancy Wake began to work as a courier for French partisans. Their hero was a maverick general, **Charles de Gaulle** (SHARL du GAWHL) (1890–1970), who formed a Free French government-in-exile

Charles de Gaulle (1890–1970) French general and statesman who led the Free French Army in resis-tance to German occu-pation. Later elected president of France.

in London to recruit an army of liberation. But in 1941 de Gaulle had few resources at his command and as yet no way to link up with the resistance within France.

War also came to North Africa and southeast Europe. Early in 1941, after a failed Italian offensive against British-dominated Egypt, German forces arrived to shore up the Italian position. Eighteen months of motorized warfare between German and British tank companies followed. Similarly, Mussolini's designs on the Balkans were undercut by his failure that same spring to conquer Greece. Again, the German high command had to divert troops to reinforce the Italian position. As a result, most of Hungary, Yugoslavia, Romania, and Greece were brought under Axis control.

Though the American president, Franklin Delano Roosevelt, privately agreed with Churchill about how much was at stake in the war, American public opinion balked at committing troops to Europe. Instead, Roosevelt declared that the United States would become the "arsenal of democracy" by negotiating a "lend lease" arrangement through which American arms were supplied to Britain without need for immediate payment.

Atlantic Charter
(1941) Agreement between Winston Churchill and Franklin D. Roosevelt before the entry of the United States into the war; reaffirmed the Wilsonian principle of national self-determination.

In the summer of 1941 Churchill and Roosevelt met aboard a ship off the coast of Newfoundland and jointly issued the **Atlantic Charter**, reaffirming the Wilsonian principle of national self-determination: *"[We] respect the right of all peoples to choose the form of government under which they will live; and . . . wish to see sovereign rights and self government restored to those who have been forcibly deprived of them."* But America's moral and material support did no more than help the British to hold on. There seemed little hope that German advances could be rolled back.

Matters looked just as bleak in East Asia. To justify attacks on the colonial possessions of the United States, the Netherlands, Britain, and France, Japanese propagandists spoke of a Greater East Asian Co-Prosperity Sphere that would free Asian peoples from Western imperialism under Japanese leadership. Having allied with Germany, in 1940 the Japanese demanded that the Vichy government give them access to ports and airfields in French Indochina. Vichy officials agreed and handed much of mainland Southeast Asia over to the Japanese. Japanese naval assaults soon gave the empire control of southern Burma, gravely threatening British-held northern Burma and British India.

Tensions between Japan and the United States were growing in the summer of 1941. The United States beefed up its Pacific command in the Philippines, put a freeze on Japanese assets in the United States, and most important, cut off petroleum and steel exports. Since the Japanese fleet depended on U.S. oil, the empire's military and industrial planners needed to find another source of supply and focused on the oil reserves of the Dutch East Indies. To get them, however, they would have to take the Philippines from the United States. Gauging that conflict was now inevitable, Japan decided to launch a preemptive surprise attack. Japanese fighters attacked the U.S. naval outpost at **Pearl Harbor** on December 7, 1941—"a date," President Roosevelt said, "which will live in infamy"—crippling much of the American battleship fleet. Simultaneously, Japan attacked American naval assets in the Philippines. The war for the Pacific had begun.

Pearl Harbor
The attack on the U.S. naval base in Hawai'i by Japanese fighter planes on December 7, 1941, bringing the United States into the Second World War.

Once attacked, the American people rallied behind their president. A few days after Pearl Harbor, the German and Italian governments also declared war on the United States, and the country began an intensive mobilization to meet Axis forces on both sides of Eurasia. While that mobilization was taking place, however, the Japanese occupied British Hong Kong, took the Philippines from the United States, and attacked the Dutch East Indies. The brutality they had shown in China during the Rape of Nanjing (see Chapter 28) was soon repeated. In the spring of 1942, for example, thousands of Filipinos and hundreds of American prisoners of war died as their captors drove them on a forced march across the Bataan (buh-TAHN) peninsula in the Japanese-occupied Philippines. Despite the rhetoric about shared prosperity, it was the quest for empire that lay at the heart of Japan's war plans.

The Allies on the Offensive, 1942–1945

Even before Japan's attack on Pearl Harbor, Hitler reneged on his secret pact with Stalin and invaded the Soviet Union. Hitler viewed Russia and the Ukraine as natural territory for the expansion of Germany, while his military planners projected that Soviet resources would be necessary to win the war. In one of the most consequential movements of the war, the German army advanced from Poland into the Soviet Union in June 1941. As a consequence of Japanese and German aggression, both the United States and the Soviet Union joined with Britain to challenge the power of the Axis, and by 1943 these **Allied powers** were on the offensive. By then, Nancy Wake had escaped Vichy France by hiking across the Pyrenees and was in England, training for the Allied counteroffensive.

Hitler's eastward thrust was successful at first, and the Germans were soon nearing Moscow and Leningrad (as the historic capital of St. Petersburg was then called). The three-year **Siege of Leningrad** was gruesome. Residents were reduced to hunting rats for food, and many starved. Escape was possible only during winter, in convoys of trucks across a frozen lake north of the city. While some escaped, others drowned in the icy waters as German aircraft strafed and bombed them. Of a population of 3 million, one-third perished.

Allied powers
Alliance of Britain, the United States, and the Soviet Union during the Second World War.

Siege of Leningrad
(1941–1944) German siege of this Soviet city that left the city without food or fuel, resulting in over a million deaths.

Siege of Leningrad As long as the German siege lasted, death was an everyday occurrence for the people of Leningrad (today's St. Petersburg). Though the German army never entered the city, they maintained a constant barrage of artillery fire that kept the residents constantly scrambling for cover. Even so, in defiance of the Germans, the "Leningrad Symphony" by the great Russian composer Dmitri Shostakovich was performed in the beleaguered city in the summer of 1942 as a symbol of endurance. (Sovfoto)

Like Napoleon, Hitler had opened a second front in Russia while Britain remained unconquered. With German supply lines stretched thin, Soviet generals were able to use the vastness of their country and the harshness of winter to their advantage. The German tanks became mired in the mud that came with spring rains. Soviet resistance to the Nazis was unmatched in its toughness and resiliency. Stalin's propagandists emphasized heroic stands against earlier invaders and rallied the Soviet peoples behind the "Great Patriotic Homeland War."

If the Germans had treated the Soviet people well, they might have found allies, such as the Ukrainians, who had suffered under Stalin's brutal dictatorship. Instead harsh treatment by the Nazi occupiers—who believed that Slavic peoples were only good for manual labor under German command—drove the various Soviet peoples together under Stalin's leadership. If Stalin's secret police suspected people of having pro-German sympathies, as happened in the Baltic states of Latvia and Estonia, they were either killed outright or sent to Siberian labor camps.

As the United States and the Soviet Union mobilized for war, momentum shifted toward the Allies. One reason for the Allied advantage in the war after 1943 was the superior coordination of the British, Americans, and Soviets in defining their strategies and sharing their communications. On the Axis side, in contrast, poor coordination meant that Hitler's forces had to rush in when Mussolini's faltered. The same was true in the Pacific, with which the Germans remained unconcerned while Britain and the United States collaborated closely in their fight with Japan.

The alliance between liberal democrats and communists was an unlikely one, made possible only by their common fascist enemies. Communists played key roles as partisans in France, Italy, and eastern Europe, and in Asia the antifascist alliance between liberal democrats and communists expanded to include both the Guomindang government of Chiang Kai-shek and communist partisans led by Mao Zedong (see Chapter 28).

Britain and the United States supplied arms to Chiang to keep up the fight against the Japanese in Burma and in China, while Mao's forces harassed the Japanese in the north. Communist forces in Vietnam harassed the Japanese as well, supplied by the British and Americans. By 1942 it was becoming clear that holding on to China and Southeast Asia required a huge Japanese investment of men and material.

The first decisive military reversal for the Axis came in North Africa, where the British finally gained the upper hand. Victory at the Battle of El Alamein in Egypt (1942) not only protected Britain's control of the Suez Canal but also secured a base for a counterattack against Italy across the Mediterranean. By 1943 British and American forces were driving northward up the Italian peninsula, aided by Italian partisans. Mussolini's forces collapsed. Though Germany propped him up until 1945, he was eventually captured by the Italian resistance. To express their contempt, Mussolini's executioners hung his body by the heels from a public balcony.

In the Pacific, the Allies also gained momentum in 1942. In early summer American aircraft sunk four of Japan's six largest aircraft carriers at the Battle of Midway. Then the United States took the offensive at Guadalcanal, the beginning of an "island-hopping" campaign to drive back the Japanese. The fighting was tough, but the huge U.S. economy was now fully geared toward military production, and new ships and airplanes rolled off assembly lines at a staggering rate, ensuring American naval dominance in the Pacific.

Perhaps the single most important turning point of the war was the **Battle of Stalingrad**. Unable to take Moscow, in late 1942 the Germans swung south toward the Soviet Union's strategic oil fields. House-by-house fighting in Stalingrad gave the Red Army time to organize a counteroffensive, and in 1943 they surrounded and annihilated the German Sixth Army. Galvanized by their victory, the Soviets launched a series of punishing attacks. In January 1944 the siege of Leningrad ended as Germans departed from the city's outskirts, and in the spring Stalin's forces drove Hitler's army out of Soviet territory altogether. Meanwhile, British and American bombing was taking a terrible toll: in the summer of 1943, the port city of Hamburg in Germany was obliterated in a firestorm that killed tens of thousands of civilians.

The Japanese were also on the defensive by 1943. The Allies retook the Burma Road, their main supply line to Chiang Kai-shek's Nationalist forces in China. Matching the Soviet thrust to drive the German army back toward Berlin, by 1944 American forces were pushing Japanese forces back toward their home islands. Local resistance in China, Vietnam, the Philippines, and the Dutch East Indies complemented British, Australian, Canadian, and American efforts.

When Churchill and Roosevelt met with Stalin for the first time, in Teheran, Iran, in 1943, they agreed to open a western front in addition to the front already opened in Italy. British and American commanders, led by General Dwight Eisenhower of the United States, began preparations for a difficult landing on the beaches of Normandy in northwestern France. Meanwhile, Soviet forces drove the German army all the way to the Polish border.

In anticipation of the Normandy invasion, Nancy Wake and her group parachuted into central France behind German lines. It was difficult and dangerous work. Once when her group lost their radio, and therefore contact with London, Wake bicycled more than a hundred miles over mountainous terrain to re-establish their communications link: *"Every kilometer I pedaled was sheer agony. I knew if I ever got off the bike, I could never get on it again. . . . I couldn't stand up, I couldn't sit down, I couldn't walk and I couldn't sleep for days."*[*]

After assisting in the Allied invasion of Normandy on D-Day, June 6, 1944, Wake reached Paris just as Allied forces drove the German army from the city she had once called home: *"Paris was liberated on 25 August, 1944, and the whole country rejoiced. . . . After defeat and years of humiliation their beautiful capital was free. The aggressors were now the hunted. . . . The collaborators seemed to have vanished into thin air and the crowds in the street went wild with joy."*[*] But there was still hard fighting to do. A final German offensive in Belgium led to significant American casualties in the Battle of the Bulge in the winter of 1944 before British and U.S. forces regained the initiative. And Nancy Wake's happiness was tempered by personal loss: the Nazis had executed her husband and many of her friends.

By early 1945 Allied forces were poised to invade Germany from both east and west. The European war ended in a final fury. As the Red Army moved into eastern Germany, Soviet troops took their vengeance by raping, looting, and executing German civilians. When British and American aircraft firebombed Dresden, civilians who fled to underground shelters suffocated as the firestorm above them sucked the

Battle of Stalingrad (1942–1943) One of the major turning points of World War II, when the Soviet army halted the German advance and annihilated the German Sixth Army. After victory at Stalingrad, the Soviets went on the offensive, driving the Germans out of Soviet territory.

---

[*]Excerpt from Nancy Wake, *The Autobiography of the Woman the Gestapo Called the White Mouse,* pp. 225–226, 255. Copyright © 1985 Pan Publishing.

oxygen from the air. Over one hundred thousand died. With Soviet troops storming Berlin, Hitler killed himself in a bunker beneath the city. The nightmare of German fascism was over. On May 8, 1945—V-E Day—Germany surrendered.

It took the rest of the summer, however, for American forces to defeat Japan. Once the United States retook the Philippines late in 1944, the path toward invasion lay open (see Map 29.2). American submarines blockaded Japan, starving its military of supplies, while U.S. aircraft dropped incendiary bombs on Tokyo and other cities, reducing them to ashes. Still, some Americans thought that it would require a massive landing of troops to force a Japanese surrender, putting hundreds of thousands of American lives at risk.

After the death of Franklin Roosevelt in 1945, Harry S. Truman (in office 1945–1953) entered the presidency faced with the dreadful decision of whether to try to

MAP 29.2 World War II in Asia and the Pacific The Japanese empire, like the Axis powers in Europe, dominated the early stages of the war in Asia, overrunning British, French, Dutch, and Chinese positions in Southeast and East Asia in 1940–1942 and threatening British India. By 1943, however, with the United States fully mobilized to fight the Pacific war, momentum shifted to the Allies. The war ended in the summer of 1945 when President Harry Truman ordered the use of the atomic weapons dropped on Hiroshima and Nagasaki. (© Cengage Learning)

end the war quickly by deploying recently tested atomic bombs. His choice to do so has been debated ever since. Atomic blasts at **Hiroshima and Nagasaki** killed hundreds of thousands, some instantly, others gradually from radiation poisoning. Meanwhile, the Soviet Union occupied Manchuria and northern Korea, raising fears of Soviet invasion. Calculating that immediate submission was Japan's best option, Emperor Hirohito (hee-ro-HEE-to), whose voice his subjects had never before heard, went on the radio and announced Japan's unconditional surrender. On September 2, 1945—V-J Day—that surrender was made official. Finally, the Second World War was over.

Hiroshima and Nagasaki (1945) Two Japanese cities devastated by atomic bombs dropped by the United States in an attempt to end the Second World War. Hundreds of thousands were killed, many by slow radiation poisoning.

Total War and Civilian Life

Total war in the twentieth century intensely involved civilians in each conflict. Even more than during the First World War, in the Second tens of millions of ordinary people saw their routines and life plans disrupted; in that sense, Nancy Wake's experience was not atypical.

In addition to witnessing the horrors of war, civilian populations were affected in myriad ways. Governmental power intensified. Newspapers, radio, and film were censored and often incorporated state-sponsored misinformation and propaganda. (See the feature "Visual Evidence in Primary Sources: Warfare and Racial Stereotypes.")

Once again colonized peoples were deeply involved in the global struggle. Many Africans, Indians, Arabs, and Southeast Asians participated directly in the war, were mobilized for wartime production, and had their destinies altered by the successes and failures of Allied and Axis armies. Many suffered tragic losses. Warfare and famine killed tens of millions of Chinese and at least 25 million Soviet citizens. During the genocide known as the Holocaust, the Nazis killed 6 million Jews in concentration camps, death camps, and by other forms of abuse and execution. Of the entire European Jewish population, over 60 percent perished, including over 90 percent of Poland's Jews. The slaughter extended to millions more people as well—homosexuals, disabled persons, Jehovah's Witnesses, and others deemed enemies of Aryan racial supremacy. Eighty percent of Europe's Roma (Gypsies) were killed.

Civilians and Total War in the United States and Europe

The American people sacrificed in the fight against fascism. Families were disrupted, sons and husbands went to war, and basic consumer goods were rationed. But almost none of the fighting occurred on American soil, and the war actually benefited American society in a number of ways. Massive state spending on munitions put the country back to work, effectively ending the Great Depression. Secure employment boosted the spirits of those who had long been unemployed, even if there was relatively little to buy.

For Americans who had long been at the bottom of the job ladder, especially women and African Americans, mobilization brought new opportunities. "Rosie the Riveter" became the symbol of women laboring on industrial production lines to produce the boots, bullets, and bombers needed by the military. Segregated African American military units, such as the famous "Tuskegee Airmen," distinguished themselves in combat, while other American blacks gained access to good industrial employment for the first time. More broadly, the camaraderie and discipline of both military and civilian life, dedicated to a successful fight against a great evil, gave an entire generation of Americans a shared sense of purpose.

The people of the Soviet Union also experienced the "Great Patriotic Homeland War" as a powerful collective endeavor; however, their suffering and sacrifice,

Warfare and Racial Stereotypes

Western democracies were not immune from the trend toward greater use of government propaganda to mobilize civilian populations during the total wars of the twentieth century. While authoritarian regimes like those in Nazi Germany and in communist societies like the Soviet Union had even greater control over what the public heard and saw, even in liberal societies wartime censors carefully checked the scripts for films and radio broadcasts and established government bureaus to feed information, and sometimes disinformation, to their citizens. They also restricted the political rights and liberties of individuals, outlawing strikes and sending workers where they were most needed.

The development and dissemination of racial stereotypes was part of government propaganda efforts during both global wars in the twentieth century. The most infamous case was Adolf Hitler's extreme anti-Semitism, as he stated clearly in *Mein Kampf* ("My Struggle"): "The personification of the devil as the symbol of all evil assumes the living shape of the Jew." In Asia the Japanese government also believed themselves a "master race" destined to rule over the "racially inferior" peoples of Korea, China, and Southeast Asia.

After the attack on Pearl Harbor, racial animosity toward people of Japanese descent increased in both Canada and the United States. Although most Japanese Americans and Japanese Canadians were citizens, governments stripped them of their property and forced them into detention camps on the assumption that their loyalty toward the Japanese emperor was stronger than that toward their adopted nations. As these illustrations show, wartime propaganda in the United States played on racial stereotypes.

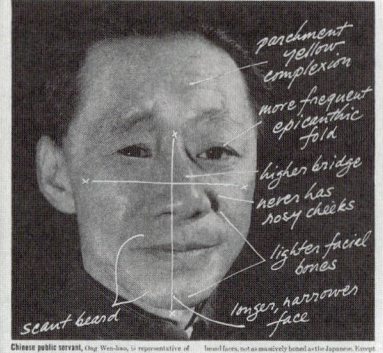
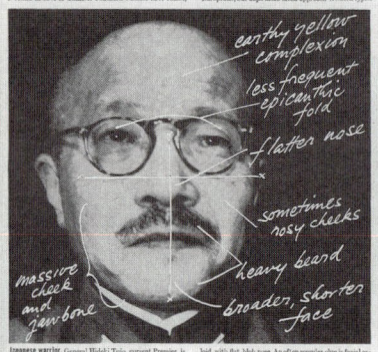

© 2012 Time Inc. reprinted by permission; top left: Carl Mydans/Getty Images; bottom left: Domonken/Black Star; bottom right: AP Images

From Life Magazine, December 22, 1941. Copyright © 1941 The Picture Collection Inc. Reprinted with permission. All rights reserved.

These images are from the December 22, 1941, issue of *Life* magazine, one of the most widely circulated magazines of the period, its success stemming from its extensive use of photographs. This issue, which appeared two weeks after the assault on Pearl Harbor, featured an American flag on the cover. These images accompanied an article entitled "How to Tell Japs from the Chinese," about assaults that had just taken place on Asians in the United States. Many Americans used the single term *Orientals* to describe all Asians, and the editors of *Life* wanted to help their audience distinguish friends (the Chinese) from the Japanese foe.

» *In these images, how is physical appearance associated with behavior?*

» *How do these images seek to explain contemporary conflicts as related to fixed, unchanging racial characteristics?*

The caption for this photo describes Ong Wen-Hao, a Chinese civil servant, as "representative of Northern Chinese anthropological group with long, fine-boned face and scant beard. Epicanthic fold of skin above eyelid is found in 85% of Chinese."

The editors make a further distinction: "Southern Chinese have round, broad faces, not as massively boned as the Japanese. Except that their skin is darker, this description fits Filipinos who are often mistaken for Japs. Chinese sometimes pass for Europeans; but Japs more often approach Western types."

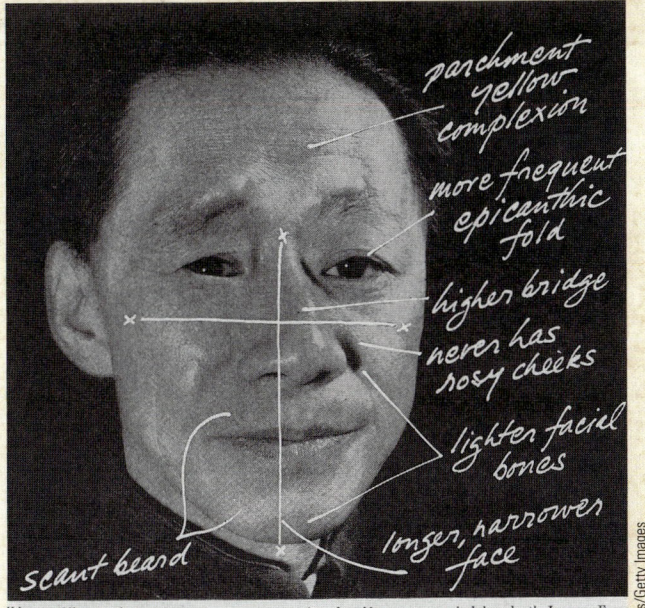

parchment yellow complexion

more frequent epicanthic fold

higher bridge

never has rosy cheeks

lighter facial bones

longer, narrower face

scant beard

Carl Mydans/Getty Images

Chinese public servant, Ong Wen-hao, is representative of North Chinese anthropological group with long, fine-boned face and scant beard. Epicanthic fold of skin above eyelid is found in 85% of Chinese. Southern Chinese have round, broad faces, not as massively boned as the Japanese. Except that their skin is darker, this description fits Filipinos who are often mistaken for Japs. Chinese sometimes pass for Europeans; but Japs more often approach Western types

In the caption, General Hideki Tojo, the Japanese premier, is described as "a Samurai, closer to type of humble Jap than highbred relatives of Imperial Household. Typical are his heavy beard, massive cheek and jaw bones. Peasant Jap is squat Mongoloid, with flat, blob nose."

The editors of *Life* claimed that "an often sounder clue" in distinguishing Chinese from Japanese individuals "is facial expression, shaped by cultural, not anthropological, factors. Chinese wear rational calm of tolerant realists. Japs, like General Tojo, show humorless intensity of ruthless mystics."

earthy yellow complexion

less frequent epicanthic fold

flatter nose

sometimes rosy cheeks

heavy beard

broader, shorter face

massive cheek and jawbone

Domonken/Black Star

Japanese warrior, General Hideki Tojo, current Premier, is a Samurai, closer to type of humble Jap than highbred relatives of Imperial Household. Typical are his heavy beard, massive cheek and jaw bones. Peasant Jap is squat Mongoloid, with flat, blob nose. An often sounder clue is facial expression, shaped by cultural, not anthropological, factors. Chinese wear rational calm of tolerant realists. Japs, like General Tojo, show humorless intensity of ruthless mystics

During the Cold War, when the Japanese were allies of the United States and communist China was an implacable enemy, these stereotypes were reversed, with the Chinese often depicted as ruthless fanatics and the Japanese as tolerant realists.

Hulton Archive/Getty Images

British War Production Total war required the complete mobilization of civilian populations behind a nation's military. As in the United States and the Soviet Union, traditional gender roles in Britain were transformed as female factory workers replaced departed servicemen. Here a British worker finalizes assembly of the nose cone of an Avro Lancaster bomber in 1943.

especially in the Siege of Leningrad, was much greater. Even before the German invasion, workers dismantled factories and moved them to interior regions. Millions of people were likewise uprooted and put to work on farms in safer interior areas. Soviet women bore a special burden, caring for children and the elderly while taking on dangerous jobs in mines and factories. Many Soviet women also served with distinction in the armed forces. By the end of the war, tens of millions of people had been killed or uprooted, the country's agricultural and industrial infrastructure destroyed. Wartime suffering left the Soviet people with a deep determination never again to allow such an invasion from the West.

The western European experience was more like the Soviet than the American one. Civilians throughout western Europe—French, Belgians, Dutch, and others—saw the war come to their own cities and villages, the horrors of war at their very doorsteps. In every nation, families were evacuated from cities under bombardment to safer rural areas, where farming families took them in. In countries under occupation by the Nazis, the slightest sign of anti-German feeling, or any display of sympathy for the Jews, could result in imprisonment, torture, and death. By war's end much of urban Europe lay in ruins.

Before 1944, the civilian population of Germany had a very different experience, with a lower level of mobilization. Since National Socialist ideology restricted German women to roles as wives and mothers—breeders of the Aryan master race—they were not asked to contribute to the war effort as British, American, and Soviet women were: the Nazis' plan was for enslaved subject peoples to do their work for them. Total war came to the German people only in the last stages of the conflict, but then it did so with a vengeance. As Allied bombs pummeled German cities, and as Soviet advances pushed German soldiers and civilians back toward Berlin, Adolf Hitler called up children and old men to reinforce his disintegrating army. In a sense, he involved the whole country in his own suicide.

The civilian experience of total war had long-term effects on Western political culture. In Europe, bitterness remained between those who resisted and those who collaborated with the Axis powers. Meanwhile, the Soviets sought to establish a zone of buffer states to insulate them from future invasion. And the people of the United States were, for the first time, fully willing to engage themselves as a great power in world affairs.

Civilians and Total War in Asia and the Colonial World

At war, the Japanese state commanded all aspects of civilian life, regulating industry and commerce, while severely restricting speech and assembly. Even so, like the Germans, most Japanese did not experience the violence of war firsthand until 1944–1945. Then Allied air assaults, and ultimately nuclear annihilation, exacted a terrible price indeed for their nation's imperialist adventures.

Elsewhere in the Asian theater of war, European colonies were caught in the crossfire between the Allied powers and Japan from the very beginning. Early in the war, Japanese forces seized the colonial territories of the British, French, Dutch, and Americans. The European powers were intent on "liberating" their colonial territories, but also on returning them to colonial rule. Local nationalists in places like Vietnam and Indonesia, however, saw the fight against the Japanese as a fight to throw off foreign rule altogether. Once the war against the Axis was over, multiple conflicts would arise between the European powers and local nationalists fighting for self-determination (see Chapter 30).

As in Europe, civilians in Asia suffered a war fought on their own soil. The Japanese regarded exploitation of Southeast Asia's natural resources as essential to their imperial mission. They treated local populations like slaves, even forcing Korean, Filipina, and other young women into prostitution to service their troops. These so-called "comfort women" suffered severe emotional scars. American, British, Canadian, and Australian prisoners of war were also cruelly treated and often

Filipina Women in Protest Memories of Japan's wartime atrocities run deep in East and Southeast Asia. These Filipina women are protesting the Japanese government's lack of restitution for the suffering of the "comfort women"—girls and women from the Philippines and other Asian countries who were forced to provide sexual services to Japanese soldiers during the war. (AFP/Getty Images)

National Memory and Historical Accountability: Germany and Japan

The German and Japanese peoples have had unequal success in coming to terms with their nations' behavior in World War II. While postwar Germans were initially reluctant to face that past honestly and openly, today most are quite frank in acknowledging their national culpability in the Nazi era. In Japan, by contrast, political and educational leaders have been less forthcoming: many young people there still know little of the excessive violence inflicted by the Japanese military on other peoples at the time.

In 1945, urban Germany was buried in rubble and refugees wandered the countryside. With top Nazi leaders dead or facing harsh sentences, many citizens focused on rebuilding their shattered lives. In East Germany, the communists presented themselves as anti-fascists with no responsibility for the Holocaust. In liberal West Germany, many lower-ranking Nazis melded into the mainstream.

Then, the postwar generation began asking difficult questions about the war of their parents and teachers. After the late 1960s, this intergenerational dialogue bore fruit. The study of Nazi criminality is now thoroughly integrated into the school curriculum. Berlin is the site of a haunting Holocaust memorial. The German government forthrightly communicates its regret for past atrocities.

The Japanese have, in general, been less forthright, preferring to see themselves as victims of a nuclear nightmare rather than as perpetrators of war crimes. It became the life work of historian Saburo Ienaga (1913–2002) to alter history textbooks to more accurately tell the story of events such as the Rape of Nanjing (see Chapter 28). Ienaga's efforts met only limited success. Opposition continues to the treatment of topics like the "comfort women" forced to serve Japanese soldiers. At times, Japan's less-than-open attitude has strained relations with neighboring countries such as China and Korea, who have demanded formal government apologies for such abuses.

For any society, confronting difficult episodes of the past can be painful. In the United States, some are angered when teachers pay close and critical attention to violent historical episodes like slavery or the conquest of Amerindians. Most educators, however, believe that historical honesty is the best policy.

died in captivity. (See the feature "World History in Today's World: National Memory and Historical Accountability: Germany and Japan.")

Hunger and hardship was the lot of Chinese civilians throughout the war. Those under Japanese occupation especially suffered, but even those living in zones controlled by Chiang Kai-shek's Guomindang Army faced shortages of food and medicine. Malnutrition was common. The lack of coordination between Chiang's Guomindang and Mao's Red Army hampered Chinese resistance to Japanese occupation, the two armies achieving little more than a temporary cease-fire. Once the Japanese were expelled, the rival armies would renew the fight for China's future.

Communist resistance also arose in neighboring Vietnam, where communist guerrillas led by Ho Chi Minh harassed Japanese occupation forces, with American and British assistance. In Southeast Asia the principal Allied concern was the Burma Road. Bitterly contested jungle warfare in Burma, engaging African and Australian troops supported by Allied bombing, caught many peasant villagers in its crossfire. Late in the war, forced replacement of food crops with industrial ones, Japanese hoarding of food, and American bombing of rail and road lines contributed to the starvation of 2 million Vietnamese.

The British were astonished when Mohandas K. Gandhi and his Indian National Congress refused to back the British empire in the war. During World War I Gandhi and the Indian National Congress had supported the British, hoping to be rewarded with concrete steps toward Indian self-government. But Congress leaders were frustrated when the British-controlled Government of India declared war on Germany and Japan without consulting Indian public opinion. Much to the disgust of British colonial officials, the Congress launched a "**Quit India**" campaign, demanding that the British leave immediately even in the midst of war. Indian nationalist Subhas Bose (soob-ahs BOZ) (1897–1945) went even further than Congress leaders, advocating an Indo-Japanese alliance against the British and traveling to Tokyo to enlist captured Indian soldiers to fight alongside the Axis powers.

British authorities once again threw Gandhi and other nationalist leaders into jail, and Bose died in a plane crash before British officials could charge him with treason. Still, the Indian army remained the bulwark of British defense in Asia, and Indian civilians continued to contribute labor and economic resources to the Allied war effort. However, as in China and Vietnam, wartime economic policies led to great hardship for people in British India. In 1943, over 2 million people died in a famine in the northeastern province of Bengal.

British war strategies also provoked a backlash in Arab lands. Egyptian nationalists were outraged when the British mobilized their forces without seeking permission from the nominally independent government. As a result, Britain had to quell demonstrations in Cairo even as it prepared for desert war with Italy and Germany. Arab nationalists were also upset at the increased Jewish immigration to Palestine. Muhammad Amin al-Husseini, the Grand Mufti of Jerusalem and leader of Palestinian Muslims, took a strongly anti-Zionist stand and, on the principle of "the enemy of my enemy is my friend," collaborated with the Nazis and ultimately sought refuge in Germany. In Iraq, the government also declared its sympathies with the Axis powers, prompting the British to invade and occupy Baghdad in the spring of 1941.

Britain's African subjects, perhaps surprisingly, showed greater loyalty to the empire. For example, the British mustered the **King's African Rifles** from West African colonies such as Nigeria and East African ones like Kenya to buttress their forces in Asia. Here was another example of total war on an international scale, with African soldiers fighting in Burmese jungles to protect India from Japanese invasion. Many of these African soldiers had never traveled more than a few days' distance from home. Those who returned after the war brought an expanded view of the world and of Africa's place in it. The liberation of Ethiopia from Italian occupation in 1941, along with the return of Hailie Selassie to his throne, became symbolic of a restoration of African dignity.

Africans supported the Allies in the name of ideals enshrined in the Atlantic Charter: liberty, freedom, and national self-determination. In South Africa, the African National Congress (see Chapter 27) specifically pointed to this charter in

"Quit India" Campaign by Mohandas K. Gandhi and the Indian National Congress during World War II to demand independence. They refused to support the British war effort and instead launched a campaign of civil disobedience demanding that the British "quit India" immediately.

King's African Rifles African regiment recruited by Britain during the Second World War; saw action in Burma, fighting against the Japanese to save India for Britain.

its calls against racial segregation and discrimination. In fact, with many white working-class men conscripted into the army and with blacks forbidden to join the military, some black South Africans found new and better job opportunities in the industrial sector, just as their counterparts did in the United States. On the other side of the racial divide, the war polarized South African whites. While mainstream politicians remained loyal to the British empire and brought South Africa into the war on the Allied side, some Afrikaner nationalists, sympathetic to national socialism, organized a pro-Axis underground movement.

Some Africans in the French empire also helped in defeating fascism, providing soldiers for Charles de Gaulle's Free French Army. While most colonial officials allied with the Vichy government, the governor of French Equatorial Africa, Félix Éboué (1884–1944), stood with de Gaulle. Éboué was from French Guiana in South America; a descendant of slaves, he had attained French citizenship through educational achievement. Under his leadership, the colonial city of Brazzaville became a staging ground for Free French recruitment of African soldiers.

As in Southeast Asia, European dominance in Africa would be strongly challenged by nationalist movements after the war's end. Though it took some time for the British and French to realize how much the world had changed, the Second World War brought an end to the age of European imperialism (see Chapter 30).

The Holocaust

Even among the many people who made great sacrifices in the war against fascism, few grasped the magnitude of Hitler's assault on the Jews of Europe. Only when the death camps were liberated by Allied forces in 1945 did the scale of the horror known as the Holocaust become clear.

Some of the most calamitous events of the twentieth century occurred when political leaders tried to turn extremist ideologies into reality. The Nazi death camps of World War II are the most infamous example. The ideology of racial superiority that drove Hitler's National Socialism played to the insecurities of Germans resentful of their losses after World War I and frightened by the upheaval of the Great Depression. Now scapegoating turned to slaughter.

The Nazis regarded the peoples of eastern Europe, especially the Slavs, as an inferior "race" destined to work under the direction of their "Aryan" superiors, the German "master race." But Hitler identified two "races" that he claimed played no useful role at all. One was the Roma, or Gypsies, a traveling people whose ancestors had come from India. Clinging to their own language and traditions, the Roma of central Europe suffered prejudice and discrimination. Hitler's other outsider group was the much larger Jewish community. Thorough assimilation into German culture and society gave the country's Jews no protection from Hitler's racial obsession.

During the 1930s, the Nazis had segregated Jews into ghettos and then herded them into labor camps. Early in 1942, Nazi officials met to devise a "final solution" to the "Jewish problem." According to the minutes of the Wannsee Conference, a bureaucracy would be set up to *"cleanse the German living space of Jews in a legal manner."* Jews *"capable of work"* would be sent to camps in Poland, *"whereby a large part will undoubtedly disappear through natural diminution."* Those who were not worked to death *"will have to be appropriately dealt with."* The "appropriate" measure for those too young, too old, or too sick to work was simply to kill them outright. Europe's Jews would be systematically liquidated in "death camps." (See the feature "Movement of Ideas Through Primary Sources: Primo Levi's Memories of Auschwitz.")

The Nazi extermination of the Jews was methodical and cold-blooded. When a death camp administrator observed that people died faster if they were already short of breath when they entered the "shower rooms" that were actually gas chambers, he applied "the industrialist's logic," and forced Jewish captives to run to the showers in a panic, saving gas as well as time. Thus, thousands could be killed in a day. Scientific rationality and industrial progress were perverted to the most horrible of ends.

Not all Jews went meekly, however. The most militant resistance was the **Warsaw Ghetto Uprising**. Shortly after occupying Warsaw, the Nazis forced the city's Jews into a fenced-off ghetto where they found no work and very little food. In 1943, as the Nazis began to remove residents for transportation to the Treblinka death camp, the sixty thousand residents of the Warsaw ghetto rose up in armed revolt. Ten thousand paid with their lives, and the Nazis killed most of the rest at Treblinka.

Before 1944, the United States retained its racially discriminatory immigration policies: in 1939, over nine hundred Jewish refugees seeking sanctuary from fascism were turned away at American ports and returned to Europe. (Many of them later died in the Holocaust.) Britain also restricted Jewish immigration, both to England and to Palestine. So where were Jewish refugees supposed to go? Some Zionists, seeking to create a Jewish state to be called Israel (see Chapter 27), formed guerrilla groups and developed an underground network to aid illegal Jewish immigration to Palestine. After 1939, however, it was almost impossible for Jews under Nazi rule to escape. Those who did so were helped by people such as Raoul Wallenberg, a Swedish diplomat who helped save thousands of Hungarian Jews from the death camps, and others like him who hid Jewish families or adopted Jewish children, putting their own lives and livelihoods at risk for the sake of common humanity. But neither resistance nor the heroism of people who tried to aid their Jewish neighbors was enough to prevent Hitler from carrying out his plans. In 1933 there had been 9.5 million Jews in Europe; by 1950 there were only 3.3 million left.

Along with 6 million Jews, the Nazis also slaughtered hundreds of thousands from other targeted groups. Viewing homosexuals as traitors to the master race, they imprisoned over one hundred thousand of them, and many died in concentration camps. Jehovah's Witnesses, who respect the primacy of their God by refusing to salute flags and other symbols of state authority, were also targeted. The Nazis executed tens of thousands of Roma, while the mentally and physically challenged of all ethnic groups were frequently sterilized and cruelly subjected to medical experiments.

The Nazi death machine continued even after it became clear that the Allies would win the war. The mass graves in the camps sickened the Allied soldiers who liberated the emaciated victims. Many Holocaust survivors found that their entire families had been killed. Sometimes, however, after scattering to different parts of the world after the war, survivors were lucky enough to find relatives who were still alive.

How could the Holocaust have happened? It is not enough to blame Hitler and the Nazis. Anti-Semitism was strong across Europe, and Nazi collaborators from France, Italy, Hungary, Poland, and elsewhere helped send Jews to the camps. Moreover, the system could not have worked without the passive acquiescence, if not the active participation, of the German people. Debates continue today about whether others could have done more to prevent the slaughter. For example, could Pope Pius XII, who sponsored humanitarian work for refugees and prisoners

Warsaw Ghetto Uprising (1943) Unsuccessful revolt of Polish Jews confined to the Warsaw ghetto, who rose up to resist being sent to the Treblinka death camp.

of war, have successfully confronted the German government? For her part Nancy Wake, appalled by the treatment of Jews in Austria before the war, did everything in her power to prevent Nazi ideas from spreading. But too many simply looked the other way.

Starting in the fall of 1945, the British and Americans initiated the Nuremberg Trials to call Nazi leaders to account for their actions. Herman Goering, the most senior Nazi official left alive, was convicted and executed, as were dozens of other top officials. Many less prominent Nazis escaped punishment; some fled into South American exile, while others stayed in Germany and retired into quiet obscurity.

Origins of the Cold War, 1945–1949

At the end of the European war, Soviet and American troops met each other at the Elbe River in Germany in a spirit of friendship and joy, celebrating their joint victory over fascism. Roosevelt envisioned that Allied cooperation would continue after the war in the new United Nations, which was founded in San Francisco in the spring of 1945. Instead, the unlikely wartime partnership of liberal democracy and communism quickly dissolved, and the world divided into two hostile camps (see Map 30.2, page 863).

The New United Nations and Postwar Challenges, 1945–1947

At the Yalta Conference on the Black Sea, held in early 1945, the most important priority for the aged and ill Franklin Delano Roosevelt was to secure Joseph Stalin's cooperation in the founding of the **United Nations (UN)** to rebuild the postwar future. Winston Churchill, also present at Yalta, was more cynical than Roosevelt about Stalin's intentions, correctly doubting the Soviet leader's pledge to allow free elections in Poland. Roosevelt's more optimistic view prevailed, however, and in the spring of 1945, the founding meeting of the UN was held in San Francisco.

United Nations (UN) Organization established near the end of the Second World War to guarantee international peace and security through permanent diplomacy. A Security Council of five members, each with veto power, was created to enhance UN authority.

The UN included a General Assembly of sovereign nations and a Security Council of the major war allies: Britain, France, China, the Soviet Union, and the United States. Since each member of the council had veto power, its decisions could only be reached through consensus. It was hoped that the Security Council's special powers would make the UN more effective than the League of Nations.

The spirit of Allied cooperation did not last. The fate of Poland was a central issue. The British and Americans had promised the Polish government-in-exile elections after the war. Stalin, however, knew that any Polish government chosen through free elections would be hostile to the Soviet Union and insisted that Poland must have a "friendly government." While the fighting continued, the Allies papered over the difference. But as soon as the war was over, it became clear that Stalin intended to occupy eastern Europe and install communist governments that would do his bidding.

By the summer of 1945, when Allied leaders met at Potsdam, the Soviet Red Army had occupied all of eastern Europe, and Roosevelt had died and been replaced by Truman. The Allies agreed on the plans for punishment of Germany, including a reduction in its size. But with Truman's distrust of Stalin, a much chillier diplomatic atmosphere prevailed at the Potsdam Conference. To American insistence that the peoples of Europe had the right to choose their own form of government through free elections, Stalin responded, *"Everyone imposes his own system as far as his army can reach."*

Europe was dividing into two opposing camps. The British, Americans, and de Gaulle's Free French controlled western Europe, while Stalin's Red Army controlled eastern Europe.

In 1946 Winston Churchill, now out of office as the war-weary British trusted the difficult task of recovery to a Labor Party government, gave a speech in the United States in which he coined the term *iron curtain* to describe the imposition of communism in the Soviet sphere of influence:

> *From Stettin in the Baltic to Trieste in the Adriatic an iron curtain has descended across the Continent. Behind that line lie all the capitals of the ancient states of Central and Eastern Europe. Warsaw, Berlin, Prague, Vienna, Budapest, Belgrade, Bucharest and Sofia; all these famous cities and the populations around them . . . are subject, in one form or another, not only to Soviet influence but to a very high and in some cases increasing measure of control from Moscow.*

Ironically, in many of these countries local communists were actually a strong political force after the war, having played important roles in the antifascist resistance. But Stalin was not interested in working with communists who had their own legitimacy and bases of power. He wanted control from the top down through men of unquestioned loyalty to Moscow, whose rule would be enforced by the continued presence of the Soviet army.

Nancy Wake witnessed one of the most tragic examples of Soviet domination when she traveled to Prague in 1947. Before the war, Czechoslovakia had been a prosperous society with a strong middle class and an emerging democratic tradition. But when Wake arrived to work at the British consulate, she found uneasiness: *"Although the Russians were not visible, the majority of Czechs I met used to walk around looking over their shoulders in case someone was listening to their conversation."*

Czechs saw themselves as a bridge between East and West. Local communists fared well in a free election held in 1946 and were part of a coalition government. But that was not good enough for Stalin, who wanted firmer control. In 1948, Czech communists loyal to Moscow seized power and ended their country's brief postwar experiment with democracy. *"Yes, the Germans had gone,"* Wake commented, *"but who would liberate the country from the liberators?"*

The United States, the Soviet Union, and the Origins of a Bipolar World

The United States and the Soviet Union were now bitter enemies, two potent "superpowers" dividing the globe in a bipolar struggle between Washington and Moscow. But full-scale war between them never developed. This was a "cold" war, often fought by proxies (smaller nations on either side) but never by the main adversaries (see Chapter 30). The deployment of nuclear weapons, first by the United States in 1945 and then by the Soviet Union in 1949, raised the stakes of total war beyond what any leader was willing to wager.

---

*Excerpt from Nancy Wake, *The Autobiography of the Woman the Gestapo Called the White Mouse*, pp. 280, 285. Copyright © 1985 Pan Publishing.

While Soviet ideology proclaimed the desirability and inevitability of socialist revolution on a global scale, Stalin was most concerned to protect the Russian core of the Soviet Union. With large, exposed land frontiers, Soviet Russia needed buffer states along its European and Asian borders to prevent invasions such as those staged by Napoleon and Hitler. Such "defensive expansion" had also been part of the grand strategy of the Russian empire (see Chapter 20).

The American outlook was quite different. After the war, Americans retained their characteristic optimism and idealism and stood ready to project their ideals—personal liberty, democracy, technological progress, and market-driven economic efficiency—onto the world stage. Some thought it was the beginning of an "American century," a belief reinforced by economic dominance in a world where the country's major industrial competitors had all suffered huge losses. But as Americans engaged the postwar world, they found impediments to this global vision: not everyone seemed to share American ideals. Moreover, cynical observers saw American idealism as a smokescreen for the expansion of American capitalism and American imperialism.

American policy was strongly influenced by the "Long Telegram" sent to Washington in 1946 by a U.S. diplomat in Moscow who advocated a policy of "containment." *"At the bottom of [the] Kremlin's neurotic view of world affairs,"* he wrote, *"is [the] traditional and instinctive Russian sense of insecurity."** If the Western powers held firm and maintained their unity, the author argued, Soviet expansionism could be contained.

Truman Doctrine
(1947) Declaration by President Harry S. Truman that the United States would aid all peoples threatened by communism. In reality, his doctrine of "containment" meant that the United States did not try to dislodge the Soviets from their sphere of influence.

In 1947, the **Truman Doctrine** expressed that concept of containment in the context of a civil war in Greece. Communist partisans who had fought the Germans for control of their homeland did not disarm at the war's end but continued fighting to bring about a communist revolution. The Greek government and army were unable to put down this rebellion on their own, and in 1947 Truman stood before a joint meeting of Congress and promised American aid to suppress the "terrorist activities" of the Greek communists, also promising aid to Greece's neighbor and traditional enemy Turkey and to any nation struggling for freedom: *"I believe that it must be the policy of the United States to support free peoples who are resisting attempted subjugation by armed minorities or by outside pressures."* Despite the implications of Truman's strong language, in fact Stalin conceded that Greece would be under Western control. For its part the United States took no direct action in response to the Soviet takeover of Czechoslovakia, implicitly acknowledging that Stalin would control "wherever his army could reach."

The Cold War stalemate was most apparent in Germany, where the Soviets occupied the eastern part of the country and the British, Americans, and French occupied the west. The capital city of Berlin, which lay within the zone of Soviet occupation, was divided into four sectors. With the breakdown of wartime collaboration between the Soviet Union and the Western powers, no agreement could be reached on Germany's future. Border tensions escalated in 1948 when the Soviets cut off access to Berlin by land and the United States responded by sending supplies by air to West Berlin in what was called the Berlin Airlift. In 1949, the rift resulted in the creation of two separate states, the Federal Republic of Germany (or West Germany) and the German Democratic Republic (or East Germany). Each side blamed the other for preventing the reunification of Germany, but in reality neither France nor the Soviet Union was unhappy with the outcome, given that German aggression had twice in a generation posed a grave

*George Kennan, the "Long Telegram," Moscow, 1946.

Sovfoto/Eastfoto/photographersdirect.com

Berlin, 1945 In April 1945, the Soviet army advanced on the German capital, supported by American and British aerial bombardment. While Adolf Hitler committed suicide in his subterranean bunker, Soviet soldiers hoisted the communist flag over the ruined city. The Red Army remained in occupation of most of eastern Europe after the war.

threat to their peace and security. As long as the Cold War lasted, the division of Germany was its symbolic battle line.

Meanwhile, the United States took an active role in rebuilding war-ravaged western Europe, most famously through the **Marshall Plan**. Although some

Marshall Plan
U.S. effort to rebuild war-ravaged Europe, named after the American secretary of state, George C. Marshall.

Americans wanted Germany to pay reparations, and others wanted the United States to withdraw from European affairs, Truman saw that the reconstruction of western European economies was essential. First, a revival of global trade, in which Europe would play a central role, was necessary for postwar American economic progress. Second, the communist parties of Italy and France were still quite strong, and continued economic difficulties might increase their popularity. In early 1948, the United States announced that $12 billion would be made available for European reconstruction.

Bretton Woods Conference
(1944) Conference that led to creation of the World Bank and the International Monetary Fund, designed to secure international capitalism by preventing global economic catastrophes.

In 1944, even before the war was over, the American-sponsored **Bretton Woods Conference** had formed a plan to prevent a repeat of the economic catastrophe that followed World War I. It created the World Bank to loan money to nations in need of a jumpstart, and the International Monetary Fund to provide emergency loans to nations in danger of insolvency. The Marshall Plan and the Bretton Woods institutions were designed to enhance the stability of a free-market international economic order. Critics pointed out that the U.S. government was creating international institutions that favored American-style capitalism.

The Soviet Union and its eastern European satellites were invited to join the Marshall Plan, but Stalin refused, not wanting to integrate communist economies into the market-based system of the West. Thus, after 1948 the Cold War division of Europe would be economic as well as political and military. While the U.S. sphere of influence consisted of market-based, industrialized economies, the Soviet Union dominated another sphere in which centralized planning shielded socialist economies from international market forces. To the weakest, least industrialized areas—Asian and African colonies, weak and dependent Latin American countries—the United States would promise development assistance, while the Soviet Union would advocate prosperity through socialist revolution.

Having undergone enormous industrial expansion during the war, the United States was in a much better position to aid its allies. The Soviet Union had suffered widespread destruction and was itself in need of reconstruction. So while the United States offered the Marshall Plan, the Soviets exploited their eastern European satellites economically. Entire factories were dismantled and moved from eastern Germany to the Soviet Union. While the United States could use a combination of military strength, diplomacy, and economic aid to gain allies during the Cold War, the Soviet Union more often relied on direct military control.

Both sides also expanded their intelligence operations, as international spy rings became a central Cold War feature. The Soviet spy agency, known by the initials KGB, worked through local proxies, such as the East German *Stasi*, to maintain tight control over its satellites while trying to infiltrate Western political, military, and intelligence communities. The United States formed the Central Intelligence Agency (CIA) out of its wartime intelligence service. This was the first time a U.S. government agency was dedicated to collecting foreign intelligence and engaging in covert operations overseas (see Chapter 30). One of the CIA's first operations paid Italian journalists to write negative stories about communist parliamentary candidates.

As we will see in the next two chapters, the Cold War divided the globe. Outside Europe, communist regimes took power in the People's Republic of China, the Democratic People's Republic of Korea, the Democratic Republic of Vietnam, and the Republic of Cuba. As British and French empires declined in

Asia and Africa, emerging new nations were often caught in the tension between the communist East and capitalist West. Some nations, such as India, were able to steer a middle course. But others, like Vietnam, Angola, Afghanistan, and Nicaragua, would be torn apart by Cold War rivalries. Two generations of humanity lived in the shadow of the Cold War, with the terrible knowledge that it could one day lead to a nuclear doomsday.

CONTEXT AND CONNECTIONS

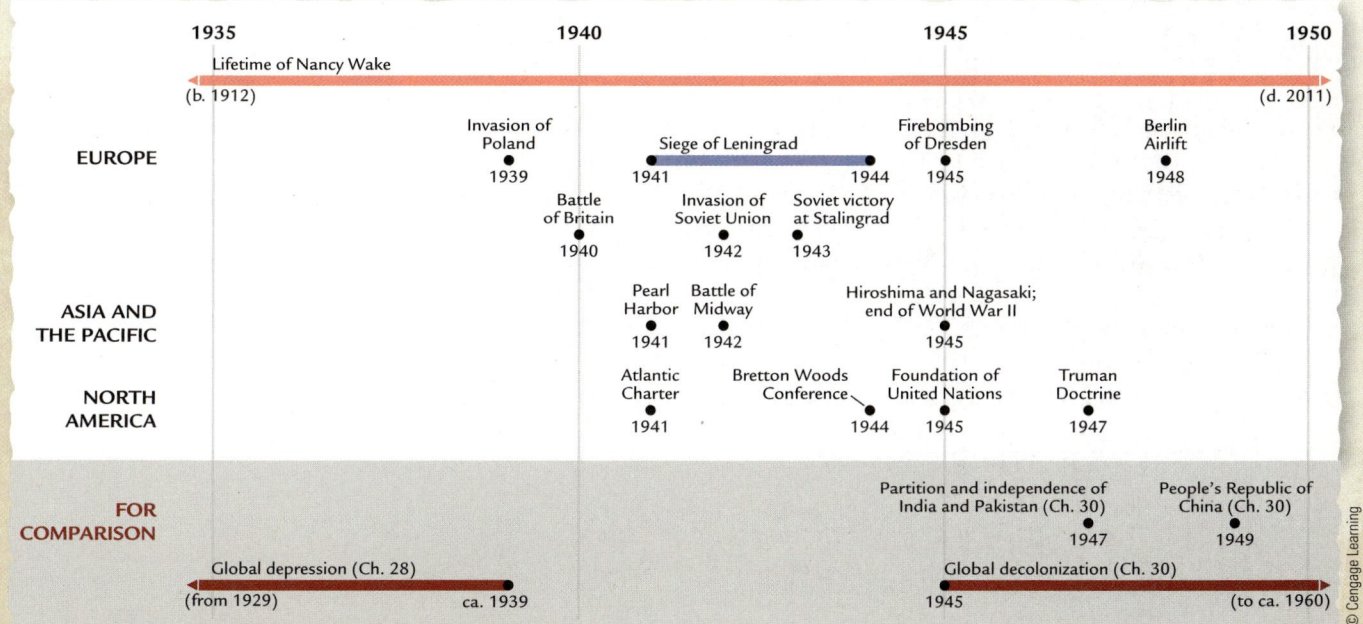

© Cengage Learning

Total War in World History

"The Second World War was the single most globalizing experience human beings have ever had." Hyperbole, perhaps, but it is difficult to think of any other series of events that have affected more people more deeply. The scale of death was unprecedented: more than 50 million all told. The number of lives sent onto entirely new trajectories in the first half of the 1940s is impossible to count. For Nancy Wake and many others who fought and survived, it was the defining period of their lives.

As the war years recede—Nancy Wake died in 2011, just weeks shy of her one-hundredth birthday—we are beginning to see the two world wars of the twentieth century as a single conflict, a single war during which hostilities were merely suspended.

Total war was the unifying theme. Both the earlier and later conflicts mobilized civilian populations as never before and hinged on the ability to sustain industrial production. In both, imperial rulers brought colonized peoples into the war. And in both, an alliance including Britain, France, the United States, and Russia battled a German-led coalition, including the Ottoman empire in the first war and Japan in the second.

The contrasts were in enlargement of scale, such as the development of a full-fledged theater of battle in East Asia during the second war. Technological developments were another contrast, with the rapidly moving fronts of the second war a marked difference from the static battle lines of the first one, and aerial bombardment now a key to success rather than a marginal tactic. Partly for that reason, civilians were much more likely to be in the direct line of fire in World War II. From China, Spain, and Ethiopia, through the London blitz, the firebombing of Dresden, and the nuclear nightmare of Hiroshima and Nagasaki, the intensity and terror of civilian bombardment increased year by year.

The Holocaust was a benchmark of evil. It was not unique: Hitler's "final solution" followed earlier twentieth-century genocides targeting the peoples of Southwest Africa and Armenians in the Ottoman empire (see Chapters 26 and 27), and it would not be the last attempt to annihilate a group of people, as later tragedies in Serbia, Cambodia, and Rwanda would show (see Chapter 31). But the Nazis' ruthlessly methodical machinery of slaughter was unprecedented, a nightmare execution of the racist logic of Social Darwinism and the purported "struggle for existence" that had for generations infected the world (see Chapters 23 and 26). The Holocaust did not, of course, cure the world of racism. But Hitler's madness was a wake-up call for humanity: at a terrible cost, racism lost much of its respectability.

Through both world wars, the international system had, in fact, been ordered around racial principles, with western Europeans in control of global empires that systematically denied rights of self-determination to colonized peoples in Africa and Asia. After 1945, that would quickly change. India, long the "jewel in the crown" of the British empire, became independent in 1947. In 1960, seventeen new African countries left the British and French empires to join the United Nations as sovereign states (see Chapter 30). But for many of the world's people, in places as diverse as Vietnam and the Congo, the road to freedom was complicated by the Cold War. The United States and the Soviet Union were unwilling to confront each other directly, since the prospect of nuclear annihilation was very real. Instead, the two sides sponsored proxy conflicts in Africa, Latin America, and Asia, undermining for decades the quest of the world's poorest and most disenfranchised for a better future. Still, however harsh the Cold War climate, the world's worst fears were never realized. Somehow, our species avoided nuclear self-destruction.

Voyages on the Web: Nancy Wake

The Voyages Map App follows the traveler's journeys using interactive study tools, including 360-degree panoramic views of historic sites, zoomable maps, audio summaries, flash cards, and quizzes.

Key Terms

Nancy Wake (824)
Axis powers (828)
Winston Churchill (828)
Charles de Gaulle (829)
Atlantic Charter (830)
Pearl Harbor (830)

Allied powers (831)
Siege of Leningrad (831)
Battle of Stalingrad (833)
Hiroshima and Nagasaki (835)
"Quit India" (841)
King's African Rifles (841)

Warsaw Ghetto Uprising (843)
United Nations (UN) (846)
Truman Doctrine (848)
Marshall Plan (849)
Bretton Woods Conference (850)

For Further Reference

Browning, Christopher. *The Origins of the Final Solution: The Evolution of Nazi Jewish Policy, 1939–1942*. Lincoln, Neb.: Bison Books, 2007.

Burleigh, Michael. *Third Reich: A New History*. New York: Hill and Wang, 2001.

Chang, Iris. *The Rape of Nanking*. New York: Basic Books, 2012.

Dower, John. *War Without Mercy: Race and Power in the Pacific War*. New York: Pantheon, 1987.

Dwork, Deborah, and Robert Jan Van Pelt. *Holocaust: A History*. New York: W. W. Norton, 2003.

Hastings, Max. *Inferno: The World at War, 1939–1945*. New York: Knopf, 2011.

Higgonet, Margaret, ed. *Behind the Lines: Gender and the Two World Wars*. New Haven: Yale University Press, 1989.

Iriye, Akira. *Power and Culture: The Japanese-American War, 1941–1945*. 2d ed. Cambridge, Mass.: Harvard University Press, 2004.

Keegan, John. *The Second World War*. New York: Penguin, 2005.

LeFeber, Walter. *The United States, Russia and the Cold War*. Updated ed. New York: McGraw-Hill, 2002.

Leffler, Melvyn P., and David S. Painter. *Origins of the Cold War: An International History*. 2d ed. New York: Routledge, 2005.

Mercatante, Stephen. *Why Germany Nearly Won: A New History of the Second World War in Europe*. Westport, Conn.: Praeger, 2012.

Morgan, Philip. *The Fall of Mussolini: Italy, the Italians, and the Second World War*. New York: Oxford University Press, 2007.

Osborne, Richard. *World War II in Colonial Africa: The Death Knell of Colonialism*. Indianapolis: Riebel-Roque, 2011.

Thurston, Robert W., and Bernd Bonwetsch, eds. *The People's War: Responses to World War II in the Soviet Union*. Champaign: University of Illinois Press, 2000.

Wake, Nancy. *The White Mouse*. Melbourne: Macmillan, 1986.

Yahil, Leni. *The Holocaust: The Fate of European Jewry*. New York: Schocken, 1987.

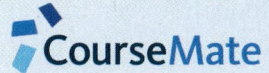 Go to the CourseMate website at **www.cengagebrain.com** for additional study tools and review materials—including audio and video clips—for this chapter.

30

The Cold War and Decolonization, 1949–1975

In 1952 Alberto Granado and **Ernesto Guevara** (1928–1967), two Argentine students with promising futures in medicine, decided to take an ambitious road trip across South America on an aging motorcycle. At first, their motive was fun and adventure, *"not setting down roots in any land or staying long enough to see the substratum of things; the outer surface would suffice."* Soon, however, their encounters with Indians, peasants, and miners changed the nature of Guevara's quest:

Ernesto ("Che") Guevara, 1960
(© Stefano Rellandini/Reuters/Corbis)

*W*e made friends with a [Chilean] couple. . . . In his simple, expressive language he recounted his three months in prison . . . his fruitless pilgrimage in search of work and his compañeros, *mysteriously disappeared and said to be somewhere at the bottom of the sea. The couple, numb with cold, huddling against each other in the desert night, was a living representation of the proletariat in any part of the world. They had not one single miserable blanket to cover themselves with, so we gave them one of ours and Alberto and I wrapped the other around us as best we could. . . . The communism gnawing at [their] entrails was no more than a natural longing for something better, a protest against persistent hunger transformed into a love for this strange doctrine, whose essence they could never grasp but whose translation, "bread for the poor," was something which they understood and, more importantly, filled them with hope.*[*]

[*]Ernesto Guevara, *The Motorcycle Diaries: Notes on a Latin American Journey,* ed. and trans. Alexandra Keeble (Melbourne: Ocean Press, 2003), pp. 75–78.

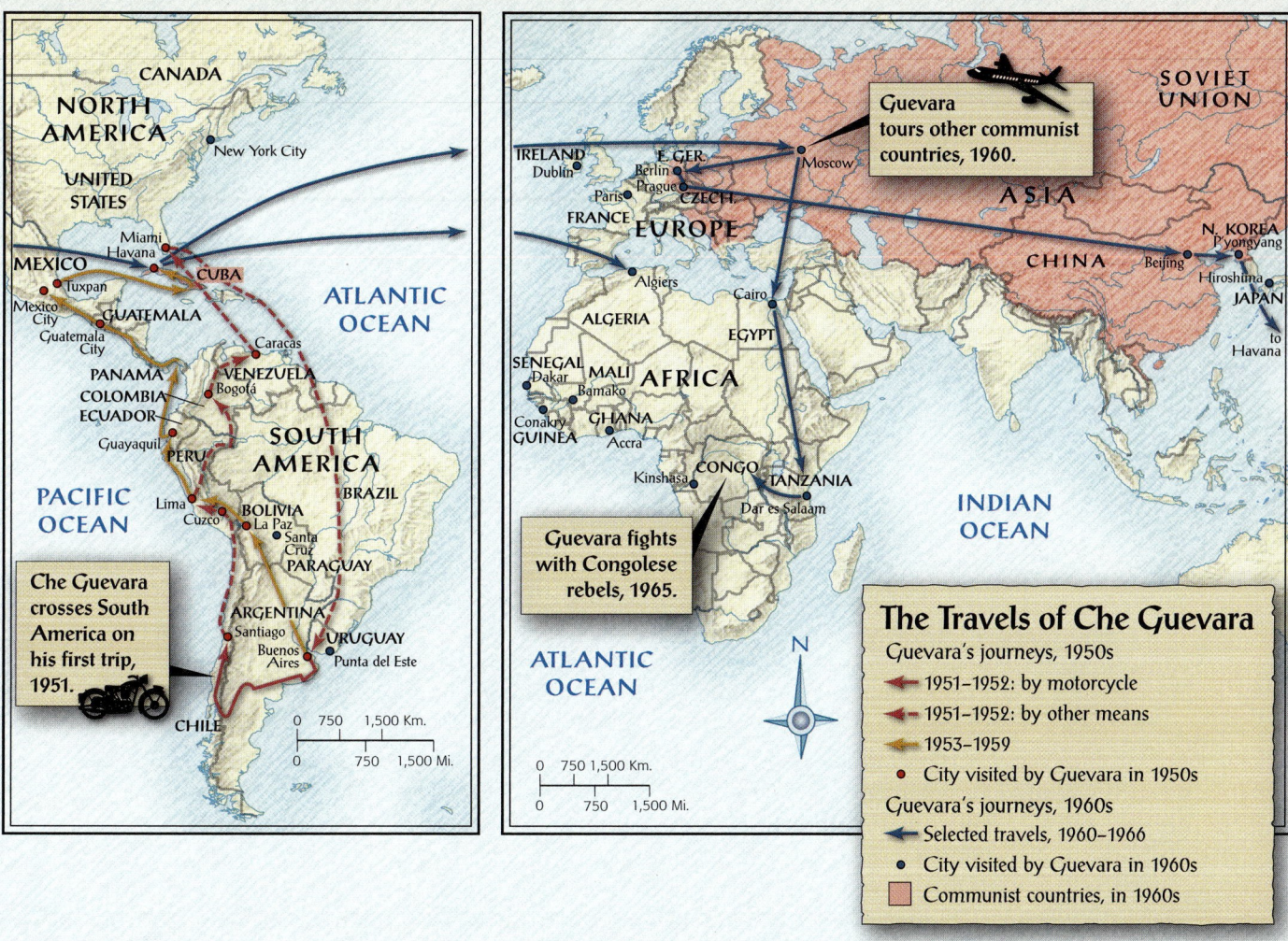

Guevara tours other communist countries, 1960.

Che Guevara crosses South America on his first trip, 1951.

Guevara fights with Congolese rebels, 1965.

The Travels of Che Guevara

Guevara's journeys, 1950s
- ← 1951–1952: by motorcycle
- ◄--- 1951–1952: by other means
- ← 1953–1959
- ● City visited by Guevara in 1950s

Guevara's journeys, 1960s
- ← Selected travels, 1960–1966
- ● City visited by Guevara in 1960s
- ▨ Communist countries, in 1960s

© Cengage Learning

Join this chapter's traveler on "Voyages," an interactive tour of historic sites and events: **www.cengagebrain.com**

By the time Ernesto returned to Buenos Aires, he was a different man and on the path to becoming "Che," the most charismatic of twentieth-century revolutionaries.

It took one more trip to change Guevara's path from that of an Argentine doctor to that of a professional revolutionary. After completing his degree, he set out on another road trip, this time with heightened political consciousness. While in Guatemala in 1954, he witnessed the overthrow of its democratically elected socialist government by a right-wing rebel army allied with the United States. Fearing arrest, Guevara fled to Mexico, where he met a group of Cuban exiles determined to overthrow their own dictator. Che joined them as a soldier and military commander, using guerrilla tactics such as quick raids and surprise ambushes to defeat the Cuban army. After the success of the Cuban Revolution in 1959, Che's fame spread around the world.

Ernesto Guevara (1928–1967) Argentinean socialist and revolutionary, called "Che," who played a crucial role in the Cuban Revolution. After serving as a Cuban government minister, he left to organize guerrilla campaigns in the Congo and Bolivia. He was executed in 1967 by the Bolivian army.

Guevara identified completely with the downtrodden, especially those in the "Third World." In 1952, a French journalist had pointed out the tripartite division of the postwar world. The capitalist United States and its allies constituted the wealthy First World, and the socialist Soviet Union and its allies were the Second World. The Third World, lacking in industry and with little voice in world affairs, made up two-thirds of the world's population. Guevara chose to speak and act on behalf of this disempowered majority, the people Frantz Fanon, another advocate of Third World revolution, called *"the wretched of the earth."*

Rather than settling down in socialist Cuba, Guevara pursued his dream of revolution in Africa and South America. In 1965 he traveled to the Congo and in 1967 to Bolivia, in both cases organizing guerrilla armies in the name of socialist revolution. But there were to be no more glorious victories: in 1967, Bolivian troops captured Che and executed him. Yet in death he became even more powerful and influential than in life. When his remains were discovered in 1998, they were sent to Cuba, where Che received a hero's burial. By then he had long been an icon of youth culture. The familiar image of "Che," reproduced on endless T-shirts and posters, became emblematic of the social and political idealism of the 1960s. As a symbol, Che was loved and admired, or hated and feared, by millions.

Guevara lived at the intersection of two great global struggles. One was the East-West division of the Cold War. The other was the North-South division between the global haves and have-nots. This was the age of decolonization, when many former colonies were moving toward national independence. Across Asia and Africa, mass political movements brought the possibility of positive change. But there, as in Latin America, the Cold War environment increased the risk that violence and authoritarianism would triumph over democracy and liberation. In many societies, the conflict between the Soviet Union and the United States dampened hopes for democracy and reinforced trends toward dictatorship.

This chapter explores the turbulent quarter century between 1949 and 1974, when dozens of new nations were born from the dissolution of European empires; when communist revolutionaries took power in mainland China; when the United States and the Soviet Union, the new "superpowers" of the Cold War era, faced off across a deep nuclear chasm; when antidemocratic political forces in strategic parts of the world found sponsorship from the American and Soviet governments; and when young people dreamed of transforming the world. For many, Che Guevara symbolized their dreams and their disappointments.

Focus Questions

» *What were the implications of successful revolutions in China and Cuba for the Cold War rivalry of the United States and the Soviet Union?*

» *How were democratization and decolonization movements in the mid-twentieth century affected by the Cold War?*

» *What was the role of youth in the global upheavals of 1965–1974?*

The Cold War and Revolution, 1949–1962

By the 1950s, the United States and Soviet Union were building huge arsenals of nuclear weapons, including hydrogen bombs many times more powerful than those dropped on Hiroshima and Nagasaki. Since any direct conflict between them threatened mutual annihilation, both sides were cautious not to push the other too far. Official U.S. policy remained one of "containment," of preventing an expansion of the Soviet sphere of influence but not intervening within it. Insults, propaganda, and espionage characterized U.S.-Soviet relations in Europe.

While the Cold War in Europe was a standoff, communist revolutions elsewhere increased the potential sphere of Soviet influence. In 1949, after the victory of the People's Army, Mao Zedong stood in Tiananmen Square in Beijing and declared the foundation of the People's Republic of China. Ten years later Fidel Castro and Che Guevara led a rebel army into Havana and founded a socialist government in Cuba, an island just 90 miles (145 km) from Florida. From the perspective of anticommunists in the United States and elsewhere, the "Soviet menace" was increasing.

The People's Republic of China, 1949–1962

Almost immediately after Japan's defeat, the competition between Chiang Kai-shek's Guomindang and Mao Zedong's Chinese Communist Party for control of China resumed (see Chapter 28). By the time war ended in 1949, the Communists were in charge of the People's Republic of China on the mainland, and Chiang Kai-shek and his Nationalist followers fled to the island of Taiwan, where they established the Republic of China (see Map 30.1).

The Communists succeeded even though the Nationalists started with a larger army, a stockpile of weapons supplied by the Allies during World War II, and control of China's largest cities. Mao's army had cultivated support among the Chinese peasantry while fighting Japanese invaders, and the People's Liberation Army had become a tough, disciplined organization. Mao used his popular base to his advantage, telling his soldiers to *"swim like fishes in the sea"* of rural China, camouflaging their activities amid the routines of village life. Since the People's Liberation Army treated Chinese peasants with greater respect than Chiang's Guomindang, they rode mass support to success.

Once in power, the Communists revolutionized China from the bottom up. They organized peasants into agricultural cooperatives, expanded educational opportunities, indoctrinated young people in youth organizations guided by the party, and enrolled workers in state-sponsored trade unions. Within the unions, the army, and other mass organizations, mandatory "thought reform" sessions focused on the study of "Mao Zedong Thought." Those accused of deviation from socialist thought were shamed and forced to publicly confess their "errors."

As under the Jacobins and Bolsheviks during earlier revolutions in France and Russia (see Chapters 22 and 27), external threats justified repressive policies. At the end of World War II, the Korean peninsula had been divided between a Soviet-backed Democratic Republic of Korea in the north and an American-allied Republic of Korea in the south. The Korean War (1950–1953) began when North Korea attacked the south. When the United States rushed to defend its South Korean ally, the mainland Chinese government feared that the United States intended to attack them as well. The People's Liberation Army then threw its massive forces

MAP 30.1 China and Taiwan After World War II, the Communist forces of Mao Zedong took the offensive against the Guomindang, or Nationalist army, of Chiang Kai-shek. The Nationalists were driven off the mainland to the island of Taiwan. In Beijing, Mao declared the creation of the People's Republic of China on October 1, 1949. The Communists and Nationalists agreed that there was only "one China," and their continuing animosity became another zone of conflict in the global Cold War. (© Cengage Learning)

into battle to reinforce the north. In the end, the south fended off invasion, but stalemate ensued along the demilitarized zone that separated the communist regime in North Korea, which allowed no freedom at all, from the stern authoritarian regime in South Korea, which allowed very little.

Initially, the People's Republic of China followed Soviet-style economic policies of state-run heavy industry and collective farming. In 1953, the Chinese adopted a Five-Year Plan and sent engineers and state planners to Russia for training. But the results were disappointing. Not only was the growth of production slower than Mao expected, but the dull, bureaucratic socialism of the U.S.S.R. did little to inspire him. Mao felt that the fire was going out of the revolution.

He decided to shake things up. In 1956, Mao launched a public call for new ideas, using the phrase *"Let a hundred flowers bloom."* China's intellectuals responded by openly criticizing the Communist Party, and even Mao himself. Either the criticism was more than Mao had expected, or perhaps he had intended all along to trick opponents out into the open, but during the savage repression of 1957, intellectuals were arrested, imprisoned, and exiled. Independent thinking was now a "rightist" deviation to be purged.

Mao saw the Communist Party as divided into two factions, which he labeled "red" and "expert." The "experts" in charge of agricultural collectivization and industrial development were becoming an elite cut off from the masses. The "red" leadership, emphasizing socialist willpower rather than technical ability, would help China catch up with the world's dominant economic powers. If only the true revolutionary potential of China's peasants and workers could be unleashed, Mao thought, the people could move mountains.

In 1958 Mao launched the **Great Leap Forward**, decreeing that the agricultural collectives should be harnessed for industrial development. Rather than relying on large steel factories, revolutionaries would set up small furnaces all across the country. The "masses" were directed to pour all their energy and enthusiasm into communal production. Meanwhile, property rights were restricted, and peasants lost access to the small plots they relied on to feed their families.

The Great Leap Forward was disastrous. The steel produced in small communal furnaces was virtually useless, and food production suffered as the farm workers wasted their energies on Mao's inefficient scheme. As many as 30 million people died in the famine that ensued. By 1961, the failure of the Great Leap Forward led the more pragmatic "experts" in the Communist Party to reduce Mao's authority behind the scenes (still publicly acknowledging his leadership) while reinstating rationality to economic planning.

Still, Mao's belief in the power of revolutionary enthusiasm would inspire a younger generation who wanted to believe that their passion for justice would allow humanity to take a "great leap forward." Che Guevara was among those attracted to the Chinese model as an alternative to both capitalism and the stodgy Soviet model of technocratic socialism.

Great Leap Forward (1958) Mao Zedong's attempt to harness the revolutionary zeal of the Chinese masses for rapid industrialization. The result was a massive economic collapse and millions of deaths from famine.

The Cuban Revolution and the Cuban Missile Crisis

In the 1950s, Cuba was an island of contrasts. Its capital, Havana, was famous for its beaches and nightclubs, where its mambo musicians fused the nation's African and Latin musical traditions. But while Cuban culture was vibrant, there was a dark side as well. The Mafia controlled Havana's casinos, and prostitution flourished. Havana was a playground for wealthy tourists, and the Cuban dictator Fulgencio Batista, supported by American business interests, allowed no democratic freedoms. Most

Cubans, the poorest of them descendants of slaves, had no access to good employment, health care, or education. They lived in desperate poverty.

Fidel Castro (b. 1926), like Ernesto Guevara, was an idealistic young man who renounced middle-class privilege in the name of revolution. In 1953, he was imprisoned for leading an attack on an army barracks, and after his release in 1955 he went into exile in Mexico City. There he formed a deep friendship with Che Guevara, newly arrived from Guatemala, where the overthrow of the democratically elected socialist government had been accomplished with the backing of the U.S. **Central Intelligence Agency (CIA)**. Che joined Castro's small rebel band for military training at a nearby secret base.

In 1956, Castro and Guevara left by boat for Cuba, finding sanctuary in the island's Sierra Maestra Mountains. Gradually they stockpiled ammunition by attacking police stations and military barracks, at the same time attracting recruits from the peasant population, whose assistance enabled them to outmaneuver their government pursuers. During two years of hard fighting, Che's medical background proved useful in tending wounded colleagues, but his most important role was as commander and tactician. Conditions were ruthless, and Guevara had no second thoughts about executing suspected government agents. Summary executions without trial or legal defense were common. Guevara himself often pulled the trigger. By 1958, the rebels were poised to attack Havana, and on New Year's Day 1959 Batista fled when Castro's forces marched triumphantly into the capital.

Neither Castro nor Guevara had ever joined the Cuban Communist Party, and many Cubans expected that the new government would redistribute wealth through a combination of socialist economics and liberal politics. But "defense of the revolution" rather than protection of civil liberties quickly became the focal point of Castro's government. The new leaders faced the threat of counterrevolution, as the pro-Batista forces that had fled to the United States lobbied for an American-backed invasion.

Initially, President Dwight Eisenhower (in office 1953–1961) hoped that Castro might be someone he could work with, and the Cuban leader toured Washington and New York seeking both public and official support. But relations deteriorated after Cuba's Agrarian Reform Law nationalized land owned by American corporations. Both corporate lobbyists and Cold War hawks soon portrayed Castro as a Soviet threat on America's doorstep. As tensions increased, Castro sent Che Guevara to Moscow and Beijing to shore up support for his regime, while the Eisenhower administration drew up plans for invasion.

In the spring of 1961, a U.S.-sponsored group of Cuban exiles stormed ashore at the island's Bay of Pigs. The new American president, John F. Kennedy (in office 1961–1963), having had strong doubts about their prospects for success, had given the Cuban counter-revolutionaries only lukewarm support. Their invasion was a debacle and validated Castro's distrust of U.S. intentions, pushing him toward more repressive policies. In addition, the United States placed an economic embargo on Cuba that made diplomacy and compromise all but impossible. Castro turned to the Soviet Union for support.

In the fall of 1962, tensions climaxed during one of the most frightening events in modern history: the **Cuban Missile Crisis**. Convinced that the United States would never let his socialist experiment proceed in peace, Castro developed ever-closer ties with the Soviet Union. Soviet premier Nikita Khrushchev (KHROOS-chev) took advantage of the situation to secretly ship nuclear missiles to Cuba. Khrushchev's action was an unusual, and very dangerous, departure from the Soviets' policy of focusing on the security of their own borders and avoiding provocations within

Fidel Castro (b. 1926) Cuban prime minister from 1959 to 1976 and president from 1976 to 2008. Led the successful Cuban Revolution in 1959, after which his nationalization policies led to deteriorating relations with the United States and increasing dependence on Soviet support.

Central Intelligence Agency (CIA) U.S. federal agency created in 1947 whose responsibilities include coordinating intelligence activities abroad as well as conducting covert operations—for example, against the Soviet Union and its allies during the Cold War.

Cuban Missile Crisis Tense 1962 confrontation between the United States and the Soviet Union over placement of nuclear missiles in Cuba. A compromise led to withdrawal of Soviet missiles from Cuba and of American missiles from Turkey.

the American sphere of influence. When American surveillance aircraft detected the missiles, Kennedy presented Khrushchev with an ultimatum: withdraw the missiles, or prepare for war. As the world stood on the brink of nuclear war, both sides blinked: Khrushchev agreed to remove Soviet missiles from Cuba, Kennedy quietly agreed to remove U.S. missiles from Turkey, and the world's people breathed a sigh of relief.

Feeling more vulnerable than ever, Castro threw himself into an even tighter alliance with Moscow. To help Cuba withstand the American trade embargo, the Soviets agreed to buy the island's entire sugar output at above-market prices and to subsidize the socialist transformation of the island with cheap fuel and agricultural machinery. By the mid-1960s, Cubans were better fed and better housed than they had been before the revolution; they also had free access to basic health care and were more likely to be able to read and write.

But underlying economic problems remained. As was common in Latin America, Cuba had long been a dependent economy, exporting agricultural produce (mostly sugar and tobacco) while importing higher-valued industrial goods. With the Soviet Union as an economic patron, Cuba's reliance on agricultural exports was as strong as ever. Economic development was further hampered by the Soviet-style command economy installed by Castro, characterized by bureaucratic inefficiency and low worker morale.

When Cuban workers agitated for higher wages, Che Guevara, as minister for industry, told them to be content with knowing that their hard work supported the glorious cause of socialism. Himself willing to work long hours for almost no material reward, Guevara thought that others should do the same. But without material rewards for workers or incentives to inspire creativity and entrepreneurship, the Cuban economy settled into lethargy. Fidel Castro's verbose four-hour speeches exhorting Cubans to rally around his slogan *"Socialism or Death!"* did nothing to help workers facing shortages of basic goods.

With "defense of the revolution" taking priority, as in the French and Russian revolutions, leaders set aside early promises of democratic liberties and equated dissent with treason. Castro's government viewed all opposition to its policies as emanating from the United States and the hostile community of Cuban émigrés in Florida. Authorities on the island executed hundreds and sent thousands to prison labor camps based on the Soviet model. Guevara, still viewing himself as a soldier even while he served as a government minister, regarded such repression as the cost of war against capitalism and American imperialism.

A romantic revolutionary idealist, Guevara could not abide the endless meetings and plodding pace of government. The country's reliance on the Soviet Union bothered him, too, his distrust heightened by the brutal Soviet suppression of popular uprisings in eastern Europe. In 1965 he left for Africa to pursue his revolutionary dreams on a global stage.

Spheres of Influence: Old Empires and New Superpowers

The Cuban Missile Crisis illustrated the dangers of one superpower intervening in the other's sphere of influence. Usually such interventions took place within a superpower's own strategic domain, as when the United States helped overthrow the democratically elected government of Guatemala in 1953 or Soviet tanks crushed a prodemocracy uprising in Hungary in 1956.

But much of the world lay outside either sphere. In Asia and Africa, European empires were supplanted by decolonization movements. How would these new nations fit into the international system? In some countries, especially in Africa, colonial powers managed to retain substantial influence even after national independence. Elsewhere, however, the power vacuum created by the decline of European empires meant that new African and Asian nations were caught up in the tensions stoked by the global bipolarity of the Cold War. Some, like the Congo and Vietnam, were pulled apart in the process.

Recognizing the danger that the superpower rivalry posed to recently decolonized nations, in 1955 a group of African and Asian leaders met to discuss ways to defend their sovereignty. Their goal in founding the Non-Aligned Movement was to avoid both neocolonial influence from Europe and, by refusing to associate themselves with either the Soviet Union or the United States, to avoid superpower intervention in their affairs. It was not a simple goal to achieve. After the French withdrawal from Vietnam, the intervention of the United States against communist forces led by Ho Chi Minh (see Chapter 27) showed how the decline of European power could lead to superpower intervention.

Superpower Interventions, 1953–1956

During the Cold War, the United States allied with the European democracies and Turkey in the North Atlantic Treaty Organization (NATO), and the Soviet Union countered with the Warsaw Pact allying eastern European nations under its sway. Both superpowers presented themselves as champions of freedom. Of course, they had different interpretations of what that meant. The Soviets, identifying colonialism and imperialism as the main barriers to liberation, supported nationalists in the Third World who were fighting to throw off European colonialism, as well as socialists fighting against American political and economic domination in Latin America. But Moscow would not tolerate similar liberation movements within its own sphere. In the Soviet Union and its satellites (see Map 30.2), movements toward self-determination and freedom of speech, association, or religion were brutally crushed.

In eastern Europe, extensive secret police networks were usually enough to keep people from openly expressing anticommunist or anti-Soviet views. In East Germany, for example, the *Stasi* planted informers at all levels of society and encouraged neighbors to spy on neighbors. But after the death of Stalin in 1953, some eastern Europeans, and even some Russians, saw an opportunity for reform when the Soviet leader, Nikita Khrushchev (in office 1953–1964), denounced the excesses of Stalinism at a Communist Party congress. Nevertheless, while Khrushchev preached limited reform, he would not tolerate popular movements for change.

When East German authorities and Soviet forces crushed demonstrations in East Berlin, it became clear that communist rule was based more on Soviet coercion than popular legitimacy. Over the next eight years, thousands of East Berliners fled to the West. Finally, in 1961, East Germany constructed the Berlin Wall to fence its people in. Now Churchill's metaphoric "iron curtain" took physical shape.

The people of Poland detested the pro-Moscow government imposed on them by Stalin after the war. Being predominantly Catholic, they resented the official atheism of the communist state. In 1956, a religious gathering attended by a million Poles turned into an antigovernment demonstration. Here the Soviet government compromised, allowing reforms such as an end to the collectivization of agriculture and some religious freedom. But it was clear that attempts to further weaken Poland's ties to the Soviet Union would not be tolerated.

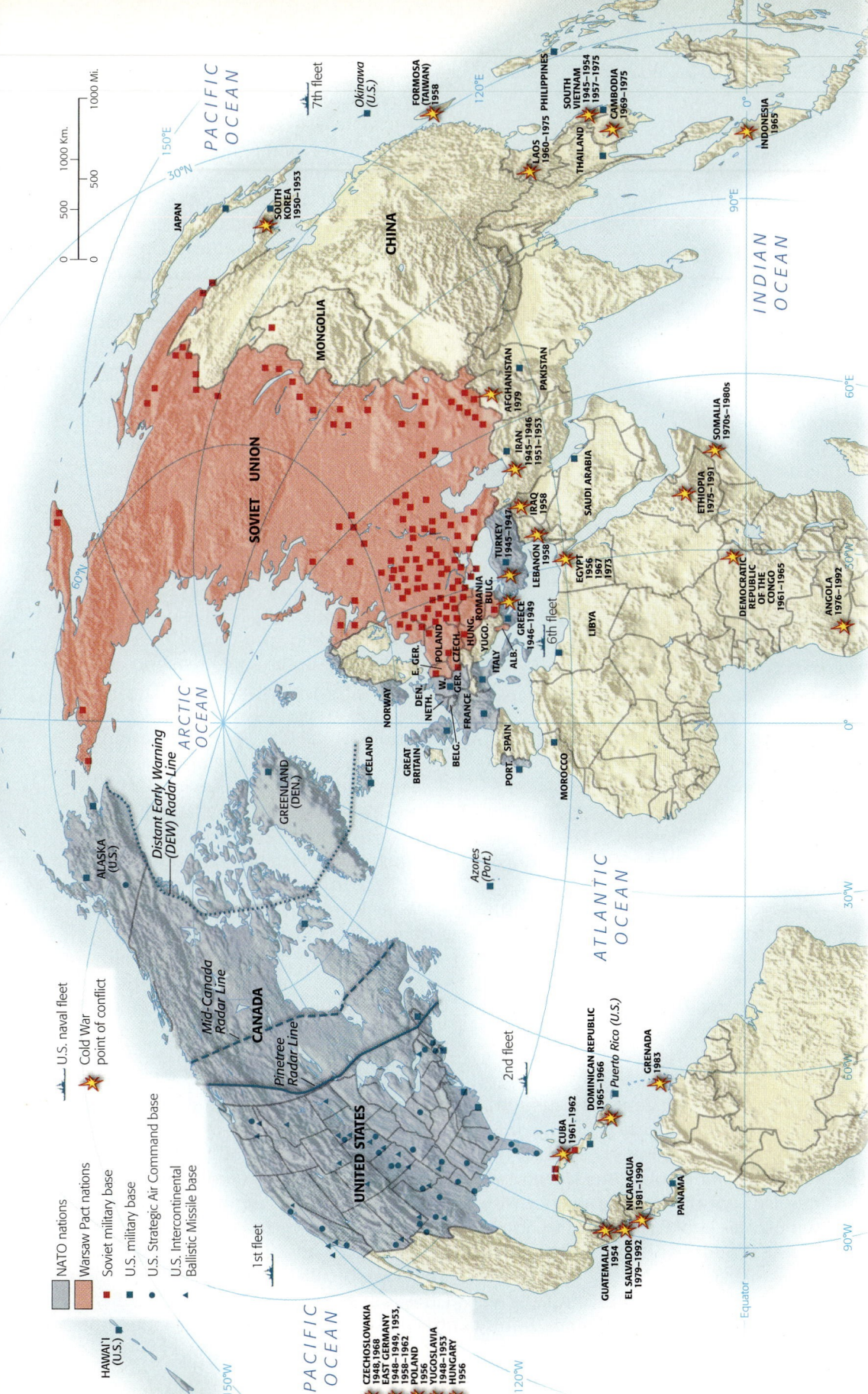

MAP 30.2 Cold War Confrontations Two military alliances, the North Atlantic Treaty Organization (NATO) led by the United States, and the Warsaw Pact dominated by the Soviet Union, were the principal antagonists in the Cold War. Fearful of mutual nuclear annihilation, however, they never engaged in direct combat. Instead, the Cold War turned hot in proxy struggles around the world—in Central America and the Caribbean, Africa, the Middle East, and Southeast and East Asia. (© Cengage Learning)

Legend:

NATO nations
Warsaw Pact nations
Soviet military base
U.S. military base
U.S. Strategic Air Command base
U.S. Intercontinental Ballistic Missile base
U.S. naval fleet
Cold War point of conflict

CZECHOSLOVAKIA 1948, 1968
EAST GERMANY 1948–1949, 1953, 1958–1962
POLAND 1956
YUGOSLAVIA 1948–1953
HUNGARY 1956

Laszlo Almasi/Reuters/Landov

The Hungarian Uprising A rebellion against their communist regime brought thousands of Hungarians onto the streets of Budapest in 1956, provoking a Soviet invasion. The Hungarians showed great courage in confronting Soviet tanks and troops, but they were bitterly disappointed when the United States and NATO provided no military support for their freedom struggle.

Hungarian Uprising (1956) Popular revolt against the Soviet-controlled government of Hungary, leading to a Soviet invasion and reimposition of communist authority.

The **Hungarian Uprising** showed the seriousness of the situation. In 1956 Hungarian students, factory workers, and middle-class professionals rose up to protest the Soviet-imposed communist dictatorship. The Hungarian government collapsed, and though leaders of the new provisional government feared a Soviet invasion, they expected support from the Western democracies. Despite Voice of America broadcasts encouraging rebellion, however, the United States failed to intervene, considering the danger of nuclear confrontation with the Soviets to be too great. Soviet tanks rolled in and crushed the Hungarian revolt with mass arrests and executions.

Americans were quick to point out the obvious contradiction between Soviet rhetoric, which equated socialism with democracy, and the Soviet practice of suppressing freedom. But U.S. practices were also at odds with American ideals. By the early 1950s, the tensions of the Cold War were leading many Americans to develop an almost paranoid fear of the Soviet Union, an attitude stoked by Senator Joseph McCarthy with his accusations of communist infiltration into the country's government. Since communism was evil, many thought, anyone who opposed Marxism-Leninism must be on the side of "freedom." The reality was that the anticommunist regimes backed by the United States were often authoritarian dictatorships.

Covert actions of the CIA often assisted authoritarian leaders who were willing to support American interests. Iran was one example. In the early 1950s, Shah Muhammad Reza Pahlavi (pahl-AH-vee), a constitutional monarch, aspired to greater power. He was checked by the Iranian parliament, led by a popular prime minister, Muhammad Mossadegh (MOH-sah-DEHK). Pahlavi, an ardent anticommunist, cultivated a close alliance with the United States. The Eisenhower administration was concerned that the Soviet Union, which had occupied northern Iran during World War II, still had designs on these oil-rich lands.

For their part, Mossadegh and his parliamentary allies were upset that Britain's Anglo-Iranian Oil Company reaped the lion's share of Iranian oil profits. Mossadegh tried to renegotiate Iran's contracts, and when negotiations failed he made plans to nationalize the oil industry. In 1953 the Iranian military, with the covert support of the CIA, arrested Mossadegh, expanding the shah's authority and fatally weakening the chances for a more democratic Iranian future. Many Iranians now saw their king as an American puppet.

The next year the United States undermined democracy in Guatemala in a similar fashion. Like other Central American countries, Guatemala had long been ruled by authoritarian dictators and had an economy dominated by foreign corporations, especially the United Fruit Company, an American company that owned vast banana plantations, the only railroad, the only port, and the country's telephone system. A small Guatemalan elite benefited, but the country was a study in inequality: 72 percent of the land was owned by 2 percent of the population.

During World War II reformist army officers seized control and organized elections. In 1946, the new democratic government promised land and labor reform, its leader arguing that democracy could not flourish in a country where resources were concentrated in so few hands. After another election in 1950, the new president, **Jacobo Arbenz** (1913–1971), reaffirmed those reformist policies. But the Eisenhower administration, thinking that the Arbenz government had been penetrated by Soviet agents, invoked the "domino theory," claiming that the "loss" of Guatemala would lead to communist victories elsewhere in the Americas. With United Fruit using high-level connections to lobby for action, the CIA supported a rebel leader who overthrew Arbenz in 1954. Guatemala's brief experiment with democracy was over as the country reverted to a dictatorship in the caudillo style.

Witnessing the overthrow of the Guatemalan government was a turning point in the life of Ernesto Guevara, who thereafter dedicated himself to revolution. Though he distrusted the Soviet Union, his experience in Central America convinced him that the United States was the greater evil.

Jacobo Arbenz (1913–1971) President of Guatemala from 1951 to 1954. A moderate socialist, Arbenz enacted comprehensive land reforms that angered Guatemalan elites and U.S. corporations. He was deposed by rebel forces backed by the United States.

Decolonization and Neocolonialism in Africa, 1945–1964

During World War II, Africans became more aware of the wider world and increasingly dissatisfied with their colonial status. The French, British, and Belgians underestimated African sentiments; entering the 1950s, colonial officials thought they were in Africa to stay. Yet by 1960, nationalist movements had freed most of the continent from colonial rule and many new African nations had been established (see Map 30.3). The Swahili word *uhuru* (oo-HOO-roo), "freedom," was heard around the world, and **Kwame Nkrumah** (1909–1972), the first president of independent Ghana after 1957, became an international symbol of African aspirations and Pan-Africanism.

But reaping the fruits of independence proved difficult. For one thing, the economic structures of colonialism remained. Economic development required capital and expertise, and both had to be imported. This situation created ideal conditions for neocolonialism: the continuation of European dominance even after independence had been attained.

The French government was a clever practitioner of neocolonialism. Even before independence, the French had laid the foundations for neocolonial control of their former African colonies. Colonial policies of "assimilation" held out the promise of French citizenship for educated Africans, creating an African elite that identified strongly with French culture. Appealing to their sentiments and responding to the rise of nationalism in the French African empire, in 1958 President Charles de Gaulle

Kwame Nkrumah (1909–1972) One of the most prominent post-war African nationalists, he emphasized Pan-African unity while leading Ghana to independence in 1957.

MAP 30.3 Decolonization In the three decades following Indian independence in 1947, the European colonial empires in Asia and Africa unraveled, adding many new "Third World" representatives to the United Nations. Their aspirations toward dignity and development were frequently thwarted, however, by Cold War politics, continued Western economic domination, poor leadership, and ethnic and religious rivalries. (© Cengage Learning)

announced a referendum to be held across French Africa. A "yes" vote meant that the former French colonies would receive control over their own internal affairs but would remain part of a larger French "community" directed from Paris. The French government would retain control over economic policy, foreign affairs, and the military. A "no" vote meant complete and immediate independence, severing all ties to France.

All but one of the colonies voted to become members of the French community. The exception was Guinea, where a radical trade union leader, Sekou Toure (SEY-koo TOO-rey), campaigned for complete independence. The French government responded to Guinea's "no" vote by withdrawing their administrators overnight, stopping economic aid, and even ripping telephones from the walls as they vacated their offices. The French message was clear: play by our rules, or suffer the consequences. Other African leaders learned the lesson and cooperated with France. There were actually more French soldiers in the Ivory Coast after independence than before. With their currencies pegged to the value of the French franc, new nations such as Senegal and Mali had little control over their own economic policies.

Elsewhere, Africans were forced to take up arms to liberate themselves, especially where Europeans had come not just as rulers but also as settlers. For instance, over a million French men and women lived in Algeria. After the Second World War, Algerian nationalists, some of whom had fought for de Gaulle's Free French Army, demanded rights equal to those of French settlers and a voice in their own governance. Harshly repressed, these nationalists formed the National Liberation Front (FLN—the French acronym) and, in 1954, began their armed struggle. It was a brutal war, with the FLN sometimes launching terrorist attacks on French civilians and the French military systematically using torture in its counterinsurgency campaign. Over time, French public opinion soured on the violence, and in 1962 an agreement recognizing Algerian independence was finally negotiated. (See the feature "Movement of Ideas Through Primary Sources: *The Wretched of the Earth*.")

Like Algeria, Kenya in East Africa was a country with a large settler population. The main nationalist leader, Jomo Kenyatta (JOH-moh ken-YAH-tuh; see Chapter 28), hoped to develop a mass organization to force the British into negotiations. But a group of African rebels took a more militant stand, forming a secret society, stealing arms from police stations, assassinating a collaborationist chief, and naming themselves the Land and Freedom Army. The British called them the Mau Mau and depicted them as "savages" who had returned to a "primitive" state of irrationality. Hopelessly outgunned by colonial forces, the rebels used their knowledge

Bettmann/Corbis

Ghana's Independence In 1957 the British colony of the Gold Coast in Africa led the way toward continental decolonization when it became the independent state of Ghana, named after an ancient African kingdom. Here Prime Minister Kwame Nkrumah (KWAH-may n-KROO-mah) waves to a massive crowd during Ghana's independence ceremony. Nkrumah provided support for other anticolonial movements on the continent, and through his emphasis on Pan-Africanism, became a spokesman for the ambitions of people of African descent around the world.

The Wretched of the Earth

Frantz Fanon (1925–1961) was an advocate of Third World revolution, guerrilla warfare, and socialism. Born on the Caribbean island of Martinique in the French West Indies, Fanon volunteered for service in the Free French Army and was wounded during the liberation of France in 1944. After training in Paris as a psychiatrist, he was stationed in North Africa. During the Algerian war Fanon's medical practice included psychiatric treatment of both French practitioners and Arab and Berber victims of torture. From this experience he concluded that colonialism was intrinsically violent and could only be removed by violence. He joined the Algerian National Liberation Front and became a prominent spokesman for their cause. Fanon was dying of leukemia in 1961 while writing his most bitter indictment of colonialism, *The Wretched of the Earth* (1961).

Sources: From Frantz Fanon, *The Wretched of the Earth* (New York: Grove, 1963), pp. 36, 39–41, 43, 45, 59, 61, 312, 315–316. Reprinted by permission; David Macy, *Frantz Fanon* (New York: Picador, 2000), p. 483.

Decolonization is the meeting of two forces, opposed to each other by their very nature. . . . Their first encounter was marked by violence and their existence together—that is to say the exploitation of the native by the settler—was carried on by dint of a great array of bayonets and cannons. . . .

The naked truth of decolonization evokes for us the searing bullets and bloodstained knives which emanate from it. For if the last shall be first, this will only come to pass after a murderous and decisive struggle between the two protagonists. . . .

The settlers' town is a strongly built town, all made of stone and steel. It is a brightly lit town; the streets are all covered with asphalt, and the garbage cans swallow all the leavings, unseen, unknown, and hardly thought about. . . . The settlers' town is a town of white people, of foreigners. . . .

The native town is a hungry town, starved for bread, of meat, of shoes, of coal, of light. The native town is a crouching village, a town on its knees, a town wallowing in the mire. . . . The look that the native turns on the settlers' town is a look of lust, a look of envy; it expresses his dreams of possession—all manner of possession: to sit at the settler's table, to sleep in the settler's bed, with his wife if possible. The colonized man is an envious man. . . .

The violence which has ruled over the ordering of the colonial world, which has ceaselessly drummed the rhythm for the destruction of native social forms and broken up without reserve the systems of reference of the economy . . . that same violence will be claimed and taken over by the native at the moment when, deciding to embody history in his own person, he surges into the forbidden quarters. . . .

As if to show the totalitarian character of colonial exploitation the settler paints the native as the quintessence of evil. Native society is not simply described as a society lacking in values. . . . The native is declared insensible to ethics; he represents not only the absence of values, but the negation of values . . . and in this sense he is the absolute evil. . . .

The violence with which the supremacy of white values is affirmed and the aggressiveness which has permeated the victory of these values over the ways of life and thought of the native mean that, in revenge, the native laughs in mockery when Western values are mentioned in front of him. . . . In the period of decolonization, the colonized masses mock at these very values, insult them, and vomit them up. . . .

[When the urban militants] get into the habit of talking to the peasants they discover that the rural masses have never ceased to pose the problem of their liberation in terms of violence, of taking back the land from the foreigners, in terms of a national struggle. Everything is simple. . . . They discover a generous people prepared to make sacrifices, willing to give of itself, impatient and with a stony pride. One can understand that the encounter between militants who are being hunted by the police and these impatient masses, who are instinctually rebellious, can produce an explosive mixture of unexpected power. . . .

Come, then, comrades, the European game has finally ended; we must find something different. We today can do everything so long as we do not imitate Europe, so long as we are not obsessed with desire to catch up with Europe. . . . European achievements, European techniques, and European style ought to no longer tempt us and to throw us off our balance.

When I search for Man in the technique and style of Europe, I see only a succession of negations of man, and an avalanche of murders. . . . It is a question of the Third World starting a new history of Man, a history which will have regard to the sometimes prodigious theses Europe has put forward, but which will also not forget Europe's crimes. . . . For Europe, for ourselves, for humanity, comrades, we must turn over a new leaf, we must work out new concepts, and try to set afoot a new man.

QUESTIONS FOR ANALYSIS

» *What is similar and what is different between Fanon's ideas and those of Mohandas K. Gandhi (see Chapter 28)?*

» *What is Fanon's critique of European society, and how does he find hope in Third World revolution?*

of the forest and the support of the local population to carry on their fight. By the late 1950s the Kenyan rebellion was contained, after over twelve thousand Africans and one hundred Europeans had been killed. The British government was now determined to make the settlers compromise with moderate African nationalists. In 1964, Jomo Kenyatta became the first president of an independent Kenya.

In southern Africa, compromise between white settlers and African nationalists was impossible. The white settlers of Rhodesia declared their independence from Britain in 1965 rather than enter into negotiations over sharing power, while in South Africa the apartheid regime was deeply entrenched. Because the Rhodesian and South African leaders were adamantly anticommunist, governments in London and Washington were usually willing to overlook their repressive policies. In response, the African National Congress, led by Nelson Mandela (see Chapter 31), had abandoned its traditional policy of nonviolence by beginning a sabotage campaign. When Mandela was arrested on charges of treason and sentenced to life in prison in 1964, hopes for transforming South Africa were at an all-time low.

Once they realized that the "winds of change" were blowing in the direction of African independence (a term used by the British prime minister in 1960 to acknowledge the inevitability of decolonization), the British and French managed the process without superpower intervention. Tragically, the same could not be said of Belgium, as the new Democratic Republic of the Congo descended into anarchy and became the site of a proxy war between the United States and the Soviet Union.

After King Leopold's reign (see Chapter 26), the Belgian government had created a tightly centralized, racially divided colonial administration. They did little to prepare Africans for independence: after eighty years of Belgian rule, only sixteen Africans in the entire Congo had university degrees. Still, with the Congo caught up in the nationalist excitement spreading across the continent, in 1960 the Belgians made hasty plans for independence, believing that the weakness of the new Congolese government would make it susceptible to neocolonial control.

Patrice Lumumba
(1925–1961) The first prime minister of the Democratic Republic of the Congo in 1960. He was deposed and assassinated by political rivals in 1961.

The Congolese National Movement won the election, and a government was formed by Prime Minister **Patrice Lumumba** (loo-MOOM-buh) (1925–1961). The independence ceremony in 1960 was fraught with tension. After the Belgian king made a patronizing speech praising his country's "civilizing mission" in Africa, Lumumba responded with a catalogue of Belgian crimes against Africans. *"Our wounds,"* he said, *"are still too fresh and painful for us to be able to erase them from our memories."* The speech made Lumumba a hero to African nationalists, but he was now regarded as a dangerous radical in Brussels and Washington.

Lumumba faced immediate challenges. African soldiers mutinied against their Belgian officers, and the mineral-rich province of Katanga seceded. When the United Nations sent in peacekeeping forces, Lumumba suspected their real purpose was to defend Western mining interests. After turning to the Soviet Union for military aid, Lumumba was branded a "communist," and—with the complicity of the CIA—he was arrested, beaten, and murdered by rivals. Rebel armies arose in several provinces. Finally Joseph Mobutu (mo-BOO-too), an army officer long on the CIA payroll, seized dictatorial power.

Che Guevara was among those who regarded Lumumba as a fallen hero and Mobutu as an American puppet. In 1965, Che joined up with Congolese rebels in the eastern part of the country. It was a disappointing experience, since the rebels were lacking in both discipline and ideological commitment: *"I felt entirely alone,"* he later wrote, *"in a way that I had never experienced before, neither in Cuba nor anywhere else, throughout my long pilgrimage across the world."*[*]

---

[*]Quoted in David Sandison, *Che Guevara* (New York: St. Martin's Griffin, 1997), pp. 105, 108.

When Che returned to Cuba in 1966, the Congo was firmly under Joseph Mobutu's authoritarian control. The United States was the main power broker in Central Africa, allied with Mobutu to secure the mineral riches of the Congo, some of which, such as cobalt, were vital to the aerospace industry.

The Bandung Generation, 1955–1965

Neocolonialism and superpower intervention were exactly what the leaders of former colonial states who met in Bandung (bahn-DOONG), Indonesia, for the first Asia-Africa conference in 1955 wished to avoid. The careers of the Indonesian, Indian, and Egyptian representatives at the Bandung Conference—leaders of large states with significantly more regional influence than countries like Guatemala or the Congo—illustrate how difficult it was to achieve their goal of nonalignment with either the United States or the Soviet Union.

Ahmed Sukarno (1901–1970) first emerged as an Indonesian nationalist fighting against Dutch colonialism in the 1920s. In 1945 he and his party declared Indonesia free of both the Dutch and the Japanese, but it was not until 1950 and the defeat of Dutch reoccupation forces that independence became a reality. The new country was a scattering of hundreds of islands across thousands of miles. Sukarno sponsored the development of an Indonesian language with a simplified grammar as a way to unify Indonesia's great diversity of peoples.

Sukarno was widely popular at first, but he had had no experience running a country. Priding himself as the key to Indonesia's development, he became erratic and declared himself "president for life" in 1963. As his popularity waned, he faced a potent communist insurgency. Suspecting that Sukarno was either sympathetic to the communists or too weak to stave them off, the Indonesian military launched a murderous crackdown in 1964 to wipe them out. In 1967 General Suharto, a military commander backed by the United States, suspended the constitution and took power. The administration of President Lyndon B. Johnson turned a blind eye to the dictatorial and corrupt aspects of Suharto's regime. As in Mobutu's Congo, the United States was glad to have a dependable ally in the struggle against communism, especially as it stepped up its attacks on neighboring North Vietnam.

India's prime minister, **Jawaharlal Nehru** (juh-wah-HER-lahl NAY-roo) (1889–1964) (see Chapter 28), was more successful than Sukarno in securing his country's nonalignment during the Cold War. Like other leaders of newly independent nations, Nehru faced tremendous problems. In the 1930s, the Muslim League had begun to challenge the dominance of the Indian National Congress by arguing for a separate Muslim nation to be carved out of British India. In 1947, when the British finally granted independence to India, they did partition their colony into two separate independent states: India and Pakistan. However, a substantial Hindu minority resided in Pakistan, and an even larger Muslim minority remained in the new state of India. In a climate of fear and uncertainty, millions of people tried desperately to cross to the country where they "belonged." In the intercommunal violence that followed, as many as 10 million people were dislocated, perhaps seventy-five thousand women were raped or abducted, and more than 1 million people lost their lives.

Despite its violent birth and the enduring challenges of poverty and illiteracy, India emerged as the world's largest democracy (see Chapter 32). Even though military tensions emerged on India's borders with Pakistan and China, Nehru kept his country stable and nonaligned by purchasing military hardware from both the United States and the Soviet Union and by building up India's own defense industries. In Pakistan, by contrast, corruption and misrule led to a military seizure of power. In 1958, Pakistan's military government entered into a defense agreement

Ahmed Sukarno (1901–1970) Leader in the struggle for Indonesian independence from the Netherlands, achieved in 1949. Indonesian military leaders, backed by the United States, thought Sukarno incapable of battling communism and removed him from power.

Jawaharlal Nehru (1889–1964) Statesman who helped negotiate the end of British colonial rule in India and served as independent India's first prime minister from 1947 to 1964. Nehru was an influential advocate of the Non-Aligned Movement, refusing to choose sides in the Cold War.

with the United States, which was concerned about India's military ties with the Soviet Union and anxious to have a reliably anticommunist ally in this strategic region. These agreements meant that, in spite of India's nonalignment, the Cold War deeply affected South Asian politics.

Another prominent figure at Bandung was **Gamal Abdel Nasser** (1918–1970). In 1952 he had led a military coup to overthrow Egypt's King Farouk, whom he saw as a pawn of foreign interests. Nasser argued that Arabs should unite to fight both European neocolonialism and American imperialism. He embraced secular Arab nationalism, while rejecting religion as a basis for politics and banning competing political parties such as the Egyptian Communist Party and the Muslim Brotherhood.

In 1954, Nasser successfully negotiated the withdrawal of British troops from the Suez Canal Zone (see Chapter 26). He also began plans for building the giant Aswan Dam on the Nile River to provide electricity for industrialization. He approached Britain and the United States for aid but refused to join an anti-Soviet alliance as a condition of their assistance. Instead, in 1956 Nasser proclaimed the nationalization of the Suez Canal to finance the dam. The British government was outraged, feeling that Nasser's action threatened its vital economic and security interests.

The Suez Crisis of 1956 deepened when the British, French, and Israelis hatched a secret plan: the British and the French would send "peace-keeping" troops to the Canal Zone in response to a prearranged Israeli incursion across the Egyptian border. However, the plan lacked American support, and the British and Israelis withdrew when faced with Egyptian opposition and international criticism. For Nasser, it was a triumph. He became a hero across the Arab world for facing down British imperialism and Israeli aggression, and the Aswan Dam was later completed with Soviet aid.

The Non-Aligned Movement The Bandung Conference in 1955 led to the creation of the Non-Aligned Movement of nations dedicated to avoiding the trap of siding with either the United States or the Soviet Union in the Cold War. Most member countries were former European colonies. Only a few, such as India, successfully managed to put "non-alignment" into practice.

Howard Sochurek/Getty Images

Gamal Abdel Nasser (1918–1970) Prime minister of Egypt from 1954 to 1956 and president from 1956 to 1970. The nationalization of the Suez Canal in 1956 made Nasser a Pan-Arab hero, though the loss of the Six-Day War to Israel in 1967 badly damaged that reputation.

Nasser's reputation in the Arab world was grounded in his support of the Palestinian cause and belligerence toward Israel. In 1947, as the British withdrew their forces from Palestine, which they had occupied under a League of Nations mandate after the First World War (see Chapter 27), diplomats at the United Nations finalized a plan to partition Palestine into separate Arab and Jewish states. In 1948, with Arab states refusing to accept the partition plan, Zionist leaders declared the independence of Israel. Egypt, Lebanon, Syria, Jordan, and Iraq immediately attacked Israel; Nasser himself fought in the Pan-Arab army.

As Arab refugees fled the fighting, some driven from their homes by Israeli soldiers, the Israelis routed the Arab armies, and the Israeli government expanded its borders beyond what the UN planners had envisioned. Shocked and humiliated, Arabs thereafter looked to Nasser as their best hope to destroy Israel and return Palestinian refugees to their native land.

Nasser's reputation, however, was severely damaged after he made a series of threatening moves that prompted a preemptive Israeli attack. In the Six-Day War of 1967, virtually the entire Egyptian air force was destroyed as Israeli forces occupied Egypt's Sinai Desert, Syria's Golan Heights, and the West Bank of the Jordan River. Israeli occupation of predominantly Arab East Jerusalem was particularly galling. U.S. support had helped make Israeli victory possible, a cause of resentment across the Muslim world. The Soviet Union gave rhetorical support to the Palestinians, but its material and military aid never came close to what the United States provided to Israel.

Sukarno, Nehru, and Nasser had all grown up in European-dominated colonial worlds and had dedicated themselves to the liberation of their peoples. While they were all aware that Cold War entanglements would compromise their ability to move their nations forward, they had different levels of success in achieving the nonalignment to which they had dedicated themselves at Bandung. Sukarno was the least successful; his fall brought to power a military dictatorship allied with the United States. Nehru was by far the most successful, maintaining India's status as a genuinely nonaligned democracy throughout this period. Nasser chose to ally Egypt with the Soviet Union simply because the Soviets were enemies of the United States, Israel's main ally.

Vietnam: The Cold War in Southeast Asia, 1956–1974

As in Indonesia, Vietnamese nationalists had to fight colonial reoccupation forces to win their independence. After helping drive the Japanese from Indochina during World War II, **Ho Chi Minh** had declared an independent Democratic Republic of Vietnam in 1945, explicitly referring to the American Declaration of Independence in asserting the right of the Vietnamese people to be free from foreign rule. That claim was disputed by France, which sent forces to re-establish colonial control.

> **Ho Chi Minh**
> (1890–1969) Vietnamese revolutionary and Marxist who led military campaigns against Japanese invaders, French colonialists, and American and South Vietnamese forces.

Ho's Viet Minh soldiers had developed tough fighting skills in the war against the Japanese. In 1954, the Viet Minh victory at Dien Bien Phu (dyen byen FOO) proved to be too much for France. French military officers told their government that they could not wage two counterinsurgencies—in Algeria and Vietnam—simultaneously. Since Algeria was home to a million French citizens, it was the greater priority, and the French withdrew from Indochina.

At the multination Geneva Conference following French withdrawal, Vietnam was temporarily partitioned into northern and southern regions, pending national elections. Fearing that Ho Chi Minh's Communists would win those elections, the United States supported the formation of a separate South Vietnamese regime led by Ngo Dinh Diem (no din dyem). Conflict between the two Vietnams intensified as the United States supplied the south with weapons and military training, while North Vietnam sponsored a southern-based rebel army, the National Front for the Liberation of South Vietnam, called Vietcong.

In 1964, President Lyndon Johnson (in office 1963–1969) sought congressional approval for launching a full-scale war against the communist regime in Hanoi, claiming that North Vietnamese ships had launched an unprovoked attack on American gunboats; in reality the American ships in the Gulf of Tonkin were within North Vietnamese waters on an intelligence-gathering mission. Congress (and the American people) believed the version of events given by their commander-in-chief

Vietnamese Protest On June 11, 1963, Thich Quang Duc, a Vietnamese Buddhist monk, burned himself to death on a Saigon street. His self-immolation was a protest of the policies of the U.S.-backed South Vietnamese government, which many Buddhists thought favored the Catholic minority. (Malcolm Browne/AP Images)

and gave Johnson authority to wage war. By 1965, there were two hundred thousand American military personnel in Vietnam.

The policy of the United States hinged on success in creating a legitimate nationalist government in South Vietnam, a goal that was never achieved. The administration of President Diem was so ineffective and corrupt that the United States supported his assassination by rivals in 1963. South Vietnam never came close to replicating the leadership that Ho Chi Minh had achieved in the north through years of fighting the Japanese and French.

Despite massive bombing attacks on North Vietnam, the Vietcong grew in strength. American soldiers were often unable to distinguish guerrilla soldiers from civilians. At home, Americans were incredulous when their troops brutally slaughtered the villagers of My Lai (mee lie) in 1969 and spread poisonous clouds of defoliating chemicals across the Vietnamese countryside. Images of burning children fleeing napalm bomb blasts sickened global audiences. In this first "televised war," images of death and destruction were transmitted around the world.

In 1968, the Vietcong took the fight straight to the South Vietnamese capital of Saigon during the Tet Offensive. In 1969, as antiwar protests spread across American college campuses and anti-American feelings arose in much of Europe, Asia,

Africa, and Latin America, the new administration of President Richard Nixon (in office 1969–1974) promised a "secret plan" to win the war: even more intensive bombing of North Vietnam and the replacement of American ground forces with South Vietnamese ones. Demoralized and corrupt, the South Vietnamese government and military were not up to the task. On April 30, 1975, after the United States withdrew its ground troops, Communist forces entered Saigon, renamed it Ho Chi Minh City, and reunified the country under their dictatorship.

Entering the Vietnam War, Americans were inclined to think of the world in simple terms: democracy was good, communism was evil, and any fight against communism was necessarily a fight for freedom. In the course of the Vietnam War, they discovered that the world was more complicated. While the Viet Minh were dedicated Marxist-Leninist revolutionaries, their movement had its roots in Vietnam's long history of resistance to foreign intrusion: China in ancient times, Japan and France more recently, and now the United States.

In Vietnam, as in Indonesia, the Congo, and many other parts of the world, the Cold War disrupted the transition from colonialism to national independence. While outcomes varied, Vietnam, Indonesia, and the Congo had one thing in common: by the mid-1970s not one of them was a democracy.

A Time of Upheaval, 1966–1974

Americans who grew up during "the Sixties" remember it as a time of political, social, and cultural turmoil. The Civil Rights Movement, under the leadership of figures like Dr. Martin Luther King, Jr., paralleled other liberation movements taking place around the world. Young people took center stage, proclaiming that the world could, and should, be made a place of peace, love, and justice. In 1963, the poet-musician Bob Dylan captured the spirit of the time:

> *Come mothers and fathers throughout the land*
> *And don't criticize what you can't understand*
> *Your sons and your daughters are beyond your command*
> *Your old road is rapidly aging*
> *Please get out of the new one if you can't lend your hand*
> *For the times they are a-changing.*[*]

This global trend toward greater youth involvement in politics and society arose among students who had come of age after the Second World War. Parents who had lived through economic depression and global war were likely to be satisfied with the relative stability and prosperity of the 1950s and early 1960s, especially in western Europe and the United States, where economic growth rates were strong and consumer goods abundant. Part of that abundance was the expansion of universities to accommodate a much larger number of students than ever before. The students' dissatisfaction with the status quo, amazing to many of their parents, was a revolution of rising expectations.

In dormitory rooms across the world, posters of Che Guevara symbolized the revolutionary fervor of youth. In most places, youth movements arose in opposition

---

[*]Bob Dylan, "The Times They Are A-Changing." Copyright © 1963, 1964 by Warner Bros. Inc.; renewed 1991, 1992 by Special Rider Music. Reprinted courtesy of Special Rider Music.

to traditional authority. In China, however, Mao Zedong harnessed the power of young people to drive his final experiment in radical revolutionary transformation.

In the end, global youth in the 1960s did not change the world. In the United States, Europe, China, and Latin America, authorities reasserted control, and the bipolarity of the Cold War continued.

The Great Proletarian Cultural Revolution, 1965–1974

After the disaster of the Great Leap Forward, the People's Republic of China returned to a more conventional planned economy. But the Soviet model of top-down economic planning had never appealed to Mao, who felt that elitists and technocrats stifled the revolutionary enthusiasm of the masses. A series of border clashes between China and the Soviet Union in 1960 further discredited the Soviet model and led to a deterioration of relations with Moscow. In 1965, Mao began a campaign to mobilize the revolutionary potential of the youth, organizing them into units called the **Red Guards**, who were taught that Mao himself was the source of all wisdom. His thoughts were collected in a "little red book" that became the bible of the Red Guard movement, waved enthusiastically in the air by the millions of young people who came to Beijing to pay homage to the "Great Helmsman."

Mao used the Red Guards to attack his enemies within the Communist Party, the "rightists" and "experts" who had resisted him during the Great Leap Forward. Soon the Red Guards had created an atmosphere of anarchy, attacking party offices, publicly humiliating their teachers, destroying cultural artifacts that linked China to its past, and harassing anyone they thought needed "re-education." Educated Chinese were sent to farms and factories to humble themselves and absorb the authentic revolutionary spirit of the masses. Many died.

By 1968 the country was in chaos and its economy was at a standstill. Pragmatic Communist leaders realized that this "Cultural Revolution" had gone too far and convinced Mao to allow the People's Liberation Army to restore governmental authority. Now, Red Guards themselves faced "downward transfer" to remote villages and labor camps. But while authorities curbed the worst excesses of the Cultural Revolution, a bitter power struggle took place behind the scenes. A radical faction called the "Gang of Four," led by Mao's wife, Jiang Qing (jyahng CHING), schemed to restore the Cultural Revolution. Jiang was a former actress who used her power to purge Chinese art and intellectual life of Western influences and to take vengeance on her many enemies. On the other side were pragmatists like Deng Xiaoping (DUNG shee-yao-PING), an "expert" who was struggling to regain his influence. With the Cultural Revolution reined in, and an aging Mao no longer in complete command, Deng and the "expert" faction gradually reasserted themselves.

The pragmatists scored a victory in 1972 when the American president Richard Nixon came to Beijing. Relations between the two countries had long been tense, partly because the Americans supported the Nationalist government of Chiang Kai-shek on the island of Taiwan, which the Communists regarded as a rebel province of China. But the Chinese were also worried about their long border with the Soviet Union, where armed confrontations had recently taken place. Although a die-hard anticommunist, Nixon judged that better relations with communist China would increase his own bargaining power with the U.S.S.R. and might help the United States extricate itself from Vietnam.

In spite of thawing relations with the United States, the restoration of party and army control, and the return of moderates to positions of influence, the

Red Guards
Young people who rallied to the cause of Maoism during the Great Proletarian Cultural Revolution. As their enthusiasm got out of control, the Red Guards spread anarchy across the People's Republic of China.

毛主席永远和我们在一起

大型彩色纪录片　　　　中央新闻纪录电影制片厂摄制　　　　中国电影发行放映公司发行

Cultural Revolution Poster Graphic art played an important role in reinforcing the cult of Mao Zedong in the 1960s. Here Mao accepts the adulation of the Chinese masses; each of the soldiers, peasants, and workers in this poster waves the "little red book" containing the essence of "Mao Zedong Thought." The caption reads: "Chairman Mao Will Be With Us Forever." (China Film Production and Project Company/International Institute of Social History, Amsterdam)

shadow of the Cultural Revolution still hung over China at the time of Mao's death in 1976. The eventual victory of Deng Xiaoping's pragmatic faction over the Gang of Four sent the People's Republic of China in a new direction, a road to economic growth that could scarcely have been imagined in the darkest days of the Cultural Revolution (see Chapter 31). The people of China had paid a terrible price for Mao's political adventures: the Great Leap Forward and the Great Proletarian Cultural Revolution had killed tens of millions of people.

1968: A Year of Revolution

In 1968, just when the Chinese Communist Party was suppressing the Red Guard movement, the political power of youth was escalating elsewhere in the world. In the United States, the "hippie" movement was in full flower. During the "summer of love" in 1967, long hair, psychedelic art and music, and slogans such as *make love, not war* emanated from college campuses. Eastern religion and consciousness-altering drugs became part of the quest to remake the mind while remaking the world. (See the feature "Visual Evidence in Primary Sources: *Sgt. Pepper's Lonely Hearts Club Band*.")

Sgt. Pepper's Lonely Hearts Club Band

Listen and compare two songs by the British group the Beatles, "I Want to Hold Your Hand" (1963) and "A Day in the Life" (1967), to get an idea of the depth and rapidity of cultural change in the mid-1960s. In a mere four years, John Lennon, Paul McCartney, George Harrison, and Ringo Starr went from pop stars adored by screaming adolescent girls to artists whose words, music, and rapidly evolving public images made them globally influential figures.

Millions anxiously anticipated the release of their new album, *Sgt. Pepper's Lonely Hearts Club Band*, on June 1, 1967. Their albums had become more complex in musical structure and more

Tribute is paid to the Rolling Stones, the Beatles' main rival on the rock music scene, and Bob Dylan, a strong influence on their musical development.

Bob Dylan

Rolling Stones tribute

Redferns/Getty Images

John Lennon's suggestion that Jesus, Gandhi, and Hitler all be included was vetoed. Lennon had been criticized the previous year for declaring that the Beatles were "more popular than Jesus," and the inclusion of Hitler would have been even more offensive. An image of Gandhi was included at the photo shoot but was later removed at the request of the record company.

ambitious in lyrical content, influenced by the highly conceptual songwriting of Bob Dylan, an opening of the imagination commonly attributed to marijuana and psychedelic drugs, and the brilliance of their producer/engineer George Martin, with his strong background in classical music. While recording *Sgt. Pepper*, the group traveled to India for training in transcendental meditation, a journey eagerly covered by the global media and one that provided further artistic stimuli.

The album lived up to expectations. No one had ever heard anything like it before. But the album was more than just a collection of songs. Eager fans sought symbolic meanings not only in the sometimes obscure lyrics but also in the visual images that adorned the large gatefold cover of the album. The Beatles were clearly playing with the idea of celebrity and shifting identities, for example, by creating the persona of "Billy Shears" as front man of the mythical Sgt. Pepper's Band, and by posing for the album cover next to wax models of themselves circa 1964. The resulting image was studied for meaning by millions of young people around the world.

Redferns/Getty Images

The inclusion of figurines of the Beatles (*a*) from Madame Tussauds wax museum highlights the transformation of the group's visual self-representation between 1964 and 1967.

Scattered among the historical figures and film stars are three Indian spiritual leaders (*b*), included at the suggestion of George Harrison. The influence of both Indian instrumentation and Hindu philosophy on Harrison can be heard on the album track "Within You Without You."

Redferns/Getty Images

Redferns/Getty Images

Famous historical figures include Karl Marx (*c*), T. E. Lawrence ("Lawrence of Arabia") (*d*), and writers Edgar Allan Poe (*e*), Lewis Carroll (*f*), and Oscar Wilde (*g*). Actors include Marlon Brando (*h*), Marilyn Monroe (*i*), and Stan Laurel (*j*).

QUESTION FOR ANALYSIS

» *Given your knowledge of 1960s popular culture, what ideas and emotions would this image have evoked at the time of its first release?*

New thinking about gender roles transformed women's rights. Even though women had achieved legal equality in much of the world, opportunities for women remained sharply limited; the common expectation was that young women need not advance in their careers because they would quickly marry and devote themselves to motherhood. In the 1960s, the founders of the modern feminist movement demanded equal social and economic rights for women. Women's sexuality became a key source of debate after 1960, when the United States followed several European nations in legalizing the birth control pill for contraceptive use. In the West a new openness about sexuality seemed to be blooming, and the term *sexual revolution* came into use.

In the United States, the hopes of feminists, civil rights advocates, and student leaders in the early 1960s were soon tempered by harsher realities. The "sexual revolution" that came with easy access to birth control pills and more liberal attitudes could be physically liberating, but also emotionally damaging. Drug use ruined lives, peace marches turned violent as protesters confronted army troops defending the Pentagon, and mass arrests followed a series of "stop the draft" demonstrations in New York. Two voices for peace and moderation—civil rights leader Martin Luther King, Jr. and Democratic presidential candidate Robert F. Kennedy—were assassinated in 1968. Violence spread through American cities.

During the 1968 Democratic National Convention, American television viewers watched in horror as Chicago police bludgeoned youthful protesters; a few months later, Republican Richard Nixon won the presidency. To those Americans appalled by the ferment of the Sixties, Nixon was an experienced, thoughtful anticommunist who would restore order. To those who dreamt of a new age of peace and justice, Nixon represented everything that was wrong with "the establishment." The nation became even more bitterly divided after Ohio Army National Guardsmen shot four student protesters to death at Kent State University in the spring of 1970.

In Europe, Paris was a major center of student unrest. As in the United States, the number of university students had risen sharply in the post-1945 period. After three college students were arrested for occupying a dean's office, students all over France rose to their defense. In May 1968, the Sorbonne University in Paris was festooned with portraits of Che Guevara and other revolutionary heroes. Student marchers, assaulted by riot police, built barricades of overturned cars and garbage cans.

Whereas in the United States most working Americans, including most union members, tended to side with the forces of "law and order," in France the major trade unions joined the protests. Two million French workers went on strike, taking over factories and proclaiming that their bosses were unnecessary. Art students expressed this philosophy on posters they plastered around Paris, with slogans such as *"Be realistic, ask for the impossible," "The boss needs you, you don't need him,"* and *"It is forbidden to forbid."*

In response, French president Charles de Gaulle appeared on television to proclaim: *"The whole French people . . . are being prevented from living a normal existence by those elements, Reds and Anarchists, that are preventing students from studying, workers from working."* But he also offered concessions: an increase in the minimum wage and new elections. De Gaulle's re-election in late 1968, like the election of Richard Nixon in the United States, made it clear that most voters wanted a return to "normal existence." After workers were appeased with new contracts, French students lost their working-class allies and the forces of "law and order" reasserted themselves.

In eastern Europe, students also played a prominent role in the **Prague Spring** of 1968, the most ambitious movement for political reform in the Soviet sphere. In 1948, Czechoslovakia had been forced by Stalin's Red Army to give up its fledgling

Prague Spring (1968) An attempt by political reformers in Czechoslovakia to reform the communist government and create "socialism with a human face." The Soviet Union invaded Czechoslovakia, ending this attempt at reform and reimposing communist orthodoxy.

democracy (see Chapter 29). By the mid-1960s, discontent with the stifling conditions of Soviet-imposed communism was growing. Early in 1968 the pressure for change escalated as workers' strikes and students' protests forced the resignation of the hardline communist leadership.

The new head of the Czechoslovak Communist Party, Alexander Dubček (DOOB-chek), promised *"socialism with a human face,"* including freedom of speech and association as well as more liberal, market-oriented economic policies. The Czech public rallied to Dubcek's cause, and students and teachers took advantage of the new atmosphere of intellectual freedom to discuss how economic justice and democratic freedoms could be achieved in their country.

Fearing that the movement toward liberalization would spread, the Soviet leadership ordered a half-million Soviet and Warsaw Pact troops into Czechoslovakia. They replaced Dubček with a more compliant Czech communist leader. There was no substantial resistance, and reformers in Czechoslovakia, as well as in Poland, Hungary, and the Soviet Union itself, were put on notice: no changes to the status quo would be allowed.

Mexico was another country where a large school-age population held higher aspirations than their parents. But while Mexican society was changing rapidly, Mexican politics were not. The Party of Institutional Revolution (PRI) was the elitist, bureaucratic, and corrupt descendant of the old National Revolutionary Party (see Chapter 27). Since the PRI did not allow free elections, Mexican advocates of political change had no choice but to go to the streets.

The tensions of 1968 began when riot police used force to break up a fight between two student groups. Over a hundred thousand students, with support from many of their teachers and parents, went on strike, marching through the city shouting *"¡Mexico, Libertad!"* ("Mexico, Liberty!"). The timing of the protests was particularly awkward. The Summer Olympic Games were to be held in Mexico City in October, and the government wanted to project a positive image to the worldwide television audience. Rather than risk being embarrassed by the strikes and protests, the government decided to crack down.

The result was the **Tlatelolco Massacre**, in which shooting broke out as thousands of people protested the closing of the National University. The government said the protesters fired first, a contention contradicted by many eyewitnesses watching from apartments lining the square. Hundreds were killed, but the Olympic Games went on as planned, and most of the world heard nothing about the bloodshed at Tlatelolco (tlah-tel-OHL-koh).

Despite their passionate commitment, student protesters in the United States, France, Czechoslovakia, and Mexico were unable to radically change the status quo. In the longer view of history, however, the impact of this generation seems unmistakable. The spirit of the 1960s informed social movements in the decades to come, bringing idealism and activism to music and the arts, educational reform, environmental sustainability, and gender equality. (See the feature "World History in Today's World: Toxic Legacies of Chemical Dumping: Minamata and Love Canal.") The cause of civil rights had been greatly advanced, with traditionally marginalized groups organizing to secure their rights, as when gays and lesbians came out to demand decriminalization as well as social and political equality.

Tlatelolco Massacre (1968) Massacre that occurred when ten thousand university students, faculty, and other supporters gathered in Tlatelolco Plaza in Mexico City to protest the closing of the Mexican National University; government forces opened fire and killed three hundred people.

Death and Dictatorship in Latin America, 1967–1975

After his failed sojourn to Central Africa, Che Guevara was still looking for a place where a dedicated band of rebels could provide the spark for revolution. In 1967, he headed for Bolivia, convinced that its corrupt government would fall swiftly once the

Toxic Legacies of Chemical Dumping: Minamata and Love Canal

In the 1950s, few government officials, industrialists, or members of the general public had much awareness of just how damaging the casual use and haphazard disposal of industrial chemicals could be. Unrestricted dumping of toxic chemicals created exceptionally dangerous living conditions for the people of Minamata, Japan, and Niagara Falls, New York.

From 1932 to 1968, the Chisso Corporation dumped an estimated 27 million tons of mercury compounds into Minamata Bay. By the mid-1950s, a spike in neurological disorders—slurred speech, blurred vision, and signs of brain disorders—became apparent. Local fishermen made the connection, but for decades Chisso did everything possible to evade responsibility. "Minamata," writes one historian, "was the proverbial canary in the coal mine of modernity, the terrifying dark side of petrochemical industrialization."[*]

Meanwhile, in upstate New York, the Hooker Chemical Corporation (now Occidental Petroleum) was disposing of toxic chemicals in an abandoned canal before filling in the land and selling it to the city of Niagara Falls for $1,

[*]Andrew L. Jenks, *Perils of Progress: Environmental Disasters in the Twentieth Century* (New York: Prentice Hall, 2005), p. 5.

disclaiming any future liability. By the 1970s, the resulting Love Canal development seemed a suburban expression of the American dream, except that homes had been built on land saturated with dioxin and other carcinogens. As these seeped to the surface, rates of cancer steadily increased. Like Chisso in Japan, Occidental marshaled its resources not to help those it had afflicted, but to hire legal teams to try to protect itself from responsibility.

More stringent government environmental oversight, spurred by changes in public attitudes, eventually forced both companies to pay up. Though Chisso paid over a billion yen (more than $10 million) in compensation to thousands of victims, the suffering continues. Middle-aged victims, some of whom lost their parents to "Minamata Disease," struggle to get by. Likewise, suffering continues in Niagara Falls. While Occidental reached a $129 million agreement to compensate Love Canal survivors, and though the site has long been fenced off, cancer rates remain high, and women report persistent reproductive problems. The terrible legacies of environmental ignorance and corporate malfeasance endure in Minamata, Niagara Falls, and other localities across the globe.

---

oppressed indigenous population rose against it. But Guevara did not attract the support he expected. Long exploited, Andeans were wary of Spanish-speaking outsiders who claimed to be fighting on their behalf. Short on rations, Che's rebel band wandered in the frigid mountains. In September 1967, Guevara was captured by Bolivian soldiers and executed as an agent of the CIA stood by.

Che's death occurred as dictatorships arose throughout Latin America, with authoritarian governments justifying repression in the name of anticommunism. Chile's relatively strong democratic tradition came under assault after an alliance of center-left and left-wing parties led by the Marxist **Salvador Allende** (uh-YEN-day) (1908–1973) won a bitterly contested election in 1970. Allende's effort to build a socialist economy was strongly opposed by Chilean businessmen and landowners, and his nationalization of the copper mines alarmed American economic interests. In the fall of 1973, with the backing of the United States, the military staged a coup. Allende committed suicide as a force commanded by General Augusto Pinochet (ah-GOOS-toh pin-oh-CHET) stormed the Presidential Palace in Santiago. Pinochet

Salvador Allende (1908–1973) Socialist leader, elected president of Chile in 1970. His government was overthrown in a U.S.-backed military coup in 1973, during which Allende took his own life.

instituted free-market economic policies and invited foreign investment. But economic liberalism was not matched by political openness, as Pinochet dismantled the institutions of Chilean democracy. Thousands of students and union leaders, like the couple Che had once met on the open road, were jailed or killed.

In the mid-1970s military governments prevailed across South America. In Argentina, thousands of students vanished, their mothers holding silent vigils for months and years for these *desaparecidos* (DEH-say-pah-re-SEE-dohs) ("disappeared ones"), not knowing that in many cases their sons and daughters had been killed, some drugged and pushed out of airplanes over the open sea. In Brazil as well, military authorities used anticommunism to limit freedom of speech and freedom of association. Successive administrations in Washington, ever fearful that communism might gain advantage in "America's own backyard" following the Cuban example, were generally supportive of the right-wing regimes that repressed popular democracy.

Détente and Challenges to Bipolarity

The strained relations between the United States and the Soviet Union played out in images from the early 1960s—Soviet premier Nikita Khrushchev banging his shoe on a table at the United Nations while angrily denouncing American imperialism, and President John F. Kennedy pledging to put American astronauts on the moon before the end of the decade. In 1957, the Soviets had launched *Sputnik* (SPUHT-nick), the first artificial satellite to orbit the earth. In response, America developed the Apollo space program, accomplishing the first manned mission to the moon in 1969. Indeed, the Cold War propelled continuous technological innovation, as each side poured huge resources into applied scientific research.

By the mid-1960s, a state of reluctant coexistence between the superpowers was becoming the norm. Both nations faced increasing challenges, domestic and foreign. While the United States was dealing with social discord related to the Civil Rights Movement and increasing opposition to the Vietnam War, in the Soviet Union poor living standards were the issue. The Soviet people had guaranteed employment, universal education, and health care, but they faced persistent shortages of consumer goods, and those available were often shoddy. Moscow was looking for some breathing space in which to develop its domestic economy.

In theory, the division between East and West, between capitalism and communism, was absolute. In reality, both the United States and the U.S.S.R. were having increasing difficulty controlling their respective blocs. It was the strained relations between Moscow and Beijing after 1960 that gave Richard Nixon an opening with the People's Republic of China. On the other side, the Western alliance was no longer subject to complete American domination. In 1957, the Treaty of Rome laid the foundation for what would become the European Economic Community. While shielded from Soviet aggression by NATO and the still powerful American military presence, in the 1960s and early 1970s western European leaders began to emerge from under the economic and political umbrella of the United States.

Although the Cold War division of the world appeared likely to remain for the foreseeable future, the two superpowers began to soften their rhetoric and seek ways to live together in a spirit of **détente** (DAY-tahnt). The greatest achievement was the Strategic Arms Limitation Treaty (SALT) of 1972, which froze the number of ballistic missiles in the possession of the United States and the Soviet Union. The specter of nuclear war never disappeared, but in the mid-1970s it began to recede.

détente
The easing of hostility between nations, specifically the movement in the 1970s to negotiate arms limitations treaties to reduce tensions between the Eastern and Western blocs during the Cold War.

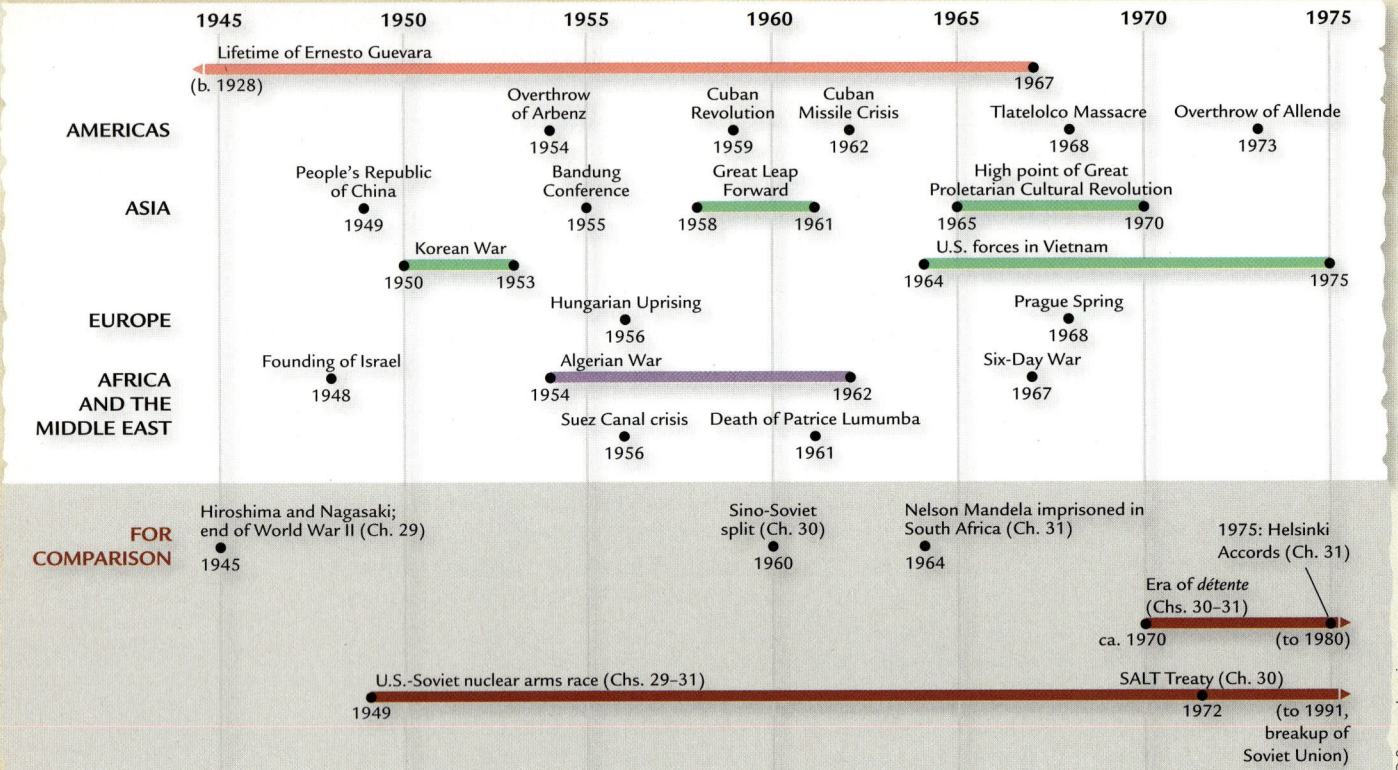

	1945	1950	1955	1960	1965	1970	1975

Lifetime of Ernesto Guevara (b. 1928) — 1967

AMERICAS
- Overthrow of Arbenz — 1954
- Cuban Revolution — 1959
- Cuban Missile Crisis — 1962
- Tlatelolco Massacre — 1968
- Overthrow of Allende — 1973

ASIA
- People's Republic of China — 1949
- Bandung Conference — 1955
- Great Leap Forward — 1958–1961
- High point of Great Proletarian Cultural Revolution — 1965–1970
- Korean War — 1950–1953
- U.S. forces in Vietnam — 1964–1975

EUROPE
- Hungarian Uprising — 1956
- Prague Spring — 1968

AFRICA AND THE MIDDLE EAST
- Founding of Israel — 1948
- Algerian War — 1954–1962
- Six-Day War — 1967
- Suez Canal crisis — 1956
- Death of Patrice Lumumba — 1961

FOR COMPARISON
- Hiroshima and Nagasaki; end of World War II (Ch. 29) — 1945
- Sino-Soviet split (Ch. 30) — 1960
- Nelson Mandela imprisoned in South Africa (Ch. 31) — 1964
- 1975: Helsinki Accords (Ch. 31)
- Era of *détente* (Chs. 30–31) — ca. 1970 (to 1980)
- U.S.-Soviet nuclear arms race (Chs. 29–31) — 1949
- SALT Treaty (Ch. 30) — 1972 (to 1991, breakup of Soviet Union)

© Cengage Learning

New Horizons Amid Cold War Constraints

Painful as it was, the Second World War had opened new vistas for humanity by upending the status quo across much of the world. Hope for liberation from confining traditions became a global theme. Still, the Cold War and the threat of nuclear annihilation cast heavy shadows over the quest for a better future.

In the Soviet sphere, little could change while Stalin was still alive. But after his death in 1953 repeated uprisings in the U.S.S.R.'s captive states, even in the face of harsh reprisals, showed an intense longing for more prosperous and open societies than those imposed through communist dictatorship. In China, Mao Zedong's willingness to risk anarchy in the name of revolution led to the disaster of the Cultural Revolution, when he called on the youth of China to liberate themselves from the past and build a socialist paradise.

In the United States traditionally marginalized groups organized for greater equality: inspired by the African American drive for civil rights, feminists and leaders of the new gay rights movement demanded recognition. And in western Europe postwar prosperity eased the scars of war, laying the foundations for European cooperation, allowing the creation of welfare states that protected all citizens from the uncertainties of life, and bringing forth (there and elsewhere) a generation with radically heightened expectations for the future.

Our attention is usually drawn to the East-West divisions of the Cold War in the three decades following the Second World War. Obviously the struggle between capitalism and communism, between liberal democracy and communist dictatorship, was crucially important. However, we should not allow a focus on superpower rivalries to obscure another critical dimension of the postwar world: the enduring "North-South" axis between the industrialized and underdeveloped worlds, a division older and more enduring than East-West bipolarity. In the Global South, including Latin America, Africa, and formerly colonized parts of Asia, superpower interventions all too often dampened hopes for development and democracy. Only after the fall of the Berlin Wall in 1989 and the end of the Cold War did many of the world's poorest nations have a clearer path toward democracy and prosperity, and even then stark global inequalities remained in the coming age of accelerated globalization (see Chapter 31).

After the fall of communism in the Soviet Union, and its transformation in China into a form of market socialism, was the legacy of Ernesto Guevara still relevant? It certainly seemed so in Cuba, where Fidel Castro and his brother Raul struggled to maintain their grip on power without the Soviet backing on which they had so long depended. In 1997, after lying for two decades in an unmarked Bolivian grave, Che's body was returned to Havana, receiving a hero's welcome and full state honors.

In the wider world, Guevara's legacy is mixed. The inequalities and injustices that drove him to a life of revolutionary combat still exist wherever the life chances of the world's poor and their children are stunted by the greed of the powerful. But Che's solution no longer attracts many followers or sympathizers. The idea that the salvation of the "wretched of the earth" will come through mass uprisings sparked by single-minded revolutionaries now seems naïve, after a century in which all such attempts—under Lenin, Mao, Castro, and others—led to cruel and stifling dictatorships. Whatever the solution, Ernesto Guevara would have agreed with the late Brazilian bishop Dom Hélder Camara that charity alone can never solve the problem of global inequality. As Camara, Brazil's "bishop of the slums," once said: "When I feed the poor, they call me a saint. When I ask why they are poor, they call me a communist."

Voyages on the Web: Ernesto Guevara

The Voyages Map App follows the traveler's journeys using interactive study tools, including 360-degree panoramic views of historic sites, zoomable maps, audio summaries, flash cards, and quizzes.

Key Terms

Ernesto Guevara (854)
Great Leap Forward (859)
Fidel Castro (860)
Central Intelligence Agency (CIA) (860)
Cuban Missile Crisis (860)
Hungarian Uprising (864)

Jacobo Arbenz (865)
Kwame Nkrumah (865)
Patrice Lumumba (870)
Ahmed Sukarno (871)
Jawaharlal Nehru (871)
Gamal Abdel Nasser (872)
Ho Chi Minh (873)

Red Guards (876)
Prague Spring (880)
Tlatelolco Massacre (881)
Salvador Allende (882)
détente (883)

For Further Reference

Ferguson, Niall, Charles S. Maier, Erez Manela, and Daniel J. Sargeant, eds. *The Shock of the Global: The 1970s in Perspective*. Cambridge, Mass.: Belknap, 2011.

Gaddis, John Lewis. *The Cold War: A New History*. New York: Penguin, 2005.

Guevara, Ernesto. *The Motorcycle Diaries: Notes on a Latin American Journey*. Alexandra Keeble, ed. and trans. Melbourne: Ocean Press, 2003.

Hart, Joseph, ed. *Che: The Life, Death and Afterlife of a Revolutionary*. New York: Thunder's Mouth Press, 2003.

Hunt, Michael. *The World Transformed: 1945 to the Present*. New York: Bedford/St. Martin's, 2004.

Jeffrey, Robin, ed. *Asia: The Winning of Independence*. London: Macmillan, 1981.

Judge, Edward H., and John W. Langdon. *The Cold War: A Global History with Documents*. 2d ed. New York: Prentice Hall, 2012.

Kurlansky, Mark. *1968: The Year That Rocked the World*. New York: Random House, 2005.

Lee, Christopher J., ed. *Making a World After Empire: The Bandung Moment and Its Political Afterlives*. Athens: Ohio University Press, 2008.

McMahon, Robert J. *The Cold War: A Very Short Introduction*. New York: Oxford University Press, 2003.

Prashad, Vijay. *The Darker Nations: A People's History of the Third World*. New York: New Press, 2007.

Spence, Jonathan. *Mao Zedong*. New York: Viking Penguin, 1999.

Stark, Steven. *Meet the Beatles: A Cultural History of the Band That Shook Youth, Gender, and the World*. New York: William Morrow, 2006.

Westad, Odd Arne. *The Global Cold War: Third World Interventions and the Making of Our Times*. New York: Cambridge University Press, 2007.

Wiener, Tim. *Legacy of Ashes: The History of the CIA*. New York: Anchor, 2008.

Zubok, Vladislav. *A Failed Empire: The Soviet Union in the Cold War from Stalin to Gorbachev*. Charlotte: University of North Carolina Press, 2008.

CourseMate

Go to the CourseMate website at **www.cengagebrain.com** for additional study tools and review materials—including audio and video clips—for this chapter.

885

31

Toward a New World Order, 1975–2000

Throughout the 1950s **Nelson Mandela** (b. 1918) had campaigned for racial justice and democracy as a member of the African National Congress (ANC). Forced underground in 1961 when the South African government banned the ANC, Mandela then traveled across Africa seeking support for the creation of a guerrilla army. After returning to South Africa, he was captured and, in 1964, tried and sentenced to life in prison.

Finally, in early 1990, after decades of repression and violence, South Africa's white leaders responded to international calls for Mandela's release. A few hours after he walked through the prison gates, he spoke before a large crowd in Cape Town and before a global television audience:

Nelson Mandela
(© David Turnley/Corbis)

Today, the majority of South Africans, black and white, recognize that apartheid has no future. . . . Negotiations on the dismantling of apartheid will have to address the overwhelming demand of our people for a democratic, nonracial, and unitary South Africa. There must be an end to white monopoly on political power and a fundamental restructuring of our political and economic systems to ensure that the inequalities of apartheid are addressed and our society thoroughly democratized. . . . I wish to quote my own words during my trial in 1964. They are as true today as they were then: "I have fought against white domination and I have fought against black domination. I have cherished the ideal of a democratic and free society in which all persons live together in harmony and with equal opportunities. It is an ideal which I hope to live for and to achieve. But if needs be, it is an ideal for which I am prepared to die."

---

*Nelson Mandela, *Nelson Mandela in His Own Words*, ed. Kader Asmal, David Chidester, and Wilmot James (New York: Little, Brown, 2003), pp. 59–62.

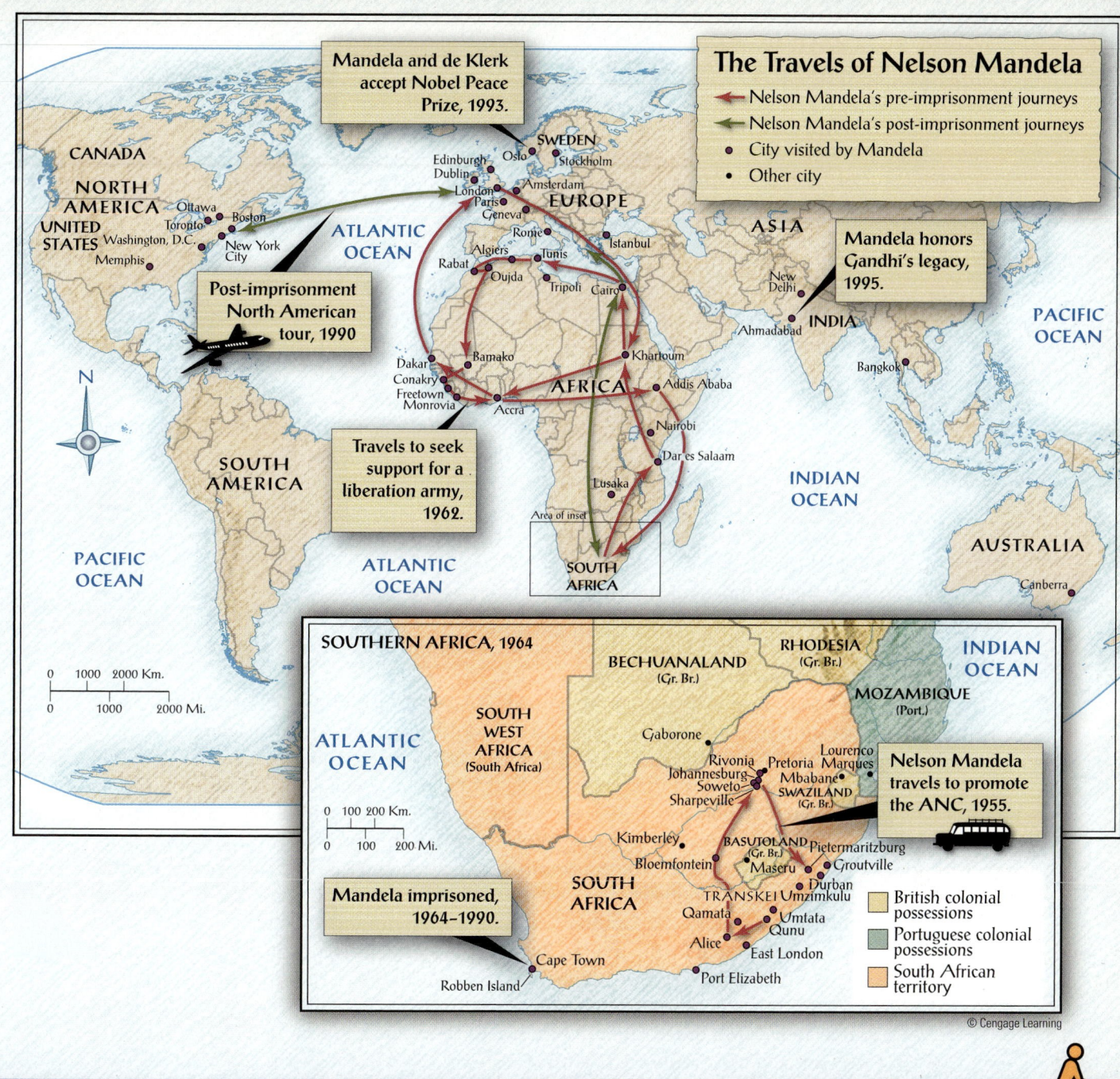

The Travels of Nelson Mandela

→ Nelson Mandela's pre-imprisonment journeys
→ Nelson Mandela's post-imprisonment journeys
• City visited by Mandela
• Other city

Mandela and de Klerk accept Nobel Peace Prize, 1993.

Post-imprisonment North American tour, 1990.

Travels to seek support for a liberation army, 1962.

Mandela honors Gandhi's legacy, 1995.

SOUTHERN AFRICA, 1964

Nelson Mandela travels to promote the ANC, 1955.

Mandela imprisoned, 1964–1990.

British colonial possessions
Portuguese colonial possessions
South African territory

© Cengage Learning

Join this chapter's traveler on "Voyages," an interactive tour of historic sites and events:
www.cengagebrain.com

None of Mandela's many journeys before and after his imprisonment were as significant as his short walk through those prison gates.

As a youth, Mandela received an early education in the history of his own Tembu people and in the protocols of the chief's court while also attending an English-language primary school. There a teacher assigned him the "proper" English name of Nelson; before that, he was called Rolihlahla ("pulling the branch of a tree," or "troublemaker"). He lived up to his African name at the all-black Methodist

Nelson Mandela
(b. 1918) South African leader of the African National Congress and opponent of apartheid. Sentenced to life in prison in 1964; released in 1990. After winning the Nobel Peace Prize in 1993, he became the country's first democratically elected president in 1994.

college he attended when he became embroiled in student politics and was expelled after leading a protest against the bad cafeteria food. In 1940 he headed for Johannesburg and earned a law degree through a correspondence course (since blacks were not allowed to attend law school).

Mandela combined his practice of law with a passion for politics, taking a leadership role in the African National Congress, the party that had, since 1912, worked for racial equality in South Africa (see Chapters 27 and 29). When their nonviolent campaign was met with police brutality and escalating repression, Mandela was set on the path that led to his imprisonment and his later triumph. In 1994 he became the country's first democratically elected president.

The world had changed dramatically in the period of Mandela's confinement. In 1964, Cold War tensions dominated international affairs. But with the collapse of the Soviet Union in the early 1990s, new possibilities emerged. Hopes for democracy spread not only across Russia and the former Soviet sphere but also in many other parts of the world, like South Africa, where Cold War alliances had empowered authoritarian regimes (see Chapter 30). For example, in the last decade of the twentieth century a wave of democratization swept Latin America. Capturing the optimism of the time, President George H. W. Bush of the United States spoke of a *"new world order."* With the stalemate of the Cold War broken, he said in 1991, the path lay open to *"a world in which freedom and respect for human rights find a home among all nations."*

Still, myriad challenges remained. Russia's transition to democracy and capitalism was a difficult one, peace in the Middle East remained elusive, and democratic elections in South Africa did not instantly or automatically remove the social and economic inequalities of apartheid. The liberal association between free trade and democratic politics was contradicted by the People's Republic of China, where market-driven economic reforms created the world's fastest-growing economy under the control of the communist government. Some critics of the United States equated "globalization" with "Americanization" and saw the "new world order" as a means of expanding American power. Among them were Islamist activists who, inspired by the Iranian Revolution, joined the struggle against what they saw as the decadent West. While the last decade of the twentieth century therefore offered hope, and in some places genuine progress toward freedom and security, the "new world order" did not offer a clear and agreed-upon road map as humanity entered the twenty-first century.

Focus Questions

» *What were the major causes of the collapse of the Soviet Union?*

» *How successful were free markets and political reforms in bringing stability and democracy to different world regions?*

» *At the end of the twentieth century, in what ways were major conflicts in the Middle East still unresolved?*

» *What were the major effects of economic globalization?*

The Late Cold War and the Collapse of the Soviet Union, 1975–1991

Abandoning Vietnam in 1975, the United States was divided and weary of war. Sensing an American lack of resolve, Soviet leaders expanded their navy and their support for rebel movements globally. In 1981, however, the United States reasserted an aggressively anti-Soviet posture, confronting the Soviet regime with the need to increase its military spending or fall behind in a renewed arms race. Meanwhile, in eastern Europe simmering discontent was threatening outright rebellion against Soviet overrule. After 1985 a new Soviet leader, Mikhail Gorbachev, initiated reforms, but it was too little, too late. In 1989 the Berlin Wall fell, and in 1991 the Soviet Union dissolved.

After Soviet communism's collapse, Germany reunified while Hungary, Poland, and other formerly communist states became stable democracies. But in Russia and some other nations that emerged from the U.S.S.R.'s breakup, establishing democratic institutions proved difficult. Where authoritarian traditions persisted, sharp inequalities attended the introduction of capitalist markets.

The United States in the Post-Vietnam Era, 1975–1990

Misadventure in Vietnam, and the resignation in 1974 of President Nixon as a result of the Watergate scandal, left U.S. society in disarray. At the same time, a steep rise in oil prices engineered by the Organization of Petroleum Exporting Countries (OPEC) shocked Americans into realizing how much their standard of living depended on foreign oil. *Stagflation* was a term coined to describe the combination of slow growth and inflation that afflicted the U.S. economy in the 1970s.

When Iranian revolutionaries seized American hostages in late 1979 and a rescue attempt the following spring failed to free them, Americans felt powerless and angry. In the 1980 presidential campaign, Republican **Ronald Reagan** (1911–2004) promised to restore American power and confidence. His sweeping victory brought a brash, nationalistic, and sternly anticommunist tone to American foreign policy. Huge tax cuts combined with sharp increases in military spending sent the federal budget into deficit. Nevertheless, after a harsh recession in 1981–1982, economic recovery provided the popular support Reagan needed for re-election in 1984.

The "Reagan Revolution" was a backlash among conservatives against what they considered the liberal excesses of the 1960s and 1970s. This modern American conservative movement embraced the ambitious agenda of turning back the stronger role the government had taken for five decades in areas such as equal rights, social welfare, regulation of financial institutions, and environmental protection.

In Europe, Reagan found a strong British ally in Conservative Prime Minister Margaret Thatcher, who was equally committed to rolling back the scope of government at home and to confronting the Soviet Union more forcefully abroad. However, many in Europe, and in the United States as well, were alarmed by Reagan's refusal to use the diplomatic language of détente. Europeans rallied for peace, and their leaders rejected Reagan's description of the Soviet Union as an "evil empire," preferring instead to continue the language of "peaceful coexistence." Reagan's harsh tone was offset by his optimism, however, and in 1986 he

Ronald Reagan (1911–2004) Fortieth president of the United States. A staunchly anticommunist Republican, he used harsh rhetoric toward the Soviet Union and increased American military spending but compromised when negotiating arms limitations agreements.

and Gorbachev met in Iceland, where they made unexpected progress on arms limitation. Even so, Reagan kept up the pressure and in 1987 traveled to Germany, where he stood before the Berlin Wall and demanded, *"Mr. Gorbachev, tear down this wall!"* Few guessed just how soon the wall would indeed come down.

From Leonid Brezhnev to Mikhail Gorbachev

The period from 1964 to 1982, when Leonid Brezhnev led the Soviet Union, was a time of relative stability for many Soviet citizens. While their standard of living was low, employment, education, and health care were guaranteed. They might never own a car, but they could take an annual vacation. While they had no freedom of speech, religion, or assembly, they did have old-age pensions that would help keep them from suffering at the end of their lives. Perhaps for those who had lived through the ravages of Stalinism and the Second World War, basic security was enough, but for the younger Soviet generation, now more aware of the higher standard of living and greater opportunity common in the West, dissatisfaction with the dull Soviet status quo was growing.

Some Russian and eastern European dissidents were emboldened to speak out more forcefully after détente with the United States led to the **Helsinki Accords**, signed in 1975. This agreement committed western Europe and the United States to recognize the borders of the communist bloc countries in return for a Soviet pledge to respect basic human rights. Among those brave enough to speak out was Russian physicist Andrei Sakharov (1921–1989), the man most responsible for the development of the Soviet hydrogen bomb.

Sakharov argued that Soviet society could advance only through greater freedom of information. Developments in computer technology proved his point. While Soviet computer scientists and mathematicians were world class, the centralized system within which they operated made it impossible for them to work as creatively as their American counterparts. In 1977, for example, Apple Corporation was founded and pioneered the individual use of computers, democratizing access to this increasingly powerful technology. In contrast, the idea that computing would be accessible to individuals apart from state control was inconceivable in Brezhnev's Soviet Union.

In 1975, Sakharov won the Nobel Peace Prize for his writings in defense of civil rights and democracy. Brezhnev prevented him from receiving the award in person, however, and cut off Sakharov's communications with the outside world by sending him into an internal exile. Soviet promises to respect human rights meant nothing in practice.

A large gap separated the Soviet Union's global ambitions from the resources generated by its inefficient economy. Brezhnev worsened the problem by making major new military commitments in the wake of the American withdrawal from Vietnam, such as expanding his country's nuclear submarine program and its Indian Ocean fleet. When the Reagan administration subsequently stepped up American military spending in the 1980s, an already overstretched Soviet Union could not keep pace.

War in Afghanistan took an especially heavy toll on Brezhnev's regime. After Afghan communists seized power in Kabul in 1978 with the help of Soviet special forces, a Soviet occupation faced tough resistance from Islamic guerrilla fighters known as *mujahaddin* (moo-jah-ha-DEEN). As the British had learned in the nineteenth century and as U.S. and NATO forces would later discover (see Chapter 32), superiority in military technology can be offset in the mountains of Afghanistan by the tenacious defense of local peoples protecting the sanctity of their villages and traditional social values. The mujahaddin, aided by the United States and

Helsinki Accords
A 1975 agreement made during the Cold War that gave recognition to the borders of communist bloc countries in eastern Europe in return for a Soviet promise, never fulfilled, to respect basic human rights.

Pakistan, used their familiarity with the land and the populace to counter superior Soviet technology. As death tolls increased, the Soviet people grew weary of the war in Afghanistan, just as Americans had with Vietnam.

When Brezhnev died in 1982, he left a difficult situation to the aging party functionaries who replaced him. Then in 1985 came a startling change when **Mikhail Gorbachev** (b. 1931) consolidated power. Knowing that real reform would be necessary to save the Soviet system, and sensing the impatience of Russia's younger generation, Gorbachev denounced what he called *"the era of stagnation"* under Brezhnev. He withdrew from Afghanistan, reached out to President Reagan in pursuit of further arms limitations, and introduced policies of *perestroika* ("restructuring") and *glasnost* ("openness"). Perestroika brought an end to massive economic centralization. While the state would still dominate, industry would now use market incentives rather than bureaucratic command to manage production. Glasnost allowed formerly taboo subjects to be discussed.

Gorbachev's new policy was tested in 1986, when officials tried to cover up the Chernobyl disaster, the worst nuclear accident in history to that time. Western observers noted a sharp spike in radiation levels, but at first Soviet officials said nothing. Both the Soviet people and their European neighbors were enraged at the attempted cover-up, and Gorbachev promised that the old pattern of Soviet lies would be replaced by honesty and openness.

Glasnost did indeed lead to greater openness. For the first time since the earliest days of the revolution, Russians were free to speak their minds and publish their opinions. The very success of glasnost proved Gorbachev's undoing, however, when the economic progress offered by perestroika failed to materialize. The Soviet people faced continuing and even worsening shortages of consumer goods, standing in long lines to secure basics like milk, bread, and eggs. The only difference from the Brezhnev era was that they were now free to complain about it. By the end of the 1980s Gorbachev's popularity was plummeting. His attempt to combine Marxism-Leninism with market reforms and political transparency was a halfway measure, doomed to failure.

The new openness of glasnost also contributed to the unraveling of the Soviet Union. When members of repressed nationalities gained a public voice for their grievances with Russian rule, the forces of repressed nationalism exploded in various Soviet republics, such as Georgia in the Caucasus Mountains and the Baltic states of Latvia, Lithuania, and Estonia. The Soviet Union began to break apart as Gorbachev agreed to a treaty giving the republics of the U.S.S.R. their de facto independence as part of a commonwealth led from Moscow (see Map 31.1). It was an awkward compromise, with authority split between Gorbachev, head of the Communist Party of the Soviet Union, and elected leaders in the separate republics.

This political fragmentation was too much for hard-line conservatives in the Communist Party, who, in the summer of 1991, attempted a coup d'état. But huge crowds rallied to protect the newly elected government of the Russian Republic. In the wake of the failed coup attempt, the Russian Federation outlawed the Communist Party of the Soviet Union. Gorbachev had failed to find a middle ground between reform and revolution, and his political career was over.

> **Mikhail Gorbachev**
> (b. 1931) Leader of the Soviet Union from 1985 to 1991 who introduced "openness" to Soviet politics and "restructuring" to the Soviet economy. Unable to control calls for even greater changes, Gorbachev presided over the collapse of the Soviet Union.

Revolution in Eastern Europe

As the Hungarian uprising in 1956 and the Prague Spring in 1968 had shown, force had been necessary to keep eastern Europe in Moscow's orbit (see Chapter 30). By the mid-1980s, however, the Soviet Union was no longer willing to intervene to prop up unpopular communist regimes in eastern Europe.

MAP 31.1 The Dissolution of the Soviet Union In the 1990s, the collapse of the Soviet Union led to the creation of new states across eastern Europe, the Caucasus Mountains, and Central Asia, regions that in the nineteenth century had been part of the Russian empire. The Baltic states of Estonia, Latvia, and Lithuania emerged as thriving democracies. Conflict was endemic in the Caucasus, however, where Russia battled separatists in Chechnya and Armenia and Azerbaijan fought for control of territory. The new nations of formerly Soviet Central Asia were dominated by strong-armed dictators. (© Cengage Learning)

In Poland, for example, the Roman Catholic majority despised the atheism of their rulers. Catholicism was a touchstone of Polish nationalism and a historical connection with the West. The surprise announcement in 1978 that the Polish cardinal Karol Wojtyla would become Pope John Paul II powerfully affirmed that feeling.

In 1980, discontent with the communist regime reached a turning point with the formation of **Solidarity**, a trade union formed by shipyard workers. Facing mounting popular pressure, the government was forced to recognize Solidarity, the first independent trade union in the Soviet bloc. In a direct challenge to the authority of the Communist Party, nearly a third of Poland's population joined Solidarity. Faced with increasing unrest, the government agreed to an election in 1989. The result was a massive victory for Solidarity and the election of its leader Lech Walesa to the position of president. The "iron curtain" was starting to crumble as events in Poland emboldened dissidents across eastern Europe.

In Czechoslovakia, the young rebels of the Prague Spring of 1968, now adults, began pushing for a new constitution. They had an additional grievance: the terrible

Solidarity
Polish trade union created in 1980 that organized opposition to Communist rule. In 1989, Solidarity leader Lech Walesa was elected president of Poland as the Communists lost their hold on power.

pollution and environmental degradation caused by communism's industrial policies. Unaccountable to public opinion, the communists had not matched western European progress in seeking to protect their nation's air, water, and forests. The police cracked down on democratic protesters led by the renowned playwright Václav Havel, but they were unable to control events: this time no Soviet forces arrived to save them. Communism's fall went so smoothly in Czechoslovakia, with the election of Václav Havel as president, that it has been called the "Velvet Revolution."

The new presidents of Poland and Czechoslovakia could not have come from more different backgrounds: Lech Walesa was a shipyard worker and labor organizer, and Havel a dramatist and intellectual. When they met as leaders of truly independent and democratic states, their complementarity was obvious, because industrial workers and artists, though from radically different backgrounds, were both groups that had been straitjacketed by the restrictions of communism. Now, no longer would Polish and Czech workers have to settle for the phony trade unions imposed on them from above by Communist Party officials, and no longer would eastern European artists have to conform to the dictates of cultural commissars.

Communism fell more suddenly and violently in Romania, where Nicolae Ceauşescu (chow-SHES-koo) had ruled with an iron fist, building sumptuous palaces and promoting family members to increase his personal control while his people went hungry. Isolated in his palace, Ceauşescu did not realize the depth of public anger. At a large public rally in the capital of Bucharest organized to reaffirm his position, Ceauşescu stepped forward to receive the accolades of the crowd; instead, he was loudly jeered. Television showed Ceauşescu's confusion as he heard, for the first time, his people's true opinion of him. His own security officials turned on him, and he and his wife were summarily executed—the end of a brutal and vain dictator who (like Benito Mussolini of Italy before him, and Saddam Hussein of Iraq later) died despised by the people he had long abused.

The most evocative image of the fall of communism in eastern Europe was the destruction of the Berlin Wall. Since 1961, the wall had symbolized the Cold War divide, but in 1989, as part of the larger wave of revolution in central Europe, huge crowds of East Berliners streamed toward it. The next year, the East German government relented and opened the gates, allowing tearful reunions of long-separated families. Soon after, the Berlin Wall was demolished in a festival of constructive mayhem by euphoric Berliners. The Cold War was truly over.

If, in retrospect, the fall of communism in Europe seems to have been inevitable, it certainly did not seem so to people at the time. In East Germany, Bulgaria, Romania, and across eastern Europe, soldiers under the command of communist officials faced the awful prospect of being ordered to fire on crowds of protesters. When they did not do so, the people's sense of relief was palpable, and their feeling of joy in victory all the more intense.

Post-Soviet Struggles for Democracy and Prosperity

The failure of the communist coup in 1991 and the fall of Mikhail Gorbachev put Russian President **Boris Yeltsin** (1931–2007) in charge of defining a new path for the country. (See the feature "Visual Evidence in Primary Sources: Tanks and Protests in Moscow and Beijing.") Advised by American economists that free markets would bring prosperity, Yeltsin instituted bold economic reforms. The immediate results, however, were disappointing. A few of the "new oligarchs," as the post-Soviet economic elite

Boris Yeltsin (1931–2007) First president of the Russian Federation, from 1991 to 1999. He rallied the people of Moscow to defend their elected government during the attempted communist coup of 1991, but his presidency was marred by financial scandals and war in Chechnya.

Tanks and Protests in Moscow and Beijing

Among the many striking images associated with the late Cold War period are these very different representations of the role that tanks played in political protests in Beijing in 1989 and Moscow in 1991. The Chinese image shows the repression of democracy, the Russian one its triumph.

As China opened up to the world in the 1980s, it was undertaking a much more successful economic restructuring than Mikhail Gorbachev's perestroika, but its leaders had done virtually nothing to emulate his program of glasnost, or "openness." By 1989 some Chinese, especially students

From April to August 1989, large crowds assembled in Beijing's Tiananmen Square to protest corruption and to advocate democracy. Under the giant banner of Chairman Mao that dominates the square, some students erected a facsimile of the Statue of Liberty. Some Communist officials were sympathetic to the protests and urged dialogue. Chairman Deng Xiaoping rejected their advice and sent in the People's Army to dislodge the protesters. Estimates on the number of those killed range from the hundreds to the thousands.

Jeff Widener/AP Images

Taken with a long-range lens from a Beijing hotel room, this photograph of a lone individual trying to stop a line of surging tanks (which eventually went around him) summed up both the heroism and futility of the Tiananmen protests. He has never been identified. In 1989, *Time* magazine declared the "Unknown Rebel" to be one of the one hundred most influential people of the twentieth century.

QUESTION FOR ANALYSIS

» *How does the manner in which the photographer has framed each of the shots affect the viewer's reactions?*

in the capital city of Beijing, thought it was time for a change. They were inspired by a visit from Gorbachev but also by ideals of democracy they associated with the United States.

By this time it was becoming clear that fundamental changes were likely to occur in the Soviet Union. Gorbachev was in danger of losing central control as nationalists began discussing separation from the U.S.S.R. After first resisting that trend, he then agreed to a compromise that would enhance the power of the individual republics, reversing the old domination from Moscow. In the summer of 1991 a group of Communist Party officials and army officers, understanding that the Soviet Union stood on the brink of dissolution, launched the August Coup to restore central authority.

Boris Yeltsin, elected president of the Russian Republic, stands on top of a tank, rallying the people of Moscow in defense of their new democratic institutions. The commander of the tank brigade had declared his loyalty to the Russian Republic and had refused to join Soviet forces against it. Contrary to the wishes of the coup plotters, this image was shown on state television and became a rallying point for further defense of democracy.

In the background is the Russian "white house," the parliament of the Russian Republic. The authority of this elected body was part of the shift away from centralized Soviet control toward newly empowered governmental institutions within the republic. After declaring a state of emergency, the coup leaders had the building shelled.

AP Images

The coup plotters were unable to muster enough military strength to overcome this resistance, which would have required a level of violence and death that was intolerable to most military commanders. Gorbachev regained his authority and declared the orders of the coup leaders null and void. It was not much of a victory, however, as the Soviet state quickly unraveled around him.

were called, grew very wealthy very suddenly when state assets were auctioned off. But they sometimes behaved more like gangsters than corporate executives, using government ties to enrich themselves and suppress competition.

Many Russians suffered when the old sureties of the Soviet system—free education and health care, guaranteed employment, old-age pensions—disappeared: the market system did not instantly make up for the loss of the security they had provided. Even as imported consumer products became widely available, few had the means to purchase them. Russia simply did not have the institutional capacity, civic traditions, and managerial expertise to shift so rapidly to a capitalist system. By the end of the 1990s, life expectancy and fertility rates were in decline, the population was shrinking, and Russians were often hungry and cold.

Yeltsin's problems were compounded by unrest in the southern Caucasus region, where Muslim guerrillas organized a separatist movement in Chechnya (CHECH-nee-yah). Though Yeltsin used massive military force against them, he was unable to suppress the uprising. Ailing, Yeltsin handed power to a former intelligence officer named Vladimir Putin in 1999.

Putin was returned to office in 2000 by a Russian electorate anxious to embrace an authority figure who promised order. Putin reined in capitalism by restoring state authority over the economy and the media, using control of oil revenues and television as bases of power. He crushed the Chechnya rebellion, stood up to the United States in global forums, and restored order to the Russian Republic. Stability was achieved, but at the expense of democracy and civil rights.

The former Central Asian republics of the U.S.S.R. faced equally difficult transitions. Located on the borderlands between China, Russia, and the Muslim world, these newly independent nations had plentiful natural resources, especially oil and gas. The potential for democracy, however, was limited because, unlike in eastern Europe, regime change came from the top down rather than through popular mobilization. Kazakhstan and Uzbekistan were typical, with independence overseen by former communist officials who paid lip service to democracy while keeping a tight rein on power and resources.

In general, the transition to liberal governance and market economics was smoother in eastern Europe. Hungary, the Czech Republic, and Poland all experienced political and economic progress in the 1990s, with a blossoming of the free associations that characterize civil society. The reunification of Germany, however, was more difficult because East Germans were much poorer than West Germans and usually lacked competitive job skills. The first decade after the fall of the Berlin Wall brought freedom and opportunity to eastern Germany, but also unemployment and insecurity.

Though it is still too soon to assess its full implications, the fall of the Soviet Union was clearly a momentous turning point in modern history. It marked not only the failure of the world's longest experiment with communism but also the breakup of the formerly great Russian empire.

The Late Cold War in Latin America and Africa: Crisis and Opportunity

During the late stages of the Cold War (1975–1990), political crises afflicted many parts of Africa and Latin America. With the collapse of the Soviet Union, however, opportunities arose to heal political divisions and bring greater democracy. In Central America, violence between leftist insurgents and military regimes aligned with Washington gave way in the 1990s to elections and new hope for democracy and stability. Likewise in southern Africa, warfare gave way to elections and the promise of a brighter future. But civil war and genocide in Central Africa demonstrated that the destructive legacies of colonialism and superpower intervention were still powerful.

From Dictatorship to Democracy in Central America

Events in Chile in 1973 were a preview of things to come. That year a group of Chilean military officers, with U.S. backing, launched a successful coup against President Salvador Allende, the leader of a left-wing coalition hostile to American mining interests (see Chapter 30). The new military dictator, General Augusto Pinochet, denounced communism, protected U.S. investments, and brought down Chile's once-powerful labor unions. American economic advisers then remade Chile's economy along free-market lines, reforms that Pinochet carried out through authoritarian means. Like dictators elsewhere, Pinochet enjoyed U.S. government support because of his anticommunist credentials. Pinochet's officers routinely tortured Chilean dissidents.

In the 1980s the main battleground between leftist rebels and military forces backed by the United States was Central America. Nicaragua, for example, had long been ruled by the Somoza family, anticommunist dictators aligned with American economic interests. Resistance to the Somoza dictatorship was organized by the rebel Sandinista National Liberation Front. When a major earthquake

Sandinistas The Sandinistas were victorious in 1979, but their control over Nicaragua was then challenged by U.S.-backed Contra rebels. The Sandinistas modeled themselves on Cuban revolutionary heroes; the soldier on the right wears a red-starred beret like that of Che Guevara.

© Jean Louis Atlan/Sygma/Corbis

occurred in 1972, the Somoza family and its friends in government stole millions of the dollars of relief aid sent to Nicaragua by international donors, pushing many Nicaraguans toward sympathy with the rebels. In 1979 the Sandinistas ousted the Somoza family and formed a new government.

After Ronald Reagan took office in 1981, the U.S. government threw its support behind anti-Sandinista insurgents known as *Contras*, led by military men associated with the previous regime. The Sandinistas then clamped down on civil liberties, following the example of Fidel Castro, who, twenty years earlier, had justified limitations on individual freedom in the name of saving the revolution.

Reagan's support for the Contras was politically divisive. In the Iran-Contra scandal, administration officials evaded congressional oversight by illegally selling arms to Iran to get funds for the Nicaraguan rebels. But the decline of Soviet power brought new possibilities for a negotiated settlement. Since Cuba's economy was undercut as Gorbachev phased out Soviet subsidies, Cuba could no longer aid the Sandinistas, and U.S. leaders no longer saw the Contras as necessary allies. Free elections were held in Nicaragua in 1989. The defeated Sandinistas respected the election results by peacefully handing over power, a major step forward for Nicaraguan democracy.

Guatemalan society was also marred by violence in the 1980s. Paramilitary death squads aligned with the right-wing government targeted hundreds of thousands of Guatemalans, mostly indigenous Maya people, suspected of collusion with rebel armies. Often the killers were children kidnapped by the army and forced into service. As many as a million refugees fled from the mountains to the cities or across the border into Mexico. Guatemalan leaders either denied their connection to the death squads or justified the violence as necessary to defeat communism. Four decades after Che Guevara had witnessed the destruction of Guatemalan democracy through American intervention (see Chapter 30), the position of the country's poor was worse than ever.

After the Cold War, the United States pressured the Guatemalan government and military to work toward a solution. But a peace deal was not brokered until 1996, when the rebels finally agreed to lay down their arms in exchange for land. For the first time since 1952 Guatemalans went to the polls to vote in free elections. Wounds from the violence remained deep, however, and a government panel was set up to investigate paramilitary atrocities.

Elsewhere in Latin America the trend was also toward democracy. In Chile, prodemocracy activists removed General Pinochet from power. In Argentina, the turning point was defeat in the Falklands War against Great Britain in 1982, when the incompetence of Argentine generals brought about irresistible calls for change. Shortly following Argentina's democratic transition, in 1985 elections swept the military from power in Brazil as well. Thus the liberation of eastern Europe from Soviet domination was paralleled in Latin America when new democratic governments replaced authoritarian ones that had, typically, been allied with the United States and had used anticommunism as a justification for repression.

In Mexico, the problem was neither military governments nor Cold War alignments, but rather the monopoly power of the Party of Institutional Revolution (PRI), which constrained Mexican political freedom and bound the country to incompetence and corruption (see Chapter 30). Finally, in 1989, a conservative opposition party won gubernatorial elections in the state of Baja California, the first time the PRI had lost control of a statehouse since the 1920s. The stage was then set for more open electoral competition at the national level. In 2000 the election of Vicente Fox of the conservative National Action Party (PAN) finally ended the PRI monopoly on Mexican presidential politics.

The Congolese Conflict and Rwandan Genocide

In Africa, the big Cold War prize had been the former Belgian Congo. America's ally Joseph Mobutu changed his name to Mobutu Sese Seko and took dictatorial control over the vast nation he renamed Zaire. In return for facilitating Western access to Zaire's strategic minerals and for allowing American use of his military bases, Mobutu received large sums of American foreign aid, which disappeared into his private accounts. His regime was so corrupt that a new term was coined to describe it: *kleptocracy*, or "government by theft."

With the fall of the Soviet Union and the release of Nelson Mandela, the United States' affiliation with Mobutu Sese Seko became an embarrassment, and in 1990 Congress cut off direct aid to Zaire and supported efforts to democratize the country. Those efforts failed for two reasons. First, the political opponents of Mobutu were themselves bitterly divided. As in the early days of the Congo (see Chapter 30), most politicians represented regions and ethnic groups rather than ideas or policies. Second, the region was destabilized by the shock of genocide in Rwanda.

The Rwandan genocide of 1994 is often presented as having "tribal" or "ethnic" roots, but Rwandans, Hutu as well as Tutsi, speak the same language, participate in the same culture, and mostly share a common Roman Catholic faith. As colonial rulers, however, the Belgians had sharply differentiated the two groups, favoring the Tutsi as local allies and giving Tutsi children preferred access to European education. These policies generated resentments that surfaced upon independence in 1960, when the previously disenfranchised Hutu took power and expelled many Tutsi. By the 1980s these Tutsi exiles had organized a rebel army in neighboring Uganda.

In 1994, Hutu death squads went on a rampage when the plane carrying the Rwandan president was shot from the sky, and within a few months nearly a million people had been slaughtered, many cut with machetes. Another million Rwandans fled to neighboring countries, as United Nations peacekeepers stood by, unwilling to intervene.

As a Tutsi army re-entered Rwanda to establish a new government, Hutu extremists who had perpetrated the horrible violence fled to refugee camps in neighboring Zaire. By this time Mobutu was old and sick and no longer able to hold the country together. As in the early 1960s, Zaire (which restored the name Democratic Republic of the Congo in 1997) fractured along ethnic and regional lines. The aftermath of Mobutu's authoritarian rule was not freedom but a nation of multiple militias verging on anarchy. Neighboring African countries compounded problems by sending in armies to back the various factions.

Although the "new world order" of democracy and civil rights did not arrive in the Democratic Republic of the Congo, after 1995 Rwanda did make strides toward restoring peace and civility. But further south the dream of African democracy rising from the ashes of Cold War conflict came closer to fulfillment.

South African Liberation

For many years little hopeful news reached Nelson Mandela in prison, as South African apartheid became more and more extreme in its suppression of the black majority. The government oversaw a "Bantu education" system that prepared blacks only for menial jobs. Residential segregation was strictly enforced: the pass law system made it illegal for blacks to be in "white" areas unless they could prove they were there for employment. Meanwhile, white South Africans enjoyed a First World standard of living.

To complete the racial separation, the South African government developed the system of **Bantustans**, arguing that Tswana, Zulu, Xhosa, and other peoples did not belong to a common South Africa but to "tribal" enclaves (Bantustans) where

Bantustans
Term used by apartheid planners for "tribal regions" in which Africans, denied citizenship in a common South Africa, were expected to live when not working for whites. They were not internationally recognized and were later reabsorbed into democratic South Africa.

they should seek their rights. The Bantustan system was developed on the foundation of the old "native reserves," where inadequate land and overcrowding had long forced blacks to seek work in white-controlled cities and mines. According to apartheid, these impoverished and scattered territories would form the basis for independent "nations." In reality, the Bantustans were simply a device to subjugate black Africans and deprive them of any hope for rights in a unified South Africa.

While African National Congress (ANC) leaders languished in jail or left South Africa to seek foreign allies, in the 1970s a new generation of leaders emerged. The Black Consciousness Movement was led by Steve Biko, who argued that black South Africans faced not only the external challenge of apartheid but also an inner challenge to surmount the psychological damage it caused. The first step toward liberation, Biko said, was for blacks to eliminate their own sense of inferiority.

Soweto Uprising
(1976) Youth demonstrations in South Africa that were met with police violence. The Soweto Uprising brought a new generation of activists, inspired by Steve Biko's Black Consciousness Movement, to the forefront of resistance to apartheid.

Many black South African youths heeded his call, culminating in the 1976 **Soweto Uprising**, in which black students protested the inferiority of their education. When marchers refused an order to disband, police fired into the crowd, killing dozens of children. As protests spread across the country, authorities responded with their usual brutality. But this time resistance endured. Black consciousness stayed alive in the Soweto generation even after 1977, when Steve Biko's jailers beat him to death.

By 1983, black trade unions, church groups, and student organizations had formed a nationwide United Democratic Front. Schoolchildren boycotted apartheid schools. Resistance on the streets became violent. Sometimes African militants cruelly executed those accused of collaboration with apartheid by putting tires around their necks and setting them ablaze. Nelson Mandela's own wife, Winnie Mandela, was implicated in the violence. In 1986 the government declared a state of emergency and sent the army into the black townships to restore order.

Critics outside South Africa argued that economic sanctions could force meaningful change. College students in the United States and Britain demanded that their institutions sell off investments in companies that did business in South Africa. In 1986 the U.S. Congress passed a comprehensive bill limiting trade with and investment in South Africa. President Reagan, viewing the South African government as an ally against communism, vetoed the economic sanctions bill, but the Democratic-controlled Congress overrode his veto.

Feeling the pressure, the South African government offered to release Mandela if he renounced the ANC. His daughter Zindzi read his response at a packed soccer stadium: *"I will remain a member of the African National Congress until the day I die. . . . Your freedom and mine cannot be separated. I will return."** Finally, as the decline of the Soviet Union undercut the government's claim that Mandela and the ANC represented a front for the creation of a Soviet-backed communist state, and as sanctions undermined an already weak economy, South African President F. W. de Klerk granted Mandela an unconditional release in 1990. Despite ongoing violence, elections were held in 1994. Mandela was easily elected president, and the ANC became the dominant political force in the new South Africa.

True to the words he had spoken at his trial in 1964, Mandela emphasized inclusiveness in his government. South Africa, christened the "rainbow nation," had a new flag, a new sense of self-identity, a multiracial Olympic team, and one of the world's most democratic constitutions. A Truth and Reconciliation Commission was instituted to uncover the abuses of apartheid, while offering amnesty to those who publicly acknowledged their crimes.

---

*Nelson Mandela, *Nelson Mandela in His Own Words,* ed. Kader Asmal, David Chidester, and Wilmot James (New York: Little, Brown, 2003), pp. 46–47.

Soweto Uprising In 1976, schoolchildren in South Africa protested the compulsory teaching of the Dutch-based Afrikaans language in their schools. When police fired into the crowd, made up mostly of teenagers, hundreds were killed and thousands injured. The Soweto generation played a central role in bringing down apartheid over the next fifteen years. (Bettman/Corbis)

But if this was the story of a new dawn for South Africa, it was also clear that the legacies of racism would take a long time to overcome. A severe crime wave and the rapid spread of HIV/AIDS posed difficult challenges for the Mandela administration. But at least all South Africans were now empowered to help find solutions. As in eastern Europe and Latin America, the end of the Cold War stalemate had brought a new era of hope. (See the feature "World History in Today's World: Sports in Post-Apartheid South Africa.")

Enduring Challenges in the Middle East

Throughout the twentieth century the Middle East had been politically unsettled, with tensions magnified by its strategic importance as a primary source of fossil fuels. Ethnic and religious rivalries combined with the involvement of external powers in a combustible mixture.

The international dimension of tension between Israel and its Arab neighbors intensified after 1973, when a brief war led Arab representatives of the **Organization of Petroleum Exporting Countries (OPEC)** to declare a boycott on oil

Organization of Petroleum Exporting Countries (OPEC) An international organization of oil-producing nations created to set production quotas in an attempt to influence prices. OPEC's policies led to a steep rise in oil prices in the early 1970s.

Sports in Post-Apartheid South Africa

Passion for organized sports is shared by most South Africans. Under apartheid, however, athletics were as polluted by racism as with any other part of South African society.

The Springboks, the national rugby team, have been a source of pride to Afrikaners for generations. But for many years international boycotts protesting apartheid locked them out of international competitions. Finally, the arrival of democracy brought them back to the world stage as hosts of the 1995 Rugby World Cup. Some blacks, still seeing the Springboks as a symbol of their long oppression, were set to root against them. President Mandela, however, successfully urged Africans to rally behind the national team to symbolize post-apartheid reconciliation (as dramatized in the 2009 film *Invictus*). When the Springboks defeated New Zealand in the final game, public rejoicing across racial lines marked an important step in the forging of the new "rainbow nation."

Africans' true passion remains football (soccer). Boys turn fields and streets into impromptu playing grounds, often playing without shoes or proper balls. Great talents developed under these trying conditions, but they had no global stage on which to display their skills, because from 1958 until 1992 South Africa's racially segregated leagues were boycotted by the international football federation. Then, in the early 1990s, a new multiracial South African Sports Federation sponsored the creation of an integrated (primarily black) national team, fondly known to its supporters as "Bafana Bafana" (in Zulu, "the boys"). A moment of glory came in 1996, when South Africa hosted the African Cup of Nations for the first time and Bafana Bafana took home the title. Global attention came in 2010, when the country became the first African nation to host the World Cup. Though Bafana Bafana failed to advance, their 2 to 1 defeat over France in the opening match sent cheering fans of all races into the streets.

Some criticized the huge sums spent on stadiums and other luxuries in a country where millions still live in great poverty, but the consensus was that the 2010 World Cup was an unqualified success, a showcase for the new South Africa and a source of pride for Africans everywhere. Like rugby, football had become a unifying force in a once deeply divided nation.

---

exports to the United States in retribution for its vast program of military aid to the Jewish state. The shock of long lines at gas pumps and greatly increased energy prices, and the global economic slowdown that followed the oil boycott of 1974, showed that the Arab-Israeli conflict could not be quarantined.

The Iranian Revolution of 1979 was an example of a predominantly Muslim nation making its voice heard on the global stage. For the first time in the postcolonial era, a state would be ruled under a constitution derived explicitly from Islamic law and tradition. Iran provided inspiration to **Islamists** (also referred to as Muslim fundamentalists) throughout the Middle East and across the Muslim world. The path toward a just society, Islamists argued, was not through absorption of Western influences and modernity but through a return to the guiding precepts of their religion. It was an explicit rejection of the secular ideologies that had dominated nineteenth- and twentieth-century global political discourse.

Islamists
Muslims who believe that laws and constitutions should be guided by Islamic principles and that religious authorities should be directly involved in governance.

The rise to power of the Islamists in Iran, and their increasing influence elsewhere, accelerated existing conflicts in the Middle East. The popular appeal of this new ideology threatened regimes founded on the principles of secular Arab nationalism, such as Egypt, Syria, Iraq, and Jordan. The Iranian Revolution also provided inspiration and support for Islamist revolutionaries in Afghanistan.

Meanwhile, the Israeli-Palestinian conflict endured. In spite of occasional signs of compromise, no resolution was forthcoming, although it seemed impossible that any meaningful "new world order" could ever be constructed without one.

Iran and Iraq

In the 1950s the shah of Iran had been supported by American intervention (see Chapter 30). For over twenty years, the shah used oil money to modernize the country while his secret police repressed the students, workers, and religious leaders who accused him of promoting decadent Western values and serving as a tool of U.S. power.

With riots and demonstrations spreading, the shah fled to the United States early in 1979. Returning from exile in Paris at the same time was **Ayatollah Khomeini** (1902–1989), whose authority was recognized by the ninety-thousand-member *ulama* (oo-leh-MAH), or community of Shi'ite religious scholars. Some of these scholars argued that while the ulama should advise political authorities on proper Islamic practice, they should not themselves wield governmental power. But Khomeini envisioned a tighter connection between religious and governmental authority. Though the radicals who seized the American embassy in Teheran and held its employees hostage were motivated more by nationalism than by religion, they responded to Khomeini's assessment of the United States as *"the great Satan."*

Ayatollah Khomeini (1902–1989) Shi'ite cleric who led the Islamic Revolution in Iran in 1979 and became Supreme Leader of the Islamic Republic of Iran.

Iranian Revolution Iranian nationalists, suspicious of both the United States and the Soviet Union, flocked to the banner of Ayatollah Khomeini to establish an Islamic Republic in 1979. Khomeini returned from exile in France as their spiritual and political leader, denouncing the United States as the "great Satan" for its longstanding support of the deposed shah. (AFP/Getty Images)

After Iraq invaded Iran, a surge of nationalism further consolidated support for Khomeini's government. The political divide between the two countries also had religious overtones. While the vast majority of Iranians are Shi'ites, in Iraq a Sunni minority had ruled over the Shi'ite majority since the days of the Ottoman empire (see Chapter 17). During eight years of brutal fighting (1980–1988), over a million people were killed. Iranian civilians and soldiers suffered terribly when the Iraqi army used chemical weapons in violation of international law.

As the war dragged on, Iran's economic problems became acute. Starved of investment capital, the economy foundered. By the 1990s employment prospects for Iran's growing population of graduates were bleak, and dissatisfaction with the regime was growing. Even with the election of a moderate reformist candidate as president in 1997, ultimate power still rested with the religious leaders who had inherited Khomeini's authority after his death in 1989.

After reaching a stalemate with Iran, Iraqi President Saddam Hussein turned his expansionist ambitions toward Kuwait, a small, oil-rich state on the Persian Gulf. Hussein considered Kuwait part of Iraq's rightful patrimony, taken away from Baghdad's control by the British in 1919 (see Chapter 27), and accused the Kuwaitis of reaching below Iraqi soil to steal its oil. Miscalculating that the United States, which had supported him in his war with Iran, would not oppose him now, Hussein invaded Kuwait in the summer of 1990 (see Map 31.2).

President George H. W. Bush reacted to Hussein's gambit by forging an international coalition against him. In the past, Hussein might have tried to counterbalance the United States by seeking an alliance with the Soviet Union, but that option no longer existed. Early in 1991, the **Persian Gulf War** began with the devastating U.S. bombing of Baghdad, after which the coalition swiftly liberated Kuwait. Hussein's army melted away under the onslaught, many killed by aerial bombardment. While the path to Baghdad was open, the Bush administration calculated that removing Hussein would upset the delicate Middle Eastern balance of power. As Americans withdrew, Hussein brutally crushed a rebellion in the largely Shi'ite south.

Afterward, the United Nations subjected Hussein's regime to sanctions intended to force his disarmament. The burden of sanctions, however, fell on the common people rather than the governing elite, and officials in the West grew skeptical about having left the regime in power (see Chapter 32). The "new world order" promised by President George H. W. Bush had yet to emerge.

Persian Gulf War (1991) War that occurred when an international coalition led by the United States expelled Iraqi forces from Kuwait. Iraq was not invaded, and Saddam Hussein remained in power.

Afghanistan and Al-Qaeda

In 1993, the administration of new U.S. President William Jefferson (Bill) Clinton became increasingly concerned about Afghanistan. In the aftermath of the Soviet withdrawal, Afghanistan came under the control of the Taliban, Islamists whose fundamentalism was even more severe than that of neighboring Iran. Women especially suffered; education for girls was eliminated completely. Mujahaddin from around the world had joined the fight against the Soviets in the 1980s, inspired by the call to holy war. After the Soviet withdrawal, some returned home to places like Egypt and Saudi Arabia determined to bring Islamic revolution to their own societies. Now some found refuge under the Taliban.

The most notorious was **Osama bin Laden** (1957–2011), son of a wealthy builder in Saudi Arabia. Though formerly allied with the United States against the Soviets, bin Laden despised the way America and the West propped up Israel and illegitimate and exploitative Middle Eastern regimes, and he decried the presence

Osama bin Laden (1957–2011) Saudi Arabian leader of the Islamist group al-Qaeda, whose goal is to replace existing governments of Muslim countries with a purified caliphate; killed by U.S. commandos in 2011.

MAP 31.2 Middle East Oil and the Arab-Israeli Conflict Not all Arabs and Arab states benefit from Middle Eastern oil reserves, which are highly concentrated in Saudi Arabia and the Persian Gulf. Farther west, Israel, born into a state of war when attacked by its Arab neighbors in 1948, ruled over significant Palestinian populations after taking the West Bank from Jordan and the Gaza Strip from Egypt during the Six-Day War in 1967. Whatever their other disagreements, Arabs have been unified in their denunciation of the Israeli occupation of the West Bank. (© Cengage Learning)

Labels appearing on the map:

Soviet occupation, 1979–1989
U.S. aid to rebels, 1980s
International and Northern Alliance forces defeat Taliban, 2001

U.S. troops, 1958, 1983–1984

U.S. arms sales, 1955–1978: $20.8 billion
Shah overthrown, 1979
American hostages taken, 1979–1981

Principal center of al-Qaeda activity, 2004–

U.S. and allies launch First U.S.-Iraq War, 1991

U.S. arms sales, 1980s, during Iran-Iraq War
Iraq invades Kuwait, 1990
Second U.S.-Iraq War, 2003

Al-Qaeda headquarters, 1992–1996

Oil embargo, 1973
Source of 17% of U.S. oil imports in 1975
Largest buyer of U.S. arms, 1978

Bombing of USS *Cole* by al-Qaeda, 2000

U.S. troops assist in relief of famine, 1992–1993.
U.S. troops withdrawn, 1994.
U.S.-backed Ethiopian invasion removes Islamist government, 2006

Members of the Organization of Petroleum Exporting Countries (OPEC)
Oil fields

ARAB-ISRAELI CONFLICT

Jewish state after UN partition of Palestine, 1947
Israel after War of 1948–1949
Area controlled by Israel after Six-Day War, 1967
Israeli-occupied area after Yom Kippur War, 1973

By Egyptian-Israeli agreements of 1975 and 1979, Israel withdrew from the Sinai in 1982. In 1981 Israel annexed the Golan Heights. Through negotiations between Israel and the PLO, Jericho and the Gaza Strip were placed under Palestinian self-rule, and Israeli troops were withdrawn in 1994. In 1994 Israel and Jordan signed an agreement opening their borders and normalizing their relations.

of American soldiers on Saudi Arabian soil. Bin Laden and his followers in al-Qaeda (el-ka-AYE-dah) first practiced terrorism to advance their cause in truck bomb attacks on American embassies in Kenya and Tanzania in 1998. In retaliation, the Clinton administration bombed southeastern Afghanistan in an unsuccessful attempt to kill bin Laden and destroy al-Qaeda's base of operations.

The Israeli-Palestinian Conflict

The unresolved Israeli-Palestinian conflict fueled Arab and Muslim resentments. A vicious cycle of violence rocked Israel and the occupied Palestinian territories in the 1970s and 1980s. Israel kept the territories it had occupied during the Six-Day War of 1967 (see Chapter 30), arguing that continued control, especially in the West Bank and Gaza, ensured Israeli security; but violence persisted. Some Israelis believed that these lands, as part of the ancient Hebrew kingdom, should be permanently annexed. To this end, the conservative Likud (lih-KOOD) Party, in power in Israel for much of the period after 1977, sponsored the construction of Jewish settlements on half of the land on the West Bank. Return of the territory to its Arab inhabitants was becoming much more difficult (see Map 31.2).

The Palestine Liberation Organization (PLO), under the leadership of Yasir Arafat (yah-SEER AHR-ah-FAT) (1929–2004), felt justified in using any means to resist the Israeli occupation, including terrorist attacks on civilians. In 1982, Israel invaded Lebanon to root out the bases from which it faced constant attacks and to drive out the PLO, which had its headquarters in Beirut. The international community was horrified by the savage attacks on Palestinian refugee camps by Lebanese militias allied with Israel. Support for Islamist organizations grew both in Lebanon, with the

Hope for Middle East Peace This 1993 handshake between Israeli Prime Minister Yitzhak Rabin and Yasir Arafat, chairman of the Palestine Liberation Organization, gave the world hope for a Middle East peace. However, negotiations for an Israeli-PLO peace accord, mediated by U.S. President Bill Clinton, proved unsuccessful. Some Israelis and their allies regarded Arafat as nothing more than a terrorist, and Rabin was later assassinated by an Israeli extremist for his role in the negotiations. (© Reuters/Corbis)

increasing influence of Hezbollah ("Party of God"), and in Palestine, where Hamas (the "Islamic Resistance Movement") arose as an alternative to the secular PLO.

Violence flared in Palestine in 1987 with the beginning of the first *intifada*, "ceaseless struggle," against the Israeli occupation of Gaza and the West Bank. The Israelis responded with security regulations restricting Palestinian mobility. Even as the intifada and the harsh Israeli response increased tensions on the ground, however, diplomatic initiatives were bearing some fruit. In 1991, under European and American sponsorship, Israeli and Palestinian diplomats met to discuss possibilities for compromise, and in 1993 the Oslo Accords laid out a mutually agreed-upon "road map" for peace based on the idea of two separate and secure nations living side by side.

President Clinton then invited Yasir Arafat and Israeli Prime Minister Yitzhak Rabin (YIT-shak rah-BEEN) to Washington, where the two men, formerly implacable enemies, shook hands before a worldwide television audience. As in South Africa, the post–Cold War climate seemed to provide the possibility of a new beginning. Those hopes were dashed, however, when Arafat refused to accept an Israeli land-for-peace offer more generous than any previously discussed. The status of Jerusalem was one sticking point, with Israelis and Palestinians both laying claim to the city as their capital. The Israelis could also not accept the Palestinian demand for a "right of return" for Arabs to the homes within Israel they had abandoned in the war of 1948 (see the feature "World History in Today's World" in Chapter 27). The "road map" had led nowhere.

The Economics of Globalization

With the fall of the Soviet Union and the Second World socialist economy, the post–World War II process of economic globalization took a huge leap forward. Expanding global trade led to unprecedented growth and international economic integration. Some Asian economies surged, with Taiwan, South Korea, and Singapore, the so-called "Asian Tigers," leading the way. Overcoming the disruptions of the Cultural Revolution (see Chapter 30), the People's Republic of China became the world's fastest-growing economy by adopting market principles. Likewise India embraced the market, purging old socialist and bureaucratic institutions to achieve stunning rates of growth (see Chapter 32).

Western Europe was consolidated when the European Economic Community transformed into the European Union (EU). By the late 1990s the EU had expanded into the former Soviet sphere to constitute one of the three major centers of the global economy along with China and the United States. At the same time, however, some pointed to the increasing inequality of economic globalization. Both within nations and between them, the benefits of economic growth were not shared equally, and the gap between the global haves and have-nots increased.

Japan and the "Asian Tigers"

Japan rose quickly from the battering it took in 1945. Under occupation by the United States, Japanese leaders renounced militarism and accepted the democratic constitution Americans drafted for them. The energy and drive that had earlier gone into empire building was now focused on domestic rebirth. Fukuzawa Yûkichi (see Chapter 24) would have been proud as Japanese products came to surpass those of Europe and the United States in both quality and price.

Several factors facilitated Japanese economic success. American military protection relieved the country of the financial burden of military spending, and close collaboration between the government bureaucracy and large corporations brought planning and coordination to the national economy. Japanese employees, famous for their work ethic, were also willing to accept policies that favored savings and corporate investment over private consumption. Old corporations, like Mitsui, and new ones, like Sony, developed organizational structures that emphasized long-term loyalty between employer and employee, leading to relatively harmonious labor relations and an absence of strikes. However, company loyalty entailed endless work hours, and many Japanese women lived confining lives, raising children while rarely seeing their husbands.

In the 1970s, Japan enjoyed a rapid increase in automobile exports, especially to the United States. Japanese models first targeted consumers of inexpensive yet well-built cars. Meanwhile, manufacturers in the United States built large vehicles of indifferent quality. After oil prices surged following the OPEC oil boycott in 1973, demand for the more fuel-efficient Japanese cars skyrocketed.

At the same time, the rising price of oil revealed vulnerabilities in the Japanese economy. In addition to being dependent on food and energy imports, Japan was subject to competition from other Asian nations that began to follow the same industrial export strategy with even lower labor costs. Japan responded to the challenge by moving away from heavy industry toward knowledge-intensive sectors such as computers and telecommunications. Backed by large government subsidies for research and development, and coordinating their efforts with the Ministry for International Trade and Industry, Japanese corporations in the 1980s increasingly focused on such high-profit activities while relocating many of their factories to countries with lower labor costs.

Then, even as American executives studied the Japanese model for business success, the bubble burst. In 1989, the Tokyo Stock Exchange collapsed. Real estate speculation, political corruption, and a banking crisis caused by bad loans were to blame. To reignite the economy, the government began to emphasize leisure and consumption over savings, hoping that the country could spend its way out of crisis; but, while the Japanese economy stabilized, Asian growth moved elsewhere.

The South Korean government emulated the export-oriented industrial model of Japan, including close coordination between the state administration and the emerging Korean *chaebols*, economic conglomerates such as Hyundai. The South Korean government was fiercely anticommunist, led by authoritarian personalities with close ties to the military, and paramilitary police often met student and worker protests with fatal force. Then in 1988, with South Korea preparing to host the Summer Olympics and the power of the Soviet Union fading, liberal political reforms were finally instituted, with a peaceful transfer of power between political parties in 1992. The liberal political equation of rule of law, democratic processes, and free markets had been achieved.

Economic growth and authoritarian government also characterized Taiwan. The island's government was dominated by exiles from the mainland who controlled the bureaucracy, the military, and the economy. As in South Korea, popular discontent grew during the 1980s, especially among those who had been born on the island and were unhappy with the political monopoly of the Guomindang, dominated by exiles from the mainland. By 1988, as part of the general trend toward democratization, free elections had laid the foundation of Taiwanese democracy. Meanwhile, the economy blossomed.

By the 1980s Taiwan, along with South Korea, Singapore, and British-ruled Hong Kong, was counted as one of the "Asian Tigers," adding high technology to its existing industrial infrastructure. South Korea became a leader in telecommunications technology, while Taiwan became a major supplier of microchips for the expanding market in home computers. Some analysts began to speak of "Confucian capitalism," based on group consensus and hierarchy rather than individualism and class conflict, as an alternative to the individualistic Western model. But no generalizations about Asian capitalism could be made without taking into account the transformation of the People's Republic of China.

Deng Xiaoping's China and Its Imitators

At the start of the nineteenth century China produced about one-third of the world's industrial output (see Table 23.1). But in 1949, after a century and a half of European economic dominance, that percentage had shrunk to less than 3 percent. The country's astonishing economic growth in the last two decades of the twentieth century restored China's historical role as a global center of manufacturing.

That turnabout resulted from the policies of **Deng Xiaoping** (1904–1997), one of the pragmatic "experts" who had opposed the excesses of the Great Leap Forward and the Cultural Revolution. After Mao's death and the defeat of the "Gang of Four" (see Chapter 30), Deng put China on a new economic path by adopting market incentives. The first step was to grant peasants their own farm plots for private production. Food production surged. Deng became a hero to millions of Chinese farming families, who could now afford small luxuries for the first time. When asked how he, a lifelong communist, justified adopting capitalist principles, Deng replied: *"It does not matter whether the cat is black or white, as long as she catches mice."* *"To get rich,"* he added, *"is glorious."*

The second stage in Deng's reforms was to provide legal and institutional mechanisms for the development of the industrial sector. In the southern region of Guangzhou, near the British-controlled territory of Hong Kong, foreign investors were invited to build manufacturing plants. In an embrace of international capitalism unthinkable under Mao, many multinational corporations moved their manufacturing operations to Guangzhou to take advantage of China's cheap labor.

Chinese banks funded local investors with connections to the Communist Party. The Red Army itself became a major economic power, controlling one of the world's largest shipping lines. As manufacturing spread from Guangzhou throughout eastern and central China, a vast flow of finished goods crossed the Pacific destined for American markets. China's cities experienced a huge construction boom, attracting millions of rural migrants. The coastal city of Shanghai became a glittering cosmopolitan center as traffic jams and billboards replaced bicycles and moralistic party posters.

Although Deng Xiaoping resigned from his post in 1987, he remained a dominant power behind the scenes until his death in 1997. During that period, both the costs and benefits of his policies became more and more apparent. A great success was the return of Hong Kong in 1997 from British to Chinese control. Communist leaders promised that the people of Hong Kong would retain their accustomed civil liberties such as rights of free speech and assembly.

The big test of Deng's legacy came in 1989. Student activists, yearning for political change to match the economic transformation of their country, organized a large antigovernment rally, erecting a replica of the Statue of Liberty in the heart of Beijing to symbolize their goal of greater freedom and an end to corruption. This student-led prodemocracy movement ended with the **Tiananmen Massacre** when communist authorities sent tanks and troops to clear the square,

Deng Xiaoping (1904–1997) Chinese Communist Party leader who brought dramatic economic reforms after the death of Mao Zedong.

Tiananmen Massacre Massacre in a public square in Beijing where, in 1989, students and workers demanded freedom and democracy. On order from the Communist Party, the Chinese military cleared Tiananmen Square with tanks and gunfire.

Dylan Martineaz/AFP/Getty Images

Hong Kong, 1997 The return of Hong Kong to China ended more than 150 years of British rule. As in India and dozens of other former colonies in prior decades, the Union Jack was lowered and "God Save the Queen" played for the final time; the flag of the People's Republic of China was then raised to mark the transfer of sovereignty. Communist leaders pledged that their "one country, two systems" policy would protect the civil liberties guaranteed by Hong Kong's unique legal system.

killing hundreds, perhaps thousands, of student activists and arresting many more.

Though some Chinese officials advocated a moderate approach and reconciliation with the students, Deng Xiaoping remembered the chaos that had accompanied student demonstrations during the Cultural Revolution and backed the hardliners who advocated a crackdown. The party leaders, well aware of how Mikhail Gorbachev's policy of glasnost had undermined communist authority in the Soviet Union, were unwilling to take a chance that tolerance for dissent would fatally undermine their authority. The Chinese Communist Party would not risk its political monopoly.

China's economic transformation also created other challenges. Environmental problems multiplied. The gap between rich and poor increased, as did imbalances between wealthier coastal regions and China's interior. As corruption spread, protests increased among the same rural population that Mao had made the center of his revolution. Still, whatever their social, political, and environmental byproducts, the economic policies of Deng Xiaoping had raised China to the status of a great power. Many Chinese felt that their country had returned to its proper historical place after two centuries of humiliation by Western powers and Japan.

China's competitive advantage was its political stability combined with low-cost labor. By the 1990s other Asian countries were also able to build up export-oriented manufacturing centers. American consumers hardly even noticed that much of their clothing and other commodities were now produced in places like Thailand, Malaysia, Indonesia, and Vietnam. For much of the twentieth century, nationalist leaders in these countries had dreamed of catching up with the West through industrialization. Now, like China, they were moving toward that goal.

The nature of the global economy, however, was shifting. Industry was being overtaken by marketing, financial services, and other "knowledge industries" as the highest value-producing activities. Chinese leaders worked to develop and borrow high technology as part the country's economic mix. But for many Asian workers, especially in Southeast Asia, industrialization brought little benefit. Young women with few skills other than manual dexterity made up much of the industrial workforce, and child labor was all too common. As global consumers demanded ever-cheaper products, wages remained low in China, Southeast Asia, and other industrial economies.

The European Union

Beginning in the 1980s, western European leaders, especially in France and Germany, sought to deepen the level of cooperation already in place throughout the European Economic Community. A European Parliament, with little real authority but great symbolic importance, was elected. Negotiations were begun to open borders, to create a single internal market free of tariffs, and to move toward a common European currency. While these negotiations were taking place, the Soviet Union began to dissolve and talk turned to the possibility of incorporating new members from the former Eastern bloc.

In 1992 the Treaty on European Union was signed at the Dutch city of Maastricht. It set a date of January 1, 1999, for the introduction of the euro (the EU's proposed currency), limited the amount of public debt that a nation could hold to be admitted to the union, and created a European Central Bank to coordinate monetary policy. Now with a clear timeline toward a common flag and common citizenship, some complained that a European "superstate" run by faceless bureaucrats in Brussels would undermine national sovereignty, and Great Britain, Denmark, and Sweden all rejected the euro, refusing to surrender control of their own currencies. But other provisions of the Maastricht Treaty were approved (see Map 31.3 on page 914).

With an internal market larger than that of the United States, and members who represented complementary economic and human resources, the European Union was a major success, accounting for over 18 percent of global exports by century's end. While each member country benefited from the new relationship, growth rates were especially high in poorer, more agricultural countries. Spain, Greece, and Portugal, all of which had suffered from authoritarian governments, became modern democracies with significantly more educated populations. Ireland was dubbed the "Celtic Tiger" for its transformation from an agrarian society to one based on strong educational foundations and prowess in high technology. The new prosperity of Portugal, Greece, Spain, and Ireland as members of the European Union was a striking and rapid change, although in the next decade concern over the debts accumulated to jump-start those economies would lead to a deep crisis for the European Union and the euro zone (see Chapter 32).

The European Union arose partly in reaction to the United States. Many Europeans saw the materialism of American society as a threat to their own more leisurely mode of life and generous social policies. In the 1990s, leaders of traditionally socialist parties, such as Tony Blair in Great Britain and Gerhard Schröder in Germany, advocated a "third way" to growth and stability. Rejecting both the relatively unfettered capitalism of the United States and the inefficiencies of state socialism, they advocated a combination of market incentives and social investment. In France, the government reflected popular feeling when it took advantage of globalization while avoiding a "new world order" of cultural Americanization. (See the feature "Movement of Ideas Through Primary Sources: The End of History?")

On balance, by the end of the twentieth century the European Union represented optimism and growth. In 2000, negotiations began to bring former Soviet satellites such as Poland, the Czech Republic, and Hungary into the EU; Turkish membership was also being discussed. To some, predominantly Muslim Turkey seemed beyond what could be called "European," though Turkey's connection with Europe had deep roots (see Chapter 28).

The End of History?

No longer able to use the familiar compass points of East-West conflict, scholars and political analysts at the end of the Cold War struggled to find ways to describe the "new world order" and to anticipate its future direction. One of the most discussed contributions to this literature in the early 1990s was Francis Fukuyama's essay "The End of History."

Fukuyama, a Japanese American, was employed by the U.S. state department when he wrote this article. At that time, in 1989, he was associated with neoconservatism, a movement that stressed the right and responsibility of the United States to unilaterally assert its power across the globe in the defense of American interests, including the promotion of American values of political freedom and economic enterprise. After the neoconservatives achieved great political influence under the administration of George W. Bush, however, Fukuyama broke with them over the issue of the Iraq War (see Chapter 32).

Source: Francis Fukuyama, "The End of History," *The National Interest*, Summer, 1989. Copyright © 1989, Francis Fukuyama. Reprinted by permission of the author.

In watching the flow of events over the past decade or so, it is hard to avoid the feeling that something very fundamental has happened in world history. The past year has seen a flood of articles commemorating the end of the Cold War, and the fact that "peace" seems to be breaking out in many regions of the world. . . . [T]he century that began full of self-confidence in the ultimate triumph of Western liberal democracy seems at its close to be returning full circle to where it started . . . to an unabashed victory of economic and political liberalism. . . .

What we may be witnessing is not just the end of the Cold War . . . but the end of history as such: that is, the end point of mankind's ideological evolution and the universalization of Western liberal democracy as the final form of human government. . . . [T]he victory of liberalism has occurred primarily in the realm of ideas or consciousness and is as yet incomplete in the real or material world. But there are powerful reasons for believing that it is the ideal that will govern the material world in the long run. . . .

The state that emerges at the end of history is liberal insofar as it recognizes and protects through a system of law man's universal right to freedom; and democratic insofar as it exists only with the consent of the governed. . . . [H]istory ended . . . in the ideals of the French or American Revolutions: while particular regimes in the real world might not implement these ideals fully, their theoretical truth is absolute and could not be improved upon. . . .

In the past century, there have been two major challenges to liberalism, those of fascism and of communism. The former saw the political weakness, materialism, anomie, and lack of community of the West as fundamental contradictions in liberal societies that could only be resolved by a strong state that forged a new "people" on the basis of national exclusiveness. Fascism was destroyed as a living ideology by World War II. This was a defeat, of course, on a very material level, but it amounted to a defeat of the idea as well. . . .

The ideological challenge mounted by the other great alternative to liberalism, communism, was far more serious. Marx . . . asserted that liberal society contained a fundamental contradiction that could not be resolved within its context, that between capital and labor, and this contradiction has constituted the chief accusation against liberalism ever since. But surely, the class issue has actually been successfully resolved in the West. . . . [T]he egalitarianism of modern America represents the essential achievement of the classless society envisioned by Marx. This is not to say that there are not rich people and poor people in the United States, or that the gap between them has not grown in recent years. But the root causes of economic inequality do not have to do with the underlying legal and social structure of our society, which remains fundamentally egalitarian and moderately redistributionist. . . .

[T]he power of the liberal idea would seem much less impressive if it had not infected the largest and oldest culture in Asia, China. . . . China could not now be described in any way as a liberal democracy. . . . But anyone familiar with the outlook and behavior of the new technocratic elite now governing China knows that Marxism and ideological principle have become virtually irrelevant as guides to policy. . . . The student demonstrations in Beijing that broke out . . . recently . . . were only the beginning of what will inevitably be mounting pressure for change in the political system as well. . . . The central issue is the fact that the People's Republic of China can no longer act as a beacon for illiberal forces around the world. . . . Maoism, rather than being the pattern for Asia's future, became an anachronism. . . .

Important as these changes in China have been, however, it is developments in the Soviet Union . . . that have put the final nail in the coffin of the Marxist-Leninist alternative to liberal democracy. . . . What has happened in the four years since Gorbachev's coming to power is a revolutionary assault on the most fundamental institutions and principles of Stalinism, and their replacement by other principles which do not amount to liberalism per se but whose only connecting thread is liberalism. . . .

[A]re there any other ideological competitors left? . . . The rise of religious fundamentalism in recent years within the Christian, Jewish, and Muslim traditions has been widely noted. . . . In the contemporary world only Islam has offered a theocratic state as a political alternative to both liberalism and communism. But the doctrine has little appeal for non-Muslims, and it is hard to believe that the movement will take on any universal significance. . . .

This does not by any means imply the end of international conflict per se. . . . There would still be a high and perhaps rising level of ethnic and nationalist violence. . . . This implies that terrorism and wars of national liberation will continue to be an important item on the international agenda. But large-scale conflict must involve large states still caught in the grip of history, and they are what appear to be passing from the scene.

The end of history will be a very sad time. The struggle for recognition, the willingness to risk one's life for a purely abstract goal, the worldwide ideological struggle that called forth daring, courage, imagination, and idealism, will be replaced by economic calculation, the endless solving of technical problems, environmental concerns, and the satisfaction of sophisticated consumer demands. In the post-historical period there will be neither art nor philosophy, just the perpetual caretaking of the museum of human history. . . . Perhaps this very prospect of centuries of boredom at the end of history will serve to get history started once again.

QUESTION FOR ANALYSIS

» *Two decades after it was written, how accurate does Francis Fukuyama's prediction seem? To what extent has the triumph of liberal democracy and free-market economics marked an "end of history"?*

MAP 31.3 The European Union The European Union (EU) developed from the more limited European Economic Community, dominated by France and the Federal Republic of Germany. The United Kingdom, Ireland, Denmark, Spain, Portugal, and Greece were added in the 1970s and 1980s. The collapse of the Soviet Union led to a dramatic EU expansion into eastern Germany, central and southeastern Europe, and the Nordic and Baltic countries. Turkey's application for membership proved controversial, while Russia has resisted the inclusion of Georgia and Ukraine.

(© Cengage Learning)

Structural Adjustment and Free Trade in the Third World

As we have seen, the "new world order" based on democracy and free markets had a mixed record in the 1990s. The challenge across much of the world, especially in Africa and Latin America, was to balance social needs, including spending on health and education, with economic liberalization policies that required steep cuts in government spending. Rising energy prices in the later 1970s and 1980s had driven many underdeveloped nations into debt, leading them to turn to the International Monetary Fund (IMF) for emergency loans to maintain their solvency. IMF officials granted such loans only on the condition that the indebted nations accept **structural adjustment** programs that required sharp cuts in government spending. IMF economists argued that state interference in markets was constraining economic activity, and that only when state expenditures were slashed could developing countries reach sustainable levels of growth.

In Mexico, structural adjustment meant cutting government subsidies on the price of maize meal. In the long run, economists argued, the "magic of the market" would align production and consumption and lead to greater prosperity. In the short run it meant a sharp rise in the price of tortillas and thus more hungry children. When the East African nation of Tanzania accepted an IMF loan in 1987, it was forced to lay off thousands of teachers to help balance its books, suspending the country's goal to provide universal primary education. Still, advocates of structural adjustment argued that, in the long term, free markets were the only way to create abundance for the people of countries like Mexico and Tanzania.

The economics of liberal free trade also guided the development and passage, in 1994, of the North American Free Trade Association (NAFTA), uniting Canada, the United States, and Mexico in a market even larger than that of the European Union. NAFTA was controversial. In the United States, critics warned that the removal of tariffs on Mexican imports would mean the loss of high-paying industrial jobs as manufacturers seeking to pay lower wages moved south of the border. In Mexico, farmers worried that they would be ruined by open competition with U.S. farmers, who were heavily subsidized by their government. Then even as previously high-wage industrial jobs moved south, rural Mexicans would flee north because of falling crop prices.

In the southern state of Chiapas, rebels calling themselves Zapatistas (after the Mexican revolutionary Emiliano Zapata; see Chapter 27) declared "war on the Mexican state" in 1994, with NAFTA as one of their principal grievances. The Zapatistas were part of a global movement of people who sought to reassert their collective welfare against the free-market onslaught and to protect their locally based cultural and political identity against the wave of globalization. As we will see, such efforts would continue into the twenty-first century. But for better or worse, capitalism was now the only game being played in the global economy.

structural adjustment Economic policy imposed by the International Monetary Fund and World Bank on debtor nations, requiring significant cuts in government spending and reduced economic intervention in markets to create conditions for long-term growth.

CONTEXT AND CONNECTIONS

Beyond the "Age of Extremes"?

Eric Hobsbawm, a prominent British historian, referred to twentieth-century world history as the "Age of Extremes." Like Nelson Mandela, Hobsbawm was born while the First World War still raged, and like Mandela he could reflect back from the year 2000 on a lifetime during which rapid and unpredictable change seemed the only constant.

When Mandela and Hobsbawm were young, radio was still a new invention, telephones were a luxury, commercial aviation was in its infancy, and the British empire was the framework for the world around them, a world in which European domination was taken for granted. At the end of the century, both men had lived long enough to witness the development of instantaneous global telecommunications, a thoroughly integrated global economy, and a population that had grown from less than 2 billion to over 6 billion persons.

In the interim, momentous events had rocked the world: the Great Depression; the rise of communism and fascism; the Second World War and the Holocaust; the development of nuclear weapons

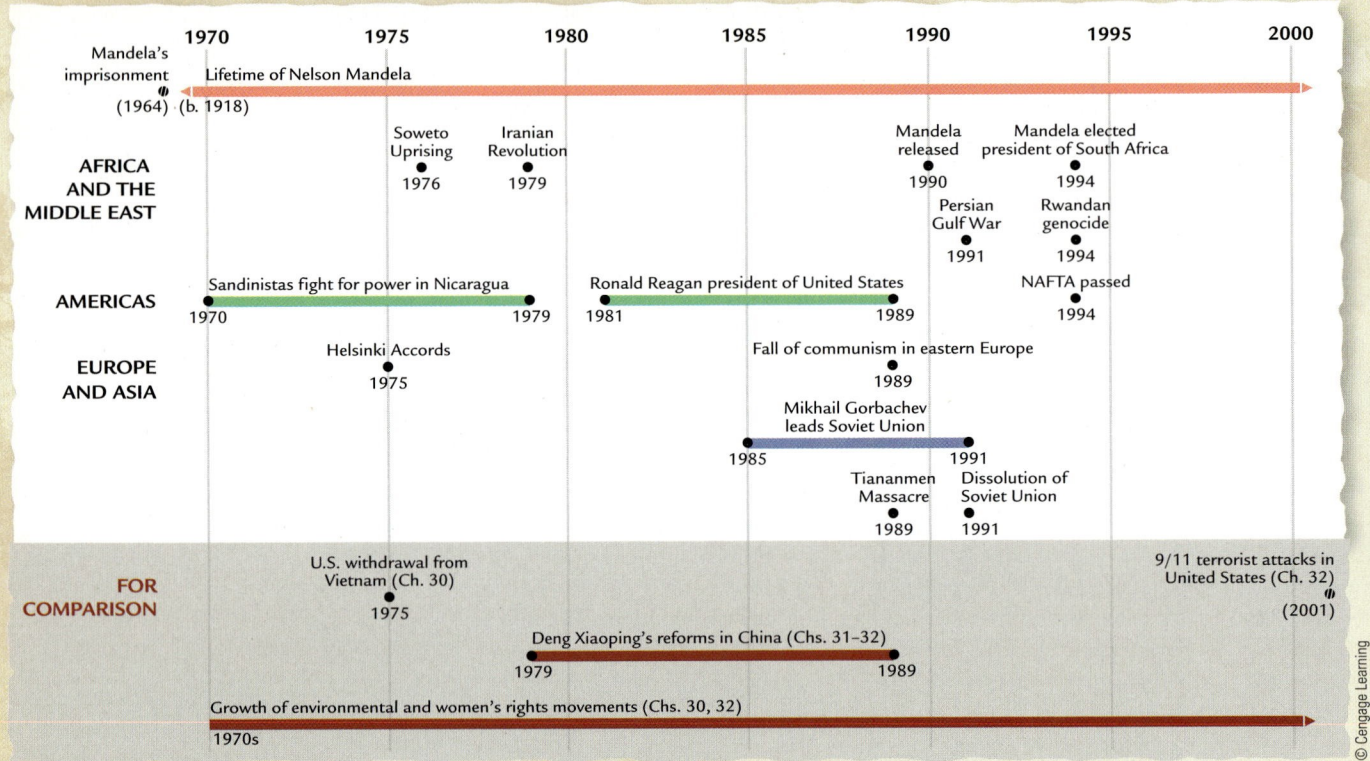

Timeline (1970–2000)

	1970	1975	1980	1985	1990	1995	2000

Mandela's imprisonment ⊕ (1964) · (b. 1918) — Lifetime of Nelson Mandela →

AFRICA AND THE MIDDLE EAST
- Soweto Uprising 1976
- Iranian Revolution 1979
- Mandela released 1990
- Mandela elected president of South Africa 1994
- Persian Gulf War 1991
- Rwandan genocide 1994

AMERICAS
- Sandinistas fight for power in Nicaragua 1970–1979
- Ronald Reagan president of United States 1981–1989
- NAFTA passed 1994

EUROPE AND ASIA
- Helsinki Accords 1975
- Fall of communism in eastern Europe 1989
- Mikhail Gorbachev leads Soviet Union 1985–1991
- Tiananmen Massacre 1989
- Dissolution of Soviet Union 1991

FOR COMPARISON
- U.S. withdrawal from Vietnam (Ch. 30) 1975
- 9/11 terrorist attacks in United States (Ch. 32) ⊕ (2001)
- Deng Xiaoping's reforms in China (Chs. 31–32) 1979–1989
- Growth of environmental and women's rights movements (Chs. 30, 32) 1970s →

and the Cold War; the collapse of the European and Soviet empires; the transformation of China and other Asian economies; and the re-creation of a brutally racist South Africa into a beacon of post–Cold War democracy and racial reconciliation. An "Age of Extremes" indeed!

The entire history of the rise and fall of the Soviet Union took place during these single lifetimes. True, communism persisted. But China and Vietnam had transformed their economies using market principles, hardly an advertisement for the superiority of Karl Marx's economic philosophy (see Chapter 23). In North Korea and Cuba, it became doubtful that communism could long survive the economic failure of their leaders. Everywhere else communism had retreated: these four nations represented all that was left of the great hopes and the great fears raised by communism in the twentieth century—a paltry legacy. The retreat was seen even in South Africa, where the Communist Party, close allies of Nelson Mandela and the African National Congress in the struggle against apartheid, now advocated private enterprise rather than state control as the key to economic growth and improvements in the lives of the African majority.

However, even as the world celebrated the dawn of a new millennium and U.S. President Bill Clinton talked of "building a bridge to the twenty-first century," new challenges appeared on the horizon. Genocide in Rwanda and other human rights abuses driven by ethnicity and religion had shown that the extreme hatreds of the old century had not been entirely left behind. More broadly, commentators observed the rise of religious extremism as a menace to secular and Enlightenment traditions. Such fears were magnified after the attacks by Islamic fundamentalists on the World Trade Center in New York and the Pentagon in Washington on September 11, 2001, and by the highly controversial U.S. invasion of Iraq a few years later. These events are too recent for proper historical analysis, but in the final chapter of this book we will attempt a survey of twenty-first-century realities in a world that has become smaller and smaller thanks to the political, economic, technological, and cultural dynamics of accelerating globalization.

Voyages on the Web: Nelson Mandela

The Voyages Map App follows the traveler's journeys using interactive study tools, including 360-degree panoramic views of historic sites, zoomable maps, audio summaries, flash cards, and quizzes.

Key Terms

Nelson Mandela (886)
Ronald Reagan (889)
Helsinki Accords (890)
Mikhail Gorbachev (891)
Solidarity (892)
Boris Yeltsin (893)

Bantustans (899)
Soweto Uprising (900)
Organization of Petroleum
    Exporting Countries (OPEC)
    (901)
Islamists (902)

Ayatollah Khomeini (903)
Persian Gulf War (904)
Osama bin Laden (904)
Deng Xiaoping (909)
Tiananmen Massacre (909)
structural adjustment (915)

For Further Reference

Barber, Benjamin. *Jihad vs. McWorld: How Globalism and Tribalism Are Reshaping the World.* New York: Times Books, 1995.

Fukuyama, Francis. *The End of History and the Last Man.* New York: Free Press, 2006.

Garthoff, Raymond. *The Great Transition: American-Soviet Relations at the End of the Cold War.* Washington, D.C.: Brookings, 1994.

Gerlach, Christian. *Extremely Violent Societies: Mass Violence in the Twentieth Century World.* New York: Cambridge University Press, 2010.

Hoffman, David. *The Oligarchs: Wealth and Power in the New Russia.* 2d ed. New York: Public Affairs, 2011.

Huntington, Samuel P. *The Clash of Civilizations: The Debate.* 2d ed. Washington, D.C.: Foreign Affairs, 2010.

Iriye, Akira, Petra Goedde, and William I. Hitchcock, eds. *The Human Rights Revolution: An International History.* New York: Oxford University Press, 2012.

Judt, Tony. *Thinking the Twentieth Century.* New York: Penguin, 2012.

Kagan, Robert. *Of Paradise and Power: America and Europe in the New World Order.* New York: Knopf, 2003.

Kenney, Padraic. *1989: Democratic Revolutions at the Cold War's End: A Brief History with Documents.* New York: Bedford/St. Martin's, 2009.

Kepel, Gilles. *The War for Muslim Minds: Islam and the West.* Cambridge, Mass.: Harvard University Press, 2004.

Mamdani, Mahmood. *Good Muslim, Bad Muslim: America, the Cold War, and the Roots of Terror.* New York: Crown, 2005.

Mandela, Nelson. *Long Walk to Freedom: The Autobiography of Nelson Mandela.* Boston: Little, Brown, 1996.

Marti, Michael. *China and the Legacy of Deng Xiaoping: From Communist Revolution to Capitalist Evolution.* Washington, D.C.: Potomac, 2002.

Sebestyn, Sebastian. *Revolution 1989: The Fall of the Soviet Empire.* New York: Vintage, 2010.

Smith, Charles D. *Palestine and the Arab-Israeli Conflict.* 7th ed. New York: Bedford/St. Martin's, 2009.

Smith, Peter H. *Democracy in Latin America: Political Change in Comparative Context.* 2d ed. New York: Oxford University Press, 2011.

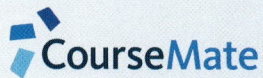

32

Voyage into the Twenty-First Century

The life of Chinese artist **Ai Weiwei** (b. 1957) exemplifies some of the best and some of the worst of contemporary China. On the one hand, Ai is a global face of the "new China," a highly respected creative talent whose works are internationally admired and whose innovative contributions to the design of the Beijing National Stadium for the 2008 Summer Olympics helped the People's Republic put its best face forward to the world.

As a firm believer in freedom of speech and the rule of law, however, Ai Weiwei (eye way way) has been subjected to constant police surveillance, had his influential blog shut down, had his Shanghai studio demolished, and in 2011 was detained for almost three months on highly suspect charges of tax evasion. His life story crystallizes the contradictions of his nation, a country whose economic renaissance over the past three decades has not yet yielded equivalent strides in political openness, legal transparency, or civil rights.

Ai has suffered deeply for his principled stands, requiring brain surgery after a severe beating by police officers that led to problems with concentration. Still, he remains optimistic. Although it is dangerous for Chinese citizens to make public statements of support, Ai was surprised and heartened by their response to his incarceration:

Ai Weiwei
(Peter Macdiarmid/Getty Images)

I [have] always thought, in modern history [the] Chinese people are like a dish of sand, never really close together. But today I think a dish of sand is a good metaphor because now we have the Internet. We don't have to be physically united. You can be an individual and have your own set of values but join others in certain struggles. There is nothing more powerful than that. On the Internet, people do

Imprisoned for three months in 2011, for alleged tax evasion.

Ai relocates to New York, 1981–1993.

ARCTIC OCEAN

ASIA

London
Berlin
EUROPE
Munich

NORTH AMERICA

New York

Los Angeles

Beijing
CHINA

Tokyo

See inset map

AFRICA

ATLANTIC OCEAN

INDIAN OCEAN

PACIFIC OCEAN

AUSTRALIA Brisbane
Sydney

SOUTH AMERICA

Rio de Janeiro

N

0   1500   3000 Km.
0   1500   3000 Mi.

Ai Weiwei and his family are sent to Shihezi, 1957–1975.

SOVIET UNION/ RUSSIA
KAZAKHSTAN
MONGOLIA
ALTAI MTS.
Shihezi
GOBI
TAKLAMAKAN
Beijing

NORTH KOREA
SOUTH KOREA

Ai is severely beaten by authorities in 2009, after revealing that shoddy school construction contributed to high student death count in 2008 earthquake.

CHINA

Chengdu

Shanghai
Hangzhou

INDIA   BANGLADESH
0   300   600 Km.
0   300   600 Mi.
BURMA
VIETNAM
LAOS

Taipei

Guangzhou
Hong Kong

Selected Travels of Ai Weiwei
← Ai Weiwei's selected journeys
○ Selected city visited by Ai
● City in which Ai has had a solo show
● City in which Ai's art has been exhibited

© Cengage Learning

Join this chapter's traveler on "Voyages," an interactive tour of historic sites and events:
www.cengagebrain.com

not know each other, they don't have common leaders, sometimes not even a common political goal. But they come together on certain issues. I think that is a miracle. It never happened in the past. Without the Internet, I would not even be Ai Weiwei today. I would just be an artist somewhere doing my shows.*

---

*"Ai Wei Wei: Shame on Me," SPIEGEL International, 11, 24, 2011; http://www.spiegel.de/international/world/0,1518,799302,00.html. Published in English, the language of the interview.

Ai Weiwei
(b. 1957) A Chinese artist, blogger, and critic of the Communist government. His arrest and detention in 2011 focused global attention on the slow pace of democratization in China.

In spite of the "Great Firewall of China"—the government's effort to regulate the Internet by blocking access to sensitive topics—the power of information technology, and especially of social networking, may yet prove too strong to control.

Ai Weiwei's father, the poet Ai Qing (eye CHING), established a pattern of both traveling for his art and suffering for it. The elder Ai traveled to Paris in the 1920s, returned to China in the 1930s, joined with Mao Zedong's Communists, and became an influential figure after the founding of the People's Republic in 1949 (see Chapter 30). Then in 1957, Mao declared an "anti-rightist" campaign against intellectuals he thought had strayed too far from the party line. Ai Qing was arrested, and for twenty years publication of his poetry was forbidden while he cleaned toilets at a "re-education" camp in the far west of the country. Ai Weiwei grew up in bleak circumstances.

Mao's death in 1976 and Deng Xiaoping's opening of China brought new possibilities. The party restored Ai Qing to official honor, and in 1980 he traveled back to France to receive a prestigious literary award. Ai Weiwei himself moved to New York in 1981, where he formed his singular artistic vision amid the city's many creative voices. When his father fell ill in 1993, Ai Weiwei returned home and created an "East Village" in Beijing, emulating the artistic community he had experienced in New York. Unlike many other émigrés, he had never changed his citizenship status: his fate was intertwined with his native land.

The timing of Ai Weiwei's arrest in April 2011 was not coincidental. During that "Arab Spring," the spirit of revolt spread across North Africa and the Middle East. Later, demonstrators would also take to the streets in Europe, India, South America, and the United States. China cracked down harshly on dissidents and intensified its surveillance. The Communist government feared that social networking technology would be used to re-create, on an even larger scale, the Tiananmen Square protests of 1989 (see Chapter 31).

Were the protests of 2011 a seismic shift, or merely a passing phase? There is no way to be sure. Our survey of world history has given us some tools for assessing the recent past, but lacking adequate perspective, we cannot evaluate the events of the past decade historically. In this final chapter, therefore, our conclusions can be only tentative as we address some of the core issues facing contemporary humanity. The authors hope that as you read this, Ai Weiwei will have attained the freedom to enrich us all with his creative vision.

Focus Questions

» *How is globalization affecting the world economy and global security?*

» *What are the most important environmental and demographic trends of the twenty-first century?*

» *To what extent is the world moving forward in gender equality, democracy, and cultural exchange?*

New Economic Players

When Ai Weiwei was a child, China's already meager contributions to the global economy were being further reduced by Mao Zedong's disastrous Great Leap

Forward (see Chapter 30). In 1981, when Ai left for the United States, the Chinese economy had just begun to benefit from Deng Xiaoping's new market model policies (see Chapter 31). By 1993, when Ai returned, the country's economy had been entirely transformed by years of sustained growth. In 2011, the year of his detention, China surpassed Japan as the world's second-largest economy, and more of its people had been lifted out of poverty than at any other time in history.

China's economic rise and the story of contemporary economic globalization therefore go hand in hand. The twenty-first century began with strong growth globally, but growth rates in China and India were spectacular, with other Asian, African, and Latin American countries showing strength as well. Economists coined the term *BRIC*—for Brazil, Russia, India, and China—to describe the world's surging growth points. Turkey has also shown exceptionally strong development in the past decade. In fact, the dramatic collapse of the financial sectors in the United States and Europe in 2008 (discussed in the next section) sent a sharp signal that the age of Western economic dominance might be coming to an end.

China and India led the way, the sheer size of their billion-plus populations guaranteeing enormous global influence. Their very different political and social systems—China a one-party communist state with a strongly centralized system, India a vibrant multiparty democracy with a less centralized federal model of governance—provided alternative models for prosperity. And while Chinese government and business leaders focused on industrial development for export, Indian leaders put a greater emphasis on high technology and the cultivation of the huge domestic market.

For India, the starting point came in 1991 when India's finance minister, **Manmohan Singh** (b. 1932), lowered business taxes and relaxed government regulations, adding further reforms in 1997. Annual economic growth rates surged toward 10 percent, and India's steel, chemical, automotive, and pharmaceutical industries, once bound by state regulation, made major strides in national, regional, and global markets. Middle-class families who once spent years waiting to buy a car could now choose among multiple models and buy on credit. At the same time, India became a major player in the software industry, especially as concerns about a "millennium virus" caused Western companies to seek inexpensive ways to back up electronic data. As a result of the government's structural reforms and the creativity of Indian entrepreneurship, growth rates remained high even in the wake of the 2008 global financial crisis, exceeding 10 percent annual growth in 2010.

While such has been the good news for India, many have been left behind. In the world's largest democracy, hundreds of millions still live without access to clean water, let alone computers. Data from India, China, Brazil, the United States, and elsewhere show a strong correlation between global economic growth and rising inequality. Critics contend that in their haste to liberalize their economies, governments have abandoned the health and educational needs of their citizens. As one economist has argued, *"The ancient question of how market forces need to be tempered for the greater good of the economy and the society is now a global one"* (see Map 32.1).[*]

In postcommunist Russia, the initial experience of free-market capitalism had been deeply destabilizing. The rapid privatization of state assets in the 1990s benefited economic insiders, instant billionaires who formed a new economic oligarchy. Vladimir Putin (see Chapter 31) played on popular disgust with the new economic regime to reassert state control over important sectors like natural gas, media, and telecommunications, magnifying his personal power and that of his

Manmohan Singh Finance minister (1991–1996) and prime minister of India (since 2004) whose liberal reforms lessened government regulation of the economy, leading to rapid economic growth.

---

[*]Robert Kuttner, "The Role of Governments in the Global Economy," in *Global Capitalism,* ed. Will Hutton and Anthony Giddens (New York: New Press, 2000), p. 163.

India's High-Technology Sector The southern Indian city of Bangalore is home to the headquarters of software giant Infosys Technologies. Though the company scaled back growth projections in 2012 in response to weaker demand for its products in Europe and the United States, its revenue for the year was still expected to top $2 billion. The beautiful Infosys campus and the middle-class lifestyles of its employees contrast sharply with the conditions faced by the hundreds of millions who have yet to share in the economic dynamism of the New India. (Dibyangshu Sarkar/AFP/Getty Images)

government in the process. As president from 1999 to 2007, Putin oversaw an economy growing at a rapid 7 percent per year, with real incomes doubling and the middle class growing.

In spite of a diversified economy driven by military sales, high technology, consumer goods, and other vibrant sectors, Putin's strategy for success has depended primarily on high energy prices. As a dominant shareholder in Russia's natural gas and oil enterprises, the government can reward its backers with rich contracts while also investing in education and infrastructure. A culture of corruption and cronyism remains deeply entrenched. In 2011, Transparency International ranked Russia 143rd out of 182 nations on its Corruption Perception Index, well below the other BRIC countries, with Russian companies "most likely to bribe" when doing business abroad.

Strong growth across Latin America since the 1990s has been another feature of contemporary global economics, with Brazil taking the lead during the presidency of Luiz Inácio Lula da Silva (in office 2003–2010). Given Brazil's history of severe income inequality and Lula's personal background in union and left-wing

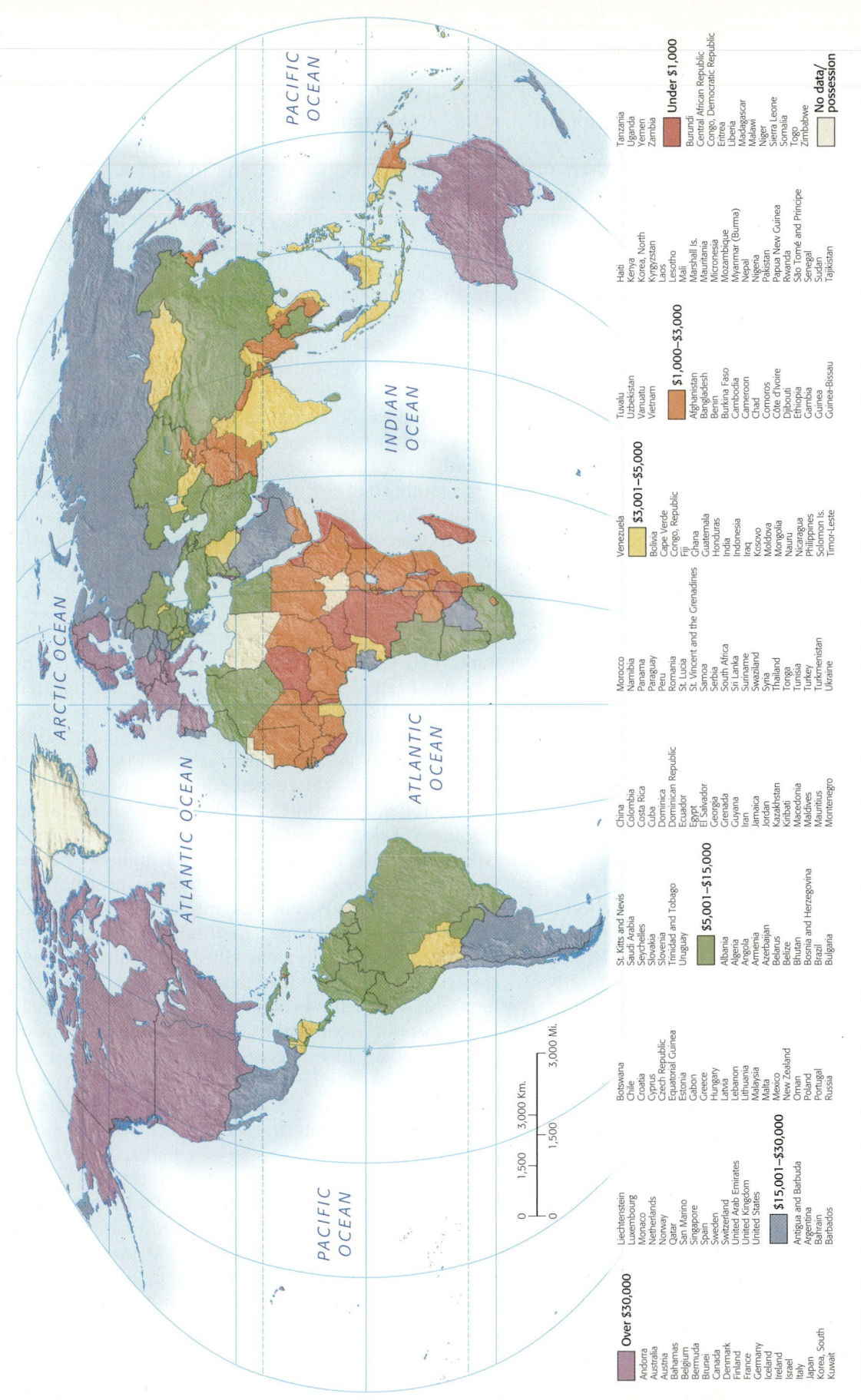

MAP 32.1 Per Capita Income In spite of recent surges in the economies of countries such as India, China, Russia, and Brazil, the global economy is still dominated by the United States, western Europe, Canada, Australia, and Japan. Per capita income gives only a rough estimate of people's quality of life, however. The United Nations Development Program (UNDP) uses a Human Development Report that takes account of a variety of factors in addition to income—such as education, health care, environmental standards, and gender equality—in its rankings. According to the UNDP, the island nation of Iceland ranks first in human development, Canada fourth, France tenth, Japan eighth, and the United States twelfth. (© Cengage Learning. *Caption data from http://hdr.undp.org/en/statistics. Map data from *The World Almanac and Book of Facts, 2008,* ed. C. Alan Joyce (World Almanac Books, 2008).

politics, many thought that he would emphasize social programs rather than market-driven strategies. To their surprise, his emphasis was on private sector growth and state-assisted infrastructure development, and in 2011 Brazil surged past Great Britain to claim sixth place on the list of the world's largest national economies. At the same time, Lula emphasized his *Fome Zero* ("Zero Hunger") program, combining governmental and private resources to bring food and clean water to Brazil's neediest.

Though not recognized in the original BRIC designation of important new economic players, Turkey seems to have earned a place. As elsewhere, liberal policies in Turkey have unshackled markets and industries from state control, leading to high growth rates and a position as the regional leader in agriculture, industry, and tourism, as well as banking and finance. Reforms driven by the Turkish government's desire to qualify for entry into the European Union (EU) were part of the reason for higher investment and growth. The ruling party, the moderately Islamist Justice and Development Party, resisted the military's traditional dominance of Turkish politics and has established a strong social base among businessmen and entrepreneurs. This shows that social conservatism grounded in religious beliefs can be compatible with strong economic performance in a predominantly Muslim society. Economic growth has also magnified Turkey's diplomatic influence in the Middle East.

The economic star status accorded to the BRIC countries and Turkey has been at the forefront of a broader global resurgence in the former Third World, the "Global South" of underdeveloped nations. With South Africa leading the way, Africa's economic performance has also been strong, although national and regional situations have varied widely. Early in 2012, the leaders of the BRIC countries recognized South Africa's prominent place by including President Jacob Zuma in a summit meeting in New Delhi, though it was clear that divisions among these five nations—especially between India and China—offset their common interests.

Perhaps the most startling economic transition in Africa has been the trend away from traditional Western sources of aid and investment and the debut of China as a leading player. In the first decade of the new century, over 1 million Chinese relocated to Africa to engage in a broad range of economic activities, most notably in the reconstruction of Africa's dilapidated roads, railroads, mines, and ports. Questions have been raised, however, about Chinese business methods and possible ulterior motives. Chinese tend to dominate the higher-skilled positions in their enterprises, often using Africans only for the least skilled jobs without training them for higher positions. Even more troubling is China's support of certain African leaders with poor human rights and corruption records in its drive to secure the African raw materials, especially metals and fossil fuels, necessary for further industrial growth. In 2006, fifty African leaders received red carpet treatment when they traveled to Beijing to participate in a Forum on China-African Cooperation, raising fears that Africa's political elites were being tempted into the same neocolonial relationship that had followed independence in many countries (see Chapter 30). Would Chinese investment benefit only the privileged few at the top of African societies?

That was a central question in Zambian elections held in 2011, in which the role of China was central to the presidential debate; the incumbent was accused of financing his campaign with Chinese funds. In a blow to China's Africa policy and an affirmation of recent moves toward more vigorous democracy on the continent, the opposition candidate won the election, with Zambian voters strongly supporting his promise to more closely oversee Chinese economic activities in the national interest.

A general trend in twenty-first-century economics toward "South-to-South" trade and investment between developing countries has been part of a general shift away from Western (and Japanese) predominance. *"The earth is flat,"* declared American commentator Thomas Friedman in a much-discussed 2005 essay. He meant that globalization now allows people anywhere in the world with access to high-speed Internet to be involved at the highest levels of the global economy. The next phase of globalization, according to Friedman, *"is going to be driven . . . by a much more diverse—non-Western, nonwhite—group of individuals."*[*] It remains to be seen whether China's persistent Internet censorship will prove compatible with the global free flow of information. India, with its open society and well-developed information technology sector, might be better placed to take advantage of a "flatter" world.

Regional trading blocs that first arose during the 1990s continue to be important, but balancing regional goals with national interests has often entailed controversy and tough bargaining. The United States, Canada, and Mexico have all had complaints about the North Atlantic Free Trade Association (NAFTA) (see Chapter 31), while political disputes have hampered the effectiveness of a proposed South American common market. (See the feature "World History in Today's World" in Chapter 22, page 636.) The European Union, the largest of the regional trade blocs by far (representing a combined economy even bigger than that of the United States), has struggled to balance the interests of more developed countries such as Germany, France, and Great Britain with the needs of weaker members such as Ireland, Spain, Portugal, and Greece.

More ambitious than regional agreements was the attempt by members of the **World Trade Organization** (WTO), founded by former signatories of the General Agreement on Tariffs and Trade (GATT), to establish rules for global trade. Organized opposition to the WTO began at once. The Global People's Network, allying environmentalists and campaigners for social justice, directs its criticism not only at the WTO but also at multinational corporations that gain from the loosening of global trade restrictions. In particular, detractors object to corporations avoiding labor protections and environmental regulations. Just as labor unions once arose in individual nations to counterbalance the power of industrialists, advocates of the Global People's Network argue for the need to reduce the excesses of multinational corporate power.

> **World Trade Organization**
> Organization founded in 1995 to establish rules for international trade, with an emphasis on lowering tariffs and other barriers to the free movement of goods.

While defenders and opponents debated the merits of free-market globalization, **Muhammad Yusuf** (b. 1940) of Bangladesh was thinking of practical solutions for those left behind. His Grameen ("Village") Bank pioneered microfinance, lending small amounts of money. Poor borrowers proved to be trustworthy clients even when they had no collateral to secure the loans, and small investments often led to big returns when they pooled their resources, energy, and ideas to start new enterprises. Yusuf's model, even if sometimes plagued by corruption, improved the lives of many Bangladeshis and showed promise as a means of spreading the benefits of free markets more widely across the globe. Still, such "bottom-up" approaches were dwarfed by the power and resources of the world's largest financial institutions.

> **Muhammad Yusuf**
> (b. 1940) Bangladeshi pioneer of microfinance whose Grameen ("Village") Bank gives small loans to the poor, usually women, to start small enterprises. His bank became a global model for microfinance, and in 2006 he was awarded the Nobel Peace Prize.

Global Financial Crisis

In the autumn of 2008, the American global financial services firm Lehman Brothers collapsed. Panic spread across world markets at the prospect of the insolvency of the entire global banking and brokerage system. The use of complex financial

---

[*]Thomas Friedman, "It's a Flat World After All," *New York Times*, April 3, 2005.

instruments called "derivatives" had allowed banks to bundle and sell inflated mortgages to third parties while masking the high risks involved, infecting the global financial system and creating a domino effect when the housing bubble burst. The New York Stock Exchange lost 22 percent of its value in a single week and, along with other international stock exchanges, continued to plunge thereafter. Memories of the Great Depression, when a stock market crash led to a general banking failure and a decade of economic misery, seemed ominously relevant.

In the short term, most economists and government leaders determined, state intervention would be necessary to quarantine the crisis and guarantee that no more major banks, those that were "too big to fail," went into bankruptcy. Thus the outgoing administration of U.S. President George W. Bush proposed and Congress passed a program to make $700 billion available to stabilize the financial services industry. In Britain as well, where the City of London parallels New York as a global financial services center, the government organized an emergency rescue operation. Many were appalled that the very people whose poor business decisions had brought the world to the brink of ruin were being "bailed out," but the measures prevented further bankruptcies among large firms.

Though a general collapse of the banking sector had been avoided, economic recession still struck, with the United States and Europe facing high unemployment and other nations finding shrinking markets for their products. A fundamental question of economic theory then took center stage. Was the best medium-term solution to use the ability of governments to borrow, cut taxes, and extend credit to stimulate a broader economic recovery? Or were government deficits at the very root of the slump, meaning that fiscal austerity rather than the expansion of government spending was necessary to restore prosperity?

In China, there was no public debate about how to respond to the global contraction that was hurting the country's exports: the Communist Party makes such decisions without public consultation. Its response was stimulus: a $580 billion plan largely focused on infrastructure development. Marxism-Leninism had little to do with the logic of this policy. Instead, Chinese leaders were following the economic advice of the renowned British economist John Maynard Keynes (1883–1946), who, at the time of the Great Depression, had argued that during recession, governments should "prime the pump" of their economies by increasing the money supply and making direct investments to restore employment. Fears of inflation and public debt should be set aside until the crisis passes.

For generations, Keynesianism was the orthodoxy of Western economics: government should spend in hard economic times and pay down debt when recovery leads to an increase in tax revenues. In the United States, Britain, and the EU, fiscal conservatives disagreed, arguing for immediate austerity measures to avoid further increases in public debt and to clear the way for private enterprise to boost growth.

In the United States and Great Britain, the response of President Barack Obama and Prime Minister Gordon Brown was economic stimulus along Keynesian lines: low interest rates, tax cuts, and increased government spending. By 2010, however, both economies were still in the doldrums, while the political calculus had changed: elections in 2010 endorsed conservatives in both countries. Obama's Democratic administration shelved plans for further stimulus spending. In Britain, new Conservative Prime Minister David Cameron focused on steep cuts in government spending to help balance the government's books.

Responses by European governments were mixed. For example, the Irish government imposed harsh austerity measures after the collapse of its own housing market, while the French implemented a $40 billion stimulus plan. In Germany, there had been no mortgage crisis or large increase in unemployment, and memories of the great inflation following World War I were still seared into the national consciousness (see Chapter 27). The German government advocated fiscal probity. These divided responses indicated that the real problem for the EU was the lack of a coordinated fiscal response, at least until the 2011 financial meltdown of Greece forced the issue.

In Greece, relatively low economic productivity paired with generous social welfare benefits created a structural imbalance brought into full relief by the global economic crisis. With its credit rating in decline, the Greek government could no longer borrow enough money to sustain the system. The Greek parliament passed sharp spending cuts (which also occurred in Spain and Italy) as a condition for an emergency fiscal support package from the EU. In the summer of 2012, it was an open question whether Greece would remain in the euro zone or depart the EU altogether.

The euro currency and the EU now faced an existential crisis. The euro had been adopted just ten years earlier by dozens of countries with very different economic systems (see Chapter 31), but no sufficiently centralized institutions had been empowered to control their fiscal policies. Would member nations now be willing to give up a much larger degree of their fiscal autonomy, and national sovereignty, to ensure the future of the euro and the EU? Great Britain, a member of the EU that had chosen not to adopt the euro, was unwilling to do so. The other EU members agreed to follow Franco-German leadership toward a strengthened Union with stronger oversight of national budgets, but achieving political consensus across and within so diverse a conglomeration of states remained a challenge.

In early 2012, with the United States poised on the brink of at least a modest recovery, world markets followed these European events closely. Whatever the outcome, the global economic crisis of 2008–2012 seems to have reinforced the twenty-first-century trend toward a more prominent international role for the BRIC countries and for developing nations more generally. While developed economies teetered on the brink of depression, growth rates in the developing world quickly recovered and remained healthy. Early in 2011, China held a huge account surplus that included $1.4 *trillion* in U.S. Treasury bonds. The long age of Western domination of the international economy seemed to be coming to an end. (See the feature "Movement of Ideas Through Primary Sources: A Post-American World?")

Global Security

On **September 11, 2001**, operatives of al-Qaeda (see Chapter 31) hijacked four jetliners in the United States and turned them into weapons of destruction. While two planes brought down both towers of the World Trade Center in New York, another caused extensive damage to the Pentagon, and the fourth plane, perhaps on its way to destroy the U.S. Capitol, crashed in a Pennsylvania field. Thousands were killed, and international sympathy for the people of the United States was nearly universal.

In response, President George W. Bush declared a "war on terror," first sending U.S. forces in October 2001 to invade Afghanistan, where the Islamist Taliban government had given sanctuary and support to Osama bin Laden, and then into Saddam Hussein's Iraq in 2003. The invasion of Afghanistan had broad international backing. Even Iran, Russia, and China—nations usually suspicious of American military ventures on or near their borders—backed the move. An international coalition, working with local anti-Taliban fighters, quickly removed the Taliban from power.

The subsequent U.S. invasion of Iraq, however, generated considerably more controversy. Unlike in 1991, when his father had assembled a broad international

September 11, 2001
Date of the al-Qaeda terrorist attacks on the United States in which two hijacked jetliners destroyed the twin towers of the World Trade Center in New York City. Another hijacked plane crashed into the Pentagon, and a fourth fell in a Pennsylvania field.

A Post-American World?

The Post-American World by Fareed Zakaria caused quite a stir. Not everyone wanted to hear his analysis of how the United States needs to adjust to a world where its influence, while still potent, has weakened. *The Post-American World* helped shape the debate about how the United States might best respond to what Zakaria calls "the rise of the rest," that is, to the challenges and opportunities of globalization.

Born in Mumbai, India, Zakaria earned his Ph.D. at Harvard before rising to prominence as a columnist for *Newsweek* and as host of CNN's *GPS* (Global Public Square). In 2007, the journal *Foreign Policy* named him one of the world's one hundred most influential public intellectuals.

Source: From THE POST-AMERICAN WORLD RELEASE 2.0 UPDATED AND EXPANDED by Fareed Zakaria. Copyright © 2011, 2008 by Fareed Zakaria. Used by permission of W. W. Norton & Company, Inc., pp. 1–3, 204, 207–208, 210, 212, 241–243, 285.

This is a book not about the decline of America but rather about the rise of everyone else. . . . We are now living through [a] great power shift [that] could be called "the rise of the rest." Over the past few decades, countries all over the world have been experiencing rates of economic growth that were once unthinkable. . . . Even the economic rupture of 2008 and 2009 could not halt or reverse this trend; in fact, the recession accelerated it. While many of the world's wealthy, industrialized economies continued to struggle with slow growth, high unemployment, and overwhelming indebtedness through 2010 and beyond, the countries that constitute "the rest" rebounded quickly. India's annual growth rate slowed to 5.7% in 2009, but hummed along at a 9.7% rate in 2010. China's GDP growth never fell below 9%. . . .

[T]he fund manager who coined the term "emerging markets," has identified the 25 companies most likely to be the world's next multinationals. His list includes four companies each from Brazil, Mexico, South Korea, and Taiwan; three from India; two from China; and one each from Argentina, Chile, Malaysia, and South Africa. . . . Look around. The tallest building in the world is now in Dubai. The world's richest man is Mexican, and its largest publicly traded corporation is Chinese. . . . Once quintessentially American icons have been appropriated by foreigners. The world's largest Ferris wheel is in Singapore. Its number one casino is not in Las Vegas but in Macao. . . . The biggest movie industry, in terms of both movies made and tickets sold, is Bollywood, not Hollywood. . . .

It might seem strange to focus on growing prosperity when there are still hundreds of millions of people living in desperate poverty. But in fact, the share of people living on a dollar a day or less plummeted from 40% in 1981 to 18% in 2004, and is estimated to fall to 12% by 2015. China's growth rate alone has lifted more than 400 million people out of poverty. . . . The 50 countries where the earth's poorest people live are basket cases that need urgent attention. In the other 142—which include China, India, Brazil, Russia, Indonesia, Turkey, Kenya, and South Africa—the poor are slowly being absorbed into productive and growing economies. For the first time ever, we are witnessing genuine global growth. This is creating an international system in which countries in all parts of the world are no longer objects or observers but players in their own right. It is the birth of a truly global order. . . .

At the politico-military level, we remain in a single-superpower world. But in all other dimensions—industrial, financial, educational, social, cultural—the distribution of power is shifting, moving away from American dominance. That does not mean we are entering an anti-American world. But we are moving into a post-American world, one defined and directed from many places and by many people. . . .

When trying to explain how America will fare in the new world, I sometimes say, "Look around." The future is already here. Over the last twenty years, globalization has been gaining breadth and depth. More countries are making goods, communications technology has been leveling the playing field, capital has been free to move across the world. And America has benefitted massively from those trends. Its economy has received hundreds of millions of dollars in investment—a rarity for a country with much capital of its own. . . .

[S]ay those who are more worried . . . "America's advantages are rapidly eroding as the country loses its scientific and technological bases." For some, the decline of science is symptomatic of a larger cultural decay. A country that once adhered to a Puritan ethic of delayed gratification has become one that revels in instant pleasures. We're losing interest in the basics—math, manufacturing, hard work, savings—and becoming a post-industrial society that specializes in consumption and leisure. . . .

[Yet] higher education is America's best industry. . . . With 5% of the world's population, the United States absolutely dominates higher education, having either 74% or 54% of the world's top fifty universities (depending which study you look at). In no other field is America's advantage so overwhelming. . . . America remains by far the most attractive destination for students, taking 30% of the total number of foreign students globally. All these advantages will not be erased easily. . . .

I went to elementary, middle, and high school in Mumbai, at an excellent institution. . . . I recall memorizing vast quantities of material, regurgitating it for exams, and then promptly forgetting it. When I went to college in the United States, I encountered a different world. While the American system is too lax on rigor and memorization—whether in math or poetry—it is much better at developing the critical faculties of the mind. . . . Other educational systems teach you to take tests; the American system teaches you to think. . . . American culture celebrates and reinforces problem solving, questioning authority, and thinking heretically. It allows people to fail and then gives them a second and third chance. It rewards self-starters and oddballs. These are bottom-up forces that cannot be produced by government fiat. . . .

America remains the sole superpower today, but it is an enfeebled one. Its economy is troubled, its currency sliding, and it faces long-term problems with its soaring entitlements and low savings. . . . In 2007, China contributed more to global growth than the United States—the first time any nation has done so since the 1930s. . . . America still dominates the world but the larger structure of unipolarity—economic, financial, cultural—is weakening. . . .

This power shift could be broadly beneficial. It is a product of good things—robust economic growth and stability around the world. And it is good for America, if approached properly. The world is going America's way. Countries are becoming more open, market friendly, and democratic. As long as we keep the forces of modernization, global interaction, and trade growing, good governance, human rights, and democracy all move forward. That movement is not always swift . . . but the direction is clear. Look at Africa, which is often seen as the most hopeless continent in the world. Today two-thirds of the continent is democratic and growing economically. . . .

These trends provide an opportunity for the United States to remain the pivotal player in a richer, more dynamic, more exciting world. . . . For America to thrive in this new and challenging era, for it to succeed amid the rise of the rest, it need fulfill only one test. It should be a place that is as inviting and exciting to the young student who enters the country as it was for this awkward eighteen-year-old a generation ago.

QUESTION FOR ANALYSIS

» *If Zakaria is correct that we now live in a "post-American world," what changes in American behaviors and attitudes are most appropriate to changing circumstances?*

consensus and military coalition to evict Iraqi forces from Kuwait (see Chapter 31), George W. Bush failed to convince much of the world that there was a connection between the harsh, secular authoritarianism of Hussein and the radical Islamism of Osama bin Laden. Many Americans, and even more members of the international community, argued that Iraq had no connection to al-Qaeda and doubted the Bush administration's claims that Iraq possessed "weapons of mass destruction."

In 2002, United Nations weapons inspectors assigned to Iraq ascertained that earlier chemical, biological, and nuclear weapons programs were no longer active. U.S. and British intelligence services, however, suggested that the UN inspectors were being deceived. With the support of British Prime Minister Tony Blair, President Bush insisted that Iraq represented an imminent threat: *"Facing clear evidence of peril, we cannot wait for the final proof—the smoking gun—that could come in the form of a mushroom cloud."* Without UN sanction, Bush assembled a "coalition of the willing" and invaded Iraq in April 2003. Saddam Hussein was quickly deposed, tried by an interim Iraqi government, and executed.

American Occupation of Baghdad In the Iraq invasion of 2003, the U.S. military quickly took the Iraqi capital. Here, a soldier has draped an American flag over the head of a Saddam Hussein statue. This flag was quickly removed and replaced with an Iraqi one. Some interpreted the American invasion as an occupation rather than a liberation of the country.

Facelly/Sipa

The region seemed less rather than more secure, however, after the removal of the authoritarian power that had held Iraq together. Although the Shi'ite majority of the country had political control for the first time in over a thousand years, Iraq remained divided not just between Kurdish, Sunni, and Shi'ite interests but also between armed Shi'ite factions (see Map 32.2). And the intervention of the United States had, ironically, created the possibility that Islamist Iran, which had historical and religious affinities with Iraq's ascendant Shi'ites, might benefit from the change of regime.

With Iraq's political future unresolved, in 2011 the United States followed the lead of coalition partners like Great Britain and began to withdraw its troops. Most Americans were now ready to end this difficult conflict after eight years of tough fighting and thousands of casualties, especially with the sense of closure that came with Osama bin Laden's death in a smoothly executed Navy Seals operation. Domestic economic issues were now the U.S. priority.

Meanwhile, Moscow and Beijing borrowed Washington's antiterror rhetoric to justify crackdowns, especially in areas with large Muslim populations, such as the Caucasus region in the southern Russian Federation and China's western Xinjiang province. (See the feature "World History in Today's World" in Chapter 20, page 559.)

Russian leaders bristled at the expansion of the North Atlantic Treaty Organization (NATO) into former Soviet satellites such as Poland. Their response came with the invasion of independent Georgia in the summer of 2008. Vladimir Putin's resurgent Russia, like the Soviet Union and the tsarist empire before it, regarded the Caucasus

Majority population
- Shia Arab
- Shia Arab/Sunni Arab
- Sunni Arab
- Sunni Arab/Sunni Kurd
- Sunni Kurd

Path of U.S./Coalition forces, March–April 2003

Sunni Triangle

Oil field

Site of major clash with Iraqi insurgents

MAP 32.2 Iraq in Transition After the regime of Saddam Hussein, dominated by Iraq's Sunni Arab minority, fell to U.S.-led forces in 2003, some Sunnis took up arms against the U.S. coalition, independent Shia Arab militias, and the now Shi'ite-dominated Iraqi government itself. By 2007, however, violence abated as an increasing number of Sunni leaders rejected the terrorist tactics of the militants and as the United States increased its troop levels. The question remained whether the Iraqi government—with a Shi'ite prime minister, Kurdish president, and Sunni leader of parliament—could effectively balance the complex regional, religious, and ethnic divisions of the country. (© Cengage Learning)

Mountain region as part of its "near abroad," where Russian interests must hold sway. The invasion was a lesson not only to Georgia, but also to any other contiguous republic contemplating membership in NATO and the EU.

Elsewhere the possibility of terrorist access to "weapons of mass destruction" rekindled Cold War–type fears of biological and even nuclear attacks on civilian populations. Even if that danger were avoided in the near term, nuclear proliferation remained a significant challenge to global security. In Europe the threat of nuclear weapons seemed to have diminished after the fall of the Soviet Union. Still, there was reason to worry that nuclear devices and technology in post-Soviet states might enter the global arms trade and find their way into the hands of extremist organizations or irresponsible governments.

Russian security anxieties had been heightened in 2007 when the United States announced plans to station antimissile defenses in eastern Europe, purportedly to contain a future Iranian nuclear threat but also with the capacity to shoot down Russian missiles. At the same time, the United States drew a firm line in the sand against Iran's nuclear program. While Teheran claimed merely to be advancing its civilian energy potential, both Republican and Democratic leaders argued that Iran was such a threat to world peace that it should not be allowed to have a civilian program that could be converted to military use. Using the same rationale, Israeli aircraft had destroyed a Syrian nuclear power plant in 2007.

The potential for a nuclear exchange between India and Pakistan was even more worrisome. Both nations (along with Israel) developed such devices while refusing to sign the international Treaty on the Non-Proliferation of Nuclear Weapons. And in 2006, the communist government of North Korea snubbed international opinion by openly testing a nuclear bomb. The death of North Korea's mercurial dictator Kim Jong-Il in 2011, which brought his untested son to power, did nothing to dampen fears that the country would continue to develop a nuclear arsenal. North Korean and Iranian scientists made substantial strides after the chief of Pakistan's nuclear program shared his technology with them. Southern, western, and northeastern Asia thus remain possible flashpoints for nuclear conflict.

Health and the Environment

With so much attention fixed on terrorism and nuclear proliferation, insufficient progress has been made on other issues also vital to long-term global security. One of the major challenges of globalization is in the area of public health. International mobility increases the risk of pandemics, as shown by the global spread in 2009 of H1N1, or swine flu, a near-relative of the flu strain that killed millions across the world in 1918–1919 (see Chapter 27). Originating in Mexico, the virus killed about fifteen thousand people worldwide, mostly in North America, South America, and Europe. Although not nearly as lethal as had originally been feared, the swine flu pandemic did remind us of the ease with which such diseases now cross international borders. Historians, mindful that epidemic diseases have never respected the borders of either nations or civilizations, began to play closer attention to earlier global pandemics such as smallpox, influenza, and cholera. (See the feature "World History in Today's World: Globalizing History.")

Virulent new strains of traditional killers like malaria, which until recently were confined to small geographic areas, now hop from continent to continent courtesy of mosquito hosts that find their way aboard jet airplanes. Apart from H1N1, other new strains of influenza, such as the avian flu virus from East Asia, threaten uncontrollable global epidemics. Meanwhile, the worldwide use of antibiotics has spawned resistant strains of bacteria. Viruses and bacteria that ignore national borders are straining health-care systems around the world.

HIV/AIDS is, of course, another case in point. When it was first diagnosed in the 1980s, the disease was associated with two particular groups, homosexual men and intravenous drug users. Today, Africa has the largest number of AIDS victims, and there are more women than men among them. For those who can afford them, medical advances have decreased suffering and extended life spans, but most of the world's HIV victims die without the benefit of any effective medical intervention.

While HIV infection rates have stabilized in wealthier nations, many global health experts fear that India and China are in danger of joining Africa as frontiers in the expansion of the disease. Estimates for 2011 put the Chinese infection rate at a relatively low 750,000 persons. However, in India the number of people living with HIV/AIDS had soared past 2.4 million. Hundreds of millions there lack access to the most basic health care, and older scourges like tuberculosis, polio, cholera, and malnutrition have yet to be effectively addressed. Yet if HIV were to spread there as quickly as it did in South Africa in the 1990s (the infection rate growing

Globalizing History

Changing circumstances often alter the questions we ask of the past, and today it has become clear that understanding our complex world requires a more global view than is provided by the histories of individual nations, regions, or civilizations. Recently, organizations such as the World History Association in North America, the European Network in Universal and Global History, and the Asian Association of World Historians have promoted international collaboration in the effort to globalize history scholarship.

A number of world history research areas have proven especially productive. For example, the study of oceans as arenas for cultural and economic interaction has illuminated the connected histories of peoples around the Atlantic, Pacific, and Indian Oceans as well as the Mediterranean Sea. Environmental factors have also loomed large, as historians have paid closer attention to the history of climate change as well as to transregional movements of diseases, food crops, plants, and animals. Human voyages have also received significant attention, both those that were smaller in scale (trading expeditions or religious pilgrimages) and mass migrations of peoples. World historians often focus on aspects of cultural diffusion, such as the movement of religious ideas, technological innovations, and artistic traditions between regions and around the world.

Apart from this emphasis on connections, world historical research often sheds new light on particular societies by looking at them in comparison with others across time and space. The comparative studies of empires, of systems of slavery, and of the dynamics of cross-cultural trade are all important examples. Yet another area of recent research, so-called "big history," zooms out to identify patterns in the human past over very large scales of time, back to the earliest history of our species about 160,000 years ago.

The task of globalizing history has produced an exceptionally dynamic and diverse research agenda, not surprising given the insistent globalization of our contemporary reality. The world history you have studied in *Voyages in World History*, informed by that research, is particularly relevant to your own twenty-first-century voyage.

---

from 1 to 25 percent of the population between 1990 and 2005), Indian society would be overwhelmed. Unlike most epidemic diseases, which are deadliest for the very young and very old, AIDS carries people away in the prime of their productive and reproductive lives, adding huge social and developmental costs.

Some health threats are compounded by global climate change. Approximately sixty thousand people die every year in natural disasters that scientists believe are related to increasing global temperatures, including a massive European heat wave in 2003, Hurricane Katrina in the United States in 2005, the huge cyclone that hit Burma in 2008, and unprecedented cycles of drought and flooding in many parts of Africa and Asia. Scientists predict that melting polar ice caps will soon disrupt the world's highly populated coastal areas, especially Bangladesh, where 55 million people would be displaced by even a modest rise in sea levels.

Global climate change is also affecting the spread of infectious diseases. The director general of the World Health Organization, Dr. Margaret Chan, argues: *"Many of the most important global killers are highly sensitive to climatic conditions. Malaria, diarrhea and malnutrition kill millions of people every year, most of them children. Without effective action to mitigate and adapt to climate change, the burden of these conditions will be greater, and they will be more difficult and more costly to control."*[*]

---

[*]Dr. Margaret Chan, "Health in a Changing Environment," http://www.who.int/mediacentre/news/statements/2007/s11/en/index.html.

Global Warming Average temperatures in the Arctic are rising twice as fast as elsewhere in the world. The rapid melting of the polar ice cap is an outcome of global warming and also a further cause: in the future there will be less snow and ice in the Arctic to absorb the sun's heat and cool the planet. The peril faced by this polar bear mother and her cubs is immediate; the threat to humanity from rising sea levels is ominous. (Johnny Johnson/Getty Images)

Kyoto Protocol
(1997) International agreement adopted in Kyoto, Japan, under the United Nations Framework Agreement on Climate Change in an effort to reduce greenhouse gas emissions linked to global warming. The Kyoto accords were not accepted by the United States.

The most significant international effort to address global warming was the **Kyoto Protocol**, an agreement adopted in 1997 under the United Nations Framework Agreement on Climate Change. For the first time, nations agreed to mandatory limits on emissions of the "greenhouse gases" that pump carbon dioxide into the atmosphere and contribute to increased temperatures. However, the United States' refusal to ratify the treaty has undermined the effectiveness of the Kyoto (kee-OH-toh) Protocol. Unlike the Europeans, the Americans refused to accept the proviso that emissions controls would be mandatory for rich countries but not for poorer but rapidly developing ones like China, India, and Brazil. Indeed, the most contentious issue, raised again at a follow-up meeting in 2011, has been the question of how to share the global burden. The largest contributors to global climate change historically have been the United States, Canada, western Europe, and Japan, but today the surging and largely unregulated Chinese and Indian economies threaten to offset progress elsewhere in the world. China and India have argued that since most greenhouse gases are still produced in the United States and Europe, those countries should shoulder the largest burden in their reduction.

Major health problems accompany rapid industrialization in China, where most cancer deaths are attributable to pollution. Though official Chinese sources frequently understate the problem, the monitoring station above the U.S. embassy in Beijing often reports hazardous levels of air pollution, and the city's international airport has sometimes been closed because of the heavy, polluted haze that limits visibility. The effects are not just local. A toxic cloud of coal smoke not only covers most of China but also drifts over neighboring countries and even across the Pacific Ocean.

Though both India and China have put significant investment into the development of renewable energies such as solar and wind power, the goal of **sustainable development**, generating prosperity without poisoning the environment, is far from attainment. The most powerful alternative energy source is nuclear power. However, many remain wary of its health and environmental consequences. In the spring of 2011, an earthquake in Japan reignited the global debate when the resulting tsunami led to the release of radiation from the Fukushima electricity plant, the worst nuclear incident since Chernobyl (see Chapter 31).

Deforestation magnifies the effect of the world's rising output of greenhouse gases. Tropical forests play a large role in cleansing the atmosphere of carbon dioxide and replenishing it with oxygen. High prices and sustained demand for tropical hardwoods from Central Africa and Indonesia, however, have led lumber companies to fell vast areas of forest, sometimes bribing politicians to evade environmental regulations. In Brazil, farmers clear the forests for agriculture; in some cases, huge tracts of sugar cane or soybeans displace biologically diverse ecosystems. (See the feature "World History in Today's World" in Chapter 25, page 721.)

Work is needed on every front to resolve the health and environmental challenges of our times: personal choices and government policies, international agreements and local initiatives, the actions of rich nations, poor ones, and those on the rise. And rising population, urbanization, and global migration make the search for solutions all the more urgent.

sustainable development
Means of increasing economic output and productivity without severe damage to the environment; for example, in the search for alternatives to fossil fuels.

Population Movement and Demography

People are on the move, both within countries and between them, usually seeking opportunity at the focal points of wealth and economic growth. That means cities. In China, for example, tens of millions have left their villages in less developed parts of the country for Beijing, Shanghai, and other urban areas: China now has twelve cities with over 2 million residents each. For the planet as a whole, 2008 was the first year when the majority of humankind lived in cities.[1]

International labor flows have been checked somewhat by the global economic slowdown after 2008 and by increasingly restrictive immigration policies across much of the world, but such movement remains robust. Globally, prospects of higher wages drive millions each year to leave their homes, though they often send much of their pay back home to support their families and intend to return there. Higher education is another inducement to movement, with Europe, the United States, and Australia as principal destinations for students. Of course, for millions of others, terrible conditions at home are the tragic inducement for movement across international borders: refugee camps are still too frequent a sight in some parts of Africa.

Immigration policies are controversial all around the world. In 2008, South African gangs killed twelve immigrants from other African countries, claiming that the outsiders were taking their jobs. In Italy, the government cracked down on illegal Roma (Gypsy) immigrants from southeastern Europe, claiming that they were responsible for an increase in crime. Since immigrants are usually willing to work for less, they can drive down wages for native workers. In the United States, immigration from Latin America has shifted the cultural and linguistic balance of American society, generating harsh anti-immigrant policies in states like Arizona and Alabama.

Religion and ethnicity often go hand in hand, and religious issues feed concerns about immigration (see Map 32.3). Many western Europeans have been alarmed by Muslim immigration to their countries, further stimulated by political unrest in the Arab world in 2011. A few years earlier, young Arabs and Africans had rioted on the desolate fringes of Paris. Conservatives called for law and order and restrictions on immigration; those with more liberal views cited racism as the cause of the riots and demanded improved educational and employment prospects for immigrant youth. In Germany in 2011, a furious debate raged when a prominent politician published an anti-immigration book in which he wrote: *"If the birth rate of the [Muslim] migrants continues to remain higher than the indigenous population, within a few generations the migrants will take over the state and society and create a nation of dunces."* Such harsh rhetoric, while not commonplace, was on the rise in many countries. (See the feature "World History in Today's World" in Chapter 28, page 802.)

In the past, time and distance would usually have ensured the gradual assimilation of immigrants into host societies. Today's transportation and communications, however, make it easy to remain connected to familial and cultural networks on the other side of the globe. Questions of whether and how to accept immigrants, and how best to create cultural and linguistic bridges to host societies, are matters of global and not merely national concern.

Total world population recently surpassed 7 billion persons, a worrisome figure if we consider the resources it takes to give each of these individuals the chance at a decent life. Demographers, experts in population science, focus as much on the distribution of populations as their total size, however. When we consider the ratio of young to old in different societies, we find a striking global imbalance. While the population of wealthier countries grows old and in some cases (for example, Italy, Japan, and Russia) fertility rates are below the level needed to replace the current population, surging growth rates in Latin America, Africa, and much of Asia have created an enormous population of young people whose ambitions exceed their chances to fulfill them. Creating opportunities to tap the creativity and intelligence of these hundreds of millions of young people is a matter of urgent concern.

One Child Policy
In China, most parents are restricted by this policy to a single child to curb population growth. The policy has led to a significant gender imbalance.

In the 1980s, leaders of the People's Republic of China adopted a radical solution to population growth. China's **One Child Policy** punishes parents who have a second child with heavy penalties and even prosecution, with enforcement being most strict in urban areas. Population growth leveled off, and within a single generation the long Chinese tradition of extended families was largely replaced by small nuclear ones. Without siblings, the younger generation receives the full attention and financial support of its parents, who usually focus on education.

As part of the One Child Policy, women who cannot pay the fine for a second pregnancy have often been forced to have abortions. That issue recently surged to the forefront when photos were posted online of one such victim, Feng Jianmei, holding her aborted baby. Microblogs such as Sina (the Chinese version of Twitter) lit up in protest, another example of the difficulty Communist officials are having in controlling public opinion in the new age of social media.

Even before the forced abortion controversy, however, the Chinese government had begun to re-examine the One Child Policy and to experiment with a more flexible approach, seeing the problems that may come with a "graying" population down the road when, as in much of Europe and Japan, fewer people of working age are available to support a rapidly increasing population of the elderly. In that sense, India and Africa have a potential demographic advantage, as long as sufficient

---

"In a Rich Irony, German Jews Defend Muslims," The Jewish Daily Forward, January 28, 2011; http://www.forward.com/articles/134701/.

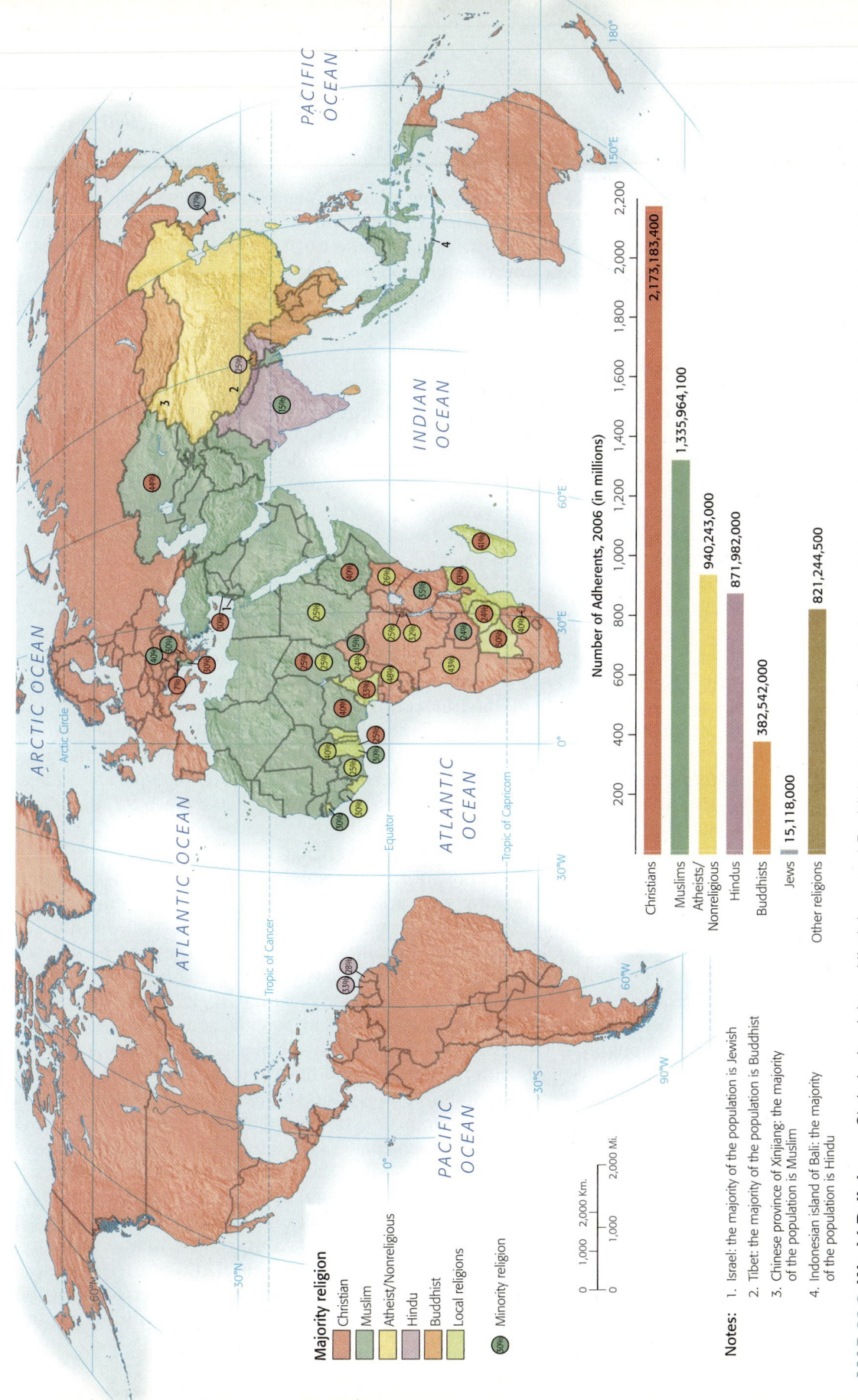

Majority religion

- Christian
- Muslim
- Atheist/Nonreligious
- Hindu
- Buddhist
- Local religions

50% Minority religion

Number of Adherents, 2006 (in millions)

Religion	Adherents
Christians	2,173,183,400
Muslims	1,335,964,100
Atheists/Nonreligious	940,243,000
Hindus	871,982,000
Buddhists	382,542,000
Jews	15,118,000
Other religions	821,244,500

Notes: 1. Israel: the majority of the population is Jewish
2. Tibet: the majority of the population is Buddhist
3. Chinese province of Xinjiang: the majority of the population is Muslim
4. Indonesian island of Bali: the majority of the population is Hindu

MAP 32.3 **World Religions** Christianity, Islam, Hinduism, and Buddhism are the four major world religions, with "atheists/nonreligious" forming a majority in Communist-ruled China. The religious map of Africa is especially complex. While Muslims predominate in the north and west, and Christians in the east and south, there is a great deal of mixing along the boundaries between them, and local religions are still strong in many areas. In much of Europe and Russia, where Christian majorities are indicated, secularism is also strong and rates of church attendance quite low. While Islam predominates in North Africa and the Middle East, the nation with the largest Muslim population in the world is Indonesia, in Southeast Asia. (© Cengage Learning)

opportunities are found for their large numbers of young people. Through immigration, affluent societies can maintain a stable mix of working-age and senior citizens.

Previously alarming predictions of uncontrolled growth have now been replaced by an understanding that when people attain greater wealth and security, they tend to have fewer children. Today, population growth is slowing not just in richer countries but also across much of the world. If current trends hold, total global population will reach equilibrium sometime later in this century, perhaps at a level of 9 billion people. The urgent question is whether the earth can sustain such numbers.

Gender Issues

No society can prosper by squandering the creative talent of half its population: women's rights are closely linked to the social and economic advancement of any culture. Overcoming legacies of male dominance and rebalancing power more evenly between men and women requires more than material prosperity, technological progress, or government intervention. Addressing patriarchal attitudes requires attention to local circumstances.

Connecting the local to the global was a hallmark of Kenyan biologist and environmental activist Dr. **Wangari Maathai** (wahn-gah-ree mah-TIE) (1940–2011). Alarmed by environmental degradation in East Africa, Maathai organized rural women into collectives to plant trees, inspiring affiliated organizations in other developing countries. However, her success, and international recognition with a Nobel Peace Prize in 2004, did not come without a fight. While women planting trees may seem like an innocuous act, and certainly not politically daring, in patriarchal Kenya it took great courage for partisans of this Green Belt Movement to organize for change. These women, Maathai explained, have learned that *"planting trees or fighting to save forests from being chopped down is part of a larger mission to create a society that respects democracy, decency, adherence to the rule of law, human rights, and the rights of women."*

In India, globalization and technological change have presented new possibilities for women, at least for those fortunate enough to have an education and employment in rapidly growing sectors like information technology, engineering, and telecommunications. But the record on improving gender relations in India, as elsewhere, is mixed. Old patriarchal attitudes remain, as shown by the persistence of the ancient **dowry system**, in which parents can arrange a marriage for their daughters only by showering gifts on the groom's family. A girl's dowry has traditionally been the largest expense faced by Indian parents, sometimes leading the poor to lifelong indebtedness. Now the greater availability of consumer goods has had an inflationary effect, with families demanding ever-greater payments in return for marriage to their sons, including refrigerators, houses, cars, and even business capital. Newspapers abound with reports of young brides murdered by their in-laws after their dowry payments have been made. Officially, there were 6,787 dowry murders in India in 2005; experts suspect that the actual number is much higher.

Because of the dowry system, the birth of a girl can seem like a tragedy, ruining the family's financial prospects. One ancient tradition has been female infanticide, leading to a long-term gender imbalance in India favoring males. Modern technology makes the process more efficient. Across India, medical clinics advertise sonogram services to determine the gender of a fetus, leading to the selective abortion of female fetuses. In the state of Punjab there are fewer than eight hundred girls for

Wangari Maathai (1940–2011) Kenyan biologist, environmentalist, and human rights campaigner who founded the Green Belt Movement in Kenya, empowering rural women to plant trees and take leadership roles. She was awarded the Nobel Peace Prize in 2004.

dowry system Traditional Indian marriage system in which a bride brings substantial gifts to the household of her new husband. Though illegal, it has expanded as the country's wealth has grown, leading to chronic indebtedness and the frequent murder of young brides.

The Greenbelt Movement, "Question and Answer Session with Prof. Wangari Maathai," http://www.greenbeltmovement.org/a.php?id=27.

Wangari Maathai The Green Belt Movement led by Wangari Maathai stresses environmental renewal, women's empowerment, and human rights. Here Dr. Maathai (*right*) plants a tree in Nairobi's Uhuru Park with U.S. Senator Barack Obama, later elected president of the United States, who traveled to Kenya in 2006 to visit his father's homeland. (Sayyid Azim/AP Images)

every thousand boys. Women's rights activists estimate that 50 million females are "missing" from the population because of selective abortion, female infanticide, and violence against young brides.

In China, a similar pattern of progress has emerged for some women (such as Liu Yang, the nation's first female astronaut) and severe maltreatment of others (including Feng Jianmei, to whom officials later apologized for her forced abortion). Despite strong legal and constitutional guarantees of equality, and a much broader range of opportunities than ever before for educated women in the booming middle class, discrimination remains rampant. As in Europe and the United States, and even more so in Japan, professional women face invisible barriers to advancement as male employers tend to favor those with whom they feel "more comfortable" as equal colleagues. Lower pay for identical work is as common in China as elsewhere.

Gender imbalances in China's population are almost as extreme as they are in India. Apart from forced abortions under the One Child Policy, some Chinese parents, feeling that they need a male heir to carry on the family line, also practice selective abortion using ultrasound technology. Demographers estimate that there are as many as 70 million more males than females in the country. Even if a more balanced male-female birth ratio is achieved in the near future, tens of millions of Chinese men face a lifetime of bachelorhood.

In the poorest parts of the world, scourges such as the systematic denial of education to girls, sex trafficking, high female death rates in childbirth, and practices like female genital mutilation are still all too common. If global leadership is key to overcoming such problems, there is hope. The 2011 Nobel Prize Committee again recognized the importance of women's leadership when it awarded the Peace Prize to Ellen Johnson Sirleaf and Leymah Gbowee of Liberia, and Tawakkul Karman of Yemen. Johnson and Gbowee both played key roles in the reconstruction of Liberian society after decades of dictatorship and civil war, Johnson serving as Africa's first democratically elected female president and Gbowee mobilizing women across regional and ethnic lines to bring peace to her war-torn country. Karman, according to the Nobel Committee, has played a leading part in the struggle for women's rights and for democracy and peace in Yemen, part of a much broader effort by Arab and Muslim women to reconcile their faith with aspirations for greater equality.

By connecting their quest for women's rights with a broader agenda of social, economic, and political improvement for their nations, these Nobel Prize winners are following in the tradition of Wangari Maathai, and also of Burmese democracy advocate Aung San Suu Kyi (awng san soo CHEE), the 1991 recipient of the award. For decades, Suu Kyi has been a model of persistence and patience in the difficult struggle for freedom in Burma (or Myanmar, as it was renamed by the secretive military officers who have ruled the country with a firm hand since 1962). After overturning election results that would have made Suu Kyi president of the country in 1990, the Burmese regime subjected her to years of house arrest. Suu Kyi was released in 2011 and elected to parliament in 2012, when the military finally allowed relatively fair elections. In the summer of 2012, she was allowed to travel to Oslo to belatedly receive her Nobel Peace Prize. Still, the Burmese military holds the keys to power, while allowing gradual reform from the top down. Elsewhere, especially in the Arab world, political change came more swiftly.

Democracy and the Year of Protest

The rising importance of women in politics showed once again when they stood front and center in the wave of prodemocracy protests that spread across much of the world in 2011. Despite positive trends at the end of the Cold War (see Chapter 31), progress toward democratization remained elusive in many nations. Beginning with revolution in Tunisia in late 2010, large-scale protests spread internationally, most notably in the mass movements in the Arab world that overthrew entrenched regimes in Egypt and Libya as well as Tunisia. Tahrir Square in Cairo was the epicenter of the Arab Spring, and, as in past revolutions, young people played a central role, their ability to organize and sustain massive demonstrations now greatly increased through the power of the Internet and social networking media. (See the feature "World History in Today's World" in Chapter 23, page 668.)

Protests in other parts of the world also featured the use of social media and the central role of young people. In democratic India, Europe, and the United States, however, the purpose was to influence government policy rather than, as in the Arab world, to provoke fundamental constitutional change.

In India, an anticorruption activist named Anna Hazare mobilized millions using Gandhian tactics of nonviolent protest to call the country's political and

The Arab Spring Cairo has long been the political and intellectual center of the Arab world, and Tahrir Square in the center of Cairo was the focal point of the Arab Spring. Protesters, including many students, used social media to organize massive demonstrations against the regime of Hosni Mubarak, who was successfully toppled in February 2011, paving the way for free elections. (Peter Macdiarmid/Getty Images)

business elite to account for squandering the nation's resources. His hunger strikes galvanized support from both the booming middle class and those who have yet to see much benefit from twenty years of economic growth. When the government proposed an anticorruption bill that he saw as inadequate, Hazare began his campaign anew. His supporters across the country chanted *"I am Anna Hazare,"* borrowing the formula of a popular Egyptian slogan from Tahrir Square. Entering 2012, the government had not yet found a way to satisfy their demands for independent oversight over government contracts and financial activities.

In the European Union, especially Spain, Greece, and Great Britain, the cause of protest was fiscal austerity imposed by governments in the wake of the 2008 financial collapse. High unemployment and steep cuts to education were the main factors bringing students and recent graduates out into the streets and plazas, though cuts in wages, pensions, and government employment brought older workers out as well. Guarantees of the welfare state, like basic social benefits and free education, taken for granted for several generations, were now being withdrawn. The fault for the troubled economies, protesters argued, lay not with the ordinary people who were being hurt, but with the political and corporate elites who had mismanaged both national and international finances.

In the United States the issue was similar: who should be held accountable for high unemployment, forsaken homes, and steep drops in educational and other social funding? Two radically different movements emerged in response. Members of Tea Party organizations claimed that government itself was to blame and argued for a radically smaller federal government and sharp cuts in spending. "Occupy Wall Street" demonstrators, in contrast, focused on corporate greed as the root of the problem. Popular mobilization outside the political party structure, they claimed, would be needed to replace corporations with people at the center of

American politics. While the Tea Party was absorbed into the Republican Party, and pushed it rightward, Occupy Wall Street remained outside the mainstream and, for all of its innovations in the use of technology and the widespread publicity that came from its encampments around the nation, had less effect on public policy.

Toward the end of 2011, Russia belatedly and dramatically joined the year of protest. For a decade it had seemed as if the iron grip of Vladimir Putin on Russian politics was unassailable, and that his United Russia Party, in spite of accusations of corruption and antidemocratic tendencies, enjoyed broad public support. However, when Putin announced that he would run once again for president in 2012, the mood was against him. In parliamentary elections, his party won barely 50 percent of the vote amid accusations of massive voter fraud. Moscow, St. Petersburg, and other Russian cities joined the growing global list of places where street protests organized through new technologies challenged the status quo. Putin's victory in the 2012 presidential election signaled that he still had considerable support, and protests subsided. Still, criticism of his authoritarian tendencies by the educated Russian middle class continued.

China remained relatively quiet. True, unrest was intense among some ethnic minorities, most dramatically in western China, where dozens of Tibetan monks set themselves on fire to protest government restrictions. But those protests did not affect the core areas of the Chinese population and economy. During the Arab Spring, Chinese leaders, having lived through youth revolutions in the late 1960s and again in 1989, clamped down even further on freedom of communication, including social media, the Internet, and freedom of assembly.

Such was the global context for the arrest and detention of Ai Weiwei. The official media, easily controlled by the government, limited its coverage of events in Tahrir Square; authorities prevented the translation of foreign news reports and even blocked the word *Egypt* from search engines. For the Communist Party, the cat-and-mouse game of providing, yet controlling and censoring, Internet and social media access was a new variable.

Perhaps it was Ai Weiwei's facility in the use of new media that made him seem dangerous enough to be detained. After a massive earthquake in Sichuan province in 2008, in which many children were killed due to the shoddy construction of their schools, Ai had led a movement to investigate the incident and publish the names of the victims. When Ai made those names known on his blog and posted them on the wall of his Beijing studio, the government was embarrassed, trying as it was to project an image of competence and control. The idea that Chinese citizens themselves would organize a relief effort and investigation into who was responsible was completely outside the bounds of what the Communist leadership would accept. When Ai traveled to a provincial capital to testify on behalf of a fellow protester, he was detained by the police and severely beaten.

Thus 2011 passed with no major challenge to the political monopoly of the Chinese Communist Party. But hundreds of small eruptions had become common across the country, often in out-of-the-way places with little media coverage, while ethnic tensions in Tibet and Xinjiang continued to fester. (See the feature "World History in Today's World" in Chapter 20, page 559.) Will the Communist Party be able to put out all of those small fires one by one, while keeping the lid on larger-scale urban protest? Perhaps it can, as long as the economy continues to grow at a rapid pace. But the lessons of history, and even the logic of Marxist philosophy, indicate that the emerging Chinese middle class will not remain content with economic benefits alone. Once-in-a-decade changes at the top of the Communist hierarchy late in 2012 present a chance for new directions, even if reforms are likely to be slow and cautious. The quest will undoubtedly continue for democracy, freedom of information, freedom of assembly, freedom of religious worship, government transparency, and the rule of law.

Global Art and Culture

Although globalization has been a mixed blessing, creating political confusion and economic anxiety for many people, the potential for cultural globalization still seems immense, as examples from the visual arts and sports indicate.

Chinese civilization, of course, is renowned for the power and longevity of its artistic traditions, but when Ai Weiwei came to New York in 1981, that global reputation had faded. The persecution of his father's generation had left the country with nothing but barren propaganda, and artists who left China rarely returned. In the past two decades all that has changed as international influences flow into and out of the country. Studios and galleries abound in the nation's cities, especially in Beijing and Shanghai, which are magnets for artistic talent equivalent to Paris, London, and New York. Art schools of the highest quality are booming, and tens of thousands of Chinese art students now study abroad. Ai Weiwei was a pioneer in this revitalization. His pieces are often deliberately provocative. When he shows himself in a series of photographs dropping and destroying an ancient vase, for example, he forces the viewer to consider the destruction of China's cultural patrimony in the rush to modernize. (See the feature "Visual Evidence in Primary Sources: The Public Art of Ai Weiwei.")

As long as art remains confined to galleries and international exhibitions, Chinese officials applaud. No longer constrained by state dictates, China's visual artists are pushing the envelope even in social and political commentary, with ironic images of Mao Zedong and sly critiques of the current Communist bureaucracy abounding. But everyone knows there are lines that must not be crossed; when artists enter the public arena as advocates of change, the hammer falls. That is the line Ai Weiwei has repeatedly tested.

While art is central to civilization, sports are a bigger part of most people's everyday lives. Here we see the creative potential of globalization as well in the international dimensions of football (or soccer). While China, the United States, and India have yet to make major contributions, almost everywhere else across Europe, Latin America, Africa, and Asia, football is king. As one writer notes: *"You could see globalization on the pitch. . . . Basque teams, under the stewardship of Welsh coaches, stocked up on Dutch and Turkish players; Moldavian squads imported Nigerians. Everywhere you looked, it suddenly seemed, national borders and national identities had been swept into the dustbin of soccer history."* The internationalization of soccer does have some negative effects, as when Africa's best players sign with European teams, depriving their fellow citizens of a chance to watch them on home turf. Still, there is a net benefit, as *"cultural alchemies . . . yielded wonderful new spectacles: The cynical, defensive-minded Italian style livened by an infusion of freewheeling Dutchmen and Brazilians; the English stiff-upper-lip style . . . tempered by a bit of continental flair, brought across the Channel in the form of French strikers."**

When South Africa hosted the World Cup in 2010, it was a triumphant celebration for the African continent, as hundreds of millions watched on media around the world and learned more about contemporary African art, music, and culture in the process. From soccer to basketball, from film to fashion, from home design to graphic novels, from hip hop to classical music—across the artistic landscape the creative potential of such cultural borrowing and mixing is limitless.

*Franklin Foer, *How Soccer Explains the World: An Unlikely Theory of Globalization* (New York: HarperCollins, 2004), pp. 2–3.

The Public Art of Ai Weiwei

Ai Weiwei's artworks vary from the small and intimate to grand public statements. His most famous large-scale work is the design he contributed to the "Bird's Nest" stadium for the Beijing Olympics. More recently Ai designed a London art pavilion to coincide with the 2012 Summer Olympics; however, China's Communist rulers did not allow him to travel to attend the gallery's opening.

International attention to Ai's arrest and detention heightened with the display of two

A video (available online) accompanied the Tate Gallery exhibition of *Sunflower Seeds*. In it Ai Weiwei explains his rationale behind the piece: to help maintain the traditional ceramics industry by employing sixteen hundred people in the production of the sunflower seeds.

Although health and safety concerns prevented it, the original intention was for visitors to the Tate Gallery to interact with the exhibit by walking among the seeds, feeling and hearing them crunch beneath their feet.

© Tate, London 2012

In the harsh days of the Cultural Revolution, sunflower seeds were small luxuries even exiles like Ai's family could enjoy and share with friends.

In communist iconography, Mao Zedong was often portrayed surrounded by sunflowers. The implication was that Mao was the sun; the beautiful sunflowers bending toward him represented the masses of loyal party members.

Each seed was laboriously hand painted and quite realistic. Ai's art blurs the distinction between natural objects and artistic creations.

impressive public installations during 2011. *Sunflower Seeds* premiered at the Tate Modern Gallery in London before moving to New York. *Circle of Animals* traveled in 2011 from São Paulo to New York, London, and Los Angeles, and in 2012 to Taipei, Houston, Princeton, and Washington; it is slated for exhibition in Pittsburgh and Tel Aviv in 2013. There are no official plans to display either of these globally recognized works in the People's Republic of China.

Circle of Animals, 2010, bronze, 12 pieces, dimensions variable, Pulitzer Fountain, New York. Photo credit: AW Asia

The artist's intention was for each installation of *Circle of Animals* to have a unique feel. In New York (shown here), for example, the heads were placed high above the spectators and behind a fountain, giving a sense of monumentality. In Los Angeles, by contrast, they were placed in a circle around a sunny courtyard, inviting visitors to pose for photographs with individual busts.

The original "zodiac heads" were looted in 1860 from the Qing Summer Palace by British forces during the Second Opium War. In an online video, Ai discusses how, as a young art student, he would visit the ruined Summer Palace. He admired the remaining stonework, but noticed that farmers were using that material to build their pigpens. During the Cultural Revolution, such reminders of the imperial past were despised by Communist authorities.

QUESTION FOR ANALYSIS

» *Examine these images, and other works by Ai Weiwei online. Though they are diverse, what common themes reveal the artist's vision?*

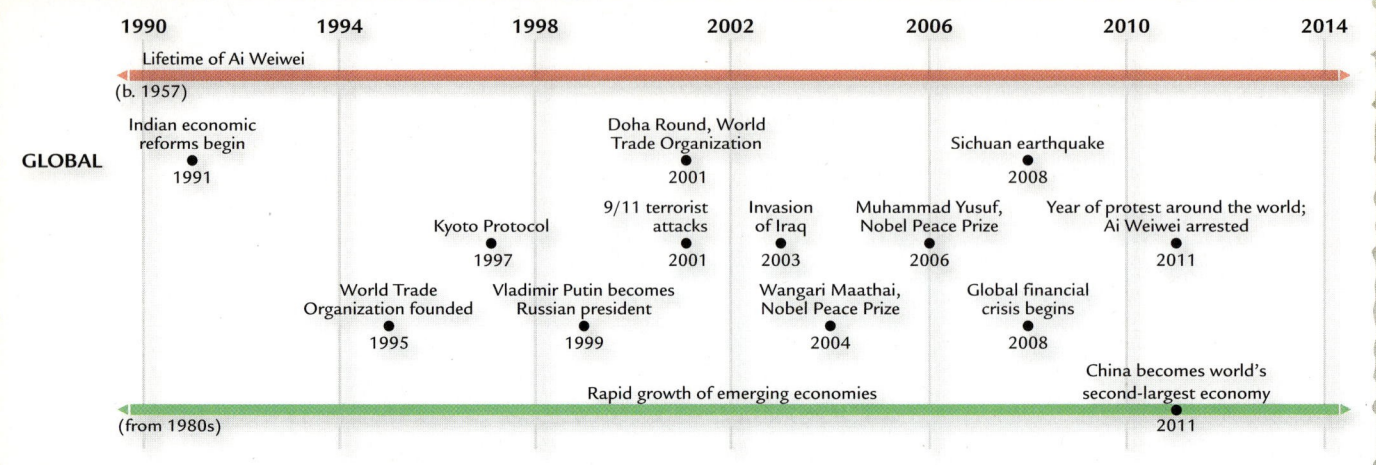

Our Future Voyage

World historians need to be adept at moving across various temporal and spatial scales, from a single moment in time to the sweep of millennia, from individual lives, like that of Ai Weiwei and other travelers featured in *Voyages in World History*, to the development and interaction of global civilizations. In this chapter, we have narrowed the temporal dimension to the very beginning of the twenty-first century, while attempting to keep the entire world in view. Now, in conclusion, we may widen our lens briefly to contextualize contemporary events in broader temporal perspective.

In these terms, the key issues are undoubtedly the interrelated ones of population, environment, and energy use. Though only 6.5 percent of the human beings who have ever lived were alive in 2011, they were having an unprecedented impact on the earth and its resources: land, water, and atmosphere. Our preindustrial ancestors relied principally on the power of their own muscles and those of domesticated animals, occasionally harnessing water, wind, and, in small quantities, coal. Since the Industrial Revolution, such constraints have been left behind. In just the past two decades, global energy use has skyrocketed by 39 percent, with growth rates highest in the new emerging economies of China (146 percent), India (91 percent), and Latin America (66 percent). While European energy consumption grew by only 7 percent during that period, the United States maintained its position as the largest per capita consumer of energy, each American using four times more than the global average. Are such growth rates sustainable? Will future conflict between global societies be sparked by competition for dwindling energy and water resources?

An optimistic view of humankind's ability to support 7 billion and more people at reasonable levels of prosperity and energy consumption might come from reflection upon the mistake of Thomas Malthus, an early-nineteenth-century pioneer of population studies. Malthus believed that Britain was headed for an inevitable crisis as population growth came to outstrip the food supply. "The power of population," he wrote, "is indefinitely greater than the power in the earth to produce subsistence for man."[*] Yet Britain escaped the Malthusian trap by harnessing new technologies and energy sources. It remains to be seen, of course, whether an equivalent burst of technological progress can replicate that success on a global scale, where the stakes are much higher than in Malthus's time.

At any rate, the human story is about much more than just production, consumption, and reproduction. Culture matters, and at least since the Enlightenment, a vision of political, intellectual, and artistic liberation has inspired dreams of a better future. Yet progress is usually charted using only mundane economic indicators, as if increased consumption alone is the key to human fulfillment. From the tiny Himalayan kingdom of Bhutan comes an alternative: the concept of "gross national happiness." In addition to material satisfaction, a measurement of spiritual and personal fulfillment includes factors such as

[*]Thomas Malthus, *An Essay on the Principle of Population*, Oxford World's Classics (New York: Oxford University Press, 2008), p. 61.

sustainable development, retention of cultural values, environmental conservation, and effective government. In 2012, the United Nations met to consider whether "gross national happiness" might be a more accurate measurement of human development than economic indicators alone.

The twenty-first century has begun with its share of political tensions and economic crises; still, across the world people and societies are striving for something more. As the human voyage continues, the African continent, where the human story began some 160,000 years ago, points the way forward. For all the challenges they have dealt with in their modern history, recent polls show that Africans are the most optimistic people on the planet. Perhaps Africans' persistent belief in and commitment to a better future for themselves and their children is a lesson for the world.

VOYAGES ON THE WEB: Ai Weiwei

The Voyages Map App follows the traveler's journeys using interactive study tools, including 360-degree panoramic views of historic sites, zoomable maps, audio summaries, flash cards, and quizzes.

KEY TERMS

Ai Weiwei (918)
Manmohan Singh (921)
World Trade Organization (925)

Muhammad Yusuf (925)
September 11, 2001 (927)
Kyoto Protocol (934)
sustainable development (935)

One Child Policy (936)
Wangari Maathai (938)
dowry system (938)

FOR FURTHER REFERENCE

Ai, Weiwei. *Ai Weiwei's Blog: Writings, Interviews, and Digital Rants, 2006–2009.* Lee Ambrozy, trans. Cambridge, Mass.: MIT Press, 2011.

Appiah, Kwame Anthony. *Cosmopolitanism: Ethics Is a World of Strangers.* New York: W. W. Norton, 2007.

Berger, Peter L., and Samuel Huntington, eds. *Many Globalizations: Cultural Diversity in the Contemporary World.* New York: Oxford University Press, 2003.

Connelly, Matthew. *Fatal Misconception: The Struggle to Control World Population.* Cambridge, Mass.: Belknap Press, 2010.

Farlow, Andrew. *Crash and Beyond: Causes and Consequences of the Global Financial Crisis.* New York: Oxford University Press, 2012.

Foer, Franklin. *How Soccer Explains the World: An Unlikely Theory of Globalization.* New York: HarperCollins, 2004.

Friedman, Thomas. *Hot, Flat and Crowded: Why We Need a Green Revolution.* Rev. ed. New York: Picador, 2009.

Maathai, Wangari. *Unbowed: A Memoir.* New York: Knopf, 2006.

Manning, Patrick. *Migration in World History.* 2d ed. New York: Routledge, 2011.

McGregor, Richard. *The Party: The Secret World of China's Communist Rulers.* New York: Harper, 2012.

Peterson, V. Spike, and Anne Sisson Runyan. *Global Gender Issues in the New Millennium.* 3d ed. Boulder, Colo.: Westview, 2009.

Sen, Amartya. *Identity and Violence: The Illusion of Destiny.* New York: Penguin, 2008.

Staab, Andreas. *The European Union Explained.* 2d ed. Bloomington: Indiana University Press, 2011.

Toft, Monica Duffy, Daniel Philpott, and Timothy Samuel Shah. *God's Century: Resurgent Religion and Global Politics.* New York: W. W. Norton, 2011.

Wright, Robin. *Rock the Casbah: Rage and Rebellion Across the Islamic World.* New York: Simon and Schuster, 2011.

Zakaria, Fareed. *The Post-American World, Version 2.0.* New York: W. W. Norton, 2011.

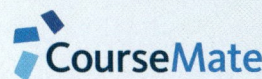

Go to the CourseMate website at **www.cengagebrain.com** for additional study tools and review materials—including audio and video clips—for this chapter.

NOTES

Chapter 1

1. John Noble Wilford, "In Ancient Skulls from Ethiopia, Familiar Faces," *New York Times*, June 12, 2003, pp. A1, A8.
2. John Noble Wilford, "Report Reignites Feud over 'Little People' as Separate Species," *New York Times*, August 22, 2006, p. F2.
3. Tom D. Dillehay et al., "Monte Verde: Seaweed, Food, Medicine, and the Peopling of South America," *Science* 320, no. 5877 (May 9, 2008): 786–789.
4. Ibid., pp. 784–786.
5. William H. Stiebing, Jr., *Ancient Near Eastern History and Culture* (New York: Longman, 2003), p. 13.

Chapter 2

1. Martha T. Roth, *Law Collections from Mesopotamia and Asia Major* (Atlanta: Scholars Press, 1997), p. 121.
2. Samuel Noah Kramer, *History Begins at Sumer: Thirty-nine Firsts in Recorded History* (Philadelphia: University of Pennsylvania Press, 1981), p. 58.
3. This book uses the chronology given in Douglas J. Brewer and Emily Teeter, *Egypt and the Egyptians* (New York: Cambridge University Press, 1999).
4. Anthony P. Sakovich, "Counting the Stones: How Many Blocks Comprise Khufu's Pyramid?" *KMT: A Modern Journal of Ancient Egypt* 13, no. 3 (Fall 2002): 53–57.
5. William H. Stiebing, Jr., *Ancient Near Eastern History and Culture* (New York: Longman, 2003), p. 127.
6. Ann Hyland, "Chariots and Cavalry," in *The Seventy Great Inventions of the Ancient World*, ed. Brian M. Fagan (London: Thames and Hudson, 2004), p. 196.
7. Lionel Casson, *Travel in the Ancient World* (Baltimore: Johns Hopkins University Press, 1994), p. 39; for a critique of the nature of the text and its date, see also Benjamin Sass, "Wenamun and His Levant—1075 BC or 925 BC?" *Ägypten und Levante* 12 (2001): 247–255.
8. William G. Dever, *Did God Have a Wife? Archaeology and Folk Religion in Ancient Israel* (Grand Rapids: William B. Eerdmans, 2005), p. 13.
9. Ibid., pp. 64–69.
10. Stiebing, p. 240.
11. William G. Dever, *What Did the Biblical Writers Know and When Did They Know It? What Archaeology Can Tell Us About the Reality of Ancient Israel* (Grand Rapids: William B. Eerdmans, 2001), p. 127.
12. Ibid., p. 118.

Chapter 3

1. Jonathan Mark Kenoyer, "Uncovering the Keys to the Lost Indus Cities," *Scientific American* 289, no.1 (July 2003): 67–75.
2. J. P. Mallory and D. Q. Adams, *Encyclopedia of Indo-European Culture* (Chicago: Fitzroy Dearborn Publishers, 1997), p. 306.
3. Richard H. Davis, "Introduction: A Brief History of Religions in India," in *Religions of Asia in Practice: An Anthology*, ed. Donald S. Lopez, Jr. (Princeton: Princeton University Press, 2002), pp. 19–30.
4. John S. Strong, "Images of Asoka: Some Indian and Sri Lankan Legends and Their Development," in *King Asoka and Buddhism: Historical and Literary Studies*, ed. A. Seneviratne (Kandy: Buddhist Publication Society, 1994), p. 99.
5. Lionel Casson, *The Periplus Maris Erythraei Text with Introduction, Translation, and Commentary* (Princeton: Princeton University Press, 1989), p. 91 (Thina); 93 (regions beyond China).

Chapter 4

1. *Chuang Tzu: Basic Writings*, trans. Burton Watson (New York: Columbia University Press, 1964), p. 41 (Perfect Man); 45 (butterfly); 115 (talking skull).
2. *Tao Te Ching: The Classic Book of Integrity and the Way*, trans. Victor Mair (New York: Bantam Books, 1990), p. 54.
3. Denis Twitchett and Michael Loewe, eds., *The Cambridge History of China*, vol. 1: *The Ch'in and Han Empires 221 B.C.–A.D. 220* (New York: Cambridge University Press, 1986), p. 61.
4. A. F. P. Hulsewé, *Remnants of Ch'in Law: An Annotated Translation of the Ch'in Legal and Administrative Rules of the Third Century B.C., Discovered in Yün-meng Prefecture, Hu-pei Province, in 1975* (Leiden: E. J. Brill, 1985), p. 205.
5. Hugh Scogin, "Between Heaven and Man: Contract and the State in Han Dynasty China," *Southern California Law Review* 63, no. 5 (1990): 1386.
6. Nancy Lee Swann, *Pan Chao: Foremost Woman Scholar of China* (New York: American Historical Association, 1932), pp. 84–85.

Chapter 5

1. Michael D. Coe, *The Maya*, 6th ed. (New York: Thames and Hudson, 1999), p. 196.
2. "By Canoe from Hawaii: Tahiti Trip to Celebrate Bicentennial," *Los Angeles Times*, May 30, 1976, p. D8.
3. Mau Piailug obituary, *Washington Post*, July 21, 2010.
4. John Flenley and Paul Bahn, *The Enigmas of Easter Island: Island on the Edge* (New York: Oxford University Press, 2002), p. 104 (the number of moai); 125–127 (Van Tilburg's experiments).
5. K. R. Howe, *The Quest for Origins: Who First Discovered and Settled the Pacific Islands* (Honolulu: University of Hawai'i Press, 2003), p. 180.

Chapter 6

1. M. Aperghis, "Population—Production—Taxation—Coinage: A Model for the Seleukid Economy," in *Hellenistic Economies*, ed. Z. H. Archibald et al. (London: Routledge, 2001), pp. 69–102, 77 (population estimate). Reference supplied by Christopher Tuplin (University of Liverpool).

2. The translation from *The Avesta* of the prayers is courtesy of Stanley Insler, Edward E. Salisbury Professor of Sanskrit and Comparative Philology at Yale University (e-mail dated September 4, 2002).

3. Lionel Casson, *Travel in the Ancient World* (Baltimore: Johns Hopkins University Press, 1974), pp. 53–54; estimates speed of the couriers and translates Herodotus, *The Histories*, trans. Aubrey de Sélincourt, further rev. ed. (New York: Penguin Books, 1954, 1996), 480, VIII: 98.

4. Richard N. Frye, *The Heritage of Persia* (New York: World Publishing Company, 1963), p. 85.

5. M. Cary and E. H. Warmington, *The Ancient Explorers* (London: Methuen, 1929), pp. 47–48.

6. Summary of the unpublished research of Shaul Shaked is courtesy of Kevin van Bladel, University of Southern California (e-mail dated June 23, 2005).

Chapter 7

1. "Slavery," in *The Oxford Companion to Classical Civilization*, ed. Simon Hornblower and Antony Sparforth (New York: Oxford University Press, 1998), p. 671.

2. "Population, Roman," in *The Oxford Companion*, pp. 561–562.

3. Ibid.

4. Morton Smith, *Jesus the Magician* (New York: Harper and Row, 1978), p. 45. Chapter 4 of this book, "What the Outsiders Said—Evidence Outside the Gospels," provides an excellent introduction to nongospel sources about Jesus. Only one nonchurch source from the first century refers to Jesus: The Jewish historian Josephus, writing sometime in 90 c.e., mentions "the brother of Jesus, the so-called Christ, James was his name." In addition to the sources discussed by Morton Smith, some scholars believe that the gospel of Thomas contains earlier versions of Jesus' sayings than those recorded in the canonical gospels, while others contend that they are later.

5. *Documents of the Christian Church*, ed. Henry Bettenson (New York: Oxford University Press, 1966), p. 35.

Chapter 8

1. Richard H. Davis, "Introduction: A Brief History of Religions in India," in *Religions of Asia in Practice: An Anthology*, ed. Donald S. Lopez, Jr. (Princeton: Princeton University Press, 2002), p. 5.

2. Robert Kaplan, *The Nothing That Is: A Natural History of Zero* (New York: Oxford University Press, 1999), p. 41.

3. Anthony Reid, "Introduction: A Time and a Place," in *Southeast Asia in the Early Modern Era: Trade, Power, and Belief* (Ithaca: Cornell University Press, 1993), p. 3.

4. Valerie Hansen, *The Open Empire: A History of China to 1600* (New York: W.W. Norton, 2000), p. 182.

Chapter 9

1. Charles Issawi, "The Area and Population of the Arab Empire: An Essay in Speculation," in *The Islamic Middle East, 700–1900: Studies in Economic and Social History*, ed. A. L. Udovitch (Princeton: Darwin Press, 1981), pp. 375–396; estimated population on p. 392.

2. Patricia Crone, *Meccan Trade and the Rise of Islam* (Piscataway, N.J.: Gorgias Press, 2004), p. 190, n104.

3. See an alternate translation in Dmitri Gutas, *Greek Thought, Arabic Culture: The Graeco-Arabic Translation Movement in Baghdad and Early Abbâsid Society (2nd–4th/8th–10th centuries)* (New York: Routledge, 1998), p. 30.

4. Richard W. Bulliet, *Conversion to Islam in the Medieval Period: An Essay in Quantitative History* (Cambridge: Harvard University Press, 1979), p. 44, graph 5.

5. Compare *The History of al-Tabari*, vol. 30: *The Abbasid Caliphate in Equilibrium*, trans. and annotated C. E. Bosworth (Albany: State University of New York Press, 1989), p. 42; romanizations changed for consistency.

6. *The Abbasid Caliphate in Equilibrium*, p. 45.

Chapter 10

1. Warren Treadgold, *A History of the Byzantine State and Society* (Stanford: Stanford University Press, 1997), pp. 196, 297.

2. Patrick J. Geary, *Before France and Germany: The Creation and Transformation of the Merovingian World* (New York: Oxford University Press, 1988), p. 115.

3. Ibid., p. 130.

Chapter 11

1. Because of differences in the calendars, Islamic years often straddle two Western years. Although most sources give the year in both the Islamic calendar and the Western, this chapter, like Chapter 9, will give only the Western equivalent.

2. Jan Vansina, *Paths in the Rainforest: Toward a History of Political Tradition in Equatorial Africa* (Madison: University of Wisconsin Press, 1990), pp. 31, 33.

3. Susan Keech McIntosh and Roderick J. McIntosh, "Cities Without Citadels: Understanding Urban Origins Along the Middle Niger," in *The Archaeology of Africa: Food, Metals and Towns*, ed. Thurstan Shaw et al. (New York: Routledge, 1993), p. 633.

4. D. T. Niane, "Mali and the Second Mandingo Expansion," in *General History of Africa* (Calif.: Heinemann and UNESCO, 1984), p. 148, n62.

5. Ralph A. Austen, "The Trans-Saharan Slave Trade: A Tentative Census," in *The Uncommon Market: Essays in the Economic History of the Atlantic Slave Trade*, ed. Henry A. Gemery and Jan S. Hogendorn (New York: Academic Press, 1979), pp. 23–69; tables on pp. 31, 66; Paul Lovejoy, *Transformations in Slavery: A History of Slavery in Africa*, 2d ed. (New York: Cambridge University Press, 2000), pp. 24–26.

6. Andrew M. Watson, "Back to Gold—and Silver," *Economic History Review* 20, no. 1 (1967): 1–34, estimate in 30–31, n1.

7. Ross E. Dunn, *The Adventures of Ibn Battuta, a Muslim Traveler of the 14th Century* (Berkeley: University of California Press, 2005), p. 45.

8. J. N. Mattock, "Ibn Battuta's Use of Ibn Jubayr's Rihla," in *Proceedings of the Ninth Congress of the Union Euro-péenne des arabisants et Islamisants*, ed. Rudolph

Peters (Leiden: E. J. Brill, 1981), pp. 209–218, estimate on p. 211.

9. Michael W. Dols, *The Black Death in the Middle East* (Princeton: Princeton University Press, 1977), p. 215.

10. Peter Garlake, *Great Zimbabwe Described and Explained* (Harare: Zimbabwe Publishing House, 1982), p. 14.

11. P. S. Garlake, *Great Zimbabwe* (New York: Stein and Day, 1973), p. 27 (size of Elliptical Building); 195 (estimate of number of laborers); 131 (excavated horde).

Chapter 12

1. Peter K. Bol, "The Sung Examination System and the Shih," *Asia Major*, 3d ser., no. 2 (1990): 149–171, statistic on 152.

2. Ellen Neskar, "Shrines to Local Former Worthies," in *Religions of China in Practice*, ed. Donald S. Lopez, Jr. (Princeton: Princeton University Press, 1996).

Chapter 13

1. R. I. Moore, *The First European Revolution, c. 970–1215* (Oxford: Blackwell, 2000), p. 30.

2. M. T. Clancy, *From Memory to Written Record*, 2d ed. (Oxford: Blackwell, 1993), pp. 120–121.

3. Barbara H. Rosenwein, *A Short History of the Middle Ages* (Peterborough, Ont.: Broadview Press, 2002), p. 168.

4. Paul Freedman, "Spices and Late-Medieval European Ideas of Scarcity and Value," *Speculum* 80, no. 4 (2005): 1209–1227.

5. Samuel K. Cohn, Jr., "The Black Death: End of a Paradigm," *American Historical Review* 107, no. 3 (June 2002): 703–738; p. 727 (Avignon death statistics).

Chapter 14

1. Joseph Fletcher, "The Mongols: Ecological and Social Perspectives," *Harvard Journal of Asiatic Studies* 46, no. 1 (1986): 1–56, explanation of tanistry on 17.

2. André Wegener Sleeswyk, "The Liao and the Displacement of Ships in the Ming Dynasty," *The Mariner's Mirror* 81 (1996): 3–13.

Chapter 15

1. Terence d'Altroy, *The Incas* (Malden, Mass.: Blackwell, 2002), p. 172.

2. Michael E. Smith, *The Aztecs* (Malden, Mass.: Blackwell, 1996), p. 62.

3. Ibid., p. 61; Noble David Cook, *Demographic Collapse: Indian Peru, 1520–1620* (Cambridge: Cambridge University Press, 1981), p. 94.

Chapter 16

1. E. Mungello, *The Great Encounter of China and the West, 1500–1800*, 2d ed. (Lanham, Md.: Rowman and Littlefield, 2005).

2. Simon Schama, *An Embarrassment of Riches: An Interpretation of Dutch Culture in the Golden Age* (New York: Vintage, 1997).

Chapter 20

1. Susan Mann, *Precious Records: Women in China's Long Eighteenth Century* (Stanford: Stanford University Press, 1997), p. 149.

2. Conrad Totman, *Early Modern Japan* (Berkeley: University of California Press, 1993).

3. Kenneth Pomeranz, *The Great Divergence: China, Europe, and the Making of the Modern World Economy* (Princeton: Princeton University Press, 2000).

Chapter 23

1. John Stuart Mill, *On Liberty* (London: Longman, Roberts and Green, 1869), p. 5.

Chapter 25

1. Cited in Thomas Bender, *A Nation Among Nations: America's Place in World History* (New York: Hill and Wang, 2006), p. 121.

Chapter 32

1. United Nations, *World Urbanization Prospects* (New York: Author, 2006).

INDEX

I-2 INDEX

Missionaries, Buddhist, 201; in China, 211
Missionaries, Catholic. *See also* Jesuits; Ricci, Matteo; in Spanish America, 425, 426; Amerindians and, 501; in Vietnam, 749
Missionaries, Christian. *See also* Ricci, Matteo; William of Rubruck; Byzantine, 282; Nestorian, 373; in Mexico, 425, 426; expelled from Japan, 456, 457; in India, 692; in China, 678, 681, 682; Protestant, 661; in Africa, 736
Mississippian peoples, 123–124
Mississippi River, 507, 646
Missouri Compromise (1820), 708–709
Mita labor system, 498
Mithra cult, 183
Mitochondrial Eve, 6
Mitsubishi Corporation, 688
Mitsui Corporation, 908
Mixed-race peoples. *See also* Johnson-Tekahionwake, Pauline; in Brazil, 427, 506–507, 725; mulattos, 502, 505, 510; in Spanish Americas, 500, 501, 502, 504–505 and illus., 512, 516, 629; in Venezuela, 630; gens de couleur, in Haiti, 627, 628, 634; mestizos, 427, 501, 502, 505 (illus.), 512, 629, 633; métis, in French Canada, 508, 706 (illus.), 723–724
Moa birds, of New Zealand, 133
Moai statues, of Easter Island, 131–132 and illus., 134
Mobutu, Joseph (Mobutu Sese Seko), 870–871, 899
Moctezuma (Aztec), 425, 426
Modernization. *See also* Westernization; in Ethiopia, 757; in Turkey, 810 (illus.)
Mogadishu, 306, 398
Mohawk Indians, 613, 703, 704, 729
Mohenjo-daro, 59 and map, 60 (illus.), 61 (illus.)
Mombasa, 306; Portuguese fort in, 439 (illus.), 524
Monarchy (kings). *See also* Chakravartan ruler; Constitutional monarchy; *specific monarchs;* Mesopotamian, 29, 54; Sumerian, 32; British Parliament and, 480, 481, 594; Nubian, 43–44; Egyptian pharoahs, 34, 37–38, 40, 41, 42–43, 54; Hebrew, 52; Mauryan India, 74, 75, 80; early China, 87, 88; Iranian, 138, 142; Parthian, 162; Roman, 169; Srivijayan, 205; Mali, 297, 298 (illus.); French, 347, 367, 478, 618; English, 347, 367; West African, 442, 444, 445 (illus.); enlightened despots, 593–594; of Siam, 757, 758 (illus.)
Monasteries and monks, Buddhist, 450, 574; in India, 68, 76, 202; in China, 200, 201, 211, 212, 216, 217, 218, 333, 336; in Japan, 450; in Java, 206–207 and illus.; in Korea, 221; in Srivijaya, 205; travels of Japanese (Ennin), 198–200, 202–203, 216; in Vietnam, 337, 874 (illus.)
Monasteries and monks, Christian: in Egypt, 192; literacy in, 262, 266; Viking

raids on, 270 (map), 271; land grants to, 347; manuscript copying, 262, 266 (illus.), 269; reforms, 356, 357–358; Rule of St. Benedict, 266, 357
Monetary system. *See also* Coins; Currency; paper, in China, 323, 340, 387; Germany hyperinflation and, 776; European Union, 911, 927
Moneylenders, Jews as, 363
Möngke Khan, 372, 379, 380, 382, 384–385
Mongkut (Siam), 757
Mongolian empire (Mongols), 370–400; Xiongnu of, 102–103; sack of Baghdad by, 253, 254; Golden Horde, 380, 386 (map), 465; Khitan and, 319; Mamluk defeat of, 304; at Möngke's court, 380–382, 384–385; nomadic ways of, 373; William of Rubruck and, 370–372; postal relay system in, 378–380, 382, 399; reign of Ögödei, 378; religion in, 373, 377; rise of Chinggis Khan in, 375–378, 399; Russia and, 465, 486; society in, 374–375; successor states, 383, 387–388; Ming China and, 395, 398; Yuan China and, 386 (map), 390–391; Zunghars, 557
Monks. *See* Monasteries and monks
Mononobu Hishikawa, 574–575 (illus.)
Monotheism: Hebrew, 48, 52; Islamic, 231; Jews and, 183
Monsoons: in China, 85; India and, 59; India Ocean trade and, 78, 438; in Southeast Asia, 205, 210
Montesquieu, Baron de, 591, 615, 621
Monte Verde (Chile), early humans in, 16–18 and illus., 123
Moriscos (Muslim converts), in Spain, 476, 501; revolt by, 474
Morocco, 170, 238; Pigeon Cave in, 8; Arab rule in, 466; Sijilmasa in, 293; Portugal and, 415, 417, 525; Songhai and, 525
Morrison, David, 113
Morsi, Muhammad, 668
Mosaics: Roman, 178–179 (illus.); in Islamic mosques, 235, 238 (illus.); in Samarkand, 388 (illus.)
Moscow, 472. *See also* Muscovy; St. Basil's Cathedral, 486 (illus.); Napoleon in, 626
Moses (Bible), 52
Mosques, 233, 362; in Africa, 295; in Damascus, 235, 238 (illus.); in Constantinople, 390, 391 (illus.), 462–464; destruction of, in India, 446; West African, 524
Mossadegh, Muhammad, 864–865
Mound-building cultures, 123–124
Movable type. *See also* Printing technology; in China, 328, 329 (illus.); in Europe, 414–415, 452; in Korea, 338–339
Movies. *See* Film industry
Muawiya, 235
Mubarak, Hosni, overthrow of, 668, 941 (illus.)

Mugabe, Robert, 748
Mughal empire (India): Indian Ocean trade and, 443, 447, 566; Islam in, 443, 446–447; religious toleration in, 446, 453–454 and illus.; women rulers in, 446–447; Aurangzeb and decline of, 566–568; British and, 552, 566, 568–570, 571 (illus.), 578, 693
Muhammad Ali (Egypt), 648, 666
Muhammad bin Tughluq, Sultan, 312–313
Muhammad (Prophet), 694, 772. *See also* Islam; Muslims; death of, 233; descendants of, 234; last sermon of, 233, 252; life and teachings of, 230–233
Mujahaddin (Afghanistan), 890, 904
Mulattos, 502, 505, 510. *See also* Mixed-race people
Multinational corporations, 925, 928; in China, 909
Mumbai (Bombay), 570, 690
Mummification: in Egypt, 39, 46–47 and illus.; in Inca Peru, 409
Mungo Man, 2–3, 10, 24, 127
Murad II (Ottoman), 392
Murasaki Shikibu, 224
Muscovy, principality of, 387, 388, 472. *See also* Moscow
Museums: in Alexandria, 160; in Athens, 155; cultural theft and, 595; Hermitage (St. Petersburg), 487 (illus.)
Music: German romanticism, 649; Argentine tango, 717; African American jazz, 764, 791; Cuban mambo, 859; Beatles, 878–879
Muskets, 466, 485
Muslim Brotherhood, in Egypt, 668, 872
Muslim fundamentalists, 902. *See also* Islamists
Muslim-Hindu relations, in India: in Mughal India, 443, 453, 567; British rule and, 692, 694, 695, 697; partition of Bengal and, 698; independence and, 871; terrorism and, 446
Muslim League (India), 812–813, 871
Muslims, 241, (map). *See also* Islam; in India, 308–309; traders, in Africa, 248, 293, 398; Crusades and, 361–362; in Spain, 363, 419; in East Africa, 288, 438, 524; trans-Sahara trade and, 418; in Malacca, 438; in Central Asia, 488; *moriscos,* in Spain, 474, 476, 501; Ottoman reforms and, 667; in China, 559, 676; prohibition against pork and, 692, 695; in Russia, 563, 564; in West Africa, 524, 742, 772 and illus.; in Malaya, 749; in Bosnia, 765, 776; in Chechnya, 896; women, 796 (*See also* Edib, Halide); in Indonesia, 937 (map); in western Europe, 936
Mussolini, Benito, 796, 800, 801–803; corporatism and, 802; invasion of Ethiopia and, 802, 820; in World War II, 830; death of, 832
Myanmar. *See* Burma (Myanmar)
Mycenaean Greece, 148
My Lai Massacre, Vietnam (1969), 874